Expectations of Life

H.O. Lancaster

Expectations of Life

A Study in the Demography, Statistics, and History of World Mortality

With 28 Illustrations

Springer-Verlag
New York Berlin Heidelberg
London Paris Tokyo Hong Kong

H.O. Lancaster, MD, DSc, FAA
Emeritus Professor of Mathematical Statistics, The University of Sydney
Sydney, Australia

Library of Congress Cataloging-in-Publication Data
Lancaster. H.O. (Henry Oliver). 1913–
    Expectations of life : a study in the demography, statistics, and history of world
mortality / H.O. Lancaster.
    p. cm.
    ISBN 0-387-97105-X
    1. Life expectancy. 2. Mortality 3. Demography. I. Title.
HB 1322.3.L36 1989
304.6′4—dc20   89-19654

Printed on acid-free paper.

Typeset by Asco Trade Typesetting Ltd., Hong Kong.
Printed and bound by Edwards Brothers, Ann Arbor, Michigan.
Printed in the United States of America.

9 8 7 6 5 4 3 2 1

ISBN 0-387-97105-X Springer-Verlag New York Berlin Heidelberg
ISBN 3-540-97105-X Springer-Verlag Berlin Heidelberg New York

Dedicated to Frank John Fenner, AC, CMG, MBE, MD, FAA, FRS, bacteriologist, virologist, and environmentalist,
and
to the memory of Thomas Carlyle Parkinson (1884–1909) and Dora Lush (1910–1943), bacteriologists.

(See page 61 for details of these latter two persons.)

Acknowledgments

I wish to thank the University of Sydney for the provision of office accommodation and administrative support, and the Australian Research Grants Scheme for its financial assistance over 4 years in the preparation of this book.

Particular thanks are due to Emeritus Professor F.J. Fenner, AC, CMG, MBE, FAA, FRS for his encouragement and comments on epidemiological aspects, especially the section on smallpox, and to Emeritus Professor Adrien Albert, AO, FAA for his advice on pharmacology and therapy, and his suggestion for the title.

Many members of the University of Sydney have provided advice and assistance, among whom should be mentioned the University Librarian, Dr. Neil Radford and his staff, Dr. Aileen Plant and Dr. Terry Dwyer of the School of Public Health and Tropical Medicine, the Department of Geography and the Department of Mathematical Statistics.

The cooperation of the Australian Bureau of Statistics is gratefully acknowledged, and the valuable contribution of Miss Brenda Heagney, Librarian of the Royal Australasian College of Physicians, for whom no assignment was ever too difficult.

I wish to thank also the Librarian of the London School of Hygiene and Tropical Medicine and the Director for room space during my visit to London.

I am indebted to the following persons and organizations who have granted permission for the use of copyright material:

Academic Press, Orlando, FL.
American Society for Microbiology, Washington, DC.
Australian Association of Gerontology, Sydney.
Australian Journal of Statistics, Canberra.
Baillière Tindall Limited, London.
British Medical Journal, London.
Dr. D.P. Burkitt, Stroud, UK.
Cambridge University Press, Cambridge.
Carnegie Endowment for International Peace, Washington, DC.
Churchill Livingstone, Edinburgh.
Clarendon Press, Oxford.
CRC Press, Inc., Boca Raton, FL.
Economic History Review (Basil Blackwell Ltd., Oxford).

Edward Arnold (Publishers) Ltd., London.
Professor D.E.C. Eversley, Huntingford, UK.
Facts on File, Inc., New York.
Her Majesty's Stationery Office, Norwich, UK.
History Project, Inc., Canberra.
Professor Y. Hofvander, International Child Health Unit, Uppsala.
Human Biology (Wayne State University Press, Detroit, MI.)
Japan Statistics Bureau, Tokyo.
John Murray (Publishers) Ltd., London.
John Wiley & Sons, Inc., New York.
Johns Hopkins University Press, Baltimore, MD.
Josiah Macy, Jr. Foundation, New York.
Journal of the Institute of Actuaries, London.
Journal of the Royal Statistical Society, London.
Journal of Tropical Medicine and Hygiene, London.
S. Karger AG, Basel.
Dr. J.P. Kreier, Ohio State University, Columbus, OH.
The Lancet Ltd., London.
Lea & Febiger, Philadelphia, PA.
Little, Brown and Company, Boston, MA.
Dr. W.P.D. Logan, Bognor Regis, UK.
Longman Group Limited, Harlow, UK.
Macmillan Press Ltd., Basingstoke, UK.
Medical Journal of Australia, Sydney.
Metron (Professor C. Benedetti, University of Rome).
New York Academy of Medicine.
Office of Population Censuses and Surveys, London.
Oxford University Press, Oxford.
Dr. R. Passmore, Edinburgh.
Population Studies, London.
The Royal College of Physicians of Edinburgh.
Scandinavian Economic History Review, Lund, Sweden.
Dr. V.H. Springett, Solihull, UK.
Statistics Sweden (Statistiska Centralbyrån), Stockholm.
Statistisk Sentralbyrå, Oslo.
Syracuse University Press, Syracuse, NY.
Dr. O. Turpeinen, Helsinki.
United Nations, New York.
The Walter and Eliza Hall Institute of Medical Research, Melbourne.
Williams & Wilkins Co., Baltimore, MD.
World Health Organization, Geneva.

   I would like to thank especially Mr. John Roberts and Mr. Peter Johnson for their work on the illustrations, and Mrs. Elsie Adler for assistance with the typing. Lastly, I would like to thank particularly my research assistant Mrs. Philippa Holy for preparation of the manuscript and bibliography, proofreading, and other tasks associated with publication.

                                                        H.O. Lancaster

Contents

Glossary of Abbreviations

BCG	Bacille Calmette-Guérin
BP	Before the present
CHD	Coronary heart disease
CVD	Cardiovascular disease
DA	Decennial average
DDT	Dichlorodiphenyl-trichlorethane
ECHO	Enteric cytopathic human orphan (virus)
EPEC	Enteropathogenic *Escherichia coli*
ETEC	Enterotoxigenic *Escherichia coli*
FAO	Food and Agriculture Organization (United Nations)
HLA	Histocompatibility leukocyte antigen
ICD	International Classification of Diseases
IDDM	Insulin-dependent diabetes mellitus
IGT	Impaired glucose tolerance
IHD	Ischemic heart disease
ILO	International Labor Organization
IM	Infant mortality
LBW	Low birth weight
LIH	Lying-in hospital
MODY	Mature onset diabetes in the young
NIDDM	Non-insulin-dependent diabetes mellitus
PAHO	Pan-American Health Organization
PAS	Para-aminosalicylic (acid)
PNM	Perinatal mortality
PYLL	Potential years of life lost
TAB	Typhoid, paratyphoid A, paratyphoid B
UN	United Nations
UNESCO	United Nations Educational, Scientific and Cultural Organization
WHO	World Health Organization

Dimensions

g	gram(s)
mg	milligram(s)
μg	microgram(s)
ng	nanogram(s)
l	liter(s)
ml	milliliter(s)
m	meter(s)
mm	millimeter(s)
μm	micron(s) (10^{-6} meters)
ppm	parts per million
rad	radiation absorbed dose
mrad	millirad(s)

Introduction

The first chapter gives partial answers to the question, how far back can we make numerical or other general statements on the mortality of man? Several books have been written on the mortality of early man, some authors even going so far as to compute expectations of life in the Old Stone Age. A reading of the texts shows that few firm facts, usually in the form of skeletal remains, are available and that the discussion depends on the extrapolation back from observations of modern primitive tribal communities. It is logical, therefore, to begin with a discussion of the general conclusions on these modern communities and to indicate how few are the independent findings on early man. But lack of observational data applies to much later periods; thus, although there have been interesting pathological investigations into naturally or artificially mummified bodies in ancient Egypt, no useful numerical statements can be made about the general population. Ancient Greece and Rome with their archeological relics and literary works give us no better information about the general mortality of the populace. It is not even practical to compute a crude death rate of the free population of the ancient world. Some genealogical records of great interest are available for the German nobility from the twelfth century on, but generalizations cannot be made for the general population because of the special risks of the nobles in both war and peace and the special advantages in famines. Parish records became available in the late sixteenth century and at a later stage merged into the official statistics of the national states, notably in Sweden. From the parish records, many details of mortality by disease, war, and famine have been obtained.

A second question to be answered is: What credence can be given to the remarks of contemporary observers, to whom neither modern methods nor well-founded theories were available? We attempt to answer this question by giving some dates of important discoveries in chapter 2. Thus, for example, we note that the techniques of freezing, supporting, and paraffin imbedding of sections of tissue for examination were available in 1843, 1853, and 1869, respectively; stains for the examination of cell structure began to be used in 1847; the compound microscope was developed commercially from 1840 onward and had reached a high degree of efficiency in 1880. On the theoretical side, systematic pathology began with the publication of Rokitansky's great text over the years 1842–1846; Rudolf Virchow announced the cell theory in 1855 and later led the application of microscopic methods to pathology. Joseph Lister in 1853 and Julius Cohnheim in 1878–1880 elucidated the sequence of events in inflammation. Since that time many advances have been made in pathology; but for us the most important advances were made in microbiology, parasitology, and related sciences. By 1840 a small number of diseases had been shown to be caused by living organisms and F.G.J. Henle had written his famous essay, but appropriate methods for the culture and identification of bacteria had yet to be developed. In this field the leaders were Ferdinand Julius Cohn, Louis Pasteur, and Robert Koch. They and their followers discovered the agents responsible for most microbial diseases in the period 1880 to 1905. Developments in the nomenclature of disease were possible only after the bacteriologic advances and the establishment of the belief in the specificity of organisms, namely, that they bred true. Moreover, this belief enabled diverse manifestations of a microbial infection to be seen as due to a single cause, for example, consumption and spinal caries, caused by the tuberculosis bacillus.

For those hoping to follow the course of individual diseases over a long period of time, the most optimistic statement can be that, notwithstanding the various revisions of the international classifications, some diseases can be traced back to 1880 and others earlier still with some confidence. Nevertheless, a warning is given that careful examination of the definitions used must be made if errors are to be avoided in making comparisons over time and between countries.

In chapter 3 some general remarks are made on the measurement of mortality and a few techniques are explained. In chapter 4 a short discussion is given on fertility and the dynamics of population growth.

In chapter 5 general properties of the infectious diseases, or more precisely the diseases of organismal origin, are treated, giving appropriate emphasis to points important in other parts of the book; thus, population size is critical for the perpetuation and fade-out of diseases with properties like measles. Some stress is laid on the importance of the zoonoses, that is, infective diseases of animals, and their transmission to man as anthropozoonoses, of which the most spectacular example has been bubonic plague; but an important if less known shared infection is epidemic influenza. The zoonoses are often responsible for variations in disease incidence between regions. We mention that the great modern pandemic of plague and the occurrence of yellow fever and malaria in the tropical areas led to experimental studies of the epidemic process in laboratories under W.W.C. Topley in England and L.T. Webster in the United States just after World War I. We believe that such experimental work has been far more successful than the mathematical theory of epidemics in leading to useful knowledge.

In chapters 6 to 34, diseases are described with few exceptions in the order of the *International Classification of Diseases*; however, influenza has been treated among the viral diseases and famine is brought back from ICD 994.2 to the chapter bearing on nutritional diseases; war has been given a separate chapter; hospital gangrene, happily not indexed in the ICD, is treated in a special section of the chapter on other bacterial diseases, ICD 030–041. In chapters 6 to 19 we discuss the various organismal diseases. There are some diseases, such as plague, malaria, tuberculosis, and measles, that have played an important role in world mortality, to which we have given additional sections with headings such as "typhus as a great pestilence," a term used to avoid the confusion introduced by the word, plague.

In chapters 32, 35, and 36 mortality rates are given for the various age groups. This has the advantage of giving easy comparisons between the diseases of childhood. In chapters 37 to 44 discussions of mortality in various countries and continents are given.

The factors in the declines of mortality are discussed in chapters 45 to 47, first the role of various forms of therapy, then general aspects of hygiene and ecology and variations between subpopulations and classes. In chapter 48 we discuss the relative importance of some diseases before and after the general declines in mortality. The epilogue gives an overall summary of the relationships between man and his diseases and accidents, from early man to the present, with some speculations on the future.

As every effort has been made to bring official mortality into contact with microbiology, epidemiology, economic history, and so on, there is an extensive bibliography, of which most entries are used in the discussions of particular topics.

Chapter 1
Mortality and the Evolution of Society

1.1 Disease and Mortality in Tribal Societies

The first questions posed by intelligent laymen to the author are the following: How far back in time can one compute mortality rates? How far back in time can one obtain counts of deaths by recognizable disease? The first of these questions is answered in this chapter and the second in Chapter 2. Of course, we cannot hope to go deeply into the various diseases and their frequencies in this chapter, but we can at least point to the deficiencies of the data and give an idea of the lost possibilities due to time and to the absence in past times of a knowledge of science combined with the lack of a strong centralized and literate bureaucracy, essential for the collection of mortality statistics.

We begin with a diversion, the study of mortality in tribal peoples, that is, in peoples living together in small isolated population units with a primitive technology (referred to as tribal man as opposed to caucasoid man) in many parts of the world. Caucasoid man earns his name from the historical fact that European man has usually, but not invariably, been the intruder in many regions of all the continents. The survey of tribal man here precedes that of early man because it is necessary to underline the absence of real knowledge and the confusion between facts and inference in many discussions of early man.

Some typical tribal peoples are the Amerindians of the Amazon valley or of Tierra del Fuego, the Australian aborigines, island peoples of the Pacific, and the Eskimo. Such tribal peoples have been studied, for example in Elliott and Whelan (1977), Gajdusek (1977a), and Black (1980), with two scientific aims, namely, to throw light on the evolution and mutation of diseases, especially those due to the respiratory viruses, and to assist in establishing models of the style of life, health, immunology, and mortality of ancient man. With respect to this last aim, it must be pointed out that after the spread of the great Asian, African, and European civilizations, the isolated communities in all the other great land masses did not enjoy the same degree of isolation as did the Australian (especially Tasmanian) and American populations before 1490, so that they inevitably carry a greater load of disease than ancient man. We consider the diseases in the order of the International Classification of Diseases (ICD), (WHO-manual, 1977/1978) the use of which for the general purposes of this book is justified elsewhere. General statements on why some diseases are likely or unlikely to be present in the tribal societies are given in §§5.2 through 5.7, and there are also commentaries on the special diseases in Chapters 6 through 19. We give a double numbering, the second referring to the chapter of the disease(s).

In the tribal societies:

(*i*.6) Among the intestinal infectious agents, only amebiasis and, perhaps, salmonella infections acquired from animal sources are present.

(*ii*.7) Tuberculosis, being an infection of long standing, may be present but is a rarity in untouched tribes.

(*iii*.8) Zoonotic bacterial diseases will appear sporadically if the tribe is located near a nidus for the particular agent, for example, plague in the Himalayan region or in central Africa, or tularemia in North America.

(*iv*.9, 10) "Other bacterial diseases," for example, leprosy, diphtheria, pertussis, acute poliomyelitis, and slow virus infection of the central nervous system will rarely be present.

(*v*.11) Chickenpox, herpes zoster, and herpes simplex A and B may be present, since these infections can persist for long periods in the body.

(*vi*.11) Smallpox, cowpox, measles, and rubella will not have been present except as a short incident in the group's existence (see Black, Pinheiro, et al., 1977).

(*vii*.12) Occasional sporadic infections may appear from the groups of arthropod-borne viral diseases, including sylvatic yellow fever.

(*viii*.14) Viral hepatitis can be perpetuated in small groups, but the other diseases due to viruses and chlamydias are either unimportant or cannot be perpetuated in a small group, for example, mumps.

(*ix*.15) Malaria can be perpetuated in small groups, but a tribe living in a temperate climate and nomadic in the warmer months would be quite free of it; louse-borne (epidemic) typhus will not occur, but other members of the rickettsioses and other arthropod-borne diseases may occur sporadically, usually as zoonoses.

(*x*.10, 26) Influenza and most other respiratory infections will either be absent or occur in intense epidemics with a clear termination.

(*xi*.16) Tribal man may be affected by leishmaniasis, trypanosomiasis, relapsing fever, and bartonellosis; moreover, trypanosomiasis may kill his cattle, for example, nagana in tropical Africa.

(*xii*.17, 18) Syphilis and gonorrhea will usually be absent, although yaws may be present.

(*xiii*.19) Hookworm disease and the common helminths may be present; occasionally, trichinosis is introduced into small primitive tribes through infected pigs; toxoplasma infections may be perpetuated.

(*xiv*.26) Tribal people do not suffer the attacks of the numerous viruses that cause upper respiratory tract infections.

(*xv*.33, 34) Deaths may be common from intertribal warfare; there may be attacks by large carnivores and venomous snakes, drownings may occur, or compound fractures may be fatal. Among natural disasters, volcanic activity may destroy villages or homelands, typhoons may submerge coral islands, local droughts or floods may destroy crops or food; even with less dramatic events, it may be difficult in a small community to smooth out the extremes of want and plenty that are brought about by chance events in the hunting and gathering band or by the sequential ripening of wild or cultivated crops.

(*xvi*.22) A small isolated community may not be able to adjust to a change in climate, for example, the Norsemen in Greenland in the fourteenth century. There may be extreme deficiency of essential elements in the soil such as iodine or sodium; there may be unusual exposures to toxins in the diet or drinking water, for example, excessive cult use of kava in the New Hebrides or intoxicating snuff in the South American Indians.

(*xvii*.22, 25, 27) Tribal man does not suffer from many diseases common in civilized, especially western European-type, societies, such as appendicitis, cholecystitis, high blood pressure, and certain cardiovascular diseases.

For studies on the diseases of tribal man, see also Black (1966, 1975); Black, Hierholzer, et al. (1974); Hoffman (1932); Nurse and Jenkins (1977); and Polunin (1967). Fractures in modern wild apes have been studied by Schultz (1939) as a comparison with tribal man.

1.2 Early Man

The evidence on mortality in man and his precursors from 100,000 years BP to the present can be summarized as in Brothwell (1967, figure 1). Before 100,000 years BP, in the paleolithic age, there are only a few skeletal remains; cranial injuries and dental-defective disease, following difficulties with mastication of coarse food, are the only findings. From 100,000 to 10,000 years BP, skeletons show evidence of fractures of bones, especially the cranial, of osteoarthroses, and of oral diseases following wearing down of teeth. It can be concluded that *little positive knowledge* besides these findings is available. Black (1980) believes that the principal causes of death in early man were abortion, infanticide, accident, and war. For other researches and monographs, see Acsádi and Nemeskéri (1970), Binford (1981), Brothwell and Sandison (1967), Dunn (1968), Hart (1984), Janssens (1970), Jarcho (1966), Landy (1977) with an extensive bibliography, Price and Brown (1985), Törő, Szabady, Nemeskéri, and Eiben (1972), Vallois (1937), Wells (1964), and Zimmermann and Kelley (1982). For paleonutrition and food crises, see Cohen (1977) and Wing and Brown (1979). A counterexample to estimates of the expectation of life at birth, suggested by such researches, is given in §3.11. For ancient diseases of the blood, see Hart (1980). For paleopathology, see Kliks (1983).

1.3 Agricultural Man and Egypt

From approximately 7,000 years BP, with increasing sizes of the human populations, the numbers of artifacts and skeletons available for study increase greatly. For example, in predynastic Egypt bodies were buried in dry sand and underwent rapid desiccation, preserving them to be examined by G.E. Smith and others before the construction of the Aswan High Dam. Other examples of natural preservation of the soft tissues of the body are supplied by the bog burials in Denmark and by bodies buried in soil with high salt content. Sandison (1980) in Cockburn and Cockburn (1980) summarizes the finds in the Egyptian mummies. There are 31 cases of tuberculosis, definitely diagnosable in Egyptian mummies, ranging in time from 3,700 to 1,000 BC according to Morse (1967) and Morse, Brothwell, and Ucko (1964). Sandison (1980) believes that the possibility of diagnosing tuberculosis in many other mummies has been overlooked. It is believed that tuberculosis was probably of the bovine type (see §7.1). No certain evidence of syphilis has been obtained. The ova of *Schistosoma hematobium* have been identified on several occasions; their earliest appearance is not stated. Gallstones have been found on

several occasions. Osteoarthritis, osteomyelitis and mastoid disease have been often identified. The helminths, *Ascaris* and *Taenia*, have also been identified.

Although so much work has been done on the pathology of the ancient Egyptians, it is impossible to make any statement on the relative importance of the diseases in causing death, nor are there any data that would assist us in calculating mortality rates by age.

1.4 Evolution of Human Disease

At the time of his differentiation from other primate species, probably in Africa, man was a hunter-gatherer. In Europe early man lived most of the time as nomad in summer and if the climate were severe he lived in closely confined caves in winter (Fiennes, 1978). Possibly population aggregates of more than a few hundred were rare. With the coming of the neolithic age, agriculture and stock rearing began; larger communities were formed and, finally, cities. There is very little evidence of pathology in the skeletal remains other than that previously mentioned in §1.2, although more is known about mode of life, nutrition, and religion from the archeological findings.

A principal cause of death in tribes around 10,000 years BP would have been accident and injury, including attacks by carnivores.

The various infections are now briefly mentioned, as possible human pathogens in the ages before the large agricultural settlements, in the order of the ICD.

Intestinal Infectious Diseases. It appears that the cholera vibrio arose in the Indian subcontinent, and cholera (ICD 001) may well have been closely limited to a few of its river systems until the time of the great movements of persons engaged in trade and war. The bacilli causing the other diseases in this subclass are closely related to normal commensals of the bowel. Moreover, the carrier state is known for many of them, and so problems of perpetuation are not as great for them as, for example, measles. It is possible that enteric fevers, dysenteries, and nonspecific bowel infections were present from the earliest times.

Tuberculosis. Possibly after the domestication of cattle, a mutation occurred in the bovine bacillus, *Mycobacterium bovis*, to the human type. Owing to its chronicity, tuberculosis would have been able to perpetuate itself in the small communities. However, it has not been present in many modern day, isolated communities, and possibly it can be thought of as a common or even true human disease only after the development of the agricultural societies.

Zoonotic Bacterial Diseases (ICD 020–027). It is possible that before historical times bubonic plague was confined to a single focus or region, either in Africa or in Asia, and played an insignificant role in human life as does the modern tularemia in America.

Other Bacterial Diseases (ICD 030–041). Møller-Christensen (1966, 1967) believes that there is no positive evidence for leprosy before AD 500. Possibly infections with any of these organisms were rare or nonexistent before the rise of the great urban populations.

Nonarthropod-borne Viral Diseases (ICD 045–049) and Viral Diseases Accompanied by Exanthem (ICD 050–057). These diseases, particularly measles and smallpox, could not have been perpetuated in the small communities (see §§5.1 and 5.2).

All Other Infective Diseases. We may briefly dismiss all the other diseases listed in ICD 045–049 and 060–139, with the exception of some diseases to which we refer throughout this monograph as the great pestilences.

Yellow Fever. There is a good evidence that the mosquito *Aedes aegypti* and yellow fever virus evolved in Africa and were carried to the Americas in slave ships. Yellow fever would have been a great risk to tribes hoping to extend their territory into the jungles of Africa.

Typhus. Man wintering in caves may well have suffered from this disease, which may be considered to have been a zoonosis at that time.

Malaria. Possibly malaria has not been a threat to nomadic man; it would often have been such to men living in the jungles or in agricultural land in the tropics and subtropics. See §15.5 for the arguments on the origin of

the disease in Africa or Asia; it seems to have been in both continents in prehistoric times.

Acute and Chronic Respiratory Infections (ICD 460–487). The common diseases of modern times such as coryza, "influenza," and lobar pneumonia may have been uncommon in the days of early man.

Further information on the evolution of organisms can be found in the chapter dealing with the particular organism and also in Chapter 5. For the evolution of man's response to microbic infection, see Chapter 31. There is no evidence that early man in a state of nature before the development of agriculture was ever submitted to such heavy rates of infection as have been observed in the great modern cities, except, perhaps, in hyperendemic malaria areas.

1.5 Mortality in the Classical World

The classical world of ancient Greece and Rome can be approached more hopefully. Hippocrates (ca 460–370 BC) and his school have left descriptions of disease syndromes that enable confident diagnoses to be made now, and this applies also to Galen in Antonine times in Rome. Some fragments of the numerous estimates of the population at the times of Roman censuses are known, so there is some evidence on population size and numbers in the army (Brunt, 1971). Gomme (1933, reprinted 1967) ends a discussion of sources and facts known on the population of Greece and, in particular, Athens by concluding that it will always be impossible to attempt a "social structure of Greece," matching similar works on modern populations. Comparatively little seems to be known about the slave population size in either Greece or Rome. Age-specific or even crude mortality rates cannot be computed for either free or slave populations for either Greece or Rome. We, therefore, can deal with only a few themes.

Bubonic Plague

According to W. Shadwell and H.L. Hennessy, writing in Vol. 21, pp. 693–705 in the 11th Edition of the *Encyclopaedia Britannica*, London, 1911; J. Mahé on pp. 641–752 of Raige-

Delorme and Dechambre, *Dictionnaire ency-clopédique des sciences médicales*, Paris, 1864–1889; and Biraben (1975/1976), there are traditions preserved in Livy (*lx, Epitome*) and more fully by Orosius (*Historia, iv*, II) that a great pestilence was present in Libya, Egypt, and Syria toward the end of the third century BC but it did not pass over into Europe. Descriptions of cases by Dioscorides and Posidonius, whose dates are not precisely known, have been preserved in Orobasios (Book 44, Chapter 17); these authors give precise descriptions of buboes that have been accepted by modern commentators as firm evidence of bubonic plague. The pestilence mentioned by Livy as occurring in 127 BC in the same areas also might well have been bubonic plague; it is said to have destroyed a million persons in Africa (the province), but no clinical observations are extant.

This interpretation of plague along the Mediterranean shores is in accord with the views of MacArthur (1952), who believes that the pestilence of ca 1320 BC mentioned in the Bible in the book of Samuel 1, *v* and *vi*, is plague. This pestilence has been much discussed. According to Hirst (1953), the word "ofalim" meaning a hill or hills in the original Hebrew was altered to "t'chorim" by later scribes of the Old Testament because of offensive sexual implications in the original word. So, in the Vulgate version and in the authorized English version, there appears the phrase, "emerods in the private parts," which has been variously interpreted as meaning buboes or hemorrhoids. This latter interpretation has inclined some commentators to believe that the pestilence was dysentery, but others believe that buboes were meant and the Revised Version of the English Bible has "tumours in their private parts," which could be interpreted without difficulty as buboes.

Smallpox

Littman and Littman (1969) have convincingly argued that the "plague of Athens," so carefully described by Thucydides, was smallpox. Farr (1885, p. 321) astutely stresses the importance of the arrival in the city of many countrymen. Littman and Littman (1973) give equally good

arguments to suggest that the Antonine plague, commencing during the reign of Marcus Aurelius in AD 165 or 166, brought home from a Persian war and lasting some years, perhaps up to the reign of Commodus in AD 189, was also due to smallpox. They believe that Galen, writing in the style of the school of Hippocrates, suppressed or thought unimportant some observations on the rash. Gilliam (1961) believes that "descriptions of pestilence in any period are likely to be highly colored and extravagent. Like battles, they tempt writers to display their talents and make the most of their material, following established patterns . . . Nevertheless, . . . it seems probable, though by no means certain, that it caused more deaths than any other epidemic during the Empire before the middle of the third century." He estimates the losses, due to smallpox in the Antonine plague, at perhaps 7–10% overall in the Empire and perhaps as high as 13–15% in Rome and some other great cities. He believes that the epidemic was serious and important but by no means decisive for the decline of the Roman Empire. Historians may be asking the wrong question. They might be better asking why the Empire lasted so long.

Malaria

Ronald Ross, after determining the method of infection with the malaria parasite through the anopheline mosquitoes, visited Greece in 1906 and was inspired by the havoc wrought there in modern times to suggest that malaria was a leading cause in the decay of the Greco-Roman civilization there in classical times. Although malaria can be diagnosed from the case histories of Hippocrates, who evidently met with cases of benign tertian and of quartan malaria but not malignant tertian malaria, Celsus in Augustan times has left us case histories, some identifiable as malignant tertian malaria. Following the suggestion of Ross (1906), classical historian W.H.S. Jones (1909) concluded from a search of the extant ancient Greek literature that the importance of malaria in Greece had increased in the centuries from Hippocrates up to the time of the fall of the western Roman Empire. Ross's conclusion on the importance of malaria has been accepted by Angelo Celli

(1933), Hackett (1937), Russell (1955), Zulueta (1973), and Bruce-Chwatt and Zulueta (1980) among modern malariologists and by McNeill (1976) among the historians.

In this discussion the climatic and ecological conditions in modern times cannot be equated with those in classical times without further enquiry. As Bruce-Chwatt and Zulueta (1980) point out, European man lived free of malaria during a great part of the Pleistocene period because the sporogonic cycle in the mosquito could not have been completed at the low temperatures. Further, according to Zulueta (1973), the most effective anopheline vectors were absent from Europe during the colder periods; indeed, after the passing of the cold periods, the two most effective vectors did not penetrate into the Aegean area, Italy, and Spain until extensive deforestation of Hellenistic and Roman times had created suitable conditions for them. There were other more technical interactions between parasite and host as explained by these authors. The general conclusion is that malignant tertian malaria was not present or prevalent before imperial times. This seems to be borne out by historical accounts of army operations which were not hampered by malarialike diseases in republican times; in the civil war, the two sides of Octavian and Anthony had large armies operating around Actium and Dyrrachium on the west coast of Greece, where malaria was later to be hyperendemic, without any malarialike diseases. Brue-Chwatt and Zulueta (1980, p. 90) state that "the three species of malaria parasites were present in Italy by the second century AD"; they are prepared to give an important, but not dominant, role to malaria. There were, surely, many other factors to consider even prior to the beginning of the second century AD as we now note. Hughes and Thirgood (1982) point out that deforestation also led to impoverishment of the soil.

War and Roman Population

A discussion by Brunt (1971) shows the difficulties of assessing the effect of war on the Italian population. He gives an estimate for 225 BC of 0.9 million Romans and, in all, 3 million free persons in Italy, excluding Cisalpine Gaul, which had a population not exceeding 1.4 million. He casts doubts on previous estimates of the losses in the great battles; thus, he puts the losses at Trasimene in 217 BC and at Cannae in 216 BC as 25 and 30 thousand, respectively. The "total mortality in the army from 218 to 203 would then have been about 120,000." Now Brunt (1971, p. 422) points out that "some 70,000 of the war casualties would in any event have died in these years," so that the net loss would have been only 50,000; but this is a fallacious method of computation, for let us add all the men given in his Table X. There are thus approximately 1 million man years at risk in the legions over the years 218 to 201 BC, inclusive. Allowing for a high rate of mortality, 2% per annum, one can set the expected peace time deaths at 2% of 1 million = 20 thousand. So, the net loss due to war in the legions would have been 100,000 and not 50,000. Brunt (1971) presumes that the loyal allies "suffered in proportion, and the rebels probably worse," as a result of famines and epidemics. To obtain an idea of the effect on the population, an average may be struck, about 120,000/16 = 7.5 thousand deaths per annum in the 16 years, 218–203. These deaths occurred in a population of 0.9 million and so represent a population loss of 8 per thousand per annum, about three times the intensity of loss occasioned in Great Britain in the 1914–1918 war, but prolonged over 16 years. Some authors have claimed that the devastations in Italy were worse in the Social War, although they were less prolonged than in the Hannibalic wars.

Mortality in the Free Population

According to Brunt (1971, p. 121) there were not more than 4.4 million free persons in Italy in 225 BC. Persons with Roman citizenship numbered 5 million in 28 BC and 6.2 million in AD 14; of these, perhaps 1 million were living abroad in 28 BC. He deduces a decline in the old Italian stocks living in Italy. In his Chapter 11, Brunt (1971) claims high mortality and family limitation, principally by infanticide, as the causes. It can be seen that even if total deaths were known it would be impossible to give even a crude death rate.

Tombstone Evidence

In view of such a lack of age-specific or crude death rates, some authors, for example, Burn (1953), have taken note of the names, sex, and ages on tombstones and considered them to be representative of the deaths in the general (free) population, really middle and lower middle class, with a high proportion of centurions, noncommissioned officers, and some auxiliary soldiers. In more modern times, these authors have linked suitable ancient data with modern data to give life tables, after making assumptions on the general level of mortality. Hopkins (1966) gives good reasons for abandoning all such attempts at the construction of life tables or calculating death rates, for it is easy to see that the deaths of children, especially infants, will be underrepresented, and that if the two parents die close together neither will be represented. Moreover, famines or wars will cause conditions unfavorable to representation and so on.

Slavery

Historians of Rome, such as Theodor Mommsen, believe that the miseries of modern slavery are but a drop compared with the ocean of Roman times. Possibly this was not so in the earlier days of Rome when only a few slaves belonged to any given familia; but, with the coming of large scale capitalism in the later republic, the lot of the slaves deteriorated. Thousands of them could then belong to the one owner or familia; many such were employed in large factories in the agricultural areas, in the galleys, and in the great pastoral estates. At night they were locked up in buildings, often partly subterranean and with windows high up in the walls. See also Westermann (1942) for industrial slavery. The slaves had often been recruited after successful military campaigns in earlier times, but later after systematic slave hunts in the present Asia Minor. Heavy penalties were inflicted for misconduct; many of the worst offenders were sent to the mines and quarries, where they survived only a few years. Others were forced or volunteered to become gladiators (Auguet, 1972). In Nero's time, according to an old law over 400 slaves were executed on one occasion because their master had been murdered. Of course, in many cases the slaves looked forward to a chance of manumission or escape, but the lot of many was hopeless, so there were instances of mass escapes sometimes reaching the magnitude of slave wars, the most famous of which, associated with the name of Spartacus, occurred in 73–71 BC; ten legions were required to combat them in 71 BC and it is believed that over 100,000 slaves were slain in battle and over 6,000 crucified in southern Italy.

Roman Patriciate

Mortality was probably also high among the Roman patricians, first, because of the necessity for military service and, second, the proscriptions of the civil wars. No holder of any of the original clan names held office in the senate after about AD 200. It is well known that no line, descendant from Augustus or his adopted son Tiberius, survived.

Nationality Struggles

During imperial times there was reluctance of the free Romans to enroll in the army. Tribal groups, principally German, were allowed to settle within the Empire to serve as troops, especially to guard the borders; some of them rose to the highest ranks. There was then jealousy between the Latin and German elements. Inroads by the barbarians continued throughout the later Empire, the Saracens, Norsemen, and Magyars being of great importance (see Petersen, 1975, p. 428).

We refer the reader to Beloch (1886, 1897) for population, Boak (1955) for manpower, and Gapp (1933) for famines of the reign of Claudius. See Gwei-Djen and Needham (1967) for disease conditions in China contemporary with Roman times and Grmek (1983) for disease at the dawn of Western civilization.

1.6 Middle Ages

After the breakdown of the western Roman world and the gradual decline of the Byzantine Empire, there are few literary sources.

Manorial Records

Much evidence on diet, malnutrition, and famine and some on mortality has been obtained by the study of records of the manor, the important center of social and economic life before 1600. Much of this material has been published in the literature of economic or general history, for example, Parain (1966), Hutchinson et al. (1977), Slicher van Bath (1963), and Le Roy Ladurie and Goy (1982).

Ecclesiastical and Legal Records

Russell (1948a), from the inquisitiones post mortem for landowners, and Campbell (1931) and Gasquet (1908), from the lists of the holders of church benefices, were able to give estimates of mortality caused by the Black Death.

Genealogical Records

Many genealogies on the noble families of Europe exist; these noble families were sufficiently numerous to ensure that the sampling errors in calculating age-specific rates are moderate. It can be argued that almost all these records refer to elite classes. Only when the parish records are available for the early modern period can the results be representative of the whole population, for the elite classes did not suffer greatly from famine, although they would have suffered death rates from war and war games much higher than those of the population at large. Nevertheless, it is of interest that the death rates of these elite classes rose during the Thirty Years War.

Guy (1845) summarizes the experience of the classes covered by *Sharpe's Peerage*, 1830, and *Debrett's Baronetage*, 1832, in those cases where the age was expressly stated or admitted of calculation, omitting those who had died by accidents, violence, poison, or in battle. We give his results in the form, epoch, number of of males observed, and estimated expectation of life at age 21 years in Table 1.6.1. Neglecting the means before AD 1500, it is clear that there had been no increase in the expectation of life of males at age 21 years between 1500 and 1745. Guy (1846) amplifies these observations separating out peerage and baronetage,

TABLE 1.6.1. Expectation of life at age 21 years among the aristocracy of England from AD 1200 through 1745.

Epoch	No. of males observed	Estimated (further) expectation of life at 21 years (years)
1200–1300	7	43.14
1300–1400	9	24.44*
1400–1500	23	48.11
1500–1550	52	50.27
1550–1600	100	47.25
1600–1650	192	42.95
1650–1700	346	41.40
1700–1745	812	43.13

*The low figure in 1300–1400 reflects the effects of the Black Death.
From Guy (1845).
Explanatory note: Guy (1845) gave "expectation of life at birth" as expectation of life at 25 years + 25 years that is, $\overset{0}{e}_0 = \overset{0}{e}_{25} + 25$, which is not admissable.

gentry, professions, and females of the upper classes. This larger experience enables us to assign local minima to 1300–1400 and 1650–1700, and maxima to the epoch 1500–1550. As Guy (1846) points out, there may be some bias upward in the figures cited in this paper because of details of collection. He cites some figures from F.G.P. Neison (1845, 1846) comparing expectation of life with sexes combined at age 30 years, in peerage and baronetage, 30.9; gentry, 31.2; professions, 33.9; agricultural laborers' friendly societies, 40.6; England, 34.1, and Liverpool friendly societies, 30.1. He believed the agricultural laborers, with their daily exercise in a pure atmosphere and with prudent and temperate habits, had the advantage over the other classes represented in his table.

Guy (1847) extends his survey to hereditary sovereigns who constitute a less satisfactory class; he excludes all who have died by accidents, violence, poison, and in battle. The sovereigns still have a less favorable experience than the aristocracy and gentry of England.

Henry (1965a) also studied the mortality of the British nobility, including all their sons and daughters. He calculated the proportions dying before 20 years of age in a table showing a plateau for the British rates of about 0.380 for the 25-year epochs included in 1625–1750. He compared these rates with his own statistics of Genevan families. The Genevan rates commence at a much higher level 0.519 and by about 1850 have fallen below the British noble levels. At this time both rates are markedly below the contemporary general rates for England and Wales. Indeed, for the epoch 1850–1899, the British noble, Genevan, and England-Wales proportions dying before age 20 years are 0.118, 0.094, and 0.305, respectively. The same rates, which we may write as $_{20}q_0$, are compared with Peller's German ruling families, 1500–1599, 0.320; 1600–1699, 0.410; 1700–1799, 0.345; 1800–1849, 0.230; 1850–1899, 0.100; and 1900–1930, 0.036. Henry (1965a) believes that the plateau effect is genuine for there is the same plateau for $_{25}q_{15}$, that is, the proportion dying between 15 and 40 years, precisely, over the years 1600–1750.

Peller (1943), studying the mortality of the German ruling families, gives a number of interesting results and comments too long to be adequately summarized here. The age-specific death rates of women in these families, married in 1500–1599 (1600–1699) are given as percentages in his Table 4 and Graph 2 as follows: under 19 years, 1.2 (0.20); 20–24, 1.4 (1.13); 25–29, 1.9 (1.73); 30–34, 1.5 (2.07); 35–39, 2.3 (2.25); 40–44, 2.9 (2.78); and 45–49, 3.6 (2.37). These rates are very high by modern standards, for example, see Table 3.7.1. In the sixteenth and seventeenth centuries, 11.3% of fertile women died from complications of childbearing.

In the same periods, stillborn plus neonatal deaths amounted together to 100 and 107.5 per thousand, respectively, with deaths counted up to the end of the first year, the corresponding rates were 193 and 246 per thousand. The rate for offspring of parents marrying in 1850–1930 was 18.5 per thousand.

Survival rates for children were low; l_{16} (see §4.1) was 0.701 in the sixteenth century and 0.617 in the seventeenth century, a time of wars including the Thirty Years War, 1618–1648. Peller (1944) finds that l_{16} was 0.64 for singletons and 0.31 for twins in the sixteenth and seventeenth centuries. Since 1800 the l_{16} were 0.85 for singletons and 0.79 for twins, with $l_0 = 1$.

Peller (1947) reports chiefly on the mortality of men. He believes that mortality in the sixteenth and seventeenth centuries was possibly at the same level as in ancient Rome. He reports in his Table 16 that 9.8% of the deaths of bachelors and 2.2% of the deaths of married men were due to war. Many comparisons are available in Peller (1948, 1965). We also refer the reader to Russell (1941) for mortality in the period AD 200–900 and to Beloch (1900) for population.

1.7 Parish Records

Although there were no general instructions on their maintenance, the parish records of medieval Europe had been improving with the progress in literacy, the easier communications, and the availability of paper, which together made possible more extensive bureaucracies and, hence, heightened the interest in local records for the central governing bodies of church and state. A need was felt at the time of the Reformation to establish statistical records on church affiliation. At the Council of Trent (1545–1563) obligatory rules were made for the recording of baptisms, marriages, and burials in all Catholic parishes. The earliest parish records in existence are said to be for Givry in Burgundy (Mols, 1954–1956; Hollingsworth, 1969). Parish registers had been inaugurated in most European countries by the end of the sixteenth century. Of course, for the successful use of the parish records as demographic data, it is necessary that the particular, usually state or national, religion should be accepted by the great majority of the population, otherwise the results may be disappointing as in the United Kingdom and in some overseas extensions of the European nations. In any case, for the collection and survival of this type of records, they must be secure from the hazards of war, civil strife, fire, and neglect. Goubert (1960) provides a notable example of analysis of such records in his *Beauvais et le Beauvaisis*. Parish records have been analyzed also to provide good demographic accounts of the devastation caused by the Thirty Years War (Franz, 1961; Keyser, 1941; Westermanns Atlas, 1956).

In Europe demographers have done much work on the old parish records. In the north many studies have been made in the nordic countries. To the east valuable data commencing in 1613 have been obtained from parishes near Stockerau, some 50 kilometers up the Danube from Vienna (Lehners, 1973). Little can be expected from east of Vienna because of the unsettled nature of the frontier area of the Turkish hegemony. To the south, for Italy, Spain, and Portugal, many records have become available. The French demographers particularly, under the influence of L. Henry (b. 1911), have obtained excellent estimates of mortality before the beginnings of the official secular centralized series; we defer discussion on them until the mortality of France is considered in a later chapter.

The churches in the seventeenth and eighteenth centuries were not only interested in the ceremonies of birth, death, and marriage, but the state religion constituted the leading bureaucracy in the state. Furthermore, the parish data could be consolidated into larger aggregates such as the diocese and further consolidated to include the whole state. Modern official statistics thus evolved in Sweden out of the parish records. Indeed, by carrying out such consolidations, the modern official statisticians have been able to extend their present day series back toward the early eighteenth century as in the countries of Norden.

Extensive data of a kind similar to parish records are available from the temple records in Japan (see Suda and Soekawa, 1983).

(See also Le Roy Ladurie and Goy, 1982, and §4.3.)

1.8 General References on Population and Mortality

In this section we give a list of general references, many of which are not explicitly referred to in the text, but that may be of use of the reader.

Biography. Many useful and enlightening biographies of medical scientists are given in the *Dictionary of Scientific Biography*, Scribners, 1970–1980; in our name index such are distinguished by an asterisk. Details of biographies of perhaps several dozen more are given in Lancaster (1982c).

History of Medicine. Clarke (1971), Debus (1974), Garrison (1933), Lyons and Petrucelli (1979), Mettler (1947), Morton (1983), Poynter (1965, 1968), Rosen (1958), Singer and Underwood (1962), Temkin (1977), Underwood (1953), Wangensteen and Wangensteen (1978), Wightman (1971), Youngson (1979).

Medical Specialties. bacteriology and microbiology: Braude, Davis, and Fierer (1986), Bulloch (1938/1960), Clark (1961), Dubos (1954), Ford (1939), Foster (1970), Lechevalier and Solotorovsky (1965), Scott (1939), Smith (1985).

clinical pathology: Foster (1961).

culture, disease and healing: Landy (1977), Rothschild and Chapman (1981).

developing countries and economic change: Easterlin (1980), Glass and Revelle (1972), Preston (1980).

disease and death: Cartwright (1972), Clegg and Clegg (1973), Silverstein (1979).

exanthemata: Rolleston (1937).

global epidemiology and mapping of disease: Doll (1984), Howe (1971), May (1961).

health and disease, speculation: Hobson (1963), Wynder, Hertzberg and Parker (1981).

infectious disease: Creighton (1891, 1894, 1965), Haeser (1862, 1882), Hecker (1832–1844), Hirsch (1883–1886), Ransome (1881–1882), Sticker (1908–1912), Winslow (1943, 1952).

medical and demographic statistics: Bernoulli (1841), Greenwood (1948b), Prinzing (1930–1931), Suessmilch (1761–1762), Westergaard (1880, 1882).

military medicine: Garrison (1929).

mortality, international comparisons: Alderson (1981), Benjamin (1966, 1973a, 1974), Chase (1969, 1972), McKeown (1971), McKeown and Record (1962), Manton and

Stallard (1984), Pressat (1972, 1978), Preston (1974, 1976, 1977a, 1980), Preston, Keyfitz, et al. (1972), Preston and Nelson (1974), Preston and Weed (1976), Stolnitz (1955, 1956a, b, 1957, 1975).

mycology: Ainsworth (1976).

parasitology: Faust (1955), Foster (1965), Garnham (1971).

pharmacy: Poynter (1968).

philosophy and ecology: Croll and Cross (1983), Dubos (passim), Ehrlich, Holdren and Holm (1971), Hobson (1963), Wynder, Hertzberg and Parker (1981).

preventive medicine: Greenwood (1948a), Howard-Jones (1980), Wain (1970).

surgery: Cartwright (1967), Wangensteen and Wangensteen (1978).

technology, medical: Daumas (1962), Reiser (1978).

therapeutics: Ackerknecht (1973).

tropical disease: Scott (1939).

World Population. Black (1789/1973), Deevey (1971), Glass and Grebenik (1965), Keyfitz and Flieger (1968), Petersen (1975), Törö, Szabady, et al. (1972), Trewartha (1969).

World Population History. Hauser and Duncan (1959), Lorimer (1959), McEvedy and Jones (1978), Petersen (1975), Reinhard, Armengaud, and Dupâquier (1961), Russell (1941, 1958), Wallace (1753, 1761).

Chapter 2
Identification and Classification of Diseases

2.1 Introduction

If the progress of mortality is to be traced over time, it is necessary to have some account of the progress in the observation and understanding of the disease processes by the contemporary observers. Although this is part of the history of medicine, we recall in this chapter some advances, dates, and persons to show the difficulties in attempting to trace back the frequencies of particular diseases into past times or to assign, now, the cause of disease in individuals or of epidemics.

The signs and symptoms had first to be described. Early observers, especially Hippocrates, recognized groups of signs and symptoms—the syndromes. After Hippocrates there was relatively little progress in the grouping of these syndromes, which may be called the taxonomy problem, into meaningful taxa (singular, taxon) until the late eighteenth century. Indeed, the history of medicine illustrates the difficulties of constructing taxa by the unaided senses; for example, the confusion between scarlatina and measles and between typhoid fever and typhus persisted into the late nineteenth century. Extensions of the ideas of Linnaeus (1707–1778) to a hierarchical classification of diseases failed. Progress in the taxonomy of diseases had to await developments in human anatomy, physiology, and pathology, which we discuss in §2.2, and the correlation of the pathological findings with the clinical observations.

It was found that many diseases were caused by organisms, and the rise of bacteriology and related sciences is mentioned in §2.3. An important consequence of the bacteriologic studies was the recognition that some diseases "bred true" and were strictly definable entities. However, even today, satisfactory definitions of disease entities are lacking in many clinical syndromes, especially in the cardiovascular and renal systems. Indeed, there still remains much work to be done in clearing up the etiology of disease not caused by infection, accident and injury, poisonings, malnutrition and starvation, and some genetic deficiencies. We give in Table 2.1.1 the authors and the dates of publication of descriptions of some well-known syndromes.

Once the disease syndromes have been established, it is necessary to name them: this is the problem of nomenclature, treated in §2.4. For the purpose of clinical medicine, science, or statistics, it is necessary to gather the syndromes or diseases together in a classification. This problem is treated generally in §2.5 and more particularly in §2.6, in which the international classifications of diseases for statistical purposes are described. This leads on to a discussion of the use of coding rules in §§2.7 and 2.8 and some illustrative examples, indicating that care must be taken in making comparisons in disease frequency over time or between countries.

2.2 Some Advances in Pathology

There had been great difficulties in characterizing individual diseases. First, the disease processes, or even their final state, were not

TABLE 2.1.1. Dates and authors of the description of some syndromes and also of some clinical aids to diagnosis.

Years	Syndrome/aid	Discoverer
1761, 1839	Percussion	Auenbrugger, Škoda
1768	Angina pectoris	Heberden
1819, 1839	Mediate auscultation	Laennec, Škoda
1827	Chronic nephritis	Bright
1832	Aortic regurgitation	Corrigan
1832	Lymphadenoma (Hodgkin's disease)	Hodgkin
1835	Exopthalmic goiter	Graves
1849	Pernicious (or Addisonian) anemia	Addison
1852,1868	Bacterial endocarditis	Kirkes, Wilks
1854	Stokes-Adams syndrome	Stokes
1855	Addison's disease (of the suprarenals)	Addison
1859	Diabetes	Pavy
1867	Clinical thermometer	Allbutt, Wunderlich
1873	Myxoedema	Gull

directly observable; the clinician could observe only the symptoms and signs of the disease, and, even so, the number of observable signs was small until recent times. Percussion and auscultation were in common use only after 1840, the sphygmomanometer was developed in the 1890s, the electrocardiogram in the 1900s, and so on with many of the biochemical and radiological tests. In any case, there could be only a limited number of such observables; moreover, in a particular patient some of the signs and symptoms of a disease might be suppressed. Studies of the function of the body in health and disease, now gathered under the headings of anatomy, physiology, and pathology, or form, function, and disease, were required. Of these subjects, pathology has the most direct interest for us here.

G.B. Morgagni (1682–1771) studied anatomy, gross and microscopic, in health and disease. By viewing the body as a mechanism, he was able to associate some diseases with particular pathological findings. His views were set out in the book *De sedibus et causis morborum per anatomen indagatis* of 1761, published in Venice, in which he reasoned that a breakdown in some part of the organism must be the seat and cause of the clinical manifestations of the disease. He also believed that external causes such as environment and occupation could be important. Morgagni, thus, can be regarded as the founder of pathological anatomy.

M. Baillie (1761–1823), in 1795, published *Morbid Anatomy of some of the most Important Parts of the Human Body*, the first English text on pathology and the first systematic study of pathology in any language. The *Nosographie philosophique* of P. Pinel (1745–1826) also used a classification primarily by site. M.F.X. Bichat (1771–1802) drew attention not to the topography of the organs but to the "membranes" in them, that is, to the tissues. He believed that tissues of the same type would be prone to the same kind of lesions in whatever organ they were situated. General anatomy and the pathology of tissues were transformed in the nineteenth century by the use of the microscope, allowing the development of histology and cytology and the study of morbid processes in the cells—cellular pathology. T.R.H. Laennec (1781–1826), a skilled anatomist and pathologist and colleague of Bichat, related the clinical findings in chest disease to the pathological changes by the development of mediate auscultation, that is, by stethoscope, in 1818.

Karl von Rokitansky (1804–1878) continued the systematization of the macroscopic appearances of diseases with the publication of the *Lehrbuch der pathologischen Anatomie* in several volumes over the years, 1842–1846. This book was based on many thousands of autopsies by the author. However, as the importance of cell structure had not yet been recognized, Rokitansky rarely used the microscope for the purpose of description and diagnosis. Moreover, his interpretations of the appearances were made under the humoral theory, that tissues or cells could develop out of the unspecialized body fluids. A more rational pathogenesis, that is, view of the development of disease, could only come after new discoveries in botany and zoology of the importance of the cell by J.M. Schleiden (1804–1881), T.A.H. Schwann (1810–1882), and R.A. von Koelliker (1817–1905), among others. In 1855 Rudolf Virchow (1821–1902) enunciated the cellular theory of pathological processes, stating that every bodily cell develops from a preexistent cell, "omnis cellula e cellula," and denying that cells can develop out of unspecialized body fluids as supposed under the humoral theory. This cellular theory led to a closer examination of the cells in health and disease, cytology, and to a more orderly conception of the development of diseases.

In 1855 the difficulties of histological examination were still great. Although leukemia had been first correctly interpreted with the aid of the microscope in 1845, methods for the fixing and cutting of sections and for staining were not available until J. von Gerlach (1820–1896), in 1847, noticed that carmine stained the nuclei of cells. He used carmine in ammoniacal solution to study the cells of the brain in 1858; such was "one of the most valuable additions to our means of investigation that has ever been discovered" according to another histologist in 1865. According to W.D. Foster (1961), among the staining fluids available by 1880 were carmine, osmic acid, indigo, silver nitrate, eosin, and logwood (now known as hematoxylin). Of the aniline dyes, eosin was the only one much used by the earlier workers. Staining with a double stain, so that cell structures could be more readily distinguished, became common and eosin-hematoxylin has been used ever since. By 1900 all the common histological techniques now in use had been developed. For the effective use of staining, methods of support for the tissues were developed, so that thin slices could be cut (sectioned) suitable for microscopic examination. The freezing of tissues was used in 1843, they were supported externally in 1853, and in 1869 paraffin embedding was introduced.

The sequence of events in inflammation was elucidated in 1857 by Joseph Lister (1827–1912) and by Julius Cohnheim (1839–1884). Although these advances gave insight into the development of diseases in the body and the reaction of the body, they sometimes gave little guide to the correct assignment of the cause of the disease. Some disease processes, such as diabetes, do not leave evident pathological changes; they must be examined by other methods such as biochemistry. For the taxonomy of fevers, see Wilson (1978); for the history of clinical pathology, see Foster (1961) and Bracegirdle (1978).

2.3 Organismal Causes of Disease

An organismal theory of infectious and contagious diseases had been current for many years before the development of effective methods of culture and identification. Although Daniel Defoe speculated on the presumably unpleasant appearance of the animalcules causing plague, there is some doubt as to the intentions of phrases used by older authors such as Fracastoro (ca 1478–1553). More specific hypotheses and firmer evidence were brought forward by M.A. Plenčič (1705–1786), who recognized the possible etiological significance of the animalcules observed under the microscope by A. van Leeuwenhoek (1632–1723). To account for his clincial observations on the importance of contagions, Plenčič (1762) believed that disease organisms are both constant and specific, so that a given animalcule always causes the same disease in a specific host. He considered that only a minute amount of material would be needed to transmit such a disease because of the numbers of animalcules in a small volume and the possibilities of rapid multiplication. Plenčič saw that such a theory could apply to men, to animals, and to plants, alike.

Later events have shown the advantages of such a general approach to the problems of infectious diseases. It happens that some of the organisms causing disease in animals and plants are readily observed microscopically and readily grown in culture; as a result, discoveries of the causes of some nonhuman diseases preceded those of the human diseases. A.M. Bassi (1773–1856), in 1833, showed that the silkworm disease known as muscardine in France was caused by a cryptogam, a fungus parasitic on the silkworm; he further showed that the disease could be spread by spores produced by the parasite. In 1839 J.L. Schoenlein (1793–1864) identified another fungus as the cause of the human skin disease, favus. H.A. de Bary (1831–1888), in 1861, found a fungus as the cause of potato blight; his arguments, as given in the *Dictionary of Scientific Biography*, appear convincing. Pasteur and his colleagues in the years about 1866 obtained an organismal cause for another disease of silkworms, pébrine.

F.G.J. Henle (1809–1885) gave a closely

reasoned statement in 1840 of the hypothesis that infectious diseases are transmitted by living organisms. Before such a doctrine could be widely accepted, it was necessary to solve four problems. First, J.J. Lister (1786–1869) developed the compound microscope in 1840 and E. Abbe (1840–1905) the homogeneous oil immersion lens in 1878. Second, Louis Pasteur (1822–1895) in the years up to 1861 showed that it was difficult to explain the presence of organisms in lesions by the hypothesis of spontaneous generation. Third, J. Lister, Pasteur, Robert Koch (1843–1910), and their followers devised methods for obtaining organisms in pure culture. Fourth, it was necessary to consider the biology of the microbes and their classification as by Ferdinand Julius Cohn (1828–1898).

It is difficult for us, now, to understand the opposition to the hypothesis of infection by organisms as the cause of disease or even to the hypothesis of contagion as mentioned in the section on puerperal sepsis, §29.4, and later in this section.

Examples of human diseases spread by organisms were discovered. Thus, bacilli were found in cases of anthrax in 1849 and leprosy in 1868. Indirect evidence was provided for other important diseases; for example, in 1819 P.F. Bretonneau (1778–1862) characterized typhoid fever by its pathological appearance, adduced evidence for it as being due to a specific transmissible agent, and showed that contact was important in its transmission. In 1865 J.A. Villemin (1827–1892) injected tuberculous material from a human case into a rabbit and produced the characteristic tubercles; fresh animals were infected from them, showing that the infection could be maintained in vivo. It was only in 1882 that R. Koch was able to stain and cultivate the tubercle bacilli in vitro by the use of novel methods.

With the new laboratory methods, the cause of all common bacteriologic infective diseases had been elucidated before 1925, mainly by the followers of Robert Koch and Louis Pasteur, for which see Table 2.3.1. In Table 2.3.2 we have given the date of discovery of the causes of a miscellaneous group of infective diseases. There is great difficulty in giving similar information for the viral diseases, as in many

cases the diseases had been established as entities, and it was known that they were due to filterable viruses long before they were actually cultivated in the laboratory.

Whether an organism can be considered as the cause of a disease is determined by its satisfying the reasoning of Henle (1840), as modified in the famous postulates of Koch (1882), who first stated them informally. We may write them as:

(*i*) The organism should be found in all cases of the disease in question, and its distribution should be in accordance with the lesions observed.

(*ii*) It occurs in no other disease as a fortuitous and nonpathogenic parasite.

(iii) The organism should be cultivated outside the body of the host repeatedly in pure culture, and the organism so isolated should reproduce the disease in other susceptible animals. (See also Koch, 1890.)

Evans (1976) points out that these rules were not to be used dogmatically; in any case, difficulties arose when the virus diseases were investigated. At first, and even after Koch's time, it was assumed that the presence of an organism was both necessary and sufficient for the disease. It was later found that healthy carriers exist for some pathogens; their presence is not sufficient for the disease. With the redefinition of many diseases caused by organisms, their presence is necessary, although technical methods may fail to demonstrate them in individual cases. In diphtheria, patients died of myocarditis, although the bacilli could not be found in the heart; it was proved that a soluble toxin could explain the difficulty. Streptococci were found in the lesions of cases of puerperal sepsis; that they were also found in the normal vaginal flora was held to be evidence against the bacterial causal hypothesis. Later, it was shown that only one group of pathogenic hemolytic streptococci was responsible for such infections and that the normal flora did not contain hemolytic streptococci, which points to the necessity of an accurate diagnosis of the organisms seen or cultivated. Technical difficulties may prevent the fulfillment of Postulate (*iii*); thus, the bacillus of leprosy has never been cultured, although its presence has been demonstrated in the human lesions and in

TABLE 2.3.1. Discoveries of the main human bacteriological* diseases—ICD 001–079.

Year	Disease	Modern name of organism	Discoverer
1849, 1876	Anthrax	*Bacillus anthracis*	Pollender, Koch
1868	Leprosy	*Mycobacterium leprae*	Hansen
1873	Relapsing fever	*Treponema recurrentis*	Obermeier
1877, 1878	Actinomycosis	*Actinomyces israeli*	Bollinger, Israel
1878, 1879, 1881	Suppuration	*Staphylococcus aureus*	Koch, Pasteur, Ogston
1879	Childbed fever	*Streptococcus pyogenes*	Pasteur
1879, 1885	Gonorrhea	*Neisseria gonorrhoeae*	Neisser, Bumm
1880, 1884	Typhoid fever	*Salmonella typhi*	Eberth, Gaffky, Klebs, Koch
1881	Suppuration	*Streptococcus pyogenes*	Ogston
1881	Rabies	*Rhabdovirus*	Pasteur
1882	Glanders	*Pseudomonas mallei*	Loeffler and Schütz
1882	Tuberculosis	*Mycobacterium tuberculosis*	Koch
1882	Pneumonia (special)	*Klebsiella aerogenes*	Friedländer
1883	Erysipelas	*Streptococcus pyogenes*	Fehleisen
1883	Cholera	*Vibrio cholerae*	Koch
1883, 1884	Diphtheria	*Corynebacterium diphtheriae*	Klebs, Loeffler
1884, 1889	Tetanus	*Clostridium tetani*	Nicolaier, Kitasato
1886	Pneumonia	*Streptococcus pneumoniae*	Fraenkel
1886	Poliomyelitis	*Poliovirus hominis*	Medin
1886, 1892	Smallpox	*Poxvirus*	Buist, Guarnieri
1887	Cerebrospinal meningitis	*Neisseria meningitidis*	Weichselbaum
1887	Scarlet fever	*Streptococcus pyogenes*	Klein
1887	Undulant fever	*Brucella melitensis*	Bruce
1888	Food poisoning	*Salmonella enteritidis*	Gaertner
1889	Soft chancre	*Haemophilus ducreyi*	Ducrey
1892	Gas gangrene	*Clostridium welchii*	Welch
1894	Bubonic plague	*Yersinia pestis*	Kitasato, Yersin
1896	Botulism	*Clostridium botulinum*	Ermengem
1896	Bacillary dysentery	*Shigella shigae*	Shiga
1900	Paratyphoid fever	*Salmonella paratyphi*	Schottmüller
1905	Syphilis	*Treponema pallidum*	Schaudinn and Hoffmann
1906	Whooping cough (pertussis)	*Bordetella pertussis*	Bordet and Gengou
1912	Tularemia	*Francisella tularensis*	McCoy and Chapin
1917	Varicella (chickenpox)	*Herpesvirus*	Paschen

*Due to organisms studied in texts of bacteriology.

armadillos. There have also been difficulties with the cultivation in vitro of protozoan parasites and viruses. The clause, insisting that the bacteria must be cultivated over several generations, was to ensure that there was not a carriage of parts of the original host to the test animals.

When it became known that some diseases were caused by filter-passing viruses, later abbreviated to viruses, it became clear that Koch's postulates were unduly strict. Rivers (1937) suggested modifying them: Postulate (*i*), a specific virus must be found associated with a disease with a degree of regularity; Postulate (*ii*), the virus must be shown to occur in the sick individual not as an incidental or accidental finding but as the cause of the disease under question; Postulate (*iii*) could not be applied because viruses need living culture media. Further, at least one natural plant disease needs the action of two viruses, and there are viruses that lie latent in both humans and animals that may cause further difficulties. There may be no susceptible laboratory animal to satisfy Postulate (*iii*).

Evans (1976) suggests that with the development of various laboratory techniques, other observations can be used, for example, if a virus is the cause of a disease, then antibodies against it will be developed in the body, so that

TABLE 2.3.2. Discoveries of miscellaneous agents of disease.

Year	Disease	Modern name of organism	Discoverer
1835	Trichinosis	*Trichinella spiralis*	Paget, Owen
1843	Hookworm disease	*Ancylostoma duodenale*	Dubini
1853	Schistosomiasis	*Schistosoma mansoni*	Bilharz
1860, 1875	Amebic dysentery	*Entamoeba histolytica*	Lambl, Loesch
1868	Filariasis	*Wuchereria bancrofti*	Wucherer
1880	Malaria	*Plasmodium falciparum*	Laveran
1901, 1903	(African) Sleeping sickness	*Trypanosoma gambiense*	Forde, Bruce, Castellani
1903	Kala azar, black death	*Leishmania donovani*	Leishman, Donovan
1905	Tick-borne relapsing fever	*Borrelia duttoni, etc.*	Dutton and Todd
1909	American trypanosomiasis	*Trypanosoma cruzi*	Chagas
1909	Bartonellosis	*Bartonella bacilliformis*	Barton
1915	Leptospirosis	*Leptospira icterohaemorrhagiae*	Inada
1916	Typhus	*Rickettsia prowazeki*	Rocha Lima
1916	Rocky Mountain spotted fever	*Rickettsia rickettsi*	Ricketts
1933	Influenza	*Orthomyxovirus influenza A*	Smith, Andrewes, and Laidlaw

a rise of antibody concentration (titer) is confirmatory evidence. Evans (1976) believes that, although Koch's postulates have been useful in the past, the general scientific community is now able to bring different considerations to the solution of the problem of causation of disease by microorganisms. As a modern instance, see Aurelian, Manak, et al. (1981). See also King (1952).

Koch's postulates were successful in persuading observers of the truth of the hypothesis that bacteria were, indeed, the cause of disease and in rejecting facile claims that a given organism was the cause of a given disease. An illuminating story of the final acceptance by William Osler (1849–1919) in 1886 of the malaria plasmodium as the cause of malaria is given in Cushing (1940) and Russell (1955). Osler was at first skeptical because of the previous reporting of micrococci that could not be cultured and successfully injected to cause new cases of disease; he was also skeptical of the claims of C.L.A. Laveran (1845–1922) who had reported ameboid forms in the blood. Nevertheless, he examined many cases of malaria, finding not only the ameboid forms but also crescentic bodies not visible in nonmalarious patients, and became convinced of the validity of Laveran's claims.

As a result of the discovery of bacterial and other parasitic causes of disease, it became possible to link together various disease syndromes according to their cause; thus, the local lesion and secondary rash of syphilis could be linked to such later manifestations as aortic aneurysm, tabes, and general paralysis of the insane; tuberculosis infection could be shown to be the cause of many syndromes such as acute miliary tuberculosis, lymph gland infections, pulmonary tuberculosis, spinal caries, among others. Another result of the bacteriologic revolution was the establishment of the doctrine that certain diseases "bred true"; indeed, it could have been of little value to classify diseases into separate entities if their properties were not constant. Without this doctrine, even the description of the development of an epidemic becomes confused as in the writings of Charles Creighton (1847–1927) (see Creighton, 1965). Nevertheless, we must allow for different syndromes to be caused by the same organisms, for example, *Streptococcus pyogenes* causes erysipelas, infection of wounds, and puerperal infections. Some of the difficulties with *Myco. tuberculosis* disappear when microscopic observations are available, when it is seen that the lesions in different organs exhibit the same sequence of microscopic changes.

The establishment of organisms as a cause of infective disease was also important for therapy. In 1891 Dimitriĭ Leonidovič Romanovskiĭ (1861–1921), using an eosin-methylene blue stain, was able to detect morphological damage in the malaria parasites of patients being treated with quinine. He stated that quinine cured malaria by damaging the parasite more than the host, a novel concept not appreciated at the time, but later to become a leading motive of P. Ehrlich, for which see §45.3.

After the triumph of parasitology and of microbiology in the years around 1880, advances could be made in many fields. First, organisms could be accepted as the cause of many diseases and note of this made in their definition; thus, fever could be seen not as a disease but as a symptom, for example, Wilson (1978). Second, the disease so defined could be seen as an entity so that an epidemic could not be imagined as starting as scarlatina and ending as measles, for example. Third, microbiology suggested that direct action against the organism might be possible. Fourth, bacteriology suggested that the chain of infection might be broken by a variety of methods. Fifth, bacteriology gave the true reason for the virtue of cleanliness.

For microbiology, see Bulloch (1938), Clark (1961), Ford (1939), and Foster (1970); for parasitology, see Faust (1955), Foster (1965), Garnham (1971), Lechevalier and Solotorovsky (1965), and Scott (1939).

2.4 Disease Nomenclature

A disease or medical nomenclature is a list or catalogue of approved terms for describing clinical or pathological observations in such a way that for each disease or syndrome a name or term can be uniquely allotted that can be recognized by other workers and recorded. The nomenclature must, therefore, be exhaustive so that every condition can be given an approved name, or it can be assigned to some suitable collection of conditions not yet fully differentiated. A definition of every approved term must be given as a guide to the conditions or syndromes to be assigned to the term. It is customary these days to consider that a nomenclature should reflect the etiology of the condition, but this is by no means essential; indeed, there can be ignorance or doubts as to the underlying cause of the condition. A nomenclature should be able to accommodate new advances by which the conditions, previously considered to be homogeneous, can be distinguished by name or by which conditions insufficiently understood can take more precise titles. W. Farr (1839) concluded that: "The advantages of a uniform statistical nomenclature, however imperfect, are so obvious, that it is surprising no attention has been paid to its enforcement in Bills of Mortality. Each disease has, in many instances, been denoted by three or four terms . . ."

A nomenclature of diseases was drawn up by a committee appointed by the Royal College of Physicians of London and published in 1869. It has been revised, roughly at 10-year intervals since that time. In 1919 the U.S. Bureau of the Census published a *Standard Nomenclature of Diseases and Pathological Conditions, Injuries, and Poisonings for the United States*, a consolidation of eight nomenclatures then in use. In 1937 the American Medical Association took over the responsibility for periodic revisions, and, as result of the Fourth National Conference on Nomenclature held in 1940, the third edition, which included a standard nomenclature of operations as well, appeared in 1942. The fourth edition was published in 1952 under the title *Standard Nomenclature of Diseases and Operations*.

On the other hand, many countries found it necessary to prepare lists of diseases for the statistical tabulation of causes of illness. A standard morbidity code was prepared by the Dominion Council of Health of Canada and published in 1936. The main subdivisions of this code represented the eighteen chapters of the Fourth Revision of the *International List of Causes of Death*, 1929, and these were subdivided into some 380 specific disease categories.

The early attempts at a classification in 1768 and 1772 by François Boissier de Sauvages de la Croix (1706–1767), the commentary on it in 1769 by William Cullen (1710–1790), and the work of Linnaeus in 1763 may be mentioned as belonging to the prehistory of the art of classifying diseases. More relevant were the researches of Philippe Pinel in 1798 and Pierre Charles Alexandre Louis (1787–1872), which bring us up to modern times. See Armitage

(1983), Faber (1923), Feinstein (1967), and King (1958) for later developments.

2.5 Classification of Disease

A statistical classification of disease will usually require a limited number of rubrics, covering the whole range of morbid conditions. A specific disease entity should have a separate rubric in the classification only when its separation is warranted because of its high frequency or its speical interest. Some rubrics in the classification will refer to groups of separate but usually related morbid conditions. Efforts to provide a statistical classification on a strictly logical arrangement of morbid conditions have often failed in the past. The various rubrics will represent a series of necessary compromises between classifications based on etiology, anatomical site, age, and circumstances of onset, as well as the quality of information available in medical reports; that is, the classification will use eclectic criteria. Every disease or morbid condition must have a definite and appropriate place of inclusion in one of the rubrics of the statistical classification; the rubrics of the classification must be exhaustive and mutually exclusive. In the theory of sets, a classification would be said to be a partition of the set of all disease causes. It is necessary to insert residual rubrics for other and miscellaneous conditions that cannot be readily classified under the more specific rubrics. The number of these miscellaneous rubrics should be kept to a minimum.

2.6 International Classifications

With the establishment of the statistical series of the national bureaus of statistics, the question of comparability soon arose. The following discussion makes use of the introduction to the 7th and 9th revisions of the *International Statistical Classification* and Lancaster (1950b). After the first International Statistical Congress at Brussels in 1853, William Farr (1807–1883) and Dr. Marc d'Espine of Geneva were requested to prepare a uniform nomenclature so that international comparability of mortality statistics might be achieved. It appears that Farr's nomenclature based on eclectic criteria

prevailed over that of d'Espine, based on general pathological criteria that were becoming obsolescent. Farr's classification was revised in 1864, 1874, 1880, and 1886 and became the basis of the *International List of Causes of Death*. As a result of a request in 1891 by the International Statistical Institute, Dr. Jacques Bertillon (1851–1922) and a committee prepared a classification of causes of death that was adopted at the meeting of the Institute at Chicago in 1893. It represented a synthesis of English, German, and Swiss classifications used by the city of Paris and was based on the principle, introduced by Farr, for distinguishing between general diseases and those localized to a particular organ or anatomical site. The classification of 161 titles could be abridged to either 44 or 99 titles. *The Bertillon Classification of Causes of Death*, as it was at first called, received general approval and was adopted by several countries as well as by many cities. The Institute at its meeting in 1899 recommended that since the classification has been adopted by all the North and South American states, it should be adopted in principle and without revision by all the statistical institutions of Europe. It further approved generally the system of decennial revisions proposed by the American Public Health Association in 1898, and it urged all statistical offices to adhere to the general agreement on classification.

The French Government convoked in 1900, 1909, 1920, 1929, and 1938 the international conferences for the revisions of the *International Classification of Causes of Death*. The first revision gave 179 rubrics and an abridged classification of 35 groups of rubrics. In 1928 the Health Organization of the League of Nations published a monograph that listed the expansion in the rubrics or titles of the 1920 *International List of Causes of Death* that would be required if the classification was to be used in the tabulation of statistics of morbidity. The Health Organization of the League of Nations was jointly responsible with the Institute for the revisions of the *International List* in 1929 and 1938, under which few changes were made to the rubrics of the list. Further, it drew up a list of causes of stillbirth. It recommended that morbidity be covered by an international list of diseases corresponding as far as possible with the list of causes of death. It also noted that the United States had studied the means of unifying the methods of selection of the main cause of death to be tabulated in those cases where two or more causes are mentioned on the death certificate, and suggested that the United States Government should set up an international committee to study the problem.

The World Health Organization has now taken over the responsibility for the revisions of the *International List* and at its first assembly endorsed the report of the Sixth Revision Conference and adopted World Health Organization Regulations No. 1, prepared on the basis of the recommendations of the Conference.

In 1948 the *Manual of the International Statistical Classification of Diseases, Injuries, and Causes of Death* (ICD) was published in two volumes. The first volume contains an introduction, a tabular list defining the content of each rubric, a model form of the medical certificate of the cause of death, and the rules for coding; the second volume is an alphabetical index of diagnostic terms coded to the appropriate rubrics.

The Sixth Decennial Revision Conference of 1948 marked the beginning of a new era in international vital and health statistics. It approved a comprehensive list suitable for mortality and morbidity purposes and agreed on international rules for selecting the underlying cause of death. It also recommended the adoption of a comprehensive program of international cooperation in the field of vital and health statistics. The dates of appearance of the most recent manuals for the revisions are sixth, 1948; seventh, 1957; eighth, 1967; ninth, 1977. There have been modifications of the numberings and for special purposes additional digits have been added, but details of changes need not concern us here. See WHO-manual (1948/1949, 1967/1969, 1977/1978).

Notwithstanding the eclectic nature of the criteria for classification, the ICD has been used in this book with only slight modification. Thus we have gastrointestinal infections in Chapter 6; tuberculosis in 7; zoonotic bacterial diseases in 8; other bacterial diseases in 9; influenza, poliomyelitis, and a few other diseases unimportant from the point of view of mortality in 10; exanthemata (skin eruptions) caused by viruses, including smallpox and measles, in 11; arthropod (commonly called insect)-borne (i.e., transmitted) diseases in 12; miscellaneous microbial diseases in 13; rickettsioses (diseases such as typhus caused by a microbe resembling a bacterium, but not being considered as such) in 14; malaria in 15; protozoan diseases in 16; venereal diseases in 17; other spirochetal diseases in 18; and helminthiases (worm diseases) in 19. This completes the chapters formally concerned with organismal causes. There follow neoplasms in 20, hormonal diseases in 21, nutritional diseases to which famine has been added in 22, and diseases of the blood systems in 23. Then there are chapters on the diseases, residual after infections and neoplasms have been taken out, in the organ systems in 24–28 and 30, with accidents and diseases associated with childbearing in 29, genetic disease in 31, infancy in 32, war in 33, and injury and accident in 34.

2.7 Coding Rules for the Classification

The pathological conditions to be included in the rubrics of the classification having been decided at each revision, it is necessary to determine which terms in use by the certifying physicians are to be included in each rubric. If medical nomenclature were uniform and standard, such a task would be simple and quite direct. However, the doctors who make out the certificates of death have been educated at different schools and in different epochs. As a result, the medical entries on death certificates are certain to be of mixed terminology. All these terms, good and bad, must be provided for as inclusions in some rubric of the statistical classification.

Since the records of death in the earlier years of certification usually contained only a single cause, a few simple rules sufficed to secure uniform selection of the cause of death. Later, as an increasingly larger proportion of the certificates of death contained multiple causes, the problem of selection became more important in securing comparable statistics. J. Bertillon, in presenting the first revision of the *International List of Causes of Death* in 1900, laid down certain principles for the selection of the primary cause of death. These principles were incorporated into the *United States Manual of Joint Causes of Death* published originally in 1914 and revised in 1925, 1933, and 1940, to conform to successive revisions of the *International List*. This manual was used by several other countries.

The General Register Office of England and Wales from 1902 to 1939 used specific rules for the selection of the underlying cause of death more flexible than those of the *United States Manual*. In 1940 it began to use the procedure of taking as the cause to be tabulated the underlying cause of death as stated by the certifying physician, except in instances where the order of entries on the medical certificate was obviously erroneous. This change in procedure had come about through the adoption in England and Wales in 1926 of a new form of medical certificate that permitted the certifying physician or surgeon to signify more clearly the order of events leading up to death.

The Fifth Decennial Revision Conference approved of the International Medical Certificate of Cause of Death and Rules for the Selection of the Underlying Cause of Death. Because some countries had experienced difficulties, the WHO Centre for Classification of Diseases, after consultation with several national offices and after experimental trials, prepared additional rules that were incorporated into the *Supplementary Interpretations and Instructions for Coding Causes of Death* (shortly called the *Addendum*), which amplified the provisions in the *Manual* and interpreted and clarified a number of points in the *Classification* without altering its structure and meaning. These rules were, whenever possible, simplified during the process of consolidation to facilitate their application. This recasting of the rules led to an extensive but largely editorial rearrangement and did not appreciably affect the substance of the rules.

2.8 General Remarks on the International Classifications

In considering the cause assigned to a death under the rules laid down by the *International List of Causes of Death* up to the introduction of the Sixth Revision, it can be noted that there had been no international agreement on a list of assignments of individual diagnostic terms to the various titles of the *International List*. Further, no guidance had been laid down for selecting a single cause to be assigned from a statement of multiple causes. The tendency was for some countries such as Australia (Lancaster, 1950b) to follow the *Manuals of Joint Causes of Death* published by the U.S. Bureau of Census in 1914, 1925, 1933, and 1940, which were rather rigid in their preferences. It must be conceded that the problem is a difficult one. Since the Sixth Revision, practices in most countries have tended to follow the lead of England and Wales and accept the judgement of the certifying physician.

The difficulties in obtaining long series in the deaths from infectious diseases, from cancer, and from violence and accidental deaths over a period since 1880 are often greatly exaggerated. In these classes, difficulties about multiple causes will not usually arise, and the clinical entities can be recognized through the different revisions of the *International List*. The same may be said of the smaller classes, but there have been extensive changes in the boundaries between the classes of cardiovascular, nervous, genitourinary, and ill-defined diseases and senility. Statements cannot be made about the progress of the causes in these classes without extensive research into the customs of the particular offices. A personal opinion is that, since the sums of the age-specific rates in this group of classes had tended to remain rather constant over a long period of time, there had often been merely interchange of assignments between them, without great changes in the real rates of mortality from individual diseases (see §25.1).

There has been a tendency to move infectious diseases from the other classes into Class I of the *International List* or *Classification*. An unfortunate example of a move in the other direction is provided by influenza.

Some examples of possible difficulties of interpretation of the coding rules are now given.

Tuberculosis. Tuberculosis had a high priority under the coding rules of the successive revisions of the *International List of Causes of Death.* Possibly there were some losses to "violence" for the earlier ages and to "cancer" in the later ages. Another source of loss might be the failure of the certifying medical officer to give the diagnosis "tuberculosis" on social grounds. There are no means of assessing the numerical importance of any of these sources of loss. It may be argued, on the other hand, that some of the cases assigned to "tuberculosis" by the coding rules were not really deaths from tuberculosis; for instance, had a diabetic died in coma and "tuberculosis" been mentioned on the death certificate, the death would have been referred, according to the coding rules before the Sixth Revision, to one of the tuberculosis rubrics, since these rules gave an unvarying preference to "tuberculosis" over "diabetes." Another disturbing factor was the increased interest in tuberculosis and the widespread use of mass radiography in the later years, from around 1940. Notwithstanding all these factors, it seems fair to conclude that the official statistics of the developed countries did give an approximate estimate of the total deaths from tuberculosis.

Diabetes. The American system of priorities used with the *International List* gives a high priority to diabetes. Thus "diabetes" would be preferred to "coronary disease" or even the more definite "coronary occlusion." It would also be preferred to the rubric "gangrene," if the terms "gangrene" and "diabetes" both appeared on the certificate. On the other hand, there are certain diseases that would be preferred to diabetes. Thus, cancer and tuberculosis, all forms of violence, and the rarer specific infectious diseases would have a higher priority than diabetes. The mortality figures for diabetes will, therefore, be a minimum estimate of the number of persons who died "with diabetes." Studies in the United States of America, Joslin, Root, et al. (1946/1959),

have also shown that only some 60% of known diabetics were finally coded to diabetes. Similar surveys in other countries would be expected to give similar results and sometimes even lower percentages.

Maternal Mortality. Coding practice with respect to the deaths from conditions related to pregnancy and childbearing have varied over the years. In some countries medical officers of health have preferred where possible to certify deaths to other rubrics; moreover, criminal abortions have often been coded to the class of accidental and violent deaths. *Acute infective diseases* and *violent and accidental causes of death* have always been given high priorities.

For certification, see Moriyama, Baum, et al. (1966).

2.9 International Agencies

The International Statistical Institute was founded in 1885 (Nixon, 1960) to facilitate cooperation between the official statisticians of different countries. It remained the leading international statistical society until the formation of the League of Nations in 1920. Although many of its functions are now carried out by the agencies of the United Nations, the Institute remains an important forum for the discussion of problems in the collection, reporting, and analysis of official statistics. Furthermore, individuals at its congresses can express opinions that might be thought quite inappropriate for publication in the journals of the United Nations or its agencies.

The Institute has done much to unify the procedures of collection and reporting of the results of the census and other official statistics. It has been closely associated with the International Commission for the Decennial Revision of the *International List of the Causes of Death*, which has met in Paris at the invitation of the French government.

The Institute publishes a regular journal, the *International Statistical Review*, and its biennial meetings are published as the *Bulletin of the International Statistical Institute* by the host country. In recent years the congresses and publications of the Institute have become increasingly concerned with distribution theory and with the theory of sampling surveys.

Of the agencies of the United Nations, the World Health Organization (WHO), the International Labor Organization (ILO), the Food and Agriculture Organization (FAO), and the United Nations Educational, Scientific and Cultural Organization (UNESCO) all publish material that is relevant to medical statistics. For a general review of WHO, the reader can consult WHO—Director-General (1970 et seq.); for its publications, there are WHO—bibliography (1958, 1964, 1969, 1974, 1980, 1984) and WHO—health statistics (1969).

Of special interest to us here are *World Health Statistics Annual* (in three volumes): Vol.I, *Vital Statistics and Causes of Death*; Vol.II, *Infectious Diseases, Cases, Deaths and Vaccinations*; Vol.III, *Health, Personnel and Hospital Establishments*; The *Chronicle of the World Health Organization* and *Technical Report Series*. Under "WHO" in the bibliography, we have included a number of publications illustrating the statistical work done by WHO.

The Population Division of the Department of Economic and Social Affairs of the United Nations publishes three series: *Population Bulletin of the United Nations*, *Population Studies, and Demographic Yearbook*, which contain much material on mortality and other medical statistics.

Of international journals not already mentioned, *Acta Genetica et Statistica Medica*, *Metron*, *Genus*, *Biometrische Zeitschrift*, *Biometrie-Praximetrie*, and *Sankhyā* (*Series B*) contain articles of medical statistical interest.

Chapter 3
Measurement of Mortality

3.1 Historical and Introductory Notes

Although there had been anticipations by Ibn Kaldun in the fourteenth century, G. Botero in 1589, Francis Bacon in 1612, and others, the first great study of mortality statistics was made by John Graunt (1620–1674) with his observations on the bills of mortality of the city of London in Graunt (1662), Hull (1899). The bills had commenced in 1517 or 1519 at the order of Henry VIII as a means of warning against increases in the incidence of plague; such use of them has been described by Mullett (1956). The bills were compiled weekly by the parishes and sent on to the Company of Parish Clerks, who combined them into a total for each year ending with the Thursday before Christmas. Causes of death were given under some 60 headings, but neither age nor sex was given. There were separate tabulations of the numbers of males and of females, christened or dying. Since plague was endemic in London and, in many years, the dominant cause of mortality, Graunt confined his main discussion to the deaths occurring in the 20 years, 1629 to 1636 and 1647 to 1658, during which England was comparatively free from the plague. He noted that it was immaterial to his purpose whether a man aged 70 years was recorded as dying from cough or from age. However, he would have liked to know the exact age in years of children who died. As this information was not available to him, he found that of 229,250 people dying in 20 years, 71,124 died from thrush, convulsions, rickets, "teeth," and worms or as "abortives," "chrysomes," infants "liver-grown," and "overlaid." He guessed that about half of 12,210 deaths due to small-pox, swine pox, measles, and worms without convulsions were also of children under 6 years of age. He concluded that 36% of all births (quick conceptions) resulted in death before the age of 6 years. Later statistics, when they became available in the early part of the nineteenth century, showed that Graunt's guess was probably a very good one. In general, Graunt (1662) demonstrated the regularity of certain vital phenomena, such as births, deaths, and marriages, the excess of male over female births and the approximately equal numbers of the sexes in the adult population, the high rate of mortality in the earliest years of life, and an urban death rate that exceeded the rural death rate. Graunt carefully examined the reliability of the data and enquired, for example, whether the apparent changes over the years were due to transfer of deaths from one disease rubric to another. His work can still be read with interest because of the great insight displayed in his criticism of the sources and the caution with which he put forward new hypotheses (see Glass, 1963, 1964; Greenwood, 1948b; and Lancaster, 1962b).

Graunt's contemporary and friend William Petty (1623–1687) also made observations on mortality and other vital statistical matters, proposing a system of censuses and registration that was far in advance of his time (see Strauss, 1954).

An early difficulty was the computation of

specific death rates or even crude death rates, since no populations at risk were available in the absence of censuses, which could not be held because of popular prejudices against them, sometimes expressed in riots, and because of the weakness of the central bureaucracies.

Graunt's life table was necessarily guesswork; nevertheless, Christiaan Huygens (1629–1695) and his brother Lodewijk derived from it an estimate of 18.22 years for the expectation of life at birth. In 1671 Johan de Witt (1625–1672) writing on life annuities, after some speculation set in effect, $l_4 = 128$, $l_{54} = 28$, $l_{64} = 14.7$, $l_{74} = 4.7$, $l_{81} = 0$; he further supposed that in each of the age intervals, 4–54, 54–64, 64–74, and 74–81 years, l_x could be approximated by a linear function. In accordance with these hypotheses, q_x increases over the intervals but at their boundaries at the ages 54, 64, and 74 years it is less than at the preceding age. De Witt's table appears closer to reality than Graunt's.

E. Halley (1656–1742) saw that life tables could be constructed on a sounder basis if data on births and the ages at death could be collected in some population in which migration was negligible; Breslau (Wrocław) was his choice. Halley's methods have been discussed in detail by Greenwood (1948b), who suggests that Halley had, in effect, the notion of the stable life table population. See also Figure 4.1.2 for his life table.

Once l_x of the life table had been computed, q_x and so m_x, the age-specific death rate were available (see §3.5). Halley, like Graunt, commented on the high mortality of the early years of life and noted that 43% of those born in Breslau about 1690 would be dead before their sixth birthday. It is remarkable that many later demographers have criticized Graunt's estimate of 36% for the same feature as being too high, yet J. Graetzer (1883) (cited by Greenwood, 1948b) found that Halley's findings agreed with those for Breslau in 1876–1880. Further, there is ample evidence from more recent studies on parish records that the death rates implied by Graunt and Halley at these ages were realistic. Better data were to become available in Sweden from the general registration system so that age-specific death rates could be calculated, and during the nineteenth century such rates became available for all European states and many of the states in the rest of the world.

L. Euler (1707–1783) obtained the stable life table population simply by multiplying the number of persons at age x in the stationary life table population by a factor, r^x, $x = 0, 1, 2, \ldots$ (see Euler, 1767/1977).

According to Dorn (1959), Pehr Wargentin (1717–1783), using the deaths registered in Sweden for 1755 to 1757 and the population registered in 1757, was the first to construct a life table for an entire nation from statistics of death and population classified by age and sex. Initially, the data collected by the registration system were treated as state secrets, but Wargentin (1766) published tables of age- and sex-specific death rates for the epoch 1755 to 1763. These tables showed the mortality rates for males to be higher than those for females. Comparable data for other non-Scandinavian countries began to become available in the nineteenth century. A list of notable works on mortality is given by Dorn (1959). Extracts and translations of works on the life table and stable population theory are given in Smith and Keyfitz (1977). (See also Pressat 1974a, WHO—mortality 1977, 1978, UN Population Studies No. 84, 1984.)

3.2 Definitions of Death

In general, there is little ambiguity about the fact of death or its registration, but there are instances in which care must be taken when international comparisons are being made.

Not all deaths in a given national state may be registrable. The statistics may, indeed, apply only to certain classes within the state. There may be areas where civil control and death registration are not yet established, because of distance or historical factors; for example, aboriginal tribes may be excluded from the regional statistics and perhaps not recorded in the national figures. Grave disturbances such as war, civil war, and natural disasters may render it impossible to ascertain and so to register deaths. Further, deaths of military personnel in war time are sometimes not published for security or policy reasons. Difficulties have also arisen from varying definitions of "birth" and "stillborn." In some countries, including notably Belgium and the Netherlands, infants who died within the first 3 days before registration were registered as "presented dead." If a public holiday intervened, the period might be extended to 6 days. The statistics of the "presented dead" are given separately in these countries, and such births and deaths do not appear otherwise in the official statistics. In Italy, however, children who are born and die before registration are registered as "stillborn," but for statistical purposes they are counted as "live births" and "infantile deaths." Signed articles on this topic and some of the implications of the divergences of practice are given by Pascua (1948) and Stowman (1947–1948d). Therefore, care must always be taken in interpreting international comparisons. Moreover, even within a given political entity, there may be provincial variations in registration practice. Difficulties arising from these varying definitions have been lessened by the publication of the following definitions and recommendations, adopted by the World Health Assembly under Article 23 of the Constitution of the World Health Organization. They are reproduced here because of their importance especially for the consideration of maternal and infantile mortality rates.

3.2.1 Live Birth

Live birth is the complete expulsion or extraction from its mother of a product of conception, irrespective of the duration of the pregnancy, that, after such separation, breathes or shows any other evidence of life, such as beating of the heart, pulsation of the umbilical cord, or definite movement of voluntary muscles, whether or not the umbilical cord has been cut or the placenta is attached. Each product of such a birth is considered live born.

3.2.2 Fetal Death

Fetal death is death prior to the complete expulsion or extraction from its mother of a product of conception, irrespective of the dura-

tion of pregnancy. The death is indicated by the fact that after such separation the fetus does not breathe or show any other evidence of life, such as beating of the heart, pulsation of the umbilical cord, or definite movement of voluntary muscles.

3.2.3 Causes of Death

The causes of death to be entered on the medical certificate of cause of death are all those diseases, morbid conditions, or injuries that either resulted in or contributed to death and the circumstances of the accident or violence that produced any such injuries.

3.2.4 Underlying Cause of Death

The underlying cause of death is (a) the disease or injury that initiated the train of events leading directly to death, or (b) the circumstances of the accident or violence that produced the fatal injury. (This latter information is for the supplementary classification, E800 to E999, of the ICD.)

3.2.5 Birthweight

The first weight of the fetus or newborn obtained after birth. This weight should be measured preferably within the first hour of life before significant postnatal weight loss has occurred.

3.2.6 Low Birthweight

Less than 2500 g (up to, and including 2499 g).

3.2.7 Gestational Age

The duration of gestation is measured from the first day of the last normal menstrual period. Gestational age is expressed in completed days or completed weeks (e.g., events occuring 280 to 286 days after the onset of the last normal menstrual period are considered to have occurred at 40 weeks of gestation). Measurements of fetal growth, as they represent continuous variables, are expressed in relation to a specific week of gestational age (e.g., the mean birthweight for 40 weeks is that obtained at 280–286 days of gestation on a weight-for-gestational age curve).

3.2.8 Preterm

Less than 37 completed weeks (less than 259 days).

3.2.9 Term

From 37 to less than 42 completed weeks (259 to 293 days).

3.2.10 Postterm

Forty-two completed weeks or more (294 days or more).

3.2.11 Maternal Mortality

A maternal death is defined as the death of a woman while pregnant or within 42 days of the termination of pregnancy, irrespective of the duration and the site of the pregnancy, from any cause related to or aggravated by the pregnancy or its management but not from accidental or incidental causes.

Maternal deaths should be subdivided into two groups:

(*i*) Direct obstetric deaths: those resulting from obstetric complications of the pregnant state (pregnancy, labor, and puerperium), from interventions, omissions, incorrect treatment, or from a chain of events resulting from any of the above.

(*ii*) Indirect obstetric deaths: those resulting from previous existing disease or disease that developed during pregnancy and that was not due to direct obstetric causes, but that was aggravated by physiologic effects of pregnancy.

In relation to the definition of WHO No. 3.2.2 above, by accepted clinical definition the embryo becomes a fetus at the end of 10 weeks. Lauritsen (1977) shows that it is possible to classify fetal deaths as early and late, for very few occur in the fifth and sixth months. Late fetal deaths are synonymous with stillbirths. Because some causes can lead to death before or after birth, it is convenient to divide the deaths of a fetus-child into prenatal deaths or stillbirths, deaths in the first month (or 4 weeks or week), and deaths in the remainder of the first year of life, and then for some purposes to combine the first two classes and so to define a perinatal death as the death of a late fetus or of an infant in the first month of life.

Doubts are sometimes expressed about the validity of using the births and infant deaths in a calendar year as a divisor for the computation of the infant mortality rates, when death may occur in a year later than that of the birth. It is easily seen that, when the infant mortality falls below 50 per thousand, a large proportion of the deaths occur in the first month, so the infant mortality rate as computed is a good measure of the mortality, before their first birthday, of those born in a given year because the numerator used includes almost all the deaths of infants born in that same year. Some computations illustrative of this remark are given by Shapiro, et al. (1968, Table 1.1).

3.3 Populations at Risk

The absolute numbers of deaths are usually not sufficient for comparison between epochs, sexes, or ages. It is necessary to reduce them to a mortality (= death) rate. Except for the computation of the infant mortality and the maternal mortality rates, mortality rates are computed as a ratio, deaths to years of life at risk. For a single calendar year, the concept of the population at risk is simple; if the death rate of the whole population is to be computed for a certain year, the midyear population may be taken as the measure of the mean number of persons alive during the year and, thus, of the total number of years lived by persons at risk in the year, or, more shortly, of the years at risk. There is usually interest in special classes of the population, for example, persons of given age group and sex. The years at risk are computed in the same way. This simple device is often extended to the 3 years surrounded a census to obtain age- and sex-specific death rates for all causes or some specified group of causes. Of course, the deaths and the years at risk used in the computations must refer in all cases to the same defined subclass of the population.

Often the mortality rates need to be computed for an epoch, a term that we will use for any stretch of time, usually a decade. In such cases the years at risk are obtained by addition of the mean populations for each of the calendar years in the epoch. The bureaus of statistics usually have some system of computing the midyear populations for the years between successive censuses and often readjust them in the light of knowledge gained at an ensuing census; the required totals can be obtained by addition. The estimates of population by the usual 5- or 10-year age groups are sufficiently accurate in any country with a well-established statistical bureau.

At ages under 5 years there may be substantial underenumeration at the census of the population at risk. It is practicable at these years to build up population numbers by single years of age by taking account of the births and the deaths by age over a number of calendar years, a device used by W. Farr. This methodology is widely used in the study of mortality from genealogical, insurance, follow-up, or occupational records.

3.4 Age-Specific Death Rates

Throughout this monograph the terms "death rates" and "mortality rates" are used synonymously. For any serious comparisons between populations, it is usually necessary to compare the death rates of classes that are similar with regard to age and sex, because populations and death rates can differ considerably in their distributions by age and sex. Experience has shown that, for most purposes, the age groups are conveniently defined by ages in years at the last birthday as follows: 0, 1 to 4, 5 to 14, 15 to 24, . . . , 65 to 74, 75 and over. There is some need to limit the number of operations to be performed and of rates to be calculated, while retaining age groups that are comparable throughout a great range of actual populations. This is because wider age groups, such as 15 to 44 years, are likely to give groups that may not be strictly comparable in age composition between, for example, a rapidly growing population and a declining population. Death rates can be made specific with respect not only to age and sex but also to disease, occupation, geographical location, economic condition, or other factors. It is always assumed in this monograph that age-specific rates are also sex specific, except in international comparisons of the infant mortality rates, which are sometimes not available by sex.

The age-specific death rates are obtained by dividing the number of deaths in a defined group of persons by the years of life experienced by the same group (i.e., the years at risk) in the same epoch. The death rates are usually given as deaths per annum per thousand, per million, or other power of 10. In other words, the death rates are decimals, and it is usually more advantageous to present them multiplied by a thousand or by a million to obtain results in whole numbers. Such a use of rates per million, although uncommon, is far more convenient from the point of view of the printer and reader than giving precisely the same figures expressed as rates per annum per 100,000 to 1 decimal place (Yule, 1934). The infant and maternal mortality rates are not age-specific mortality rates, but are analogous to case fatality rates. For an analysis of mortality in a single area over time (i.e., between epochs) and for comparisons between areas or countries, the age-specific death rates are usually preferred to other measures. Indeed, William Farr (Farr, 1885 p. 123) said that the age-specific death rates were facts and all other measures were inferences based on some concept such as the life table population.

The calculation of the rates is discussed in the usual actuarial and medical statistical texts and also in the official statistical publications of many countries and in the international publications of the United Nations and World Health Organizations. Benjamin (1968), Greenwood (1928), Grove and Hetzel (1968), Lancaster (1951c), Larsson (1965), Linder and Grove (1943), Spiegelman (1955), UN/WHO-mortality (1970), and Yule (1934) are useful references.

3.5 Relation Between m_x and q_x

Mortality is sometimes observed in the form of survival from one age to a higher; for example, the infant mortality rate purports to give the probability of dying between birth and the attainment of 1 year precisely. In the analysis of insurance or genealogical records and follow-up enquiries, individuals are observed over stretches of time and so p_x, the probability of surviving from precise age x to precise age $x + 1$, can be estimated directly. In all such cases, it is supposed that l persons attain the precise age x and that they are observed for the duration of 1 year. Then $q_x l_x = (1 - p_x) l_x$ may be expected to die in that time. It can also be supposed with a good degree of approximation, except in the first years of life or at very high ages, that deaths are distributed evenly throughout the year so that each person dying lives on an average half a year in that year. There are $l - lq$ who live a complete year by the hypothesis made, so the number of years experienced is given by the sum, $l - lq + \frac{1}{2} = l - \frac{1}{2}lq$. By the mode of definition of the age specific death rate,

$$m = q/(1 - \tfrac{1}{2}q), \text{ and} \qquad (3.5.1)$$

$$q = m/(1 + \tfrac{1}{2}m). \qquad (3.5.2)$$

It is easily verified that m/q differs from unity by no more than 2.5% up to age 70 years in the life tables.

3.6 Standard Errors of a Mortality Rate

Standard errors of death rates can be computed by assuming the (Bernoullian) hypothesis of the independence of deaths of different persons. The usual statistical theory leads to a simple rule for the standard error of an estimated death rate, $\hat{M}$ for example.

$$SE_{\hat{M}} = \hat{M}/\sqrt{D}, \qquad (3.6.1)$$

where the rate has been founded on D deaths. In practice standard errors are not appended to the estimates of the rates. It is convenient to remember equation (3.6.1) above, since the number of deaths is often easy to find. UN-historical (1979) distinguishes those rates based on less than 31 deaths and so, by (3.6.1), having a standard error of more than $100/\sqrt{30}$ or 18% but less than a unit at rates below 10 per 10,000.

The main causes of the failure of the independence hypothesis are the infective diseases and accident and injury because the events leading to death may not be independent, for example, in cataclysms, large civilian disasters, civil war, and war, among others. It is consequently difficult to devise a statistical test or rule by which the beginning of a decline in the death rates in a time series can be determined; yet, demographers and social scientists often give a date of such a beginning and tie it up with particular social or other events suggested by the presumed date. Perhaps the only solu-

TABLE 3.6.1. The beginning of a persistent decline in the death rates.

Country	Sex	0	1–4	5–14	15–24	25–34	35–44	45–54	55–64	65–74
France*	M	1896	1861	1861	1896	1886	1901	1911	1911	1911
	F	1896	1861	1861	1891	1886	1901	1911	1911	1911
Sweden†	M	1841	1871	1871	1881	1881	1881	1861	1851	1851
	F	1841	1871	1881	1921	1881	1881	1841	1841	1841
Norway‡	M	1896	1886	1896	1901	1906	1921	1921	1921	1921
	F	1896	1886	1896	1906	1906	1921	1921	1921	1921
United Kingdom§	M	1901	1901	1861	1866	1871	1876	1896	1896	1896
	F	1901	1901	1891	1866	1871	1876	1876	1901	1891
Australia‖	M		1870							
	F		1870		All other ages not later than 1891					
New Zealand¶	M	1881		1881	1881	1886	1881	1881	1886	—#
	F	1881		1881	1886	1886	1886	1886	1906	1921

Sources of data but not of conclusions:
* Bourgeois-Pichat, 1965.
† Historisk Statistik, 1955.
‡ Backer, 1961; estimation rendered difficult by choice of ages and influenza epidemic.
§ Greenwood, 1936.
‖ Lancaster, 1951c, 1956c,d, 1957a.
¶ Lancaster and Donovan, 1967a.
# No decline noted.

TABLE 3.7.1. Age-specific death rates (deaths per 10,000 per annum).

Country	Year	All ages	0	1–4	5–9	10–14	15–19	20–24	25–34	35–44	45–54	55–64	65–74
						Males							
England and Wales	1948	115	384	19	9	6	12	16	19	31	84	219	504
	1985	120	106	5	2	3	7	8	8	18	54	172	450
Scotland	1948	122	519	25	11	10	14	21	23	42	102	239	525
	1985	126	103	4	3	3	8	9	10	24	70	210	520
Northern Ireland	1948	116	555	27	8	8	15	16	23	42	107	195	509
	1985	106	106	6	2	3	9	12	10	21	71	198	510
Ireland (Eire)	1951	149	515	28	9	6	13	20	26	41	96	228	572
	1983	102	104	7	3	2	9	13	10	20	64	198	497
Norway	1948	91	268*	15*	13	8	15	20	23	31	61	133	330
	1984	112	83	6	2	2	8	12	10	18	52	146	384
Denmark	1948	89	365†	15†	9	6	11	17	19	29	65	150	381
	1985	121	91	4	4	4	8	11	14	22	64	173	421
Sweden	1948	100	274	15	7	6	13	18	19	28	64	156	397
	1985	121	137	3	2	2	6	9	10	18	48	133	346
Finland	1948	124	608	38	16	15	28	47	53	66	139	298	628
	1985	105	66	3	3	3	9	12	16	30	77	201	478
France	1948	133	615	33	10	8	14	22	29	48	101	214	485
	1985	107	99	5	3	3	9	16	16	28	71	164	367
Japan	1948	125	730	111	26	15	34	70	73	78	124	262†	650†
	1985	69	59	6	3	2	7	8	8	18	50	110	290
Australia	1948	110	319	20	9	8	14	19	18	33	90	231	536
	1983	79	105	6	3	3	11	15	13	18	56	156	394
New Zealand	1948‖	101	256	19	7	7	12	18	16	26	74	195	466
	1985	89	122	5	4	4	15	16	14	20	59	169	311
United States	1948	111	384‡	16‡	8	8	15	20	23	48	115	247	537
	1984	94	120	6	3	3	11	17	18	28	68	172	394
Canada	1950	104	382§	16§	10	8	14	17	18	33	83	203	456
	1985	80	86	5	3	3	10	14	14	20	54	148	372

tion to this problem in the age-specific death rates is a common-sense one, namely, to select the first epoch at which the rate is lower than in the preceding epoch and after which the rate in each successive epoch is less than in its predecessor. It is unfortunate that the influenza epidemic of 1918 occurred at an interesting point of the decline of many time series on rates; common sense suggests that this epoch be ignored as "atypical." Based on these principles, the epochs of the beginning of the fall in age-specific rates are given in Table 3.6.1.

3.7 Age-specific Death Rates

In UN-historical (1979) the death rates are given by age and sex for those nations providing the data from 1948 to 1976. Here, as in §3.11, for convenience *we write death rates per 10,000 per annum as an asterisked integer*, for example, 7*. Many countries in 1948 were still suffering from the disorganizations occasioned by war and so were not able to give complete statistical information. In some instances the death rates for 0 and 1–4 years were not given

TABLE 3.7.1. *Continued.*

Country	Year	All ages	0	1–4	5–9	10–14	15–19	20–24	25–34	35–44	45–54	55–64	65–74
							Females						
England and Wales	1948	101	296	16	6	6	11	16	17	24	54	123	332
	1985	117	83	4	2	2	3	3	5	12	34	96	241
Scotland	1948	113	372	19	9	9	20	26	30	33	65	150	406
	1985	124	88	4	2	2	3	3	6	14	40	120	300
Northern Ireland	1948	107	381	25	7	8	16	18	23	38	75	151	431
	1985	99	86	4	3	2	3	4	6	12	38	103	278
Ireland (Eire)	1951	137	387	24	7	7	13	21	25	40	75	180	482
	1983	86	89	5	2	1	3	4	5	12	38	106	276
Norway	1948	87	222*	14*	7	5	8	12	14	23	43	95	275
	1984	93	83	5	1	1	3	3	4	10	26	67	178
Denmark	1948	83	262†	12†	6	4	7	10	15	24	51	119	331
	1985	107	70	4	2	2	3	4	6	16	44	100	224
Sweden	1948	97	194	12	5	4	7	11	13	23	50	121	352
	1985	104	119	3	1	2	3	3	6	10	26	66	174
Finland	1948	100	465	34	10	10	22	29	32	37	60	145	423
	1985	92	58	2	2	1	3	3	5	11	26	70	219
France	1948	115	466	29	8	6	11	17	22	30	56	122	316
	1985	94	73	4	2	2	4	5	6	13	28	61	158
Japan	1948	112	632	107	23	16	36	66	64	67	96	182†	459†
	1985	56	51	4	2	1	2	3	5	10	24	54	154
Australia	1948	89	245	15	6	5	5	9	15	28	62	137	360
	1983	64	88	5	2	2	4	5	6	11	32	79	202
New Zealand	1948‖	81	188	14	6	5	9	13	16	24	68	190	463
	1985	78	96	6	3	3	5	6	7	14	39	94	238
United States	1948	85	296‡	14‡	6	5	9	12	16	32	68	148	376
	1984	79	97	5	2	2	5	6	7	14	38	92	214
Canada	1950	83	309§	14§	7	6	8	10	13	27	56	131	346
	1985	63	71	4	2	2	4	4	5	11	31	75	238

Data modified from tables in UN-historical (1979) and UN Demographic Yearbook (1986), copyright (c) (1979) and (1986), respectively, United Nations. Reproduced by permission.

When the rates were not available for the stated year, we have used rates from the closest possible year as follows: * 1952; † 1950; ‡ 1949; § 1956.

‖ Europeans only.

separately and so we have used the corresponding rates from the first year available without adjustment. Space and convenience have forced us to defer the corresponding tables for some other nations to Chapters 37–42.

In Table 3.7.1 we have given, for either sex and for the earliest and latest years of the UN table, the crude death rate, the death rates at ages in years 0 (infant mortality rate),

1–4 (early childhood), then for four 5-year age groups, and five 10-year age groups bringing the table up to 75 years; we have deferred the rates at ages over 75 years to §36.7. It will be recalled that in many countries the infant mortality rate had fallen below 900* before the war, so unsatisfactory social and medical conditions had caused them to appear to be unduly high in 1948. As an example of a country not so

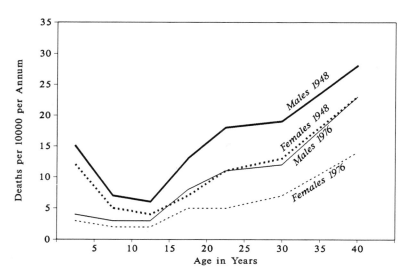

FIGURE 3.7.1. Death rates in Sweden.

troubled, we have given in Figure 3.7.1 the Swedish death rates for either sex in the years 1948 and 1976, confining attention to ages 1–40 years. Such a comparison in age and time can be treated in two ways.

Calendar Method

The shape of the curve of mortality m_x can now be deduced for a calendar year or an epoch. It commences high in infancy but has already fallen considerably in early childhood, 1–4 years. In 1976 Swedish female rates, little affected by accident and injury in early adult life, are at a minimal level from 1–14 years, indeed, 3* (i.e., 3 per 10,000 per annum), 2*, 2*, 5*, 5* at ages 1–4, 5–9, 10–14, 15–19, and 20–24 years, respectively, and 7* and 14* at ages 25–34 and 35–44 years, respectively. The rates then continue to rise throughout life; for some countries there is a local maximum at approximately 20 years, usually due in recent times to accident and injury in males, for which also see §§35.2 and 35.3.

Historical Narrative Method

This name was assigned by Case (1956). Whereas the calendar method takes the calendar year as fixed, this second method considers the age as fixed. The UN table from which Table 3.7.1 was constructed had entries for years 1948 to 1985; we could run down any column by this method. Our summary Table 3.7.1 makes only a single comparison between the first and last years; in the original table, the calendar method analyzes a row of entries and the historical narrative method a column of entries. It is clear that there have been striking improvements at all ages 0–74 years. Such comparisons can be made in greater detail from the original table and from national statistics in the later chapters; the method is commonly used to determine the progress of individual diseases.

It is evident from the table that the curve of mortality in females has become almost horizontal from 2 to 45 years; further analysis by cause would show that if deaths from injury and accident were excluded, the same would hold for the male rates.

3.8 Generation or Cohort Analysis of Death Rates

A third method of analysis is the cohort or generation methods, in which rates are given for persons born in a given epoch and followed throughout life. Thus Andvord (1921, 1930) interpreted the similarity of shape of the curves of death rates for tuberculosis, observed in the different cohorts, as meaning that the behavior of the rates in a cohort depended strongly on the rate in children. He stressed the importance of childhood infection for the later health of the child and so for the death rates in the cohort at later times (i.e., at higher ages). Brownlee (1916a) had already applied the generation method to analyze the long-time series of tuberculosis death rates for England and Wales, and had found that the shape of the curve of the death rates for a generation was more constant than that given by the calendar method. Derrick (1927) independently adopted the method and so did Greenwood (1936), although the opinion of Greenwood (1927) had been unfavorable to the method; Frost (1939) is a readable account that has been very influential. See also Cramér and Wold (1935) and Lancaster (1950c, 1982a, 1983).

The generation (or cohort) method can be described in general terms as follows. With laboratory animals, a given cohort of mice can be followed through life to give an order of dying out, *Absterbeordnung* of German authors, but this procedure is usually impracticable in longer-living animals such as man. But in man, we can suppose that a table has been formed of death rates given by year (row) and age (column) commencing at some origin, such as zero, and carried through for many years. Then the death rates of a given cohort, for example, born in the year 0, can be determined from the table of death rates, the rates for this cohort being at positions $(0,0)$, $(1,1)$, $(2,2)$, . . . in the table. Similarly for a cohort beginning life in year y, the appropriate rates are found at positions $(y, 0)$, $(y + 1, 1)$, $(y + 2, 2)$, . . . , $(y + k, k)$, ... The general shapes of the curves of death rates by age obtained by the first (or calendar) and third (or generation) methods will be the same in an era of stationary death rates, but if rates are changing they are possibly not the same; especially is this so if the death rates from individual causes are studied.

The death rate, Z, can be considered at the age X, the year of birth Y, and the calendar year T. In symbols,

$$Z = Z(X, Y, T), \qquad (3.8.1)$$

and for a given individual or persons born at the same time,

$$T = X + Y. \qquad (3.8.2)$$

The first or calendar method (i.e., ordinary actuarial method) considers a fixed value of T, namely t, and the death rate, Z, is a function of $X = t - Y$, t fixed. The cohort method considers a fixed cohort born at $Y = y$ and then $X = T - y$, T variable but y fixed. The death rates imagined to be laid out in the table, with X as the column and T as the row variable, could be replaced by a surface with a third variable Z, where Z is a function of X and T. The graph of the death rates can then be obtained from the surface by taking appropriate slices or sections of the surface.

If the death rates are independent of the epoch t, then the horizontal sections taken along $T = t$ are the same for every t; the diagonal sections have the same form (after correcting for the interval lengths representing a year of age in the two sections). In the absence of this independence or, in other words, when the death rates are in a state of change, the horizontal and diagonal sections may appear quite dissimilar.

Attempts have been made to give some kind of acknowledgement to the role of the year of birth as well as the age by writing as a possible hypothesis,

$$Z(X, Y, T) = Z_1(X)Z_2(Y), \qquad (3.8.3)$$

as in Kermack, McKendrick, and McKinlay (1934a, b). Plotted on a logarithmic scale, the successive curves of mortality are the same shape but displaced vertically. Such an exact relationship could hold, in the special case of an infective disease acquired in childhood; $Z_2(Y)$ would then represent the proportion infected and $Z_1(X)$ would measure the case fatality at each age imagined not to vary with the epoch. It is possibly more realistic to suppose that these different response capabilities against the disease at different ages have a preponderant effect on the shape of the generation curves but that some modification due to the external environment, including treatment of the epoch, may also modify the curve.

For a disease of long standing with a marked age distribution of deaths observed by the calendar method, a decrease in the incidence of the disease will appear to transfer the mortality to the older age groups, and, conversely, an increase will appear to bring the mortality down into the younger age groups. These points will be illustrated in later sections on tuberculosis and lung cancer in §§7.5 and 20.10.

Many examples of the analysis of death rates are available in the various national and international official publications and in the journal literature, especially the *Journal of Hygiene* and the journals of the Royal Statistical Society, the Institute of Actuaries, and the Faculty of Actuaries, *Population*, and *Population Studies*.

For general discussion, see also Pressat (1981). For generations since 1840, see Jacobson (1964); for USA, see US National Center (1972).

3.9 Standardization of the Death Rates

Standardization determines the number of deaths that would occur per annum in a standard population, conveniently of a million individuals, if it were exposed at every age group to the same mortality risks (rates) as obtained in the observed population. The procedure can be used when it is thought desirable to have a single measure of mortality that will summarize the mortality and yet be independent of the age distributions of the populations compared, for example, in testing whether the incidence of cancer is increasing over time in a population. Standardization is no longer thought of as "correcting" the death rates to conform with some standard, especially a life table population, and, so, as being more biological. If the death rates from an experience are standardized on to the stationary life table population, calculated from the same rates, the reciprocal of the standardized rate is equal to the expectation of life at birth; this result does not hold for the other standardized rates. Since such bio-

logical interpretations are not generally available, the standardized rates are best seen to be weighted averages, and then the merits of the simple standardization of Yule (1934) are evident, certainly for diseases with mortality falling on the younger age groups.

Weights commonly used are of the form P_i for the ith age group. The directly standardized rates are then of the form,

$$R = \Sigma P_i M_i / \Sigma P_i, \qquad (3.9.1)$$

where M_i is the death rate of the ith age group.

P_i may be population numbers in (i) an actual population, for example, England and Wales, 1901; (ii) a conglomerate actual population, such as WHO standard population; (iii) a life table population, for example, males in Australia, 1933; (iv) Yule's population, unit frequency for each year of life, 0–64 years, zero frequency above that age.

The details of direct standardization are available in Lancaster (1974) and many other books of medical statistics and demography; Alderson (1981) has used standardization to compare the mortalities by cause in many different countries.

3.10 Forecasting the Mortality Rates

Forecast mortality rates serve in estimations of population numbers in future years and, more rarely, as a test of a particular hypothesis. Age- and sex-specific rates are used. The commonest technique is to fit a straight line to the rate or the logarithm of the rates for a given age and sex. Sometimes the fit of a straight line to the logarithm of the rates is good, and satisfactory results are obtained from the extrapolation. This is the method of extrapolating down a column of the rates as given in a table such as 41.3.1. An alternative method is to assume that the shape of the curve of the mortality rates for a cohort has a given form; then, if the first few years of experience are known, the remainder can be forecast by taking simple proportions.

A more detailed biological method is to consider for each age group the possible effects of projected public health measures or therapy on the mortality from individual diseases. Thus, we might assume a negligible mortality from tuberculosis, no change in the mortality from cancers generally, but an increase in the mortality from lung cancer, and so on. These estimated rates can be summed to give the projected death rate.

Examples of forecasting mortality are provided by Cramér and Wold (1935), Greenwood (1936), Kermack, McKendrick, and McKinlay (1934a,b), Knibbs (1917), Pollard (1949), Pressat (1974b), Selby (1974), and WHO—forecast (1974). (See also Preston (1974, 1975, 1976), of which the latest evaluates postwar mortality projections.)

3.11 Crude Death Rates

Although the use of the crude death rates to study secular changes in the incidence of cancer has led to many false conclusions, the only information available in studies of past times, primitive communities, or some modern communities may be the crude death rates. For brevity, it is assumed that the rates written in this section are deaths per 10,000 per annum and *this latter phrase is replaced by an asterisk* as in §3.7.

Some norms can be established. Table 3.11.1 shows the crude death rates for 1751–1980, averaged over decennia from the rates given in the yearbooks of the various countries and, more conveniently, in Mitchell (1975).

Examination of Table 3.11.1 indicates that in the years 1751–1800, the averaged crude death rates for Sweden were usually in the range 220* to 280*, with rates never below 220*; this was so for Finland and Norway as well. The European populations in 1801–1850 were generally increasing; in this era the crude death rates had fallen but were rarely below 200*, except in Norway. In 1851–1900 the crude death rates throughout Europe had fallen further, but infections, especially among children, prevented falls to much below 200*. In 1901–1950 declines in mortality from the infectious diseases (taken here to mean all such diseases whether in Class 1 of the ICD or not) led to crude death rates in the vicinity of 120*. This process continued and rates below 100* were quite common after 1950; this phenomenon was possible because the populations were young in the

sense that there were lower proportions of the aged groups in them than would be implied in a stationary life table constructed from the current rates of mortality. Indeed, in such a stationary life table a crude death rate of y^* would imply an expectation of life at birth of $10,000/y^*$; a crude death rate of 100* would therefore imply an expectation of life at birth of 100 years. In many countries, in accord with theoretical population dynamics, the crude death rate is increasing within recent years. In the future one could expect it to stabilize in the neighborhood of 140* because the actual populations are coming to resemble the stationary life table population, since the fertility rates are not greatly different from those of stationary life table population, for example, those consistent with zero population growth.

The crude death rate in a population cannot remain at levels over about 450* since the upper limit of an average for the crude birth rate cannot be greater than 450*, for such a high rate would ensure a great number of children to the population; a population will thus decline if its crude death rate is above 450*. In older times, besides the years of normal high rate of mortality, there were years of abnormal mortality due to famine and/or war, so that most countries would have had an average crude death rate, years of serious epidemic, famine, and war excluded, not greater than 350*. McNamara (1982) stating that "these figures are crude approximations that probably reflect the lowest levels of mortality in their time," gives expectations of life at birth as follows, to which we append the implied crude death rate obtained as a reciprocal: prehistoric era, 18–25 years, 556*–400*; Egyptian era, 22 years, 455*; Greek and Roman era, 25–30 years, 400*–333*; late Roman era, 35 years, 286*. The prehistoric and Egyptian estimates for the crude death (population) rate are too high without qualification and if we use her qualification that they represent the "lowest" level of mortality, the crude death rates for the remaining eras are also too high.

Large variations from year to year may result from (*i*) infections; (*ii*) war and civil strife; (*iii*) famines; (*iv*) catastrophes. The size of the excess will sometimes be partly concealed be-

TABLE 3.11.1. Crude death rates per ten thousand per annumn.

	1751–1760	1761–1770	1771–1780	1781–1790	1791–1800	1801–1810	1811–1820
Denmark	—	—	—	—	—	238	220
Finland	301	304	249	298	266	319	265
Norway	242	276	262	252	223	252	212
Sweden	272	276	289	279	253	282	258

	1821–1830	1831–1840	1841–1850	1851–1860	1861–1870	1871–1880	1881–1890	1891–1900	1901–1910	1911–1920	1921–1930	1931–1940	1941–1950	1951–1960	1961–1970	1971–1980
Austria	286	326	333	314	307	316	295	266	233	214*	152	137†	127†	124	128	125
Belgium	—	259	243	225	234	226	207	192	164	151	132	128	134†	120	121	119
England & Wales	—	—	224	222	225	214	191	182	154	144	121	123	123†	116	117	119
France	252	248	233	239	237	237	221	215	194	185	170	158	148†	120	109	104
Ireland	—	—	—	—	170‡	188	181	183	174	167	145	142	140†	122	116	105
Netherlands	—	—	262	257	251	242	210	184	152	133	102	89	96†	76	80	82
Scotland	—	—	—	208	221	217	192	185	166	154	138	134	132†	121	121	123
Spain	—	—	—	—	308	304§	318	295	251	235	191	172	130†	95	86	82
Switzerland	—	—	—	—	—	234	208	190	168	146	123	117	111†	100	93	90
Denmark	219	232	204	206	198	194	185	175	142	130	115	107	97†	91	98	103
Finland	249	283	234	287	322	222	211	200	187	189	149	140	136†	93	94	94
Iceland	—	306	299	281	316	240	244	178	162	142	127	107	91†	71	70	67
Norway	189	202	181	171	180	171	171	163	142	138	113	104	98†	87	97	100
Sweden	236	228	206	217	202	183	170	164	149	143	121	117	104†	97	101	107
Australia	—	—	—	—	166	157	153	130	112	108	94	93	99†	90	88	80
New Zealand	—	—	—	—	—	116‖	104	98	98	100	86	87	98†	91	88	83
Japan	—	—	—	—	—	—	—	—	—	220¶	207	175	136#	82	70	63

*Excluding 1914–1917;
†excluding 1940–1945;
‡7 years only;
§1878–1880 only;
‖1877–1880 only;
¶1912–1920;
#1941–1943 and 1947–1950.

Sources: Data from B.R. Mitchell.
   European Historical Statistics, 1750–1970, pp. 104–124. Copyright (c) 1975, The Macmillan Press Ltd. Reprinted with permission.
   UN Demographic Yearbooks.
   Yearbooks of Iceland, Australia, and New Zealand.

cause the deaths have been entered into 2 consecutive years rather than into a single year as would happen if the special events occurred in midyear. Of course, with small populations the variation in the rates will be greater than with large, for example, in counties or subdivisions, especially if small, isolated populations suffer from infections introduced from abroad. After a year of particularly heavy mortality, the rate may fall below its "local average" value because of several factors; first, in the year of high mortality the aged and the young may have been particularly susceptible to the famine, infections, or war causing the high mortality, so in the next year these age groups will have lower representation in the population and will contribute less than expected to the deaths; second, if the cause in the year of high mortality were measles or smallpox, the epidemic would leave the population immune to it in the following year; third, low rates of marriage and conception in the bad year would leave fewer infants at risk in the following years.

For an easy comparison of the falls in the crude death rates, some averaging is necessary to avoid or reduce the variations due to epidemics, famines, and war. Backer (1961, Table 143) gives a tabulation of the crude death rates of nine European states by quinquennia. Similarly, the data of the official publications could be averaged into appropriate 10-year rates, or constructed more conveniently from Mitchell (1975).

Specific commentary is made on such data in Chapters 37, 39, and 41; in particular, we give years in which certain infections were active. In general, there have been great falls in the crude death rates in the countries considered beginning around 1880. Since the declines in mortality were especially due to the infectious diseases, they had an effect similar to that of an increase in the birth rate, so that the declines of mortality delayed the aging of the population, very largely brought about by declining fertility rates. In the latest decade, after 1971, there is evidence that the crude death rates are increasing now, or will do so in a few years in most of the countries surveyed, because of the aging of the populations; rises up to 150* are to be expected, 150* being the reciprocal of the expectation of life multiplied by 10,000. See Stowman (1947–1948a,b) for postwar death rates.

Chapter 4
Dynamics of Population Growth

4.1 Life Tables

Mortality, fertility, and migration are the three important components of population growth. In this chapter the theory of population dynamics is considered as a field of application of mortality statistics.

It is an unfortunate historical accident that life tables have usually been constructed by actuaries who have developed many procedures involving the theory of interpolation; as a result, textbook descriptions have often been difficult to read by novices to the field. Since many of these procedures turn out to be irrelevant for biological purposes, we make no further reference to them. The primary aim of a life table is to calculate the survivorship from birth, or any other particular age, of individuals submitted to observed or theoretical conditions. With a short-lived animal such as the mouse, it is practical to calculate such survivorship (or order of dying out, as the Germans have called it, or the curve of l_x of the actuaries).

Figure 4.1.1 shows an order of dying out of 269 mice introduced into a cage; birth cannot be used since mice in captivity are cannibalistic. There are few losses in the cage initially but the curve becomes steeper after age 400 days.

Of course, it would be inconvenient, if different life tables were compared, to have different starting points, l_0, so that l_0 is usually chosen as a power of 10, commonly $10^5 = 100,000$, thus avoiding decimals; but for theoretical work and demography, it is conve-

nient to set $l_0 = 1$ and then l_x is the proportion of persons surviving to age x years precisely.

In Figure 4.1.2 we show three life tables with the survivorship given as a percentage. Graunt's (1662) table is highly speculative but the table of Halley (1693), reprinted in Halley, Haygarth, et al. (1973), was constructed from tables of ages at death, for which see §3.1. These two classic life tables are compared with a modern life table of 1947 in which the drop due to infant mortality can still be represented graphically without ambiguity. The two classic graphs show an enormously higher loss by death (lower survivorship) at the younger ages than do the modern tables (or graphs), for example, the graph for Australian males in 1947 (see also Glass, 1950).

The use of the life tables is fundamental in studies of human mortality, population size, and fertility, but they are also of use in follow-up studies as in diabetic or surgical clinics. We make use of them in the remaining sections of this chapter.

More formally, the life table is a mathematical model giving the survivorship, l_x, in a population subjected to a schedule of mortality rates, $\{m_x\}$ say, or experience, as the actuaries call it, throughout life. Usually x takes only integer values, 0, 1, 2, . . . but this limitation is not essential. Here we set l_0 equal to unity. Then

$$l_{x+1} = l_x \, p_x, \quad l_0 = 1. \qquad (4.1.1)$$

The schedule $\{m_x\}$ is given, where

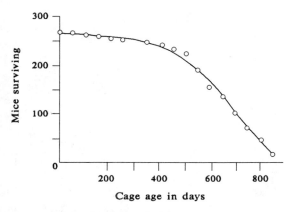

FIGURE 4.1.1. An order of dying out.
Hill's normal mice (after Greenwood, 1928).

(In captivity mice are often cannibalistic, so age is calculated not from birth but from entry into the cage.)

Copyright (c) 1951, *The Medical Journal of Australia*, reprinted with permission.

From Lancaster (1951*e*).

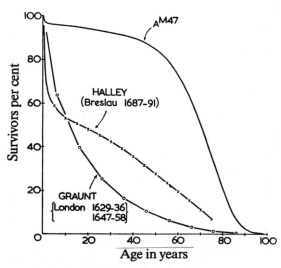

FIGURE 4.1.2. Two classical life tables compared with a modern life table (Australian males, 1947).

Copyright (c) 1951, *The Medical Journal of Australia*, reprinted with permission.

From Lancaster (1951*e*).

$$m_x = \text{deaths}/(\text{number of person-years at risk}),$$
$$(4.1.2)$$

the death rate. In §§3.3 to 3.5, we have already defined p_x as the probability of an individual of precise age, x years, surviving to precise age, $x + 1$ years, and given the relation between m_x and q_x. It is evident from the definitions that

$$p_x + q_x = 1, \text{ for every } x, \qquad (4.1.3)$$

since the individual must die in the interval or survive through it.

The data available will usually be the rates of mortality $\{m_x\}$ observed in some population at a given epoch, that is, age-specific rates of the calendar method, but life tables can also be constructed using generation death rates as by Case (1956) and Lancaster (1959*b*). Indeed, the generation life tables give a satisfactory answer to those who have criticized the calendar life tables (i.e., those constructed on the basis of death rates in a single year or epoch) on the grounds that unless the death rates by age are unchanging from year to year, no group of individuals has ever passed through life submitted to the rates of mortality holding in the given epoch.

Examples of graphs of m_x, or, alternatively, of q_x because they cannot be distinguished graphically, are given in Figure 4.1.3. Such a graph begins at a high point due to the infant mortality, declines to a minimum about the age of 11 years, rises then throughout life, with the exception that it may show a local maximum at ages around 20 years or early adult life, usually due to accident and injury in males and to childbearing and tuberculosis in females, for which see §35.3. From the middle twenties throughout the remainder of life, the curve of q_x or m_x has been in the past well represented by a straight line, when a semilogarithmic scale is used as in Figure 4.1.3, the Makeham-Gompertz law of §4.2.

Figure 4.1.4 gives graphs of the values of l_x for either sex, the survivorship curve. In modern experience the graph falls slightly before age 1 year and then more slowly; as the death rates are relatively low up to the age of 50 years, the curve of l_x has fallen only slightly before that age. With the death rates increasing with age, the curve becomes steeper in the seventies and early eighties and then flattens

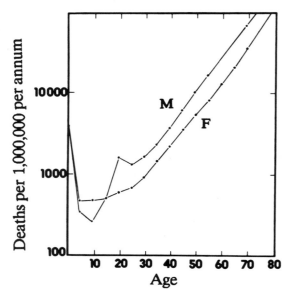

FIGURE 4.1.3. Mortality rates by age, q_x or m_x approximately, Australia, 1947.

Copyright (c) 1951, *The Medical Journal of Australia*, reprinted with permission.

From Lancaster (1951*e*)

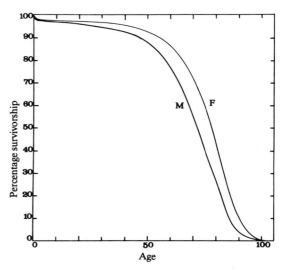

FIGURE 4.1.4. Survivorship in the life tables, l_x, Australia, 1947.

Copyright (c) 1951, *The Medical Journal of Australia*, reprinted with permission.

From Lancaster (1951*e*).

out because the numbers at risk have fallen; by the age of 100 years there are few survivors. If log l_x, rather than l_x, is plotted, this flattening of the curve does not occur because the differential coefficient of log l_x is $-\mu_x$, where μ_x is the instantaneous death rate to be defined later in this section, and μ_x, like q_x, increases with age at these high ages.

The proportion of deaths, d_x, at age x in the life table is evidently given by

$$d_x = l_x - l_{x+1}, \text{ and so} \qquad (4.1.4)$$

$$l_x = d_x + l_{x+1} \qquad (4.1.5)$$

moreover, by a repeated application of (4.1.5)

$$l_x = d_x + d_{x+1} + d_{x+2} + \ldots , \qquad (4.1.6)$$

as is evident from the fact that the survivors to age x ultimately all die. The maximum of the death curve, the modal age at death, occurs at about 72 years for males and about 82 for females in Figure 4.1.5, and this also would be approximately true for many modern life tables and actual populations.

The complete expectation of life, usually known as the expectation of life, is the average length of life that a person aged precisely x years will live in the life table and is written $\overset{0}{e}_x$. The years lived by the l_x individuals of precise age x can be computed. First, there will be $l_{x+1} + l_{x+2} + l_{x+3} + \ldots$ complete years as the survivors reach their successive birthdays; second, if it is assumed that an individual lives on an average half a year in the year of death, there will be $\frac{1}{2}l_x$ years lived by individuals in these incomplete years. It follows that

$$\overset{0}{e}_x = (\tfrac{1}{2}l_x + l_{x+1} + l_{x+2} + l_{x+3} + \ldots)/l_x. \quad (4.1.7)$$

$\overset{0}{e}_0$ is the expectation of life at birth; it is much used and misunderstood by popularizing authors. A graph of $\overset{0}{e}_x$ is given as Fig. 4.1.6. It will be noted that the expectation of life is possibly not a maximum at birth; $\overset{0}{e}_x$ increases with increasing x at points at which the instantaneous mortality rate exceeds the reciprocal of $\overset{0}{e}_x$. This feature of $\overset{0}{e}_x$ increasing in the first year of life is not as marked in the modern life tables as it was in the older tables or in the tables in areas with high infant and child death

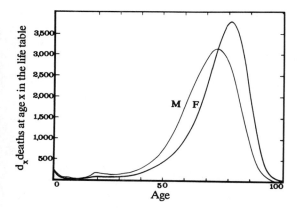

FIGURE 4.1.5. Deaths in the life tables, d_x, Australia, 1947.

From Lancaster (1951e)

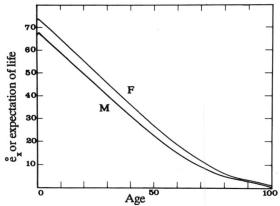

FIGURE 4.1.6. The complete expectation of life, $\overset{0}{e}_x$, Australia, 1947.

From Lancaster (1951e).

rates. Thus, the graph of $\overset{0}{e}_x$ attained its maximum at approximately the age of 10 years in some of the tables constructed in the nineteenth and the early twentieth centuries. If, and only if, $l_x = l_{x+1}$, then $\overset{0}{e}_x = \overset{0}{e}_{x+1} + 1$.

For some purposes, it is convenient to think of the age not only at the integer values of x, that is, at the birthdays, but also as a function of age as a continuous variable. The curve of q_x is smooth, so it can be approximated closely by a differentiable function curve. Making this assumption, it is possible to introduce μ_x, the force of mortality or instantaneous death rate. We then have

$$\log l_x = -\int_0^x \mu_t \, dt \qquad (4.1.8)$$

where the logarithms are the natural logarithm taken to the base e, and e is the symbol of the exponential of common mathematical analysis. Except at the extremes of life, μ_x approximates quite closely to m_x; μ_x and m_x are analogous to an instantaneous velocity and a velocity calculated over a fixed time, respectively. From (4.1.8)

$$l_x = \exp\left[-\int_0^x \mu_t \, dt\right]. \qquad (4.1.9)$$

Further,

$$d_x = l_x - l_{x+1} \qquad (4.1.10)$$

and, as before, $q_x = d_x/l_x$, $p_x = 1 - q_x$.

$$\overset{0}{e}_x = \int_0^\infty l_{x+t} \, dt/l_x. \qquad (4.1.11)$$

In this notation it can be proved that $\overset{0}{e}_x$ is an increasing function at any age x, if, and only if, $\mu_x > 1/\overset{0}{e}_x$, and so approximately that the death rate is greater than the reciprocal of $\overset{0}{e}_x$, the expectation of life at birth.

For modern applications of the life tables in ecology and population, see §4.4. For applications to human survival, see Greenwood (1922a), Gross and Clark (1975), Kalbfleisch and Prentice (1980), Nelson (1982), and Seal (1978). For England and Wales in the nineteenth century, see Hayward (1901); for general treatment of life tables, see Dublin, Lotka, and Spiegelman (1949); for maximum life span, see Walford (1983). For expectations of life at ages 0, 1, 15, 45, and 65 years and proportions dying at later ages for broad groupings of causes, see WHO-vital statistics (1985). For medical factors affecting the expectation of life, see Brackenridge (1977). For the biology of the life table, see Pearl (1922). For tables of mortality in the seventeenth and eighteenth centuries, see Béhar (1976).

4.2 Laws of Mortality

Some approximations to the curve of l_x were early adopted to simplify the computation of life assurances and annuities. A. de Moivre (1667–1754), in de Moivre (1725), noted that a satisfactory approximation could be obtained by the assumption that the curve of l_x was linear over a span of years in the form

$$l_x - l_{x+t} = at \qquad (4.2.1)$$

where a was constant. By the subdivision of the total life span and the use of several constants, good approximations could be obtained. According to Westergaard (1932, p. 46), Isaac de Graaf in 1729 believed that the vital power of man diminished with age and could be approximated in the present notation by

$$q_x = \left(\frac{x}{92}\right)^n, \quad p_x = 1 - \left(\frac{x}{92}\right)^n \qquad (4.2.2)$$

where x is the age; and with $n = 5$, a fair approximation could be obtained to de Witt's table of mortality. The hypothesis implies that all the survivors have disappeared from the table by age 92 years. B. Gompertz (1779–1865) made the hypothesis on the force of mortality,

$$\mu_x = B\, c^x = B\, e^{x \log c}$$
$$= B \exp [x \log c], \quad c > 1. \qquad (4.2.3)$$

From the definition of μ_x and an integration, it can be shown that (4.2.3) is equivalent to

$$l_x = \text{constant} \times \exp [-B \exp(x \log c)]. \qquad (4.2.4)$$

Gompertz (1820, 1825, 1860–1861, 1862) thought of the constant c as measuring a life destroying force. The later generalizations of this law can be summarized after the manner of Greenwood (1928),

$$\mu_x = A + \sum_i B_i\, \phi_i(x) + \sum_j g_j \exp [h_j\, \psi_j(x)]$$
$$= A + S_1 + S_2, \text{ say.} \qquad (4.2.5)$$

Gompertz (1825) set $A = 0 = S_1$ and $S_2 = B \exp [x \log c]$ in this formulation. Makeham (1860) modified the original formula by taking a non-zero A. Makeham (1890) took a non-zero A, $S_1 = Bx$ and $S_2 = g \exp [hx]$. See also Greenwood and Irwin (1939) and Burnet (1952) for other numerical relations.

Brownlee (1919) found that Makeham's formula implies that the substances or capacities on which life depends decay according to the law of the unimolecular reaction, that is that the amounts present at the end of equal intervals of time can be represented by the terms of a geometrical progression.

For a later version see Strehler and Mildwan (1960).

With Greenwood (1928), we must admit that excellent fits to data have been obtained and doubt that any biological significance can be read into the actual values of the constants estimated in the fitting. We make no use of the theory in this monograph.

Number mysticism applied to health created in 1633 the belief that the human body had a 7-year cycle and every seventh year was critical to health, with particular danger at 49 and 63 (see Westergaard, 1932, pp. 32, 33); Kaspar Neumann (1648–1715) proved that the phases of the moon had no influence on health.

(See also Goldstein, 1971, and Taylor, 1961.)

4.3 Fertility

In demography, fertility is used in the sense of offspring born, whereas fecundity is used to refer to the potential of bearing children; in particular, a group of fecund women may be infertile. Fertility and mortality determine the size and structure by age and sex in any closed population. Measures of fertility can be defined analogous to the various death rates. The crude birth rate is defined by

(number of births in the population in a year)/
(mean population for the year) (4.3.1)

or by

(number of births in a population)/
(years at risk) (4.3.2)

where births and years lived refer to events in the same defined population over the same period.

The age-specific fertility rates, written f_x, apply to specified classes within the population, usually births to females of a specified age group, and so

$$f_x = \text{(number of births)} / \text{(years at risk)}, \qquad (4.3.3)$$

where births to females and years at risk refer to the same age class over the same period. Sometimes only the female births are counted, a convention we shall follow here. The rates may be combined to form measures of interest, namely, the gross reproduction rate (GRR),

$$\text{GRR} = \Sigma f_x, \qquad (4.3.4)$$

and the net reproduction rate (NRR),

$$\text{NRR} = \Sigma l_x f_x, \text{ with the convention } l_0 = 1, \qquad (4.3.5)$$

where summation is over the positive integers, effectively in most countries, $x = 15, 16, 17, \ldots, 45$. The GRR takes no account of mortality; $\{l_x\}$ in (4.3.5) is calculated from the current schedule of mortality rates $\{m_x\}$ in the same population. The curve of the f_x plotted against the age is only slightly asymmetrical and a good approximation is given by

$$\text{NRR} = \text{GRR} \times l_{m^*}, \qquad (4.3.6)$$

where m^* is the mean age of mothers at the birth of a child. It can be assumed that f_x takes values not only for years but for smaller stretches of time, analogously to the use of μ_x in place of m_x for the death rates. The formulas given above can then be written as

$$\text{GRR} = \int_0^\infty f_x \, dx, \qquad (4.3.7)$$

and

$$\text{NRR} = \int_0^\infty f_x \, l_x \, dx. \qquad (4.3.8)$$

We define

$$R_s = \int_0^\infty x^s f_x \, l_x \, dx, \quad s = 0, 1, 2, 3, \ldots \qquad (4.3.9)$$

The net reproduction rate is R_0. It thus measures the mean number of female offspring born to a female passing through life, subject to the given schedules of mortality and fertility.

It measures the ratio between the numbers in successive generations in a mathematical model in which the females are imagined to be submitted to fixed schedules of $\{f_x\}$ and $\{m_x\}$.

The long-term implications of such constant schedules of fertility and mortality can be worked out by mathematical analysis (see Lancaster, 1974). The main result of the theory is that for any initial age distribution of the population, after a sufficiently long time the population attains a stable age distribution and the total size increases exponentially with time so that

$$P(t) = \text{constant} \times e^{\rho t}, \qquad (4.3.10)$$

where ρ, the intrinsic rate of increase, is defined by

$$1 = R_0 \int_0^\infty e^{-\rho y} f_y \, l_y \, dy. \qquad (4.3.11)$$

The stable age distribution is given by

$$g(y) = e^{-\rho y} l_y / \int_0^\infty e^{-\rho y} l_y \, dy. \qquad (4.3.12)$$

If $\rho = 0$, the population is stationary. More generally,

$$\rho \simeq \log_e R_0 / m^*. \qquad (4.3.13)$$

(4.3.6) is often useful in putting limits on the fertility in empirical stationary distributions if the mortality is known, and conversely. For example, if the population of a country has been approximately stationary over a period and $l_{m^*} = 0.6$, it will be necessary to assume that the gross fertility rate is approximately 1.7.

There is a theory of the survival of physical aggregates that has many points in common with the theory of human population dynamics and is known as reliability theory (e.g., Gross and Clark, 1975). The density function, $f(x)$, of this theory is d_x regarded as a continuous variable of age. The survivorship function is defined as the complement of l_x, $S(x) = 1 - l_x$. Evidently $f(x)$ is the derivative of $S(x)$. $\lambda(x)$ the hazard function is the instantaneous death rate, μ_x. The death density conditional on the individual reaching age t is given by

$$\lambda(x \mid t) = f(x) / l_t \qquad (4.3.14)$$

TABLE 4.3.1. Life table functions in England and Wales.

Epoch	Complete expectation of life				Survivorship*	
	$\overset{0}{e}_0$		$\overset{0}{e}_{60}$		l_{25}	
	Males	Females	Males	Females	Males	Females
1841	40.19	42.18	13.59	14.40	623*	643
1838–1844	40.36	42.04	13.60	14.49	626	644
1838–1854	39.91	41.85	13.53	14.34	624	644
1871–1880	41.35	44.62	13.14	14.24	657	685
1881–1890	43.66	47.18	12.88	14.10	694	725
1891–1900	44.13	47.77	12.93	14.10	694	725
1901–1910	48.53	52.38	13.49	15.01	745	774
1910–1912	51.50	55.35	13.78	15.48	779	804
1920–1922	55.62	59.58	14.36	16.22	822	846
1930–1932	58.74	62.88	14.43	16.50	858	881
1948[†]	66.4	71.2	15.8	19.0	934	946
1950–1952	66.4	71.5	14.8	18.1	945	959
1960–1962	68.1	74.0	15.1	19.1	958	971
1970–1972	69.0	75.2	15.4	20.0	964	976
1977–1979	70.3	76.3	15.9	20.5	971	981

* Survivors from 1,000 at birth.
[†] The series of English Life Tables was broken because of war in 1939–1945.
From Registrar-General of England and Wales.

TABLE 4.3.2. Life table functions in Australia.

Epoch	Complete expectation of life				Survivorship*	
	$\overset{0}{e}_0$		$\overset{0}{e}_{60}$		l_{25}	
	Males	Females	Males	Females	Males	Females
1881–1890	47.20	50.84	13.77	15.39	737*	768
1891–1900	51.08	54.76	13.99	15.86	782	807
1901–1910	55.20	58.84	14.35	16.20	828	849
1920–1922	59.15	63.31	15.08	17.17	863	886
1932–1934	63.48	67.14	15.57	17.74	907	924
1946–1948	66.07	70.63	15.36	18.11	938	954
1953–1955	67.14	72.75	15.47	18.78	946	964
1960–1962	67.92	74.18	15.60	19.51	954	969
1965–1967[†]	67.63	74.15	15.27	19.52	955	972
1970–1972[†]	67.81	74.60	15.35	19.74	956	973
1975–1977[†]	69.56	76.56	16.40	21.04	962	978

* Survivors from 1,000 at birth.
[†] Includes full-blood aboriginals.
From Demography (Australia).

and, of course, the integral of $\lambda(x,t)$ is unity. The hazard function, or conditional mortality rate, is relevant in mortality studies on migrants, in follow-ups after therapeutical procedures, and in studies on mice, the latter of which can usually only be studied after introduction into the cage (Greenwood, 1928).

In view of equation (4.3.6) above, we give now as tables 4.3.1–4 values of l_{25} as observed in life tables. It is convenient to give values at age 25 years for females, although this may not be the true value of m^*, the mean age of mother at parturition; however, l_{25} will differ very little from l_{m^*}.

TABLE 4.3.3. Life table functions in Norway.

| Epoch | Complete expectation of life | | | | Survivorship* | |
| | $\overset{0}{e}_0$ | | $\overset{0}{e}_{60}$ | | l_{25} | |
	Males	Females	Males	Females	Males	Females
1821–1830	45.0	48.0	15.2	15.8	—	—
1831–1840	41.8	45.6	13.8	14.8	—	—
1841–1850	44.5	47.9	14.4	15.2	—	—
1856–1865	47.4	50.0	15.2	16.2	702*	730
1871–1880	48.3	51.3	15.6	16.7	715	746
1881–1890	48.7	51.2	16.1	17.2	710	737
1891–1900	50.41	54.14	16.39	17.46	737	775
1901–1910	54.82	57.70	16.80	17.85	791	818
1911–1920	55.62	58.71	16.98	17.78	804	832
1921–1930	60.98	63.84	16.97	18.16	865	884
1931–1940	64.08	67.55	17.22	18.38	897	919
1946–1950	69.25	72.65	18.39	19.45	933	953
1951–1955	71.11	74.70	18.52	19.93	950	967
1956–1960	71.32	75.57	18.12	20.06	956	972
1961–1965	71.03	75.97	17.60	20.06	961	976
1966–1970	71.09	76.83	17.33	20.64	966	979
1971–1975	71.41	77.68	17.44	21.18	968	982
1978–1979	72.27	78.73	17.71	21.92	974[†]	985[†]

* Survivors from 1,000 at birth.
[†] 1976–1980.
Norway Statistical Yearbook 1981, pp. 33, 34.
Last two columns by courtesy of G.S. Lettenstrøm, Statistisk Sentralbyrå, Oslo. Data unavailable for 1821–1850.

TABLE 4.3.4. Life table functions in Japan.

| Epoch | Complete expectation of life | | | | Survivorship* | |
| | $\overset{0}{e}_0$ | | $\overset{0}{e}_{60}$ | | l_{25} | |
	Males	Females	Males	Females	Males	Females
1891–1898	42.8	44.3	12.8	14.2	668*	678
1899–1903	43.97	44.85	12.76	14.32	683	682
1921–1925	42.06	43.20	11.87	14.12	658	653
1935–1936	46.92	49.63	12.55	15.07	725	732
1947	50.06	53.96	12.83	15.39	776	791
1950–1952	59.57	62.97	14.36	16.81	875	885
1955	63.60	67.75	14.97	17.72	912	926
1960	65.32	70.19	14.84	17.83	932	948
1965	67.74	72.92	15.20	18.42	956	969
1970	69.31	74.66	15.93	19.27	964	977
1976	72.15	77.35	17.59	20.95	974	983

* Survivors from 1,000 at birth.
Japan Statistical Yearbook, 1978.

Famine amenorrhea. Fertility falls under famine conditions for a variety of reasons, but Meuvret (1946, 1965) noticed that there was a low rate of conception at the height of famines by a careful comparison between indicators of famine and times of birth. Ruwet (1954) and Goubert (1954) noted similar low rates during the famines of 1693–1694 in Liège and in the parishes of Beauvais, respectively. Le Roy Ladurie (1969, 1972, 1979) has reviewed the whole question with the aid of observations made during and immediately after the wars of 1914–1918 and 1939–1945 in European countries, Smith (1947a), for example. Strikingly high rates of amenorrhea have been reported from young women; sometimes confirmatory pathological evidence has also been reported; further, the syndrome has been terminated in many instances with restoration of adequate food supplies.

The contraceptive effect of breast feeding is underestimated in modern times in the developed world, where demand feeding is not always practiced and where the mother is not living on restricted rations. Short (1983, 1984) believes that demand feeding is usually necessary to give continuous hormonal stimulus. For conditions of the mother, see Royston (1982), and for the prevalence and duration distribution of breast feeding, see WHO-breast feeding (1982). (See also Dobbing, 1985.)

4.4 Life Table Populations

Life table populations are mathematical models constructed by assuming an influx of births at the rate of $B(t)$ per annum in an idealized (theoretically given) population. If age in the life table is taken to be a continuous function or a function defined at discrete points of time if the age variable is taken to be discrete, then $B(t)$ may be considered to be a continuous function. After the influx by birth into the model, the individuals are assumed to be submitted to a schedule of death rates given by some hypothesis or observed in some actual population. At time t the number of individuals at age x is proportional to $B(t-x)l_x$. If the variables are taken to be continuous, the graph of the age distribution, $g(x)$, is given by

$$g_t(x) = B(t-x)l_x, \quad x > 0, \qquad (4.4.1)$$

or if l_x is only defined for integer values,

$$g_t(x) = \tfrac{1}{2}(B(t-x)l_x + B(t-x-1)l_{x+1}); \qquad (4.4.2)$$

in this second case, a slight correction has to be made for $x = 0$ and possibly for other x since it cannot be assumed that deaths occur evenly throughout the year in the first, and possibly other, years of life. In each case $B(t)$ can be scaled so that the total population is unity, a million, or other convenient power of 10. The scaling factor can be obtained by an integration in (4.4.1) and a summation in (4.4.2). When $B(t) = B(0)$, a constant, the population stays at a fixed size, independent of the time; it is then said to be a stationary life table population. In Figure 4.4.1 we give the stationary life table populations calculated from Australian mortality data centered on 1886 and 1947, respectively. Following the usual conventions, age is given by the ordinate and population numbers by bars to the left (right) for males (females). Such a figure is usually termed a "population pyramid." The slopes of the edges of the pyramids are proportional to d_x of the corresponding life table. In the 1886 tables there are rapid declines in the population numbers as age increases from birth to age 10 years, then a decline, slow at first but increasing with age, up to a maximum at approximately 70 years, and then decreasing; in fact, the changes are those in l_x as already detailed in §4.1. The numbers of aged in the later life table population (stippled) are relatively much greater than in the earlier (not stippled). It is important to note that l_x is a strictly decreasing function of x and a stationary population pyramid cannot be undermined. It may be also noted that improvements in mortality will always increase the proportion of the aged in a stationary life table population; this is possibly not so in actual population pyramids, a point to be made later with Figure 4.4.2.

Life table population pyramids can also be constructed when the births in year t, $B(t)$, are not constant. If

$$B(t) = \exp(t\rho) \times \text{constant}, \qquad (4.4.3)$$

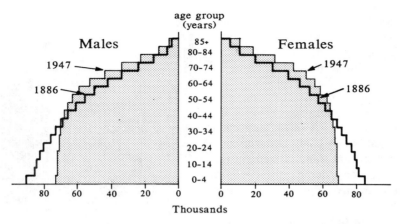

FIGURE 4.4.1. Stationary life table populations constructed from Australian data, 1886 and 1947.

Copyright (c) 1954, *The Medical Journal of Australia*, reprinted with permission.

From Lancaster (1954g)

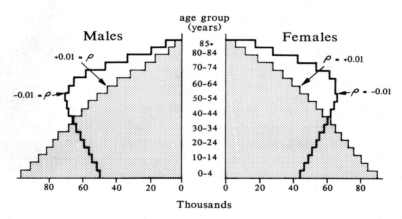

FIGURE 4.4.2. Two stable life table populations constructed from the mortality rates existing in Australia in 1947. In one the births are increasing by 1% every year, that is, $\rho = 0.01$; in the other, decreasing by 1% every year, that is, $\rho = -0.01$.

Copyright (c) 1954, *The Medical Journal of Australia*, reprinted with permission.

From Lancaster (1954g)

the table is said to be a stable life table population, where ρ, the intrinsic rate of increase, can be positive, negative, or zero. In this last case we would have again a stationary life table population.

In Figure 4.4.2, we give population pyramids of two stable life table populations subject to the same mortality schedules, increasing or decreasing at the rate of 1% per annum, or, in the notation above, the births are proportional to $\exp(\rho t)$ with $\rho = \pm 0.01$. The stippled areas represent the increasing populations; age is read off vertically and the numbers of persons in the quinquennial age groups are represented by the horizontal distances. Males (females) are given on the left (right). The lengths fall off rapidly with age since the persons aged x are representatives of a birth cohort x years previously and their numbers are proportional to $B(-x)l_x = \exp(-0.01x)l_x$. In any rapidly growing life table population, the numbers at any fixed epoch fall off rapidly with age. In the declining population the lengths are proportional to $B(-x)l_x = \exp(0.01x)l_x$, and so the lengths are increasing up to the age at which $\exp(0.01) = q_x$, in modern tables about 50 years or later. Figure 4.4.2 is designed especially to show that aging in an existent population could be brought about solely by changes in the birth rate. Since Figure 4.4.1 shows that aging could be brought about by changes in the mortality rates, it is clear that some judgement and consideration of the past demographic experience of a population are required before stating a cause of aging in it.

The births in a life table population can be defined in a manner, different from the above, by assuming a schedule of fertility rates, scaled to give account of female births only, $\{f_x\}$. A general result can be stated.

In the life table populations (i.e., in a mathematical model) if the schedules of mortality $\{m_x\}$ and fertility $\{f_x\}$ are given and, so, are fixed and independent of the time, the population ultimately becomes increasing, stationary, or decreasing, according to whether the net reproduction rate is greater than, equal to, or less than unity (see Lancaster, 1974). Modern research has shown that this effect can be observed in actual populations if the age-specific mortality and fertility rates remain approximately constant over several generations. See also the comment of Humphreys (1883), who found that the observed distributions of population of England and Wales at the times of the censuses of 1861 and 1871 approximated closely to those of the stationary life table populations calculated from mortality data at the corresponding times.

For population dynamics, see also Anderson (1982), Anderson and May (1979, 1982a,c), and Sladen and Bang (1969). For a popularization, see Lancaster (1973a).

4.5 Age Distributions in Actual Populations

In Figure 4.5.1 a famous example of aging in a population is given, that of Sweden; population pyramids are shown for the years 1920, 1935, and 1950. It is clear that fertility rates

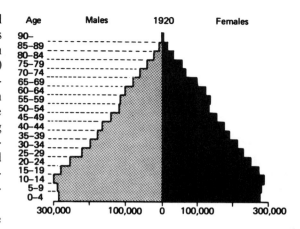
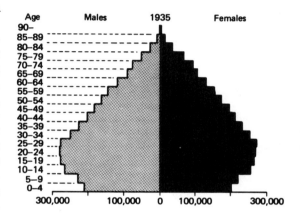
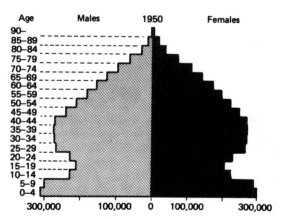

FIGURE 4.5.1. Population Pyramids for Sweden. From *Historisk Statistik for Sverige, Befolkning, 1720–1950*. Statistiska Centralbyrån (1955).

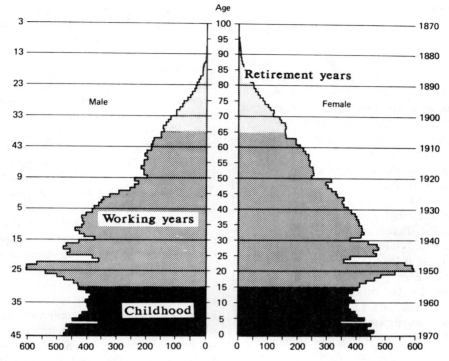

FIGURE 4.5.2. Population pyramid of Japan, 1970. Reproduced from the *Japan Statistical Yearbook for 1971*.

had already begun to decline around 1910, and slight undermining is present in 1920, but is far more marked in 1935; after 1935 the fertility rates increased, and there are now classes of deficient numbers at ages from 10 to 25 years.

The Japanese population pyramid in 1970 is given in Figure 4.5.2. There is a deficit of males at ages in the vicinity of 50 years, the effect of World War II, and at ages around 25 years, the effects of the low birth rates at the time of World War II. It is clear from these figures from Sweden and Japan that fertility effects are more evident than mortality effects. Nevertheless, by examining the ratio of males to females by age, it is often possible to detect the effects of the differential mortality produced by war. Although there are usually excesses of females over males at high ages in modern populations because of the more favorable female death rates throughout life, if the ratio differs from that suggested by life table studies, one can often conclude that the variation is due to war.

See also Coale (1956, 1963, 1972) and Coale and Demeny (1983) for applications of life table theory to population distribution changes due to mortality declines and other factors.

4.6 Social Consequences of Changes in Mortality

Changes in mortality rates will have effects on social and other factors in the general population. These effects can usually be worked out in mathematical models of populations, but some care has to be used if such computations are carried out so as to be predictions in actual populations.

Orphanhood

Rates for paternal and/or maternal orphanhood of a child reaching his or her xth birthday are given in Lancaster (1954g) and Lotka (1931).

Population Size

Population growth will obviously be faster if mortality rates fall. Let us apply the mortality rates of Table 4.3.1–4.3.4 to mathematical models in which fertility rates are supposed to be held constant but in which the mortality rates hold, as in the first epoch of each table, and then are replaced by the mortality rates of the last epoch of each table. The net reproduction rate can be approximated by the use of (4.3.6); for example, in England and Wales we would obtain the NRR as the GRR multiplied by 0.643, that is, l_{25} for females in 1841, and then, after the change in rates, as GRR multiplied by 0.981, that is, l_{25} for females in 1977–1979, so, the NRR would be increased by a factor of $0.981/0.643 = 1.53$ corresponding to an increase of 53%. Similar ratios would be obtained for the other pairs of initial and terminal l_{25}: Australia 1.27, Norway 1.35, and Japan 1.45, corresponding to percentage increases of 27%, 35%, and 45%, respectively.

Population Distribution

Declines in mortality applied to a mathematical model in which the fertility and mortality schedules are such as to produce a stationary population will lead to an aging of the population if the fertility schedule is changed so as to produce, again, a stationary population, but general statements cannot be made without some hypothesis regarding the change in fertility rates. In actual populations, because mortality changes occur first in infancy and childhood, the first effect of a change in mortality rates is usually a lowering of the average age in the population—a somewhat paradoxical result.

In actual populations of the developed world in recent times, changes in fertility have caused greater changes in size and age distribution than have changes in mortality. The Royal Commission on Population (1949–1950) gave its view that without catastrophic changes in the birth or death rates, the proportion of persons in the population at ages 15–64 years would remain at the level 62–66% for any projection forward of the fertility and death rates of England and Wales into the next hundred years or so. It is clear, then, that the improvement in the mortality rates does not impose an impossible burden on the state, which will be expected to be responsible for the care of the aged and will have to help either by pensions, hospital care, or otherwise.

It is possible that many of the more pessimistic views on the problem of aging emanate from those working in teaching hospitals. Sheldon (1948), working in Wolverhampton, England, noted that biased views might result, for "the degree of self-selection imposed by the population on itself in regard to its approach to doctors inevitably gives anything other than a random sample a considerable bias."

The consequences or values of declines in mortality are often discussed with the aid of the life table; the use of the complete expectation of life at birth, $\overset{0}{e}_0$ of the life table, has led to many misunderstandings. Romeder and McWhinney (1977) and Walsh and Warren (1979) have computed changes in the expectation of life or potential years of life lost (PYLL) under changing mortality rates; one may remark that if the disappearance of a disease killing at age 1 year saves a life, it does not add $(70 - 1.5)$ years but a more complicated expression $(\overset{0}{e}_1^* - 1.5)$ years where the asterisk implies $\overset{0}{e}_1^*$ has been computed with the death rates for the given disease removed from m_x and the life table curtailed at age 70 years.

For value of human life, see Linnerooth (1979) and Williamson (1984); for aging of population, see Grinblat (1982), Siegel and Hoover (1982) (world), Lopez and Hanada (1982), and Meegama (1982) (developing countries). For world population prospects, see UN Population Studies No. 86 (1985); for problems of rapid population growth, see Study Committee of the National Academy of Sciences (1971). For the modern rise of population, see McKeown (1976). (See also, for aging throughout the world, §36.7.)

Chapter 5
Infectious Diseases

5.1 Introduction

Some general properties of the infectious diseases, or, more precisely, the diseases of organismal origin, are now treated, with emphasis on numerical and epidemiologic details. Material for the quantitative study of epidemics has been available in the various countries only in recent times; for example, the *London Bills of Mortality* had first been published about 1518 after the aggregation of parish records and were continued until the collection of such data became the duty of the Registrar-General of England and Wales. Tables of mortality from smallpox, tuberculosis, and measles can be constructed from these data from about 1615 or 1630 up to the present time, which we discuss in the relevant sections below. Deaths from all causes combined became available from the nordic countries after about 1729; further, great epidemics of measles, scarlet fever, whooping cough, and smallpox were recorded in Sweden. Many such observations have been published in the works of Haeser, Hecker, Hirsch, and Creighton, which we list in §1.8, but these volumes are tending now to date because in recent times much work has been done in this field. Monographs, which treat each disease historically and on a worldwide basis, are now available on individual diseases such as smallpox and plague; there are also governmental serials and reports and the publications of the World Health Organization. We have made much use of Christie (1980) for the clinical description of infective diseases. The various editions of the *Principles of Bacteriology, Virology, and Immunity* of W.W.C. Topley (1886–1944) and G.S. Wilson (1895–1988) have been preeminent in the field and have given due attention to the epidemiologic and vital-statistical side of their work, but there has been a great expansion of knowledge between the appearance of the first edition in 1929 and the seventh edition in 1983–1984, which has entailed restriction of space for some vital-statistical information. We have used principally the sixth edition in these early chapters, but have checked wherever necessary to see that our conclusions are consistent with the seventh edition of 1983–1984, and references are given to the authors of the chapters in it. See Wilson (1984*a*).

5.2 Fade-out of Epidemics

The behavior of many epidemic diseases, especially the extremes of perpetuation and fade-out, is dependent on population size. Measles is often considered as a convenient example of an infection peculiar to mankind. The fundamental properties of this virus infection were established by Panum (1847), who noted the length of the incubation period, the almost universal susceptibility to it, and the existence of a solid immunity to a second attack.

Assuming such properties for an infectious disease, the behavior of an epidemic in a small closed community can be considered. In a model of the disease we imagine a fresh case to be introduced into a community of N susceptibles; although no fresh case may occur, usually there will be n further cases with n not being greater than N, since we have supposed a solid immunity so that no individual suffers a second attack. For simplicity of exposition, it is assumed that the time between the appearance of the disease in one patient and its appearance in a second patient infected from him is a constant, so that we can speak of generations of the disease. There will be a chain of infections, $n_1, n_2, \ldots$ in the first, second, $\ldots$ generations of the infection and $n_1 + n_2 + \ldots = n \leq N$. Under various hypotheses, computations of the numbers of cases in each generation can be made, see Greenwood (1931). These computations are practicable for small communities such as sibships and small schools, but with larger communities, the possible sequences are too numerous for convenience of computation if it is desired to assign probabilities to each.

These models can be applied in the real world. Thus, in Boston, Wilson (1947) and Wilson, Bennett, Allen, and Worcester (1939) observed that the first case in a sibship was usually an older child who attended school or had other opportunities to become infected. A larger subunit of a population is the residential school, in which there may be many susceptibles. Such epidemics have been studied by Cheeseman (1950). The family and the school are examples of partially closed subunits in the populations. Their importance was well brought out by Halliday (1928) studying the incidence of infectious diseases in Glasgow. He noted that in the congested "often slum" areas, children played in a common courtyard or "land," and this could determine an extended family or partially closed community into which the more mobile older children could introduce new infections, thus exposing the younger children to a much greater risk of infection than would be experienced by those living in better conditions in less-congested housing estates. This difference in the number of contacts caused differences in the ages of acquisition of the common childhood infections. As the case fatality rates were higher at the younger ages, gradients in incidence and case fatality rates were evident. In the con-

gested areas and housing estates, measles was essentially a disease of infants; in the better residential areas, it was a disease of school children, and in the houses of the well-to-do public school class, it was a disease of later childhood, 14 to 18 years, the disease being often contracted at boarding school.

Another type of small closed communities has been provided by the sailing ships in the days of large overseas migrations. Congestion on board ships greatly enhanced the ease of the spread of infections, and the chain of infections on a ship would be short, perhaps only one, two, or three generations of the epidemic occurring before the susceptibles were exhausted. In particular, a ship leaving England, for instance, would be quite unlikely to carry the infection direct to Australia or the west coast of America. However, the ships would call at some South American port for fresh food and then proceed on to Capetown and Australia. At these ports the population might be too small to perpetuate an epidemic but would provide a risk of infection for the passengers of the ships, so, from time to time, there might be infections reintroduced at these intermediate ports and then conveyed on by ship to the next port and finally Australia, for example. Indeed, according to Donovan (1970a), measles was first introduced into Australia in this way in 1834, 46 years after the first European settlement.

We attempt to give some estimate of the minimum size of a closed community required for the perpetuation of an epidemic, in other words, to avoid "fade-out." To simplify the discussion, we assume that the incubation period is 14 days and that one case is infective only for a short time at the end of this period. We consider a small, closed human community, an island, perhaps, with an annual birth rate of 25 per 1,000, to determine the smallest population that could perpetuate the epidemic of measles indefinitely. If the epidemic were deliberately and rigidly controlled, 2 new cases would be required roughly every fortnight to avoid accidents to the cases or chance failure of the virus to pass from person to person. About 50 new cases would be required per annum and, so, the population would need to be approximately 2,000; but under ordinary natural field conditions, this regularity would not be observed and there would be some outbreaks with many cases, so the estimate of the critical size for perpetuation would have to be greatly raised.

In a country in which measles is endemic, a city can be regarded as being almost a closed unit of population because there is relatively little migration of children. Bartlett (1960) gave a useful table showing the fade-out of measles from cities of less than 300,000. This phenomenon was rare in the cited experience for larger cities.

It has come as a surprise to many that the critical population size for perpetuation of measles is so large, although excellent data on the Australian epidemics have long been available in Cumpston (1927). There was a fade-out in the Australian colonies as a whole after the epidemic of 1834, and there have been many fade-outs in the individual colonies since that time (Lancaster, 1967b). Moreover, works on the history of epidemics show that measles and smallpox have faded out from even larger demographic units (see Table 11.7.1). Indeed, the epidemiologic behavior of influenza suggests that thousands of millions of humans cannot support indefinitely a pandemic of influenza of a given strain.

It is clear that measles, rubella, and smallpox could not have been perpetuated as human diseases before the establishment of the great riverine communities. As pointed out by Burnet and White (1972), this has evolutionary implications for measles, the virus of which may have arisen by mutation from some virus of another species within historic times.

The foregoing probabilistic reasoning is received with reluctance by the bacteriologists. The person-to-person progress of measles infection is obviously a "chancy" matter, in other words, probabilistic. However, even the effect of the injection of bacilli in huge numbers directly into the tissues is subject to chance; thus, the second edition of Topley and Wilson (1936, Table LX) shows that only 15% of mice became infected when a dosage of 10^3 B. typhi-

TABLE 5.2.1. Incubation period of notifiable diseases.

Disease	Incubation period in days
Amebic dysentery	Variable
Anthrax	2–3
Bacillary dysentery	$\frac{1}{2}$–7 (1–2)*
Chicken pox	7–23 (approx. 18)
Diphtheria	1–6 (2–3)
Infective hepatitis	25–35
Influenza	1–3
Malaria, *vivax*	14
Malaria, *falciparum*	12
Malaria, *quartan*	18–40
Measles	10–11
Meningococcal meningitis	<7
Mumps	7–23 (17–18)
Paratyphoid	7–10
Pneumonia	1–2
Poliomyelitis	9–13
Rabies	10–700 (50–60)
Rheumatic fever	7–35
Rocky Mountain spotted fever	2–14
Rubella	10–20 (17–18)
Scarlet fever	2–5
Smallpox	8–12
Syphilis	10–70 (approx. 30)
Tetanus	2–40 (5–10)
Tuberculosis	100 possibly
Tularemia	1–10
Typhoid fever	5–40 (10–14)
Typhus fever	8–12
Undulant fever	5–30 (14)
Whooping cough	7–14

*The numbers in parentheses are the most likely times. See Pullen (1950, p. 63), Christie (1980), Sartwell (1950, 1966).

murium was injected subcutaneously, and 50%, with a dosage of 10^9. Further, the result of injecting a known amount of toxin into experimental animals is also a chance event, which is implicit in the theory of bioassay, so that not only the event of infection is a chance event but also the amount of toxin released into the circulation by a diphtheria infection and the response of the body to it.

In Table 5.2.1 we give the incubation period of various notifiable infectious diseases. These incubation periods are relevant for calculation of the time in which an epidemic can reach its maximum intensity and also for the perpetuation of the epidemic. See also Armenian and Lilienfeld (1983).

5.3 Perpetuation of Virus Epidemics

Fade-out, one extreme case of epidemic behavior, has just been considered. We now turn to the other extreme, namely, perpetuation, limiting the discussion mainly to virus diseases; some of the argument is applicable to bacterial or other organismal diseases. Virus diseases are subject to two constraints, namely, they cannot multiply except in living cells and they are unable to survive outside the body of some living host. We may follow the general discussions of Matumoto (1969) and Yorke, Nathanson, Pianigiana, and Martin (1979). Human virus infections may be confined to the single host species, as in measles and rubella; they may be vector-borne with the single vertebrate host, as in dengue and urban yellow fever; there may be multiple vertebrate hosts, as in jungle yellow fever and, perhaps, influenza. The human population is not involved in the perpetuation of infections by the arboviruses, arenaviruses, and rabies, which are zoonoses with man as an accidental host; of course, a similar theory can be applied to animal hosts. Some of the models of perpetuation are now detailed.

Perpetuation by Short Cycle. Measles evokes a strong response from man and is only perpetuated by a relatively rapid transmission from man to man. It cannot survive long outside the host, so close contact between members of the herd is essential; the communicable period is short and a solid immunity is induced and, in effect, all previous cases have been removed from the population. Moreover, an epidemic does not usually exhaust all the susceptibles. Thus, empirical studies (Matumoto, 1969) have shown that if measles is introduced into a community with a proportion of about 40% of susceptibles this will be reduced to about 20%. Smallpox and mumps behave similarly, but rubella and varicella have additional modes of perpetuation. The incubation and infectious periods of influenza are both 48 hours, shorter than in the diseases already mentioned, so the

minimal size of population can be expected to be higher; indeed, for virulent strains, it appears to be higher than the human population of the world. Poliovirus is also perpetuated by the short cycle method, infection being from the bowel or nasopharyngeal excretions to the upper respiratory tract of the new host. The incubation period is shorter than in measles, but the virus is excreted at irregular intervals in the feces for some weeks. Poliovirus does not excite such a strong immunologic reaction as measles, so that the poliovirus can be reacquired later and again be excreted; few persons suffer from overt disease.

Transmission via the Placenta. Rubella can infect the fetus in utero, and the infection can persist until after birth and then cause fresh infections.

Perpetuation by Chronic Infections. Herpes simplex virus is maintained as a chronic, often inapparent, infection with the common lesions appearing only after some incident, such as a cold or pneumonia. Varicella also can become a latent chronic infection of the nerve fibers; many years later the virus may become active, multiply, and appear in the vesicles of herpes zoster (see §11.4). It can then pass into the air and be the source of another case of varicella. Thus, varicella has become permanently established in Iceland, although measles has never become so. Black (1966) estimated the critical size as only 1,000 for the perpetuation of varicella; clearly a stochastic (or chance) process is involved here. It is possible for no infected case to become a latent chronic carrier of the virus, in which case there is fade-out.

Perpetuation by Long Time of Incubation. The cycle of infection can be prolonged as in the so-called slow-virus infections, which include the disease "kuru" and, perhaps, other chronic human diseases of the central nervous system.

Perpetuation by Vertebrate Reservoir. Yellow fever has a reservoir of jungle yellow fever and is a disease of primates and some other vertebrates.

Perpetuation by Mosquitoes. Dengue can be perpetuated in mosquitoes in hot humid weather.

Perpetuation by Ticks. Tick vectors can maintain virus over long periods, and the virus, for example, of relapsing fever, can be transmitted transovarially to the tick offspring.

Perpetuation in Resistant Hosts. If a disease has several hosts, it can readily be perpetuated if it causes a chronic disease in at least one of them. Among nonvirus diseases this mode of perpetuation is very important for plague.

The shorter generation times of animal species other than man permit a smaller critical size of population for perpetuation in them than in man. On the other hand, although measles occurs in monkeys exposed to human infections, sylvatic measles does not occur since the primate community groups tend to be too small for perpetuation.

Man's mobility, longevity, and large population size render him susceptible to many diseases, although the equilibrium of a virus with properties similar to those of measles with man is delicate. If its power of infecting new cases is high and its cycle short, it may well exhaust all the susceptibles; on the other hand, if its powers are less, it may fade out without exhausting all the susceptibles. This suggests that comparatively small changes in the environment or conditions of passage of the parasite from person to person may greatly alter the epidemic behavior of the disease, for example, may lead to seasonal incidence and/or fade-out. It may also render the disease susceptible to eradication programs, as in the case of smallpox.

The considerations of this and the previous section show that an epidemic may fade out under fixed conditions of infective agent, host, and environment without any changes in any one of these three components. It is, thus, idle to require that some outside agency has been effective, for example, a measles epidemic in a community or an influenza pandemic may end, plague may fade out in the rats, and so on. The end of such epidemics or epizootics will obviously be difficult to observe.

5.4 Island Epidemics

There have been many studies of intense epidemics of measles and some other infections in island communities and in some partially isolated communities on the continents. The epidemics in the northern countries of Europe have been well documented, for which see §11.7. Greenland, the Faeroes, Iceland, and northern Norway and Sweden are all within easy sailing distance of the great continental centers of population, from which returning residents, government officials, visitors, seamen, and others could introduce infections. Similar problems did not exist in the Pacific Ocean until measles was endemic on those shores from which cruises were made into the isolated islands. An unhappy consequence of an Australian epidemic of measles in 1875 was the introduction of measles into Fiji; a party of Fijians had been entertained in Sydney at Government House and other places where they came into contact with an infectious case of measles (Squire, 1875–1877, Corney, 1883–1884). Unfortunately, they were conveyed back to Fiji by fast steamer and were met on their arrival by welcoming parties from the various islands of the group. After the ensuing celebrations, the parties dispersed to their homes throughout the islands, carrying their infections with them and causing a disastrous epidemic in which some 10% to 20% of the islanders perished. See §11.7 for a discussion of high case fatality rates in similar incidents.

Black (1966) gives the endemicity measure of islands as the percentage of months in which measles occurred. Hawaii, with a population of more than half a million, was the only island with an endemicity of 100%; Guam was second with 80%, then Fiji with 64%, Iceland with 61%, and Bermuda with 51%; but of the 19 islands considered, no other endemicities exceeded 32%, and several values were below 10%. Black points out that Guam and Bermuda have the special feature of frequent interchange of millitary personnel, so that their experience is not typical of an island community. See Carroll (1975) for experience on Pacific atolls and Shine (1970) for St. Helena.

It appears from experience of fever hospitals, that they may help to perpetuate epidemics of measles. Nurses are recruited often from country areas and become infected, their nursing friends visit them and become infected, and so a chain of infections can be established independently of the state of the epidemic in the city or country; but, of course, the hospital chain may contribute at any stage to further cases in the community. For Australian experience in measles and in rubella, see Lancaster (1952c, 1967b, measles; 1951g, 1954f, 1954h, rubella) and Lancaster and Pickering (1952e) for rubella in New Zealand. It may be noted that fade-outs of rubella epidemics in Australia and New Zealand created the conditions for rubella infections in pregnant women leading to congenital defects.

See also Black (1966), Black, Hierholzer, et al. (1974), Cliff, et al. (1981), Parker (1964), and Tyrrell (1977).

5.5 Vector-borne Infections

Although intelligent guesses had been made as to the role of insects in the transmission of disease, Busvine (1980a) believes that no standard textbook of medicine had given any specific reference to this role before 1871. Patrick Manson, in 1878, described the development of the nematode worm *Wuchereria bancrofti* in the body of a mosquito, and later he showed that the mosquito is the vector of filariasis. In 1895 David Bruce (1855–1931) proved that a biting fly of the genus *Glossina* was the vector of nagana, a fatal African disease of horses and cattle, and later that *Glossina* species were also the vectors of the human sleeping sickness. Ronald Ross, in 1897, announced that anopheline mosquitoes carried malaria, an important discovery to be confirmed and amplified by Italian workers.

A disease agent is said to be vector-borne (often written as transmissible) if the infecting agent is usually spread by vectors (insects, arthropods). If the disease is spread only by vectors, it is said to be strictly vector-borne, otherwise, it is said to be facultatively vector-borne; for example, plague considered as a human disease is facultatively vector-borne since it can be spread by the human flea, *Pulex irritans*, and as a respiratory disease without the intervention of the flea as a vector. Yellow fever, typhus, and malaria are strictly vector-borne. We are excluding from consideration here, of course, experimental transmission and

accidental transmission by syringe in treatment or in drug injection.

Arthropods transmit pathogens mechanically or biologically. In mechanical transmission, the vector carries the infective agent without any development in the agent; usually, this is a case of interrupted feeding as in transmission by the domestic fly. There are three varieties of biological, that is, vector, transmission: (*i*) the organisms undergo cyclical changes and multiply, (*ii*) the organisms undergo cyclical changes but do not multiply, and (*iii*) the organisms undergo no cyclical changes but multiply. These three modes are known as cyclopropagative, cyclodevelopmental, and propagative transmission. Examples of the three types are malaria as in §15.1, bancroftian filariasis as in §19.4, and bubonic plague as in §8.2, respectively.

Many human diseases are now known to be vector-borne; of these a convenient table is available in Beaver, Jung and Cupp (1984, pp. 558–563) that lists the taxonomic group of the species, the pathogenic agent, the role of the arthropod, and the method of human exposure. Malaria and bartonellosis may be the only vector-borne human diseases for which no animal host is known (see also Stanley, 1980).

Most of the vector-borne diseases of man being anthropozoonoses, as defined in §5.6, it is necessary for us to consider briefly the general conditions for the spread of a vector-borne zoonosis, a problem in animal ecology.

5.6 Zoonoses

A zoonosis is a disease of animals. The agents of many zoonoses do not infect man, those that do are called anthropozoonoses. However, in writings about human diseases, these human infections are usually without ambiguity referred to as zoonoses. In this section the zoonoses are considered in general terms, free of any considerations that they may infect man.

Many zoonoses are vector-borne and this fact gives them a geographical distribution, for both host and vector will require special conditions for survival. So Pavlovsky (1963, 1966) lays down propositions as follows: (*i*) a cycle of infection in vector-borne diseases is normally host → vector → host, whereby the vector acquires the infection by taking up the host's blood. The totality of environment and living matter is known as a biogeocenose; (*ii*) the cycle in (*i*) occurs only under favorable natural conditions, especially of climate, for example, the developmental cycle in the body of the vector may only occur under certain conditions of temperature and humidity; (*iii*) viewed as a zoonosis, a vector-borne disease usually has a distinct, often quite marked, geographical distribution; an area in which transmission occurs is called a nidus; changes in the nidus can make great changes in the enzootic or epizootic behaviors; (*iv*) a nidus may contain several vectors for the same disease, and several diseases can be spread by the same vector; (*v*) a nidus has limits only when the cycle of infection occurs strictly within its boundaries. Thus, a burrow that supports an enzootic of sylvatic plague is a nidus, but the vector may be more widely spread and then the nidus is wider, as in the case of tick-borne encephalitis.

The climate, the arthropod vector and the vertebrate host species, and the presence of a suitable organism determine the geographical distribution of a vector-borne disease. Usually the distribution is limited; in the temperate regions, especially, it may be spotty and even highly focal; in the hot, wet continental masses there may be many vectors and host species and the disease may be widespread. Of course, the arctic areas do not support vector-borne zoonoses.

Man is not necessary for the perpetuation of a zoonosis in any nidus, although man has often transported both vector and vertebrate host; examples are provided by the transport by ship of mosquitoes infected with yellow fever and the transport of rats and/or fleas infected with the plague bacillus along land or sea routes. Moreover, man often transforms the ecology of an area by engineering works; thus, irrigation in the Yakima Valley in the State of Washington resulted in a great increase in the populations of the mosquito *Culex tarsalis*, birds, man and, at the same time, St. Louis western equine virus. Many deaths resulted until the mosquito population was controlled. See also Stanley (1980) and Stanley and Alpers (1975). Conversely, engineering or other human works can often control vector-borne diseases.

5.7 Anthropozoonoses

Zoonoses can be transmitted from animal to man with or without the aid of arthropod vectors. It is convenient to list the infections passing from animals to man in the order suggested by the International Classification of Diseases (ICD).

ICD 003. Salmonella infections from human and/or animal sources are often carried mechanically by filth flies, such as the common house flies, and arthropods, as well as by water, milk, and other contaminated foods.

ICD 010. Bovine tuberculosis is an anthropozoonosis since it is a natural infection of cattle; it is conveyed to the humans in milk and sometimes by cough spray.

ICD 020–027. These zoonotic bacterial diseases are spread to man in a variety of ways. Plague (020) has been the most important of them; man is infected in the first place by a rodent flea but, as is pointed out in §8.2, the disease may be borne by the human flea, *Pulex irritans*, as vector, or the infection may be spread by cough spray as in pneumonic plague. Tularemia (021) is transmitted to humans in many cases by ticks but sometimes directly from infected animals or their tissues. Anthrax (022), brucellosis (023), glanders (024), and melioidosis (025) are not transmitted by vectors; rat-bite fever (026) is transmitted by the bite; the "other zoonotic bacterial diseases" are not transmitted by vectors. Of the arthropod-borne viral diseases (060–066), yellow fever (060), transmitted to man by *Aedes* and other genera of mosquitoes, is the only one of importance in causing deaths. Rabies (071) is transmitted by the bite, usually, of a rabid dog. The subclass, *Rickettsioses* and other arthropod-borne diseases (080–088), contains a number of important diseases that are vector-borne and the agents of which are anthropozoonoses or have closely related species causing zoonoses. Classical typhus is a good example of a disease thought of as a peculiarly human disease, although reservoirs of infections exist in domestic animals in some countries. Species of *Plasmodium* other than those infecting man are well known as infecting other vertebrates. Similar remarks apply to the *Leishmania* and *Trypanosoma*; it is usually found that related groups of diseases occur in related groups of hosts.

For further reading, see also Acha and Szyfres (1980), Fiennes (1967), Garnham (1971), and Steele (1982). For diseases of man acquired from his pets, see Bisseru (1967) and Zeuner (1963).

5.8 Experimental Epidemiology

Epidemics have been observed from ancient times. Little understanding of epidemics was possible before the rise of bacteriology and parasitology, although Hippocrates had made a beginning. However, the great epidemics of the nineteenth century, such as cholera in Europe, the plague pandemic commencing in 1891, and the epidemics of yellow fever during the construction of the Panama Canal led to a heightened interest in epidemics, for they posed problems of great practical interest, and deeper understanding of them as processes was essential. W.W.C. Topley had witnessed part of the great typhus epidemic at the end of World War I during his war service in Greece; he was dissatisfied with the works of the classical authors, writing on the great epidemics of the past, who had either written before the rise of bacteriology or who had failed to acknowledge the importance of bacteriology for the interpretations of those epidemics.

Topley (1919) stated that "any tenable theory must thus explain the constant presence of a specific cause of disease through long periods of time, the periodic reappearance of the disease in epidemic form and the characteristic form of each such wave of disease in its rise, crest, and subsidence, leading to another disease-free period."

There were great problems to be overcome. First, laboratory work was required to identify the infective agent. Second, the mode of transmission of the infective agent had to be deter-

mined. Third, it was necessary to obtain general understanding of the epidemic processes, possibly by resort to animal experimentation. It may also be noted that in field work under the second heading, there was often grave danger to the investigators; thus, there were fatalities in the study of yellow fever, typhus, and cholera.

It is practicable and ethical, however, to carry out experiments on animals. Animals that are small and easy to accommodate in the laboratory and of short life span are to be preferred; mice, indeed, have a life span of about one-thirtieth that of the human, so that experiments are readily carried over a number of generations. Infections, lethal or dangerous to the mouse, can be studied without undue risk to the investigator. The mice can be subjected to postmortem or other required investigation at any point of the disease, and artificial immunization can be tested out in a way neither ethical nor practicable in a human experimental group. Important centers of experimental epidemiology were set up under W.W.C. Topley in England (see Greenwood, 1932, 1935, and Greenwood, Hill, Topley, and Wilson, 1936) and L.T. Webster in the United States just after 1920 (see Webster, 1946). Mice were the subjects in England, various animals in the United States. Webster's group also considered the genetic effects of infection.

F.J. Fenner (b. 1914) studied a laboratory epidemic of mousepox in the tradition of the English workers in the late forties, but later was able to extend his methods to the natural epizootic of myxomatosis among rabbits in the wild in Australia under favorable conditions. The results are summed up in Fenner and Ratcliffe (1965). It appears from their work that if the properties of the host or parasite change, a new equilibrium may be attainable; milder (i.e., less virulent) strains of myxomatosis virus had arisen and persisted in the epizootic of Australian rabbits and the resistance of the rabbits had increased.

Similar evidence of virulence in human disease is difficult to obtain. The reason why scarlatina was such a lethal disease in the nineteenth century, as judged by case fatality rates or population mortality rates, is still uncertain; in other diseases, different races of the same bacterial or viral species are known to have different virulence, for example, diphtheria and poliomyelitis (see §§9.3 and 10.1).

The need to use animals in the study of human infections has led to interesting ad hoc studies with wide implications. Thus, Meyer, Brooks, Douglas, and Rogers (1962) were investigating the viruses found in rhesus and other monkeys that disturbed later studies on them; they found that jungle rhesus monkeys captured in India were not infected with measles because simian communities are not large enough to perpetuate an epizootic, but after capture the monkeys were held for some days in close proximity to human dwellings and, so, in close contact with human infections, especially of children. After this holding in the village, the monkeys were transported by train with much opportunity to pass the disease on to other monkeys. In air freighting over a thousand might be carried on the same plane with consequent favorable conditions for further spread. It was thus found that the majority of monkeys transported to the United States from India had been infected with measles. It also appeared, incidentally, that epidemics could be perpetuated in holding centers (the equivalent of islands) by the continued introduction of new susceptibles.

For unplanned experiments or observations on humans, see §5.10. For medical ecology, see le Riche and Milner (1971), Lancaster (1963), and the references in §5.9, which follows.

5.9 Mathematical Theory of Epidemics

W. Farr (1839) can be said to have begun the theoretical study of the rise and fall of epidemics with his hypothesis that an expression, $A \exp [-B (x - C)^2]$, where A, B, and C are constants, could approximate to the weekly numbers of deaths in an epizootic. This was suggested to him by the recent statement on infectious diseases by Henle, which led him to believe that epidemics must be orderly processes subject to scientific laws. The hypothesis implied that the epidemic wave would be symmetrical and bounded but gave very little insight into the mechanism.

A striking feature of the incidence of deaths from or notifications of measles in London was a 2-year cycle, which persisted into recent times as the graph of P. Stocks (1942), given as Figure 11.7.2, shows. To explain this cycle, William Hamer (1862–1936) carried out computations in which he assumed that the rate of new infections was proportionate to the number of susceptibles, obtaining a cyclical curve of the number of infections, maintained by immigration and births (Hamer, 1906). His model was deterministic in the sense that he assumed that the number of new infections would be equal to the expectation. Deterministic models were also proposed by A.J. Lotka, Ronald Ross, H.E. Soper, John Brownlee, and others. Some of these models give insight into epidemic behavior but often suggest that epidemics continue until all the susceptibles have been exhausted, which is contrary to experience.

On the theoretical side, A.G. McKendrick (1926) considered a stochastic model for populations of any size and Greenwood (1931) a stochastic model for epidemics in small groups, such as families, schools, or institutions. The probabilities of all possible epidemics (compositions of n into non-zero parts) can be computed by elementary methods when the numbers are not too large. An account of the later development of these theories is available in Bailey (1975).

On the other hand, it is worthy of note that there is no reference in the sixth edition of Topley and Wilson (1975) to mathematical theory developed since the second edition, even though they give far more vital statistics than other such handbooks. One can agree with the authors' implied conclusions that the difficult mathematical theory has had little effect on practical epidemiology. However, this distaste of the theory leads them not to consider the importance of population size in the epidemiology of such diseases as measles, and particularly rubella and congenital malformations; in this case it is readily shown that population size is a critical factor in the development of an epidemic involving many adult females, some of whom may be in the critical months of pregnancy. One can, therefore, deplore the gap, in both outlook and references, between these representatives of mathematical epidemiology and of field and laboratory epidemiology. A solution seems to lie in formulations less mathematically ambitious than the theory in which, for example, all the properties of an epidemic are expressed by a set of differential equations with three parameters, only one of which is concerned with the external physical or biologic conditions. For the general reader, Sladen and Bang (1969) goes some way toward bridging the gap although it has more general aims. Some articles in the *American Journal of Epidemiology* are also helping to develop and apply generalizations in epidemiology with the aid of mathematical notions and techniques. See also Abbey (1952), Anderson and May (1979, 1982*a,b,c*), Anderson (1982), Greenwood (1946), and A.D.M. Smith (1983).

5.10 Infections of Epidemiologists, Morbid Anatomists, and Laboratory Workers

Infections of laboratory workers can occur as a result of accidents, a breakdown of normal laboratory conditions, carelessness, or of other unavoidable risks in handling dangerous cultures or tissues. Some remarks on the dangers from certain diseases are listed in Topley and Wilson (1975) in the following pages: tuberculosis, 1729; glanders, 1857; cholera, 1867; scarlatina, 1911; dysentery, 2045; brucellosis, 2175, 2180; tularemia, 2144; relapsing fever, 2299; murine and classical typhus, 1196, 2347; psittacosis, 2375; smallpox, 2390; bartonellosis, 2289. It is likely that many tuberculosis infections have not been counted as laboratory infections because it is a chronic disease. There have been many cases of laboratory infections from cholera; L. Thuillier, Pasteur's assistant, died in Egypt; M.J. von Pettenkofer (1818–1901) and his assistant R. Emmerich deliberately swallowed cultures of cholera vibrio, the former suffering only a mild attack, but the latter a very severe attack, (Kisskalt, 1929). Typhus has also been important as a laboratory infection. Wain (1970) names eight persons dying from yellow fever. Sulkin and Pike (1951), after a questionnaire survey of American (U.S.A.) laboratories, obtained notices of 1342 laboratory-acquired infections with 39 deaths, a case fatality of 3.0%. Sixty-nine different agents were involved, but brucellosis, tuberculosis, tularemia, typhoid fever, and streptococcal infections accounted for 31% of all infections; rickettsioses for 14.9%. See also Pike (1976, 1979).

Of some 300 bacteriologists given in a biographical note by Bulloch (1938), no less than 8 had died of infections contracted in the course of their work.

Busvine (1980*a*) points out that work on the vectors of disease is particularly dangerous to the investigators, since the vectors have to be studied in the field under natural conditions, as in typhus, plague, and tularemia.

In the autopsy room there has always been danger from high concentrations of bacilli in the air, especially the tubercle bacillus. However, the pyogenic organisms, especially the hemolytic streptococci, if they are inoculated into the body of the operator either on an instrument or a spicule of bone, have caused many deaths in the operator and even his later patients when the lesion was localized. The death of J. Kolletschka after receiving an accidental wound at an autopsy on a case of puerperal infection weighed heavily with I.P. Semmelweis, investigating causes of puerperal fever. Deaths of bacteriologists infected directly or indirectly from specimens or cultures have been detailed by Kisskalt (1929).

Ackerknecht (1948*a*) gives a list of about 30 anticontagionists who submitted themselves to various inoculations and experiments; of these only three died. The unfortunate personal and scientific consequences of the inoculation of John Hunter (1728–1793) (see §17.2) may be also recalled.

For modern reviews of laboratory safety, see Fuscaldo, Erlick, and Hindman (1980) and Collins (1983), of which the latter has many useful tables and an extensive bibliography.

Of special interest to us here are the cases of two of the epidemiologists to whom we have dedicated this book. Thomas Carlyle Parkinson (b. February 17, 1884), after a brilliant undergraduate medical career at the University of Sydney, inhaled plague bacilli from a culture, which he was making as part of a project to provide a vaccine against bubonic plague at the Lister Institute, London, and died of pneumonic plague on February 4, 1909. Dora Lush (b. July 31, 1910), investigating scrub typhus (then, after malaria, the foremost medical military problem in the Southwest Pacific) at the Walter and Eliza Hall Institute, Melbourne, when distracted by a sudden movement of an animal being inoculated, accidentally inoculated herself with a rickettsial preparation and died of scrub typhus as a result on May 20, 1943. In his Annual Report to the Institute, F.M. Burnet wrote of her that "she was the most outstandingly competent bacteriologist with whom I have ever worked."

5.11 Seasonal Variation in the Infectious Diseases

The reason for seasonal variation in the incidence and deaths from some infectious diseases is evident, for example, in malaria it will usually depend on the multiplication of the vectors; but in some of the peculiarly human diseases the reasons are not so evident. Seasonal variation has been much studied in the British and American schools. Thus, for the three diseases, measles, chickenpox, and mumps, seasonality appears to depend on the large seasonal variation in the contact rates, according to London and Yorke (1973). Simulation experiments showed that if the incubation periods were longer, the epidemic would appear annually; if the infectivity were slightly higher, the disease would die out, at least locally, and no regular sequence of epidemics would be observed. Yorke, et al. (1979, p.104) state that seasonality remains essentially unexplained.

Many diseases, such as the venereal diseases, depend on a core of efficient transmitters. Similarly, mobile school children are the principal transmitters of the common infectious diseases.

5.12 Genealogy of the Infections Peculiar to Man

The anthropozoonoses and the zoonoses have been briefly reviewed in §§5.6 and 5.7. It is possible that too much stress has been laid in the past on the species specificity of infections, that is, some infective species is characteristic of some particular host species.

Suppose A^* is a free living organism or a parasite or commensal of some particular class of living organisms. Then by a first hypothesis there may be a mutation to A causing an infection in some hosts, h_A, say; further mutations to B may occur leading to diseases in hosts, h_B. There may be overlap between h_A and h_B; further mutations in A or B to $C, D, \ldots$ may occur. An alternate hypothesis would be that there are a number of distinct mutations from A^* to $A_1, A_2, \ldots$ say. Perhaps the most notorious example of this second hypothesis has occurred in relation to the infections by trypanosomes of man and other animals, whereby trypanosomes morphologically indistinguishable have been assigned to different genera. The trypanosomes are also instructive as it is thought that they were originally parasites of certain arthropods and acquired the ability to infect vertebrates, too. From one point of view they are parasites of arthropods using their vertebrate hosts to spread from site to site; from the other, they are parasites of vertebrates with arthropods spreading the infection from one vertebrate to another of the same species. In the trypanosomiases, there is a choice of evolutionary hypotheses; if it is assumed that trypanosomes were originally parasites of arthropods, then there may have been mutations to species infecting certain species or genera of vertebrates, $A, B, \ldots, C$, say, without secondary mutations, or there may be secondary mutations to species of trypanosomes that only infected $A^*, B^*, \ldots, C^*$ single species or genera of vertebrates.

Similar considerations apply to tuberculosis. There are free living bacteria related to *Myco. tuberculosis*. Some such bacteria may have become parasitic on animals. This may have happened several times or, once established in one group of animals, the mycobacteria may have evolved so as to prefer different hosts, as we have mentioned in the two hypotheses above. Bovine tuberculosis is now a zoonosis, but there may once have been a progenitor of the human type that was parasitic on the ungulates but whose descendants are now no longer capable of perpetuating a zoonosis. See §7.1 for the identity of species of the two types.

There is now some evidence suggesting that new strains of influenza virus causing pandemics may originate in Central Asia where there are nonhuman types of virus sharing antigens with influenza A viruses. It is hypothesized that there may be an exchange of genetic material with such virus (a hybridization) so that the new virus has the power to infect humans already immune to past strains of the virus. The new virus is maintained for a few years in the human population but there is no perpetuation (see §5.13).

With the examples of trypanosomiasis, tuberculosis, and influenza in mind, we may examine the properties of infections peculiar to man. Measles has already been treated in §5.3. It can be perpetuated in man only because the human population of the world is large and this factor of size prevents it becoming established in monkeys, which are fully susceptible. Leprosy is perpetuated by its long persistence in the individual infected cases. *Corynebacterium diphtheriae* seems to have few relatives causing diseases in animals other than man; its perpetuation seems to depend on the existence of nontoxic varieties in the throats of normal carriers. Cholera is only maintained in areas with a dense population, a high absolute humidity, and decaying vegetation, the conditions, indeed, of a river delta or river with low banks in a wet tropical area, so that the vibrios can remain in a suitable moist warm site until they can once again be ingested by man. Meningococci are normal commensals in the nasopharynx, where they normally do not cause disease; under conditions not well understood, but including crowding, severe epidemics may arise. Gonorrhea is perpetuated by chronic cases. Staphylococci and streptococci can exist as commensals and, so, the diseases caused by them can be perpetuated. The enteric infections are perpetuated by carriers; perhaps 80%

of long term carriers have an infection of the gallbladder. Dysentery infections are perpetuated by carriers.

For the origin of infective diseases, see Cockburn (1961a, 1963, 1977), Dubos (1958), and the sections on the individual diseases. For host-virus interaction, see Bang (1974) and Anderson and May (1982a,c).

5.13 Secular Changes in the Lethality of Human Infections

An organism (parasite) of an important infectious disease must have two properties, infectivity, or the power to spread from host to host, and virulence, or the power to do damage to the host. These two properties are not always or even usually able to be assessed separately, so it is convenient to combine them for the moment in a single property lethality. Lethality is a property of the organism; resistance is the name for all those properties of the host, both of the individual and of the organization of the herd, tending to overcome the organism. It is desirable to determine whether long term events in the struggle between parasite and host are due to changes in the parasite and, so, to its lethality; sometimes we will have case fatality rates, at other times only estimates of the numbers of deaths. The reader is referred to the discussion on pages 1686–1690 of Topley and Wilson (1975). We consider now the lethality of some important diseases, principally those that we have termed the great pestilences.

Cholera (ICD 001). It is known that there is some heterogeneity in the species of *Vibrio* causing the disease as defined by the ICD. If we are judging lethality by the effects on the patients, we have to note that a malnourished destitute Indian picked up in the streets of Calcutta after a sudden collapse cannot be equated to a bacteriologically diagnosed contact among European air passengers passing through the country. Perhaps the question has to be posed more precisely, and then it is seen that it is unanswerable; and perhaps the same conclusion would be reached for any of the bowel infections in ICD 001–009.

Tuberculosis (ICD 010–018). Although Topley and Wilson (1975) state that "the disease is of ancient origin and has preserved its individuality throughout the centuries", there is some doubt as to the epoch in which it could be said that this organism is *Mycobacterium tuberculosis* and that it had separated out from the parent stock of *Myco. bovis*. All we know is that Hippocrates described cases, easily diagnosable from his description, of pulmonary tuberculosis and that spinal caries has been diagnosed in Egyptian mummies. There seems to be no way of testing the properties of the bacillus of the "epidemic" in the British population; on the other hand, it has often been claimed that tuberculosis has brought about genetic changes in the European populations, strengthening resistance (see §7.5).

Zoonotic Bacterial Diseases (ICD 020–027). Only plague needs to be considered; unfortunately, here Topley and Wilson (1975, p. 2136) state that "rats from a plague-infected area are more resistant to experimental inoculation than those from non-infected areas" and that "the young of resistant animals are said to enjoy a high degree of natural immunity." In the following paragraph they imply that the finding of no plague in several thousand rats caught each night for 2 years in Bombay and over 3,500 caught in Paris implied that "a strain of rats is evolved having a greater degree of natural [presumably genetic] resistance to plague infection than that of the original susceptible animals." Others might well say that the negative findings merely showed that the plague had failed to be perpetuated in the rats, that is, plague was enzootic in neither Bombay nor Paris. Plague has been almost universally fatal in its pneumonic form, and mild variants have not been noted in the bubonic form.

Leprosy (ICD 030). There is a widely held belief, which can hardly be contested, that changes have occurred in human resistance rather than in bacterial lethality. Chaussinand (1959) believes that there is a cross immunity between leprosy and tuberculosis, so that leprosy can extend only into countries with a minimum of tuberculosis experience.

Diphtheria (ICD 032). Here is a clear case. The infecting organism has three main groups of variants of known difference in case fatality (McLeod, 1943). The relative frequencies of the strains have been observed to change from year to year (see §9.3).

Whooping Cough (ICD 033). No evidence for heterogeneity or secular change is forthcoming.

Streptococcal Sore Throat and Scarlatina (ICD 034). Scarlatina (scarlet fever) was a major cause of mortality in European countries; evidence for epidemics in eighteenth-century Sweden is available. In England and Wales in 1861–1870 the annual death rate from scarlatina was 2617 per 1,000,000 per annum; by 1921–1930 the rate was down to 73 per 1,000,000. Similar experiences have been reported from other countries in Europe, North America, and Australia. A relation of type prevalence to population mortality rates is suspected but no clear case has been made.

Acute Poliomyelitis (ICD 045). There are several strains of varying lethality but no general statement can be made. It has often appeared in a new country at the time of improved hygiene, and its lethality depends not only on the strain but also on the age at infection.

Smallpox (ICD 050). Secular changes have been evident since there are two forms of the disease, the classical *Variola major* and *Variola minor* or Alastrim (see §11.1).

Measles (ICD 055). Measles has varied greatly in its lethality (measured by case fatality rates or by population age-specific rates), but it is concluded in §11.7 that this is due to social and other changes in the human population rather than to changes in the virus.

Rubella (ICD 056). Changes in the virus are not required to explain the newly observed epidemics of congenital defects.

There appears to be no evidence for secular changes in the lethality of louse-borne typhus (ICD 080), malaria (084), leishmaniasis (085), trypanosomiasis (086), relapsing fever (087). Syphilis (ICD 090–097) is too controversial in its origins for any statement to be made on secular changes in it. Certainly, among morphologically indistinguishable strains there is wide variation in the lethality throughout the world at any given epoch.

There are many types of *Streptococcus pneumoniae* responsible for lobar pneumonia (ICD 481).

Influenza (ICD 487). *Influenzavirus A* circulating in the community is usually slightly different from that of previous years. This is not so with pandemic strains. Sometimes the pandemic virus strains are thought to be identical with or closely related to strains of approximately 60 years previously. Such new pandemic strains could have arisen from circulating strains or they may have formed by hybridization with some avian or other animal strain. Kilbourne (1975b, p. 513) gives a diagram in which a human virus with certain genetic properties H_3 and N_2 hybridizes with an animal virus with corresponding genetic properties H_4N_4, where H_4 and N_4 are powerful forms of the hemoglutinin and neuraminidase properties. The human virus with properties H_4N_4 now has the power to cause pandemics. It may well be that there exist genetic properties, H_4', H_4'', ... and N_4', N_4'', ... that result in distinct pandemic strains. According to Sisley (1891), workers traditionally believed that influenza pandemics originated in China, and that the progress of a recent pandemic could be traced from the East reaching Bokhara in May, 1889, St. Petersburg in October, 1889, and London in December, 1889, although other cases had been noted in England in October, arriving perhaps by a faster sea route (see also §31.4).

5.14 The Control of Herd Infection (Crowd Diseases)

As Topley and Wilson (1975) write in the section with the above title, the scientific and laboratory studies on herd infection and herd immunity have modified many of our conceptions of the administrative control of disease.

Isolation and quarantine had been regarded as important weapons against the infections in the past. Indeed, in special cases such as typhus, they have had some success. Combined with immunoprophylaxis, they have been successful in the eradication of smallpox from the world. Smallpox has the properties: (*i*) the cases are readily detectable, (*ii*), the mode of spread is known, (*iii*) there are no animal reservoirs, (*iv*) the carrier state is unknown, (*v*) there is a solid and lasting immunity, (*vi*) there is a high case fatality, and (*vii*) there is a relatively safe prophylactic, namely, vaccination. Number (*vi*) ensured a continued interest in the public health campaign against the disease, and the low ratio of deaths from prophylaxis to deaths from the disease has secured the cooperation of governments and peoples alike in the campaign. Numbers (*ii*), (*iii*), (*iv*), and (*v*) ensured that the campaign could be directed at the isolation of cases and the vaccination of contact with hopes of final success; (*i*) ensured that almost all cases would come into the campaign.

However, measles with properties similar to those of smallpox is still a cause of serious mortality in the poorer regions of the world, but it could hardly be usefully eradicated in one part of the globe.

Many other infections could not be considered for such a program, even with a limited area in mind. For example, there are many carriers of the meningococcus causing meningitis and the streptococcus of scarlet fever. If cases only are isolated, there can be little effect on the course of the epidemic.

Quarantine can only succeed if it is complete. The carrier and atypical case can defeat a quarantine system. Under modern conditions of travel, especially by air, quarantine is likely to prove ineffective. Greenwood and Topley (1925) failed to show any effect due to isolation practices on the incidence rates of scarlet fever. They concluded that the value of the isolation hospital must be judged by the benefits it conferred on its patients and that it had had little effect on the health of the community as a whole.

5.15 Generalities on Infectious Diseases

In this monograph we attempt to follow the ICD as closely as possible, but it is convenient to consider tuberculosis and syphilis (including tabes dorsalis and general paresis) in separate groupings because of their numerical importance and chronicity. In the Australian series of Lancaster (1952, et seq.), some other diseases were included in this grouping of infectious diseases, for example, nonepidemic encephalitis and nonmeningococcal meningitis from the diseases of the nervous system, gastroenteritis and hydatid disease from the alimentary system, and a few other minor changes were made. These practices agree with the spirit of the Ninth Revision of the ICD and the former *International List of Causes of Death*. Even so, many microbial diseases still remain in other systems, that is, nervous, cardiovascular, respiratory, alimentary, genitourinary, puerperal, cutaneous, and musculoskeletal systems, in which context it is easiest to consider them. Later, when we are examining the declines of mortality, we will distinguish between the various categories: tuberculosis, syphilis, all other diseases in Class 1, and infectious diseases occurring in classes other than Class 1.

For the history of epidemiology, see Lilienfeld (1980). Perhaps the new annual series, Rubin and Damjanov (1984), may be relevant to this monograph.

Chapter 6
Intestinal Infectious Diseases

6.1 Introduction

We begin now a systematic study of mortality by cause, following the order of the rubric number of the Ninth Revision, 1975, of the *International Classification of Diseases* (ICD). Thus, we begin with the infectious or organismal diseases. It is necessary to give, if only for the ease of remembering, some character to the disease rubrics, so we give the description of each disease with its ICD number and, where relevant, define the inclusions to and exclusions from the particular rubric according to the rules accompanying the ICD. For the infectious diseases we give the name of the infective organism and some of its properties. There follows a necessarily brief account of the pathology of the disease. It is sometimes important to mention the time of the differentiation of the disease from others resembling it because before we have knowledge of the accurate differentiation between diseases, we cannot expect to know which organism was responsible for the disease. The descriptions of the diseases in the order of the ICD entails the mention of rubrics that cause but few deaths, and, so, if we adhered to the rule of one rubric to a section, there would be an undue number of sections. Occasionally, therefore, we have combined the discussion of a number of rubrics into one section. On the other hand, we have not followed the breakdown of the ICD classification of tuberculosis by principal site of the disease, but have given sections of interest or importance about race, certification, country, and so on,

which would be unnecessary in the description of other diseases.

6.2 Cholera

ICD 001. Fourth digit (organism): 0, *V. cholerae*; 1, *V. cholerae eltor*; 9, unspecified.

Cholera is defined as a diarrheal disease due to *V. cholerae* or *V. cholerae eltor*. Pathologically, cholera is an enteritis associated with a great loss of fluid into the small intestine and with usually characteristic "rice-water" stools provoked by an enterotoxin according to De (1961) and Craig (1980); the general symptoms follow from the dehydration of the body and the loss of electrolytes from the circulatory system. It is now known that other vibrios and bacteria can cause syndromes similar to that of cholera, known as paracholera or choleralike states. Such states will be referred, according to the rules of the ICD, to other rubrics when the causal organism has been identified.

The disease was studied by European observers in the nineteenth century. The presence of vibrios was reported by F. Pacini (1812–1883) and others in Italy and England, but convincing evidence that the vibrios were the causative organism was first provided in 1882 and 1883 by Robert Koch, who was able to observe and culture the vibrios in acute cases but, of course, was not able to complete the proof by feeding them to new subjects.

Cholera had been the subject of some classical researches in 1849 and 1854 by J. Snow (1936) and W. Budd (1849) in England, and others, that had the effect of suggesting effective public health measures before the organismal nature had been established. In the great London epidemic of 1854, Snow established that there were many more deaths, 7 per 1,000 per annum, in the areas with water supplied by the Southwark and Vauxhall Water Works Company, which, as noted in §6.12, drew its water from the Thames at a site polluted by the city, than in the areas supplied by the Lambeth Waterworks Company, which drew its water from above the weir at Teddington, with 0.6 deaths per 1,000 per annum. Snow also traced an epidemic to a well fouled by leakage from a nearby sewage pipe. The effectiveness of filtration of the water supply was later displayed by the events of the Hamburg cholera epidemic of 1892. There were 18,000 cases with 8,200 deaths in the main city area, which was supplied by unfiltered water from the River Elbe taken above the city; in Altona, which drew its water from below the city but filtered it, there were only 516 cases; and in Wandsbeck, which had an independent, filtered water supply, there were very few cases.

The modes of infection are given in detail in Pollitzer (1959, p. 846) as direct contact, water, food and drink, and flies. Of these, the spread by water, whether from waterworks, rivers, irrigation channels, tanks, ponds, springs, wells, shipboard water supply, or even melted ice or snow, is the most important. The spread by water, food, and drink is detailed by Felsenfeld (1967), who mentions infection directly from untreated water and indirectly from ice and water used for washing raw vegetables, and from contaminated utensils, vegetables, soft drinks, and cooked food. It has been believed that the vibrios do not multiply in nature outside the human body and, so, require a dense population for perpetuation, and that hot humid climates favor the infection. Professor F.J. Fenner (1983, personal communication) points out that recent experience in Queensland, Australia, suggests strongly that cholera vibrios can survive and probably multiply in water under suitable conditions. Epidemics often arise at the end of a dry season or spell when the rain washes the human excreta into wells and streams.

Water-borne epidemics are usually explosive with many cases appearing in a short time without warning. Case or carrier infections are also possible and, of course, are the means of spread between cities, countries, or other areas, often referred to as chain infection. With the rapid transport in the modern world, it is possible for cholera infections to be spread to any part of the world. It is even possible for aircraft as part of routine to eject into the clouds fluids contaminated with feces and, so, to give rise to infections in areas with no apparent connection with cholera-infected areas.

Endemic cholera is confined to the great river deltas, especially of the Ganges and Brahmaputra. According to Felsenfeld (1967), the requirements for endemicity are a dense population, high absolute humidity, and decaying vegetation. According to Pollitzer (1959), epidemic cholera is a disease of the warmer climates and had failed to obtain a foothold north of 50°N or south of 3°N, that is, in the humid riverine areas of the ancient world; however, more recently, in 1970, it has appeared in Africa (Stock, 1976).

The spread of the disease has often been aided by the many millions of pilgrimages undertaken each year within India and to Mecca. The disease has spread by maritime commerce to southern and western India, to Ceylon, and to Eastern Asian countries; from the great Indian seaports, it has been carried to other littorals of the Indian Ocean and to the New World; but it has also spread by land routes to Uttar Pradesh, Pakistan, Afghanistan, Persia, and Turkey, and then into Europe.

Since infection is spread to the healthy persons by water, food, or linen, prophylactic measures include an efficient water supply, proper disposal of the infectious discharges and fomites from the patient, control of flies, proper food inspection, and control of travelers. Water, ice, fresh vegetables, and all food must be properly policed. Excreta and garbage must be carefully disposed of. Contacts and pilgrims must be prevented from spreading the disease, and, in the longer term, health education is necessary.

The case fatality of cholera had been high, up to 60% in some Indian epidemics. This rate can be reduced by the replacement of water and salts by oral administration and, in severe cases, by the intravenous injection of appropriate fluid to restore the normal blood volume and electrolytic balance (following the works of Phillips, 1964), by good nursing, and by chemotherapy. The stated case fatality rates would not apply to cases diagnosed by modern methods, with the aid of which subclinical (i.e., inapparent) cases are often found.

Standard works, not already mentioned, are Barua and Burrows (1974), Bushnell and Brookhyser (1965), Ouchterlony and Holmgren (1980), Remington and Klein (1983), and Wilson (1984d).

6.3 Cholera as a Great Pestilence

There is much doubt about the time of the first appearance of cholera as an epidemic or endemic disease. There are suggestions of its presence in India at the time of Alexander the Great. Certainly it was present in severe epidemic form in AD 1503 shortly after the visit of Vasco da Gama to India, from which time unmistakable descriptions of the disease are known. Before 1817 cholera had not spread west into Europe, although there are some suggestions that on occasion it had spread east into China. From 1817 onward it is customary, following Pollitzer (1959), to describe six pandemics commencing 1817, 1826, 1852, 1863, 1881, and 1889, and to add a seventh commencing in 1961.

The first of these pandemics began in the hinterland of Bengal between the Ganges and the Brahmaputra and reached Calcutta in early August, 1817. In 1818 the disease spread to Nepal and toward the Punjab, where it arrived in 1820. Burma and Thailand were invaded by the land route in 1819. Cholera reached Malacca in 1820 and, soon after, Penang and Singapore. It reached China by the sea in 1820. The farthest points reached were Alexandretta in Turkey, Astrahan on the Caspian Sea, Tbilisi in Georgia, the Malaccas, Java, Northern China, and Japan.

The second pandemic commenced in 1826, spread westward along the Ganges and Jumna Rivers, and in 1827 invaded the Punjab. In 1829 cholera was already active in Afghanistan, Persia, Bokhara, Hiva. The infection was then carried by caravans to Orenburg in southeast European Russia at the end of August, 1829. The infection reached Moscow by the autumn of 1830. In the spring of 1831 cholera spread to St. Petersburg and the Baltic provinces, as well as Archangel, and into Poland. It was introduced by Polish and Russian contingents into Galicia, whence it spread to Vienna in August, 1831. After its arrival in the Baltic ports, cholera was carried by ship to other ports in Europe, Canada, and the United States; some observers believe that it reached the western coast of the United States. By 1834 all the European states had suffered from epidemics. In 1835 French troops carried the disease to Algeria. Egypt, Sudan, and Abyssinia had already been affected.

The third pandemic, lasted from 1852 to 1859 but was less general than the second; there were, however, outbreaks in Réunion, Mauritius, and the eastern African littoral.

The fourth pandemic, lasting from 1863 to 1875, reached Europe by new routes over Arabia into Egypt, Constantinople, Italy, and southern France. The fifth pandemic, 1881 to 1896, caused far fewer deaths than those preceding, especially in Europe. The great cities by this time had developed municipal water supplies free, or relatively so, from human excreta. The bacteriologic revolution reinforced appropriate public health activities. Thus, importation of the disease from a steamer reaching New York in 1887 from Marseilles was averted by rapid diagnosis by laboratory means and appropriate isolation methods. Serious outbreaks occured in South America in 1886–1888. The sixth pandemic, 1899 to 1923, began with a great epidemic in India that spread through Afghanistan and Persia to Russia. Over 4,000 persons died among the pilgrims in Mecca in February, 1902. There were some 150,000 deaths in Russia in 1902–1913 and there were further large epidemics, especially in 1915 and 1920–1922. See also Biraud and Kaul (1947–1948).

The seventh pandemic of cholera began during 1961 in Sulawesi, Celebes, where the *eltor* variety had been known to be present since

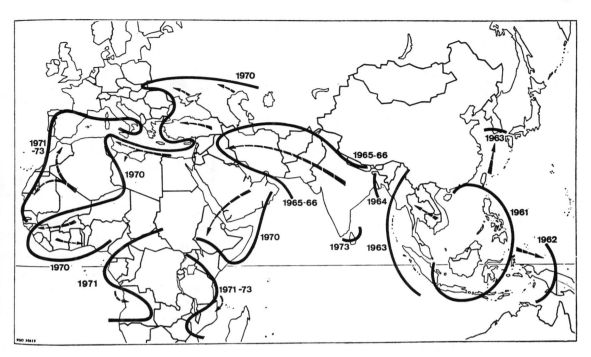

FIGURE 6.3.1. The global spread of cholera in the seventh pandemic, up to 1973. This began in the Celebes in 1961 and was still in progress in 1974; the vibrio concerned is the *eltor* biotype. (From WHO *Wkly Epidem. Rec.* No. 27, 1974, 229–231.)

1938. After some hesitation, it was generally agreed that the *eltor* variety produces a true cholera. In 1962 it had spread to neighboring islands, in 1963 to the Asian continent, and in 1970 to Europe and Africa. See Figure 6.3.1 for a map of its spread. According to Mukerjee, Basu, and Bhattacharya (1965), the *eltor* variety tends to displace the classical cholera vibrio as the cause of cholera in the classical endemic areas; they provide a useful map for the spread through Asia up to 1965. Kamal (1974) divides the pandemic into a first period, 1961–1962, when the infection spread through the East Indies and Southeast Asia, a second, 1963–1969, when there was pandemic involvement of the Asian states, and a third period, beginning in 1970, when the disease spread to southern Europe. The infection was carried by students and others to Sierra Leone and Liberia and, so, throughout the wet African tropics, where it has become endemic in many areas. Stock (1976) has given a detailed account of its diffusion through many river systems in Africa.

We may summarize the main findings of Pollitzer (1959), assisted by S. Swaroop, in their Chapter 2 on world incidence. First, of all deaths from cholera throughout the world in 1950–1954, 75.48%, 22.57%, and 1.93% occurred, respectively, in India, Pakistan, and Burma. Their Figure 1 shows the area of high endemicity is in the Ganges-Brahmaputra river system with the large delta area now included in Bangladesh. Their Figures 1 and 4 show that the areas of high mortality rates from cholera are in the aforementioned river system, including the delta, and in the area corresponding roughly to the Brahmani, Mahanadi, Godavari, Kistna, and Cauvery rivers, in that order, to the southern end of the east coast and the Narvada and Tapti rivers on the west coast of the Indian peninsula. Consistent with this, their Table 13 shows the great bulk of the deaths in India occured in four provinces during 1910–1954, namely, 2.95 million in Bengal, 2.60 million in Bihar and Orissa, 1.72 million in the United Provinces, 1.46 million in the Madras Presidency, with a total of 10.22 million in all "British" India. Their Figure 11 shows a general decline in the annual cholera death rate in Bengal from 1891 to 1954, beginning with a rate of 3 per 1,000 and ending with a rate of 0.3 per 1,000 per annum; a notably high rate was 3.6 per 1,000 per annum in 1943, the year of the great famine, with rates of approximately 1 per 1,000 in 1942 and 1944. Their Table 15 shows that the cholera death rate in Bengal fell from an average of 2.73 per 1,000 per annum in 1901–1910 to 1.27 in 1934–1943. Individual provinces, however, could have rates up to 4.14 per 1,000 in Howrah in the earlier period and 2.51 in Bakargani in the later period. Cholera deaths in various countries are given in Pollitzer (1959, Table 6). In this century the greatest number of annual deaths in the present India and Pakistan, combined, was 0.81 million in 1900. In their Table 6 countries with an important number of deaths were India and Pakistan, Burma, Indochina, Korea, Singapore, Taiwan, Japan, and the Philippines. Russia suffered several large epidemics with 0.47 million cases in 1831, 1.74 million cases in 1848, 0.62 million cases in 1892, and 0.21 million cases in 1921 during the civil strife.

For endemic areas throughout the world, see Swaroop and Pollitzer (1952). For the experience of cholera in America, see Chambers (1938), Heyningen and Seal (1983), and Rosenberg (1962, 1972). For English experience, see Pelling (1978).

6.4 Enteric Fevers

ICD 002. Typhoid and paratyphoid fevers. Fourth digit (species of *Salmonella*): 0, *typhi*; 1, *paratyphi A*; 2, *paratyphi B*; 3, *paratyphi C*; 9, *paratyphi* unspecified.

Enteric fever was known to Hippocrates, who, during two successive autumns, met with many cases of a fever of continuous type and characterized by diarrhea, offensive watery stools, bilious vomiting, tympanites, abdominal pain, red rashes, epistaxis, sleeplessness, and a tendency to delirium, subsultus (twitching), and coma; there were irregular remissions, lengthy durations, and increasing emaciation. The disease was also known to Galen,

according to Gay (1918). Such syndromes, easily recognized by a modern observer as of typhoid fever, were studied again in detail in the seventeenth century. First, enteric fever had to be separated out from simple enteritis, and, second, it had to be differentiated from other continued fevers. Thomas Willis (1621–1675) attempted, in particular, to distinguish typhoid fever (i.e., enteric fever) from typhus on clinical grounds. The pathological lesions were described by French observers early in the nineteenth century, among whom P.F. Bretonneau demonstrated the special lesions in the Peyer's patches in the ileum (small intestine) and defended the concept of a specific transmissible agent or, at least, poison. The French observers also distinguished the disease from simple gastroenteritis on pathological grounds. Many workers gave evidence for the distinction between typhoid fever and typhus but the clearest demonstrations were given by W.W. Gerhard (1809–1872) in 1837 in the United States and by J. Schoenlein in Germany in 1839; Schoenlein referred to the two diseases as *typhus exanthematicus* and *typhus abdominalis*, respectively, names that persisted for many years in the German literature. However, much confusion remained in the minds of the clinicians, certainly of the English speaking clinicians, until William Jenner (1815–1898) gave a close analysis of the continued fevers in Britain in the years 1849 to 1851. In the prebacteriologic era, William Budd (1811–1880) described the essential epidemiology of enteric fever, namely, the multiplication of the agent in the living body, the excretion of the infected material in the feces, the infection of other members of the family, and the role of contamination of water and milk. See Dolman (1970) for references.

Enteric fever is essentially a septicemia due to *Salmonella typhi*, *Salm. sendai*, and *Salm. paratyphi* of types *A*, *B*, and *C*, with a clinical syndrome resembling that given by Hippocrates. The syndromes caused by the other salmonellae cannot be sharply differentiated clinically from the enteric fevers as just defined; septicemia can be caused by other salmonellae, mentioned later in §6.6, and some of the other organisms produce the "typhoid state," that is, delirium with subsultus or plucking at the blankets. On the other hand, *Salm. typhi* can cause localized lesions in the bones, for example, more characteristic of the other salmonellae. The salmonellae of enteric fever can be isolated from the rose spots of the cutaneous eruption, from the blood, the urine, and the feces of cases. The bacilli may be excreted by precocious carriers before the disease develops, by clinical and subclinical cases, and by symptomless excretors. Although *Salm. paratyphi B* has been isolated from animals and has caused meat- and milk-borne epidemics, the organisms of enteric fever are almost entirely restricted to man.

The pathogenesis of a typhoid infection has been worked out by clinical observation and animal experimentation (Gay, 1918) and by experiments in human volunteers (Hornick, Greisman, et al., 1970). After an infective dose has been received, most of the typhoid bacilli are excreted or destroyed in the alimentary tract; however, some pass through the wall of the alimentary tract to the mesenteric lymph glands, probably in the ileum. They later pass to the liver and spleen, where they multiply, and later many bacilli escape into the blood (i.e., cause a bacteremia). As a result, there is an invasion of the intestine chiefly through the gallbladder and the bile duct. The characteristic lesions in the Peyer's patches in the ileum result from an inflammatory reaction to the bacilli, followed by necrosis and ulceration into the gut lumen, and sometimes by a perforation into the peritoneal cavity, this last event being almost invariably fatal before the advent of chemotherapy. Infection of the gallbladder may cause acute cholecystitis. Of course, there are degrees of severity of the disease and some of the signs and symptoms of the fully developed syndrome may not be present; thus, it is possible to have typhoid fever without the presence of the distinctive lesions in the small intestine, the Peyer's patches. Subclinical attacks are known, so that the salmonellae may be recovered on occasion in healthy carriers. A chronic carrier state is also known, usually maintained by a chronic infection of the gallbladder.

The incubation period is usually 10–14 days but wider variation is possible. The onset of the disease is insidious with malaise, chills, headaches, and generalized aches in the muscles and joints. Diarrhea can be severe but is not common, vomiting may occur, and anorexia is usually present. The temperature rises to between 38.8°C and 40°C. Complications include relapse, intestinal perforation in 0.7% to 4.7% of cases, pneumonia, thrombophlebitis, and bone abscesses. The disease in children is often atypical; gastroenteritic symptoms may be present in them.

Treatment is by chloramphenicol, but perforation and intestinal hemorrhages may occur. Christie (1980) does not consider that prior antityphoid immunization alters the prognosis. Case fatality rates of the order of 17% are cited by Gay (1918) for European cases. For the years 1915–1924, Godfrey (1928) found that in the State of New York the case fatality rate from typhoid was 13%, varying from 11% to 17%. At ages under 5, 5 to 9, . . . , 35 to 39, the percentage case fatality rates were 8.4, 4.4, 6.4, 10.2, 12.5, 13.5, 16.4, and 15.2, with a steady rise to 22.8 at age 55 to 59. The crude death rate from typhoid varied throughout the State from 30 per 1,000,000 per annum in New York City to approximately 84 per 1,000,000 in towns with populations of 10,000 to 20,000. He considered the differences between areas to be due to the differences in hygiene in the delivery of water and milk. See Huckstep (1962), Olitzki (1972), and Parker (1984*f*).

6.5 Enteric Fever as a Great Pestilence

Gay (1918) remarked that typhoid fever (i.e., enteric fever) had been one of the great causes of death and disability and was still so. Scientific studies had led to a complete conception of the disease process and practical results of great significance. "No human disease, under varying conditions of life, in war and in peace, has been more rapidly checked, and none gives greater promise of eventual complete suppression." He point out that in the United States typhoid fever still ranked fifth among the infective diseases as a cause of death, being

TABLE 6.5.1. Enteric fever in England and Wales: deaths per 1,000,000 per annum.

Epoch	All ages*	0–4	5–9	10–14	15–19	20–24	25–34	35–44	45–54	55–64	65–74	75 and over
					Males							
1871–1880	324	398	309	274	377	432	311	259	273	291	341	259
1881–1890	215	131	170	192	300	338	273	202	177	166	132	71
1891–1900	202	85	120	152	279	347	296	227	174	137	87	36
1901–1910	109	32	52	71	137	179	178	142	104	80	40	17
1911–1920	41	8	16	26	52	62	62	57	48	36	21	5
1921–1930	11	3	5	8	14	16	16	14	13	14	11	3
					Females							
1871–1880	319	405	366	352	438	336	280	239	230	248	256	187
1881–1890	184	128	189	226	281	234	197	165	136	122	99	55
1891–1900	151	80	134	172	233	205	186	154	117	90	54	24
1901–1910	74	30	59	81	100	99	97	86	67	50	29	10
1911–1920	28	8	20	27	41	43	37	33	27	25	13	6
1921–1930	10	3	5	9	14	14	12	12	13	10	8	4

*Standardized on to the population of England and Wales as enumerated in 1901.
From the Registrar-General's Decennial Supplement (1952, Part 3, Table 12).

exceeded in importance by tuberculosis, pneumonia, infantile diarrhea, and diphtheria.

An example of the importance of the enteric fevers in a densely populated region is provided by the experience of England and Wales over the period 1870 to 1930 (Table 6.5.1). In any epoch the mortality rate has a maximum (or local maximum) at the ages 20–24 years; for any given age the rates have been declining. In 1871–1880 typhoid deaths at all ages were about 1.4% of the total deaths from all causes and at ages 15–19 years for males about 5.6% of the total mortality.

Gay (1918) says that the case fatality rate for typhoid fever is about 10% in America. He cites Murchison's statistics from the London Fever Hospital giving a case fatality rate of 17% and this was approximately equal to that of the best hospitals in France, Germany, and England, so that some sort of estimate of incidence can be made from the mortality rates.

Enteric fever was controlled in England and Wales by the application of the campaign against filth, even though the campaign, initially, was not motivated by a belief in the bacterial etiology. In §6.12 the history of the supply of water to London is briefly reviewed, and it is shown that a water supply of assured quantity and quality was obtained for London only after

the Public Health Act of 1875. In many of the provincial centers such a supply would have been later.

Gay (1918) gives a confirmation of the importance of the water supplies for the decline in the enteric fever death rates. Thus, he shows crude mortality rates, expressed here in deaths per 1,000,000 per annum as follows. In the first category we have Munich and Vienna with a rate of 40; water from mountain springs had been brought into Vienna in 1870–1873 at the instance of J. Škoda (1805–1881) and into Munich during the years 1867–1883 at the instance of M.J. von Pettenkofer. In the second category we have Berlin, Zurich, Hamburg, Paris, and London, in that order, using filtered water with a rate approximately 96. Of 66 American cities listed, 5 had filtered water with a mean mortality of 162, 4 had ground water and large wells with a rate of 181, 11 had impounding reservoirs with protected watersheds with a rate of 185, 7 had a protected river or stream supply with a rate of 185, 8 had a supply from small lakes with a rate of 193, 7 had great lakes subject to pollution with a rate of 331, 5 had mixed surface and underground water with a rate of 457, and, finally, 19 had river water subject to pollution with a rate of 616. A later figure of Gay (1918, p. 18) shows that of 7 cities changing their water supply all registered falls in mortality rates. With improved city water supplies in the United States, mortality rates in the rural areas exceeded those in the urban areas; Gay gives a graph for New York State that shows the comparison quite clearly.

Typhoid fever was a problem in the armies, according to Gay (1918), both in peace and war. Thus, in Munich the deaths per 1,000,000 for the garrison were 11,100, 5,670, and 4,660 per annum in the three decades commencing in 1851, 1861, and 1871, respectively, but by 1880 the new water supply had been introduced and the mortality rate was 198 for 1881–1890.

In campaigns the death rates would be much higher; Prinzing (1916) gives details of 8,908 deaths out of 24,473 patients in the Russian troops in Caucasia in the Russo-Turkish war of 1878–1879 and of 383 deaths in a garrison of 13,500 English troops in the siege of Ladysmith, South Africa, and many other examples. In some of these examples, no doubt, other factors were operating such as closeness of contact and a breakdown of food hygiene, but, here again, the water supply would have been an important factor.

In World War I, active immunization was introduced. Mortality rates from enteric fever were kept low, but it is by no means clear from the statistics whether the active immunization was the effective cause of the low rates; possibly its effect was negligible.

Milk is a vehicle of infection in some cases, and food can be infected in handling as pointed out in §6.13. Shellfish have been important in the spread of enteric fever, and, indeed, caused over 25,000 deaths in France during the 15 years before 1934. The disposal of excreta in the great European cities was often defective, as is pointed out in §6.15.

It may be concluded that the important measures of control were the provision of an adequate water supply, the proper disposal of excreta, and the protection of food and milk from infection.

The remarks of Ashcroft (1964) are relevant to a historical survey of typhoid fevers. He has four models of infection: (i) hygiene is very bad and Salm. typhi is ubiquitous; infection occurs in infancy or early childhood and is either symptomless or unrecognized; (ii) hygiene is poor and Salm. typhi is common; first infections occur in childhood rather than in infancy and are recognizable, although often mild, (iii) hygiene is not uniformly good; outbreaks may involve all age groups, (iv) hygiene is excellent; Salm. typhi and typhoid are both rare, for example, in Northern Europe, America, and Australasia.

A problem in countries with a high standard of hygiene is to determine the means of perpetuation of the human epidemic. Some excretors are only temporary; these may be convalescents or symptomless carriers. After infection or at the end of a clinical attack, there is a steady decline in the percentage of carriers up to approximately 3 months; if infection persists so long, it may persist indefinitely. It is found that many of these chronic carriers have an infection of the gallbladder with the organism and that the carrier state can be terminated by cholecystectomy.

By the 1920s in England, for example, the major problems of enteric fever had been solved, so it was often the task of the medical officers of health merely to determine at which link in the chain the hygiene had broken down (Greenwood, 1935; Scott, 1934). Food handlers became less important partly as the result of better education and partly because of public health action on the safety of food; for example, measures were taken to ensure that uncooked vegetables, shellfish, ice creams, and so on were not contaminated in processing.

The role of active immunization was important, possibly, only in special circumstances of high risk. Chemotherapy has been of some value in later years.

For incidence in the world, see WHO-typhoid (1950) and van Oye (1964). For incidence in Europe, see Stowman (1947–1948c). For experience on the goldfields, see §47.9. See Luckin (1984) for enteric fever in London 1851–1900, Parker (1984f) for a general survey, and Wilson (1984a) for accounts of epidemiologic investigation of a widespread epidemic in the "Home Counties" of England in 1941 and 1942, in which phage-typing indicated that all cases were infected from a single source, milk supplied by a farmer who carried the bacillus. Another epidemic could be traced to tinned meat infected in the Argentine.

6.6 Other Salmonella Infections

ICD 003. Fourth digit: 0, gastroenteritis; 1, septicemia; 2, localized infections; 8, other.

Although they have been much less important in causing deaths than the enteric groups, some other salmonellae can give rise to entericlike or septic infections. They are often associated with osteomyelitis or abscesses in the internal organs, particularly if there has been local trauma. They can be regarded as zoonotic.

Fenner (1971) pointed out that there had been an increased incidence in salmonellosis because of increased international trade, the importation of infected fodder for domestic animals, the use of detergents with consequent interference with the function of septic tanks, and the consumption of half-frozen industrial foods. Further, the custom of feeding antibiotics to animals to promote their well-being is leading to the rise of dangerous strains of salmonella.

For drug resistant salmonellae, see Cohen and Tauxe (1986).

6.7 Bacillary Dysenteries

ICD 004. Shigellosis (includes bacillary dysenteries). Fourth digit (species of *Shigella*): 0, *dysenteriae*; 1, *flexneri*; 2, *boydii*, 3, *sonnei*; 8, other.

Dysentery is an inflammation of the large bowel with consequent passage of blood and mucus in the stools. After the demonstration of parasitic amebae by Loesch in 1875, dysentery had been regarded as a single, well-defined disease; at the turn of the century, Shiga in Japan, Flexner in the Philippines, and Kruse in Germany isolated causative bacteria, now classed in the genus *Shigella*.

Bacterial dysentery is common in both temperate and tropical regions, whenever the hygienic conditions are bad; it is therefore a disease of war, famine, jails, mental hospitals, and institutions. On occasion, these bacteria have been shown to be responsible for over 50% of deaths from diarrhea of infants under 6 months of age and almost all the deaths of infants at ages 6 months to 2 years in Georgia and New Mexico (see Topley and Wilson, 1975, p. 2042), whereas in Asia, Africa, and other Latin American countries the proportions may be less.

The most severe attacks of bacillary dysentery are due to *S. dysenteriae* (Shiga's bacillus). In some series it is said to have a case fatality of 50%. Cases can occur without blood and with or without mucus. Bacillary dysentery is spread from the feces of a human case or carrier by water, fruit, or food, but especially by flies.

See Parker (1984*g*), Roelants and Williams (1982).

6.8 Other Food Poisonings (Bacterial)

ICD 005. Fourth digit: 0, staphylococcal food poisoning; 1, botulism; 2, food poisoning due to *Clostridium perfringens* (*Cl. welchii*); 3, due to other clostridia; 4, due to *Vibrio parahaemolyticus*; 8, other; 9, unspecified.

Botulism (from Latin, botulus = sausage) is an intoxication caused by eating food in which *Cl. botulinum* has multiplied and produced the characteristic neurotoxin, usually after preservation with insufficient heating to kill the spores. The foods are commonly canned vegetables and fruits, but meats and fish have been implicated. The case fatality of botulism is high. However, it depends largely on the treatment of the preserved food before eating; Christie (1980) quotes a series of 1,000 cases in France in which the case fatality rate was only 2% since the food had been reheated before eating. Case fatality rates have been much higher in many of the other reported series. The value of serotherapy is dubious. Botulism is not a common disease; according to Gangarosa (1969), less than 10 deaths were reported annually from the United States in 1950–1959 (see also the surveys of Meyer, 1956, and Petty, 1965). There is now little danger in manufactured tinned foods, but still some in improperly prepared home preserves (Gilbert, Roberts, and Smith, 1984).

Poisoning may follow the ingestion of meat contaminated by *Cl. welchii* but deaths in this rubric are few, only seven deaths in Great Britain in this century.

For neurotoxin of botulism, see Sugiyama (1980). Botulism can also occur in infection of wounds and as an infant disease (Arnon, 1980).

Staphylococcus aureus develops an enterotoxin in a wide variety of foods and, so, causes acute gastrointestinal symptoms, but few deaths. See Parker (1984*d*) for a table of relative incidence of food poisonings in England and Wales.

6.9 Amebiasis

ICD 006. Infections due to *Endamoeba histolytica*. Fourth digit classifies by site.

Amebiasis, infection with *E. histolytica*, is a bowel infection often associated with dysentery. An important complication is liver abscess. Transmission of the disease is by infected food, especially in those countries where human excretions are used as fertilizer. Amebic infection can be water-borne, as in the Chicago epidemic of 1933 in which the source of drinking water in a hotel was found to be fouled by a leak from the toilet system (Bundesen, Connolly, et al., 1936). The ameba was falsely blamed for many deaths in the Gallipoli campaign of 1915.

The case fatality from the disease is low, only 35 deaths from 27,755 cases in the United States armed forces in World War II, according to Shaffer, Shlaes, and Radke (1965). For the USA civil population, see Juniper (1971). For more general accounts, see Albach and Booden (1978), Cheng (1973), Elsdon-Dew (1968, 1971), and Faust (1954). For amebic liver abscess, see Peters, Gitlin, and Libke (1981).

6.10 Other Protozoal Intestinal Diseases

ICD 007. Fourth digit: 0, balantidiasis; 1, giardiasis; 2, coccidiosis; 3, intestinal trichomoniasis; 4, other protozoal; 9, unspecified.

These infections tend to be nuisances rather than diseases, although giardiasis (Desai and Chandra, 1982; Erlandsen and Meyer, 1984; P.D. Smith, 1985; and J.W. Smith and Wolfe, 1980) and balantidiasis (Zaman, 1978) are considered more seriously, recently, especially as adding to the load of infections in infancy and childhood.

Beaver, Jung, and Cupp (1984) mention *Naegleria fowleri* and *Acanthamoeba culbertsoni* as examples of pathogenic free-living amebae that can cause serious disease, usually an amebic meningoencephalitis with a very high case fatality rate. *Naegleria* meningoencephalitis is usually fatal within a week from onset; treatment is usually unsuccessful. Infection is from swimming pools or thermal waters.

6.11 Gastroenteritis and Related Diseases as a Great Pestilence

ICD 008. Intestinal infections due to other organisms. Fourth digit by cause: 0, *Escherichia coli*; 1, *Enterobacterium arizona*; 2, *Aerobacter aerogenes*; 3, *Proteus*; 4, other specified bacteria; 5, unspecified bacterial enteritis; 6, specified virus; 8, other organism.

ICD 009. Ill-defined intestinal infections.

Since it may be impossible to state the cause of the epidemics, we may include other salmonella infections, shigellosis, amebiasis, and other protozoal intestinal diseases already discussed in §§6.4, 6.6, 6.7, and 6.10. So, we discuss here the infective bowel diseases, especially of infants and children, having in mind the many deaths caused by them in the developed countries, formerly, and in the developing countries, now. Moreover, this group of diseases is important in hospitals, mental asylums (Parker, 1984*b*), homes for the elderly, and in times of famine.

First we consider an infection that has become important in the developed world. It is only in recent times that strains of the common intestinal bacillus, *Escherichia coli*, have been shown to posses special properties of toxin production (ETEC) or other enteropathogenic properties (EPEC) giving rise to gastroenteritis. See, for example, Christie (1980), Gross (1984), Holme, Holmgren, et al. (1981), Parker (1984*g*), Sack (1975), and Sussman (1985). *Esch. coli* is a Gram-negative motile rod about

3 μm long and 0.6 μm in diameter. It is easily grown on common or special plate media. It is usually easily killed by heat; it can survive outside the human body. Epidemiologically, (*i*) only some strains cause gastroenteritis; (*ii*) the illness occurs most frequently in infants; (*iii*) infection, as distinct from illness, is very common; (*iv*) pathogenic strains vary, even over short periods of time, in their disease-producing properties. The evidence incriminating these strains of *Esch. coli* is epidemiologic; thus, the introduction of a case of infantile diarrhea into a nursery or hospital ward may be followed by many cases of diarrhea, each of which shows the same type of *Esch. coli*. The organism can be spread from case to case by contamination of feeding bottles, but it can also be spread by sweeping or mopping; these are some of the methods of spread under fair conditions of hygiene, but under bad hygienic conditions, one can easily imagine, it can be spread by flies, movements of children between families, contamination of milk, food, or water, and so on.

Pathological findings, even in fatal cases of the disease, are often not obvious; changes in the gastrointestinal tract may be hard to detect. The intestinal mucosa often appears normal, but sometimes there are areas of localized capillary engorgement; there is no gross inflammation and no ulceration of the mucosa—this recalls the lack of local pathological signs in cholera. There may be liver changes such as fatty degeneration or necrosis, which may be accompanied by jaundice. Rarely, mucosal ulceration, diffuse hemorrhages, abscesses, and peritonitis have been found at autopsy. The clinical signs are dominated by the loss of fluid from diarrhea. Treatment is largely by general nursing support and, where such help is available, by restoring the balance of the minerals, especially sodium chloride, in the blood. Antibiotics and chemotherapy play little part. We may recall the fancy of Daniel Defoe who believed that the causal organism of bubonic plague would have a terrifying and horrible appearance. Yet, in the present case, a group of bacilli closely resembling a predominant form of the commensals in the human intestine has produced a steady stream of deaths

in each generation, possibly without pause, since man began to live in large communities.

Now it is difficult to reconcile the description of the disease given above as occurring in modern developed countries with the actual statistical realities of the disease in Australia, England and Wales, the Scandinavian countries, or the United States during the nineteenth century and the early third of this century. Yet, the national statistics show that at least 2% of all deaths were due to gastroenteritis, infantile diarrhea, and such causes in those times. For example, the contributions to the infant mortality in Australia for males (females) were 24(20), 18(15), 11(8), 3(2), and 2(1) deaths per 1,000 live births in the epochs 1908–1910, 1911–1920, 1921–1930, 1931–1940, and 1941–1950, respectively. It is to be noted that in Australia in the earliest epoch above, over 2% of all persons born died of gastroenteritis in their first year (see §32.7). In Puffer and Serrano (1973, Table 72) we find gastroenteritis in the first year of life as the underlying cause of deaths per 1,000 births in various epochs ending in 1970, by country, as follows: Chaco and San Juan provinces, Argentina, 28 and 22; Bolivia 16; Recife, Ribeirão Prêto, and São Paulo, Brazil, 38, 17, and 20; Cali, Cartagena, and Medellin, Colombia, 17, 12, and 15; and Monterey, Mexico, 18. If we take these figures as representative of countries in poor states of hygiene and economic circumstance, it is evident that gastroenteritis well deserves the appellation of pestilence.

Good nutrition is by no means protective against such infections, as is shown by the high attack rates of well-nourished travelers (Lee and Kean, 1978).

Mata, Kronmal, and Villegas (1980, p. 10) state that although malnutrition is an associated or underlying cause of death due to diarrheal disease, diarrhea is a primary factor in the genesis of malnutrition. Mata (1978) showed that in the Guatemalan villages diarrhea was the cause of 10% of all infant deaths and of 16% and 25% of deaths at age 1 and ages 2 to 3 years, respectively. Nichols and Soriano (1977) and Rohde and Northrup (1976) in Elliott and Knight (1976) estimated that 10 million or 5–18 million, respectively, of children under 5 years throughout the world would die of diarrhea; overall morbidity could be 100-fold greater. Mata, Kronmal, and Villegas (1980, p. 5) give the mechanisms by which bowel infections affect host nutrition: (*i*) food consumption is reduced because attendants believe that this restriction is necessary; (*ii*) digestion is affected by a variety of mechanisms such as loss of appetite, increased peristalsis, and interference with enzymatic reactions; (*iii*) absorption is hindered by the epithelium being covered by *Giardia* or damaged by bacteria and rotaviruses or by microbes and parasites using the nutrients or by them releasing substances which reduce the intake of sodium; (*iv*) there may be hypersecretion of fluids into the bowel; and (*v*) there may be gross imbalance of magnesium, potassium, and phosphate.

For the interaction of diarrhea and malnutrition, see Bellanti (1983), Chen and Scrimshaw (1983), Harries (1976), and §22.16. See also Holme, Holmgren, et al. (1981) and Tomkins (1984) for prospects for treatment and control; Cukor and Blacklow (1984), Estes, Graham, et al. (1983), and Holmes (1979) for human viral gastroenteritis; Blaser, Taylor, et al. (1983) and Gross (1984) for *Campylobacter* as a cause of diarrheal diseases.

6.12 Water Supply

The mortality from bowel infections has fallen in the developed countries and in some of the developing countries as a result of improvements of the hygiene of water, milk and food supplies, and of excreta and garbage disposals. It is therefore appropriate to discuss historical aspects of these problems of supply and disposal here, although they have some importance in other infections.

Bacteriologically pure water can be obtained by the desalination process, but the source of almost all present water supplies is rain. Collected under favorable conditions, water may be free from human fecal contamination. Rain water can be collected at ground level in tanks; it may be collected by streams flowing into rivers, lakes, and reservoirs; it also sinks into pervious geological formations such as soil, alluvium, sand, gravel, and limestone. These sources can be tapped by wells. Sometimes these wells are securely protected by a cover or by other means to prevent fouling. Boreholes of small diameter can tap deep water-bearing strata to obtain water adeqately filtered by the passage through a sufficient depth of soil and can readily be protected because of the small cross-sectional area. Water can be obtained from infiltration galleries, which are tunnels near rivers, used to collect clean ground water by a natural filtration. Once the great cities are established, these methods become inadequate for the supply of a sufficiently pure and abundant supply of water, and some more formal system is required with purification by straining, sedimentation, coagulation, sand filtration, and disinfection usually by chlorine or ozone.

An interesting general history of water supplies has been given by Robins (1946) and some technological details are given in Daumas (1962). As a special example in an ancient European city, we consider London, with the aid of Kent (1951). Conduits brought water to London in the latter half of the thirteenth century; at that time such conduits were controlled by the City, and were often built as a result of a gift of wealthy citizens; distribution to the populace was by water-bearers. Later, in 1581, a waterwheel was erected at London Bridge. In 1609–1613 a canal, later to be known as New River, was constructed to bring water some 40 miles from the north-northwesterly direction. London is surrounded by rather flat country, so that extension to more distant sources would be difficult. Some pumping was necessary for further extensions at later times; however, the early steam power pumps were too expensive on fuel for their pumping to be economical. The Thames itself served as the principal source of water for a long time, although its quality was, in general, poor; the choice of intake point was often unfortunate, as in 1827 one London waterworks took in water from the Thames only 3 meters from the outfall of a sewer. In 1829 the Chelsea Waterworks introduced sand filtration by a suitable arrangement of large stones, small stones, gravel, and sand, on top of which a film of diatoms, green algae, and other organisms gradually built up; this invention later spread to many other cities. The Lambeth Waterworks Company was the first to take in water above the tideway at Teddington Weir and, so, avoid the pollution of the supply by the city. In East London a Cornish mining pump brought water from the River Lee. After 1861 the Kent Waterworks, serving suburbs southeast of the Thames, obtained all its water from deep wells. The Grand Junction Waterworks Company, established in 1811, used stone pipes but replaced them with castiron in 1812. The Southwark and Vauxhall Company, established in 1845, had works at Battersea. The Metropolitan Water Act of 1852 obliged all metropolitan water companies to filter their water. A more general control of water supplies and of sanitary conditions in England followed the Public Health Act of 1875, which is said to have reduced the typhoid fever rate to less than half its former size. The Metropolitan Water Board took control of London's water supply in 1903, after the Act of 1902. The difference between purities of two water supplies was a vital point in Snow's (1936) reasoning in 1849 that cholera was conveyed by water (see also Dickinson, 1954).

Similar problems of supply arose in other countries; for example, Blake (1956) states that in 1790 American cities drew their water almost exclusively from springs, wells, and cisterns, sources that became steadily more inadequate in quantity and quality as the population grew. By 1860 . . . most cities had learned a great lesson . . . at whatever expense or difficulty they must impound the waters of outlying lakes and rivers and bring this life giving stream . . . into the very homes of their citizens. See Gay (1918). In Australia the European settlement was made at Sydney Cove in 1788 near a pleasant stream supplying good water. In a few years this had become fouled with persons washing in it and with drainage from latrines, slaughter houses, and tanneries, despite attempts to keep the watershed free of pollution. Further, the digging of many wells led to a cessation of flow of the stream in the months of low rainfall. Similar sequences of events have been observed in mining areas, particularly alluvial gold mining areas, where many thousands of miners are

suddenly concentrated on a small stretch of stream. In Sydney water was brought in from nearby lagoons and swamps, and finally it was necessary to bring water from dams constructed on distant rivers.

It may be observed in conclusion that an abundant supply of pure water is necessary not only to prevent the passage of bowel infections such as cholera and typhoid fever from person to person and for the establishment of a water closet system but also for personal hygiene, the washing of clothes, and the preparation of food.

The account above holds for temperate climates and economically and educationally well-developed communities. There are more difficulties in such areas as the riverine communities of Southeast Asia where water is abundant, but the river is used for a great variety of purposes, that is, drinking water, industrial passage way, swimming, washing, and, above all, sewage disposal.

The problems of the pollution of the water supplies of a modern city may be exemplified by the Thames; Warner (1979) notes that the Royal Commission on Environmental Pollution was especially concerned with deoxygenation. The problem is that 25 m^3 per second of the water held above the weir at Teddington must be supplied for drinking water and ordinary civil use; it is also considered that 9 m^3 per second must pass over the weir to keep the estuary purged. In the dry summers of 1975 and 1976 this latter flow could not be sustained. For many years sewage had been allowed to enter the river without proper oxidation; as a result, there had been less than 10% saturation of dissolved oxygen in the water below London Bridge in the epoch 1930–1970. Completion of the sewage treatment works in 1975 ensured that the oxygen saturation did not fall below 30%, even after the two dry summers of 1975 and 1976.

The entry of halogenated organic compounds into the water of cities is now being reduced by restricting their manufacture and discharge into the environment.

For general reviews of water supply and health, see Feacham, et al. (1983), Garrison (1966b), Lelyfeld and Zoeteman (1981), N.

Smith (1976), Urbistondo (1985), Water Development (1978), and WHO-water (1976).

6.13 Milk as a Vehicle of Infection

Milk, collected under hygienic conditions from healthy cows, contains few bacteria. Under less-favorable conditions, there are many possible sources of contamination. The udder itself may be diseased or its exterior contaminated from the environment. The milking equipment may be contaminated by air, dust, or by human contact; this last can be of considerable importance if the milker is an intestinal carrier of typhoid, paratyphoid, dysentry, or food poisoning bacilli, if he is a nose and throat carrier of hemolytic streptococci or diphtheria bacilli, or if he is an open case of tuberculosis. In the developed world pasteurization of milk has been widely adopted because the milk is held several days before sale to the consumer, so that infections at source in the dairy are no longer important clinically; but milk can be contaminated after delivery by faulty handling and by flies. The principal diseases spread by milk are human and bovine tuberculosis, brucellosis, sore throat and scarlet fever due to streptococci, food poisoning due to staphylococci, diphtheria, typhoid-paratyphoid fevers, dysentery, and enteritis of infancy. The protection of milk after delivery to the consumer is a leading factor in the reduction of infant and child mortality.

For diseases, see WHO-milk (1962) and, especially, Kaplan, Abdussalam, and Bijlenga (1962). For popular and technical accounts of the tracing of the sources of milk-borne epidemics, see Sun (1985a) and G.S. Wilson (1984a).

6.14 Food Hygiene

The hygiene of food has varied with the culture, standards being relatively high in the Hebrew, Greek, and Roman worlds but low in the ages after the collapse of the Roman Empire. In the developed world much of the food is consumed far from its point of production, and, so, many possibilities exist for its contamination. In the last hundred years, that is, since the bacteriologic revolution, much has been learned about the preservation of food and its protection from poisons and infections deleterious to the consumer.

Infection of the food can occur during production, processing, distribution, and serving. Important organisms include: vibrios, salmonellas, shigellas, endamebas, and miscellaneous bowel organisms, such as staphylococcus and the clostridia of species *botulinum*, *welchii*, and *necroticans*, which produce a specific toxin in the food and hence cause a poisoning rather than an infection, hepatitis A virus, the round worm *Trichinella spiralis* of "measly" pork, *Echinococcus* species of hydatid disease, and the slow virus of kuru disease. For an elaboration of the above, see Felsenfeld (1967), Riemann (1969), Hobbs (1974), Roberts (1981), Jelliffe and Jelliffe (1982), and, especially, Fannin (1982) and Hornabrook (1982).

From a mortality point of view, the principal aims are to prevent the passage of infectious organisms into the food and to prevent their multiplication in it. Much food can be rendered effectively sterile by cooking or by pasteurization; refrigeration slows the multiplication of bacteria and reduces the possibility of food poisoning. However, food may be contaminated by food handlers, and there are many classic incidents of this in Topley and Wilson (1975) and elsewhere. To avoid such poisonings and infections, there are many health laws and policing procedures in the modern state. In particular, since the infections are of the gastrointestinal tract, food handlers must be trained in washing their hands, especially after going to the toilet, and in using no-touch techniques to avoid accidental soiling of the food. Proper plumbing, such as washbasins and sinks, should be installed.

See Melosi (1982) for the transformation of the disposal of garbage over the last hundred years and Hinton (1918) for animal nuisances.

6.15 Disposal of Excreta

The disposal of excreta becomes an important problem as soon as population density rises since excreta constitute a source of bacteria for the spread of diseases, especially gastrointestinal. Although water closets had been used in ancient times, as in Mohenjo-Daro, Knossos, the Greek states, and many Roman cities, it was not until the late nineteenth century that they came into general use in Europe.

There had been little progress in the development of proper drainage systems in the great cities before 1800. The first large sewer was constructed in New York City in 1805. Construction of large sewers was begun in Paris in 1833 and in Hamburg in 1842. Sewer systems for Brooklyn and for Chicago were designed in 1857 and 1858. Excreta were legally admitted to the sewers of London in 1815, of Boston in 1833, and of Paris in 1880. The nuisances caused by the admission of excreta to the sewers led to special studies and the crea-

tion of the Metropolitan Sewerage Commission of London in 1847–1848, for example. Proper disposal systems were installed in 1844 in Hamburg, 1854–1865 in London, and 1837–1863 in Paris. Shocking conditions for the disposal of excreta were recorded by the reports of the Health of Towns Commission in many of the English cities. Flies, of course, had ready access to the cesspools or middens, and liquid contents from these passed into the underground water, thus fouling the drinking water of the wells. Many special details are available in Corfield (1870, 1871), Latham (1878), Smith (1973), and Stewart and Jenkins (1969). For a general review of sanitation and disease, see Feacham, Bradley, Garelick, Mara, et al. (1983).

Chapter 7
Tuberculosis

7.1 History and Pathology

ICD 010–018. Infection by *Mycobacterium tuberculosis*, whether human or not. Third and fourth digits by site; fifth digit by isolation of bacillus.

Tuberculosis is an infectious disease affecting man at all ages, causing lesions in all organs, and having all grades of severity. It is an ancient disease; for example, bone tuberculosis in the form of spinal caries or cold abscesses of the vertebrae has been observed in Egyptian mummies; the pulmonary form was known to the Hindus in 500 BC and was later described by Hippocrates.

Tuberculosis seems only to have become common in the modern highly developed world with the possibilities of large densely populated cities under conditions of poor hygiene, nutrition, and housing. Tuberculosis can now be defined as disease caused by *Myco. tuberculosis*, although it was difficult to see all its various manifestations, for example, in its pulmonary and bone forms noted above, as due to the same cause in the prebacteriologic era. The first step was taken in 1865 by J.A. Villemin, who injected tuberculous material from a human case and produced the characteristic tubercles in rabbits; fresh animals could be infected from them. The problem of etiology was solved in 1882 by Robert Koch with the aid of novel staining and cultivation methods to demonstrate the presence of the bacilli in lesions and to obtain them in pure culture on artificial media. From these cultures, bacilli could be in-

jected into susceptible animals, producing the disease and fulfilling Koch's postulates, as we should now say.

Many species of *Mycobacteria* are now known, of which only *Myco. tuberculosis* and *Myco. bovis*, variously regarded as belonging to separate species or as variants of a single species, are causes of human mortality. For further details we refer the reader to Topley and Wilson (1975, 1983–1984), Grange (1984), and Barksdale and Kim (1977). The bovine type of human tuberculosis could be considered among the zoonoses, but it is included in the ICD with the human type for convenience, party because of the difficulties in distinguishing between the two. Bovine tuberculosis is a rare cause of pulmonary disease in the adult; when it occurs, it is usually an occupational disease of persons attending cattle under unfavorable hygienic conditions. Bovine tuberculosis has been a very important cause of infant and child death in the past. Indeed, Myers and Steele (1969) quote a report of Park, Krumwiede, et al. (1910–1911) which states that of 1,511 cases in an American experience of generalized tuberculosis in children, 66% were due to the bovine type of the bacillus. The relative importance of the bovine type varies considerably in different countries and even within countries.

The characteristic lesion of the disease is the tubercle, seen microscopically to be a collection of epithelioid and lymphoid cells grouped around the invading bacilli. If the disease progresses, these lesions may go on to local cure, leaving small areas of fibrosis; but they may enlarge and coalesce causing the death of neighboring tissue cells, and there may be extensive damage with a breakdown of the structure of the tissue and the formation of small abscesses, which may be too large for the body to reabsorb and repair. The results of these processes may be seen macroscopically as areas of caseation, that is, of areas of amorphous cheeselike remnants, after the normal structure has been broken down. Such areas may be quite extensive and form an abscess, which is said to be *cold* because heat, a usual sign of inflammation, may not be evident. In the lungs such a breakdown of susceptible tissue leads to ulceration of the small arteries and, so, to hemorrhages into the bronchial system, clinically observable as hemoptyses or the coughing up of blood, which is such a characteristic feature of the disease. The ulceration leads also to a discharge of the caseous material into the bronchi and, thence, by the sputum into the outside world. This is the principal mode of spread of the infection due to the human type of the bacillus. Moreover, extensive caseation may occur in other organs without direct access to the exterior of the body; thus, areas of caseation may form in the vertebrae and the contents may track along natural channels such as the muscle sheaths to be discharged through an ulcer in the skin far removed from the original abscess, for example, in the thigh.

The spread of the human type of the disease depends on open cases, namely, those who pass the bacillus into the surrounding atmosphere in the form of cough spray or sputum, to be inhaled or ingested by susceptibles. The bacillus is well adapted to spreading in this manner for it can survive drying even for years. Moreover, an infection of an individual can persist throughout a lifetime and, after a recrudescence of the disease, the subject may become an open case and lead to other individuals becoming infected.

In adults in a European-type community the pulmonary type of infection may be sufficient to cause death. Otherwise, grave forms of the disease may follow when the infection becomes widely disseminated in the body as acute miliary tuberculosis, named so because of the many lesions throughout the body about the size of a millet seed. Another grave complication is acute meningeal tuberculosis, an infection of the covering of the brain. In children, particularly, there may be lesions in the lymphatic glands and in the intestines leading to much wasting and even death.

Clinically, there are several types of the disease. First, in primary pulmonary tuberculosis, signs of the infection in the lung may be evident clinically and by X rays. The attack may be mild leading on to spontaneous cure. Occasionally, it leads on to meningitis or other forms of tuberculosis. Second, adult or reinfection type is characterized by an insidious onset. Third, nonpulmonary tuberculosis occurs in other parts of the body, such as the meninges, bones, joints, lymphatic nodes, or more generally in the whole body. Attacks of tuberculosis disease of the first type are referred to as exogenous, and those of the second type are usually thought to be endogenous and due to the reactivation in some partly healed lesion, although there has been much argument about the actual frequency of exogenous infections. See §7.6.

It is now considered that infections are acquired, usually early in life and often from a family contact, and lead to a "primary infection," usually inapparent. There may be a long, latent time before the infection becomes apparent. Then, at some later time, the defenses break down and lead to active disease. This idea is consistent with the concept of Andvord (1921, 1930) of tuberculosis as a "childhood" disease and with the usual interpretations of the generation death rates and of certain follow-ups of tuberculin-tested children (Comstock, 1975).

For history of the disease, see Cummins (1950), Keers (1978), Myers (1974), and Pièry and Roshem (1931). For bovine tuberculosis, see Myers and Steele (1969).

7.2 Certification and Assignment

Tuberculosis, under the rules for assignment of the *International List of Causes of Death* in its original and revised forms, always had high priority and was to be preferred to almost any other form or causes of death appearing on the death certificate, with the exceptions of cancer, violence, accident, and certain rare infections. So, if the diagnosis of tuberculosis was noted on the death certificate, the death would with almost complete certainty be assigned to one of the rubrics of the *International List* dealing with tuberculosis, although possibly there would have been some losses to violent causes at the younger ages and to cancer at the higher ages. See §2.8. for a detailed discussion. In conclusion, it is probably true that the official statistics have given a good and significant answer to the problem of estimating how many persons die of tuberculosis.

7.3 Age-specific Death Rates for Australia

Excellent time series are now available for many countries of the world, extending over a hundred years in many cases. Space permits only the analysis of a few countries, and we choose Australia as representative in many ways of the worldwide experience in the developed countries and use its rates as an example of the methods. We then pass on in the next section to discuss the statistics of England and Wales as representative of a long European experience, on which much commentary is available.

The rates may be considered for an epoch and for either sex, for instance, males in 1911 to 1920 in Australia. In Table 7.3.1 and Figure 7.3.1 there is initially a high rate for the ages under 5 years, namely, 387 per 1,000,000 per annum. The rate then falls to 109 per 1,000,000 per annum at ages 5 to 14 years; from this minimum the rates rise for successive 10-year age groups, 15–24, 25–34, . . . 55–64, to 529, 1,104, 1,365, 1,587, and 1,612; the curve of the rates thus climbs sharply in early adult life, flattens out to reach a maximum at about the age of 60 years, and finally falls in the higher age groups. The female rates follow a similar course with age, although with a rather sharper and earlier maximum at about the age of 30 years. In later epochs the position of the maximum is at higher ages still, for males in 1941 to 1950 at 70

years and in 1961 to 1970 at over 75 years. The maxima in females for the epochs 1911 to 1920, 1941 to 1950, and 1961 to 1970 were at ages 30, 30, and over 75 years, respectively. These changes in the position of the maxima can only be explained satisfactorily after a consideration of the cohort or generation method.

A second method of analysis is to follow the rates in a given sex and age group over a time series, in other words, to consider Table 7.3.1 by columns. It is evident from this table that there have been marked declines in the death rates at all ages. The declines begin earlier in the younger age groups and then are evident in the older age groups until, in the later years, tuberculosis is no longer an important cause of death in Australia at any age, a surprising conclusion to the "white plague," as tuberculosis used to be called.

The third method of analysis has already been described in general terms in §3.8; it is now used to explain the progress of the death rates from tuberculosis. Some demographers had been uneasy at the assumption in the construction of a life table by the actuaries, who took the rates in a particular epoch as being those of a group passing through life. K.F. Andvord (1921, 1930), a Norwegian clinician, first gave clinical interest to the cohort method; he believed that tuberculosis should be regarded as a disease of childhood with late effects possibly persisting throughout life and so used the cohort method of analysis. This novel idea has been attacked by some epidemiologists, but is now generally accepted. In Figure 7.3.2 the death rates of successive cohorts are plotted, that is, groups of persons born in the same epoch, for example, 1861–1870, 1871–1880, and so on. The rates for the earlier cohorts for the epochs before 1900 are not given in Table 7.3.1, for reasons of space; but the male cohort of 1901–1910 has a high mortality rate, about 533 per 1,000,000 per annum, represented by the rate in 1908–1910 at ages 0–4 years; the rate then falls to 108 in 1911–1920, and then 373, 447, 435, 209, 126, and 57 per 1,000,000 per annum at ages 15–24, 25–34, . . .65–74 years, respectively, with a maximum at about the age of 30 years. Similar findings are shown graphically for both sexes in Figure 7.3.2. In

TABLE 7.3.1. Mortality rates in Australia from tuberculosis (all forms)*.

Age in years	0–4	5–14	15–24	25–34	35–44	45–54	55–64	65–74	75+
				Males					
1908–1910	533	157	582	1,150	1,548	1,720	1,988	1,704	861
1911–1920	387	108	529	1,104	1,365	1,587	1,612	1,276	651
1921–1930	244	67	373	844	1,056	1,337	1,335	1,138	648
1931–1940	155	41	197	447	707	982	1,225	1,089	677
1941–1950	88	24	98	230	435	774	1,095	1,314	898
1951–1960	13	3	11	36	84	209	441	666	727
1961–1970	3	0	1	3	16	53	126	285	494
1971–1980	1	0	0	1	4	13	23	57	121
				Females					
1908–1910	418	172	934	1,383	1,215	956	939	857	468
1911–1920	332	128	762	1,074	935	745	664	605	358
1921–1930	217	76	642	866	667	562	488	478	339
1931–1940	133	47	373	607	469	338	372	390	336
1941–1950	77	33	190	344	311	242	242	333	298
1951–1960	19	2	15	43	67	65	70	114	164
1961–1970	2	1	0	3	11	21	30	46	79
1971–1980	1	0	0	1	2	5	10	14	23
				Masculinity rates[†]					
1908–1910	128	91	62	83	127	180	212	199	184
1911–1920	117	84	69	103	146	213	243	211	182
1921–1930	112	88	58	97	158	238	274	238	191
1931–1940	117	87	53	74	151	291	329	279	201
1941–1950	114	73	52	67	140	320	452	395	301
1951–1960				‡	125	322	630	584	443
1961–1970				‡	145	252	420	620	625
1971–1980‡									

* Deaths per 1,000,000 per annum.
[†] 100 × (male death rates)/(female death rates).
‡ Not computed (numbers too small).
From Lancaster and Gordon (1987).

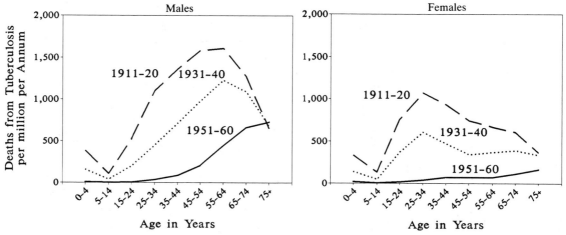

FIGURE 7.3.1. Death rates from tuberculosis (all forms) by epochs in Australia (1971–1980 rates are too low for inclusion).

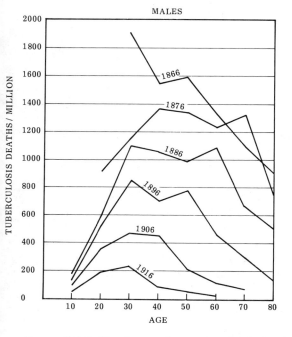

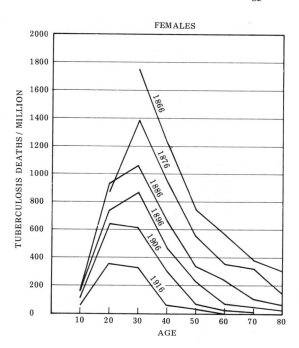

FIGURE 7.3.2. Death rates from tuberculosis (all forms) in Australia studied by the generation (or cohort) method. Arithmetic grid. (Rates at the youngest ages cannot be shown.)

the cohorts the maxima in the rates are obtained in the age group 25–34 years, approximately at age 30 years, and then the rates decline for the rest of the life of the cohort. The curves are often plotted on a semilogarithmic scale; they are of the same general shape for the different cohorts and appear as if each were merely a copy of the same curve displaced vertically at variable distances. There is a regular tendency for the later graphs to be at a lower level than the earlier. As was mentioned in §3.8, this means that the death rate at age X in the cohort of persons born in epoch Y can be expressed as a product of a function of X and a function of Y. The interpretation of this observation is that the death rates of a cohort are largely determined by the value in childhood. In other words, the conditions in the environment, including therapy, have not changed rapidly enough to affect the shape of the curve. It can now be seen that the changes in the shapes of the curves in Fig. 7.3.1 can be explained. In a given epoch the oldest persons have experienced the highest rate of tuberculosis infection in their childhood and have ben-

efited very little by changes in the environment, including therapy, except for those cohorts surviving after 1950. The later cohorts have begun their lives under increasingly favorable conditions and this advantage has persisted with them throughout. In particular, it can be noted that the latest calendar rates are the most recent rates taken one from each cohort. See §5.8.

Of course, the nice relations mentioned in the last paragraph may be upset if the external conditions are altered greatly as by war, famine, or malnutrition. Moreover, they have not been greatly altered by changes in therapy; effective therapy was only available from approximately 1950 onward and the infection and morbidity rates of childhood had already fallen greatly.

The cohort method brings a satisfying order into the behavior of the death rates as can be seen in the similar graphs for the different cohorts. It is also consistent with clinical experience according to the notion that most adult cases in the European-type experience are *endogenous*, that is, recrudescent after an earlier infection. Exact agreement of rates estimated on a generation basis cannot be expected, for it would suggest that all events in the outside world are irrelevant to the progress of disease in individuals.

Table 7.3.1 shows the masculinities of the death rates by age in the different epochs as a percentage. After 1950 the rates at ages under 45 years depend on deaths, too few to give good estimates of ratio. Masculinity has been high at ages 0–4 years and then low up to the age of 35 years. This is a feature differing from the English experience, which will be discussed in the following section. After age 35 years the masculinities increase with age and there is a general tendency for this to be more evident in the later epochs. It is possibly explicable by occupational factors and the greater tendency of elderly males to become derelicts.

7.4 Tuberculosis in England and Wales

A commentary is now given on the progress in tuberculosis mortality in England and Wales. The number of deaths from tuberculosis are available for London from 1631 until 1838 in the Bills of Mortality, which were superseded in 1838 by the reports of the Registrar-General of England and Wales. Before 1701 population figures were not available for the calculation of death rates, so Brownlee (1916a, 1918) calculated the ratios of tuberculosis deaths to all deaths in the Bills. Brownlee (1916a) justified this method of expressing the rates in the earlier years by showing that the two methods gave similar results when applied to the years after 1838. We give a curve of what can be considered to be the ratio of tuberculosis to all deaths in England and Wales as Figure 7.4.1. This curve begins at 15% in 1631, rises to a maximum of 22% just after 1651, falls to a minimum of 12% just after 1725, and finally rises to a maximum of 25% in 1802, from which year the curve continues to fall; after 1838 the curves of the ratio and of the crude death rate from tuberculosis are practically parallel. The fall of both curves continues into the most recent years.

It is of interest that the reproduction of the figures of Brownlee (1916a) by Sydenstricker (1927, 1974) led to the posthumous publication of Frost (1939), an analysis of Massachusetts data by the generation method. Neither of these latter two authors recognized that Brownlee (1916a) had already introduced the generation method of analysis.

Using Brownlee's estimate, we note that

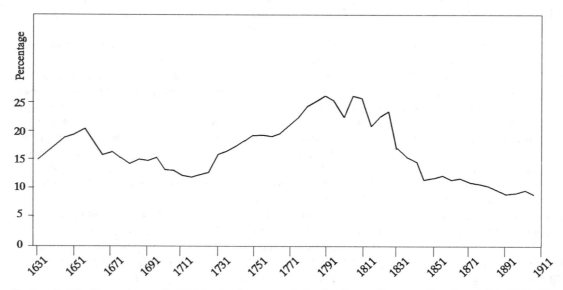

FIGURE 7.4.1. Percentage of phthisis deaths to total deaths from all causes London 1631–1910. From Brownlee (1918)

after 1802 the curve of the tuberculosis crude death rate is almost linear for many years, but in this century it flattens out since its absolute value is relatively low, although, proportionally to the height of the curve the annual decline steadily becomes steeper; and this is so if the data are plotted on a semilogarithmic (or ratio) grid. Topley and Wilson (1975, Table 58.1) give the death rates from 1851 to 1967, noting that the proportionate decrease in the death rates between 1949 and 1959 was as great as that between the years 1855 and 1945, and they attribute the accelerated declines to the use of effective chemotherapy. These authors reject any cohort interpretation of the changes.

A more detailed series of the age-specific death rates from tuberculosis in England and Wales is given in Table 7.4.1. An analysis by the calendar method shows that in the epochs before 1920 there is a high death rate in infancy and then a minimum in the childhood decade; the rates then rise rapidly to a high level in early adult life and remain high up to the age of 75 years. The maximum has tended to appear at rather later ages, and there has only been slight mortality at the younger ages in the more

TABLE 7.4.1. Tuberculosis in England and Wales (deaths per 1,000,000 per annum).

Epoch	All ages*	0–4	5–9	10–14	15–19	20–24	25–34	35–44	45–54	55–64	65–74	75 and over
					Males							
1851–1860	3,477	6,323	1,225	1,102	2,636	4,245	4,163	4,119	3,957	3,479	2,573	1,061
1861–1870	3,357	6,018	1,029	899	2,382	4,031	4,206	4,244	3,969	3,433	2,174	740
1871–1880	3,080	5,798	900	748	1,857	3,219	3,785	4,198	3,928	3,285	2,025	650
1881–1890	2,656	5,004	817	630	1,510	2,516	3,164	3,685	3,611	3,027	1,913	732
1891–1900	2,285	4,347	705	521	1,234	2,102	2,541	3,251	3,296	2,768	1,706	629
1901–1910	1,891	3,129	636	463	997	1,744	2,158	2,622	2,934	2,574	1,686	668
1911–1920	1,550	1,942	589	499	1,068	1,558	1,840	2,204	2,335	2,135	1,390	585
1921–1930	1,110	1,059	343	300	835	1,387	1,401	1,636	1,725	1,452	957	394
1936†	825	520	173‡		494	946	922	1,053	1,353	1,281	790	398§
1946	NA	68	22	23	239	481	615	687	1,020	1,165	768	340§‖
1956	177	7	1	2	7	4	71	113	231	456	640	463§‖
1966	48			NA			11	27	76	189	324	408¶
1976	19			NA			1	7	34	65	122	258¶
					Females							
1851–1860	3,483	5,232	1,201	1,595	3,731	4,430	4,690	4,293	3,236	2,523	1,783	834
1861–1870	3,177	4,917	939	1,300	3,300	4,087	4,482	3,988	2,954	2,178	1,354	528
1871–1880	2,701	4,663	830	1,099	2,577	3,253	3,631	3,475	2,535	1,866	1,193	452
1881–1890	2,251	3,987	874	1,030	2,052	2,495	2,932	2,846	2,146	1,597	1,058	452
1891–1900	1,780	3,516	744	818	1,555	1,788	2,086	2,264	1,753	1,344	906	427
1901–1910	1,424	2,636	698	710	1,250	1,425	1,651	1,710	1,449	1,186	894	494
1911–1920	1,218	1,619	618	748	1,416	1,526	1,484	1,401	1,156	943	750	437
1921–1930	887	874	352	461	1,238	1,467	1,228	941	734	624	498	318
1936†	570	476	184‡		807	1,164	848	594	458	417	356	252§
1946	NA	60	25	69	468	842	662	382	261	242	207	119§‖
1956	68	4	1	0	6	35	80	79	62	70	111	125§‖
1966	28			NA			8	26	35	49	67	96¶
1976	15			NA			3	6	19	30	32	60¶

* 1851–1930, standardized on to the population of England and Wales as enumerated in 1901. From the Registrar-General's Decennial Supplement (1952, Part 3, Table 12).
§ From Annual Reports of the Registrar-General.
‖ Pulmonary tuberculosis only.
¶ From World Health Statistics Annual.
† From 1936, crude death rates by sex.
‡ 5–14 years.

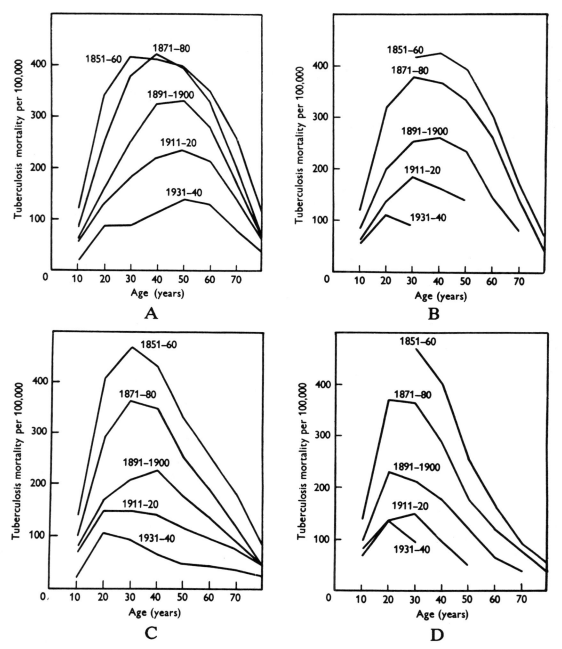

FIGURE 7.4.2. (A.) England and Wales (males). Tuberculosis mortality at various ages in the decennia 1851–1860, 1871–1880, 1891–1900, 1911–1920, and 1931–1940. (B.) England and Wales (males). Tuberculosis mortality at various ages of the cohorts age 25–34 years in 1851–1860, 1871–1880, 1891–1900, 1911–1920, and 1931–1940. (C.) England and Wales (females). Tuberculosis mortality at various ages in the decennia 1851–1860, 1871–1880, 1891– 1900, 1911–1920, and 1931–1940. (D.) England and Wales (females). Tuberculosis mortality at various ages of the cohorts age 25–34 years in 1851– 1860, 1871–1880, 1891–1900, 1911–1920, and 1931– 1940. From V.H. Springett, "A comparative study of tuberculosis mortality rates." *Journal of Hygiene* 48 (1950) p. 373, Cambridge University Press. We refer the cohorts back to the mid-year of birth, so 1851–60 becomes 1826 = 1856 − 30.

recent epochs. Examining the table by columns shows that there have been great declines at all ages over all the epochs.

Figure 7.4.2 shows graphs, labelled B and D, of the rates analyzed by the cohort method for males and females respectively, compared with the calendar analysis in A and C. The shapes of the various cohorts are similar. There is no evidence of a postponement of the mortality to later life in males, as is suggested by the calendar analysis, which, indeed, was noted by Brownlee (1916a). There have been slight changes in the positions of the maxima of the males, with those of the cohorts of 1846, 1886 and 1906 being earlier than the preceding one. For males the maximum of the curve appears at ages 35–44 years for the cohort of 1826; for the cohorts of 1846 and 1886 the maximum is at ages 25–34; in the cohort of 1906 of Springett (1950) in Figure 7.4.2 the maximum has been at ages 15–24 years. The females have had maxima in the 15–24 year group with the exceptions of the cohorts of 1826 and 1886. For females the curves have been rather more peaked than for males. This consistency of the position of the maximum is due to the sharp peak in mortality in young adult life in the earlier epochs, whether the rates are examined by the calendar or cohort method. The progress of the rates agrees well with the analysis of Springett (1950, 1952). It is evident that the cohort curves had begun to be displaced downward earlier than the cohort of 1856, the first for which full data are available.

Analysis of English data by Springett (1952) found that in females the attack rates, the notification rates, and the mortality rates were all greatest at young adult life, but the mortality rates in males were highest in the older age groups. He concluded that the deaths at high ages were the late effects of infections acquired many years earlier. He states:

There is no difficulty in appreciating that a large part of the tuberculosis mortality in males in later life is due to a final breakdown of disease originally acquired many years earlier. This is not to say that fresh disease never occurs in these older age-groups. Despite the present form of the tuberculosis mortality curve [that is by the calendar method], there has never yet been a group of men who experienced a greater tuberculosis mortality at ages over 45 than they had experienced at young adult ages,

that is, for a cohort the rates over 45 years of age have always been less than the rates at young adult ages.

It is necessary to consider the reasons for the decline in mortality from tuberculosis. For the infections with the bovine type of bacillus, it appears that active measures to lessen infection of the milk of cows and then the killing of the bacilli, when present, by routine boiling or pasteurization of milk are sufficient causes for the passing of bovine tuberculosis and, hence, a good deal of the morbidity and mortality from tuberculosis in infancy and childhood. It is not easy to give such a satisfying account for the human type of the disease. Many authorities stress genetic aspects; tuberculosis is, according to them, a long-standing epidemic in which selection is playing its role in weeding out those less fit to withstand the effects of tuberculosis infection. Although it must be admitted that differences in immunity can be demonstrated in animal species, the evidence is more equivocal in the humans. We may conclude that there may have been some changes in genetic constitution, but the rates have fallen so rapidly in recent times that other factors, hygienic, social, and environmental, must be considered as responsible for the observed declines in the death rates.

Nutrition. As Topley and Wilson (1975) point out, tuberculosis is one of the few infectious diseases that is seriously influenced by malnutrition under conditions holding in the developed world. Increases in the death rates have often been noted in famines and in wars.

Housing. Overcrowding can be expected to be of importance as it leads to increased frequency of the passage of organisms between persons.

Alcoholism. This acts in a number of ways, leading to malnutrition, for example. Tuberculosis is a common disease of derelicts.

Social Habits. Spitting, especially in confined spaces such as trains, may have assisted the spread of the bacillus.

Wages. The incidence of tuberculosis seems to be negatively correlated with the level of real wages.

Much of the decline in mortality had already occurred before the establishment of effective remedies.

Bignall (1971), referring to England and Wales, states: "Extrapolation suggests that there will only be about 1,200 notifications in 1980. By 1990 it is probable that the disease will be no commoner than non-tuberculous meningitis is now, and by 2010 it should be of interest to the medical historian only."

For history, see Cummins (1950) and Pièry and Roshem (1931); for progress in the disease in England and Wales, Heaf and Rusby (1968), Logan and Benjamin (1957), Philip, Willoughby, Collis, and Greewood (1928), and Stocks (1949). See also Brownlee (1920) for mortality by city and region.

7.5 Tuberculosis in Newly Exposed Populations

In animal experimentation and observation, differences have been found in the reaction to tuberculosis infections both between species and within species. The evidence for genetic differences in the human species is more difficult to assess. Twin studies on the clinical outcomes in human monozygotic and dizygotic twins have lent some support to the existence of hereditary factors within given communities. It is, thus, not unreasonable to assume that there are genetic differences between populations.

Whatever may be the reasons for the differences in resistance between populations, the case incidence and the case fatality rates may be very high when tuberculosis is first introduced. The disease may follow a rapid course with enlargements of the lymph glands, ulcerations of the intestine, tuberculous meningitis, and generalized spread of the disease in the adults as well as in children. These acute forms and epidemic spread are in marked contrast to the more chronic forms of the disease in adults, usually seen in the developed communities where pulmonary tuberculosis is the common adult form of the disease. Thus McDougall

(1949, p. 263) cites R. Arima and I. Ishihara who reported in 1928 an epidemic of tuberculosis among 23 Japanese girls attending a course of instruction in tailoring; of these girls, aged 15 to 19 years, 9 developed active tuberculosis and 8 died; there were also secondary infections of friends and relatives of these girls. The Prophit Survey carried out by Daniels, Ridehalgh, Springett, and Hall (1948) showed that the Irish and Welsh nurses working at certain English hospitals fared less well than English nurses at the same hospitals whether they had a Mantoux test showing previous infection with the bacillus or not, the morbidity rates being in the ratio 2.5 to 1.

In the contacts between the invading or intruding races (the caucasoids of §1.1) and the tribal peoples, the reasons for the lack of resistance in the tribal people to their initial introduction to the disease are less easy to ascertain. The tribal people do not always meet the disease under favorable conditions; they may first meet it while serving as military auxiliaries or as laborers on developmental projects, where the hygienic conditions may be much inferior to those enjoyed by the caucasoids or by themselves previously. See also Torchia (1977) for a study of tuberculosis in the American negroes and Wilcocks (1962) for tuberculosis of man in the tropics.

Control is possible through an amelioration of working and other social conditions mentioned above and by the use of the BCG (i.e., Bacille Calmette-Guérin) vaccine, for which see Mande (1968), Eickhoff (1977), and Fox (1984).

7.6 Personal Factors

(i) Age at Infection. The evidence for infection by age has been obtained by postmortem examinations and surveys using the Mantoux test in the living. There are great difficulties of interpretation of the results from either type of enquiry. The populations examined were not homogeneous in their hygienic experience, and the Mantoux surveys were only carried out on a sufficiently large scale when the incidence of the disease was declining, that is, after 1930. Moreover, it was not always recognized that

the subjects examined were not representative of the population at large. Thus, postmortem surveys were carried out on the public hospital or dispensary populations that would have included principally the lower economic groups. In the European cities postmortem studies showed that almost 100% of the population at age 20 years would already have had an infection with the bacillus, although clinical signs and symptoms might have been absent. The evidence of the Mantoux surveys in American college students would have shown rather lower rates. In the period after 1945 surveys would have been available showing the rate of tuberculosis infection by single years of life from infancy into early adult life. However, notwithstanding the difficulties of comparison between times, nations, and classes, it would be possible to state that there were many infections in individuals who had never had the signs or symptoms of tuberculous disease. Further, under the hygienic conditions holding in the great European cities in the period before 1940, most persons would have been infected before reaching adult life.

(ii) Size of the Infecting Dose. The size of the infecting dose has been a matter of considerable research and discussion. The following summarizes some of the leading views. The subject inhales tubercle bacilli, many of which are dead or in a damaged condition, in dust or fine aerial particles. Often, as in the case of domestic infections, there will be repeated inhalation of the bacilli. Usually, however, there is only one primary lung lesion, usually at the apex of a lung. There is some reason to think that a massive initial dose is rather more dangerous than repeated small doses. The primary infection may pass without any signs or symptoms. The disease may become active at some later stage because of overwork, acute infections with other organisms, various stresses, poor nutrition, poverty, or other unfavorable factors. This activation is usually due to the infection that has already been established in the body, an endogenous infection.

(iii) Tuberculosis of Infancy and Early Childhood. Tuberculosis death rates by the broader age groups showed high tuberculosis death rate in the first 5 years of life, relative to that in the next 10 years of life. Analyzed by single years of life as in Lancaster (1950*d*, figure 2) the rates of the two sexes were about equal at ages 0 and 1 years. There were two sources of infection, one, from open cases within the family and, two, from milk infected with the bovine type bacillus (but sometimes with human type bacilli). The resistance to the organism was low in infancy, and tuberculosis was an acute disease with meningitis being the usual terminal lesion; other forms were lymphadenitis, enteritis, and acute miliary tuberculosis.

(iv) Sex. The male death rates from the disease may be divided by the female death rates at the corresponding ages to obtain a "masculinity" after multiplication by a convenient figure, 100, to avoid decimals, as in Table 7.3.1 for Australia over a number of epochs. It is evident that the masculinity is over unity in the first 5 years of life, but at ages 5 to 14 years it has fallen, and then it rises steadily throughout life. The increases in the mortality rates for both sexes in early adult life can only be partly due to the increased opportunities for infection as the individual moves out into the world, so that other factors must be invoked and these have acted on the two sexes rather differently in most countries (see Comstock, 1975). The rates tend to rise earlier in the females than in the males after the low rates in childhood; in England this was the subject of the enquiries of Hill (1936) and Daniels, Ridehalgh, Springett, and Hall (1948). The true reasons for the behavior of the masculinity rates are not well understood although much has been written on the subject. The high rates of mortality in both sexes in young adult life was formerly a cause, especially for the females, of the local maximum in the total death rate that occurred in both sexes.

(v) Pregnancy. There has been a widespread clinical view that pregnancy is an unfavorable factor. It has seemed to many that pregnancy activates a preexisting infection, which becomes more acute. The statistical evidence for this opinion is rather equivocal as it is difficult to find sutiable controls for comparison. The pregnancy and the confinement may change

other operative factors, such as the economic condition of the mother; most experts concede that pregnancy is an unfavorable factor without taking the view that it is uniformly a disaster to the subject.

(vi) Diabetes. It has been found in studies on diabetes clinics that the incidence of tuberculosis deaths is greater than would be expected in the population at large (see §21.3).

(vii) Silicosis and Other Pneumoconioses. Mortality studies of occupations have shown that tuberculosis is a common and dangerous complication of silicosis (Sydenstricker, 1974). The presence of silica in the tissues favors the spread of the bacillus. It is known that the inhalation of silica at certain particle sizes is critical; other dusts do not have the same effect, for coal miners often have lungs colored strongly with coal dust but do not suffer from an unduly high rate of tuberculous disease. Silicosis leads to high death rates in some occupations. Silicosis tuberculosis is obviously a generation, not a calendar, effect. Preventive efforts will not have their effects until many years later.

(viii) Schizophrenia and Other Mental Disorders. Since the times of John Howard and William Farr, unfavorable conditions of health in mental institutions have been known to lead to high death rates, including high rates from tuberculosis; moreover, in modern times high rates still persist. Deegan, Culp, and Beck (1942) found that the death rates from tuberculosis in mental institutions were 12 times that in the general population of New York City. See also Alström (1942) for the Scandinavian experience.

7.7 General Hygienic Factors

We give a brief summary of the importance of environmental or general hygienic factors that can be grouped under headings not completely mutually exclusive. We note that there is a vast literature on the subject, and that we can only briefly touch on what are very important practical problems in public health (see Hart and Wright, 1939).

(i) Climate. For many years the treatment of mild cases of tuberculosis had been carried out in sanatoriums in the Alps. There seems to be no definite evidence in favor of such sites, possibly their value was that they offered mild climatic conditions with pleasant, peaceful but interesting surroundings. High tubercular death rates have been found in a great variety of climates from Greenland to the tropics. The smaller dosages of solar ultraviolet light at high latitudes leads to an increased incidence of bone tuberculosis in infancy and childhood.

(ii) Population Density. It is necessary to define population densities calculated on not too wide a stretch of territory for there may be great diversity of densities in the territory. To take an extreme example, the inhabitants of an arid country may be all or nearly all concentrated in a few cities or towns, favored by climatic conditions, nearness to the ocean, and so on, and in the cities and towns crowding may be intense. Crowding has its effect in enabling infections to pass readily from person to person, from open cases to new subjects, for example, within households from parents and grandparents to child.

(iii) Employment and Occupation. Tuberculosis death rates are known to be high in some occupations, but comparisons between trades are rendered difficult by conscious or unconscious selection, for example, the health of underground miners may be more favorable than that of others employed in surface jobs in the mining industry because only the most fit go down into the mines. Some consideration has also to be given to the fact that the disease itself lowers the economic status of the subject, thus possibly reversing the causal connection. There is often a selection at entry into an occupation, the tuberculosis initial rates being low in those occupations requiring heavy physical labor, so that some other occupations will have a spuriously high initial rate. Sydenstricker (1974, p. 353) illustrates this effect very well with the experience of workers in "mines and quarries," who have low initial death rates but after the age of fifty years have higher rates than those in the other classes, except for those working in "marble and stone." Similarly, if migration is easy between cities, the cities with

high levels of heavy industries will recruit high levels of physically fit young men.

Notwithstanding such reservations, there are occupations in which the worker is exposed to special risks; he may be exposed to high concentrations of fine silica dust in the air breathed. Underground miners, excluding coal miners, are especially exposed, so are pottery workers, stone cutters, cutlers, and grinders. The ensuing damage to the lung is known as silicosis. Although silicosis itself is a serious disease, its importance lies in that it is often complicated by pulmonary tuberculosis. The related condition, asbestosis, is also sometimes complicated by tuberculosis but anthracosis does not have the property of leading to tuberculosis. Postmortem room attendants are exposed to special hazards of high infection rates, so also, to a lesser degree, are nurses.

The rates in a trade or profession may be high because the tradesman works in an area of defective ventilation and so can readily be infected from open cases if they are present. Some trades are lower paid than others and the high rate of tuberculosis may be a reflection of economic circumstances.

(iv) General Economic Conditions. There is general agreement that poor economic conditions lead to high tuberculosis death rates. Various kinds of observations have been made on this point. Time series for the United States and for England and Wales are given by McDougall (1949, pp. 347–348), showing that the rates are high in years of low economic activity and in the years of World War I. The various Registrar-General's Decennial Supplements, for example, 1951, show a great increase in the death rates as we pass from the highest economic class to the lowest; similarly, there is a striking increase in the rates as we pass from the best or most affluent suburbs to the poorest suburbs. Insurance companies have found that large policy holders suffer less from tuberculosis than do the small policy holders; similarly, in England, those receiving poor relief had high tuberculosis death rates.

It is possible that low economic conditions have an effect especially through defective housing, diet, and rest.

(v) Housing. Crowded housing is particularly important because it leads to high rates of infection in infancy and childhood. Surveys in England and Wales and also Scotland have shown the importance of overcrowding. Greenwood (1926), cited in McDougall (1949, pp. 355–356), gives a general review of the findings and difficulties of interpretation of such surveys. In Sweden the introduction of double windows led to closer contact of persons and, so, to probably higher infection risks (Greenwood, 1924).

(vi) Nutrition. First class protein deficiency in the diet appears to be of great importance and to be the explanation of why Vitamin A has been thought to have a favorable effect on the disease.

(vii) War. The death rates from tuberculosis have been observed to rise in many countries in times of war, for example, in Germany after World War I. It is believed that the cause is a decline in nutritional standards. See Helweg-Larsen, Hoffmeyer, et al. (1952*b*) and Mollison (1946) for concentration camp experience.

(viii) Urbanization. A marked and increasing gradient is shown by Greenwood (1924, Tables 8 and 10) for the mortality from tuberculosis in passing from the country to the city in Sweden for the four decades beginning with 1861–1870. (See Sydenstricker, 1929, and §7.9.)

7.8 Reasons for the Declines in Mortality

Once bovine tuberculosis had been recognized as a serious health hazard, it was easy to eliminate it as a human disease by the pasteurization of dairy products, especially milk, which is the vehicle of the infection among children. Another important step was the development of tuberculosis-free dairy herds. It was easy to have these measures adopted because there is also good commercial merit in preserving milk more effectively and developing better herds. There has also been bacteriologic surveillance of milk supplies.

For the disease caused by the human bacillus, the importance of the various factors in the

decline of mortality is difficult to estimate because of the universality of the disease, its long
duration, and the sophisticated means required
for its diagnosis.

Before 1945 there was no effective antibacterial therapy. Surgical measures such as artificial
pneumothorax to rest the lung have played
little part in the declines in mortality; nursing
was largely palliative; we have to look elsewhere to the more general factors. The cycle of
tuberculosis infection is weak at two points;
first, the bacillus becomes locked up in closed
lesions within the body; second, the presence
of many bacilli in the air is not sufficient to infect susceptibles with certainty. General factors such as nutrition, conditions of work, and
living conditions seem to be important in healing the primary lesion and preventing breakdown and the development of open lesions in
later stages. There had been lessened risks of
infection in public places due to better education and prejudices against indiscriminate spitting in more recent times; here, the obsoles-
cence of the short clay pipe was recalled by
Udny Yule in his discussion on Greenwood
(1936).

By 1930 specific public health measures had
been directed against the two weak points
mentioned above. Programs adopted against
primary tuberculosis included (i) finding the
infected children and keeping them under
observation, (ii) seeking the source of infection
of each child reactor, (iii) breaking the tuberculosis contact, (iv) examining all adults in contact with school children, (v) following up positive reactors with X ray examinations, and (vi)
working for the elimination of bovine tuberculosis in cattle. Conditions of work have been
improved with special emphasis on pneumoconiosis in mining, proper ventilation in all
trades, and the correct disposal of infective
material in hospitals, pathology laboratories,
and laundries.

Vaccination with the Calmette-Guérin bacillus (BCG) has been successful in guarding susceptible groups. No value can be attached to
the use of other immunological methods.

After 1945 effective treatment by chemotherapy and antibiotics became available, for
example, isoniazid, paraaminosalicylic acid,

streptomycin, and, more recently, rifamycin.
Such therapy has proved particularly effective
in the childhood infections and in the primary
pulmonary tuberculosis of adults; but it should
be noted that such therapy had taken place in
the developed countries. These agents have
greatly aided the suppression of the excretion
of tubercle bacilli and, so, help to break the
cycle of infections. See also WHO-tuberculosis
(1980), Waksman (1964), and Grange (1984),
who gives references to modern therapy.

7.9 Tuberculosis as a Great Pestilence

It is probable that deaths from tuberculosis,
recorded in the official statistics, correspond
closely to those of persons actually dying of the
disease in any developed country. McDougall
(1949, p. 3) gives some examples of countries
in which this correspondence did not hold. In
the developed world the importance of tuberculosis is not to be measured from recent experience but from that of prewar or earlier
epochs.

Tuberculosis has often been referred to as
the "white plague" (Dubos and Dubos, 1952)
and the experience of areas such as England
and Wales, in which Brownlee (1916a) found
over a long stretch of time about one quarter of
all deaths at ages 15–44 years were due to it,
shows that the title is well deserved. Indeed,
tuberculosis has been responsible in England
and Wales in the nineteenth century for more
deaths than any other bacterial disease. Its importance has been enhanced by the fact that
the main burden of the mortality has fallen on
the years of productive and reproductive life in
both sexes. In most countries there has been a
low masculinity in young adult life and a high
masculinity at the higher ages. Many states
have experienced a rise in tuberculosis rates at
the beginning of industrialization and then falls
commencing in this century when the conditions of urban life have been ameliorated. Increases in mortality have been observed when
conditions deteriorate as in war and famine.
The surveys of Bulla (1977a, b), McDougall
(1949, 1950), and Yelton (1946) show that
there is great variation in the incidence between countries. Thus, McDougall (1949) gives

the crude death rates per 100,000 per annum for the years around 1940 as Belgium, 44; Denmark, 26; England and Wales, 44; France, 84; Ireland, 66; Italy, 119; Netherlands, 34; Norway, 68; Sweden, 57; Switzerland, 53; Portugal, 98; Argentine, 90; Chile, 112; Uruguay, 107; Japan, 90; Canada, 51; United States (total), 36; United States (colored), 82; Australia, 36; and New Zealand (excluding Maoris), 30.

In §§7.2 and 7.3, the statistics for tuberculosis have been given in detail for Australia and for England and Wales, respectively. Springett (1950) has given tables and graphs of the experience of England and Wales, Scotland, Ireland, Norway, towns of Denmark, Sweden, Paris, and Massachusetts.

For the United States, Doege (1965) has given calendar and cohort analyses of the tuberculosis statistics and Grigg (1958) has given historical details.

The Swedish demographers, notably Axel Gustav Sundbärg (1857–1914), have been able to obtain tuberculosis death rates by age back to 1751; Greenwood (1924) has made use of these statistics to compare the historical progress of the disease with that in England and Wales. Greenwood (1924) notes that the crude death rates for phthisis (i.e., pulmonary tuberculosis) in Sweden (Stockholm) by decennia 1751–1760 to 1821–1830 were 2.13 (7.32), 2.06 (6.98), 2.08 (7.44), 2.31 (8.77), 2.40 (8.50), 2.51 (8.37), 2.69 (8.72), and 2.77 (9.31) per 1,000 per annum. Greenwood (1924, Table 10) shows that there has been an upward gradient of the crude death rates from tuberculosis in passing from the small country villages of less than 2,000 to the cities of more than 100,000 inhabitants, presumably only Stockholm, namely, in deaths per 1,000 per annum, for 1861–1870, 1.99 to 3.93; for 1871–1880, 2.26 to 3.39; for 1881–1890, 2.26 to 3.39; and for 1891–1900, 2.27 to 2.95. Swedish observers, especially, blame the growing industrialization. Greenwood (1924) adds that the introduction of "unsalted" stock to urban life added to the mortality.

We may cite some statistics from Backer (1961, Table 76); in Norway at ages 15–19 years, for each quinquennium of the stretch 1891–1935, the proportion of deaths from tuberculosis was more than 50% of those from all causes with two exceptions for the males and with no exception for the females, at ages 20–29 years there was one exception for each sex, and the same at ages 30–39. Notwithstanding increases in mortality from other causes at ages over 40 years, the percentages were still high, for example, the percentages for males (females) in the years 1899–1902, 1919–1922, 1931–1935, and 1951–1955 were 35 (36), 29 (29), 26 (23), and 10 (7) at ages 40–49; 20 (24), 14 (16), 11 (10), 5 (3) at ages 50–59; and 10 (11), 7 (7), 6 (5), 3 (2) at ages 60–69 years (Backer, 1961, Table 105).

Backer (1961) makes the following comments:

Tuberculosis which was an important cause of death among children 1–4 years at the beginning of this century claims at present only very few victims. In 1921–25 one third of all deaths was due to tuberculosis, in 1936–40 12 per cent and in 1951–55 only 3 per cent. The fall in the mortality of tuberculosis in childhood can partly be explained by the improved standard of life in Norway since 1900, particularly to the organized preventive measures against the disease. The general adoption of BCG vaccination in the 1920s has evidently reduced the chances of small children of becoming infected. Improved medical treatment of the infected has also helped bringing down the mortality from tuberculosis among infants and children 1–4 years.

"The dominating cause of death of young adults in Norway has till recently been tuberculosis. Table 76, page 125, shows the trend 1871–1955 of mortality of this disease together with that of all other diseases and of violent causes. From 1871 to 1900 the mortality of tuberculosis among adults was increasing, while the mortality of other diseases shows a declining tendency. In the first decades of the present century only a slight reduction of the tuberculosis mortality was registered particularly between 15 and 30 years, and the relative importance of this disease as a cause of death among young adults continued to increase. In 1921–25 tuberculosis was responsible for 70 per cent of all deaths from diseases in the age group 15–29 years and about 50 per cent in the age group 30–39 years. Since 1920 there has been a progressive decline in the tuberculosis mortality in all age groups in particular after 1945. At present tuberculosis plays a negligible part as a cause of death in the age group 15–19 years. Between 20 and 40 years, however, tuberculosis, is still one of the most important causes of death, responsible for 17–20 per cent of all deaths from diseases among males and 16–18 per cent among females.

"The improvement of the general mortality in the middle and older age groups is essentially due to the considerable reduction of the mortality of tuberculosis, pneumonia including influenza, and other infections.

"Before the second world war the level of the general mortality rates among young adults in the different parts of the country was to a great extent determined by the prevailing tuberculosis mortality and for the males also by the frequency of violent deaths."

Tuberculosis showed a marked urban/rural gradient in Finland with a crude death rate of 4.77 per 1,000 per annum in the towns and 2.10 per 1,000 in the rural districts according to Turpeinen (1973), who cites a series of Bachman and Savonen (1934) for 1771–1929.

For a popular account, see Dubos (1949). For countries other than England and Wales and Australia, see Scotland §37.3, France §38.3, Greenland §39.2, Norway §39.5, Sweden, §39.7, and Japan §40.2.

Chapter 8
Zoonotic Bacterial Diseases

8.1 Introduction

Some general problems of the zoonoses are conveniently treated here, although the infective agents belong to many species, causing many of the diseases of ICD 060–088, perhaps more than a hundred in all. Many of the zoonoses are vector-borne, an aspect that has already been treated in §5.5. It is probable that some infections, now considered as peculiar to man, have originated as infections of animals. Once the cycle of infection has been established in man, it may happen that an animal reservoir is no longer needed to perpetuate the infection; further, if such changes in the organism have occurred that it no longer causes natural infections in animals, it is classed as an epidemic or human disease rather than a zoonosis. Such a disease is measles, which possibly is a mutation from the distemper group of animal virus infections; cases can be made even for influenza and classical typhus as zoonoses.

Rabies, cowpox, and anthrax were early recognized as animal diseases that attacked man incidentally during the progress of the infection in the animal population, but it was only in the 1890s that plague was seen to be a zoonosis. Bovine tuberculosis, a zoonosis, is excluded in the ICD from the zoonoses for convenience and because of the difficulty in separating bovine from human types without adequate bacteriologic resources. There are variations in the degree of pathogenicity to man and animal hosts; plague, anthrax, and rabies are obviously highly pathogenic to both; some, such as

brucellosis, leptospirosis, and Q-fever, are more pathogenic to man than to the animal hosts; some diseases of animals, for example, foot and mouth disease, have a low pathogenicity for man, myxomatosis has none. In some zoonoses man-to-man infections are possible, for example, pneumonic and bubonic plague, pulmonary cases of bovine tuberculosis, the gambian form of trypanosomiasis, and the transplacental infection of the fetus with *Listeria* or *Toxoplasma*.

As will be seen in the case of plague, an epidemic (or epizootic) is unstable if it always causes an acute disease with death or immunity as outcomes. There will be, usually, some host species in which the infection causes a mild disease and in which the infection is enzootic. Usually the host species will have a limited geographical distribution, a zoonotic nidus. See §§5.6 and 5.7.

8.2 Plague

ICD 020 Inclusion: infection with *Yersinia pestis*, epidemic and bubonic plague; pneumonic plague.

Plague is an acute infective disease of man due to the bacillus, *Y. pestis*. It is spread to man by the bite of a flea to give bubonic plague, characterized by a small puncture site and infection and swelling of the lymph glands draining the site. These swellings are the buboes; they may go to suppuration and ulceration. Bacteremia and septicemia usually follow. There is an incubation period of approximately 2 to 5 days. This common form of the disease, namely, bubonic plague, has had high case fatalities, possibly about 60% under natural conditions or before the advent of chemotherapy. Under exceptional conditions the infection may spread from man to man as a respiratory infection, pneumonic plague, with an incubation period from 1 to 5 days, and associated with a very high case fatality, formerly close to 100%. Plague may also be acquired from wild rodents; these cases, usually of the bubonic form, are referred to as wild-rodent or sylvatic plague. Sylvatic plague now exists on all the continents except Australia and Europe. It is probable that before the Christian era there were established niduses of plague in both the foothills of the Himalayas and in Africa. Possibly some fluctuating balance between susceptible and resistant rodents on the one hand and the plague bacillus on the other had been established in those areas.

The nature of the perpetuation of plague in the wild has been revealed by the work of Evgeniĭ Nikanorovič Pavlovsky (1884–1965) and his school in the Soviet Union and by a group of workers sponsored by the World Health Organization. According to Baltzard, Bahmanyar, et al. (1960), in a nidus perpetuating plague in Iranian Kurdistan there was a complex interaction between the plague bacillus and four species of wild rodents of the genus *Meriones*, of which two were highly resistant and two were highly susceptible. "The existence [i.e. perpetuation] of plague in Kurdistan . . . arises from a balance between resistant and susceptible species mingling in nature; its continued presence in the same place [nidus] is linked with the sedentary habits of the resistant species which have deep, permanent burrows acting as reservoirs of infected fleas." The chain of infections is maintained by the chronicity of the disease in some of the species of *Meriones* and the fact that the wild rodents live in burrows in which the hosts and their ectoparasites can survive throughout the winter. Possibly similar conditions exist in niduses in other parts of the world. Pollitzer (1960, pp. 387–400) gives lists of the species of wild rodents and their locales from many different areas.

The presence of such foci of enzootic or sylvatic plagues is noticed when farmers, hunters, sportsmen, surveyors, and other are infected by the bite of an infected ectoparasite. From such a primary human case, a minor human epidemic can be initiated with the human flea, *Pulex irritans*, spreading the infection. A similar train of events can occur in the western United States where *Y. pestis* has become enzootic on the ground squirrels during the third great pandemic.

Under suitable meteorological conditions, the infection may spread from such an enzootic focus among wild rodents to rats, particularly the wild brown rat and the more domesticated black rat, and become epizootic among them with rat fleas as vectors. The rats may spread the disease by moving from area to area, although this seems to be a slow process, or by being conveyed by humans, especially along trade routes. Fleas already infected may also travel long distances in merchandise or personal belongings before causing fresh infections among the rats. In particular, if an infected rat reaches a large city, an epizootic among the rats may occur and conditions will be conducive to human infections. In a city the rat epizootic may persist for some time, even many years. Yet, the disease is essentially unstable among both the brown and black rats, for it is an acute disease leading to death or recovery and immunity. The presence of the more resistant brown *R. norvegicus* appears to be essential for the maintenance of the rat enzootic, see Baltzard (1960) and Topley and Wilson (1975, p. 2123, Figure 72.1); the black *R. rattus* is far too susceptible to the disease to perpetuate it over a period of years. Certainly, man also is too susceptible to perpetuate the infection. But man has been important in providing vehicles for the rapid carriage of diseased rats and rat fleas over long distances, for example, from Europe to America and to Java.

Before the present pandemic, commencing in the 1890s, there were few clear ideas of the nature of the human disease. However, as we have seen in §2.3, epidemiologic theory and appropriate laboratory techniques were available for the study of the disease when it appeared in Hong Kong in 1894. The causative organism was found in human tissues by S.

Kitasato (1852–1931) and A.J.E. Yersin (1863–1943) in 1894. P.P.E. Roux (1853–1933), in 1897, first clearly stated that plague is primarily a disease of rats. M. Ogata, in 1897, demonstrated the organisms in fleas from infected rats. P.L. Simond (1858–1947) showed that the likely chain of infection was from rat to rat and that sometimes man became infected from the rat; man-to-man infection was believed to be far less common. It was recognized that plague was an anthropozoonosis. Experiments to prove the spread of plague by fleas were at first inconclusive. A difficulty was the marked species preference of fleas. Thus, the human flea *Pulex irritans* does not attack rats, although members of the genera, *Nosophylla* and *Xenopsylla*, especially *X. cheopis*, will bite either rat or man. A.W. Bacot (1866–1922) established that the efficiency of these rat fleas for spreading plague is enhanced by the fact that after feeding the provenriculus may become completely or partially blocked by an overgrowth of plague bacilli. The flea in this state becomes hungry and attacks fresh hosts with great avidity, regurgitating the bacterial growths. Since plague is a zoonosis of the rats, when the disease reaches a city, there is often a preepidemic phase with the observation of a few cases separated sometimes by rather long intervals of time. Then, with the intensification of the epizootic, more cases appear, often centered on some feature that favors rats, such as grain stores, warehouses, and shops. Human case-to-case infection with plague is quite uncommon in these urban epidemics in India. It is evident that a social gradient may appear, with those in unsanitary dwellings suffering higher rates. New cases may appear in distant parts of the city without intermediary human cases, the infection being spread by rats or rat fleas. The spread over long distances is usually by means of human transport, for example, by ship from Hong Kong to the west coast of America or to Australia.

Following the report of the English Plague Commission (1906) and, so, generalizing the Indian experience, it has been generally accepted that plague is transmitted so inefficiently by human ectoparasites that the transmission of plague in human epidemics is from rat to man; consequently, the human epidemics have been regarded as epiphenomena in which the plague bacilli in human cases do not participate in any chain of infection except in very rare cases of intrafamily infection or pneumonic plague. The views of the earlier workers are set out in detail by Hirst (1953). Although experimental work seemed to support the thesis that human ectoparasites were of small importance, Rodenwaldt (1953) believed that they must have been the principal transmitters of plague in the epidemic of 1575 in Venice. In modern times epidemics in the absence of rats and of rat fleas have been studied. Baltazard, Bahmanyar, et al. (1960) make the following statement:

Evidence is adduced showing that epidemics of bubonic plague in this focus, where there are no domestic rodents or "liaison rodents", are due to inter-human transmission by the human flea, *Pulex irritans*, starting with rare cases of plague contracted in the fields. Such inter-human plague, originating in villages, tends to die out rapidly in view of the scanty population of the villages, the long distances between them, and the paucity and poverty of the means of communication. Nevertheless, when imported into an urban area with a denser human population, plague immediately becomes the terrifying disease it was during the Middle Ages.

And Baltazard (1960) writes:

Plague can become epidemic only when there is interhuman transmission by human ectoparasites, as is shown by the existence in the Middle East of plague epidemics in the absence of rats and the non-epidemic nature of the disease in India, despite the presence of rats and of *Xenopsylla cheopis* in numbers never reached in any country or at any time. The great slaughter caused by plague in olden days was all due to transmission by human ectoparasites, but the duration of the epidemics must have been dependent on the existence of a large murine background . . . The outbreaks in antiquity were exactly similar to the type of plague studied and described in Morocco [by the author and his colleagues].

Plague is usually thought of as a tropical disease, but its highest incidence in India occurs in the cooler months when the mean temperature is between 10°C and 30°C and the air has a high relative humidity. Such conditions are attainable in Northern Europe, and, indeed, the second of the great pandemics, in the fourteenth century, involved Norway, Sweden, and, later, Iceland.

Since there is septicemia in human plague, it is not surprising that the organisms reach the lungs and may pass into the air finally by coughing. Inhalation of such infective material may result in pneumonic plague in others. Pneumonic plague has a short incubation period and was, formerly, almost inevitably fatal. Pneumonic plague is spread independently of rats; rather special conditions of crowding are necessary for an epidemic to appear. Striking epidemics of pneumonic plague have been reported from Manchuria, Transbaikalia, and the Kirghiz steppes.

Plague can be controlled by measures:
(*i*) the rat-proofing of buildings and ships and the catching and poisoning of rats;
(*ii*) the flea-control of merchandise, domestic hygiene, and the use of DDT;
(*iii*) the notification, isolation, and evacuation of cases of the disease.

Treatment with antibiotics and chemotherapy are available. Tetracycline is the drug of choice. The case fatality of treated cases is less than 5%.

For general reviews and texts, see Butler (1983), Hirst (1953), and Pollitzer (1954). Smith and Wilson (1984*b*) give the geographical distribution of varieties of *Y. pestis* infecting man but state that these varieties are of no clinical or diagnostic importance. For plague in the Americas, see Rail (1985).

8.3 Bubonic Plague as a Great Pestilence

In §1.5 we have mentioned a great pestilence in Egypt, Libya, and Syria in the third century BC, which can be confidently diagnosed as bubonic plague from classical literary sources. Even earlier, in 1320 BC, there had been the plague of the Philistines that, some authorities have argued, was probably bubonic. Two other pestilences, which may well have been bubonic, occurred in ca 127 BC and AD 66. Since that time there have been three well-attested pandemics, commencing in 541, 1346, and 1894, respectively.

There are difficulties to be overcome in interpreting historical events by the light of epidemiologic theory (*i*) the paucity of literary resources, (*ii*) uncertainty as to the geographical distributions of the commensal rats at various historic times, and (*iii*) the propriety of applying, to the behavior of the disease in medieval or early modern Europe, models that have been constructed from the experience of plague in India during the early years of this century.

As to the second difficulty, *R. rattus* and *R. norvegicus* are believed to have evolved from *Rattus rattus roquei* (Sody) of Java, according to Schwarz (1960). After dispersion from Java, the black rat, *R. rattus*, was early native to Asia Minor and the Orient and was brought into Europe at the time of the Crusades. It may have had a temporary sojourn in Ireland in the ninth century. Other authors state that *R. norvegicus* was not known in Europe until approximately 1553 and in America until 1775. However, McArthur (1952) gives accounts of the existence of rats not at all consistent with the above statement; thus, rats were found in the excavations at Pompeii; and *R. rattus* and *R. norvegicus* were possibly both present in first century Rome. Shrewsbury (1970) is able to solve this problem by stating that if plague is present, *R. rattus* must have been present; but this generalization is false because Baltazard and his colleagues have observed epidemics in the absence of rats, for which see the following.

As to the third difficulty, the observers of the Indian Plague Commission found that the human flea was far less efficient than the rat flea in transmitting plague; as a result, it was considered that the human flea, *Pulex irritans*, could play no important part in human plague epidemics. However, localized epidemics of sylvatic plague occur in which it is not disputed that transmission is by the human flea. In recent times rather more extensive epidemics of plague have been studied in Morocco and Madagascar in which rats had played no part; moreover, the epidemics have seemed to be limited by the size of the human population. We, therefore, can hold the view that intense epidemics occurring during the Justinian and medieval pandemics might well have been mediated by the human flea and other human ectoparasites. See also the previous section.

Justinian's Pandemic

The literary sources are much fuller than for the pandemics of classical times. Thus, according to the account of Gregory of Tours, cited by Deaux (1969), typical lesions appearing in the groin or armpit were followed by death in 2 or 3 days. No one, indeed, doubts that the disease was bubonic plague. Possibly the best account is given by Biraben (1975–1976, pp. 27–48) together with literary sources and a bibliography. His first map (Biraben, 1975–1976, p. 34) shows the disease arriving by sea at Pelusium, Egypt, in AD 541 and then spreading to Carthage, Spain, Antioch, Atropatene, Constantinople, and Illyria in 542 and to Rome and to Trèves via Marseilles in 543. In later maps Biraben (1975–1976) shows further apparent advances and retreats until the last European outbreak in Naples, Italy, in 767. Of course, we cannot expect to obtain information about the progress along the North African coast or around the Caspian Sea. Modern historians, for example, the *Cambridge Mediaeval History*, have paid less attention to this pandemic than its importance warrants, although Edward Gibbon, in Chapter 43 of his *Decline and Fall of the Roman Empire*, notes that the disease spread from Pelusium, Egypt, to Syria, Persia and the Indies, along the coasts of Africa, and to the ports of Europe. Gibbon quotes Procopius as believing that the spread was from the trade routes to the surrounding country. Gibbon believes that the plague swept away perhaps half the inhabitants of the Byzantine Empire in the years from AD 542 to 565; perhaps, 100 million persons died.

On the social side Russell (1968) points out that there had been prosperity in Greece and the Balkans and in Egypt and the populations had been increasing immediately before the outbreak of the plague. The deaths at Constantinople are said to have been 5,000 a day over some months and even reached a height of 10,000 on one day with deaths totalling 300,000 in AD 541. Russell (1968) believes that losses in an "ordinary" area would have been 20–25% for the first epidemic of 541–544 and, then, taking account of later epidemics, the total decline in population for the period 541–700 would have been 50–60%. Russell (1968) concludes that the plague had an important, even critical, effect on the decline of culture, prosperity, and military power in the Byzantine Empire.

Black Death

The Black Death, or Great Plague, the second of the great pandemics of plague adequately recorded, originated in Central Asia, according to tombstone evidence, and then was spread along trade routes until it appeared on the shores of the Black Sea in 1346. From the Black Sea the infection was spread to Constantinople and then to Genoa, Venice, and other European ports, and reached England in 1348. See the maps in Biraben (1975–1976, pp. 88–89). The Great Plague took about 3 years to sweep over Europe and was followed by further waves up to about 1388. In 1402 plague was carried to Iceland; as a result the population, possibly 120,000 in 1402, fell to 40,000 by 1404; plague was again introduced by British ships and raged in 1493–1495 (Jonsson, 1944). In his Annex IV, Biraben (1975–1976, pp. 375–449) gives a table of the dates and places of known epidemics from 541 to 1850 in Europe and the Near East. We can only note a few points. The second pandemic was perpetuated in Western Europe, until 1712 in Sweden and Denmark, 1720 in Marseilles and surrounding country, 1739–1740 in Debreczen, Hungary, again in Marseilles in 1786, 1716 in Bruck, Austria, 1798 in Szarograd, Poland, 1828 in Odessa, Russia, and 1841 in Constantinople. Indeed, as we pass toward the niduses of Iranian Kurdistan and the Caspian Sea, there is a general tendency for the plague to be endemic and epidemic almost up to the time of the third pandemic.

Estimates of the mortality due to the plague have been made from various sources; for example, Campbell (1931) cites the deaths of 255 church incumbents of the rank of bishop or higher to 435 survivors through the time in which the Black Death reigned in the land of the particular see, so that their mortality was 36% for the epidemic. Russell (1948a) was also able to give mortality rates, from the records of the "inquisitiones post-mortem," conducted when the ownership of land was being settled. Further, from manorial documents it appears that less than one-tenth of the population survived in some parts of England (Rees, 1923). England and Italy may have lost as much as half their population. Many demographers have thought that the accounts of mortality had been exaggerated, but they have been confirmed by the numerical data of Gasquet (1908), Russell (1948a), and Biraben (1975–1976).

Helleiner (1967) believes that the population of Europe in 1500 was still less than its size in 1300 or 1340; he mentions a well-documented account of the deaths in the city of Bremen, where the immediate toll of the plague was not less than 40%. The demographic aftermath appears now to have been more serious than previously thought, and the population of Europe in 1400 was possibly only half its size in 1340. The decline of European populations continued for approximately 80 years; since 1430 the European population has grown steadily (Russell, 1958).

The two pandemics commencing in 541 and 1346 caused huge losses of life and disturbances to the civil order, constituting the greatest demographic events of the past 2,000 years, (see Renouard, 1948, Russell, 1966, Saltmarsh, 1941, and Thrupp, 1965, 1966).

Bubonic Plague, 1894–

It may well be that the division of the experience of human plague into pandemics is artificial, although, perhaps, for Europe useful, as plague does appear to have been absent from all European states in the late nineteenth century. The date 1894 refers to when the plague reached Hong Kong. Thus, Simpson (1905) reports that M.E. Rocher had seen a great number of cases in Yúnnán with typical onset and a case fatality of more than 50% ; in some localities the deaths amounted to about 4–6% of the population, whereas in other areas the popu-

lation was "completely decimated." Simpson (1905, p. 53) gives a map showing the geographical incidence of the epidemic in the years 1871–1873. It was noted that the first sign of the disease in an epidemic form was a sickness and mortality among rats. There was some evidence that some portion of Yúnnán had been an endemic center for at least 100 years. A Chinese author, dying in 1809, speaks of a friend dying of this "queer rat epidemic." Dr. Lowry, British medical officer to the Customs at Beihai (Pakhoi), reports that plague had been endemic there from 1867 with yearly recrudescences in the spring. Beihai appears to have been free of plague from 1884 to 1894, although in these years plague was endemic in other Chinese cities. The first recorded case of plague in Guǎngzhōu (Canton) occurred on January 16, 1894, and was one of seven cases seen by Dr. Mary Niles up to May 2. She is quoted by Simpson (1905) as saying "it has been noticeable to the people that rats in infected houses have died. . . in the house, where she took the disease thirteen dead rats were swept out one morning." It was only toward the end of March, 1894, that the disease began to attract attention; Dr. A. Rennie then reported that the case fatality rate was high, indeed over 80%, in a Mohammedan quarter of the city. Deaths up to the middle of June were some 40,000. It was remarked that the chief sufferers were the poor, over-crowded, and badly housed. In 1894 the deaths from plague in Canton were estimated as between 80,000 and 100,000. The deaths in Hong Kong did not exceed 3,000. Here it was that S. Kitasato on June 14, 1894, and A.J.E. Yersin a few weeks later discovered the plague bacillus. Much of the coastal strip of south China then became infected and it was noted that the chief ravages in China were limited to that strip. In March, 1896, plague reached Bombay, from which it had been absent since 1702 or a period of 194 years, although plague was said to be endemic in Mesopotamia in 1891–1892. After a silent period with no human cases, the first human cases appeared in August, 1896, with the diagnosis confirmed microscopically on October 13 by W. Haffkine; rats were dying in numbers, although the significance of this was not appreciated. Rats then began dying in other parts of the city and were followed by human cases of plague. After a few months of low incidence, the mortality rose to a maximum in the 2d and 3d weeks of February, 1897, and then fell to the level of October, 1896, in May. There was an exodus from the city of almost half the inhabitants and, so, localities outside Bombay became infected. Early in March, 1897, the Government of Bombay took over control of the epidemic. Simpson (1905, pp. 70–71) shows maps in which 4,751 deaths are recorded in Bombay up to June, 1897; as for the other cities, there had been more than 100 deaths in only a few and in the majority there were less than 10. Between June, 1897, and June, 1898, 61,000 deaths occurred as against 29,000 in the first year. In the year ending June, 1899, the deaths reached 115,000 for the southern part of the Bombay Presidency. Soon the disease was spreading to other parts of India and the annual deaths rose from 30,000 in its first year to a little less than a million in 1903. A table is given in Simpson (1905, p. 72) for the various provinces of India up to that time. In §40.3, we give a table showing the

annual deaths from plague in India for a more extended time.

In Simpson (1905) the curves of the weekly deaths of rats and of man throughout the year are compared; a similar curve for weekly deaths of *R. norvegicus*, *R. rattus*, and man is given in Topley and Wilson (1975, p. 2123). It is evident that the epizootic on *R. norvegicus* commences in early December and has a maximum in February and March, the epizootic on *R. rattus* follows 10 days later, and it is succeeded by the epidemic on man; this can be interpreted as due to plague being perpetuated principally by *R. norvegicus*, which suffers an epizootic as soon as meteorological conditions are appropriate, the infections then spread to *R. rattus* and then to man. It is evident from the second graph that deaths in the nonepizootic time (i.e., season) are predominantly of *R. norvegicus*.

With the mortality in India and China becoming less, the pandemic of plague might well be said to have ended. Now we have plague endemic in all continents with the exception of Australia and Europe (see Figure 8.3.1). In the other continents plague has become a nuisance

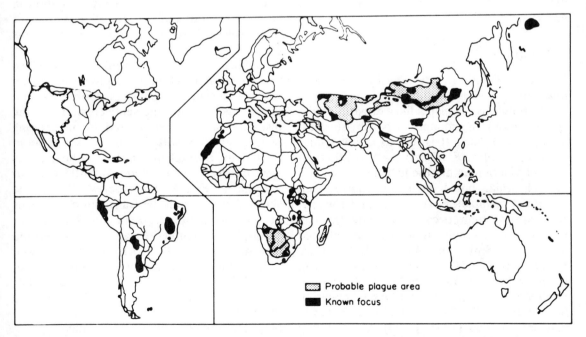

FIGURE 8.3.1. Known and probable foci of plague in 1976. From Manson-Bahr and Apted (1982), p. 336.

rather than a serious problem, although it is a surprise to find that plague deaths have continued to occur in Vietnam with about 5,000 deaths per annum in the years before 1968 (see also WHO-plague, 1979, 1980, and Davis, 1953).

With such exceptions, human plague is controllable, and there are efficient antibiotics and chemotherapeutics to treat cases. Rats can be controlled in the cities; ship and other transport can be made rat-free. The enzootic areas may be cleared (Fenjuk, 1960). Bubonic plague, therefore, presents no great threat to a modern state in time of peace.

For accounts of the plague by country, see Biraben (1975–1976), but also: England and Wales, Sutherland (1972), Shrewsbury (1970 reviewed by Morris, 1971), Bell (1951), Hollingsworth and Hollingsworth (1971), and Potter (1880); France 1720–1722, Biraben (1972); Venice, Preto (1978); United States, Zentner (1942); India, Seal (1960). For a popularization, see Ziegler (1969). For plague in the twentieth century, see Gregg (1985).

For references to countries, see Australia §41.3, America §42.2, Sweden §39.7, Iceland §39.3, France §38.3, Scotland §37.3; for urbanization §47.4, tropics §46.2, and World War II §33.18.

8.4 Tularemia

ICD 021 Inclusion: infection by *Francisella tularensis*.

Tularemia is a plaguelike disease, widespread among the rodents of North America, Europe, and Asia. It is due to a tiny Gramnegative bacillus, *F. tularensis*. It was first described as a human disease in Tulare, a county of California, but human cases have been described in Japan, Soviet Asia, and Europe. Infection of man occurs indirectly through tick bites or contamination from an infected animal, (G. Smith and Wilson, 1984*b*). Case fatality was 358/8022 or approximately 5% in the American experience before 1938; the case fatality rates in Europe and Asia appear to have been 1% to 2% according to J. Zidon in van der Hoeden (1964, p. 83). Case fatality rates after treatment with streptomycin or a tetracycline are now low. Since the organism can pass through the intact skin or mucous membranes, it is very dangerous to laboratory workers.

In the Soviet Union and southern Europe, tularemia is spread widely among rodents in a great variety of climatic conditions, and man can be infected in a variety of ways such as by the bite of an ectoparasite, the inhalation of dust containing infected material, the eating of contaminated fresh vegatables, and so on (see Pavlovsky, 1966). Treatment is by chloramphenicol and the tetracyclines.

8.5 Anthrax

ICD 022 Inclusion: infections with *B. anthracis*.

Anthrax is an acute zoonosis due to the large spore-bearing Gram-positive *Bacillus anthracis*. Wilson and G. Smith (1984*c*) give an order of susceptibility of animals: first, the herbivores including cattle, sheep, goats, buffalo, horses, camels, reindeer, and elephants; second, dog, cat, rat, and man; third, pigs, which are resistant; and then, fourth, birds, which are highly resistant.

B. anthracis is capable of multiplication in warm moist soils and of persisting as spores for more than 12 years according to van Ness (1971).

The disease is of interest in having been the first bacterial infection of man to be associated with its causative organism, possibly because of its large size and the septicemia. Thus, the disease could be propagated by inoculating healthy animals with blood, as was demonstrated by Barthélemy in 1823. The bacillus was observed in the blood of cattle dead of anthrax by F.A.A. Pollender. C.J. Davaine showed that it could be transmitted by means of the inoculation of a minute quantity of blood; he also found the organism in sheep and in a human case. R. Koch, in 1877, showed that the three postulates of §2.3 were satisfied, thus giving a satisfactory proof that the bacillus was the cause of the disease; he also described the formation of spores and, thus, explained how stock could be infected from fields.

Man is only incidentally infected in the country from fresh cases of the disease and in cities from spores in industrial products, such as in the industrial treatment of animal skins and hair. Infection is by an abrasion leading to a "malignant pustule" or by inhalation leading to an acute pulmonary disease (see also Whitford, 1979).

Topley and Wilson (1975) cite an estimate, made by E. Kauker and Z. Kettle, of annual incidence in the world of about 9,000 cases in the years before 1968. Van der Hoeden (1964) cites an estimate by H.N. Glassman, in 1958, who believed that there are between 20,000 and 100,000 cases of anthrax per annum throughout the world. It is evident from his table (van der Hoeden, 1964, p. 207, Table XIX) that in many developed countries anthrax is now well controlled.

The incidence in the developed world has been greatly reduced by appropriate legislation on the disposal of carcasses and the use of skins of animals dying of the disease. In the British experience the case fatality rate had been approximately 10% to 20% before the advent of chemotherapy and 1% to 2% since that time. Penicillin is the drug of choice.

8.6 Brucellosis

ICD 023. Inclusion: fever, Malta, Mediterranean, or undulant.

The genus *Brucella* includes several species of small Gram-negative bacilli, naturally parasitic on ungulates; *melitensis*, *abortus*, and *suis* are described by G.S. Wilson and G. Smith (1984*d*) (see also Young, 1983).

The human disease, a low fever with almost regular remissions, had been recognized in the Mediterranean area from the time of Hippocrates; it was only separated from other continued fevers by J.A. Marston in 1859, according to Dalrymple-Champeneys (1960) and Spink (1956). It was a leading cause of invalidity and mortality in the naval personnel stationed at Malta. Subsequent studies have shown that the human infection is acquired by the ingestion of raw goats' milk containing *Brucella melitensis*. Related diseases due to *Br. abortus* and *Br. suis* are acquired by the ingestion of raw cows' milk and of improperly

handled pig carcasses. Brucella infections in man are now known to be worldwide, the species depending on the animal host. Case fatality rates from infections with *Br. melitensis* were formerly about 2% and are now lower, after treatment with tetracyclines and streptomycin, although treatment is still said to be unsatisfactory. Population mortality rates have fallen greatly because of the decline in incidence rates (van der Hoeden, 1964, pp. 96, 110, Tables XII, XIV are relevant). The average incidence rates in army and naval personnel in Malta were reduced to approximately 3% of the rates holding in 1900–1905 after a prohibition on the use of raw goats' milk. Civilian incidence rates per annum were still high in 1951–1956 in Malta. For all forms of brucellosis, rates amended from van der Hoeden (1964, Table XIV) would be per 100,000 per annum: Italy 182, Malta 172, Greece 87, Mexico 40, France 22, and United States 13. It is clear that much could be done to improve the rates in Malta, Italy, and Greece. For brucellosis in France, see Cantaloube (1911) and §38.3.

8.7 Glanders and Melioidosis

Glanders

ICD 024 Infections due to *Pseudomonas mallei*.

Glanders, a zoonosis of the horse and some other ungulates, is due to *Ps. mallei*, a Gram-negative bacillus. The disease has been not uncommon among horses, especially in times of special stress such as war, with crowding of horses. It has spread to many other animals in captivity. The disease in man, usually acquired in occupations bringing man into close contact with infected animals, particularly the horse, may be acute or chronic, and it may be localized in the respiratory organs or skin and subcutaneous tissues. In acute cases there is mucopurulent discharge from the nose and great prostration; there may be a generalized skin eruption. Death can occur within 10 days. Sulfadiazine is probably an effective cure. It has been a rather rare human disease with a high case fatality, but is now of little importance in

Europe or in those countries where the horse has been displaced from use in transport. Veterinary services have eradicated the chronic contagious disease of horses, mules, and asses in Europe and in many Asian countries.

Melioidosis

ICD 025 Infections due to *Ps. pseudomallei*.

Melioidosis is a disease resembling glanders, caused by *Ps. pseudomallei*. The disease occurs naturally in rats and other rodents and man is infected from them. It is a negligible cause of mortality in man.

See Parker (1984*e*) and Wilkinson (1981).

8.8 Rat-bite Fever

ICD 026 Fourth digit: 0, spirillary fever due to *Spirillum minus*; 1, streptobacillary fever due to *Streptobacillus moniliformis*.

Rat-bite fever is an irregularly relapsing septicemic fever characterized by arthritis and cutaneous eruptions, spread to man by the bite of a rat or, sometimes, a cat. Spirillary fever (also known as *sodoku*) has a case fatality rate of 2% to 10%. Salvarsan is partly effective and so is penicillin. Streptobacillary fever (Haverhill fever) appears to be a more severe disease with a case fatality rate of perhaps 10% without modern treatment. Penicillin and tetracyclines are recommended for treatment. Infections with either type of organism are not common except under abnormal conditions such as famine or trench warfare. See Wilson and Coghlan (1984).

8.9 Other Zoonotic Bacterial Diseases

ICD 027 Fourth digit: 0, listeriosis; 1, infection with *Erysipelothrix*; 2, pasteurellosis; 8, other.

Listeria monocytogenes is a Gram-positive, coccoid or rod-shaped organism with a tendency to the formation of long filaments. It gives rise to epizootics in a variety of wild animals. In man it can cause abortion or perinatal death or severe disease leading to permanent brain damage. The source and route of infections in humans are not yet known, although it appears to be transmitted across the placenta, usually from a mother showing few signs or symptoms.

Erysipelothrix is a thin nonmotile Gram-positive rod. *E. insidiosa* causes swine erysipelas. Most human infections have been contracted by those handling meat, slaughter products, and manure, and by veterinarians, and have been local or arthritic. Case fatality rates appear to be low.

See G. Smith and Wilson (1984*a*).

Chapter 9
Other Bacterial Diseases

9.1 Leprosy, a Great Pestilence

ICD 030. Inclusion: leprosy, Hansen's disease, infections due to *Mycobacterium leprae*.

Leprosy is a chronic bacterial disease due to infection with *Myco. leprae*. It has an incubation period of 2 to 4 years and a variable course progressing to a spontaneous cure or perhaps lasting a whole lifetime. Human leprosy occurs in two forms, tuberculoid leprosy with few lesions containing few bacilli and lepromatous leprosy with multiple lesions where the bacilli grow without inhibition because of defective cell-mediated immunity.

Leprosy is not now a direct cause of death if therapy is available, but patients may die of complications and intercurrent infections. In past years the lepers, segregated from the rest of the population, possibly suffered much higher total mortality rates than the other members of the general population. The mode of infection is not known for certain; the chief mode of exit of the bacilli from the body of infected cases is by the upper respiratory tract. It was formerly believed that the chief mode of entry was from skin-to-skin contact through abrasions; entry via the nasal mucosa is now believed to be more likely (Waters, 1984). *Myco. leprae* has never been cultured. Great advances have been made recently because susceptible animals have been found; in 1960 limited multiplication of the bacillus in the footpads of mice was obtained, and in 1971 it was found that some nine-banded armadillos could be infected; growth of the bacillus in these two animals is facilitated if they are "immunologically compromised" as by thymectomy. Further, under such conditions a syndrome like the human lepromatous leprosy was produced.

According to Skinsnes (1973), leprosy dates back to ca 1500 BC in India, ca 1400–1300 BC in Palestine, ca 1300–1000 BC in Egypt, and possibly much further in China. It may have entered the nortern Mediterranean littoral in ca 480 BC following the conquests of Darius and Xerxes. Osteologic evidence shows that it existed in Egypt, France, and England certainly as far back as the sixth and seventh centuries AD. Leprosy reached its greatest prevalence in Europe in the years AD 1000–1400, following dissemination during the Crusades, with 200 lazar houses in France, 285 in England, 19 in Scotland, 2 in Wales, and 20 in Ireland. In the sixteenth century leprosy spread from Portugal to Brazil; in the sixteenth to eighteenth centuries it spread from Spain to Colombia, Equador, Cuba, Mexico, and southern United States. In 1865 leprosy was noted in the New Hebrides and, so, it had become worldwide. Its decline in Europe began after the Black Death and authors have speculated on a possible connection. It may be that social conditions improved with the smaller populations in Europe after the Black Death.

Leprosy has been well documented in Norway. Its virtual disappearance from that country over the years 1850 to 1920 has been discussed by Irgens (1981). Leprosy prevalence rates had been relatively low in the eastern districts of Norway, that is, southern Norway east

of 8° east. Important factors in the high prevalence rates in the west of Norway were high
humidity, overcrowding, malnutrition, and
proverty. Spread within families was important; in such family infections the primary was
usually male and often he had worked under
unhygienic conditions in the fisheries in either
west or north Norway, but the secondary cases
in the family tended to be younger with equal
rates for the sexes. This origin of family cases
was lessened in importance by the great
emigration of young men to America in 1891–
1900. As a summary of Irgens (1981), leprosy
passes with some difficulty from case to case;
passage is especially favored by conditions of
high humidity and low hygiene.

The prevalence of leprosy in Europe had
fallen by 1900, although it has lingered on in
southern and eastern Europe; indeed, there
were an estimated 3,000 cases of leprosy in
Portugal in 1964. The disappearance of the disease from Great Britain was said to be due to
a restriction of skin-to-skin contact of lepers
with the general population and to the gradual improvement in the state of society under
which such contacts were lessened. Leprosy
was introduced to the Americas by the explorers and the slave trade. It remains as a serious
problem in the Latin American countries. As
we have seen above, leprosy had already
reached Africa, India, and China long before
the Christian era. In the nineteenth century it
became endemic on many Pacific islands and
probably spread from the East Indies to the
northern shores of Australia where it became
endemic in the native inhabitants.

For rates before 1952, see Pizzi (1952). For
modern prevalence, probably almost always
understated in the hot tropics, see Bechelli and
Dominguez (1966), who give rates per 1,000
for the latest period as India, 6; China, 3;
Egypt, 2; Indonesia, 1; Thailand, 7; Ceylon, 1;
Nigeria, 18; Philippines, 1; and Burma, 25.
Sansarricq (1981) quotes estimated leprosy
cases in millions by WHO regions as Africa,
3.5; Americas, 0.4; Southeast Asia, 4.5;
Europe, 0.025; eastern Mediterranean, 0.016;
and western Pacific, 2.0, a total of nearly 11
million. Rates of known prevalence per 1,000
and population in millions in the states with a

leprosy problem are 0.3 to 0.9, 403; 1.0 to 4.9,
878; 5.0 to 9.9, 80; 10.0 to 19.9, 22.4; and 20 +,
5.4. So, there has been little change in the estimates of total world prevalence, about, 10–15
million, although Skinsnes (1982) gives a graph
showing great falls among a number of states in
Southeast Asia possessing a total population of
140 million. He also reports a fall in prevalence
in China from 600,000 in 1950 to 200,000 in
1984.

There has been a rise in the resistance of the
leprosy bacillus to drugs and, particularly, to
dapsone, a sulfone drug; the latest advice of
WHO is to give a number of drugs, including
dapsone and rifampicin, in succession. It must
be remembered that of about 10 million lepers
in the world only about 18% are estimated to
be under treatment (Bechelli and Dominguez,
1966). BCG vaccine campaigns have been
effective (Bechelli, Gallego Garbajosa, et al.,
1973). For world incidence, see Noorden and
Lopez Bravo (1986).

The leprosy becillus has many unusual properties (see Fine, 1982; and Skinsnes, 1982); for
its general epidemiology, see G.S. Wilson and
G. Smith (1984a); see also Dharmendra
(1985).

9.2 Diseases due to Other *Mycobacteria*

ICD 031. Exclusions: tuberculosis, leprosy.
Fourth digit by site and species: 0, pulmonary:
avium, intracellulare (Battey bacillus), *kansasii*; 1, cutaneous: *marinum, ulcerans*; 8, other
species.

These diseases are causes of illness rather
than death. *Ulcerans* and *marinum* cause skin
lesions; *intracellulare* and *kansasii* have been
reported from cases of lung conditions resembling tuberculosis and of lymphadenitis. See
Collins, Grange, et al. (1984) and Grange
(1984).

9.3 Diphtheria

ICD 032. Inclusion: infections by *Corynebacterium diphtheriae*. Fourth digit by site.

Diphtheria is an acute infective disease due
to *C. diphtheriae* and, rarely, to *C. ulcerans*.

The disease usually presents as a sore throat with a characteristic acute ulceration in the pharynx and/or larynx. It may present as a cutaneous ulcer (tropical ulcer) or as a wound infection. Diphtheria kills commonly either through the action of a soluble toxin on the heart or through respiratory complications when the larynx is affected.

C. diphtheriae occurs in three types distinguishable by cultural properties and known as *gravis, intermedius*, and *mitis* and first clearly differentiated by Anderson, Cooper, McLeod, and Thomson (1931). Case fatality rates vary with the type; initially it was supposed that there was variation in the order suggested by the names. However, although tables in McLeod (1943) show that this continued to be usually so, there have been further divisions in the three types and some of the *mitis* subtypes are also associated with high case fatalities. *C. gravis* has been found to be the predominant type in almost all epidemics associated with many deaths. Authorities agree that there is heterogeneity in the virulence of the bacillus. See also Collier (1975) for the mode of action of toxin.

According to Andrewes, Bulloch, et al. (1923), a classic authority, diphtheria was known to the ancient world. In modern times it caused severe epidemics in Spain from 1583 onward and spread to other European countries. Bretonneau, in 1826, stated that the essential pathological lesion was the pseudo-membrane in the pharynx or elsewhere. After Bretonneau, much good clinical and pathological research was done, particularly by the French observers. In 1884 F. Loeffler discovered the bacteria, grew them in culture, and produced lesions in animals resembling those in man. In 1890 E. Behring and his co-workers showed that animals inoculated with modified diphtheria bacilli could produce curative antitoxin. In 1894, under the guidance of E. Roux, antitoxin was produced commercially.

Diphtheria is spread possibly chiefly via the respiratory system; on occasion it has been spread through the use of unpasteurized milk; diphtheritic tropical ulcer is possibly a contact disease. There is no definite urban/rural differential, but crowding seems to be of importance, and there have been numerous epidemics in institutions such as schools; military operations have been impeded by epidemics among the troops.

In Table 9.3.1 the cases of diphtheria in some countries of Europe and Oceania are given by year. It is evident that the incidence varies irregularly from year to year. It may be that the relative frequencies of the three types have also varied, and this proposition has been used to explain some of the irregularities in the mortality.

TABLE 9.3.1. Diphtheria cases reported in various countries from 1941 to 1951.

Country	Cases by year										
	1941	1942	1943	1944	1945	1946	1947	1948	1949	1950	1951
United States	17,987	16,260	14,811	14,150	18,669	16,354	12,405	9,610	8,027	5,931	4,138
Canada	2,866	2,955	2,804	3,233	2,786	2,535	1,550	898	799	425	247
Japan	40,442	44,431	63,761	94,274	85,833	49,166	28,346	16,198	14,825	12,515	10,743
Austria	14,320	15,678	22,425	15,361	14,392	16,812	12,389	10,846	10,845	9,059	7,414
Denmark	917	1,661	2,530	3,353	2,677	987	408	157	77	61	31
France	19,719	30,607	47,736	40,313	45,541	22,869	11,911	7,235	5,237	3,950	2,689
Greece	984	810	637	697	1,503	2,011	1,558	1,272	1,765	2,713	1,732
Italy	21,161	30,099	31,816	22,404	26,542	19,874	16,889	12,036	12,906	13,934	12,954
Norway	2,605	8,451	22,732	14,202	7,850	3,740	1,267	601	285	246	133
Sweden	280	1,284	2,457	3,348	2,245	790	309	171	65	43	31
Australia	8,567	5,482	7,034	5,145	3,916	3,018	2,151	1,945	1,558	1,252	1,084
New Zealand (total popln)	397	583	845	713	1,075	1,683	546	166	89	56	64

Source: WHO-diphtheria (1952).

TABLE 9.3.2. Deaths from diphtheria, scarlet fever. and typhoid fever in England and Wales, 1871–1924.

Year	Diphtheria	Scarlet fever	Typhoid fever
1871–1880*	2,943	17,423	7,842
1881–1890*	4,473	9,177	5,401
1891–1900*	8,067	4,829	5,340
1901–1910*	6,092	3,608	3,097
1911–1920*	5,058	1,706	1,278
1920	5,648	1,430	537
1921	4,772	1,305	613
1922	4,075	1,382	465
1923	2,722	993	450
1924	2,501	888	496

*Annual average.
Modified after MacIntyre (1926).

The data of Goodall, Greenwood, and Russell (1929) on patients admitted to the Eastern Fever Hospital, Homerton, London, may be taken as typical of the experience before the introduction of widespread active immunization campaigns; the authors note that in the more recent years a larger proportion of cases notified were admitted to hospital. Their Table XII shows that admissions were 644 in 1895 and increased to 1,454 in 1901, 1,027 in 1902, 705 in 1903, 967 in 1904, and then declined to about 400 per year in the years 1911 to 1914. At ages 0–5 the case fatality rates were 28%, 17%, 15%, and 12% in the epochs 1895–1899, 1900–1904, 1905–1909, and 1910–1914, respectively. Thus, there were declines in both case incidence and case fatality rates over these years. Such variations can also be seen in the longer experience displayed in Table 9.3.1

MacIntyre (1926) gives average annual deaths in England and Wales as in Table 9.3.2, and comments:

It is just over 30 years since antitoxin was discovered for the treatment of diphtheria, and it may be of interest to take a brief review of the results obtained with it and the progress which has been made in our methods of administration. For the first few years after its introduction in 1894 the serum used was often of uncertain strength and the dosage, according to our present standard, was very small; but in spite of this the results obtained were very definite, as shown by the improvement of patients after injec-

tion and the marked decrease in the case mortality. . . . However, after 30 years' experience, during which antitoxin has been extensively used, we find that diphtheria still causes a large number of deaths in this country every year. And in comparing the deaths in 1924 with the number registered from the disease in 1871 we find that the decrease has been very small. Also, if we compare diphtheria in this respect with scarlet fever and typhoid fever, we find that during the past 54 years a much more marked and progressive fall has occurred in the annual deaths from these two diseases than from diphtheria.

Th. Madsen and S. Madsen (1956) give the experience of Denmark in some detail; Thorvald Madsen, indeed, had helped to prepare the first antidiphtheritic serum in Denmark, available in the summer of 1895; he notes the case fatality rates in Copenhagen had already fallen before the availability of serum, some months in 1894 passing without a single diphtheritic death. Also, case fatality rates had fallen in Stockholm before serum had been introduced, being 38.3% 34.7%, 20.3%, and 9.0% in the four quarters of 1894. In Norway, also, serotherapy was introduced at a time of rapidly declining death rates. Madsen and Madsen (1956) believe that much of the decline in the mortality around 1895 was due to changes in the type of diphtheria bacillus prevalent at the time. S. Madsen says in Part II of the cited article that "diphtheria was defeated by immunization and not by serum therapy." A public clinic for immunization was opened in 1928 in Copenhagen, but it was a long time before immunization became widespread, the reasons being that diphtheria case fatalities were low and clinicians were wary of the vaccine. In 1941 prophylactic immunization was introduced free of charge for children between the ages of 1 and 15 years. Incidence of diphtheria was low in Denmark in the 1930s; in 1940 there were 860 cases with 44 deaths. The incidence then rose to a maximum of 3,353 recorded cases with 255 deaths in 1944, and then there was an uninterrupted fall in incidence. S. Madsen concludes that the fall in the incidence of diphtheria following the 1942–1946 epidemic was not entirely due to immunization against diphtheria but also to the natural fall of the epidemic.

It appears that the *intermedius* type was dominant in the 1930s but *gravis* and *mitis* (which can be clinically virulent) types predominated in the 1940s. It is believed that no deaths occurred in Copenhagen's Blegdamshospital in adequately immunized patients after 1945.

The secular incidences of both the disease and the bacillary types have fluctuated widely as has been shown in the two tables and discussion above; see also Wright (1939) for types of organism and case fatalities in English cities. We have to apportion the credit for the practical disappearance of the disease from developed countries between passive immunization (i.e., serotherapy), active immunization, and changes in the nature of the infecting agent.

The influence of passive immunization treatment, or serotherapy, on the mortality from diphtheria has been usually thought by epidemiologists and commentators, for example, Bourgeois-Pichat (1964), to be of great importance, although there had been no serious controlled clinical trial except by Fibiger (1898); the Danish statistician, G. Rasch, cited by Madsen and Madsen (1956), believes that even Fibiger's trial cannot be used with confidence to make the required comparison, although case fatality rates were 3.5% in the treated and 12.2% in the untreated cases. Some therapists had put these doubts to a trial. Thus, Bingel (1918) found that there was no evident superiority of the antidiphtheritic horse serum over normal horse serum in a trial involving 900 cases of the disease. Variations on this experiment were carried out by other observers but no clear cut decision was obtained.

Friedberger (1928) reported from the Rudolf-Virchow Hospital in Berlin that the case fatality rate reached 36.3% in August, 1927, in spite of early injections of large doses of antitoxin. Similar outbreaks had occurred in the cities of the Rhine Valley. The reviewer of this article, J.D. Rolleston in the *Bulletin of Hygiene*, (vol. 3, 1928, p. 976), remarks that

the paper is remarkable as being an attempt by a prominent epidemiologist to discredit the value of diphtheria antitoxin. . . . No one who, like the reviewer, has had a prolonged and intimate acquaintance with diphtheria can subscribe to the author's views.

This seems to be an unjustified criticism since two other reports on the same page of the *Bulletin* have case fatality rates of 23.5% in 1927 (E. Techoueyres in a French hospital) and 8.7%, 17.4%, and 12.8% in the 3 years 1926–1928 (U. Friedemann at the R.-Virchow Hospital).

Some explanation of these varied opinions has been given in the review of McLeod (1943). Tables are given therein of the incidence of the three main types throughout the regions monitoring the bacillary types, namely Great Britain, central Europe, and Australia. His general conclusion is that the type frequencies have varied over time and that the failure of serotherapy had been associated with an undue proportion of the more dangerous forms of the disease, namely, those caused by the *gravis* and *mitis* types of bacilli. Two quotations may be given from pages 1 and 3 of McLeod (1943):

Not only are there these numerous records of unusually severe diphtheria, but there is no doubt that in many of these outbreaks the results of serum treatment have been singularly disappointing notwithstanding the great advances in the potency of antitoxic serum . . . cases . . . have died notwithstanding large doses of serum on the first day of disease. *This must mean that with certain varieties of diphtheria in certain patients it will always be impossible to give serum in time to be of use—that is so long as we are limited to the forms of antiserum now available.*

G.S. Wilson and G. Smith (1984b) believe that serotherapy is of value to the individual patient and that it has had some effect in lowering the case fatality but that "it would be wrong to ascribe to it any substantial part in the decline in mortality that occurred in many European countries" in 1894–1900, for instance. We can agree with this statement and extend the years in any country up to the introduction of a vigorous active immunization campaign.

The present freedom from serious diphtheria mortality is due to the immunization campaigns carried out by governmental agencies under such rules as set out by G.S. Wilson and

G. Smith (1984*b*), who believe that diphtheria toxoid immunization is best carried out toward the end of infancy; however, for convenience and economy of operations toxoid is often combined with pertussis vaccine and given early in infancy at 2–4 months of age. Controlled experiments have shown that incidence is reduced in the ratio 2:7 and mortality in the ratio 1:25. Logan (1950*a*) showed that on the basis of the experience 1866–1940, the immunization campaign of 1940 onward was successful in allowing only 67 deaths in England and Wales against an expected 1,427 deaths in 1949.

For the human herd, if immunization procedures cover more than 70% of the population, spread of the bacillus is impeded and the infection tends to die out; but, it seems, even this may not prevent the spread of particularly virulent *gravis* type.

In summary, diphtheria is caused by groups of *Corynebacterium diphtheriae*, labeled *gravis, intermedius*, and *mitis*, of various degrees of virulence. Case fatality rates vary between epidemics because of this heterogeneity in the causal organisms. The role of serotherapy is ambiguous; it probably has done some good. After active immunization campaigns, the deaths from diptheria have been few.

At the centenary of the discovery of the diphtheria bacillus, the *Journal of Hygiene* invited authors to write on its history. The points made are of interest. Pappenheimer (1984) notes that all diphtheria toxins so far analyzed have the same chemical structure, namely, sequence of amino acids; this suggests that toxic corynebacteria have only evolved recently, perhaps in the last millenium. Groman (1984) discusses the "conversion" of the corynebacteria, so that they produce toxin, by corynephages, living particles smaller than a bacillus. Dixon (1984) and Kwantes (1984) give graphs of the decline in deaths from diphtheria in North America and Europe, respectively, and assign the virtual elimination to the effects of toxoid campaigns.

For further details of the mortality from diphtheria, see: England and Wales, Stocks (1941); world, WHO-diphtheria (1952); years 1894–1940, L. Martin (1919) and Russell (1943). For corynebacteria, see Barksdale (1970).

9.4 Whooping Cough

ICD 033. Inclusion: infections by *Bordetella*. Fourth digit, (species): 0, *pertussis*; 1, *parapertussis*; 8, other.

Whooping cough or pertussis is an infectious disease caused by the small Gram-negative bacillus, *Bord. pertussis*, (Munoz and Bergman, 1977). The date of the first appearance of the disease in Europe is controversial; the earliest references to it appear to be in 1578 and 1658. There is an incubation period of 7–10 days, then a catarrhal stage, passing on after 1–2 weeks to a paroxysmal stage in which the irritating cough passes over into the characteristic whooping paroxysm; the complete attack lasts about 6 weeks. Bronchopneumonia may complicate the disease. Collapse of parts of the lung may follow blockage of a bronchus by mucus and this may cause bronchopneumonia and/or pass on into a chronic stage; a final result may be bronchiectasis. The deaths assigned to this rubric will include cases of bronchopneumonia if whooping cough has been mentioned on the death certificate, but later deaths from bronchiectasis will not be included, even if pertussis has been mentioned, since the practice of the statisticians responsible for the design of the ICD was rather to ignore very long-standing diseases that have arisen either in infancy or congenitally.

Pertussis is a disease usually of early childhood. Thus, from the *Registrar-General's Statistical Review of England and Wales for the six years, 1940–1945*, Vol. 1, Table XLV, it is evident that about 80% of the notifications were of children under the age of 5 years. Further, the case fatality rates were very much higher in infancy than at higher ages, for example, the case fatality rates in England and Wales at ages 0, 1 and 2, and 3 and 4 were for males (females) 63 (73), 9 (13), and 1 (3) in 1944, with case notification rates of 14 (15), 19 (22), and 21 (24) per 1000. See also §37.3.

Pertussis is remarkable in being one of the few infective diseases to have a low masculinity for the death rates. The reasons for this low masculinity are not understood. The subject was discussed at a meeting of the Royal Statistical Society (Hill, 1933), at which it was shown that this low masculinity was a feature of the mortality in all countries under a variety of climatic and hygienic conditions.

Pertussis has been a serious cause of mortality in childhood in the past—perhaps 3 to 5 per 1,000 of all children born would die of the disease in the years at the beginning of this century.

From the *Fourth Epidemiological Report of the League of Nations* 1926, we quote after Hill (1933):

The opinion, often met with and reflected in the regulations for notification of these diseases, that whooping-cough and measles are less important than scarlet fever and diphtheria, evidently dates from the latter half of the nineteenth century, when the two latter diseases caused many more deaths than they do now, and when mortality under two years of age was so heavy as to leave less in evidence such causes as measles and whooping-cough.

Cases of pertussis in adults occur in young parents and nursing attendants. In children deaths related to pertussis are due principally to bronchitis, pneumonia, and exhaustion.

A late complication of the disease is bronchiectasis. Although pertussis is not the only cause of bronchiectasis, the sex incidence is worthy of note. Thus, Lancaster (1952a), in Sydney, found that in a hospital admitting only children under the age of 15 years, 57 of the cases were males and 107 females; in a nearby general hospital for persons over the age of 15 years, 130 were males and 206 females. Thus, there were low masculinities in both series, 0.53 and 0.63, indicating that pertussis was a predominant cause of bronchiectasis of childhood and adulthood at that time.

The mortality rate from pertussis has greatly fallen. As causes of this decline, improved hygiene, better care of premature infants, a lessened number of infants weakened by other diseases such as gastroenteritis, and, recently, the inoculation of infants and the use of antibiotics and chemotherapy may all be cited. The antibiotics are particularly useful if pneumonia due to other organisms develops. Much can

also be done to prevent the onset of bronchiectasis by the prompt treatment of collapsed areas of lung. Notwithstanding all these points, it must be conceded that the greater part of the decline of mortality occurred before the advent of effective therapy. It is possible that the most important factors were the general improvement in child welfare, the lowered risks of infection brought about by improved housing, and, perhaps, a lowered infection rate from other debilitating diseases such as gastroenteritis and otitis media; indeed, it is clear from the case fatality rates that any factor preventing or reducing infection in the first year of life would be expected to reduce greatly the mortality from the disease. It is suggested in Topley and Wilson (1975) and J.W.G. Smith (1984b) that vaccine prophylaxis may be of comparatively little value. A complication of vaccine prophylaxis is provocation poliomyelitis in which poliomyelitis causes paralysis in the limb closest to the site of inoculation (McCloskey, 1950). See also WHO-whooping cough (1952) and Sekura, Moss, and Vaughan (1985).

Whooping cough can still be a dangerous disease; indeed, Morley, Woodland, and Martin (1966) report a case fatality rate of 6.5% in an African village study and even higher in patients admitted to hospital. Miller, Alderslade, and Ross (1982) are in favor of vaccinations against pertussis.

9.5 Streptococcal Sore Throat and Scarlatina

ICD 034. Fourth digit: 0, sore throat; 1, scarlatina. Inclusion: septic sore throat; with rash scarlet fever or scarlatina.

The *Streptococci* pathogenic to man belong almost entirely to the species *pyogenes* and *pneumoniae*. Members of the *pyogenes* species have been classified by cultural and serological properties into the Lancefield groups and the infections important to man are caused by members of Group A. They cause a diversity of diseases, assigned as follows: Streptococcal sore throat and scarlatina to ICD 034, erysipelas to 035, the nonsuppurative complications, nephritis to 580 and rheumatic fever to 390. See also §9.11, §29.5, and Chapter 30.

Streptococcal respiratory infection is a disease of temperate and cold climates occurring mainly in the winter and spring and causing a fever and symptoms referable to the pharyngeal region. The infecting *Streptococci* belong to Group A and can be subdivided serologically into some 50 types. Some strains produce an erythrogenic toxin, which produces the characteristic rash of scarlet fever. The natural habitat of Group A is the lymphoid tissues of the oropharynx and the usual portal of entry is the respiratory tract. Transmission of the organism is by intimate contact and there is no evidence that it is carried by fomites and very little that air-borne transmission is important.

Clinically, there is an incubation period of 1 to 6, usually 2 to 3, days. Sore throat and fever come on rapidly. Other diagnostic features are the rash and appearance of the tongue. There is a variable degree of toxemia, sometimes extreme. The causes of death include toxemia, septicemia, meningitis, and other localized septic conditions. Acute nephritis may occur approximarely 18 to 21 days after infection and can be fatal; if there is recovery there may be no permanent damage to the kidneys. Acute rheumatism may follow either scarlet fever or acute streptococcal throat infections; it may be followed by chronic endocarditis and valvular damage.

The behavior of scarlet fever in England and Wales is discussed in Goodall, Greenwood, and Russell (1929); their Table I shows that there were considerable annual variations in admissions to a fever hospital, the Eastern Hospital, London; thus, there were 2,175 admissions in 1896, 204 and 186 in the years 1901 and 1902, then over 1,500 in each of the years 1905 to 1908. Few cases occurred in infants; their Table II shows in each of the first 7 years of life 122, 691, 1,541, 2,075, 2,423, 2,438, and 2,130 cases; their Diagram 1 shows that the incidence was greatest in the autumn. Their Table IIA shows percentage case fatality rates of 35.25, 15.34, 8.89, 7.18, 4.33, 2.42, and 2.30 for the first 7 years of life and an overall percentage case fatality rate of 3.61. Thus, scarlet fever was a serious disease even as late as 1895–1914.

According to Woods (1933), also studying scarlet fever in England and Wales, mortality from the disease has varied greatly since the eighteenth century. Thus Robert Willan (1757–1812) referred many times to the gravity of scarlet fever at that time. In the early nineteenth century it was a mild disease. However, after 1830 it became "the leading cause of death among the infectious diseases of childhood" in the words of Creighton (1965). The mortality reached a peak in 1863 when the deaths per 1,000 per annum of children under age 15 years were almost 4.0; in 1871–1880 and 1876–1880 they were 2.0 and 1.8 per 1,000. After 1880 a decline was observed that continued down to 1926–1930, the latest period of Woods (1933), when they were only 0.055 per 1,000. Woods (1933) mentions a number of hypotheses for the declines in mortality, such as the amelioration of poor social conditions, and low rainfall and gives data showing that they cannot have been generally important; declines were greater in the case fatality rates than in the incidence.

Scarlatina was, indeed, one of the great epidemic scourges in the nineteenth century in many countries. Thus, it is clear from the graphs of Ransome (1881–1882) and the official statistics of Sweden that scarlatina was a very important cause of mortality, there, over a long period of time, going back to the eighteenth century. The epidemic features were also noted in Australia by Cumpston (1927); according to him, the first case of scarlet fever in Australia was observed in Tasmania in 1833, and cases were observed in Victoria and New South Wales in 1841. There is doubt as to when the first cases occurred in other states but it may be stated that it was some years before definite cases were recorded. In 1875, 985 died from scarlatina in Victoria and in the following year, 2,240. As 1,541 deaths also occurred from measles in Victoria in 1875, there was a considerable rise in the crude death rate for the year. In this century only influenza in 1919 was able to cause a comparable jump in the crude death rate. By 1908 scarlatina had already become a minor cause of mortality in Australia.

The decline in the death rates from scarlet fever has occurred in many countries; it cannot be ascribed to progress in medical science, with the possible exception of the improvement about 1940 that may have been partly due to the use of the sulphonamide drugs; however, by 1940 the disease had already become a minor source of mortality, with low incidence and low case fatality rates. It may be that the virulent strains operating in previous centuries are now no longer circulating, for no other adequate explanation has ever been given. See Parker (1978, 1984c).

Few deaths occurred in past years at ages over 15 years. Mortality rates by age and sex are given in later chapters on the mortality of childhood.

For further remarks on scarlet fever see: England and Wales, Stocks (1941); world, WHO-scarlet fever (1951, 1952).

9.6 Erysipelas

ICD 035. Exclusions: postpartum or puerperal erysipleas (670).

Erysipelas is an acute, spreading inflammation of the skin; it was formerly common but is rare nowadays. It is due to some types of *Streptococcus pyogenes* and may be preceded by sore throat. A single attack confers no protection against later attacks. In earlier ICD classifications erysipelas would have been included among the infective diseases of the skin.

A partial summary of the article of Russell (1933) on the statistical data available in England and Wales in the era before chemotherapy is now given to show the importance of erysipelas as a cause of death. His Table 1 shows that the notified *cases* were centered about 650 per 1,000,000 per annum in the years 1912–1915. They then fell to a minimum of 321 in 1923 and rose again to 460 per 1,000,000 per annum in 1930. His Table 2 gives the *deaths* per 1,000,000 per annum in the general population as 95, 69, 42, 32, 23, and 21 in the six decennia 1871–1880, . . . , 1921–1930. The mortality had evidently declined over the years 1871 to 1930 before the advent of chemotherapy. His Table 3 gives the age-specific death rates for each sex; there is a minimum rate at ages 5–10 years followed by a marked increase with age; the male rates are higher than the female. His Table 4 shows a marked gradient in the standardized

annual rates per 1,000,000 for males (females) from 12 (12) in the rural districts, 16 (14) in the urban districts, 23 (18) in the county boroughs, and 25 (21) in London. His Diagram 1 shows a marked seasonal gradient with excess of mortality for the months November to April. In London and Glasgow mortality rates were positively correlated with overcrowding; so, there was a good case for erysipelas mortality being associated with socioeconomic conditions.

Erysipelas was thus responsible for a small, but not negligible, share of the mortality of approximately 0.5% in the earlier years. Its importance had declined before chemotherapy was available. After chemotherapy erysipelas became negligible as a cause of death.

Erysipelas formerly had a more extended meaning; for example, Nunneley (1841) uses it as we would use septic infection.

Among pathogenic organisms, the streptococci are versatile in their production of diverse disease syndromes; so we mention here the monographs on them by Skinner and Quesnel (1978) and Holm and Christensen (1982); although, excluding *Str. pneumoniae*, almost all streptococci causing human disease belong to Group A, there are many different types in that Group; Parker (1978) mentions that rheumatic fever and acute glomerulonephritis rarely occur together, and Maxted (1978) mentions that rheumatic fever follows throat infections but rarely skin infections. See also Parker (1984c).

9.7 Meningococcal Infections

ICD 036. Fourth digit by site.

The clinical syndrome, cerebrospinal fever, was first described by G. Vieusseux (1746–1814) in 1805 after an epidemic in Geneva. It was later reported form Massachusetts and Prussia. The organism is a Gram-negative coccus, *Neisseria meningitidis*. Many of the epidemics reported have occurred in military establishments; others have occurred in jails, barracks, ships, and domiciliary schools.

Meningitis is an inflammatory reaction of the meninges, the membranes surrounding the brain and spinal cord. Many agents can cause such inflammations: bacteria, viruses, fungi, and protozoa. Meningitis may be secondary to some general disease such as tuberculosis, lobar pneumonia, typhoid fever, general septicemia, syphilis, and virus diseases, when it will be included in the diagnosis of the particular disease, or to some local disease such as septic internal otitis or osteomyelitis. An especially important cause in infants is an infection of a meningocele; in such cases the diagnosis will refer back to the underlying disease according to the rules of the ICD.

There was much loss from the corresponding rubric in the assignment of the causes of death before 1930, for bacteriologic methods were not widely used to differentiate the various forms of meningitis.

The organism can vegetate in the nasopharynx without causing symptoms. Indeed, there is a high carrier rate during epidemics. The epidemics are due to a high proportion of persons carrying the organism and to a relatively high proportion of passage of the organisms from the nasopharynx to the meninges. Overcrowding leads to the high carrier rate, and some meteorological conditions lead to a dry unhealthy state of the nasal mucosa, which facilitates the passage of the organisms through the mucosa and finally to the meninges. The large proportion of the reported epidemics occurring in troops is remarkable. In 1966 more than half the cases occurred in Africa, especially in the hot, dry area of 8° to 16° north of the equator.

Antibiotics and chemotherapy are effective in treatment, reducing the case fatality rate to about 5%.

For world statistics, see WHO-meningitis (1952) and Peltola (1983); for pathogenicity, de Voe (1982). See Wilson (1984c) for a discussion of the general topic of bacterial meningitis.

9.8 Tetanus

ICD 037. Exclusions: tetanus neonatorum, 771.3; puerperal tetanus, 670.9; tetanus after abortion, 634.0; tetanus after ectopic or molar pregnancy, 639.0.

Tetanus is an infective disease due to the spore forming anerobic bacillus, *Clostridium tetani*. It results from the contamination of a wound or raw surface with spores of the organism, from an introduction of them into the body in penetrating wounds, or sometimes by operative, including obstetrical, procedures. It multiplies in anaerobic sites associated with wounds and produces its effects by the development of a soluble toxin. The bacillus has been found in the feces of many herbivores and carnivores and in that of man. It is believed, however, that it does not multiply in the intestine but in soil, especially soil rich in animal manure.

Human deaths from tetanus fall into three main classes:

(*i*) tetanus neonatorum
(*ii*) obstetrical tetanus
(*iii*) tetanus of wounds, civil and war.

Tetanus neonatorum probably has not been confused with "tetany" in the classification of the deaths by the official statisticians. In the past it has been an important cause of mortality in neonates. In neonates the case fatality rate is said to be about 80% by Adams, Laurence, and Smith (1969), and in some underdeveloped countries tetanus many account for up to 70% of neonatal deaths, according to the same authors. It was responsible for the deaths of 30% of neonates in parts of temperate Scotland in the late eighteenth century but has been eliminated by adequate training of the midwives. In some countries the cord may be ritually smeared with dung. It is now a negligible cause of mortality in the developed countries.

Obstetrical cases occur after parturition or abortion. Case fatalities of puerperal tetanus may be as high as 90%

Tetanus spores enter the body in various ways; war wounds, injuries and accidents of civil life, operations and the treatment of wounds are evident examples. However, there are other examples such as ear-piercing, ritual circumcision, and the injection of vaccines or drugs. The age and sex distributions of the disease can often be explained by the social customs, for example, tetanus rates may be relatively high in those age groups not wearing shoes or in soldiers wounded in areas of contaminated soil as on the western front in the

1914–1918 war. Case fatality rates on this front were lowered by the routine use of prophylactic doses of antitoxin.

In World War II active immunization with toxoid was effective in reducing case incidence and fatality rates. In civilian life since that time, the incidence has been reduced by the use of toxoid, usually in the form of a triple vaccine (see Lancaster, 1953*b*).

See also: review, Bytchenko (1966); history, Chalian (1940); analysis of toxin, Bizzini (1979).

J.W.G. Smith (1984*a*) believes that the prognosis of tetanus is very grave, whatever the treatment, if it follows the clinical signs; he believes, moreover, that there is no conclusive proof of the therapeutic usefulness of antitoxin.

9.9 Septicemia

ICD 038. Exclusions: septicemia or infections during pregnancy, labor and the puerperium, after abortion, and after operation. Fourth digit: bacterial species.

Deaths are possibly rarely assigned to this rubric. Before chemotherapy was available, such deaths would have been assigned probably to infections of bone, skin, and the subcutaneous tissues.

9.10 Actinomycosis and Other Miscellaneous Bacterial Diseases

ICD 039. Inclusion: infection by *Actinomyces* (*israelii*).

Actinomycosis is a disease caused by *Nocardia madurae* and other actinomyces-like organisms, that is, aerobic branching filamentous organisms. It is not a common cause of disease or mortality in man. See Bronner and Bronner (1971) Chandler, Kaplan and Ajello (1980), Heite (1967), Sykes and Skinner (1973), Topley and Wilson (1983), and Wilson (1984*b*).

ICD 040. Fourth digit by disease: 0, gas (bacillus) gangrene, malignant edema, clostridial myositis due to infections by *Clostridium* species; 1, rhinoscleroma; 2, Whipple's disease or intestinal lipodystrophy; 3, necrobacillosis; 8, other bacterial.

Deaths now classified to ICD 040 would usually be infections of wounds with severe muscle destruction as in the conditions of warfare in 1914–1918 and in war or hospitals in past centuries, discussed in §9.11 below.

We are not concerned with ICD 041.

For staphylococcus, see Easmon and Adlam (1983). For staphylococcal toxin syndrome, see Todd (1985).

9.11 Wound Infections

It is a tribute to modern surgery, or perhaps bacteriology, for example, Koch (1880), that there is no satisfactory indication in the most recent edition of the ICD as to the appropriate rubric for "hospital gangrene." Indeed, it is difficult for us, now, to imagine the unsatisfactory conditions of surgery and obstetrics in the days before Nightingale and Lister. There was a lack of trained nursing and dressing staff. Gross overcrowding often existed in the hospitals. Some ward practices were quite unsound. A notorious practice was to do a round of the wards, "cleansing" the wounds in turn with a common sponge and common bucket; the wounds would be washed in turn with the sponge wrung out in the bucket after each patient, an unhygienic practice widely spread among the great hospitals; see Wangensteen and Wangensteen (1978, p. 335). Worst of all, there was no generally accepted theory of contagion to show that such practices were necessarily bad. Nevertheless, there were many who were shocked by such procedures and recommended cleanliness. The military surgeon John Hennen (1779–1828) is quoted in Cantlie (1974*b*, pp. 374–375) as saying, "With cold water, one is never at a loss for a remedy." See also Hennen (1820). Similarly, Charles White (1728–1813), a Manchester surgeon, greatly improved the cleanliness and discipline of a hospital and P.G. Cederschjöld (1782–1848), in 1833, insisted on boiled individual sponges for the use of parturients. There was, in fact, a "cold water" school of surgeons who believed in cleanliness and the use of cold water previously boiled (see Cartwright, 1967, p. 85, and Tait, 1890) and who aimed to obtain healing of wounds by first intention. Some surgeons using these methods obtained good results even before 1860. There were other surgeons working in such a way as to protect the wounds from infection; Edward Bennion (obit 1844, aet. 87) of Shropshire thus brought the ends of broken bones of a compound fracture into apposition and covered the wound with lint saturated with a compound of benzoin, retaining it as long as possible. Wangensteen and Wangensteen (1978) cite this and other examples of the use of successful methods, which were not gathered together because of a lack of an overall theoretical system. They also give modern examples of the difficulties in sterilizing surgical instruments, dressings, sheets, and other fomites.

In military hospitals conditions were aggravated by crowding, low quality and deficient numbers of medical assistants, shortage of equipment, and so on. The expectations of surgeons were low. As Cantlie (1974b p. 390), writes "Hunter said he had seen wounds heal by first intention but Longmore declared he had never seen such a case; all went septic. His account of the dreaded complication of hospital gangrene shows how extensive was the acquaintance of military surgeons with the disease, and Hennen's unique experience of treating nearly 1,000 cases in the hospital at Bilbao during the Peninsular War was probably the largest number dealt with by a British surgeon; after the battle of Vitoria there was a total of 1,614 cases of whom 518 died."

We may follow the eminent surgeon and bacteriologist, Theodor Billroth (1829–1894) in his description of hospital gangrene in Billroth and von Winiwarter (1883, pp. 368–373). Some wounds, as well as some sites of recent operation, being treated in hospital, might be healing, that is, granulating and cicatrizing, when they became diseased in a peculiar manner without known cause. In some cases the granulating surface changed partially or entirely to a yellow smeary pulp, sometimes easily detachable or at other times adherent. This change extended also to the surrounding skin which became rosy-red turning later to a dirty yellowish gray. The process might extend superficially or involve deeper structures such as the muscles; the disease often progressed to

death. Billroth noted that many surgeons of his time had not seen cases of the disease. Others considered it to be due to gross neglect, dirty dressings, and so on; some surgeons believed that it was peculiar to hospitals and did not occur elsewhere. Billroth had no doubt that in every case streptococci and micrococci could be found in the wound but pointed out that no proof had been given that they were causal. This was written before the epoch-making works of R. Koch on the etiology of traumatic infective diseases in 1878.

The actual causal organisms of hospital gangrene have never been established. Meleney (1924) described a "streptococcal gangrene" with a clinical picture closely resembling that of hospital gangrene; Miles (1967) says that the organism may have been "large-celled clostridia." Possibly no such identification is possible for the disease has not occurred since the development of bacteriologic techniques for identifying it. Although the causal organisms were not known, it was evident to many military surgeons that overcrowding of the wounded was a serious matter and in the Peninsular War they had not favored general hospitals; medical policy was to have the wounded treated in the regimental hospitals because of fear of hospital gangrene. Bacteriologic theory suggests that the chance of a dangerous strain of bacteria being introduced into a hospital was increased with the greater intake, and within the hospital spread was aided by unsatisfactory hygienic conditions, especially the use of the common sponge.

Infections of wounds also appeared in civil hospitals and were seen by Joseph Lister as the greatest problem of surgery. A colleague and chemist had advised him of the recent work of Louis Pasteur, in the years 1861 to 1864, on the existence of microscopic life in the air, which could cause fermentations and putrefactions, and Lister recognized the possible analogies with disease processes. Lister's methods were a corollary to the germ theory of wound infection. He aimed to prevent the access of environmental organisms to the surgical wound by means of an antiseptic (5% phenol was a favorite) and perhaps kill them in situ. The new methods constituted a great advance,

TABLE 9.11.1. Case fatalities of amputations in the British Isles.

Site	Number of beds in hospital									
	Over 300		201–300		101–200		26–100		25 or less	
	A	C	A	C	A	C	A	C	A	C
Thigh	935	465	298	359	431	304	241	244	34	206
Leg	613	440	261	264	483	234	266	180	55	145
Arm	297	370	138	297	239	205	133	150	27	74
Forearm	244	164	106	100	217	78	121	58	27	11

A: Number of amputations,
C: Case fatality per 1,000.
Data from Simpson (1868–1869), reprinted in (1871–1872, pp. 338, 393, 394, 397).

although bacteriology was not yet sufficiently developed to give the Listerian methods a firm theoretical basis.

Pasteur had long recognized the applications of bacteriology to medicine but other problems had prevented him from entering the field. As early as 1874 and again in a lecture in 1878, as cited in Geison (1974, p. 389), Pasteur stated the necessity. . . . to use none but perfectly clean instruments, lint, bandages, and sponges heated previously to 130°C to 150°C, water subjected to a temperature of 110°C to 120°C, and to work with hands cleansed with the greatest care. Moreover, Pasteur's most famous assistant, C.E. Chamberland (1851–1908) carried out many experiments on sterilization by heat and by filtration. According to Delaunay (1971), he considered that the atmosphere was not the chief vehicle of infectious germs but that soiled objects, clothing, and the hands of surgeons and their assistants were of great importance.

With efficient sterilization and training of theatre and general hospital staff, it was possible to hinder the passage of bacteria from person to person and to proceed to the ideal of working in a germ-free atmosphere. E.G.B. von Bergmann (1836–1907) and other surgeons developed the new techniques of aseptic surgery with the aim of excluding bacteria; the instruments and dressings were now sterilized; sterile gowns, masks, and rubber gloves were worn by the surgeon and his assistants; the air entering the theatre was filtered; and care was taken to prevent the introduction of infective material into the theatre and to eliminate such material without soiling the surroundings of the operation. By about 1905 such aseptic methods were available in all the advanced centres of surgery.

In Table 9.11.1 an example is given of the dangers of sepsis in the larger hospitals before the establishment of antiseptic methods; in it the case fatality rates have been classified by Simpson (1868–1869, 1871–1872) according to hospital size (i.e., number of beds). It might have been expected that patients would have been better off in the great hospitals because of the possibilities of specialism and the greater experience of the surgeons there, but the contrary was the case; for each site of amputation, there is a marked gradient in the case fatality rates favorable to the smaller hospitals. As Simpson points out, a successful operation carried out by a surgeon in a great hospital might well lead to death by sepsis after a few days in the dangerous hospital atmosphere.

It can be seen that advances in antiseptic and aseptic techniques have greatly lessened the mortality of wounds sustained in war or in civil life, in operations involving incisions, and, so, in all major surgery. As a result of these advances, compound fractures are less likely to lead to death or to chronic septic conditions, especially osteomyelitis. Advances in combatting septic infections have had effects on deaths in ICD Classes 12, 13, and 17, namely, diseases of the skin and subcutaneous tissue, diseases of the musculoskeletal system and connective tissue, and injury and poisoning, and, further, in those classes in which operations with incisions have to be performed.

Besides those persons already cited, Erichsen (1859, 1874), Beck, Greenfield, McCarthy, and Ralfe (1879), Ogston (1881), and Watson Cheyne (1886) were concerned with sepsis in hospitals, the last three using the newly developed bacteriologic techniques. Much work was done on the bacteriology of wounds in World War I, for example, Committee upon Anaerobic Bacteria and Infections (1919); for later work, see MacLennan (1962) and Willis (1969). Poynter (1967) surveys the scientific milieu before and in Lister's time and the development of the notion of asepsis. Klainer and Beisel (1969) review the passage of organisms, not necessarily thought of as pathogenic, into incisions and wounds. Wangensteen (1970) reviews the priorities of Semmelweis and Lister. See also §33.7.

Ovariotomy is an operation in a sterile field, as we would now say. Tait (1890) and the citations 33 and 34 of Wangensteen and Wangensteen (1978, pp. 235, 644) show that before 1878 Tait had performed 50 ovariotomies with 19 deaths (case fatality 38%); he had used Listerian methods early in his career but abandoned them for "scrupulous attention to cleanliness"; later he was able to report 139 consecutive ovariotomies in 1884–1885 without

a death; but Tait (1890) derides the belief in the bacterial causation of sepsis.

Pyogenic infections do not fit easily into the ICD classification or into a classification by bacterial species. We have treated them in this and the following section and in Chapter 30 and elsewhere. See Parker (1984a, b, c, d, e); Duerden (1984), J.W.G. Smith and G. Smith (1984). For some historical notes, see Youngson (1979). For the *Clostridia*, see Willis (1969).

9.12 Legionnaires' Disease

The causative organism of this new disease is *Legionella pneumophila*, a Gram-negative bacterium, 2 to 6μm in length, sluggishly motile with flagellum. *Legionella* species are aquatic bacteria found in lakes, streams, and ponds, and they are able to maintain themselves over a wide range of temperature with an optimum at 45°C and a maximum of 70°C. Because of these special properties, all cooling towers will contain legionellae at some concentration. *Legionella pneumophila* can infect man by water ingested or air inspired. The result of infection is a fever and often pneumonia, sometimes with death following. See Broome and Fraser (1979), Thornsberry, Balows, et al. (1984), Wilson (1984e), and Meyer (1983).

Chapter 10
Diseases due to Viruses and Chlamydias

10.1 Acute Poliomyelitis

ICD 045. Acute poliomyelitis. Fourth digit: 0, bulbar; 1, with other paralysis; 2, nonparalytic.

Poliomyelitis is an acute infective disease due to *Poliovirus hominis*, an enterovirus, of three numbered types, infecting the human. The primary site of infection is the alimentary tract, infection passing from person to person by the fecal-oral route, especially under conditions of low hygiene; young children are frequently the means of spreading the infection, and there is rapid spread throughout a family after its introduction. The virus multiplies in the lymphoid tissues and follicles of the pharynx and small intestine or in the superficial mucosal cells of the same areas. The virus may persist in the intestine for many weeks; 50% of cases are still excreting the virus at the end of 3 weeks. Epidemics tend to appear in late summer. Some epidemics have been caused by contamination of the water supply by sewage.

Virulent strains are able to cause a viremia and then obtain access to the central nervous system by vascular channels or along the nerves from the peripheral nervous ganglia. The invasion of the brain is a relatively late event in the progress of the disease; the anterior horn cells of the spinal cord and the motor cortex of the brain are attacked; but there are many more infections than cases with paralyses; as Fenner and White (1976) say; "paralysis is a relatively infrequent complication of an otherwise trivial infection."

It is necessary to add that the disease pre-viously caused distressing long-term effects on the patients and some deaths; nevertheless, the death rates from poliomyelitis suggest that in the past an undue emphasis was placed on the importance of the disease by laity and public health authorities alike. Attention was distracted from such diseases as pertussis and measles as causes of death and morbidity.

The probability of neural cell death and consequent paralysis is affected by various factors. Among those not protected by prior infection or immunization, paralysis is more frequent and severe in adults than in children. Injections, notably triple antigen or pertussis alone (McCloskey, 1950), predispose to paralysis in that limb, as already mentioned in §9.4, and tonsillectomy predisposes to bulbar poliomyelitis. Fatigue and local trauma are also factors predisposing to paralysis.

The first recorded outbreak is said to have occurred in St. Helena about 1830. Small epidemics were reported in Europe in the middle of the nineteenth century, and a large epidemic, in Sweden in 1887.

Because of the mode of spread by water and close contact, higher rates of infection might be expected in regions of poor hygiene, although epidemics of paralysis were first noted in regions of better hygiene. The explanation of this apparent paradox is that paralysis is much more likely to occur in infections at the older ages. Thus, in regions of poor hygiene, almost all infants will have had the infection; after such infection, the child will be immune, and in areas of poor hygiene the paralytic cases will

TABLE 10.1.1. Poliomyelitis morbidity in Europe and Oceania (annual mean of cases).

	1941–1945	1946–1950	1951–1955	1956–1960	1961–1965	1966–1970	1971–1975
Austria	334	1,191	607	644	70	1	1
Belgium	225	164	475	395	79	3	1
Denmark	984	703	1,614	72	77	1	0
Finland	302	227	342	306	7	0	0
Ireland	1,750	2,527	3,342	4,796	2,121	93	11
Norway	743	574	981	140	36	8	5
Sweden	1,766	1,432	1,526	213	28	1	1
England and Wales	824	5,843	4,381	2,706	317	24	2
Australia	336	1,201	2,187	331	151	1	2
New Zealand	54	313	413	225	44	1	0

Source: Paccaud (1979).

occur sporadically. In areas of better hygiene, smaller families, and more favorable conditions generally, the individual may escape infection until later childhood or adult life, and paralytic cases with the possibility of invalidity and death will appear. There is also the possibility that the virulence of strains of the poliovirus may have changed, for it is known that the present strains differ in their virulence.

Study of the history of the disease is hampered by the failure of the official statisticians to separate poliomyelitis from other diseases. Thus, deaths in Australia from poliomyelitis can be studied only since 1921, for up to that time deaths certified as due to poliomyelitis were assigned, according to the rules of the ICD, to a rubric that included neuritis and neuralgia or to a rubric including other diseases of the spinal cord.

The cases by year for some countries are given in Table 10.1.1. It is evident that cases have occurred in epidemics at irregular intervals.

Only palliative treatment has been available. The inactivated vaccine of Salk, introduced after 1955, provided considerable protection. Attenuated live virus vaccine (Sabin) was introduced in many countries of the world after 1960 and has been successful in protecting populations.

For a history of the disease, see Paul (1971); for world incidence, see Paccaud (1979), WHO-poliomyelitis (1951, 1953), Freyche (1952), and Assaad and Ljungars-Esteves (1984); for eradication, see Nathanson (1984).

See also Gamble (1984, Figure 99.1), who shows what is perhaps the longest possible time series of the incidence of poliomyelitis, namely, in the United States from 1910 to 1960, after which complete control was attained.

10.2 Slow Virus Infection of the Central Nervous System

ICD 046. Fourth digit by disease: 0, kuru; 1, Jakob-Creutzfeldt disease; 2, subacute sclerosing panencephalitis; 3, progressive multifocal leukoencephalopathy; 8, other.

We take definitions of these diseases from Fenner and White (1976). For a general discussion, see Kimberlin (1984).

Kuru is a disease of the central nervous system characterized by cerebellar degeneration, leading to ataxia, tremors, incoordination, dementia, and death within a year. It is caused by a slow virus and is spread by cannibalism, the ritual eating of dead relatives. Women and children were affected but adult males took no part in the ceremonies. See Gajdusek (1977a, b), Gajdusek and Alpers (1965), and Gajudsek, Gibbs, and Alpers (1965). Kuru is similar to Jakob-Creutzfeldt disease in which the patient, usually middle aged, becomes incoordinated and demented and dies within 9–18 months (Brown, 1980).

Subacute sclerosing panencephalitis has now been shown to be due to measles virus and is not properly to be referred here.

Progressive multifocal leukoencephalopathy is a demyelination of neurons accompanied by proliferation of giant bizarre astrocytes due to a papovavirus, usually fatal within a year.

None of these diseases causes a significant number of deaths in any population.

See also Prusiner and Hadlow (1979) and Stroop and Baringer (1982). For the control and eradication of exotic viruses, see Murphy (1979).

10.3 Meningitis due to Enterovirus

ICD 047. Inclusion: abacterial, aseptic and viral. Fourth digit; 0, coxsackie virus; 1, ECHO virus; 8, other.

ICD 048. Other Enterovirus Diseases of the Central Nervous System. Inclusion: Boston exanthem.

ICD 049. Other Non–arthropod-borne Viral Diseases of the Central Nervous System. Fourth digit: 0, lymphocytic choriomeningitis; 1, meningitis due to adenovirus; 8, other.

Most infections with these viruses are sub-clinical. Deaths are rare. See Gamble (1984) and Madeley (1984) for discussion of these diseases and for references.

10.4 Influenza as a Disease

ICD 487. Exclusions: *Hemophilus influenzae* (a bacterial disease), infection not otherwise specified (041.5), meningitis (320.0), pneumonia (482.2). Fourth digit: 0, with pneumonia; 1, with other respiratory manifestations; 2, with other manifestations.

We break here from the ICD assignment of influenza to ICD 487 in the diseases of the respiratory system, which may be regarded as a historical anomaly.

It appears that there are two types of disease diagnosed as influenza. To make secular comparisons, it is necessary to define the important form of disease or epidemic influenza after the manner of Stuart-Harris (1965) as follows: influenza is an acute febrile illness, with a sudden onset during 1 or 2 days, accompanied by pyrexia, headache, shivering, and cough, and often complicated by acute bronchitis or pneumonia. Of course, in an epidemic, not all cases will display the full syndrome, but most of the signs and symptoms should be observed

in a large proportion of cases, at least; for example, as in Stuart-Harris (1953, p. 10, Table 1), where in 84 cases the percentages showing the signs were: sudden onset 75, malaise 91, headache 87, anorexia 77, shivering 74, coryza or nasal obstruction 73, cough 71, and so on. The incubation period is 2–3 days and the patient may remain intermittently infective for a week. For an epidemic to be judged as influenza, since the setting up of a worldwide surveillance system in 1947 for the identification of the virus, it would also be required that the virus had been cultured and typed during the epidemic.

Schild (1984) remarks that there are few physical signs in the patient enabling the clinician to make a firm diagnosis of influenza as against other respiratory tract infections. Diagnosis is usually made with the knowledge that the disease is epidemic at the time. He says that unequivocal identification is entirely dependent on virus isolation or appropriate laboratory tests of serum antibodies.

For the pathogenesis of epidemic influenza, the reader may be referred to the accounts of Stuart-Harris and Schild (1976) or Schild (1984). The virus multiplies in the respiratory epithelium for 2 to 6 days causing epithelial necrosis, there may be dissemination by the blood, and the virus is excreted from a day before the onset of symptoms up to 7 days after onset. In complicated cases there are findings such as productive cough, substernal soreness, chest tightness, and wheezing, with corresponding chest signs. Only about 10% of persons with influenza suffered from acute bronchitis or pneumonia in recent epidemics; these complications are relatively common in persons with chronic pulmonary or cardiovascular disorders.

Burnet and Clark (1942) believe that the speed of infection and the area of epithelium involved are important factors in the severity of the disease. As in virus or other infections, the physical state of the patient before infection is also important; case fatality rates in the aged tend to be high; the supposed high rates in young adult life in the pandemic of 1919, mentioned in particular by Greenwood (1920), can be accounted for by the method of calculation, namely, by relating the deaths from influenza to deaths from all causes in the same age group. For a review of the severity of influenza epidemics, see Glezen (1982). Pneumonia can occur with dyspnea, chest pain of pleural type, and mucoid or frothy sputum. Consolidation of the lungs may occur, and resolution is slower than with ordinary pneumonia. Indeed, respiratory failure with extensive edema of the lungs seems to have been the common mode of death in the 1918–1919 pandemic. Pneumonia can occur as a secondary bacterial infection (Douglas, 1975). It has been generally believed that *H. influenzae* was an important secondary invader in the pandemic of 1918–1919; but in later epidemics, the secondary invaders have been usually the *Streptococcus pneumoniae* or sometimes the staphylococci. Although antibiotics are inactive against the virus, their routine administration may reduce case fatality by acting against the secondary invaders.

Killed-virus vaccinations have been used in the past, but there seems to be no great faith in their efficacy. Schild (1984) believes that live attenuated virus strains may be used in the future.

For a bibliography of influenza 1930–1959, see Loosli, Portnoy, et al. (1978).

10.5 Types of Influenza Virus

Influenza virus occurs in types known as A, B, and C: A was discovered in a London epidemic of 1932, B, discovered in a New York epidemic of 1940, and C, discovered in an American epidemic of 1949. The last mentioned plays little part in human influenza epidemics. Within these types, there can be variations; thus, there are variations in influenza A virus, and these have come to be known as types A0, A1, A2, . . .; more recent serological finds divide them further, according to the specific toxic factors associated with the properties of hemagglutinin (H) and neuraminidase, (N), respectively, and designated by notations such as H_1N_2. Such variations in influenza A virus have important implications for the great epidemics and pandemics of influenza. It is now believed that there are a

finite (i.e., limited) number of antigens on the surface of the influenza virus, and that some variations in virulence are due to an alteration of the proportions of these antigens; this phenomenon is known as antigenic "drift." Some Hs or Ns as defined above have been found in influenza virus isolations over periods of 10 or even 20 years (Schild, 1984).

A more important change is "genetic shift." There has been much speculation as to how the antigenic constitution of the virus changes qualitatively, that is, how new genes appear in it, and it becomes capable of initiating a further epidemic. A possible explanation is given in §5.13, namely, that there is a genetic inflow from nonhuman sources. Schild (1984) gives tables of antigens of influenza A viruses recovered from avian sources. Recoveries of influenza A virus have also been made from swine and horses. Indeed, "swine" viruses have been recovered from both pigs and persons on a farm in Wisconsin; this increases the plausibility of an argument that human and nonhuman viruses could coexist in the one individual, either man or animal, and that there could be genetic recombination, during this double infection, with the production of a new virulent strain.

10.6 Antigenic Tracers and Pandemics of Influenza

In each pandemic since 1889 secondary waves have been observed (Kilbourne, 1975b). Such a secondary wave was observed in England and Wales during the pandemic of 1918, as we show in the next section. The phenomenon may well be a stochastic or chance event, since the properties of the disease seemed not to be altered in the secondary waves; further, in the United States the secondary waves of the 1957 epidemic were consistently limited to areas in which large numbers of people were crowded together.

Authors, including Stuart-Harris (1970), Beveridge (1977), and Fiennes (1978), have attempted to classify outbreaks of influenza as epidemic or pandemic. Possibly the use of the word pandemic should be taken to mean something similar to "widespread in several continents," since it is known that some pandemics did not appear in all regions of the world. With this remark in mind, we can mention pandemic years and areas of known epidemics as follows: 1729–1730, widespread in Europe; 1732–1733, Plymouth in England, Moscow, Connecticut; 1761–1762, North America and Europe; 1767, North America and Europe; 1775–1776, Europe and Near and Far East; 1781–1782, China, India, Europe, North America; 1788, all of Europe; 1789, America; 1800–1802, Europe, China, Brazil; 1830–1833, worldwide; 1847–1848, Europe and the Americas; 1889–1890, 1892, 1918–1919, 1946, 1957, 1968, all worldwide. Indeed, under modern conditions of travel, every appearance of a new strain becomes a pandemic, although few deaths may follow. It may well be, as Greenwood (1920) appears to believe, that some of the epidemics reported in the classical accounts of Creighton, Hirsch, Hecker, and Haeser, listed in §1.8, were aberrant forms of influenza or even influenza described in terms that cannot be confidently identified as influenza.

That the 1889 pandemic commenced in Central Asia now seems undisputed. The origin of the 1918 pandemic is more doubtful, but influenza of high virulence seems first to have been noted in Sierra Leone, West Africa, in August 1918, followed by autumn epidemics in Spain and Europe. It is also known that a severe epidemic occurred in Chongqing (Chungking), China, in July 1918, suggesting that "a strain of Asiatic origin reaching France with Chinese labourers or otherwise was responsible for the new type of disease which became visible in May and June," according to Burnet and Clark (1942).

For the 1957 influenza pandemic, cases were first observed in Guìzhōu (Kweichow) Province near the southern border of China in March 1957 and then in most of the countries of the world; the disease reached Newfoundland, Argentina, and neighboring states in South America and West Africa in August 1957, according to the map of Stuart-Harris and Schild (1976), originally from UNESCO. The figure also serves as a model of influenza pandemics in general, namely, the development of a new strain of influenza A virus, usually in Asia, and its spread throughout the world. It comes as a surprise that in an era of fast air travel, the virus was so late in reaching some regions, such as Argentina and Newfoundland.

The key reference to the epidemics before 1896 is Leichtenstern (1912); Thompson (1890) gives a historical survey. Vaughan (1921, Table I) lists many epidemics and Jordan (1927) gives some details of the 1918–1919 pandemic.

Besides the straight out literary approach to the history of influenza, it is possible to obtain information from serological surveys of persons of different ages, for an individual forms antibodies against the type current at the time of his first infection; he also forms antibodies against virus types he may meet later. These antibodies remain as markers to the individual's past experience and have permitted some plausible speculations about the epidemics of the past, in particular, those of 1889–1892 and 1918–1919. It appears that the same strain of virus is incapable of provoking a second epidemic in a population in which there remains a substantial proportion of persons immune to it, so it has become possible to give, as in Davenport (1982, p. 375), tables of the prevalent subtypes of the influenza A viruses for 1874–1889, 1890–1901, 1902–1917, 1918–1928, 1929, 1933–1943, 1947–1957, 1957–1968, 1968–1978, 1976, and 1977. From 1933–1943 onward the actual viruses have been typed; before that date the antigenic subtypes have been inferred by serological methods. Of course, the differences in these subtypes suggest variations in their virulence.

Similar tables are available in Kilbourne (1975a,b) and in Schild (1984). Laver (1983) is a report to a symposium on the epidemics and the origins of their viral types. See also Francis and Maassab (1965), Stuart-Harris and Schild (1976), and a symposium reported in *Philos. Trans. R. Soc. London B*288 (1980). For the 1952–1953 pandemic, see WHO-influenza (1953); for pathogenicity, see Sweet and Smith (1980). Bradley, Massey, et al. (1951) and Stuart-Harris (1973) have given accounts of the 1951 and 1969–1970 epidemics in England and Wales. For excess mortality in winter as caused by influenza, see Glezen, Payne, et al. (1982).

TABLE 10.7.1. Influenza in England and Wales by year (deaths per 1,000,000 persons per annum).

	0	1	2	3	4	5	6	7	8	9
183–									53	57
184–	66	104	55	—*	—	—	—	285	459	92
185–	78	122	76	99	58	193	55	73	93	57
186–	58	38	45	45	39	29	31	29	14	32
187–	27	15	12	12	10	19	8	8	8	10
188–	7	4	3	4	3	5	3	3	3	2
189–	157	574	534	325	220	422	121	195	330	389
190–	504	174	224	190	169	205	184	267	288	254
191–	182	120	147	175	161	293	252	213	3129	1217
192–	282	237	563	220	489	327	229	567	196	734
193–	126	330	300	520	127	167	141	418	108	194
194–	286	177	88	333	103	70	130	79	29	130
195–	89	361	40	147	41	67	59	150	53	173
196–	24	154	71	68	22	17	76	18	96	98
197–	149	14	61	69	25	29	137	26	27	17

*1843–1846 rates are not available.
Up to 1949 the rates agree with Martin (1950); after 1949, the rates are from WHO or are computed from deaths given by the Registrar-General.
Rates in the epidemic years are italicized.

For mortality, see Dauer and Serfling (1961). For pandemics, 1700–1900, see Patterson (1986). For a general text, see Kilbourne (1987).

10.7 Influenza in England and Wales

The experience of England and Wales may be taken as an example of the behavior of influenza in a large community. Greenwood (1920) can be used as a guide to the history of influenza in England and Wales up to that time. In the years 1675 and 1679, there were epidemic coughs followed by pleurisies and pneumonias. Four outbreaks of influenza occurred in the years 1728–1752, inclusive, and one in 1762; 1782, 1803, 1831, 1833, and 1837 were all years epidemic for influenza.

The annual series of deaths from influenza of the Registrar-General is available from 1838 to the present time with the exception of the years 1843–1846. Parts of this series have been given in the form of rates by Newsholme (1918, 1918–1919), Greenwood (1920), and Martin (1950), and the series is now extended up to the present time in Table 10.7.1. See Stocks (1935).

An epidemic from the 48th week, (late November) 1847, to the 6th week, (February) 1848, is estimated to have been responsible for an excess of 7,000 deaths over the normal annual number, the excess influenza deaths on a per capita basis being about two thirds of that in London, 1918–1919. In 1889 England and Wales had been free from pandemic influenza for perhaps 30 years, although influenza had been pandemic in Europe and North America in 1874–1875 and in North America in the previous year, but in the 3 years 1891–1893 there was a total excess of more than 4,000 deaths in London above the expected number of about 1,800.

Martin (1950) gives a table showing that the week of maximum mortality could be as early as December and as late as the end of March and that the early maxima were not necessarily in the years of maximum mortality. Table 10.7.1 shows that during 1847–1867 the crude rate per 1,000,000 was usually in the range of 30 to 100, but the rates were 285, 459, 122, and 193 in 1847, 1848, 1851, and 1855, respectively. From 1868–1889, rates only exceeded 15 in the years 1869, 1870, and 1875. In 1890–1895, the rates were 157, 574, 534, 325, 220, and 422. There is good evidence from serological surveys that the 1889–1892 epidemic was caused

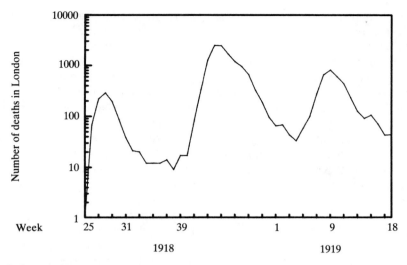

FIGURE 10.7.1. Influenza Deaths in London 1918–1919.

by influenza A. In the period 1896–1948, the rates exceeded 300 per 1,000,000 in 1898, 1899, 1900, 1918, 1919, 1922, 1924, 1925, 1927, 1929, 1931, 1932, 1933, 1937, and 1943; in 1918 and 1919, the rates were 3,129 and 1,217 per 1,000,000 per annum, about one quarter and one tenth of the crude rate for deaths from all causes in a "normal" year.

From Newsholme (1918) and Greenwood (1920), the weekly deaths from influenza are available from the 25th week of 1918 up to the 18th week of 1919; they have been plotted as Figure 10.7.1 The curve of deaths has local maxima (i.e., peaks) in the 28th and 44th weeks of 1918 and the 9th week of 1919; or there were in the London epidemic three waves of mortality, in the 27th–29th weeks, June to July 1918, in the 41st–51st weeks, October to December 1918, and from the 6th–16th weeks, February to April 1919. In the first wave, observers were surprised to find the mortality high in the younger age groups; this feature was noted again in the second wave. In the second wave, symptoms and case fatality rates were more severe than in the first. F.W.E. Andrewes (1920) believed that *H.*(then *Pf.*) *influenzae* acted as an important secondary invader as also did the hemolytic streptococcus. Although it was surmized by Andrewes that the primary cause was a filter-

passing virus, this could only be established after a susceptible laboratory animal, the ferret, had been found. Greenwood (1920) was impressed with the epidemic wave form, the apparent suddenness and undoubted rapidity of evolution of the epidemic, the high mortality of the younger age groups, and the lack of social gradients in mortality evident in previous epidemics.

The Registrar-General of England and Wales reports on p. lxiv of his Annual Report No. 81 for 1918 as follows:

The great epidemic which commenced in June increased the deaths from this cause from 5,000–10,000 usually recorded in a year to no less than 112,329 corresponding to a death rate of 3,129 per million living; and in addition led to a large increase in the deaths attributed to diseases of the lungs, including tuberculosis. . . The total deaths attributable to the epidemic during 1918 have already (p. xxix) been estimated at 132,000.

On his p. lxvi, the Registrar-General notes that deaths of females at ages 15–35 years from tuberculosis were increased by some 60%. On p. lxxxiv, he reports that the death rates for all females from all forms of pneumonia in the 3rd and 4th quarters of 1919 were 776 and 2,347, against average rates of 467 and 872 per 1,000,000 averaged over the years 1911–1917.

In the Registrar-General's Report for 1919, his No. 82, the deaths assigned to influenza numbered 44,801: males, 23,198, and females, 21,603. The mortality (i.e., crude death rate) amounted to 1,217 per 1,000,000 living.

Some comparisons can be made with normal mortality. The Registrar-General in his 82nd Report (1920, Table 3) gave the rates, standardized on to the population with the age distribution of 1901. From all causes the standardized rates per 1,000 per annum were for year, males, females, and persons as follows: 1914 15.1, 12.4, 13.7; 1915, 16.5, 13.2, 14.8; 1916, 15.4, 11.7, 13.4; 1917, 15.9, 11.4, 13.5; 1918, 19.8, 14.6, 17.1; 1919, 14.8, 11.9, 13.3. Some other commentary on the epidemic is provided.

Greenwood (1920) gives tables for deaths and death rates in Scotland and in Ireland and believes, as does Low (1920a), that there are no substantial differences from the corresponding rates in England and Wales. Housworth and Langmuir (1974) found that the excess of deaths in winter over those in summer in the epoch 1957–1966 was usually to be explained by excess influenza deaths.

10.8 Influenza in Continental Europe

The epidemics in the capitals or large cities of the various states reached their maximum weekly mortality almost simultaneously with Vienna, Prague, Trieste, and Budapest in the week ending October 19, 1918, and Paris, Berlin, Hamburg, Dresden, Breslau, Munich, and Berne in the week ending October 26. Most states had an early summer wave in June–July 1918, a second wave reaching its peak in October, and a third wave in early 1919. It seems that the notification of cases, except perhaps in special institutional reports, was not reliable. Thus, the death rates in Stockholm and Göteborg from influenza up to November 16, 1918, were 2.635 and 3.219 per 1,000 of population, respectively. But great discrepancies were evident between the two cities with respect to case fatalities, 7.3% and 0.6% in the first wave, centered in August, and 29.4% and 4.2% in the second wave, centered in October.

In Norway, during the second half of 1918, there were 774 deaths in Christiania with a population of 259,627 or 2.981 influenza deaths per 1,000 inhabitants. In Bergen, with a population of 80,000, influenza deaths numbered 302, giving a death rate of 3.775.

In Denmark there were 4,150 deaths during 1918 in a population of 3.018 million, a rate of 1.375 per 1,000.

There were 600 influenza deaths in the vicinity of Reykjavik in 1918. Even if this is taken to refer to the whole Icelandic population of about 120,000, the death rate is 5 per 1,000 population.

Perhaps it would be fair to conclude from the European figures that in a European country, not in a state of war or civil strife, the expected mortality rate from the influenza pandemic of 1918–19 would be about 2 to 3 per 1,000, and this agrees with the experiences in Australia, New Zealand, and the United States.

10.9 Influenza in Australia

The Australian influenza of 1919 was described by Cumpston (1919) in a publication much praised by Greenwood (1920). Cumpston (1919) noted that 1820, 1826, 1836, 1847, 1852, 1860, 1885, 1891, 1899, and 1907 were years of unusually high mortality. In 1918, also, deaths in Australia from influenza were higher than expected. Although ships from abroad with active cases arrived at Australian ports during 1918, there was no spread from the ships to the Australian population.

The first pandemic cases occurred in Victoria in January 1919, according to Cumpston (1919), and he maintained that there was no demonstrable connection with the arrival of any ship. Burnet and Clark (1942) were able to detect three epidemic waves in that state. From Victoria the disease spread to other states. In any period, except that including 1919, the age distribution of influenza has a characteristic form. The mortality is high in the first 5 years, especially in infancy, it falls to a minimum in early adult life, and then rises continuously throughout life. Excepting the rises from 1908–1910 to the 1911–1920 period, the mortality at all ages has tended to fall. In fact, at all ages except early childhood, the mortality rates in the period, 1941–1945, tend to be less than one third those of 1908–1910.

To indicate the severity of the epidemic, the crude death rates per 1,000,000 per annum from influenza were 2,617 for males and 1,825 for females in 1919 in Australia; the deaths from influenza were about one quarter for males and one fifth for females of the expected deaths from all causes under nonepidemic conditions.

10.10 Influenza in North America

In Canada statistics were not available for all provinces, but from the data of Low (1920a) the death rates can be computed for some provinces as follows: Ontario 3.77 and Saskatchewan 4.03 per 1,000.

Low (19920a, p. 280) writes of epidemics among the Eskimos: "From Sandwich Bay it was reported that 20 per cent of the population had died during the epidemic. At Hebron, the most northern of the Labrador villages, with a population of 220, only 70 survived, and at Okak, 50 miles south of Hebron, of 266 inhabitants, there were only 59 left, all the deaths being due to influenza and its complications."

In the United States, according to Low (1920a), fevers, probably influenza, were noted in February and March 1918 at a military camp at Fort Oglethorpe, Georgia, and in April and May 1918 in Norfolk and Louisiana; mortality was low. There was much speculation in the medical literature at the time whether the epidemic in the United States had originated there or abroad. The table of Low (1920a, p. 286), indicates that the first number of deaths from pneumonia, which was clearly above what was to be expected from past experience, occurred on September 14 for Boston, September 21 for New York, September 28 for Washington, DC, Philadelphia, and Chicago, October 5 for Los Angeles and Baltimore, October 12 for Kansas City, MO, and October 19 for Cleveland. Also (Low, 1920a, p. 287), there is a curious distribution of mortality by size of city, with cities of more than half a million having a mortality rate of 4 per 1,000 and those of less than 50,000 having rates of about 5.5 per 1,000; in the middle-sized cities, from

75,000 to 375,000, the rates were rather lower. Possibly this gradation is downward from the big cities, and the persons really at risk in the smaller cities include also the surrounding countryside.

In New York State for 1918, the death rate certified as due to influenza was 2.497; the death rate from all pneumonia was 3.281 per 1,000; probably, only the excess above the base level (i.e., from earlier years) for pneumonia should be added in, say 1.500, and then the rate would come to about 4 per 1,000. See Jordan (1927) and Crosby (1976) for the pandemic of 1918 and Dauer and Serfling (1961) for the pandemics of 1957–1958 and 1959–1960. See also Sydenstricker (1918, 1921) and Frost (1920).

There were 6,270 deaths from influenza in the 304,854-strong American Indian population between October 1, 1918, and March 31, 1919, an influenza death rate of 20.6 per 1,000, much higher than the death rates of the Europeans.

In Mexico deaths from influenza were estimated at 432,000 or even half a million. The highest mortality occurred in Michoacon with 48 deaths and the lowest in Colima with 11.6 deaths per 1,000.

10.11 Influenza in the Developing World

There is good reason to believe that the case fatality and the (population) mortality rates could be much higher in the developing world than in Europe, the United States, Canada, and Australia.

According to James (1920), 1% of the population of Swaziland and 4%–5% of the population of Bechuanaland had died of influenza in 1918. In South Africa 8 per 1,000 of the European and 27 per 1,000 of the non-European populations died from influenza in 1918. Among native miners, mortality was particularly high at about 97 per 1,000. Of other African states or colonies, the influenza mortality was 56 per 1,000 in Gambia, about 25 per 1,000 in Somaliland, and it appears that mortality rates were much higher than those in Europe.

St. Helena escaped the pandemic of 1918.

Also, Mauritius escaped it, but in 1919 there were 12,085 deaths from all causes against an expected number of about 2,500 in the period May 1 to October 31, so there were about 9,500 deaths from influenza in a population of 0.36 million, a mortality rate of close to 2.5%.

In Fiji the influenza death rates were Europeans 14, half-castes 28, Indians 42, Fijians 57, and others 69 per 1,000.

In the South Pacific islands, there were high death rates in those island groups subject to New Zealand authority, apparently because there was traffic between them and New Zealand and also because of the trans-Pacific passenger lines. The island groups subject to Australia, the Gilbert and Ellice Islands, New Hebrides, Norfolk Island, Solomon Islands, British and German New Guinea, and New Caledonia, entirely escaped infection. "This group of islands entirely escaped influenza infection, a result which is ascribed by the French Authorities and by the local British Administration to the strict outward quarantine precautions which were taken by the Australian Quarantine Service in respect of all vessels leaving Australia for these island groups" (James, 1920, p. 361).

Jordan (1927) estimates the deaths in the pandemic, which we have rounded and give as thousands, as follows: North and Central America 1,076; Latin America 327; Europe 2,163; Asia 15,757; Australia, Netherlands East Indies, and Oceania 965; Africa and Madagascar 1,354; a total of 21,642 thousands or 21.642 million deaths, which corresponds roughly to the result obtained by assuming a mortality rate of about 10 per 1,000 world inhabitants.

10.12 Myths of Influenza

The influenza pandemic of 1918–1919 caused such a shock to the civilized world that many myths have arisen.

Influenza and War Deaths

It is often stated that the number of deaths from influenza in 1918 exceeded the number of deaths caused by the war of 1914–1918. This can only be considered so if deaths from the whole world at all ages are counted against deaths in the armed forces of Europe. Such a comparison is almost meaningless.

War as a Cause of the Influenza Pandemic

Various theories have been formulated to explain the 1918–1919 pandemic by the conditions of the European populations at the end of 4 years of war. Certainly great epidemics of typhus, relapsing fever and malaria, and of less lethal diseases, such as trench fever, were favored by the conditions, but influenza needed a new strain as has been explained in §5.13.

Periodicity of Influenza

It is often stated that the pandemics of influenza may show periodicity. Measles, under certain demographic conditions in great cities such as London, does have a periodicity, but it appears that influenza is more infective than measles and such a balance is unknown for it. If it is accepted that a pandemic of influenza is due to a newly formed type of virus, there may be only a finite number of possible and probable types. Let us suppose that these types are of forms, A, B, C, . . . and that each causes an immunity to further attack within the lifetime of survivors from a pandemic so that successive pandemics will be due to types A, B, C, . . . in that order. Any particular type, for instance, A, will not be able to cause a second pandemic for probably 30 to 40 years because the proportion of immunes will be high, preventing spread within the population; with the dying out of the survivors after this time, the proportion of immunes will fall, making the passage of a similar strain easier. On the other hand, the mechanism that produces the strain has a low probability of doing so in any one year, and so the period will be 30 to 40 years plus some waiting time. But a second strain, B, will be able to follow A at any time and then it will be free to recur after a further 30 to 40 years, and so on. Perhaps this reasoning is consistent with the observations cited in Kilbourne (1975a) in which the strain of 1957 resembled that of 1889 and the strain of 1968 resembled that of 1900.

Endemicity

There is no evidence for a strain of influenza virus to be endemic in one community.

Hemophilus Influenzae

This is not a causal organism for influenza; moreover, its frequency does not seem to vary with epidemics (see Kilbourne, 1975a, p. 402).

Possible Future Epidemiology

See McKenzie (1980) and Dowdle and LaPatra (1983).

Chapter 11
Viral Diseases Accompanied by Exanthem

11.1 Smallpox or Variola

ICD 050. Fourth digit: 0, *Variola major*, all forms; 1, *Alastrim, Variola minor*; 2, modified; 9, unspecified.

Smallpox, or variola, was a disease caused by *Poxvirus variolae*; it is now extinct. See Fenner, Henderson, et al. (1988) and Baxby (1984). Spread was usually by inhalation from particles of epithelium from the mouth and pharynx during the first week of the disease and rarely from scab material later. Infection was also possible from material such as clothes contaminated by the patient. Deliberate infection, variolation, was often carried out in the times before vaccination, sometimes by inoculation and other times by inhalation of dried crusts from the vesicles. The incubation period was usually 12 days with a range of 9 to 15 days. The infectious period began at the onset of fever and was maximal about 4 days later. See the figures in Dixon (1962, pp. 297–299) for graphical displays of these properties, and Behbehani (1983) for a history of the disease up to its eradication.

Classical smallpox, *Variola major*, was a disease with very severe toxemic symptoms and a characteristic skin rash; it had a case fatality rate of perhaps 30% in an unvaccinated population. The case fatality was especially high in young children, pregnant women, and elderly adults. A variant of the disease, with a case fatality rate of less than 0.6%, *Variola minor* or *Alastrim*, appeared in the United States in 1896 and was dominant there from about 1900 until the elimination of endemic smallpox in the early 1940s. This variant caused endemic disease in the United Kingdom, between 1920 and 1934, and was the only form of smallpox in parts of Africa (Ethiopia and Somalia) in the 1970s, during the process of eradication.

Montezambert (1901) had reported a widespread epidemic in the United States and Canada in 1900–1901 with a case fatality of 0.13%, that is, 157 deaths in 11,964 cases. Korte (1904) reported an epidemic in South Africa in the same year. It is evident that this or other variants have occurred on many occasions. For example, Edward Jenner in 1772 noted an epidemic of what he termed swine pox and local practitioners recognized as a distinct entity with mild symptoms and low case fatality. *Variola minor* was observed in England in 1928 and in the Annual Report of the Ministry of Health for 1929 was so named, according to Dixon (1962). Smallpox is now believed to possess a wide spectrum of clinical severities (Baxby, 1984).

Marsden (1948) summarized the experience over 1928 and later years; out of 13,686 cases observed, only 34 patients died, with a case fatality rate of 0.25%; of those dying, the *Variola minor* attack was considered to be only a contributing cause of death in 13 cases. Topley and Wilson (1975) give case fatality rates as 10% to 30% for the major disease and 0.1% to 0.3% for the minor disease.

11.2 Smallpox as a Great Pestilence

Smallpox could not have existed as a peculiarly human disease before the establishment of large human populations, as mentioned in §5.2. For detailed historical remarks, the reader is referred to the monograph by Fenner, Henderson, et al. (1988). Smallpox may have been present in Egypt in 1160 BC, for Rameses V is thought to have died of it. Ko Hung, in China, gave an accurate description of smallpox in AD 340. After the discussion of Littman and Littman (1969), it is reasonable to believe that the Plague of Athens in 430 BC described by Thucydides was indeed smallpox. Further, the great pestilence of many years duration, known as the Antonine Plague was, at least in great part, smallpox, according to Littman and Littman (1973), who have examined Galen's description in detail. See also Longrigg (1980) and Langmuir, Worthen, et al. (1985).

Smallpox is believed to have caused a great number of deaths in the early campaigns during the expansion of Islam from AD 622 onward. An accurate description of the disease was given by Rhazes in Baghdad about AD 900. There is still some doubt as to when smallpox was first epidemic in England and Wales, but it is known that Queen Elizabeth almost died of it in 1562, and there are numerous references to the disease in later times; Queen Mary died of smallpox in 1694 and her nephew, the Duke of Gloucester, in 1700. It was introduced into the Americas in 1507 and caused great epidemics and mortality among the various native peoples. The origins of the first two outbreaks of smallpox (1789 and 1829–1831) in Australia are uncertain, according to Fenner (1984), who notes that the only observers who kept records were, of course, colonists; but there is some evidence that all three outbreaks (1789, 1829, and 1867) were introduced across the northern coastline from infections in the Dutch East Indies.

In England and other European countries, smallpox remained endemic in the large cities for long periods, but epidemic outbreaks occurred in towns and villages, often after importation through the ports.

Smallpox was the first disease whose course was altered by what we would now call an immunologic method, namely, the provocation of a solid immunity by inoculation and vaccination. Inoculation, or the artificial infection of persons by means of injection of the matter from pustules of active sufferers from the disease, was by incision or scarification and the use of impregnated thread, an ivory point, or pustule fluid. Dixon (1962) believes that no community had carried out a systematic inoculation campaign as a preventive measure before those in England and America after 1720. That work may be consulted for many further details, as also Blake (1953, 1959) for a readable account of the problems of mass inoculation in the city of Boston, Massachusetts. Drake (1965) cites an interesting instance from Norway in 1772, where a country minister (parson) from the bishopric of Bergen had inoculated 562 persons, of whom 4 had died, while in neighboring parishes, during the same period, 326 persons who had not been inoculated caught smallpox and of these 87 died. The practice was not common elsewhere in Norway.

The value of inoculation in the control of the disease in the eighteenth century is difficult to assess. The case fatality and scarring was less in the disease acquired by inoculation than in the disease naturally acquired, but such cases could give rise to severe smallpox in susceptible contacts. It was possibly only in persons especially at risk that the discomforts and risks of inoculation were less than those of the natural disease; such classes included the aristocratic and commercial classes prone to travel, the army, and populations submitted to a high risk during the course of an epidemic; and we add that the custom of inoculating the slave girls, later to be introduced into the Turkish harems or brothels, at the time of their minimum economic importance was the inspiration for the introduction of the practice into Europe.

The second method, vaccination, was to prove far more practicable and more free from therapeutic accidents than inoculation. In 1796 Edward Jenner injected cowpox material from

TABLE 11.2.1. Deaths in London from smallpox.

Year	0	1	2	3	4	5	6	7	8	9
162–										72
163–	40	58	531	72	1,354	293	127			
164–								139	400	1,190
165–	184	525	1,279	139	812	1,294	823	835	409	1,523
166–	354	1,246	768	411	1,233	655	38	1,196	1,987	951
167–	1,465	696	1,116	853	2,507	997	359	1,678	1,798	1,967
168–	689	2,982	1,408	2,096	1,560	2,496	1,062	1,551*	1,318	1,389
169–	778	1,241	1,592	1,164	1,683	784	196	634	1,813	890
170–	1,031	1,095	311	898	1,501	1,095	721	1,078	1,687	1,024
171–	3,138	915	1,943	1,614	2,810	1,057	2,427	2,211	1,884	3,229
172–	1,440	2,375	2,167	3,271	1,227	3,188	1,519	2,379	2,105	2,849
173–	1,914	2,640	1,197	1,370	2,688	1,594	3,014	2,084	1,590	1,690
174–	2,725	1,977	1,429	2,029	1,633	1,206	3,236	1,380	1,789	2,625
175–	1,229	998	3,538	774	2,359	1,988	1,608	3,296	1,273	2,596
176–	2,187	1,525	2,743	3,582	2,382	2,498	2,334	2,188	3,028	1,968
177–	1,986	1,660	3,992	1,039	2,479	2,669	1,728	2,567	1,425	2,493
178–	871	3,500	636	1,550	1,759	1,999	1,210	2,418	1,101	2,077
179–	1,617	1,747	1,568	2,382	1,913	1,040	3,548	522	2,337	1,111
180–	2,409	1,461	1,579	1,202	622	1,685	1,158	1,297	1,169	1,163
181–	1,198	751	1,287	898	638	725	653	1,051	421	712
182–	792	508	604	774	725	1,299	503	616	598	736
183–	627	563								521
184–		1,053	360	438	1,804	909	257	955	1,620	1,158
185–	499	1,062	1,159	211	694	1,039	531	156	242	275
186–	898	217	366	1,996	547	640	1,391	1,345	597	450
187–	973	7,912	1,786	113	57	46	736	2,551	1,417	
188–	475	2,371								

*For the years 1687–1700, inclusive, measles deaths are included with the deaths from smallpox.
Data from Guy (1882a).

a sore on the hand of a milkmaid into a boy, the process now known as vaccination. Seven weeks later he inoculated the boy with smallpox material and no disease followed. By 1799 vaccinations were being carried out in Hanover and Vienna and the procedure became common or at least practised in many parts of the world.

With the theory of the previous section and other modern findings in view, we can attempt to assess the importance of smallpox for mortality in the past few centuries, at least. There are long series available from England and Wales and from the Scandinavian countries. It is convenient to treat the former series first and then to pass on to the Swedish series. It must be noted that smallpox has never become as universal as measles.

We may consider the history of smallpox in London with the aid of Table 11.2.1, which is a table of Guy (1882a), modified. Guy (1882a) concluded that no smallpox epidemic in the nineteenth century caused more than 10% of the deaths from all causes; there were greater smallpox epidemics in the eighteenth century than in the seventeenth; some of the most severe smallpox epidemics occurred late in the century, causing 16.9% of all deaths in 1781 and 18.4% in 1796; the lowest recorded proportion of smallpox to all deaths was 0.3% in 1666, following the great plague of 1665; epidemics, defined as causing more than 10% of all deaths in a year, had frequencies per year of 0.32 in the eighteenth century and 0.20 in the seventeenth century; epidemic outbreaks occurred in several years running only during the eighteenth century.

An inspection of Table 11.2.1 further shows that about 3% of all deaths in London in the years 1629 to 1800 were due to smallpox. If the

Table 11.2.2. Mortality from smallpox in England and Wales. (deaths per 1,000,000 per annum).

Epoch	0–4	5–9	10–14	15–19	20–24	25–34	35–44	45–54	55–64	65–74	75 and over
					Males						
1861–1870	642	150	57	92	181	137	98	68	48	38	30
1871–1880	529	302	136	207	379	301	212	145	86	61	48
1881–1890	82	35	25	43	70	72	60	44	28	26	30
1891–1900	29	10	3	6	12	19	24	20	15	18	12
1901–1910	21	8	6	7	11	16	25	27	18	17	17
1911–1920	0	1	0	0	0	1	0	1	1	0	—
1921–1930	2	0*	0	0	0	0	0	1	1	3	7
					Females						
1861–1870	634	140	56	80	95	70	50	32	25	16	16
1871–1880	508	268	139	190	231	184	128	81	58	34	26
1881–1890	77	31	27	40	49	43	29	22	14	10	12
1891–1900	30	9	3	5	10	13	12	7	5	4	5
1901–1910	24	7	6	6	7	10	12	8	6	7	4
1911–1920	1	0	—	0	0	0	1	1	0	0	—
1921–1930	2	0	1	0	0	0	0	0	0	1	1

*Rates based on less than 20 deaths are distinguished by underlining.
From the Registrar-General's Decennial Supplement (1952, Part 3, Table 12).

case fatality rate is supposed to be $y\%$, then $3 \times 100 \times y^{-1}\%$ of persons dying would have suffered a smallpox attack. With case fatalities assumed to be 30%, 20% 10%, and 5%, the proportions of persons contracting the disease during their lifetime would have been 10% 15%, 30%, and 60%, respectively. However, the realistic case fatality rate would have been 30%, in which case only 10% would have contracted the disease.

We give as Table 11.2.2 the death rates from smallpox in England and Wales over the years around the end of the series of Guy (1882a).

The statistics of Tables 11.2.1 and 11.2.2 should be read in conjunction with some historical notes. The Vaccination Act was passed in England in 1840 to "extend the practice of vaccination" by empowering local authorities to contract with registered medical practitioners to perform vaccination without charge to the patient. A second Vaccination Act in 1853 made it compulsory to vaccinate infants within 3 months of birth. Dixon (1962, Figure 226) shows that approximately 75% of infants in England were vaccinated in the period 1880 to 1910. Morbidity and some slight mortality are associated with vaccination, and the degree of protection is not absolute and tends to fall some years after vaccination. The use of calf lymph in place of arm-to-arm vaccination was effective in reducing infections with other organisms, including syphilis, and was made compulsory in the 1898 Vaccination Act in England.

Razzell (1977) believes that the incidence of smallpox and the number of deaths from smallpox were greater in England, generally, than are suggested by Table 11.2.1 for the period before 1730. He believes also that there was an increase in the case fatality of the disease between 1574 and 1730, with peaks in 1670–1690 and 1710–1730. In a survey of cities and parishes, it appears that in some years the deaths from smallpox could form up to 31% of the total deaths. In another table, he finds that the deaths from smallpox reached 15% to 20% of the number of deaths. He also finds that in the period 1778 to 1798, there were sometimes over 50% of the persons in the town inoculated.

The percentages of deaths due to smallpox to all deaths were much higher in Sweden than in London during the latter half of the eighteenth century. These percentages are given in

TABLE 11.2.3. Sweden: Deaths from smallpox and from combined typhus and typhoid fever. Proportions of the same with respect to total deaths. Vaccinations.

Years	N of deaths from smallpox	% of Total deaths	N of vaccinated	% of Vaccinated to children born alive	N of Deaths from typhus and typhoid fever	% of Last column to total deaths
1751–1755	35,415	14.76	—	—	16,495	6.87
1756–1760	32,681	12.37	—	—	26,140	9.89
1761–1765	36,041	12.81	—	—	32,587	11.59
1766–1770	34,361	13.02	—	—	23,685	8.98
1771–1775	25,267	7.59	—	—	48,833	14.68
1776–1780	28,529	11.11	—	—	21,487	8.36
1781–1785	25,412	8.55	—	—	27,926	9.39
1786–1790	20,561	6.89	—	—	44,981	15.07
1791–1795	17,847	6.37	—	—	26,504	9.46
1796–1800	23,381	7.83	—	—	23,513	7.88
1801–1805	11,604	3.99	47,258	13	30,376	10.47
1806–1810	8,653	2.28	93,595	25	58,135	15.32
1811–1815	2.429	0.74	175,632	44	32,629	9.97
1816–1820	1,541	0.49	289,797	70	29,825	9.57
1821–1825	1,948	0.66	345,114	74	23,025	7.82
1826–1830	1,639	0.46	314,860	68	39,629	11.14
1831–1835	3,873	1.14	340,721	73	—	—
1836–1840	4,888	1.41	353,792	77	—	—
1841–1845	316	0.09	363,286	74	—	—
1846–1850	1,803	0.51	413,445	79	—	—
1851–1855	4,546	1.18	457,656	81	—	—

Reprinted from Table Z of Hendriks (1862).

Table 11.2.3. Before 1800, the percentages were all high by London standards but were tending to fall. We note that during 1751–1775, there were 163,765 deaths from smallpox and 1,382,108 deaths from all causes, so 11.84% of all deaths were due to smallpox. During 1776–1800, the numbers were 115,730 and 1,431,425, respectively, and the smallpox deaths constituted 8.08% of all deaths.

In Sweden, Norway, and England, the proportions of deaths due to smallpox fell around the year 1800, and some critics have believed that vaccination was already having an effect. From the statistics of vaccinations, this seems unlikely. McKeown and Record (1962) postulate a change in virulence of the virus, which is a plausible but unprovable hypothesis.

In other countries, vigorous campaigns were also carried out, hampered in the early years of the nineteenth century by the shortage of trained medical personnel. Drake (1965) gives a table of vaccinations for Norway for the years 1802–1810 and then for the next 5 decades as 16%, 31%, 48%, 58%, 75%, and 82%, respectively, of live births; at the end of this period about 80% of children were vaccinated in infancy. Yet, the cover was irregular, so that smallpox could be perpetuated in Norway. It is reported that smallpox deaths occurred in every year up to 1915, but of course there is no proof that it was not reintroduced from abroad.

It may be remarked that in the western European countries and in North America, the death rates from smallpox declined, but severe epidemics could occur in disturbed times (see Prinzing, 1916, for examples); by 1900 smallpox was a minor problem in these countries. Throughout the world, it was declining, and by the end of World War II, hygienists were be-

TABLE 11.2.4. The eradication of smallpox (number of cases per year).

	1939	1955	1965	1966	1967	1968	1969	1970	1971	1972	1973	1974	1975	1976	1977–1979
Africa															
Benin	58	16	168	490	815	367	58	—	—	—	—	—	—	—	—
Botswana	3	—	—	—	1	—	—	—	36	1,059	27	—	—	—	—
Ethiopia	201	2,662	124	358	466	426	197	722	26,329	16,999	5,414	4,439	3,935	915	—
Uganda	—	101	1,351	614	365	55	9	2	19	16	—	—	—	—	—
America															
Brazil	86	2,580	3,417	3,623	4,514	4,372	7,407	1,771	19	—	—	—	—	—	—
Asia															
Afghanistan	...	1,411	72	66	334	739	250	1,044	736	236	25	—	—	—	—
Bangladesh	...	1,926	316	3,207	6,648	9,039	1,925	1,473	—	10,754	32,711	16,485	13,798	—	—
India	133,616	41,837	33,402	32,616	84,902	35,179	19,281	12,773	16,190	27,407	88,114	188,003	1,436	—	—
Nepal	...	....	70	164	110	249	163	76	215	399	277	1,549	95	—	—
Pakistan	...	3,330	1,285	2,936	6,084	1,836	3,520	3,192	5,808	7,053	9,258	7,859	—	—	—

... Not available.

— No cases.

Data from *The Global Eradication of Smallpox, Final Report of the Global Commission for the Certification of Smallpox Eradication,* WHO, Geneva, 1980.

ginning to see the possibility of its eradication. See Fabre (1947–1948).

In general, it may be concluded that in the developed countries a policy of almost universal vaccination and the isolation of cases with vaccination of possible contacts and quarantine policies had been successful in clearing smallpox from many countries. Twenty-eight countries were considered endemic areas of smallpox in 1945, and 14 in 1970. There were remarkable declines between 1962 and 1970 in the number of smallpox cases.

In 1966, WHO resolved to eradicate smallpox from the world. That hope has now been realized. In Table 11.2.4 the deaths are listed for some of the countries reporting cases after 1955; there are still seven countries listed in 1973 with deaths, but after 1976 all countries were free of the disease. Progress was reported in *WHO Chronicle* at Vol. 29 (1975) 134–139, Vol. 30 (1976) 152–157, and Vol. 31 (1977) 4–8; in the first, smallpox persisted only in India, Bangladesh, and Ethiopia; in the second, it was noted that smallpox had been eradicated from Asia; in the third, a photograph of a boy from Bangladesh, the last known case of *Variola major* in the world, was given. It was reported that 22 cases of a disease similar to *Variola minor* had been reported during September and October 1976 from Somalia, and it was believed to be the sole remaining country with smallpox cases. Details of the global eradication campaign are available in the *Final Report of the Global Commission for the Certification of Smallpox Eradication* (WHO-smallpox, 1980), Fenner (1980, 1984), Fenner, Henderson, et al. (1988), and for India, in Basu, Jezek, and Ward (1979).

It became the general opinion of such observers as Downie (1965) and the members of the WHO Smallpox Eradication Unit that smallpox is less contagious than measles or chickenpox. Further, it has an incubation period of 12 days and low infectivity during the preeruptive stage. Therefore, it is a slowly spreading disease, spread by those who have not been vaccinated; so, it is carried from hut to hut by unvaccinated school-age children. Since few areas or villages are affected at one time and a case rarely infects more than five further

cases, isolation of cases and vaccination of neighborhood children are practicable. These methods were found to be superior to the older aim of obtaining universal vaccination, pursued by national health authorities.

Murray (1951) and WHO-smallpox (1953, 1955, 1975) have given figures for world incidence of smallpox in its last few years. Namfua, Kim, and Mosley (1978) give estimates of the gains in expectation of life in developing countries. Sweitzer and Ikeda (1927) describe a sharp epidemic in Minneapolis in 1924–1925. Hopkins (1983a) gives much historical detail, including accounts of the disastrous Amerindian epidemics (see §43.3).

11.3 Cowpox and Paravaccinia

ICD 051. Fourth digit: 0, cowpox (generalized vaccinia from vaccination goes to 999.0); 1, pseudocowpox; 2, contagious pustular dermatitis, orf; 9, unspecified paravaccinia.

Poxvirus variolae is closely related to the vaccine (*P. officinale*), cowpox (*P. bovis*), and ectromelia (*P. muris*) viruses. *P. officinale* is possibly originally derived from *P. bovis*, although Baxby (1981, p. 192) believes that it may be derived from horsepox or perhaps some strain from another animal. See also Baxby (1979, 1984).

Vaccination against smallpox was not entirely without risk, although such complications as sepsis, tetanus, and syphilis could be avoided under modern aseptic conditions. The most lethal complication of vaccination was progressive vaccinia (*vaccinia necrosum*) that occurred in persons with disorders of cellular immunity. Generalized vaccinia usually occurred in immunologically normal individuals and was rarely fatal. *Eczema vaccinatum* was an important complication, mainly because it occurred in children infected by contact with a vaccine.

Since complications are less frequent and also less lethal in young children, it has become customary to classify the remaining lesions into encephalopathy at ages younger than 2 years and encephalomyelitis at ages older than 2 years. Fenner, Henderson, et al. (1988, Table 7.8) show that in surveys conducted over the years 1924–1968, there were about 20 cases of encephalopathy per 1,000,000 vaccinations at ages younger than 2 years, with some variation between surveys. At ages older than 2 years, the rates of encephalomyelitis were around 250 per 1,000,000 vaccinations, with quite large differences between surveys. Their survey overlaps with that of Wilson (1967, Tables 5 and 6). His Table 5 shows a clear increase with age in the case rates per 1,000,000 vaccinated, for example, 68, 154, 1313 at ages 2–3, 4–5, 6–11 in Düsseldorf, 1948, and 140, 275, and 1055 in Holland, 1930–1943 at corresponding ages. As the case fatality of encephalomyelitis is approximately 30%, it follows that the mortality associated with vaccination, for persons over the age of 2 years, was approximately 75 per 1,000,000, not a negligible figure for a merely prophylactic treatment.

11.4 Chickenpox and Herpes Zoster

ICD 052 and 053. Inclusions: diseases due to *Herpesvirus varicellae*, chickenpox, varicella, herpes zoster.

Chickenpox (varicella) and herpes zoster are different forms of the same disease due to *Herpesvirus varicellae*.

Varicella is a common fever with rash, having an incubation period of 15 to 18 days. An attack is followed usually by a solid immunity. Although the disease causes little mortality in previously healthy subjects, it may be a dangerous disease to the young, the very old, and those in a state of ill health or malnutrition; thus, in a virgin soil epidemic from central Africa, Millous (1936) reported a case fatality rate of 19%.

Herpes zoster is now known to be a late complication of varicella. The credit for the first complete and well-argued case for the identity of the two diseases goes to Garland (1943), according to the authoritative review of Gordon (1962); see also Hope-Simpson (1954), Gold and Nankervis (1973), and §5.3 for a treatment of the varicella–herpes-zoster problem of perpetuation of a virus infection.

In some cases of apparent recovery from varicella, particles of the virus lie dormant in the cells of the dorsal root ganglia of the spinal nerves; many years later they may become acti-vated and multiply, the infective agents passing down along the nerve sheath and appearing in vesicles, some similar to those of varicella, in the distribution of some spinal nerve. This is herpes zoster. The matter in the vesicles is infective and the cycle may begin again in a new subject. For reviews of the virus and the diseases, see Roizman (1982–1985), Watson (1984), and Weller (1982).

11.5 Herpes Simplex

ICD 054. Exclusion: congenital herpes simplex, 771.2. This is not a frequent cause of mortality.

Herpesvirus hominis is a common infection of man (Rawls, 1973; Kaplan, 1973; and Rapp and Jerkovsky, 1973). It has the capacity to lie dormant in the tissues for long periods of time. There are two serotypes. The first causes minor disease such as "cold sore" in the lip in adults but can be fatal to infants. The second type can be transmitted as a venereal disease and may be the cause of some cervical cancers. See Figueroa and Rapp (1980) and Watson (1984). For genital herpes, see Becker and Nahmias (1985).

11.6 Measles

ICD 055. Inclusion: morbilli, roseola, rubeola, measles.

The virus of measles belongs to the family *Paramyxoviridae*; its nearest relatives among the animal viruses are those of canine distemper and rinderpest, all three belonging to the genus *Morbillivirus*. See Fraser and Martin (1978) and Sellers (1984c). Because of the difficulties of perpetuation in the small human populations before the development of the great agricultural and riverine civilizations, it is believed, on grounds brought forward in §5.13, that the human virus has evolved from a virus enzootic in some nonhuman vertebrate species (see Gastel, 1973). The measles virus seems to have a single antigenic type. Measles is endemic throughout the world in the great centers of population; or, rather, the disease has long been pandemic. The time of its appearance as a human disease is unknown, although there is a description of it by Rhazes (ca 860–932), who believed the disease had been described in AD 68. Sellers (1984c) says that it was known in the first century BC. There is no clear evidence of measles in the English experience before approximately AD 1500, although T. Sydenham (1624–1689) gave a precise account of the disease in 1675. Wilson (1962) points out that after 1629, measles and smallpox were listed separately in the London Bills of Mortality, but rubella and the more important scarlatina were only differentiated consistently from the end of the nineteenth century.

The clinical features of measles are as follows. The incubation period is 10–14 days, and there is an infective period of a few days at the onset of symptoms; there is no carrier state. A solid immunity follows an attack of the disease, lasting for 65 years in some cases, according to Panum (1847); second attacks are rare. There is a high attack rate, that is, a high proportion of susceptibles exposed to the infection, show overt signs of the disease, especially in virgin soil type of epidemics in the Arctic region, on islands, and in isolated areas (see Christensen, et al., 1953, Peart and Nagler, 1954, and also §5.4).

Complications of the disease are: otitis media; bronchopneumonia (giant cell pneumonia); postinfectional encephalitis at a rate of from 1 in 1,000 to 1 in 400; subacute sclerosing panencephalitis (about 1 case per 1,000,000 of population per annum in England and Wales) (Kimberlin, 1984); multiple sclerosis with a low rate per measles infection case (Black, 1982); and enteritis, under unfavorable conditions of nutrition. For a general review of associated diseases, see Morgan and Rapp (1977). Deaths are now uncommon under normal conditions in the developed world, where they are due to the respiratory and neurological causes. In the experience in the great urban masses of Europe, the maximum case fatality tends to occur in the last 6 months of infancy. In the nineteenth century the case fatality rate of measles in England and Wales would have been approximately 2%. This comes as a surprise to modern clinicians, but under unfavorable conditions in the underdeveloped world,

far higher case fatality rates have been reported in the recent past and measles is often a leading cause of mortality, as we shall see in the next section. See also §37.3. For the spread of measles within the family, see E.B. Wilson (1947) and Wilson, Bennett, et al. (1939).

Treatment is supportive and for complications arising. A live vaccine against measles is now available and has been used extensively in the United States, sometimes combined with rubella vaccine.

11.7 Measles as a Great Pestilence

This heading will come as a surprise to many observers in the developed world, in which the status of measles has sunk during this century to a mere nuisance, whereas, even in the nineteenth century, measles caused many deaths in England and Wales, Scotland, the European states, and in their extensions overseas, such as Australia. There appears to be no good evidence that the virus is less virulent than formerly or that the genetic abilities of the populations to resist it have risen.

As a representative of measles mortality in a great city, the deaths in London given in Table 11.7.1 may be considered. From 1629 to 1879, the figures are taken from Guy (1882a). In 1629 London was a city of 130,000, approximately. Years of high mortality tended to be followed by a year of low mortality, for example, in 1670–1675 the deaths were 295, 7, 118, 15, 795, 1; but this regular alternation is not a constant feature of Guy's table. The picture will be confused if an epidemic begins in the last quarter of the calendar year; to avoid this difficulty Stocks, (1942) began his year on October 1. So 1936 begins October 1, 1935, and runs through to September 30, 1936. With this convention, Stocks (1942) states that in the period 1921–1940, "epidemics never commenced later than the first quarter and such an event has been of rare occurrence throughout the present century." In Table 11.7.2, the convention given above is used. The alternation of years in the table of Stocks (1942) is regular with the single exception of the two consecutive high years in 1917 and 1918. Before and including 1917, the deaths are high in the odd

TABLE 11.7.1. Deaths in London from measles, 1629–1939.

Year	0	1	2	3	4	5	6	7	8	9
162–										42
163–	2	3	80	21	33	27	12			
164–								5	92	3
165–	33	33	62	8	52	11	153	15	80	6
166–	74	188	20	42	311	7	3	83	200	15
167–	295	7	118	15	795	1	83	87	93	117
168–	49	121	50	39	6	197	25	*		
169–										
170–		4	27	51	12	319	361	37	126	89
171–	181	97	77	61	139	30	270	35	492	243
172–	213	238	114	231	118	70	256	72	82	41
173–	311	102	30	605	20	10	169	127	216	326
174–	46	42	981	17	5	14	250	81	10	106
175–	321	21	111	253	12	423	156	24	696	316
176–	175	394	122	610	65	54	482	80	409	90
177–	325	115	211	199	121	283	153	145	388	99
178–	272	201	170	185	29	20	793	84	55	534
179–	119	156	450	248	172	328	307	222	196	223
180–	395	136	559	438	619	523	530	452	1,386	106
181–	1,031	235	427	550	817	711	1,106	725	728	695
182–	720	547	712	573	966	743	774	525	736	578
183–	479	750								
184–		973	1,293	1,442	1,182	2,318	747	1,778	1,144	1,154
185–	980	1,297	595	978	1,409	878	1,479	1,341	2,369	1,330
186–	2,090	1,062	2,334	1,634	2,788	1,290	2,220	1,143	1,962	1,456
187–	1,449	1,427	1,680	2,149	1,680	1,408	1,720	2,387	1,500	2,475
188–	1,501	2,533								
189–										
190–										
191–		3,274†	1,151	2,306	958	2,676	712	1,819	1,935	303
192–	1,113	157	1,656	154	1,539	117	1,170	53	1,480	112
193–	1,113	56	885	62	906	10	596	15	245	2

*For the years 1687–1700, inclusive, measles deaths are included with deaths from smallpox (see Table 11.2.1).
†Period October 1910 to September 1911, and so on with the succeeding years.
  Data from Guy (1882a) and Stocks (1942).

years, and from 1918 onward, the deaths are high in the even years. In Birmingham's experience deaths were high in the odd years throughout. In Liverpool, Manchester, Leeds, and New York, similar tendencies towards alternation are evident but there is less regularity. Less regularity appears in the experience of Glasgow in Table 37.3.1.

The explanation of this alternation appears to be as follows. In a large city in which measles is endemic, perhaps 90% of the population over the age of 5 years has already been attacked by measles and thus plays no part in the epidemic process except to dampen down the rate of transfer of the infection between persons. The susceptibles consist almost entirely of infants and children of ages 1 to 4 years, the toddlers. It will be principally the toddlers who transmit the infection, for they are mobile and often still susceptible. In an epidemic year, the susceptible toddlers will be infected and will transmit the disease to other toddlers and to the infants. This process goes on until the proportion of susceptibles among the toddlers falls so greatly that one case on an average infects less than one susceptible. The weekly number of cases declines, there is reduced probability that infants will be infected, and in the second year there are few cases. However, births are occurring and infants pass through infancy, becoming toddlers in the third year, so the weekly numbers can again in-

TABLE 11.7.2. Measles in England.

Period Oct.–Sept.	London A.C. (deaths)	Birmingham (deaths)	Liverpool (deaths)	Manchester (deaths)	Leeds (deaths)	Sheffield (deaths)	New York* (cases in hundreds)
1910–1911	3,274	328	359(311)*	376	149	861	255
1911–1912	1,151	124	589(846)*	482	133	30	390
1912–1913	2,306	826	607(319)*	291	138	453	293
1913–1914	958	174	350(521)*	231	151	395	258
1914–1915	2,676	555	440(255)*	492	115	645	382
1915–1916	712	87	236	175	174	216	216
1916–1917	1,819	356	423	315	183	157	275
1917–1918	1,935	47	409	125	493	27	287
1918–1919	303	189	61	106	22	196	82
1919–1920	1,113	81	462	251	183	64	351
1920–1921	157	225	111	2	7	87	77
1921–1922	1,656	62	369	326	25	160	406
1922–1923	154	194	279	107	175	9	140
1923–1924	1,539	71	203	376	41	114	336
1924–1925	117	104	412	56	39	15	95
1925–1926	1,170	62	184	236	12	87	397
1926–1927	53	146	342	18	122	5	21
1927–1928	1,480	32	138	270	15	138	350
1928–1929	112	194	451	29	107	8	25
1929–1930	1,113	25	96	175	1	69	236
1930–1931	56	199	451	18	47	6	265
1931–1932	885	22	287	172	57	44	104
1932–1933	62	110	292	9	7	1	362
1933–1934	906	25	246	133	103	25	50
1934–1935	10	49	78	9	3	11	285
1935–1936	596	35	248	204	50	54	365
1936–1937	15	74	2	8	8	3	121
1937–1938	245	7	224	96	19	26	346
1938–1939	2	17	3	1	3	3	37
1939–1940	5(29)*	2(10)*	31(136)*	19(28)	5(8)*	3(9)*	105

*Calendar year totals, also given (in brackets) for Liverpool in 1911–1915 and all towns in 1940, when epidemics tended to commence in the second or third quarters.

After Stocks (1942, p. 265).

Note: A.C. = administrative countries.

crease. This alternation of years is facilitated also by the seasonal incidence of the disease, the reasons for which are still not understood. It is possible that the periodicity of measles has been overstressed by authors concentrating on the epidemics in London; J. Brownlee (1915) was a great offender. He professed to find different strains of virus with different lengths of cycle. We accept the reality of the 2-year cycle in London, but there are good reasons against accepting a cycle length that is not an integral multiplier of the year; for let the cycle be of length m/n years, where m and n have no common factor, then the month of greatest in-

cidence will have a cycle of the same length and the time of greatest incidence will appear to have the distribution, uniform on the points $[(km + a) \bmod n]/n$. This is contrary to the experience of Stocks (1942), cited above; so, such hypotheses must be rejected.

A good commentary on the mortality from measles in England and Wales is provided by Brincker (1938, Table 1). The male rates tend to be higher than the female. The maximal mortality is at age 1 year. The rates had fallen greatly from the epoch 1851–1860 to the epoch 1931–1935. Brincker (1938) further shows that the London mortality rates are higher than the

TABLE 11.7.3. Measles in England and Wales. Corrected notification and fatality rates by sex and age (civilians), 1946 to 1949.

Ages	1946		1947		1948		1949	
	M	F	M	F	M	F	M	F
	Notifications* per 10,000 living							
0–	94	103	189	201	205	217	199	211
1–	271	264	622	629	629	631	618	612
3–	366	365	880	882	861	872	811	830
5–	218	224	530	532	523	532	480	485
10–	22	24	53	59	39	41	35	39
15–	1	1	3	4	2	2	2	2
All ages	43	36	101	88	99	88	95	84
	Deaths per 10,000 notifications*							
0–	130	125	167	130	64	65	60	55
1–	20	18	32	30	12	13	12	12
3–	6	3	6	6	4	3	2	4
5–	3	2	3	3	2	3	3	3
10–	—	6	1	4	5	9	6	2
15–	32	18	5	21	23	22	26	35
All ages	13	12	17	16	8	8	8	8

* Fully corrected for diagnosis revision.
  From Registrar-General of England and Wales (1950).

New York rates. There is an urban/rural gradient of mortality, the rates for 1922–1930 for London, County Boroughs, other Urban Districts, and Rural Districts being 198, 164, 93, and 48 per 100,000 population, respectively. For each of these latter three categories, there was also a marked gradient from north to south, with rates higher in the north. It can be estimated from his Table 1 that approximately 2% of all children born in London in the epoch 1851–1900 would die of measles before the age of 15 years. These high case fatality rates of young children are unfamiliar to modern observers in the developed countries.

An important feature of measles mortality in the great urban centers is that the maximum incidence is at ages 3 to 4 years and the maximum case fatality rates are at 6 to 11 months, the rates declining into adult life. A maximum mortality rate usually occurs at age 1 year. Table 11.7.3 gives such figures for England and Wales in 1946–1949.

At the other extreme of population density, there will be periods of no infections in island communities and then brief epidemics when measles is introduced from without, which we have already discussed in §5.4. An intermediate situation has existed in the Australasian colonies and states, which is illustrated by Table 11.7.4, with data principally taken from Cumpston (1927). It is clear that Western Australia was not large enough to perpetuate an epidemic. Although there is a tendency for years of high death rates from measles to be followed by low, it would be idle to pretend that there is a tendency toward cycles of regular length in such populations as provided by the colonies or states of Australia. A remarkable feature was the slow spread of the disease from Victoria in 1850 to the other colonies; it reached New South Wales in 1853, Tasmania in 1854, Queensland in 1857, South Australia in 1859, and Western Australia in 1860.

For a world-wide view of the disease, we cite now opinions from the symposium reported in the *American Journal of Diseases of Children*, volume 103. Wilson (1962) notes that after 1629, measles and smallpox were well differ-

TABLE 11.7.4. Deaths from measles in Australasia by state (colony) and year.

Years	N.S.W.	Vic.	Qld.	S.A.	W.A.	Tas.	N.Z.
1860	348	274	—	1	9	—	—
1861	46	252	—	111	48	—	—
1862	4	20	—	104	0	—	—
1863	0	8	—	0	0	—	—
1864	0	7	—	0	0	—	—
1865	1	11	—	0	0	—	—
1866	0	427	—	0	0	—	—
1867	462	630	—	112	0	—	—
1868	1	24	—	17	0	0	—
1869	2	24	—	0	0	0	—
1870	0	3	—	1	0	0	—
1871	0	4	—	0	0	2	—
1872	1	7	—	0	0	1	1
1873	0	1	—	1	0	0	14
1874	62	256	1	280	0	0	55
1875	752	1,541	178	75	0	129	289
1876	35	5	33	5	0	1	2
1877	2	6	1	1	0	2	1
1878	1	5	1	2	0	0	2
1879	3	3	1	1	0	0	1
1880	270	252	0	9	1	0	4
1881	88	62	3	72	0	45	113
1882	10	15	32	11	0	0	86
1883	47	7	59	12	30	0	15
1884	45	233	6	139	95	1	31
1885	10	69	2	6	4	20	1
1886	6	20	1	3	0	1	49
1887	52	78	0	2	0	0	28
1888	218	30	3	1	0	0	5
1889	13	19	0	1	0	0	2
1890	7	1	0	1	0	0	1
1891	10	4	0	0	0	0	1
1892	2	1	1	0	0	0	0
1893	730	659	186	261	21	35	511
1894	143	32	113	28	6	14	14
1895	2	0	2	2	0	0	0
1896	4	3	0	0	0	1	1
1897	3	7	0	0	1	0	1
1898	510	671	138	54	34	45	57
1899	209	34	116	27	5	13	137
1900	10	112	7	2	1	0	9
1901	37	50	1	5	45	0	6
1902	107	50	4	235	19	1	134
1903	16	21	44	5	3	0	143
1904	21	0	5	0	1	0	10
1905	29	79	1	0	1	3	8
1906	17	7	5	1	5	4	12
1907	90	41	20	5	6	1	101
1908	32	20	39	14	27	4	19
1909	11	4	7	1	9	2	26
1910	99	32	11	0	2	0	1

TABLE 11.7.4. *Continued.*

Years	N.S.W.	Vic.	Qld.	S.A.	W.A.	Tas.	N.Z.
1911	44	74	39	16	10	12	41
1912	371	87	54	15	0	13	15
1913	51	45	51	20	9	11	26
1914	19	105	14	11	6	0	33
1915	324	32	65	37	20	3	64
1916	73	19	104	20	16	5	93
1917	30	15	16	11	13	1	17
1918	76	7	1	1	3	2	15
1919	8	25	7	9	0	1	3
1920	189	220	54	15	17	17	122
1921	31	5	11	14	21	0	47
1922	11	2	9	4	2	0	1
1923	120	81	13	1	1	6	7
1924	36	7	33	0	39	4	52
1925	30	46	9	45	0	0	11
1926	90	14	3	0	0	0	13
1927	20	51	35	7	0	0	29
1928	162	12	7	2	3	15	12
1929	66	45	5	8	18	1	1
1930	100	34	3	7	1	0	2
1931	29	15	0	1	0	0	8
1932	14	17	0	1	0	3	0
1933	45	13	36	11	0	0	17
1934	34	25	10	8	0	0	46
1935	83	20	1	0	18	7	1
1936	22	1	12	0	1	7	3
1937	8	1	6	0	0	3	4
1938	0	0	9	0	0	1	163
1939	100	66	11	11	1	4	8
1940	22	14	21	30	29	9	1
1941	8	2	8	1	0	0	4
1942	130	72	17	8	11	7	31
1943	13	4	82	3	5	0	7
1944	4	0	2	4	0	1	0
1945	5	15	2	1	0	2	10
1946	37	13	12	15	30	2	16
1947	7	15	12	2	0	0	1
1948	49	9	4	8	1	7	4
1949	23	12	5	5	9	2	24

From Lancaster (1967*b*).

entiated and points to high incidence rates in childhood in the United Kingdom leading to an almost completely immune population older than 15 years of age. He remarks on a mortality rate of 318 per 1,000,000 per annum at the beginning of the century and a more recent rate of 2. Langmuir (1962) gave evidence of a fall in the crude death rates in the United States from approximately 100 per 1,000,000 per annum in 1912, that is, almost 1% of the total mortality, to about 2 per 1,000,000 per annum in 1962. Taneja, Ghai, and Bhakoo (1962) stress the contemporary high morbidity and mortality in India and the importance of adequate nutrition; approximately one quarter of the cases of bronchopneumonia admitted to hospital were due to measles. Morley (1962) and Morley, Woodland, and Martin (1963) show that the maximum case incidence was in the second year of life in Nigeria; about 25% of children admitted to hospital with measles died, malnutritional states were often initiated by an attack of measles, and preexistent malnutrition was associated with high case fatality rates. See also McGregor (1964) for Gambian experience. From Brazil, Moraes (1962) reported considerable falls in the mortality from measles over the years, from 229 in 1901 to 36 in 1958 per 1,000,000 per annum. Ristori, Boccardo, et al. (1962) showed that the mortality from measles in Chile had increased greatly over the years 1951 to 1960; it was the most severe infectious disease in Chile accounting for 2.3% of all deaths and 51% of deaths due to communicable diseases; there was a greater mortality in the southern regions. Rolleston (1937) gives references to many island or virgin soil type of epidemics. See also Babbott and Gordon (1954) and Whitelegge (1892–1893).

The high case fatality rates in island epidemics have often been used to support the hypothesis that the Europeans or urbanized populations are genetically better fitted to deal with these diseases than those populations that have been free of such infectious diseases, but the comparison may not be valid; for in the intense island epidemics, there are usually multiple cases within families and the whole community life may be in disarray. Also, there may be a lack of even the simplest medical and supportive care, particularly of sufficient calories in the diet, according to Morley (1980), a situation quite different from that in the populated areas of Europe where the adults, in particular, would have been immune. See Neel (1977), who believes that excess mortality is perhaps 80% nongenetic in origin.

We may conclude that measles was an important cause of mortality in the European states, certainly in the seventeenth to nineteenth centuries, being responsible for some 2% of all deaths in the areas of dense population. Under present day conditions in the developed world, it has become an unimportant cause of mortality. However, in less developed areas, such as Latin America, India,

and Africa, it may still cause many deaths, see Black (1982), WHO-measles (1952), and Borgoño (1983). Measles has also caused disastrous epidemics in islands and other isolated areas. Case fatality rates have varied greatly over the years, as in the United Kingdom and also between countries; this phenomenon appears not to be due to changes in the virus but rather to the circumstances under which the disease is acquired. For the feasibility of eradication in the United States see Hinman, Brandling-Bennett, et al. (1980), who conclude that measles is not presently indigenous in most of the United States and that the elimination of measles transmission is both "feasible and imminent." For vaccines, see Beale (1977) and Greenwood and Whittle (1981). For measles in Aberdeen, Scotland, see G.N. Wilson (1905); in tribal societies, see Black, Pinheiro, et al. (1977); in urban areas, §47.4; and in tropics, §46.2. For measles by country, see England and Wales, §37.2; Scotland, §37.3; France, §38.3, §38.4; Greenland, §39.2; Iceland, §39.3; Faeroes, §39.4; Norway, §39.7; Sweden, §39.7; Finland, §39.8; Japan, §40.2; Australia, §41.3; Maori New Zealand, §41.4; Oceania, §5.4, §41.6; America, §42.2, §42.3; and United States, §42.8.

11.8 Rubella and Other Viral Exanthemata

ICD 056. Inclusion: German measles. Exclusion: Congenital rubella (771.0).

Rubella is a mild infectious disease, characterized by a rash and enlargement of the lymph nodes, especially the posterior cervical. For its clinical features, see Horstmann (1982). It is caused by a virus, the sole member of the genus *Rubivirus*. Although its epidemiology resembles that of measles, the virus of rubella appears to have no close relatives (Banatvala and Best, 1984).

In large populations rubella is endemic and tends to be a disease of childhood. Under conditions in which adults are infected, it can cause congenital malformations if infection occurs at the critical times in early pregnancy. It is therefore a cause of congenital malformations occurring in epidemic form; and hence causes a slight burden of deaths following the malformations. Rubella was reported by Gregg (1941) to cause congenital cataract, and others showed that it also caused deafness, cardiac malformations, and so on, see §31.1. Since the time of its description in 1840, rubella had not been observed to cause any worthwhile disease in either the patient or the fetus; it was suggested that there must have been a mutation. However, the work of Lancaster (1951*g*, 1952*e* (with Pickering), 1954*h*) showed that mutation was an unnecessary hypothesis and that epidemics could be traced by institutional data back to 1898 in Western Australia and to 1899 in New South Wales and New Zealand. Since that time there has been much study on the epidemiology of the acute exanthemata in small populations, see §§5.2 to 5.4. It is now recognized that the age distribution of rubella and measles in small isolated populations can be quite different from that in the great populated land masses. Symposia and reviews of rubella and the congenital defects caused by it are available; see a symposium on many aspects of the disease, including congenital malformations, in *American Journal of the Medical Sciences*, **110** (1965) 345–476; also Ingalls, Babbott, et al. (1960), Ingalls, Plotkin, et al. (1967), and Neva, Alford, et al. (1964). See also references in §5.4. For the value of vaccination, see André (1979), Banatvala (1977), and Preblud, Serdula, et al. (1980).

ICD 057. Fourth digit: 0, erythema infectiosum (fifth disease); exanthema subitum (sixth disease).

These are negligible causes of mortality.

11.9 Nature of Viruses

It is convenient to discuss here the nature of viruses and their importance to humans, leaving the interested reader to read further among the authors in Topley and Wilson (1984). We begin with Brown (1984*a*). It was shown in 1892 that some infectious agents could pass through a filter that held up the smallest bacterium. In 1898 there was speculation on the nature of "contagium vivum fluidum" and why it was only infective for those organs of the plant that were growing, why the agent must be incorporated into the living protoplasm of the cell to propagate, and why it cannot multiply outside the cell. Many examples of such "filter-passing agents" (later shortened to "virus") were discovered in plants, animals, and bacteria.

In 1935 tobacco mosaic virus was obtained in crystalline form; later it could be concluded that viruses are nucleoproteins and that it is a matter of definition whether they are alive or not. Brown (1984*a*) gives the following properties by which viruses can be distinguished from "other living things."

1. Possession of only one type of nucleic acid, either DNA or RNA, but not both.
2. Reproduction solely from nucleic acid, whereas other agents grow from the sum of their constituents and reproduce by division.
3. Inability to undergo binary fission.
4. Lack of genetic information for the synthesis of essential cellular systems.
5. Use of ribosomes of their host cells.

A history of virology has been given by Waterson and Wilkinson (1978). Brown (1984*b*) briefly reviews the classification of viruses and gives a number of important references. Almeida (1984) then discusses the morphology; Skehel (1984), the mode of replication; and Pringle (1984), the genetics of the viruses. Some striking photographs of virus particles are given with magnifications of up to 800,000 in Almeida's article.

Beale (1984) points out that there has been a notable reduction in the impact of viruses on man largely because of improved methods of sanitary control. It has long been known that the severity of poliomyelitis and mumps has increased with age, as explained in §§10.1 and 13.3; but now other diseases, chiefly viruses, are known to have this property. Thus, the delay of onset of infection of the Epstein-Barr virus and the hepatitis viruses has led in the first case to outbreaks of infectious mononucleosis and in the second case to outbreaks of hepatitis, especially among military personnel in World War II and in later wars in Korea and Vietnam.

That the virus must enter the host's cells to

cause an infection shows that chemotherapy and passive serotherapy will be ineffective if given after the beginning of symptoms; moreover, viral infections have a short duration, so usually all the replication is complete before the therapy can be applied. Methods of prophylaxis have been more successful, as in smallpox and poliomyelitis, in which attenuated live vaccines are used; in some cases killed vaccines have been used. It must be noted that there are usually risks in using live vaccines and these must be weighed against the protection afforded. A striking instance of this is the increasing reluctance of the pharmaceutical firms to prepare vaccines because of medicolegal problems (Dolin, 1985). In place of attenuation, live vaccines of the virus may be given by an unusual route; this procedure has been used for animals in modern times and was previously the mode of prophylaxis against smallpox, namely, by inoculation.

Serotherapy and chemotherapy have sometimes been used with success in prophylaxis. Although much hope is held for the future, there is, as yet, very little active therapy specific against viruses. For problems of antiviral therapy, see Stuart-Harris and Oxford (1984) and Oxford and Öberg (1985).

Chapter 12
Arthropod-borne Viral Diseases

12.1 Yellow Fever

ICD 060. Fourth digit: 0, sylvatic; 1, urban.

Arthropod-borne virus is now usually written arbovirus. The genus *Flavivirus* belongs to the family *Togaviridae* (Simpson, 1984*a*).

Yellow fever is an acute disease caused by *Flavivirus febricius*. Classical cases were characterized by headache, myalgia, and prostration, followed by hepatomegaly, jaundice, vomiting, hemorrhagic signs, oliguria, and albuminuria. Milder cases are known with symptoms similar to influenza. Pathologically, the disease is a hemorrhagic fever with hepatitis and nephritis.

Carter (1931), after extensive search of old American colonial records, concluded that the first dependable description of yellow fever was of the cases in the Yucatan epidemic of 1648, long before the disease was recognized in Africa in 1778 at St. Louis on the coast of Senegal and at Bulam in Portuguese Guinea in 1793. Carlos Finlay (1833–1915) suggested in 1881 that it was spread by *Aedes aegypti*. Interest in the disease heightened at the time of the building of the Panama Canal, and it was one of the triumphs of modern medicine for Walter Reed (1851–1902) and his colleagues to determine the mode of spread and effective methods of control of the disease.

It seems very probable that yellow fever had its origin in Africa, as R.M. Taylor (1951) maintains, for there is an antigenic unity of all the strains of yellow fever virus isolated,

suggesting that it evolved in a single region. There had been no contact between the Amerindians and the Old World except through the northern near-Arctic regions until post-Columbian times, and so the origin was either Africa or America. The disease appears to have been longer established in Africa, for African monkeys and the native west Africans are more resistant to the attack of the virus than are South American monkeys and the Amerindians, respectively. This is shown by the lower case fatality rates of the west Africans and the severe mortality observed when an epizootic occurs in an American monkey population. The virus had to be transported across the Atlantic by ship in the days of sail, when the length of passage was longer than the infective period of the host. *Aedes aegypti* has been observed in recent times to accommodate itself to life on board ship, since it is a domestic species with larval forms developing in domestic containers, such as hollows in tree trunks, empty bottles, or tins containing water; on ship board it is able to breed in casks or other receptacles. Now there still exist in Africa primitive forms or races of *Aedes aegypti* that do not attack man and are adapted to forest rather than domestic habitats. Some of these developed into the domestic races in Africa but there are no such jungle races in America. R.M. Taylor (1951) concludes that yellow fever existed in Africa but escaped detection because in West Africa there were few Europeans among whom only could yellow fever be recognized; moreover,

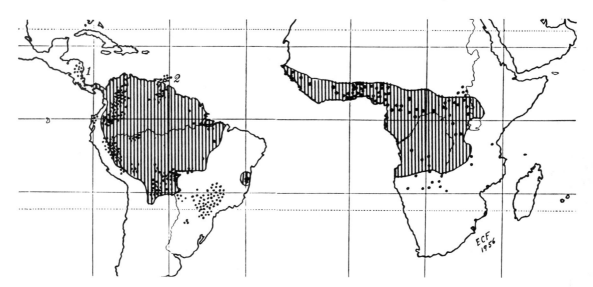

FIGURE 12.1.1. Map showing yellow fever enzootic foci (vertical lines) in tropical America and Africa, and epidemics in communities within and outside

enzootic areas (dots) for the period 1946–1955. (Original adaptation by Faust and Russell, 1964, Fig. 315, p. 845, from WHO and other sources.)

there was much malaria in the places endemic for yellow fever, and there is, in any case, a paucity of historical records from these areas.

The disease is spread by mosquitoes in two cycles; in the urban cycle of man-mosquito-man the vector is *Aedes aegypti* (synonym, *argenteus*) and in the sylvatic cycle, primate-mosquito-primate, there are several mosquito vectors, and man is infected in the cycle primate-mosquito-man. Human epidemics are believed to result from an infection transmitted from an animal in the sylvatic, or jungle, cycle. From the primary human case, the infection is spread by mosquitoes, almost always *Aedes aegypti*, to other humans. *Aedes aegypti*, fed on a patient during the first 3 days of the fever, becomes capable of transmitting the disease after about 12 days and remains infected throughout its life. The infection is enzootic in tropical Africa and in the tropical Americas. The disease is not enzootic or endemic in any area subject to winter frosts, as the mosquito population falls in winter (see Figure 12.1.1).

Case fatality rates are high; in Bermuda in 1864, 14 officers and 173 men died in an epidemic, corresponding to case fatality rates of 18.9% and 14.9%, respectively.

No specific therapy is available, but it is like-

ly, from experiences without their use, that nursing and supportive therapy are helpful. Control of the *Aedes aegypti* mosquito breeding has been very successful against urban epidemics and it has been claimed that campaigns have freed large regions of South America from the *Aedes*. Little can be done against the mosquitoes in the sylvatic cycle; vaccination of the exposed human population is advisable in such areas.

12.2 Yellow Fever as a Great Pestilence

It simplifies the discussion of the epidemiology of yellow fever to acknowledge it as a zoonosis, in which the hosts belong to the primates and some other animal orders, that is transmitted from host to host by a variety of mosquito genera but particularly by the *Aedes* species. Indeed, the infection can be thought of as being of the mosquitoes with the animal hosts permitting passage between mosquitoes. In highly endemic areas, most adults would be immune to yellow fever because they would have contracted the disease in childhood. Infants would be protected for a few months, because of antibodies received from their mother, but would contract the disease in early childhood; in such communities yellow fever would cause the deaths of perhaps 1% of all children born. In such areas yellow fever used to be considered as a disease of newcomers or immigrants, for example, in Havana, Cuba.

Although yellow fever is endemic only within the tropics, the presence of *Aedes aegypti* on ships in the days of sail enabled it to cause important epidemics in the northern temperate zone. Thus, there have been severe intense epidemics in Gibraltar, several of which are mentioned in §33.13. Boyce (1951) gives examples of the importance of yellow fever as measured by deaths by years along the Atlantic coast of the United States; for Philadelphia 220, 1699; 240, 1741; 4,044, 1793; 1,292, 1797; 3,506, 1798; 1,015, 1799; and 3,900 in 1803. It was noted that the newcomers from Europe contracted this disease, whereas those from the West Indies remained free. New York had some large epidemics, 370 deaths in 1668, 606 in 1803, and 538 in 1856.

Yellow fever played a large part in ruining the attempt of de Lesseps to build the Panama Canal, where deaths were about 30% per annum in the European workforce; the immigrants were not immunes and they produced domestic conditions suitable for breeding of the vector of urban epidemics, *Aedes aegypti*. Once a case was introduced there was a great chance of an epidemic following. In military campaigns, case fatality appears to have been higher than is suggested by the rule of James Carroll, cited in Strode (1951, p. 398), that it should not exceed 20%. Scott (1939, p. 281) mentions that the French army attacking rebels in Haiti in 1800 lost 23,000 men out of a total strength of 30,000.

Control of the disease began in America, for which we may follow the account of Strode (1951). American troops occupied Cuba in 1899; only seven deaths from yellow fever were reported in the first 7 months. In August Spanish immigrants began to migrate into the city, 12,000 arriving before the end of the year; an epidemic was already under way in December 1899 and continued through 1900; it was unaffected by the general hygienic measures applied. At the beginning of 1901, the new theory

of mosquito transmission of the disease was put to the test; little was known at that time of the bionomics (life history) of *Aedes*. Each case was protected from bites of mosquitoes by being immediately removed in a carefully screened ambulance to a hospital. As soon as the patient was removed, the house was fumigated to kill any mosquitoes that may have bitten the patient. Action was then taken against mosquito breeding throughout the city. These measures were effective; for the 10 years preceding the occupation of Havana there had been an average of 500 deaths per annum; there were still 310 deaths per year in 1900. However, under the measures begun in February 1901, yellow fever rapidly disappeared. Deaths by month, commencing February 1901, were 7,5,1,0,0; 0,1,2,1,0; 0,0, and no further cases occurred. This was the first conquest of the disease by hygienic measures. In Rio de Janeiro, a similar campaign was begun in March 1903, and for the years 1903 to 1909 deaths from yellow fever were 584, 48, 289, 49, 39, 4, and 0, the last case occurring in 1908. Other South American states followed with campaigns in the large cities. Gorgas (1915) estimated that during their attempt to construct the canal through the Panama Isthmus, the French lost yearly by death one third of their employees. Gorgas was placed in charge of a campaign to prevent a similar disaster. He was at first overimpressed with the success of the fumigation campaign in Cuba, which he had supervised; in 1904 there were 6,000 persons in Colón, 24,000 in the city of Panama, and about 10,000 scattered in 22 villages along the railroad. After a sharp epidemic in June 1905, Gorgas was given complete control. In the autumn of 1905, the incidence of yellow fever fell rapidly and the last case in the city of Panama occurred in November 1905, and the last case in Colón, in May 1906. After that there were no further cases originating in the isthmus for many years. An outbreak occurred in New Orleans, with deaths 57, 220, 111, 58, and 6 in the months July through November 1905. These epidemics and their conquests all dealt with the urban type of the disease.

We give as Table 12.2.1 the deaths from yellow fever before and after control measures

TABLE 12.2.1. Yellow fever deaths and control in American region.

	Havana (300)*	Vera Cruz (45)*	Isthmus of Panama (400)*	Rio de Janeiro (1,000)*	Para (200)*	Manaos (60)*	Guayaquil[†] (54.5)*
				Deaths			
1873	1,244	—	—	3,659	—	—	—
1874	1,425	—	—	828	—	—	—
1875	1,101	—	—	1,292	—	—	—
1876	1,619	—	—	3,476	—	—	—
1877	1,374	—	—	282	—	—	—
1878	1,559	—	—	1,176	—	—	—
1879	1,444	—	—	974	—	—	—
1880	645	—	—	1,625	—	—	—
1881	485	—	11	257	—	—	—
1882	729	—	36	89	—	—	—
1883	849	—	26	1,608	—	—	—
1884	511	—	128	863	—	—	—
1885	165	—	199	445	—	—	—
1886	167	—	308	1,449	—	—	—
1887	532	—	216	137	—	—	—
1888	468	—	102	747	—	—	—
1889	303	—	15	2,156	—	—	—
1890	308	—	1	719	—	—	—
1891	356	—	202	4,456	—	—	—
1892	357	—	51	4,312	—	—	—
1893	496	131	8	825	—	—	—
1894	382	209	29	852	—	—	—
1895	553	142	[‡]	818	—	—	—
1896	1,282	[‡]	[‡]	2,929	—	—	—
1897	858	[‡]	[‡]	159	—	—	—
1898	136	[‡]	[‡]	1,078	—	—	—
1899	103	127	[‡]	731	—	—	—
1900	310[§]	594	15	344	—	—	—
1901	18	261	2	299	—	—	—
1902	—	103	22	984	—	—	—
1903	—	285	46	584	—	85	—
1904	—	375[§]	5	48	98	56	—
1905	22	12	62[§]	289[§]	183	157	116
1906	12	23	1[‖]	49	149	117	275
1907	5	12	—	39	166	170	120
1908	1	1	—	4	213	117	103
1909	—	20	1[‖]	—	140	61	228
1910	—	3	2[‖]	—	358[§]	173	113
1911	—	—	—	2[‖]	49	210	102
1912	—	—	2[‖]	3[‖]	3	96[§]	166
1913	—	—	—	3[‖]	4	39	123
1914	—	—	—	1[‖]	—	—	21
1915	—	—	2[‖]	—	—	—	144
1916	—	—	—	—	—	—	152
1917	—	—	—	—	—	—	65

*Estimated population (in thousands).
[†]No control instituted.
[‡]Number not ascertained.
[§]Year of inauguration of control.
[‖]Imported instances.
Data from Low (1920*b*, pp. 252–253).

had been instituted in some Latin American cities. WHO-yellow fever (1971) gives tables and maps of the incidence of yellow fever in the Americas and Africa, 1950–1959. It is evident that in Africa cases only occur from about 17°N to 5°S, whereas in America occurrence is from 18°N to 40°S. Many of the cases are singletons, evidently of the sylvatic type. In their Table 1, with annual data for countries, it is mentioned that an estimated 3,000 deaths occurred in Ethiopia in 1961, *Ae. africanus* and *Ae. luteocephalus* were the vectors. There were 88 deaths in Sudan in 1959 and 60 deaths in Nigeria in 1969. In Brazil there were 46 deaths in 1951, 221 in 1952, and a total of about 140 in other years. Peru and Colombia had deaths in many years, with a maximum number of 53. Venezuela had deaths in many years but not more than 10 in any one year. See also Soper (1955) and Brès (1970).

Yellow fever has had an importance quite small in comparison with the other great pestilences, and it may be said to be of importance only under special circumstances in hot humid conditions with abnormal numbers of *Aedes*-type mosquitoes present. Nevertheless, it has been responsible for many memorable epidemics, for example, in the construction of the Panama Canal and in war. In the nineteenth century, yellow fever and malaria were responsible for the naming of the Guinea coast as the "white man's grave," see §§33.5, 33.13, and Cantlie (1974*a*, p. 441).

Yellow fever can still cause great epidemics; Simpson (1984*a*, p. 246) cites over 15,000 deaths in Ethiopia in 1960–1962 and several hundred deaths in Senegal in 1965.

12.3 Dengue

ICD 061.

Dengue fever is spread by *Aedes* mosquitoes and it has a wide distribution in the tropics and warm subtropical areas (Simpson, 1984*a*). In many regions it has had a low case fatality. Monkeys are reservoir hosts (and probably always important as the ultimate source) in west Africa and Malaysia. In Thailand hemolytic forms of the disease (ICD 065.4) have a serious case fatality rate.

12.4 Other Vector-borne Virus Infections

ICD 062–066.

A World Health Organization definition in 1967 is cited by Simpson (1984*a*) as follows:

An arthropod-borne or arbovirus has been defined as a virus that is maintained in nature principally through biological transmission between susceptible vertebrate hosts by haematophagous arthropods; arboviruses multiply and produce viraemia in the vertebrate, multiply in the tissues of arthropods and are passed on to new vertebrates by the bites of arthropods after a period of extrinsic incubation.

He further remarks that all arboviruses, with perhaps a very few exceptions such as dengue, ICD 061, and O'nyong nyong, ICD 066.3, are actual or potential zoonoses, being maintained in nature by hosts other than man. Although these viruses seem to be well adapted to their natural nonhuman hosts, usually causing little disease, they can infect man; the infection may be inapparent or cause a few symptoms such as a fleeting fever or mild arthritis, or it may cause severe disease such as encephalitis or hemorrhagic manifestations.

For convenience of reference, we list the arthropod-borne virus (arbovirus) infections in Table 12.4.1, modified from Stuart-Harris (1984*a*, Table 85.2) Together with the virus identified by its informal name, Table 12.4.1 gives the reservoir cycle of host and vector, the genus of the vector, and the ICD number. We now make some brief remarks on the incidence of human cases, with the aid of Simpson (1984*a*) for the *Togaviridae*, Porterfield (1984) for the *Bunyaviridae*, and Sellers (1984*b*) for the *Reoviridae*.

Eastern and Western Equine Encephalitis. These zoonoses are important causes of death in horses, but outbreaks in man are usually small, with encephalitis occurring in children, sometimes leading to death. Areas affected by Eastern equine encephalitis include the eastern seabord of the United States, the West Indies, and South America down to Argentina. Human cases of Western equine encephalitis have occurred in North America and Brazil.

TABLE 12.4.1. Vector-borne infections.

Family and virus	Reservoir	Vector (genus, etc.)	ICD (9th rev.)
Togaviridae			
(i) *Alphavirus*			
Eastern, western	Avian-mosquito	*Aedes, Culex*	062.1,.2
Venezuelan equine encephalitis	Avian-mosquito	*Aedes, Culex*	066.2
African-Chikungunya, etc.	Monkeys, (?) birds, rodents	Various (mosquito)	066.3
Australian-Ross River	Avian-mosquito	Culicine	062.8
(ii) *Flavivirus*			
(a) Mosquito-borne			
Jungle yellow fever	Monkeys,-mosquito	*Aedes*	060
Urban yellow fever	Man-mosquito	*Aedes*	060
Dengue	Man-mosquito	*Aedes*	061
St. Louis, Japanese B	Avian-mosquito	*Culex*	062.0,.3
Murray Valley encephalitis	Avian-mosquito	Culicine	062.4
West Nile encephalitis	Avian-mosquito	Culicine	066.3
(b) Tick-borne			
Far East-Russian encephalitis	Wild animals-ticks	Ixodid	063.0
Central European encephalitis	Goats-ticks	Ixodid	063.2
Louping ill	Sheep-ticks	Ixodid	063.1
Powassan encephalitis	Rodents-ticks	Ixodid	063.8
Kyasanur Forest encephalitis	Monkeys-ticks	*Haemaphysalis*	065.2
Omsk hemorrhagic fever	Muskrats-ticks	*Dermacentor*	065.1
Bunyaviridae			
Bunyavirus			
California encephalitis group	Rodents-mosquito	*Aedes*	065.5
Crimean-Congo hemorrhagic fever	Small mammals-ticks	*Hyalomma*	065.0
Rift Valley fever	Sheep, goats-mosquito	*Aedes, Culex*	066.3
Sandfly or *Phlebotomus* fever	Man-sandfly	*Phlebotomus*	061
Reoviridae (*Orbivirus*)			
Colorado tick fever	Rodents, ground squirrels-ticks	*Dermacentor*	066.1

Adapted from Table 85.2, p. 140, Vol. 4, of Topley and Wilson (1984) in the article by Stuart-Harris.

Venezuelan Encephalitis. This is a severe zoonosis of horses; in 1971 in an epizootic involving Texas, Guatemala, and Costa Rica, there were over 200,000 deaths of horses. Simpson (1984a) states that only about 4% of human cases suffer encephalitis but the case fatality rates in such cases are about 20% giving an overall case fatality of about 0.8%.

Chikungunya Disease. The virus was first isolated in the Newala district of Tanzania but it has since been found in many cities of the Indi-

an subcontinent. It has been estimated that 0.3 million cases appeared in the Madras population of 2 million in 1964; the principal symptoms were fever and very severe pains in the limbs and spine. Monkeys are probably the reservoir host in Africa, but little is known of its hosts in India.

St. Louis Encephalitis. In the late summer of 1933, there were over a thousand cases of encephalitis in St. Louis, MO, with a case fatality rate of 20% and a markedly higher incidence and case fatality in the elderly.

Japanese B Encephalitis. This is a disease of "maritime Siberia," Japan, China, the Philippines, Indonesia, and eastern India. According to Okuno (1978), in the years 1946–1965 there were about 3,000 to 5,000 cases annually in Japan, with 1,000 to 2,000 deaths; children and persons over 50 years were particularly affected. Its true incidence and mortality outside Japan have been difficult to estimate. He gives a table with deaths in Japan 1,600, 744, 1,349 in 1956, 1957, and 1958, respectively, falling to 27, 2, and 6 in 1973, 1974, d 1975, respectively, and remarks that this decline could have possibly been due to changes in agricultural practices by which the vector population was greatly reduced. The disease was first noted in 1871 and established as a zoonosis in the 1950s; there was an epizootic of equine encephalitis in 1947.

Murray Valley Encephalitis (Previously Australian X Disease). This disease resembles Japanese B encephalitis clinically; it occurs in many areas of Australia and New Guinea. Several deaths have occurred, chiefly in children.

West Nile Virus. Spread widely around the Mediterranean Sea, West Nile virus has caused febrile illness of man, principally in young children.

Far East Russian (or Russian Spring-summer) Encephalitis. This disease is confined mainly to the eastern USSR but cases do occur as far west as Leningrad; case fatalities are said to be as high as 30% in some epidemics. There may be bulbar paralysis, and residual paralyses may occur in up to 5% of cases.

Central European Encephalitis (Biphasic Milk Fever). This disease occurs in the Balkans and Czechoslovakia and in more northerly European states. Human infection occurs from goats' milk. The disease is much milder than the Far East version mentioned above.

Louping Ill. This is a disease of sheep. Most human infections have been in the laboratories.

Powassan and Kyasanur Encephalitis. These are rare human diseases of the Canada-United States and Mysore, India, regions.

Omsk Hemorrhagic Fever. This is a disease of muskrats in the vicinity of Omsk, and human cases have been reported only among those with close contact with the muskrats; it is a severe hemorrhagic disease in man.

California Encephalitis. This must be a rather mild disease, since 40% of persons in certain parts of Wisconsin show antibodies to this group of viruses; there are few deaths.

Congo-Crimean Hemorrhagic Fever. This disease has a wide distribution from the Crimea through Iraq and Pakistan and central and south Africa; case fatality rates are high, possibly 15% to 30%; it may occur as a nosocomial disease with even higher case fatality.

Rift Valley Fever. This is a major epizootic in domestic animals, mainly sheep and goats; in 1977 there were 600 human deaths from the disease in Egypt due to spread from the epizootic by *Culex* mosquitoes to man.

Phlebotomus or Sandfly Fever. This acute infectious disease of man, endemic in the Mediterranean area, has a quite negligible case fatality.

Colorado Tick Fever. This is a zoonosis of wild rodents in northwestern United States and southwestern Canada, and the disease is transmitted to humans by tick bites; some deaths in humans have been recorded.

Chapter 13

Miscellaneous Diseases due to Viruses and Chlamydias

13.1 Viral Hepatitis

ICD 070. Fourth digit is by viral type and mention of hepatic coma. Excluded from this rubric is hepatitis symptomatic of another disease, in particular, due to herpes, yellow fever, coxsackie, mumps, and some other exotic viruses.

Clinically, infectious or viral hepatitis is a disease characterized by malaise, fever, sometimes vomiting, abdominal pain, and jaundice; the liver is often enlarged and tender. The disease has a variable course from a few days up to 3 to 6 months. Morbidity rates are up to 50% of the exposed population. Case fatality rates are usually low.

The hepatitis of this rubric is due to three groups known as Hepatitis A, B, and not-A not-B viruses. We refer the reader to Gerety (1981) and Gitnick (1984) for this last heterogeneous group.

Hepatitis A

This is caused by an RNA virus, Hepatitis A, belonging to the family of *Picornavirus* (*Enterovirus* 72), which may be an enterovirus; it may have a reservoir host among the primates. In epidemics it is spread by the intestinal-oral route, including by contaminated food or water. As an infection in normal times, Hepatitis A is seen most commonly in infancy and childhood. With improving hygiene, the age distribution of patients has tended to move up to older ages. There is no evidence of chronic persistence (Howard, 1984). Hepatitis A is typically a mild disease and notifications may form only about 5% of actual infections. It does not seem to be associated with long-term effects such as cirrhosis of the liver or neoplasms. See also Gerety (1984).

Hepatitis B

This is due to the DNA virus, Hepatitis B. It is not closely related to Hepatitis A virus except in so far as both are causes of hepatitis; moreover, it is a far more dangerous disease and it is persistent leading to Cirrhosis. Howard (1984) gives estimates that there are some 176 million carriers of Hepatitis B virus in the world, ranging from 0.1% in northern Europe to 5% in the countries bordering the Mediterranean Sea and to 15% in the tropical regions. Although it was first discovered as a contaminant of blood and blood products and as a result of illicit drug taking, for which see Parker (1984*b*), it has become evident that there must be other more important modes of transmission from case to case, for in the tropical areas it has been found that an important proportion of children can be shown to be carrying the virus or to have been infected by it. In the underdeveloped world virus B is naturally transmitted, perhaps by insect vectors, with up to 50% of some populations in Asia and Africa attacked. Virus B is probably important as a cause of primary hepatocellular carcinoma in China and Africa, see §20.6, and it is regarded as potentially a great risk to health in all communities. See also Gerety (1985).

See Zuckermann (1979) for a history of

hepatitis, Luermann (1885) for an early epidemic of hepatitis following vaccination, Francis and Maynard (1979) on the mode of transmission and the severity of the diseases, Millman, Eisenstein, and Blumberg (1984) for the prophylactic vaccination against Hepatitis B virus.

13.2 Rabies

ICD 071. Inclusion: hydrophobia, lyssa.

Rabies is a virus disease of dogs, cats, bats, and other carnivorous wild animals, endemic in all continents except Australia and Antarctica. The usual mode of spread is by bite. No reservoir host, namely, one in which the disease is not highly lethal, is known to exist. Turner (1984) gives a table that suggests that over 90% of all human exposures follow from domestic pets; further, man is not highly susceptible to the virus, for the probability of human rabies after the bite of a known rabid dog averages about 15%. The probability varies with the site of the bite, the presence of clothing, and whether the animal is secreting virus at the time.

For the disease in man, the reported incubation period varies from 9 days to a year, more usually about 15 days, varying with the distance of the site of entry from the central nervous system and the size of the bite. The earliest symptoms are those of fever and are followed in about a week's time by severe mental disturbances including paralyses, the latter of which are usually a fore-runner of coma, which may be brief or last for months and is almost invariably fatal. The acute laryngeal spasms after the patient has tried to drink and the disease itself have been termed hydrophobia. Once symptoms appear in man, the disease is almost universally fatal.

No therapy, except active immunization, is available. Doubts remain on the efficacy of treatment. Steele (1975) quotes a report of Pottevin in 1898 that showed 96 deaths occurring in 20,166 persons treated by Pasteur's methods, a case fatality rate of 0.46%. Recent figures from India state that about 0.5% of cases treated, die. Semple (1919) prepared a dead carbolized vaccine and secured a case fatality rate of only 0.19% in 2,009 Europeans treated in India. It is believed that if immunization is complete before the virus reaches the central nervous system the patient survives but otherwise, dies; hence, bites of the extremities are less dangerous than those of the face. Semple (1919, pp. 336, 372) gives results of treatment in pre-Pasteurian days and in more recent times. Although Semple's killed vaccine is still in use in some countries, neurological complications follow its use, perhaps up to 1 in 500. The reader is referred to Wilson (1967) for a discussion. Improved vaccines are being prepared.

Control is difficult but has been successful in England and Wales by quarantine measures and muzzling of dogs; all cases of human rabies occurring there between 1955 and 1980 had been imported. Urban rabies can be controlled by the slaughter of domestic animals (Shimada, 1971) but the control of sylvatic rabies is more difficult. Indeed, Tierkel (1972) reported that there had been "no real depression in the number of human rabies cases" in Asia generally and gave an estimate of 15,000 human cases per annum in India's population of 525 million. For general reviews, see the texts of Baer (1975), Nagano and Davenport (1972), and the conference of Kuwert, et al. (1985).

13.3 Miscellaneous Diseases due to Viruses and Chlamydias

ICD 072. Mumps is an acute generalized infection with symptoms usually referable to the salivary, particulary the parotid, glands, to the gonads, and to the pancreas. Most cases occur in the spring. Infectiousness is less than measles or chickenpox. The disease is usually benign and deaths are rare. Complications and severity of the disease tend to increase with the age of the patient. Thus, it can be a great nuisance in military camps and other places where susceptibles are gathered. Effective live vaccines are available (Sellers, 1984c).

ICD 073. Ornithosis. Inclusions: parrot fever, psittacosis. This is an avian zoonosis, due to *Chlamydia psittaci*, known to affect over a hundred avian species. It has been often spread to man, usually by inhalation of dust from the wings of affected birds. It occurs as an industrial disease. It has a variable severity in man but is not a cause of much mortality.

ICD 074. Specific diseases due to Coxsackie viruses. The disease caused by these viruses is usually mild. See Gamble (1984).

ICD 075. Infectious mononucleosis. Inclusion: glandular fever, moncytic angina, Pfeiffer's disease. Glandular fever is an acute infection of insidious onset associated with fever, enlargement of the lymphatic nodes and spleen, sore throat, and a rubellalike rash. It is caused by a herpesvirus, the Epstein-Barr virus. Infection is by intimate contact, as in kissing, and by blood transfusion (Watson, 1984). Although the disease can cause invalidity for some months, deaths are rare. See also Roizman (1982–1985), Klein (1973), Klein and Klein (1984), and Henle, Henle, and Lennette (1979).

ICD 076 and 077. Trachoma and other diseases of the conjunctiva. These two rubrics are not associated with deaths. *Chlamydia trichomatis* (several serotypes) is the leading cause.

13.4 Other Diseases due to Viruses and Chlamydias

ICD 078.

Many of these diseases are mild and cause no mortality; others have high case fatalities; many have a limited geographical distribution. We consider them in the order of the ICD fourth digit.

0. Molluscum Contagiosum. This is an infectious human disease due to an RNA virus, characterized by the production of small, pearly, flesh-colored skin nodules. Transmission is by direct contact, by fomites, or sexually (Baxby, 1984). The virus is listed by Wyke (1984) as causing nodular epidermal hyperplasia.

1. Viral Warts. These are due to papilloma viruses of the *Papovaviridae* family. These viruses are under suspicion as oncogenic, especially for cancer of the uterine cervix.

2. Sweating Fever (inclusions miliary fever and sweating disease). The inclusions for this rubric do not seem to be defined.

3. Cat-scratch Fever. This is characterized by a suppurative subacute enlargement of one or more lymph nodes. Its cause is believed to be a pleomorphic Gram-negative bacillus, which has not yet been cultivated (Wilson, 1984e). Spontaneous cure is the rule.

4. Foot and Mouth Disease. Human infection with foot and mouth disease is rare but appears to be mild (Sellers, 1984a).

5. Cytomegalic Inclusion Disease. This is characterized by greatly enlarged cells containing acidophilic intranuclear and cytoplasmic inclusion bodies in salivary glands, liver, pancreas, kidney, and other human tissues. The disease was first recognized about 25 years ago in postmortems on infants; in the past decade it has been acknowledged as the most common infectious cause of perinatal brain damage, the main cause of morbidity and death in organ transplantations, and as a terminal complication in some malignancies (Watson, 1984).

6. Hemorrhagic Nephrosonephritis. This rubric seems identical with Korean hemorrhagic fever of Porterfield (1984).

7. Arenaviral Hemorrhagic Disease. There are several zoonoses of wild rodents caused by arenaviruses. They are transmitted to man, probably, by saliva or urine. The "Junin" virus of the Argentine is seasonal in its attack on man, human cases occurring at the time of the maize harvest and being associated with case fatality rates of 3%–20%, (Simpson, 1984b). Bolivian hemorrhagic fever is due to the "Machupo" virus with case fatality rates of 3%–30%.

8. Other. Lassa fever. This is a chronic infection or zoonosis of rodents in West Africa. Humans are infected through articles soiled by rodent urine; the incubation period is 3 to 16 days. It is a severe human infection and is now notorious for appearing in nonendemic areas. Marburg and Ebola fevers. These are related, but distinct, viruses indigenous to Africa and causing severe hemorrhagic disease in man. They are zoonoses of vervet (*Cercopithecus*) monkeys in Uganda (Stuart-Harris, 1984a); from monkeys in Marburg there were 25 known infections with 7 deaths. At one African hospital 41 deaths occurred among 76 infected members of the staff. In 1976 there were two notable epidemics; in the Sudan there were 151 deaths out of 284 known cases, a case fatality of 53%, and in Zaire the case fatality rate was 88% with 318 known cases (Simpson, 1984c). In hospitals spread is by person-to-person contact, by syringe, and by blood transfusion. Ticks or other ectoparasites may be responsible in the wild.

See Schachter (1978), Schachter and Grossman (1981), and Collier and Ridgway (1984) for the *Chlamydias*.

ICD 079 is not a rubric for primary classification.

13.5 AIDS—Acquired Immune Deficiency Syndrome

This disease is now believed to be due to a retrovirus (Wyke, 1984). Similar organisms are found in equatorial Africa, affecting men and women equally; these retroviruses are not associated there with Kaposi's sarcoma, which is a complication of Western-style AIDS. The AIDS virus attacks the T4 lymphocytes, that is, those white blood cells that are specifically involved in immune processes against the entry of foreign proteins or parasites into the body. Presenting symptoms are sometimes enlarged lymph glands, leukemia-like blood picture, oral thrush, pneumonia or other infection or malignant growth, or a combination of such or other symptoms and signs caused by the breakdown of the defenses of the immune system. Once signs or symptoms have developed, the case fatality is high. There is as yet no effective remedy. Indeed, if the retrovirus developed in Africa, its introduction into the Western world met circumstances favoring its propagation: the spread between promiscuous homosexuals, the shared use of syringes in drug abuse, and the high incidence of blood transfusion with possible pooling of donors' bloods.

Since many of the factors responsible for the spread of the disease have been questioned, the recent review of Curran, Morgan, et al. (1985) can be examined. Of 12,767 adult cases of the disease, diagnosed before January 1983 in the United States, more than 73% were in homosexual or bisexual men (12% of whom had also used intravenous drugs) and 17% occurred in heterosexual men or women who used intravenous drugs. An additional 1.5% of patients with no other risk factors had received a transfusion of whole blood or of some of its components within 5 years of diagnosis and 0.7% were persons with hemophilia who had received clotting factor concentrates. One percent were heterosexual partners of AIDS patients or of persons with increased AIDS risks; another 6.4% could not be classified by recognized risk factors, but a large proportion of these were born outside the United States. At least half a million persons have already been infected in the United States to the present time, 1985. To the risk factors, and so mode of transmission, above can be added passage from mother to newborn child. Measures have been undertaken to control the giving of blood, and sometimes blood extracts for special purposes can be sterilized by heat, but control of sexual transmission is more difficult; the number of sexual partners should be reduced. Needles for intravenous drug taking should not be shared.

The disease has been reviewed by Armstrong (1984) and Selikoff, Teirstein, and Hirschman (1984). Vaeth (1985) has reviewed cancer and AIDS. More popular accounts are given by Marx (1982) and Norman (1985). For AIDS in Africa, see Quinn, Mann, et al. (1986). For an authoritative text, see de Vita, Hellman, et al. (1985). For an international perspective, see Piot, Plummer, et al. (1988). For an update, see US National Academy of Sciences (1988). For the *Science* series of discussions, see Kulstad (1989).

Chapter 14
Rickettsioses

14.1 Louse-borne Typhus

ICD 080. Inclusion: classical, epidemic, louse-borne, or exanthematic typhus, i.e., infections with *Rickettsia prowazeki*.

It may be remarked that Brill's disease might be classified in this rubric with greater propriety than in ICD 081, as it is believed always to be a recrudescence of classical typhus.

Classical or epidemic typhus is caused by *R. prowazeki* and is now said to be invariably transmitted by the louse, *Pediculus corporis*. The disease attacks the blood capillaries particularly and the symptoms are explicable by these lesions. It is an acute systematic infection, commencing after an incubation period of 10 to 14 days with an abrupt onset of shivering, malaise, headache, muscular pains, pyrexia, and anorexia. On about the fifth day a pink macular rash appears (spotted fever). There is enlargement of the spleen. The fever may become remittent but prostration is extreme. In favorable cases, the temperature falls on about the fourteenth day and, although weakness persists for some time, recovery is usually complete. Zinsser (1935) believed that the first adequately described and identifiable case occurred in Spain in 1489. Typhus was confused with typhoid fever until William W. Gerhard noted in 1837 at autopsy that in typhus cases from ships there were no lesions of the Peyer's patches in the small intestine. William Jenner in 1850 confirmed Gerhard's work and did much to establish the clinical signs and progress of the two diseases. Until there was a universal recognition of the distinction, it had been customary to refer to typhus and typhoid fever as exanthematic and abdominal typhus, respectively. Although James Lind (1716–1794) in 1740 was convinced that typhus infection was carried on the bodies of man, on clothes, and on other household furniture, it was only in 1909 that Charles Nicolle (1866–1936) identified the rickettsiae in louse feces and established the importance of the louse in the transmission of the disease. The body or head louse ingests blood of a patient and excretes rickettsiae in the feces, so that transmission to a new person through the skin follows scratching. Inhalation is a much less frequent mode of transmission. See Figure 14.1.1 for worldwide distribution of louse-borne and murine typhus and Burgdorfer and Anacker (1981) for a general review of the genus *Rickettsia* and the diseases caused by its members. See also Zdrodovskiĭ and Golinevich (1960), Marmion (1984), and Faust and Russell (1964).

There is a marked age gradient in the case fatality rates, varying from less than 5% younger than 20 years of age to 50% at age 50 years and practically 100% over age 60 years. In famine and conditions of general stress the case fatalities can be still higher.

Treatment of typhus is by antibiotics and chemotherapy. Prevention now consists in measures against lice, for example, the washing and ironing of clothes, the cleaning or cutting of hair, and the use of insecticides. It is said that the first typhus epidemic to be

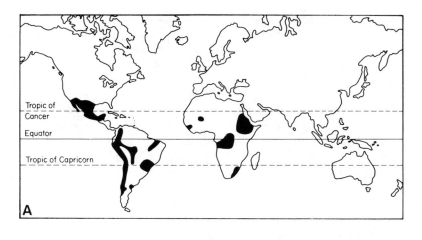

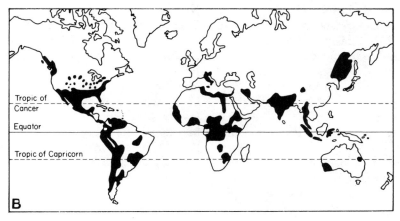

FIGURE 14.1.1. A: Distribution of epidemic louse-borne typhus. B: Distribution of endemic flea-borne typhus. From Manson-Bahr and Apted (1982, pp. 436, 440).

aborted in winter time was in Italy in 1943, when DDT was successfully used against the louse. See also for lice control, PAHO/WHO (1973).

14.2 Typhus as a Great Pestilence

Typhus has caused many notable epidemics in times of war, civil disturbance, and famine and so constantly that when "plague" is mentioned as having occurred at such times, it is as well to check that it was not typhus. Typhus has often been accompanied by relapsing fever, also louse-borne, in such epidemics. We have first to explain the presence of typhus during such events.

First, the disease may persist in jails and prisons at times in which it is not present in the population at large. Second, the disease can persist through interepidemic times by lying in a dormant state in human tissues, as is discussed in §14.3 under Brill's disease. This mode of perpetuation was first demonstrated by H. Zinsser in 1934, when he found that a usually mild form of typhus, observed sporadically in the northeastern coastal towns of the United States, was caused by *R. prowazeki*, which had with great probability been acquired in Russia or Poland before the patient's migration to the United States. Other authors have maintained that typhus infections may lie latent in the tissues until a famine or other incident breaks down the body's resistance. Third, typhus can also persist in the louse or in dried feces and be initially transmitted by inhalation. Woodward (1973) mentions that a French naval squadron under the Duc d'Anville suffered from an infectious fever (typhus) and left blankets at Chubucto near Halifax, Nova Scotia, during the summer of 1746 when they returned to Europe. In the winter Mimack Indians used these blankets and clothes and the whole nation was "virtually wiped out" by the ensuing epidemic. The infection would have been kept alive by lice or in their feces in the blankets in the period between the departure of the squadron and the start of the epidemic. Fourth, *R. prowazeki* has been isolated from such animals as cattle, sheep, camels, and goats, in which it is transmitted by ticks, and this may be an important factor in perpetuating the disease in some countries, so that it should possibly be thought of as a zoonosis.

Although the etiology of typhus was unknown, prevention of the disease was possible before the modern era of insecticides and chemotherapy; thus, at the time of the Thirty Years War, strict measures were adopted by the German cities to prevent the spread of disease. If cases had occurred within the city, the house was quarantined, the clothes and beds used by the patients were burned, and fumigations took place in the streets and squares. Strangers from infected places were not allowed to enter the city, incoming effects were disinfected, and money boiled in vinegar; often patients were isolated in houses outside the city. Under such regimes typhus might be accidentally admitted into the city but comparatively few persons might be infected. Snyder (1965), in Horsfall and Tamm (1965), believed that a description by Fracastoro in 1546 is sufficiently clear to identify typhus. It appears that typhus had been endemic in the Turkish armies earlier. In 1489 there were 17,000 deaths in the Spanish Army at the siege of Granada, about six times the number killed in combat with the Moors. Thirty thousand soldiers of the French Army besieging Naples in 1528 were "struck down." From the Balkan campaigns of the sixteenth century, the disease was disseminated to the rest of Europe and so became known as the "morbus hungaricus". Sinclair and Maxcy (1925) report that, according to a Spanish observer, there was a severe epidemic in the highlands of Mexico in 1576 and 1577 during which more than 2,000,000 Indians died. Whether the disease existed in America before the Spanish conquests is not known.

Many examples of typhus epidemics associated with war are mentioned by Prinzing (1916), for example, in the Thirty Years War, the Napoleonic wars in which typhus was a major factor in Napoleon's defeat in his Russian campaign of 1812 (Drew, 1965), and in the Great Northern War with an ensuing civilian epidemic in Sweden in 1829. After the Napoleonic wars, there were also over 700,000 cases of typhus in Ireland in 1816 to 1819 among a population of 6 million inhabitants. Typhus and relapsing fever were again active in Ireland at the time of the famines, especially after September 1846; the former disease was known as "black fever" and the latter "yellow fever." MacArthur (1956) believes that typhus had always been more prevalent in the western than in the eastern counties; movements from the west to the east, brought about by famine, created conditions for heavy infestation by lice and for their exchange.

There were 285 deaths from typhus in the British Army in the Crimea from 1854 to 1856, according to Cantlie (1974b). In the Franco-German war of 1870–1871, typhus is said not to have occurred because of the hygienic measures taken against the disease, although there were cases in the civilian population. Typhus was not important on the Western Front in World War I, although there was a large epidemic in Serbia. It is believed that 126 out of 400 Serbian doctors died from typhus in the epidemic beginning in Serbia in 1915. In the civilian population the case fatality rate was 60% or even 70%. Strong, et al. (1920) report that in less than 6 months, over 150,000 Serbians died of typhus. Further, there were epidemics on the Eastern Front, and these caused many deaths in the ensuing wars of intervention and civil disturbances in Russia and in the bordering states of eastern Europe— perhaps 30 million cases with 3 million deaths in Russia between 1918 and 1922.

In times of war troops often carried infections into the towns. At the close of the Great Northern War, infection was spread throughout Sweden by discharged troops. Similarly, in times of famine there would be a breakdown of civil order; there would be migration of numerous persons in the hope that they would reach areas where food was available, and, in such cases, there was often a herding together for shelter and mutual protection or from segregation forced by the civil authorities. There would be apathy among the refugees and lack of cleaning facilities leading to high rates of lice infestation. All that would be needed for an epidemic of typhus under such conditions was the introduction of infected lice from cases or the presence of a latent carrier.

In the civilian populations, typhus was no longer an important cause of death in the general experience of western Europe after 1825 in areas not devastated by wars or famine, see Table 11.2.3. However, an extensive epidemic of typhus occurred in London in 1838 with over 13,000 deaths, and this was made the subject of a report, Chadwick (1842, 1965), by Edwin Chadwick (1800–1890), who stressed the importance of poverty. Similarly, there was an epidemic in 1848 in Upper Silesia, which had a subject Polish-speaking population; here also, R. Virchow's report stressed the importance of poverty; indeed, Virchow did not believe typhus was contagious until many years later, see Ackerknecht (1953, pp. 14–15, 124, 125).

Typhus is associated with conditions of crowding and poor personal hygiene in jails (jail fever), military campaigns (§§33.13 and 33.15) navies, merchantmen, migrating groups fleeing from war zones, or famine (§22.10), and any group living under such conditions. Some notorious incidents, called Black Assizes, have been discussed by MacArthur (1927). The Assizes are legal gatherings in England, where judges, together with their assistants, pass from city to city holding court. Famous outbreaks of disease, almost certainly principally due to typhus, have occurred and we can speak of the Black Assizes of Cambridge 1522, Oxford 1577, Exeter 1589, Taunton 1730, and Old Bailey 1750, among others. The Assize at Ox-

ford in 1577 was attended by a great crowd. From prisoners the infection spread to officials in the court; both judges died, together with the sheriff, undersheriff, six Justices of the Peace, and all members of the Grand Jury, except one or two; 100 members of the University died and, in all, the recorded death roll was 510. The Exeter epidemic of 1589 later spread all over Devonshire. After the Assize of Old Bailey in 1750, it was decided to ventilate the court. Seven out of 11 builders making the new constructions contracted jail fever. See also §16.6.

For typhus in London, 1851–1900, see Luckin (1984).

14.3 Other Rickettsioses

ICD 081. Fourth digit: 0, murine (endemic) typhus, flea-borne typhus; 1, Brill's disease, Brill-Zinsser disease, recrudescent typhus; 2, scrub typhus, Japanese river fever, Kedani fever, mite-borne typhus, tsutsugamushi.

Murine Typhus

This is a mild form of typhus caused by *Rickettsia mooseri*, closely related to *R. prowazeki*. It is a disease of rats with the rat louse, *Polyplax spinulosus*, and the rat flea, *Xenopsylla cheopis*, as the principal vectors in the rat cycle; *X. cheopis* is responsible for passing it on to man. Murine typhus is not spread from man to man and has a low case fatality rate, less than 1%

Brill's Disease

Zinsser (1934) isolated *R. prowazeki* from cases of Brill's disease; he suggested that typhus could persist in interepidemic periods as an inapparent infection, which could break down under unfavorable conditions to initiate a new epidemic. Price, Emerson, et al. (1958) later found that 30% of migrants to the United States from eastern and southeastern Europe before 1930 were seropositive for classical typhus; of over a thousand such positives, in no case had the disease passed on to another member of the family. This disease might be more appropriately classified in ICD 080.

Scrub or Mite Typhus

This is a disease caused by *Rickettsia tsutsuga-mushi*, occurring in a variety of climatic zones in a roughly triangular area with West Pakistan, Japan, and Queensland in Australia as vertices. It is transmitted through the bite of larvae of trombiculid mites of the genus *Lepto-tromnidium*. Since the larva only bites once, the disease has been transmitted transovarially from the mother mite.

The disease is characterized by an abrupt onset of fever and headache after an incubation period of 7 to 10 days. The symptoms are similar to those of classical typhus. The case fatality may vary in different areas. During World War II, scrub typhus was widespread among military forces operating in the southeast Asian and southwest Pacific zones. Case fatality rates were reported varying between 0.6% and 35%, 2.5% for all Pacific war zones for the US forces, and 9.1% for Australian forces in New Guinea, deaths 258 and 259, cases 10,526 and 2,839. Case-to-case infections do not occur. Successful prevention was attained by the application of mite repellent to clothes, especially gaiters, according to Philip (1948).

Tick-borne Rickettsioses

ICD 082. Fourth digit: 0, spotted fevers, Rocky Mountain spotted fever, São Paulo fever; 1, Boutonneuse fevers, African, Indian, Kenyan, or Mediterranean tick typhus, Marseilles fever; 2, North Asian or Siberian tick fever; 3, Queensland tick typhus; 8, other.

These fevers are often referred to as spotted fevers. The infective agents are 0, *Rickettsia rickettsi*; 1, *R. conori*; 2, *R. siberica*; 3, *R. australis*. Genera of ticks are 0, *Dermacentor*; 1, Ixodid ticks, *Amblyomma*, *Rhipicephalus*, *Boöphilus* and *Haemaphysalis*; 2, *Dermacentor* and *Haemaphysalis*; 3, *Ixodes*. See Aikawa (1966) and Hoogstraal (1970).

Other Minor Rickettsioses

ICD 083. Fourth digit: 0, Q-fever; 1, trench fever; 2, rickettsial pox; 8, other.

Q-fever, caused by *R. burneti*, is now known to occur in many countries, infecting sheep, goats, cattle, and men. The route of infection varies and is often inhalation. Case fatality rates are low. Trench fever, caused by *R. quintana* and spread by the louse, is a sharp fever with headaches and severe pains in the bones and muscles. Considerable outbreaks occurred on the Western Front in World War I and on the Eastern Front in World War II. However, case fatality is low and little mortality has been due to these rickettsioses.

For reviews and history of Q-fever, see Baca and Paretsky (1983) and Wentworth (1955). For relapsing fever, see Johnson (1976) and Burgdorfer (1976). For the rickettsioses in Africa, see Freyche and Deutschman (1950). See also Spink (1979). For rickettsial diseases of the Far East, see Rapmund (1984).

Chapter 15
Malaria

15.1 General Epidemiology

ICD 084. Inclusions: malaria.

Exclusion: congenital malaria (771.2). Note: subcategories 084.0–084.6 exclude the listed conditions with mention of pernicious complications (084.8; 084.9), which are due always to *falciparum* infections.

Fourth digit: 0, *falciparum*; 1, *vivax*; 2, *quartan*; 3, *ovale*; 4, other; 5, mixed; 6, unspecified; 7, induced; 8, blackwater fever; 9, other pernicious complications of malaria.

Malaria in man is a disease due to infection by protozoa of the genus *Plasmodium*, namely, (*i*) *P. ovale*, causing a tertian fever, occurring principally in central Africa, although it has reported from southern Asia and the East Indies; (*ii*) *P. malariae* spread throughout the tropics and subtropics and causing a quartan fever; (*iii*) *P. vivax*, having a wide geographical distribution and causing benign tertian malaria; and (*iv*) *P. falciparum*, largely confined to the tropics and causing an irregular subtertian fever. The life cycles of the four species of *Plasmodium* share essential features. Mortality from malaria is almost always due to infections with *P. falciparum*, subtertian malaria, so we confine our attention almost entirely to it.

The life cycle of the parasite, always of the genus *Plasmodium*, can be said to begin when the mosquito ingests blood from a patient containing the two sexual forms (gametocytes) of the parasite. After fertilization, the resulting cell penetrates the stomach wall of the mosquito and develops beneath the lining membrane into a large cyst containing the infective form of the parasite, namely, the sporozoites. After 7–20 days the cysts rupture and the sporozoites migrate, many reaching the salivary glands. The infected mosquito may now bite a second host, injecting sporozoites into the host's tissues during the blood meal. The cycle within man now follows; first, the sporozoites disappear from the blood and undergo development for some 5–7 days; the new forms enter the general circulation and commence the asexual life cycle. This cycle consists of the invasion of a red blood cell by a malaria parasite, its development, and then division into organisms of a new generation of parasite, and with that the asexual cycle is completed. After a variable number of generations or cycles, sexual forms are produced that do not develop further in the host but may do so after ingestion by a mosquito biting the host to give rise to sporozoites. See Figure 15.1.1.

There is thus an alternation of cycles between the host and the mosquito. In any epidemiologic study of malaria, it is necessary to determine the species of *Anopheles* that is (are) the vector(s) of the parasite. The habits of these different species of vector vary considerably. Generalizations about the spread of malaria in one area may not be applicable to other, different types of area; for example, in one area the vector may breed in swamps, in another area the vector may breed in small pools of water.

See Bruce-Chwatt (1980), Manson-Bahr

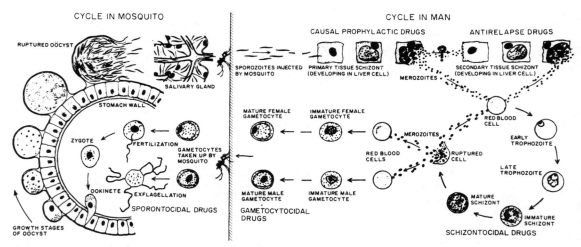

CYCLE IN MOSQUITO   CYCLE IN MAN

FIGURE 15.1.1. Diagrammatic presentation of the life cycle of human malaria parasites and the nomenclature of drug groups acting against different stages of the life cycle. From Kreier (1977, Vol. III, p. 499). Adapted from a World Health Organization publication.

(1963), and Manson-Bahr and Apted (1982); for *Plasmodium* species, see McCutchan, Dame, et al. (1984).

Of four species of *Plasmodium*, *P. ovale* is rare and *P. malariae* is distributed widely, although the proportion of cases due to it usually does not exceed 2%. Clinical experience has shown that the relative incidence of *falciparum* and *vivax* malaria varies; a good example of this is given by Boyd (1949, Figure 228, p. 779). Along the island chain, Jamaica to the Leeward Islands at 10°N, *falciparum* malaria ranges from 75% to 98%; throughout tropical South America *falciparum* proportions vary around 50%, and then the proportions fall steadily in the subtropical region to zero at 29°S. Such observations can be classified as by James and Christophers (1922).

(*i*) Tropical zone. This is marked by a preponderance of *falciparum* malaria, and *vivax* malaria is seen only in young children; there are only moderate seasonal intermissions of epidemics. Infection rates are potentially high and infection occurs in infancy; this is followed by a high immunity among the older indigenes. Epidemics are thus only noted among the immigrants; severe clinical manifestations occur only in the infants and the migrants from nonmalarious areas.

(*ii*) Subtropical zone. From the Tropic of Cancer to 40°N, *falciparum* malaria occurs in late summer and autumn, an effect especially noted by Italian authors as estivo-autumnal. After a winter pause, *vivax* infections occur in early summer and are followed by the estivo-autumnal epidemics of *falciparum* malaria. This zone includes the Mediterranean littoral and Palestine; Egypt with its low rainfall is relatively free of malaria. The zone also includes the lower course of the Euphrates, the hills of Iran, the plains of Turkestan, northern India, and the valley of the Chángjiāng (Yangtze); the zone formerly included southern United States. A less marked zone exists between the Tropic of Capricorn and 40°S.

(*iii*) Temperate zone. This extends from 40°N to the limits set by the mean summer isothermal lines at 60°N. The corresponding southern temperate zone has always been free of malaria. In the northern temperate zone, malaria was almost totally *vivax*; malaria was limited to fenland, reclaimed sea bed, and the margins of lakes, and the hills were malaria free. There are limits due to altitude; in the tropical zone, malaria can be present as high as 2,773 m at Quito on the equator and at still higher levels in southern India. In the temperate zone even a moderate elevation will prevent malarial endemicity.

See WHO-malaria (1969, 1975a, 1983) for

the distribution of the various types throughout the world.

15.2 Historical Remarks

Some landmarks in the development of ideas on malaria are now recounted to illustrate how recent are the methods of diagnosis of the parasite and the separation of malaria from other continued fevers. In approximately 1620, the Countess of Cinchon, wife of the Viceroy of Peru, was cured by a remedy made from a Peruvian bark. The active principle is now known as quinine, named in honour of the Countess. Giovanni Maria Lancisi (1654–1720) in 1717 stressed that the fevers in a neighborhood of Rome could only be overcome by draining the Pontine Marshes. In 1880 C.L.A. Laveran first gave a detailed description of malaria parasites seen in the blood in stained and unstained preparations. Camillo Golgi (1844–1926) in 1889 distinguished the parasites of quartan from those of tertian malaria and noted that the segmentation of the larger parasitic forms in the blood commenced slightly before the onset of fever. In 1891 D.L. Romanovskiĭ devised a stain of eosin and methylene blue that was easy to apply and greatly aided the microscopic diagnosis of malaria and , indeed, of other parasites. Ettore Marchiafava (1847–1935) and Amico Bignami (1862–1929) in 1892 distinguished between *P. vivax* and *P. falciparum* morphologically and between *vivax, falciparum*, and *malariae* clinically. Patrick Manson (1844–1922) in 1894 stated that the function of certain crescentic bodies seen in the blood in *falciparum* malaria was to spread the disease outside the body. Arguing from an analogy with the mode of spread of filariasis, which he had already solved, he made the hypothesis that the crescentic bodies were removed by some suctorial insect and then underwent changes yielding flagellated bodies in the insect's body that later were the source of infection of further cases. Ronald Ross (1857–1932) in 1898 reported finding flagellated bodies in the mosquito's stomach, and finally sporozoites in the mosquito's salivary glands. Giovanni Battista Grassi (1854–1925) also described the mosquito as the vector of malaria.

Nobel Prizes in Medicine and Physiology were awarded to Ross in 1902 and to Laveran in 1907; these awards underline the difficulties to be overcome and the importance of the disease.

The great compendium on malaria is Boyd (1949). See also Kreier (1980), Rieckmann and Silverman (1977), and for some historical notes, Ackerknecht (1945). For a popularization, see Alvarado and Bruce-Chwatt (1962). See §45.2 for Johnson.

15.3 Pathology

Infection is acquired naturally by the bite of a mosquito but it can also be acquired through the injection of blood from a case, active or latent, of malaria during the course of blood transfusion, drug addiction, or therapy; it can also be acquired in utero by the fetus.

The pathogenesis depends on the destruction of the infected blood cells by the malaria parasite with consequent disturbance of the oxygen supply to the tissues, on the aggregation of parasitized cells in the smaller blood vessels, and on the discharges of protein from the parasites liberated by the breakdown of the red cells and from the red cells themselves. The spleen and liver enlarge as a result, and in chronic cases death may occur from rupture of the spleen. The severest complication is blackwater fever or malarial hemoglobinuria, now much rarer than formerly, an attack often being precipitated by quinine therapy. Massive hemolysis is followed by renal anoxia and failure of the glomerular flow; methemoglobin is passed in the urine, hence, the name of the syndrome. Other pernicious attacks are classifiable into types (a) septicemic, or toxic, with numerous parasites in the blood, (b) cerebral, (c) algid with shocklike symptoms, and (d) renal. The relative frequencies of the these types are 30%, 55%, 14%, and 1%

The demonstration of malaria parasites in the blood films is the chief method of clinical diagnosis. The intensity of community infection is measured by the proportion of children with a blood film positive for malaria, or, more conveniently, the proportion of enlarged spleens in the children of the community.

15.4 Treatment and Suppression

Quinine was for a long time the sole effective therapy against malaria but, with the development of new chemotherapy in the 1930s, it has become obsolete. A number of drugs and regimens are now available for therapy and chemoprophylaxis such as sulfonamide, 4-aminoquinolines, 8-aminoquinolines, diguanides, pyrimidines, and acridines. Of these, atebrin (mepacrine hydrochloride) is an acridine yellow dye used very successfully in World War II, especially in Burma and New Guinea, but it also has become obsolete. However, with its aid, troops could remain free of malaria in hyperendemic regions. See Bruce-Chwatt (1971), Bruce-Chwatt, Black, et al. (1981), and §45.3.

15.5 Malaria as a Great Pestilence

Although malaria has not caused disasters on the scale of bubonic plague in the European population, on a worldwide view it has been the greatest of all the pestilences (or plagues) of man. Indeed, reaction to it is reflected in the existence of "abnormal" hemoglobins (Stuckey, 1966) and red cell sickling, which would have been great rarities now in any population not submitted to a long process of malarialization. We must, therefore, review the possible history of malaria with the aid, especially, of Boyd (1949), Bruce-Chwatt (1965), Bruce-Chwatt and Zulueta (1980), Coatney, Collins, et al. (1971), Garnham (1963, 1966), and Manson-Bahr (1963).

The many common properties of simian and human malaria suggest a long association going back to a common ancestral population of lemurs and monkeys that Garnham (1963) places in the early Tertiary Age, 60 million years ago. Garnham (1963) considered that benign tertian malaria originated about 30 million years ago among lower monkeys and malignant tertian malaria about 2.5 million years ago near the time of development of the higher apes and

man. Authorities differ as to the sites of these developments, whether it was in tropical Africa or tropical Asia (Coatney, et al., 1971, favoring Asia). However, there can be little doubt as to a long association of malaria and man in the Old World, that is, Europe, Africa, and Asia. Perhaps man in Europe was free of malaria during most of the Pleistocene period. During the glacial periods, conditions for the development of malaria in Europe would have been unfavorable, especially for the most lethal of the human malarial parasites, namely, *P. falciparum*; conditions would also have been unfavorable for the mosquito vectors. Cro-Magnon man living at the time of the last glaciation would have been free of malaria. It is probable that malaria did not spread throughout Europe immediately after the passing of the last Ice Age because man was nomadic, especially in summer, and few in numbers, and these factors would militate against successful parasitization by the malaria parasites; moreover, the present known mosquito vectors probably did not become installed in Europe before the extensive deforestations of Hellenistic and Roman times (see §1.5). Bruce-Chwatt and Zulueta (1980) believe that only *P. malariae* and *P. vivax* were present in Europe in the neolithic and bronze ages.

There is still considerable debate as to whether malaria existed in the Americas in pre-Columbian times. If it existed, Bruce-Chwatt (1965) believes that it would have had a very patchy distribution in the coastal areas away from the centers of civilization in the highland areas.

Even in recent times it has been a leading cause of death; thus, Russell (1955) estimated that there were about 350 million cases annually with an estimated case fatality rate of 1%. Similarly, Bruce-Chwatt (1979) estimated that 1741 million live in areas once malarious and, of these, 381 million are still subjected to endemic malaria; a further 710 million live in areas partially controlled.

In holoendemic (i.e., with most intense transmission) areas, a person may be bitten by an infected mosquito every 10 days on an average. Such a high risk rate ensures that everyone is infected in the first year of life, and almost all children have enlarged spleens and detectable parasites in the blood. Livingstone (1971) finds, from an inspection of relevant statistics, that the crude death rate from malaria in holoendemic areas is about 10–15 per 1,000 per annum, although this is larger than any malarial death rate recorded in official statistics. Under such conditions, any genetic trait that favors the individual will be positive selected. The sickle cell gene (hemoglobin S) is thus favored if it appears in a holoendemic area; in the Bwamba in Uganda, the sickle cell gene frequency is 0.195 and the proportion of heterozygotes is $2(0.195)(0.805) = 0.314$ or 31.4%. The proportion of homozygotes is $0.038 = 3.8\%$. Out of 1,000 persons born in such a community we have 38 homozygous and 314 heterozygous for the S-hemoglobin gene. Now assume that all 38 homozygous die before reaching adulthood, then out of $314 + 38 = 352$ persons in such a community, fewer die than out of 352 normal persons, that is, the subpopulation carrying the S-hemoglobin gene can compensate for an additional 38 deaths of the homozygotes. The proportion of deaths from malaria in the normals must be at least equal to $38/352 > 10\%$.

We give some more specific data on the disease by continents. The classic account of malaria considered as a wordwide disease is Boyd (1949), to which many experts have contributed including Hackett (1949*a*) on the general distribution, Faust (1949) on the incidence in North America, Gabaldon (1949) on the West Indies and South America, Hackett (1949*b*) on Europe, the near East, and North Africa, Wilson (1949) on central and south Africa, Covell (1949) on the Far East, and Lambert (1949) on Australia and the South Pacific. The difficulty in estimating the importance of malaria as a cause of death is that the health and statistical services in the countries worst affected are, or at least have been, most defective principally because of poverty. As an example of the difficulties, we may consider figures in *Annual Epidemiological and Vital Statistics (WHO)* for the year 1954 and list for some of the countries the reported numbers of cases and deaths as follows: Gabon 12,310, 8; Middle Congo 50,623, 62; Ubangi-Chari 16,911, 30; Chad 10,826, 15; Upper Volta 24,531, 67; Belgian Congo 747,488, 2,032; Kenya 18,050, 586; Madagascar 218,128, 498; Colombia 73,906, 2,041; Mexico 48,521, 19,437; Panama 2,849, 93; El Salvador 5,737, 852; and United States 715, 24. It follows from these figures that the case fatality rates in 1954 were 0.1% to 0.4% in the African countries, whereas they were 3% to 15% in the American countries. It is evident that the *WHO Yearbooks* give little information of value on the incidence and case fatality of malaria and, similarly, for the *Weekly Epidemiological Reports (WHO)*. We are therefore obliged to cite secondary literature in §15.9 below. Sources often are concerned not with mortality figures in themselves but with the success of the eradication or control programs.

In severely affected (holoendemic) areas, almost all children born into the community become infected in infancy or early childhood; a child may die directly as a result of the infection; if not he/she will have an enhanced risk of mortality from other causes because of the malarial debilitation. Infant mortality had been known to be approximately twice as high in the malarious areas of India as in the nonmalarious. In these holoendemic areas there are no epidemics of malaria; it is constantly present.

In some other areas, malaria is capable of causing sharp epidemics on the introduction of the parasite or an efficient mosquito vector or because of changed meteorological conditions. Thus, in a population of 47,000 in Port Louis, Mauritius, 6,000 deaths occurred during a malaria epidemic in 1867. In the Punjab in the months of October and November 1898, there were 307,000 deaths as against an expected normal number of 100,000. In Ceylon 80,000 persons died from malaria in 7 months of 1934–1935. When *A. gambiae* was introduced accidentally into Brazil in 1938, over 100,000 cases with 14,000 deaths from malaria occurred within 7 months. The examples are cited by Pampana and Russell (1955). These authors give a review of malaria as a world health problem.

It is clear that malaria has profound effects on many aspects of the demography of a country; in particular, it affects the birth rate by causing abortions and stillbirths. Campaigns are reported in which the birth rate rose as a result of antimalarial measures, but sometimes it is unaffected. Malaria will also affect the general economic efficiency of the population. Pampana and Russell (1955) give examples of huge financial losses from malaria, for example, in the United States in the first decade of this century. See also Payne, Grab, et al. (1976) and Bruce-Chwatt (1979). For the world malaria situation in 1983, 1984, see WHO-malaria (1985, 1986); for present and future, see Bruce-Chwatt (1987).

15.6 Oceania

New Zealand and Polynesia have been free of endemic malaria. Black (1972) believes that malaria occasionally occurred in northern Australia before 1788; in north Queensland there was some trade with New Guinea, and there is a known historical case that points to the possibilities of malaria being introduced in pre-European days. Further west there were many visits from Indonesia; as a result, some malarial outbreaks occurred after 1800, and it is probable that sporadic cases and even epidemics of *falciparum* malaria occurred before that time. With more extensive contact after 1800 and the introduction of Asian fishermen and miners, there were larger outbreaks with up to about 70 deaths on the whole continent in the 1890s. During World War II, cases occurred in troops returning from New Guinea, and there were minor epidemics in north Queensland.

15.7 Europe

In §1.5, we have mentioned the incidence of malaria in Europe during Roman times and have concluded that the pernicious form of the disease had not been described before the time of Celsus (14 BC–AD 37) and only in imperial Roman times was malaria a cause of significant mortality.

Malaria in Europe has been much studied, for example, Hackett (1937, 1949*a*, *b*), Bruce-Chwatt and Zulueta (1980), and Zulueta (1973). It is possible here, only to pick out iso-lated features and incidents in a brief summary. In the Balkans, because of the lack of continuous official or hygienic records, it seems customary to call on the experience of armies of the great European powers to indicate the true extent of the malarial infections.

The 40°N parallel cuts Spain and Sardinia roughly in halves, passes through the heel of Italy, and then southern Albania and Greece just south of Mt. Olympus, so that much of Europe lies in the temperate zone as defined in §15.1. Some of the areas north of 40°N have had the subtropical type of experience. Indeed, such is the case for the northern half of Sardinia, the coastal strip near Rome, the valleys of the rivers draining the Macedonian highlands, the Danube basin below the Iron Gate, and the western shore of the Black Sea. Marshes and areas of rice cultivation are special hazards.

We begin with Greece, part of which clearly had had an experience subtropical, as defined in §15.1 As pointed out in §1.5, an analysis of the literary sources from Homer onward suggests that, although Attica and Boeotia may have been highly malarious in the fourth century BC, malaria, especially that due to *P. falciparum*, spread over the greater part of Greece at the beginning of the first millenium AD, causing death and debility of inhabitants, desolation of whole districts, and the decay of agriculture and trade. There follows a long period of foreign domination and darkness, for which estimates of malaria endemicity can only be speculative. Indeed, the importance of malaria only became recognized by western Europe when European armies assisted the Greeks in their wars of liberation and suffered severe losses from malaria from 1821 onward. Numerical data became available in the 1890s when there were over 40,000 admissions to the military hospitals in Greece over 5 years. Ronald Ross received information that there were over 960,000 cases of malaria in Greece with almost 6,000 deaths in 1905. In 1906 antimalarial measures were instituted, but much malaria remained, and the Allied and German sides suffered heavy losses in the Macedonian campaign during the war of 1914–1918. See §33.17. During 1921–1932, deaths in Greece due to malaria varied between 3,400 and 7,800 per annum, constituting about 5.6% of total mortality. During the 1930s there were some large reclamation schemes, altering the course of rivers and draining marshes, and quinine prophylaxis was instituted. After World War II, more control measures were available with insecticide sprayings and better prophylactic drugs. The mortality rate fell from 313 per 1,000,000 in 1930–1939 to 0.6 in 1954–1955. After 1965 there was a flattening out of the curve of cases per annum and it was observed that there were undue numbers from Macedonia and Lesbos; special attention was devoted to these areas and by 1973 endemic malaria in Greece had been reduced to practically zero; the table in Bruce-Chwatt and Zulueta (1980, p. 42) shows that no new indigenous case of malaria was reported after 1960.

The subtropical zone of the classification in §15.1 does not stop at 40°N, for Thrace in northern Greece and the valleys of the Vardar and Struma in Macedonia have been highly malarious, including areas in Yugoslavia, Greece, and Bulgaria. European Turkey was highly malarious and there was much malaria on Gallipoli at 40°N in World War I. The southern Bulgarian coast at 42°N–43°N was hypo- or mesoendemic with some hyperendemic foci, whereas the northern coastal plain at 43°N–44°N was said to be hypoendemic; nevertheless, this was the coast on which the Russian army fighting in Bulgaria in 1877–1878 had over half their forces simultaneously sick. Similarly, in Romania the Dobrogea area, 44°N–45.4°N, has been declared a severe endemic area; thus, in 1945–1946 the local incidence of infection varied from 50%–70% in some localities with *falciparum* accounting for 66% of infections; the malaria mortality reached the very high figure of 2 deaths per 1,000 of population in the epidemic. In Romania, in 1892–1897 there had been a rate of 200,000 cases per year and early in this century, 420,000. In the southwestern province Oltenita, including part of the Danubian lowlands, there were 4,500 cases of malaria in 1912, and in 1923 there were 40,000 cases with some 2,000 deaths, with *falciparum* being dominant. In this later outbreak, the importance of the cultivation of rice for malaria endemicity was noted. In 1945–1946, there were over 600,000 cases of malaria in Romania.

Further up the Danube at 46°N in southeast Hungary and in Yugoslavia, the problem was not so severe, with *falciparum* proportions falling to 10% of all malaria cases.

From Greece we may examine the malaria experience along the northern Mediterranean littoral to the west. Albania, largely between 40°N and 42°N, had been highly malarious, with Austrian and Italian armies suffering severely in the 1914–1918 war. It was one of the regions with marked deforestation, erosion, and formation of freshwater lagoons. Antimalarial measures were begun in the early 1930s, especially the salinification of lagoons; the campaign was intensified after 1947 and by 1966 the country suffered little.

In Yugoslavia, malaria has been of special importance in Macedonia, where the incidence of enlarged spleen in children was up to 80% in some areas, indicative of holoendemicity. *Vivax* infections in March to July were replaced by *falciparum* infections from August to November. The Allied Army advanced up the River Vardar from Salonika during World War I; in the autumn of 1916, the French had only half their force fit, and approximately one quarter of the British force suffered from malaria; the German forces suffered rather less. Two other provinces, Montenegro and Serbia, had highly malarious areas, coastal in the first case and on the upper Morava River in the other.

Italy is of interest because of the literary records in ancient, medieval, and modern times and because there were scientists in close proximity to the Pontine Marshes, which together with southern Calabria (toe of Italy), Sicily, and Sardinia, were the only areas with a tropical type experience, for which see Bruce-Chwatt and Zulueta (1980). These authors show that deaths from malaria were already falling by the turn of the century but consider that this fall was accelerated by the provision of quinine prophylaxis and, less so, by the reclamation of marshy areas and resettlement of populations (*bonifica integrale* or bonification). The decline in deaths was halted by World War I but began again with about 200 deaths per 1,000,000 in 1920; by 1940 the rate was almost negligible. The necessary programs were neglected during 1939–1945 but after the war, DDT, synthetic antimalarial drugs, and land reclamation rapidly eradicated malaria. An intensive campaign also reduced the number of cases from over 16,000 to 4 in 6 years in Sardinia.

In France malaria is said to have accounted for 6.3 per 1,000 of all deaths in 1855–1857. *Falciparum* malaria has been transmitted only in the south. It is agreed by French authors that by 1900 malaria had ceased to be a public health problem in France. Corsica has been highly malarious; 10% of the French garrison are said to have died every year from various fevers; the mean annual case rate among the garrison at Ajaccio was 200 per 1,000. Reclamation works, bed nets, the screening of houses, and, especially, quinine prophylaxis were applied at the end of the nineteenth century to reduce the mortality. After World War II, malaria was practically abolished from Corsica.

In Spain, deaths were 168, 217, 299, 338, and 526 in 1936 through 1940; 1,278, 1,781, 1,307, 523, and 201 in 1941 through 1945; 275 in 1946 and thereafter declined to a last death in 1959; this was remarkable as it was almost entirely due to therapy.

In the remaining states of western Europe *falciparum* malaria has played little part. The reader is referred to Chapter 14 of Bruce-Chwatt and Zulueta (1980) for a description of the events in Poland and southern USSR.

See also Vasiliev and Segal (1960) for Russia.

15.8 North America

There is good agreement that, although anopheline mosquitoes were present, malaria was not endemic in America until the arrival of the Europeans. Before 1880, malaria was endemic in some of the western Canadian provinces, and sporadic epidemics ocurred on the northern banks of the St. Lawrence River, but after 1892 it became limited to the western shores of Lakes Erie and Ontario and seems to have died out soon after. See also Dunn (1965).

According to Faust (1949), it was only after African slave labor was brought in to develop rice cultivation in the Carolinas, to fell the forests, and clear the land, that malaria was present in appreciable proportions among the negro slaves or white susceptible populations. Around 1850, malaria was endemic in most of the eastern half of the United States and in some scattered areas in the western half. Its endemicity was greatest up the great Mississippi-Missouri system and along the southeast coast from Alabama to Maryland.

Mortality rates per 1,000,000 in the years around 1860 were Missouri, 1,120; Illinois, 370; Iowa, 790; Wisconsin, 570; and Minnesota, 260. Malaria became a special problem for the Federal (northern) troops in the Civil War; Faust (1949) gives case rates of 391 in 1862 to 536 in 1864 per 1,000 mean strength in the Federal army for the years 1862–1865. Malaria was taken to the north by the returning Federal troops. Far greater losses were incurred in the fertile land of the south, where the land was allowed to lie fallow. Malaria and hookworm were major causes of slow economic recovery until the turn of the century. Maxcy (1923) is cited for death rates per 1,000,000 as follows: Michigan, 200 in 1880s, 1 or lower in 1915; and, similarly, Missouri, 170 in 1910, 40 in 1920; Indiana, 100 in 1900, 7 in 1920; Kentucky, 100 in 1910, 10 in 1920. *Falciparum* malaria has been common in the south and was long a great cause of mortality, especially among the negroes. See also Faust (1945) and §42.5.

In Mexico, with a chiefly moist tropical environment, high rates of malaria mortality were experienced along both east and west coasts, south of 26°N, with very high rates of 8 per 1,000 per annum on the Pacific coast at 16°N near the Golfo de Tehuantepec and 17 per 1,000 in northeast Guatemala to 0.6 in the highlands in the years 1931–1939, according to Faust (1949). See Garcia-Martin (1972) for the status of malaria eradication in the Americas at the end of 1970. See also Friedlander (1977) for the effects of malaria on demography. For malaria in Latin America, see Chapter 43.

15.9 Southeast Asia

According to Harinasuta (1983), malaria is still a leading public health problem in Southeast Asia and a cause of considerable morbidity and mortality. The control of areas near the semi-forested and hilly regions, where the cultivation of rice has recently been extended, has been especially difficult. In these countries, embracing some 340 million, the population is largely, perhaps 80%–85%, rural. Campaigns of residual house spraying against the anopheline vectors and of detection and treatment of malaria cases were successful in 1950–1970 in reducing the morbidity and mortality throughout the region; but since 1971 the incidence has increased gradually at first, but markedly in 1976–1980.

Burma

Here, malaria is the greatest public health problem; infections with *P. falciparum* dominate, being three times as common as those with *P. vivax*. Resistances have developed of parasite to chloroquine and of anopheline mosquito to DDT. In 1979 the position had improved and the slide-positive rate was 1.2%; 7% of the population were living in malaria-free areas, whereas the remainder were receiving protection by drugs, DDT house spraying, and other activities.

Thailand

Here, great problems have resulted from large-scale population movements. In 1980 the slide-positive rate was 8 per 1,000 and the mortality rate was 80 per 1,000,000; in 1947 the mortality rate had been almost 3,000 per 1,000,000; further, malaria death rates per 1,000,000 per annum were 2,015, 302, 101, 125, 158, 97, and 82 in 1949, 1969, 1970, 1971, 1974, 1978, and 1979, respectively. The campaigns have been more successful in the flat, flooded rice fields and agricultural areas than in the semiforested areas near the borders with the neighboring states. Special features in some areas have been the early rising of rubber tappers, the creation of breeding grounds by gem mining, drug resistance, less community participation in DDT house spraying, and inefficiency in the administration.

Vietnam

Here, again, malaria is a great public health problem; according to WHO reports, the slide-positive rates were 15%–20% in 1975 and 5.1% in 1979.

Kampuchea

Little information is available except that malaria incidence is very high. Political instability, military operations, and lack of security have led to grave difficulties for antimalarial programs.

Laos

Little is known about malaria campaigns and incidence.

Malaysia

There have been great reductions in the number of cases. Sabah has no problem of control, whereas the malaria infection rate is about 1% in Sarawak.

Philippines

Malaria is a problem on the fringes of the forest where new settlers are living in temporary huts and dwellings, often without walls.

Indonesia

Some progress has been made but the positive slide rate was still about 1.5% in 1979.

Singapore

Cases here all come from abroad.

In general terms, the difficulties of control can be grouped under the headings (*i*) internal migration of people, (*ii*) movement across national boundaries, (*iii*) habits of the people, for example, staying outdoors in the early evening, (*iv*) failure of community participation, (*v*) conditions of temporary huts and houses, for example, open huts have no walls on which DDT can be sprayed, (*vi*) drug-resistant *P. falciparum*, (*vii*) chemotherapy, for instance, difficulties in persuading persons to take the drugs at the right time, (*viii*) insecticide resistance of vector mosquitoes, (*ix*) changes of habit of the vector mosquitoes, and (*x*) finance.

15.10 Eradication and Control

After the development of effective therapy and powerful insecticides, together with the gaining of much knowledge of the bionomics of the vector *Anopheline* species and skills in the necessary engineering works, it was considered desirable by expert committees of WHO that an attempt should be made to eradicate malaria from the world, even from regions where it had been a grave cause of mortality for many centuries. If eradication were not possible, then it was considered that control, namely, to hold the rates of morbidity and mortality at acceptable limits, would be (see Yekutiel, 1980).

In the spirit of these aims, Gabaldon and Berti (1954) reported the control of malaria in Venezuela; for example, in one area there had been 6,819 clinically diagnosed cases in 1950 and 182 in 1953. There had been, in the meantime, clinical treatment of cases, the use of pesticides against the *Anopheline* vectors, and appropriate engineering works. In more favorably placed countries, it has been possible, as we have seen above, to eradicate malaria from Australia, from Europe, and from the United States.

A map in Faust and Russell (1964, p. 262) shows the geographical distribution of malaria throughout the world before 1946, prior to the widespread use of residual insecticides in control. Malaria is present throughout the wet tropics. The northern limit of endemic malaria is at about 32°N on the west coast of North America, approximately at the border of Mexico and the United States. To the east of the Rocky Mountains and their extensions, the northern limit is at about 40°N in the valleys of the Mississippi and Missouri rivers. In Europe, France and the extreme north of Italy are free, so are Hungary and Transylvania in Romania; a small strip of Poland is shown as malarious,

as is most of the Ukraine and part of southern Russia to about 55°N. The dividing line between malarious and nonmalarious areas runs south, skirting the west coast of the Aral Sea, then through northeast Afghanistan easterly but to the south of the Himalayas, then from the northern districts of Burma in a roughly northeasterly direction to North Korea, and through Honshu, Japan, roughly at 36°N. In South America the dividing line runs northwest from approximately 30°S on the eastern coast to 23°S on the western coast; in Africa the Tropic of Capricorn is the dividing line. Madagascar and mauritius are malarious and there is a thin potentially malarious coastal strip of northern and northeastern Australia extending down to near the Tropic of Capricorn.

In Faust and Russell (1964, Figure 7.6), it can be seen that in 1963, Australia is free of malaria and that Africa and South America are free up to the Tropic of Capricorn. The United States, Panama, and most of the island groups of the West Indies are free of malaria; so, too, are Europe, the Soviet Asian territories, and Japan. No statement is made for mainland China. Taiwan, Mauritius (partly), and Singapore are now free of malaria.

Yekutiel (1980) gives the position as of December, 1973. Peru, Venezuela, and much of the eastern coastlands of Brazil have become free; so, also, have the Ryukyu Islands, Taiwan, and much of southern India.

The value of the global eradication campaign can be estimated in some areas as shown in Table 15.10.1, modified slightly after Gramiccia and Hempel (1972), in which they compare rates of mortality from malaria in 1955 and in 1967/1968, the first year being a target year before large-scale antimalarial measures were implemented; the year 1967/1968 was the most recent year for which data were available.

In Table 15.10.2, the crude mortality (all causes) rates per 10,000 and the crude mortality (malaria) rates per 1,000,000 are given for a number of countries. There have been great declines in the rates between 1955 and 1967/1968.

Table 15.10.3 shows great reductions in the mortality and morbidity rates for selected Asian countries.

TABLE 15.10.1 Malaria death rates for the years 1955 and 1967–1968 in selected countries.

	1955			1967/1968*					
	(1)	(2)	(3)	(4)	(5)	(6)	(7)	(8)	(9)
	Malaria deaths	Popln in thousands	Malaria death rate per million	Malaria deaths	Popln in thousands	Malaria death rate per million	Reduction in % of malaria death rate[#]	Year control activity started	Year eradication program or attack phase started
America group 1									
El Salvador	955	2,135	447	206	3,266	63	86	1949	1955
Honduras	2,538	1,595	1,591	145[†]	2,333[†]	62[†]	96	1949	1958
Mexico	19,639	30,557	643	29	47,267	1	100		1956
Nicaragua	1,694	1,218	1,391	340	1,842	185	87	1949	1958
Panama	110	919	120	21	1,372	15	88	1952	1957
Colombia	1,822	13,172	138	1,127[†]	19,191[†]	59[†]	57	1952	1956
Ecuador	1,411	3,752	376	140[†]	5,508[†]	25[†]	93		1957
Total	28,169	53,348	528	2,008	80,779	25	95		
America group 2									
Costa Rica	150	1,028	146	13[†]	1,590[†]	8[†]	94	1949	1957
Domin. Rep.	848	2,541	334	5	4,029	1	100	1952	1958
Brit. Hond.	9	78	115	0	116	0	100	1949	1957
St. Lucia	53	79	671	0	108	0	100		1956
Guyana	6	486	12	0[†]	698[†]	0	100		1959
Paraguay	55	782	70	18	1,159	2	77	1952	1957/1967[¶]
Venezuela	18	6,089	3	3	9,689	0	90		1945
Surinam	3	234	13	0[†]	363[†]	0[†]	100	1952	1958
Total	1,142	11,317	101	39	17,749	2	98		
Asia									
Ceylon	268	8,723	31	4[†]	11,952[†]	0[†]	99	1945	1958
India	196,000[§]	394,200[§]	497[§]	2,203[‖]	525,607[‖]	4[‖]	99	1952	1958
Philippines	3,714	23,568	158	1,061	35,963	29	82	1953	1958
Syria[‡]	45	3,861	12	0	5,701	0	100	1952	1956
Thailand	14,520	22,975	632	3,308	33,206	104	84	1949	1956
Total	214,547	450,654	476	6,576	612,429	11	98		

* Whenever available, 1968 data have been recorded, otherwise 1967 data have been used. The totals and the percentage reduction in malaria death rates have been calculated on the latest available figures.

[†] 1967 data.

[‡] Number of deaths from patients attending clinical centers only.

[§] Estimated data for 1956, obtained from extrapolations from sample surveys of the National Malaria Control Programme giving an estimated number of 19,600,000 cases for the year. Malaria deaths are estimated at 1% of the malaria cases.

[‖] Estimated deaths, calculated as 1% of malaria cases reported from the National Malaria Eradication Programme.

[¶] Malaria eradication program activities were suspended in 1960 owing to insufficient funds: An epidemic developed. The program started again in 1967.

[#] Calculated as: $100 - \left[\dfrac{(6)}{(3)} \times 100 \right]$

From Gramiccia and Hempel (1972).

TABLE 15.10.2. General mortality and malaria mortality for the years 1955 and 1967 in selected countries.

	General mortality (per 10,000 popln.)		Malaria mortality (per 1,000,000 popln.)	
	1955	*1967*	*1955*	*1967*
America group 1				
El Salvador	142	92	447	73
Honduras	119	84	1,591	62
Mexico	136	92	643	1
Nicaragua	92	80	1,391	146
Panama	91	67	120	16
Colombia	128	94	138	59
Ecuador	155	106	376	25
America group 2				
Costa Rica	113	69	146	8
Domin. Rep.	91	76	334	12
Brit. Hond.	108	71	115	0
St. Lucia	119	—	671	0
Guyana	119	82	12	0
Paraguay	—	42	70	35
Venezuela	96	66	3	0
Surinam	92	—	13	0
Asia				
Ceylon	108	75	31	0
Philippines	90	69	156	33
Syria	47	46	12	0
Thailand	83	74	632	129

The proportion of mortality due to malaria can be obtained as (malaria rate)/(100 × general mortality rate).
From Gramiccia and Hempel (1972).

TABLE 15.10.3. Malaria morbidity (per 10,000 population) and malaria mortality (per 1,000,000 population) in selected countries in 1955 and 1967/8 in Asia.

Country	1955			1967/1968			Reduction in %	
	+ve cases	Morbidity	Mortality	+ve cases	Morbidity	Mortality	Morbidity	Mortality
Ceylon	11,191	13	31	3,466[†]	3[†]	0[†]	77	99
Philippines	79,707	34	156	14,904	4	29	88	81
Syria	69,252	18	7	3,007	1	0	97	100
Thailand	45,106[*]	2[*]	332[*]	89,057	3	104	—	69

[*] 1959.
[†] 1967.
From Gramiccia and Hempel (1972).

TABLE 15.10.4. Malaria morbidity in some countries before and at the end of the eradication program.

Continent	Country and stage* of program	Year	Number of cases of malaria
The Americas	Dominican Republic, M + C	1950	17,310
		1973	418
	Jamaica, M	1954	4,417
		1969	nil
	Venezuela, M + C + A	1943	817,115
		1958	800
Africa	Mauritius, M	1948	46,400
		1968	14[†]
Asia	Taiwan, M	1954	1,000,000
		1969	9[†]
	Iraq, M + C + A	1950	537,286
		1973	3,783
	Turkey, M + C + A	1950	1,888,000
		1973	9,828
Europe	Bulgaria, M	1946	144,631
		1969	10[†]
	Romania, M	1948	388,200
		1969	4[†]
	Spain, M	1950	19,644
		1969	28[†]
	Yugoslavia, M	1937	169,545
		1969	15[†]

*Stage of program in the last year quoted.
 M = Maintenance phase; C = Consolidation phase; A = Attack phase.
[†]All cases reported in countries in maintenance phase were imported or induced.
Data from Brown, et al. (1976), Wright, et al. (1972), and WHO-malaria (1975b).

From Yekutiel (1980), p. 71. (With permission from S. Karger AG, Basel.)

In Table 15.10.4 are some results given chiefly by Brown, Haworth, and Zahar (1976) and Wright, Fritz, and Haworth (1972) in a table by Yekutiel (1980), showing rates of malaria morbidity before and after eradication campaigns. It is evident that the disease can be controlled and even eradicated in some countries.

15.11 Malaria Postscript

Of all the great pestilences, malaria has been the most difficult to control. For a recent picture, 1982, we may summarize WHO-malaria (1984). Throughout the world, with total population 4,574 million in 1982, there were 6.5 million cases reported as against 7.8 million cases in 1981; but reporting throughout the world was of varying efficiency, and the reported overall incidence is strongly influenced by the resurgence of malaria in Southeast Asia and the inclusion of China within the reporting area in 1977. Of the world population in 1982, 28% lived in areas where malaria had never been endemic or from whence it had disappeared without specific antimalarial measures, 18% lived where malaria had been eliminated in recent decades, 46% lived in areas where antimalarial measures had reduced the incidence in varying degrees, and 8% lived in areas in which no specific antimalarial measures had been undertaken, except, perhaps, in certain cities.

In Africa, north of the Sahara, 73 million lived in areas formerly malarious out of a total population of 96 million. Imported cases occurred in Egypt. In Africa, south of the Sahara, 47 million out of a total of 397 million population lived in areas where malaria had never existed or had been eliminated. In the remaining 350 million, antimalarial measures had been insufficient to check the incidence.

In the area north of Mexico and, so, in the United States and Canada, with a total population of 257 million, cases of malaria were few and were either imported or occurred as congenital or infections by syringe and blood transfusion. Of 127 million population in Central America, 22 million lived in areas from which malaria had been eliminated and 24 million lived in areas where the risk was limited. Some improvement had occurred in the area in which the remaining 81 million lived. We mention some problems and some researches.

Drug Resistance

Strains of *falciparum* malaria resistant to drugs have arisen. See Wernsdorfer (1984) for a popularizing account of the problem and Rieckmann (1983) for the need for safe and effective drugs, and also Bruce-Chwatt, Black, et al. (1981). For recent researches on Qinghaosu (Artemisinin), an antimalarial drug from China, see Klayman (1985).

Immunology

With theoretical advances in immunology and the possibility of gene manipulations, attention is being directed toward the making of effective vaccines (Taylor and Siddiqui, 1982, and Kolata, 1985a).

Mode of Action of the Parasite

More intense research is being devoted to the mode of attack of the parasite on the red cell (Evered and Whelan, 1983, and Weatherall, Abdalla, et al., 1983).

WHO-Publications

The state of malaria in the world has been reviewed by WHO-malaria (1974, 1975a, 1978, 1983, 1984, 1985, 1986). Conferences on malaria are being held (e.g., Lepes, 1974).

Thalassemia

Even if malaria were eradicated, there would be a considerable problem caused by the anomalous hemoglobins, for example, thalassemia, that will increase in relative importance as a cause of mortality, especially in children.

Chapter 16
Other Arthropod-borne Diseases

16.1 Leishmaniasis

ICD 085. Fourth digit: 0, visceral leishmaniasis, or kala azar, caused by *Leishmania donovani*; 1, urban cutaneous leishmaniasis or oriental sore, caused by *L. tropica*; 2, Asian desert cutaneous, caused by *L. tropica major*; 3, Ethiopian cutaneous, caused by *L. ethiopica*; 4, American cutaneous, caused by *L. mexicana*; 5, American mucocutaneous, caused by *L. braziliense*; 9, unspecified.

Leishmania species are parasitic in certain vertebrate hosts, including man, other primates, rodents, and canids. Sandflies of the genus *Phlebotomus*, in which the organisms are mobile extracellular inhabitants of the lumen of the gut, are vectors of the parasite. In the vertebrate host, the parasite is a small ovoid or roundish organism measuring 2–4 μm, so the long diameter is rather less than one half of that of a red cell. After being introduced into the vertebrate body by the sandfly vector, the parasites multiply in the reticuloendothelial cells of the liver, spleen, lymph glands, and bone marrow. The infective cycle is completed by the sandfly vector biting and becoming infected from a concentration of the parasites in the subdermis.

There are two forms of visceral leishmaniasis caused by *Leishmania donovani*. In the Mediterranean region it is an anthropozoonosis, primarily infecting dogs and only occasionally humans, but in India, it appears to be essentially human since no nonhuman host has been demonstrated. In other parts of Asia the

dog acts as a reservoir host. Visceral leishmaniasis, or kala azar, is characterized by fever of long duration, anemia, low blood-white-cell count, and by enlargement of the liver and spleen. There is wasting and serious imbalance of the serum proteins. The disease untreated is almost uniformly fatal.

The diseases mentioned in ICD 085.1–085.4, although milder, are sometimes associated with considerable morbidity.

American leishmaniasis, espundia, or mucocutaneous leishmaniasis is again a severe disease. The causative organism is *L. braziliense* although many protozoologists say that this species is identical with *L. donovani*, the species of Indian or Mediterranean leishmaniasis. In any case, it is generally agreed that the *Leishmania* strains causing the South American forms of the disease are heterogeneous; there is doubt as to whether these differences warrant race or species status. The disease may be purely cutaneous or mucocutaneous. The general signs and symptoms are not as severe as in the Indian or Mediterranean types, but the mucocutaneous ulcerations may invade vital organs, especially in the regions surrounding the nasopharynx, and so lead to death.

Kala azar, or visceral leishmaniasis, is an important cause of death especially in the principal endemic areas, Assam and Bengal. Epidemics may occur as at Dum Dum, India, in 1900. There was an epidemic of kala azar in Bengal following the famine of 1943, with a peak in 1946, according to Faust and Russell (1964); it was believed to be more virulent than

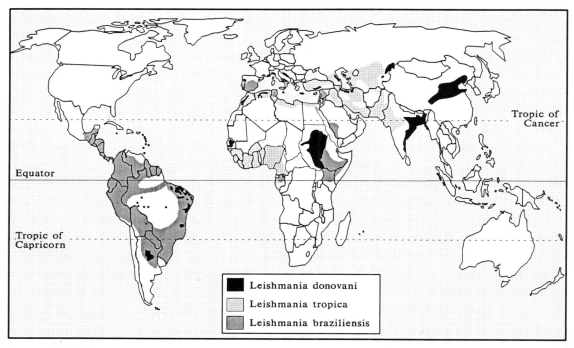

FIGURE 16.1.1. World distribution of leishmania infections as of 1955. After Faust and Russell (1964, p. 108).

usual because of a large proportion of susceptible children under the age of 15 years and because of lowered resistance associated with famine and war conditions.

In Catania, Sicily, the annual incidence of the Mediterranean form was said to be 1 per 1,000 of population, and in Malta the rate was about 0.3 per 1,000, according to Theodor (1964).

In South America leishmaniasis cases occur in many areas; children under the age of 4 years are the most affected group. The disease is said to resemble the Indian form when *L. donovani* is the agent. Cutaneous leishmaniasis in South America is reviewed by Convit and Pinardi (1974).

Subclinical cases of all forms of leishmaniasis are common in the endemic areas, see Figure 16.1.1.

General surveys are available in Adler (1964), Elliott, O'Connor, and Wolstenholme (1974), Theodor (1964), and Zuckerman and Lainson (1977). See also Faust and Russell (1964) for clinical descriptions.

A substantial epidemic with 70,000 cases occurred in Northern Bihar in 1971–1977 with a maximum prevalence of 0.44% in the affected villages (D.H. Smith, Manson-Bahr, and Chance, 1984).

16.2 Trypanosomiasis

ICD 086. Fourth digit: 0–2, Chagas' disease with site of involvement; 3, Gambian trypanosomiasis; 4, Rhodesian trypanosomiasis; 5, African trypanosomiasis; 9, unspecified.

Trypanosomes are flagellated protozoa, which, like the *Leishmania* species, are believed to have evolved from parasites or commensals of arthropods, see Lambrecht (1967) and, more generally, Hoare (1972). The human diseases are spread by reduviid bugs in America and by species of the genus of biting flies, *Glossina*, in Africa. As Baker (1974) remarks, the organisms of western African sleeping sickness, *Trypanosoma brucei gambiense*, and of eastern African sleeping sickness, *Trypanosoma brucei rhodesiense*, have been regarded as two separate species, but now the prevailing view is that they are subspecies or even "clinical races" of their presumed ancestral species, *T. brucei*, which by definition does not infect man. *Trypanosoma brucei* causes a severe zoonosis among the ungulates in which it is perpetuated. *Trypanosoma brucei gambiense* can only be perpetuated if there is close and repeated contact between man and the appropriate *Glossina* (tsetse fly) species; infections of ungulates are regarded as adventitious. *Trypanosoma brucei rhodesiense* is perpetuated in the ungulates with close and repeated contact with appropriate *Glossina* species; infection of man is regarded as adventitious, although it is believed that the cycle *Glossina*-man-*Glossina*-ungulate is possible and would be a factor in perpetuation. Evolution of the *T.b. rhodesiense* is believed to have occurred recently, perhaps in the past hundred years. We defer until later discussion of the American trypanosomiasis.

The trypanosomes are introduced into the skin from the proboscis of an infected tsetse fly; a local inflammatory action is set up that subsides in a week or two, and the trypanosomes then gain entrance to the blood and cause a parasitemia. They do not invade tissue cells but they have injurious effects on them. The characteristic disease symptoms occur when the trypanosomes enter the subarachnoid spaces and the nervous tissue of the brain. As Faust and Russell (1964) describe, there is an incubation period of 2 to 23 days, usually 6 to 14 days, then a period when the trypanosomes are predominantly in the blood stream, a period when they are predominantly in the lymph nodes, and finally there is an invasion of the central nervous system. The third of these stages is characterized by fever and enlargement of the lymph nodes, especially of the posterior triangle of the neck. In the fourth stage there are neuralgic pains, weakness, headache, mental dullness and other neurological signs, followed by a deepening coma and death.

The *rhodesiense* form of the disease is the more acute and usually ends in death in the first year; the *gambiense* form is milder and may end in death after several years.

The third form of human trypanosomiasis is Chagas' disease or American trypanosomiasis due to *T. cruzi*. Chagas' disease became an anthropozoonosis when the insect vectors became adapted to human buildings.

It is possible that *T. cruzi* can enter the human body through the intact skin, although the common mode of entry seems to result from deposition of semiliquid feces of the bug on exposed mucous surfaces, particularly at the corner of the eye or around the nose or lips. The organisms multiply in the adipose cells immediately below the point of entry. For about 3 days they multiply as leishmania forms, then they infect the local lymph nodes, and finally become generalized by passing to the satellite lymph nodes, the lymph system, and blood stream. The pathology consists essentially in the destruction of the reticuloendothelial and other tissue cells. Any organ can be invaded, including the central nervous system. The symptoms are variable. The minimum incubation period is 7 to 14 days; a parasitemia develops about 2 to 3 weeks after infection. In the acute form, usually found in children, there is high fever and the deposition of mucoid material in the tissues, causing tumefaction. The first symptom is often edema of an eye; lymph nodes, spleen, and liver are usually enlarged. Fever is present. There may be typhoidlike mental states; meningeal or encephalitic signs may be present. Death may occur in 4 to 8 weeks. Chronic infection follows in those who do not die. The prognosis is always grave since there is no certain cure; spontaneous recovery is rare. The parasite can survive up to 12 years.

For trypanosomiasis of South Asia, see Weinman (1977).

16.3 American Trypanosomiasis as a Great Pestilence

American trypanosomiasis or Chagas' disease was originally a zoonosis of wild mammals in the two Americas with reduviid bugs as the vector. About 150 species of wild mammals from seven orders have been incriminated as reservoir hosts of *T. cruzi*; some dozen species of the subfamily *Triatomidae* (family *Reduviidae*) are known to be important vectors of the infection to humans. Now, as a human disease, Chagas' disease occurs principally in rural areas and endemicity is related closely to low socioeconomic conditions. The different vectors prefer different conditions. Thus, houses built of adobe, mud, or cane provide numerous cracks and crevices in wall or partition in which the bugs can shelter. Other vectors prefer thatched roofs of palm leaves or grass. Some can stay hidden from predators in the earthen floors within or under houses. Vectors can often find appropriate shelter within large towns or cities where domestic animals are kept, especially dogs, cats, and guinea pigs. See Fife (1977).

Transmission of the disease by blood transfusion is becoming common. Somewhat rarer is transmission by a damaged placenta, but in 500 deliveries in Bahia there were 2% of transplacental infections. There is evidence that some infections occur via the food. See Marsden (1983).

WHO-Chagas' disease (1960) reported that 35 million persons were exposed to infection with *T. cruzi* and that, in areas where surveys had been carried out, infection rates averaged 20%. They concluded that about 7 million persons were infected. The committee believed that the case fatality rate was approximately 10%, probably higher in the first years of life. The distribution of *T. cruzi* infections in man and animals is given in Figure 16.3.1.

Marsden (1984), in reviewing the prevalence of human *T. cruzi* infections, estimates the infected might number as many as 6 million in Brazil and 1 million, each, in Argentina and Venezuela, figures not greatly different from those of WHO-Chagas' disease (1960) already quoted. The chief method of control is to break the nexus between the bugs and the human population but this is difficult in rural areas.

16.4 African Trypanosomiasis as a Great Pestilence

Although African trypanosomiasis in man has been responsible for far fewer deaths than, for instance, bubonic plague, it has been responsible for great epizootics and enzootics among ungulates in Africa between the latitudes 15°N

FIGURE 16.3.1. Distribution of *Trypanosoma cruzi* infection (Chagas' disease) in the Americas as of 1955. Adapted by E.C. Faust from Dr. Emmanuel Dias (1953), with supplementary information from Dr. L. Mazzotti. From Faust and Russell (1964, p. 148).

and 15°S, for which see Figure 16.4.1. Good accounts are given of the epidemics in Ford (1971), Duggan (1970), de Raadt and Seed (1977), and Mulligan (1970). As an example, we mention briefly the account of Ford (1971) on the epidemiologic history of Nyanza province in Kenya. Before 1890 there were flourishing populations of people and cattle from the Nile around the northeast shores of Lake Victoria to the Kuja River. Around 1890 there was an extensive epizootic of rinderpest with probable severe reduction of cattle and other ungulates; in 1891–1893 there was a smallpox epidemic and an invasion of chigger fleas; in 1896 an epidemic of trypanosomiasis began in Bukoli; there was a severe famine in 1898–1900. By 1900 the epidemic of trypanosomiasis had become well established, and in 1903 the causal organism was identified as *T.b. gambiense*. There were probably 100,000 deaths in the province in the years 1900–1907.

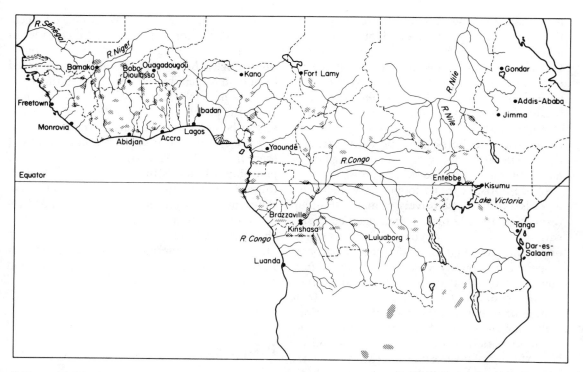

FIGURE 16.4.1. The occurrence of African trypanosomiasis. From Manson-Bahr and Apted (1982, p. 72).

There were voluntary evacuations of population from the affected areas in Bunyoli and Kavirondo, and in 1908 compulsory evacuations were made from a 2-mile strip of shore line. By 1910 the epidemic was over in Nyanza province but continued in western Uganda, that is, on the northwestern shores of Lake Victoria. Famine was present in 1918, and influenza in 1919–1920. It is recorded that there were 105 able-bodied men in Bunyoli in 1920 as against a reputed 17,000 before the epidemics. Endemic trypanosomiasis persisted along the Kenya lake shore, with gradually falling incidence elsewhere; in 1940 there was a second epidemic of trypanosomiasis of the Rhodesian form, terminating in 1944.

In the areas of Africa supporting epidemics of trypanosomiasis, related, if not identical, trypanosomes have caused epizootics among the ungulates, both wild and domestic, of a disease, nagana, due to *T. brucei*, with severe effects on the domestic herds, and there have been difficulties in obtaining protein for human consumption and losses of sources of animal traction.

Measures against human contact with the tsetse flies have been suggested, such as appropriate clearing of vegetation near the river courses, the use of insecticides, and removal of the dwellings from the haunts of the tsetse fly.

See Wilcocks (1962, pp. 59–90) for a lucid summary of the human problems of the disease and Molyneux, de Raadt, and Seed (1984) for a review of new findings.

16.5 Relapsing Fever

ICD 087. Fourth digit by arthropod vector: 0, louse-borne; 1, tick-borne.

Louse-borne Relapsing Fever. The discovery of the causative organism, *Borrelia recurrentis*, in 1868 by Otto Hugo Franz Obermeier (1843–1873) was the first purely human example of a living contagium vivum. Murchison (1862) believes that the disease could be reliably identified from descriptions about 1750. *Borrelia* is a slender spirochete of 3 to 25 μm in length that multiplies by transverse fission; it is ingested with the blood of a patient by the common body louse, *Pediculus humanus*, which becomes infective after about a week; infection of a new host is effected by a passage through an abrasion of the skin or, perhaps, through intact skin after a louse carrying the organisms has been crushed on the skin.

Louse-borne (or cosmopolitan) relapsing fever is a disease exclusively of man. No other reservoir host is known. It had been confused with typhus until the discovery of the causative organism, although the difference had been suspected on purely clinical grounds. Often epidemics of the two diseases are concurrent in famine or troubled times, as in the Irish famine or in the Russian wars of intervention. Relapsing fever is characterized by an incubation period of about 5 to 8 days and an abrupt onset of fever with shivering, headache, body pains, and temperatures of up to 40°C. Jaundice appears in about 50% of cases. Relapses occur in nearly half the cases. The case fatality is usually about 5% but in times of famine, war, and civil disturbance it may be as high as 70%.

Treatment is by antibiotics; prevention is effected by measures against the louse.

Tick-borne Relapsing Fever. This disease is caused by various species of *B. duttoni* in East Africa, *B. persica* in Asia, *B. hispanica* in Spain and Spanish Africa, *B. crocidurae* in Senegal, *B. turicatae*, *B. parkeri* and *B. hermsi* in North America. It occurs naturally in rodents, pigs, porcupines, opossums, and armadillos and is transmitted by ticks of the genus *Ornithodorus*. In humans, after an incubation period of 2 to 14 days, there are usually three or more spells of fever, each lasting 1 to 4 days, occurring at short intervals. The temperature is higher than in the louse-borne disease and various paralyses occur with greater frequency. Treatment is now by antibiotics. Prevention can be attained by measures against the ticks, see Felsenfeld (1971).

Borrelia duttoni infections can be perpetuated in ticks by transovarial infection, that is, the infection can be carried over to the next generation; this is not surprising, as it is considered that *Borrelia* species have evolved from parasites of ticks. *Borrelia recurrentis* is transmitted from man to man by the louse, but in the louse there is no such transovarial infection. There arises the problem as to how *Borrelia recurrentis* can be perpetuated, since no reservoir host is known, it has no transovarial infection, and there is no chronic carrier state in man. A plausible solution is that *B. recurrentis* and *B. duttoni* are not distinct species but, at most, different races transmitted by different arthropods; on occasion, *B. duttoni* is transmitted by the louse and thus renews the man-louse-man chain. For the relapsing fevers, see Burgdorfer (1976), Felsenfeld (1965), Geigy (1968), and Wilson and Coghlan (1984).

16.6 Relapsing Fever as a Great Pestilence

Relapsing fever can cause many deaths in times of war, civil commotion, or famine. In Europe epidemic typhus and relapsing fever are both transmitted by the louse; they have therefore tended to occur together in epidemics in disturbed times. Before laboratory diagnosis was possible, they were often confused; nevertheless, the two diseases can usually be distinguished on purely clinical grounds. Relapsing fever tends to be associated with jaundice, sudden onset, sharp crises, and relapses, whereas typhus is associated with rashes and almost invariably severe mental symptoms. These differences are especially evident in epidemics when numerous cases are seen. Individual cases may possibly be confused; moreover, simultaneous infection is possible.

MacArthur (1956, 1957) has given accounts of the famine fevers in Ireland. In 1846 epidemics of fever were of both kinds. The doctors there had become accustomed to typhus as the usual fever and reported from some areas that their cases were "of a new and extraordinary nature." There were districts in which one of the fevers predominated. Some class distinctions were noted. In the "better classes" relapsing fever was almost unknown, and where a fever case did occur the disease was not transmitted to other members of the household, whereas in the poorer classes the infection would run through the whole family. Since the fever in the "better classes" was almost always typhus fever, the case fatality rates were high. A notable example is provided by the 473 medical officers appointed by the board of health to special fever duties during the Irish famine; one out of every 13 died at his post, principally from typhus. MacArthur (1957) believed that there had been many epidemics of relapsing fever in Ireland; the earliest mentioned was in the era of the Justinian bubonic plague.

Gaud and Morgan (1947–1948) and Gaud, Khalil, and Vaucel (1947–1948) have described a modern epidemic of a louse-borne relapsing fever. Cases were first noted in Sfax, Tunisia, in October 1943 that were carried in from the Fezzan region. In the last quarter of 1942, cases had been noted among the nomadic tribe of Megarha who wander through the region between Djebel Sôda and the Chiati Valley in Tripolitania. The epidemic spread up to Sfax and Bizerte in Tunisia and then traveled along the north coast of Africa to Fez and Rabat in April and May 1945. Official estimates for most areas appear to have been too low, but cases have been estimated at probably more than 20% of the population in Tunisia and the case fatality rates as 5%–10%. Gaud, Khalil, and Vaucel (1947–1948, p. 95) give a table of an epidemic in Egypt with over 100,000 cases; and cases were observed in the neighboring countries in the middle east and in Spain and Portugal. See also Bryceson, Parry, Perine, et al. (1970).

Another epidemic, commencing in Kouroussa, Guinea, in 1921, perhaps after its introduction by soldiers returning home after World War I or the dispersal of them on demobilization at Kouroussa, spread to Upper Volta, Niger, Nigeria, Chad, and the Sudan. Along a 500-km stretch of the Niger centered on Mopti, it was estimated that there were nearly 100,000 cases, of whom 15,000 died, according to D. Scott (1965).

16.7 Other Arthropod-borne Diseases

ICD 088. Fourth digit: 0, Bartonellosis.

Oroya fever and verruga peruana are two stages of the disease caused by *Bartonella bacilliformis*. Bartonellosis is limited in a strip approximately 160 by 1,600 kilometers to the tropical zone of western South America, namely, Peru, Colombia, and Ecuador. Within this strip, the disease is limited to areas at altitudes 670 to 2,650 meters. It is borne by sandfly vectors of the genus *Phlebotomus* and their bionomics determine the restrictions on height. No animal reservoir of the infection has yet been determined. The infection may lead to a wart (verrucca) or to an acute general disease with fever and anemia due to extensive hemolysis of the red cells, associated with a case fatality rate of some 40%. In endemic regions, it seems to be an almost universal infection of infancy and childhood, survivors being permanently immune (Beaver, Jung, and Cupp, 1984).

Several intensive epidemics have been reported; 7,000 deaths occurred in the building of the railway from Lima to Oroya, according to Strong et al. (1915a, b), cited by Weinmann and Kreier (1977), and 4,000 deaths occurred in a population of 100,000 in Colombia in 1938, according to Weinmann (1944). Treatment with antibiotics and tetracyclines is effective. Prophylaxis is directed against the vector *Phlebotomus verrucarum*, a sandfly. See also Wilson (1984e).

Babesiosis is not listed in the ICD index. It is due to a protozoan *Babesia bigemina*, the first parasitic protozoan to be shown to be transmitted by an arthropod vector; Ristic and Lewis (1977) cite T. Smith and F.L. Kilbourne for the demonstration in 1893 of a tick vector. The disease is a zoonosis. *Babesia*, perhaps after the trypanosomes, are the most frequently found mammalian erythrocytic protozoa, and have a wide range of vectors. Infection of man is accidental and rare and a large percentage of cases reported have been in splenectomized individuals. See Garnham (1971, pp. 103, 104, 113) and Beaver, Jung, and Cupp (1984, p. 205) for human cases.

Chapter 17
Syphilis and Other Venereal Diseases

17.1 Syphilis

ICD 090–097. Inclusions: 090, congenital; 091, symptomatic early; 092, latent early; 093, cardiovascular; 094, neurological; 095, other late symptomatic; 096, latent late; 097, other and unspecified.

Syphilis is a disease due to the *Treponema pallidum*. Although syphilis is an infective disease, its late complications have been referred by the rules of the ICD to rubrics other than those of Class I. The rules assigned more of the deaths to syphilis in later revisions (the fifth and the sixth) than in earlier revisions. In all revisions there had been a rubric in the class of infectious diseases, to which deaths from congenital syphilis, acute syphilitic disease, therapeutic accidents, and the like, would be assigned. However, before the fifth decennial revision of the list in 1938, deaths from locomotor ataxia (tabes dorsalis) and general paralysis of the insane were assigned to rubrics in the class of diseases of the nervous system. Deaths from aneurysm of the aorta were assigned by the fourth revision of the list in 1929 to a rubric "aneurysm" and cannot be identified positively as syphilitic. In accordance with the fifth and sixth revisions of the list, unqualified "aneurysm" is taken to mean syphilitic aneurysm. For the purposes of Table 17.1.1, taken from Lancaster and Gordon (1987), it has seemed preferable to omit the deaths from aneurysm.

The disease is spread, principally, as a venereal disease by sexual contacts and as a congenital disease by infection through the placenta. However, it has also been spread by unsterile instruments, such as in cupping operations or vaccinations. In modern times it has appeared as a complication of intravenous therapy or drug abuse. It has also been transmitted in either direction between infant and wet nurse. Syphilis is transmitted usually by direct, but sometimes by indirect, contact. The treponema enters the body through minute cracks in the skin or mucous membranes; it can exist only for a short time outside the body. A primary sore or chancre first appears 2 to 3 weeks after infection, and, even in the first few hours, the spirochetes can be found in other parts of the body; the primary sore heals, and this is followed by general symptoms with some fever, enlargement of the lymph nodes, rashes on the skin, and some ulcerations on the mucous membranes. This is called the second stage, usually about 6–12 weeks from infection and the risk of transmitting the infection is then high. This is following by a third or latent stage. After a variable time the fourth stage is reached in which the principal lesions are like abscesses and may cause ulceration on the skin or mucous membranes. Any organ or tissue can be attacked in the fourth stage, in which mortality occurs principally after the appearance of the late complications, namely, aneurysm of the aorta and other cardiovascular syphilis, tabes dorsalis, and general paralysis of the insane. See Nicholas and Beerman (1967), Wilkinson (1984*b*).

Treatment of syphilis by mercury was used

TABLE 17.1.1. Mortality in Australia from syphilis* (deaths per 1,000,000 per annum).

Epoch	All ages	Age in years								
		0–4	5–14	15–24	25–34	35–44	45–54	55–64	65–74	75+
		Males								
1908–1910	121	279	2	10	42	188	282	305	255	242
1911–1920	117	191	4	13	59	177	298	298	257	146
1921–1930	87	80	5	7	36	143	221	247	236	131
1931–1940	74	40	2	5	18	92	178	246	238	156
1941–1950	37	14	1	3	6	26	80	129	143	93
1951–1960	9	3	0	0	2	6	29	109	175	161
1961–1970	—	2	0	0	0	2	5	23	61	68
1971–1980	1	1	0	0	0	0	1	3	11	18
		Females								
1908–1910	46	196	4	7	15	42	63	65	78	127
1911–1920	38	155	3	8	13	40	63	64	29	43
1921–1930	26	70	2	5	12	29	52	47	51	39
1931–1940	19	30	2	4	9	21	37	46	46	28
1941–1950	10	9	1	1	3	8	23	30	28	14
1951–1960	2	1	0	0	1	2	9	22	35	67
1961–1970	—	1	0	0	0	1	3	8	18	19
1971–1980	1	2	0	0	0	0	1	1	4	4

* Excluding aneurysm of the aorta.
From Lancaster and Gordon (1987).

before AD 1500 and inunction was the method of choice, but the margin between the effective and toxic doses was too narrow. There were many cases of mercurial poisoning with ulcerations, gangrene of the mouth, loss of teeth, and mental signs. This toxicity led to the abandonment of mercury and the exhibition of guaiacum, sarsaparilla, and other vegetable products. Even syphilization, the inoculation of syphilis in imitation of variolation, was tried in the period 1850 to 1880. In 1837 potassium iodide was introduced with some success and has remained valuable in the later stages. However, after 1850 treatment with mercury became standard with slow and intermittent dosage by inunction, with the beginning of salivation (ptyalism) as the danger sign to cease treatment. The arsephenamines were introduced in 1915, as a result of Ehrlich's work, and they continued to be the standard treatment until they were superseded by penicillin from about 1940 and now, on occasion, by other antibiotics and chemotherapy. For the spirochetes, see Holt (1978).

17.2 Syphilis as a Great Pestilence

The origin of syphilis in Europe is still much in doubt. One view is that the treponemal diseases, syphilis, yaws, pinta, and endemic non-venereal syphilis form variations of a single disease that has affected man on all the major continental masses for many thousands of years. See Zimmerman (1935) and Goodman (1943).

Since syphilis does not appear to have been known in the acute epidemic form in Europe before the time of Columbus, and recorded clinical observations show that after the time of the return of Columbus, acute and novel forms of the disease appeared in Spain, it has been suggested that syphilis originated in America, but there appears to be no firm evidence for the American origin. The reader is referred to Crosby (1969), Cockburn (1961a), and Weisman (1966).

In the early cases of the new disease, acute abscesses and ulcerations and even deaths were noted. The disease signs and symptoms seem to have become modified with the passage of time and to have evolved into those of the disease as it now appears in Europe and elsewhere. The first great epidemic of the disease occurred after the capitulation of Naples to Charles VIII of France in 1495. Infection spread through Charles' army and the civilians of Naples. Military reasons and disease compelled Charles to retreat to Lyons in November 1495 and to disband his army. As a result, syphilis was carried by troops to all the countries of Europe.

It broke out in Italy as an acute epidemic in 1495 and then quickly spread to France, Switzerland, and Germany. It had reached Bristol in 1496 and many other British cities the following year, according to Abraham (1944). The disease was spread by the crew from Vasco da Gama's ship and appeared in India in 1498 and in China in 1505. This tradition is against the hypothesis that syphilis was already established as an endemic disease throughout the world in pre-Columbian times.

The medical and pathological views on the disease were in a confused state until the early twentieth century, that is, until the demonstration of the treponema in the lesions and the development of the Wassermann and other serological tests. First, syphilis and gonorrhea were thought to be due to the same cause, a false hypothesis strengthened by the self-inoculation experiment of John Hunter. Second, it was not recognized that syphilis was contagious after the first stage. Third, there was no clear idea of the later chronic (third) stage of the disease and of the fourth stage in which there were cardiovascular lesions (aortic aneurysms), neurological lesions (tabes and general paralysis of the insane), and gummata; neither was it understood that a fetus could be infected in utero from a mother who showed no signs of the disease.

There are great difficulties in estimating the mortality in previous centuries, that is, the sixteenth to the nineteenth. Brown, Donohue, et al. (1970) cite some attempts by Boeck and Bruusgard and by T. Gjestland to estimate the prognosis of patients in Oslo, infected in 1890 to 1910, who had not received treatments for their infections. They concluded that untreated

syphilitics exceeded the expected mortality rates by 53% in males and 63% in females; cardiovascular syphilis developed in 13.6% of males and 7.6% of females; neurosyphilis developed in 9.4% of males and 5.0% of females; 23% had clinical or autopsy evidence of serious syphilitic pathology. P.D. Rosahn (1960) is cited as publishing similar findings on an American population.

Nabarro (1954) gives a detailed description of congenital syphilis. In his Figure 18, he gives a comparison of the fates of 1,001 pregnancies of 150 syphilitic mothers with those of 826 pregnancies of 150 nonsyphilitic mothers; of the former, 390 were healthy children, 92 resulted in miscarriages, 80 in stillbirths, 229 in infant death, and 210 in children with syphilitic disease. Nabarro (1954, pp. 36, 37) cites William Osler as giving similar emphasis to the importance of congenital disease and his tables show continuous declines in the contribution of syphilis to the infant mortality rates in the United States from 1933 to 1950 and rates in England and Wales, falling from 1918 to 1949, with the exception of a rise in the war years. Nabarro (1954) also cites G.D. Kettlewell who found in 1923 that 8% of 1,000 school children in Plymouth, England, exhibited signs of the disease.

Brown, Donohue, et al. (1970, Appendix A) give death rates of syphilis and its sequelae for the United States in selected years from 1900 to 1965. There have been striking declines at all ages, as shown in their Table A.II.6. In 1939 the infant mortality rate from syphilis was over 2 per 1,000 for either sex for white infants, but by 1965 this rate had fallen to 0.03 per 1,000, as given in their Table A.II.7. See also Brandt (1985).

We can examine as an example the mortality from syphilis and its sequelae, omitting aneurysm, in Australia in Table 17.1.1. There is some mortality in the age group 0–4 years; however, this is principally in the first year of life; indeed, the rates per 1,000,000 at age 0 are 1149 (822), 733 (610), 329 (296), 171 (123), 74 (50), 36 (23), and 16 (7) for males (females) in the epochs 1908–1910, 1911–1920, 1921–1930, 1931–1940, 1941–1945, 1946–1950, and 1951–1953, according to Lancaster (1956c). This mortality is due to congenital syphilis acquired in utero. The declines in these rates over time are marked and are due to control of syphilitic infections, to routine testing in prenatal examinations of the mother, and effective treatment by arsephenamines when the Wassermann reaction is positive.

In the Australian statistics in any period in Table 17.1.1 for instance from 1911 to 1920, the mortality at ages under 5 years is higher than in the next age group. The mortality then increases throughout life until about the age of 65 years, after which there is a decline. In early adult life mortality is possibly due to acute and congenital syphilis. Finally, in later adult life tabes dorsalis (progressive locomotor ataxia) and general paralysis of the insane are the predominant forms.

There is at every age in every period a high masculinity; that is, the male rates are higher than the corresponding female rates. In adult life, this can well be interpreted as reflecting social habits and the relative female immunity to syphilitic infections, but in childhood, only the second of these can be of importance. When any age group is considered, there have been definite declines in mortality at all ages. The declines at ages under 5 years are especially notable. In comparable epochs the rates for white males and females in the United States appear to be approximately double those in Australia. In the Australian experience, in the epochs 1908–1910 and 1911–1920, syphilis caused less than 1% of male deaths and 0.5% of female deaths, but by 1961–1970 these proportions had been reduced to about 1/120 of all deaths in males and 1/250 in females. See also for statistics, WHO-venereal (1954).

On a wider view of the developed world, we can summarize the available data as follows. Syphilis appeared as a new disease, or as a new form of an existent disease, a few years before 1500 and spread in a great pandemic throughout Europe and, soon afterwards, into Asia. It must have been responsible for much greater rates of mortality in Europe over four centuries than appear from twentieth century statistics, as have been quoted above or are available elsewhere. It must have been an important cause of abortion and infant mortality and of

cardiovascular and neurological disease. Authors, writing in the late nineteenth century, possibly assigned congenital syphilis as a cause for many disease conditions now known to be due to other causes, for example, rickets, but many lesions are characteristic of syphilis. Syphilis probably was more important in the city than in the country. Over most of its pandemic history, syphilis was treated with mercury and other less-potent drugs inefficiently. It has been controlled in the developed world, first, by correct mercurial treatment, then, after 1915, by the arsephenamines, and finally, after 1940, by antibiotics and chemotherapy.

See also Dennie (1962) and Hackett (1963, 1967) for historical details, Johnson (1976, 1977) for reviews of the spirochetes, and Fitzgerald (1981) for the pathogenesis and immunology of syphilis.

17.3 Gonococcal Infections and Other Venereal Diseases

ICD 098. Gonococcal infections.

Few deaths are assigned to gonorrhea as a cause. See Barnes and Holmes (1984), Wilkinson (1984a), and Skinner, Walker, and Smith (1977) for current perspectives.

ICD 099. Fourth digit by disease: 0, chancroid; 1, lymphogranuloma inguinale; 2, granuloma inguinale; 3, Reiter's disease; 4, other nongonococcal urethritis; 8, other.

0. Chancroid. Soft chancre or ulcus molle is a nonsyphilitic ulceration of the external genitalia due to *Haemophilus ducreyi*, sometimes associated with buboes. It is a cause of morbidity rather than mortality. Treatment is by sulfonamides or antibiotics (Wilson, 1984e).

1. Lymphogranuloma Inguinale. This is a venereal disease with trivial lesions in the male, sometimes with severe ulcerations going on to scarring in the female, but not a cause of mortality. The organism is *Chlamydia trachomatis* (several serotypes, L-1, L-2, L-3). Treatment is by the tetracyclines. Schachter (1978) and Collier and Ridgway (1984).

2. Granuloma Inguinale. This disease is characterized by a slowly progressive ulceration of the tissues in the genital region. A bacterial agent, *Donovania granulomatis*, has been described. Streptomycin, aureomycin, and terramycin are effective treatments. See Wilson (1984*e*). Gajdusek (1977*a*) gives examples of the effects of this and the preceding disease in causing depopulation in tribal societies.

3. Reiter's Disease. Negligible for mortality.

4. Nongonococcal Urethritis is often due to *Chlamydia trachomatis* (several serotypes) (Schachter, 1978).

For the incidence, see WHO-venereal (1954); for therapy, see Washington, Mandell, and Wiesner (1982).

Chapter 18
Other Spirochetal Diseases and the Mycoses

18.1 Leptospirosis

ICD 100.

Leptospires infect many wild vertebrates throughout the world. All pathogenic leptospires are now said to belong to the one species, *L. interrogans* (Topley and Wilson, 1983/1984). Van der Hoeden (1964, pp. 252–260, 268, 269) gives tables of the *Leptospira* species and the species of the host; orders naturally infected include *Marsupialia*, *Insectivora*, *Chiroptera*, *Edentata*, *Lagomorpha*, *Rodentia*, *Carnivora*, and *Artiodactyla*. Indeed, leptospirosis seems to be one of the most widespread of all the zoonoses. It is also one of the most widespread of all the anthropozoonoses. Man is an incidental host, usually infected from mud, soil, or water contaminated by urine carrying leptospires. Thus, man is infected when at his occupations, sports, hobbies, or war. Leptospirosis sometimes leads to a severe disease. The incubation period of the disease is usually 7 to 13 days. The clinical signs are variable, but severe cases usually have jaundice with fever, neutrophil leucocytosis, renal signs, and hemorrhages; any of the major body systems may be attacked. Case fatality is often high. Treatment with antibiotics, particularly penicillin, is effective if delivered early in the disease.

Incidence rates can be diminished by the use of protective clothing, particularly boots, and by the control of animals. They have been reduced in occupations such as rice farming, mining, underground sewage work, and fish cleaning, by personal and environmental hygiene, and also, in some cases, by vaccine prophylaxis. See Wilson and Coghlan (1984).

18.2 Miscellaneous Spirochetal Infections

Vincent's Angina ICD 101

Under peacetime conditions, Vincent's angina, a necrotic ulcerative disease of the nose, mouth, and throat, can be a troublesome, but rarely fatal, disease. In wartime it can become epidemic and cause deaths. See Wilson and Coghlan (1984).

Yaws ICD 102

Yaws is a widespread disease of the wet tropics in regions of poor personal hygiene and low standards of living. It is due to *Treponema pertenue*, morphologically indistinguishable from *Tr. pallidum*, the causal organism of syphilis. However, yaws is not transmitted sexually. Infection usually occurs in childhood by contagion or possibly insects. Case fatality is low and many subclinical attacks occur. For world incidence, see Figure 18.2.1. For control, see WHO-yaws (1953) and for paleopathology, see Stewart and Spoehr (1952).

Pinta ICD 103

Pinta is a contagious inoculable disease caused by *Tr. carateum*. It is confined almost entirely to the tropical zone of the two Americas.

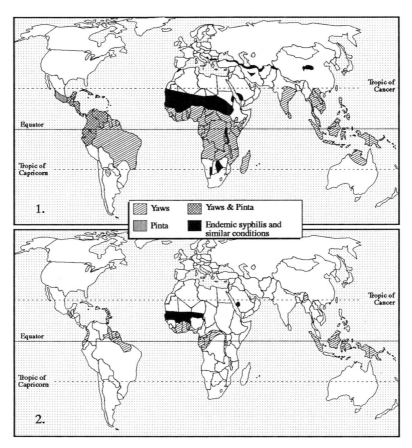

FIGURE 18.2.1. Geographical distribution of the endemic treponematoses. 1. In the early 1950s. 2. In the early 1980s. After Perine, et al. (1984, pp. 4, 5).

For general reviews of yaws and pinta, see Wilkinson (1984*b*) and Perine, et al. (1984).

Other Spirochetal Infections ICD 104

This includes endemic syphilis, spread by contact and caused by a treponema. For Lyme disease, see Wilson (1984*e*).

18.3 Mycoses and Miscellaneous Infectious and Parasitic Diseases

For the subclass ICD 110–118 Mycoses, see Chandler, Kaplan, and Ajello (1980); for candidiasis see Bodey and Fainstein (1985) and for histoplasmosis (ICD 115) see Sweany (1960). For helminthiases (ICD 120–129), see Beaver, Jung, and Cupp (1984) and Manson-Bahr and Apted (1982). For ICD 131–136 Other Infec-

tious and Parasitic Diseases, we omit those rubrics not associated with many deaths. We consider ICD 120, 121, 122, and 125, which are associated with many deaths or have other special interest, in Chapter 19.

ICD 130 Toxoplasma. There is a high prevalence, about 50%, of asymptomatic toxoplasmosis in the United States, according to Krick and Remington (1978). The infection is acquired by eating raw or undercooked meat; it is a zoonosis. Reservoirs of infection are in mice and rats and the oocysts of the parasite may be introduced into foods via infections of cats. Toxoplasmosis acquired by the mother during pregnancy may be fatal to the fetus, approximately 4 per 1,000 pregnancies in the United States; it can cause serious symptoms and death in the newborn infant.

Chapter 19
Helminthiases

19.1 Schistosomiasis

ICD 120. Fourth digit by species and site: 0, *haematobium*; 1, *mansoni*; 2, *japonicum*; 3, cutaneous (cercarial dermatitis); 8, other.

The worms parasitizing man belong to five phyla (i) the flatworms or *Platyhelminthes*, including the exclusively parasitic flukes (*Trematoda*), (ii) the true round worms (*Nematoda*), (iii) hair snakes (*Nematomorpha*), (iv) thorny headed worms (*Acanthocephala*), (v) leeches (*Hirudinea*). From a mortality point of view, the schistosomes of the class *Trematoda* are the most important.

The schistosomes have a complicated life cycle, egg → miracidium → sporocyst → cercaria → schistosomulum → adult schistosome → egg. For diagrams of the stages, see Beaver, Jung, and Cupp (1984) or Manson-Bahr and Apted (1982). In the human infections, eggs passed out in the urine or feces hatch as soon as the urine or feces is diluted sufficiently with water and become miracidia, which swim about in the water; on coming in contact with the snail, a miracidium enters the soft tissues and in the course of 5 to 7 weeks develops as a sporocyst, capable of multiplication within the snail to further sporocysts, and finally these become cercariae. The cercaria, the stage infective for the mammalian host, swims in the water. After contact with the skin of a mammal, the cercariae cast off their tails and penetrate down to the cutaneous capillary beds with the aid of glandular secretions, which break down the mammalian proteins, and enter small veins. They are now called schistosomula.

This penetration of the human skin forms the first stage of the human diseases, a dermatitis, especially marked 24 to 36 hours from the penetration of the cercariae.

The progress of the schistosomula is still subject to doubt, but one version is that they develop in the lungs and squeeze through into the pulmonary veins and are distributed to the general systemic circulation; but, in any case, most of them reach a site characteristic of the species, *Sch. mansoni* and *Sch. japonicum* in the portal veins and *Sch. haematobium* in the veins of the bladder. In the lungs the developing schistosomula may cause small hemorrhages, sometimes observed as hemoptyses, the second stage of the human disease.

Arriving at their final destination in the mesenteric veins (for *Sch. mansoni* or *Sch. japonicum*), the adult worms set up inflammatory changes, observed as a hepatitis, the third stage of the disease. The hepatitis subsides and there is irritation in the mesenteric venules, the fourth stage of the disease. The female schistosomula enter the gynecophoral canal of the male and thus fertilization of the ova is assured. The eggs accumulate in sausage-shaped chains in groups of the smaller mesenteric venules, which become damaged, and the eggs escape into the submucosal tissues with the production of macroscopic pseudotubercles; ulceration of the intestinal wall follows, the eggs are passed in the feces, and the life cycle begins anew; this is the fifth stage. Already damage had been done to intestinal wall, lungs, and liver in *Sch. mansoni* and *Sch. japonicum* infections and to the bladder in *Sch.*

haematobium infections. In the sixth stage of the disease, there is a marked increase in the number of circulating eosinophil leucocytes as the sensitizing pathological process develops as a result of the absorption of toxic products from the worms.

Many symptoms occur; in the first stage we have already noted an urticaria or dermatitis. There is, later, recurrent daily fever, epigastric pain, and enlarged and painful liver and spleen. The basis of these symptoms is the infiltration of the eggs in the tissues around the veins of the liver and also in the intestinal wall (or alternatively, bladder wall). Granulomata develop and there is later scarring; the liver is at first enlarged and then decreases in size when the granulomata are replaced by scar tissue. The spleen may enlarge greatly, especially in infections due to *Sch. japonicum*. Symptoms of weakness and anemia appear. Infected children are retarded in physical and mental development. The worms may persist for a long time, the record being 47 years, but many die in the first few years. Some hundreds of cases of cerebral involvement in schistosomiasis japonica have been reported since 1889, with a wide range of symptomatology.

To be of value, treatment must be applied early in all the human schistosome infections. Prognosis is grave if liver, bladder, or intestinal symptoms have occurred.

Prevention is by breaking the chain of infections by (*i*) control of feces or urine disposal, (*ii*) eradication of the molluscan hosts, for example, by water management (the cycle can be broken by drying out canals in some cases) and molluscicides, (*iii*) avoidance of infective water, and (*iv*) treatment of early cases.

19.2 Schistosomiasis as a Great Pestilence

Schistosoma mansoni has a wide distribution in the Nile delta, the wet tropics of Africa, and the east coast of Madagascar, although it is not common in the Nile valley between Cairo and Khartoum. It is the only human blood fluke in America and is common in northeastern Brazil; it is endemic near the coast in Venezuela and highly so in Dutch Guiana. It also occurs in the West Indies. See Figure 19.2.1 for the distribution.

Sch. haematobium is widely distributed in Africa. See Beaver, Jung, and Cupp (1984) and Manson-Bahr and Apted (1982).

Wilcocks (1962) gives a popularizing lecture on the epidemiology of schistosomiasis in Africa, where the *mansoni* and *haematobium* species are the principal causes of the disease; the latter is said to be less harmful than the former in Africans; both species are said to be serious infections. The distribution of each is determined principally by that of the snail infected, which in turn is determined by the method of supplying water. The older traditional method of irrigation was to divide the fields into large basins in which the flood water was maintained long enough for the silt to settle out, after which the water was drawn off into the receding river; basin irrigation was thus seasonal. The Nile was later controlled by the construction of dams and water was supplied to the fields by ramifying canals. This is perennial irrigation; the canals never dry effectively, and the system is much more favorable to the snail populations, leading to great increases in schistosome prevalence. Thus, in one area with basin irrigation, the prevalence of *Sch. haematobium* remained at 10%, whereas in a comparable area, transferred to the perennial system, it rose to 90%. Wilcocks (1962) gives a table that makes these points. A survey in 1937 showed *haematobium* incidence of 60% in three areas with perennial irrigation and 5% with basin irrigation. *Mansoni* incidence was 60% in the northeast region of the Nile delta, 6% in the south of the Nile delta (both perennial irrigation), and absent from the Nile valley south from the delta. But there are other factors. Incidence rates are correlated with density of population and the proximity to water. Water, in pools, shallow canals, and so on, has a strong attraction for little boys who inevitably urinate into it, and so the boys form the main source and the main target for the miracidia of *Sch. haematobium* infections; in some areas of Egypt, almost all boys have hematuria at some time. *Sch. mansoni* can also be transmitted in the same way, as there may be feces on the perineum. For *Sch. mansoni*, the main require-

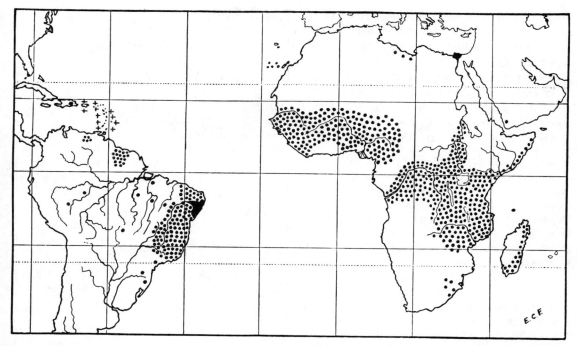

FIGURE 19.2.1. Map of Africa, South America, and the West Indies, showing endemic foci of infection with *Schistosoma mansoni*. The solid black areas in the delta region of the Nile River and in northeast-

ern Brazil indicate areas of hyperendemicity. The foci in the Lesser Antilles are shown by a +. (Original, Faust.) From Beaver, Jung, and Cupp (1984, p. 428).

ment is that human feces must contaminate fresh water. This occurs where it is the custom to defecate in the small irrigation canals. At other times, feces is washed by rain into ponds or small streams or canals, so an important factor is the distance of the village from the nearest canal.

Given that there are about 200 million persons infected with schistosomes throughout the world, the question arises how the infections contribute to mortality. Any numerical answer to this problem is difficult to obtain. Perhaps only in Egypt has there been adequate research toward answering the question, so we make use of Egyptian data.

Schistosomiasis in Egypt. We briefly mention the estimates of prevalence given by Abdel-Wahab (1982). He cites J.A. Scott, who estimated that in 1937, out of 15.23 million persons in Egypt, 7.15 million were infected with schistosomes, that is, 47% of the population,

and that a further million would be added after the expected changes in irrigation schemes in Upper Egypt. Estimates of prevalence of 20 million in 1974 and 16 million in 1976 are cited, but estimates by other authors are higher. Abdel-Wahab (1982) points out that with the great variation in prevalence between areas, more careful planning would be needed to give a correct estimate. In villages of the Nile delta, *Sch. mansoni* prevalence rates of up to 74% have been reported. Further, *Sch. haematobium* prevalence rates of 80% have been reported in some areas near Luxor. In some areas there have been great changes in prevalence over the years. Thus, in Qalyobia (Qalyub), near Cairo, the prevalence rates for *Sch. mansoni* and *Sch. haematobium* were, respectively, 12.5% and 38.4% in 1952 and 40.5% and 27.0% in 1977. Quite spectacular changes are reported from Difra in the Nile delta, 3.2% and 74.3% in 1935 and 73.0% and 2.2% in 1979 for the prevalence rates of *Sch.*

mansoni and *Sch. haematobium*, respectively; thus, there has been a fall in the *haematobium* prevalence but a 23-fold increase in the *mansoni* prevalence in Difra.

It was possible to make estimates of the rate of loss of an infection; at ages 0–4 years, the rate of losing the infection was 0.544 per annum in an area near Alexandria.

Abdel-Wahab (1982, p. 87) states:

With *S. mansoni* infection, the gastrointestinal symptoms were more common as compared to the occurrence of these symptoms in *S. haematobium* infection, the difference being statistically significant. Hepatosplenomegaly occurred more frequently in those heavily infected with *S. mansoni*. In this latter group, the hemoglobin level and the nutritional states were more affected.

Abdel-Wahab (1982, p.89) concludes:

Schistosomiasis rarely exists as the sole infection or disease-state in many areas in Egypt. Malnutrition, enteric diseases, viral hepatitis, malaria, filariasis, amebiasis, and other diseases and states of ill health, more often coexist in schistosome-infected individuals than not. Elucidation of these interrelationships could have significance for public health programs.

Reprinted with permission from M.F. Abdel-Wahab, *Schistosomiasis in Egypt.* Copyright 1982, CRC Press, Inc., Boca Raton, FL.

Schistosomiasis japonica or Oriental Blood Fluke. The great bulk of the world's schistosome infections occur in the Far East, for which see Figure 19.2.2, especially the Chángjiāng (Yangtze) basin, south and southeastern China, with some infections in Japan and the Philippines. The distribution and control of schistosomiasis japonica are complicated by the existence of animal reservoir hosts, namely, dogs, cats, rats, mice, field mice, cattle, water buffaloes, pigs, horses, sheep, and goats. Infections are by miracidia developing in snails living in water polluted by these reservoir hosts and by man. The danger from wet ploughing with buffaloes is evident. According to Yokogawa (1976*a, b*), the prevalence rates in Japan have fallen notably. Thus, eggs were detected in only 124 of approximately 19,000 persons in endemic areas on Honshu; on Kyushu, eggs had been detected in 156 (73%) of 214 people

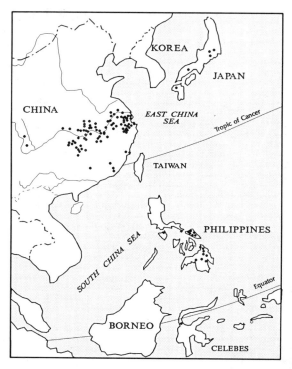

FIGURE 19.2.2. Endemic foci of infection with *Schistosoma japonicum* in Japan, China, Taiwan, the Philippines, and Celebes approximately 1955. After Beaver, Jung, and Cupp (1984, p. 417).

in 1948, whereas eggs were detected in only 6 (1.2%) of 467 persons in 1971; of these positives, none was younger than 36 years. For progress in China, see Mao and Shao (1982).

Control of schistosomiasis japonica is made difficult by the use of human night soil as fertilizer and by promiscuous defecation of the human population. Farmers and boatmen are principally affected, as are others coming into contact with polluted water, such as children wading and women washing. The reservoir hosts, especially cows and buffaloes used in agriculture, dogs, and field rats, are important in control.

Two other species pathogenic to man are *Sch. intercalatum*, whose epidemiologic importance is unknown, and *Sch. mekongi*, which resembles *Sch. japonicum* in clinical features.

The great problem is to assess the damage done to the community by high schistosome prevalence rates. Studies are now underway comparing the health of the schistosome-infected with controls in the same population (Mahmoud, 1984).

For the global distribution of schistosomiasis, see also Ansari (1973), Doumenge and Mott (1984), Mostofi (1967), Nash (1982), and WHO-schistosomiasis (1959, 1980).

19.3 Other *Trematode* Infections

ICD 121. Fourth digit by parasite: 0, opisthorchiasis; 1, clonorchiasis; 2, paragonimiasis; 3, fascioliasis; 4, fasciolopsiasis; 5, metagonimiasis; 6, heterophysiasis; 8, other.

For descriptions of the helminthiases of man, see Beaver, Jung, and Cupp (1984) and Manson-Bahr and Apted (1982). Generally speaking, although the parasitic helminths are the cause of a great deal of ill health, there are comparatively few deaths attributed to them.

Opisthorchis felineus and *O. viverrini* have life histories similar to those of the schistosomes, in that the eggs become miracidia and infect snails; after further development, cercariae leave the snails and attack fish. Infection of man or other definitive host, such as dog, cat, fox, swine, and rodent, is acquired by eating raw fish. Human infections with *O. felineus* are frequent in central Siberia and generally on the great rivers of the steppes and eastern Europe. *O. viverrini* is of importance in Southeast Asia.

Clonorchis sinensis, similarly after a life cycle involving snails, infects fish. Human infection follows ingestion of raw fish. The larvae of *Clonorchis sinensis* reach the distal bile ducts and mature, causing proliferative and inflammatory lesions in the walls of the bile ducts. Heavy infections may be followed by cirrhosis of the liver. The disease is widely spread with endemic areas in Japan, Korea, most of China excluding the northwest, Taiwan, and Vietnam. There are many reservoir hosts including the dog and cat. Prevalence rates in the human host have fallen in the endemic areas.

Paragonimus westermani causes an infection, principally of the lung in man, with abscess formation and persistent pneumonialike conditions, leading to scarring. Man acquires the infection by eating raw crabs and crayfish.

Man is only one of many definitive hosts. The most heavily endemic regions are central China, Korea, Japan, Philippines, and Taiwan.

Fasciola hepatica is a liver fluke of sheep. The infective form may be ingested either on watercress or in water. Deaths from the resulting disease are rare; symptoms follow from hemorrhages.

Fasciolopsis buski is an intestinal parasite of man and pigs throughout the Orient. Infection occurs by ingesting the encysted form on the water nut *Trapa natans*. It can cause severe bowel disturbance. The number of cases is few in India and Southeast Asia.

Species of the trematode family *Heterophyidae*, especially *Heterophyes* and *Metagonimus*, cause infections of the bowel but the course is benign.

19.4 Echinococciasis

ICD 122. Inclusions: echinococciasis, hydatid disease, hydatidosis, due to *Echinococcus granulosus* and *E. multilocularis*.

The adult tapeworm is a small worm (4–6 mm long) living attached to the mucosa of the fore part of the small intestine of the dog, wolf, or other wild canine. The eggs are passed in the animal's feces and are ingested on the grass by a herbivore. The eggs develop into oncospheres that are capable of penetrating the intestinal wall of the herbivore, usually settling in the liver but sometimes passing to other organs where they develop into the hydatid cysts, in which the scolex (or head) of the tapeworm becomes developed. The cycle is completed by the carnivore devouring the infested flesh, after which the tapeworm develops to maturity in the gut of the carnivore. Witenberg (1964) defines three cycles (*i*) sylvatic, in which both carnivore and herbivore are wild, (*ii*) pastoral, involving wild or domestic carnivores and domestic stock (or man), (*iii*) synanthropic, mainly affecting dogs and other domestic animals (or man). However, he points out that the mainstay of hydatid disease in man is the pastoral cycle, with large flocks, usually of sheep. The sheep dogs eat the offal of slaughtered or other dead sheep. The infested

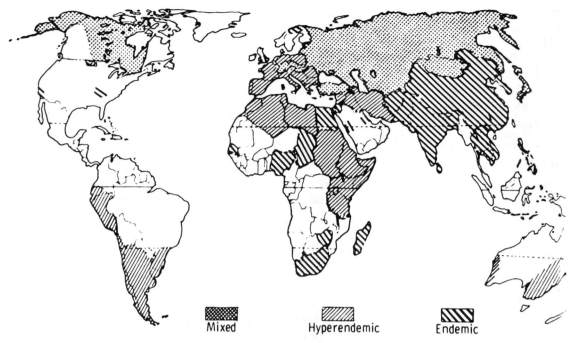

FIGURE 19.4.1. Global distribution of human and animal hydatidosis. Single lines represent Echinococcus granulosus and crossed lines the coexistence of both *E. granulosus* and *E. multilocularis* infections. From Matossian, et al. (1977).

dog 'disseminates eggs of the parasite in the field or in the vicinity of human habitations. Hydatid infestation is worldwide but the incidence in man varies, for which see Figure 19.4.1.

In Iceland the disease has been very common. Thus, autopsies carried out in Iceland from 1932 to 1950 showed that hydatid cysts were present in 15% of those subjects born before 1861, and there were 22%, 15%, 3%, 0%, 0%, and 1% in those born during the decades beginning 1861, 1871, ... , 1911, respectively. Beard (1973) found that hydatid infections had almost been eliminated from Iceland by control of slaughtering, dogs, and dog feeding through which the cycle dog→ sheep → dog was broken; dogs had been reduced by a dog tax and were not fed uncooked offal.

The hydatid cysts in man are found principally in the liver (approximately 70%) and lungs (approximately 20%), but sometimes in other organs. The cysts grow slowly and with time may wither and die. They do not produce

any specific toxin. Their effects are through pressure, as a rule; an individual cyst may have a volume of several liters. A cyst may rupture causing anaphylactic shock and sometimes death, or in the peritoneal or pleural cavities the rupture may lead to the development of many new cysts.

The treatment of the disease is surgical with injection of disinfectant substances into the cyst and relief of obstructions. The crude death rates from hydatid disease in Australia have been of the order of 10 per 1,000,000 per annum, according to Lancaster (1954*b*), with a tendency to decline.

Australia has not shared the fortune of Iceland in the reduction of the incidence of the disease. The canine rates of infection have remained high, and it is possible that any declines of mortality in the rates are due to the increasing urbanization. White (1958) may be consulted for more details on the rates.

For the biology and disease due to the *Echinococcus*, see Thompson (1986).

19.5 Other *Cestode* Infections

ICD 123. 0, *Taenia solium*; 1, cysticerciasis; 2, *Taenia saginata*; 3, taeniasis unspecified; 4, Diphyllobothriasis, intestinal; 5, sparganosis; 6, hymenolepiasis; 8, other; 9, unspecified.

ICD 124. Trichinellosis.

Taenia is the generic name of the common tapeworm. *Taenia solium* is a "bladder worm" in the tissues of the pig and a "tapeworm" in the small intestine of man. The "head," or scolex, is attached to the mucosa of the small intestine. The tapeworm develops in length by forming new segments (or proglottids), the most mature of which are at the end of the "tape" and break off to be passed out in the feces. The eggs break free from the proglottids and later they may be ingested by the pig, in which they develop as "bladder worm" or cysticercus in the tissues. The cysticercus is globular and contains the rudiment of a head or scolex, which is capable of developing into the mature tapeworm. In the human infection, the adult *Taenia solium* causes slight irritation at the site of attachment and sometimes even intestinal obstruction. The cysticercus stage in the tissues of man is an irritant, and the human body reacts by forming a fibrous capsule about it. Symptoms appear when the cysticercus begins to die and the body reacts. As the cysticercus can occur in any organ, it can produce severe symptoms, for example, epilepsy or other mental symptoms.

T. saginata has a wider natural distribution than *T. solium* and appears in all the states of Europe.

Diphyllobothrium latum is a common human infection in Europe and competes with the body for vitamin B12, and so infection with it is a dangerous complication of pernicious anemia.

For trichinellosis, see Kim, et al. (1985).

19.6 Filariasis and Dracontiasis

ICD 125, Fourth digit by species: 0, Bancroftian filariasis; 1, Malayan filariasis; 2, loiasis; 3, onchocerciasis; 4, dipetalonemiasis; 5, *Mansonella ozzardi* infection; 6, other specified filariasis; 7, dracontiasis; 9, unspecified filariasis.

Sasa (1976) groups these diseases together as human filariasis; he gives many maps and statistics of incidence throughout the countries of the world. There are complicated life cycles for each kind of filaria, for which the reader may be referred to Manson-Bahr and Apted (1982) and Beaver, Jung, and Cupp (1984).

We may consider filariasis as the most widely distributed of these diseases and also important historically because its known life cycle gave an impetus to the theory that other diseases, notably malaria, might be borne by mosquitoes. The parasitic cause is *Wuchereria bancrofti*; in this species of nematodes the adult male worms are about 40 mm long and the females 80–100 mm long. They live in the lymph glands or tissues; the females are viviparous. The young microfilariae, of length, 244–296 μm, are found in the connective tissues or in the blood, awaiting passage to another host. *W. bancrofti* microfilariae show the remarkable property of swarming, that is , appearing in the peripheral blood, believed to be an adaptation to the time of biting of a mosquito, usually *Culex pipiens quinquefasciatus*. In the mosquito, the microfilariae develop further and, after about 10 days, migrate to the labella of the mosquito. They escape through the tip of it during feeding of the mosquito and then are ready to enter the skin of the new host by active penetration.

The infestation causes irritation and inflammation of the lymph channels and glands together with a "filarial fever." The adult worms block lymph channels; these blockages may lead to local swellings, low grade inflammatory changes, and finally an elephantoid condition, in which the skin is thickened and wrinkled covering swollen tissues. There are striking photographs of the clinical state in the texts mentioned above.

Treatment is by antimonials and arsenicals but the prognosis is bad. Prevention is by anti-mosquito methods. See also Dissanaike (1984).

Onchocerciasis. This is a debilitating rather than a killing disease, known as river disease. In many parts of west and equatorial Africa, more than 50% of the population may be infected with 4%–10% blind. These high frequencies can reduce the efficiency of the work force and so cause great economic loss and lead to ruin of agricultural communities; it may also cause great difficulties in construction of dams. See Manson-Bahr and Apted (1982, Figure 10.14) for the areas most severely affected. The organism, *Onchocerca volvulus*, is a filarialike helminth. The adult female worms measure up to 50 cm in length, the males being about a tenth as long. They live together in tangled masses causing the formation of nodules in the skin of the human host. Microfilariae are produced, which are taken up by black flies of the genus *Simulium* and injected into fresh hosts in whom they grow to adult size. The females produce perhaps a million microfilariae in a lifetime of up to 15 years. The great importance of the infection is that the microfilariae may migrate into the eyes and so cause deterioration of sight and finally blindness. Suramin, a chemotherapeutic drug, is effective but has undesirable side effects. The simulium fly has a long range, sometimes over 200 km, and control is difficult. See also Awadzi and Duke (1984).

Guinea Worm. The embryo of *Dracunculus medinensis* is 500–750 μm long and 17 μm broad; in the water they are swallowed by a cyclops and develop in its body in about 5 weeks. When 1 mm in length, they become infective and man is infected by swallowing the cyclops in drinking water. The adult takes a year to develop. The gravid female migrates to foot or leg, usually, where she finally becomes attached to the skin and discharges her embryoes. The winding up and extraction of the female's body has been known since classical times. Prevention consists of providing good drinking water, free of cyclops. Chemotherapy has side effects. The disease could be eradicated (Hopkins, 1983*b*).

19.7 Hookworm and other Intestinal Helminthiases

ICD 126. Ancylostomiasis and necatoriasis (i.e., hookworm disease).
   ICD 127. Other intestinal helminthiases.

Hookworm Disease. The common hookworms are the round worms (*Nematodes*), *Ancylostoma duodenale*, and *Necator americanus*. In adult life they live attached to the mucosa in the duodenum and jejunum, that is, upper small intestine. Their life span can be measured in years. Hookworms pass eggs in the feces, which can hatch, under suitable conditions of moisture and warmth, into larvae. The larvae penetrate the skin of the human host and pass into the bloodstream and so to the lungs. Here, they leave the blood vessels and are coughed up and swallowed and reach the jejunum; once there, they suck blood from the vessels of the jejunum, and this loss of blood brings about the main pathology, an anemia.

Endemicity of hookworm infection depends on (1) continuous infection of the human population, since there are no reservoir hosts, (2) defecation hygiene, which ensures that the eggs are deposited in sites appropriate for their development, (3) shade and sandy humus, and (4) opportunity for the larvae to come in contact with the skin of man. Long dry periods are unfavorable to the continuation of the cycle, as the larvae climb up blades of grass waiting for an opportunity to penetrate human skin; if none such occurs, they crawl down into the soil again. The conditions are, of course, unfavorable to successful infection by the larvae if shoes are worn. The chain of infection is also broken if there is proper sanitary disposal of feces. Hookworm is obviously a disease of poor unhygienic persons living in a tropical or semitropical climate with a sufficient rainfall. The conditions, equivalent to the four above, have often been fulfilled in coal mines, and so miners' anemia was well known in England in former times. Some authors believe that only malaria and malnutrition have been more important than hookworm disease in bringing about misery and lowering living standards; further, hookworm reacts with these other diseases, enhancing their effects.

With the knowledge of the life cycles of the hookworms, the risks of infection have been lowered by sanitary disposal of feces and the wearing of shoes; moreover, therapy is effective in clearing up individual infections.

Strongyloides stercoralis. This worm has several ways of perpetuating itself. First, it has a cycle of the hookworm type, with the adult in the ileum yielding an egg or ovum to pass out in the feces, become a larva developing in the soil, and then penetrate the skin of a new host; second, under conditions of sufficient moisture, it can pass through the whole life cycle in the soil; third, it can pass through its life cycle without leaving the host (autoinfection). Strongyloides can generate severe disease with pathology in many organs, especially under conditions of stress, as in wartime, and in conditions of low nutrition, cancer, severe burns, among others. See Beaver, Jung, and Cupp (1984).

For the treatment of soil-transmitted helminths, see Rossignol (1984).

19.8 Progress in Parasitology and Control

Parasitology has come to mean the study of diseases caused by organisms that are not bacterial or viral. Its field thus includes the helminths and the protozoa, including malaria, with which we have dealt in Chapter 15, and the amebae and other intestinal protozoa treated in §§6.9 and 6.10. Manson (1899) grouped diseases into those with a geographical distribution (i.e., possessing a nidus as described in §5.6) and others, referred to as cosmopolitan or bacterial. Discussions of disease by authors in Canada, England and Wales, Scandinavia, and, in general, northwest Europe, and in their extensions overseas, such as Australia and New Zealand can afford to omit parasitology, whereas authors in the United States and the rest of the countries of the world must consider the problems of parasitology in any review of health or mortality. General reviews of the progress in parasitology are given in Chernin (1977), Hoeppli (1959), Moore, Collins, and Young (1976), Taylor and Muller (1978), Warren and Bowers (1983), Warren and Purcell (1982), and Worboys (1983).

We now discuss the various parasitic infections with the aid of Davis (1983), Harinasuta (1983), and Walsh (1983).

Malaria. See Chapter 15, especially §15.10.

Amebiasis. See §6.9. New effective drugs are available, but there are still many grave defects in hygiene, such as faulty water supply with drinking water fouled by seepage from sewer pipes.

Soil-transmitted Helminthiasis. See §19.7. Progress in lessening the load of hookworm disease is hindered by the agricultural nature of the population in much of the developing world, whereby many workers are barefooted and subject to infection from the soil in the case of hookworm and strongyloides infections, with the intermediate stage of the helminth developing easily in the wet soil conditions. Ascariasis and trichuriasis infections are common in such hot, wet and unhygienic conditions; prevalence rates are variable but may be as high as 80%. These infections are a burden on health, especially of children. *Strongyloides* causes gastrointestinal upsets and the prevalence is said to be in the range of 0.1%–8.0% in Southeast Asia. For the above soil-transmitted helminths, the campaigns are proper disposal of feces, mass treatment of the population with effective drugs, and hygienic education of the population.

Ascaris, *Trichuris*, and hookworm infections still persist in the south of the United States. *Strongyloides* infection has increased, partly because of troops returning from World War II. *Trichinella* prevalence in the United States was estimated to be 4.4 million cases in 1972, as against 21.1 million in 1949; the prevalence of tapeworm has also declined. The persistence of these diseases into recent times in a wealthy country illustrates the difficulties in reducing their incidence in the developing world. There is little *Echinococcus* in the United States (excepting Alaska). Cases of schistosomiasis in the United States are usually Puerto Ricans in whom the prevalence is about 10%.

Toxoplasmosis exists in chronic asymptomatic form in over one third of the population of the United States. It is important as a cause of lymphadenopathy, for lethal infections in the immunologically compromised patient, as a cause of about 3,000 congenitally defective infants per annum in the United States, and as a cause of chronic ocular inflammation. See Feldman (1982) for its epidemiology. Walsh (1983) concludes that there is "an enormous burden of worm and protozoan infections" in the United States and, we add, in the developing world. For major parasitic infections, see WHO-parasitic (1986); for the abundance of hook-worms, see Schad, Nawalinski, and Kochar (1983).

Chapter 20
Neoplastic Diseases

20.1 Definitions

A neoplasm can be defined as an autonomous new growth of tissue; or more fully, a neoplasm is a new growth of body tissue that originates from the body, grows spontaneously, possesses an atypical structure, does not subserve the uses of the organism, and reaches no definite termination of its growth. Modern theory would eliminate such a phrase as "arising spontaneously," since there are known causes of many neoplasms, or interpret it as meaning "not arising as a normal development of the body." Nevertheless, even if a neoplasm is initiated by an external cause, it may continue to develop after the disappearance of that cause, for example, after exposure to ionizing radiation, X ray, or ultraviolet light; thus, a malignant neoplasm displays an autonomy. The essential unit of a neoplasm is the living cell and each such cell is a descendant of a normal cell. Thus, a neoplasm is distinct from an infection or inflammatory process in which we find not only cells descended from normal body cells but also extraneous units, the infecting agent. Here again qualifications are necessary, for Burkitt's lymphoma is generated by the oncogenic (i.e., carcinogenic) virus of Epstein-Barr.

Neoplasms are classified into benign and malignant chiefly by their ability to invade other tissues. Benign neoplasms can cause death, however, by local pressure effects such as in the skull, in the prostate, or by hemorrhages from the uterus. Malignant neoplasms can cause death in many ways as a result of the invasion and destruction of vital tissues.

Malignancy may be preceded by demonstrable changes in the tissues, which do not inevitably lead to it; these are the precursors of Correa (1982), who gives reasons for studying them as follows: (*i*) such cellular changes may give some understanding of the process of carcinogenesis; (*ii*) abnormal proteins produced by the precursor lesions may help in determining persons at risk; (*iii*) the progression of precursors may help to identify causes of neoplasia; (*iv*) the precursors may explain the long latent period between acting cause and development of neoplasia; (*v*) the precursors may be more readily treated than the fully developed malignancy. Correa (1982) gives detailed illustrative examples of precursor lesions in carcinomata of the uterine cervix, of the stomach, and of the colon.

20.2 Historical Notes

A definition of neoplasms and rules for distinguishing them from other classes of diseases could only be made after the appropriate advances had been made in microscopic anatomy and pathology, of which we may recall the description of the tissues commencing with Bichat's work, the cell theory of Schwann, and its application to pathology by Virchow, as mentioned in §2.2. Johannes Mueller (1801–1858) had collaborated with Schwann and Virchow, his students, and in 1838 published *Über den feineren Bau und die Formen der krankhaf-*

ten Geschwülste, in which he found neoplasms to be composed of cells with nucleus and nucleolus and their various types to be distinguished only by different proportions and groupings of cell masses and stroma. The publication in *Virchows Archiv* in 1872 of "Die Entwicklung der Carcinoma" by Wilhelm von Waldeyer-Hartz (1836–1921) traced the origin of cancer of the stomach, liver, and kidney to the epithelial cells of the organs, which brings us up to the modern ideas on the histological diagnosis of the neoplasms.

No clear ideas on the etiology of neoplasms could be formed until the etiology of the infectious diseases had been solved; indeed, many tumors arise during the course of the infectious diseases, for example, tuberculosis and hydatidosis. Further, it may be difficult to distinguish microscopically between, say, the blood pictures of leukemia and the acute infections.

Although the pathology of neoplasms has only recently been understood, some of the clinical syndromes associated with some of them have been so striking that we can, with certainty, consider some landmarks in cancer epidemiology beginning in the early eighteenth century. Thus, in 1700 Bernardino Ramazzini (1633–1714) described breast cancer as an occupational disease of nuns; many subsequent investigations have shown that breast cancer is more common in the unmarried and childless women than in those who have borne children. In 1775 Percivall Pott (1714–1788) described cancer of the scrotum in chimney sweeps and evidently reckoned that if a large proportion of cases occurred in a small proportion of the general population, there must be a causal relation (but see also §20.3).

Although B. Ramazzini and Percivall Pott gave such clear examples of cancer being associated with life style and environmental conditions, the hypothesis that cancer was due either to chronic infections or to degenerative changes had dominated medical thought on its etiology up to the 1920s. In recent times the rise of clinical epidemiology has led to a search for genetic, social, chemical, physical, and other factors.

See Peller (1979) and Harris and Autrup (1983).

20.3 Electromagnetic Radiation and Radioactivity

Although the "cause of cancer" is still unknown, modern epidemiology has revealed a number of causes or associated factors. A brief discussion of a list of such factors, which is neither exhaustive nor mutually exclusive, is given in this and the succeeding sections. See Interdisciplinary Panel on Carcinogenicity (1984).

Solar Radiation of Light and Heat. The amount of sunlight of a given wavelength, not absorbed by the atmosphere, received per unit of horizontal area, is given by

$$1_\psi = 1_0 \cos \psi \qquad (20.3.1)$$

where 1_ψ is the amount of sunlight that is received when the sun is at an angle ψ from the zenith, so that, although the sun is above the horizon for an average of 12 hours per day at every point on the globe, the total dosage of visible and infrared light per unit of horizontal area varies considerably from equator to pole.

Visible Light and Radiation of Longer Wavelengths. These radiations appear not to be oncogenic.

Ultraviolet Light. The dosage of the ultraviolet light received at sea level varies more than that of visible light because of its absorption by ozone in the upper atmosphere at a height of approximately 40 km; (20.3.1) no longer holds because of a well-known physical law by which more ultraviolet light is absorbed if the sun's rays pass through the ozone-containing layer obliquely. Some ultraviolet light is refracted by small particles above and in the ozone layer and passes more directly through it. All these physical effects result in a great variation in the dosage of ultraviolet light with the height of the sun. The dosage averaged out over a day, therefore, depends largely on the number of hours that the sun spends high in the sky. The daily dosage thus depends on season and latitude. Until recently, there were difficulties in measuring ultraviolet light dosage; but now, Paltridge and Barton (1978) have given maps of erythemal ultraviolet radiation for various months of the year for Australia, which show great differences between the doses at Darwin, 12°S, and at Hobart, 43°S. Their model underestimates the radiation dosage when the sun is low in the sky, but this underestimate is a small fraction of the total dosage. Similar surveys have been carried out in the United States, and relevant graphs are available in Scotto, Fears, and Fraumeni (1982). It may be noted that only in Australia and the United States can comparisons on fair-skinned individuals in one country be made over a sufficient spread of ultraviolet light dosages. The large doses of ultraviolet light at low latitudes produce skin cancers and melanoma, for which see §20.14. See also Blum (1959a, b), Boice and Land (1982), Burton, Kates, and White (1978), Schulze and Grafe (1969), and WHO-ultraviolet (1979).

Natural Ionizing Radiation. Ionizing radiation from natural sources received is about 125 mrad per annum. This dosage is relatively constant throughout the world, although there are some deviations from the mean at great heights above sea level where cosmic (i.e., extraterrestrial) radiation doses are higher, since these wavelengths are filtered out by the earth's atmosphere, and in some areas where there is radiation from rocks or other geological formations. Natural radioactive rocks or clays incorporated into buildings may produce mild increases in the amount of radiation received. Natural radiation is received also from the degradation products of uranium in dust and air, for example, potassium-40, carbon-14 and radium, thorium, and their daughter products.

There is some doubt as to the effect of low dosages of radiation, and there seems to be some opinion that fewer cases (e.g., mutations, diseases) would be caused by a low average dose to a population than would be caused by the same total dose administered to a few persons. The investigation of this problem, namely, to test the effect of small increments of radiation dosage to the "natural" levels, which also appears in the study of chemical hazards, is difficult because huge numbers of experimental animals would be required to test

any hypothesis, and the observed effects are so slight numerically that they are difficult to distinguish from the naturally caused disease.

X Rays. The introduction of the use of X rays for clinical diagnostic purposes led to high dosages of radiation to the hands of physicians and technicians; by 1914 it was possible to find over 100 cases of skin cancer due to this cause. Proper shielding of the equipment and improvements in the photographic plates minimized morbidity from this source. Moreover, whole-body radiation provoked leukemia in American physicians and, in particular, radiologists; indeed, these latter suffered about 9 times the rates in the general population. See Miller (1975), Peller and Pick (1952), and Boice and Land (1982). Thus, there could be occupational hazards from both local and whole-body radiation. There were hazards for patients, also, for Stewart, Webb, and Hewitt (1958) showed that irradiation of the fetus during diagnostic X rays approximately doubled the risk of leukemia in the later child, and Court Brown and Doll (1965) found that patients with ankylosing spondylitis treated by X rays exhibited a tenfold excess of mortality from leukemia compared with the general population. Later practice has shown that the diagnostic and occupational hazards are largely avoidable by shielding and the construction of more efficient X ray machines. Further, X radiation is used now therapeutically only in the treatment of cancers.

Radioactive Substances. The existence of special health hazards to miners in the regions of Schneeberg and Joachimsthal had long been known. In 1879 F.H. Härting and Walther Hesse (1846–1911) found that 75% of deaths in 150 miners were due to malignant disease of the lung. This was the first time an *internal* cancer had been shown to be caused by exposure to an external chemical or physical carcinogen, probably in this case uranium disintegration products. Uranium ores have been incriminated in other mines. See also Peller (1939).

The isolation in 1898 of radium and the later application of radioactive substances in industry led to further problems. In Orange, New Jersey, watch dials were painted with a preparation containing radium and mesothorium to make them luminescent. The operators, "pointing" their brushes with their tongues, received doses of the radioactive material that became concentrated in their bones; 41 deaths from osteogenic sarcoma are known to have occurred in the first decade of this century in a total of 800 women, see Martland and Humphries (1929), Martland (1931), and Polednak, Stehney, and Rowland (1978). These tragic events have been overshadowed by the results of the explosions of atomic bombs over Hiroshima and Nagasaki, Japan. It is believed that the survivors suffered a risk of leukemia increased sevenfold by radiation and a peak incidence 7 years after the explosion. References to the original articles are available in Miller (1975). See also Beebe (1979) and Boice and Land (1982).

Occupational exposure to ionizing radiation occurs in diagnostic work in medical, dental, veterinary, research, educational, and atomic-physical occupations. In science and education, few persons have been involved and the exposure is usually well controlled; in medicine, the chief danger is from gamma-ray sources; subsonic flights are likely to add no more than 300 mrad per year to the dosage of regular crews; in atomic energy, about 10% of workers receive more than 1 rad per year. The general public is exposed to some sources; for example, television sets yield a mean dosage of 1 mrad per year; fluoroscopic shoe fitting causes a trivial part of the dosage received from all sources. Special sections of the public have received higher dosages as medical patients in diagnostic radiology and in therapy; thus, there are well-attested examples, for which see the bibliography of Norwood (1975). Sievert, Swedjemark, and Wilson (1966) give the "total commitment to the bone-marrow due to to nuclear weapon testing up to the end of 1961" as 70 mrad. They further give, as the dose commitment to all generations, from fallout from nuclear testing, 111 and 154 mrad to the gonads and marrow, respectively, and from all sources, 1500 and 1700 mrad (approximately).

For an encyclopedia of medical radiology, see Zuppinger (1966). For cancer mortality of uranium miners and millers, see Wagoner, Archer, et al. (1964). For accident at Juarez, see Marshall (1984). For mutagenesis, see Denniston (1982). For quantification of environmental risk, see Castellani (1985).

20.4 Tobacco

Tobacco is a product of plants of the genus *Nicotiana*; *N. tabacum* is the almost universal plant, but *N. rustica* is grown in India and the Soviet Union. The cultivation of tobacco by European settlers in colonial America began in the sixteenth century. Its introduction into European society met with some objections, and in 1604 King James I of England issued a condemnation of its use. It is difficult to say who first drew proper attention to the health aspects of smoking, that is, who pointed to possible pathology without drawing some social or moral lesson.

John Hill (?1707–1775) believed that the appearance of cancer of the nose in two patients was due to the taking of snuff. Redmond (1970) believes that Hill has a clear priority for pointing to tobacco or other carcinogen as a cause of cancer.

According to the introduction of US Surgeon-General (1979), J.J. Holland, early in the eighteenth century, and S.T. Soemmerring, in 1795, drew attention to the relation between cancer of the lip and the use of tobacco. Another report in 1859 from Montpellier, France, showed that of the 68 patients with cancers of the lips and mouth, all used tobacco and 66 of them smoked short-stemmed clay pipes. Broders (1920) reported on the association of cancer of the lip with the smoking of tobacco in clay pipes.

The clinical surveys of Mueller (1939), Wynder and Graham (1950), and Doll and Hill (1950, 1952, 1954, 1956, 1964) gave strong evidence that cigarette smoking was the most important cause of cancer of the lung. Later work has reinforced their conclusions, and it is now recognized that tobacco is the leading source of chemical carcinogens, with cancers usually produced by the smoking of cigarettes, cigars, and pipes but sometimes produced without smoking as in tobacco chewing. Further, tobacco is of importance in the production of cancers of the respiratory tract, generally, and also of the bladder, kidney, and pancreas. It also has a powerful synergistic effect, for example, in the production of lung cancer in asbestos workers.

Since the areas of contact with tobacco in the mouth are those most affected by cancer, it is evident that tobacco contains carcinogens; the most important are tobacco-specific nitrosamines such as N'-nitrosonicotine, which are formed from alkaloids during the tobacco curing and fermentation processes, according to Wynder and Hoffmann (1964, 1982). These nitrosamines have been found in amounts from 3 to 90 ppm in chewing tobacco and snuff. Other carcinogens are produced in the process of smoking. They reach the lung, not as gases, but in particulate matter held in suspension in the inspired air. The harmful constituents of cigarette smoke and its particulate matter have been listed in Tables 15 and 19 in the US Surgeon-General (1979, §14). The compounds judged most likely to contribute to the health hazards of smoking are 50–2500 μg of nicotine per cigarette and 500–35,000 μg of tar. Of the tar constituents, there are 10–50 ng of benzo-(a)pyrene and 0.6 ng of methylchrysene, and these are the most important complete initiators of neoplasms; there are also 50–200 ng of pyrene, 50–300 ng of methylpyrenes, 100–260 ng of fluoranthene, and 60 ng of benzoperylenes per cigarette. In this latter group, compounds do not initiate neoplasms on their own but act as cocarcinogens, enhancing the effect of compounds in the first group.

The nicotine in tobacco products is the principal constituent responsible for cigarette smokers' pharmacological responses. It is a stimulant at the sympathetic and parasympathetic ganglia. It is the habit-forming constituent of tobacco, although the evidence is said not to be conclusive.

Tobacco is further discussed in relation to cardiovascular diseases in §25.4.

20.5 Chemical Agents

Many chemical carcinogens other than tobacco are now known. See reviews by Doll (1979), Doll and McLean (1979), and Nicolini (1982).

Alcohol. Alcohol is a much less potent carcinogen than is tobacco but sometimes appears to act as an associated cause of cancer of the esophagus and upper alimentary tract. Tuyns (1982, Tables 2 and 3) gives remarkable examples of the high relative risks for cancers of the mouth and of the esophagus, when the subjects have a high intake of both alcohol and tobacco. It is pointed out that an increased risk of cancer of the mouth is also associated with the Plummer-Vinson syndrome. In any case, the action of alcohol may be mediated by associated micronutrient deficiencies (Armstrong, McMichael, and MacLennan, 1982).

Metals. Some metals or their compounds may be carcinogenic. Tomatis, Breslow, and Bartsch (1982, Tables 1 and 3) list those chemical substances that have been shown to be carcinogenic for humans from the 20 monographs of the International Agency for Research on Cancer, to which we add short commentaries, as follows:
(a) Chromium and certain chromium compounds. Inhalation leads to cancers of the lung and nasal cavities.
(b) Nickel. Nickel inhaled in the refining process also leads to cancers of the lung and nasal cavities; see also Doll (1958) and Mastromatteo (1967).
(c) Beryllium and cadmium. These are probably carcinogenic.

The survey of Roe and M.C. Lancaster (1964) suggests that the risks from the nonradioactive metals may be exaggerated by some authors. See §20.3 for radioactive minerals and chemicals.

Other Inorganic Substances. Arsenic in compounds, usually taken medicinally, can cause cancers of the skin and lungs.

Organic Compounds. There are many synthetic and natural organic compounds with carcinogenic properties. Benzpyrene and related substances are carcinogens occurring in soot and tobacco smoke. Many aniline dye compounds are carcinogens, first noted by Ludwig Rehn (1849–1930) in 1895 as a cause of cancer of the bladder. Tomatis, Breslow, and Bartsch (1982, Table 2) list 4-aminobiphenyl, benzidine, and 2-naphthylamine as bladder carcinogens.

Drugs. See §20.6

Minerals, Nonradioactive. Cancers, especially of the lung, have been attributed to the inhalation of asbestos. Here, the physical shape of the crystals and the synergistic action of cigarette smoking appear to be of importance, see Selikoff, Bader, et al. (1967), Selikoff, Hammond, and Churg (1968), and Enterline (1978).

Carcinogens in Food. Higginson, Terracini, and Agthe (1975) believe that many potential carcinogens have been or are now present in the diet. In only very few cases have any of these factors been identified as causes of a major cancer hazard, although such hazards are suspected in the cases of the esophagus, stomach, bowel, and liver. They state that little is known of the total carcinogenic load and it may be well to err on the side of prudence. In particular, levels of potentially carcinogenic substances in food should be kept as low as possible, weighing lessened risks against increased costs. Long latent periods in the production of cancers by these agents make the estimates of carcinogenicity difficult to obtain. See McBean and Speckman (1982) and Wogan (1969).

Carcinogenic substances can be produced in food contaminated during storage by fungi, especially some strains of *Aspergillus flavus*; these are the aflatoxins; they produce hepatomas in several countries in Africa and Asia and may be responsible for cancers of the liver, see Hambraeus (1982).

Dietary Deficiencies. Dietary deficiencies have not been shown to be important as initiators of cancer but may be so in the therapy of cancer. Iron deficiency is a factor in the etiology of cancer of the buccal mucosa, tongue, and esophagus. Variations in the incidence of gastric carcinoma between countries may be due to dietary differences, including methods of cooking. High intakes of fats may be associated with colonic cancer. Deficiencies in fiber content may lead to colonic cancer, partly because in persons on a low fiber diet, there is a slow passage of the contents through the colon enabling

unfavorable chemical reactions to occur, especially in the presence of nitrites, producing carcinogens. See Armstrong, McMichael, and MacLennan (1982), Doll and Armstrong (1981), Newell and Ellison (1981), and Roe (1983). For excess salt in the diet, see §22.14. For chemical mutagenesis, see Bora, Douglas, and Nestleman (1982). For macronutrients in diet, see Reddy and Cohen (1986).

20.6 Miscellaneous Causes

Viruses

Many well known workers believe that most cancers will be proved to be due to a virus; this may ultimately be a matter of definition. Evans (1982b) states that the three strongest candidates for human cancer are the Epstein-Barr virus, *Herpes simplex* type 2 virus, and Hepatitis B viruses—all DNA viruses. We now summarize the account of Wyke (1984). Only one family of RNA-containing viruses, the retroviruses, have been implicated in the production of neoplasia (oncogenesis), and its members resemble closely the DNA-containing viruses at a stage in their life cycle. A DNA virus may invade cells and be unable to complete its cycle of replication; in many cases the neoplastic cells produced by the virus infection carry all or part of the viral DNA into their chromosomal DNA; these parts of the viral DNA are passed on in cell division in the same way as normal cell genes, a phenomenon known as "integration." The process of virus oncogenesis can be divided into three stages: (*i*) the virus obtains a stable presence of its DNA in the cell, (*ii*) certain factors determine whether the presence of viral DNA initiates a neoplasm, and (*iii*) the neoplastic cell and its descendants survive and multiply to form a neoplastic tumor. Wyke (1984) gives two tables of oncogenic viruses, from which we select only entries of human importance. In his Table 104.1, there is a sole entry, namely, a human T-cell leukemia virus produces an "adult T-cell leukemia-lymphoma." In his Table 104.2 of oncogenic DNA-containing viruses, there are noted: papilloma viruses causing cutaneous, genital, and laryngeal warts; JC and BK papovaviruses causing neuroectodermal tumors; *Herpes simplex* 1 causing (with considerable doubt) squamous cell carcinoma; *Herpes simplex* 2 causing (with reasonable doubt) cervical carcinoma; Epstein-Barr virus causing Burkitt's lymphoma and nasopharyngeal carcinoma; *Cytomegalovirus* causing hepatocellular carcinoma; hepatitis B group causing hepatocellular carcinoma; and *Molluscum contagiosum* causing nodular epidermal hyperplasia. Of all these, the hepatitis B virus is easily the most important; indeed, Wyke (1984, p. 525) remarks that the primary hepatocellular carcinoma is very common in parts of Africa and Southeast Asia causing perhaps 500,000 to 1,000,000 deaths annually worldwide in adults, young as well as old, and this neoplasm may be the most common fatal neoplasm of man. See also Giraldo and Beth (1980–1984), Williams, O'Conor, et al. (1984), and Henle, Henle, and Lennette (1979).

Chronic Infections

Cancers were formerly considered to be initiated in association with syphilitic gummata; cervical cancer was said to follow chronic infections after trauma of the cervix uteri. Although much less importance is assigned to chronic infections now than formerly, cancer of the bladder has been caused in Africa and the Middle East by chronic parasitism with the fluke, *Schistosoma haematobium*; workers wading in water acquire the infection from the cercaria of the fluke, which passes part of its life cycle in the snail, see Burton (1982) and Mustacchi and Shimkin (1958). Malaria has also been postulated as a factor in African Burkitt's lymphoma, see Evans (1982*b*, p. 373).

Chronic Irritations

Much stress was formerly laid on chronic irritation, for example, jagged teeth in cancer of the tongue and clay pipes in cancer of the lip.

Burns and Other Traumata

Burns have on occasion been blamed for initiating a cancer. Other traumata seem to be unimportant, except perhaps in melanoma of the foot in the dark-skinned races.

Drugs and Hormones

Stolley and Hibberd (1982, Table 1) list drugs and hormones together with the site of neoplasm as follows: diethylstilbestrol, vagina (transplacental), breast, and uterus; conjugated estrogens, uterus; androgens (17-methyl substituted), liver; arsenicals, skin; chlornaphazine (aniline dye derivative), bladder; alkylating agents, leukemia and lymphoma; immunosuppressive and antimetabolite agents, reticulum cell sarcoma; radiopharmaceuticals, osteosarcoma and hepatocellular carcinoma.

Cancer of the breast is more common in nulliparae than in multiparae.

Genetics

A few Mendelian traits or diseases are sometimes complicated by cancer. Such autosomal recessive syndromes include ataxia telangiectasia, Fanconi anemia, xeroderma pigmentosum, Bloom syndrome, and Werner syndrome. Autosomal dominant types include neurofibromatosis and familial polyposis of the colon, see Swift (1982) and Bergsma (1976).

Genes may also act indirectly; thus, skin color is a genetic character, and fair skins are associated with melanoma and other skin cancers. Other hereditary factors of importance may be less evident.

There appears to be familial predisposition to neoplasia, according to Anderson (1982); this may be due in part to common environment and in part to common genetic make-up, for example, ultraviolet light and skin color. Other examples of the interaction of genetic make-up and environment are given by Strong (1982).

For occupation, see §20.8 and §47.7.

20.7 Statistics of Neoplasms

The ICD bases its classification largely on anatomical site, but cell type is used to separate malignant neoplasms of the skin into 172, melanoma, and 173, other, and to classify the leukemias in rubrics 204 to 207; sex is used to separate neoplasms of the breast into 174, female, and 175, male.

Only an outline of the importance of neoplasms as causes of death can be given here. The discussion will be largely on malignant neoplasms, since the benign neoplasms cause but little mortality. The malignant neoplasms were previously often referred to as cancers. Leukemia was not included in the cancers of the *International List* but is included in the neoplasms of the ICD.

Cancer had a high priority under the rules for classifying deaths of the statistical offices. Even in the most recent revisions, in which rigid rules for classification are no longer given, there is a tendency to favor cancer as a cause of death, especially if it appears that other causes mentioned are terminal or complicating features of the cancer. Over most of the period studied, the appearance of the word "cancer" on a death certificate would ensure that the death would be assigned to a cancer rubric by the statisticians, for it would be preferred to practically any disease other than the rarer infective diseases or violence. There has been, perhaps, only a small loss because of deliberate failure of the certifying physician to diagnose cancer on social grounds. More serious losses have occurred in the past, particularly at older ages, through the common use of vague terms such as "senility" and "death due to natural causes."

It is difficult to assess the effects of some changes in clinical attitudes and techniques on the death rates as recorded. First, surgical treatment can now be attempted in a greater range of cases than was possible in earlier years; there has thus been a great extension of the clinical techniques of endoscopy and biopsy, the laboratory techniques of radiology and pathology, and attempts to deliver treatment as early as possible. Second, there has been increased interest in the etiology of the neoplasms, expressed often in the formation of cancer registries to follow the progress of cancer patients and to measure the cancer load on the community.

We give as an illustration the death rates from all neoplasms in England and Wales in Table 20.7.1 by sex and the commonly used age groups. Attention may be conveniently focused on a given epoch, for instance, 1921 to 1930. It is evident from the table that there is great variation in the rate with age.

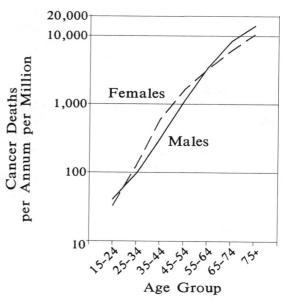

FIGURE 20.7.2. Cancer mortality by age in Australia 1908–1980. Trends of the age-specific mortality rates for cancer in Australia. Rate per 1,000,000 per annum. Semilogarithmic grid. Copyright (c) 1950, *The Medical Journal of Australia*, reprinted (and projected) with permission.

In Figure 20.7.1, the death rates in 1931 to 1940 from malignant neoplasms in Australia are plotted against age for both sexes. It is evident that these death rates increase steadily with age, and the graph of the logarithm of the death rates is approximately linear for either sex. Discussion of the attempts to relate such a linear relation to appropriate hypotheses or mathematical models can be found in Arley (1961), Armitage and Doll (1961), Bryan (1961), and Tucker (1961).

Many mistakes in interpreting cancer statistics have been made in the past through a neglect of the age factor. Age-specific death rates for malignant neoplasms vary markedly, so that crude death rates yield particularly misleading comparisons between different countries or different epochs. Thus, the crude death rates in Australia from malignant neoplasms for the first 8 decades of this century have been, per 1,000,000 per annum, for males (females): 724 (715), 808 (771), 950 (907), 1123 (1069), 1219 (1226), 1245 (1149), 1495 (1244), and 1684 (1308), whereas the age-specific mor-

TABLE 20.7.1. Cancer in England and Wales (Deaths per 1,000,000 per annum).

Epoch	All ages*	0–4	5–9	10–14	15–19	20–24	25–34	35–44	45–54	55–64	65–74	75 and over
					Males							
1851–1860	207	21	9	8	16	27	62	175	422	932	1,503	1,738
1861–1870	225	13	8	7	18	26	60	205	539	1,206	1,874	2,269
1871–1880	333	13	7	8	16	27	71	240	706	1,593	2,605	2,989
1881–1890	465	21	11	12	23	37	80	299	1,002	2,302	3,758	3,926
1891–1900	639	33	18	19	32	51	99	384	1,300	3,160	5,325	5,824
1901–1910	784	36	18	17	31	53	109	414	1,549	3,904	6,683	7,874
1911–1920	897	35	17	18	35	54	110	422	1,680	4,439	8,002	9,731
1921–1930	1,000	35	19	18	37	57	115	416	1,629	4,768	9,405	12,641
1936	1,612	51		21¶		50#	137	452	1,632	4,721	10,179	15,190†
1956	2,274	109‖		75¶		101#	178	561	2,019	5,885	11,102	16,962†‡
1976	2,771	NA		69¶		92#	177	433	1,890	5,810	13,279	22,281§
					Females							
1851–1860	440	23	9	9	18	29	140	595	1,283	1,857	2,355	2,326
1861–1870	522	13	7	7	16	32	161	670	1,539	2,302	2,806	2,798
1871–1880	619	12	7	7	14	27	174	793	1,764	2,765	3,524	3,520
1881–1890	739	19	9	10	18	33	173	855	2,051	3,375	4,531	4,601
1891–1900	882	28	14	14	27	39	175	891	2,323	4,099	5,829	6,377
1901–1910	942	29	13	15	27	39	170	846	2,321	4,410	6,658	7,901
1911–1920	959	29	13	14	28	40	156	790	2,266	4,380	7,114	9,191
1921–1930	980	32	16	15	27	44	159	762	2,150	4,281	7,548	11,023
1936	1,636	36		15¶		43#	168	734	2,045	4,019	7,508	12,157†
1956	1,891	100‖		61¶		71#	201	697	1,809	3,559	6,250	10,350†‡
1976	2,272	NA		51¶		69#	161	679	2,075	4,005	6,619	11,464§

* 1851–1930, standardized on to the population of England and Wales as enumerated in 1901. From the Registrar-General's Decennial Supplement (1952, Part 3, Table 12).
† From Annual Reports of the Registrar-General.
‡ Rates for 75–84 years. The male (female) rate at 85+ was 18038 (13682).
§ From World Health Statistics Annual.
‖ Age 0.
¶ Ages 5–14 years.
# Ages 15–24 years.

tality rates for Australia, given in tables 36.2.1 to 36.7.1, for the same epochs show no such dramatic rise; indeed, the female age-specific rates have tended to fall as have the male rates for malignant neoplasms other than those of the respiratory system. The principal cause of the increase in the *crude* death rates from malignant neoplasms during this century has been the aging of the populations.

Sex also has an important bearing on the cancer rates. Thus, in Figure 20.7.1, the death rates are higher for males than for females at ages other than 25–55 years. Some of these differences have an explanation that can be related directly to the organs of sex, see Lancas-ter (1950e). Cancers of the uterus and then cancers of the female breast cause mortality at an earlier stage in life than many of the other major cancers, whereas cancer of the prostate tends to occur at older ages. However, there are other differences in the rates between the sexes for other cancers, where sex might not be thought to be relevant. Cancers of the buccal cavity, stomach, rectum, and skin are more common in males, cancers of the intestine and liver are more common in females. Examples could be multiplied. In some cases a plausible cause for this difference can be found; thus, in Australia cancer of the skin and melanoma are more common in males than in females, pre-

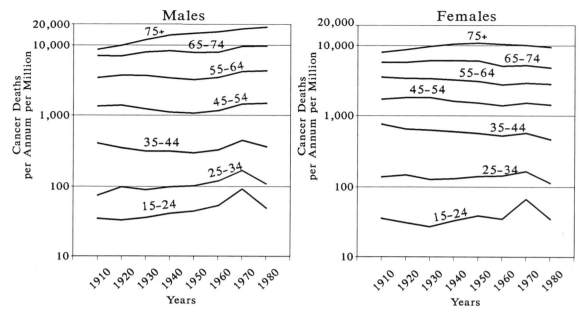

FIGURE 20.7.2. Cancer mortality by age in Australia 1908–1980. Trends of the age-specific mortality rates for cancer in Australia. Rate per 1,000,000 per annum. Semilogarithmic grid. Copyright (c) 1950, *The Medical Journal of Australia*, reprinted (and projected) with permission.

sumably because of the greater exposure in outdoor occupations and sports.

The age-specific rates from malignant neoplasms for Australia can be obtained from §§35.1 to 35.3 and 36.2 to 36.7. They are plotted as Figure 20.7.2. The increases in the rates before 1930 are possibly artifacts, as more cancers have been diagnosed and assigned as such in the later years. There have been increases after 1940 in the male rates at ages older than 25 years, principally because of increases in lung cancer. There have been declines at age 25 to 44 years in females, principally because of improvements in the rates from cervical cancer.

For a popularization, see Kolata (1985b). For cancer in developing countries, see Parkin (1986).

20.8 General Topics

Although cancer causes a large proportion of the mortality in the developed world, it can only be given a short analysis here by site, part-

ly because it has not played a large part in the decline of mortality and partly because there are now large reviews of the epidemiology and statistics throughout the world. Before going on to the special sites, we mention here some topics in the study of cancer, with the aid principally of authors in Schottenfeld and Fraumeni (1982), to which the reader is referred for tables and graphs.

Experimental Studies

Although many leads on the carcinogenicity of substances have been obtained by epidemiologic methods, there is often a need for verification by animal experiment; further, there is a need to test new substances, usually synthetic, for safety. Animal experiments are expensive, and so the relation between mutagenicity and carcinogenicity is used, whereby the substances are tested on bacterial cultures for mutagenicity. A detailed discussion on the relevance of the mutagenesis tests and the animal experiments is given in Tomatis, Breslow, and Bartsch (1982).

Air and Water Pollution

As Shy and Struba (1982) point out, some evidence suggests that air pollution in the great cities may increase the incidence of lung cancer; in industry and mining, there is a similar problem because of the combustion products of fossil fuels; correlations have been reported between lung cancer rates and indexes of atmospheric pollution. Although there is good evidence for the carcinogenicity of high concentrations of coal tar products and asbestos, such as have been found in some industries, the evidence for them or other products in the air of the cities is much weaker. Similarly, relationships between water pollution and the cancers of the gastrointestinal system and bladder have been investigated. See also §6.12 and Doll and McLean (1979). For the effect of urbanization, see Greenberg (1983) and Kraybill and Mehlman (1977).

Occupation

Observations of persons in their occupational setting are good sources of the effects of chemical and physical hazards. Härting and Hesse (1879) is a classical account of lung cancer in workers of uranium ores. Decouflé (1982) details several further examples: cancer of the bladder in the aniline dye industries, cancer of the lung after inhalation of asbestos, and cancer of the lung in the chromate producing industry. Many of the agents only produce the cancer after long latent periods; thus, mineral oils produce lesions only after many years of exposure. Cancers may be produced at multiple sites; industrial cancers may only appear after retirement. These factors have been responsible for the delay in the recognition of risks. Some occupational cancer data have been obtained from general national vital statistics records, hospital records, and general cancer surveys. See §20.3 for occupational risks from radioactive substances. For reports of occupational cancers, see also the *Cancer Yearbook*, Vainio, Sorsa, and Hemminki (1979), Alderson (1986), and Peto and Schneiderman (1981).

Familial Predisposition

This is a difficult topic. There are inherited diseases, such as retinoblastoma and xeroderma pigmentosum, in which cancers obviously have a familial predisposition. There is also inherited polyposis of the colon, which is associated with cancers of the colon. A less obvious cause is skin color, for the fair-skinned families will contain more than their share of skin cancers. For a general discussion, see D.E. Anderson (1982).

Migrant Studies

Haenszel (1982) points out the advantages of studying migrants into the United States, whose upbringing and previous environment may have differed greatly from those of United States citizens.

Survival of Patients

Although it comes under criticism, there appears to be no more satisfactory way of measuring the efficacy of treatment than the survival rates for 5 years or other lengths of time. Myers and Hankey (1982) give tables in a set of American hospitals of the 5-year relative survival rate, comparing rates in 1960–1963 with those of 1970–1973; among white male patients, survival rates rose from 7% to 9% for lung cancer; for prostatic cancer, the rates rose from 50% to 63%, whereas little change was noted for patients with cancers of the stomach, pancreas, or brain. Notable increases were registered for men with cancers of the bladder, kidney, colon, rectum, and larynx; for "non-Hodgkin's disease" or lymphatic leukemia, the success rates were high. Similar results were obtained with white women.

For international comparisons, see:
World: Clemmesen (1965); Doll, Muir, et al. (1970); Mould (1983); Muir and Nectoux (1982); Schottenfeld and Fraumeni (1982); Segi, Kurihara, and Matsuyama (1969); Waterhouse, Shanmugaratnam, et al. (1982); and WHO-neoplasms (1963, 1970, 1974).
Europe: Campbell (1980); Campbell, Chiang, and Hansluwka (1980); Hansluwka (1978); and

Schinz and Reich (1959). England and Wales: McKenzie, Case, and Pearson (1957) and Schinz and Reich (1959).

USSR: Napalkov, Tserkovny, et al. (1983).

USA: See §42.9.

Japan: Segi, Fukushima, et al. (1955).

For persons at high risk, see Fraumeni (1975).

20.9 Lip, Oral Cavity, and Pharynx

ICD 140–149.

The mortality from cancers of this subclass is now unimportant numerically in the western countries, but there is great variation in the incidence rates between the countries of the world.

Lip

Squamous cell cancer is a common tumor of fair-skinned persons exposed to large doses of ultraviolet light; thus, in Australia at the beginning of this century there were many cases of untreated cancers that had progressed so far as to require not only local excision but block dissection of the glands of the neck; correct therapy, especially radium plaques to the primary lesion, has rendered these operations superfluous (Lancaster, 1954d).

Oral Cavity and Pharynx

These cancers are relatively common in some of the Asian countries where betel nut is chewed, often reinforced with tobacco. In the southern states of the United States much snuff is taken, especially by women. Risk factors noted by Mahboubi and Sayed (1982) include alcohol, especially when combined with heavy smoking, nutritional deficiencies, and occupational factors, particularly when increased dosage of ultraviolet light is implied. In the past, undue weight has been given to syphilis and to poor dentition (jagged teeth) as etiologic factors.

20.10 Digestive Organs and Peritoneum

ICD 150–159.

Esophagus

Cancer of the esophagus is not a rare cancer; in Australia it has appeared with crude death rates of approximately 50 and 18 per 1,000,000 per annum for males and females, respectively. It has a marked geographical distribution. In Day and Muñoz (1982, Table 1), we find standardized rates per 1,000,000 per annum for males (females) in New Zealand, 38 (18); Rhodesia (Zimbabwe), 64 (22); Singapore, 200 (64); and Bombay, India, 152 (108); whereas most European countries lie within the range 10 to 50 per 1,000,000 per annum for either sex. In Kazakstan there are areas with rates of over 800 per 1,000,000 per annum. In Singapore the rates of the Chinese vary with both birthplace and place of origin of family. In Brittany high rates are associated with alcohol and tobacco consumption. See also for etiology, Wynder and Bross (1961).

Stomach

Cancer of the stomach was noted in Lancaster (1954d) to be first in frequency among cancers in either sex in Australia during 1931–1940. In the decade 1951–1960, in males the mortality from lung cancer and in females the mortality from breast cancer exceeded the death rates from cancer of the stomach. In Table 5 and Figure 3 of that article, there are evident substantial declines in the mortality from cancer of the stomach at all ages under 65 years in both sexes, although there are substantial increases at ages over 75 years. The reasons for these declines are obscure. It is difficult to find another site to which cancers, previously diagnosed as of the stomach, have been transferred. Moreover, the same declines have been noted in other countries such as the United States (Gordon, Crittenden, and Haenszel, 1961). Certainly few authors would be prepared to ascribe the improvement to surgery; the results of follow-up surveys, such as Berkson, Walters, et al. (1952), Ederer, Cutler, et al. (1960), Griswold, Wilder, et al. (1955), and Harnett (1952), show that the surgical or other treatment of cancer of the stomach has never been sufficiently successful to account for the declines in mortality. Nomura (1982) points out that cancer of the stomach has the poorest 5-year relative survival rate after pancreatic and lung cancers.

With respect to other stomach lesions, there seems to be no definite relationship of cancer to either polyps or gastric ulcer; there may be some genetic background to some diffuse stomach cancers in subjects of blood type A. There is general agreement that foods manipulated by smoking, salting, or other means of chemical preservation, such as by nitrates and nitrites, should be avoided. Perhaps, fresh fruit and vitamin C are partly protective against some of the above factors. For the general epidemiology of the disease, see Nomura (1982), Wynder (1967), and Wynder, Kmet, et al. (1963).

Pancreas

The recorded death rates from cancer of the pancreas have increased over the decades of the survey of Lancaster (1954c). It is difficult to ascertain whether these increases, as shown in Table 1 of that article, are real or due to transfers of some deaths from cancers of other sites. The same article showed that diabetes developed in patients with pancreatic cancer, and conversely, pancreatic cancer appeared in the patients of a large diabetic clinic with a frequency greater than the expected. Mack (1982) cites other similar surveys and conclusions; he also points to the absence of any clearly established etiologic factors for pancreatic cancer. For international trends, see Aoki and Ogawa (1978).

Liver

Many official statistical series show declines in death rates from cancer of the liver, probably spurious, because in earlier times, secondary deposits were often regarded as evidence of primary disease. Indeed, primary liver cancer is relatively uncommon in the western world; see, for example, Aoki (1978) and Falk (1982). The latter points out that it is a leading cause of deaths from cancer in many parts of Africa and Asia. About 75% of cases are said to be associated with a preexistent cirrhosis of the liver; leading etiologic agents are hepatitis B virus, alcohol, and aflatoxin. Falk (1982) gives tables showing the remarkable variations throughout the world in mortality from primary cancer of the liver. See §20.6 for an explanation and Anthony (1984), Ayoola (1984), and Uwaifo and Bababunmi (1984).

Small intestine

Cancers are rare. See Lightdale, Koepsell, and Sherlock (1982).

Large Intestine

There have been increases in the rates in many countries of the western world, including Australia, particularly of cancers of the colon. See Correa and Haenszel (1975) and Schottenfeld and Winawer (1982) for international comparisons. Burkitt (1975a) remarks that "no other form of cancer is so closely related to economic development and modern western civilization as cancer of the colon and rectum"; in Burkitt (1975a, Figure 10.4), he gives a comparison of death rates, standardized over the males at ages 35 to 64 years, for many different populations, which is consistent with the hypothesis. It is hypothesized that cancer of the colon is secondary to the production of carcinogens in the colon by bacteria, with concentrations rising when the rate of passage through the bowel is slow, see Burkitt (1980), Modan and Lubin (1980), and §22.14. For persons at risk, see Fraumeni and Mulvihill (1975).

20.11 Respiratory System

ICD 160–165.

ICD 160: nasal cavities, middle ear, and accessory sinuses.

ICD 161: larynx.

ICD 162, 163, 164, 165: trachea and all respiratory and intrathoracic organs.

Nasopharynx

Shanmugaratnam (1982, Figure 1) illustrates the variation in incidence rates of nasopharyngeal cancer throughout the world, with very high rates for the ethnic Chinese of the Californian Bay area, Singapore, and Hawaii; further, in Cantonese clinics it constitutes 57% of all cancers, but only 4% to 8% in northern clinics. This variation is almost entirely due to undifferentiated carcinoma, although it is possible that some of the squamous cell and nonkeratinizing carcinomata are due to the same causes. The cause of this tumor is not known, although the Epstein-Barr virus and HLA antigen may be relevant.

Larynx

Death rates from cancer of the larynx in Australia are available in Lancaster (1953*d*). For a given epoch, there is the usual increase of the rates with age. Over the period 1908–1950, slight falls in the rates at ages 45 to 64 years and some rises at ages over 75 years have occurred, but neither movement is large. The rates at each age have remained practically stationary for females. There is a pronounced degree of masculinity of the rates, the male to female ratio being over five. Tobacco and alcohol, and also asbestos, are believe to be important etiologic factors (Austin, 1982 and Wynder, Bross, and Day, 1956).

Lung

It is convenient to class cancer of the bronchus and lung together as cancer of the lung. Little is lost by supposing that all deaths in the cancers of the respiratory system, indeed in ICD 161–165, are due to either cancer of the larynx (ICD 161) or cancer of the "lung," that is, of the trachea, lung, and pleura; of course, it is necessary to exclude cases of cancer secondary to cancers of other organs.

Cancer of the lung is now the most important cancer of the western world; it may be used to point to some of the difficulties in estimating the reality of increasing importance of any cancer. In the early years of this century there had begun an aging of the population. As a result, many papers appeared suggesting great increases of mortality in all forms of cancer. It was clear that comparisons must be made using the age-specific death rates. The official statistics of many countries around 1930 were beginning to show increases in the mortality from

lung cancers, for example, in Australia at ages 65 to 74 years males had mortality rates per 1,000,000 of 70, 69, 203, 356, and 950, in the five decades 1911–1920, . . ., 1951–1960 (Lancaster, 1953*d*, 1962*a*), but little change in many other cancer incidences. An anomaly was soon noticed in the statistics for cancer of the lung. Whereas, if the death rates were considered for an epoch, most cancers would show a regular increase with age, the mortality from lung cancer showed a local maximum at some age below 75 years; for example, in the epoch 1940–1945, according to the *Registrar-General's Statistical Review for England and Wales* (1949), the death rates from cancer of the bronchus, lung, and pleura were 144, 555, 1116, 1050, and 571 at ages 35 to 44, 45 to 54, 55 to 64, 65 to 74, and 75 and over, with a local maximum in the age group 55 to 64 years. Such phenomena were shown by Kennaway and Waller (1953/1954) to be due to successive cohorts having increasingly high death rates; for, if the etiology of cancer of the lung is due to a carcinogen (cigarette smoking) acting over many years and there has been an increasing hazard to successive generations, when the death rates are displayed by the generation (cohort) method, the anomaly disappears, for the death rates of each cohort increase approximately linearly throughout life, when a semilogarithmic grid is used, in the same way as do those of other important cancers.

The etiology of lung cancer was investigated first by Mueller (1939), who found in a clinical survey that there were 3 (14) nonsmokers, 27 (41) light smokers, and 56 (31) heavy smokers out of 86 (86) patients with (without) cancer of the lung; or, in other words, those with cancer tended to have smoked more than those without (i.e., the controls). Wynder and Graham (1950, 1951) and Doll and Hill (1950, 1952, 1954, 1956, 1964), with larger series of cases and controls, made a strong case for tobacco, especially as in cigarette smoking, being the major etiologic factor in the modern increases in lung cancer death rates. This hypothesis has been vehemently disputed in some statistical circles but is now almost universally accepted; see Wynder (1972) and Wynder and Goodman

(1983). The treatment of lung cancer is unsatisfactory, with 5-year survival rates of 6% in 1950–1954 and 9% in 1970–1973 in surgical clinics of the United States, according to Fraumeni and Blot (1982), who remark also that of persons suffering from lung cancer in the United States in the years before 1980, tobacco was responsible in 80% of males and 40% of females.

Another cause of lung cancer in the United States, especially in the shipbuilding industry, is asbestos. There is a strong synergism with cigarette smoking, a table of Hammond, Selikoff, and Seidman (1979) showing a high relative risk for the combined causes (53.2). Other occupational factors, listed by Fraumeni and Blot (1982), are exposure to radon as in uranium mines, mustard gas, polycyclic aromatic hydrocarbons, chloromethyl ethers, chromium, nickel, and inorganic arsenic.

The etiology of cancer of the lung has been extensively investigated: first, by questionnaires or retrospective methods, second, by prospective methods, and third, by animal experimentation. All methods show that cancer of the lung can be caused by cigarette smoking or contact with tobacco derivatives and that there is a dose-incidence relationship.

Interesting comparisons can be made between Mormons, who do not smoke, and persons of other religious persuasions, who do, as in Utah, see Cairns, Lyon, and Skolnick (1980) and Lyon, Gardner, and West (1980); similar comparisons are available between Seventh Day Adventists and control populations in the United States, as in Phillips, Kuzma, and Lotz (1980) and Wynder, Lemon, and Bross (1959). The Mormons and Seventh Day Adventists have notably lower death rates from lung cancer than the other religious groups (i.e., non-Mormon or non-Seventh Day Adventist).

See for further references, Fraumeni and Blot (1982) and the extensive bibliographies of US Public Health Service (1972, 1974), US Surgeon-General (1979, 1982), US Office on Smoking and Health (1983), and Mass, et al. (1985). For the etiology of lung cancer in the United States see Haenszel (1966) and for quantitative estimates of avoidable risks of cancer in the United States, see Doll and Peto (1981); world comparisons are given by Benjamin (1977).

20.12 Genitourinary System

Uterus

ICD 179, 180, 182. It is impossible to give the cancers of the cervix and of the body separately from the official statistics of, perhaps, most countries; it can be assumed, however, from clinical knowledge that most of the deaths under 65 years from uterine cancer are from cancers of the cervix. There have been some moderate declines in Australia under the age of 55 years (Lancaster, 1951d). It can be shown that all the declines in mortality from neoplasms at ages under 45 years in females have been associated with cancer of the uterus. A number of follow-up studies have shown that therapy is successful in this disease, for example, in Australia, Fowler and McCall (1949) and Schlink (1960). Follow-up often can be carried out in the absence of a formal registry or clinic if the need is felt.

Gagnon (1950), studying the causes of death in nuns, showed that the disease was rare in virgins; see also Fraumeni, Lloyd, and Smith (1969). Later studies have indicated that the risk of cervical cancer is strongly correlated with age at first coitus; where such age is below 20 years, the risk of uterine cancer is increased threefold. See Cramer (1982) for a more detailed discussion on the relevance of number of pregnancies, promiscuity, Herpes genitalis and other infections, and the circumcision status of the spouse; he suggests that the causation may be multifactorial. Some recent studies have pointed to the possibility that modern promiscuity has caused increased rates at the younger ages. See de Palo, Rilke, et al. (1986) for herpes and papilloma.

For cancer of the body of the uterus, see de Waard (1982), who gives evidence of increased incidence in some areas, probably because of the prescription of estrogens for menopausal and postmenopausal women.

Ovary

ICD 183. The death rates in Australia from cancer of the ovary have risen. Similar increases have occurred in other countries and have been commented on by the Registrar-General of England and Wales (1949), Gordon, Crittenden, and Haenszel (1961), and Muir and Nectoux (1978). The estimate of Weiss (1982) that cancer of the ovary will cause the death of 1% to 2% of all white women appears to be high; he comments that little is known of the etiology.

Choriocarcinoma

ICD 181. This is not a common cancer; it arises from a maldevelopment of a female embryo. From ages 15 to 34 years, the incidence is around 8 per 10,000 births, at ages 35 to 39, 40 to 44, 45 to 49, and 50 to 54 years it is 9, 18, 234, and 636 per 10,000 births, respectively, according to data from the Registrar-General of England and Wales. See Bagshawe and Lawler (1982) for further details and Bracken, Brinton, et al. (1984) for a review.

Other Genital Cancers

ICD 184. Numerically, the other genital cancers of females are not important, according to Lancaster (1951d, 1958a).

Prostate

ICD 185. The death rates from cancer of the prostate are given in Lancaster (1952b, 1955a). There have been considerable increases in the mortality rates in Australia at ages over 65 years. Whether this increase is due to changes in diagnosis is difficult to determine, but clinical opinion suggests that this cancer would be diagnosed more efficiently in recent years. The most likely rubric of the ICD from which transfers might have occurred is "diseases of the prostate," which was not further divided before the Fifth Revision, after which it was subdivided into "hypertrophy of the prostate" and "other diseases of the prostate." But for the years 1941–1945 there were 2,658 deaths from hypertrophy and 412 deaths from other diseases of the prostate in Australia, so that the rubric can be taken to refer almost entirely to hypertrophy of the prostate. From Lancaster (1955a) it appears that there has been little change in the death rates from this cause, except for a slight increase at ages over 65 years, so it cannot be expected that transfers from this rubric were responsible for the apparent increase in the cancer rates; we may conclude that the increase in the rates of prostatic cancer is real. In Lancaster (1952b, Table 3) it is shown that the incidence in unmarried men is less than in married, so rates may depend on sexual activity. Little is known about the etiology (Greenwald, 1982).

Breast

ICD 175. Before 1930, cancer of the male breast had been usually classed with cancers of the skin. Lancaster (1952b, Table 4) shows that it had been and is now a rare cause of death.

Other Male Genital Organs

ICD 187. These are relatively rare cancers; rates can be found in the papers quoted above and discussions, as follow: testis, Schottenfeld and Warshauer (1982) and penis, Hall and Schottenfeld (1982).

Bladder and Kidney

ICD 188, 189. Cancers of the bladder and of the kidneys are among the less common cancers. There have been some increases in the rates given in Lancaster (1955a, Table 8), the comparison being made between 1931–1940 and 1941–1946. See Staszewski (1980a,b) and Morrison and Cole (1982) for international comparisons of cancers of the bladder and kidney.

20.13 Female Breast

ICD 174.

Cancers of the breast and uterus are among the most common cancers of the female. They are responsible for the excess of the female cancer death rates over those of the males at ages 25 to 55 years; they provide an interesting test case for the control of cancer by early diagnosis, since the breast and cervix are readily accessible to clinical examination and the criteria for diagnosis are well established.

The death rates from cancers of the breast have been almost stationary over the period 1908–1945 in Australia at the younger ages under 55 years, but at the older ages there have been steady increases. These features can be traced back to earlier Australian experience; similar experience in the United States has been noted by Gordon, Crittenden, and Haenszel (1961). In many other countries concern has been expressed about similar trends. It is often argued that earlier treatment would lead to more cures. Even at this time, there is doubt as to the roles of surgery and radiotherapy in the treatment of the disease. M. Page (1948), in his Presidential Address to the Royal College of Surgeons, notes that the confident opinions of surgeons are not always based on adequate follow-up series. Others have expressed the view, with more enthusiasm than information, that earlier diagnosis when the cancer was well localized would lead to more complete removal of the growth. On the other hand, McKinnon (1949, 1950, 1952) has discussed in detail the official statistics for the province of Ontario, for Massachusetts, and for England and Wales. In Ontario and Massachusetts, intensive campaigns, carried through with energy, have been successful in bringing the patient to the doctor at an earlier stage, and they have succeeded in reducing the time between the first visit to the doctor and the commencement of treatment, and yet no effective reduction in the cancer death rate has ensued. See the follow-up series of Berkson, Harrington, et al. (1957). The problem of treatment certainly cannot be regarded as solved.

See Kelsey (1979) and Petrakis, Ernster, and King (1982) for a general discussion of the etiology, Logan (1975) for some international comparisons, Myers and Hankey (1982) and Kolata (1985c) for some improvements in survival rates, and Kolata (1985b) for a summary of recent opinion on efficacy of treatment.

20.14 Melanoma and Other Neoplasms of the Skin

It had long been known that persons exposed to the weather suffered an undue incidence of keratoses and carcinomata of the skin. Among the first to suggest that rodent ulcer (basal cell carcinoma) and squamous carcinoma were due to insolation was Dubreuilh (1907), after studying cases in southern France. In Australia the problem of skin cancers was important, for there was a large fair-skinned population living at lower latitudes than similar fair-skinned populations in Europe, especially the British Isles, and it was evident to Australian dermatologists that incidence of skin carcinomata was greatly in excess of that in the British Isles. These dermatologists assumed therefore that insolation was the cause of the excess, without specifying the wavelength of the active component, although there had been no proper verification of the hypothesis. Findlay (1928), motivated by this hypothesis, submitted mice to ultraviolet light for periods exceeding 9 months to obtain papilloma and malignant epitheliomata of the skin; he found that there was a synergism between ultraviolet light and the application of tars to the skin. Further experimental work was carried out by Blum (1959a, b), who was aware of the clinical importance of the filtering out of the ultraviolet light by the ozone layer of the atmosphere, although the importance of this was not appreciated by the dermatologists, who continued to think of the hours of sunlight, without mention of the height of the sun, as the important parameter. That ultraviolet light is the cause of the skin cancers is now universally accepted (Scotto and Fraumeni, 1982). See also §20.3.

Estimates of mortality from skin cancer are subject to some doubt. Cancer of the lip should be included; however, it is combined with cancers of the tongue in cancers of the buccal cavity, for which Lancaster (1954d, Table 3) shows death rates in the years 1908 to 1920 of around 570, 1,080, and 1,600 per 1,000,000 for males in Australia at ages 55–64, 65–74, and 75 and over, respectively; these rates are 8 to 10 times higher than the corresponding rates for females. On the clinical side, there were major operations for removal of the primary and block dissections of the glands of the neck. The rates fell markedly after 1920 as a result of earlier treatment and the use of radium. In Australia for the years 1908 to 1920, the death rates from cancer of the skin for males were around 110, 270, and 830 at ages 55–64, 65–74, and 75 and over, respectively, in Lancaster (1954e, Table I) with declines in later epochs not well marked. Indeed, because of the chronic nature of most cancers of the skin, the official statistics may not be a good guide to the incidence of the disease.

It is a remarkable fact that, although ultraviolet light had long been accepted as the cause of skin cancers and fair skin was accepted as being relatively common in melanoma patients, ultraviolet light had not been suggested as the cause of melanoma. This was changed by Australian experience. McGovern (1952, 1977) found that melanoma tended to be more frequent on the exposed areas of skin and suggested that insolation might be the cause. Lancaster (1954e) noted that the crude death rate from melanoma in Australia was more than twice the corresponding English rate, and later Lancaster (1956b) showed that within Australia the incidence of melanoma was higher in the lower latitudes. Indeed, the deaths per 1,000,000 per annum for the Australian States in 1951–1953, with the latitude of the capital cities, males (females), were as follows: Queensland 27°, 28(17); Western Australia 32°, 13(17); New South Wales 34°, 17(13); South Australia 35°, 15(10); Victoria 38°, 8(8); and Tasmania 43°, 7(9). Similar comparisons could be made in two other countries; thus, the North Island of New Zealand has a higher melanoma death rate than the South Island, and the southern states of the United States have a higher rate than the northern. Much work is now being carried out in Australia on the effect of sunlight on the skin, especially in Western Australia, for example, Holman, Mulroney, and Armstrong (1980).

This general relation between latitude and melanoma incidence appears to hold generally throughout those countries of the world where the incidence in fair-skinned races can be measured. There has been much argument over two anomalies. In Queensland the melanoma incidence in the dry inland, more-northern zone, where there is not so much exposure to the sun in sport, is less than in the coastal zone, where the bulk of the population is more southerly and may be taken to be, on the average, on the latitude of the capital city; possibly, the reason for this apparent anomaly is that people surf on the coast and expose themselves far more to the sun than do those of the inland zone. In Sweden the ultraviolet dosage comes almost entirely from the diffracted rays, is consequently low, and does not vary greatly by region; the differences between regions in incidence rates are small and may not be correctly estimated because other effects, relative to them, are not small. See Lee (1982).

Melanoma incidence is increasing in Australia as can be seen in Table 20.14.1.

See Jensen and Bolander (1980) for international comparisons and MacKie (1983) for recent advances. For a clinical survey, see Lancaster (1957b).

20.15 Leukemia and Hodgkin's Disease

ICD 200–208.

Leukemia

Leukemia is an unusual malignant disease, in that deaths occur at all ages. With the decline of death rates from all other causes, it has assumed greater relative importance in childhood and young adult life. It occurs in three forms, acute, chronic granulocytic, and chronic lymphatic. See Heath (1982) and Gunz (1980) for etiology.

Radiation received occupationally by physicians was recognized in the 1940s as a possible cause of leukemia, for example, see Henshaw and Hawkins (1944). With appropriate safeguards there is little of such leukemia. The explosion of the atomic bombs at Hiroshima and Nagasaki 1945 has led to many investigations, of which we mention Brill, Tomonaga, and Heyssel (1962); in particular, it has been shown

TABLE 20.14.1. Mortality rates in Australia from melanoma.*

Age in years	15–24	25–34	35–44	45–54	55–64	65–74	75+
				Males			
1931–1940	3	7	8	13	22	28	34
1941–1950	3	10	12	18	25	26	44
1951–1960	7	18	29	38	37	55	84
1961–1970	7	23	40	56	76	90	117
1971–1980	6	24	42	69	106	145	175
				Females			
1931–1940	2	6	6	12	14	19	33
1941–1950	2	8	14	15	22	24	44
1951–1960	5	14	23	26	32	38	62
1961–1970	3	16	31	42	48	54	92
1971–1980	4	15	26	46	61	78	108

* Deaths per million per annum.
From Lancaster (1956b, 1987)

that risk of leukemia increases with dosage received. Leukemia has also followed therapeutic radiology (Court Brown and Doll, 1965) and irradiation as a fetus (Diamond, Schmerler, and Lilienfeld, 1973). Some leukemias in animals are known to be caused by viruses, but no such virus-leukemia has been found in man. Treatment of leukemia has proved disappointing. For worldwide comparisons, see Kessler and Lilienfeld (1969).

Hodgkin's Disease

This is a malignant neoplasm of the lymph nodes. It may be a mix of several such diseases, as its age distribution curve is bimodal. The incidence rate in the United States in the mid-1970s was 32 per 1,000,000 per annum. See Correa (1977), Grufferman (1982), Grufferman and Delzell (1984), WHO-Hodgkin's disease (1955), and Beebe, Kato, and Land (1978).

Miscellaneous

Burkitt's lymphoma is the most common cancer of children in tropical Africa and lowland Niugini, according to Morrow (1982); an important necessary, but not sufficient, causal agent is the Epstein-Barr virus. See also Alderson (1980), Linet (1985), Osunkoya (1982), de-The (1979), Williams (1984), Williams, John-son, et al. (1984), and Williams, O'Conor, et al. (1984).

For cancer of the eye, see Hakulinen, Teppo, et al. (1978).

20.16 General Conclusions on Cancer Incidence

There have been great changes in the attitudes towards cancer. We have seen in §§20.2 and 20.4 that causes of cancer have been known for many years, for example, chimney sweep cancer in 1775, miners' cancer in 1879, skin cancers in 1907 (as in §20.14), watchmakers' osteosarcoma in 1929, and aniline dye cancer of the bladder in 1895; nevertheless, the clinical teaching of the 1930s treated cancer as a degenerative disease of the aged, the incidence of which was little affected by the environment. There was much stress on chronic irritations, such as by jagged teeth and clay pipes, and on chronic infections, such as syphilis. There had been a general impression in the era 1900 to 1920 that cancer incidence was on the increase. Many authors showed that false conclusions were being drawn and that, if age-specific death rates rather than crude death rates, were considered, the mortality and/or incidence rates were not increasing.

This apparently stable era of the death rates was soon to be ended. In 1939 it was reported that the incidence of lung cancer was higher in smokers than nonsmokers. Developments were possibly inhibited by the coming of World War II, but this clue was followed up by other surveys into the cigarette-lung cancer relationship and by more general studies into etiology, such as by geographic pathology. Cancer incidence was found to vary not only between countries but within countries. Here advantage was taken of the existence of large identifiable religious groups in the United States, which could be compared with other groups differing only in religion and life style from them; the incidence of certain cancers between ethnic groups could also be measured in the United States. The increased interest in the diseases of the countries of Africa, in particular, led to many comprisons between ethnic groups. It became clear that some cancers, for example, of the colon, were much rarer in the negroes of Africa than in the white population of the United States and other developed countries and even were rarer than in negroes in the United States living in the American life style. These discoveries and the rise of epidemiology in the study of diseases, not necessarily infective in origin, have led to a great number of careful studies into the etiology of cancer. It is now recognized that by control of the environment, the incidence of cancer can be greatly reduced; indeed, estimates have been made that proper control could reduce cancer incidences to a small fraction of the present load.

Nonmelanotic cancer of the skin can be cured by therapy, but the cure rate from surgery is usually not good for any of the major cancers, for example, cancer of the breast, stomach, lung, colon and pancreas, and melanoma. On the other hand, it is known that changes of personal habits, namely smoking, diet, and exposure to sunlight, could effectively reduce the incidence of lung cancer, cancer of the colon, and melanoma, respectively. So, there is much to be gained by the control of environmental factors.

If we exclude cancer of the lung and melanoma, we conclude that cancer mortality has been relatively stable in the period for which statistics have been available and that, although it has been a major cause of death, its burden on the developed world has shown little decline over the past 80 years.

Chapter 21
Endocrine Diseases

21.1 Disorders of the Thyroid Gland

ICD 240–246. ICD 240, simple and unspecified goiter; 241, nontoxic nodular goiter; 242, thyrotoxicosis; 243, 244, congenital and acquired hypothyroidism; 245, thyroiditis; 246: other.

There was formerly a high incidence of simple goiter in mountainous or other areas with a shortage of iodine in the soil. These days, the origin of food eaten is not usually confined to the particular area, so goiter in these areas is of less importance; prophylaxis against simple goiter is the addition of small quantities of iodine salts (iodates) to the diet, usually in common salt. Occasionally, dosage with iodates precipitates an attack of thyrotoxicosis.

Of these rubrics, only 242, thyrotoxicosis, is associated with significant mortality—about one-thousandth of the deaths from all causes in 1911–1920 in Australia. Usually, there is a masculinity ratio of 1 to 7 or 1 to 10. The cause of the disease is not known. Treatment is by a chemical blockade of thyroid hormone synthesis or by surgical ablation of much of the gland substance; case fatality rates have fallen since World War II, and the population mortality rate has fallen to possibly only a third of its former level.

For endemic goiter, see WHO-goiter (1960).

21.2 Diabetes: Genetics and Epidemiology

ICD 250. Fourth digit is used for various complications. Exclusion: neonatal diabetes (775.1); hemochromatosis (275.0).

Diabetes is a disease characterized by hyperglycemia and, some authors add, due to a relative or absolute lack of insulin. Formerly, authors have distinguished two types of the disease, a "thin" type with onset in childhood and youth and a "fat" type with onset in late adult life, often preceded by obesity. The etiology and genetics of the disease have been clarified by Keen (1982) and Schernthaner (1982) in the Serono Symposium (Koebberling and Tattersall, 1982).

There are two main types,

(i) insulin-dependent diabetes mellitus (IDDM), in which there is a predominantly juvenile onset;

(ii) non–insulin-dependent diabetes mellitus (NIDDM), in which onset is usually above the age of 40 years. There is a subtype, mature onset diabetes in the young (MODY), for those whose onset comes early although their syndrome is of non–insulin-dependent type. There are also types secondary to other distinctive disorders, for example, secondary to destruction of the islets of Langerhans, to other endocrinopathies, or to toxic effects of drugs. Hyperglycemic symptoms may appear in pregnancy, and these cases will need to be reclassified after pregnancy.

The criteria for the diagnosis of diabetes mellitus and another category, impaired glucose tolerance (IGT), are set out by Keen (1982); there is good agreement by authorities on the level of fasting blood glucose, namely, 140 mg per 100 ml. Impaired glucose tolerance is a necessary category because some normal persons have blood glucose levels overlapping the set limits. It appears that both IDDM and NIDDM classes are heterogeneous, which has been established through family, twin, metabolic, immunologic, and HLA-disease associations (Keen, 1982). This new classification admits that a diabeteslike syndrome may be secondary to another disease, for example, hemochromatosis, cancer of the pancreas. See also Bennett (1983).

With such exclusions, diabetes mellitus is due to an inherited defect. Moreover, there are now two distinct types of disease, IDDM and NIDDM, as mentioned above. Possibly in a state of nature or in societies where food is not abundant, the NIDDM gene is not a handicap to its possessors. So, a theory on the "thrifty genotype" proposed by J.V. Neel in 1962 has to be modified, according to Neel et al. (1982), to cover only the gene for the juvenile type of disease (IDDM). The problem is how a genetic defect with the generally adverse impact on survival and reproduction of diabetes mellitus could attain the high frequency observed; the solution is to call on a genetic polymorphism. In any case, it is reasonable to ask whether such a common gene is always unfavorable. Steinberg and Wilder (1952) and Aschner and Post (1956–1957) point out that diabetic children are often precocious in development, that women, later to become diabetic, have a high fertility, and that under primitive conditions the doubly recessive may be able to cope better with periods of conditions of near-starvation. In other words, possibly only since the coming of agriculture and regular and abundant food supplies, has the gene had a low survival value. It is quite unreasonable, in the present state of knowledge, to deplore the effective treatment of diabetes on genetic grounds.

Wilkerson and Krall (1947, 1953) and Wilkerson, Krall, and Butler (1959) tested 3,516 of the 4,983 inhabitants of a New England (USA) community and concluded that at least 3.5% of persons would ultimately develop diabetes. Such evidence for a high gene frequency in diabetes came as a surprise to many, but later surveys have confirmed the findings (Remein, 1959). Walker (1964) in Birmingham, England, estimated that 6.2% would be a minimum figure.

Surveys of clinic patients, as by Joslin, Root, et al. (1959), Joslin and Wilson (1950), and Lancaster and Maddox (Lancaster, 1950a, 1958b), have shown that the most common age at onset is about 60 years and that there is a majority of females. Treatment has been effective, although the mortality rates in clinic populations still remain higher than those of the general population from which they are drawn.

It has thus appeared that diabetes is a common disease, for which an effective treatment is known. It is understandable that it has been chosen as the subject of some theoretical speculations on the change in gene frequencies due to modern treatment. However, the effect of treatment cannot have had time to affect the genetic frequencies. It is only 60 years since the introduction of insulin, and successful pregnancies in diabetic women, even in the years since 1945, have not been numerous. Moreover, many diabetics have been past their reproductive years at the commencement of their treatment.

Trowell (1975, 1977a) brings forward data to support the hypothesis that fiber-depleted starchy foods are diabetogenic and fiber-rich starchy foods are protective. He also gives some interesting data comparative over time and country.

The National Diabetes Data Group (1985) gives mortality rates for the United States by age, sex, epoch, and other factors, and also mortality rates for Latin American groups, in an impressive volume. See Volk and Arquilla (1985) for the diabetic pancreas, Jackson (1971) for variations by race and country, Jackson (1978), and Friedman and Fialkow (1980) for the genetics of diabetes.

21.3 Diabetes: Statistics

Diabetes may cause death directly or through complications or it may merely be present in a person dying. Therefore, there is considerable difference of opinion as to what constitutes a death due to diabetes. Although some national death certificates have been drawn up with the English certificates as a model, the procedure for assigning priorities of an American manual has often been used; thus, diabetes has had a high priority in many statistical offices. As a cause of death, diabetes would thus be preferred in Australian statistical offices to coronary disease or the more definite coronary occlusion. Gangrene would be considered to be a complication of diabetes, in accordance with clinical thought. However, cancer and tuberculosis, all forms of violence, and the rarer, specific infective disease would all be preferred to diabetes. The official statistics give therefore only a minimum figure for the number of persons who died "with diabetes" (Moriyama, 1948). Joslin, Root, et al. (1946) believed that diabetes was assigned as the cause of death in only about 60% of the deaths of diabetics in American states such as Massachusetts. The conclusions of Lancaster and Maddox (Lancaster, 1950a, 1958b) were that only about one-third of the deaths of patients in a Sydney diabetic clinic were finally assigned to "diabetes." In over one-half of the deaths of such clinic patients, diabetes was not mentioned by the certifying physician.

A deeper question is where the line can be drawn between arteriosclerosis with diabetes and diabetes leading to arteriosclerosis. There has been a suggestion that diabetes would be better grouped in the ICD with the arteriosclerotic diseases. This would entail an additional digit so that it could be determined whether diabetes was present or not. Moreover, it would minimize the importance of the genetics. A rather better solution seems to be to divide the diabetic deaths according to whether death was due to a diabetic complication, such as coma or gangrene, arteriosclerosis, and septic infections, or to an apparently unrelated cause, such as violence or tuberculosis. Even this latter disease raises a difficult problem. Tuberculosis has been a relatively common cause of death of diabetics in Australia at a time when tuberculosis had become an uncommon cause of death

TABLE 21.3.1. Diabetes in England and Wales (deaths per 1,000,000 per annum).

Epoch	All ages*	0–4	5–9	10–14	15–19	20–24	25–34	35–44	45–54	55–64	65–74	75 and over	85 and over
						Males							
1861–1870	43	3	5	10	22	24	44	55	83	136	181	121	
1871–1880	54	1	4	10	24	34	48	69	96	182	248	172	
1881–1890	74	5	7	14	26	35	59	79	135	282	399	315	
1891–1900	90	5	7	16	32	43	57	87	161	347	559	474	
1901–1910	104	4	10	19	36	46	59	78	160	415	731	720	
1911–1920	107	7	13	23	41	46	64	82	146	399	765	839	
1921–1930	90	6	11	19	30	32	43	52	105	324	753	979	
1961[†]	59			3[‡]		3[‡]	10	19	37	76	286	705[§]	870
1981[‖]	83	2		0[‡]		3[‡]	7	20	43	111	330	851	
						Females							
1861–1870	21	2	4	8	13	14	22	30	37	58	62	38	
1871–1880	28	2	4	10	14	18	27	35	50	88	107	68	
1881–1890	46	3	6	15	22	27	36	51	82	161	208	181	
1891–1900	64	3	8	17	25	31	42	56	112	258	380	312	
1901–1910	84	5	10	20	27	35	51	63	129	357	574	473	
1911–1920	91	7	12	25	29	37	50	65	129	367	664	644	
1921–1930	98	4	11	21	26	29	36	53	121	421	839	894	
1961[†]	106			4[‡]		4[‡]	7	9	28	123	429	846[§]	898
1981[‖]	103	1		1[‡]		1[‡]	4	9	25	95	270	774	

* 1861–1930, standardized on to the population of England and Wales as enumerated in 1901. From the Registrar-General's Decennial Supplement (1952, Part 3, Table 12).
[†] From the Registrar-General's Report for 1961.
[‡] Age groups 5–14, 15–24 years.
[§] 75–84 years.
[‖] From the Registrar-General's Report for 1981.

in the nondiabetics. Diabetes in many of these cases could be regarded therefore as the fundamental cause leading up to death, and tuberculosis could be treated as a special complication of diabetes; such deaths could be assigned by the official statisticians to the class of diabetes, and tuberculosis would then be treated in the same way as the ordinary septic complications of diabetic gangrene and carbuncles.

As an example of the progress of the mortality from diabetes in a modern developed country, we give in Table 21.3.1 the death rates from diabetes in England and Wales. Reading the table by columns, it is evident that great decreases in mortality have occurred, especially in the younger age groups. Above the age of 65 years, there have been some apparent increases. Fixing attention on any given period, for example, 1921 to 1930, the table shows a marked increase in the rates with age. There is also a low masculinity of the rates at ages, 35 to 74 years. These mortality findings from the official statistics are in general agreement with the usual clinical findings such as of Joslin, Root et al. (1959). See also Marks (1966).

To determine the modes of death in known diabetics, Lancaster (1958b) reviewed the death certificates of 894 patients from a clinic in Sydney, Australia. Unspecified diabetic complications, such as coma and gangrene, accounted for 135 deaths. Naturally, arterial degeneration ranked high as a cause of death,

and it was possible to show that the 439 deaths from it were many more than might be expected from this cause in the experience of the general population. Forty-eight deaths were due to tuberculosis, which points to the importance of early diagnosis by X ray in such susceptible populations. Seven patients died with hemochromatosis, 39 patients died with purulent infections or intercurrent acute infections. In the females, there were 15 deaths from cancer of the breast and 9 from cancer of the uterus, as against expected numbers of 7 and 5. Other clinics have also reported such high cancer rates. However, even more striking were the 10 deaths from cancer of the pancreas compared with an expected 1.25, possibly due to destruction of the cells producing insulin.

For death rates from diabetes in England and Wales 1861–1942, see Stocks (1944). For international comparisons, see WHO-diabetes (1955), and for discussion of diabetes etiology, see Stanbury, Wyngaarden, et al. (1976).

21.4 Other Endocrine Diseases

In brief notation, we have ICD 251, disorders of pancreatic secretion, not diabetic; 252, parathyroid; 253, pituitary; 254, thymus; 255, adrenal; 256, ovarian; 257, testicular; 258, polyglandular; 259, other.

These rubrics are associated with few deaths. For a historical survey of the endocrine diseases, see L.G. Wilson (1984).

Chapter 22

Food, Malnutrition, Avitaminoses, and Famine

22.1 Evolution of Human Nutrition

Nutrition has so many diverse influences on mortality that an attempt must be made to summarize its history. Lee and DeVore (1968*b*) point out that "cultural" man has spent most of his time as a hunter-gatherer, for it is only in the past 10,000 years that he has domesticated plants and animals for food; further, of all cultural men over the past 2 million years, it is estimated that more than 90% have lived as hunters and gatherers, about 6% have lived by agriculture, and the remainder have lived in industrial society. Attempts have been made to assess the activities of ancient man with the aid of observations on modern hunter-gatherers, but criticisms of this approach have been made, for many of the modern hunter-gatherers appear to be descendants of agricultural man forced back from the more fertile lands by others with more highly developed technology. Authors have therefore turned their attention particularly to the Eskimos, Bushmen, and Australian aborigines. Indeed, the Australian aborigines had had very little cultural contact with the outside world before the coming of the Europeans 200 years ago. Harlan (1975) concludes from his studies that the emphasis is on gathering, from which many "hunters" obtained their principal food, for the rewards of hunting are variable; it is time consuming and seems often to be undertaken chiefly as a sport. Gathering has the additional advantage that it can be carried out by the women and children of the tribe.

Gathering, by definition, includes the seeking not only of seeds and roots but also of rodents, lizards, eggs, insects, grubs, worms, tortoises, and shellfish; moreover, the gathering does not take up too much time, 2 to 5 hours a day (Lozoff and Brittenham, 1977) or even less (Harlan, 1975) being sufficient. These authors and Truswell (1977) agree that hunter-gatherers do not suffer from malnutrition. Detailed analysis has shown that plant sources contribute 60%–80% of the calorie intake of the gatherers. Of course, gathering becomes more difficult as a complete way of life in the high latitudes and Harlan (1975) finds that 44°N and 44°S can be taken as useful limits for the gatherers, citing the Eskimos as the extreme example of hunters, with a diet entirely composed of fish and meat. Before the development of agriculture, most men lived predominantly on plant foods, always qualitatively good and only rarely in short supply, in what was in many ways a "golden age", enjoyed by some 10 million men until about 10,000 to 12,000 years ago, according to Lee and De-Vore (1968*a*). There were some disadvantages; thus, among certain modern Bushmen, breast milk is the predominant food over the first year and continues sometimes for 3 years; supplements in forms of melons, roots, and perhaps nuts are introduced in the first year, but the child suffers from not being able to chew enough in the early part of the second year. These Bushmen, by our standards, are mildly undernourished but not qualitatively malnourished; as compensations, they do not suffer obesity, they have very little dental caries, there is no hypertension, serum cholesterols are low, there is no coronary heart disease, and old age is attainable. Perhaps this can be extrapolated back to 10,000 BP, together with the suggestion that the tribes had not yet been forced off the most fertile land.

Then, with unknowable motives, almost certainly overpopulation in some areas, man began to domesticate plants and animals for food production.

As Stamler (1979) points out, man in many regions, such as the Fertile Crescent of the Middle East and the Nile flood plain, in the Far East, Central America, and elsewhere, made decisive steps toward food production and became a farmer and a herder. So began the progression toward the diets of the modern world, typified by the United States today. For the first time, dairy products, cereals, breads, alcoholic beverages, and salt were freely available. The new agriculture permitted larger populations to live together and the societies lost their homogeneity. Aristocracies and priesthoods arose who enjoyed luxury diets, resembling our own and leading to a similar pathology, for Egyptian mummies often reveal gross atherosclerosis in the aorta, and the Roman aristocracy is reported to have suffered angina pectoris and sudden death (Leibowitz, 1970). As the Bible has it, they lived "off the fat of the land." These luxury diets were not available to the general populace; the common diets were in ancient Egypt bread and beer, and in ancient Rome coarse bread, grain pastes, and polenta-like porridge made from millet. From those times down to the present, the staple foods have been bread, rice, potatoes, and beans. At the present time, in the developing world of Africa, Asia, and the Americas, more than 60% of the calories are supplied by these starchy foods, with insufficient first class protein; as a result, the inhabitants suffer from malnutrition or undernutrition, with consequent failures of bodily development and vitamin deficiencies. Often, too, they suffer from apathy and other constitutional symptoms, which we observe in more definite form in famines; but in rural settings, they are remarkably free of some diseases of the cardiovascular

and alimentary systems that are common in the western world.

There are many entries to nutrition in the general index. For the hunter-gatherers, see Nurse and Jenkins (1977); see Wing and Brown (1979) for paleonutrition and Simmonds (1976) for the evolution of crop plants. Walcher and Kretchmer (1981) believe that food was an important factor in the evolution of man. Gilbert and Mielke (1985) analyze prehistoric diets. Darby, Ghalioungui, and Grivetti (1977) give an account of nutrition, especially in ancient Egypt. Burnett (1966), Drummond and Wilbraham (1957), Finberg (1972), and C.A. Wilson (1974) give descriptions of the Englishman's food. More general references are Birch and Parker (1980), Heiser (1981), Lowenberg, Todhunter, et al. (1974), McCay (1973), and Walcher, Kretchmer, and Barnett (1976). See also Miller (1979) for the prevalence of nutritional problems throughout the world.

22.2 Production and Transport of Food in Europe

Since much of our analysis is concerned with mortality in Europe, we begin with some remarks on food there. The quantity of food is believed to have been a limiting factor in the growth of population in Europe for many centuries. This is properly the subject of study in economic and agricultural history, but it is necessary to make mention here of some problems in the production and transport of food.

Although the system of long distance transportation of grain, particularly from Egypt and other colonies to Rome, built up during imperial times, was lost after the break-up of the Empire, Roman agricultural practices were continued throughout the Middle Ages, especially in southern Europe. These techniques were used with varying degrees of skill and management in the villas (or later manors), which were the centers of economic life. For much of the Middle Ages, agricultural technique was primitive and inefficient. Génicot (1966) believes that agricultural techniques improved little in western Europe during the later Middle Ages. There was also a great lack of fertilizer before modern times—animal dung and in some cases human nightsoil from the towns were for a long time the chief sources.

According to Parain (1966), the yield of crops to seeds planted was no more than 2 or 2.5 to 1 in western Europe in the ninth and tenth centuries, much below later averages such as on the lands of the Bishop of Winchester in the thirteenth and fourteenth centuries, which were about 4 to 1. Other estimates by Slicher van Bath (1963, 1977) of the ratios are: during the fourteenth century, for wheat 3.8 to 1, barley 3.2, rye 4.0, oats 2.5, and peas 3.5; during the period 1504–1537, for wheat 6.6, rye 8.1, and oats 4.4; during the period 1802–1851, the ratios appear to be higher, although he does not give any average figure. With a 2 to 1 ratio between crop and seed, half the land planted is being used to raise seed for the next season. Under such conditions of poor agricultural technology and deficiencies in the supply of fertilizer, the bad seasons, severe prolonged winters, or cold wet summers in Europe inevitably led to dearth and famine. Moreover, in the absence of adequate stores, a bad harvest would gravely deplete the stocks to provide seed for the next season and would leave a reduced amount for the local population until the next season's crop had been gathered. Only slow recovery could therefore be made after a bad season. It is evident also that these low crop to seed ratios would have increased the difficulties of migration.

In the fifteenth century, the increasing use of power and the division of labor made possible the large city, in which most inhabitants worked for a money wage and were fed, usually, from the surrounding country; but because the radius within which grain could be carted economically to a central market was about 20 km (for which see Parry, 1967, p. 156), it was necessary for the larger cities to import food by sea and river. Here again, before 1500 there were limits of distance, and the Mediterranean area, for example, was almost self-sufficient. After 1500 there was an increase generally in the amount of food transported between European countries.

Thus, in the early sixteenth century there was much trade between the Baltic countries and the north German Hansa and the ports of the Netherlands, especially in grain, salt, and salt fish. Fisheries were extended to the Dogger Bank and the seas near Scotland and Iceland, and later in the century there were imports of fish from New England and Newfoundland (Michell, 1977). With the establishment of the American colonies, sugar could be imported, but at first little grain (Glamann, 1977). This ability to import food over long distances by ship and later by rail has been important in lessening the harsh effects of localized failures of the grain harvests.

22.3 Destruction of Food during Growth, Transport, and Storage

During growth, the food crops may be destroyed or the yield greatly diminished by excessively cold winters, as in Sweden, mentioned by Jutikkala (1955), or by drought in the tropical areas. They can be destroyed by such natural disasters as excessive rain, floods, hurricanes, and tsunamis following earthquakes. Hailstorms or falls of volcanic ash can cause local destruction of crops. Floods and inundations on a vast scale have occured in India and in the areas around the Bay of Bengal and in China, causing huge losses of crops. Plant diseases, such as potato blight in the Irish famine, can cause widespread damage to crops. Monocultures make populations particularly vulnerable to such diseases (Adams, Ellingboe and Rossman, 1971). Among insect pests, the effects of the locust, especially in China, are well known. In wars and civil wars, crops may be deliberately destroyed—in fact, the destruction of crops in classical times forced the inhabitants to enter into battle. In Saxon England, for example, fortified depots for the storage of grain were constructed, including one at Surbiton (= South Barley Ton). Great distress would follow any requisition, seizure, or destruction of such stores; fire also was always a hazard, whether in peace or war.

Even in modern times, the storage of food presents great difficulties according to Ordish (1952), Pirie (1961), and Herford (1961); perhaps one-quarter of all food is destroyed in storage. Herford (1961) cites a study by the United Nations, which demonstrated a loss of 35% of cereals and pulses during storage each year in six South American republics. Moreover, 10% of the wheat harvested in the great plains of the United States was lost in storage.

Brown (1981), in an overall world survey of growth, reports that in 1960 the world reserve of food was 102 days, and 285 kg of grain per head of population was produced, and that for 1980 the corresponding figures were 40 days and 324 kg of grain per head.

22.4 Secular Changes in Climate

Because the production of harvests is dependent on the weather, it is natural to turn to considerations of climate. For example, in the long series of annual rainfalls, is the weather of one season independent of that of the next? In one season is the weather in, for instance, Britain independent of that in Finland? The answer to each question is negative. Indeed, there are secular changes in climate, but the physical causes are still a matter of controversy. There are two main theories: one, championed especially by Budyko (1974, 1982), is that volcanic dust in periods of especial vulcanological activity increases the earth's albedo, that is, the reflection back into space by particles in the upper atmosphere; the second group of hypotheses, favored by physicists and astronomers, is that changes in the obliquity of the earth or in the ellipticity of its orbit or in the sun's output of heat or other astronomical events are responsible, for example, McCormac (1983) and Saltzman (1983). Secular changes in climate have indeed been important, especially in northern Europe. The existence of the great Ice Ages is well known, but climatic variation in historical times has been a much neglected topic, even in scientific circles, until recently. There have been at least eight important climatic phases since the foundation of the earliest civilizations, modified after Lamb (1966, 1972, 1977, 1982) as follows:

(*i*) A severe cold period including the disappearance of the last major ice sheet in Scandinavia about 8000–7000 BC, and passing into (*ii*)

(*ii*) 4000–2000 BC, the postglacial climate optimum.

(*iii*) A period of decline, 2000 BC–AD 400.

(*iv*) An optimum of climate, AD 400–1200.

(*v*) A period of decline, AD 1200–1400

(*vi*) Partial recovery, AD 1400–1550.

(*vii*) The Little Ice Age, AD 1550–1850.

(*viii*) Partial recovery, AD 1850–.

The average winter temperature in a given area for some decades might be 3° higher in the optimal times than in the unfavorable. Of course, instrumental readings are only available over the past 300 years, but it has been possible to correlate temperature within this time with other observable features, such as water freezing inside or outside houses, the behavior of crops, the dates of the declarations of wine harvest (Le Roy Ladurie, 1973), the type of vegetation, tree rings, the height of the tree line above sea level, the length of glaciers, and then to interpret old records and physical remains.

These climatic changes can be illustrated by historical events. We note the optimum of climate between AD 400 and 1200, with a peak about AD 800–1000, coinciding with a surge of population. Vineyards were found in England as far north as Herefordshire. This implies summer temperatures perhaps 1°C to 2°C higher than today, freedom from May frosts, and good Septembers. The Norsemen settled Iceland in AD 870 to 930 and Greenland in AD 985 in this climatic optimum. The early Norse burials in Greenland were deep in ground, which is now permanently frozen, and in that era the north-west passage had probably been open, and Greenland could be circumnavigated. Indeed, the eastern coast of Greenland is believed to have been colonized by the Eskimos migrating around its northern shores.

From 1400 to 1550 there was a partial recovery, and this is the period of the successful ocean exploration and the introduction of southern fruits into England. There followed the "Little Ice Age" of 1550–1850, so the attempts at the northeast and northwest passages in 1553 and 1585 were made in an unfavorable epoch. Tree growth rings were narrow in the 1690s. Records exist of the abandonment of farms in Iceland because of glaciers advancing over them in 1709, and the growing of cereals was discontinued there only to be resumed in the 1920s. Changes in the same direction were noted in other lands such as Norway, the regions around the Alps (for which see the striking photos of Le Roy Ladurie, 1973), and the higher land in the British Isles. In a lighter vein, the Thames froze over eight times in the 1600s and six times in the 1700s (Lamb, 1966); one such year was 1684, immortalized in *Lorna Doone*. An auxiliary German cruiser, *Komet*, ran the northeast passage in 1940, a time almost coinciding with the optimum of the recent partial recovery. See also Bryson (1974).

In the climate of the north, during the epochs of climatic deterioration, the fields in winter were often covered by ice, so spring would be delayed, and there would not be enough warm weather to permit ripening of the grain. Even when these long term effects were not evident, there could be crop failures. In Finland, as is strikingly shown in Sømme (1968, Figure 9.10), there was total crop failure in 1952, roughly north of a line through 63°N, which was the mean position of an isoline showing a total of daily minimum temperature deficits of 5°C below freezing point in July through August 1952. Incidentally most of Tavastland and all of Nyland, to be mentioned in §22.6, lie below this line.

See also Takahashi and Yoshina (1978), Blaxter and Fowden (1982), and Wigley, et al. (1981).

22.5 Starvation as a Clinical State

ICD 994.2

Starvation occurs when the food ingested is insufficient to maintain life. In starvation, the body can call upon its reserves, especially of fat in the subcutaneous adipose tissue and elsewhere and of protein in the liver and muscles. With the depletion of these reserves, the subject becomes emaciated; indeed, a patient weighing less than two-thirds of his normal weight is in a dangerous condition. This emaciation is often partly obscured by edema as, for example, in the Irish famine of 1845–1847. The intestinal walls become very thin because

of loss of substance and, in particular, the atrophy of the intestinal glands. Diarrhea with consequent excessive loss of water occurs because of ulceration of the bowel wall. This diarrhea is not infective (Aykroyd, 1971) but its presence has led to the false conclusion that epidemics follow famines. Psychological disturbances, such as confusion and disorientation and apathy are common. The apathy may become extreme. It does not appear that starvation itself leads to an increased susceptibility to infections (Scrimshaw, Taylor and Gordon, 1968), except perhaps the bowel infections, although Foege (1971) cites a measles epidemic in Nigeria, during a famine in 1965 and 1966, with high case fatality rates. The avitaminoses usually do not play an important part in famines because the activity of the body declines in starvation. Scurvy was important in the Irish famine because maize, which is deficient in Vitamin C, was imported to replace the potato; lack of this vitamin caused many deaths in California at the time of the gold rushes of the nineteenth century, according to Pirie (1969). See also Hess (1982). It is now recognized that the very young and the very old persons, pregnant women, and nursing mothers are especially vulnerable to the effects of starvation. The very young are especially vulnerable to protein deficiency and may die even when total calories are adequate, for example, from kwashiorkor. Table 22.5.1 shows the great mortality among children and the aged in a famine in the Punjab, India, in the 1930s (Passmore, 1951). See also Keys, Brožek, et al. (1950).

In famine, there is a migration of healthy persons away from the affected areas, which may explain the diminished number of adult

TABLE 22.5.1. Total deaths in the Hissar district.

	1934–1938 (Annual average)	1939
Under 10 years	11,044	21,160
10–59 years	11,378	9,771
60 years and over	2,372	6,836
	24,794	37,767

Data obtained by Passmore (1951) from Col. C.M. Nicol, formerly Director of Public Health in the Punjab.

deaths in the famine years (see Table 22.5.1). There may be a breakdown of the work and sometimes of the whole social structure. Special features may appear, such as the ergot infections of wheat, rye, and barley leading to human intoxications, the "mal des ardents" or "feu sacré", as in 1358. Many observers, such as Meuvret (1946), have commented on the ingestion of unsuitable substances during famines. Utterström (1955) mentions that in the Swedish famine of 1697, people ate bark and ground hay, straw, and chaff into bread; but these are mild aberrations. The marrow of dead animals or even of human corpses maybe consumed (e.g., Read, 1974). A modern incident, reported by Dean (1961), was the intoxication by insecticides in Turkey, when members of the population ate cereal seeds treated with insecticides that had been supplied to famine areas. For a review, see Waterlow (1981).

22.6 Cold Climate Famines

Only the northern hemisphere can provide populations with the history and statistical series to illustrate the importance of climatic change on mortality. Thus, in the period of decline of AD 1200–1400, mentioned in §22.4, the Norse settlements in Greenland perished in the late fourteenth century. Other details are given in §39.2. In the northern European areas, crop failures could be due to cold preventing the beginnings of growth of the crop before winter and undue length of winter. In the southern areas, such as France and England, famine was more likely to be caused by cool wet summers, in which crops failed to ripen. In 1315–1317, in England and in Flanders, there were widespread famines—there were 2,794 deaths in Ypres during 6 months of 1316 out of a total population of perhaps 25,000 persons (Lucas, 1930). It is difficult to obtain precise information on famine mortality for this early period. Russell (1948a) says there were 10 years of great dearth in England in 1087, 1151, 1189, 1196, 1205, 1224, 1294, 1314, 1315, and 1321 but doubts that great numbers of British died because of lack of food in the worst of famine years; further, he believes that

the climate of England was milder than that of the continent. A bibliography of the famines recorded up to 1450 in the German-speaking lands is available in Curschmann (1900/1970), recently reprinted. A more general discussion was given by Walford (1878–1879/1970). Possibly, we can only argue for the period AD 1200–1400 by analogy with later official series or parish data.

More records are available for the Little Ice Age of 1550–1850. There is good evidence that the bad winters often occurred simultaneously throughout the northern countries, followed by years of dearth; for example, 1696 was a year of famine in Scotland, for which see Trevelyan (1944, p. 432) and in the parishes of Beauvais, studied by Goubert (1960). For Finland, Jutikkala (1955) reports a great famine from deaths recorded in 13 parishes of the provinces of Tavastland, lying almost entirely south of the 64°N parallel, and of Nyland, in the south lying below 61°N; thus, they were relatively favorably placed. In 1697, in a population initially about 20,000, the deaths numbered 5,643, so the crude mortality rate was 28% per annum. Indirect methods of assessment show this rate was consistent with population losses derived from head counts for the poll tax in both 1694 and 1707, which indicated a loss of 30% of the population. In more recent times, the crops failed in 1807, and this was followed by 2 years of high crude death rates, namely, 61.5 in 1808 and 59.1 deaths per 1,000 in 1809. See also Utterström (1955). As Turpeinen (1979a) points out, the relationship between crop failure and famine is less clear in later times. Infant mortality rates are particularly sensitive indicators of famine conditions.

Iceland has been affected in the same way by secular changes, although the conditions in the worst year, 1783–1784, were complicated by the volcanic eruption of Laki and a loss of sunlight from the resulting dust in the atmosphere; the infant mortality was as high as 70%, and the continued existence of the colony was in doubt. In §39.3 we give some years of crop failures followed by very high crude mortality rates.

Although the data are incomplete, we can agree with the general conclusions of Jutikkala

(1955); the growth of population in the European states, between the late Middle Ages and the industrial revolution, was marked by irregular fluctuations; population tended to outgrow food supply; then there would be epidemics or famines that would restore the balance.

22.7 Hot Climate Famines

In India the great cause of famine has been the failure of the monsoonal rains, with the distress increased by the lack of water storage. The Bihar famine of 1966–1967, see Government of Bihar (1973), has been studied thoroughly by Ramalingaswami, Deo, et al. (1971) and Berg (1971). This Indian state had a population of 53 million persons in 1967, with 694 persons to the square mile (460 to the square kilometer). Only 7% of the gross sown area has assured irrigation; the rivers run rapidly and empty quickly. The year 1965 yielded deficient rain, then there were floods in north Bihar and drought in south Bihar, the annual production fell to less than half its usual amount. Scarcity in 1966 changed into famine in 1967:

Prices began to rise, thefts increased, the social structure began to crumble, hooliganism and indiscipline were on the increase. The scarcity of food was so great that people gathered around railway sidings and grain chutes in order to collect individual pieces of grain from the dust. Those who were relatively fit migrated to adjoining industrial areas leaving behind the aged, the infirm and the sick. In one district alone, 40,000 people left the district in search of food and job. The agrarian structure was greatly disturbed. Sale of land was on the increase, the sale of cattle also increased. One could buy a cow for less than Rs. 10. Even the seed that the farmers stored for the next sowing season was consumed. Beggars increased in numbers, mortgage of land was in evidence. The scarcity of water was most acute. There was a cry for water everywhere. A general state of alarm existed. Starvation deaths in thousands were predicted around the corner. There was a pathetic submission to deprivation. The village drums and music died out. People became sullen and listless. Each day that passed, one felt relieved by the time of dusk that one more day in this long famine had gone by. The splendid wild life of South Bihar faced extinction. As the hill streams dried up, tigers and panthers frequented the remaining water holes. The fast-vanishing Indian gazelle showed up at water points in full view of people. One could see as one drove through this vast expanse of South Bihar an unending stretch of parched and dry fields.

(Ramalingaswami, Deo, et al., 1971.) Happily, aid was at hand and there were relatively few deaths. It appears that the failure of the monsoon rains may be patchy, so that neighboring districts can receive quite diverse rainfall in a year.

See §44.3 for famines in Africa.

22.8 Famines and War

War operations leading to famines include deliberate and accidental destuction of the crops and granaries, blockades of a country, sieges of cities, requisitions of crops, grain, and seed, the recruitment of the farmers, and the breakdown of the social system. Much disorder may be provoked by armed bands, often in the pay of one combatant in a war, leading to wilful damage of food, crops, or farm houses. See also §§33.12 and 33.14.

22.9 Famines due to Other Natural Causes

In §§22.6 and 22.7 two important classes of famines have been mentioned. We add some more natural causes here.

(i) *Earthquakes and Volcanic Action.* Earthquakes can affect large regions and damage or destroy as much as one-third of the structures in a country, for example, in Guatemala in 1976; however, structures rather than food were destroyed and the problem was to restore the structures storing food, the bridges, and also the marketing facilities. Volcanic action was partly responsible for the great famine of 1783 in Iceland. Tsunamis are due to volcanic action but are more conveniently dealt with as floods.

(ii) *Floods.* Tsunamis may cause destruction of crops, as in Andra Pradesh, India, in November 1977, where the area of destruction was 30 km long and 15km wide. The effects of the tsunami were aggravated by floods due to rain, leading to extensive damage of over 200,000 hectares. Flooding was the initial cause of famine in Bangladesh in 1974. The dead numbered 27,000 persons and 1.2 million were fed in gruel kitchens. Floods have often produced widespread damage in Africa, India, and China, especially on the great rivers. In China the dangers are aggravated by some parts of the river course being higher than the surrounding plain, and the resulting famines may be overshadowed by the enormous loss of life by drowning (Latter, 1969).

(*iii*) *Droughts*. Droughts occur in all continents in the marginal lands that are susceptible to the years of low rainfall. The Sahelian experience is the most notable of recent droughts, see chapter 44. It is pointed out by several authors that drought does not necessarily lead to famine, especially if the drought area lies in a much larger political entity, as in India.

(*iv*) *Insect and Other Animal Pests*. Locust swarms may consume or destroy all plants in their way. Worms may destroy growing plants.

(*v*) *Plant Diseases*. Potato blight may destroy crops over wide areas, as in the Irish famine, for example. See Carefoot and Sprott (1969).

(*vi*) *Diseases of Animals*. See §16.4 for rinderpest of cattle and trypanosomiasis of domestic and wild animals.

22.10 Famines and Epidemics

A "crisis of subsistence" is defined by an exceptional increase in the price of grain and a sudden coincident increase in deaths and decrease in births (Meuvret, 1946). Demographers have been eager to associate crises of subsistence with epidemics as direct cause and effect. Although not holding that epidemics necessarily follow from famine, we can see how the upset of social order following famines or crises of subsistence can bring about conditions favoring epidemics. Thus, in medieval and modern times of famine, we find in the parish registers many deaths of wanderers from other parishes, who had hoped to escape to a famine-free area (Meuvret, 1946); they would not know that famine existed over a wide area and their condition would be miserable, for the towns would not admit them because they would bring more mouths to feed and perhaps

infection. It seems that the sequence of events was often as follows: an actual shortage or prediction of grain shortage was followed by a rise in prices and consequent difficulties for the poor in obtaining grain; there would be wanderings and a dispersion of infections that otherwise might have remained quite localized; typhus, bowel infections, measles, and other common infections would be spread in this way. It appears from the parish records of the Beauvaisis that the very old and the young were most affected (Goubert, 1960). The infant mortality could rise to 70% and childhood mortality was also very high.

We may now consider specific groups of diseases.

(*i*) *Bowel Diseases*. As pointed out in §22.5, diarrhea, even accompanied by blood, is a common finding in starvation but it is not infective. However, the atrophy of the lymphoid system in starvation, as noted by Porter (1889) in the 1876–1878 famine in Madras, no doubt increases the case fatalities of the infections that do occur. Thus, over 13,000 deaths were listed from diarrhea and dysentery, about 7,000 died from dropsy, debility, privation, ulcer, among others, about 1,500 from cholera, 400 from smallpox, and 500 from fevers, among 22,939 dying in relief camps. Cholera, of course, rarely is a factor in famines outside India.

(*ii*) *Louse-borne Infections*. Apathy, crowding, and lack of bathing facilities usually have led to gross louse infestations in famines in the colder climates; such conditions are conducive to the louse-borne diseases, particularly typhus and relapsing fever in endemic areas; the initial infections may come from clinical cases or relapsed cases. Deaths from these diseases were important in the Irish famines of the 1840s; and were even more so in the Russian famines; thus, in the 4 years, 1919–1922, there were 2.2, 2.7, 0.5, and 1.5 million cases, according to Bang (1981, Figure 5). Gantt (1928) reported that, when the average calories per head fell to 1,500 per day, the prevalence of all types of infection rose to over 50%. Lack of bathing was an important factor in raising infection rates.

(*iii*) *Bubonic Plague*. Demographers have often assumed that the outbreak of any serious epidemic with a high case fatality was bubonic plague, even if bubonic plague were not endemic in the area. With the hypothesis that infection was almost always from rat to man, it could not be seen why bubonic plagues could occur as acute incidents in nonendemic areas. However, now that human ectoparasites are recognized as carriers of bubonic plague, the idea that bubonic plague can follow famine is more plausible.

(*iv*) *Pneumonias*. Deaths from pneumonia and acute lung diseases are often common in famines and indeed caused 9% of the deaths in the Madras famine of 1876–1878.

(*v*) *Measles*. Recently, measles has been believed to be a particular problem of famines (Foege, 1971). We must distinguish here between an increased case fatality rate and an increased incidence rate and concede that increased case fatality rates are to be expected in many diseases during famines.

(*vi*) *Tuberculosis*. The course of a tuberculosis infection is known to be unfavorably affected by a poor diet, so an increased number of tuberculosis suffers and deaths may be evident in a famine. Possibly the great majority of the infections antedated the particular famine. It was undoubtedly important in the Madras famine, although recognition of the disease was difficult because of the famine conditions. Keys, Brožek, et al. (1950) point out that in such conditions, the importance of tuberculosis became apparent only after louse-borne disease had been eliminated. Gontzea (1974) called tuberculosis and famine the twin sisters of poverty. See also Helweg-Larsen, Hoffmeyer, et al. (1952*b*).

22.11 General Remarks on Famine

Dando (1980) defines famine as "a protracted shortage of total food in a restricted geographical area, causing widespread disease and deaths from starvation." We have already given in §§22.6–22.9 various causes of famine; Blix, Hofvander, and Vahlquist (1971), Cuny (1981), Dalrymple (1964), Dando (1980, 1981), Mellor and Gavian (1987), Ramalingaswami, Deo, et al. (1971), and many other authorities have pointed out that there is usually

failure in the government as well. Thus, the government may fail to react because of the failure of communications, as in the Bengal disaster of 1943–1944, when the existence of the famine was only realized in the capital when refugees drifted into Calcutta and died in the streets. Governments are often reluctant now, as in the past, to admit to the existence of a famine and so delay the sending of their own aid and the relief measures from neighbors or international agencies.

In many famines or dearths, there have been unequal distributions of food; sometimes it may be diverted to or reserved for the military in times of war and sometimes it may be hoarded for use or speculation. Sometimes food has even been transported out of famine areas for profit as in the Irish famine. Jutikkala (1955) notes that in the famine in Finland of 1596, the central government failed to give help, "the Crown should not lose a single öre or half-peck of grain," which he deplores but he remarks that successful aid would have aggravated the position over future years. However, some of the errors in the management of famines appear to have been errors of judgement.

Lee and DeVore (1976) point out that famine was probably unknown to the hunter-gatherers who had constituted the human population before the development of agriculture, for their population density was usually well below the carrying capacity of the territory occupied. But population increases led to the evolution of agriculture, a sedentary agricultural life, and further population increases. Large populations, dependent on food from a fixed area not readily increased in size, then became exposed to the danger of famine, resulting from causes acting on this area, possibly war, flood, droughts, or cold wet summers.

Much information is available on the effects of famine in Europe. According to Le Roy Ladurie (1966), cited by Glamann (1977, p. 187), the peasant world of France and Belgium was stable from the fifteenth to the nineteenth centuries, whether measured by sowings or by area. Yields per acre were constant. A greater population therefore meant less food per head. Le Roy Ladurie and Goy (1982) have made these statements more precise by an examination of tithes and other revenues over the period 1320–1813. Le Roy Ladurie concludes (Le Roy Ladurie, 1966, p. 191) that the facts clearly justify the pessimistic theories of Malthus and Ricardo.

The European population size was limited by total food supply, directly, through deaths from starvation in famine, and indirectly, by a greater susceptibility to disease, especially of the infants. There are checks through diminished fertility; first, marriages are delayed; second, ovulation is suppressed by lactation more strongly when the nutritional status of the mother is low; third, possibly there is an increase in abortions and miscarriages during famines; and fourth, infanticide may be practised.

For world nutritional determinants, see Bourne (1985).

22.12 Statistics of Famines

Leading sources of historical data on famines are two papers read to the Statistical Society in 1878 and 1879, and reprinted as Walford (1970); for the special case of India, there are Loveday (1914) and Bhatia (1967); see also May and Jarcho (1961) and Learmonth (1978). Tabulations from these sources are available in Dando (1980, pp. 114–116). In general, it can be said that direct numerical measures of the severity of famines are not and perhaps have never been available before the time of the parochial records in the seventeenth century. They are also not available, even in modern times, for some famines that naturally occur under conditions of war and social upheaval. When official statistics are available, deaths in a famine will be reflected in the crude death rates; usually, crude death rates of more than 40 per 1,000 per annum are associated with war and/or famine. The parish data are of importance because they usually give information on famine, as in Goubert (1960, 1965a).

We mention famine in various sections as follows: Scotland, §37.3; Eire, §37.5; France, §38.2; Norden, Chapter 39; India, §40.3; Africa, Chapter 44.

To be more definite, we give an account of famines in England and Wales, making use of Walford (1970) and the classification by era of Dando (1980). In the first or Romano-British period, AD 10 to 450, Walford (1970) lists famine years as follows: England, 54, 104, 107, 119, 160, 173, 272, 288, 310, 325, and 439; Wales, 107, 119, 151, 259, 272, 288, 298, 325, and 439; Scotland, 104, 228, 238, and 306. This is the period containing the Roman occupation, beginning with the invasion under Claudius in AD 43 and ending with the withdrawal of the Roman legions during the last quarter of the fourth century. In this period, the effects of war and separatism are evident causes in the sense that a widely recognized government could have transferred food stores from area to area in time of need; indeed, in these famines, the records or annals only mention physical causes twice, namely for the years 107 and 173; in all other cases, disturbed social conditions are listed as the "cause" of the famine.

In the Anglo-Saxon period, 450–1066, social disruption and raids from the Picts and Scots had reduced the Romano-British civilization to chaos; help was at first supplied by the Saxons, but they soon saw opportunities for taking over the divided land. This led at first to some orderly government, but the sixth to ninth centuries were times of incessant warfare and the resulting separatism, fear, and distrust led to irregular agriculture with but a small margin of reserves of grain between seasons. Shortages in the bad seasons then could not be covered from the stores, and supplies could not be brought in from other areas because of separatism, expressed in local feuds and wars. This period includes the Viking invasions. According to Thompson (1966, p. 762), the greatest privation of the British peasant was famine.

In the Norman period, 1066–1485, England was unified under William the Conqueror, but the price was great, as the quotations of Simeon of Durham show (Hassall, 1962, pp. 297, 298). William used famine as a weapon; after campaigns against dissidents in the north, with destruction of farms, a great famine arose in Northumbria and adjacent provinces, and, as Simeon says, "men . . . devoured human flesh . . . and whatever custom abhors . . . human corpses in the streets . . . no one was left to bury them . . . the land . . . deprived of anyone to cultivate it for nine years . . . an extensive solitude prevailed . . ." Such incidents, although on a smaller scale, continued until Edward I reestablished royal (i.e., centralized) power; even so, in 1277 a contrived famine compelled the Welsh rebel Llewelyn to surrender. Famines in 1314 and 1316, contemporary with the famine of 1315 in Ypres, France, were so severe as to affect the king's household; in 1235, deaths numbering 20,000 are said to have occurred in London.

The modern period, 1485–1850, begins with the consolidation of the central power by Henry VII with a relative freedom from famine. In the reign of Henry VIII, the growth of large holdings resulted in a class of landless rural laborers; by this time, there were larger cities with a money economy, and so, greater possibilities of unemployment and of lessened responsibility for the needy. Debasement of the currency and resulting inflation contributed to economic mismanagement; for example, much land was thrown out of cultivation, perhaps as much as two-thirds in some bishoprics in the reign of Edward VI, 1547–1553. The reign of James I, 1603–1625, was free of famines in England and Wales; from that time onward there were no great famines in England and Wales. The above account considers chiefly the effects of war and social and economic factors. England was not affected as badly as Scotland in years of climatic deterioration, 1200–1400 and 1550–1850. Drummond and Wilbraham (1957) comment that in 1700–1750 "the years of wet summers, droughts and bad harvests can be counted on the fingers of one hand". In 1764–1775, there was a disastrous sequence of wet seasons and bad harvests with grave dearth in 1765. Again in 1793–1795, there was disastrous weather. Rye and barley breads began to pass out of fashion. Wheat began to take over in the southern counties, but in the north cereals grown were wheat 50% and barley and oats 25% each. Potatoes were firmly established north of the "coal line" by 1770. Turnips, introduced for winter fodder, enabled more stock to be kept over winter.

For food supply and population growth, see Passmore (1962); for general remarks on famine, see Aykroyd (1974), Berg (1973), Biswas and Biswas (1979), the symposium, Blix, Hofvander, and Vahlquist (1971), and Robson (1981). See Wheatcroft (1984) for famine in Saratov, Russia, 1918–1920.

22.13 Avitaminoses

General references: Barker and Bender (1980–1982); Davidson, Passmore, et al. (1979); Hess (1982); McCollum (1956); and Scrimshaw (1966).

The vitamins are food substances, now of known chemical constitution, that are necessary for the efficient working of the body but that do not contribute directly to the calories produced by the body. They are in adequate supply for the hunter-gatherers and usually for the general population of the developed world, but their absence or deficiency in the diets of many special classes of persons has led to many illnesses and deaths; among these classes are infants, old people caring for themselves, victims of famines, pioneering groups in developing countries, polar explorers, soldiers, especialy "native" troops, merchant seamen, naval men, alcoholics, the chronically ill, persons on unbalanced diets, and inmates of residential schools, prisons, or mental asylums. We will see that some of the avitaminoses are, indeed, associated with special groups of those classes mentioned.

Vitamin A Deficiency

ICD 264. Fourth digit: clinical conditions.

Fat-soluble vitamin A is formed in the body as retinol from the pigment B-carotene found in carrots and other plants. Deficiency of vitamin A rarely causes disease in the absence of other deficiencies; it can result from deficiency in the diet or from malabsorption syndromes, liver diseases, diabetes, or other diseases causing malabsorption. Severe forms of the disease caused by deficiency of vitamin A tend to be grouped together as xerophthalmia. The deficiency arises usually at the end of a seasonal shortage of green, leafy vegetables, during famines, in prisons, or under conditions of privation. The most susceptible age group covers the last few months of infancy and early childhood. Dryness of the skin is common but generalized defects of the mucous membranes do not occur.

Hypermedication can cause severe symptoms and so can the eating of polar bear or dog livers, in which vitamin A is highly concentrated. See Barker (1982).

Thiamin and Niacin Deficiency States

ICD 265. Fourth digit: 0, beri-beri; 1, other and unspecified thiamin deficiencies; 2, pellagra.
(*a*) *Thiamin Deficiency*. The richest sources of thiamin are cereals, yeast, pork, and legumes, although most of the thiamin is lost in milling for white flour or for polished rice. Nuts and eggs are rich in thiamin, meat other than pork is moderately rich, and milk is poor.

Thiamin deficiency leads to beri-beri, falling into three groups: chronic dry atrophic variety, chiefly characterized by multiple peripheral neuritis; mild and subacute form of the above; and acute fulminating disease, in which cardiac failure is a leading symptom (wet beri-beri). Widespread beri-beri dates only from the introduction of machine milling of wheat and rice in the nineteenth century. According to Sinclair (1982), at p. 114 of Barker and Bender (1982) the conquest of beri-beri began when K. Takaki supplemented the rice diet of Japanese sailors with fish, vegetables, meat, and barley in 1882. Christiaan Eijkman (1858–1930) showed that chickens would develop the paralytic disease if fed on polished rice, a result confirmed by other experiments on animal and human populations. Populations at risk are those on a restricted diet such as laborers, pioneering or construction men on a salted meat and damper type of diet, persons in institutions such as homes for the elderly and asylums, prisoners of war, chronic alcoholics, and persons suffering from other diseases, especially of the gastrointestinal tract. Infantile beri-beri was formerly a common cause of death in the Far East.
(*b*) *Niacin Deficiency*. Niacin, nicotinamide or

pyridine-3-carboxylic acid, is the anti-pellagra vitamin. Pellagra is endemic in maize-eating areas, in which there has often been a deficiency of tryptophan in the diet; it is characterized by dermatitis, diarrhea, and dementia, the skin being unduly sensitive to the sun or other trauma or injuries. Bender (1980, p. 326) mentions that the disease was unknown in Europe before the introduction of maize but by the nineteenth century, pellagra was common in the maize-growing areas of southern and eastern Europe, as well as in north Africa, especially Egypt. After an outbreak of rinderpest in South Africa, killing most of the cattle, there was a marked change in the diet of the Bantu and other races, whereby they consumed less milk products and more maize, which became the common weaning food for children. Pellagra followed; even now, up to half of the general run of patients attending clinics show signs of pellagra. A similar problem is met with in Hyderabad. India. Pellagra became important in the southern United States after the Civil War; see Sydenstricker (1958) for details of incidence and conquest, especially by Joseph Goldberger (1874–1929) and his colleagues. Prophylaxis is possible by correct preparation of the maize, as by the Amerinds. Treatment is by foods rich in niacin or tryptophan and by niacin. See Roe (1973) for a readable account of the history of the disease. See also Carpenter (1981).

Deficiency of Other Components of the B-complex

ICD 266. Fourth digit: 0, ariboflavinosis; 1, vitamin B6 (= pyridoxine) deficiency; 2, other B-complex deficiencies (excluding deficiency anemias).

These diseases have an importance less from the mortality point of view than some of the other deficiency diseases.

(*a*) *Ariboflavinosis*. This is characterized by angular stomatitis, glossitis, seborrheic dermatitis about nose and scrotum, and vascularization of the cornea. It is due to a deficiency of riboflavin, widely distributed in natural foods. Good sources are yeast, milk, white of egg, kidney, liver, heart, and meat, fish, and poultry. Prophylaxis is a suitable diet. Treatment is by riboflavin.

(*b*) *Vitamin B6 (=pyridoxine) Deficiency.* This can cause weakness, nervousness, and insomnia.

(*c*) *Other B-complex Deficiencies.* Vitamin B12 or Cobalamin is a complex molecule containing tightly bound cobalt. Deficiency can result in anemia, both pernicious and other. Its role is discussed under ICD 281 in §23.1. It can also cause glossitis, diarrhea, and other gastrointestinal abnormalities; an important change is the demyelination of tracts in the posterior lateral column of the spinal cord, causing subacute combined degeneration. B12 deficiency occurs in strict vegetarians; the most numerous of these are Hindu vegetarians. The untreated disease is fatal in strict vegetarians, but *Torula* yeast is effective in arresting the course of the disease.

Ascorbic Acid Deficiency

ICD 267. Inclusion: scurvy.

Vitamin C, or ascorbic acid, is present in fruit juices, potato, germinating pulses, or cereals. Maximum incidence of the deficiency state occurs in the spring as a rule. There is a peak of incidence at ages 6 to 12 months in infants on artificial diets containing insufficient vitamin C and a further peak in middle and old age groups who care for themselves. There are special occupational hazards among polar explorers, merchant seamen, naval men, pioneering groups in the developing countries, prisoners in jails, and victims of famines. See Watt, Freeman and Bynum (1981) for experience of seamen.

As Davidson, Passmore, et al. (1979) point out, when long sea voyages began with Vasco da Gama in 1497, scurvy became a great source of invalidity and mortality. Da Gama lost 100 out of 160 of his crew members, and for the next 300 years, control of scurvy was always important for the success of the voyages. Captain James Lancaster in 1600 clearly demonstrated the efficacy of lemon juice during the voyage to India. The publication of *A treatise of the scurvy* in 1753 by James Lind was a not-

able event. In the voyage of 1772–1775 of James Cook no man was lost because of scurvy. There is a good description of the disease and interesting historical notes in Drummond and Wilbraham (1957, pp. 133–146, 259–270, 390–396), in Hess (1982), and Carpenter (1986). See also §§32.1 and 33.15.

Scurvy is now readily treated by ascorbic acid, that is, vitamin C, either synthetic or obtained from natural sources. In infants, mash made from just under the skin of boiled potatoes had been found to be a convenient source. See also Bender (1982), Counsell and Hornig (1981), and Tickner and Medvei (1958).

Vitamin D Deficiency

ICD 268. Fourth digit: 0, rickets, active; 1, rickets, late effects; 2 osteomalacia.

Vitamin D, usually ergo- or cholecalciferol, is necessary for the adequate absorption of calcium and phosphates from the intestine and the development of bones. Vitamin D is a fat soluble vitamin, obtainable from milk, cream, butter, and eggs, in a diet that may be or has been too expensive for many families; it can be synthesized from cholesterol by the body, with the aid of the ultraviolet light of normal sunlight. Rickets is the disease appearing in infancy and childhood, and osteomalacia is the same disease appearing in later life. The essential pathology is the failure of the support structures in the bone and of the epiphyseal cartilege cells to mature properly. The clinical result is softened bones and displacements of the epiphyses (i.e., growing zones of the bones).

Rickets has tended to be a disease of great industrial cities in which the poor are unable to obtain the appropriate food and the ultraviolet light is absorbed by the buildings and smoke. Glasgow, Vienna, and Lahore have had especially high prevalence of rickets. Further, ultraviolet light dosage varies considerably with latitude, northern European cities being at a great disadvantage. The condition may be aggravated by a high cereal content in the diet, which may have an inhibitory effect on the absorption of calcium. Rachitic children do not die directly of the disease but they are weaklings more prone to other diseases, especially bronchopneumonia. Pelvic malformations, resulting from the disease, have been important in malpositions and difficult birth, causing mortality in the mother and infant and birth injuries to the infant. Vitamin D deficiency appears also to be a factor in bone tuberculosis of children and in multiple sclerosis.

Treatment is by vitamin D concentrates, especially codliver oil, and ultraviolet light, especially by exposure to sunlight. Prophylaxis comprises the same methods.

The two diseases are not great causes of mortality but are associated with debilitated states from other causes.

22.14 Dietetic Errors and Excesses

An alternative title, food and killer diseases, for example, Berkson and Stamler (1981), seems to have been devised to bring attention not to famines, or the avitaminoses, or to malnutrition, as ordinarily understood, but to the denatured food of western style, particularly its low content of plant fiber (Burkitt and Trowell, 1975 and Blix, 1964). The errors and excesses discussed here have relevance for diseases of the cardiovascular and alimentary systems.

Dietary Fiber

We may follow the Select Committee on Nutrition (1977). Fibers can be classified into three types, (*i*) vegetable fibers, which are highly fermentable with low indigestible residue, (*ii*) brans, which are less fermentable, and (*iii*) such chemically purified fibers as wood cellulose, which are relatively unfermentable. A fourth category of soluble substances, including pectins and gums, may not be true fibers but are considered part of the dietary fiber complex because they behave similarly to (*ii*) and (*iii*) in the diet. P.J. van Soest (1977), in this report, points out that pectin, gums, cellulose, hemicellulose, and lignin, constituting the fiber residue of the diet, have not been studied systematically and that grossly inaccurate methods have been used to measure the fiber content of food.

The important fibers are the brans, which

represent an indigestible fraction produced by the cereals as a result of an aging process; they differ from the fibers of the dicotyledonous plants, which can be regarded as less mature and more readily digestible. Important nutritional properties of fiber are bulk, density, hydration capacity, binding properties, and fermentability. Bulk, increased by hydration capacity and binding properties, favors faster transit of food through the alimentary system. The degree of fermentation depends partly on the rate of passage of the fiber through the bowel and reduces the fecal bulk. Trowell (1977*b*) believes that high fiber content of the diet increases fecal bulk, decreases transit times and intraluminar pressure, and decreases deoxycholate absorption. The result is that a rural African passes a bulky soft stool and his alimentary transit time averages 35–45 hours. Western man passes a small firm stool, often accompanied by much straining, and his transit time is 50–70 hours. Associated with such factors, western man has high rates of diverticulosis, irritable bowel syndrome, appendicitis, hemorrhoids, benign and malignant tumors of the large bowel, and hiatus hernia. For some reservations on this theory, see McLaren (1982). Trowell (1981, p. 31) gives a table showing that the principal cereals have a calorie value of about 350 per 100 g. The percentage fiber content of wheat is 1.6–2.1 at 100% extraction, 0.4–0.9 at 85% extraction, and trace to 0.2 at 70% extraction. Bran has a fiber content of 10.5%–13.5%. Whole maize has a fiber content of 2%, millet 2.0%–3%, depending on variety, rice 2%, and rye, as baked, 1.5%. Only in recent times, since 1860, have there been the means to remove a high proportion of the fiber from the various grains, for example, to produce white flour or polished rice; similarly, the separation of sucrose from the fiber in sugar beet is recent. Modan and Lubin (1980, p. 129) give a table summarizing the various possible protective properties of fiber; in particular, they remark that adequate fiber makes for an important shortening of the intestinal transit time, with a reduced conversion of bile salts to potentially carcinogenic sterols. Further, the amount of cholesterol is reduced by binding and excretion. There is also a lower anaerobic/aerobic ratio in the intestinal flora, which in turn affects bile salt degradation, although the details of the effects on the formation of cholesterol gallstones have not yet been worked out.

The removal of fiber from foodstuffs and the consequent abundance of cheap sugars has another set of effects—on appetite, particularly, stressed by Cleave and Campbell (1966), Cleave (1973, 1974), and Trowell, Burkitt, et al. (1985). Overconsumption of food can be divided into two parts. First, the presence of fiber leads to a feeling of satiety, so the use of wholemeal bread would reduce calories taken in bread; second, the desire for sweetness is not well satisfied unless the sugar is taken in association with fiber as in sweet fruits and vegetables. Nevertheless, according to McLaren (1982), the annual per capita sugar consumption in the United States has remained rather constant over the last 60 years, and deaths from coronary heart disease increased "dramatically" between 1945 and the early 1960s but have fallen steadily since.

Salt Excess

Joossens (1980) believes that excess consumption of common salt increases the blood pressure and hence the risk of stroke. It also increases the risk of gastric carcinoma, thus leading to a positive correlation between the rates of the two diseases in the countries of the world. See §25.5.

Diseases favorably affected by a high fiber diet are diabetes, cancer of the colon, obesity and so heart disease, hypertension (salt important here), gallstones, appendicitis, hemorrhoids, and hernia.

22.15 Miscellaneous Toxicants in Food

There is a general review of toxicants in food given by Jelliffe and Jelliffe (1982). In it, Hambraeus (1982) classifies the naturally occurring toxicants as follows:

1. Natural components of natural food products (inherent toxins):
   a. simple components, that is, carbohydrates, fatty acids, proteins and amino acids, and vitamins;
   b. complex components that have specific antimetabolic effects, that is, antivitamins, goitrogens, chelates, vasoactive and psychoactive factors, carcinogens, and other potential antinutrients.
2. Natural contaminants of natural food products (acquired toxins):
   a. toxicants of microbiological origin;
   b. nonmicrobiological toxicants, that is, minerals and toxicants consumed by animals used as food sources,

Lactose intolerance and mushroom poisoning are examples of 1a and 1b, respectively. Mortality from the sources of the first class is unusual, and the most important sources are of microbiological origin. Direct infection of man has already been discussed in the earlier sections of chapter 6 and poisonings by the products of organisms in §6.8. Aflatoxins have been mentioned in §20.5. For mycotoxins, see Wogan (1969). Ergot, produced by a parasitic fungus from cereals, most often rye, has caused sharp epidemics of the disease known as "St. Anthony's fire" (Barger, 1931); the disease seems to have been common in the Middle Ages but an epidemic has been reported as late as 1951 by Wilson and Hayes (1973). No allowance has been made in the ICD for ergotism other than iatrogenic. There has been much debate about the toxicants in the environment. Hambraeus (1982) points out that the most important source of environmental contamination among chemicals is tobacco smoke, see §§20.4, 25.4 and 26.4.

With the rise of technology, natural contamination has tended to become of less importance than the by-products of mining and industry. Lead was already known to be toxic in Roman times, (Nriagu, 1983, Wedeen, 1984, and Scarborough, 1984), and in modern times it appears in electric batteries, paints, antiknock additives of gasoline, and solders in tinned food containers. Its importance, or rather the source of contamination with lead, has been hotly debated. Cadmium is also highly toxic but cases of poisoning seem to have been reported chiefly from Japan. See Lindsay and Sherlock (1982).

Mercury and its compounds have been

known to cause disease since ancient times; the symptoms of mercurialism include insomnia, shyness, nervousness, tremor, and dizziness; in severe cases there is salivation, gingivitis, and signs of kidney disease (the nephrotic syndrome). It has caused pink disease in infants through the use of teething powders containing mercury compounds—a disease that has been eradicated by the abandonment of these powders. Mercury is also combined in organic compounds, organomercurials, that are used as pesticides. Lawther (1979) cites an incident in which in the winter of 1971–1972 in Iraq, 6,000 patients were admitted to hospital, of whom more than 500 died, after eating bread made from grain treated with methyl or ethyl mercury. Methyl mercury, released by industry into Minamata Bay and into the Agana River, Japan, was absorbed by fish that were later eaten; by 1971, 260 cases of poisoning by methyl mercury had been reported in Minamata and Niigata, of which 55 were fatal. See also Harada (1982) and Tsubaki and Irukayama (1977).

An unsolved, perhaps unsolvable, problem is the effect in low concentrations in the environment and in food of substances that are toxic in higher concentrations.

For a detailed account of the adverse effects of foods, see Jelliffe and Jelliffe (1982), from which three accounts have been used above. See also Hathcock (1982) and its succeeding volumes and Roberts (1981). For the toxicology of trace elements, see Goyer and Mehlman (1977).

22.16 Interactions of Nutrition and Infection

There is much evidence for the importance of infections as a cause of malnutrition; there is equally evidence going the other way, although it cannot be as easily interpreted. The general social and natural environments are also of great importance, and there are interactions between factors; in particular, generalizations made on observations in the developed countries may be irrelevant or far less important in the developing countries and vice versa.

There is much conclusive evidence that almost all infections produce changes for the worse in nutritional status. One of the leading changes is the breakdown or loss of the proteins in the blood and tissues, particularly the muscles; these changes are easily measured by the output of nitrogen compounds through the kidneys. Thus, it was found early that there was a great nitrogen output in enteric fever, and as a result, high protein diets were recommended for the disease. Gastroenteritis has severe effects on nutrition, for which see §6.11 and also Chen and Scrimshaw (1983), Harries (1976), Bellanti (1983), and Elliott and Knight (1976). Disturbance of the protein balance persists until after clinical recovery. Infections also interfere with the absorption and metabolism of the vitamins. Scrimshaw, Taylor, and Gordon (1968, p. 59) conclude with the remark, "Infections so consistently worsen nutritional status that they must be taken into account in all clinical problems and public health programs that involve persons whose diet is inadequate or whose nutritional status is suboptimal."

Possibly, state of nutrition has more influence on the case fatality rates than on the incidence rates; in diarrheal disease, for example, well-fed travelers suffer from alimentary infections but have low case fatality rates; similarly, gastrointestinal diseases cause higher case fatality rates in badly nourished than in well-nourished children. We return to "weaning diarrhea" in Chapter 32.

In §7.4 it is noted that death rates from tuberculosis rise during times of malnutrition as in times of war and famine.

The classic descriptions of the onset of cholera were given on Indian subjects, many already in a poor state of nutrition; the onset was far more dramatic than those of modern airline passengers whose nutrition was presumably good. In §§11.4 and 11.7, high case fatality rates are reported for chickenpox and measles under conditions of poor nutrition.

Stinnett (1983) might be a good place at which to start for readers on this topic, as there are many descriptions of the actions of the immune system, the effects of nutrition on the body metabolism, protein-calorie malnutrition, and host defense; it is evident that much high-grade work has been done and that the interaction between dietary factors is of importance; but it is yet too early to be able to point out the relation between given nutrients (e.g., amino acids) and given host immune responses. As Stinnett (1983) writes, "clearly nutrition impacts upon the immune system. The mechanisms, however, are not so clear." He concludes that on a world scale, malnutrition is usually a political, not a medical, problem. See also Weinberg (1978).

22.17 Breast Feeding

For infants and their mothers in the developing world, there are three important and interrelated problems: malnutrition, infection, and superabundant fertility, with pregnancies often ill-timed, closely spaced, and too frequent. These three problems do not occur in isolation, for they are often associated with poor sanitation, low educational level, and poor socioeconomic conditions, including a paucity of health and social services, according to WHO-breast feeding (1982). The authors, who are members of the Division of Family Health, WHO, give statistics of the prevalence of breast feeding determined by WHO surveys, by country, and

continent, and sometimes in special subclasses of the populations. In Africa nearly all the infants are breast-fed, usually for an extended period of time, with an average of 14 to 33 months; supplementation takes place early, at about 3 months, but the lowest breast-fed proportion at 6 months was 54% in an elite group in Cairo. In middle and western south Asia, the average length of breast feeding is 1 to 2 years. Among the poor in Bangladesh, supplementation is delayed into the second year.

In the United States the initial prevalence rates fell to an all-time low of 26% in 1975 but recovered to 54% in 1980. At 5 to 6 months the breast-fed prevalence was 25% in 1982.

Rates in Australia and New Zealand are much higher and are rising. Elites in the developing world tend to follow the trends in the developed world.

In Latin America the initial rate of breast feeding is high but the durations are less than in Africa.

See Chapters 6, 32, 37–44 for the gastrointestinal diseases, infant mortality, and remarks by country, for example, Finland §39.8. For protein-energy malnutrition, see Keller and Fillmore (1983). *Annales de Démographie historique*, 1983 contains many articles touching on aspects of this problem.

Chapter 23

Diseases of the Blood and Blood-forming Organs

23.1 Iron and Other Deficiency Anemias

The rubrics of this class, ICD 280–289, do not cover an important proportion of the deaths.

Iron deficiency anemias, ICD 280. Although deaths are assigned to this rubric, the anemia is usually secondary to some more important condition.

Other deficiency anemias ICD 281. Fourth digit (by etiology): 0, pernicious; 1, other vitamin B12 deficiency; 2, folate deficiency anemia; 3, other specified megaloblastic; 4, protein deficiency; 8, associated with other specified nutritional deficiency.

Of these diseases, pernicious anemia is the most important cause of mortality in the developed world. The etiology is not well established, but it is known that there is an intrinsic factor, the absence of which interferes with the absorption of vitamin B12, the extrinsic factor. Similar syndromes are produced by known agents preventing absorption, for example, gastrectomy, tapeworm infestation, celiac disease, tropical sprue, and gastric carcinoma; deaths will be referred to the fourth digit, 1, or to the primary disease, elsewhere in the classification. The fourth digits refer to dietary deficiencies, which to some degree mimic the pernicious anemia syndrome.

Pernicious anemia, or Addison's disease, is associated with neurologial disorders entitled subacute combined degeneration; untreated, it has an unfavorable prognosis, an expectation of life of only 1–3 years at the time of diagnosis. Following the researches of Minot and Murphy, treatment by raw liver was initated in the late 1920s. The active principle is now known as Vitamin B12 (Castle, 1980). This treatment restored the expectation of life almost up to that of healthy persons. Official statistics, the age of onset, and familial aspects are considered in detail by Chanarin (1969, 1980). For a review, see Kapadia and Donaldson (1985).

Although hematology plays an important part in clinical medicine, the changes in the blood are usually only symptomatic, and the death of the patient is assigned to the particular disease. Leukemia may be considered as a disease of the blood and blood-forming organs, but deaths due to it are assigned to the class of neoplasms by the rules covering the ICD. For an interesting popularization by a leading hematologist, see Wintrobe (1980a, b, c).

Although it is not justified by the ICD classification, the other chapters in Wintrobe (1980a) may be noted here. We give a list of subjects and authors; the complete reference to each can be found in the bibliography. The other chapters are: plasma, Janeway; blood groups, Diamond; lymphocytes, Ford; red cells, Beutler; life span of red cells, Dacie; iron and heme, London; spleen, Crosby; blood cell lineage, Lajtha; bone marrow, Tavassoli.

A standard reference for the human blood groups is Race and Sanger (1975). For infections at blood transfusion, see Dodd and Barker (1985).

23.2 Hereditary Hemolytic Anemias

ICD 282. Fourth digit gives type of disease listed below.

Hereditary spherocytosis (282.0) is confined almost entirely to the "north caucasian" type of Europeans; the defective shape of the red cell appears with a frequency of 50 per 1,000,000 in the British Isles and an estimate of 220 per 1,000,000 in the United States. On occasion, the defect leads to severe hemolytic anemias. See Dacie (1980).

Hereditary elliptocytosis (282.1) is a defect of the red cells, perhaps rarer than spherocytosis. Severe anemia sometimes appears.

Anemia due to disorders of glutathione metabolism (282.2) can come about as a consequence of the hereditary deficiency of an enzyme that prevents oxidative denaturation of the hemoglobin by a variety of substances. The most important of these disorders is glucose-6-phosphate dehydrogenase (G6PD) deficiency. See Beutler (1980) and Luzatto and Battistuzzi (1985).

Other hemolytic anemias due to enzyme deficiency (282.3) seem to be less important.

Thalassemia (282.4) is due to the production of abnormal forms of hemoglobin, labeled C, E, G, and A_2, or the persistence of high concentration of a fetal form, labeled F in the technical literature. It is common on the Mediterranean littoral and has been studied in patients there and in migrants, particularly Italian and Greek, to the United States. See Weatherall (1980).

Sickle cell hemoglobinopathy (282.5 and 282.6) has been studied in the Negro population of America. It is due to a hereditary defect by which normal hemoglobin is replaced by hemoglobin-S. The gene for the defect has a high concentration in sub-Saharan Africa and a more patchy distribution in Madagascar and in the Mediterranean and Persian Gulf areas. See Edelstein (1986).

In the homozygous form, these two latter hereditary diseases are dangerous, and without the aid of modern medicine, few patients reach adult life. See Hercules, Schechter, et al. (1974) and Conley (1980).

The remaining rubrics of this class are the names of rare blood diseases and syndromes or of syndromes secondary to causes acting elsewhere, so they need not be discussed further here. The evolutionary aspects of sickle cell anemia and, by implication, of thalassemia are studied in the next section.

23.3 Sickle Cell Anemia as a Balanced Polymorphism

Sickle cell anemia is a defect of the hemoglobin of the red blood cell transmitted as a Mendelian recessive. The cells take on a typical sickle shape when exposed to low-oxygen tension. In the heterozygote, sickling is present but there are usually no symptoms; in the homozygote, sickling is present and there is usually severe anemia. It is said that under natural conditions in Africa the homozygote rarely attains adult life. The gene has a significant incidence in eastern Spain, southern Italy and Greece, in sub-Saharan Africa and Madagascar, in the Persian Gulf area, and in parts of India, with the heaviest incidence in the African areas.

It may be asked how the gene has attained such high frequencies in these populations if the homozygote rarely attains adult life. Opinion now favors the view of Allison (1954), made at the suggestion of J.B.S. Haldane, that the high gene frequency is an example of "balanced polymorphism," for the heterozygotes, possessing both normal and abnormal hemoglobins in their red cells, enjoy an immunity to malaria, which has been hyperendemic in those areas in which the gene appears first to have become common. Of course, the gene is of no value to the negroes who have migrated or been transported to nonmalarious areas such as the United States, in which it has the appearance of a lethal recessive (or dominant). Lehmann and Raper (1956) found a 40% frequency among the adult people of the Bwamba and estimated that this suggested a selective advantage of 25% over the homozygotes without the gene. Considered as part of a world wide survey, sickle-cell anemia is not of great numerical importance but it is a great cause of death in childhood in certain regions, since the monozygotes (with proportional frequency p^2)

all die before reaching adult life. In the Bwamba $p = 0.4$, so that the homozygotes form a proportion $p^2 = 0.16$ of the population; 16% of all children born die before the age of about 15 years from sickle cell anemia.

The example shows that balanced polymorphism in the human species is real. The balance of the gene for sickling can be compared with that of the diabetes gene, for which the evidence, although good, cannot be tested experimentally or in the field. It also points to the care that should be taken in attaching adjectives of approval or disapproval to genes. Some genes are clearly only disadvantageous with respect to some environments. See also Weatherall and Clegg (1981).

See §31.3 for the mode of inheritance of the hemoglobin anomalies. Some, perhaps even all, of the blood group systems may be polymorphisms. See Mourant, Kopeć, et al. (1978).

23.4 Miscellaneous Blood Diseases

Coagulation Defects

ICD 286. Hemophilia and Christmas disease are two related bleeding disorders with a combined incidence of about 1 in every 100,000, the first being about nine times more common than the second; each is a sex-linked genetic trait associated with a deficiency, usually labeled VIII or IX. The major symptom is excessive bleeding on injury, either external or internal; the bleeding may cause death or it may cause further symptoms by bleeding into a joint, causing arthroses and leading to contractures and deformities. In past times, these disorders usually led to death in early adult life from massive or continued hemorrhages. Blood transfusions have led to a better prognosis, but transfusions lead to other problems, such as infective hepatitis and recently to AIDS. For a recent symposium on hemophilia, see Seligsohn, Rimon, and Horoszowski (1981).

Vitamin K

Vitamin K deficiency is a cause of bleeding of the newborn and of patients with advanced liver disease. For the general causes of bleeding, see Ratnoff (1980).

Purpura and Other Hemorrhagic Conditions

ICD 287. See Spaet (1980).

Diseases of White Blood Cells

ICD 288. For leukemia, specifically excluded by the ICD from this class, see §20.16. For the physiology of these cells, see Craddock (1980). Other diseases primarily affecting these cells are rare causes of death.

Other Diseases of the Blood and Blood-forming Organs

ICD 289. For polycythemia of high altitudes, see Winslow (1984) and Erslev (1980).

Chapter 24

Disorders and Diseases of the Nervous System

24.1 Introduction

The ICD devotes two classes, 5 and 6, to mental disorders and to diseases of the nervous system and sense organs. We combine them here as there is little mortality directly assignable to the first, and some difficulty must be present in determining, for example, that migraine is an organic disease rather than a mental disorder or that senile dementia is a mental disorder rather than a disease. The rubrics of class 5 with their ICD numbers are as follows: 290, senile and presenile organic psychotic conditions; 291, alcoholic psychoses; 292, drug psychoses; 293, transient organic psychotic conditions; 294, other organic psychotic conditions (chronic); 295, schizophrenic psychoses; 296, affective psychoses (manic-depressive psychosis). Rubrics ICD 297–319 are largely concerned with symptoms rather than with fully developed diseases and so are not considered further.

Class 6 of the ICD is divided into inflammatory diseases (ICD 320–326), hereditary and degenerative diseases (ICD 330–337), other diseases of the central nervous system (ICD 340–349), disorders of the peripheral nervous system (ICD 350–359), diseases of the eye and adnexa (ICD 360–379), and diseases of the ear and mastoid process (ICD 380–389). Cerebrovascular disease is now classed as a part of disease of the cardiovascular system, so that care has to be taken in making secular comparisons.

To make some comparisons over time, we consider the crude death rates per 1,000,000 of causes for males (females) in class 2, Diseases of the Nervous System and of the Organs of Special Sense in Australia, 1911 to 1920, classified according to the rules of the second revision of the *International List of Causes of Death*: 60, encephalitis, 18 (13); 61, meningitis, 182 (129); 62, locomotor ataxia, 25 (4); 63, other diseases of the spinal cord, 66 (45); 64, cerebral hemorrhage, apoplexy, 446 (430), later transferred to a subclass of the Diseases of the Circulatory System; 65, softening of the brain, 21 (20); 66, paralysis without specified cause, 79 (61); 67, general paralysis of the insane, 51 (9); 68, other forms of mental alienation, 16 (19); 69, epilepsy, 48 (37); 70 and 71, convulsions, over and under 5 years of age, 84 (75); 72, chorea, 1 (2); 73, neuritis and neuralgia, 6 (7); 74, Other diseases of the nervous system, 54 (45); 75, diseases of the eye, 0 (0); 76, diseases of the ear, 8 (5); total for class 2 (second revision), 1,108 (902). Of these, locomotor ataxia and general paralysis of the insane have now been transferred to 094, "neurosyphilis" of the ninth revision. Cerebral hemorrhage has been transferred to 431 and 432 of the ninth revision, softening of the brain to 434.9 and so to the class of Diseases of the Circulatory System. Convulsions, 70 and 71, whether under or over age 5 years, have almost disappeared as a disease; certainly, at ages under 5 years they were a reaction to an infectious disease with fever. The ninth revision of the ICD still retains inflammatory diseases of the nervous system as a subclass of class 6.

There have been marked declines of mortality rates in this subclass. See Goldberg and Kurland (1962). For meningitis, see §9.7 and Wilson (1984c).

24.2 Alcoholism

ICD 291. Alcoholic psychoses.

As Bradley (1980) points out, by alcohol we usually mean ethanol or ethyl alcohol, for there are many monohydroxy derivatives of aliphatic hydrocarbons, many of which are in common use. All are toxic to man, with symptoms ranging from irritations of the eyes and mucous membranes, headaches, dizziness, and flushing to vomiting and from mental depression to anesthesia, coma, and death. Only ethanol permits regular human consumption. It is no longer used as a therapeutic agent or anesthetic.

Alcohol has a depressant effect on the central nervous system and affects behavior principally by releasing the subject from inhibitions. Cutaneous vasodilation and the subjective feeling of warmth is possibly due to an action on the central nervous system. Alcohol promotes the secretion of acid gastric juice. Alcohol metabolism takes place largely in the liver, acetaldehyde being produced as a by-product, see Berry and Pentreath (1980).

Most alcoholic beverages contain fusel oil, a mixture of hydroxylated hydrocarbons, that can produce chronic alcoholic hepatitis (including postnecrotic cirrhosis) and cancers of the esophagus and forestomach in animals. Other alcoholic drinks contain polycyclic aromatic hydrocarbons, for example, nitrosamines in beer.

Pathological effects follow high alcohol intakes:

(i) liver: fatty liver, hepatic necrosis, iron overload and cirrhosis, and hematoma; these effects are aggravated by dietary deficiency (See §27.6);

(ii) kidney: fatty changes;

(iii) nervous system: in acute alcohol poisoning, fits, hypoglycemia, head injury, anorexia, and pressure palsies; in chronic alcohol poisoning, acute myopathy, Wernicke-Korsakov syndrome, disturbances secondary to liver disease, head injury, and dementia (see also Truswell and Apeagyei, 1982);

(iv) pancreas: "inflammatory disease" of the pancreas;

(v) suicide: self poisoning (see §34.13);

(vi) head injuries;

(vii) disturbances of nutrition: the surface of the gastrointestinal tract can be damaged. There may be inefficient absorption of the necessary vitamins; alcohol supplies many calories accompanied by none of the usual accessory factors, such as vitamins, and so may result in various deficiency states. The effect of alcohol on malnutrition will vary with social status and food habits. Figueroa, Sargent, et al. (1952–1953) found that of alcoholics examined, 5.8% were pellagrins in 1942 and 2.6% in 1953. Some authors believe that mild malnutrition did not exceed 20% in the American environment of 1960 and frank deficiency rates were less than 3%, possibly due to fortification of foods with B-complex vitamins, better economic status, and freer availability of foods. Further, chronic alcoholics are intermittent drinkers and build up reserves. Their chief deficiencies are of protein, water-soluble vitamins, especially the B-complex, and magnesium, potassium, and zinc (see also Avogari, Sitori, and Tremoli 1979);

(viii) effects on the fetus: it is known from clinical studies and animal experimentation that large doses of alcohol consumed throughout pregnancy have a deleterious effect on the offspring, especially on growth and mental development; the effects of smaller doses are not clear (Lee and Leichter, 1982);

(ix) alcoholism occurs in derelicts, whether by cause or effects;

(x) for carcinogenesis, see §20.5.

Besides the personal effects just mentioned, the alcoholic is prone to injury and accident, including suicide; here, the clouding of judgement appears to be more important than the loss of motor skills. The family is affected through the diversion of funds to pay for the alcohol; the alcoholic may show a lack of care for his family, and there may be a breakdown of the family; these factors were much more important in the working-class families of nineteenth century England and Wales and are more so also in the developing world than in, for instance, an upper-class family in twentieth century England and Wales. Similar grave social effects of alcohol are observed especially in the "septic fringes" of the great cities in the developing world.

Finally, alcohol causes great losses to the community from automobile accidents, from breakdown of the social order, and from the necessary diversion of funds from other causes to assist the alcoholic or repair damage, to him, his family, and the community.

It is difficult to assess the effects of alcohol on the mortality rates by either follow-up study or official statistics. Thus, Schmidt and de Lint (1972) followed up, until the end of 1964, 5,359 men and 1,119 women, who had sought treatment for alcoholism between 1951 and 1963; these patients were mostly from Ontario. Comparing their mortality rates with those of the general population, deaths from alcoholism were 24.00 (33.33) times more than the general male (female) rates for the same epoch, cirrhosis of the liver 11.49 (25.00), suicides 6.02 (8.69), peptic ulcer 3.55 (6.66), accidents 2.52 (12.40), and all causes 2.02 (3.19) times more.

Out of 82 deaths from accidents in the two sexes of alcoholics, 20 were poisonings, 18 were from falls, and 13 were by fire; further, there were 3 from homicide. Possibly the derelict class of alcoholics did not become members of the clinic. Their proportional ratios would be much higher than those given.

Ledermann and Metz (1960) found that alcoholics had 10% more accidents than controls between 10 AM and midday, in a group of 3,500 workers in a metallurgical enterprise followed over a period of 13 months.

In whole populations, Ledermann and Tabah (1951) believe that the high masculinity of the death rates at ages 36 to 50 years in France owes much to alcohol. Contrary to the experience in the Scandinavian countries, for example, where alcoholism has raged under its most violent forms, French alcoholism is widely spread and moderate; nevertheless, France still has the largest per capita consumption of alcohol in the world. Ledermann and Tabah (1951) give tables and graphs to relate the masculinity ratio, namely, the male rate of mortal-

ity from all causes at ages 35–49 years divided by the corresponding female rate, to the average consumption of alcohol; the conclusions drawn assume that the great part of drinking is done by the males. For comparison, the ratio is shown to have decreased in Sweden from 1.38 in 1841–1855 to 1.19 in 1891–1900 after antialcoholic measures, resulting in less alcohol consumption per head, had been initiated in 1885; similar declines were noted in Denmark after antialcoholic measures in 1917. The authors conclude that alcohol is an important factor in the masculinity rates of deaths from all causes. Lederman (1956, 1958, 1964) has continued these studies.

Although there are great difficulties in assigning a numerical estimate to the effect of alcoholism on mortality, Sundby (1967), Valverius (1981), Sundbärg (1907/1970). Sjostrand and Sahlin (1924) discussing the paper of Greenwood (1924), Meurk (1932) and Åkesson (1931) all stressed the importance for Swedish mortality of the fall in alcohol consumption.

For suicide in alcoholism, see Prinzing (1895) and Ritson (1977). For suicide and alcoholism in England and Wales, see Glatt (1958) and McLeod (1967). For the psychopharmacology of alcoholism, see Sandler (1980). See Nace (1984) for a review of alcoholism in the United States by age, race, and sex, and the prospects of treatment.

For international trends in production and consumption see Walsh and Grant (1985).

24.3 Drug Dependence and Pathology

Drug dependence, other than on caffeine, alcohol, and tobacco, has become a topic of great social interest and importance. Heroin-related deaths appear to be greatest in Washington, D.C., where the mortality was 88 per 1,000,000 in 1980 and 174 per 1,000,000 per annum in 1981. The important subsidiary factors were alcohol abuse and quinine adulteration of the drug, which led to temporarily extremely high concentrations in the blood (Ruttenberg and Luke, 1984). Grundmann (1976) reports glomerulonephritis as an important sequela. Grundmann (1980), Jick (1980) and Schmähl and Habs (1980) report on drug-induced pathology, illness, and cancer.

Cannabis and cannabinoids. These drugs are believed to have mutagenic and carcinogenic effects; so far, there is no strong evidence for teratogenicity, although lasting behavioral effects have been noted in humans and animals when the mother has been exposed to cannabis during pregnancy. Jones (1983) concludes that cannabis under certain conditions is harmful.

Hughes, Canavan, et al. (1983) give tables of the extent of drug abuse by drug, number of persons treated, and country. The statistics of reported abusers are dominated by entries from the Americas in millions: amphetamines 2.1, barbiturates 4.2, coca/cocaine 6.0, cannabis 24.6, hallucinogens 2.0, heroin 0.46, other opiates 0.47, total 39.8.

See Gottschalk, McGuire, et al. (1980) for drug abuse deaths in nine cities and Kozel and Adams (1986) for an overview of the epidemiology. See also Statistics—alcohol and drug use (1985).

24.4 Epilepsy

ICD 345. Exclusions: progressive myoclonic epilepsy (333.2). The rule is not stated, but epileptiform convulsions secondary to multiple sclerosis, acute infections, brain tumors, or cerebrovascular disease would be assigned to the cause.

The cause of some 75% of patients suffering repeated attacks of the characteristic epileptiform convulsions cannot be determined; this is ideopathic, as opposed to symptomatic, epilepsy.

WHO-epilepsy (1955) points out that epilepsy, although rarely in itself a cause of death, appears in nearly all lists of causes of death, national or international. According to a table, the prevalence of epilepsy was about 4 per 1,000 in Denmark in 1953, Finland in 1954, and England and Wales in 1951–1952, with deaths assigned to epilepsy being about 20 per 1,000,000 per annum. It can be estimated that for England and Wales for 1951–1952, there were 824 deaths in a year in a population of 176,000 epileptics—a load of more than 5 per 1,000 per annum to be added to the total mor-

tality rate for persons in the community. In the countries surveyed by WHO-epilepsy (1955) there was a general tendency for the deaths and the crude death rates to fall over the years 1900 to 1954. The deaths tend to be scattered through all ages in either sex. The epileptic attacks can be controlled by anticonvulsants. Probably there is a real decline in the prevalence and mortality rates.

See Ward, Penry, and Purpura (1983) and Aird, Masland, and Woodbury (1984) for general texts on epilepsy.

24.5 The Psychoses

ICD 290, senile and presenile organic psychotic conditions; 291 and 292, alcoholic and drug psychoses, already discussed; 293, transient and 294, other psychotic (chronic) conditions; 295, schizophrenic psychosis; 296, affective psychosis; 297, paranoid states; 298, other nonorganic psychoses; 299, psychoses with origin specific to childhood; ICD 300–316, nonpsychotic mental disorders, and 317–319, mental retardation are symptomatic, rather than organic, disease diagnoses. Few of these conditions, ICD 290–319, will be certified as the cause of death, but we may consider the effect, on the mortality rates, of psychosis and asylum committal. It is remarked that in the largely agricultural populations of the past, it was possible to find a place for many types of psychotics who would, in an industrial society, be committed to an asylum for the sake of their own welfare and the safety of the state. We mention that few modern states have wished for or could afford sufficient manpower and resources to maintain an atmosphere as satisfactory as a hospital or even a well-run workhouse. There are special hazards.

(i) The staff. Many psychotics have violent incidents and may attack others, including the attendants. The attendants have responded in the past by harsh disciplinary measures and violence, including retaliatory attacks; for example, I.P. Semmelweis was beaten up and died within a fortnight of admission to a mental institution.

(ii) Other inmates. There is often danger of

attack from other psychotics, especially schizophrenics.

(*iii*) The inmate himself. Suicide is a common end in many forms of psychosis, for example, in schizophrenia, depression, and paranoia; it is a symptom of the disease, paranoia. The inmate may be careless of his own safety with respect to fires and electrical appliances, and he may endanger others by setting fire to the asylum.

(*iv*) Hygiene. The inmate may be negligent of such hygienic habits as the correct disposal of excrement, the maintenance of personal cleanliness, and the care of food. These are particularly dangerous failings because asylums are often crowded. Bowel infections are especially common; in former times, typhus would have been a special hazard.

We can therefore expect the rates of mortality in an asylum to be high. See Farr (1885/1975, pp. 425–438) for the difficult problem of ascertaining a measure of mortality of inmates and of comparing it with that of the general population. See also WHO-schizophrenia (1975) and Gottesman, Shields, and Hanson (1982). See WHO-paralysis agitans (1955) for statistics on mortality and Lieberman (1974) for a general review. For Alzheimer's disease, see Price, Whitehouse, and Struble (1985).

24.6 Multiple Sclerosis

ICD 340

There is a marked gradation of rates by latitude; Kurland and Reed (1964) give the prevalence rates per 1,000,000 as 42, 41, 38, 30, and 13 at latitudes 50°N, 42°N, 40°N, 37°N, and 30°N in Winnipeg, Boston, Denver, San Francisco, and New Orleans, respectively, suggesting a gradient in incidence according to ultraviolet light dosage. Detels, Visscher, et al. (1978) and Sutherland (1969) study the age at migration from Europe, presumably from areas of low ultraviolet light dosage, to the United States and Australia, respectively. There is also a relationship between the disease and previous infection with measles and perhaps other viruses, Black (1982), Carp, Warner, and Merz (1978), and ter Meulen and Carter (1984). See also Scheinberg and Raine (1984).

Chapter 25
Cardiovascular Diseases

25.1 Cardiovascular-related or Combined Classes of Disease

Although the mortality from diseases of the cardiovascular system has come to be relatively more important as the death rates from the infections have declined, it is difficult to make satisfactory comparisons over the epochs of a survey of any country, for there have been several transfers of some types of death from one class of the ICD to another, as well as changes in the ideas of etiology and diagnosis. In the earlier epochs there were still a large number of deaths assigned to "senility" and other vague and ill-defined causes. There has been a definite policy not to accept such ill-defined causes, and the certifying physicians have responded by assigning deaths of the elderly to more definite rubrics, such as arteriosclerosis, chronic nephritis, cerebral hemorrhage, and coronary disease. There also has been an increased tendency to consider arteriosclerosis as a fundamental cause leading up to death. However, there have been other changes not due to the policies of the certifying physicians. Between the third and fourth decades of this century, that is, at the time of the Fourth Revision, there was some transfer of deaths with the combined diagnosis of "chronic nephritis" and "arteriosclerosis" from the genitourinary system to the cardiovascular.

To avoid these difficulties, Lancaster (1979) produced two sets of tables, which we now consider. First, the deaths in the four classes,

neurological, cardiovascular, genitourinary, and indefinite, were combined to give rates of a single combined class, which could be followed through for Australia from 1908–1910 by decades until the present time. We give such death rates for males and females in the age group 65–74 years for the individual classes and the combined class in Table 25.1.1. Although cardiovascular death rates have tended to increase in each sex during the epochs considered, the death rates from the combined class have tended to decrease during the same epochs.

Death rates from cardiovascular diseases during a more restricted set of epochs are given for age and sex groupings in Table 25.1.2. In any epoch, after a decline at childhood ages, 5–14 years, the death rates rise steadily throughout life; from age 25 onward there are high masculinities for the rates. At fixed ages, the death rates have remained rather constant with a clear tendency to be lower in the more recent epochs. For a more recent period, according to Uemura and Piša (1985), the age-standardized death rates at ages 40–69 years in Australia declined by 13.6% in the first half and by 21.4% in the second half of the period 1971–1982 and declined by 32% for the whole period, a striking decrease.

For the first few years of life, the deaths assigned to cardiovascular causes are chiefly congenital in origin; in later childhood, they were formerly due to acute rheumatism, and from later childhood up to 45 years of age, they were chiefly due to acute and chronic forms of

TABLE 25.1.1. Mortality in Australia in persons aged 65–74 Years for cardiovascular-related classes individually and combined.

Cause	Deaths per 1,000,000 per annum							
	1908–1910	1911–1920	1921–1930	1931–1940	1941–1950	1951–1960	1961–1970	1971–1975
Males								
Nervous	5,853	5,547	4,746	3,541	5,671	7,075	4,636	694
Cardiovascular	12,357	11,950	13,153	19,365	22,574	24,047	27,460	28,682
Genitourinary	5,711	5,444	5,269	4,938	3,810	1,694	1,087	683
Combined classes*	31,716	30,702	27,665	29,705	33,052	33,104	33,303	30,162
Females								
Nervous	5,867	5,502	4,930	3,807	6,145	6,616	3,894	433
Cardiovascular	10,178	9,291	10,160	13,795	13,510	12,633	14,430	15,845
Genitourinary	2,508	2,322	2,833	2,928	1,946	653	630	446
Combined classes*	24,067	22,513	20,771	21,706	22,176	20,066	19,042	16,799

*Combined classes: subtotals of nervous, cardiovascular, genitourinary, and ill-defined (including senility) causes of deaths. Modified after Lancaster (1979, Table 3). Note that the contributions from senility and other ill-defined diseases have not been included as a class, so that the totals of the combined classes are more than the sum of the three classes tabulated.

TABLE 25.1.2. Age-specific death rates from cardiovascular disease in Australia.

Epoch	Deaths per million per annum at ages (years)								
	0–4	5–14	15–24	25–34	35–44	45–54	55–64	65–74	75+
Males									
1941–1950	38	37	90	176	664	2,906	8,848	22,574	59,935
1951–1960	40	22	63	161	733	3,128	9,823	24,135	65,069
1961–1967	22	13	41	135	869	3,643	10,494	25,854	63,848
1971–1975*	19	6	23	101	771	3,243	9,758	22,875	62,432
Females									
1941–1950	39	37	84	153	417	1,574	4,006	13,510	49,114
1951–1960	35	27	48	106	330	1,140	3,993	12,725	50,712
1961–1967	22	8	34	89	298	1,108	3,964	13,158	48,380
1971–1975*	24	6	15	49	268	937	3,325	11,124	46,075

*Class 7 of the International Classification of Diseases less Rubrics 430–438, cerebrovascular diseases.
From Lancaster (1979).

rheumatic disease. Over the age of 45 years, rheumatic disease as a cause of heart disorder becomes less common, and hypertensive and arteriosclerotic diseases predominate.

Under the age of 45 years there have been worthwhile declines in mortality. As many of the deaths from subacute bacterial endocarditis were due to disease superimposed on a pre-existing rheumatic valvular lesion, it may be said that the improvements for under the age of 45 years are due almost entirely to changes in the mortality and morbidity from acute rheumatic fever and its sequelae.

Over the age of 45 years, for reasons already

stated, the position is different. Although in unpublished tabulations for females there were only moderate increases between the epochs 1921–1930 and 1931–1940, or, in other words, between the classifications of the third and fourth revisions of the ICD, males at every age over 45 years showed a substantial increase in the rates. These disparities between the sexes have persisted.

For congenital heart disease, see Rashkind (1982).

For the death rates by age and sex for the cardiovascular system we give in Table 25.1.3, as the experience of a single country, the

TABLE 25.1.3. Mortality rates in Australia from diseases of the circulatory system.*

Age in years	0–4	5–14	15–24	25–34	35–44	45–54	55–64	65–74	75+
					Males				
1908–1910	125	114	235	315	812	1,841	4,885	12,357	23,573
1911–1920	97	139	224	349	773	1,997	5,157	11,950	25,587
1921–1930	65	92	145	249	624	1,859	5,133	13,153	31,182
1931–1940	48	57	114	202	639	2,363	7,282	19,365	51,302
1941–1950	38	37	90	177	665	2,906	8,849	22,574	59,936
1951–1960	36	11	46	144	693	3,058	9,714	24,047	65,058
1961–1970	25	11	31	124	867	3,685	10,945	27,460	71,382
1971–1980	25	11	41	139	825	3,445	10,176	25,626	74,955
					Females				
1908–1910	125	156	247	367	736	1,431	3,685	10,178	19,857
1911–1920	83	138	244	395	697	1,491	3,453	9,291	21,283
1921–1930	57	92	146	267	565	1,300	3,506	10,160	27,507
1931–1940	46	61	122	195	496	1,484	4,337	13,795	43,960
1941–1950	39	37	84	153	417	1,351	4,006	13,510	49,114
1951–1960	31	14	36	86	285	1,061	3,875	12,633	50,666
1961–1970	24	8	27	77	314	1,155	4,196	14,430	55,708
1971–1980	26	9	27	85	392	1,310	4,103	13,799	63,341
					Masculinity rates[†]				
1908–1910	100	73	95	86	110	129	133	121	119
1911–1920	117	101	92	88	111	134	149	129	120
1921–1930	114	100	99	93	110	143	146	129	113
1931–1940	104	93	93	104	129	159	168	140	117
1941–1950	97	100	107	116	159	215	221	167	122
1951–1960	116	79	128	167	243	288	251	190	128
1961–1970	104	138	115	161	276	319	261	190	128
1971–1980	96	122	152	164	210	263	248	186	118

*Deaths per 1,000,000 per annum.
[†] 100 × (male death rates)/(female death rates).
From Lancaster and Gordon (1987).

Australian figures for the 8 decades of this century. There have been striking declines at ages up to 34 years for males and to 44 years for females, chiefly due to the decline of the rheumatic diseases. At ages 45–54 the female rates have declined to a local minimum in 1921–1930 and then risen in 1931–1940, and then risen in the last two decades. At ages 55–64 years, the female rates have been rather stable, but the male rates have doubled over the 8 decades. Similarly, the male rates have doubled over the 8 decades at ages 65–74 years. Over 75 years of age the rates of each sex have trebled over the same decades, with the masculinity rates remaining within the vicinity of 120. The rates at these oldest ages have been affected by coding practices, especially the treatment of the virtual abolition of deaths due to ill-defined causes, and presumably also by the coming of the antibiotics and chemotherapy, which altered the frequency of the deaths from respiratory disease.

In summary, the increases of the male rates at ages 45–64 years and the consequent rises of the masculinity rates for deaths from the cardiovascular system have been a striking feature of the Australian experience up to 1970, but some declines can be noted after that date. The interpretation of the rise and fall of masculinity rates is more difficult.

25.2 Rheumatic Fever and Its Sequelae

ICD 390–392, acute rheumatic fever; ICD 393–398, chronic rheumatic fever.

It is difficult to follow the progress of mortality from acute rheumatism and its sequelae over the 8 epochs of a survey on Australian mortality, as there have been changes in the rubrics; thus, in the epoch 1908–1910, deaths certified as being of persons in the acute phase of the initial attack or of a relapse were assigned to rubric 47, "acute articular rheumatism." Rubrics 77 and 78 contained deaths due to acute pericarditis and acute endocarditis. The same classification was used in 1911–1930. More chronic forms of the disease were probably included under "organic diseases of the heart." In 1931–1950, rubric 92a–c included chronic valvular disease of the heart. It appears that if the death rates between 5 and 45 years are considered, there have been substantial declines from the rheumatic diseases, since deaths at these ages in the earlier epochs would be partly due to infections of congenital valve defects but mostly due to the effects of rheumatic infection. Chronic valvular lesions would have been almost entirely rheumatic in origin, and subacute bacterial endocarditis would also be usually on a heart valve damaged by rheumatic infection. Wilson and Geraci (1983) report that the cure rate of infective endocarditis is over 85%. For rheumatic fever, see Stollerman (1975) and for bacterial endocarditis, see Perry (1936) and Parker (1978, 1984a).

25.3 Atheroma and Serum Lipids

With the aid of Stamler (1973), we introduce the important disease, atherosclerosis and the lesion atheroscleroma, a term applied in the old pathology to any noninflammatory cyst or sac surrounded by hard walls containing soft mushy material; the Greek athere means mush of the consistency of groats or gruel, and skleros, hard. Atheroma is commonly seen in the elderly in the developed countries, most readily in the aorta, the greatest blood vessel. Such was observed in 1727 in an aorta, and the internal coat was said to be in several places ruptured, lacerated, and rotten like fruit. In 1775 Albrecht von Haller (1708–1777), in a brief essay, stressed the atheromatous property more than the hardness of the wall of the atheroma; R. Virchow and his school established atherosclerosis as a pathologic identity, with stress on the cholesterol-lipid (Greek: chole = bile, steros = solid), or mushy, content. During 1908 to 1912, an animal model was produced, in the course of dietetic experiments for other purposes, by feeding eggs, milk, and meat to rabbits, food obviously rich in cholesterol. This suggested that the human lesions might well be associated with hypercholesterolemia (i.e., high levels of cholesterol in the blood stream). By this time, atherosclerosis had been observed in diverse diseases, including hypothyroidism, uncontrolled diabetes, and nephrosis. Thus, diet was seen not to be the sole cause. In the 1920s it was found that hypercholesterolemia occurred often in those with cardiac infarction. Up to this time autopsies had usually been carried out on Europeans, but with increased interest in the pathology of Africa, Asia, and Latin America, workers found that atherosclerosis was uncommon among the chiefly vegetable-consuming populations of the undeveloped world. Raab (1932) and Rosenthal (1934) both stressed the importance of diets, rich in cholesterol and the related vitamin D in the western style of life, but poor in these same ingredients in the undeveloped world. These observations were multiplied after World War II.

Analyses of WHO and FAO Data

International comparisons of diet and frequencies of the disease were made with the aid of statistical multivariate techniques. Ten data sets had been published by 1979; all 10 show statistically significant correlation between CHD [coronary heart disease], measured at middle age, and dietary constituents, such as total calories, total fat, animal fat, saturated fat, total protein, animal protein, and sucrose, and negative correlation of CHD with vegetable protein, vegetable fat, and total carbohydrates (expressed as a fraction of total calories). Because many of these correlation coefficients are high, and because the variables (other than CHD) are highly correlated among themselves, the second order correlations (that is, of the form: correlation of X and Y with Z held constant) can be positive, zero, or negative. The correlation coefficient between CHD and cigarette smoking is positive and high. We conclude that CHD is significantly correlated (in the statistical sense) with some factors associated with cholesterol and also with tobacco consumption.

International Comparisons of Postmortem Findings

The incidence of atherosclerosis as seen in autopsy material can be compared between countries. Here results similar to those with CHD have been reported.

International Comparisons of Living Population Samples

Here again the same general conclusions are reached. In countries with high scores for CHD there would be high scores for serum cholesterol.

International Studies of the Effects of Emigration

The most satisfactory investigations cited by Stamler (1973) were the comparisons between Japanese in Japan and Japanese in western countries and between Japanese migrants to the United States and Japanese in their home country.

There have also been intranational studies. Thus, there was a regression in atherosclerosis in those countries subjected to famine, near famine, or severe rationing during each of the two World Wars or immediately after. In the United Kingdom there was a correlation between CHD and egg consumption over the years 1921–1966. Within countries there are marked differences between subgroups, for example, religious, in the consumption of the lipids, and correlated differences between the levels of CHD.

For the effects of diet on cardiovascular disease, see Hegyeli (1983), Glueck, Larsen, et al. (1981), Vlodaver, Amplatz, et al. (1976). For the Framingham Study, see Dawber (1980). Glueck and Tsang (1979) point out that atherosclerosis may begin in infancy.

25.4 Tobacco

Although the effects of tobacco (largely through cigarette smoking) on the lung, producing cancer, are well known, as in §20.4, the even greater importance numerically of its effects on the cardiovascular system is little known. To correct this we may quote from the US Surgeon-General (1979, §1, p. 12) as follows:

Although mortality ratios are particularly high among cigarette smokers for such diseases as lung cancer, chronic obstructive lung disease, and cancer of the larynx, coronary heart disease is the chief contributor to the excess mortality among cigarette smokers. Lung cancer and chronic obstructive lung disease, in that order, follow after coronary heart disease in accounting for the excess mortality. Pipe and cigar smoking are associated with elevated mortality ratios for cancers of the upper respiratory tract, including cancer of the oral cavity, the larynx, and the esophagus.

US Surgeon-General (1979, §1, p. 11) uses the mortality ratio, that is, the ratio of the death rate for a given age-sex group and the death rate for the whole population, to describe the importance of smoking on health. He reports, after a review of the relevant literature, as follows. The cigarette smokers have mortality rates raised by about 70% above the general population, that is, have a mortality ratio of 1.7. The mortality ratio of smokers increases with the amount smoked. Heavy smokers of two packs a day have a mortality ratio of 2.0. Overall mortality ratios are proportional to the duration of cigarette smoking, so that overall mortality ratios are higher for those who began smoking earlier. Overall mortality ratios are higher among inhalers than among noninhaling smokers. Although mortality ratios are highest at the younger ages and decline with increasing age, the excess mortality rate due to cigarette smoking increases with age. The overall mortality ratios of former cigarette smokers decline as the length of the period of discontinuation increases. Cigar smoking is not without risk. The excess mortality is proportional to the number of cigars smoked per day. Pipe smoking alone seems to have a slight effect in increasing overall mortality. Prospective study data imply that the life expectancy is importantly shortened by cigarette smoking; for example, a 32-year-old, two-pack-a-day smoker has a life expectation about 8 years shorter than a nonsmoker of the same age. Overall mortality ratios increase with the "tar" and nicotine content of the cigarette. The prospective studies have shown that the mortality ratios for female cigarette smokers are somewhat less than those for male smokers. When variables other than sex are fixed, females and males probably suffer equal increases in mortality rates and ratios. For a bibliography, see US Office on Smoking and Health (1983).

Buerger (1908) described "thromboangiitis obliterans: a study of the vascular lesions leading to presenile spontaneous gangrene," for which he gave evidence incriminating tobacco as a cause. Juergens (1980) has described the disease but it is not certain that there is a clear division between Buerger's disease and atherosclerosis obliterans; if not, it could be said that tobacco is a powerful synergic factor in the incidence of atherosclerosis obliterans. For mortality from coronary heart disease, see Wald (1976). For the increasing rates of myocardial infarction, see Johannson, Vedin, et al. (1983) and Margulies (1983). For the effect of tobacco smoking, see Wilhelmsson, Vedin, et al. (1981).

25.5 Hypertension

Hypertension is perhaps the only disease or syndrome characterized by a single measurement. Meyer (1980) cites an accepted WHO definition by which an adult is said to be hypertensive if the systolic arterial pressure [i.e., upper limit of the blood pressure as measured] is above 160 mm of mercury and/or the diastolic arterial pressure [i.e., lower limit of the blood pressure as measured] is above 95 mm of mercury. The adult is said to be nor-

motensive if the systolic and diastolic pressures are below 140 and 90 mm of mercury, respectively. The "borderline" cases have systolic pressures of 140 to 160 and/or diastolic pressures of 90 to 95 mm of mercury, respectively. The definitions are simple but imperfect, for in the western world the blood pressures tend to rise throughout life. Further, in the western world a diastolic pressure of 100 mm or a systolic pressure of 165 mm of mercury in a person of 70 years is not held to be hypertensive.

Some forms of hypertension are secondary to another disease, for example, chronic nephritis, myxedema, and toxemia of pregnancy; otherwise, hypertension is said to be essential or primary. The cause of essential hypertension is unknown. No genetic mechanism has been demonstrated. Essential hypertension is unique to man, indeed almost unique to western man, for it has been shown that native tribesmen do not suffer from the disease. It has been considered that diet must be a leading cause of the disease, but it has not been possible to characterize the responsible factors.

Overeating and obesity show positive correlation with hypertension in surveys in western populations. Therefore, it is interesting to note the absence of increasing weight with age in adulthood in the primitive societies. A. Keys (1981) gives tables from his seven-countries study showing that weight is not a determining factor of mortality in middle age.

A reasonable case can be made for salt as an etiologic factor in hypertension; (massive) feeding with salt can lead to induction of hypertension in animals. Primitive peoples eat less salt than western man; hypertension is more common in those parts of the western world where larger amounts of salt are consumed; when persons leave the tribal areas to enjoy the food of the western life, their blood pressure rises. Excess body weight may be principally due to increased sodium retention. See, for example, Trowell (1981), Joossens (1980), Trowell and Burkitt (1981a, b), Diehl and Mannerberg (1981), and Dodson and Humphreys (1981), but see also the anomalous findings of McCarron, Morris, et al. (1984).

We conclude that the cause of essential hypertension is still unknown, but that salt retention, high fat diet, obesity, some endocrine factors, some neurogenic factors, and the western life style, generally, may all be important factors in some individuals.

The pathogenesis and pathology of the disease are obscure. The most striking anomaly is the existence in the arterioles of alternating zones of constriction and dilatation. In the foci of dilatation, there may be an exudation of plasma into the media of the wall of the arteriole and small hemorrhages may occur; these are clinically evident in the arterioles of the fundus of the eye. In the media of the arterioles, the smooth muscle cell appears edematous and there is a fibrohyaline infiltration and degeneration of the intercellular spaces.

For the epidemiology of hypertension, see also Kesteloot and Joossens (1980), MacMahon and Leeder (1984), Stallones (1965), and Lambert (1975).

25.6 Coronary Heart Disease

Hypertension. Studies show that in middle age, coronary heart disease is twice as common in hypertensives as in normotensives. Treatment of hypertension has clear cut benefit in lowering the risk of hemorrhagic cerebrovascular accidents but its value in lowering coronary heart disease risk is not so clear; recent surveys of 1978 and 1979, respectively, have shown rather more definite positive value.

Diabetes. Diabetes seems to be a risk factor because of the atherosclerosis usually present.

Inactivity. Various surveys in the 1970s have shown physical inactivity to be a hazard, perhaps increasing the risk factor threefold. Low energy output, heavy smoking, and hypertension increased the risk twentyfold in three surveys. The evidence on the benefits of exercise is difficult to refute. See Paffenbarger, Hyde et al. (1986).

Endocrine. Hypothyroidism is a risk factor probably associated with raised blood cholesterol levels. Estrogen, whether administered to males with carcinoma of the prostate or to females as a contraceptive pill, increases the risk of coronary heart disease.

Atheroma and Serum Lipids. See §25.3.

Tobacco. See §25.4.

Diet. See §25.3.

Therapy. The classical therapy of coronary heart disease is rest followed by carefully graduated exercise. In recent times, by-pass surgery has been used to compensate for the lack of flow through the thrombosed arteries; this is widely used in the developed countries. More radical is cardiac transplantation. Hunt and Stinson (1981) believe that a patient undergoing heart transplantation can be hopeful of a successful outcome; rejection of the transplant is the chief worry but the authors believe that the immunologic problems may be soluble. Aitkin, Laird, and Francis (1983) believe that the statistical follow-up of patients is not always fairly given and so are pessimistic of success for the operation. Many others, including the author, feel that the results obtained from operation are not commensurate with the undesirable features introduced into hospital practice by the routines necessary for the gathering of organs from patients dying; relatives may well feel that the interests of the patient are no longer paramount.

Prophylaxis. Hjerman, Velve Byre, et al. (1981) found decreased incidence of deaths from coronary occlusion in a group modifying their diet and smoking.

25.7 Coronary or Ischemic Heart Disease—Statistics

There are great difficulties in following the death rates from any of the cardiovascular diseases over a long stretch of time, and we cannot relate the changes unambiguously to given causes, as has been possible in the treatment of the infectious diseases. This is all the more unfortunate as cardiovascular diseases are now the most common cause of death in the developed world and are subject to much public discussion. The large literature on the epidemiology of cardiovascular disease has not yet brought the subject into definitive form. Therefore, we can do no more than point to

TABLE 25.7.1. Cardiovascular disease in 1975 at ages 40 to 69 years (age-standardized mortality rates per 100,000).

Country	All causes		Cardiovascular diseases		Cardiovascular diseases less Cerebrovascular		Cerebrovascular disease		Ischemic heart disease	
	M	F	M	F	M	F	M	F	M	F
Canada	1,288	652	619	238	552	187	67	51	473	143
United States	1,438	723	703	284	625	227	78	57	528	171
Israel	1,090	797	541	362	438	259	103	103	370	193
Japan	1,024	568	379	210	150	83	229	127	69	29
Austria	1,427	702	570	245	449	175	122	70	308	89
Belgium	1,409	702	553	228	455	163	97	65	312	84
Bulgaria	1,267	749	546	362	337	191	208	171	237	110
Czechoslovakia	1,611	769	707	326	524	209	183	117	410	129
Denmark	1,164	675	530	202	468	157	61	45	400	114
Finland	1,707	651	913	293	790	207	123	86	673	142
France	1,346	574	380	147	282	95	98	52	152	37
Federal Republic of Germany	1,416	704	556	221	453	161	102	60	325	81
Hungary	1,540	842	670	360	513	262	157	98	328	125
Ireland	1,393	818	708	322	594	223	113	98	508	168
Italy	1,274	610	476	224	363	154	113	70	226	63
Netherlands	1,184	551	506	176	436	128	70	48	363	87
Norway	1,092	526	535	179	465	122	70	57	398	86
Poland	1,478	711	606	273	531	219	75	55	229	56
Romania	1,281	779	547	375	392	252	154	122	146	64
Sweden	1,040	548	491	181	424	130	67	51	368	102
Switzerland	1,100	523	420	161	359	124	61	38	226	50
UK: England and Wales	1,355	720	696	277	596	204	100	74	498	138
UK: Northern Ireland	1,519	818	848	369	720	266	129	103	614	189
UK: Scotland	1,626	872	857	379	706	264	151	115	615	202
Yugoslavia	1,344	794	515	334	389	232	126	102	180	70
Australia	1,374	702	726	318	615	230	111	89	534	180
New Zealand	1,376	738	724	308	630	214	94	94	545	167

Data from Piša and Uemura (1982).

recent changes in the death rates and cite some recent opinions on them.

According to Rosenberg and Klebba (1979), the standardized death rates for the major cardiovascular diseases declined over the years 1950–1976 form 4,256 to 2,844 deaths per 1,000,000 per annum, a decrease of 33%. Over the same years, the death rates from malignant neoplasms increased from 1,254 to 1,323 deaths per 1,000,000 per annum, an increase of 5.5%; death rates from accidents and injuries declined from 739 to 672, although there is no definite trend; deaths, excluding these three groupings, decreased from 2,166 to 1,436, a decline of about 34%.

One-third of all deaths in the United States are caused by "ischemic" (or "coronary") heart disease, according to Rosenberg and Klebba (1979). For their comparisons, these authors used rates standardized on to populations as enumerated at the US Census of 1940. In their Figure 1, death rates were behaving as follows: all causes falling, malignant neoplasms remaining steady, accident and injury tending to decrease but reaching a maximum in 1969, major cardiovascular disease falling by approximately a quarter, all other diseases also declining by a quarter. In their Figure 2 the progress of the major cardiovascular diseases, treated as a whole, seemed unaffected by the changes from the introduction of the seventh revision in 1958 and of the eighth revision in 1968; indeed, all the components suffered little change from the introduction of the seventh revision. On

TABLE 25.7.2. Mortality from all causes—England and Wales (deaths per 1,000,000 per annum).

Year	All	40–44	45–49	50–54	55–59	60–64	65–69	Standardized rate
				Males by age in years				
1968	12,409	3,019	5,086	9,220	16,023	26,897	44,087	14,673
1969	12,486	3,011	5,577	9,290	16,082	27,829	45,648	15,093
1970	12,297	2,943	5,246	9,093	15,939	26,608	43,963	14,597
1971	12,148	2,970	5,330	9,004	15,157	25,526	41,618	14,060
1972	12,600	2,875	5,415	9,237	15,594	25,979	42,996	14,392
1973	12,400	2,892	5,382	9,007	15,723	25,075	41,533	14,078
1974	12,335	2,832	5,242	9,168	15,420	24,670	40,926	13,896
1975	12,280	2,680	5,088	9,060	14,553	24,406	40,147	13,548
1976	12,538	2,657	4,886	8,997	14,736	24,882	40,296	13,605
1977	12,113	2,545	4,817	8,752	14,143	23,916	38,928	13,137
				Females by age in years				
1968	11,358	2,072	3,386	5,273	7,950	12,935	21,268	7,571
1969	11,279	2,236	3,502	5,413	8,228	13,089	21,999	7,801
1970	11,215	2,106	3,494	5,253	7,912	12,708	21,252	7,555
1971	11,104	2,011	3,483	5,206	7,923	12,272	19,862	7,312
1972	11,569	2,012	3,479	5,393	8,225	12,623	20,512	7,519
1973	11,518	1,998	3,468	5,210	8,025	12,298	20,380	7,385
1974	11,479	1,936	3,407	5,282	8,156	12,361	19,970	7,361
1975	11,435	1,913	3,256	5,214	7,842	12,238	19,618	7,205
1976	11,838	1,890	3,247	5,282	7,784	12,566	19,792	7,267
1977	11,357	1,769	3,145	4,983	7,691	12,169	19,243	7,034

Data from Piša and Uemura (1982).

the introduction of the eighth revision, rates from "other major cardiovascular diseases" (residual grouping) fell from 510 to 320; hypertensive heart disease, with and without renal disease, decreased from about 230 to 100; ischemic heart disease rose from 2,100 to 2,400; all these rates are per 1,000,000 per annum. In particular, these observations show that any series purporting to display the progress of hypertensive disease must make note of the effect of the change from the seventh to the eighth revision. In Rosenberg and Klebba (1979, Figure 3), the standardized rates for white males are highest, followed by all other male, all other female, and white female. Their Figures 4–8 show that the rates by age are not increasing at ages under 45 years; they are increasing for white males at ages 75–84 years and more so for white females at the same ages; in general, the rates at 45–74 are decreasing in such a way as to decrease the differences between races and between sexes. Havlik and

Feinleib (1979), reporting on their conference, gave as the major conclusions (i) the decrease in the heart disease mortality is real, (ii) the declines are due to primary prevention through changes in risk factors and improved medical care, although not entirely so, and (iii) precise quantification of the causes of the declines requires further studies, especially a documentation of nonfatal coronary events.

More extended tabulations are available. Ischemic heart disease (IHD), as Table 1 of Piša and Uemura (1982) and our reproduction of it, Table 25.7.1, indicates, is the leading single cause of death among men in most industrialized countries. The reliability of the data reported by the 27 member states of WHO has been checked by relating the national death rates provided against the notifications of acute myocardial infarction reported to Myocardial Infarction Community Registers. There seems to be a constant ratio between death rates and incidence rates of about 4 to

TABLE 25.7.3. Mortality from all cardiovascular diseases—England and Wales* (deaths per 1,000,000 per annum).

Year	All	40–44	45–49	50–54	55–59	60–64	65–69	Standardized rate
				Males by age in years				
1968	6,017	1,333	2,441	4,487	7,838	13,022	21,786	7,141
1969	5,998	1,274	2,677	4,572	7,739	13,328	22,164	7,260
1970	5,932	1,264	2,603	4,570	7,812	12,866	21,716	7,142
1971	6,023	1,324	2,715	4,613	7,579	12,763	21,429	7,099
1972	6,232	1,306	2,801	4,795	7,876	13,012	21,929	7,287
1973	6,120	1,291	2,744	4,734	7,832	12,656	21,242	7,128
1974	6,119	1,289	2,650	4,812	7,824	12,536	21,006	7,080
1975	6,104	1,230	2,568	4,815	7,507	12,464	20,693	6,956
1976	6,085	1,145	2,438	4,579	7,583	12,530	20,515	6,870
1977	5,986	1,175	2,428	4,581	7,439	12,142	20,179	6,759
				Females by age in years				
1968	6,098	518	910	1,611	2,806	5,714	10,904	3,063
1969	6,034	515	942	1,661	2,829	5,594	11,007	3,077
1970	5,951	511	906	1,618	2,732	5,483	10,609	2,985
1971	5,996	492	903	1,557	2,795	5,252	10,083	2,889
1972	6,237	488	889	1,634	2,911	5,384	10,278	2,960
1973	6,185	466	900	1,547	2,796	5,301	10,209	2,903
1974	6,147	458	909	1,581	2,840	5,322	9,928	2,888
1975	6,078	419	832	1,514	2,713	5,096	9,688	2,774
1976	6,126	450	842	1,479	2,679	5,202	9,516	2,765
1977	5,929	404	826	1,437	2,610	4,980	9,195	2,666

*A80–A88, ICD 390–458, 8th revision.
Data from Piša and Uemura (1982).

10; the two statistics therefore have a satisfactorily high correlation. Further, comparisons have been made over the years 1968–1977, when the eighth revision of the ICD was being used. The populations studied were usually not sufficiently large to avoid the appearance of random fluctuations, but fluctuations have been reduced by taking standardized death rates for consideration.

There are considerable variations in total cardiovascular disease mortality at ages 40–69 for 1975; the highest rates are approximately double the lowest; per 100,000 per annum for males (females) the rates are: Finland 913 (293), Scotland 857 (379), Northern Ireland 848 (369), Australia 726 (318), . . . France 380 (147), and Japan 379 (210), the order decided by the male rate.

The rankings of the IHD rates are similar to, but not exactly the same as, the rates by cardiovascular disease: Finland 673 (142), Scotland 615 (202), Northern Ireland 614 (189), Australia 534 (180), . . . France 152 (37), and Japan 69 (29). The order of cerebrovascular disease deaths is rather different: Japan 229 (127), Bulgaria 208 (171), Czechoslovakia 183 (117), Hungary 157 (98), . . . Sweden 67 (51), Denmark 61 (45), and Switzerland 61 (38).

For the male mortality rates from ischemic heart disease there have been over the 10 years, diminution in Australia, Belgium, Canada, Finland, Israel, Japan, New Zealand, Norway, and the United States, with increases in Bulgaria, Denmark, France, Ireland, Hungary, Poland, Romania, Sweden, Northern Ireland, and Yugoslavia, and no change in the remainder. When an increasing trend occurred in IHD mortality, such trend was often highest in the younger age groups.

We give in Table 25.7.2 the death rates in

TABLE 25.7.4. Mortality from ischemic heart disease—England and Wales* (deaths per 1,000,000 per annum).

Year	All	40–44	45–49	50–54	55–59	60–64	65–69	Standardized rate
				Males by age in years				
1968	3,374	950	1,773	3,233	5,537	8,610	13,492	4,775
1969	3,405	893	1,952	3,281	5,415	8,948	13,869	4,877
1970	3,392	917	1,894	3,409	5,598	8,663	13,721	4,870
1971	3,498	981	2,039	3,446	5,482	8,716	13,660	4,899
1972	3,669	951	2,138	3,659	5,765	8,987	14,176	5,096
1973	3,644	932	2,101	3,600	5,744	8,852	13,901	5,021
1974	3,670	964	2,027	3,686	5,737	8,835	13,832	5,018
1975	3,707	918	2,013	3,750	5,590	8,825	13,750	4,984
1976	3,735	856	1,885	3,529	5,769	8,908	13,609	4,930
1977	3,738	883	1,876	3,551	5,647	8,731	13,675	4,900
				Females by age in years				
1968	2,357	158	269	584	1,146	2,605	5,193	1,326
1969	2,335	155	285	624	1,194	2,638	5,258	1,356
1970	2,324	142	272	586	1,207	2,617	5,067	1,322
1971	2,392	137	296	624	1,227	2,543	4,961	1,314
1972	2,548	146	333	666	1,358	2,722	5,157	1,400
1973	2,563	164	365	662	1,322	2,742	5,221	1,412
1974	2,589	164	343	663	1,400	2,758	5,123	1,413
1975	2,599	147	325	672	1,367	2,644	5,114	1,385
1976	2,682	169	341	667	1,339	2,762	5,087	1,400
1977	2,635	143	325	664	1,326	2,648	4,974	1,361

*A83, ICD 410–414, 8th revision.
Data from Pisǎ and Uemura (1982).

England and Wales from all causes 1968–1977. At the ages given, there are declines of 5% to 6% for males and females. In Table 25.7.3 the mortality from all cardiovascular disease in England and Wales is given. The relative declines of mortality from these diseases are of the same order of magnitude as those from all causes. In Table 25.7.4 we give the death rates from ischemic heart disease; there seem to be no definite trends in the rates for either sex. The same conclusion can be drawn from Table 25.7.5, showing mortality from cardiovascular diseases (excluding cerebrovascular disease), except at ages 40–44 years, where the decline may be variously interpreted as being due to the waning of rheumatic diseases or the effects of new life styles in the years before 1968.

We give now some examples of the commentaries on the death rates from the cardiovascular diseases. Walker (1977) notes that the US Surgeon-General (1964) warned of the health hazards of tobacco consumption and that a few months later the American Heart Association recommended changes in the general American diet. A decline in the coronary heart disease death rates began in the same year and continued up to 1975, as the rates had behaved in the Scandinavian countries after changes in diet during World War II. Walker (1977, Table 1) shows declines in each 10-year age group during the years 1963–1975 of the order of 25% up to age 75 and around 16% at the oldest ages; similarly, there were declines in the age-specific death rates from cerebrovascular diseases during the period 1963–1975, averaging more than 25%. These were the first declines in coronary mortality in the United States.

In Dwyer and Hetzel (1980, Figures 1 and 2), are the age-standardized death rates by age and sex from coronary heart disease and hyper-

TABLE 25.7.5. Mortality from cardiovascular diseases (excluding cerebrovascular disease—England and Wales* (deaths per 1,000,000 per annum).

Year	All	40–44	45–49	50–54	55–59	60–64	65–69	Standardized rate
				Males by age in years				
1968	4,675	1,171	2,163	3,926	6,705	10,735	17,286	5,940
1969	4,682	1,125	2,371	3,987	6,598	11,121	17,755	6,072
1970	4,637	1,126	2,283	4,012	6,745	10,791	17,383	5,997
1971	4,715	1,187	2,415	4,074	6,586	10,682	17,236	5,988
1972	4,898	1,165	2,491	4,256	6,856	10,984	17,775	6,181
1973	4,820	1,136	2,447	4,189	6,797	10,719	17,241	6,048
1974	4,855	1,147	2,366	4,295	6,797	10,693	17,130	6,039
1975	4,869	1,084	2,302	4,313	6,585	10,583	17,033	5,956
1976	4,884	1,019	2,187	4,096	6,718	10,785	16,893	5,914
1977	4,823	1,039	2,150	4,096	6,569	10,451	16,735	5,822
				Females by age in years				
1968	4,149	373	608	1,110	1,943	4,007	7,690	2,141
1969	4,100	352	641	1,164	2,031	4,034	7,828	2,187
1970	4,025	344	590	1,095	1,921	3,933	7,511	2,095
1971	4,050	334	614	1,086	1,981	3,764	7,132	2,040
1972	4,247	333	630	1,143	2,120	3,978	7,367	2,133
1973	4,225	312	633	1,107	2,044	3,916	7,381	2,103
1974	4,223	325	636	1,093	2,133	3,927	7,189	2,099
1975	4,198	287	570	1,082	2,039	3,803	7,120	2,036
1976	4,273	308	591	1,054	1,981	3,948	7,018	2,038
1977	4,123	261	579	1,021	1,938	3,719	6,796	1,956

*A80–A84 and A86–A88, ICD 390–429 and 440–458, 8th revision.
Data from Piša and Uemura (1982).

tension, respectively, during the years 1950–1975; here, we quote their figures as rates per 1,000,000 per annum. For hypertension, there were declines for both the United States and Australia from just under 3,000 in 1950 to half that figure in 1975. The rate in the United Kingdom began at 2,500 in 1950 and fell to about 1,200 in 1975. For coronary heart disease, the death rates for males at ages 35–74 began to decline in the years 1966 in Australia, 1968 in the United States, and 1972 in England and Wales; the death rates for the females began to decrease at the same time. The authors believe that the changes in these three countries "correlate to some extent with life style changes, particularly in relation to diet and smoking."

For international comparisons, see also Epstein and Piša (1979), Keys (1970, 1981), Keys, et al. (1980), Levy, Rifkind, et al. (1979), Puf-

fer and Verhoestraete (1958), and Stamler (1979). For reviews of the declines in mortality, see Thom and Kannel (1981). For individual countries, see Great Britain: Dwyer and Hetzel (1980), Florey, Melia, et al. (1978), and Rose, Reid, et al. (1977). Japan and Japanese in the United States: Kagan, Harris, et al. (1974), Kato, Tillotson, et al. (1973), Robertson, Kato, Gordon, et al. (1977), and Robertson, Kato, Rhoads, et al. (1977). New Zealand: Bonita and Beaglehole (1982). Finland: Pyörälä and Valkonen (1981). Norway: Gundersen (1967). Sweden: Böttiger and Carlson (1981), Vedin, Wilhelmsson, et al. (1970), and Wilhelmsen (1981). United States (including subpopulations): Borhani (1966), Cooper, Stamler, et al. (1978), Moriyama, Krueger, et al. (1971), Phillips, Lemon and Kuzma (1978), and Wynder, Lemon, and Bross (1959), the latter two dealing with Seventh Day Adventists. For recent research, see Levy and Mosko-witz (1982), Levy, Rifkind, et al. (1979), and McCarron, Morris, et al. (1984). For sudden cardiac death, see USA/USSR Joint Symposium (1980). For bad prognosis in females, see Wenger (1985).

25.8 Cerebrovascular Disease

We study the mortality from cerebrovascular disease with the aid of the review of Ostfeld (1980). The physical effects following an occlusion of a vessel can vary considerably, according to the extent of the anastomosis of the blood vessels; thus, thrombotic occlusion of one common carotid or one internal carotid artery may produce no infarct, or one so small as to go undetected. Some occlusions of the middle cerebral artery may cause only minor disturbances of speech apprehension and production; so, changes in any motor or sensory function may be missed by incomplete clinical examinations. There are four causes of stroke: thrombosis, embolism, intracerebral hemorrhage, and subarachnoid hemorrhage. There are great variations in the signs and symptoms of each kind, and correct diagnosis requires high diagnostic skill. Coronary heart disease and thrombotic cerebrovascular disease have, in common, atherosclerosis as a leading cause, but there is difference in their age distributions, strokes tending to occur at older ages. So far, the diagnostic knowledge or technique for coronary disease is much more advanced than for stroke.

Ostfeld (1980) cites a survey of 198 deaths at ages 65–74 years from stroke: 80% were cerebral infarctions, 12% hemorrhages, 1% emboli, and 7% (actually 8%) uncertain types, including subarachnoid hemorrhages. There are large relative errors in the estimation of these latter three, and this is borne out by the figures for five surveys given by him. Ostfeld (1980, Table 1) shows that stroke incidence increases with age, is higher in males than in females, and is substantially higher in United States blacks than in United States whites.

Throughout the world, the Japanese in the United States and the United States blacks exhibit the most elevated rates. Diabetes is often a predisposing cause; cigarette smoking has no important effect; heart disease (especially hypertension, left ventricular hypertrophy, and coronary heart disease) are important predisposing causes.

During the years 1940–1976, standardized death rates from cerebrovascular disease in the United States declined steadily until 1967; after some slight discontinuities due to the introduction of the eighth revision of the ICD in 1968, the rates decreased more rapidly until 1973 and then quite steeply during 1974–1976. The rates in 1940 were highest in the nonwhite females, then nonwhite males, white males, and white females. After about 1963, the order was nonwhite males, nonwhite females, white males, and white females, and the rates had fallen by almost one-half in each of these four classes. The causes of these striking declines are obscure; possibly, diagnosis, coding practice, treatment (chiefly against hypertension), and life style all had some part to play.

Comparisons can be made between the industrialized nations of the world over the stretch 1968–1977, with the aid of Piša and Uemura (1982), from whom we have constructed Table 25.8.1, the table of age-specific mortality rates from cerebrovascular disease in England and Wales. The rates at 40–49 years have shown no marked tendency to decline; at these ages, hemorrhages from the circle of Willis may be the leading cause. At ages 60–69 years, the rates have fallen substantially, perhaps by up to a quarter of the initial rates.

25.9 Overview

It is difficult to give an account of the progress of the cardiovascular diseases from the nineteenth century to the present time, although the infective subclasses of the diseases can be described.

Rheumatic Heart Diseases. These may have been diseases new to human experience after the rise of the streptococci, which may well have been of importance only since the development of large populations or even since the development of the great hospitals. Rheumatic heart diseases were already declin-

TABLE 25.8.1. Mortality from cerebrovascular disease—England and Wales* (deaths per 1,000,000 per annum).

Year	All	40–44	45–49	50–54	55–59	60–64	65–69	Standardized rate
				Males by age in years				
1968	1,342	162	278	561	1,133	2,287	4,501	1,201
1969	1,315	148	306	585	1,141	2,208	4,410	1,188
1970	1,294	138	320	558	1,067	2,075	4,334	1,145
1971	1,308	137	300	539	993	2,081	4,194	1,110
1972	1,334	141	310	539	1,021	2,028	4,154	1,105
1973	1,300	154	298	545	1,034	1,937	4,001	1,079
1974	1,263	142	284	517	1,026	1,843	3,877	1,041
1975	1,236	146	266	501	922	1,881	3,660	999
1976	1,201	126	251	483	864	1,744	3,623	956
1977	1,163	137	278	485	870	1,691	3,444	937
				Females by age in years				
1968	1,949	146	302	501	863	1,706	3,214	922
1969	1,934	164	300	497	797	1,559	3,179	889
1970	1,926	167	316	523	811	1,550	3,098	890
1971	1,946	158	289	471	814	1,488	2,951	848
1972	1,990	155	259	491	791	1,405	2,911	826
1973	1,960	154	267	440	752	1,385	2,829	799
1974	1,924	133	273	489	707	1,395	2,739	789
1975	1,880	132	262	432	673	1,293	2,568	737
1976	1,853	142	251	424	698	1,254	2,497	726
1977	1,806	143	247	416	671	1,261	2,399	710

*A85, ICD 430–438, 8th revision.
Data from Piša and Uemura (1982).

ing in the 1930s, but the coming of the sulfonamides, chemotherapy, and the antibiotics greatly reduced their importance.

Subacute Bacterial Endocarditis. This disease was often secondary to rheumatic heart disease or a congenital valve defect; it has been controlled by effective therapy.

Cardiovascular and Neurological Syphilis. These diseases are not included in the cardiovascular diseases by the rules of the ICD and are discussed in our chapter 17. Chemotherapy and antibiotics have been the causes of declines in the various syphilitic syndromes.

Cerebrovascular Diseases. Here again, it has been difficult to give long series and to show whether there have been interesting long-term trends.

Atherosclerosis, lipids, diet, hypertension, salt, tobacco, and life style have all been important factors as we have seen above in §§25.3 to 25.5. Other factors are no doubt important, but comparisons between subpopulations or populations of countries have been made difficult by the high correlations between the variables. It is possible that, with changes of life style, including diet and tobacco consumption, the incidence of cardiovascular disease became heavy in the 1930s and perhaps increased into the 1960s. There is evidence that it had begun to decrease in the 1970s in some countries, with declines of more than 30% in the 10 years, 1972–1982, but the results are not entirely free of controversy. In the popularizations of the problems, the sizes of the increases have been greatly exaggerated by the use of ratios of cardiovascular to all deaths, in which case the declines in the death rates from infective diseases give the appearance of an increase in the importance of the cardiovascular diseases.

Chapter 26
Respiratory Diseases

26.1 Introduction

Class 8. ICD 460–519. The class of Disease of the Respiratory System of the ICD includes the infective and inflammatory diseases of the nose and throat, lungs, pleura, the respiratory passages generally, and the mediastinum, not listed elsewhere as specific infective diseases, influenza, and certain noninfective diseases. The class does not, for example, include disease due to tuberculosis or pertussis; it does not include the cancers and lesions secondary to cardiovascular disease. The diseases included may be characterized briefly as asthma, the pneumoconioses, and the nonspecific infections of the respiratory system, the pneumonias and bronchopneumonia. Even asthma, which is fundamentally not infective, will often have an infective component either as a provoking agent or a complication. There has been some loss of the deaths from pneumoconiosis, since if tuberculosis is present at the time of death, it will be preferred, according to the rules, as the cause of death. Comparisons show that the diseases assigned to this class have remained constant over the various revisions. The deaths over the years before 1950 were almost entirely due to infections.

In this monograph, as in Table 26.1.1, and in Lancaster (1953c), we have taken influenza deaths out of the class of respiratory disease and included them in the totals for "infective diseases." To fix the ideas, we give as Table 26.1.1 the progress of the age-specific death rates from these residual causes in Australia over the 8 decades of this century, which can be taken to be lobar pneumonia and pneumonia unspecified, since influenza has been removed. In §41.3 we also give the rates standardized on to several populations. For a particular epoch, there are relatively high death rates in infancy and early childhood, then a minimum at ages 5 to 14 years, followed by a steady rise throughout life. For a fixed age group, declines in the rates become evident shortly after 1920. For some international comparisons, see Bouvier and Guidevaux (1979), the value of which is greatly reduced by the lack of proper information by age.

26.2 Miscellaneous Respiratory Diseases

Acute Respiratory Infections. ICD 460–466. Exclusions: diphtheria (032), whooping cough (033), streptococcal sore throat and scarlatina (034), pneumonia and influenza (480–487), and some other specific diseases.

Various bacteria and viruses are capable of attacking the mucosa of the upper respiratory tract, which responds by the inflammatory process, so there may be swelling, surface secretion, sneezing, catarrh in some degree, and symptoms depending on the part of the tract affected. It is now known that these acute infections are caused largely by rhinoviruses, adenoviruses, and coronaviruses (Stott and Garwes, 1984). For administrative purposes the physician is led to diagnose rhinitis, pharyngitis, laryngitis, tracheitis, and bronchitis, or

TABLE 26.1.1. Mortality rates in Australia from diseases of the respiratory system.[*][†]

Age in years	0–4	5–14	15–24	25–34	35–44	45–54	55–64	65–74	75+
	Males								
1908–1910	2,662	161	218	335	719	1,290	2,475	6,794	17,249
1911–1920	2,781	173	248	424	817	1,501	2,750	6,062	19,165
1921–1930	2,458	146	198	289	625	1,357	2,399	5,115	16,597
1931–1940	1,833	130	150	204	432	913	2,061	4,189	13,597
1941–1950	1,250	69	72	90	199	548	1,442	3,585	11,797
1951–1960	692	44	45	60	137	419	1,429	3,859	12,419
1961–1970	565	27	31	43	114	375	1,445	4,713	14,330
1971–1980	289	19	29	37	91	341	1,234	4,259	14,319
	Females								
1908–1910	2,112	147	158	262	462	715	1,431	5,307	15,256
1911–1920	2,273	159	175	297	437	678	1,444	4,719	16,473
1921–1930	2,028	137	155	244	400	577	1,203	3,719	14,973
1931–1940	1,487	116	125	190	296	471	947	2,765	11,248
1941–1950	1,031	69	82	103	165	318	646	1,982	9,570
1951–1960	585	42	52	67	111	192	445	1,286	7,158
1961–1970	456	25	24	40	82	169	372	1,061	5,979
1971–1980	216	14	24	33	71	192	437	1,042	4,954
	Masculinity rates[‡]								
1908–1910	126	110	138	128	156	180	173	128	113
1911–1920	122	109	142	143	187	221	190	128	116
1921–1930	121	107	128	118	156	235	199	138	111
1931–1940	123	112	120	107	146	194	218	152	121
1941–1950	121	100	88	87	121	172	223	181	123
1951–1960	118	105	87	90	123	218	321	300	173
1961–1970	124	108	129	107	139	222	388	444	240
1971–1980	134	136	121	112	128	178	282	409	289

*Deaths per 1,000,000 per annum.
†Excluding influenza.
‡100 × (male death rates)/(female death rates).
From Lancaster and Gordon (1987).

even upper respiratory tract infections; but, of course, these terms give no hint as to the etiology. There is a prospect of treatment by new antiviral agents or by vaccination with killed or attenuated strains, but probably these infections will remain a mere nuisance except in special cases, such as in the London fog (Logan, 1956) or hospital cross infections (Hall, 1983).

Other Disease of the Upper Respiratory Tract. ICD 470–478. The rubrics of this subclass cover conditions usually associated with little mortality. Some are associated with infections of the nasal sinuses although those of the

mastoid sinus are referred to ICD 383. The few diseases in this group likely to cause death are usually due to secondary bacterial invaders. For the etiology of diseases in this section, see J.W.G. Smith (1984b) and G. Smith (1984). For diseases caused in isolated communities, see Tyrrell (1977).

26.3 Pneumonia

The mortality due to Diseases of the Respiratory System, as defined by the ICD, is effectively due to pneumonia, once influenza has been transferred to the class of Infectious and Parasitic Dieases. Pneumonia of the earlier revisions of the ICD was equivalent to lobar pneumonia and pneumonia unspecified of the later revisions. It is convenient to run through the etiology in the order of the ICD.

Pneumonia due to Viruses Other than Influenza. ICD 480. The virus diseases mentioned in §26.2 rarely go on to pneumonia and the same applies to the parainfluenza virus (Sellers, 1984c), except perhaps when the patient is incompetent immunologically, as in the elderly or chronically ill.

Pneumococcal and Other Bacterial Pneumonia. ICD 481 and 482. These two rubrics cover the disease known as primary lobar pneumonia. This is a classical disease, characterized by acute onset, with fever often accompanied by rigor, a cough with bloody sputum, and pain in the chest. In favorable cases the course is usually resolved in the dramatic change known as crisis, occurring 5 to 10 days after the onset, whereby there is a sudden reduction of temperature together with great improvement in the general condition of the patient. In unfavorable cases such resolution may not occur and death may follow from local complications such as lung abscess, bronchiectasis, empyema, and pericarditis or, after spread via the blood to other organs, from meningitis, endocarditis or other septic lesion, or finally from exhaustion. Pathologically, pneumonia is an inflammation of the lung with outpouring of fluid into the lung substance filling the alveoli and bronchioles, leading to a consolidation in one or more lobes of the lungs, detectable by the well-known classical signs, by radiology, or by ultrasound methods.

It has been found that in about 90% of cases of lobar pneumonia occurring in or being admitted to hospitals, the causal organism is *Str. pneumoniae*, to which we refer as the pneumococcus. Moreover, at least 85 distinct types have been described; of these, type 3 is usually regarded as the most lethal, and the types of low number tend to occur more frequently than those of high number. Many of these types were often first described after being obtained from healthy carriers; indeed, even type 3 is so obtained. So, we consider what factors are associated with the incidence of the disease and with high case fatalities.

Some attacks seem to be associated with the gathering together of army recruits or South African negro miners, who may have had no previous experience of the types; similarly, the incidence may be high during famine, as in §22.10; but the reasons for the disease appearing, rather than the new pneumococcus becoming a harmless member of the nasopharyngeal flora, are not at all clear. More definite are the factors that may be especially important for high case fatalities. Osler (1897a) states that very few fatal cases occurred in previously robust, healthy adults; thus, the case fatality in over 40,000 cases occurring in troops of the German army was only 3.6%; the case fatalities varied among children in various series from 1.9% to 3.3%; in the elderly, however, Osler cites case fatalities of 50% to 60%; Osler says "So fatal is it that to die of pneumonia in this country is said to be the natural end of elderly people"; other bad prognostic features were debilitation by other diseases or by poor food or alcoholism. For the admissions to hospital in the United States and England, Osler (1897a) obtained case fatalities, all ranging between 25% to 38%. The severity of the toxemia is an important element in the outcome of the disease, and death may occur with the consolidation of a single lobe. It has, since Osler's time, been determined that the striking clinical event known as the crisis is due to the body's immune system overcoming the toxic substances produced by the pneumococcus.

As to the seriousness of lobar pneumonia, Osler (1899) wrote "among diseases there is not one which requires to be more fully and carefully prevented than pneumonia—the most common as well as the most serious acute infection of this country, with a mortality exceeding that of all the other acute fevers put together, measles, scarlet fever, diphtheria, whooping cough, typhoid fever and dysentery." Thus, Osler regarded pneumonia as the "captain of the men of death" as he was later to write in the fourth edition of his famous textbook of medicine in 1901, and eminently worthy to be studied by his students (Osler, 1897b).

As to treatment, serum treatment was early attempted but a great difficulty was the multiplicity of strains; the sulfonamides were shown to be effective in 1938, but they were super-seded by antibiotics, especially the penicillins, as soon as they became freely available. Strains of pneumococci resistant to the penicillins and some other antibiotics have been reported. Austrian (1975), quoting the above remarks of Osler, states that, notwithstanding the 4 decades of the use of antimicrobial drugs, there is little to indicate any decline in the attack rates; indeed, evidence from several hospitals shows that as many patients are being admitted with bacteremic pneumococcal pneumonia in the early 1970s as were admitted 40 years earlier. Austrian (1975) also believes that the decline in the annual number of deaths from pneumonia in the United States has been disappointing; many deaths in the latest epoch have resulted from irreversible injury to the patient prior to the commencement of specific anti-pneumococcal therapy. Austrian and Gold (1964) report case fatality rates of 17%, or 57 deaths in 338 cases, among those treated with bactericidal drugs; they estimate conservatively that there were in the early 1960s in the United States "150,000 to 300,000 cases of pneumococcal pneumonia per annum, a fourth to a third of which are accompanied by bacteremia." They further estimate that 9,000 to 18,000 deaths have occurred from infections with a certain half dozen of the pneumococcal types. The case fatality rate varies with the pneumococcal type. Thus, with type 3 pneumococcus in bacteremic cases it is 51%, whereas with type 1 it is 8%. These authors do not think that an agent much more effective than penicillin will be found. Case fatalities in bacteremic pneumonia, moreover, vary considerably with age; thus, for cases treated with penicillin, there are 2 deaths out of 36 cases at ages 12–29 years, or 6%, 11 deaths out of 142 cases at ages 30–49 years, or 8%, and 44 deaths out of 160 cases at ages over 50, or 27.5%, the experience being in the years immediately prior to 1964. In 1929–1935 the corresponding case fatality rates were 79 out of 120, or 66%, 292 out of 391, or 74%, and 322 out of 345, or 93%. No controls, contemporary with the treated cases, could be used for obvious ethical reasons. It seems safe to agree with the authors that therapy was effective and that age has a considerable effect on prognosis as measured by the case fatality rate. It should be noted that all cases in the therapeutics series were bacteremic before entry into the trials. Austrian (1968) gives the current status of bacterial pneumonia as seen in the United States in the late 1960s.

Bacteremia is common in the early stages but is of bad prognosis if it persists. J.W.G. Smith (1984b) states that 80% to 90% of cases of lobar pneumonia are caused by the pneumococcus *Str. pneumoniae*, and the remainder by a variety of organisms such as *Str. pyogenes*, *Staph. aureus*, *Haemophilus influenzae*, and *Klebsiella pneumoniae* (Friedländer's bacillus). The members of the species *Str. pneumoniae* can be grouped into over 85 numbered types by serological methods, of which most of the virulent strains have a number less than 24, and of which type 3 is usually regarded as the most lethal.

Of other species, the *Staphylococcus aureus* and *Klebsiella pneumoniae* (Friedländer's bacillus) are possibly the most lethal, with case fatality rates untreated of more than 70%. The foregoing and certain Gram-negative bacilli of the genera, *Pseudomonas*, *Escherichia*, and *Serratia*, among others, give rise to dangerous nosocomial respiratory infections and, what is worse, are often drug resistant.

Therapeutic problems remain. Since case fatalities of pneumonia are still not negligible, it is possible to manufacture vaccine against the capsular polysacharides, although there are many relevant types, see Austrian (1977). Untreated *Klebsiella* pneumonia has a very high case fatality rate that in some treated series may reach 50%. Legionnaires' disease is associated with high case fatalities of 15%–20%.

For examples of pneumonia complicating the treatment of fractures, see Greenwood and Candy (1911). For pneumonia in the developing world, see §44.4. For a popularization, see Austrian (1985).

26.4 Other Respiratory Diseases

The remaining diseases in the respiratory class, ICD 490–519, can be found detailed in the ICD manual. Some points of interest are mentioned.

Bronchitis, Acute and Chronic. ICD 490, 491

These diseases are often associated with asthma. By definition, except perhaps in children, they will not be associated with much mortality.

Emphysema. ICD 492

Emphysema is usually secondary to some other disease so there are many exclusions. Two great causes are pneumoconiosis and cigarette smoking. Few deaths will be referred to this rubric. See §25.4.

Asthma. ICD 493

This disease has a large genetic component and is often complicated by chronic bronchitis. Deaths that are certified as being due to an infective complication of asthma will be assigned by the statistician to this rubric. Cardiac asthma will be classified however with deaths of the cardiovascular system. There has been increasing interest in the etiology and the mortality from bronchial asthma. When the mortality from infectious diseases and the pneumonias was high, asthma as a cause of mortality tended to be rather underestimated, and it is possible that deaths in childhood, formerly assigned to the pneumonias, were at least partly due to this cause. At the younger ages there has been some tendency for the death rates from asthma to increase since 1940. This has occasioned some concern among clinicians and its cause remains obscure. Gandevia (1968) points out that the increases in mortality have been particularly evident over the years 1964 to 1966 in males and in the younger age groups in Australia; increases had been observed earlier in England about 1960 according to Speizer, Doll, and Heaf (1968). Gandevia (1968) believes that the increase in mortality may be due to changing methods of therapy; the adrenalinelike substances in pressurized aerosols are suspect, but the evidence is not yet convincing.

From an evolutionary point of view, "asthma" genes appear to have a high frequency in the population. Possibly this is an example of a polymorphism, the implications of which have

not yet been explored. See also Bernstein (1981).

Bronchiectasis. ICD 494

Bronchiectasis can be a late complication of pertussis or measles, in particular, among the infections and of operations such as tooth extraction. This disease was not allotted any separate rubric until the seventh revision of the International Classification, so that it cannot be traced through as a cause of mortality. There are clinical grounds for believing that the disease is now less common than formerly. Explanations are possibly the fall in the incidence of pertussis and measles, which in earlier days would often attack children, weakened by other diseases or unsatisfactory care, and the more careful attention to surgical detail during the extraction of teeth under anesthesia or the removal of foreign bodies. Some case of bronchiectasis can, of course, be detected early by a careful diagnosis of the cause of residual coughs after infections in young people and be treated and hence no longer proceed on to the advanced forms of the disease. See Lancaster (1952a).

Extrinsic Allergic Alveolitis, ICD 495, and Chronic Airways Obstruction, ICD 496

These are of little interest. See Melia and Swan (1986) for statistics of bronchitis, asthma, and emphysema.

Pneumoconiosis. ICD 500–508

This is group of diseases characterized by the deposition of inhaled particulate matter in the substance of the lung for example, coal dust in anthracosis, fine sandy or rocky particles in silicosis, and asbestos in asbestosis. Silicosis is often associated with tuberculosis; anthracosis is not associated with tuberculosis and appears to be relatively unimportant. Asbestosis, due to the inhalation of certain fibrous silicates, especially crocidolite, was first established as a diffuse pulmonary fibrosis in 1900. Owing to the long latent period, the establishment of asbestos as a cause of cancer was delayed until its use had been greatly extended in shipbuilding and sound proofing in houses; it is now known to be especially dangerous when associated with cigarette smoking. Although public health legislation in many countries has greatly reduced the occupational risks from the inhalation of the dusts mentioned, it is difficult to make proper comparisons of the mortality caused by them over the decades. See also §47.1 for the Cornish metal miners.

The reader is referred to the texts of Weill and Turner-Warwick (1981), Gee, Morgan, and Brooks (1984), and Brooks, Lockey, and Harber (1981) for occupational lung diseases. In the latter volume, there are chapters: asbestos, Casey, Rom, and Moatamed (1981); nonasbestos fibrous minerals, Lockey (1981); nonfibrous minerals, Lapp (1981); and irritant gases, Summer and Haponik (1981). See also for tobacco smoke, Weill and Diem (1978) and for industrial pulmonary disease in Great Britain, Meiklejohn (1960).

Other Diseases of the Respiratory System. ICD 510–519

Most of the terms covered here are unimportant or secondary to more important diseases. For chronic respiratory disease in the United States, see Moriyama (1966).

Chapter 27
Digestive Diseases

27.1 Introduction

ICD 520–579. Diseases of the Digestive System. ICD 520–529, diseases of the oral cavity, salivary glands, and jaws, and ICD 530, diseases of the esophagus, may be omitted from a mortality survey without important numerical loss.

A group of diseases can be followed through from the earlier revisions of the ICD up to the ninth revision by the following considerations. This class has not included typhoid, dysentery, or tuberculosis in any revision; but it has included diarrhea and enteritis, hookworm, and hydatid disease. These are clearly more logically and conveniently classed with the other infective diseases. This policy was adopted by Lancaster (1956a) and continued, so that the death rates in Table 27.1.1 are roughly comparable over the epochs considered. However, some deaths of an ill-defined cause still remained in the class in the earlier revisions; thus, in Australia for the epoch 1911 to 1920, there were 3,014 deaths at ages under 5 years, with "hernia, intestinal obstruction" yielding 36.7% of the deaths, "other diseases of the stomach," 36.2%, "diseases of the pharynx," 5.9%, and "simple peritonitis," 4.7%. It appears probable that many of these latter three rubrics were infections of the digestive tract, such as gastroenteritis and upper respiratory tract infections.

We can regard the progress of mortality in these diseases of the digestive system as a test of the value of surgery in reducing mortality, for in a modern general hospital much of the surgical effort goes into their treatment. Ranked as to the efficiency of surgical treatment, these diseases hold an intermediate position between accidents and the cancers, for although surgical techniques have improved and there have been substantial declines in mortality from appendicitis, the declines in the mortality from peptic ulcer and gallbladder disease have not been great, relative either to their initial values in 1908–1910 or to the total decline in mortality.

In Table 27.1.1 are given the death rates by age and sex for the diseases of the digestive system, as defined by the ICD. It is evident that there have been declines at all ages, although at the ages older than 75 years, the decline is less marked.

Rubrics in this class associated with serious mortality rates are treated in later sections.

27.2 Dietary Fiber and Diseases of the Digestive System

Recent work, as presented in Burkitt (1973b), Burkitt and Trowell (1975), Trowell and Burkitt (1981a), and Spiller and Kay (1980), for example, and also in §§20.10 and 22.14, has made it evident that nutrition, especially the amount of fiber in the diet, plays an important role in the etiology of the diseases of the digestive system. Other references are included in later sections of this chapter. Burkitt (1981) and Brodribb (1980) have reviewed the importance of dietary fiber for surgical diseases of

TABLE 27.1.1. Mortality rates in Australia from diseases of the digestive system.*

Age in years	0–4	5–14	15–24	25–34	35–44	45–54	55–64	65–74	75+
					Males				
1908–1910	432	186	194	236	424	781	1,378	2,746	3,962
1911–1920	616	140	188	237	408	764	1,264	2,030	3,692
1921–1930	440	115	189	213	391	736	1,253	1,830	3,086
1931–1940	309	111	157	191	380	727	1,186	1,911	2,930
1941–1950	241	75	67	96	232	592	1,128	1,814	3,105
1951–1960	144	20	27	55	153	413	915	1,681	3,293
1961–1970	199	12	16	34	129	338	668	1,342	3,015
1971–1980	38	4	9	33	148	441	713	1,147	2,530
					Females				
1908–1910	318	157	186	268	408	682	1,297	2,402	3,817
1911–1920	456	154	156	239	383	616	1,025	2,004	3,888
1921–1930	327	120	123	192	316	544	900	1,607	3,125
1931–1940	231	96	92	146	243	450	761	1,336	2,794
1941–1950	162	63	63	90	169	337	609	1,083	2,323
1951–1960	98	20	29	50	115	230	468	904	2,284
1961–1970	157	11	17	28	74	185	317	730	2,187
1971–1980	31	3	8	20	64	175	332	586	1,893

*Deaths per 1,000,000 per annum.
From Lancaster and Gordon (1987).

the large bowel and diverticulosis. For the role of bacteria in the inflammatory diseases of this group, namely, appendicitis, cholecystitis, and peritonitis, see Parker (1984a).

27.3 Peptic Ulceration

ICD 531, gastric ulcer; 532, duodenal ulcer; 533, peptic ulcer, site unspecified.

Peptic ulceration occurs in the mucosal lining of those parts of the digestive tract containing acid and pepsin. The lesions are called erosions if they do not extend through the muscular layer and ulcers if they do. Acute ulcerations are erosions, chronic lesions are ulcers. In populations with western-style diets, there is high masculinity in the incidence of duodenal ulcer and higher still in that of gastric ulcer. The etiology is not fully understood. Genetic factors have been determined; smoking is definitely a determining factor in some cases; diet has not been fully established as a factor; some drugs, especially aspirin, have been incriminated. About 80% of all peptic ulcers are duodenal, and about 10% of persons suffer from duodenal ulcers during their life on a western-style diet. Leading causes of death are hemorrhage and perforation into the peritoneal cavity.

The age-specific death rates for Australia from peptic ulcer are given in Table 27.3.1. Few deaths occur before the age of 25 years. The masculinities of the death rates are high and have been rising. There have also been increases in the death rates at ages above 65 years.

27.4 Appendicitis

ICD 540–543.

The proximate precipitating cause for an attack of acute appendicitis seems usually to be a fecalith within, or some obstruction of, the appendiceal lumen. Bacterial invasion of the walls of the appendix follows. The appendix becomes red and swollen, and the overlying coat (or peritoneum) becomes inflamed, thus, giving rise to characteristic symptoms. In a se-

TABLE 27.3.1. Mortality rates in Australia from peptic ulceration.*

Age in years	0–4	5–14	15–24	25–34	35–44	45–54	55–64	65–74	75+	All Ages
					Males					
1908–1910	0	2	6	10	25	57	78	92	143	20
1911–1920	3	1	5	19	39	63	81	84	130	26
1921–1930	3	0	9	37	94	160	209	242	207	65
1931–1940	3	0	6	33	118	247	374	461	558	111
1941–1950	1	0	2	18	70	209	408	590	795	122
1951–1960	1	0	3	10	45	136	318	613	1,123	106
1961–1970	1	0	1	7	28	80	195	420	988	73
1971–1980	1	0	1	4	15	58	130	307	866	56
					Females					
1908–1910	3	1	29	31	42	51	47	56	76	26
1911–1920	3	1	12	22	38	28	46	72	87	21
1921–1930	3	1	5	12	29	54	85	120	143	25
1931–1940	2	1	3	8	21	43	88	154	234	29
1941–1950	1	1	2	7	19	33	63	149	289	30
1951–1960	2	0	3	10	23	40	67	141	362	36
1961–1970	0	1	1	5	14	32	47	120	396	32
1971–1980	0	0	0	1	7	18	49	112	447	33

*Deaths per 1,000,000 per annum.
Data from Australian Bureau of Statistics.

vere attack, the inflammation leads to localized gangrene of the wall of the appendix and the formation of a local abscess or general peritonitis.

There have been marked variations in the incidence of acute appendicitis over time and place. According to Short (1920–1921) there had been abscesses in the right iliac fossa reported 33 times between 1820 and 1840 and 102 times between 1840 and 1860, widely distributed in Europe and North America. Short (1920–1921) contrasted the high incidence of appendicitis in well-to-do boys at an English boarding school with the lower incidence in an orphanage. He made similar comparisons between Romanian urban and rural populations. He particularly blamed the popularization of white flour, without, however, stressing its low fiber content. Many similar comparisons have been made by other authors. Burkitt (1975b) gives a sequence of events that would appear consistent with the hypothesis that high fiber diet protects against appendicitis; in particular, with these high fiber diets, fecaliths (i.e., hard concretions in the colon) do not form,

and occlusion of the lumen of the appendix, which is associated with fecaliths, does not occur.

The distribution of appendicitis is markedly affected by geography. It has its highest incidence in Europe, North America, and in countries with the general European food customs such as Australia, New Zealand, and South Africa. On the other hand, as Burkitt (1975b) points out, appendicitis is still very rare in rural Africa; however, in urban areas of Africa in which western customs have been largely adopted, the incidence is rising. The incidence is also high in the negro population of the northern United States, but in the southern States it is lower in the negroes than in the whites. Increased incidence was also noted in African troops provided with European food in World War II.

The mortality rates from appendicitis in Australia are given in Table 27.4.1. There have been declines in the rates at all ages younger than 75 years. For the rates considered in an epoch, there are local maxima for males at ages 15 to 24 years in all epochs and for females at

TABLE 27.4.1. Mortality rates in Australia from appendicitis.*

Age in years	0–4	5–14	15–24	25–34	35–44	45–54	55–64	65–74	75+	All Ages
					Males					
1908–1910	19	105	113	81	70	83	93	97	77	85
1911–1920	19	70	108	86	87	100	117	100	93	83
1921–1930	32	63	110	83	91	120	145	145	137	91
1931–1940	46	64	101	86	97	130	165	207	188	102
1941–1950	32	32	38	35	47	71	104	145	169	55
1951–1960	11	9	10	11	12	24	39	75	112	20
1961–1970	4	3	3	3	4	9	17	37	84	9
1971–1980	1	1	1	1	2	3	7	17	42	4
					Females					
1908–1910	22	72	79	64	53	63	58	84	51	62
1911–1920	17	70	67	54	55	72	52	79	62	58
1921–1930	21	57	56	51	54	77	79	94	85	57
1931–1940	33	49	43	39	40	70	100	109	140	55
1941–1950	18	28	24	18	19	31	50	70	112	31
1951–1960	5	10	8	5	7	8	19	34	70	12
1961–1970	3	3	3	2	2	4	6	15	48	6
1971–1980	1	1	1	1	1	2	4	10	29	3

*Deaths per 1,000,000 per annum.
Data from Australian Bureau of Statistics.

the same ages or at ages 5 to 14 years. It can be assumed that incidence rates are high at ages 10 to 24 years.

Among some clinical surveys, Lie (1963) cites case fatality rates of 150 (simple acute appendicitis), 765 (acute appendicitis with general peritonitis), and 81 (acute appendicitis with abscess formation) per 1,000 in London Hospital experience in 1900–1904; and corresponding rates of 17, 200, and 33 per 1,000 in 1912–1913; whereas Officer Brown is cited with rates of 14, 164, and 65 in Melbourne, Australia, in 1926–1930. Lie (1963) also cites later English experience with further declines in the case fatality rates, which indeed approached the rates of minor operations under anesthetic. Peltokallio and Tykkä (1981) give case fatality rates for all acute appendicitis in Finland per 1,000 as 44.4 in 1920–1930, 5.6 in 1951–1955, 2.6 in 1953–1969, and 2.9 in 1969–1974. For the same periods, the case fatality rates for acute (but not perforative) and for perforative cases were 10.4 and 238.8, 0.9 and 32.7, 1.1 and 13.6, and 1.4 and 9.1. The ratio of the number of acute to the number of perfora-

tive cases rose over the years studied and was approximately 7 to 1. Prognosis depended almost entirely on the presence of perforation, and the ensuing disease was more fatal to the elderly.

The case fatality rates and the population mortality rates can be interpreted as follows. Appendicitis can be regarded as a bacterial infection following the obstruction or occlusion of the appendiceal lumen by a fecalith. Only after the adoption of low fiber diets has appendicitis been a serious cause of mortality. In the western world the incidence of the disease possibly reached its maximum by 1910. Since that time, operative and diagnostic methods have succeeded in reducing the case fatality rates dramatically and, in the absence of a further rise in incidence, the population mortality rates. Little interest has been shown in attacking the underlying dietary cause. It seems evident that appendicitis in a modern, developed country could be reduced to a trivial cause of mortality.

For further statistics, see Young and Russell (1939).

27.5 Miscellaneous Diseases of the Abdominal Cavity

ICD 550–553, hernia of abdominal cavity; 555–558, noninfective enteritis and colitis; 560–569, other diseases of intestines.

The age-specific death rates from hernia and intestinal obstruction are given in Lancaster (1956a, Table 6). There is a marked masculinity at ages 0 to 4 years in every decade, owing to the predominance of inguinal hernias. Masculinity is less marked at the older ages. There have been declines in the mortality at all ages.

For diverticulosis and colon dysfunction, see Eastwood, Brydon, and Tadesse (1980), Painter and Burkitt (1975), Spiller and Amen (1976), and Spiller and Kay (1980).

27.6 Hepatitis and Cirrhosis of the Liver

ICD 570, acute and subacute necrosis of the liver; 571, chronic liver disease and cirrhosis; 572, liver abscess and sequelae of chronic liver diseases; 573, other diseases of the liver; note ICD 275, hemochromatosis.

In §24.2 some mention has been made of pathological changes induced by excessive alcohol intake and of these, liver disease in important. We can regard ICD 570 and 571 as different stages of one disease; acute changes in the liver take place after excessive intake of alcohol, and if these episodes are frequent there is permanent damage, with extensive scarring and destruction of cells resulting in cirrhosis. Williams and Davis (1977) point out that the mortality rate from cirrhosis is from 7 to 13 times higher in alcoholics than in those who do not drink to excess. Among alcoholics, more lesions are seen in the liver. Schmidt (1977, Table 1) shows that there is great variation between countries in the death rates associated with cirrhosis, 57 per 1,000,000 per annum in England and Wales and 572 per 1,000,000 in France. His Table 2 shows great increases over time in the rates, and his Table 3, great preponderance of the male rates. His Table 9 shows that the death rates of persons over age 27 in Ontario, Canada, from cirrhosis, cancer of the lung, and suicide were, respec-

tively, 76, 192, and 136 in 1950 and 214, 510, and 212 per 1,000,000 per annum in 1972. His Figure 8 shows that cirrhosis deaths and the consumption of alcohol per capita over the years 1954–1973 in the United Kingdom have a correlation of 0.98, very high indeed, See also Masse, Juillan, and Chisloup (1976).

For hemochromatosis, see Valberg and Ghent (1985). Note Hepatitis B virus as a cause of cirrhosis (see §13.1).

27.7 Gallbladder and Related Diseases

ICD 574, cholelithiasis; 575, other disorders of the gallbladder, principally cholecystitis, and other pathological conditions arising from cholelithiasis; 576, other disorders of the biliary tract, not already included; 579, sprue.

It is now generally accepted that cholelithiasis is the fundamental disease and that the predominant constituent of gallstones in the western world is cholesterol. Acute cholecystitis is to be regarded as a local infection, usually *Esch. coli* and sometimes *Streptococci*, according to Parker (1984a, f), set up as a result of the trauma caused by the stones, such as damage to the epithelium of the gallbladder and the cystic (i.e., gallbladder) duct by the spasm of the muscles pushing the stone and by the effective blocking of the cystic duct by stones.

Routine autopsy statistics show that gallstones had formed in 70% of women and 35% of men by the age of 70 years in Sweden, according to N.H. Sternby (cited by Heaton, 1975). Similar, but less spectacular, statistics are available from other western countries. It seems reasonable to believe that the incidence of cholelithiasis increased in any population with increasing urbanization. Thus, autopsy incidence of gallstones in Finland was 0.2% in 1879. Further, the condition believed to be a disease of sedentary persons by Osler (1921) has now spread to all classes of the western urbanized populations. Among the developing countries, cholesterol stones are a rarity in Africa and in Asia; in India, they have been diagnosed far more often in the upper classes and this has been the case in many other countries. In summary, Heaton (1975) notes that cholelithiasis is essentially a disease of modern western civilization, that there has been an increasing incidence since World War II, and in some western countries the probability of gallstones having formed during the lifetime of a woman is greater than one-half.

See also Holland and Heaton (1972) and Heaton (1981). For the epidemiology of chronic alimentary disease, see Langman (1979).

ICD 579 Sprue. Tropical sprue is a syndrome among residents or visitors to the tropics, characterized by chronic diarrhea and other debilitating symptoms together with malabsorption. There is no clear evidence on causative factors or treatment. See Baker (1982).

Chapter 28
Genitourinary Diseases

28.1 Nephritis

Only the subclass, Nephritis, nephrotic syndrome, and nephrosis, ICD 580–589, provides an important contribution to mortality. Other subclasses contain diseases of the urinary system, 590–599; male genital organs, 600–608; the breast, 610–611; and inflammatory and other diseases of the female pelvic organs, 614–616 and 617–629.

ICD 580–589. The rubrics in this subclass refer to stages in glomerulonephritis. Typically, there is an attack in childhood or early adult life of pharyngitis due to *Streptococcus pyogenes* type A, followed in 1–4 weeks, but usually in 10–14 days, by an acute nephritis, in which the symptoms and signs may include malaise, anorexia, headache, proteinuria, hematuria, oliguria, edema of feet and ankles, and high blood pressure. This acute attack may clear up either immediately or after several further attacks or it may lead on to a nephrotic stage characterized by heavy proteinuria, hypoalbuminemia, hypercholesterolemia, and edema as leading signs before hypertension has set in; this stage may lead on to chronic nephritis and complete renal failure; the patient is now pale and sallow, easily fatigued, suffers anorexia and nausea, has edema, nitrogen retention and uremia, and other signs and symptoms of the nephrotic stage. Hypertension is almost invariable, leading to cardiovascular disease. See Kerr (1977) for a description of the disease and Parker (1978, 1984c) for its bacteriology.

There have always been difficulties about the classification of the nephritides, for which see Greenwood and Russell (1937), and they are not yet resolved. Moreover, in the past 50 years, there have been suggestions that ascending infections, namely pyelonephritis, can give a histological picture indistinguishable from the classical glomerulonephritis. See Witting (1976).

The association of chronic nephritis and hypertension led to the concept of cardiorenal disease; many death certificates once assigned to the renal system would, according to more recent revisions of the rules, now be assigned to the class of cardiovascular diseases. This is a feature that has rendered difficult any accurate comparisons of either genitourinary or cardiovascular disease incidences over time. See §25.1. We have used the idea of a composite class containing classes 5, 6, 7, 10, and 16 for making comparisons over epochs especially at the older ages, for which see chapter 36.

28.2 Other Genitourinary Diseases

ICD 590–599. The diseases in ICD 590 are infections of the lower urinary tract that may be associated with an infection spreading into the kidney itself. The leading infecting organisms usually come from the alimentary canal, for example, *Escherichia coli* or other Gram-negative bacillus. We have noted earlier that such an ascending infection can cause a nephritis with symptoms indistinguishable from glomerulonephritis. Other rubrics in this sub-

TABLE 28.1.1. Mortality rates in Australia from diseases of the genitourinary system.*

Age in years	0–4	5–14	15–24	25–34	35–44	45–54	55–64	65–74	75+
				Males					
1908–1910	112	36	122	169	474	1,022	2,371	5,711	11,952
1911–1920	137	46	133	231	417	1,055	2,350	5,444	12,474
1921–1930	103	45	117	196	362	863	2,100	5,269	12,991
1931–1940	104	28	99	160	318	764	1,841	4,938	14,325
1941–1950	65	33	66	134	227	576	1,379	3,810	12,614
1951–1960	33	13	40	71	130	261	599	1,694	6,394
1961–1970	19	5	18	34	66	158	380	1,087	4,099
1971–1980	8	2	5	10	24	69	178	568	2,586
				Females					
1908–1910	109	44	159	297	508	787	1,463	2,508	3,438
1911–1920	99	48	174	308	429	717	1,279	2,322	3,888
1921–1930	103	43	159	297	470	728	1,306	2,833	5,300
1931–1940	93	42	138	250	439	703	1,215	2,928	6,722
1941–1950	41	31	71	164	311	546	857	1,946	5,569
1951–1960	24	15	31	67	155	257	362	653	1,675
1961–1970	12	7	13	42	114	234	360	630	1,641
1971–1980	6	2	5	11	46	113	214	396	1,362

*Deaths per 1,000,000 per annum.
From Lancaster and Gordon (1987).

class are of less importance from a mortality point of view. For renal stone, see Blacklock (1981). For the bacteriology, see Parker (1984a). Hyperplasia of the prostate, ICD 600, is the other entry in this class of importance to us. Here enlargement of the prostate causes obstruction to the passage of urine and leads to infection of the bladder; operation may be needed. In Australia, 1911–1920, this rubric was responsible for more than 10% of male deaths in this class, and in 1980, about 12%.

There are few deaths associated with other rubrics in this class. Diseases in this class have caused a not unimportant contribution to the death rates in the earlier years, for which see Table 28.1.1. Perhaps, at the younger ages, the changes should be assigned to the decline in the incidence of acute nephritis, which in many cases was due to an immune reaction after an infection with streptococci. At older ages the changes could be assigned to improved management of enlarged prostates.

Fatal infections (or toxic shock) due to generalized staphylococcal infections have followed the use of intravaginal tampons (Parker, 1984d).

Chapter 29
Pregnancy, Childbirth, and the Puerperium

29.1 Definitions

ICD 630–676. See §3.2 for the definition of maternal deaths.

There are two types of measure for mortality from causes in this class, conveniently referred to as maternal mortality. First, we can take deaths from these causes and relate them to the years at risk of persons of the appropriate ages to obtain a (population) mortality rate as we would do for any other class or rubric. Second, the deaths can be referred to the actual numbers of women at risk, namely, those counted as confinements, to obtain a rate analogous to the case fatality rate of an infective disease, for instance, as in the lower part of Table 29.1.1. Before the number of abortions became important, this traditional maternal mortality rate served a useful purpose. The reader is referred to Roht, Sherwin, and Henderson (1974) for a discussion of the point.

There has been some diversity in the definition of a death to be referred to this class. In New South Wales, Australia, accidental, therapeutic, and criminal abortions have all been included in the class of puerperal deaths since 1893. After the fifth revision of 1938 of the ICD, these practices were adopted generally throughout the countries of the world. These international differences must be borne in mind when making comparisons before 1938. There had been an attempt, particularly in England and Wales, to admit as few deaths as possible into the puerperal group of causes, since the maternal mortality was used as a measure of hygiene of the different cities or coun-ties. These practices led to many misunderstandings. For example, Campbell (1924), in her chapter written with M. Greenwood on international comparisons, drew attention to the wide disparity between the English and colonial rates, at the same time pointing out that some European countries with lower rates may not have counted all their deaths. Tandy (1935) found that Australian and United States practices were comparable, but that about 13% of their deaths assigned to puerperal causes would have been referred to other rubrics under English practice.

As can be seen in the following, the maternal mortality rates have fallen to very low levels in the developed countries within recent years. Few hints can be obtained by studying recent statistics as to what were the causes of death in the developed world in past years, whether it be in the 1950s, 1890s, or in earlier times. On the other hand, the causes of death are usually unavailable from earlier times; so a compromise has to be struck. The main discussion of causes therefore is centered on the rates in the first 60 years of this century. The dominant cause of high mortality in the present developed world was always childbed fever (puerperal sepsis), as will be shown later.

29.2 Mortality Statistics in New South Wales

M. Dublin (1936) and McKinlay (1929, 1947) had commented on the worldwide lack of data on the effects of age and parity on the maternal mortality rates. Indeed, the only surveys they

TABLE 29.1.1. Puerperal causes in general mortality, England and Wales (deaths per 1,000,000 per annum).

	All ages*	15–19	20–24	25–34	35–44	45–54
			Females			
1861–1870	341	162	634	925	891	60
1871–1880	350	168	681	949	890	53
1881–1890	318	129	604	892	806	43
1891–1900	301	99	543	879	756	41
1901–1910	206	67	366	607	520	26
1911–1920	157	54	280	471	384	19
1921–1930	140	40	249	432	332	17
1961†	12		26‡	35	28	1

*1861–1930, standardized on to the population of England and Wales as enumerated in 1901. From the Registrar-General's Decennial Supplement (1952, Part 3, Table 12, p. 95).
†From the Registrar-General's Annual Report for the year 1961.
‡15–24 years.

			Maternal mortality per 100,000 confinements.					
	All ages	15–19	20–24	25–29	30–34	35–39	40–44	45 and over
1940–1045	69	46	41	55	79	113	143	244

From the Registrar-General's Report for the years 1940–1945.

could cite were Duncan (1871) on Scotland for a single calendar year, 1866, and Coghlan (1898, 1899, 1900) for New South Wales, Australia, where the coding practices had been consistent over the years 1894–1937 with the rules of the fifth revision in 1938 of the ICD. Lancaster (1951a) could give statistics of the maternal mortality of married women for New South Wales for the period 1901–1948. For a typical epoch, 1901–1907, the rate at any fixed age was highest for primiparae and lowest for 1-parae or at older ages for 2-parae. Thus, for females at ages 25–29 years, the maternal mortality rates were

Rate	Issue
9.2	0
4.1	1
5.4	2
5.1	3 and 4
4.9	5, 6 and 7

For a fixed parity, there is a fall in the rate passing from under 20 to 20–24 years of age; from this age, there is a general tendency to increase with age, with particularly high rates at ages older than 40 years. The maternal mortality rates for primiparae (no previous issue) were 8.2, 7.2, 9.2, 14.5, 14.5, and 28.9 at ages under 20 years, 20–24, . . . , 35–39, and over 40 years. For the same age groups, the 1-parae (one previous issue) rates were 4.0, 3.3, 4.1, 5.7, 12.0, and 10.7 per 1,000.

Table 29.2.1 is given as an example of the mortality by cause in the developed world and a short commentary on it.

Abortion. No distinction has been made here between different forms of abortion. At no age is this factor important in the mortality of the primiparae. The statistics, of course, give a rather biased picture, for only married women are being discussed. A single woman falling pregnant will not as a rule marry and then induce an abortion, nor will a married woman as a rule attempt to induce one in her first pregnancy, but if later pregnancies occur at too short an interval she may. In each parity group the mortality from abortion increases with age. At confinements beyond the first, abortion accounts for some 30% of the mortality.

TABLE 29.2.1. Maternal mortality in New South Wales, 1943–1948, by parity and cause for two age groups.

Cause code number	Age group	Mortality rate per 100,000 confinements of women with previous issue			
		0	1 or 2	3 or 4	5 or more
140, 141	25 to 34	10	38	83	79
(Abortions)	35 and over	14	65	101	181
142	25 to 34	19	12	0	0
(Ectopic gestation)	35 and over	42	39	31	0
143, 146	25 to 34	31	19	30	56
(Hemorrhages)	35 and over	97	55	70	148
144, 148	25 to 34	94	30	49	56
(Toxemias)	35 and over	249	85	78	107
147	25 to 34	54	23	34	68
(Infections)	35 and over	194	85	79	41
Total*	25 to 34	240	142	227	281
	35 and over	762	379	421	559

*The totals do not add correctly because deaths in 145, 149, and 150 have not been included in the table.
Data from Australian Bureau of Statistics (NSW Branch).

Ectopic Gestation. This cause is more important in the earlier pregnancies. At a given parity the mortality is greater with age.

Hemorrhages. At all age groups, the mortality from hemorrhages is higher for the primiparae than for the women with previous issue of from one to four, possibly due to greater frequency of shock and delayed labor in first births. The rate rises however for the later confinements. This is probably associated with the increased frequency of placenta previa at higher parities. There is a marked increase with age in the death rate from hemorrhage in any parity group.

Toxemias. Similar conclusions can be drawn from the death rates from toxemias as from the hemorrhages. It seems that these two factors are between them responsible for the characteristic dip in mortality for women at each age with a previous issue of one or two.

Infections. The death rates for infections are highest for the first birth, and this is probably related to the greater need for instrumentation and other operative procedures because of delay and other difficulties in labor.

29.3 Maternal Mortality in England and Wales

Boxall (1893) gives the maternal mortality rates for the years 1847–1891 and notes that the mean was 4.85 per 1,000 confinements and that the annual rates exceeded 6 per 1,000 in only 2 years, 1848 and 1874. Approximately one-fifth of the mortality was due to puerperal sepsis in most years, but this proportion could rise in bad years. Before 1860 the mortality was slightly less in the provinces than in London, 5.00 as against 5.47, but after 1860 it was greater in the provinces, 4.89 against 3.74 per 1,000.

The rates for England and Wales seem not to have been affected by the high rates in the lying-in hospitals, for they suffered few of those terrible epidemics of the great European metropolitan lying-in hospitals. Farr (1885/1975, p. 273) wrote:

Childbirth is of course a physiological process, and under favourable conditions, where the mother has been previously taken proper care of, is attended with little danger. Unfortunately English mothers do not escape scatheless; nor can this be expected under existing circumstances; 3,875 mothers died during 1870 of the consequences of childbirth. But there is evidence of improvement. In the four years 1847–1850 no less than 59 mothers died to every 10,000 children born alive; in the four years 1867–1870 the deaths had sunk to 45. The error of collecting poor lying-in women into hospitals has been discovered, and to some extent discouraged; medical men have adopted wiser measures; they have taken greater precautions against infection, and midwives have been better taught. Still there is great room for improvement.

Rather more shortly, the maternal mortality from all causes was 5.9 per 1,000 in 1847–1850 and 4.5 per 1,000 in 1867–1870.

Bonney (1918–1919) complained about "the continued high maternal mortality" in the United Kingdom. He gave a long series of annual rates and pointed out that there had been little improvement over the years 1856–1917 in the maternal mortality rate; sepsis, toxemia and related diseases, hemorrhage, and embolism were the problems, in that order. Notwithstanding improvements in bacteriologic knowledge, there had been only a slight improvement in the death rates from puerperal sepsis. Full surgical skill and aseptic and antiseptic rigor were required.

Campbell (1924) stated that the contagious nature of the disease had been "fairly well recognised in this country" and that measures had been taken to prevent the spread of infection. The application of cleanliness and antiseptics had led to the practical disappearance of puerperal fever from lying-in hospitals, but there had been rather less success in the private practice of midwifery. Campbell (1927) notes that there were 694,563 births and 2,860 deaths of mothers in England and Wales in 1926. Campbell's list of causes of death and their contributions to the maternal mortality rate can be given as rates per 100,000 as follows: all causes, 412; puerperal sepsis, 160; puerperal convulsions, 58; puerperal hemorrhages, 49; other accidents of childbirth, 49; puerperal embolism and sudden death, 25; puerperal nephritis, uremia, and Bright's disease, 25; other accidents of pregnancy, 21; ectopic gestation, 14, and abortion, 12; all other causes, 6. Her table shows that there were slight improvements over the years 1911–1926 (Campbell, 1927, p. 2).

From 1923 to 1932 the maternal mortality rates for England and Wales were, per 10,000: 38, 39, 41; 41, 41, 42, 42, 42; 40 and 40 in 1932. After 1932 the tables of the Registrar-General make it more convenient to use the rates with abortion excluded, making a reduction of about 6 per 10,000 in the total maternal mortality rate. With these exclusions, deaths (deaths from sepsis) per 10,000 births in England and Wales were: 37(15) in 1933, 34(13) in 1935; 32(12), 28(8), 27(7), 26(6), 22(6) in 1940; 22(5), 20(4), 18(4), 15(3), 15(2) in 1945; 12(2), 10(2), 9(1), 8(1), 7(1) in 1950; 7(1), 6(1), 6(1), 6(1), 5(1) in 1955; 4(1), 4(1), 4(1), 3(1), 3(0) in 1960; 3(0), 3(0), 2(0), 2(0), 2(0) in 1965. An inspection of the tables by cause of death of the Registrar-General leads to conclusions not unlike those reported for the United States in §29.5, to follow. See also Gemmell, Logan, and Benjamin (1954), Johnstone (1950), Munro-Kerr, Johnstone, and Phillips (1954), Peckham (1935), Playfair (1882), Spencer (1927a, b), and UK Ministry of Health (1932). For virus infections in pregnancy and the puerperium, see Hurley (1983). For the lack of influence of bacteriology on mortality before 1935, see Loudon (1986a, b).

29.4 Maternal Mortality in the Hospitals

Maternal mortality in the hospitals is an important test of the commonly used hypothesis that the rise of modern medicine was a significant factor in the fall in the mortality rates generally, and in particular, that hospitals took a leading part in this progress, for which see §45.11.

Hospitals had been founded in the great European cities to give mothers, among others, shelter and medical attention. See §45.8. But hospitalization brought new problems, especially childbed fever. Churchill (1850) points out that although sporadic cases of the disease had been noted by Hippocrates and later authors, epidemics had not been reported before M. Peu, who stated that a "prodigious number" had died in the Hôtel-Dieu of Paris in 1664 following their confinements. Churchill cites a better attested example in

TABLE 29.4.1. Maternal mortality rates for the Rotunda Lying-in Hospital, Dublin, (rates per 1,000 confinements).

	0	1	2	3	4	5	6	7	8	9
175–								18	18	12
176–	7	17	11	18	20	11	4	16	24	12
177–	12	7	6	19	31	7	9	8	11	8
178–	6	6	6	13	9	6	6	7	16	17
179–	8	16	6	11	13	5	6	8	5	6
180–	10	17	13	22	8	5	10	5	5	7
181–	10	9	16	25	10	6	5	9	16	29
182–	28	8	4	23	8	9	33	13	15	16
183–	5	6	5	6	17	18	20	13	21	12
184–	17	11	10	10	6	25	8	28	19	18

93 years; 159, 749 puerperae; 1,966 deaths; mat. mort.: 12.3 per 1,000.
Source: C.E.M. Levy in Semmelweis (1861).

which of 20 women confined in February 1746, scarcely one recovered. Other such incidents occurred at the Hôtel-Dieu. In Britain in 1760, the first such epidemic was recorded, 11 years after the institution of lying-in hospitals, at the British Lying-in Hospital, London. Epidemics in Ireland also can be cited, especially in the years 1767–1768 and 1773–1774. It was said that from the end of February 1773 at the Rotunda Hospital, Dublin, almost every woman delivered was seized with puerperal fever, and all of those infected died; it was noted that the disease did not exist in the town.

A long series of maternal mortality rates is given in Table 29.4.1 for the Rotunda Hospital, Dublin; the rates from 1757 up to 1819 were perhaps about 50% higher than the rates in national populations of the early twentieth century. In the later years they were a good deal higher. These high rates in the hospitals were noted by such observers as Charles White (1728–1813), Alexander Gordon (1752–1799), Thomas Nunneley (1809–1870), and Oliver Wendell Holmes (1809–1894). Thus, White (1773) wrote: "most, if not all, those disorders which are usually disposed to be peculiarly incident to the puerperal state are either the effects of mismanagement by the accoucheur or nurses, or else arise from the patient's own imprudence; they may, in general, be truly said to be fabricated, and may always, except in lying-in hospitals, be avoided." He also cited

incidents that suggested that the accoucheur himself might be the cause of spreading the disease.

In Churchill (1850, p. 398) we find that Gordon (1795) stated: "This disease seized such women only as were visited, or delivered by a practitioner, or taken care of by a nurse, who had previously attended patients affected with the disease." . . . In short, "I had evident proofs of its infectious nature, and that the infection was as readily communicated as that of the small-pox or measles, and operated more speedily than any other infection with which I am acquainted." He gave a table of 77 cases, in many of which the channel of propagation was evident, and in some cases he regrets that he was the conveyer. He then enumerated a number of instances in which the disease had been conveyed by midwives and others to the neighboring villages, and declared that "these facts fully prove that the cause of the puerperal fever, of which I treat, was a specific contagion, or infection, altogether unconnected with a noxious constitution of the atmosphere." Gordon knew that his findings and hypotheses were not consistent with the prevailing academic view of epidemic (in the original sense of an effect falling on the people) disease being due to specified or unspecified atmospheric, worldwide, or cosmic effects. Nunneley (1841, p. 89) writes: "If this [the truth of the facts stated that depend on the respectability and reputation of the narrators] be admitted, and I cannot imagine that it will be rejected, I see not how we can avoid what appears to me to be the inevitable conclusion, namely, that puerperal fever is only one form of a diffused inflammatory action, which, when it is exhibited upon the surface of the body, is called erysipelas." He justifies this conclusion by the following: (*i*) and (*ii*) similarity of constitutional symptoms and postmortem findings; (*iii*) similarity of the indications for treatment; (*iv*) erysipelas and childbed fever appear in epidemics simultaneously (here he cites a number of authors, Gordon, Hey, Osiander, West, Ingleby, Ferguson, Hutchison, and Locock, of whom Locock had noted many coincidences of childbed fever in the hospital and erysipelas in the nurses and servants); (*v*) both forms of disease arise under the same circumstances and prevail at the same seasons of the year and during the same kind of weather; he notes that M. Vesou had attributed the epidemic of 1664 entirely to the fact that the lying-in wards were situated above wards with many wounded; (*vi*) pus is deposited in various parts of the body; (*vii*) "erysipelas" follows autopsy wounds in childbed fever; (*viii*) the two diseases often coincide in one patient; and (*ix*) childbed fever and erysipelas may produce each other in a second person.

Holmes (1843) gave some specific examples of contagion. Women delivered on March 20, April 9, 10, 11, 27, and 28, and May 8 were the only deliveries attended by a certain physician in that time; the first five died, the last two suffered symptoms but recovered; the physician had cut his finger at an autopsy on March 19. Holmes (1843) cited the work of both C. White and A. Gordon. He adduced further evidence. Thus, a midwife in Manchester delivered in the first instance a woman who died in childbirth; of the following 30 successive deliveries by this same midwife, 16 contracted puerperal fever and all died; the incidence of the fever was not unduly high in Manchester at this time. Holmes (1843) reported other such striking sequences. He also cited a death of an obstetrician performing an autopsy on a case of puerperal fever. Regrettably, some evidence of a connection between puerperal fever and erysipelas led to controversy rather than to a strengthening of belief in his argument, see Minor (1874). Academic obstetricians, such as Professors Meigs and Hodge, were not all impressed by Holmes's evidence, according to Holmes (1855) in an introduction to a reprint of his earlier article. See Ackerknecht (1948*a*) for the anticontagionist doctrine.

The Allgemeines Krankenhaus in Vienna was founded in 1784 by Dr. Gerhard van Swieten, backed by Maria Theresa four years after her husband's death. The hospital was well equipped; 20,000 patients were admitted annually, and there were 76 medical men on the staff. J.L. Boër (1751–1835) was appointed in 1789 as director of the obstetrical wards, which are referred to in the tables as the Imperial and Royal Lying-in Hospital. He had returned from a tour of France and Great Britain, where he saw T. Denman (1733–1815), C. White, and others at work. He decided to follow White's methods in Vienna, and did so to such good effect that in the preanatomic days, 1784–1822, that is, before the institution of K. von Rokitansky's pathology laboratory, there were 71,395 deliveries with 897 deaths, a maternal mortality rate of 13 per 1,000, for which see Table 29.4.2. He retired in 1822, perhaps partly due to pressure from his colleagues because of his conservatism.

These examples show that the high maternal rates of mortality in hospitals were really iatrogenic and not the natural lot of women. We give now some rates from lying-in hospitals (LIH) and from national or other sources in Table 29.4.3. It is evident, from the official statistics of England and Wales, that a maternal mortality rate of less than 6 per 1,000 was possible throughout the latter half of the nineteenth century, a rate compatible with that of a modern state, for example, New South Wales in Australia for 1931–1937. The rates for French private patients before 1850 were somewhat higher, 9 per 1,000, and for German noble patients, 17 per 1,000. The smaller lying-in hospitals could average from 6 to 17 per 1,000, but the larger ones usually had a much higher average.

In Vienna at the Imperial and Royal Hospital, after the retirement of Boër, the maternal

TABLE 29.4.2. Maternal mortality* in the Imperial and Royal Lying-in Hospital from 16 August 1784, (deaths per 1,000 confinements).

	0	1	2	3	4	5	6	7	8	9
178–					21	14	4	4	4	6
179–	8	6	9	26	4	21	12	2	2	10
180–	20	8	4	7	4	4	7	6	8	14
181–	8	19	6	11	32	7	5	9	22	50
182–	25	17	8	74	49	48	81	22	36	46
183–	40	66	32	52	84	56	80	86	39	50
184–	64	60	121	77	54	46	81	30	13	

*Table XVII of Semmelweis (1861) as translated by F.P. Murphy.
1784–1822, the preanatomic years, 71,395 deliveries with 897 deaths, mortality rate 13 per 1,000.
1823–1832, postanatomic years, 28,245 deliveries with 1,509 deaths, mortality rate 53 per 1,000.

TABLE 29.4.3. Maternal mortalities.

Years	Institution or country	Maternal deaths/10,000 confinements	Authority
1749–1846	British LIH*	134	Levy[†]
1757–1849	Dublin (Rotunda) LIH	123	Levy
1828–1842	Queen Charlotte LIH	169	Levy
1829–1846	General LIH	387	Levy
1833–1846	Coombe LIH	119	Levy
1847–1854	Registrar-General, England and Wales	54	W. Farr (1885, p. 273)
1847–1850	English LIHs	59	W. Farr
1847–1891	Registrar-General, England and Wales[‡]	48.5	Boxall (1893)
Before 1860	French hospitals	340	Le Fort[§]
Before 1860	French private	90	Le Fort
1850–1900	German noble families	174	Peller (1943)
1867–1870	English LIHs	45	W. Farr, (1885)
1931–1937	Australia (New South Wales)	56	Lancaster (1951a)

*LIH: Lying-in hospital.
[†]Levy: Professor of Obstetrics at Copenhagen, in Semmelweis (1861). For Dublin, see also Browne (1947).
[‡]See §29.1 for international comparisons.
[§]Cited by Wangensteen and Wangensteen (1978, p. 347); Le Fort was later to oppose Pasteur's germ theory (Wangensteen and Wangensteen, 1978, p. 420).

mortality rate jumped to 74 per 1,000 and the average for the years 1823–1832 was 53 per 1,000. High rates continued there until Ignaz Philipp Semmelweis (1818–1865) in 1847 compared the rates in the two divisions, created in 1840. For 1840–1846 the rates were 99 per 1,000 in the first division (attended by trainee obstetricians), much higher than 33 per 1,000 in the second division (attended by nurses and midwives). Indeed, in the first division the rates for the years 1840–1849 were 90; 77, 158, 89, 82, 68; 114, 50, 13, 20 deaths per 1,000 confinements. These extremely high rates, almost 1 in 6 in the highest years, would imply that, if they were continuous and general, about half the females would have died from childbirth-related diseases during their reproductive life. During the years 1841–1846, even the rates in the second division were high by the standards of Table 29.4.3. Semmelweis (1861) had been able to show that the atmospheric hypothesis was irrelevant against opposition from the conservative members of the staff. His hypothesis was that "childbed fever [is] a resorption fever, dependent on the resorption of a decomposed animal-organic matter, and the first result of the resorption is a disintegration of the blood, and after this the exudates." He suggested that the transmission of "decomposed animal-organic matter" from the autopsy room to the uterus was the link to be attacked. He set about reducing such transmission by insisting on the washing of hands in a "liquid chloride," or later "chlorinated lime," solution. The mortality rate fell for the months June to December 1847 to 30 deaths per 1,000 parturients. In 1848, as a result of the chlorine washings, rates were approximately 13 per 1,000 in both divisions. Semmelweis carried out experiments, painting the cervix of parturient rabbits with material from human endometritis; disease resembling puerperal fever was so produced. The successful therapeutic test however does not prove, as is sometimes stated, his hypothesis.

Semmelweis shows in other places that he believes that infection could be spread from septic diseases, although he would say this was because decomposing animal-organic matter had been generated. His hypothesis therefore departs in important respects from the bacteriologic hypothesis erected on conclusions from bacteriologic studies (Pasteur, 1878, and Mackie, McLachlan, and Percival, 1929). Semmelweis (1861, p. 106) states "childbed fever is accordingly not a species of disease, but a variety of pyemia," but a reading of the text shows that this argument is circular.

It appears that Semmelweis accepted the doctrines of Johann Justus von Liebig (1803–1873) on the etiology of infection; Liebig believed that fermentation is caused by chemical substances capable of evoking in another substance, with which it is in contact, the same changes as it is, itself, undergoing. William Farr and John Snow were favorably and not unfavorably disposed, respectively, to such a hypothesis. Liebig never admitted that organisms were responsible for fermentations or infections, even after Pasteur's work on yeast fermentation. Statistical analysis would be quite unable to distinguish the hypotheses of bacterial infection and Liebig's chemical sub-

stances. It is therefore gratuitous to assume that Semmelweis was in favor of bacterial hypotheses or stimulated bacteriologic research.

Semmelweis, a Hungarian who had appeared in the uniform of the revolutionary guards during the revolution of 1848, was not reappointed to control the wards. Later he took up positions in Budapest and reduced the mortality to a level of about 13 per 1,000 in the maternity hospital of St. Rochus, about which there must remain considerable doubts after some of his exclusions of cases. He seems not to have developed the theory further by 1861. He gives an opinion that the cause of death does not affect the power of the "decomposed animal-organic matter" derived from autopsy material, although this is brought into doubt by the fates of his animals, 4 and 5, which were inoculated with matter from case(s) of marasmus, for which see Semmelweis (1861, pp. 76–80). He did not believe that childbed fever was contagious. Many authors have since put modern bacteriologic ideas into their interpretations of Semmelweis's writings. Semmelweis died in a mental asylum after a beating by his attendants, for which see Semmelweis (1966).

Simpson (1851) attacked the hypothesis of Semmelweis, published later in 1861, that autoinfection plays some considerable role (1 death per 100 confinements). Although Semmelweis had accepted the resemblance of childbed fever to surgical fever following a suggestion of the physician, Carl Haller, he did not go on to consider the implications, as did Simpson (1851) who "believed that generally, if not always, the material which, when carried from one subject to another, could produce puerperal or surgical fever in a newly inoculable subject, was an *inflammatory secretion*, just as the inoculable matter of small-pox, cow-pox, syphilis, & c., was an inflammatory secretion." Simpson (1851) believed that (*i*) autopsy material from subjects dead of puerperal fever, (*ii*) secretions from such patients, even when still alive, (*iii*) inflammatory effusions of erysipelas, (*iv*) exhalations from a patient, and (*v*) fomites were all dangerous; that (*vi*) crowding in hospital and (*vii*) general epidemic tendency might be important; and further, (*viii*) there might be no obvious relation to a previous disease. Simpson (1851) thought that the Viennese doctors might find other sequences in which erysipelas could be incriminated. See also Simpson (1850).

The bacteriologic proof of the hypothesis was given by Pasteur (1878), and we can say that the hypotheses of C. White, A. Gordon, T.C. Nunneley, O.W. Holmes, and J.Y. Simpson were vindicated, even though they had necessarily to be incomplete; but Semmelweis and, even more so, his enemies make many statements inconsistent with the bacteriologic hypothesis, which could only be established after bacteriology had been developed by Pasteur (1878). Garrigues (1889), looking back, cites Mayrhofer, Recklinghausen, Waldeyer, Orth, Heiberg, Haussmann, Spillmann, Kehrer, Hugh Miller, and Pasteur as leading to the bacteriologic hypothesis. Of these authors, Karl Mayrhofer (1837–1882) had described vibrios in the lochial discharges in 1863 and had brought about successful antisepsis in division one in Vienna. See also the detailed accounts of Lesky (1964, 1972, 1976), who regrettably overlooks some of the faulty reasonings of Semmelweis (1861, e.g. pp. 194, 109) that the infection can be generated from the cadavers of animals and that autoinfection is a frequent cause.

See also Hirst (1889), Kehrer (1952), Routh (1848), Parker (1978, 1984c), and Youngson (1979).

[The quotations and tabular data from Semmelweis (1861), *The Etiology, the Concept and the Prophylaxis of Childbed Fever*, transl. by F.P. Murphy, *Medical Classics*, Vol. 5, (c) 1940–41, The Williams & Wilkins Co., Baltimore, are reprinted with permission.]

29.5 Progress in Maternal Mortality

It can be seen that puerperal sepsis was a great problem by the 1820s in the large hospitals, but much less so in the rural areas. White, Gordon, Nunneley, and Holmes, among others, had substantially proved that the disease was contagious by 1843; the maternal mortality rates were almost constant over the epoch 1847–1900 in England, as we have seen in Table 29.4.3. The disappointment of Bonney (1918–1919) and of Campbell (1924, 1927) has already been noted in §29.3. Yet, by this time, medical opinion had accepted the truth of the bacteriologic hypothesis, although the knowledge was not enough to secure asepsis and antisepsis of a sufficiently high order. The replacement of untrained midwives by midwives, either male and usually medically qualified or female and trained as nurses, was not followed by immediate declines in mortality rates, a fact noted by Peller (1943) and Graham (1950). Fortunately, the change to academically and technically trained personnel led to reexaminations of the problems of the various diseases and accidents by the methods of bacteriology, and other medical sciences, and to the use of modern hospital disciplines. An example of the change in attitudes is also provided by the Committee Abstract (1933) of the Committee on Maternal Mortality in New York City, which led to the formation of hospital committees to investigate the cause of each maternal death and fix responsibility for it, an application of quality control theory.

Shapiro, Schlesinger, and Nesbitt (1968) show that for the United States there is little change in the level of the maternal mortality rates from 1915 to 1936 at approximately 60 per 10,000, but from 1936 to 1956 there is a rapid decline to 4 per 10,000, which the authors attribute to an increased interest in the causes of maternal mortality after the publication of the report. Around 1936 there was an increase in hospitalization, sulfonamides became available for the control of infections, and blood and blood substitutes came into general use for the treatment of hemorrhage. The total rate per 10,000 had decreased to 20.7 in 1945, then to 8.3 in 1950, and 4.1 in 1956. The authors show the total rates for 1939–1941, 1949–1951, and 1959–1961 as, respectively, 36.4, 8.3, and 3.7 per 10,000. There is thus a decline of 28.1 per 10,000 between the first two epochs and 4.6 between the second and third epochs. These two declines can be partitioned by cause as follows: sepsis, 7.9 and 0.8; toxemias, 6.1 and 2.0; hemorrhages, 3.2 and 0.8; ectopic pregnancies, 1.0 and 0.3; all forms of abortion, 5.9 and 0.2; and other complications, 4.0 and 0.5; sepsis was the predominant cause of death from abortion. For mortality 1750 to 1950, see Leavitt (1986).

The progress of maternal mortality is conveniently measured by a study of the individual causes.

Puerperal Sepsis. The great epidemics of the lying-in hospitals have been abolished. Puerperal sepsis has been reduced by excluding the infective organisms by rigid rules for obstetric, diagnostic, and operative procedures, such as the avoidance whenever possible of the manual removal of the placenta and unnecessary vaginal examinations before and during labor. It became the custom also to situate obstetrical wards away from the general hospitals. When infection has occurred in the recent decades, effective chemotherapy and antibiotic therapy have been available.

Hemorrhage. This is more readily controlled with the use of such drugs as ergotamine and pituitrin and special prophylactic care of placenta previa, including Cesarian section.

Toxemia. The toxemias have largely been controlled by dietary means and rest.

Ectopic Pregnancy. This has been controlled by a better understanding of the cause and its

diagnosis and an appreciation of it as a surgical emergency.

Abortion. The principal risk of death from abortion is sepsis; after legalization and with better surgery, the risk of infection is less and the sepsis can be treated with chemotherapy and antibiotics.

Many of the conditions noted above can be detected early by regular attendance at prenatal clinics, for example, toxemia and pelvic deformity. A special case is provided by obstruction to labor by malformed pelvis. In former days this was often due to rickets. Fortunately, with better child nutrition, such gross malformations have become rare. Possibly, too, the modern woman approaches pregnancy and labor in far better physical condition than formerly. In general, the development of prenatal clinics enabled special care to be taken of cases at special risk.

Maternal mortality rates are now of the order of 0.1 per 1,000 throughout the developed world, as appears in Table 29.5.1, constructed from the 1981 *UN Demographic Yearbook*, in which rates calculated from less than 31 deaths are distinguished by a sign. We have marked the first of these signs by an asterisk

TABLE 29.5.1. Maternal mortalities rates (deaths per 1,000,000 confinements).

	1971	1972	1973	1974	1975	1976	1977	1978	1979	1980
Austria	304	250*	224	195	171	218	187	152	127	77
Bulgaria	339	297	343	295	277	234	345	279	126*	211
Czechoslovakia	177	175	138	151	183	90*	135	97	129	—
Denmark	53*	40	28	70	55	30	48	80	118	17
England & Wales	169	155	130	126	127	134	130	114	116	107
G.D.R.‡	409	299	266	201	231	220	183	211	234	—
G.F.R.†	504	428	459	340	396	363	340	255	220	206
Hungary	352	431	377	387	267	199	197	220	156*	209
Norway	198*	62	33	67	71	131	98	19	136	118
Sweden	79*	71	27	73	19	40	114	64	10	—
Switzerland	270*	219	183	118	127	81	41	182	111	—
Australia	185	125	113*	114	56	132	80	66	81	98
New Zealand	217*	158	230	169	230	109	185	98	115	—
United States	206	187	152	147	129	123	112	96	—	—

*The first year in which the number of deaths fell below 31 per annum. To the right of this point the standard error will be greater than 18% of the true mean.
†Federal Republic of Germany.
‡German Democratic Republic.
UN Demographic Yearbook (1981, p. 318). Copyright (1981), United Nations. Reproduced by permission.

and note that for most of the countries, the years to the right of the asterisk will also be associated with less than 31 deaths. Denmark averaged 3.6 deaths per annum over the 10 years, 1971–1980. See also Istituto Centrale di Statistica (1934) and Institute of Medicine (1973); United States: Rochat (1981) and W. Smith (1987); world: Tietze (1977). For maternal mortality in rural Sweden, see Högberg and Broström (1985).

Chapter 30

Diseases of the Skin and Supporting Tissue

30.1 Diseases of Skin and Subcutaneous Tissue

ICD 680–709. 680–686, infections; 690–698, other inflammatory conditions; 700–709, other diseases.

This class is not now of any importance from the point of view of the number of deaths caused. It retains its place in the ICD because of its importance in morbidity and hospital statistics. It is clear from Table 30.1.1 that the deaths caused by it, about 0.5% of the total deaths in Australia in 1911–1920, were due to infections, possibly principally due to staphylo-cocci and streptococci. Modern observers will find it odd to note deaths occurring as complications of furuncle. Mortality from this class of diseases is now rare. The reductions are due partly to improved cleanliness in more recent times but principally to improved surgery, especially the use of chemotherapeutics and antibiotics. For epidemiology, see Greenbaum and Beerman (1965). See §9.11 for wounds, and note that erysipelas is treated in §9.6. For staphylococcal and streptococcal lesions in these two classes, see Parker (1984c, d). For a text on dermatology, see Moschella and Hurley (1985).

TABLE 30.1.1. Diseases of the skin and supporting tissue in Australia, 1911–1920.

Rubric no.	Disease rubric	Deaths per 1,000,000 per year	
		Males	Females
142*	Gangrene	27	24
143	Furuncle	6	3
144	Acute abscess	18	13
145	Other diseases of the skin and adnexa	10	10
	Total Skin and Adnexa[†]	61	49
146*	Nontuberculous arthropathy	13	7
147	Arthropathy of joints (excluding tuberculosis and rheumatism)	3	2
148	Amputations	1	0
149	Other diseases of organs of locomotion	1	0
	Total organs of locomotion[‡]	17	9
	Total All Causes	12,117	9,337

* Rubric number according to the second revision of the International List of Causes of Death.
† Corresponds to ICD 680–709.
‡ Corresponds to ICD 710–739.
Data from Demography (Australia).

30.2 Diseases of the Musculoskeletal System and Connective Tissue

ICD 710–739. 710–719, arthropathies and related disorders; 720–724, dorsopathies; 725–729, rheumatism, excluding the back; 730–739, osteopathies, chondropathies, and acquired musculoskeletal deformities.

These diseases were causes of few deaths in Australia in 1911–1920, as can be seen in Table 30.1.1, with about 0.1% of deaths assigned to them as the leading cause. The class is of more importance in morbidity. See Jeffrey and Ball (1963), WHO-rheumatic (1963), and Lawrence and Shulman (1985).

Chapter 31
Congenital Anomalies and Human Genetics

31.1 Causes of Congenital Anomalies

ICD 740–759. Classification by organ affected.

The causes of congenital and genetic defects are now given.

(*i*) *Infectious Causes.* Rubella can cause lethal malformations, see Dudgeon (1976) and Rutstein, Nickerson, and Heald (1952). Cardiovascular lethal defects include persistent ductus arteriosus and various atrophies and stenoses of arteries and valves, the tetralogy of Fallot, and myocardial damage. Defects in other systems such as microcephaly and panencephalitis are rather less important. As an example of the mortality load, there were 64,000 deaths in the United States for 1970–1980 with an average of 2 per 1,000 births.

Toxoplasma causes 3,000 congenitally defective children annually in the United States. See Feldman (1982). Cytomegalovirus is also a well-attested cause of congenital defect, 1.3% of infants being infected before birth, according to Wright (1973). Numerically, these latter two are much less important than rubella as a cause of infant deaths.

(*ii*) *Genetic Causes of Congenital Defects.* (a) Genes, whether they are dominant or recessive, at a single locus or at a few loci producing effects are known as major genes or genes of large effects. These major genes are more important than the multifactorial genetic systems for mortality and for structural defects during infancy and childhood. The total birth frequency of dangerous major genes is as much as 1%.

The characteristic family pattern given by a dominant condition, dangerous to life, is that the first patient in the family is a sporadic case with unaffected parents, for example, in Apert acrocephalosyndactyly, almost all cases are sporadic and few are known to have had children, and in tuberous sclerosis, some 80% of patients appear sporadically. Some dominant major genes, dangerous to health and life, cause an onset late in life; Huntington's chorea often develops late in life, and so, many patients reproduce; indeed, pedigrees of this disease over many generations are known. Many dominants show remarkable variation in the severity of the disease, that is, in penetrance, so that an individual heterozygous for porphyria variegata may only be detected by special biochemical tests. Recessive conditions appear most commonly in consanguineous marriages—usually cousin marriages, and this is especially so if the gene is rare.

There may be difficulties in defining a syndrome due to genetic causes, according to Opitz, Jürgen, et al (1979). Sometimes a single gene can cause a number of different defects (pleiotropy), only some of which may be present in some subjects; this variation may conceal an identity of cause of different syndromes. On the other hand, false syndromes have often been defined that include the results of coincidences or associations, that is, the syndrome does not represent pleiotropy or other developmentally and/or functionally correlated manifestations of a single cause, such as

Mendelian mutation, chromosome abnormality, or teratogenic agent. See also Carter (1976*a*, *b*, 1981), Carter and MacCarthy (1951), Janerich and Polednak (1983), and Leck (1981*b*). (b) Multifactorial gene systems determine many characters, such as height, in the normal individual. The study of the effects of such multifactorial gene systems has not progressed very far, but they do not seem to play an important part in the mortality at birth and early life. (c) Chromosome syndromes. In these syndromes there is no defect in the genes, but the chromosomes may appear in abnormal numbers. Thus, there may be a trisomy of a certain autosome, so that three chromosomes are present instead of the normal pair. A trisomy can occur at chromosome 18 (Edwards syndrome), at chromosome 13 (Patau syndrome), or at chromosome 21 (Down syndrome, or mongolism). Chromosome anomalies can also occur in the sex chromosomes; thus, in the Klinefelter syndrome there is an additional sex chromosome with the formula XXY instead of the normal XY; XYY, XXX, and XO syndromes also occur; here, XO signifies that there is no Y chromosome. Most chromosomal anomalies lead to serious defects of development, especially if they occur in an autosomal chromosome. Most infants with trisomy 13 or trisomy 18 die in the first year of life and the survivors suffer great physical and mental handicaps. The expectation of life at birth for mongoloid children (Down syndrome, or trisomy 21) is low, although it has improved since the advent of antibiotics and chemotherapy, as the subject is abnormally susceptible to intercurrent infections. Prognosis is rather better in the sex chromosome anomalies, except in the Turner XO syndrome in which there is a more profound effect on body development with webbed neck, skeletal deformities, fibrous ovaries, and lack of proper growth.

(*iii*) *Maternal Disease.* Congenital malformations appear in about 5% of births to diabetic mothers. Less important maternal diseases are endemic cretinism, as in Zaire and Niugini, and phenylketonuria. See Carter (1950).

(*iv*) *Irradiation.* Medical diagnostic or other radiation of less than 5 rads of X rays poses a negligible threat. For fetal loss induced, see Brent (1980) and Porter and Hook (1980).

(*v*) *Hyperthermia.* This has been suggested as a cause of some defects. The suggestion is supported by animal experimentation.

(*vi*) *Natural Environmental Substances.* These appear to be unimportant.

(*vii*) *Addictive Drugs.* In general their importance has not been established. Caffeine has no effect. The case for tobacco smoking has not been supported by convincing evidence. Large amounts of alcohol drunk by the mother in early pregnancy increase the infant mortality rates.

(*viii*) *Pharmaceutical Drugs.* Thalidomide has been important. Doll (1971) gives examples: (a) phocomelia (congenital defects of limbs) caused by thalidomide medication of the mother, see §45.12; (b) primary pulmonary hypertension caused by the weight reducer, aminorex fumarate; (c) deaths in asthma by the excessive use of aerosols containing sympathomimetic drugs related to adrenalin; (d) thromboembolism, following the taking of oral contraceptives; and (e) malignant neoplasms, following the use of arsenical compounds, radioactive materials, and coal tar derivatives.

(*ix*) *Industrial Chemicals.* Mercury appears to be the most dangerous. See Sullivan and Barlow (1979).

(*x*) *Blood Group Incompatibility.* See §32.6.

We have used the conclusions of Kalter and Warkany (1983) and Warkany and Kalter (1961) in causes (*iii*) through (*viii*) above. These authors conclude that the rate of chromosomal abnormalities and malformations, combined, is 1.8 per 1,000 live births; taking the frequency of congenital malformations as 30 per 1,000, about 6% of all serious malformations in live-born children are associated with major chromosomal abnormalities. These figures are negligibly higher when stillbirths are included. These authors conclude that the etiology of most congenital defects remains unknown but the deaths due to congenital defects now constitute about 21% of all infant deaths and it is difficult to reduce them. See also Bergsma (1976).

TABLE 31.2.1. Deaths from congenital anomalies in infancy in Australia.*

Period	Males	Females	Masculinity of rates
1908–1910	3.08	2.60	118
1911–1920	4.01	3.17	127
1921–1930	4.71	3.68	128
1931–1940	5.07	3.92	129
1941–1950	4.36	3.74	116
1951–1960	4.16	3.58	116
1961–1970	3.76	3.27	115
1971–1980	3.46	3.18	109

*Deaths per 1,000 live births.
Data from Australian Bureau of Statistics.

31.2 Statistics of Congenital Anomalies

Death rates from congenital anomalies in Australia are given in Table 31.2.1, from which it is evident that the rate of deaths in the first year of life, computed as an infant mortality rate, has remained relatively stable over the years of the series, in the vicinity of 4 per 1,000 births. The masculinities for total deaths in the class have been approximately 120%, although these masculinities vary between individual causes.

It was believed in 1951 that many congenital abnormalities might be due to infective causes other than rubella and that the resulting epidemicity might be detectable by statistical methods. This hypothesis was not supported by the official data (Lancaster, 1951f), even when the deaths from cardiovascular defects were classified by month for 1941, a known year of epidemic births of the deaf from rubella. Some clinical data on hare-lip and cleft palate also failed to show epidemicity.

Carter (1976b Table 1) gives the frequency per 1,000 total live births and the approximate sex ratio in Great Britain as follows: spina bifida cystica, 2.5, 0.6; anencephaly, 2.0, 0.3; congenital heart defects, 6.0, 1.0; pyloric stenosis, 3.0, 4.0; cleft lip and/or cleft palate, 1.0, 1.8; and congenital dislocation of the hip, 1.0, 0.14. Note that the frequency is an incidence and not a mortality rate. See the texts by Wil-

son and Fraser (1977–1978) and Weinstein (1976), the review of Taffel (1978) of United States experience, and the general review of Ingalls and Klingberg (1965).

31.3 Human Diseases Caused by Major Genes

Of diseases due to genetic causes, the most important possibly is diabetes, for the genetics of which, see §21.2. For the limited regions of malarial hyperendemicity, the hemoglobin anomalies, for which, see §15.5, will continue to be of even greater importance. These high incidences of genes, unfavorable to survival under modern conditions of adequate nutrition and freedom from malaria, exist because such polymorphisms were of selective value in past ages, in which the heterozygote was fitter than either homozygote under the given environmental conditions of low nutrition or of hyperendemicity of malaria, respectively. For the general theory of such polymorphisms, see Motulsky (1960) and Vogel and Motulsky (1982). Two other important diseases that appear to have a genetic cause are schizophrenia and epilepsy, although the actual mechanism of inheritance is still in doubt; but the diseases determined by major genes probably have had little effect on mortality as a whole.

With the aid of Nora and Fraser (1974), human diseases or defects due to genetic causes, together with their ICD number, are now listed.

Among autosomal dominant diseases there are: deafness, cardiac disease and freckles (Leopard syndrome) not listed in the ICD; Huntington's chorea, 333.4; myotonic dystrophy (Steinert's disease), 359.2; osteogenesis imperfecta, 756.5; polyposis of the colon (intestinal polyposis I), 211.3; and tuberous sclerosis, 759.5. Without regard to mortality, it is appropriate to add here also sickle cell trait, 282.6; and thalassemia minor, 282.4.

Among autosomal recessive diseases there are: homocystinuria, 270.4; sickle cell anemia, 282.6; α- and β- thalassemias, 282.4; cretinism, 243; chondroectodermal dysplasia (Ellis-van Creveld syndrome), 756.5; hepatolenticular degeneration (Wilson's disease), 275.1; leprechaunism (Donohue's syndrome), 259.8; cystic disease of the pancreas, 277.0; Leyden-Moebius syndrome, 359.1; recessive muscular dystrophy with arthrogryposis, 728.3; and premature senility, 259.8.

Among sex-linked (X-linked) diseases there are: hemophilia A (classic form), 286.0; hemophilia B (Christmas disease), 286.1; and Duchenne muscular dystrophy, 359.1.

Among diseases that appear to be based on multifactorial gene systems there are: anencephaly, 740; spina bifida, 741; diabetes mellitus, 250;and epilepsy, 345.1.

31.4 Genetics of Resistance to Infective Diseases

The hypothesis that there exist specific genetic factors important for the incidence of and resistance to infective diseases is not new. Thus, the high case fatalities observed in island (or virgin soil) epidemics of measles, such as in Fiji in 1875, have been interpreted to support the hypothesis that Europeans or members of other urbanized populations are better fitted genetically to deal with measles than populations that have been free of the disease, a weeding out of the unfit in Darwinian terms. There are good reasons for not accepting this as a valid natural experiment; in the intense island epidemics, there are usually multiple cases within the family, including the parents, so that even food, water, and rest are not available to the patient—a situation not comparable with European urban experience,where cases would be chiefly occuring among the young. Neel (1977) believes that the excess mortality in the island epidemics can be at most 20% genetic in origin. A better comparison might be with healthy young prisoners of war in, for instance, the American Civil War, as in §33.11, where the case fatality rate was high.

Watt (1813) is often cited by modern authors, for example, Wilson (1962), for his remarks on the incidence of measles in Glasgow, mentioned in §37.3. A quotation of some length from Watt (1813) is available in Farr (1885, pp. 321, 322), who remarks that "it is, however, by no means proved that the general mortality under unfavourable sanitary conditions is much reduced by rendering a child insusceptible of one type, while he remains exposed to all other types of zymotic disease." Watt (1813) considered whether, for example, a child who had had smallpox was less likely to succumb to measles, and if so whether under given (but not defined) conditions the total death rate might remain constant, even though one cause had been removed.Farr appears to consider this a valid problem. Drake (1969) notes the same phenomenon in Sweden. From Table 37.3.1 it appears that measles deaths in Glasgow of 168 in 1802, 99 in 1805, 787 in 1808, 267 in 1811, and 304 in 1812 were more numerous than in any year before 1800; this may well have been a chance phenomenon; moreover, at this time Glasgow was undergoing a rapid expansion of population and influx of susceptibles.

It is known from experimental work that the ability to resist parasites is at least partly genetic in some species, and so it is reasonable to expect that populations tend to become genetically resistant to their pathogens. Sometimes such resistance may depend on a gene at a single locus. Thus, Sladen and Bang (1969, p. 7) state that resistance in mice to arbovirus B infection is determined at one locus and resistance is dominant; the Princeton strain of mice was resistant and the C3H strain was susceptible; on the other hand, with mousehepatitis, the C3H strain had recessive resistance and P dominant susceptibility, but the resistance to this disease was controlled by genes at another locus. They conclude after appropriate crossing experiments that, in mice at any rate, there is no general gene for resistance against viruses.

In the human population, an example of fitness depending on a gene at a single locus is the protection against malaria afforded by the gene for S-hemoglobin. See §§15.5 and 23.3. It is clear that this protection is bought at a high cost. Moreover, few such protective gene systems have been described.

The balance between parasite and host is sometimes more complex than has just been assumed, namely, that the infective agent is fixed in its properties. Myxomatosis has many of the properties of the acute human exanthemata; in particular, it has difficulty in perpetuation as an enzoosis because it may destroy its host population. In a large scale enzootic, Ferner and Ratcliffe (1965) have demonstrated the evolution of less lethal forms of the myxoma virus. Parallels in human genetics have not been determined with certainty. Perhaps measles has not been exposed to the same risk of extinction, for it can or could move from country to country in the past, although it has no alternative host. The appearances of alastrim or variola minor cannot be considered as a mutation favorable to the organism, as it has not been perpetuated any more successfully than smallpox itself. Bubonic plague appears to have maintained its high case fatality rates over many centuries in man; this may well be because the epizootics in any region, not belonging to its niduses, are not perpetuated. Indeed, because bubonic plague is perpetuated in the niduses as a chronic or subacute disease, all the epizootics and epidemics caused by the bubonic plague bacillus are, from an ecological point of view, only epiphenomena or at most vehicles for the transfer of the infection to new niduses; it can be said that the balance has been obtained only in the niduses and not in either man or the common rats.

Many authors have given their opinions that any declines in mortality from the levels holding at the end of the nineteenth century would have a disastrous effect on the genetic constitution of the population. This view has often been expressed during the discussions on mortality in the Royal Statistical Society and in the eugenic writings of Karl Pearson and others. A milder form of hypothesis appears in Dubos (1961). It must be admitted that there may be truth in the hypothesis that protection against infective disease has been obtained by genetic selection and that a relaxation of pressure may lead to a weakening of the defence mechanisms; but, in any case, a very short time has elapsed since the general decline of mortality began in Europe, perhaps four generations. Can gross changes in genetic composition of the human population have occurred in such a short experience? Few striking findings of a similar nature appear to have been noticed in gene frequencies in *Drosophila* or *Mus* in such a small number of generations. It is possible that improvements in therapy in the past have had negligible effects on the average genetic fitness of the urbanized communities. It seems prudent to wait for more precise information from genetic science and to note that, although the problems of genetic resistance against diseases can be studied in small laboratory animals, there are difficulties in the long-lived human populations—in particular, the confounding of effects due to nature and to nurture (e.g., common effects of environment such as socioeconomic circumstances). For the coevolution of climate and life, see Schneider and Londer (1984).

31.5 Balance of Human Genes

The balance of the genes in the human species, as a result of mutations occurring naturally or induced by manmade changes in the environment, is now studied, after the manner of Vogel (1979), who had in mind the essay of Muller (1950) on the possible increase of deleterious genes in the human population.

Mutations can be subdivided into two kinds: (*i*) numerical and structural chromosome aberrations and (*ii*) gene or point mutations, where the mutation occurs in the base sequence of the DNA, and the number and visible structure of the chromosomes are intact. The interest here is in mutations in germ cells; mutations in somatic cells have special important in the genesis of cancer.

It is possible that the structural or numerical type of mutation does not add to the gene pool. Some examples are given. Down syndrome is due to a trisomy of autosome 21, that is, an excess of a chromosome to the pair corresponding to the 21st chromosome. Sex is determined by the presence or absence of Y in the sex chromosome; Klinefelter syndrome, with type XXY, occurs in males with an excess of one X-chromosome; Turner syndrome with a defect of one X, with type OX, occurs in females. The carriers of such abnormalities are usually too severely handicapped to produce children, and the mutated gene is wiped out in one generation. Nielsen and Sillesen (1975) have shown that somewhat more than one in 200 newborn infants have such a numerical or structural chromosome aberration occurring in one of the parents; in very few instances the aberration is balanced in the parent but causes an abnormality in the child. Other evidence confirms that there is a great loss of zygotes and embryos during intrauterine life.

Muller (1950) had gene or point mutations primarily in mind. Some of the earliest evidence for mutation rates came from family studies on the incidence of hemophilia and other diseases caused by mutations in the X chromosomes or on the incidence of defects caused by dominant autosomal genes. Vogel (1979) believes that the diseases already studied may give an estimate of the rate of mutation too high for other diseases or defects.

A few autosomal-recessive genes have a high frequency, 2% for the phenylketonuria gene and 3% to 5% for the cystic fibrosis of the pancreas disease. Most other defective recessive genes appear to have a lower frequency. Recessives are to be detected especially in consanguineous marriages. It has been hoped that such studies would lead to good estimates of their frequencies; but the results have been disappointing perhaps because the homozygous recessive genes are often lethal at an early stage of development. In most cases the heterozygous state for defective genes leads to a normal life.

So far the discussion has been on conditions or diseases caused by a gene at a single site. There are diseases caused by numbers of defective genes. For convenience, these fall into three main groups: (i) congenital malformations not caused by a single gene, (ii) constitutional diseases, for example, diabetes, rheumatic diseases, and heart diseases, (iii) mental deficiency and mental illness. However, there is little firm knowledge on the genetics of these three classes of disease. For mutation in human populations, see Crow and Denniston (1985), Denniston (1982), and Bora, Douglas and Nestleman (1982).

31.6 Positive Eugenic Measures

It is becoming clear that the incidence of few diseases can be affected by positive genetic measures. Some diseases caused by dominant genes can or could be controlled by genetics, for example, Huntington's chorea, but diseases caused by recessives pose very great difficulties. The general problem has been discussed by Penrose (1963) and by WHO-genetics (1964). Penrose (1963) points also to an obvious limitation of positive eugenics, namely, that a strain bred for one purpose may not be suitable for another; he also shows that not all effective therapy is dysgenic in its effect. For example, the negroes in America, no longer at risk to malaria infection, appear to be losing their sickle cell genes because the homozygotes suffer from a severe form of anemia, whereas in Africa the heterozygotes had been at an advantage over either form of homozygote, since they were partly protected from malaria. See §15.5.

In recent years in the developed countries, by screenings of fetuses known to be at high risk of abnormality, anomalies can often be diagnosed and the fetus aborted. Such changes in technique will have an effect on the statistical frequencies of genes in the population and mortality from the particular disease.

Chapter 32
Perinatal and Infant Mortality

32.1 Introduction

In this chapter, it is convenient to discuss all causes of death in the first year of life, and not limit the discussion to "certain conditions originating in the perinatal period" as in the ninth revision of the ICD, 760–779. Sometimes this policy will cause overlap with other chapters.

Perinatal mortality can only be obtained over a relatively short stretch of time in most series.

We make no attempt to divide deaths into those due to endogenous and exogenous causes, for it is evident from inspection of recent total mortality rates that the deaths from endogenous causes must be less than 10 per 1,000 in the first month of life and then less than 3 per 10,000 per annum throughout the rest of childhood. Clearly, endogenous mortality was an insignificant part of the total mortality throughout childhood in the world before 1900 and is now in many parts of the underdeveloped world.

Further, the statistics on infant mortality that are available for study come from the developed world or from special studies in the underdeveloped world, so the effects of many causes, important in some places or during some epochs, can neither be studied nor can appropriate comparisons be made. We suggest briefly some factors disturbing comparisons.

Endemic Infectious Causes

Throughout the wet tropics, malaria has played an important role in producing high infantile mortality rates. More localized examples are provided by infant botulism in Niugini and bartonellosis in the South American highlands.

Dietary Difficulties of the Infant

Francis Glisson (1597–1677) in 1668 recognized scurvy in infants but for a long time it was confused with rickets. Thomas Barlow (1845–1945) in 1883 gave an accurate description of infantile scurvy showing that the lesions, swollen and bleeding gums, and tenderness of long bones, were the same as in the adult form. By 1904 it was clear that it was especially associated with artificial feeding because very few breast-fed children had developed scurvy. It became clear that the antiscurvy factor in milk was destroyed by the heat, by the storage of commercial milk, and sometimes by the addition of potassium carbonates. There were great increases in infantile scurvy and other food deficiencies during World War I. See Smith (1947a, b) for examples from the Netherlands in World War II, and see also §32.4. But, even if the child has survived, there may be a lack of suitable foods at the time of weaning, and weanling diarrhea may ensue, for which see chapter 6 of Scrimshaw, Taylor, et al. (1968).

Infanticide and Gross Neglect

Infanticide may occur under harsh conditions of life. The reader is referred to Hausfater and Hrdy (1984). Extremes of neglect may occur; for example, under conditions of subsistence farming, the mother working in the fields may leave the infant in the care of an older sib; other economic conditions producing the same effect are well known.

Corsini (1984) concludes that the practice of abandoning children became increasingly widespread in Europe up to the nineteenth century. According to the records of the Hospital of the Innocents (l'Ospedale degli Innocenti) of Florence for the years 1762–1764 and 1809–1811, most of the legitimate children were taken back by their parents; of the others, three quarters died before reaching adulthood. The boys tended to be entrusted to peasant nurses and two-thirds of them remained in the country; the remainder became apprentices in the city at the age of 10 years; the girls were taken back by the hospital, which took care of them into their adult life and assisted them to marry by promising a dowry. Molin (1984) notes that children were abandoned in springtime, and girls were more likely to be abandoned than boys in the cities. For related themes see other articles in the same volume of the *Annales de Démographie historique*, for example, infanticide in Belgium (Leboutte, 1984).

For general references on infant mortality see: history, Boulanger and Tabutin (1980); history of infant welfare, Solomons (1958); social and biological factors, Morris, et al. (1955); maternal risk and health care, Institute of Medicine (1973); life cycle of the family, WHO-infant (1976); effects of infant and child mortality on fertility, Preston (1977*b*), and Ben-Porath (1980); autopsies, Molz (1973); migration and war, Ben-Porath (1980), Bergues (1948), and Bergues, Aries, et al. (1959).

32.2 Prenatal Death and Genetic Defects

Prenatal death until comparatively lately was curiously separated from infant mortality. An early exponent of the view that these subjects were closely related was Peller (1943), who used the term perinatal mortality to show that the early postnatal deaths and the late fetal deaths often had common causes.

Mortality commences at an early stage in development; thus, there are losses even before the embryo has become implanted in the uterine wall, but little precise knowledge of cause is available at these very early stages. A beginning has to be made at the stage of recognizable pregnancies in the second and third months. Lauritsen (1977) states that about 15% of all recognized pregnancies terminate in spontaneous abortions. From his own and other studies, he shows that about 51% of fetuses, aborted in the second and third months, had chromosomal anomalies, 41% had such in the fourth month, 12% in the fifth month, and 7% in the sixth month, and some 5% of the perinatal deaths and 0.58% of the deaths of newborn infants are to be added to these. From these figures, it can be deduced that not less than 5% of all conceptions terminate in deaths due to diagnosable genetic defects. It may well be that the true incidence is rather higher. Vogel (1979) uses this discussion to show that the problem of the build-up of hereditary diseases under favorable conditions and with relaxed selection pressure may not be as severe as was suggested by H.J. Muller (1950). Vogel (1979) gives a table showing the estimated incidence of death or severe disease due to spontaneous mutations: chromosome aberrations, numerical and structural, around 0.5% in the newborn, over 5% if miscarriages are included; dominant and X-linked diseases, less than 0.5%; autosomal recessive hereditary diseases and lethal genes, unknown; multifactorial diseases (malformations, constitutional diseases, and mental retardation or illness), 1%.

The sex ratio of fetal death in three surveys cited by Lauritsen (1977) were 0.82, 0.91, and 0.96, but he is inclined not to treat these ratios as departing from unity; indeed, false conclusions have been drawn from studies in the past that were based on ordinary anatomical diagnosis; moreover, diagnosis, even with modern cytological methods, still depends on assumptions.

See also Holland (1922) for the causes of death of fetuses. Modern surveys in the same country would not give results representative of deaths in such an "early" epoch.

For genetic wastage, see Boué, Boué, et al. (1985).

32.3 Stillbirths and Infant Deaths by Age

In only a few countries is it possible to give a comparison of stillbirth rates over a long stretch of time. They are available for England and Wales from 1931. According to Leck (1981a, Figure 2, p. 929), stillbirths have decreased from 40 per 1,000 births in 1931–1935 to 13 in 1961–1965 and 12 in 1971–1975; early neonatal deaths from 20 to 11 and then to 9 in 1971–1975; late neonatal deaths from 8 to 2 and then to less than 1 in 1971–1975; and postneonatal deaths from 30 to 6 and 6 per 1,000 births. Whereas early neonatal deaths were about two thirds of the postneonatal deaths in 1931–1935 in the developed world, in 1971–1975 they were about one-half in excess. The explanation is that congenital anomalies, ICD 740–759, complications of pregnancy and childbirth, ICD 760–772, and anoxic and hypoxic conditions and immaturity, ICD 776–777, have remained important, although the infective diseases, ICD 001–136 and 466–491, have been almost completely controlled.

In the following, much use has been made of the survey of Butler and Alberman (1969), carried out on infants born in the first week of March 1958 and stillbirths and multiple births occurring in March, April, and May 1958 in England and Wales and Scotland. Many references below will be to chapters appearing in the final report of this survey. Leck (1981a) gives many useful tables and graphs of the mortality of infants and children (up to 15 years) and is a useful summary of British experience. Leck (1981b) describes such modern problems of pediatrics as perinatal mortality by cause, common malformations, malformations due to rubella and thalidomide, and retrolental fibroplasia, which latter condition follows exposure of immature infants to high oxygen concentrations. This distribution of problems should be compared, or rather contrasted, with the distribution of problems in, for instance, the first decade of this century as given in Table 32.9.3.

From Baird and Thomson (1969b, Table 12.6), with the use of a perinatal rate of 32.0 per 1,000 from Baird and Thomson (1969a), the causes of perinatal death per 1,000 legitimate single births in the control week of 1958 were as follows: toxemia, 4.0; mechanical causes, 4.2; unexplained death in babies weighing more than 2500 g, 4.5, serological incompatibility, 1.4; malformations, 6.0; unexplained death in babies weighing 2500 g. or less, 5.7; antepartum hemorrhage, 4.5; and miscellaneous, 1.6—a total of 32.0.

The leading causes of stillbirth, observed in the same survey of 1958, were important in the following order: fetal distress, multiple births, malformations, and Rh-immunization, and in the ratios 959:152:136:90, according to Gruenwald (1969).

For the effects of masculinity on the infant mortality rates in an earlier survey, see Greenwood and Newbold (1925); for postneonatal mortality, see Pharoah and Morris (1979).

For sudden death syndrome, see Peterson (1984). For stillbirths, see Wilbur (1913).

32.4 Risks to the Development of Fetus and Infant

The embryo-fetus is at risk in utero from a number of factors. In §31.1 we have already mentioned genetic and chromosomal difficulties. We pass over the difficulties of implantation, for which statistics are scanty, and abortions, spontaneous or induced.

Some factors are now mentioned that have an importance varying greatly between communities.

(a) *Maternal Nutrition.* An extreme of maternal nutrition is famine. In the first trimester, famine conditions cause failures of implantation, raise stillbirth and early neonatal death rates, and cause later central nervous system disorders; they may also give rise to a low birth-weight syndrome due to prematurity rather than to a retardation of growth. Famine conditions in the third trimester cause an excess of deaths after the first week up to about 3 months after birth, according to Susser and Stein (1977), who had worked on famine conditions in the Netherlands. Puffer and Serrano (1973), writing on conditions in Latin America, have also stressed the importance of good maternal nutrition to prevent low birth weight and prematurity; they remark also that low maternal nutrition states may contribute to permanent deficits in growth. Anemia is likely to be associated with the malnutrition. A rapid succession of pregnancies can lead to a lower state of health and physiological well-being in the mother. After the birth of a new baby, the previous child will no longer be breast fed and so will suffer malnutrition.

(b) *Multiple Pregnancy*. The disability of a fetus in a multiple pregnancy seems to be due to the fetus receiving less nutriment than would a singleton, which causes retardation in growth in the last trimester. Moreover, the pregnancy is likely to terminate early because one effective stimulus to the commencement of labor is the distension of the uterus. Stanley (1977) cites data from McKeown and Record (1952) that shows the mean weights to be 3.38 kg for a singleton, 2.40 kg for a twin, 1.82 kg for a triplet, and 1.40 kg for a quadruplet. It is clear that many twins will be in a class with increased neonatal death rates and that triplets will be in a class of very high death rates. See also Butler, Alberman, et al. (1969a) and US National Center (1967c).

(c) *Maternal Infections*. In §31.1 we have already mentioned infections of the mother. It should be noted that during puerperal sepsis, the fetus could be infected. When maternal mortality from sepsis was high, as in the hospital epidemics (Semmelweis, 1861), there was also great perinatal mortality from sepsis. Rare specific infections by Venezuelan equine encephalitis and several ECHO viruses are mentioned by Sever (1980). In isolated communities, after the introduction of measles infections, there may be stillbirths and abortions. Congenital syphilis is still a problem with perhaps 300–400 new cases appearing in the United States annually; these may result in abortions and stillbirths. Active tuberculosis was said to be of bad prognosis to mother and child, alike.

(d) *Other Maternal Diseases*. Prematurity is common in hypertensive disease of pregnancy,

and it is usually noted that the infant is small with respect to gestational age. An important predisposing cause is overweight in mothers; heavier mothers suffer toxemia and hypertension death rates six times those of lighter mothers. In surveys, anemia in mothers was shown to be increasingly common with increasing age and parity and with low social class and economic status.

Antepartum hemorrhage is divided into placenta previa, accidental hemorrhage, and of unknown cause. A striking increase of placenta previa occurs with increasing age of the mother. (See chapter 3 of Butler and Alberman, 1969.)

(e) *Radiation*. In animal experiments, ionizing radiation causes congenital malformations, growth retardation, and embryonic death. By analogy, it is supposed that the same holds true in human populations. The risks at dosages less than 5 rad appear to be very low (Brent, 1980), so most modern diagnostic examinations do not represent a hazard to the fetus.

(f) *Iatrogenic Causes*. There are also iatrogenic causes of infant mortality, especially elective cesarean section and elective induction of labor, other than those undertaken for the treatment of an emergency arising in the current pregnancy. In the former type of induction, Niswander (1977) cites a prematurity index of about 10% with repeat cesarian section. In another personal series, he mentions 15 deaths out of 100 low-weight births in a series of 2,682 inductions. Some drugs against hyperemesis, such as thalidomide (Lenz and Knapp, 1962) and some tranquilizers, have led to congenital malformations. Diuretic drugs cause increased perinatal mortality (Berg, 1979), but it is difficult to distinguish mortality due to the drug from the effect of the maternal disease. See Kalter and Warkany (1983).

(g) *Miscellaneous*. Cigarette smoking leads to fetuses lighter than their presumed gestational weight.

For chemically induced birth defects and perinatal epidemiology, see Schardein (1985) and Bracken (1984).

TABLE 32.5.1. Neonatal deaths in California 1959–1966.

Group	Weight (g)	Gestation (weeks)	Neonatal death rate per 1,000
1	<1,500	all	726
2	1,501–2,500	<37	138
3	1,501–2,500	37+	50
4	>2,500	<37	15
5	>2,500	37+	4
Total	—	—	12

Berg (1979).

32.5 Prematurity

It has long been observed that prematurity is an unfavorable factor; with the great decline in infant mortalities, its relative importance has increased in those countries in which the bulk of the mortality falls in the early neonatal period. Yerushalmy (1938) showed the great importance of prematurity in a study of the New York statistics for 1936. We give in Table 32.5.1 the neonatal death rate by weight in a later series from California of Berg (1979). There is a steep gradient with weight. Above 2,500 g, the infant is well fitted to cope with the environment; over this weight, moreover, the risk of damage to the brain is much less and tentorial tears are rare with good obstetrics. Butler and Alberman (1969) give combined stillbirth-early neonatal rates of mortality of 227 per 1,000 at weights under 2,501 g, 28 at 2,501 to 3,000 g, 12 at 3,001 to 4,000 g, and 16 at weights over 4,000 g; of those under 2,001 g, the rates were 625 per 1,000 for singletons born in the control week of 1958.

There have been several special series of investigations on the effects of prematurity on neonatal mortality. It is pointed out by Baird (1977) that very few national epidemiologic studies of low birth weight (LBW) have been carried out because it is difficult to obtain accurate information on the various factors. We might add that these studies can only occur, as a rule, in those countries in which the perinatal death rates have already decreased to low levels, but we may suppose that factors so isolated were important in the past in those countries and are so in countries with less developed health services now. The mother's height, presumably conditional on the given ethnic stock (or genetic frequencies of the population), is the most important single factor influencing the birth weight of the infant (Baird, 1977). Under such conditions, height is highly dependent on social status. In Britain the high rates of perinatal mortality (PNM) by area were closely linked with socioeconomic (or environmental) factors. In Aberdeen the PNM fell by 50% between 1948 and 1972. It fell steadily during that time in the "obstetric" cause group, except in fourth or later births, because more than half the women in this parity group still elected to have a home confinement. In later times there has been an increasing use of induction of labor to avoid difficult births, and this has been successful in lowering mortality at weights over 2,500 g. Other authors and discussants in Reed and Stanley (1977) were in general agreement with the findings that social conditions were of importance, although some preferred other indicators of prosperity such as weight.

Leck (1981a, Table 12) shows that only 40% and 55% of infants of birth weight less than 1,500 g at two London hospitals survived to leave the hospital. Alberman (1974) gives the stillbirth and neonatal mortality for England and Wales, 1953–1971. For low birth weight, see Chase (1977), Committee to Study... Low Birthweight (1985), Gibson and McKeown (1950–1952), Hoffman, Lundin, et al. (1977), Lancaster (1956c), Scardovi (1960), US National Center (1965d, e, f) WHO-family health (1980), WHO-perinatal (1980), Yerushalmy (1967), Yerushalmy, van den Berg, et al. (1965), and Stanley (1977). For normal birth weights, see Macfarlane and Mugford (1984a, b).

32.6 Pathological Causes of Neonatal Deaths

The pathological causes of deaths are now detailed following Baird and Thomson (1969b) writing on mortality in the United Kingdom in 1958. Emphasis on the different factors tends to vary over the years and under differing social conditions.

(a) *Toxemia.* Death rates are high in primiparae and in women aged over 35 years. Although regimens of treatment are available for mother and infant, the reason for the declines is predominantly the effective prophylactic methods.

(b) *Mechanical Causes.* (i) Deliveries by the vertex. Trauma is greater in primiparae, especially those over the age of 35 years. (ii) Other mechanical causes of death. This group consists chiefly of deliveries complicated by abnormal presentations and by compressions of the cord.

(c) *Deaths of Uncertain Origin (Infants Mature by Weight).* These are deaths of mature infants, where neither the course of the pregnancy nor of the labor affords sufficient explanation, but such deaths are often associated with older age and primiparity or merely high parity. Prophylaxis is by surgical induction or by cesarian section, in an emergency.

(d) *Rhesus Incompatibility.* A necessary condition for the disease is high parity because there has to be immunization of the mother during a previous pregnancy. See also Muschel (1966).

(e) *Malformations.* Malformations of the central nervous system are more common in the lower socioeconomic groups. No definite gradients are detectable in the other types of malformation. See Butler, Alberman, Schutt, et al. (1969) and Penrose (1963).

(f) *Deaths of Uncertain Origin (due to Prematurity).* These are deaths of infants of low weight but with no history of an obvious cause, such as difficult birth.

(g) *Antepartum Hemorrhage.* In about 60% of cases the cause is unknown, and there is a fetal case fatality rate of about 8%; in placenta previa the case fatality rate is about 13% in one quoted series.

(h) *Sudden Death Syndrome.* The child dies or is found dead with no apparent cause. Sometimes a respiratory infection is reported. Formerly, it was believed that many such deaths were due to overlying, especially when deaths occurred on payday. In some regions, infant botulism may be an important cause, according to Arnon, Downs, and Chin (1981). See also Guntheroth (1982) and Peterson (1980, 1984).

Baird and Thomson (1969b, Table 12.6) assign the deaths for single legitimate births in their British series to categories as follows: toxemia, 12.6%; mechanical causes, 13.1%; mature unexplained, 14.1%; rhesus incompatibility, 4.3%; premature unexplained, 17.9%; malformations, 18.8%; antepartum hemorrhage, 14.2%; and remainder (maternal disease, infection, or other defined causes and not stated or inadequate), 5.1%. See §32.3 earlier for expression of these percentages as rates. They report that the older age of the mother and poor social status were of importance in this final group of causes. See also Butler, Alberman, et al. (1969b). For systemic infections of the newborn, see Parker (1984a); for staphylococcal disease of the newborn, see Parker (1984d).

32.7 Malnutrition and Bowel Infection

It has been shown in earlier sections that the chief hazards to the fetus and the neonatal infant are genetic anomalies, other developmental anomalies, birth trauma, and the state of health of the mother. By the end of the first 4 weeks, there remain two chief problems to the infant, adequate nutrition and freedom from infection, especially of the bowel.

Nutrition is usually assured for the infant if the mother is in a good state of health and nutrition and does not have too many duties other than the care of the infant to perform. In times of dearth or famine, for example, Antonov (1947), the infant may suffer greatly because there is a failure of the supply of maternal milk and substitutes are, or have been, usually impossible to obtain. Infant mortality rates have been observed to be high in such conditions of dearth. Less extreme conditions occur when the mother is forced to go out to work or, in the country, to work in the fields as has been noted by Turpeinen (1979b) in his study on Finnish infant mortality. The same effect is observed when there have been previous children who use up the mother's time and energy and cause pressure on the economic resources of the family. These general social factors are still important even in the developed countries, for example, Baird and Thomson (1969a, b), but are, of course, more apparent when mortality is considered in undeveloped areas by modern epidemiologic methods, as in Puffer and Serrano (1973). These general social and economic conditions express themselves in the adequacy of breast feeding. Although, in the developed countries, artificial milk can now be prepared that provides the protein and other constituents necessary for the child's development, and there is careful monitoring of such manufactures to ensure freedom from deleterious chemical constituents and freedom from bacilli, authoritative opinion, for example, Jelliffe and Jelliffe (1971, 1978), is that there are considerable differences between the milks of different species and that important differences still persist, even after careful modifications. An interesting example of the effect of breast feeding, in this case by wet nurses, was provided by the strikingly low infant mortality of German noble families, reported by Peller (1943) and detailed in a later section.

Artificial feeding, besides adding to the possibility of infection, brings about a change of intestinal flora and leads to the dominance of *Escherichia coli* in the bowel (Bullen, 1976). This may favor infection with pathogenic variants of *E. coli*. In the developing world or in classes with a low standard of hygiene, there are additional opportunities for infection, whether carried by flies, unclean utensils, or by hands preparing the artificial milk. The dilution of the artificial milk is also important.

Such effects of the infection as anorexia and vomiting are often aggravated by unsatisfactory treatments, whereby both food and fluids are withheld. The infection may interfere with the intake of correct nourishment and the absorption of food. The secretory powers of the bowel may be lost; the balances of magnesium, potassium, and phosphate in the body may be upset; particularly, intestinal infections reduce the intake of protein and calories

during the critical period of the onset of malnutrition and mortality in childhood, Mata, Kronmal, Garcia, et al. (1976).

In modern communities, such features can still be observed, as in Guatemala, where Mata, Kronmal, and Villegas (1980) found that the incidence rate per 100 person-years in a cohort of 45 children observed from birth was diarrhea, 483; diarrhea with mucus, 236; and dysentery, 73. In 3 years, these children had suffered 1,050 diarrhea-dysentery, 847 respiratory, 119 communicable diseases of childhood (various febrile exanthemata and whooping cough, principally), and 187 miscellaneous attacks of disease. Such experiences generalized to the world at large would mean over 2,000 million cases per annum. These authors also give deaths per 1,000,000 per annum from diarrhea and percentages of total deaths which these represent, for various countries in 1968, 1969, or 1970 as follows: United Arab Republic , 4,687, 34; Guatemala, 4,166; 24; El Salvador, 2,050, 21; Mexico, 1,506, 15; Colombia, 921, 12; Costa Rica, 691, 11; Sri Lanka, 462, 6; Cuba, 181, 3; Yugoslavia, 99, 1; Japan, 4, 0.7; Hungary, 3, 0.3; Sweden, 1, 0; Switzerland, 0.3, 0. Their Table 10 and Figure 6 show a marked decline in the rates and proportionate mortality for Costa Rica, so that the deaths per 1,000,000 per annum have decreased from about 4,000 in 1928–1932 to about 300 in 1973–1977. In Costa Rica the correlation between infant death rates and the death rate in the general population from diarrheal diseases was high, 0.96, and indeed the diarrheal diseases caused 95% of infant deaths.

We may detail the conclusions of Puffer and Serrano (1973) on infant mortality in Latin America:

(*i*) Nutritional deficiency was the most serious health problem and this is to be coupled with low birth weight.
(*ii*) The peak of mortality from nutritional deficiency was, in many cases, the third and fourth month of life.
(*iii*) Multiple causation of mortality was evident, for example, bad nutrition, infection, and the effects of complications of pregnancy and childbirth.

(iv) In undeveloped countries there may be grave deficiencies in the official statistics with resulting understatment of mortality rates.

(v) Among infectious diseases, diarrhea was first and measles second in importance. Frequency of infectious causes tended to be understated by about 20%.

(vi) Low birth weight was a principal association with high mortality in the neonatal period.

(vii) Congenital anomalies were higher than expected, and it is evident that many of these must depend on environmental causes.

(viii) Malignant neoplasms were understated in the official statistics. Sudden unexplained death was more common among the infants of mothers under 20 years of age.

(ix) Child mortality was higher in the rural districts.

(x) Reproductive wastage tended to be correlated with that of previous pregnancies of the mother.

(xi) Breast feeding was protective, especially against nutritional and diarrheal diseases.

(xii) Prenatal care of mothers reduced the infant mortality.

(xiii) Education of the mother was a useful predictor of mortality.

(xiv) Piped water supply deficiencies appeared to be important.

For perinatal infections, see Ciba Foundation (1980), Elliott and Knight (1976), and Ogra (1984). For iron deficiency, see Agarwal (1984).

32.8 Infancy in the German Nobility

Peller (1943) in his studies of the German noble families gave mortality by age of infants. In his Table 3, the first-week mortality of infants is given as 89, 75, 47, 34, 12, and 5 per 1,000 for the births in the sixteenth, seventeenth, and eighteenth centuries, and 1800–1849, 1850–1899, and 1900–1930, respectively. The rates for deaths in the first week combined with stillbirths were given as 100, 107, and 77 for the sixteenth, seventeenth, and eighteenth centuries, 63 for 1800–1849 per 1,000. For infants born to mothers marrying in the years 1850–1930, the same combined rate was 19 per 1,000.

Further, according to Peller (1943), for the sixteenth, seventeenth, and eighteenth centuries, and 1800–1849, 1850–1899, and 1900–1930, the infant mortality rates of children born alive were 193, 246, 153, 96, 41, and 8 per 1,000. He remarks that the seventeenth century, containing the Thirty Years War (1618–1648), was a time of turmoil and relatively low living standards for every class of the community. In the seventeenth and eighteenth centuries, the noble families were free of the summer epidemics because of their use of wet nurses, and they suffered no summer peak of infantile mortality.

Peller (1943) concluded that in the decades from 1870–1940, the health conditions in the general population of many countries improved so much that the children in the general population of school ages were not far behind the children of the most privileged European families in 1900–1936. This was also true for those children who had survived the first week after birth, but stillbirth rates and mortality rates in the first week of life were markedly in favor of the noble families.

32.9 Progress in Infant Mortality

The progress of infant mortality (IM) can be traced, from the high rates of 1881–1890 to the most recent completed decade, conveniently with the aid of Austrilian data, for which a breakdown by sex and cause is available for the 8 decades of this century. In Table 32.9.1, it is

TABLE 32.9.1. Infant mortality in Australia (deaths per 1,000 live births).

Epoch	Male	Female	Both Sexes	Masculinity*
1881–1890	130.5	114.1	122.5	114
1891–1900	118.8	101.9	110.5	117
1901–1910	94.4	79.0	86.9	119
1911–1920	74.7	60.0	67.5	124
1921–1930	61.0	48.6	55.0	125
1931–1940	44.6	35.2	40.0	127
1941–1950	34.0	26.9	30.5	126
1951–1960	24.5	19.6	22.1	125
1961–1970	21.0	16.3	18.7	129
1971–1980	16.0	12.5	14.3	128

*100 × (male death rates)/(female death rates)
From Lancaster (1956c) and Demography (Australia).

TABLE 32.9.2. Infant mortality rates (deaths per 1,000 live births).

	1885	1895	1905	1915	1925	1935	1945	1955	1965	1975
Austria	255	241	231	218	119	99	162	46	28	20
Belgium	150	172	147	125	100	85	100	41	24	16
England and Wales	138	161	128	110	75	57	46	25	19	16
France	161	177	135	123	95	72	114	39	22	14
Ireland	95	104	95	92	68	68	71	37	25	18
Scotland	121	133	116	126	91	77	56	30	23	17
Spain	192	—*	161	152	137	109	85	51	30	19
Switzerland	173	159	129	90	58	48	41	26	18	11
Denmark	128	137	120	93	80	71	48	25	19	10
Finland	162	129	135	110	85	67	63	30	18	10
Iceland	149	124	107	66	45	68	34	22	15	12
Norway	93	96	82	67	50	44	36	21	17	11
Sweden	114	95	88	76	56	46	30	17	13	9
Australia	123[†]	101	82	68	53	40	29	22	18	14
New Zealand	89	88	68	50	40	32	28	24	20	16

*Unavailable.

[†]For years 1881–1890.

Sources: Data from B.R. Mitchell, *European Historical Statistics, 1750–1970*, pp. 127–132. Copyright 1975, The Macmillan Press Ltd., reprinted with permission.
UN Demographic Yearbooks.
Yearbooks of Iceland, Australia, New Zealand.

evident that the IM rates have declined steadily over the 10 decades; in absolute terms, the rates of decline were greatest in the years around 1900, a gain of about 20 deaths per 1,000 between the 2 successive decades; the relative declines were greatest in the years about 1950, about 28% for males and 27% for females between the decades. For comparison with other international series, the IM rate for all live births is also given; this is approximately the average of the male and female rates. The masculinity of the IM rates was less than 120 until 1920, and since then it has increased toward 130.

In Table 32.9.2 the IM rates are detailed for a number of countries with long series; in 1885 the Australian and New Zealand rates were among the lowest in the world, and there was a considerable variance between countries, but in recent years there has been an approximate equalization in the developed world. In 1975 no Nordic country had a rate exceeding 12 per 1,000 and the IM rate did not exceed 20 in the other developed countries. In 1885 there was a greater dispersion; Austria, Spain, Switzerland, and Finland all had high rates. By 1914

the rates in Austria had decreased to a level below 200, not shown in the table, but wartime conditions delayed further declines. In general, it can be said that the declines in the IM rates began around the turn of the century; in some countries the rates rose during World War I and again, as a result of World War II. Infections and conditions of dearth were responsible for the great fluctuations from year to year in the times before 1885, especially in the Nordic countries; thus, IM rates between 275 and 654 were experienced in Iceland during the period 1838–1847. In all the Nordic countries, except Iceland, the IM rates were higher in 1868 than in either of the 2 neighboring years, 145 in Denmark, 392 in Finland, 126 in Norway, and 168 in Sweden, whereas in Iceland the rates were 232, 263, 319, and 198 in the years 1867–1870. For the countries represented in Table 32.9.2, conditions in the two World Wars thus produced less disturbance to the IM rates than did the famines or dearths of 1867–1868.

It is convenient now to use the Australian data on deaths by cause, with the aid of Table 32.9.3 and the discussion of Lancaster (1956c). Most of the remarks are of quite general ap-

TABLE 32.9.3. Infant mortality in Australia by cause (deaths per 1,000,000 live births).

	gastro-intestinal disease	tuberculosis	congenital syphilis	diphtheria	pertussis	scarlatina	erysipelas	meningitis	tetanus	acute poliomyelitis	measles	rubella
						Males						
1908–1910	25,182	967	1,149	279	1,735	57	154	1,633	324	—*	222	—
1911–1920	20,050	530	733	381	1,456	15	195	1,763	246	—	360	—
1921–1930	11,932	319	329	345	1,358	38	199	876	84	16	224	—
1931–1940	3,517	192	171	201	1,009	22	85	465	20	12	84	—
1941–1950	2,318	100	50	95	413	2	11	504	27	9	99	—
1951–1960	1,093	23	9	9	51	0	4	303	9	12	26	—
1961–1970	513	2	10	0	9	2	1	41	2	1	16	3
1971–1980	306	2	7	1	3	1	0	24	0	0	6	7
						Females						
1908–1910	21,120	744	822	246	1,987	18	162	1,578	258	—	180	—
1911–1920	16,190	419	610	279	1,751	22	171	1,381	163	—	277	—
1921–1930	9,263	286	296	263	1,672	25	187	673	48	23	147	—
1931–1940	2,647	148	123	190	1,250	25	93	336	14	18	90	—
1941–1950	1,652	102	35	61	509	1	2	417	15	11	90	—
1951–1960	873	28	6	12	59	1	3	249	3	10	26	—
1961–1970	440	2	5	1	10	2	0	33	0	0	16	2
1971–1980	251	1	9	0	8	0	1	17	0	0	9	3

	neoplasms	encephalitis, brain abscess	nervous system	circulatory	respiratory	genitourinary	malformations	peculiar to first year‡	infections of skin, bones, etc.	accident, injury	all causes
						Males					
1908–1910	97	23	4,556	279	8,072	273	3,077	28,726	597	2,025	81,940
1911–1920	49	67	2,766	179	7,359	286	4,014	32,243	457	981	74,670
1921–1930	76	134	1,423	123	7,125	245	4,713	29,403	461	767	60,990
1931–1940	93	59	596	77	5,726	261	5,069	24,989	306	918	44,648
1941–1950	91	90	421	79	4,085	134	4,356	19,670	190	788	33,975
1951–1960	107	33	222	94	2,234	78	4,275	15,074	300	677	24,471
1961–1970	81	—†	382	93	2,457	58	3,756	12,012	38	723	20,966
1971–1980	68	—	255	77	1,181	23	3,458	9,557	14	506	16,021
						Females					
1908–1910	48	0	3,409	198	6,266	210	2,563	22,711	456	1,494	68,164
1911–1920	40	49	2,063	116	6,069	190	3,171	25,418	351	832	60,027
1921–1930	40	98	1,086	84	5,933	212	3,681	22,913	355	691	48,645
1931–1940	90	33	397	67	4,531	186	3,915	19,417	255	798	35,186
1941–1950	100	71	312	54	3,385	74	3,745	15,149	141	581	26,936
1951–1960	83	27	183	64	1,854	43	3,664	11,624	204	535	19,576
1961–1970	82	—†	299	73	1,953	32	3,274	8,884	35	547	16,281
1971–1980	45	—	194	78	837	17	3,185	6,974	11	415	12,479

* Not separately listed.
† Included in nervous.
‡ This column includes deaths due to prematurity, exposure, trauma, . . . , usually occurring in the first week.
From Lancaster (1956c) and Demography (Australia).

plication to the other countries in the developed world.

Gastrointestinal Diseases. These diseases were of prime importance in the declines in the total IM rate. The most important infective disease of infancy has been gastroenteritis. The dysenteries and the salmonella infections have been, perhaps, of less importance, although it has always been difficult to differentiate these diseases in infancy from gastroenteritis; indeed, it may be stated that the difference is often only one of definition. Dysentery appears, in Australia at least, not to have been important at this age. Some of the factors underlying the decline in gastroenteritis mortality have been such public health measures as better water supplies, fly control and hygienic disposal of excreta, and educational programs, direct and indirect, on the handling of foods in the home, for example, in the preparation of artificial milk substitutes. In more recent times, there has been a great diffusion of knowledge on hygiene through the schools and also by such persons as nurses returning to civil life. Further, the germ theory of disease has been established as part of general knowledge in the population since the early years of this century. See §6.11 for a discussion of the causative organisms, and also Holme, Holmgren, Merson, and Möllby (1981) and Remington and Klein (1983).

Tuberculosis. Little is known regarding the relative frequencies of bovine and human types of tuberculosis as causes of IM in most countries; but see §7.1 for the United States, Lancaster (1950d) for Australia, and UK Ministry of Health (1931) for England and Wales. It is probable that the human type has been predominant in Australia. Tuberculosis in infancy is usually tuberculous meningitis. Certainly, treatment in the earlier epochs and probably in all epochs has been ineffective, so that other causes for the declines in mortality must be sought. Pasteurization of milk has certainly been an important factor for reducing the load of bovine tuberculosis and possibly also of the human tuberculosis infections. Public health and veterinary action against tuberculous cattle has also been of importance. Changes in social conditions and public health action against the spread of bacilli from known carriers of the disease have also been effective.

Measles, pertussis, scarlatina, and diphtheria are the four principal specific infective diseases spread by the nose and throat. The effects of such factors, as better care and better nourishment of children, smaller families, and the absence of other debilitating infections, must all be considered.

Diphtheria. The importance of diphtheria, never a leading cause of death at this age, has declined. We may recall the discussion of the values of serum therapy and toxoid prophylaxis in §9.3, especially Table 9.3.2.

Pertussis. The contribution to the IM rate of pertussis has declined from about 1.8 per 1,000 in 1908–1910 to a negligible amount in 1971–1980; see §9.4, Lancaster (1952a), and Burnet (1952). In each period the masculinity has been low, aproximately 80. It is evident that immunization cannot be held responsible for the decline that took place before its introduction; moreover, specific therapy was not available.

Scarlatina. Scarlatina was not a great cause of infant mortality in Australia over the years 1908–1980, although there had been a great epidemic in Victoria in 1875–1876 causing more than 3,000 deaths among a population of about 0.79 million; see Lancaster (1960a), Cumpston (1927), and §9.5.

Erysipelas. Erysipelas has not been an important cause of death at this age. There is a sharp decline, as for scarlatina also, around 1940, and this may have been due to the increasing use of sulfonamide drugs.

Meningitis. The absence of decline in meningitis rates around 1940 appears to negate the previous statement on the therapy of erysipelas, but the incidence of meningitis rose during the war years.

Tetanus. Tetanus appears to have caused deaths; the official statisticians have believed that such a certification is not a confusion with "tetany." Presumably the immediate cause of the tetanus is an infected cord.

Acute Poliomyelitis. Contrary to popular belief, this disease has not been a great cause of death at any age.

Measles. Measles has a high case fatality rate in infancy.

Rubella. A few deaths have been certified as due to this cause in recent years.

Neoplasms. These are rare causes of death in infancy.

Nervous System. Infective disease of the nervous system includes otitis media, and also encephalitis and brain abscess, shown separately in Table 32.9.3. Possibly many of the deaths were certified as "convulsions," and so were really due to some infection of undetermined site; but clearly the diseases certified as the causes of deaths in this class have been important in declines in IM rates.

Cardiovascular Diseases. These have not been important in infancy but have tended to decline.

Respiratory Diseases. These have been important causes of death, especially in infants either prematurely born or weakened by disease, exposure, or reduced nutrition.

Alimentary Diseases. Even when gastroenteritis has been subtracted out of the diseases of the alimentary system, the residue "other alimentary diseases" has been important for the IM rates. The IM rates for this class have fallen to about one-tenth of the earliest rates.

Genitourinary Diseases. There have been steady declines in the IM rates, again to about one-tenth of the earliest rates.

Congenital Malformations. The rates have been rather steady over the 8 epochs. This has resulted in their becoming relatively more important as a cause of infant death, from about 4% of the IM rates in the early epochs to almost 25% in the most recent.

Conditions Originating in the Puerperium. These deaths are due to a large number of causes, listed as ICD 760–779, including difficulties caused by illness of the mother, difficulties in the birth, and immaturity. See §32.6.

Accident and Injury. Infant mortality rates have greatly diminished; in the early epochs there would have been deaths from neglect and exposure, sometimes criminal.

There are many references in other chapters to infant mortality, especially in chapters 37 to 44, by country. For IM in Norway and England and Wales, see US National Center (1967*a*) and Macfarlane and Mugford (1984*a*, *b*). For New York City, see Pakter and Nelson (1974).

32.10 Infant Mortality in the Parishes

Infant mortality (IM) rates can often be obtained in the parish records after the middle of the sixteenth century, where the age-specific death rates of childhood or the probability of survival to adult life cannot be computed. Goubert (1960, 1965*a*) found that the IM rates in the seventeenth century could approach 400 per 1,000 in some parishes of Beauvais. Many parish records are also available from the Nordic countries. We can give here only some illustrative examples from Belgium, England, Finland, France, and Iceland in Table 32.10.1. See Béhar (1964) and also the sections on countries, especially France in §38.2.

32.11 Developed Countries in Former Times

England and Wales

Some estimates of infant mortality have already been given in §32.10. Although Graunt (1662) did not have age at death recorded in the bills of mortality, he found that, of 229, 250 people dying in 20 years, the causes in 71,124 deaths were thrush, convulsions, rickets, "teeth," and worms, or as "abortives," "chrysomes," infants "liver-grown," and "overlaid." He guessed that about half of 12,210 deaths due to smallpox, swinepox, measles, and worms without convulsions were also of children under 6 years of age. He concluded that 36% of all births (quick conceptions) resulted in death before the age of 6 years. Later statistics, when they became available in the early part of the nineteenth century, showed that Graunt's guess was probably a very good one. Edmonds (1835–1836) was unable to

TABLE 32.10.1. Infant mortality in the parishes.

Region	Epoch	Rate*	Author
Belgium, East Flanders			
Elversele	1650–1699	151	Deprez, 1969
	1700–1749	152	Deprez, 1969
	1750–1796	215	Deprez, 1969
Levendegem	1700–1719	206.7	Deprez, 1969
	1720–1739	193.9	Deprez, 1969
	1740–1759	204.2	Deprez, 1969
	1760–1779	228.1	Deprez, 1969
	1780–1796	220.9	Deprez, 1969
England			
8 Parishes	1550–1599	130	Schofield and Wrigley, 1979
	1600–1649	124	Schofield and Wrigley, 1979
Aldgate, London	1583–1599	299	Forbes, 1971
Nth Shropshire	1561–1610	207	Jones, 1976, 1980
	1611–1660	174	Jones, 1976, 1980
	1661–1710	191	Jones, 1976, 1980
	1711–1760	155	Jones, 1976, 1980
	1761–1770	102	Jones, 1976, 1980
Leicester	1839–1844	197	Levine, 1976
Finland	1751–1755	223	Turpeinen, 1979b
	1801–1805	196	Turpeinen, 1979b
	1851–1855	176	Turpeinen, 1979b
France			
Various Parishes	17th century	<250 (usually)	L. Henry cited by Goubert, 1965a
	ca 1750	170	L. Henry, 1976
	1656–1735	288 (min).	Goubert, 1965a
Iceland	1841, 1842, 1844, 1845	302	Schleisner, 1851

*Per 1,000 live births.

obtain the infant mortality but gave the probability of survival to 5 years as 0.255, 0.370, 0.485, 0.587, and 0.682 for the epochs 1730–1749, 1750–1769. . ., 1810–1829, respectively, in London, which can be compared with 0.832 for 1911–1915. These astonishing figures are accepted by Farr (1885, p. 195). According to Farr, among the principal causes of infant mortality are improper and insufficient food, bad management, the use of opiates, neglect, early marriages, and the debility of the mothers; we can see that these causes are not mutually independent. Farr believes that a high death rate is largely due to "bad sanitary arrangements"; the causes of death more directly due to neglect and mismanagement are convulsions, diarrhea, and atrophy. Illegitimacy was a great underlying factor of death. In a given city, or urban district, comparisons can be made; thus, the IM rates in 1875 of legitimate and illegitimate infants per 1,000 (legitimate and illegitimate births respectively) were 187 and 547 in the urban district of Radford, and in Driffield, 168 and 596. Similarly, in the City of Glasgow the corresponding rates per 1,000 were 152 and 286. Farr concludes that the IM rates in every city could potentially be reduced to the level of the rate, 118 per 1,000 live births, in the healthy districts. On this point, Brend, in Chalmers, Brend, Findlay, and Brownlee (1918), compares the IM rates per 1,000 for 1914 in various cities: Bath 59,

Canterbury 60, Oxford 72, St. Albans 52, Leyton 79, Walthamstow 77, Tunbridge Wells 79, Hornsey 58, and East Ham 76, and in the seaside towns, Bournemouth 72, Eastbourne 61, Hastings 64, Southend 69, Poole 77, Dover 76, Folkstone 62, and Worthing 60. He concludes, on his p. 18, that the most important factor in the differences may be the polluted atmosphere. On his p. 19, he compares the contributions of different pathologies to the IM rate per 1,000 in England and Wales, northern country boroughs, and southern districts: respiratory diseases 26, 35, and 14; measles 2.1, 3.8, and 0.3; diarrhea and enteritis 17, 24, and 6, and so on, and notes that the differences in the total IM rates are due largely to the differences in respiratory disease and diarrhea-enteritis. Brend does not appear to see that the differences must be the greater for the easier passage of organisms in the city. Infant mortality rates from premature births have a social gradient from 14 in the top class to 20 in the lowest; congenital malformations is rather constant over the classes and the subclass of atrophy, debility, and marasmus, again has a gradient, with upper social class 6 and lowest social class 10 per 1,000. Findlay finds that housing conditions are important; indeed, in the city of Liverpool the IM rates were 154, 125, 132, 139, and 133 in the 5 years 1911–1915, whereas in its new suburb Port Sunlight, the IM rates were for the same years 52, 81, 104, 74, and 101. He says that little progress can be made by the clinics if the child has to spend its time in unhygienic home surroundings. Findlay mentions that the number of deaths assigned to prematurity and congenital defects is rather constant, causing, between them about 31% of all infant deaths. These include deaths from marasmus (wasting) due to some inherent defect of metabolism; other causes of marasmus are environmental; indeed, some are due to tuberculosis, from the ingestion of tuberculous milk, and others, to chronic pneumonia and infection of the urinary tract. In Glasgow the deaths of children from this group are estimated as 8% to 16% by the hospital, as against 31% by the official statistics.

Brownlee finishes off this special report with some observations on the physiological processes of the developing child, with the aid of some graduations, which do not help to clarify the problems. Indeed, the whole report can be read as a social document, showing that infant mortality was then due to respiratory, gastrointestinal and tuberculous infections, faulty nutrition, and neglect, conclusions unacceptable to contemporaries.

For infanticide, see Behlmer (1979). For some comparison with continental authors, see Greenwood and Brown (1912).

32.12 International and Secular Comparisons

The infant mortality rate has long enjoyed a reputation as a useful measure of the hygiene of a state, city, region, or other demographic unit, because it can be computed without the use of census data. Countries of the world vary in the length and regularity of their series. Thus, the rates for Sweden and Norway are available from 1721 onward, whereas the rates for some of the other states are available only for the years in this century; some are even incomplete this century because of war, civil strife, changes of national boundaries or, perhaps only lack of consolidation of data collected in different areas in the country.

The Swedish rates fluctuated around 200 per 1,000 in the years 1750–1810 and then decreased to about 150 in 1850. They then began a steady decline, reaching 99 in 1900; for 1905, 1910, 1915, . . . the rates were 88, 75, 76, 63, 56; 55, 46, 39, 30, 21; 17, 17, 13, 11, 9; and 7 in 1980.

In UN Population Studies (1954), straight lines are fitted to national curves of the infant mortality rates between 1915 and 1949 and it is calculated that they have fallen by about $0.028 \times$ rate each year, that is, the curve of logarithm of the rate was practically linear between 1915 and 1949, or the rate was decreasing in a geometric progression, being halved in 25 years. This linearity must be regarded as an accident, and the estimated parameter as a convenient way to describe the decrease in the rates.

Detailed annual rates for infant mortality are given in Mitchell (1975).

See also WHO-infant (1970), WHO-perinatal (1970, 1972, 1976, 1978, 1980), WHO-perinatal and child (1976), Bracken (1984), and Foster (1981).

For infant and perinatal mortality by country, see:

United States: US National Center for Health Statistics (1965*b*, *c*); W. Smith (1987)

United States up to 1963: US National Center (1966*c*)

Belgium: (by month) Vilquin (1978)

Brazil: Yunes (1981)

Czechoslovakia: US National Center (1969)

Denmark: US National Center (1967*b*)

developing world: Béhar (1964); Département de Démographie, Louvain (1979); Morley (1978); Palloni (1981)

England and Wales: Grundy and Lewis-Faning (1957); Special Committee (1913); Special Report (1918); Thompson (1984); US National Center (1968*c*); Wohl (1983)

Europe and United States: Chase (1967)

central and eastern Europe: Pongracz (1972)

Mediterranean basin: Biraben and Henry (1957)

Netherland: US National Center (1968*b*)

Norway: US National Center (1967*a*)

Scotland: US National Center (1966*a*)

Sierra Leone: WHO-infant (1981)

Sweden: Nybølle (1931)

world: Stowman (1947–1948*d*); Vallin (1976*a*, *b*).

Chapter 33
War

33.1 Introduction

A treatment of the role of wars in the development of mortality can hardly be avoided, although there are great difficulties in obtaining and reducing the necessary data.

Records of the actual losses in the armies are only obtainable after the War of the Spanish Succession; in the period 1714–1848, reliable data apply only to the greater battles, engagements, and sieges. After 1848, the military history section of the general staff has usually compiled comprehensive monographs on the various campaigns of the armed forces. So, even approximately correct data for the battles in the period 1600–1848 are usually not available. In earlier times, few records were kept of the killing and wounding of civilians and of the famines and epidemics resulting from war. Some indirect evidence has been adduced by the study of parish records, which permits estimates to be made of the total casualties in some areas, as in §33.4. Possibly such accurate estimates are not to be hoped for with respect to earlier wars.

We make some general remarks on the literature used in this chapter. War is part of history; so some volumes consulted are Ropp (1959), Howard (1976), and Delbrueck (1975); now that the role of history is in a state of change, Parker (1979), writing in the *Companion Volume to The New Cambridge Modern History*, is of interest as, by implication, is the chapter on population in the same volume. On the losses in war, Urlanis (1960, 1971) is unavailable to us; the two volumes Parkinson

(1977) and Singer and Small (1972) are disappointing; but Wright (1965) has several chapters that include many tables of great comparative interest, and is possibly the most useful book for our purposes. In general, the Carnegie Endowment for International Peace series are also disappointing, for there is no overall plan so that countries can be compared, although Kohn and Meyendorff (1932) and Meerwarth (1932) have been useful; written under the same auspices, Bodart (1916), Prinzing (1916), Dumas (1923), and Westergaard (1923) have been particularly so. Prinzing (1916) is more useful than the widely quoted Zinsser (1935), which contains surprisingly few facts. See also Garrison (1929) for general medical history. The medical histories of the British Army and Navy have been written in two admirable series Cantile (1974*a*, *b*), and Keevil (1957/1958) and Lloyd and Coulter (1961/1963). For generalities on war, see Levy (1983) and Nettleship, Givens, and Nettleship (1975).

MacNalty and Mellor (1968) give the principal medical lessons of World War II for the countries of the British Empire. Ziegler (1971) is a bibliography of books in English on war, 1945–1965. For the impact of war on population, see Hauser (1942).

33.2 Development of the Technique of War

The methods of warfare have determined the size of armies, so we begin with a discussion of some changing techniques after the style of

TABLE 33.2.1. European army sizes, 1470–1760 (in thousands).

Date (circa)	Spanish Monarchy	Dutch Republic	France	England	Sweden	Russia
1475	20	—	40	25	—	—
1555	150	—	50	20	—	—
1595	200	20	80	30	15	—
1635	300	50	150	—	45	35
1655	100	—	100	70	70	—
1675	70	110	120	15	63	130
1705	50	100	400	87	100	170
1760	98	36	247	199	85	146

Source: G. Parker, 'The "Military Revolution, 1560–1660"—a myth?', *Journal of Modern History*, XLVIII (1976), p. 206; and Lloyd's *Lists of the forces of the states of Europe* (London, 1761).
From G. Parker, "Warfare", p. 205. *Companion Volume to Vol. 13, The New Cambridge Modern History.* Copyright Cambridge Univ. Press, 1979, reprinted with permission.

Parker (1979) and Hackett (1983). First, the development of the large siege cannon, made of cast iron from the 1380s and of bronze from the 1420s, rendered the thin high walls of the castles of the Middle Ages quite indefensible. Second, to counter such bombardment, a new style of fortification was developed—the *trace italienne*, a circuit of low thick walls, punctuated by quadrilateral bastions. War then became a struggle for the the castles that dominated the countryside. However, the castles with the new defense could not be taken easily; they had to be reduced by exhaustion and starvation.

At sea, the development of heavy artillery brought about changes—artillery bombardment replaced ramming and boarding in naval battles.

After 1550, the musket was introduced; it was capable of killing a man at 300 meters. For most of the Middle Ages heavy cavalry had dominated the battles. Heavily armed knights had won great battles at Antioch in 1098, Bouvines in 1214, and Roosbeke in 1382, for example, but they could be beaten by volleys of arrows or pikemen, suitably deployed. Further, the heavy cavalry was expensive and necessarily few. These considerations brought about an increase in the proportion of infantry in the armies. Except for some inventions such as the mortar in the 1580s, the light field gun in the 1620s, the flintlock musket in the 1630s, and the socket bayonet in the 1670s, the mode of European warfare remained rather fixed un-

til the nineteenth century, although the sizes of the armies and navies increased greatly between the fifteenth and eighteenth centuries, as is shown by estimates of the national armies in Table 33.2.1. The Dutch, English, and French navies greatly increased in size. The growth in sizes of armies and navies ceased early in the eighteenth century but began again at the time of the revolutionary wars in France.

33.3 Mortality of Soldiers in War

As Bodart (1916) points out, the losses in war of greatest interest to the official annalists or historians are those of the armed forces. The casualties are the killed, the wounded not taken prisoners, and those taken prisoners wounded or not. The recorded "missing" may include both types of losses, on the one hand the dead and wounded who could not be found, and on the other, prisoners whose fates remained unknown to their comrades, as well as deserters and dispersed troops. The fate of the "missing" is generally not known until long after the end of the war. Often they are erroneously counted with the dead.

Bodart (1916) quotes an analysis of the 30 greatest battles of the sixteenth century; the losses in killed and wounded were 10% for the victors and 40% for the defeated army of their respective, effective strengths. The numbers of those killed greatly exceeded those of the wounded, and few prisoners were taken. The main part of the armies of France, Spain, the

Empire, and Venice were mercenaries. Battles were decided in hand-to-hand combat, and the victors killed as many as possible of the vanquished, with the exception of knights, nobles, and higher officers, from whom a high ransom might be extorted. In the sixteenth century, moreover, the religious and civil wars were, as always, bloodier than wars between states and nations. Thus, the battles of the Peasants' Wars (1524–1525) frequently ended in the complete extermination of the peasant armies, and in the Huguenot Wars also the slaughter was great.

For wars before 1848, general statistics are not available, but the loss of officers is or may be given exactly, many states publishing lists of their names. Contrary to widespread views, officers of an army almost always show a much higher percentage of casualties than do the men. This is especially a feature of battles in the open field, in sea fights, in storming fortified places, and in crossing rivers in the face of the enemy. For the social consequences of such differential mortality in World War I, see Winter (1977); for Sweden, see Tiselius (1904).

In recent battles before World War I about 22% of the casualties on an average are deaths. If the percentages are higher than this figure, some explanation is usually required. In the naval battles there are the destructive effects of the enemy's artillery on large numbers of men confined within a small space, death by drowning if the ship is sunk, stranded, or rammed, death by suffocation and burns after a fire or magazine explosion; thus, in the naval battle at Abukir in 1798 the French lost 2,000 killed and 1,100 wounded, at Trafalgar in 1805 the Franco-Spanish loss was 5,000 killed and 3,000 wounded, and at Tsushima in 1905 Russian losses were 3,500 killed and 7,500 wounded. Death by drowning has sometimes played a great part in land battles; thus, the French lost 10,000 killed and an equal number wounded at the crossing of the Beresina in 1812. Large losses from drowning have often occurred when the defeated army has been driven into the sea or a river.

See also Beebe and de Bakey (1952) and Small and Singer (1982). For losses in the French Army under the First Empire, see Houdaille (1972). For the navies and sailors, see §33.15.

33.4 War and Population in 1618–1648

We choose the Thirty Years War, 1618–1648, as an example of the effects of war on the population; it can be examined without too much partisan bias. Many monographs are available for study from a copious documentation on the numbers of hearths, communicants, births, and deaths, from the commissions of enquiry about 1650, from records of land tax, and others. The studies of Franz (1940/1961) and Keyser (1941) have been the basis of the modern views on population changes due to that war. Beller (1970), Pagès (1970) and Perroy (1951) give standard accounts of the war, and pictorial records and text are available in Langer (1980).

The map in *Westermanns Atlas zur Weltgeschichte* of 1956 (p. 107), summarizing the results of Franz (1940/1961) and Keyser (1941), shows areas in Silesia, Mecklenburgh, the Pfalz, Württemberg, and western Bavaria, in which more than two-thirds of the population had been lost. Losses between the Rhine and the Elbe varied from one- to two-thirds of the total population. Indeed, the population losses over a large area of Europe were relatively greater than those due to the Black Death anywhere in the fourteenth century.

Actual losses by battle were not a large proportion of the total. In the major battles of the war, each side would have a force of the order of 20,000 to 30,000. Large citizen armies were a later development of the Napoleonic Wars.

Direct military causes were the punitive and "prophylactic" killings. Thus, at the battle of the River Lech on April 15, 1632, Gustavus Adolphus achieved a spectacular victory. After the battle, his army devastated Bavaria, slaughtering many peasants, partly to weaken the enemy and partly as revenge for the devastation of the Protestant north, according to Beller (1970).

The civil population was sometimes caught up in the actual operations of the war. Thus, we see later in §33.12 that almost 20,000 civilians lost their lives at the siege and fall of Magdeburg in 1631.

There were great losses of population, however, in areas that were not theaters of war operations. Thus, the population of Württemberg fell from 450,000 to 100,000, although it was only a zone of passage. Troops taking up winter quarters would make raids to seize food supplies, which would provoke replies from some of the people, and this would lead to reprisals. Homes would be destroyed and farms abandoned. Crops would not be sown because of loss of the seed and, perhaps, the absence of the active men from the country. The confiscation of the food would lead to famine and the building up of stocks would be slow. It has been stated that hardly more than 6,000 of the 35,000 Bohemian villages remained standing.

33.5 Soldiers in Barracks

Medical statistics on the troops were first compiled for the British Army after the Director General of Army Medical Services, General James McGrigor (1771–1858) had instituted a series of returns on illness. These were analyzed by Henry Marshall (1775–1851), Inspector-General of Hospitals, "the father of medical statistics," who was influential in informing public opinion on the state of health in the army in war and peace.

We begin with Annesley, Tulloch, et al. (1840) who reported on the mortality of European troops in the Madras Presidency, 1793–1838. In this period, 1793–1805, 1810, 1811, 1817–1819, and 1824–1826 were the years of campaigns or wars, whereas 1806–1809, 1812–1816, 1820–1823, and 1827–1838 were the years of peace; the mortality rates per 1,000 per annum were 83 in the years of war and 57 in the years of peace. The mortalities are given in Table 33.5.1 by single years of experience. Annesley, Tulloch, et al. (1840) comment on these figures as follows:

with regard to the proportion of deaths between seasons of peace and war in India, there are grounds for believing that deaths from wounds are by no means

TABLE 33.5.1. Deaths per 1,000 per annum of European troops serving in the Madras Presidency.

Years	0	1	2	3	4	5	6	7	8	9
179–	—	—	—	61	46	41	47	50	51	143
180–	78	96	50	119	96	64	80	77	70	59
181–	56	80	77	63	52	51	45	56	97	68
182–	56	57	63	49	134	120	104	71	53	35
183–	32	45	55	71	61	32	34	54	37	—

Mean strengths: 1793–1800: 5,600; 1801–1809: 8,700; 1810–1821: 12,500; 1822–1830: 11,000; 1831–1838: 10,000. Modified after Annesley, Tulloch, et al. (1840).

so numerous as might be expected, and that the greater proportion of deaths during warfare chiefly arises from disease caused by vicissitudes of climate and other evils, to which the troops are necessarily exposed upon active service.

The mortality rates per 1,000 per annum of the native troops were much lower; beginning with the year 1822, they were 12, 14, 21, 34; 25, 16, 14, 11, 10; 13, 16, 22, 17, 12; 21, 18, and finally 20 in 1838. The higher rates of 21, 34, and 25 in 1824, 1825, and 1826 were war years. However, the rates in the war years average less than 150% of those in the peace years.

More general statistics, compiled by Henry Marshall, Alexander Murray Tulloch, Graham Balfour, and others, and cited in Cantlie (1974a, p. 441), are given in Table 33.5.2. The annual mortality rates per 1,000 per annum were 668 on the Gold Coast, 483 in Sierra Leone, both affected greatly by yellow fever and malaria, 121 in Jamaica, 78 in Windward and Leeward Islands, and 70 in Ceylon. These are enormous rates of mortality at the ages of young adult life, which usually did not exceed 5 per 1,000 per annum in more settled countries at that time. Moreover, in these areas the mortality rates of European soldiers exceeded those of the locally recruited.

At epochs after 1860, the rates for British troops in the foreign stations were lower, as is shown in Table 33.5.3, although the rates were relatively high in west Africa (incorporated into Cape and St. Helena before 1888). See also §6.5 for the mortality from typhoid in barracks at Munich, 1851–1880. For suicide of British troops, see Millar (1874).

33.6 Military Medical Services

We may consider two main themes on the treatment of the sick or wounded soldier: first, the administration, conservation, and morale-building aspects of a medical service attached to the army; and second, the humanitarian aspects of care to the sick and especially to the wounded.

The conditions of the troops in the Roman armies were regulated by Augustus; normally, the troops enlisted and many of the legions had a markedly regional aspect. There were no married quarters, and marriages were not permitted during the period of service. Rates of pay were fixed, and at the completion of a term of service the soldier received a grant of land and Roman citizenship. Cases of invalidity were sometimes awarded pensions, in other times kept on as members of the unit. On the medical side, careful attention was paid to the state of hygiene of the camps, especially the supply of good clean water; camps were not located near unwholesome marshes. Surgeons were appointed to the legions and other lower formations; each camp had a well-founded *valetudinarium* with wards and attendants for the sick.

These orderly arrangements collapsed with the breakdown of the Roman empire. In medieval times there were no regular arrangements for medical services, but under favorable conditions, sick and wounded would be treated by such local religious bodies as the hostels, convents, and abbeys. Further, in medieval times, the administration was not centralized and the troops were under the command of their own feudal chief, so there could be no thought of a medical service.

For the mortality of soliders in war before the days of consolidated statistical returns, we briefly summarize from Cantlie (1974a). At the time of the great victories during the reign of Edward III, at Crécy in 1346 and Poitiers in 1356, there was only one superior surgeon noted at Crécy on the English side, but there were also inferior surgeons or barbers taken from the ranks and reckoned as private soldiers. These latter rendered first aid to the

TABLE 33.5.2. Morbidity and mortality in British troops at home and overseas.

	Annual admissions per 1,000	Annual mortality per 1,000
Windward and Leeward Islands*	1,903	78
Jamaica*	1,812	121
United Kingdom[†]	929	14
Gibraltar[‡]	966	21
Malta*	1,142	16
Canada*	1,097	16
Sierra Leone[§]	2,978	483
Gold Coast[‖]	—	668
Cape of Good Hope[‡]	991	14
Ceylon*	1,678	70
Burma[¶]	1,587	45

The beginning years were:
* 1817.
[†]1830.
[‡]1818.
[§]1819.
[‖]1823.
[¶]1827.

The observations in each area ended with the year 1836. Modified after Cantlie, 1974a, p. 442.

TABLE 33.5.3. Health of the troops of British army (deaths per 1,000 per annum).

	1860–1869	1870–1879	1879–1888	1889–1898
United Kingdom	10	13	6	4
West Indies	12	11	15	9
Cape and St. Helena	11	39	38	7
West Africa	—	—	—	45
Ceylon	24	15	14	10
China	43	14	10	11
Bengal	31 ⎫			
Madras	23 ⎬	19	16	16
Bombay	23 ⎭			

After Cantlie, 1974b, pp. 366–369.

common soldiery during and after the battle, but their abilities were limited. The severely wounded had no chance of recovery, and it was therefore customary for their comrades quietly to slit their throats on the field of battle and put them out of their pain. For the slightly wounded there was help at the nearest religious house, where they were attended by monks or nuns. Those men whose wounds required a considerable time to recover were dismissed with a small pecuniary provision to carry them home.

During the reign of Henry V, the invasion of France was commenced at Harfleur, which was reduced after breaches had been made in the walls by cannons reputed to be able to cut down a man at half a mile. These more powerful weapons made larger wounds, broke bones causing compound fractures, and introduced foreign material, such as metal and gunpowder, into the body. At first it was believed that the wounds would have to be cauterized, but later practice was milder and more conservative, largely under the influence of Ambroise Paré (ca. 1510–1590).

With the rise of the modern states and national armies, the general problems of welfare of the troops, the treatment of their diseases and injuries, invalidity, and retirement benefits all tended to be neglected. In particular, insufficient attention had been paid to the fate of the soldiers wounded or captured during the battle. However, there were exceptions. In 1587, during Elizabeth's reign, consideration was given to the removal of the wounded from the field of battle to a place where they could be treated by a surgeon; the use of special carriages and men for this purpose, it was thought, would raise morale and avoid the need to release active combatants from duty to carry them away. This suggestion was neglected by the authorities, and even in the Crimean War in 1854 positive orders were given that the fighting ranks must not be depleted by wounded men being carried out of the battle by their comrades. We may quote from Cantlie (1974a), writing on the war of the American Revolution.

Philadelphia was occupied on the 25th September 1777. A fortnight later Washington attempted a surprise attack on Germantown, some 10 miles to the north of Philadelphia, but was beaten off at the cost of over 500 British casualties while that of the Americans again exceeded 1,000 in killed, wounded and prisoners. A local resident tells us he saw a hospital being improvised in a stable, where the surgeons were beginning to arrange long tables made of doors on which to lay the wounded, friends and foes alike, for amputation. Here it is pleasant to recall that in all the many instances in the war when wounded prisoners were under treatment the opposing medical forces were invited to collaborate in a manner which transcended the bitterness of the struggle.

Richardson (1974, p. 4) recalls that

At Dettingen in 1743, John Dalrymple, the Earl of Stair, anticipated the Geneva Convention by more than a hundred years. Sir John Pringle (1761), his physician, tells us that the Earl 'proposed to the Duke de Noailles, of whose humanity he was well assured that the hospitals on both sides should be considered as sanctuaries for the sick, and mutually protected. This was readily agreed to by the French General. . . . This agreement was strictly observed on both sides all that campaign; and tho' it has been since neglected, yet we may hope, that on future occasions, the contending parties will make it a precedent.'

Florence Nightingale (1820–1910) revolutionized the treatment of the sick and wounded during the Crimean War; and in the ensuing peace continued her interest in the welfare of the troops and was particularly powerful in influencing a succession of governments. Her work was widely known and admired on the continent. See also §§9.11, 45.8, and 45.9.

In general, it may be said that there were few effective medical services in the modern armies until the twentieth century; and there was no generally accepted theory of how or why medical care should be delivered to the common soldier. In the British Army, there were no regular full-time medical officers, and in time of war there was no centralized command system for the medical services. A great difficulty was that, especially in the higher posts in the army, the medical officers and the combatant officers did not come from the same social classes, and communication was difficult; especially, it was difficult for the ideas of medical officers to affect policy.

For military sanitary statistics, see Willcox (1918).

33.7 Battle Casualties and the Treatment of Wounds

This is a large topic. The reader is referred to Cantlie (1974*a*, *b*), Cartwright (1967), Cope (1958), Graham (1939), Hennen (1820), Meade (1968), and Wangensteen and Wangensteen (1978, especially pp. 497–525) for many historical details and references.

War Surgery before 1800

In earlier times dislocations could be reduced and some hemorrhages stemmed. The missile could be removed. Most wounds became infected and healing was consequently slow; there would have been a high case fatality. See also §33.6.

Infection of Wounds

In pre-Listerian days infection was very common; it was believed that wounds never healed by first intention, that is, without suppuration. When battles became larger and large numbers of patients were assembled in hospitals, the possibility of pathogenic bacteria being present increased. There was much morbidity and mortality as a result of the infections. Large epidemics of hospital gangrene occurred, for which see §9.11. Treatment of wounds by Listerian methods was introduced in the Franco-Prussian War and had become standard by the time of the Russo-Turkish War of 1876–1877, where the methods of C. Reyher were successful. Success was achieved in the Boer War of 1899–1902 by similar methods, but the experience there proved to be misleading; in it most of the wounds were caused by high-velocity Mauser bullets, which did comparatively little damage if they did not pass through an artery or vital organ; further, there was little contamination of the wound by soil, and the battles tended to be fought over open, uncultivated, and dry country.

Debridement or Toilet of the Wound

Contrary to the conditions of warfare in the Boer War, there was trench warfare in 1914–1918; troops were operating in conditions of squalor in the mud of cultivated, highly manured, farmlands with the soil containing many pathogenic bacteria, especially the *Clostridia*. Wounds were often due to shrapnel, carrying bacteria-rich soil into the wounds. Antiseptics applied failed to reach the bacteria and, in any case, were of the general protoplasmic poison types, that is, they could not be applied in sufficient concentration to kill the bacteria without doing great damage to the body cells. The solution, reached with the aid of the bacteriologists, was to remove devitalized tissue; this procedure is now called debridement, although this word has the sense of leaving channels open. The second procedure was to leave open badly contaminated wounds, to irrigate the wounds with suitable fluids, such as hypertonic salines or solution of hypochloride of calcium, and to adopt rigid aseptic techniques. Indeed, the hemolytic streptococci in wounds were usually acquired in "ward" infections. For an extensive treatment of the researches made in World War I, see Official History (1922–1924), and for World War II, see Cope (1953).

Chemo- and Antibiotic Therapy

Until the introduction of the sulfonamides in 1935, there was no antiseptic capable of attacking the bacteria in tissues of the body; in World War II, the sulfonamides were used throughout and in 1944 penicillin also was available. Case fatality rates were therefore greatly reduced, and dangerous hospital epidemics of gangrene were avoided altogether.

Supportive Methods

It had been found in 1937 that blood could be stored for up to a week in a condition suitable for use in transfusions. This permitted the use of transfusions on a massive scale in World War II. In general, the treatment of shock was greatly improved in World War II.

Mobility of Casualties and Medical Help

The evacuation of casualties from front lines to a base was improved during World War I and greatly extended in World War II with the use of air transport. First aid had long been available in the front line, but it was evident that the sooner surgical treatment could be applied, the better it would be for the casualty. Forward operating teams were first used by Vera I. Gedroĭts, a Russian surgeon, who brought a well-equipped ambulance train close up to the battle line in the Russo-Japanese War (1904–1905); the principle was in use in both World Wars, in the second of which specialists, such as neurological surgeons, operated in mobile teams as far forward as practicable.

For gas warfare, see Paxman and Harris (1982) and §33.17.

33.8 Illnesses of Soldiers

We give the Crimean War as an example of the illnesses of soldiers because it was adequately documented and medicine had made no great progress toward treatment, other than rest and good nursing.

According to Cantlie (1974b), current medical theory regarded all disease to be due to one or more of the following,

(a) endemic causes, such as changes in temperature and weather;
(b) exhalations and miasmas from the ground;
(c) pollution of atmosphere from defective ventilation and sanitation;
(d) hardship and exposure;
(e) lack of nutritious food, causing bowel irritation.

The principal cause of sick wastage in the British army occurred under the heading "diseases of the stomach and bowels" with 63,339 admissions and 10,462 deaths. The admissions (deaths) from diarrhea, dysentery and cholera were 44,164 (3,651), 7,882 (2,543), and 7,575 (4,513), respectively, see Table 33.8.1.

Cantlie (1974b) goes on to enumerate the principal causes of death from disease:

(a) Diarrhea with three epidemic periods, July to August 1854, October 1854 to February 1855, and June to August 1856. The first and third of these epidemics were due to infection of the food by flies; the winter epidemic was due to bowel infection aggravated by lowered resistance from overwork, deplorable working conditions, and a shortage of warm clothing; by the second winter these conditions had been

TABLE 33.8.1. Crimean War sick wastage.

Disease cause	Cases	Deaths	Case fatality per 100
Diarrhea	44,164	3,651	8
Dysentery	7,882	2,543	32
Cholera	7,575	4,513	60
Fevers			
Intermittent	2,406	60	2
Common continued	25,013	2,790	11
Remittent	2,957	311	11
Typhus	828	285	34
Scurvy	2,096	176	8
Frostbite and gangrene	2,398	463	19
Wounds	12,094	1,724	14

Modified after Cantlie, 1974b, pp. 185–190.

ameliorated and the figures were strikingly lower.

(b) Dysentery was diagnosed only when blood and mucus appeared in the stools. The peak incidences occurred at the time of the second epidemic of diarrhea and in July to September 1855.

(c) Cholera appeared in two great epidemics with a case fatality of 60%.

(d) Fevers occurred with admissions (deaths) as follows: intermittent 2,406 (60); common continued 25,013 (2,790); remittent 2,957 (311); and typhus 828 (285), respectively. Intermittent and remittent fever included chiefly malaria; common continued fever included the enteric fevers, sandfly fever, dengue, tertian malaria and relapsing fever.

(e) Scurvy was diagnosed in 2,096 cases and was due to the diet of salt meat and biscuits, without fresh vegetables. Treatment was by lime juice. A new scale of diet lessened the incidence in the latter part of the war.

(f) Frostbite and gangrene caused 2,398 admissions and 463 deaths, a case fatality rate of 19.2%. The incidence was much higher in the first winter.

(g) Wounds occurred in 12,094 cases with a case fatality of about 14%.

(h) Tetanus caused only 29 deaths throughout the whole campaign.

(j) Amputations were performed in 1,027 cases of the wounds mentioned above in (g). The case fatality overall was 28%. However, the case fatality for large amputations from the knee to the hip varied from 55% to 100%. There were 150 secondary amputations with a case fatality of 51%.

(*k*) Officers enjoyed better health than the other ranks because of better living conditions and food, although they shared the hardships of trench life.

For the United States Civil War, see Steiner (1968); for an early statistical account of losses in the British Army, see Tulloch (1841) and Balfour (1872).

33.9 Prisoners of War

In the early history of warfare there had been no recognition of the status of "prisoner of war;" a captive was usually promptly dispatched on the field of battle; although in some epochs, such as in the Roman conquests of Julius Caesar, rather more humane treatment was sometimes available. Until quite recent times the older practices persisted; thus, in the Middle Ages, those not considered worthy of keeping for a ransom were usually slain. However, in the sixteenth and seventeenth centuries, philosophers on war began to express thoughts on the amelioration of the lot of prisoners. Grotius in 1625 expressed the view that the captors had the right to enslave their prisoners but advocated exchange and ransom instead. The Treaty of Westphalia in 1648 led to the release of prisoners without ransom. Montesquieu in 1748 wrote that the only right of the captor in war was to prevent the prisoner doing harm. Around 1800, treaties began to be signed between nations on the treatment of prisoners, and treatment generally improved, although, as the *Encyclopaedia Britannica* in 1968 puts it, "observations of the principles in the Civil War and in the Franco-Prussian War left much to be desired." In 1874 a conference in Brussels, Belgium, drew up rules that were not subsequently ratified. There were still no firm treaties during World War I, although the Geneva Convention of 1929 was ratified by France, Germany, Great Britain, the United States, and many other countries, but not by Japan or the Soviet Union. A further Geneva Convention was agreed to in 1949.

During World War II, tuberculosis rates in German prisoner of war camps were high, the highest being among the Russian prisoners, next, among the French, and lowest, among the British. It is believed that these differences were due to the diet and living conditions of the three groups, the Russians being given lower rations and not receiving Red Cross parcels. Of course, conditions were much worse in the concentration camps, with tuberculosis case rates estimated at 20%–40%, see Green and Covell (1953).

See also Daniels (1981) for conditions in American concentration camps in World War II.

33.10 Red Cross and Crescent

The work of Florence Nightingale was a great inspiration to Jean Henri Dunant (1828–1910), a Swiss industrialist later to be hailed as the founder of the International Red Cross, as his letter to the *London Times* of August 7, 1872, testified. He resolved to give help and to observe in the war between France and Italy, on the one side, and Austria-Hungary on the other. Dunant was present immediately after the battle of Solferino on June 24, 1859, and he organized medical and nursing care for the thousands of wounded men. Dunant (1862) suggested that relief societies should be organized in every country. As a result, a committee representing 14 countries met in Geneva on October 26–29, 1863, and after a diplomatic conference in 1864, the Convention of Geneva was published, protecting the wounded soldier in war. Later revisions of the Convention in 1907, 1929, and 1949 were concerned with the protection of victims of warfare at sea and prisoners of war. In the original Convention, Miss Nightingale was an active agent, for she had been asked by the War Office to prepare "Instructions" for the two British representatives, Drs. Longmore and Rutherford, at the congress (see Cook, 1913, p. 71, vol. 2). The purpose of the Convention was to neutralize the wounded under the supervision of the Red Cross. Societies, formed under the aegis of the International Red Cross, were soon organized throughout Europe and extended to Islam under the title of Red Crescent. The Red Cross (or Crescent) has found many new functions in recent times.

It is pointed out that the International Red Cross did not and could not solve the problems of the soldier in barracks or on campaign. This was a problem for the medical services.

33.11 Civil War

Bodart (1916) states that the Vendéan insurrection was the most severe of all of France's civil wars; beginning in 1793, the revolt was an attempt to restore the old regime, and it required 4 years and 400,000 men to put it down. Royalist prisoners, taken with arms in their possession, were massacred or executed; it was a war of extermination, resulting in the depopulation of several departments. Fifteen of the republican generals were killed, and all of the Vendéan leaders were killed in action or executed. Battle losses were high; four battles cost the republicans 32%, 17%, 16%, and 10% of their effectives; the Vendéans lost 86% at Savenay, 70% (=15,000) at le Mans, and 20% (=8,000) at Cholet. It is believed that the total losses of men were several hundred thousand.

In the months, March to April 1871, the national, or Versailles, army waged a war against the Communards holding Paris. The rebels had organized an army of almost 9,000 officers and 205,000 men. Their losses totaled 15,000 killed or wounded outside the fortifications and 25,000 in the streets and barricades; 41,000 rebels were taken prisoner, of whom 3,000 died in prision, 270 were executed, and 7,500 were deported. See Table 33.11.1 for futher details.

Perhaps the best examples of the hazards of being a prisoner of war are provided by the experiences in the United States Civil War of 1861–1865, in which the two sides were not differentiated by race or by culture. Many good accounts of these experiences are available, but we take two tables from Prinzing (1916). Table 33.11.2 gives the experience of Northern troops held as prisoners in Andersonville in 1864 between March 1 and August 31. From an average number of 19,453 prisoners, 7,712 died in these few months, amounting to a rate of 792.8 per 1,000 per annum (i.e., 79% approx-

TABLE 33.11.1. Communard insurrection, Paris, March to May 1871.

	Insurgents	Versailles army
Strength	214,000	100,000
Losses	15,000 killed outside*†	159 officers killed
	25,000 killed in street fighting	554 officers wounded
		<5,000 killed*
	41,000 taken prisoner, of whom	10,000 wounded
	3,000 died in prison	
	270 were executed	
	7,500 were deported	

* Killed is abbreviation for "killed or died of wounds."
† Outside is abbreviation for "outside fortifications."
Source: Bodart, 1916.

TABLE 33.11.2. Deaths of Northern troops held as prisoners in Andersonville, 1864.

Cause of death	Deaths (all told)	Annual rate per 1000
Typhoid fever, typhus fever	199	20.5
Malaria	119	12.2
Smallpox, measles, scarlet fever, erysipelas	80	8.2
Diarrhea, dysentery	4,529	465.6
Scurvy	999	102.8
Bronchitis	90	9.2
Inflammation of the lungs and pleurisy	266	27.4
Other diseases	844	86.7
Wounds and uncertain maladies	586	60.2
Total	7,712	792.8

Source: Prinzing, 1916, p. 181, from Barnes, 1870–1888.

imately). Less than 1,500 died of wounds and uncertain maladies, the rest died from infections and scurvy, with diarrhea and dysentery accounting for more than half the deaths.

The experience in the Northern prisons was rather better. The average number in the prisons was 40,815 and there were 19,060 deaths. There were 230.7 deaths per 1,000 per annum. Wounds, uncertain maladies, and "other diseases" accounted for 2,000 deaths other than the infections and scurvy. Scurvy caused a much lower mortality in the Northern prisons, as did dysentery and diarrhea. See Table 33.11.3.

TABLE 33.11.3. Deaths of Southern troops held in prisons of the Northern states.

Cause of death	Deaths (all told)	Annual rate per 1000
Typhoid fever, typhus fever	1,109	13.6
Malaria	1,026	12.6
Smallpox, measles, scarlet fever, erysipelas	3,453	42.3
Diarrhea, dysentery	5,965	73.0
Scurvy	351	4.3
Bronchitis	133	1.6
Inflammation of the lungs and pleurisy	5,042	61.7
Other diseases	1,729	21.3
Wounds and uncertain maladies	252	0.3
Total	19,060	230.7

Source: Prinzing, 1916, p. 181, from Barnes, 1870–1888.

Conditions for the prisoner of war during civil wars are usually worse than in an international war because his captors will make moral judgments against him; they know also that he might receive sympathetic treatment from his countrymen if he escapes and so become an additional opponent; finally, there will be great difficulties in finding a secure jail.

The lot of prisoners in concentration camps during an aberrant form of civil war (genocide) has been studied by Mollison (1946) from the point of view of famine and by Helweg-Larsen, Hoffmeyer, et al. (1952a, b) with special reference to famine and tuberculosis.

33.12 Civilians in Sieges

A siege of a city usually follows a retreat of an army and its entry into the city together with its wounded; the army is very often in disorder and without supplies; civilians from the nearby countryside also arrive, usually destitute. The leading danger to the civilians is hunger, certainly this is so in a long siege. Food is rationed; the bread soon begins to deteriorate, and there is a great lack of milk, fats, salt, and vegetables. Infants and children are the first to be affected by this lack of food. At a later stage scurvy may appear and cause many deaths.

In sieges it is difficult to maintain the usual hygienic measures. Access to springs or small streams is denied by the enemy. If the source of drinking water is a river, severe pollution results from the mere presence of the besieging army. The disposal of refuse or excreta becomes difficult. There may be insufficient space to bury the dead bodies of people or of animals, and there is no fuel to dispose of them by burning; in some sieges, it has been reported that the corpses and carcases have been left lying in the open. Fuel is not available for combating the cold. Overcrowding is often great, partly because of the influx of persons and partly because of the loss of suburbs or the destruction of shelter by enemy action. Overcrowding, bad hygiene, and food shortages thus set the stage for epidemics.

As examples, Westergaard (1916) gives accounts of the sieges of Mantua in 1796–1797, Danzig in 1813, Torgau in 1813, Mayence in 1813–1814, Paris in 1870–1871, and Port Arthur in 1904. Of these, the siege of Paris from September 18, 1870, to February 4, 1871, has been well documented. The average number of deaths in a time of peace, from September 4, 1867, to March 17, 1869, are available; indeed, they totalled 24,148; in the corresponding siege period there were 75,167 deaths, that is, more than three times the number in the same weeks in an average prewar year. At the beginning of the siege there were approximately 2 million persons in Paris. A severe smallpox epidemic was already present in the city, with 116, 168, and 158 deaths in the first 3 weeks recorded in the table of Westergaard (1916); the epidemic abated only after the armistice; there were over 300 deaths in each week from early October until late January. Typhoid fever increased from about 40 deaths per week at the beginning to more than 300 at the end of the siege. Dysentery increased but caused more than 50 deaths in 3 weeks only during the siege. Diarrhea was more important, increasing to 140 deaths per week in the last 5 weeks of the siege. Pneumonia caused about 50 deaths per week at the beginning, increasing in numbers as the siege progressed until there were more than 400 in the last few weeks. Bronchitis similarly increased from about 50 per week to more than 450 in each of the last 4 weeks of the siege. It is probable that the elderly were heavily represented among the deaths from pneumonia and bronchitis.

The siege of Paris is a good example because proper statistics are available for causes of death, but Paris was fortunate in many ways—it was garrisoned by other Frenchmen, and the civilians were not subjected to prolonged bombardment or to great fires; happily, it was not surrendered to the enemy. Many other cities did not have such good fortune. In preindustrial times, the city would have obtained most of its food from within 5 or, at most, 10 miles; a siege then would lead to the commandeering of all grain in the area and the destruction of houses and of stock. Moreover, with the low ratio of crop to seed, it would be difficult to commence the sowing of the next harvest, and famine would often result. The siege of Danzig in 1813 shows how the civilians can suffer if the garrison is foreign. In the siege of Mayence in 1813–1814 about one tenth of the population died from typhus, introduced into the city by sick soldiers. Another well-known example is Magdeburg. Tilly and his lieutenant, Pappenheim, took Magdeburg on the Elbe by storm on May 20, 1631. The troops sought revenge for their long preparation and hardships and, although the townspeople had hindered the garrison in its preparations, there was a general massacre of the inhabitants and the lighting of fires that consumed almost the whole town, including stored provisions. Almost all 20,000 inhabitants perished.

For civilians in war in the seventeenth century, see Gutmann (1977). For medical aspects of the siege of Leningrad, see Brožek, Wells, and Keys (1946), and Goure (1962).

33.13 War and the Great Pestilences

Demographers and historians have often expressed the view that there is some connection between famine, war, and epidemics. Thus, in modern times, few persons question the notion that World War I caused or, at least, had a great effect on the ensuing influenza epidemic. According to modern epidemiologic theory, for which see §10.5, any pandemic of influenza is due to some recombination of virus genes, perhaps usually in Asia among animals, giving

rise to a new strain of the virus with special properties of virulence and toxicity; this new strain spreads to man, then from man to man in this focus, and finally to the world at large. Such an example does not disprove the notion that wars have important effects on the progress of epidemics, but evidently each disease must be analyzed in detail, and it must be shown that the war has changed conditions so as to favor the spread of the disease. We list some examples of plagues or epidemics associated with war.

(*i*) *Bubonic Plague.* Many historians of war have assumed that severe epidemics had been bubonic plague. Prinzing (1916) believes that bubonic plague did appear in 1630–1636, during the Thirty Years War, and gives an important table (Prinzing, 1916, p. 78); he also believes that other historians had often mistaken typhus for plague; relapsing fever also was probably often so confused. It may be remarked that modern opinion on the transmission of plague by human ectoparasites makes it plausible that plague has been of more importance than was sometimes conceded by those accepting the theory of the almost universal transmission to man by the rat fleas.

(*ii*) *Cholera.* The incidence of cholera is increased by armies massing under unhygienic conditions in an endemic area. The disease is often spread widely by the opening up of freer communications (e.g., Barua and Burrows, 1974), for example, between the classic endemic areas in India and Persia and also by the dispersal of troops at the end of a campaign.

(*iii*) *Dysentery.* The same considerations as for cholera apply for dysentery, although dysentery can adapt to a greater variety of social and climatic conditions. If war is associated with famine, then other disease syndromes are often attributed to dysentery.

(*iv*) *Enteric Fever.* The enteric bacilli can exist in a chronic carrier state, so that epidemics of enteric fever can erupt in any community in which the hygienic conditions, especially the water supply, decline. Enteric fever was a leading cause of illness in the Boer War campaigns and in the associated concentration camps. In

TABLE 33.13.1. Enteric fever deaths.

Force or army	War	Year	Size of force	Cases of enteric	Deaths from enteric
American	Spanish-American	1898	107,973	20,738	1,580
German	Franco-German	1870	1,146,000	73,393	6,965
Russian (in Caucasus)	Russo-Turkish	1877–1878	246,000	24,475	8,900
British*	South African	1899–1902	557,653	57,684	8,022

*Corrected.

Data from *Official History of the War* (1922–1924), *Medical Services, Diseases of the War*, vol. 1, p. 12.

the United States Civil War of 1861–1865, 13.58 per 1,000 white troops and 19.8 per 1,000 per annum colored troops died of typhoid, according to a table in Westergaard (1916, p. 177). We give some other examples in Table 33.13.1, from which it will be noted that, excepting the German experience, more that 1% of the total force involved in each war died of enteric fevers.

(*v*) *Measles.* In former times, it is possible that measles had not been experienced by the great bulk of the population, as in times of peace there was limited movement between districts. There was always a danger that it would be introduced into a population consisting principally of susceptibles and cause an explosive epidemic. Certainly, the recruitment of troops by an army would bring large numbers of susceptibles into close contact and could be one way in which a war breaks down the barriers to the passage of the measles virus. Death rates from measles in the United States Civil War were approximately 1.8 per 1,000 per annum averaged over the whole war, according to Westergaard (1916).

(*vi*) *Smallpox.* Considerations of the same kind apply to smallpox in past centuries; of course, case fatality rates would have been higher in smallpox, and the disease more dangerous to the civilian population. In modern times armies have taken care to vaccinate the troops, so that smallpox has usually not been an important factor in campaigns since 1871. It is no longer even a civilian problem since its eradication. For the earlier times, see Westergaard (1916) and Guy (1882*b*). See also §43.1 and Hopkins (1983*a*).

(*vii*) *Typhus and* (*viii*) *Relapsing Fever.* These have been important in all the great wars, especially among the defeated armies and the civilians. These diseases are discussed with respect to famine in §22.9. Typhus has often spread to the civilian populations during the wars and the later demobilization, with troops introducing the infection into previously untouched areas.

(*ix*) *Malaria.* Epidemics appear among troops from nonendemic areas campaigning in endemic areas, such as the eastern Mediterranean littoral (Christophers, 1939) or in hyperendemic areas, such as western Africa, Burma, Malaysia, and the East Indies. After campaigns in southeastern Europe during World War I, troops returning home carried malaria to England, to Emden on the north German coast where 5,000 cases occurred, and to Russia where there was a disastrous epidemic, extending even to Archangel within the Arctic Circle. As Russell (1955, p. 185) points out, war nearly always intensifies the rate of passage of the malaria parasite. On the medical side, there may be a breakdown of therapy, prophylaxis, and control. Disruption of the community may lead to unsatisfactory accommodation in abandoned buildings; there may be local crowding. Movements of troops and civilians may bring in malarious persons. The ecology of the mosquito may be disturbed; previously zoophilic species may attack man. New breeding places may be created by opening up jungle areas and damage to drainage systems, and pools may be formed in bomb craters. Under modern conditions, sometimes the reverse can be the case and the malaria incidence may be actually reduced by the army authorities.

(x) *Yellow Fever*. Some terrible epidemics of yellow fever are recorded by Cantlie (1974a, p. 74), from which we choose that occurring in the disastrous West Indian campaign of 1740–1742 and two in Gibraltar. In the war against Spain, an expedition of 6,000 men was planned to leave Spithead, England, in June 1740; in fact, all the soldiers were embarked in August 1740 and fed on ship's rations until November when the ships sailed. Already, by the time of departure, 60 deaths had occurred from scurvy and a further 100 deaths occurred on the voyage. In Jamaica 3,000 American colonial troops joined the expedition. In Jamaica there were 600 more deaths and 1,500 more were on the sick list. It was then determined to attack Carthagena, on the mainland now in modern Colombia. The naval force was able to enter the harbor and the troops were disembarked. After an undue delay, an assault on the city was repulsed with severe loss; yellow fever appeared, and great numbers of the sick were sent aboard the transports. Between April 18 and 21, 1741, the number of active troops had dwindled from 6,600 to 3,200. There were some 3,000 sick to be treated on the ships. On May 5 the fleet sailed to Jamaica. Within a month 1,100 more had died and deaths continued at the rate of 100 per week. Between October 26, 1740, and February 26, 1742, deaths were 284 among the officers and over 10,000 among other ranks, yellow fever being the leading cause of death. Of the force that had sailed from Spithead, 9 out of every 10 had died (Cantlie, 1974a, p. 78).

During the siege of Gibraltar in 1804, in an epidemic of yellow fever, 54 officers and 864 of other ranks died, nearly a quarter of the garrison; deaths among the civilians approached 5,000. Boyce (1951) mentions that 899 died in the epidemic of 1813. Again in 1828, there were 432 deaths from yellow fever in a garrison of 3,600, a mortality of 12%. Here it was observed that the progress of the epidemic of yellow fever was arrested, as it is always found to be, by the setting in of a cold wind from the north, which of course interfered with the breeding of the mosquitoes.

33.14 War and Famine

Famine has always been one of the most feared consequences of war. How famine comes about has already been discussed briefly in §22.8 and in §§33.4 and 33.12. See also the Aleutian famines after the slaughter of the menfolk in §42.3.

Gutmann (1977) maintains that for civilians in the seventeenth century, conditions were at their worst in times of war and bad weather, in war alone, in epidemics, and in harvest failures; further, war brought disease to them.

With advances in transportation methods in times of peace, civilian populations in Europe had become dependent on imported grains. In World Wars I and II there were naval blockades affecting the United Kingdom and some of the continental states. According to Bell (1937), the numbers of deaths attributed to prolonged hunger in Germany were 88,235, 121,114, 259,627, and 293,760 during the years 1915, 1916, 1917, and 1918, respectively. Hoover (1960) mentions that in the summer of 1916, the Allied armies had been halted in the Somme offensive and the war on the western front had settled down to the attrition of trench warfare. The blockade had cut off all overseas supplies to the Central Powers and had put blockade pressure on border neutrals; the Central Powers had diverted agricultural manpower to their armies, fertilizers to explosives, and manufactures from agricultural products to munitions. Armies and munition workers had to be provided with full rations, farmers also took their normal diet, and so the noncombatant urban population suffered most. See Foster (1983) for army disaster relief.

Famine conditions held in much of the Soviet Union after World War II and in western Russia in World War I, which was followed by the civil war (Wars of Intervention). Fortunately, much grain could be imported from the United States after each; for examples of aid after World War I, see Hoover (1961) and Fisher (1927). For famine conditions in the Netherlands during World War II, see Stein, Susser, et al. (1975). For loss of resources, see Vincent (1947). For starvation as a mode of warfare, see Mudge (1970).

33.15 Navy and Air Force

Scurvy

The leading problem of the navies of Europe, after the development of sea-going ships and the undertaking of long voyages, was scurvy, which we have already studied in §22.13, where references are made to some famous incidents of scurvy on the long voyages. In the first 2 years of James Lind's administration of the Haslar Hospital (of the Royal Navy), there were 1,146 cases of scurvy out of 5,734 total admissions. Lind is reported by his biographer, Bullough (1973), to have said that "the number of seamen in time of war who died by shipwreck, capture, famine, fire or sword" was only a small proportion compared with those who died by "ship diseases and the usual maladies of the intemperate." Bullough (1973) also notes that 1,512 were killed in action, whereas 133,708 men in all were lost to the British Navy by disease or desertion during the Seven Years War, 1756–1763.

Tuberculosis

According to Brooks (1952), tuberculosis had been recognized for many generations to be a principal naval medical problem; in particular, he cites the remarks of Sheldon Francis Dudley (1884–1956), who believed the invaliding rate for this disease to be about 2 per 1,000 per annum as far back as reliable statistics are available. There is a special risk in navies because large numbers of men may be brought into intimate contact with open cases. In World War II, screening was used to reduce the inflow of tuberculosis cases into the Royal Navy and to detect cases in the service as early as possible, thus reducing the risk of infection of the susceptibles.

Malaria

Ships patrolling rivers or near the shore in malarious countries often suffered high malaria rates. An example is given from Bruce-Chwatt and Bruce-Chwatt (1980) of naval ships patrolling against the slave traders in West Africa in the era 1807–1857 in which the squadron was nicknamed the "coffin squadron" and suffered a malaria mortality rate of 55 per 1,000 per annum.

Typhus

Typhus was a special risk in the navy, especially in the conveyance of troops to and from theaters of war. See Cantlie (1974a, b).

A history of medicine and the (British) Royal Navy has been given by Keevil (1957/1958) and Lloyd and Coulter (1961/1963); Coulter (1954/1956) and McNee (1952) give the history for World War II. Lloyd (1965) gives reprints of some medical classics by James Lind, Gilbert Blane, and Thomas Trotter. Watt, Freeman, and Bynum (1981) give accounts of the influence of nutrition on many naval, exploratory, and commercial voyages. For health, see Allison (1943), Balfour (1872), and Dudley (1931).

For the medical problems of the Royal Air Force, see Green and Covell (1953, pp. 30–52), where the chief emphasis is on physiological problems, for example, the effect of diet on night vision.

33.16 World War I, Total Military Casualties

World War I may be said to have commenced on July 28, 1914, when Austria-Hungary declared war on Serbia; Germany declared war on Russia on August 1, 1914. Other European declarations followed within the next few days, but many nations declared war much later, as late as July 19, 1918, in one Latin American state. Russia ceased fighting in 1917 and Austria-Hungary on November 3, 1918, and an armistice was declared on the western front on November 11, 1918.

We first consider military losses for the various countries involved.

France. France suffered the greatest military losses of life, computed on a per capita basis, for which see Table 33.16.1. Total mobilized forces were 7.935 million European and 0.475 million colonial and north African troops, a total of 8.410 million; of these, dead and mis-

TABLE 33.16.1. Losses in World War I.
(France)

	Dead	Missing	Total dead and missing
Army to Armistice Day	1,093,800	260,600	1,354,400
Army from Armistice Day to June 1, 1919	28,600	. . .	28,600
Total army	1,122,400	260,600	1,383,000*
Naval losses	5521	4994	10,515
Total armed forces	1,127,921	265,594	1,393,515†

*36,800 officers and 1,346,200 other ranks.
†Total forces consisted of 7.935 million European and 0.475 million colonial troops.
After Hersch (1925–1927).

TABLE 33.16.2. Losses in World War I.
(British Empire)

	Dead	Enlistments up to Armistice Day
British Isles	702,410	5,704,416
British in India	2393	1,440,437
Indian troops	62,056	
Canada	56,639	628,964
Australia	59,330	412,953
New Zealand	16,711	128,525
Union of South Africa	7,121	136,070
Newfoundland	1,204	134,837
Other Colonies	507	
Total	908,371	8,586,202

After Hersch (1925–1927).

TABLE 33.16.3. Losses in World War I.
(United States of America)

Mode of death	No.
Killed in battle	35,560
Died of wounds	14,720
Died of illness	57,460
Died of other causes	7,920
Total	115,660

After Hersch (1925–1927).

TABLE 33.16.4. Losses in World War I.
(Allies, South and West)

Country	Dead and missing (in thousands)
France and its Colonies	1,394
British Empire	950
Italy	700
Belgium	40
Serbia and Montenegro	325
Romania	250
Greece	100
Portugal	8
United States of America	116
Total	3,883

After Hersch (1925–1927).

sing were 1.383 million, almost exactly one in six (16.6%) of the troops mobilized.

British Empire. Enlistments were 8.586 million from the British Empire, including 1.440 million from India. Of these, there were 0.908 million dead and missing, see Table 33.16.2.

United States. The United States did not enter the war until April 6, 1917, but had mobilized and trained a large army for dispatch to Europe, which accounts for the relatively high proportion of the enlisted dying of illness, see Table 33.16.3.

Allies, South and West. This classification follows Hersch (1925–1927) and includes the western and southern European states, the British Empire abroad, and the United States, yielding 3.883 million dead and missing; see Table 33.16.4.

Russian Empire and the Soviets. In Table 33.16.5, we give the losses of the Russian Empire in the war before the cessation of hostilities on the Russian front. The Russian campaigns in World War I and the ensuing civil war (Wars of Intervention) were notable for the outbreaks of four of our "great pestilences"; see Table 33.16.6.

Central Powers. In Table 33.16.7 we give the approximate losses of the Central Powers. It is evident that Germany and Austria-Hungary had great losses. For Germany, a breakdown

TABLE 33.16.5. Losses in World War I.
(Russian Empire, 1914–1917)

Mode of death	No.
Killed	664,890
Died of wounds with their units	18,378
Died of wounds in the hospitals	300,000
Died of diseases in the hospitals	130,000
Died in captivity	285,000
Sudden deaths	7,196
Reported missing	200,000
Died of gas	6,340
Additional losses from the Caucasian front	50,000
Total dead and missing	1,661,840
Losses in "round figures"	1,660,000

Modified after Kohn and Meyendorff (1932, Table 76), in which there is a discussion of the validity of the statistics.

TABLE 33.16.6. Cases of epidemic disease in World War I.
(Russian Empire and Soviet Armies)

	Registered cases	
Epidemic Disease	Russian Armed forces 1914–1917	Red army 1918–1920
Smallpox	2,708	5,749
Cholera	30,810	22,465
Relapsing fever	75,429	780,870
Typhus	21,093	522,458

After Hersch (1925–1927). Hersch gives a total for the Red Army, inconsistent with the above figures, which are indeed estimates in some cases.

by age is given in Table 33.16.8, which is possibly not greatly different from the breakdowns of other European nations. In Table 33.16.9, constructed from Hersch (1925–1927, p. 131), comparisons are made between the war losses and the population of men aged 15–49 years at the commencement of the war.

See Willcox (1923, 1928) for confirmation, largely, of the statistics of Hersch (1925–1927); also Vedel-Petersen (1923). For United States losses, see Ayres (1919), and for British losses, Greenwood (1942).

TABLE 33.16.7. Losses in World War I.

Country	Dead and missing (in millions)
Germany	2.0
Austria-Hungary	1.2
Bulgaria	0.1
Turkey	0.5
Total	3.8

After Hersch (1925–1927).

TABLE 33.16.8. Losses in World War I.
(Germany)

Age group	Total military deaths	Percentage by age
15 to 19	155,953	9.22
20 to 24	674,331	39.86
25 to 29	389,904	23.05
30 to 34	247,760	14.64
35 to 39	147,657	8.72
40 to 44	58,600	3.46
45 and over	17,036	1.01
Unknown	690	0.04
Total	1,691,931	100

Deaths by calendar year for 1914 to 1919 were: 241,343; 434,034; 340,468; 281,905; 379,777; and 14,314. Data from Meerwarth (1932); there is an inconsistency in the original table from the treatment of the entry at ages 15 to 19 in 1915.

33.17 Diseases of World War I

It would not be possible to describe the incidence of every disease in every army taking part in World War I, so we describe their importance in one force with a varied experience, namely, the armies of Great Britain, with the aid of the *Official History of the War, Medical Services* (1922–1924), especially vols. 1 and 2 on the *Diseases of the War* and the volume on *Pathology*. The history of World War I is of interest because for the first time the underlying causes of disease and death could be analyzed by modern methods, although specific therapy, for example, chemotherapy, was not yet available, neither were effective insecti-

TABLE 33.16.9. Losses in World War I.
(Deaths and proportions of deaths to prewar adult male populations)

Country	Men aged 15–49 years before the war (in thousands)	Soldiers killed in the war	
		Totals (in thousands)	Deaths per 1,000 men aged 15–49 years
France	9,981	1,320	132
United Kingdom	11,539	744	64
England and Wales	9,252	641	69
Scotland	1,193	83	70
Ireland	1,094	20	18
Italy	7,767	700	90
Belgium	1,924	40	21
Serbia and Montenegro	1,216*	325	267
Romania	1,809*	250	138
Greece	1,384*	100	72
Portugal	1,315	8	6
Germany	16,316	2,000	123
Austria-Hungary	12,176	1,200	99
Bulgaria	989	100	101
Turkey	3,303*	500	151
Former Russian Empire	39,075	5,350	137
Soviet Russia	32,117	5,000	156
Poland	4,128*	250	61
Other territories	2,830	100	35
All above countries	108,794	12,637	116
United States of America	25,541	116	5

*One-quarter of the total population.
After Hersch (1925–1927).

cides. The reader is referred back to §§33.7 and 33.13 and to the general sections on the specific diseases, for example, cholera, typhus, meningococcal meningitis, and especially §§9.8 and 9.11. We now run through the diseases of special interest in war in the order of the ICD.

Cholera. In July 1914, cholera occurred in the Russian provinces bordering on Galicia; cases appeared in the Austro-Hungarian army in eastern Galicia on September 20, 1914, and by September 1915 there had been 26,000 cases with 15,000 deaths; moreover, the infection had spread through the Austrian army operating in Serbia, with 12,000 cases at a daily average of 200 to 300. Cases also occurred in the German army cooperating with the Austrians but were not numerous, 0.65 per 1,000 of their force. At about the same time, the infection

was widespread in Turkey and the countries to the south east, now known as Syria, Iraq, and Palestine; 2,852 cases occurred in the British army engaged in Mesopotamia. Cases also occurred in the civilian population of the region, and they in turn infected the water containers and shallow wells, leading to further infections of troops newly arrived in the course of the campaign. In hot dry surroundings it was difficult to maintain correct water discipline.

Enteric Fever. After the experiences in the South African (Boer) War, for which see §33.13, enteric fever was greatly feared by the British sanitarians. Hygienic precautions usually prevented such high death rates in World War I; only in East Africa in 1917 and 1918 and in Mesopotamia 1916–1918 did the death rate per year of average "ration strength" exceed 1%. Before the war enteric fever had been endemic in every theater; paratyphoid B had been rare in England but common in the areas around Flanders, central Europe, and Macedonia, whereas paratyphoid A had been isolated only in seaports or places in contact with India and Africa; changes in incidence of the three types occurred during the war. Case fatality rates as percent from enteric fever were: France 3.8, Salonika 3.9, Egypt 6.4, Mesopotamia 8.7, Italy 10.6, and East Africa 27.4, but deaths per 1,000 average ration strength per year 1914–1919 were much lower, about 0.02, 0.1, 0.2, 0.7, 0.15, and 0.7, respectively. In East Africa the conditions were harsh and some cases were perhaps complicated by concurrent malaria and relapsing fever.

Bacillary Dysentery. In 1917 the incidences of dysentery per 1,000 ration strength were in France 4, East Africa 487, Salonika 29, Egypt 23, and Mesopotamia 60. Dysentery was responsible for a considerable proportion of the casualties evacuated from Gallipoli. Cases due to the Shiga type (now *Shigella dysenteriae*) had the gravest prognoses. Dysentery was also responsible for considerable morbidity.

Amebic Dysentery. Amebic dysentery accounted for about 7% of all clinical dysenteries in the British eastern theaters of war but only a minor percentage in France and Flanders. Later work suggests that about 10% of cases of dysentery evacuated from Gallipoli may have been amebic; original estimates had been much higher. It came as a surprise that the carrier rates in the troops were higher than expected and that even in the civil population of England they could have been as high as 4% or more.

Tuberculosis. This disease is not described in the volume *Diseases of the War* but in the volume *Pathology*, S.L. Cummins points out the difficulty of assessing its true importance. He mentions how in autopsies of troops in the United States Civil War, tuberculosis of the lungs had been found in cases that were dying of pneumonia, "paroxysmal and continuous" fevers, and diarrhea and dysentery, and that there may have been as many as 6,000 cases of

tuberculosis among the 37,000 white troops dying of intestinal disorders in that war. In World War I, British army orders required that men showing any sign of tuberculous disease should be rejected on enlistment; but this order was weakened in 1917 to pass men with no symptoms of tuberculosis in the previous two years. Cummins concludes that the tuberculosis in British troops can be regarded as the breakdown of well-established lesions and not as infections acquired during war service; in other words, war upset the balance between preexisting infection and acquired resistance. Chest wounds, unless they directly involved the "latent focus" of infections, did not add to the tuberculosis load. An interesting observation was that the Indian soldiers, who had been little exposed to tuberculosis before World War I and were accustomed in India to drink milk, acquired bovine tuberculosis infections in France after drinking unboiled milk because there was much bovine tuberculosis in the dairy herds. Indeed, the Indians suffered from glandular and abdominal forms of tuberculosis, the forms of tuberculosis suffered by British children after bovine type of infection. In Flanders and France in 1918, deaths per 1,000 ration strength per annum were for troops by nationality as follows: British and dominion troops 0.04, Portuguese 1.0, Chinese native labor corps 1.3, Indian troops 1.7, Indian native labor corps 5.3, South African labor corps, (kaffirs) 22.2, and Cape Colony labor corps ("Cape boys") 10.4. A table shows that Maori, South African labor corps, and British West Indian labor corps showed many lesions in the abdomen and glands. Cummins concludes his chapter on his p. 483 with the remark that "amongst these primitive races, gathered from remote countries, tuberculosis was not . . . an 'environmental' disease but an acutely infectious and rapidly fatal malady . . ." although, he remarks, they were "comparable in age, in the calorie value of their food and in their conditions of housing or shelter while in France [with the European troops]."

Zoonotic Bacterial Diseases. There were few if any infections of this ICD subclass.

Other Bacterial Diseases. Wound infections

have already been discussed in §33.7 and in §§9.8 and 9.11.

Meningococcal Infections. There were 1,928 deaths among troops and 3,955 deaths among civilians in the United Kingdom during the years 1914–1918. See §9.7 for the effects of crowding on the incidence of this disease.

Tetanus. According to the *Official History*, tetanus had been an important cause of mortality in the hospitalized wounded; thus, tetanus occurred in over 10 per 1,000 of the wounded in the Peninsular campaigns of the Napoleonic Wars with case fatality rates of 85% or more; the incidence in the Crimean (1853–1856) and United States Civil (1861–1865) Wars was only 2 per 1,000 wounded; and in the Franco-Prussian War, 3.5 per 1,000 wounded. Further, in the Nile Expedition of 1898, the South African (Boer) War, and the Russo-Japanese War, tetanus appeared very rarely. In the British forces in France and Belgium, there was a break of continuity in the records but the *Official History* gives an estimate of 2,529 cases; there were peaks in the incidence rates per 1,000 wounded (but not gassed) in August to October 1914 and January to June 1916, but throughout 1917 and 1918 the incidence rates were usually 1 per 1,000 or less; the case fatality rates were 1254/2529 or approximately 50%, but the author (S.L. Cummins) of the chapter in the *Official History* believed that the severity of the wounds was often the real cause of death and, indeed, the case fatality is less if the interval after wounding is long; the prophylactic use of antitoxic serum was given as a cause of the decline of the case fatality rates.

Streptococcal Diseases. See §33.18.

Poliomyelitis and Other Virus Diseases of ICD 046–049. These diseases are not mentioned in the *Official History*.

Smallpox. With universal vaccination, smallpox was absent from the British forces.

Measles, Rubella, Yellow Fever and Other Diseases ICD 051–079. These were at most causes of few deaths.

Typhus. The *Official History* recalls that from 1870 until the outbreak of war in 1914, typhus was almost unknown in Western Europe. Its association with overcrowding in houses, malnutrition, and squalor were well known but they were subordinate to the transfer of the infection by lice. C.-J.-H. Nicolle was the first to apply this information to the control of typhus in Tunis, where typhus was endemic, reducing the annual number of deaths from 836 in 1906 to 3 in 1914 by the disinfection of all infected personnel, clothing, bedding, and rooms. British troops suffered little from the disease even in endemic areas. In Russian Poland the average annual number of cases before 1914 was almost 2,000. Russian prisoners conveyed typhus to Germany and Austria; severe epidemics occurred in the prisoner of war camps, with some thousands of cases. Southern Serbia and Austrian Galicia and Styria were endemic areas. The chief extension of the disease was caused by the Austrian invasion of Serbia in 1914. The Serbian army had been quite free of typhus until after the retreat of the Austrian army from Valijevo, in which the Serbs took 40,000 prisoners and 3,000 sick and wounded, many of whom were suffering from typhus; 100 cases were reported by the end of 1914 and 1,100 by the end of January 1915. There were 3,000 cases in hospital by the end of February and case fatality rates were 30%; estimates of the total number of deaths ranged from 100,000 to 135,000 including almost two-thirds of the Austrian prisoners. Preventive measures were set in progress on March 16, 1915, under the advice of a British Sanitary Mission; the measures included suspension of all rail traffic, stoppage of leave from the army, and, above all, delousing, especially of clothes in barrel disinfectors. The number of new cases was reduced to one-half in 2 weeks and one-fifth in 4 weeks. Daily admissions to all hospitals were 1,500 on March 16, 230 cases on April 16, and 100 by May 31. The epidemic was reported to be ended by May 27, and the British mission was recalled on June 1. Very few more cases occurred in the Serbian army throughout the remainder of the war. There was no typhus on Gallipoli but cases occurred in Palestine and Egypt. Only five cases occurred in France and Italy.

Trench Fever. This fever, due to *Rickettsia quintana* (ICD 083.1), is transmitted by the human louse. It was first described in 1915, at first as a mild and short fever; later, relapsing cases became numerous, and it may be said that trench fever was a great cause of morbidity with little, if any, mortality.

Malaria. As the *Official History* (1922–1924) has it in vol. 1 of *Diseases of the War* (p. 227):

Of all diseases responsible for casualties during the war malaria probably holds first place. To realise this fully one has only to look at the figures for admissions for malaria for the three years 1916, 1917 and 1918. In Macedonia they reached the total of about 160,000; in Egypt, about 35,000; in East Africa 107,000 between June 3rd, 1916 and October 27th, 1917; and in Mesopotamia about 20,000. Other places, such as the Cameroons, German South-West Africa, France, and even England itself, contributed to the total, but the numbers are insignificant in comparison with these figures.

In Greece the British army arrived at Salonika at the end of 1915; fortunately, the malaria season was well over, and there was no transmission over the winter months. Initially, the troops were stationed in the hills around Salonika and to the north of it. In 1916 the Allies operated in the valleys of the Vardar and the Struma Rivers. Some steps were taken against mosquito breeding and perhaps were sufficient for the hilly country, but at the end of June 1916 the forces occupied the lowlands of the Struma south of Lake Butkovo, highly malarious country with five species of *Anopheles* occupying all the appropriate niches. The admissions to hospital per 1,000 of strength are given by the *Official History* (1922–1924) by six-month intervals commencing November 1, 1915, as 0.24, 237.28, 56.83, 277.85, 162.75, and 253.82 and ending October 31, 1918. Admissions to hospital formed only a part of the total incidence, as many cases were treated in their own unit or field hospital. In the winter of 1916, out of 977 men examined, 216 were infected with *vivax* malaria, 24 with *falciparum*, and 1 with *malariae*; these men were not suffering from clinical malaria at the time, and *falciparum* figures are relatively low because it was winter time, when it tends to

disappear from the blood. Admissions for *falciparum* malaria were about 8,000 in October 1971 and about 3,000 in October 1918. In the British "Army of the Black Sea," formed after the Armistice of November 1918 and operating to the south of the Caucasus, it was found that if sites of camps were chosen on the hills, relatively little malaria would be suffered. In Palestine and Egypt malaria became of great importance after the initiation of active operations in 1917–1918 in Palestine. In East Africa the area around Dar-es-Salaam was highly malarious; the admissions and deaths were for officers 3,036 and 10, and for men 104,666 and 639. Malaria accounted for more than 57% of hospital admissions. Similar conditions were found in the Cameroons in West Africa. Malaria in Mesopotamia was not as serious a disease as in the theaters already mentioned.

Leishmaniasis. This disease is not mentioned in the *Official History*.

Trypanosomiasis. Some cases of trypanosomiasis were met in the British army operating in East Africa.

Relapsing Fever. Louse-borne relapsing fever was experienced in 1917–1918 in Mesopotamia and by some native laborers working in Marseilles. The African tick-borne relapsing fever was met in German East Africa, where it was a principal cause of mortality among the Belgian troops. For the spread of this disease after war, see §16.6.

Dengue. This is a minor cause of morbidity.

Venereal Diseases. From the point of view of the army, syphilis was an acute disease. It was treated with arsphenamine "606" given in a series of injections, spaced as shortly as was consistent with safety. There was a low rate of complications from the therapy. Gonorrhea was a cause of morbidity.

Leptospirosis. This disease was responsible for a number of cases and deaths in British, French, and German troops on the western front. The case fatality was believed to be no more than 4%. The cause of "campaign jaundice" with similar symptoms had not been established in 1924.

Avitaminoses. Scurvy occurred principally among Indian troops in Mesopotamia in 1916; there were 11,455 cases with 24 deaths in the second half of 1916; the corresponding figures for the full years 1917 and 1918 were 2,199 and 5 and 825 and 2, respectively. Indian troops were paid in money and bought food from their contractors, obtaining a diet unsatisfactory in comparison with a normal British diet; further, the campaigns were fought in unpopulated areas with no supply of fresh fruit or vegetables. Limited outbreaks of beri-beri occurred in Chinese and Indian labor corps, in Chinese sailors, and in British troops at Gallipoli and Mudros; in Mesopotamia there were over 500 admissions from beri-beri, chiefly among the British troops, with 9 deaths. Pellagra was reported in 8.5% of Turkish prisoners of war held in Egypt; among 317,000 British and Indian troops in the Egyptian Expeditionary Force, there was only 1 case. An investigation showed that pellagra was already present in many of the Turks before capture; it is noted that the cause of pellagra had not been established at that time.

Protein-calorie Deficiency. This disease, known under many names, was first recorded at Lille, France, in October 1914, then under German occupation. Later, it was noted in British prisoners released from German camps and in the civil populations of the Central Powers.

Neurasthenia and War Neuroses. These were common forms of invalidity but not death.

Cardiovascular System. There were no special new organic diseases but soldier's heart (a functional disorder) was not uncommon; neurasthenic symptoms were often focused on the cardiovascular system.

Influenza. The *Official History* noted that "ordinary influenza" had never been absent from the various army commands in the United Kingdom; indeed, there had been 36,072 admissions in 1916 and 28,980 in 1917 with incidence higher in winter than in the summer.

Table 33.17.1 gives influenza admissions among troops in the United Kingdom from January, 1918 to the end of September, 1919, with peaks in the months of June-July and October-November, 1918 and February, 1919. Similarly, in the British commands in France there was an epidemic beginning in June and ending in August, 1918. About October 12, 1918 the new wave of epidemic began in the commands in France and weekly admissions and deaths from that date until March 8, 1919 are given in Table 33.17.1.

The behavior of the epidemic was similar to that in the civilian population in London, Copenhagen, and in Europe, generally. In all, in the British armies in France, there were 112,274 admissions to hospital with 5,483 deaths, a case fatality of 4.9%. In the forces abroad, the epidemic in Mesopotamia was notable with a case fatality of 6.5%.

Nephritis. The *Official History* notes that nephritis had not been especially observed in former wars, except in the United States Civil War during 1862 and 1863. Case incidence was 1.5 per 1,000 and there were, in all, 14,000 cases. It was of the order of 0.5 per 1,000 in the British troops in France throughout most of the months of 1915–1917.

Gas Warfare. With the development of the great chemical industry of Germany, it was easy to manufacture such gases as chlorine and phosgene for use in war. There are useful tables in the *Official History* (1922–1924) in *Medical Services, Diseases of the War*, vol. 2, for example, their Table 1, p. 254, gives the names of the gases, their chemical formulas and physical properties, and the nation using them. The *Official History* (Table 1, p. 271) summarizes the method of use, the gas, and the available means of protection for periods beginning on the late afternoon of April 22, 1915. Early cloud-gas attacks could not be made to generate sufficiently high local concentrations and were unduly affected by wind direction; indeed, the German attacks using cloud-gas were greatly hampered by the prevailing wind direction, and they could only depend on a favorable wind for a few days in the spring. Therefore, they turned their attention to delivery by

TABLE 33.17.1 Influenza in the British army, 1918–1919.

Commands in the United Kingdom			
Month	Admissions	Month	Admissions
January, 1918	3,158	January, 1919	4,547
February, 1918	2,356	February, 1919	13,752
March, 1918	3,483	March, 1919	7,709
April, 1918	2,306	April, 1919	2,954
May, 1918	4,737	May, 1919	1,017
June, 1918	31,138	June, 1919	416
July, 1918	25,480	July, 1919	381
August, 1918	3,358	August, 1919	281
September, 1918	2,738	September, 1919	365
October, 1918	30,097		
November, 1918	23,021		
December, 1918	6,910		

Commands in France					
Week ending	Admissions	Deaths	Week ending	Admissions	Deaths
Oct. 12th 1918	1,776	—	Dec. 28th 1918	2,579	73
Oct. 19th 1918	3,080	2	Jan. 4th 1919	2,768	34
Oct. 26th 1918	9,280	314	Jan. 11th 1919	2,195	32
Nov. 2nd 1918	13,203	701	Jan. 18th 1919	1,888	33
Nov. 9th 1918	11,877	878	Jan. 25th 1919	1,563	40
Nov. 16th 1918	7,389	689	Feb. 1st 1919	2,354	69
Nov. 23rd 1918	8,008	546	Feb. 8th 1919	3,074	104
Nov. 30th 1918	8,206	526	Feb. 15th 1919	4,011	144
Dec. 7th 1918	7,087	412	Feb. 22nd 1919	5,768	212
Dec. 14th 1918	6,033	213	Mar. 1st 1919	3,502	200
Dec. 21st 1918	3,919	121	Mar. 8th 1919	2,714	140

From *Official History of the War* (1922–1924), *Medical Services, Diseases of the War*, vol. 1, pp. 174–175.

projectile, and, after the first serious bombardment on the night of July 14–15, 1916, the Germans depended on intense gas-shell bombardment. The lung-irritant gases, chlorine, phosgene, chloropicrin, and others, caused great edema of the lungs and hence obstruction to the circulation of the blood. In the late stages of the war between 70% and 80% of all gas-casualty admissions to hospital were due to phosgene. This gas was vesicant and caused lesions of the skin as well as the lungs. Phosgene was sometimes used in association with chlorine. According to the *Official History* (see chart opposite p. 308), figures of deaths and casualties for the cloud-gas attacks in 1915 and 1916 were not always available; excluding these, there were 4,207 gas casualties up to July 14, 1916, with case fatalities of 24%. In the second period called "lethal," July 15, 1916, to July 12, 1917, there were 8,806 gas-shell casualties with case fatalities of 6%; a variety of poison gases was used, including lachrymatory, in a variety of projectiles sometimes also armed with explosives. From July 13, 1917, to the end of the war, there were 160,970 casualties with a case fatality rate of 2.6%. Before July 1917, the number of British gas casualties per week had not exceeded 1,000; there were between 6,000 and 7,000 casualties in at least 1 week of July 1917 and March, April, August, and September 1918, with gas casualties of more than 6,000 in 2 weeks of March 1918. See Haber (1986).

For an atlas of casualties, see Banks and Martin (1970); for historical studies of war casualties, Klingberg (1945).

TABLE 33.18.1. Battle deaths per 1,000,000 population of nation.

	World War I	World War II	
Grand Total	14,137	10,912	
United States	1,313	3,141	
United Kingdom	19,654	5,684	
Belgium	11,513	1,143	
France	32,927	5,109	Before June 22, 1940
Portugal	1,129		
Italy/Sardinia	18,466	401	On Allied side
		1,376	On Central Powers side
Yugoslavia/Serbia	10,667	325	
Greece	1,852	1,408	
Romania	47,183	14,500	Before August 23, 1944
		500	After September 9, 1944
Russia (USSR)	10,494	43,988	
Japan	6	14,164	
Germany/Prussia	26,866	44,416	Includes Austria
Austria/Hungary	22,642	—	
Bulgaria	2,917	159	On Allied side
		1,429	On Central Powers side
Turkey	17,568		
Canada		3,447	
Brazil		25	
Netherlands		713	
Poland		9,169	
Norway		690	
Ethiopia		500	
South Africa		870	
China		2,495	
Mongolia		5,000	
Australia		4,324	
New Zealand		10,813	
Hungary		4,348	
Finland		10,769	

From J.D. Singer and M. Small, *The Wages of War, 1816–1965*, Table 4.2. Copyright John Wiley & Sons, Inc., 1972, reprinted with permission.

33.18 World War II

World War II may be said to have begun on September 1, 1939, when Germany invaded Poland. This was followed by declarations of war on Germany by Great Britain and France on September 3, 1939. The end of the war was proclaimed by US President Harry Truman as Victory in Europe Day, May 8, 1945, and the Soviet announced the end of the European war on May 9, 1945. The United States declared war on Japan on December 8, 1941; Germany and Italy declared war on the United States on December 11; the Japanese ceased fighting on August 14, 1945, and the United States accepted the formal surrender of Japan on September 2, 1945.

In Table 33.18.1 we give, from Singer and Small (1972), estimates of the battle casualties of the different nations in World Wars I and II. Here, rounded off to the battle casualties per 1,000 population of the nations, are some illustrative comparisons between World War I (and II) rates: United States, 1.3 (3.1); United Kingdom, 20 (5.7); Belgium, 12 (1.1); France, 33 (5.1); Serbia, Yugoslavia, 11 (0.3); Romania, 47 (14); Russia or Soviet, 10.5 (44); Japan, 0.01 (14.2); Germany (Prussia) 27 (44). The second Yugoslavian figure evidently does not include the huge losses of the partisan warfare. Although early in World War II it appeared that there would not be the great and continued carnage of the western front of World War I, with France and Belgium being overrun without trench warfare, yet the sieges of Leningrad, Moscow, and Stalingrad produced great casualty lists; rather fewer casualties occurred in the battles in the north of France, Belgium, the Netherlands, and Germany itself.

On the medical side, the cause of nearly all bacterial diseases had been discovered before World War I, and the identities of the virus causes of disease had been established in the interwar years. Moreover, epidemiologic knowledge of the various important infective diseases had been deepened and extended by researches in Europe and in America, in particular, often carried out in association with the armed forces. Important advances had also been made in chemotherapy, including antibiotic therapy, for which see Andrus, Bronk, et al. (1948). Possibly the best guides to the medical problems of World War II are the series under the general editorship of MacNalty (1952–   ), especially Cope (1952, 1953) and Green and Covell (1953), who between them give an excellent bibliography.

Cholera. Little fighting was carried out in the main regions of endemic cholera; outbreaks occurred in prisoner of war camps in Thailand, and there were epidemics in the civil population of India.

Enteric Fever. Case fatality rates were still high in World War II, indeed, 11.5% of 279 cases in the Middle East Force in 1943–1944 but the admission rate was low, about 0.8 per 1,000 per annum. Cope (1952, p. 33) believed that the prophylactic vaccines were more powerful after 1934, when case incidence rates fell in the Indian Army. There were improvements in sanitation.

Bacillary Dysentery. The carrier rate can be high and can be maintained over long periods of time, and so infection can follow general contamination of water or local spread by food handlers. Finally, it was seen that therapy with

sulfonamides would be the principal weapon, sulfaguanidine for the British and sulfadiazine for the Americans.

Amebiasis. Cope (1952, p. 205) states that in most British theaters of war, the intestinal form of this disease appeared in 5% to 15% of all cases showing dysenteric symptoms. Emetine remained the drug of choice and was especially useful in the complication of liver abscess.

Tuberculosis. See §33.15 for the naval experience. Tuberculosis was still an important disease in 1940. Accrding to Green and Covell (1953, pp. 140–147), there had been a rise in the tuberculosis death rates in the years 1939–1941 in the civil population of the United Kingdom. A mass radiography survey showed significant lesions in 1% to 1.5% of the London-employed groups, and 0.3% to 0.4% were in need of immediate treatment. The rates in mental institutions were about three times as high. In England and Wales more than 1,300 persons died of nonpulmonary tuberculosis of bovine origin during 1944. Daniels, Ridehalgh, et al. (1948) in the Prophit Survey recommended BCG immunization of young persons exposed to special risk. In the American services, about 3 per 1,000 men inducted were found to have minimal active pulmonary tuberculosis (Andrus, Bronk, et al., 1948).

Bubonic Plague. Before 1941 much work had been done on the value of vaccination, serotherapy, and chemotherapy. However, bubonic plague was not experienced in the actual theaters of war.

Cerebrospinal Fever. An epidemic of meningococcal meningitis occurring early in the war in the United Kingdom was treated by means of sulfonamide drugs with low case fatality rates (Green and Covell, 1953, p. 220); this form of meningitis therefore caused much less damage than in 1915–1917.

Tetanus. Active immunization with tetanus toxoid was successful. See Cope (1952, pp. 441–450).

Influenza. No useful vaccine had been prepared before the end of the war. The feared pandemic did not appear.

Streptococcal Diseases.

Among diseases of possible or probable streptococcal etiology encountered in the United States Army during World War 1 (1 April 1917 to 31 December 1919) in Europe and the United States, the following admissions were reported: valvular heart disease 16,850; acute articular rheumatism 23,818; muscular rheumatism 11,328; scarlet fever 11,189; erysipelas 2,426; acute nephritis 2,002; and chronic nephritis 2,958,

as well as cases of acute tonsillitis and otitis media (Andrus, Bronk, et al., 1948, p. 26) By World War II, the incidence of streptococcal diseases had fallen, largely as a result of chemotherapy.

Wounds and Injuries. The speed of the German advance into France in 1940 meant that large numbers of wounded had to be transported to the United Kingdom before they could receive adequate attention; the result was that there were many cases of gas gangrene of the muscles and other forms of wound infections. Much research had already been carried out before the war, and it was known that *Clostridum welchii* produces a potent exotoxin, and further that crushing and devitalization of tissue, especially muscle, and deposition of soil in the wounded area permit germination of the gas gangrene anerobes, the *Clostridia*. *Clostridium welchii* kills by its exotoxin; *Cl. septicum* is able to kill by means of a generalized infection. More generally, infection of the wound could best be prevented by early and adequate surgical operation, including the opening up of "dead spaces" in the tissues, the removal of foreign bodies, the trimming of the walls of the cavity (debridement), relief of tension around the wound, and the provision of free drainage with the conservation of as much skin and viable tissue as possible, see Green and Covell (1953, p. 58). In the early years of the war sulfonamides were used both locally in the wound and by mouth; penicillin became generally available in 1944 to the Allied forces. The importance of hospital infections became evident

and preventive measures were introduced. For an extensive review of wounds and injuries in warfare, see Green and Covell (1953, pp. 53–137) and Cope (1953).

Encephalitis. Endemic zoonoses existed in some nations. In peace-time United States various types of viral encephalitis had been experienced, for example, St. Louis since 1933. See Andrus, Bronk, et al. (1948). Surveys of mosquito vectors were carried out before the war, with a view toward control if military training or operations occurred in the enzootic areas or if new viruses, particularly Japanese B, were introduced.

Hepatitis. Hepatitis A virus was responsible for a good deal of invalidity but little mortality; see Green and Covell (1953, pp. 150–155) at which time the virology had not yet been worked out.

Typhus Fever. Typhus was known to be present in Italy before the American landings. By the end of November 1943, there had been more than 40 cases of typhus reported in Naples. At first adequate amounts of DDT were not available, and so delousing began on December 12, 1943; the homes of all reported cases were visited and all contacts were dusted. See Wiltse (1965, p. 362) and Soper, Davis, et al. (1947). By December 24, 1943, it was possible to commence extensive delousing of air raid shelters and persons, more than 3,000,000 applications being made in the Naples area between mid-December 1943 and the end of May 1944. See Conn (1965, p. 362) for references. See also §14.3 for scrub (or mite) typhus, important in the Pacific theater.

Malaria. As is pointed out in Green and Covell (1953, p. 155), malaria presented a serious problem to the armed forces in a number of theaters in the hot, wet tropics: the southwest Pacific area, southeast Asia, the Middle East, Sicily, and southern Italy. The rate of admission to hospital for malaria for European troops was 278 per 1,000 per annum, greatly in excess of the rates for venereal disease, 81; bacillary dysentery, 65; amebic dysentery, 26; schistosomiasis, 24; and jaundice, 7. In the southwest Pacific area, the rate of admission to hospital for malaria began even higher, and malaria threatened the very continuance of the campaign. Initially there were three *drugs*, quinine, mepacrine, and pamaquin; the latter two were effective suppressants. The first measure was to ensure, by strict discipline, that the troops took their suppressant. Research was carried out in Australia, the United Kingdom, India, and America to devise the most successful suppressant and curative effects. Fortunately, DDT, or dichloro-diphenyl-trichlorethane, had been recognized as an *insecticide* and was used against the anopheline mosquitoes throughout the war. An effective *insect repellent*, dimethyl phthalate, was available in large quantity and used with success. The *mosquitoes* were attacked in their breeding places; much research had to be applied to the establishment of the identity of the malaria vectors and to their bionomics (i.e., way of life) so that their life cycle could be broken and, if necessary, their haunts could be avoided. The malariologists were consulted,

even at the planning stage of new campaigns. The net result of all these endeavors was that armies could be kept in the field even in holoendemic areas (i.e., the most malarious areas) such as New Guinea, the East Indies, and west Africa.

Venereal Disease. It can be said that venereal disease in the American army in Italy was a nuisance rather than a cause of death or even morbidity, see Conn (1965, pp. 257–258 and 411–412).

Nutrition, Malnutrition, and Starvation. See §22.8 and §§33.12, 33.14, and 33.17. The two great famines were during the siege of Leningrad and in Bengal during 1943. Various famine or starvation syndromes are reported in Green and Covell (1953). For civilian health and medical services, see MacNalty (1953–1955). For the health of the Army, see War Office (1948), and for casualties and medical statistics, see Mellor (1972). For American Forces, see Reister (1976).

Chapter 34
Injury and Poisoning

34.1 Definitions

In the ninth revision of the ICD, deaths, which can be referred to briefly as violent deaths or deaths from violence or from injury, accident, or poisoning, are grouped together in class 17 as caused by "Injury and Poisoning". These violent causes include such "external" causes of death as drownings, falls, suffocation, accidental poisonings, suicide, homicide, judicial executions, and casualties in civil strife or war.

The definitions of this class have varied over the successive revisions. In particular, in the ninth revision it includes those deaths assigned to the class of "Chronic Poisonings" before the sixth revision of the *International List* in 1948. Deaths from chronic alcoholism, however, are still to be assigned to the class of nervous diseases. Deaths from criminal abortion had often been referred to the class of violence but the rules of the ICD now assign such deaths to class 11. Deaths from tetanus in trivial wounds are referred to the class of infective diseases, but these various definitions have not been numerically important.

The ninth revision in 1975 of the ICD gives two classifications of deaths in the class of "Injury and Poisoning"—by anatomic site and by cause of the injury. We are following this second or "E" classification. Casualties of war have already been discussed in the preceding chapter.

Deaths from violence are important from the community point of view because they occur so frequently in youth and early adult life, when the community has already made its investment in the individual in the form of education and maintenance in childhood, but when the individual's contribution to the community has not yet been made.

It is evident that the mortality from injuries is dependent on the culture, state of technology, and many other factors in the make-up of the community. Dublin and Lotka (1937) have always paid a great deal of attention to violent causes in their reviews of the mortality experience of the policy holders of the Metropolitan Life Insurance Company of New York. They point out that the one unifying feature of many of these deaths, which include suicides, homicides, accidental poisonings, and external violence, is a lowered appreciation of the sanctity of human life. Therefore, ultimately the prevention of a proportion of these deaths is a moral problem. The state has always regarded this group of deaths as important, for it has appeared to be one in which administrative action and legislation might be effective in prevention. Therefore, in any list of deaths, care must be taken to see that violence, if it is the initiating cause, is not overlooked. For such reasons, the assignment rules of the *International List* and of the ICD have always given a high priority to the causes in this class.

34.2 All Injury and Poisoning (Violence)

Mortality of all violent causes (excluding war) is considered as a whole in this section, leaving a consideration of causes to the later sections.

TABLE 34.2.1 Mortality rates in Australia from injury and poisoning.*

Age in years	0–4	5–14	15–24	25–34	35–44	45–54	55–64	65–74	75+
					Males				
1908–1910	1,000	446	809	996	1,411	1,757	2,341	2,593	3,487
1911–1920	748	429	793	1,069	1,276	1,697	2,039	2,364	3,361
1921–1930	670	402	844	984	1,128	1,436	1,711	1,989	3,238
1931–1940	661	394	937	889	978	1,231	1,532	1,851	3,534
1941–1950	587	363	768	645	771	977	1,284	1,742	3,716
1951–1960	515	277	1,172	1,009	920	1,068	1,351	1,753	3,889
1961–1970	454	242	1,156	969	1,006	1,131	1,288	1,609	3,247
1971–1980	402	213	1,302	862	835	922	994	1,202	2,830
					Females				
1908–1910	803	230	199	196	255	310	455	1,002	2,477
1911–1920	602	166	174	207	239	301	374	674	2,486
1921–1930	488	167	165	186	210	285	360	630	2,311
1931–1940	486	140	177	184	204	280	346	728	3,103
1941–1950	375	129	144	144	172	238	334	698	3,621
1951–1960	362	118	184	176	227	326	418	740	3,796
1961–1970	339	115	292	248	337	467	544	830	3,036
1971–1980	286	108	333	239	286	371	430	597	2,474
					Masculinity rates[†]				
1908–1910	125	194	407	508	553	567	515	259	141
1911–1920	124	258	456	516	534	564	545	351	135
1921–1930	137	241	512	529	537	504	475	316	140
1931–1940	136	281	529	483	479	440	443	254	114
1941–1950	157	281	533	448	448	411	384	250	103
1951–1960	142	235	637	573	405	328	323	237	102
1961–1970	134	210	396	391	299	242	237	194	107
1971–1980	141	197	391	361	292	249	231	201	114

*Deaths per 1,000,000 per annum.
[†] 100 × (male death rates)/(female death rates).
From Lancaster and Gordon (1987).

In Tables 34.2.1 and 34.2.2 we give the age-specific mortality rates from violence so defined for Australia and for England and Wales.

For a given epoch, there is a local maximum in the rates at ages 0–4 years; the rates then decline to a minimum at ages 5–14 years in both sexes. In males, before 1920, the rates then continued to increase throughout life; after 1930, there is a local maximum at ages 15–24 years, becoming increasingly evident in the later epochs. This local maximum at ages 15–24 years is less evident in females but is present in each epoch after 1940. After the local maximum there is a dip to a local minimum and then a steady rise in the rates throughout life. An explanation, given in detail by Lancaster (1952d, 1957c, 1964a) and in §34.4, is the dominance of deaths from road accidents at young adult life.

Comparing the rates by columns, there have been great improvements, the rates decreasing at ages under 15 years to less than one-half of their initial values. At ages over 35 years there have been declines in the mortality rates. At almost all ages in both sexes there have been minima during the epoch 1941–1950, due to petrol (gasoline) rationing in both Australia and England and Wales during World War II and immediately after. At ages 15–24 and 25–34 years, there have been steady increases in the death rates after 1950.

We summarize these observations by saying

TABLE 34.2.2. Violence other than suicide in England and Wales (deaths per 1,000,000 per annum).

	All ages*	0–4	5–9	10–14	15–19	20–24	25–34	35–44	45–54	55–64	65–74	75 and over
					Males							
1861–1870	1,064	1,421	598	750	824	953	983	1,130	1,279	1,500	1,657	2,244
1871–1880	993	1,290	520	579	725	850	911	1,074	1,272	1,529	1,769	2,495
1881–1890	829	1,199	440	415	560	605	693	897	1,100	1,353	1,661	2,374
1891–1900	790	1,361	396	336	484	541	611	815	1,053	1,310	1,621	2,374
1901–1910	670	1,231	329	258	411	464	525	662	860	1,100	1,310	2,239
1911–1920	729	998	392	299	561	832	704	695	799	998	1,325	2,399
1921–1930	523	683	375	241	418	506	426	447	570	772	1,103	2,407
1931–1935	770	697	370	228	533	739	602	640	921	1,271	1,599	3,358[†]
1946	622	688	328	251	414	565	453	478	582	864	1,213	2,612[†]
1956	604	392	173	151	410	608	442	428	578	874	1,259	3,320[†]
1966	601	867[‡]	266[‡]	194[‡]		680[‡]	464	478	566	721	968	2,890[§‖]
1975	486	431[‡]	198[‡]	198[‡]		610[‡]	431	418	473	555	707	2,025[§‖]
					Females							
1861–1870	314	1,111	315	131	113	86	98	135	197	314	636	2,210
1871–1880	304	1,031	241	106	96	77	96	152	233	379	724	2,271
1881–1890	284	964	196	85	82	72	91	139	229	374	749	2,231
1891–1900	313	1,144	238	82	78	68	92	144	235	388	774	2,323
1901–1910	282	1,059	226	78	69	66	79	118	198	314	664	2,238
1911–1920	255	833	231	95	86	78	76	103	170	276	642	2,305
1921–1930	201	487	182	70	93	84	69	81	133	254	608	2,453
1931–1935	346	505	201	81	142	155	161	194	297	443	878	3,044[†]
1946	326	494	149	70	83	86	116	152	225	351	661	2,725[†]
1956	383	284	87	52	76	91	101	140	260	412	764	3,242[†]
1966	421	654[‡]	185[‡]	77[‡]		147[‡]	138	188	298	398	763	2,920[§‖]
1975	365	427[‡]	127[‡]	52[‡]		163[‡]	155	180	259	361	545	2,323[§‖]

*1861–1930, standardized on to the population of England and Wales as enumerated in 1901. From the Registrar-General's Decennial Supplement (1952, Part 3, Table 12, p. 96).
†From the Registrar-General's Statistical Review for the year 1956.
‡Age groups 0, 1–4, 5–14, 15–24 years.
§From World Health Statistics Annual.
‖Includes suicide.

that the age-specific mortality rates decreased as pioneering or grave industrial and urban conditions improved, but that at young adult and early parentage ages, increased use of the automobile brought greater mortality rates from violence.

Perhaps it is worthy of note that some of the effects of high risks from automobiles have been greatly lessened by improved surgical techniques.

See the injury fact book of Baker, O'Neill and Karpf (1984). For violent deaths in France and international comparisons, see Chesnais (1976a); for the United Kingdom, see Greenwood and Candy (1911), Hair (1971), and Walford (1881); for Australia, see Lancaster (1952d, 1957c, 1960b, 1964a); for America, see National Academy (1985b).

34.3 Railway Accidents

ICD E800–807.

A railway accident is a transport accident involving a railway train or other railway vehicle, whether in motion or not; excluded are accidents in repair shops, in roundhouses, on turntables, or on railway premises but not involving a train or other railway vehicle. Thus, the vital statistics do not yield the number of railwaymen injured at work.

Deaths can be numerous in a collapse of a bridge or other large accident. For an account of such disasters in the United Kingdom, see Rolt (1955) and Hamilton (1967).

34.4 Motor and Other Road Vehicle Accidents

ICD E810–829 and E846–848.

Deaths from injury and poisoning vary with the economic and technological development of the society, and so their importance for mortality varies greatly. Motor vehicle deaths are a new feature. Thus, C.F. Benz made the first motor car or automobile, that is, carriage driven by the internal combustion machine, in 1885; the first collision occurred in 1892; two deaths were recorded in Great Britain in 1896 and one in the United States in 1899. Automobiles at first were used in transport, in the trades and in the professions, and also by the wealthy; by the 1920s, mass-production methods allowed them to be produced more cheaply, but the output was slowed down by the Great Depression, and the use of cars in civilian life during World War II decreased in most countries because of petrol (gasoline) rationing. After 1950 the number of automobiles increased greatly throughout the developed world. These changes are faithfuly reproduced in the Australian age-specific death rates from violence in Table 34.2.1.

There are great variations in the death rates by age and sex, for example, in America for the year 1959, Norman (1962) gives the deaths of drivers per 1,000,000 per annum at ages under 20 as 891, then by five-year age groups, 20–24, etc., as follows: 575, 505, 433, 471, and 474; 409 at ages 50–54; 404, 461, 519, and 528 at ages 70–74; 538 at ages 75 and older, with a minimum at ages 50–60 years.

Alcohol is believed to be an important factor. Norman (1962) cites series in which 47% of pedestrians killed had a blood-alcohol level above 50 mg/100 ml. Of those killed in single vehicle accidents involving neither other vehicles nor pedestrians, 49% of the drivers had blood-alcohol levels of more than 150 mg/100 ml at death and a further 20% had levels between 50 mg and 150 mg/100 ml.

Norman (1962) gives many comparisons by age and sex within the United States and also, in his Table 3, some crude death rates per 1,000,000 per annum for various countries: Canada, 560; United States, 725; Federal Republic of Germany, 779; Austria, 1,022; Belgium, 474; Denmark, 363; France, 407; Netherlands, 285; England and Wales, 386; Sweden, 284; Australia, 826; and New Zealand, 540.

Much has been written on automobile accidents; see §35.3. We give now some further references: research on road safety, Behr (1963); France since 1953, Vallin and Chesnais (1975) and for 1968–1977, Chesnais and Vallin (1977); England and Wales 1904–1923, Edge (1926); per person mile, Garwood and Jeffcoate (1960); accidents and homicide, Iskrant and Joliet (1968); automobiles and health, Ryan (1980); motor vehicle accidents 1950–1962, WHO-accidents (1965).

34.5 Water Transport Accidents and Drowning

ICD E830–838 and E910.

Drowning, an important form of accidental death, does not fit in well with either the general ICD or its supplementary (i.e., E) classification. It is also the mode of death in many of the disasters, once given a separate rubric as cataclysm, in the *International List*. Drowning appears in many settings, from domestic drownings in bath or swimming pool to huge numbers of casualties in shipping and natural disasters.

The clinical aspects of drowning have been considered by Donald (1955). In fresh water, it is believed that involuntary inspiration occurs from 1 to 2 minutes after immersion; glottic spasm may prevent the lungs from being flooded immediately, but if fresh water enters the lungs, there is an immediate and marked absorption of the fluid into the circulation, leading to hemodilution and to hemolysis. There is an upset of the normal potassium/sodium balance in the blood and, in a few minutes, ventricular fibrillation ensues; probably the aspiration of any marked quantity of fresh water into the lungs is fatal. In salt-water drowning, because the sea-water concentration of salts is greater than that of the circulation, there is some hemoconcentration but no upset of the potassium/sodium ratio that would lead to ventricular fibrillation; death in salt-water drowning is due to prolonged and severe myocardial anoxia. Therefore, although respiration may have ceased, there is a hope of resuscitation in salt-water drownings because the heart action may not have ceased. Cold exhaustion may be an important contributing cause of death, see Keatinge (1981).

Among natural disasters, perhaps between 1 and 2 million persons died in the floods due to rain in Hénán (Honan) Province, China, in June 1931, following floods on the Chángjiāng (Yangtze) and Huang (Yellow) Rivers. In a typhoon in Haiphong, North Vietnam, on October 8, 1881, 300,000 are reported to have died; 215,000 died in the Andaman Islands in the Bay of Bengal in 1876 as a result of a tsunami of seismic origin. Most of the 36,417 casualties following the eruption of Krakatoa on August 27, 1883, were due to the ensuing tsunami. A storm in the English Channel on November 26, 1703, led to the loss of 8,000 lives by drowning. Some 1,917 lives were lost in Longarone, Italy, on October 9, 1963, following the destruction of the Vaiont dam, and 532 lives were lost after a dam burst in the Subansiri Valley, Assam, on August 23, 1950; both these disasters followed seismic activity.

In Iceland, Greenland, Norway, Scotland, the north of England, and, indeed, all the countries bordering the North Sea and North Atlantic, and in the neighboring islands, drowning was a great occupational hazard. It is estimated that 2% of all deaths in Scotland during the early nineteenth century were due to drowning, and rates were even higher in Iceland and the Faeroes, as we show in Table 39.4.1.

As was remarked by Meurk (1932), the mechanization of shipping led to a decline of occupational mortality of sailors and fishermen. However, the introduction of strange machinery and higher speeds in modern transport led to fresh problems, which now have been largely solved. As Ayers (1969) points out, many of the disasters were caused by inadequacies of construction, seamanship, charts, weather information, and navigation. He mentions large water-transport accidents of modern times, roughly after the introduction of steam. The hazards of the steam engine were at first not properly appreciated. Many explosions occurred on ships, in the United States, especially, as a result; in 1865, in the explosion and fire on the Mississippi steamboat *Sultana*, 1,500 persons lost their lives. In 1912 the *Titanic* was making full speed, at least 21 knots, without any special precautions, through an area in which icebergs had been reported; the weather was clear and the sea was calm when she collided with an iceberg and subsequently sank with a loss of more than 1,500 persons out of 2,223 on board; the total lifeboat capacity was only 1,176 persons. A conference in 1914 recommended the use of fixed routes in the North Atlantic, and such standards were later confirmed by a convention in 1929. After 1948, traffic separation rules were laid down for the areas around Great Britain, in the Straits of Gibraltar, the Red Sea, the Persian Gulf, and elsewhere. Radar has now become widely used to avoid collisions, but in the early years following World War II, collisions occurred between ships, each provided with radar. A collision of oil tankers, *Esso Massachusetts* and *S.S. Alva Cape*, in New York harbor led to 33 deaths, with 4 more deaths attributed to a spark following the release of carbon dioxide to reduce the risk of explosion on the *Alva Cape* during an attempt at salvage.

34.6 Air and Space Transport Accidents

ICD E840–845.

Tye (1969, Table 1), surveying the safety of air travel, shows that unscheduled flights flew under less favorable conditions than the scheduled; more than half the accidents occurred on the approach to land; often the airport was less well equipped with landing and navigational aids than the major airports; the presence of mountains near the airport contributed to accidents. Thirty percent of the accidents were associated with the airworthiness of the aircraft and 70% with operational matters. In 5 accidents out of 13, the aircraft was not on the correct course. Tye (1969, figure 3) gives the millions of miles per fatal accident as just under unity in 1920 with an almost tenfold improvement in the 4 decades up to 1960. From Tye (1969, Table 2), it appears that the average number of flying hours per fatality was about 360,000 in 1960, corresponding to approximately 40 years.

According to the *Civil Aviation Authority*, Table 7, CAA Paper 77027, London, 1978, fatal passenger accidents occurred rather less than 1 per 1,000,000 jet aircraft flying hours in the world during 1970–1976; in North America there were 0.6 accidents per 1,000,000 stage flights in the years 1970–1976, thus showing even lower rates.

Ramsden (1976, pp. 19–22) gives several tables; in 1963–1972, the number of fatal crashes is detailed by country per 1,000,000 revenue flights (i.e. commercial flights): Netherlands, 0; Australia, 0.785; Scandinavia, 1.348; United States, 1.680; . . . ; India, 16.238; and an unnamed Middle East country, 38.000. Eddy, Potter, and Page (1976) give tables of safety by country and by airline and a list of fatal crashes with analyses of cause of crash. See also, for fatal civil accidents, Stevens (1970).

34.7 Accidental Poisoning by Solid, Liquid, and Gaseous Substances (not in the course of therapy)

ICD E860–869. Accidental poisoning by alcohol, cleansing materials, disinfectant, paints, petroleum products, plant foods and fertilizers, corrosives and caustics, foodstuffs, gases, whether by pipeline or utility outlet, and other like materials.

Deaths will be excluded from this subclass if they occur as a complication of some disease, such as cancer, appearing after an interval.

Jelliffe and Jelliffe (1982) have chapters dealing with natural plant poisonings, for example, aflatoxicosis, coturnism, Ackee poisoning, Lathyrism, Djenkol bean, and mushrooms. See Hambraeus (1982), in particular, for a general survey of food toxicants; Barger (1931) for a bibliography of ergotism; Reilly (1980) for a general text on metallic poisonings; and Hunter, Bomford, and Russel (1940) for the general, and Harada (1982) for the special, problem of organomercury poisoning at Minamata. Dean (1961) gives an account of an epidemic of poisoning caused by a pesticide in wheat seed, provided for planting. Warner (1979) gives a review of sources and extent of environmental pollution of the accident at Seveso, Italy, in which the herbicide, trichlorophenol, was spilled into the environment. These events have been overshadowed by the leakage of methylisocyanate gas from a factory in Bhopal, a city of 0.9 million, on December 3, 1984, causing more than 2,500 deaths. See Shrivastava (1987).

This subclass causes deaths, particularly in children, under conditions of famine and other breakdowns of society and when sophisticated chemical substances are used by primitive societies.

A review of industrial accidents has been given by Hale and Hale (1972) and of dangerous materials by Sax (1979).

34.8 Therapeutic Misadventures

ICD E850–858 include accidental overdose of drug and wrong drug given or taken in error, the final digit classifying by type of drug. E870–879 include accidents in the technique of administration of drug or biologic substance, such as accidental puncture during injection or contamination of drug; in particular, E870–872 include breakdowns in operative or aseptic technique. E873 includes overdosage of drugs, for example, of hypnotics or of vitamins A and D; many effective drugs given in large doses are dangerous. E930–949 include all those states brought about by individual peculiarities in reaction when drugs, medicaments, and biologic substances cause untoward reaction, even though they have been administered in a correct manner. This section evidently includes iatrogenic disease, the adjective not appearing in the index to the ICD.

Possibly few deaths occur in modern medicine and surgery from iatrogenic disease, but it is easy to see that it was an important factor in the past. Thus, blood letting caused or precipitated many deaths from exhaustion or sepsis, excessive mercurial treatment for syphilis in the early sixteenth century often led to mercury poisoning, and patients in the nineteenth century were submitted to high risk of infections of wounds after amputations, for which see §9.11. See also §45.12.

34.9 Accidental Falls

ICD E880–888. Last digit, nature and origin.

Roughly E884 and E885 correspond to E900–904 of the seventh revision of the ICD; the (English) Registrar-General's Report for 1961 (1963, Table 109) shows that death rates in these five rubrics, combined, were, for males (females), 1,083 (1,765) per 1,000,000 per annum at ages older than 75 years in England and Wales in 1961, dominating rates of 1,470 (2,191) from "all accidents in the home and residential institutions" according to the seventh revision. An important difference in rates between the sexes is the greater frequency of fractures of the femur in the elderly females. For domestic accidents, see also Backett (1965).

34.10 Accidents Caused by Fire and Flames

ICD E890–899. Last digit determined largely by nature of the fire.

In the United States, 1959–1961, fires and explosions were the third leading cause of accidental deaths according to Iskrant and Joliet (1968). They were relatively important in children 1–14 years old. Many deaths occurred due to the use and misuse of flammable materials. More than 80% of deaths occurred in the home and 4% in industry. Causation includes fire originating in cooking or heating, smoking and the use of matches, defective electrical fittings, fires in rubbish, and flammable liquids and gases.

For fires and firefighters, see Morris (1955); for infections following burns, see Parker (1984b).

34.11 Accidents Due to Natural and Environmental Factors and Other Catastrophes

ICD E900–909.

There is great difficulty in devising a classification that is useful for ordinary clinical and hospital practice and also gives a proper role to the great natural disasters. Further, dam or bridge failure may be initiated by seismic disturbances; there could be doubt as to whether the cause should be laid to natural event or to faulty design. We discuss briefly the chief headings, and then pass on to the major cataclysms. It may be stated that, although spectacularly large disasters have occurred due to causes in this subclass, the effects averaged out over the population of the whole world do not greatly increase the death rates, for which see the following. See also Bemmelen (1956), Bignell, Peters, and Pym (1977), and Canning (1976). E900. Excessive heat can occur as a privation in a hot climate or industrially. It does not account for many deaths.
E901. Excessive cold can occur as a privation, as a result of exposure, or in the process of drowning, especially from ships in water at high latitudes. Prolonged excessive cold has led to the destruction of the community of Norsemen in Greenland in the fourteenth century, see §39.2 and also to the "cold" famines, see §22.5. E902 and 903: abnormal levels or changes in air pressure and travel and motion are included for clinical purposes. E904: hunger, thirst, exposure, and neglect, see chapters 22 and 32. E905 and 906: injuries and poisonings inflicted by plants and animals are usually minor causes of mortality. We treat E907, 908, and 909, together, as causes of deaths due to unusual events resulting from storms, floods, seismic disturbances, and lightning. Much interest, for example, Seaman, Leivesley, and Hogg (1984), has recently been shown in this type of cataclysm, the effects of which are often aggravated by human, including administrative, failure, but can be partly mitigated by prompt and well-informed human intervention. See Saylor and Gordon (1957) and Western (1972).

Seismic and Volcanic Disturbances

These appear as earthquakes, volcanic eruptions, and tsunamis (tidal waves), with such
secondary effects as land and mud slides and
floods from dams and levee failures, see Bolt,
Horn, Macdonald, and Scott (1975), Båth
(1967), and Latter (1969). Latter (1969, Figure
1) plots the sites of earthquakes by magnitude
in the first 40 days of 1964. Almost all the
points fall along or near a line passing down the
east coast of Asia and then turning down
through the Philippines, Niugini, and the
Solomon Islands to New Zealand, and another
down the west coast of the Americas; but
deaths have quite a different distribution; thus,
for the years, 1951–1964, although there were
large populations at risk and many deaths in
Japan, western and northern China, Mexico,
and Peru, there are not many other large
population masses near the principal seismic
zones outlined above, so that there were many
more deaths in the Himalaya-Mediterranean
zone between Burma and Morocco including
Italy, which is less seismically disturbed than
the two zones mentioned above. Ambraseys
(1969) gives an average of 14,000 persons
killed per annum for the world during the
period January 1951 to June 1965. This gives
slightly more than 4 deaths per 1,000,000 person years per annum, which may be considered
a mean figure in a period when no especially
devastating single earthquake occurred. With
increasing urbanization, deaths have been
numerous where large numbers of persons are
congregated in unsatisfactory town buildings,
for example, in Messina in 1908 or in Tokyo
in 1923. Tokyo and San Francisco improved
their building standards and water supplies
as a result of major earthquakes.

Volcanic eruptions are restricted to a smaller
area than earthquakes but are potentially more
dangerous, for huge sheets of lavas may be discharged through fracture zones, opened up in
the earth's crust, to spread over large areas,
and these incidents are the most dangerous
volcanic phenomena. In recent times a huge
eruption occurred in Katmai, Alaska, in 1912
in thinly populated country, so that few lives
were lost. A famous incident was the destruction by a *nuée ardente* from Mont Pelée of St.
Pierre, Martinique, in 1902, killing 28,000 to
40,000 persons. Such burning waves of gases
may, under the influence of gravity, speed
down valleys at the rate of 160 km per hour.
High casualties may also be caused by hot
mudflows in areas of high rainfall, as in Indonesia; volcanic action may also lead to the
sudden release of water dammed up by ice in
valleys; such accidents have often occurred in
Iceland, Chile, Alaska, Kamchatka, and elsewhere. The eruption of Laki in Iceland in 1783
caused many of its casualties by falls of ash that
destroyed farms, crops, and stock, leading later to starvation. The greatest seismic event in
the last 10,000 years is reported by Stothers
(1984) to have occurred at Mount Tambora,
Sumbawa, Indonesia, April 10 and 11, 1815,
with a volume of 40–90 km^3 solid rock equivalent for the ash. Resulting tsunamis were not
large. Most casualties occurred as the direct result of the fall of ash and flow of lava. The ash
resulted in a decrease of mean summer temperatures in the northern hemisphere of 0.4°C to
0.7°C in 1816.

Underwater earthquakes may cause tsunamis (i.e., tidal waves) as in the explosion of
Krakatoa in 1883, Simkin and Fiske (1983),
and in the eruption of the Santorini volcano
about 1400 BC, Sparks (1979); perhaps
100,000 persons were killed at that time. Krakatoa caused waves reaching a height of 41
meters; a great earthquake off the coast of
Honshu on March 3, 1933, caused waves of 23
meters in height and over 3,000 casualties.
Tables of great seismic disturbances are given
in Latter (1969) and in Bolt, Horn, Macdonald, and Scott (1975). See also Blong (1984),
Chen, Kam-ling, et al. (1988), Iida and Iwasaki
(1983), Kates, Haas, et al. (1973), Milne
(1911), Montandon (1959), Naranjo, Sigurdsson, et al. (1986), Turner (1928), Vallaux
(1924), and Voight (1978).

Bridge Disasters

Shirley-Smith (1969) gives details of the
reasons for bridge failures; thus, an accumula-
tion of ice upstream led to damage to the
Niagara Falls Bridge in 1897. Ships may collide

with the piers or pylons of the bridge; floods may scour the foundations of bridges; wind forces may destroy bridges, such as the Tay Bridge in 1879 and the Tacoma Narrows Bridge in 1940. Brittle fracture may occur at low temperatures; concrete bridges may fail because of bad workmanship; metal fatigue may sometimes be a factor. See also Scott (1976) and Thompson (1982).

Dam Disasters

These cause greater loss of life than failure of bridges. Failures may occur due to overtopping during flood, foundation failure through geologic faults, and seepage of water through the dam or its foundation. But there may be disasters even if the dam remains intact; thus, a landslide into the Vaiont Dam in Italy set in train a huge wave that passed over the top of the dam, destroyed several villages, and caused the deaths of more than 2,000 persons. The concrete may fail, as in the Eigiau Dam in North Wales in 1923. The de Tere Vega Dam on the Douro River in Spain collapsed during its first filling because of a blowout beneath its base, causing a heavy loss of life. See also Gruner (1963), Morgan (1971), and National Academy (1985a).

Lightning

Lightning causes rather less than 1 death per 1,000,000 per annum. The physical and medical aspects have been treated by Schonland (1950) and Spencer (1932). See also Marshall (1973).

For great disasters, see Drackett (1977) and Sigma (1986); for disaster technology bibliography, Manning (1976); for geography of calamities, Montandon (1924); for human factors, McFarland (1957) and Perrow (1984); for disasters and the mass media, National Academy (1980); for health effects, Logue, Melick, et al. (1981); for the effects of natural disasters on tribal societies, Gajdusek (1977a); for nuclear disasters, Mazuzan and Walker (1985), Meehan (1984), and Perrow (1984); for nontraumatic sudden death (no other convenient place is given in the E classification of the ICD), see Kuller (1966).

34.12 Accidents Caused by Suffocation and Foreign Bodies, and Other Accidents

ICD E910–915 and E916–929.

E910 has been treated in §34.5. E911 and 912 comprise deaths due to inhalation of food and other objects, causing obstruction of the respiratory tract or suffocation. E913 comprises accidental mechanical suffocation. E914 and 915 include the entry of foreign bodies into the eye or other orifice. E916–929 comprise other accidents, including those involving collisions with objects or persons, machinery, cutting instruments, firearms, explosives, hot objects and steam, electrical currents, and radiation. There is also overexertion and strenuous movements and other, or unspecified, environmental and accidental causes. Of these accidents and injuries, ionizing radiation is discussed in §20.3.

34.13 Suicide and Self-inflicted Injury

ICD E950–959. The final digit is concerned with mode of injury, namely, poisonings and other injuries. A fourth digit is available to give further subdivision of these modes. The rules of the ICD do not refer the case back to the psychosis, such as schizophrenia or depressive disease, but evidently merely follow the death certificate.

The crude death rates of suicide per annum for the two sexes, combined, tend to be below, sometimes much below, about 0.1 per 1,000 for the undeveloped countries and usually more than those rates for the developed countries, with especially high rates for Austria, Denmark, Finland, France, Hungary, Japan, Sweden, and Switzerland. Many references can be found in Gibbs (1968), the discussion being largely based on psychoanalysis.

Table 34.13.1 gives the rates from suicide in England and Wales. The commentary of the Registrar-General on the table, with deaths up to 1961, noted that few suicides occurred at ages under 15 years, and that there was an excess of male over female rates at every age group. The rates increase with age throughout life for the males, but tend to decrease after

TABLE 34.13.1. Suicide in England and Wales (death rates per 1,000,000 living).

	All ages	0–9	10–14	15–19	20–24	25–34	35–44	45–54	55–64	65–74	75 and over
					Males						
1901–1910	157	1	4	36	91	152	252	397	523	508	382
1911–1920	130	—	3	32	69	122	196	278	389	405	350
1921–1930	166	—	2	31	78	111	211	346	487	513	438
1931–1935	196	0	2	40	96	140	210	379	542	533	483
1936–1940	172	—	2	32	89	118	177	284	462	477	466
1941–1945	126	—	3	43	72	100	128	185	271	347	382
1951	135	—	6	24	53	78	120	213	303	410	477
1956	149	—	2	25	65	94	130	221	350	426	490
1961	135	—	1	34	71	108	147	203	283	331	388
1966*	121	—	—		68[†]	103	147	179	232	265	309
1981*	114	—	—		70[†]	145	152	173	180	165	220
					Females						
1901–1910	49	—	3	34	45	56	81	109	108	88	49
1911–1920	47	—	2	30	41	50	74	100	102	81	52
1921–1930	63	—	1	25	43	57	87	135	143	108	63
1931–1935	80	—	0	23	49	77	108	154	166	134	84
1936–1940	79	—	1	14	38	65	99	155	166	142	89
1941–1945	62	—	1	9	22	52	77	108	128	117	73
1951	72	—	—	9	20	38	66	135	160	167	105
1956	90	—	1	11	27	49	71	156	203	217	141
1961	91	—	1	14	32	55	93	157	194	192	130
1966*	88	—	—		30[†]	62	93	148	161	196	145
1981*	65	—	—		21[†]	47	70	105	116	140	105

*From World Health Statistics Annual.
[†] 15–24 years.
From Annual Reports of the Registrar-General (1956, 1961).

age 65 for the females. Until 1961 there had been a downward trend in the rates for young persons.

In England and Wales, crude death rates from suicide per 1,000,000 are approximately 150 (50) for males (females) in 1901–1910; for 1951–1960 they are about 145 (85). There were dips in the rates of males during each war; for 1911–1920 the yearly rates were 152, 153, 147, 157, 113; 115, 100, 114, 136, and 134, and for 1936–1950, they were 176, 175, 180, 168, 159; 135, 125, 134, 135, 136; 144, 137, 145, 147, and 136. These dips are variously explained by authors as due to the excitement of war and to the difficulties of obtaining alcohol in wartime. From Table 34.13.1, it is seen that the dips in the rates over the war years are greatest at ages over 45 years for males and over 35 for females.

During 1957–1961 in England and Wales, the preferred modes of suicide per 1,000 males (females) were: domestic gas poisoning, 450 (539); other poisoning, 156 (254); hanging or strangulation, 151 (60); drowning, 81 (92); firearms or explosives, 60 (5); cutting or piercing instruments, 38 (11); jumping from high places, 22 (20); and other agents, 42 (19).

Possibly the most appropriate general reference is to Dublin (1963). For the validity and reliability of the statistics of suicide, see Sainsbury (1983). For the effects of alcohol and drugs on suicide rates, see Prinzing (1895), Ritson (1977), and §§24.2 and 24.5. For student suicides, see Rook (1959) and Schneidman (1972). For comparative rates by country, see Brooke (1974) and Ruzicka (1976). For individual countries, see: England and Wales, Sainsbury (1955) and Ogle (1886a); Finland,

Verkko (1951); France, Chesnais (1976*b*) and Daric (1956); Sweden, Dahlgren (1945) and Wicksell (1934).

34.14 Homicide

ICD E960–969. The final digit denotes the means of killing.

Homicide is a small but not negligible mode of death. Iskrant and Joliet (1968) cite an annual rate of 47 per 1,000,000 for the years 1959–1961 in the United States and give many comparisons by age, sex, color, and social class. Rates varied by state with Georgia, 121; Alabama, 118; Mississippi, 113; District of Columbia, 112; and with Vermont, New Hampshire, Massachusetts, and Iowa all below 14 per 1,000,000.

For England and Wales, see Gibson and Klein (1961).

34.15 Legal Intervention

ICD E970–978.

These rubrics include all injuries inflicted by the police or other law-enforcing agents, including military on duty, in the course of arresting or attempting to arrest lawbreakers, suppressing disturbances, maintaining order, and other legal action. It excludes injuries caused by civil insurrections.

It would be invidious to carry out a survey of mortality due to legal intervention in the various states of the world. We can only express the hope that the numbers dying in these rubrics will decline. We compare the secular changes in the rates from some of them. First, we can dismiss the tradition that there were numerous executions in England and Wales during the nineteenth century. Guy (1875) gives a table for England and Wales of the executions for murder, the principal capital offence, for the 70 years 1805–1874; executions number 853, a yearly average of 12.3. He then standardizes the rates on to a population of 20 million and obtains what we may express as rates per 1,000,000 per annum for 10-year periods, namely 1.25 in 1805–1814, 1.40, 0.89, 0.68, 0.51, 0.68, 0.46 in 1865–1874, showing a general decrease. Of 2,614 cases for murder

trial in the 39 years 1836–1874, 40 were not prosecuted, for 241, no bill was found, 1,212 were found not guilty at trial; a total of 1,493 were thus acquitted; 225 were acquitted as insane, 126 were found or declared insane, leaving 770 sentenced to death, and of these 431 were executed, an average of 12 per year for England and Wales in the years 1836–1874.

Prisons as places of punishment are comparatively modern institutions. In 1597, "An Act for the Punishment of Rogues, Vagabonds and Sturdy Beggars" was passed in the English Parliament, whereby beggars were to be returned to their birthplace and there kept in jail or house of correction until they could be put to work. Later, especially in the eighteenth century, debtors formed a large part of the jail population. Otherwise, in English history prisons were regarded as holding places before trial. Felonies were punishable by death, or later by transportation; misdemeanors were punished by the stocks, the pillory, fines, or by whipping. Farr (in McCulloch 1837, reprinted in Farr, 1885, p. 418) remarked that considerable misapprehension prevails respecting the mortality in prisons, because the deaths have been divided by the committals to obtain a rate that is then treated as a death rate per annum. Both French and English commentators thus took undue pride in spuriously low rates. Farr, in the absence of numbers at risk, took the mean prison population to be equal to those in prison at the time of the taking of reports. He assumed that the prisoners were 20–30 years of age and found that their death rates were 60% more than the death rates for England and Wales at the same ages. When cholera was present in England in 1832, Farr further noted that the death rates of prisoners were nearly three times the general death rates in England at the same age, which were little affected by the cholera. Moreover, prisoners rarely labor under any serious disease at the time of their committal. Their death rates in the first year were about five times those of persons entering the Equitable Assurance Society between the ages of 20 and 40 years. Moreover, the death rates on the hulks were almost nine times those of Society members. Farr points out that only eight criminals were executed in England and

Wales in the year 1837, whereas the average number of deaths in prison more than that expected, if the rates were equal to those of the population at large, was 51; then he concludes that the present system (i.e., 1838) of imprisonment destroys 10 times as many lives as the executioner. Later he gives death rates per 1,000 per annum for prisoners in their 1st, 2nd, . . . , 5th years as 13, 36, 52, 57, and 44 (the last estimate being based on only four deaths). Farr (1885) cites W. Baly, writing in 1845, that fever now never raged in the jails as a contagious disease as it had done formerly. Fevers and bowel complaints were common diseases in the prison populations. Farr points out that there were excessive numbers of deaths from tuberculosis. It can be assumed that the death rates in prison in the past have usually been higher than those in the population at large, when comparisons are made by age groups, but that there were great differences in former times, that is, in England before 1850.

Hinde (1951) remarks that the prisoners lacked sufficient food and drink, sufficient light or air, proper sanitation, washing facilities, or suitable clothing; they were also crowded. The principal diseases are now mentioned.

Typhus had well earned its title of jail fever. The prisoners were obviously lousy and herded together, the classical conditions for typhus. Among other outbreaks, at the "Black" Assize in Oxford in 1577, judges, jurors, and the general public were infected with typhus, about 300 persons dying in Oxford and another 200 sickening there but dying elsewhere. Of course, the jail would have been crowded with prisoners awaiting trial by the traveling judges. It may well be that the prisons of those days provided a "hard core" for infections with typhus. See §14.2.

Tuberculosis also was a great cause of death in the jails. Diarrhea, dysentery, and typhoid fever were also prevalent and leading causes of death. John Howard (1726–1790) commented in 1777 on the high incidence of scurvy in prisons.

In the developed world, the conditions of hygiene and nutrition have improved greatly in the past 100 years; appointment of medical officers, full- and part-time, to the prison staff and management has greatly assisted in the process of cleaning up the prisons; free use of statistics has aided this process.

The United Kingdom, like other European nations, hoped to solve the problems of their prisons by transportation. Bateson (1969) gives the deaths for the transportations to Australia; he gives deaths from the time of embarkation and numbers arriving in Australia; we give number embarked, deaths, and "voyage fatality per 1,000" for 1788–1800, 1,441, 51, 35; 1801–1810, 1,302, 30, 23; 1811–1820, 1,927, 28, 15; 1821–1830, 4,140, 41, 10; 1831–1840, 7,655, 321, 41; 1841–1850, 6,937, 102, 15; 1851–1853, 1,854, 16, 8. The causes of death included scurvy, typhus from which 95 persons out of 300 died on one transport, dysentery, and cholera as part of the English epidemic of 1832; smallpox appeared in one ship but caused no deaths. The "case fatality" was often high in the earliest period, especially when there was no medical supervision; but after the appointment of surgeons-superintendent it was lower, with many ships reaching Australia without deaths. For general conditions in the prisons of England and Wales, see Blom-Cooper (1975), Griffiths (1884), and Webb and Webb (1922); in America, Ohlin (1973); in England and Wales, during transport, and in Australia, Hughes (1987).

34.16 Fatal Injury of Undetermined Purpose

ICD E980–989. final digit determines the instrument of injury.

This is a small subclass, which is not analyzed here.

Insect bites seem to have no place in the E classification of the ICD. Busvine (1976) notes that more people die in the United States from wasp and bee stings than from poisonous snakes (rattlesnakes, coral snakes, among others). The numbers are trivial, less than 40 per annum. On the other hand, many deaths are caused by diseases, including malaria, typhus, and plague, transmitted by arthropods (colloquially insects).

Sporting injuries, not classified by the ICD, presumably would be classified here if we exclude automobile accidents, flying accidents, drownings, falls from heights, serious fractures, and others. In medieval times sporting injuries were confined to the upper classes almost entirely, especially in jousts and other war games and in hunting, but now there is a far greater spread by class. See Jokl (1985) and Kraus and Conroy (1984).

Chapter 35
Child and Early Adult Mortality

35.1 Early Childhood: 1–4 Years

The mortality of infancy has already been examined in chapter 32; the mortality of childhood and early adult life, that is, up to age 25 years, is examined in this chapter.

Long series of mortality rates are available only for countries of the developed world. Although there were, in the nineteenth century, great differences between countries and even between subpopulations in them, rich and poor or urban and rural for example, many of these differences have tended to disappear as the death rates in the young ages, 0 to 25 years, have decreased during this century. Therefore, generalizations can be made regarding the causes of the declines in mortality for the developed world. Long series have not as a rule been available for countries of the present developing world, and there are special problems in them, such as endemic diseases, especially malaria, and the common bowel diseases. For the developing world, we therefore refer the reader to the chapters on Africa, Asia, and the Americas.

Even in the developed world, there seem to be few tabulations of mortality by cause for a given age group through a long stretch of years; here we make use of the series from 1861 to 1930 of the Registrar-General of England and Wales. The continuity of these decennial series was ended with the difficulties created by World War II and their publication has not been resumed. In some ways this reduces their value but little, for since 1930 mortality from the classical infective diseases of childhood has almost disappeared. Another series in Australia goes back to 1908–1910, but has the advantage of bringing the statistics up to the latest completed decennium. These series are reproduced as Tables 35.1.1 and 35.1.2 and are used as illustrations, as there has been much discussion, regarding the English series in particular, in the medical literature. It is pointed out that the rates for England and Wales are at ages 0–4 years in Table 35.1.1, whereas the Australian rates are for ages 1–4 years in Table 35.1.2.

For total mortality at these ages in England and Wales we do not have to hand appropriate data, but from the life tables (England and Wales, 1841, 1838–1854, and 1871–1880) we have l_1 for males (females), 84,066 (86,740); 83,641 (86,529); and 84,142 (87,127); and l_5, 72,912 (75,557); 72,372 (75,055); and 73,407 (76,262); so that the corresponding probabilities of a child at age 1 dying before his (her) 5th birthday are 0.1327 (0.1289), 0.1347 (0.1317), and 0.1276 (0.1247).

Table 35.1.2 gives the death rates of early childhood in Australia, by causes important at these ages, since 1908. The total rates have been declining since about 1880. From Table 35.1.2, it can be seen that in 1908–1910, the total death rate for males was 7,209 per 1,000,000 per annum, with death rates from individual causes as follows: intestinal infections 1,869, respiratory diseases 1,193, violence 708, diphtheria 683, meningitis 514, tuberculosis 411, other nervous diseases 404, pertusis 235,

TABLE 35.1.1. Mortality of infancy and early childhood, England and Wales* 0–4 years† (deaths per 1,000,000 per annum).

Epoch	All causes	Enteric fever	Diarrhea	Tuberculosis	Diphtheria	Croup	Pertussis	Scarlatina	Smallpox	Measles	Encephalitis	Influenza	Bronchitis and pneumonia	Nephritis	Violence, less suicide
Males															
1851–1860	72,433	—	—	6,323	—	—	—	—	—	—	—	—	—	—	1,421
1861–1870	73,471	—	6,657	6,018	760	1,705	3,408	4,765	642	3,080	—	—	9,515	71	1,290
1871–1880	68,419	398	5,304	5,798	474	1,136	3,323	3,606	529	2,653	—	—	11,686	135	1,199
1881–1890	61,607	131	8,388	5,004	687	984	3,062	1,710	82	3,266	—	28	13,587	184	1,361
1891–1900	62,710	85	6,765	4,347	1,388	388	2,786	855	29	3,368	1,625	322	12,783	174	1,231
1901–1910	50,027	32	4,552	3,129	961	103	2,170	586	21	2,695	1,498	180	9,371	148	998
1911–1920	37,817	8	4,638	1,942	724	9	1,527	246	0	2,546	1,129	668	8,261	121	934
1921–1930	25,146	3	2,204	1,059	473	1	1,134	124	2	1,204	663	405	6,272	63	683
Females															
1851–1860	62,744	—	—	5,232	—	—	—	—	—	—	—	—	—	—	1,111
1861–1870	63,710	—	5,728	4,917	781	1,494	4,157	4,523	634	2,942	—	—	8,005	48	1,031
1871–1880	58,344	405	4,516	4,663	475	966	4,011	3,402	508	2,504	—	—	9,750	97	964
1881–1890	51,941	128	7,208	3,987	692	828	3,668	1,625	77	2,989	—	23	11,287	152	1,144
1891–1900	52,797	80	5,658	3,516	1,337	326	3,385	833	30	3,126	1,303	255	10,595	143	1,059
1901–1910	41,866	30	3,687	2,636	942	84	2,683	553	24	2,507	1,229	141	7,778	122	833
1911–1920	31,377	8	3,751	1,619	682	7	1,936	243	1	2,342	922	618	6,827	111	767
1921–1930	20,231	3	1,633	874	454	1	1,398	118	2	1,073	547	327	5,059	51	487

*Data from Registrar-General of England and Wales (1952).
†Note that the age group is 0–4 years in this Table and 1–4 in Table 35.1.2.

alimentary diseases 179, measles 128, and scarlatina 79. By the years 1971–1980, most of these diseases were no longer important causes of deaths, and the total death rate was 817 for males, with leading causes: violence 376, congenital defects 103, neoplasms 81, respiratory 71, nervous 50, and intestinal infections 32. Even greater declines have occurred in the female rates, as can be seen in Table 35.1.2. The total death rates of 1908–1910 imply that about 2.3% of male and 2.2% of female children reaching their first birthday would fail to reach their fifth. The rates in the 1971–1980 decennium would imply that only 0.32% of male and 0.25% of female children would fail to survive over the same years. Individual causes of the declines are now briefly discussed, in the manner of Lancaster (1956d). For a detailed discussion of the individual diseases, the reader is referred back to the earlier chapters, especially 6 to 11. See also Backer (1961).

Infections of the Bowel. Typhoid and paratyphoid fever and dysentery have been of little apparent importance as causes of death in early childhood. However, it may be that difficulties of definition and diagnosis arise, especially in the earlier times, making differentiation from gastroenteritis problematical. Gastroenteritis has been the most important of all diseases in early childhood until recent times. Of individual causes, it has contributed most to the general decline in total mortality. In fact, over one-third of the decline in total mortality has been due to the decline in gastroenteritis mortality. In England and Wales the greatest rates were in 1881–1890. Chemotherapy and antibiotics cannot be regarded as the cause of this decline. See §6.11.

Tuberculosis. Tuberculosis was of great importance in the earlier periods, especially in the form of tuberculous meningitis. There has

TABLE 35.1.2. Mortality of early childhood in Australia 1–4 years (deaths per 1,000,000 per annum).

Epoch	All causes	Intestinal infections	Tuberculosis	Diphtheria	Pertussis	Scarlatina	Meningitis	Tetanus	Poliomyelitis	Measles	Neoplasms	Nervous	Circulatory	Respiratory	Digestive	Congenital	Injury and poisoning
Males																	
1908–1910	7,209	1,869	411	683	235	79	514	19	—*	128	70	404	81	1,193	179	74	708
1911–1920	7,345	1,676	318	833	221	57	503	21	—	289	64	376	66	1,370	227	98	627
1921–1930	5,485	1,096	218	564	193	63	234	23	12	142	73	219	48	1,199	195	83	628
1931–1940	3,822	415	142	442	126	38	113	23	28	82	71	110	40	862	182	115	580
1941–1950	2,560	178	81	165	40	8	80	20	13	56	145	99	22	476	132	136	501
1951–1960	1,539	75	10	13	3	0	43	7	9	19	195	53	23	309	64	157	473
1961–1970	1,041	69	3	1	0	0	10	1	0	10	104	75	15	171	25	103	379
1971–1980	817	32	1	0	0	0	4	0	0	2	81	50	13	71	10	103	376
Females																	
1908–1910	6,675	1,725	342	570	303	76	456	12	—*	99	70	436	110	1,061	177	46	639
1911–1920	6,654	1,519	292	791	290	61	418	17	—	257	49	369	70	1,179	188	89	507
1921–1930	4,742	940	197	489	256	73	175	8	18	132	65	180	49	1,020	167	85	428
1931–1940	3,339	394	127	411	187	44	84	13	19	78	101	104	40	743	148	115	397
1941–1950	2,104	168	68	147	65	8	50	9	8	58	121	92	31	390	98	142	294
1951–1960	1,276	72	17	10	5	1	33	4	7	17	181	51	26	249	103	137	317
1961–1970	868	62	2	1	1	0	6	0	0	14	86	56	17	145	20	105	283
1971–1980	632	30	0	0	0	0	3	0	0	3	62	36	14	66	7	91	255

*Not separately listed.
Data from Demography (Australia) and Lancaster (passim).

been a pronounced decline in the rates to a negligible level. Here again we note that these declines began before the advent of adequate public health measures or therapy. Indeed, the English rates began to decline before 1870.

Diphtheria. The great bulk of the deaths from diphtheria has usually occurred in early childhood and in the early school years. For early childhood in Australia, in Table 35.1.2, the rates are highest in 1911–1920, when they were about 800 per 1,000,000 per annum. Since then there has been a remarkable decline. There seems to be some reason for believing that immunization has played a part in the latter part of the declines, after 1940. Neither the immunization, which could have been effective only after 1930, nor the potent therapeutic serum, which was in common use after 1920, can explain the general decline in diphtheria mortality. Moreover, it is noted that the relative decrease in pertussis mortality has been almost as rapid as that of diphtheria, if we were

to measure the decline on a logarithmic scale (or ratio chart), and yet no specific therapy has been available for pertussis. See §9.3.

Pertussis. Pertussis, in the earlier periods, was an important cause of death in early childhood. In the most recent periods it was an uncommon cause of death. In every period the masculinity is low. Pertussis is practically the only disease of numerical importance that more heavily affects the females at this age. The explanation of course is still unknown. Case fatality rates and prevalance rates in England are both higher for females, as is shown by the tables of the *Registrar-General's Statistical Review of England and Wales.* Similar data are not available for the Australian experience. The case fatality rates reveal a pronounced decline with increasing age. Pertussis is a disease whose killing power will be considerably diminished by any factor that tends to delay the age of infection. It is thus very sensitive to general social conditions and hygiene. See §9.4.

Scarlatina. Since 1908, scarlatina has not been a major cause of mortality in Australia. The decline in the death rates was greatly accelerated after 1931. There were, however, great epidemics of scarlatina in Australia in the 1870s, with over 2,000 deaths in Victoria during 1875 and 1876, many of whom would have been children aged 1–4 years. In England and Wales, scarlatina was a leading cause of death at these ages until 1910.

Poliomyelitis. This disease has been relatively unimportant as a cause of mortality at these ages; no definite trend is discernible.

Measles. Measles has been prevalent in irregularly spaced epidemics in Australia. The years 1908–1910 happened to be years of low prevalence. There is therefore, in Table 35.1.2, an increase in the rates in passing from the period 1908–1910 to the next period, 1911–1920. Since then there has been a steady decrease in the rates. In London there has been a tendency to have a 2-year periodicity, and the same is true of many other large cities; the English cities did not all have the same year of local maxima. See §11.7.

Infective Disease of the Nervous System. Meningitis, in Table 35.1.2, includes all forms of simple—that is, nontuberculous—meningitis. The reduction in the rate from this group has been almost as great as in the rates from diphtheria. It should be noted that the most important part of the decline occurred before the introduction of chemotherapy or antibiotics, and that an increase even occurred in the rates during the war years at a time when chemotherapy was being used. Encephalitis and brain abscess have been numerically of less importance than the simple meningitis group, and a decline in the rates is again evident.

Other Diseases of the Nervous System. As defined here for Table 35.1.2, these include all the rubrics of the class of the same name of the *International List of Causes of Death*, except meningitis, brain abscess, or encephalitis. There have been considerable declines in the mortality from the residue of diseases so defined. However, the group comprising convulsions of children aged under 5 years is

included, and there are reasons for believing that convulsions were often secondary to undiagnosed acute infective disease and otitis media. Thus, here again the decline may be in infective causes.

Diseases of the Cardiovascular System. Deaths from the rheumatic diseases are not yet important at this age, so few deaths have been reported.

Influenza and Diseases of the Respiratory System. Influenza has been a relatively unimportant cause of death. There has been no general tendency for the rates to decrease. The rates in the period 1911–1920 are high because of the pandemic of influenza in the years 1918–1919. Diseases of the respiratory system are really bronchitis and the pneumonias. There has been a decline in the mortality from these causes, more rapid since 1940. This is possibly due to the introduction of chemotherapy and antibiotics. For global statistics see Leowski (1986).

Diseases of the Alimentary System. Because we have already taken out gastroenteritis from the class of alimentary diseases in the *International List of Causes of Death*, the residue consists chiefly of deaths from hernia, from intestinal obstruction, and from appendicitis. See also Lebenthal (1984) for chronic diarrhea.

Injury and Poisoning. There have been some declines from these causes. In England and Wales the rates in 1921–1930 are about half those of 1851–1860; in Australia the rates in 1971–1980 are again about half those of 1908–1910.

With the virtual disappearance of deaths from the infections at these ages, whether in class I or elsewhere in the ICD, deaths from cancers (principally, the leukemias) and from violence have assumed greater relative importance in recent times; yet, there have been improvements in the death rates from violence (i.e., injury and accidents).

For further references, see world: Dyson (1977), Rouquette and Corone (1965); developing countries: Gordon, Wyon, and Ascoli (1967); England and Wales: Registrar-General of England and Wales (1982), Pel (1962),

TABLE 35.2.1. Mortality of the school years in England and Wales* 5–14 years† (deaths per 1,000,000 per annum).

Epoch	All causes	Enteric	Diarrhea	Tuberculosis	Diphtheria	Croup	Pertussis	Scarlatina	Smallpox	Measles	Encephalitis	Respiratory	Rheumatic	Appendicitis	Nephritis	Violence
						Males										
1851–1860	6,696	—	—	1,163	—	—	—	—	—	—	—	—	—	—	—	674
1861–1870	6,336	—	97	964	224	140	64	1,350	104	128	—	297	—	—	43	549
1871–1880	5,206	292	80	824	164	118	58	942	219	110	—	338	—	—	70	428
1881–1890	3,378	181	87	723	228	118	52	454	30	140	—	332	84	—	75	366
1891–1900	2,779	136	130	613	363	44	38	213	6	113	265	301	83	—	64	293
1901–1910	2,922	62	42	549	290	11	28	168	7	85	180	316	81	89	57	346
1911–1920	2,963	21	40	544	283	1	26	85	0	115	124	321	70	105	59	348
1921–1930	2,085	6	24	321	210	0	17	46	0	52	101	231	71	88	42	318
						Females										
1851–1860	6,737	—	—	1,398	—	—	—	—	—	—	—	—	—	—	—	224
1861–1870	6,151	—	101	1,119	308	122	97	1,346	98	144	—	306	—	—	28	174
1871–1880	4,972	359	85	964	216	103	83	907	204	120	—	344	—	—	51	140
1881–1890	4,184	208	86	952	296	108	80	463	29	153	—	333	86	—	60	160
1891–1900	3,468	153	112	781	440	38	61	221	6	126	254	299	92	—	53	152
1901–1910	2,889	70	48	704	349	10	47	171	6	99	171	314	95	62	52	163
1911–1920	2,962	24	46	683	340	1	38	93	0	120	123	315	79	85	53	165
1921–1930	1,981	7	26	407	244	0	24	54	0	53	97	206	85	71	41	126

*Data from Registrar-General of England and Wales (1952).
†The rates given are the arithmetic means for the two age groups at 5–9 and 10–14 years.

Gale (1945, 1959), Macfarlane and Mugford (1984a,b); 1570–1653, Finlay (1978); the Americas: WHO-America (1974), and Baum and Arriaga (1981); Netherlands: van Gelderen (1955); Sierra Leone: WHO-infant (1981); accidents: Marcusson and Oehmisch (1977); cancer: Li (1982) and West (1984); chronic lung disease: Gordis (1973); infections: Leck (1981a,b); pediatrics: Morley (1978).

35.2 Childhood, the School Years: 5–14 Years

Mortality rates are lower in the school years of childhood than at any other time of life. Indeed, the deaths are so few at ages around 11 years that sampling variation may make it difficult to estimate the age at which the mortality rate attains its minimum. Moreover, the rates in any epoch have often been approximately constant, especially for females older than 8–

13 years. We may consider the Australian rates in Table 35.2.2. Notable declines in mortality rates have occurred at these school ages, the rates in 1971–1980 being about one-fifth of those in 1908–1910 in Australia. The declines in the class of injury and poisoning have been less rapid than in the other classes, and so injury and poisoning account for almost one-half of the total deaths in males and rather less than half of the total deaths in females in 1971–1980 in Australia.

An analysis is now given of the Australian rates of mortality at ages 5–14 years, during the eight epochs of the Table.

Tuberculosis. The adult forms of tuberculosis were just commencing at the older ages of this age group in 1908–1910; the rates have declined to zero in the latest epoch.

Diphtheria. At these ages diphtheria had been a leading cause of death among the infections in 1908–1910; deaths from this cause have be-

TABLE 35.2.2. Mortality of the school years in Australia 5–14 years (deaths per 1,000,000 per annum).

Epoch	All causes	Gastroenteritis	Typhoid	Tuberculosis	Diphtheria	Pertussis	Scarlatina	Meningitis and encephalitis	Tetanus	Poliomyelitis	Measles	Influenza	All neoplasms	Nervous	Circulatory	Respiratory	Alimentary	Injury and poisoning
							Males											
1908–1910	1,979	55	74	157	197	13	18	132	46	—*	10	16	44	89	114	161	186	446
1911–1920	1,971	56	35	108	245	5	21	125	38	—	34	43	37	96	139	173	140	429
1921–1930	1,562	32	16	67	97	8	17	75	32	12	18	18	45	88	92	146	115	402
1931–1940	1,368	21	4	41	110	5	10	43	31	24	13	21	70	62	57	130	111	394
1941–1950	1,021	16	0	24	46	1	4	32	28	16	9	7	104	49	37	69	75	363
1951–1960	606	5	0	3	6	0	0	6	10	13	3	2	115	38	22	42	25	277
1961–1970	481	0	0	0	0	0	0	2	2	0	1	0	79	28	16	32	10	243
1971–1980	379	0	0	0	0	0	0	1	0	0	2	0	58	18	11	19	4	213
							Females											
1908–1910	1,725	73	87	172	223	15	37	91	10	—*	19	14	23	79	156	147	157	230
1911–1920	1,711	54	47	128	295	10	31	99	10	—	33	47	21	83	138	159	154	166
1921–1930	1,241	27	22	76	113	8	23	59	12	9	16	18	29	74	92	137	120	167
1931–1940	993	19	4	47	112	7	15	32	9	15	16	17	49	51	61	112	96	140
1941–1950	705	11	0	33	40	1	5	22	8	12	12	6	78	32	37	69	63	129
1951–1960	413	5	0	2	7	0	0	6	4	8	3	2	93	32	27	39	25	118
1961–1970	316	0	0	1	0	0	0	1	0	0	1	0	64	21	14	29	10	115
1971–1980	253	0	0	0	0	0	0	0	0	0	1	0	50	17	9	14	3	108

*Not separately listed.
Data from Demography (Australia) and Lancaster (passim).

come negligible in the later periods. See §35.1 and also §9.3 for further details.

Scarlatina. By 1908 scarlatina had ceased to be the great cause of mortality it had been in the nineteenth century. See §35.1.

Measles. Mortality from measles has been low at these ages.

Poliomyelitis. Death rates from poliomyelitis from 1921, when it was first separately mentioned, to 1960, when its mortality and morbidity became negligible after the introduction of immunization campaigns, were about 15 per 1,000,000 per annum and so about 1% of the total mortality burden.

Cardiovascular Diseases. Mortality rates have declined, but it is difficult to be certain of a possible interpretation. The deaths in earlier years were diagnosed as being due to pericarditis, acute endocarditis, or, more usually, organic disease of the heart; it may be that many of these cases were rheumatic in origin.

Respiratory Diseases. There have been great declines; indeed, the same relative declines as in the total mortality rate at these childhood years.

Alimentary Diseases. There have been declines in death rates due to appendicitis, possibly due to improved diagnosis and therapy.

Injury and Poisoning. These now account for more than 50% of male and 40% of female mortality. The declines in mortality in this class have been disappointing, especially in view of the improvements in therapy (surgery). There has been an enquiry into the Australian data, by Clements (1955).

We may look at Table 35.2.1 as a kind of prehistory of Table 35.2.2. Clearly there had already been great declines of mortality before 1930. In 1921–1930, the total mortality for England and Wales for either sex was about 40% higher than the corresponding Australian rate. Enteric or typhoid fever was marginally lower than in Australia for the common years of the table; but the Australian rates were markedly better for tuberculosis. In both tables there is a low masculinity of the tuberculosis death rates, and this has been the subject of many discussions, such as Hill (1936). The diphtheria rate for either sex was higher in 1921–1930 than in 1871–1880, and the rates had not dropped a great deal after 1900, by which time passive serotherapy had become available in England and Wales. Scarlatina rates, on the other hand, had decreased steadily from 1870, and this was responsible for about one-third of the total decline, yet there were no specific remedies against it. It is clear that declines in the death rates from tuberculosis and scarlatina, combined, accounted for almost half the declines in the total mortality between the epochs 1861–1870 and 1921–1930. See Lancaster (1957a).

For England and Wales, see Macfarlane and Mugford (1984a,b).

35.3 Young Adults: 15–24 Years

Mortality of young adults, that is, at ages 15 to 24 years is of interest from several points of view. First, the individual reaches his (her) maximum economic value in that he (she) has completed his (her) education and years of no income, and so has an expectation of many years of service to the community. Second, there is a purely technical interest in that, contrary to deductions from general principles, there is a local maximum for the death rate at these ages. Third, the death rates may be studied at this age as part of a general survey. The first interest we leave to the economists and sociologists.

In many experiences, such as Bailey (1868), Fox (1859), Sutton (1872), Eijkman (1921), van Pesch (1885), and Martin (1935), it was evident that there was a local maximum in the mortality rates at early adult life, providing counterexamples to the theory of the smooth ascending curves of the actuaries, such as that of Makeham (1867), given in §4.2. This maximum has also appeared in a number of official experiences, such as of Germany in 1891–1900 and 1924–1926 and of France in 1898–1903 and 1920–1923, Sweden in 1901–1910, and Japan

in 1899–1903. Sutter and Tabah (1952) show a maximum at age 20 years in France in 1933–1938. Many tables of mortality show a weak form of this effect, whereby the increase in the death rates becomes constant for a number of successive years of a particular experience, and then the increase becomes more rapid, so that the graph of the death rates becomes horizontal for some successive ages. This phenomenon is not a new one, for in historical studies on the German ruling families, Peller (1947, Section F, Table I), gives a higher mortality rate at ages 25–29 years than in the next two age groups for 1480–1579; in his three periods covering 1580–1879, the rate at 20–24 is higher than at 25–29. Similar features are not present in females in young adult life, but in his Table II, Peller gives lower figures for the three 5-year age groups 35–49 years than for the two 5-year age groups 25–34 years, and comments that in 1780–1879 mortality in late adult life had greatly improved, whereas the mortality from infections and puerperal diseases had not improved. Russell (1948a, Tables 8.5 and 8.6, p.182), in his study of the British medieval population, also gives tables of mortality rates with a mode for the group 25–29 years in males. In the eras covered by these two studies, warfare may be said to have been endemic, and so each successive group of young men faced the risks of death in war or war games.

In Table 35.3.1, the death rates for the leading causes of death for young adults in England and Wales are given by decades for the years 1851–1930. It appears that the declines in the total rates for both sexes began about 1860. Comparisons by cause can only be made beginning at the 1861–1870 decade. The total death rates per million per annum for males (females) were 7,330 (7,308) in 1861–1870 and 3,012 (2,752) in 1921–1930, and the corresponding tuberculosis death rates were 3,206 (3,894) and 1,111 (1,352). Subtraction of the later from the earlier rates shows that the declines were: total, 4,318 (4,556); tuberculosis, 2,095 (2,542); enteric fevers and diarrheas, 444 (435); violence, 326 (-2); puerperal, 0 (254); smallpox, 136 (88); and respiratory, 122 (136). These diseases combined accounted for 3,123

TABLE 35.3.1. Mortality of young adults in England and Wales* 15–24 years† (deaths per 1,000,000 per annum).

Epoch	All causes	Enteric fever	Diarrhea	Tuberculosis	Diphtheria	Scarlatina	Influenza	Encephalitis	Smallpox	Diabetes	Rheumatism	Respiratory‡	Appendicitis	Nephritis	Childbearing	Suicide	Violence	Epilepsy
Males																		
1851–1860	7,759	—	—	3,442	—	—	—	—	—	—	—	—	—	—	—	—	888	—
1861–1870	7,330	—	82	3,206	46	114	—	—	136	23	—	378	—	55	—	44	788	—
1871–1880	6,308	404	64	2,538	24	81	—	—	293	29	—	420	—	80	—	44	582	—
1881–1890	5,024	319	82	2,013	28	33	8	—	56	30	102	407	—	96	—	48	512	91
1891–1900	4,424	313	123	1,668	28	30	110	116	9	36	88	376	—	88	—	59	438	72
1901–1910	3,634	158	27	1,320	16	26	61	77	8	41	72	414	92	80	—	64	696	72
1911–1920	4,188	57	26	1,313	17	16	410	58	0	44	52	424	95	84	—	50	698	80
1921–1930	3,012	15	9	1,111	10	10	110	52	0	31	46	256	90	68	—	54	462	58
Females																		
1851–1860	7,958	—	—	4,080	—	—	—	—	—	—	—	—	—	—	—	—	100	—
1861–1870	7,308	—	94	3,894	51	131	—	—	88	14	—	276	—	44	398	31	86	—
1871–1880	6,132	387	74	2,915	30	86	—	—	210	16	—	295	—	78	424	30	77	—
1881–1890	4,981	257	60	2,274	29	34	6	—	44	24	105	255	—	97	366	37	73	91
1891–1900	4,063	219	82	1,672	29	26	86	104	8	28	96	237	—	88	321	39	68	67
1901–1910	3,196	100	22	1,338	15	22	46	74	6	31	74	238	54	80	218	40	82	58
1911–1920	3,540	42	22	1,471	16	12	428	50	0	33	63	240	65	82	177	35	83	54
1921–1930	2,752	14	12	1,352	13	10	82	44	0	30	58	140	53	64	144	34	88	40

*Data from Registrar-General of England and Wales (1952).
†The rates given are the arithmetic means for the two age groups at 15–19 and 20–24 years.
‡Respiratory = bronchitis + pneumonia + pleurisy.

(3,453) of the total declines, about 75% of the decline of the females and slightly less of the males. In the time series of the mortality of England and Wales, we can be confident that few of the deaths in 1861–1870 were not due to infective causes. Geary (1952) has given a review of the mortality of young adults in more modern times with international comparisons. These decennial series of the Registrar-General unfortunately terminate at 1930.

In Australia the mortality of young adults can be considered by cause, as in Table 35.3.2 constructed from the tables of Lancaster (*passim*).

Enteric Fever. In the first epoch, 1908–1910, enteric was still an important cause of death at these ages in either sex; the rates showed a high masculinity because of the greater exposure of males to occupational hazards under pioneering conditions. See also Cumpston and McCallum (1927).

Tuberculosis. The death rates from tuberculosis in the earlier decades were high in both sexes, with a low masculinity; the cause of this low masculinity in Australia, as in many other countries, has never been determined.

Meningitis. These diseases were important in the epoch, 1911–1920, probably due to the crowding together of young adult males in training camps.

Influenza. Influenza was of importance only in the epoch 1911–1920, and almost all deaths from it would have occurred during the epidemic of 1919.

Poliomyelitis. This disease was the cause of few deaths at these ages.

Circulatory Diseases. There have been steady decreases in the diseases under this heading, possibly due to the declines in the rheumatic group of fevers.

TABLE 35.3.2. Mortality of young adults in Australia 15–24 years (deaths per 1,000,000 per annum).

Epoch	All causes	Enteric fevers	Tuberculosis	Meningitis	Influenza	Poliomyelitis	Other infectious*	Neoplasms	Diabetes	Circulatory	Respiratory	Appendicitis	Alimentary	Genitourinary	Childbearing	Injury and poisoning
						Males										
1908–1910	3,036	306	582	55	15	—†	133	54	25	235	218	113	81	122	—	809
1911–1920	3,128	176	529	126	177	—	126	51	35	224	248	108	80	133	—	793
1921–1930	2,468	60	373	36	35	5	84	55	26	145	198	110	79	117	—	844
1931–1940	2,097	12	197	21	31	11	63	80	14	114	150	101	56	99	—	937
1941–1950	1,489	2	98	24	6	17	38	86	10	90	72	38	29	66	—	768
1951–1960	1,642	0	11	2	4	20	30	106	5	63	41	10	19	40	—	1,172
1961–1970	1,489	0	1	0	0	0	95	96	2	31	31	0	16	19	—	1,156
1971–1980	1,588	0	0	0	0	0	57	82	2	40	29	0	9	10	—	1,304
						Females										
1908–1910	2,934	201	934	53	19	—†	96	57	22	247	158	79	107	159	291	199
1911–1920	2,761	118	762	61	154	—	103	45	26	244	175	67	156	174	301	174
1921–1930	2,175	42	642	23	30	3	76	45	30	146	155	56	67	159	291	165
1931–1940	1,642	9	373	9	24	7	43	67	22	122	125	43	49	138	238	177
1941–1950	1,036	1	190	13	3	10	37	70	17	84	82	24	39	71	136	144
1951–1960	605	0	15	1	5	11	29	67	7	48	40	8	22	31	47	184
1961–1970	564	0	0	0	0	0	70	70	4	8	24	0	17	13	22	292
1971–1980	528	0	0	0	0	0	40	67	3	27	24	0	8	11	6	334

*Total class I, less enteric fever, tuberculosis, and polio, and, where relevant, less meningitis and influenza not included in class I.
†Not separately listed.
Data from Demography (Australia) and Lancaster (passim).

Respiratory Diseases. Deaths from influenza have already been removed, the residue of deaths being due to the pneumonias. There have been steady declines from 1920 onward, hastened by the introduction of sulfonamides and later antibiotics.

Genitourinary Diseases. In young adults genitourinary disease consists almost entirely of acute and chronic nephritis. Possibly, the declines in the earlier years were due to declines in the infection rates from scarlatina.

Alimentary Diseases. There have been steady declines in the mortality rates from these diseases, especially evident in the rates from appendicitis; possibly, the principal cause for the declines in this class is improved surgery.

Puerperal Causes. There have been remarkable declines in the mortality from these causes. See §29.2.

Injury and Poisoning. The mortality from violent and accidental causes, which may be briefly described as violence, has always been an important part of mortality at this age, especially for males. With the decline in mortality from other causes, violence has become increasingly important relatively, until, in the latest period, it accounts for more than 70% of all mortality. Although the female rates have shown little change, the male rates show an increase in the latest period and, indeed, are as high as at any time since 1908. The rates in the epoch 1941–1950 may be regarded as being spuriously low, owing to the wartime practices. About 60% of the accidental and violent deaths at this age are due to motor vehicle accidents in either sex, about 10% are due to suicide, and about 10% are due to drownings. For recent trends in the United States, see Weiss (1976). For motor vehicles, see Havard (1979) and Chang (1984).

Chapter 36
Mortality by Age and Sex: The Adult Ages

36.1 Introduction

For convenience of exposition, the experience of the developed world only is being considered in this chapter. In every epoch the death rates from the infections, excluding tuberculosis and syphilis, are much lighter at ages above 25 years than at younger ages. Some of these differences are due to the solid immunity that follows some of the infections, for example, measles; others are due to immunologic changes following experience with a number of infections by which the body is able to cope with other diseases sufficiently closely related. In any case, growth has ceased, and the body is at full strength to withstand the infections and the environment. The result is that there is an almost negligible adult mortality in the developed world from such specific infections as diphtheria, scarlatina, measles and whooping cough, and the infectious respiratory and gastrointestinal diseases that have played such an important part in childhood.

In the earlier epochs of this century, tuberculosis was still an important cause of mortality at adult ages, but, as we have pointed out in chapter 7, it has become progressively less important with the declines beginning first at the younger ages. Syphilis mortality appears at older ages from the neurological and cardiovascular complications of the disease. There have been declines in mortality from injury and poisoning. Perhaps the Australian figures exaggerate these declines with the passing of pioneering conditions in Australia. In some of the age groups we have formed, as in Lancaster (1965, 1978, 1979), a composite class of the mental, nervous, cardiovascular, genitourinary, and ill-defined causes, as there have been some changes in assignments between the classes. Little can be made of the differences between epochs until the last 3 decades. Perhaps, it is fair to state that we cannot be certain about the progress of the "diseases of the circulatory system" of the ninth revision of the ICD during the epochs before 1950.

In conclusion, we refer the reader to Table 3.7.1 in which it is evident that the total death rates by age and sex for the countries of the developed world in 1985 do not differ greatly. The aim of the tables in this chapter is to show how the rates have declined in one such country, Australia. Our choice is due to the difficulties in obtaining such tables by classes of causes of death from other countries, to the absence of interference from wars, and to the detailed commentaries available for some diseases. We now run through the age groups in this chapter with emphasis on the changes of mortality during the last 80 years. For international comparisons of total mortality rates, see Table 3.7.1 and Ovčarov and Bystrova (1978) for trends in the age group 35–64 years between 1950 and 1973. Some commentary is also available in chapters 37–44, especially §§37.2 and 39.7, namely, for England and Wales and for Sweden.

TABLE 36.2.1. Mortality of young parentage in Australia 25–34 years (deaths per 1,000,000 per annum).

Epoch	All causes	Infections	Tuberculosis	Syphilis	Malignant neoplasms	Other neoplasms and leukemia	Other general*	Blood forming	Rheumatism	Diabetes	Respiratory	Nervous	Cardiovascular	Alimentary	Genitourinary	Childbearing	Skin, cellular, and bones	Congenital malformations	Violence (including poisoning)	Ill-defined
							Males													
1908–1910	4,404	597	1,150	41	74	15	44	17	22	42	335	220	315	236	169	—	28	0	1,043	54
1911–1920	5,050	983	1,104	58	98	19	53	17	26	49	424	209	349	237	231	—	23	0	1,115	55
1921–1930	3,509	215	844	35	89	24	33	13	28	31	289	172	248	213	196	—	29	1	1,011	36
1931–1940	2,656	142	447	18	98	58	20	9	30	19	204	116	202	191	160	—	28	9	895	10
1941–1950	1,778	65	230	6	101	54	9	7	12	14	90	107	177	96	134	—	8	5	653	8
1951–1960	1,729	51	34	2	115	60	6	3	24	10	57	107	138	53	68	—	5	18	968	10
1961–1970	1,548	13	3	0	168	5†	29	4	21	10	43	58	124	34	34	—	2	17	969	12
1971–1980	1,345	10	1	0	109	44	5	3	0	8	37	54	139	33	10	—	3	13	862	15
							Females													
1908–1910	4,616	360	1,383	15	138	38	73	77	24	28	262	179	367	268	297	824	29	0	210	45
1911–1920	4,574	627	1,074	14	148	42	85	45	30	42	297	176	395	239	308	765	17	0	221	47
1921–1930	3,505	199	866	12	127	38	71	22	29	34	244	154	267	192	297	703	25	0	192	32
1931–1940	2,657	120	607	9	130	56	49	15	31	20	190	99	195	146	250	519	21	6	188	5
1941–1950	1,762	63	344	3	140	59	32	10	15	22	103	100	153	90	164	291	8	7	149	8
1951–1960	980	43	43	1	142	54	13	8	20	9	67	83	86	50	67	94	7	12	176	8
1961–1970	814	13	3	0	165	9†	33	5	22	8	40	51	77	28	42	39	7	16	248	8
1971–1980	631	7	1	0	114	32	7	2	0	8	33	33	85	20	11	12	6	12	239	8

*Diseases in classes III and IV of the ninth revision of the ICD not otherwise accounted for.
†For 1961–1970, leukemia is included in malignant neoplasms.
Data from Demography (Australia) and Lancaster (passim).

36.2 Young Parentage: 25–34 Years

There seems to be no generally accepted term for groupings by age, in particular, the ages 25–34 and 35–44 years. It is convenient to call these two age groups *young* and *mature parentage*.

Infections (roughly class 1 of the ICD, less tuberculosis and syphilis, but including influenza). After the age of 25 years, the "infections," as they are briefly called in Table 36.2.1, have played a part in mortality much less important than in infancy, childhood, and young adult life. In the earliest epoch, 1908–1910, the death rates from these infections were for males (females) 597 (360) per 1,000,000 per annum, and after 1920, the rates decreased until by 1940 they were less than a quarter of the rates in the first epoch. A rise occurred in the rates because of the influenza epidemic of 1919; from influenza there were 37 (25), 448 (374), and 42 (58) deaths per 1,000,000 for males (females) in 1908–1910, 1911–1920, and 1921–1930, respectively, after which there

were few deaths from influenza in this age group. Enteric fevers were declining in importance over the same 3 decades, the death rates per 1,000,000 per annum for males (females) being 345 (183), 1908–1910; 216 (89), 1911–1920; and 53 (31), 1921–1930.

Tuberculosis. The maximum of tuberculosis rates in any cohort declined in early parentage, throughout, but, as is explained in §§7.4 and 7.5, the maximum rates in any calendar period continued to occur in progressively older age groups until the practical disappearance of tuberculosis. Declines for both sexes in young parentage were steady until 1940, and since that time the death rates have been reduced to negligible sizes.

Syphilis and Other Venereal Diseases. These diseases have caused few deaths in any epoch at these ages.

Malignant and Other Neoplasms, including Leukemia. The rates at these ages had remained steady at about 120 for males and 180 for females per 1,000,000 per annum. Some increases have occurred after 1950.

Diabetes. Diabetes at these ages has never been a common cause of death; the rates have declined from about 1930 onward.

Diseases, Other General and of the Blood and Blood-forming Organs. This group of diseases has been the cause of little mortality, but the death rates from them have declined.

Rheumatism. The death rates from cardiovascular rheumatism have declined, especially since the coming of chemotherapy and antibiotics.

Mental and Nervous Disorders. Deaths at these ages were due principally to the infections, especially meningitis, including the meningococcal forms. With the disappearance of deaths from infections, the death rates from these two classes have become stabilized and are now due to such noninfective causes as psychosis.

Cardiovascular Diseases. Acute rheumatism was mentioned earlier. There have been substantial declines in mortality, probably due to the decline of the rheumatic diseases and subacute bacterial endocarditis.

Respiratory Diseases. Deaths in the earlier epochs were principally due to the pneumonias and bronchitis. A small rise in death rates due to the influenza epidemic occurred in 1919, but there have been steady declines since.

Alimentary System. The rates in 1908–1910 were 236 (268) for males (females) per 1,000,000 per annum and in 1971–1980, were 33 (20). In 1911–1920, more than 40% of the deaths were listed under appendicitis and typhlitis and simple peritonitis, possibly usually a complication of the first. A substantial part of the decline would have been due to improvements in diagnosis and operative techniques.

Genitourinary Diseases. In 1911–1920, more than three-quarters of these deaths were due to chronic nephritis and more than one-tenth were due to acute nephritis. The table shows clearly the great improvements in the mortality from acute and chronic nephritis.

Diseases of Childbearing. There have been striking declines from 291 per 1,000,000 per annum in 1941–1950 to 12 in 1971–1980. See §29.2.

Skin and Cellular Tissue, Bones. Mortality in young parentage in these systems has never been high; the diseases have usually been infections with the common bacteria, often as a complication of trauma.

Injury and Poisoning. In 1911–1920, the principal causes of death in this class were motor vehicle accidents, suicide, drownings, and accidents in mines and quarries. The rates are spuriously low in 1941–1950 because of wartime registration practices and also petrol (gasoline) rationing.

36.3 Mature Parentage: 35–44 Years

Infections. The enteric fevers and influenza were leading causes of death in this group in the earlier epochs; the rates per 1,000,000 per annum in 1908–1910, 1911–1920, and 1921–1930 were for males (females) from enteric fever 242 (133), 144 (69), and 53 (28), and from influenza 58 (59), 546 (322), and 83 (88). For the importance of infections at this age, see Table 36.3.1.

Tuberculosis. Tuberculosis was a leading cause of death at these ages in both sexes throughout the earlier epochs. For males it was exceeded as a cause of death by violence after 1910, but for females only after 1950.

Syphilis and Other Venereal Diseases. In the earlier epochs, the late effects of syphilis were evident, causing about 2% of the mortality in males; after 1940, with more effective therapy, there was little mortality in either sex at these ages.

Malignant and Other Neoplasms, Including Leukemia. At this age there is a low masculinity because cancer of the cervix is an important cause of death; the rates for males show some slight tendency to increase in the later epochs; the rates for females have shown declines,

TABLE 36.3.1. Mortality of mature parentage in Australia 35–44 years (deaths per 1,000,000 per annum).

Epoch	All causes	Infections	Tuberculosis	Syphilis	Malignant neoplasms	Other neoplasms and leukemia	Other general*	Blood forming	Rheumatism	Diabetes	Respiratory	Nervous	Cardiovascular	Alimentary	Genitourinary	Childbearing	Skin, cellular, and bones	Violence (including poisoning)	Ill-defined
							Males												
1908–1910	7,540	579	1,548	188	408	14	48	54	43	69	719	411	812	424	474	—	36	1,553	141
1911–1920	7,450	946	1,365	177	351	21	60	45	33	71	817	398	773	408	417	—	34	1,406	128
1921–1930	5,632	312	1,056	143	314	33	41	31	29	44	625	305	624	391	362	—	38	1,198	86
1931–1940	4,569	184	707	92	316	90	32	16	29	39	432	225	639	380	318	—	34	1,001	32
1941–1950	3,421	94	435	26	295	81	18	12	24	31	199	245	665	232	227	—	11	801	23
1951–1960†	2,993	52	84	6	325	93	12	6	41	18	137	277	693	153	130	—	10	920	15
1961–1970†	3,050	18	16	2	443	10‡	82	7	50	30	114	165	867	129	66	—	7	1,006	19
1971–1980†	2,553	20	4	0	429	70	14	3	0	28	91	97	825	148	24	—	6	835	20
							Females												
1908–1910	6,440	401	1,215	42	765	92	93	86	30	62	462	407	736	408	508	713	31	307	88
1911–1920	5,843	583	935	40	648	84	114	70	38	62	437	346	697	383	429	595	23	270	88
1921–1930	4,821	251	667	29	625	98	94	52	35	55	400	309	565	316	470	540	29	225	60
1931–1940	3,876	156	469	21	596	133	78	24	38	51	296	219	496	243	439	365	21	213	11
1941–1950	2,951	77	311	8	562	108	47	16	22	35	165	293	417	169	311	200	9	184	13
1951–1960†	2,089	37	67	2	519	88	20	13	46	17	111	280	285	115	155	69	11	227	7
1961–1970†	1,905	17	11	0	568	16‡	64	9	46	18	82	167	314	74	114	29	11	337	12
1971–1980†	1,523	13	2	0	510	51	12	4	0	18	71	69	392	64	46	8	12	286	14

*Diseases in classes III and IV of the ninth revision of the ICD not otherwise accounted for.
†Malformations accounted for 21 (19) deaths in 1951–1960, 19 (14) deaths in 1961–1970, and 12 (14) deaths in 1971–1980 for males (females).
‡For 1961–1970, leukemia is included in malignant neoplasms.
Data from Demography (Australia) and Lancaster (passim).

probably due to both hygienic and therapeutic causes. See Lancaster (1951*d*) and §20.12.

Diabetes. The rates have decreased from earlier to later epochs, more so in the females so there is a high masculinity in the later epochs.

Other General Diseases. These have not been important causes of mortality.

Rheumatism. Possibly, at these ages the diagnosis of acute rheumatism as a cardiovascular disease is not relevant. There appears not to be any definite trend.

Mental and Nervous Diseases. Remarks apply as in §36.2.

Cardiovascular Diseases. There were some declines in the male rates over the years 1921–1950, but then, an increase to the initial level; the female rates continued to decrease until 1960, after which there has been a slight increase to a rate about 60% of the initial level.

Composite Class of Diseases. For definition see §36.1. The male rates for this composite class decreased until 1940 and then remained practically stationary; the female rates have declined until the most recent epoch.

Respiratory Diseases. There have been steady and substantial declines in mortality, which are almost entirely due to declines in the mortality from the pneumonias; possibly, there is some decline in the deaths from pneumoconioses in the males because there is only a small difference between the rates of the sexes in the most recent epoch.

Alimentary Diseases. There are substantial declines.

Genitourinary Diseases. The principal disease in this class at these ages is chronic nephritis. There have been substantial declines.

Childbearing. By 1930 the death rate from these causes had already decreased to half the rate of the first epoch. Part of the decrease was due to a decline in the fertility at these ages, and part to improved obstetric practice reflected in a reduction in the maternal mortality; note that the population mortality rate is the product of the fertility rate and the maternal mortality rate.

Injury and Poisoning. Male death rates declined to a minimum in 1941–1950 and have increased slightly since; the rate in the latest epoch is about two-thirds of that in the earliest. The female death rates had a similar minimum but have varied little.

36.4 Early Middle Age: 45–54 Years

Infections, tuberculosis, and syphilis have contributed between them to roughly one-half and one-third of the total decline in the mortality rates in the males and females, respectively. Remarks apply as in §36.3.

Neoplasms make a contribution of more than 10% to the total mortality for each sex for every period. There is again a low masculinity for the cancer death rates because of the importance of cancer of the cervix in the females.

There had been declines in rates from neoplasms, with a minimum in 1941–1950 for males and in 1951–1960 for females. In both sexes there has been a notable decline in the death rates from cancer of the stomach, for which see Lancaster (1954*d*). The rise in the male rates can be explained as due principally to an increased incidence of cancer of the lung (ICD 160–163).

Death rates in the respiratory diseases, chiefly the pneumonias and bronchitis, have decreased steadily since 1920, but are not negligible even in 1951–1960. The masculinity has been high.

Death rates from the diseases of the nervous system have declined little during the epochs until 1961–1970.

There have been declines in the females from diseases of the cardiovascular system, but important increases in the male rates.

There have been declines in the death rates from the alimentary and genitourinary diseases. For the great difficulties in interpreting

TABLE 36.4.1. Mortality of early middle age in Australia 45–54 years (deaths per 1,000,000 per annum).

Epoch	All causes	Infections	Tuberculosis	Syphilis	Malignant neoplasms	Other neoplasms and leukemia	Other general*	Blood forming	Rheumatism	Diabetes	Respiratory	Nervous	Cardiovascular	Alimentary	Genitourinary	Childbearing	Skin, cellular, and bones	Violence (including poisoning)	Senility and ill-defined
							Males												
1908–1910	12,692	714	1,720	282	1,337	51	77	137	47	110	1,290	910	1,841	781	1,022	—	82	1,757	338
1911–1920	13,346	988	1,587	298	1,396	40	80	136	58	132	1,500	995	1,997	764	1,055	—	62	1,910	347
1921–1930	11,009	431	1,337	221	1,231	57	64	108	41	115	1,357	750	1,859	736	863	—	61	1,545	232
1931–1940	9,623	282	982	178	1,106	145	52	30	43	92	913	523	2,363	727	764	—	52	1,271	94
1941–1950	8,954	150	774	80	1,074	165	34	19	17	93	548	800	2,906	592	576	—	22	1,039	61
1951–1960†	7,972	82	209	29	1,156	176	27	17	75	56	419	843	3,058	413	261	—	22	1,068	29
1961–1970†	8,127	31	53	6	1,450	21‡	167	15	94	73	375	449	3,685	338	158	—	26	1,131	29
1971–1980	7,284	43	13	1	1,480	147	34	7	1	70	341	209	3,445	441	69	—	19	922	38
							Females												
1908–1910	8,975	480	956	63	1,718	141	103	114	72	146	715	886	1,431	688	787	42	63	310	208
1911–1920	8,983	649	745	64	1,805	112	131	155	64	179	678	966	1,491	616	717	31	38	352	190
1921–1930	7,861	335	561	52	1,807	143	148	127	57	171	577	805	1,300	544	728	32	43	310	122
1931–1940	6,947	211	338	37	1,614	206	155	52	56	172	471	620	1,484	450	703	20	35	287	32
1941–1950	6,248	105	242	23	1,530	182	80	34	24	132	318	1,037	1,351	337	546	9	17	258	22
1951–1960†	4,983	73	65	9	1,387	153	31	28	86	66	192	952	1,061	230	257	3	24	326	16
1961–1970†	4,658	25	21	3	1,520	29‡	114	15	114	52	169	484	1,155	185	234	2	24	467	18
1971–1980	4,000	29	5	1	1,426	113	38	9	1	48	192	125	1,310	175	113	0	26	371	18

*Diseases in classes III and IV of the ninth revision of the ICD not otherwise accounted for.
†Malformations accounted for 33 (25) deaths in 1951–1960 and 26 (27) deaths in 1961–1970 for males (females).
‡For 1961–1970, leukemia is included in malignant neoplasms.
Data from Demography (Australia) and Lancaster (passim).

these decreases, see §§27.3 and 28.1, which also have a discussion of the "composite class" of diseases, between which there have been interchanges in diagnosis and statistical classification.

Death rates from injury and poisoning have declined considerably for males; the rates have started at a much lower level in females and have remained low; masculinity of the rates has been high in every epoch. See Table 36.4.1.

36.5 Late Middle Age: 55–64 Years

At the older ages the relative declines become less, but in absolute terms the declines are not much less than at the younger adult ages.

Other infections, tuberculosis, and syphilis (including tabes and general paralysis of the insane but excluding aneurysm of the aorta), together with the respiratory diseases, are sufficient to account for the declines in mortality.

Death rates from all forms of cancer have remained almost constant in males and have declined in females. From a supplementary

tabulation, death rates from all neoplasms, other than cancer of the lung, have made some improvement, but there has been a marked increase in the male death rates from lung cancer, from 36 per 1,000,000 per annum in 1908–1910 to 950 per 1,000,000 per annum in 1951–1960; notwithstanding much propaganda to the contrary, few observers now believe that this increase is not real. Contrary to some opinion, females at these ages had not smoked as heavily as had their male contemporaries, and, until the latest periods, the female death rates from cancer of the lung have been rather low. Death rates from neoplasms (other than respiratory) have shown moderate declines in both sexes. See Table 36.5.1.

There have been substantial declines in deaths from the respiratory diseases in both sexes.

Death rates in the "composite class" have increased substantially in males and declined in females.

There have also been substantial declines in the deaths from injury and accident in males.

TABLE 36.5.1. Mortality of late middle age in Australia 55–64 years (deaths per 1,000,000 per annum).

Epoch	All causes	Infections	Tuberculosis	Syphilis	Malignant neoplasms	Other neoplasms and leukemia	Other general*	Blood forming	Rheumatism	Diabetes	Respiratory	Nervous	Cardiovascular	Alimentary	Genitourinary	Skin, cellular, and bones	Violence (including poisoning)	Ill-defined (including malformations)
Males																		
1908–1910	25,191	1,160	1,988	305	3,468	87	66	233	114	389	2,475	2,382	4,884	1,378	2,370	152	2,593	1,190
1911–1920	25,465	1,151	1,612	299	3,762	67	125	294	130	307	2,750	2,499	5,157	1,264	2,350	144	2,283	1,269
1921–1930	22,443	672	1,335	246	3,736	97	76	247	97	316	2,399	1,937	5,133	1,253	2,100	127	1,834	839
1931–1940	21,858	455	1,225	246	3,445	217	70	108	65	335	2,060	1,355	7,282	1,186	1,841	84	1,580	303
1941–1950	22,063	240	1,095	129	3,242	238	54	61	39	312	1,442	2,282	8,849	1,128	1,379	38	1,352	182
1951–1960	21,754	152	441	109	3,511	349	60	58	119	203	1,429	2,588	9,714	915	599	54	1,351	102
1961–1970	21,554	43	126	23	4,255	36†	284	44	189	257	1,445	1,408	10,945	668	380	78	1,288	77
1971–1980	18,874	63	23	3	4,339	347	59	28	1	248	1,234	338	10,176	713	178	59	994	40
Females																		
1908–1910	18,136	856	939	65	3,558	181	79	257	173	549	1,431	2,233	3,685	1,297	1,463	140	506	734
1911–1920	16,861	984	664	64	3,447	127	122	263	159	529	1,444	2,162	3,453	1,025	1,279	108	420	609
1921–1930	15,379	515	488	48	3,401	120	160	271	128	545	1,203	1,943	3,506	900	1,306	83	382	382
1931–1940	14,433	328	372	46	3,253	184	178	119	103	628	947	1,437	4,337	761	1,215	52	357	114
1941–1950	13,533	153	242	30	3,124	200	136	73	52	587	646	2,367	4,006	609	857	34	351	63
1951–1960	11,711	110	70	22	2,751	244	70	71	136	296	445	2,269	3,875	468	362	58	418	49
1961–1970	10,802	37	30	8	2,932	38†	168	40	214	263	372	1,155	4,196	317	360	76	544	56
1971–1980	9,284	43	10	1	2,860	259	55	28	1	180	437	221	4,103	332	214	69	430	19

*Diseases in classes III and IV of the ninth revision of the ICD not otherwise accounted for.
†For 1961–1970, leukemia is included in malignant neoplasms.
Data from Demography (Australia) and Lancaster (passim).

TABLE 36.6.1. Mortality of retirement age in Australia 65–74 years (deaths per 1,000,000 per annum).

Epoch	All causes	Infections	Tuberculosis	Syphilis	Malignant neoplasms	Other neoplasms and leukemia	Other general*	Blood forming	Rheumatism	Diabetes	Respiratory	Nervous	Cardiovascular	Alimentary	Genitourinary	Skin, cellular, and bones	Violence	Ill-defined
							Males											
1908–1910	57,751	2,766	1,703	254	7,058	122	305	290	397	656	6,794	5,853	12,357	2,746	5,711	463	2,503	7,796
1911–1920	53,796	2,015	1,276	257	7,006	103	335	306	322	634	6,062	5,547	11,950	2,030	5,444	382	2,364	7,762
1921–1930	49,042	1,203	1,137	235	7,982	142	257	369	213	647	5,115	4,746	13,153	1,830	5,269	259	1,989	4,497
1931–1940	50,000	817	1,089	238	8,574	250	135	263	167	838	4,188	3,541	19,365	1,911	4,938	172	1,851	1,862
1941–1950	51,638	449	1,314	143	7,871	317	136	181	103	837	3,585	5,671	22,574	1,814	3,810	93	1,742	998
1951–1960	51,167	273	666	175	7,893	540	93	179	190	591	3,859	7,075	24,047	1,681	1,694	147	1,753	312
1961–1970	52,946	98	285	61	9,614	64†	466	137	281	775	4,713	4,636	27,460	1,342	1,087	165	1,609	152
1971–1980	45,346	118	57	11	9,756	783	132	86	3	712	4,259	634	25,623	1,147	568	158	1,202	78
							Females											
1908–1910	44,400	2,474	856	78	5,766	291	135	196	347	1,002	5,307	5,867	10,178	2,402	2,508	470	1,002	5,515
1911–1920	40,964	2,111	605	29	5,756	193	192	341	447	1,064	4,719	5,502	9,291	2,004	2,322	314	673	5,398
1921–1930	37,110	1,134	478	51	6,090	195	215	455	298	1,266	3,718	4,930	10,160	1,606	2,833	209	630	2,848
1931–1940	36,449	714	390	46	6,072	204	218	311	268	1,579	2,764	3,807	13,510	1,336	2,928	110	728	1,176
1941–1950	35,221	334	333	28	6,013	257	185	218	156	1,676	1,982	6,145	13,510	1,083	1,946	87	698	575
1951–1960	30,483	178	114	35	5,095	390	126	190	216	979	1,286	6,616	12,633	904	653	143	740	187
1961–1970	28,879	71	46	18	5,221	55†	266	127	316	887	1,061	3,894	14,430	730	630	181	830	116
1971–1980	23,362	85	14	4	4,859	492	117	62	3	649	1,042	401	13,795	586	396	178	597	57

* Diseases in classes III and IV of the ninth revision of the ICD not otherwise accounted for.
† For 1961–1970, leukemia is included in malignant neoplasms.
Data from Demography (Australia) and Lancaster (passim).

36.6 Retirement Age: 65–74 Years

At these high ages, the total death rates show a marked and increasing masculinity throughout; see Table 36.6.1.

Death rates in the composite class now account for about 60% of the deaths, with the percentage tending to increase over time. Tuberculosis death rates have fallen, proportionately, more rapidly in the females than in the males, with the masculinity increasing from about 200 to more than 550. Possible factors in these changes in the male rates are occupation, dereliction, and the excesses of smoking and alcohol.

Other infections have been an important cause of death but had declined in importance, even before chemotherapy had been introduced.

Death rates from syphilis have not declined as rapidly as might have been expected in the presence of effective therapy.

The death rates from neoplasms have increased in males and declined in females. These differences are almost entirely due to the markedly increasing rates from cancer of the lung.

Deaths from respiratory diseases have fallen in both sexes but much more rapidly in the females, masculinity being 128 in 1911–1920 and 300 in 1951–1960; possibly the same factors as mentioned earlier for tuberculosis are active.

Death rates from the composite class have risen in the males and fallen substantially in females.

Death rates from injury and poisoning have decreased in both sexes, but the special female problem of fracture of the neck of the femur makes reduction of mortality at these older ages difficult. See Sheldon (1960).

For international trends, see Myers (1978).

36.7 Old Age: 75 Years and Older

At these high ages, the populations at risk have probably changed in age distribution, there being a tendency in the later epochs for the

TABLE 36.7.1. Mortality of old age in Australia 75 years and older (deaths per 1,000,000 per annum).

Epoch	All causes	Infections	Tuberculosis	Syphilis	Malignant neoplasms	Other neoplasms and leukemia	Other general*	Blood forming	Rheumatism	Diabetes	Respiratory	Nervous	Cardiovascular	Alimentary	Genitourinary	Skin, cellular, and bones	Violence	Senility and ill-defined
							Males											
1908–1910	142,677	6,655	839	242	8,674	143	66	221	662	574	17,249	12,316	23,573	3,961	11,952	1,512	3,487	50,456
1911–1920	153,520	5,449	650	146	9,990	102	173	242	784	818	19,165	11,979	25,587	3,692	12,474	1,518	3,361	57,288
1921–1930	134,684	3,609	647	132	11,950	154	137	266	493	862	16,597	10,998	31,182	3,086	12,991	1,138	3,238	37,145
1931–1940	132,421	2,154	677	155	14,085	255	114	420	356	1,435	13,597	8,547	51,301	2,930	14,325	359	3,534	18,143
1941–1950	137,491	1,092	898	93	14,806	327	83	493	321	1,614	11,797	13,782	59,936	3,105	12,614	253	3,716	12,535
1951–1960	136,199	765	727	161	15,605	643	174	563	390	1,239	12,419	19,668	65,058	3,293	6,394	446	3,889	4,737
1961–1970	133,535	213	494	68	17,148	85†	792	447	446	1,730	14,330	14,167	71,382	3,015	4,099	515	3,247	1,321
1971–1980	122,619	356	121	18	18,216	1,410	248	377	6	1,801	14,319	1,741	74,949	2,530	2,586	447	2,830	587
							Females											
1908–1910	119,489	6,737	468	127	8,001	430	101	190	872	948	15,256	12,184	19,857	3,819	3,438	1,277	2,477	43,303
1911–1920	129,588	5,822	358	44	8,719	321	162	190	853	1,084	16,473	12,641	21,283	3,888	3,888	1,255	2,486	50,123
1921–1930	117,348	3,602	339	39	9,777	306	221	330	714	1,339	14,973	12,770	27,507	3,125	5,300	919	2,311	33,763
1931–1940	112,654	2,077	336	28	10,538	264	227	442	670	2,266	11,248	10,145	43,960	2,794	6,722	292	3,102	17,536
1941–1950	114,146	1,180	296	14	10,815	315	179	608	556	2,568	9,505	16,720	48,780	2,307	5,531	247	3,596	10,913
1951–1960	107,827	637	164	67	10,395	499	230	692	491	1,818	7,158	22,373	50,665	2,284	1,675	524	3,796	4,330
1961–1970	99,859	184	79	19	10,095	83†	665	465	547	2,031	5,979	15,095	55,708	2,187	1,641	631	3,036	1,387
1971–1980	89,531	291	23	4	9,429	883	263	340	3	1,730	4,954	1,291	63,337	1,893	1,362	635	2,474	589

*Diseases in classes III and IV of the ninth revision of the ICD not otherwise accounted for.
†For 1961–1970, leukemia is included in malignant neoplasms.
Data from Demography (Australia) and Lancaster (passim).

subgroups of the oldest age to have greater representation. It is possible, therefore, that the declines in mortality, noted below, would be greater if the death rates were computed for, for instance, 5-year subgroups and were then standardized on to given populations in the usual manner. See Table 36.7.1.

At these ages the death rates are high. 123 (90) per 1,000 per annum in Australia, 1971–1980. There have been discussions as to whether the rates continue to rise with age or whether there is a ceiling; 500 per 1,000 per annum has been cited; such a ceiling would make more plausible the 146 years believed to have been attained by the Dane, Drakenburg. See the references at the end of this section for such speculation.

All Causes. There has been a general downward trend in the death rates for each sex, more evident in the females; some disturbances appear in the epoch 1911–1920 from the influenza epidemic and possibly World War I, and in the epoch 1941–1950 possibly due to

World War II. The death rates for males (females) were 143 (119) per 1,000 per annum in 1908–1910 and 123 (90) in 1971–1980, and so there have been declines of about one-sixth (one quarter) of the initial rates.

Infections (class I of the ICD, less tuberculosis and venereal diseases). The death rates for males (females) have decreased from 6.6 (6.7) to 0.4 (0.3) per 1,000 per annum.

Tuberculosis. Relative to the death rates from other causes, tuberculosis has not been an important cause of death (less than 4% in either sex) at these ages. However, there have been large declines relative to the initial values, especially in females.

Syphilis. The remarks on tuberculosis apply to syphilis.

Malignant Neoplasms. Because of certifying practices, we comment only on the epochs after 1930. In females, the rates have been rather steady since 1930 at about 10 per 1,000 per annum, but in males there has been an increase from 14 per 1,000 per annum in 1931–1940 to 18 per 1,000 per annum in 1971–1980. The great contributing cause for this increase is cancer of the lung, which has affected the males far more than the females; a subsidiary cause is in assignment, previously made to the class of Senility and Other Ill-defined Causes.

Diabetes. Death rates from diabetes have increased for the males but decreased for the females.

Respiratory Diseases. In 1931–1940, the death rates from respiratory diseases were for males (females) 13.6 (11.2) per 1,000 per annum, whereas in 1971–1980 they were 14.3 (6.0). Pneumonia was called by the clinicians the "old person's friend" at this age because of its reputation for carrying off old and decrepit persons without pain or distress! See §26.3.

Cardiovascular Diseases. Making comparisons similar to those for the respiratory diseases, we find that the values were 51.3 (44.0) in 1931–1940 and 74.9 (63.3) in 1971–1980, showing an increase in both sexes, some part of which was spurious, being carried over from the next class.

Senility and Other Ill-defined Causes. With the same comparisons, the rates were 18.1 (17.5) in 1931–1940 and 0.6 (0.6) in 1971–1980. Thus, although these decreases were large, they were not sufficiently large to account for the increases in the cardiovascular and neoplastic rates, and it seems reasonable to accept that there have been real increases in the death rates at old age from malignant neoplasms, respiratory diseases, and cardiovascular diseases.

Injury and Poisoning. The rates had been rather stable until 1960, after which they have declined.

Life Span, Centenarians, and Extreme Old Age. This is a field in which the data have been of doubtful value, and it has been the task of authors to free the literature of doubtful cases of longevity; see Barrett (1985), Bowerman (1939), Greenwood and Irwin (1939), Humphrey (1970), Leaf (1973), Pearl (1919), Segerberg (1982), Vincent (1951, 1973), and Westergaard (1899).

See, for bibliography of aging, Mundkur, Yurchyshyn, et al. (1978); for biology of aging, Hayflick (1973); for life span, Dublin, Lotka, and Spiegelman (1949), Hershey (1974), and Walford (1983).

Lopez and Hanada (1982) give a survey of the death rates at older ages in various countries of the developed world. They point out that the aging of these populations is largely due to changes in the fertility rates, but that the aging has caused increased interest in the health of the elderly. Lopez and Hanada (1982, Table 1) give the age-specific mortality rates for 5-year age groups for 1975–1978 for males and females, separately. There are wide discrepancies between the highest and lowest rates, usually about 40% of the lowest. There are also large excesses of the male rates over the female rates. In their Table 2, there are large differences; $\overset{\circ}{e}_{60}$ for males varies from 14.9 to 18.7, $\overset{\circ}{e}_{80}$ for males varies from 5.0 to 7.0; similarly $\overset{\circ}{e}_{60}$ for females varies from 18.5 to 22.7 and $\overset{\circ}{e}_{80}$ from 6.0 to 9.2 years. Their Table 3 gives changes of expectation of life between 1950–1954 and 1975–1978; there was an actual decline in the male $\overset{\circ}{e}_{60}$ between these epochs in more than one-third of the countries surveyed. See also Myers (1978).

See for: life extension, Pearson and Shaw (1982); biology of senescence, Comfort (1956). See also §4.6.

36.8 Sex Differential in Mortality

There have been many methods of comparing the mortalities of the two sexes. It is possibly best to consider the age-specific mortalities; the expectation of life at birth gives an often misleading view of the problem, as it is greatly affected by the events in early life. It is possible for one sex to have a more favorable mortality rate at every age.

To give definiteness to the discussion, we define the (sex) differential index of the mortalities as

100 (male age-specific death rate) / (female age-specific death rate for the same age group).

In the experience of Australia, as given in Table 41.3.2, no instance of the differential is lower than 100 and this value is attained for the 25–34 year age group in the two epochs covering the years 1921–1940. In infancy and early childhood, the differential began at 113 in 1881–1890 and has steadily increased to 129 in the latest epoch, 1971–1980. At the school ages, 5–14 years, the differential has increased steadily from 108 to 151 over the same epochs. At young adult life, the differential began at 133 but decreased to 111 in 1901–1910, possibly due to the passing of the pioneering years, and stayed at 113 for the two epochs before 1930; then the values of the differential in the last five epochs are 128, 144, 271, 265, and 301 (in 1971–1980), and this can be almost entirely accounted for by the increase in mortality from automobile injuries; for total injury and poisoning see. Table 34.2.1 for huge values of the differential; at ages 15–24 years in the epoch 1951–1960 it was 637!

Considering the rates by cause, we see from Table 35.1.2 that the female death rates are usually lower at ages 1–4 years with the exception of pertussis, for which see §9.4. At the school years, ages 5–14, the male attributes are beginning to show a high differential for death rates from accident and injury, and in every epoch the differential is around 200. There are no other major causes of death with such high values of the differential in childhood. At young adult life, we have already mentioned "injury and poisoning" as the major cause of death and of the high differentials in the later epochs. In the earlier epochs there was some mortality associated in the females with childbearing, but also there was a low differential due to tuberculosis and perhaps to difficulties of the menarche. This feature becomes more marked the earlier the statistics; the cause of tuberculosis rates being higher in the females in young adult life has never been convincingly established, although difficulties at the time of the menarche were formerly used to explain it. Anemia was common in young women in the earlier times and it is believed that this was aggravated by pregnancies. See §35.3 and also Hill (1936).

From the age group 25–34 years upward, the contribution to the sex differential of injury and poisoning tends to decrease with successive epochs and, in any case, becomes relatively smaller. Other diseases become of great importance, namely, cardiovascular diseases, lung cancer, and respiratory diseases, all three strongly influenced by tobacco (especially cigarette) smoking. The general effect is that the sex differentials at ages, 25–34, 35–44, . . . , 65–74 years begin in 1881–1890 at 111, 110, 130, 138, and 123, respectively, and end in 1971–1980 at 214, 168, 182, 203, and 195, respectively, whereas at ages older than 75 years the differential has increased from 110 to 137.

It is difficult to make general statements, although the work of many authors, cited in Retherford (1975), shows that inferior male longevity prevails widely throughout the animal kingdom; however, whether studies on species beyond the mammals is relevant to human experience is doubtful. In a human society without sex differences in automobile behavior and occupational risks, and with no tobacco smoking, a plausible case can be made that there would be little difference in longevity or, rather, in the age-specific mortality rates between the sexes. The sex differentials depend very strongly on the society in which they are observed. When we leave the Western world, we find great sex differentials in the Eskimos or Aleuts, for example, due to high mortality from drownings and related hunting accidents. In the developing world recently, and perhaps more importantly in the past, the females carried out much of the work in the fields and had their general well-being disturbed by high fertility rates. Under such conditions the sex differentials might well be low (i.e., in favor of the males); differential rates of infanticide would act in the same manner.

In considering sex differentials in mortality, the effects of occupation have to be considered, especially trauma, but also long-term effects, such as silicosis in the mining industries. Chronic alcoholism and dereliction can also be of importance, for there is more difficulty in accepting elderly men into the home. Suicide rates are higher in men. In developing countries there may be special problems such as anemia, Royston (1982). Tabutin (1978) has discussed the excess mortality in Europe before 1940. A general review has been given by Wingard (1984).

In conclusion, generalizations on this topic are difficult to establish. The sex differential can have a biologic foundation in some cases, but life style and socioeconomic factors may be dominant in others. For international comparisons, see Hammoud (1977).

Chapter 37
The British Isles

37.1 Introduction

Chapters 37 to 44 detail the mortality by country. There is unequal coverage of countries in this monograph for several reasons.

Length of Series. Some countries have long official series, for example, Sweden and England and Wales; other countries, such as Norway, have been able to reconstruct series by going back before their foundation as an independent state and separating out the statistics within their present boundaries from those of their former paramount state.

Parish Records. Some countries have substantial collections of parish records, which have been analyzed by modern demographers, for example, Sweden, France, and Scotland.

Commentaries. There have been numerous commentaries made of the mortalities of some countries, for example, Sweden, France, and England and Wales.

Completeness of Cover. It is a fact that time series cannot be constructed for some countries covering all the area within the given boundaries. This is so for the United States.

Availability of Primary Data and Commentaries. An author is limited by the material locally available to him; the same applies to commentaries.

Diversity of Experience. The justification for a discussion of individual countries is the diversity of conditions, climatic, social, economic,

and historic, in the countries of the world. Although the mortality rates in Europe, the United States, Canada, Japan, Australia, and New Zealand may not differ greatly in the decades after 1960, there are still great differences between the experiences of the developed and developing worlds. Also, the mortalities of the developing world cannot be equated with those of the developed world some centuries ago, for example, malaria has been a dominant cause of death in west Africa, but has no parallel in the British Isles.

For an atlas of disease, see Howe (1963, 1972); for secular changes in mortality, Rhodes (1941) and W. Taylor (1951); for international comparisons, WHO-developed (1974), WHO-Europe (1952), and WHO-world (1980); for mortality by social class, Pamuk (1985).

37.2 England and Wales

Although much has been written on the mortality of England and Wales, there is no monograph covering the field in detail, and it is difficult to select from the vast store of information. The earliest records are the genealogies studied by Guy (1845, 1846), Henry (1965a), already cited in §1.6, and by Hollingsworth (1957, 1965a,b). To estimate mortality from the bubonic plague of 1348 onward, a variety of sources has been used: legal records on inheritance by Russell (1948a), manorial records by Rees (1923), and church and other professional archives by Gasquet (1908) and Campbell (1931); but numerical results for the general population in any region or parish cannot be obtained before 1600.

A beginning can be made at the initiation of the London Bills of Mortality. Fear of the plague led Henry VIII of England, probably in 1517 or 1519, to order the compilation of lists of persons dying from the plague. In the society of the time it was natural for the parish clerks to be responsible for the primary collections of names and vital events. We quote the words of Graunt (1662):

When any one dies, then, either by tolling, or ringing of a Bell, or by bespeaking of a grave of the Sexton, the same is known to the Searchers, corresponding with the said Sexton. The searchers, hereupon (who are ancient Matrons sworn to their Office) repair to the place, where the dead Corps lies, and by view of the same, and by other enquiries, then examine by what Disease, or Casualty the Corps died. Hereupon they make their report to the Parish Clerk.

The parish clerks would then make weekly summaries that were sent on to the Company of Parish Clerks; each year, on the Thursday before Christmas, annual totals were given; see also §3.1. Copies of Bills of Mortality for 1532 and 1535 are extant. It is probable that, when fear of the plague was not great, the publication of the Bills was suspended, although the information was collected and recorded. It is possible that such was the case from 1563 onward. It was early recognized that the publication of lists of cases of the plague was not enough and that the compilation of the numbers of deaths by other causes was necessary as a check. Most English registers were begun because of Thomas Cromwell's Ordinance of 1538, but a few were earlier. The keeping of parish registers in England was required by law but was not enforced. Their completeness depended on the industry of the incumbent and clerical staff. In England the parish records after the Reformation do not cover the whole population; the reasons are slackness on the part of the authorities at local or higher level, nonconformity, and anticlericalism. The Bills continued to be published by the parish clerks until 1849, by which time the Registrar-General had begun a new series of Bills that rendered the older series superfluous.

In recent years there has been a revival of interest in the British parish records, for example, Barham (1841), Cassedy (1973), Clarkson (1975), Forbes (1971), Glass and Eversley (1965), Glass and Revelle (1972), Jones (1976), Loschky (1967), Webster (1979), Wrigley (1968), and Wrigley, Schofield, et al. (1981).

From William Farr stems a very valuable tradition of comment on the figures in the *Annual Report of the Registrar-General*, followed by later official statisticians such as N.A. Humphreys, W. Ogle, T.A. Welton, R. Dudfield, T.H.C. Stevenson, V.P.A. Derrick, and P. Stocks. Actuaries, epidemiologists, sociologists, and academic statisticians have also made valuable contributions to the discussion of the official vital statistics, among whom E. Chadwick, F.G.P. Neison, W.A. Guy, G. Udny Yule, M. Greenwood, A. Bradford Hill, A. Newsholme, W.P. Elderton, and A.H. Bailey are especially mentioned. In fact, the *Journal of the (Royal, after 1887) Statistical Society* might be regarded as a supplement to the official statistics, especially in its first hundred volumes. It should be noted that many of the leading themes in mortality statistics, such as occupational and social class differences in mortality, life table methods, and the effects of crowding and urban-rural differences, originated with Farr, or were further developed by him. Farr, for example, compared the mortality of the "healthy counties" with that of the industrial areas; for he optimistically, but correctly, believed that the mortality rates in the whole country could be reduced to those in the "healthy counties," since the mortality from some diseases was shown by the comparison to be preventible (see Lewis-Faning, 1930).

The publications for England and Wales include *Registrar-General's Statistical Review of England and Wales - Part I, Medical; Part II, Civil; Part III, Commentaries, etc.* There are also various occasional publications of the Registrar-General, the most important for us are the *Registrar-General's Decennial Reports on the Census* and *Studies on Medical and Population Subjects*, especially valuable for the relations between socioeconomic factors and

TABLE 37.2.1. Mortality from all causes in England and Wales (deaths per 1,000,000 per annum).

	All ages*	0–4	5–9	10–14	15–19	20–24	25–34	35–44	45–54	55–64	65–74	75–84	85 and over
					Males								
1841–1850	NA	NA	9,170	5,130	7,050	9,510	9,940	12,900	18,200	31,800	67,500	148,300	312,300
1851–1860	22,136	72,433	8,510	4,881	6,689	8,829	9,574	12,481	17,956	30,855	65,332	165,398‡	
1861–1870	22,592	73,471	8,189	4,483	6,185	8,475	9,941	13,481	19,264	33,142	67,119	165,462	
1871–1880	21,832	68,419	6,705	3,707	5,254	7,361	9,343	13,796	20,070	34,875	69,721	169,301	
1881–1890	20,016	61,607	5,345	2,952	4,317	5,732	7,767	12,395	19,374	34,706	70,462	162,674	
1891–1900	19,526	62,710	4,309	2,448	3,789	5,060	6,757	11,498	18,946	34,949	70,386	160,086	
1901–1910	16,598	50,027	3,504	2,054	3,089	4,180	5,565	9,154	16,217	31,806	64,847	152,454	
1911–1920	14,944	37,817	3,612	2,231	3,659	4,716	5,923	8,296	14,441	29,068	63,547	153,571	
1921–1930	11,765	25,146	2,516	1,654	2,618	3,405	3,856	6,342	11,592	24,620	58,241	149,843	
1931–1940	13,100	—†	2,130	1,360	2,300	3,080	3,200	5,170	11,100	24,300	56,800	137,500	285,800
1941–1950	14,100	—	1,280	950	1,790	2,720	2,720	3,930	9,160	22,700	51,600	120,200	234,700
1951–1960	12,400	—	520	440	870	1,180	1,280	2,580	7,630	22,200	54,200	124,700	251,000
1966	12,388	—	—	916	433	1,049	1,058	2,429	7,263	21,439	53,563	140,383‡	
1976	12,538	—	—	640	324	923	936	2,095	6,985	19,719	50,719	136,659‡	
					Females								
1841–1850	NA	NA	8,900	5,440	7,890	9,090	10,600	12,900	16,000	28,400	61,000	135,900	293,300
1851–1860	20,261	62,744	8,418	5,056	7,385	8,530	9,925	12,147	15,198	27,007	58,656	155,455‡	
1861–1870	20,184	63,710	7,796	4,506	6,645	7,971	9,721	12,065	15,647	27,915	59,120	154,932	
1871–1880	18,979	58,344	6,228	3,717	5,453	6,810	8,611	11,628	15,622	28,671	61,020	156,123	
1881–1890	17,340	51,941	5,259	3,109	4,423	5,539	7,375	10,584	15,109	28,467	60,413	148,054	
1891–1900	16,733	52,797	4,370	2,566	3,665	4,461	6,082	9,593	14,741	28,438	60,723	146,464	
1901–1910	13,945	41,866	3,612	2,166	2,892	3,499	4,744	7,529	12,508	24,848	53,928	136,204	
1911–1920	12,166	31,377	3,588	2,337	3,213	3,867	4,782	6,423	10,900	21,508	49,644	132,798	
1921–1930	9,518	20,231	2,329	1,633	2,484	3,020	3,453	4,855	8,608	18,319	44,886	129,021	
1931–1940	11,500	—†	1,900	1,260	2,040	2,630	2,880	4,070	7,710	16,700	42,300	107,900	249,100
1941–1950	11,000	—	970	760	1,400	1,970	2,110	2,910	5,960	13,400	35,200	93,300	207,900
1951–1960	10,900	—	360	300	430	610	950	1,970	4,670	11,400	31,800	89,200	216,800
1966	11,141	—	—	753	273	427	686	1,705	4,416	10,284	28,562	103,373‡	
1976	11,838	—	—	459	226	377	568	1,468	4,298	10,186	26,168	101,284‡	

* 1851–1930, standardized on to the population of England and Wales as enumerated in 1901. From Registrar-General's Decennial Supplement (1952, Part 3, Table 12, p.85).

1841–1850 amd 1931–1960 from the Registrar-General's Statistical Review of England and Wales for the year 1969. To make these rates comparable with those before 1930, appropriate zeros have been added.

1966 and 1976 from World Health Statistics Annual.

†Not readily available for comparison.

‡1851–1930, 1966, and 1976: ages 75 and over.

mortality. See also Glass (1951, 1963, 1964, 1965a,b, 1973a,b).

The Medical Research Council publishes a Special Report Series, which has contained many monographs of statistical interest. Much discussion of the official medical statistics has appeared in the *Journal of the Royal Statistical Society*. Among other journals worthy of mention here are *Journal of Hygiene, Bulletin* (later *Abstracts*) *of Hygiene, British Journal of Preventive and Social Medicine*, and *Journal of the Institute of Actuaries*. See also Pemberton (1971).

We now give as Table 37.2.1 the age-specific mortality rates for England and Wales, noting that later observers would have access to a longer stretch than earlier observers. Humphreys (1883) commented on the rates from 1841–1845 to 1876–1880. At ages younger than 35 years, definite declines in the mortality were evident in the most recent quinquennium. The declines were more marked in the female. His later tables showed that these declines were such as to increase the expectation of life at birth by about 2 years. Further, there was implied an increased proportion of persons of the working ages in the stationary life table population, as it would now be termed, which could be expected to be of economic importance. At the foot of his p.197 he noted that

in a population with fairly constant birth and death-rates and a consequently fairly constant excess of births over deaths, the age distribution (as may be mathematically proved) assumes, after a certain period, fixed proportions,

presumably thinking of Euler (1767/1977). He goes on to say that "these conditions are in the main applicable to the English population" and that the age distributions as shown at the censuses of 1861 and 1871 were almost identical with the stationary life table population based on the contemporary rates.

It is of some historical interest that neither Humphreys nor anyone taking part in the discussion suggested that the declines in mortality were due to improvements in medical therapy. Humphreys (1883, p.206) hoped that his conclusions

should also, by showing the effect of recent sanitary progress upon the death rate, serve to strengthen the hands of sanitary authorities, and of medical officers of health, in their struggle against the vast amount of apathy still existing in health matters. Medical Officers of Health of large towns would find the Life Table method described in this paper useful for displaying in an effective manner the amount of the waste of life still taking place in our urban populations.

Some speakers pointed out that the recent declines might be part of a cyclical change but, on the other hand, they had occurred during a period of rapid urbanization, which made the declines all the more worthy of note because the urban death rates had formerly been greatly in excess of the rural.

Greenwood (1924) gives many tables of interest for making urban-rural comparisons in England and Wales and between England and Wales and Sweden, but is less satisfactory for the secular comparisons in England and Wales alone than is Greenwood (1936), who writes:

At the beginning of Queen Victoria's reign the general stock of hygienic knowledge, the attitude of both medical men and laymen towards the prevention of disease, did not differ fundamentally from that of their great-grandparents. What was thought, said and done when cholera came in 1831 differed in no significant way from what was actually thought and said and would have been done if plague had reached England in 1720. The epidemic did not teach the College of Physicians much, but it undoubtedly did give disease a publicity value, and led to the beginning of a national system for at least trying to control disease. In Simon's classical treatise on English Sanitary Institutions one finds a complete account of the evolution of the system, beginning with the Consultative Board of Health of 1831, proceeding through committees and commissions to the legislation of 1848 and the General Board of Health to the Medical Department of the Privy Council, and finally to the Local Government Board, which expanded in our generation into a Ministry of Health. The legislative landmarks of the nineteenth century were the Public Health Act of 1848 and the consolidating Act of 1875.

This was the evolution of specific hygienic action, but we must take with it changes which were only in part motivated by medical and hygienic arguments; they were more effectively quickened by the growth of humanity which Simon ranked among the 'New Momenta' of hygienic progress. Among these was legislative control of industrial conditions. Before the reign of Queen Victoria all such legislation was directed to mitigating the conditions of life of children, little white slaves, and none of it had much practical value until, in 1833, inspection was enacted. Women first received some small measure of protection in 1842 (Mines and Collieries Act), and in 1844 their hours of labour in factories were regulated. The Ten Hours' Act of 1847 did indirectly limit the working hours of adult males. So that children of 5–15 began to receive some protection in 1831–40, adults about 10 years later.

So far as concerns direct hygienic improvements other than limitation of hours of labour, no important legislative expression of reform is to be found before the rather complicated Factory Act of 1867, almost the only nineteenth-century measure in which the influence of scientific research (that of Greenhow) can be distinctly traced. The Metalliferous Mines Regulation Act of 1872 was also partly inspired by research into the aetiology of a particular occupational hazard - miners' phthisis. More than 20 years passed before, in consequence of an Act of 1895, medical notification of certain occupational poisonings and diseases was required and a medical inspector of factories was appointed.

Logan (1950*b*, Figure 1) compares the total mortality in England and Wales at each age for the epochs 1947, 1921–1925, and 1846–1850 and there are evidently great changes, especially at the younger ages. He comments on the passing of mortality from the acute infectious diseases, although in 1947 tuberculosis was still an important cause of death.

The reduction or elimination of some of the infectious diseases can be related directly to definite preventive measures such as vaccination (smallpox), immunization (diphtheria) and improved sanitation (cholera and typhoid). The prevalence or the fatality of other diseases have declined because of less specific measures associated with a higher standard of living - better food, clothing and housing, purer air, earlier and fuller medical attention.

Greenwood (1936) believed that children began to be protected from the worst effects of the industrial revolution in the decade 1831–1840 and adults in the next decade. Mortality at ages 5–20 years was already declining before 1870, at ages 20–35 about 1877, and at ages 45–55 about 1900; at 65 years and older, the change was still barely perceptible in 1936; infant mortality began to decline around 1900. It is possible that beneficial changes in public health were partly nullified by the increasing urbanization from 1851 to 1930.

Many authors have believed hospitalization was of importance in reducing mortality. From contemporary evidence, such as Guy (1856, 1867), Steele (1877), and Clendenning (1844), it appears unlikely that the cover by hospital was ever sufficiently complete, either geographically or by disease, to affect the general trend of mortality. Also other accounts of hospital sepsis and hygienic conditions do not suggest that the case fatality was greatly lower in hospital patients. It appears that Griffith's (1926) citation from *The Gold-Headed Cane* of MacMichael (1827) is greatly out of context, for, from reading of that book or other sources, it is evident that the physicians before 1800 were concerned chiefly with complaints, such as apoplexy and other diseases of the elderly, that even now do not yield readily to treatment. See also §45.11. Mortality did not decline until the infectious diseases began to be controlled. The first great diseases to be brought under control were smallpox with the aid of Jennerian vaccination and cholera and typhoid by public health measures. The importance of some other infections, notably scarlatina, as causes of mortality became less toward the end of the nineteenth century for reasons that are not understood. However, the mortality rates before 1835 still remain conjectural, even after much research. The relative contributions of mortality and fertility to the surge of population in Great Britain at the time of the industrial revolution cannot yet be stated with certainty; neither can the mortality rates be given by age and sex for these earlier times.

Now that the great pestilences of the past (excepting influenza) and the common infections of the developed world have been overcome, the changing patterns of communicable disease can be considered in England and Wales, as observed by officers of health and their bacteriologists, with the aid of Galbraith, Forbes, and Mayon-White (1980).

Newly Recognized Diseases

Campylobacter Enteritis. *Campylobacter fetus* (subspecies *jejuni*) is now the most common pathogen, 5%, (although some other series give higher percentages) isolated from the feces of patients with sporadic acute diarrheal illness; the incubation period of the disease is 2 to 5 days, and there is diarrhea with pain, sometimes acute. *Campylobacter* may well have been a cause of many such illnesses for many years. See also §6.11.

Enterovirus. The enterovirus attacks neonates and may cause death.

Giardiasis. Once regarded as harmless, *Giardia lamblia* is now believed to cause an acute enteritis, 7 to 14 days after exposure; the infection may become chronic. See §6.10.

Legionnaires' Disease. Cases have been noted in recent years. See §9.12.

Primary Amebic Meningoencephalitis. Infections occur after energetic swimming or diving in polluted waters. After an incubation period of 3 to 7 days, a purulent meningoencephalitis may result, usually fatal within 24 to 72 hours. Over 100 cases have been reported worldwide, 6 of which have been from England and Wales. The organisms involved are *Acanthamoeba culbertsoni* and *Naegleria fowleri.* See §6.10.

Viral Hemorrhagic Fevers. Lassa fever has occurred chiefly in air passengers from West Africa. Marburg and Ebola virus diseases have not yet (1980) occurred in England and Wales.

Group B Streptococci. These now infect neonates and the more common, septicemic form has a case fatality rate of 50%.

Low Grade Pathogens. Immunosuppression, used in organ transplantation, and chemotherapy have led to infections in intensive care units by organisms otherwise harmless; *Pseudomonas, Klebsiella, Enterobacter, Serratia, Pneumocystis, Toxoplasma, Candida,* and *Cryptococcus* are among the genera represented. *Pseudomonas aeruginosa* is especially dangerous in cases of burns. Such are often referred to as opportunistic organisms.

Disappearing and Declining Diseases

Cholera. There were 20 imported cases in 1970–1978 without a single secondary case.

Enteric Fevers. Cases observed in England and Wales during 1960–1979 were almost always imported.

Dysentery. Notifications fell from an average of about 30,000 per annum in 1960–1964 to less than 3,000 in 1978 and 1979. The dominant bacillus changed from *Shigella sonnei* to *S. flexneri.*

Brucellosis. Notifications of brucellosis, due to *Br. abortus*, decreased from about 300 per year around 1970 to about 40 in the years 1978 and 1979. An eradication program was begun in 1979.

Diphtheria. There had been a total of 19 deaths in the years 1960–1963 and 11 deaths in 1964–1979. Immunization acceptance rates had been maintained at more than 70% since the early sixties.

Pertussis. Increased use (acceptance) of the vaccine reduced the notification rates.

Tetanus. Primary immunization by toxoid and a reinforcing dose on reaching school age seem all that is necessary to maintain the mortality at a low rate.

Staphylococcus aureus. Penicillin-resistant strains caused many hospital infections in the 1950s, but this tendency has been controlled by penicillinase-resistant antibiotics.

Poliomyelitis. In 1960–1963 361 nonparalytic and 1,185 paralytic cases of poliomyelitis were reported.

Smallpox. From 1960 to 1979 there were 28 deaths, including 26 in 1962.

Measles. Notifications decreased from 160,000 and 766,000 in 1960 and 1961 to less than 80,000 in 1979. A live vaccine campaign was begun in 1968, but the vaccination (acceptance) rates remain around 50%.

Increasing Infectious Diseases

Food Poisoning. This is due mainly to canned

or salted preserved food. *Salm. typhimurium* rates were almost stable during 1960–1979; other types were increasing in frequency.

Sexually Transmitted Diseases. There have been important increases in the rates for syphilis, gonorrhea, and nonspecific genital infections of men.

The mortality statistics of England and Wales are quoted extensively throughout this monograph. We give subject with chapter and section numbers. Cholera, §6.2; enteric fevers, §6.5; tuberculosis, §7.4 and §7.6; plague, §8.3; diphtheria, §9.3; pertussis, §9.4; scarlatina, §9.5; erysipelas, §9.6; wound infections, §9.11; influenza, §10.7; smallpox, §§11.1 and 11.2; measles, §§11.6 and 11.7; typhus, §14.2; neoplasms, §20.7; diabetes, §§21.2 and 21.3; famine, §22.12; cardiovascular, §25.7; maternal, §29.3; perinatal and infant, 32 and 33 various; suicide, §34.13; homicide, §34.14; legal intervention, §34.15; infancy and childhood, §35.1; childhood, §35.2; young adults, §35.3; parish records, §36.1; and population growth, §45.11.

We give now some additional references, classifying them by centuries or other convenient methods. Wherever possible we have transferred reference to a specific disease into the relevant section among the causes of death.

References to England and Wales

Anglo-Saxon: epidemics, Bonser (1944).
Medieval: Bonser (1963).
Fifteenth century: epidemics, Gottfried (1978).
Tudor times: Copeman (1960), Forbes (1971).
1541–1871: Wrigley and Schofield (1981).
1563–1801: Hertfordshire, Munby (1964).
1570–1653: child mortality, Finlay (1978).
Sixteenth century: Forbes (1979), Webster (1979).
Seventeenth century: London, Debus (1974), Jones and Judges (1935), Morris (1751); urban-rural differences, Short (1750); pre-industrial, Wrigley (1968); pathology, Rather (1974).
Eighteenth century: early industrial England, Benjamin (1973*b*), Brownlee (1916*b*, 1925), McKeown and Brown (1965), Percival

(1789), Percival and Heberden (1789, 1801), Razzell (1965), Wrigley (1968).
Nineteenth century: general, Farr (1837, 1885), Wall (1973*a,c*);
by districts: Parsons (1898–1899, 1899–1900), Welton (1875, 1897, 1911, 1916*a,b*, 1917); urban, Sargant (1866), Wall (1973*b*), Woods and Woodward (1984*a,b*), Woodward (1984); Birmingham, Woods (1984*b*); Bradford, Thompson (1984); London, Booth (1902/1903), Mayhew (1851); Manchester, Pooley, and Pooley (1984).
mortality: patterns, Woods (1984*a*); loss and gain, Ransome (1877), Welton (1875, 1880, 1911); declines, McKeown and Record (1962); commentary, Farr (1885); sociological, Wrigley (1972); review, Phillips (1908); Friendly Societies, Ratcliffe (1850).
pauperism and relief: Corfield (1870), Yule (1895/1896).
population and history: Hicks (1942), Wrigley (1969).
public health and hygiene: Greenhow (1858, 1859), Wohl (1983).
Society of Friends: Fox (1859).
tuberculosis and general: Cronjé (1984).
urban sanitary reform early nineteenth century: Hennock (1957).
working class: Engels (1892/1971).
Twentieth century:
1900–1950: Stocks (1950).
1931–1961: Fox and Goldblatt (1982), US National Center (1965*a*).
modern rise of population: McKeown (1976), Razzell (1974).
mortality: causes, McKeown (1978); changes, Welton (1911, 1916*a*); interpretation of decline, McKeown, Record, and Turner (1975); local, Welton (1916*b*, 1917); by occupation and social class, Stevenson (1921, 1923, 1928), Tabah (1955); atlas of mortality, Gardner, et al. (1984); infants and children, Macfarlane and Mugford (1984*a,b*).
research in country practice: Pickles (1939).

37.3 Scotland

A census of Scotland by means of parish counts was made in 1755 by Alexander Webster (1707–1784), whose report has been reprinted with comments by Kyd (1975). John Sinclair (1754–1835) collected much information in his *Statistical Account of Scotland* in 21 volumes (Sinclair, 1791–1799, 1831), a great work of which later commentators have made much use. These two and other sources, particularly the Old Parochial Registers, are rich in information on parish records. Deaths by cause became available for the whole of Scotland in 1855, after compulsory registration of death. At later censuses the annual figures have been further consolidated over the decades. The official statistics of Scotland have been developed largely independent of those of England and Wales. There are *Annual Reports of the Registrar-General* and reports of the Government Actuary. Additional commentary is available in the *Health Bulletin*; we note also the *Transactions of the Faculty of Actuaries*.

The health problems of the large cities, Glasgow and Edinburgh, resembled those of many other great European cities, including London; but there are many rural areas, including the islands, where isolation has affected the epidemiology of the acute infectious diseases, a topic on which little is available in the literature. Further, Scotland has a more rigrous climate and has been more susceptible to dearth and famine than England. We therefore select a few topics for discussion.

Cholera. Cowan (1840) pointed out that there had been 3,166 deaths from 6,208 cases of cholera during 9 months in the years 1832–1833, so that the case fatality rate was a little more than 50%. He wrote that contemporaries, belittling the influence of epidemics on mortality, maintained that the intruding disease attracted deaths that would in other years be assigned elsewhere; he was able to destroy their argument by showing that the 1832 deaths (with cholera excluded) exceeded the deaths in 1831.

Bubonic Plague. Plague disappeared from Scotland after a widespread epidemic during the years 1644–1649; details are available from Old Parochial Registers in Flinn (1977), in which it is estimated that Edinburgh may have lost a quarter of its population. Aberdeen less

TABLE 37.3.1. Smallpox deaths in Glasgow by year.

	0	1	2	3	4	5	6	7	8	9
178–				155	425	218	348	410	399	366
179–	336	607	202	389	235	402	177	354	309	370
180–	257	245	156	194	213	56	28	97	51	159
181–	28	109	78							

Measles deaths in Glasgow by year.

	0	1	2	3	4	5	6	7	8	9
178–				66	1	0	2	23	1	23
179–	33	4	58	5	7	46	92	5	3	43
180–	21	8	168	45	27	99	56	16	787	44
181–	19	267	304							

Notes: The population of Glasgow was: 1785, 46,000; 1791, 67,000; 1801, 84,000; 1811, 110,000.
It was first enumerated by age in 1819.
Data from Cleland (1823).

than a fifth, Perth more than Edinburgh. For the whole of Scotland death from plague was 20,000 to 30,000. It may be that the weather conditions and the absence of both suitable wild rodents and alternative hosts in large cities made the perpetuation of plague more difficult in Scotland than in London, which had a warmer climate and a greater population of rats.

Smallpox. This was a great cause of death in the eighteenth century, endemic in Edinburgh and Glasgow for most of the century; from these centers the infection would spread to the country areas. Inoculation, never widespread, was used between 1733 and 1800. Flinn (1977, p.292) estimated that about one-sixth of all deaths in Scotland in the late eighteenth century was due to smallpox. In areas of endemicity, the disease affected principally those younger than five years. In Table 37.3.1, there is a substantial decline in the deaths, from an average of about 300 annually during the years 1783–1800 to somewhat less than 100 in the years 1804–1812, the latter period indicating the positive effects of a vaccination campaign. But there were disappointments.

Smallpox in 1835–1839 was causing more deaths than before 1801; vaccination had not been carried out. Cowan (1840) wrote:

The increasing prevalence of small-pox should attract the attention of the public. It is a disease which has caused a mortality during the last few years inferior only to that of typhus and measles, and it is one which could be eradicated, under proper management, at a trifling expense, less indeed than the sum paid from the poors' rate for the coffins of its victims. The rate of mortality from small-pox is assumed upon good authority to be 1 in 5 of those attacked.

Measles. Table 37.3.1 shows that measles was an important cause of death in Glasgow. It may well be that its passage from child to child in later years was made easier by an increase in the density of population of young children. According to a table in Flinn (1977, p. 293), measles was responsible for about 4% of all deaths in Scotland in the eighteenth century, implying a case fatality of more than 4%. At the foot of that page there is evidence that epidemic behavior then, especially a social gradient in the death rates, was similar to that in this century reported by Halliday (1928), for which see §5.2. See also for Aberdeen, G.N. Wilson (1905).

Childhood Deaths from Acute Specific Infective Disease. Glasgow was not a large city in the first half of the nineteenth century, but there were very crowded poorer parts of the city in which passage of organisms between persons was easy. Smallpox, measles, scarlet fever, and whooping cough caused many deaths there. Flinn (1977, Table 5.6.1) gives the percentage of deaths in three periods, 1800–1810, 1836–1842, and 1855–1865 as 7.5, 6.6, and 3.1 for measles and 6.6, 5.0, and 1.9 for smallpox. It is clear that, because each person has only one attack from measles and smallpox, such proportions would imply a minimum estimate of case fatalities of 6% and 4% for measles and smallpox during the early half of the nineteenth century—enormous figures for measles by modern standards. Whooping cough during the same three epochs caused an average of 6% of all deaths.

Replacement of Diseases. Although we have access to Watt (1813) only at second hand through Cleland (1823) and others and no access to Chalmers (1930), with the aid of later writers, we can comment on the theory developed by Watt (1813), who had been investigating chincough (pertussis) and the mortality of infancy and childhood. Thus, Cleland (1823) compared the numbers of childhood deaths from smallpox and measles, namely, 2,107 and 217, during 7 years before the introduction of smallpox vaccination with 795 and 1,198 deaths in the 7 years after the introduction. This argument was also used with respect to cholera, mentioned earlier in this section. In the light of Watt's theory, the apparent replacement of smallpox by measles could be explained by the deaths of children inherently incapable of surviving and so dying as a result of the dominant or prevalent disease. See the discussion of this point in Farr (1885, pp. 321–322), who cites Watt as follows:

From every circumstance which had come under my observation, the efficacy of vaccine inoculation appeared certain. The experience of 13 years' pretty extensive practice had confirmed me fully in this opinion. But still the question recurred, how are we to account for the same or nearly the same number of deaths under 10 years of age? As no new disease has appeared, the deficiency occasioned by the want of the small-pox must have been made up by a greater mortality among the other diseases of children. Has it been equally divided among them, or has a greater share fallen to some than to others?

['An inquiry into the relative mortality of the principal diseases of children in Glasgow.' Appendix to *Treatise on Chincough*, pp. 334–336. By Robert Watt, M.D. (1813).] Farr (1885) points out that the births in Glasgow were increasing over the years considered by Watt and so his method exaggerates the increase of deaths from other diseases. We may add that the presumed increase of crowding in Glasgow led to an increased passage of infections and hence to greater mortality; moreover, the deaths from measles, in particular, have been prone to great swings, and we may offer these various considerations as an acceptable alternative to the notion of replacement of diseases.

Typhus. Cowan (1840) says that the progress of the epidemic fevers has been slow "unless extreme destitution has existed"; especially is

TABLE 37.3.2. The proportional mortality of a few of the principal fatal diseases in 1000 deaths from all causes, 1846–1848.

	Edinburgh	Leith	Glasgow	Dundee	Paisley	Greenock	Aberdeen	Perth
Consumption	119	103	171	130	208	143	62	128
Typhus fever	163	102	113	114	122	220	73	86
Scarlet fever	34	56	43	31	19	35	16	29
Measles	27	19	61	61	30	8	12	38
Whooping cough	37	35	52	44	38	19	9	37
Smallpox	17	24	38	37	20	20	13	24
Croup	12	14	22	22	15	19	3	23
Brain diseases	83	81	61	71	34	73	33	83
Heart diseases	18	19	7	12	6	14	2	8

Table 23 of Stark (1851). Reprinted from *J. Statist. Soc. (London)* 14, 48–87.

TABLE 37.3.3. Deaths in Glasgow, 1835–1839*.

Cause of death						Age last birthday				
	All ages	0	1	2–4	5–9	10–19	20–29	30–39	40–49	50+
Smallpox	2,196	747	641	545	111	56	74	16	6	
Measles	2,482	520	866	863	200	23	9	1	1	
Scarlet fever	1,056	97	176	405	272	70	20	9	4	3
Fever	4,788			752†				4036†		

*Population of Glasgow 1791, 1801, . . ., 1831: 67,000; 84,000; 110,000; 147,000, and 202,000.
Hospital beds in Glasgow 1816–1829, 230; 1829–1832, 330; 1832–1840, 455.
Admissions of smallpox patients to the Infirmary by year for 1835, 1836, . . ., 1839: 72, 110, 55 (estimate), 35, 59; total, 331.
† Fever deaths given only as under and over 10 years.
Data from Cowan (1840).

this true of "contagious fever" [evidently typhus], for which the selfish fears and benevolence of the population provide only temporary respite. He is particularly concerned with the filth of the poorer parts of the city. "In 1817 to 1819, when contagious fever first prevailed to an alarming extent, its ravages were preceded by two bad harvests and want of employment for the labouring poor. . ." For typhus in Edinburgh 1816–1819, see L.G. Wilson (1978).

Tuberculosis. See chapter 7 for a general discussion on tuberculosis that applies equally to Scotland.

Influenza. See the remark of Greenwood (1920) that the progress of the influenza epidemic of 1918 had features corresponding to those in England and Wales.

To illustrate the dominance of the infectious diseases in the years 1838–1841 in the towns and cities of Scotland, we reproduce Table 23 of Stark (1851) as our Table 37.3.2 and data from Cowan (1840) as Table 37.3.3. See also Cowan (1838).

Infant Mortality. In Table 37.3.4, it is evident that there was no decline in the infant mortality for Scotland as a whole from 1855 to 1900. There is a gradient down from the principal towns to the mainland-rural and the insular-rural; indeed the crude mortalities in the principal towns are nearly double those of the insular-rural. See alo Douglas (1966).

TABLE 37.3.4. Infant deaths per 1000 births.

Year	All Scotland	Principal towns*	Mainland-rural†	Insular-rural
1855–1860	120	158	95	89
1861–1870	121	151	100	83
1871–1880	123	150	91	81
1881–1890	119	140	89	72
1891–1900	128	147	95	76

* Before 1870, also including large towns.
† Before 1870, also including small towns.
From Table 22 of the Annual Report of the Registrar-General of Scotland for 1907.

Urban-rural Differences. From the same Annual Report (1907, Table 29), the birth, death, and marriage rates per 1,000 in the insular-rural areas were 33, 20, and 6 for 1860 and 22, 18, and 4 for 1900; the corresponding rates for the principal towns were 38, 30, and 9 for 1860 and 31, 20, and 9 for 1900, suggesting a lighter mortality in the insular-rural areas, although there had been extensive migration of young persons from the islands to the cities; this is confirmed by the age pyramids shown in Kyd (1975, pp.xxxvi and xxxvii). It may well be that the effects of the measles and smallpox epidemics in the great cities were aggravated by the migration of families from the rural areas susceptible to the disease, children and adults alike.

Obstetrics. Alexander Gordon was able to establish the contagious nature of puerperal sepsis, with the investigation possibly made easier by the small size of the population. See §29.4 and Duncan (1869–1870, 1871).

Famine. Scotland is sufficiently far north to suffer from cold weather famines. The worst of these occurred in 1696, and in the following 7 years, and in 1709; 1740–1742, 1772, 1782, 1783, and 1793 were again years of dearth. Salaman (1949, p.364) gives dates for the introduction of the potato into the Highlands; he dismisses the mention of a traveler, Martin Martin, to the Hebrides in 1695 who had reported seeing a potato crop. Salaman regards 1722 as a doubtful first entry of potato cropping into a parish in Inverness; by no later than 1760, the potato had been introduced into the counties of Inverness, Ross, Perth, and Sutherland, and by 1771 it was already a staple food

of the Hebrides and other islands. By 1790, Salaman (1949) writes: "there was but one parish in the mainland of Scotland in which it is recorded that the potato was not grown." By 1794 the potato had gained its ascendance because oat and pea crops had failed, and it was then the staple food of the community for 9 months of the year. In 1835 the potato crop failed badly because of a cold, wet season and in some places, as in Skye, there was famine. The potato blight may have occurred in a few spots in 1843 and, Salaman (1949) believes, in various parts of Scotland in 1844. In 1845 the blight spread rather erratically over Scotland, some of the northern areas escaping without great loss; but in 1846 the blight was quite general, destroying the growing crops. By March 1847 distress was widespread in the Highlands where three quarters of the food supply had been lost; three quarters of the people of the Hebrides were "absolutely destitute." In the Lowlands the distress was not so great; there the potato never attained the same ascendance as in the Highlands. Never was the proportion of population in Scotland affected as much as in Ireland. It is recorded that many of the wealthy landlords did much for the tenants or clansmen, and there were great sums of money provided by church and other charities. The net result however was that there was great migration from the Highlands. Salaman (1949) believes that hunger and suffering were widespread throughout the Highlands but few persons actually died of starvation.

Brotherston (1952) notes many interesting details in his study of the early public health movement in Scotland. Malaria had been an important cause of invalidity up to 1780, but by 1840 it was no longer endemic. He gives little credit to inoculation against smallpox and states that smallpox reached its highest peak as a killer after inoculation had become an established practice. He believes that the increases in mortality after 1820 were due to increasing poverty and overcrowding and chiefly due to increases in the lowest classes, indeed, the "flood of Irish" who poured into Edinburgh from 1818 onward, attracted by work on the construction of the Forth-Clyde Junction Canal. They inhabited the lowest classes of buildings "even byres and stables, never before considered habitable." Similar events were occurring in Glasgow, where the population was increasing, although the accommodation was decreasing, partly because some dwellings had been pulled down and replaced by warehouses and factories. Typhus and relapsing fevers were responsible for more deaths in 1847 than was cholera in 1848 or 1849. Relapsing fever was epidemic in 1816–1817, 1827–1828 and 1837–1838; in 1842–1844 it affected vast numbers, and was prevalent again in 1847–1848, although it was an unimportant source of mortality in that era.

For the Western Isles, see MacCulloch (1819); for general and rural-urban comparisons, see Stark (1857, 1869–1870).

37.4 Northern Ireland

Until partition in 1922, all Ireland came under the same Registrar-General. We have given age-specfic rates in Table 3.7.1 for 2 years since 1945 to show the progress, but we do not analyze the statistics further.

37.5 Ireland (Eire)

The history of population growth and, by implication, mortality in Ireland owes much to Connell (1950, and his other works). A bibliography of these topics might well begin with the memorial volume to him by Goldstrom and Clarkson (1981). Clarkson (1981) gives estimates of the population of Ireland by Connell (1950) and his own (called hypothetical in his table) in thousands as follows—year, Con-

nell's estimate, Clarkson's estimate: *1687*, 2,167, 1,690; *1725*, 3,042, 2,221; *1753*, 3,191, 2,274; *1791*, 4,753, 4,417. To these we may append census counts (thousands) 6,802 in 1821, 8,175 in 1841 and 6,552 in 1851. See also Vaughan and Fitzpatrick (1978). Disturbing factors in the growth between 1687 and 1821 were widespread famines in 1727–1730 and 1740–1741 and severe dearths in the 1750s. It is evident that there had been a rapid population growth, a quadrupling of the population in 134 years, between 1687 and 1821. Razzell (1967) has confirmed the view of the Irish census of 1841 that Irish age-specific death rates during the 1830s were lower than those of England and Wales over the same period for ages younger than 35 years. Clarkson (1981) mentions the possibility that food supplies became more regular and urbanization was less in Ireland than in England and Wales; Dublin, Cork, and Belfast had populations of 233,000, 80,000, and 75,000 by 1841; and few Irish towns were larger than 6,000 at that time. Cullen (1981) gives evidence that the diet of the Irish was far more varied than has usually been supposed; in particular, although the potato had been grown since early in the seventeenth century, heavy potato consumption in classes above the poorest came late in the eighteenth century and was associated with the export of grains to England.

Many famines have been reported in Ireland, for which see Salaman (1949) and MacArthur (1956), both of which illustrate the variety of causes operating. Thus, a great mortality of cattle in AD 699 and 700 led to a great famine in which cannibalism is reported, that was followed by a famine pestilence. In some famine years the weather was wet throughout the growing season; in other years early wet was followed by drought. A very severe winter in AD 1115 caused great destruction of cattle, leading to famine; a pestilence followed. Floods damaged the crops in other years. In more recent times severe winter frosts destroyed the potatoes in the ground.

Localized famines have been caused by deliberate military actions during the wars with names and dates: Edward Bruce 1315–1318, Desmond 1597–1601, Cromwellian 1649–1652,

Williamite 1689–1691. These wars and the consequences of the ensuing occupation pauperized the great bulk of the population.

All these other famines and famine causes are overshadowed by the events of 1845–1847, see Edwards and Williams (1956) and Cousens (1960, 1963, 1964–1965), when the crop was struck by the potato blight, an infection by a fungus, *Phytophthora infestans*. This infection attacked and destroyed fields of potatoes, turning the display of green leaves to one of blackened and withered stalks. From the tops, the infection spread to the tubers, which soon became stained and began to rot. Failures of the potato crop had previously been local and scattered, now every area was affected; but those on higher land or in drier districts were affected less. It was later evident that this was part of a general infection of potatoes throughout Europe. On September 12, 1845, it was announced in the press that the potato blight had arrived in Ireland. However, the earlier varieties had been spared. The crop of 1846 suffered even more severely. The famine began in early 1846. The government, expecting the 1846 crop to be adequate, concluded its relief work by August 15, 1846; but it was soon found that the whole crop was rotting. An inspection party from Westminster in June 1847 met terrible scenes of disaster.

The population of Ireland was 8,175,000 in 1841 and 6,552,000 in 1851, but by then there had been some natural increase. The Census Commission estimated that Ireland was poorer by 2.5 million persons by death or emigration. O'Rourke (1875), cited by Vaughan and Fitzpatrick (1978), estimated the loss as 2.75 million. Dysentery accounted for 25,000 deaths in 1847. In 1848 there were more than 30,000 deaths from cholera—part of a European epidemic. Typhus was a more serious cause of death with more than 7,000 in a normal year, 65,000 in 1817–1819, according to Barker and Cheyne (1821), 17,000 in 1846, 57,000 in 1847, 46,000 in 1848, 40,000 in 1849, and 23,500 in 1850. Relative to population size, the losses during the famine years were comparable with those at the time of the Black Death.

MacArthur (1956) gives typhus, relapsing fever (often confused with typhus), dysentery, cholera, and scurvy as important causes of death. There is good evidence that typhus became important in May 1847, although there had been some increases in the previous year. Relapsing fever also began to be epidemic about the same time. This author states that there was no true cholera during the famine years until December 1848, when the epidemic then prevalent in Europe invaded Ireland. The dysentery epidemic commenced early in 1847 before that of typhus. Scurvy was a feature of the famine, as the potato is an excellent source of Vitamin C. In one area, Ballygar in Galway, the diseases appeared in the following order: scurvy, dysentery, famine dropsy, typhus, and relapsing fever. Then as soon as a mixed diet was available, the other diseases became less evident, but in the winter of 1848 typhus reappeared.

Food was imported with the aid of government grants and private subscriptions. Grain was brought over from America, where sympathy moved the government to convert men-of-war to carry it. Maize had been imported before the famine, but it appears likely that with an increased consumption in 1845 and successive years, cases of pellagra occurred, Crawford (1981).

Emigration to England and to the United States was on a scale not witnessed before. Deaths on the voyage and in the first few weeks after landing were numerous. Thus, 136 died

TABLE 37.5.1. Emigration from Ireland to Canada.

Out of 89,738 emigrants embarked	
Deaths on the passage	5,293
at the quarantine station	3,452
at the Quebec Emigrant Hospital	1,041
at the Montreal Emigrant Hospital	3,579
at Kingston and Toronto	1,965
	15,330

From C. Trevelyan (1848, p.144)

out of 493 passengers crossing on the Erin Queen, 246 out of 522 on the Avon, 267 out of 476 on the Virginia, and 500 out of 600 on some unnamed ship, according to d'Alton (1910, Vol.5, p.209). Many died after landing in America (see also §42.6). Trevelyan (1848) has given statistics of emigrants leaving for Canada, which we cite as Table 37.5.1.

See also for economic history, O'Brien (1918, 1919, 1921); "land war" in Ireland, Godkin (1870); poor in Limerick, Griffin (1841); famine, Woodham-Smith (1962), Johnson (1957–1958); slums in Dublin, Wall (1973b).

Chapter 38
Continental Europe

38.1 France

According to Vincent (1947), a census of the French kingdom was prescribed in 1693, a time of severe food shortage. France was divided into *généralités*, with chief royal agents, the *intendants*, who were ordered in 1697 to prepare reports (*mémoires*) on (a) the number of towns, (b) the number of men in each, (c) the number of parishes and their populations, (d) factories and workmen, (e) training of workmen, (f) labor turnover, and (g) declines or increases of population. The answers were given in the *Projet d'une dîme royale* by Sébastien de Vauban, Marshal of France.

The Institut national de la Statistique et des Études économiques publishes annually *l'Annuaire statistique de la France* (formerly *Statistique générale de la France*) and also *Bulletin de la Statistique générale de la France*. The Institut national d'Études démographiques publishes *Population* and occasional publications *Cahiers de Travaux et Documents*. La Société statistique de Paris publishes *Journal de la Société statistique de Paris*.

38.2 Parish Mortality in France

Goubert (1960, 1965a,b, 1968) points out that demographic information about France is partly complete after 1750, whereas prior to that time it is still scanty. His conclusions in Goubert (1965a), which we cite, are founded largely on his own studies in Beauvais and on those of L. Henry, in particular the study on the parish of Crulai in Normandy published in Gautier and Henry (1958). In the absence of reliable censuses or any centralized statistical system, Goubert's conclusions are based on parish records. In the parishes there was a general tendency for the annual number of baptisms to increase during the sixteenth century, although there were great crises of subsistence in 1545, 1566, 1586–1587, and 1597 in Saint-Lambert des Levées, in which years the annual baptisms decreased to less than 100, compared with a more common number of about 140 in the better years.

After discussing a number of such parish series, Goubert decided that neither the subsistence crises nor the Wars of Religion were sufficient to halt the population growth in the sixteenth century; in some areas the population may have doubled. The increase of population seems to have been most intense in the prosperous areas, particularly those providing hemp and linen cloth for export to Spain. Baptisms and births definitely increased during the wars, except during the decade 1590–1599, when they declined almost everywhere to various degrees. It appears that civilian losses in the religious wars have been exaggerated by historians. General crisis of subsistence occurred in 1591, 1597, and 1598.

The seventeenth century was darkened in the years before 1670 by the Thirty Years War, 1618–1648, and by the damage caused by thieving and pillaging armies. Plague was still endemic and sometimes caused large numbers of deaths, but these setbacks were insufficient to prevent an upsurge in the number of births. Goubert (1968) states that the following is a sound assessment for the years 1660–1704:

(*i*) the crude birth rate was almost 40 per 1,000 in the country;

(*ii*) the masculinity of births, avoiding sampling errors, was in general the same as in more modern times, although there sometimes appear to be systematic differences;

(*iii*) the twinning rate was about the same as in the twentieth century;

(*iv*) illegitimacy was quite low in the countryside, often less than 1%;

(*v*) nearly one quarter of the children died in the first year of life;

(*vi*) perhaps only 50% of children reached age 20 years, that is, $l_{20} = 0.5$, $l_0 = 1$;

(*vii*) the marriage rate was high, and the celibacy rate was low;

(*viii*) women did not begin to bear children until an older age;

(*ix*) marital fertility was about once in 30 months;

(*x*) the average number of births per completed family was between 4 and 5;

(*xi*) the rate of replacement of the generations fluctuated about unity.

For the seventeenth century as a whole, Goubert notes that children died chiefly in the summer and early autumn, presumably from gastrointestinal disorders, and old people died mainly from respiratory infections in the winter. Most epidemics struck between May and October. Famine deaths occurred throughout the year, and its effects were often difficult to separate from the epidemics. In some areas there were great epidemics of "dysentery," possibly associated with dietary defects, principally affecting the children. The demographic crises were evidently due to many diverse causes; between 1640 and 1740, they seem to have been associated with shortage of grain, made evident by high prices; in these, mortality among infants and children was particularly high, and there were reductions in conceptions and births. There would thus be a gap in the childbearing-age classes of 30 years later. Goubert believes that too much emphasis

should not be placed on cyclical changes in population; on the contrary, events in the long run are determined by what happens in the short run, and we add "if long term climatic changes are not evident."

A rather arbitrary selection of references is now given, classified by time and geographical area.

Middle Ages. Demography of villages, Higounet-Naval (1980); in Provence, Baratier (1961).

Sixteenth and Seventeenth Centuries: demographic crises in the south of the Paris region (1560–1670), Moriceau (1980); St. Trond in 1635, Ruwet (1957); Sainghin-en-Mélantois (1665–1851), Deniel and Henry (1965); infant mortality in late seventeenth century, Bourdelais and Raulot (1976); demographic crises 1590–1790, Ruwet (1954).

Eighteenth Century: Anjou, Lebrun (1971); doctors, climate, and epidemics, Desaive, Goubert, et al. (1972); Duravel, Leymond (1967); Sainghin-en-Mélantois, Deniel and Henry (1965); population of France, Henry (1965*b*); hospitals, Greenbaum (1975); infant mortality variations, Bideau, Brunet, and Desbos (1978); epidemics in Brittany, Goubert (1972); disease and doctors in Brittany, Goubert (1974); infant mortality, 1774–1794, Galliano (1966).

Nineteenth Century: hygiene in France, 1815–1848, Ackerknecht (1948*b*); population of France, Pouthas (1956); inequality in mortality, Vedrenne-Villeneuve (1961); infant mortality in Paris, van de Walle (1974); Sainghin-en-Mélantois, Deniel and Henry (1965); infancy, Bideau, Brunet, and Desbos (1978); urban French mortality, Preston and van de Walle (1978).

Parishes: villes et villages en France (ancienne), articles in *Annales de Démographie historique* (1969); in the sixteenth century, Goubert (1965*b*); epidemics in Haute Bretagne (1770–1789), Lebrun (1977); Sologne orléanaise (1670–1870), Poitou (1978).

38.3 Statistics of Infections, France

The role of the infective diseases may be considered roughly in the order of the ICD.

Cholera. In March 1832 cholera appeared in Calais and then in Paris, 51 of the 86 departments becoming infected. Again it was active in southern France in 1834, and an epidemic occurred in Marseilles in December 1839, terminating at the end of March; in June–July another epidemic killed 1,500 persons. All of France was said to be involved in 1849, according to Pollitzer (1959). In 1854 cholera was present in southern France. In September 1865 it appeared in Paris but there were "only about 10,000 victims" in the whole of France. In July 1865 it was noted in Marseilles, and in 1892 it appeared in northern France including Paris.

Enteric Fever. This group of diseases was early recognized as an entity, dothinentérie, by Bretonneau in 1819, who demonstrated the Peyer's patches and defended the concept of a specific transmissible agent; he also described the progress of an epidemic. He is said also to have suspected that typhus (a petechial pyrexia with a more rapid course) was often mistaken for enteric fever. J. Bertillon's series of deaths in Paris in Levasseur (1889–1892, vol. 2, p. 116) is of interest; for the years 1865–1887, the enteric deaths were 65; 53, 48, 51, 54, 132 (in 1870); 243, 54, 56, 43, 53; 102, 61, 40, 53, 59; 87, 143, 88, 67, 58; 42, and 61 (in 1887). The deaths were especially numerous in 1870 at the time of the siege of Paris and in the following year. The mortality rates in Paris for 1882–1886, that is, between the censuses of 1881 and 1886, were 823 per 1,000,000 per annum.

Dysentery and Diarrhea. The death rate from "diarrhée, athrepsie, and entérite" in Paris, 1882–1886, was 2,181 per 1,000,000 per annum (Levasseur, 1889–1892, vol. 2, p. 117).

Tuberculosis. As we have noted in §7.1, J.A. Villemin in 1865 injected tuberculous material from a human case, producing the characteristic lesions in rabbits. Louis (1844) did much to clarify the knowledge of the progress of the disease. Pulmonary and other forms of tuberculosis caused 4,841 deaths per 1,000,000 per annum in Paris during 1882–1886 and was the leading cause of death. For cities (other than Paris) of population greater than 20,000, the tuberculosis rate was 3,863; for cities of 10,000 to 20,000 inhabitants, the tuberculosis death rate was 2,639 per 1,000,000 per annum. Tuberculosis in Paris was indeed responsible for 20.4% of the total mortality, but in the two other city groups it was 15.2% and 10.6%, according to pp. 116–117 of Levasseur. Springett (1950) has given the tuberculosis death rates for Paris for 5 quinquennia over the years 1889–1933, showing that the maxima for the successive generations from 1876 have fallen into the 15–24 age group from the original 35–44 age group for males. The maximum for females in the 1876 generation was at ages 25–34 but fell into the 15–24 age group in the later generations. The generation method also explains the maximum at the oldest age in 1929–1933.

The later progress of tuberculosis in France can be traced in Moine and Oudet (1947), cited in Springett (1950). For the history, see also Pièry and Roshen (1931).

Bubonic Plague. Biraben (1975–1976) has given a detailed account of the bubonic plague (the Black Death). The pandemic of Justinian's time reached Arles and the Lyonnais in AD 541; in AD 571, it is mentioned as being in Lyon, Brioude, Bourges, Châlon-sur-Saône, Dijon, Clermont, and Randan; in 580, 581, and 582 it is mentioned in Marseilles and Arles, and in 654, in Marseilles. Now these are some of the extant mentions of it; the reality may well be that small epizootics were happening among the rats throughout the whole epoch 543–654, occasionally perhaps causing a few human cases until finally the epizootic came to an end. See §8.3 for a description of plague by Gregory the Great of Tours. Bubonic plague appeared again as the Black Death in November 1347 at Marseilles and in August 1348 at Paris; by the end of 1348 it had spread to most of France. The outbreak in 1720–1722 is often cited as the end of the Black Death in France, but it was active again in 1786, although by this time the epizootic was probably absent from most of western Europe.

Brucellosis. An epizootic of goats, causing abortions and severe febrile illness in human beings, occurred in southern France in December 1908 and January 1909, on which classic observations were made by Paul Cantaloube (1911). See also Spink (1956).

Anthrax. This zoonosis has been an important cause of mortality in stock and not a rare human disease in France. The causal organism was observed by F.A.A. Pollender and C.J. Davaine. Pasteur did classic work on the disease. For its control, See §8.5.

Diphtheria. Bretonneau in 1821 published his observations on an epidemic of diphtheria in Tours during the years 1818–1820. He recognized the false membrane, usually on the tonsils, but possibly elsewhere in the nasopharynx, and the toxic symptoms that appeared independently of the site of the membrane. He regarded the disease as contagious and was the first to perform a tracheotomy. In Paris, deaths per 100,000 persons per annum from 1865–1887 were 53; 45, 36, 41, 41, 27; 30, 62, 64, 53, 67; 79, 121, 93, 84, 94; 99, 100, 84, 69, 73; 67, 70, and in 1882–1886, the mortality rate was 85.9 per 100,000 per annum.

Whooping Cough. In 1882–1886, the crude annual mortality rate was 160 per 1,000,000, so whooping cough was indeed an important cause of infant and child mortality.

Scarlatina. This caused about half the mortality of whooping cough.

Wound Infections. In §9.11 we have already quoted the views of Pasteur in 1874 on the necessity for sterilizing instruments, lint, bandages, sponges, and other equipments before treating a wound, and mentioned that C.E. Chamberland carried out many experiments to devise efficient sterilization. Their work would have been greatly appreciated by the d'Alembert of 1765, whom we quote in §45.8. See Wangensteen and Wangensteen (1978, pp. 398–401).

Influenza. Levasseur (1889/1892, footnote, p. 116) mentioned that Paris had been ravaged by influenza from November 1889 to February 1890. In the first week of 1890, the number of deaths was raised to 2,683, whereas it had only been 977 in the previous week (in 1889).

Smallpox. Smallpox was still a disease to be feared in the nineteenth century, for vaccination was not universal; the death rates per 100,000 per annum are given on p.116 of Levasseur for the years 1865–1887 as 42; 32, 17, 33, 36, 521 (in 1870); 149, 5, 1, 2, 13; 19, 7, 4, 43, 99; 44, 28, 20, 3, 8; 9, 17. There was a great increase of the rates with the siege of Paris beginning in 1870 and ending in 1871, with resultant crowding in from the country and disorganization of life; but the general level of rates was high in this post-Jennerian era.

Measles. The death rates in Paris from measles per 100,000 per annum, according to Levasseur, were for the years 1865–1887: 19; 45, 34, 34, 27, 42; 32, 31, 30, 33, 34; 44, 33, 32, 43, 44; 40, 45, 49, 67, ?; ?, ?. Levasseur has marked these last three entries with queries. Note that there is no evidence of periodicity in this series. In 1882–1886 the rate was 55.9, so there had been some tendency for the rates to increase.

Rabies. Rabies is endemic in northern France but causes little human mortality.

Yellow Fever. There were outbreaks in the south of France between 1700 and 1900.

Malaria. Bruce-Chwatt and Zulueta (1980, pp. 67–81) give a history of malaria in France with many references. They point to the Camargue and the delta of the Rhône. The region became extremely unhealthy after the raids of the Saracens and remained so until the last quarter of the nineteenth century; Aigues-Mortes lost many of its inhabitants as a result of malaria and other diseases. The southwest coast of France in the valley of the Garonne and in the neighborhood of Bordeaux, where swamps and pools were maintained for the breeding of leeches, was highly malarious. The areas mentioned later provide excellent examples of the possibilities of "bonification" with drainage of swamps and reforestation being important methods. Malaria was a problem throughout France and it was endemic in Alsace and Lorraine. Peruvian bark was introduced in 1664 and its use became general after 1679. The isolation of quinine in 1820 by J.B. Caventou and J. Pelletier was a great step forward, greatly facilitating treatment. A. Laveran in Constantine (Algeria) in 1880 first saw the flagellated form of the malaria parasites in human blood. Bruce-Chwatt and Zulueta (1980) cite an author who believed that intermittent fever (malaria) caused 0.63% of all deaths in France in the years 1855–1857. *Falciparum* malaria was endemic only in the south of France. The authors cite many examples of the bad effects of war on malaria incidence.

38.4 Mortality in France

Space does not permit us to give such a detailed account of the mortality of France as, for example, we have given for England and Wales, and neither is our access to the literature as easy. Therefore, we confine this section to a commentary on some aspects of the literature.

Bourgeois-Pichat (1951, 1965) shows that the demographic experience of France from 1700 to 1775 can be summarized by assuming constant age-specific mortality rates for the period and an annual increase in population of 4 per 1,000. From 1805 onward, he is able to supply tables and graphs of the age-specific rates by sex for the years up to 1950. Thus, from Bourgeois-Pichat (1965, Tables 2 and 3), we find the infant mortality rates per 1,000 for males (females) were in 1805–1807, 207 (176); 1820–1822, 200 (176); 1840–1842, 172 (150); 1860–1862, 182 (156); 1880–1882, 184 (155); 1900–1902, 159 (132); 1920–1922, 118 (97); 1947–1950, 62 (49), with a continuous decrease first appearing in 1895–1897. At ages 1–4 years, the age–specific death rates were 1805–1807, 40 (39); 1820–1822, 37 (36); 1840–1842, 35 (34); 1860–1862, 33 (32); 1880–1882, 28 (27); 1900–1902, 17 (17); 1920–1922, 12 (12); 1947–1950, 3 (3), with a continuous decrease beginning in 1885–1887.

Bourgeois-Pichat (1965) remarks

Since the beginning of the nineteenth century, the mortality rates for each of the 3 age-groups 1–4, 5–14 and 15–24, have followed a very similar pattern:

a slow decline until 1890, after which it became more rapid as the discoveries of Pasteur began to have their effect. Table 6 shows, for the age-group 1–14, how the decline was distributed among the various epidemic diseases.

The reader will note the progressive disappearance of diphtheria, as a result of the perfecting of anti-diphtheria serum in 1895.

It appears that the statement in the first paragraph is rather optimistic about the direct effect of Pasteur's discoveries, and that in the second is a gross overstatement of the value of diphtheria antitoxin, for a discussion of which see §9.3. However, let us consider the death rates per 1,000 per annum for persons aged 1–4 years in Paris for the four epochs, 1886–1890, 1891–1895, 1896–1900, and 1901–1905. For diphtheria (measles) the rates are 10.9 (7.6), 6.5 (4.8), 1.7 (4.3), and 2.2 (2.7). There is a large drop from the first to the second of these epochs, before the perfection of the diphtheria antitoxin, and then a relatively greater fall to the third epoch; but then there is an actual increase (about 30%) passing to the fourth epoch, when the rate for diphtheria was about one-fifth of that in the first epoch. The measles rate declines over the same four epochs to about one-third of its initial value. Scarlet fever rates decline with 1.0, 0.6, 0.5, and 0.3 in the same four epochs. Infant mortality was declining from about 1896. Bourgeois-Pichat (1965, Table 7) is of interest, for it shows that if Geneva before 1789 can be compared with 1817–1821 in Paris, then the percentage of deaths from smallpox at ages under 1 year, 1–4, 5–14, and 15–24 years declined from 5, 26, 15, and 2, respectively, to 1, 7, 11, and 2, respectively. This shows that vaccination was important in lowering death rates.

Bourgeois-Pichat (1965) comments that improvement at the older ages was not as great as at ages younger than 24 years. A masculinity appears in all these rates after 1860. He believes that tuberculosis, natural genetic frailty, and alcohol consumption in males are all important factors in these differences between the sexes.

Monnier (1974) gives a brief summary of the changes in mortality after the conclusion of World War II. The crude death rates decreased from 13.1 per 1,000 per annum in 1946–1950 to 10.7 in 1971. His Figure 1 shows that age-specific rates (all causes combined) have decreased at all ages for females, but at ages 55–59 the male rates have remained stationary. The masculinity for the death rates is over 100 at all ages; it is higher in 1966–1970 than in 1946–1950 at all ages. Indeed in 1966–1970, the masculinity is above 200 between the ages of 15 and 70 years. There has been little diminution in $_{25}q_{35}$ (i.e., the probability of death within 25 years of persons aged precisely 35 years). The expectation of life for males at age 60 years had an increase of about 1 year between 1955 and 1960, but, besides this sole increase, they have had little change, whereas the females at the same age have gained about 5 years. Deaths from influenza in 1953, 1957, 1960, and 1969 for France were approximately 13,000, 12,000, 12,000, and 15,000, respectively. Of Monnier's tables, A gives $\overset{\circ}{e}_0$ by 5-year periods from 1861–1970 and annually from 1946–1971, B gives neonatal and infant mortality rates 1935–1972, C gives life table functions by single years of age, and D gives infant mortality and $\overset{\circ}{e}_0$ by sex and Département.

The following are references on general mortality in France.

Mortality rates: Villermé (1828); mortality since World War II: Pressat (1954), Vallin (1974); generation death rates since 1899: Vallin (1972); 1968–1974 by cause: Vallin and Nizard (1978); campaign against death: INED/PUF (1984), Vallin and Lopez (1985); report on French demographic condition: Institut national d'Études démographiques (1977); masculinity: Garros and Bouvier (1978); Paris social mortality gradient: Stevenson (1921); maladies and deaths: Grmek (1969); historical: Goubert (1976); infant mortality in the north, Girard, Henry, and Nistri (1959); infant mortality, measurement, Bourgeois (1946), Bourgeois-Pichat (1951); 1968–1972: Zbořilová (1977); adult mortality: Ledermann (1946); influenza at Bordeaux, 1918: Guillaume (1978); alcoholism: Ledermann (1956, 1958, 1964), Ledermann and Tabah (1951), Ledermann and Metz (1960); automobile deaths: Vallin and Chesnais (1975); effects of war: Vin-

cent (1946); bibliography 1792–1879: Bégin (1879).

38.5 Other European States

It is impractical to give a discussion in detail of the other European states, that is, excluding the British Isles, France, and the Scandinavian countries. Nevertheless, they have come under discussion in various parts of the text, as may be seen from the index. We give in Table 38.5.1 the age- and sex-specific death rates for two postwar epochs for countries not discussed in detail in the text. For them, a few references that have been collected are classified by country.

Belgium

Infant mortality: André and Gyselings (1971), Masuy-Stroobart (1983); demography: Quetelet (1827); nineteenth century demography: André and Pereira-Roque (1974); life tables: Quetelet (1849, 1870); mortality trends: Gabriel (1955).

Czechoslovakia

Infant mortality: Zbořilová (1977); mortality: US National Center for Health Statistics (1969).

Germany

Dresden Bills of Mortality: Sprengell (1733); great European towns: Sprengell (1723); urban mortality: Peller (1920); the years gained: Imhof (1981); man and body: Imhof (1983); infant and maternal mortality: Imhof (1984); sixteenth and twentieth centuries: Imhof (1985a); mortality problems: Imhof (1985b).

Hungary

epidemics to 1831: Schultweiss and Tardy (1966); increasing mortality: Compton (1985); mortality and population: McKeown, Brown, and Record (1972).

Italy

sixteenth century: Belletini (1980); demographic history: Beloch (1937–1961).

TABLE 38.5.1. Age specific death rates (deaths per 10,000 per annum).

Country	Year	All ages	0	1–4	5–9	10–14	15–19	20–24	25–34	35–44	45–54	55–64	65–74
							Males						
Austria	1950	136	796	30	10	8	18	23	23	41	98	231	538
	1976	129	197	8	4	4	16	18	19	34	80	189	521
Belgium	1950	135	629	22	7	7	13	19	24	40	100	233	513
	1976	130	195	8*	4	4	12	14	13	25	71	204	530
Bulgaria	1953	98	194	54	13	11	19	25	23	35	74	—	—
	1976	109	314	13*	5	5	9	12	15	27	70	170	468
Czechoslovakia	1958	100	330	15	6	6	12	17	17	28	75	214	519
	1975	124	239	8	5	4	10	14	17	36	86	224	584
France	1948	133	615	33	10	8	14	22	29	48	101	214	485
	1976	112	140	7	4	4	12	18	16	32	84	197	439
G.D.R[†]	1950	133	877	37	15	11	19	28	27	43	82	187	463
	1976	137	167	7	5	4	11	16	15	29	72	186	530
G.F.R.[‡]	1950	115	680	26	9	8	14	20	23	36	83	192	470
	1977	119	173	8	5	4	13	17	15	29	73	183	497
Greece	1951	79	481	32	14	8	11	23	26	34	71	159	356
	1976	94	260	7	4	4	8	10	11	18	49	142	349
Hungary	1949	123	1,077	46	15	12	21	35	36	53	102	214	498
	1977	134	294	7	4	4	11	14	18	40	97	215	553
Italy	1949	110	729	50*	13	11	15	21	23	37	84	183	416
	1976	107	205	6	4	4	10	11	11	24	72	177	446
Netherlands	1948	78	324	22	8	7	10	22	15	24	58	140	375
	1977	89	109	6	4	3	9	10	8	19	56	161	430
Poland	1955	103	969	35*	11	9	15	22	26	41	90	249	594
	1976	98	278	9	5	4	10	17	22	42	95	207	515
Portugal	1948	137	1,312	143	24	14	26	50	45	70	119	223	530
	1975	116	424	21	9	7	16	23	23	43	89	198	480
Romania	1956	104	960	53	12	11	15	21	22	35	81	212	546
	1976	100	415	23*	8	6	11	14	17	32	72	174	460
Spain	1948	119	1,032	85	17	14	27	51	48	61	112	216	517
	1974	90	160	9	5	4	9	12	14	27	64	164	452
Switzerland	1948	112	419	25	12	9	13	19	21	35	88	209	538
	1977	96	122	6	4	4	10	17	13	21	57	147	397
Yugoslavia	1950	140	1,317	110	23	16	28	47	48	60	114	235	499
	1975	92	436	17	6	5	8	13	17	32	77	189	478
							Females						
Austria	1950	113	612	27	8	6	11	15	17	29	61	137	393
	1976	124	157	6	3	2	5	6	7	16	39	97	281
Belgium	1950	117	531	25	9	8	11	16	21	30	61	143	389
	1976	113	147	7*	3	3	5	5	7	15	39	91	271
Bulgaria	1953	86	770	57	12	9	16	21	21	28	47	124	397
	1976	93	231	11*	4	4	4	6	7	14	39	99	323
Czechoslovakia	1958	87	251	13	4	3	6	7	9	19	45	115	357
	1975	105	183	6	4	3	4	4	6	15	41	106	322
France	1948	115	466	29	8	6	11	17	22	30	56	122	316
	1976	99	105	6	3	2	5	6	7	15	35	75	199
G.D.R[†]	1950	109	690	31	10	7	13	19	23	31	48	113	340
	1976	142	123	6	3	3	5	6	7	16	41	100	318
G.F.R.[‡]	1950	99	527	22	7	5	9	13	16	26	55	133	397
	1977	111	135	6	3	2	6	6	7	15	38	88	252
Greece	1951	72	465	28	10	6	11	17	20	27	48	103	273
	1976	85	205	7	3	3	4	5	6	11	27	73	223

TABLE 38.5.1. (continued).

Country	Year	All ages	0	1–4	5–9	10–14	15–19	20–24	25–34	35–44	45–54	55–64	65–74
Hungary	1949	107	863	41	13	10	20	28	28	36	67	153	419
	1977	117	232	6	3	2	4	5	8	19	49	116	330
Italy	1949	100	626	49*	11	9	13	16	20	29	55	130	380
	1976	90	163	5	3	3	4	4	6	13	34	82	230
Netherlands	1948	70	251	18	5	4	6	8	12	21	46	112	336
	1977	70	80	5	3	2	3	4	5	12	32	72	201
Poland	1955	105	765	32*	9	6	9	13	15	27	54	85	193
	1976	80	209	7	4	2	4	5	7	16	40	98	283
Portugal	1948	123	1,193	139	20	15	27	34	34	44	69	174	363
	1975	93	332	18	6	4	5	6	8	17	39	91	274
Romania	1956	96	824	53	11	8	10	14	18	29	60	145	439
	1976	92	355	19*	5	4	6	8	10	18	42	107	326
Spain	1948	101	845	79	15	13	23	34	33	42	67	135	406
	1974	80	123	7	4	3	4	5	7	14	34	83	262
Switzerland	1948	104	319	20	7	6	9	13	18	27	59	141	406
	1977	81	95	5	3	1	5	4	5	10	28	67	193
Yugoslavia	1950	123	1,139	110	20	15	27	40	44	47	75	168	401
	1975	82	392	17	5	3	5	6	8	18	41	109	325

*Data not available in the UN tables, so data from a nearby year used.
†German Democratic Republic.
‡German Federal Republic.
Data from UN–historical (1979). Copyright (1979), United Nations. Reproduced by permission.

Netherlands

Infant mortality: US National Center for Health Statistics (1968*b*).

Soviet Union

1958–1959 life tables: Myers (1965), Pressat (1963); increasing mortality: Dinkel (1985).

Spain

Plague and epidemics in late sixteenth century: Bennassar (1969).

Switzerland

Geneva: Perrenoud (1978, 1979), Valpy (1851); population history since the end of the Middle Ages: Bickel (1947).

Chapter 39
Norden

39.1 Norden: The Northern Countries

Norden is a convenient term used by geographers for the northern or nordic countries of Europe, comprising an easternmost member, Finland, the three Scandinavian members, Denmark, Norway, and Sweden and a western group, the Faeroe Islands, Iceland, and Greenland. The Faeroe Islands and Greenland are dependencies of Denmark. Of interest to us here are the high latitudes, relative isolation, and absence in the past of large urban aggregates of population. Table 39.1.1 gives the population sizes and the latitude of the principal city in each country.

There have been changes of borders between the states, but in the official statistical publications, past vital events such as births, deaths, and the marriages are given for the countries within their present boundaries. The Nordic Council and Nordic Statistical Secretariat now produce a *Yearbook of Nordic Statistics*, for example, Vol. 17 in 1978, *Nordiska Rådet* (1978). See also Sømme (1968) for a beautiful geography text. *Skandinavisk Aktuarietidskrift* had been published by the nordic actuaries since 1917; recently, it has been replaced by the *Scandinavian Journal of Statistics* and the *Scandinavian Actuarial Journal*. Many medical, statistical, and genetical monographs have been published as supplements to the leading nordic journals (*Acta*).

Norden has been greatly affected by changes in climate. In the climatic optimum about AD 800 to 1000 the seas were calmer, and the growing of crops and cattle breeding could be carried out in lands where they would now be uneconomic. All these countries are vulnerable to a fall in the mean temperature and suffered considerable hardships during the Little Ice Age of 1550–1850. Famine has caused many deaths in Norden, especially in the more northerly regions, even since 1850. Specific examples are given below for the individual countries. See Utterström (1954, 1955, 1961).

Before 1850 only Copenhagen could have been called a large city. There is a relatively homogeneous population within each of the countries. The censuses of 1950 showed 2,500 Lapps in Finland, 10,200 in Sweden, and 9,000 in Norway, where, however, only those having Lappish as their home language were recorded as Lapps; in 1930, with different definitions, 19,100 Lapps were enumerated in Norway. In Finland there was a Swedish minority of 331,000 in 1960, about 8% of the population. Finns in Sweden in 1966 were about 47,000. In Greenland there is a Danish minority of about 8%.

The relative isolation has meant that some infective diseases, especially measles and smallpox, have caused intensive epidemics with many deaths. This effect has been especially important in the Faeroe Islands, Iceland, and Greenland, and a number of such "virgin soil" epidemics have been reported principally by Danish observers.

TABLE 39.1.1. Population in Norden.

Country	Latitude of principal city	Population (in thousands)							
		1800	1850	1900	1940	1950	1960	1970	1980
Denmark*	56°N	929[†]	1,415	2,450[‡]	3,844	4,281	4,585	4,951	5,120
Faeroe Islands	62°N	5[†]	8	15[‡]	27	32	35	39	40
Finland	60°N	833	1,637	2,656	3,696	4,030	4,446	4,598	4,788
Greenland	64°N	6[§]	8[‖]	12[¶]	19	24	33	47	50
Iceland	64°N	47	59	78	121	144	176	205	231
Norway	60°N	883	1,400	2,240	2,982	3,280	3,595	3,888	4,092
Sweden	59°N	2,347	3,483	5,136	6,371	7,042	7,498	8,081	8,310

* Excluding Faeroe Islands.
[†] 1801.
[‡] 1901.
[§] 1805.
[‖] 1834.
[¶] 1901 and excluding North Greenland.
Data, except the second and final columns, from the Nordisk statistisk Årsbok (Yearbook of Nordic Statistics), vol. 11, p. 28, Stockholm, 1972.

39.2 Greenland

The Norsemen settled in Greenland during the climatic optimum in 985 or 986. At the height of their prosperity, they numbered about 3,000 on 280 farms in the presently named districts of Julianehaab and Godthaab. At this time the Eskimos were migrating south and the two groups were in contact near Diskofjord. Cattle breeding and fishing were the main occupations of the Norsemen. From 1200 onward the climate deteriorated, and the breeding of cattle became difficult; the last Norse vessel is said to have returned from Greenland to Iceland in 1410. Skeletal remains, investigated in recent years, indicate that malnutrition and famine, rather than conquest by the Eskimos, may have caused their final extinction. It is believed that the Norsemen never learned to live on the ice in the Eskimo style. It is of interest that some of the Norse burials were made in ground, now permafrost. The dissolution of this civilization seems to have been entirely due to climatic changes.

Greenland is now inhabited by the Eskimos, who have had some admixture with European stock. Denmark assumed sovereignty over Greenland in 1729 and formally incorporated it into Denmark in 1953. The first census was held in 1805. Estimates of population are 30,000 in 1700, 20,000 in 1746, 7,000 in 1764, 5,122 in 1789, 6,046 in 1805, 7,356 in 1834, 9,586 in 1870, 11,190 in 1901, and 24,018 in 1951. On the east coast, there are now only two settlements with 612 inhabitants at Angmassalik and 247 at Scoresbysund in 1960. The population of North Greenland near Thule was 560.

The mortality data on Greenland are few. Bertelsen (1920–1921) gave a table of death rates for 1851–1900 that is reprinted as Table 39.2.1 It is evident that the death rates at all ages are much higher than the contemporary European rates and that there are sex differentials at all ages. Without further enquiry, one can only suggest that this high masculinity reflects the hazards of hunting and fishing in harsh conditions. Nørregaard and Schmidt (1975) calculate the expectation of life at birth for females at various epochs as 20.3 years in 1834, 16.8 in 1840, 29.3 in 1845, 26.8 in 1855, 14.1 in 1860, 20.1 in 1881, 23.5 in 1890, 35.8 in 1901, 31.8 in 1911, 20.6 in 1921, 35.9 in 1930, and 32.7 in 1945; these figures are strikingly low, and if we observe the masculinities in Table 39.2.1, it is clear that the expectations

TABLE 39.2.1. Mortality rates in Greenland (deaths per 1,000 per annum).

Age	North Greenland 1861–1900		South Greenland 1861–1900	
	M	F	M	F
0–4	55	48	95	84
5–9	11	11	12	11
10–14	10	6	10	8
15–19	18	8	24	11
20–24	30	17	38	18
25–29	27	14	41	18
30–34	31	22	30	24
35–39	27	24	34	28
40–44	29	22	42	30
45–49	43	23	53	33
50–54	59	35	71	47
55–59	61	50	85	64
60–64	111	74	109	79
65–69	138	75	117	113
70–74	250	119	283	254
75–79	400	194	?	425
80–84	?	350	?	?

Data from Bertelsen (1920–1921)

for males would be even less. Nørregaard and Schmidt (1975) report that there were moderate rates of mortality round the turn of the century associated with a stable and secure supply of food and with an absence of epidemics. Influenza epidemics were reported for 1860 and 1920. Measles epidemics, occurring in 1945, 1951, 1953, and 1954, have been reported by Fog-Poulsen (1957), Christensen, et al. (1953), and Bech (1962). Bertelsen (1920–1921) remarks that only a very rough estimate of the numbers of deaths by cause can be made. About one-third of the total is due to tuberculosis, another third falls on children younger than 5 years of age, one-sixth is due to accidents and deaths at birth, and the remaining sixth is due to epilepsy, carbuncles, cancer, and other disease. About 5 per 1,000 per annum of males die from accidents, about 80% of these being drownings. Westergaard (1880) gives comparisons between the general mortalities in Greenland and Denmark.

For Eskimos, see also Fortuine (1971), Malaurie, Tabah, and Sutter (1952), Schaefer (1981), and Stefansson (1958); for tuberculosis, see Iversen (1971). For the separation of

the Eskimos from the Aleuts ca 10,000 BP and for their migrations, see Laughlin, Jørgensen, and Frøhlich (1979).

39.3 Iceland

At the time of the settlement by Norsemen and Celts in AD 870–930, Iceland was "wooded between coast and mountain," but much of this cover has since been lost through grazing, by sheep principally, and tree felling. Natural climatic changes and vulcanism have aided this denudation so that less than 20,000 km² is not bare. Barley disappeared at the end of the sixteenth century and has not yet been reestablished; other cereals have not been grown. The food supply has thus depended on the raising of sheep and cattle, with the aid of stored hay, and fishing in fresh and ocean waters, including whale fishing.

Estimates of the population are given as 30,000 in AD 930, 75,000 in AD 1100, and 75,000 in AD 1300. Although Iceland has been a poor country, the population has been highly literate. The first census, indeed the first in modern Europe, was held in 1703; the population was enumerated as 50,358 in 1703, 47,240 in 1801, 59,157 in 1850, 70,927 in 1890, and 213,070 in 1973.

The most serious disaster was the epidemic of bubonic plague; surprisingly, the Black Death did not reach Iceland until 1402, when the population was possibly 120,000; in 1404, it had decreased to 40,000. Plague was again introduced by English ships and raged in 1493–1495.

A series of volcanic eruptions with great destruction of life, farms, churches, houses, and stock occurred in the eighteenth century (Bjarnar, 1965). The culmination of the series was the eruption of Laki in 1783, which resulted in the deaths of almost 80% of the horses and sheep and 50% of the cattle from lack of fodder; as a result, the population decreased by over 9,000 in the 2 years 1784 and 1785.

Civil disturbances occurred in the late fourteenth century. Finally, the islanders were overcome by the forces of Christian III of Denmark in 1541 and again in 1550.

More important than either the volcanic disturbances or the civil strife was the deterioration of the climate, which set in from about 1550. According to Lamb (1966), the 1590s, the 1690s and 1780s were years of dearth in Scotland and Scandinavia generally. Thus, Thorsteinsson (1929) says that in the 1690s the polar ice had drifted close against the shores, the fisheries had entirely failed, and many livestock had succumbed to the severity of the winters. Many paupers had died. In 1701 there had been 7 years of scarcity and the previous year had been the worst. Winters were very severe also in 1751–1757, but the climate improved somewhat, late in the century. Before the disappearance of whales from the North Atlantic Ocean, some mitigation of famines was possible because meat could be obtained by the killing of whales in the bays, but by the beginning of the nineteenth century, this emergency source of food had disappeared. According to Bryson (1974), there were 5 famine years between 1250 and 1390, 12 between 975 and 1500, and 37 between 1500 and 1804, only 3 of which occurred in the sixteenth century.

Deaths from drownings have been a special feature of the mortality in Iceland, but much has been done to reduce the number of these deaths by the provision of modern equipment in the fishing fleets, warning systems, and other aids to navigation.

Iceland has been able to reduce an originally high incidence of hydatid infection in sheep and men by effective public health measures, including the exclusion of dogs, the intermediate host of the parasite, from the island.

Iceland was an isolated area before the modern era of fast sea and air transport; moreover, the population was not large enough to perpetuate such diseases as smallpox and measles. It therefore has provided classic examples of island epidemics (see §5.4), already recognized by Schleisner (1851) and Jonsson (1944), for example; and Iceland has records of incidence of all the common infective diseases going back to 1811. Schleisner (1851) found that 134 years in the period 1306–1846 were epidemic years. Typhus prevailed almost every year, and there was also a typhuslike fever (probably relapsing fever) occurring in famine years. Mild influenza was endemic; but a severe form occurred about once in 9 years. Typhus was also regarded as endemic. Smallpox raged 19 times, often for successive years, 3 times in the fourteenth century, once in the fifteenth, 5 times in the sixteenth, 5 times in the seventeenth, 4 times in the eighteenth, and once in the nineteenth century, that is, 1801–1846. It is said to have caused 18,000 deaths in 1707 out of a population of 52,000 inhabitants. Dixon (1962) states that there were 1,600 deaths from smallpox in 1310–1311.

Schleisner (1851) wrote that measles had been brought to Iceland "three years ago," which possibly should be interpreted as 1846, 3 years before writing the paper in 1849; in 1846 the infant mortality was 654 per 1,000 and the crude death rate 55.8 per 1,000 per annum. Measles had not been present for 60 years. Schleisner (1851) remarks that the disease was spread by contagion, an observation made possible because of the mountains intersecting the country. In recent times measles was present, with 2 and 25 cases in 1895 and 1896; from 1903 to 1910, there were reported cases of 3, 802, 36, 7, 6,492, 905, 27, and 2. It was absent in 1911 and again in 1914 and 1915; there were 22 cases in 1912, 5 in 1913, 4,535 (92 deaths) in 1916, and 401 (26 deaths) in 1917. It seems evident that measles was reintroduced several times without producing epidemics, even though there were many susceptibles. See also Babbott and Gordon (1954).

Rubella has caused epidemics of births of children with congenital cataract and deafness, which have been reported by Sigurjonsson (1961, 1962), who related them to appropriate epidemics of rubella. See also Sigurdsson and Tomasson (1968). Rubella appears to have been present in more years than measles.

Varicella is better adapted to persist in island communities because of the possibility of it lying dormant and then erupting as herpes zoster; it has been present every year.

Scarlet fever and whooping cough occurred in epidemics with gaps of perhaps 20 or more years and were quite unknown in the intervening periods.

In 1528 and 1551 an epidemic, called "sárásott" by the Icelanders, occurred, which

Schleisner (1851) believed was syphilis. Syphilis was said to be no longer endemic in Iceland in 1846. Typhus was mentioned as a severe epidemic 15 times, influenza, 15 times, dysentery, 5 times, and diseases occasioned by famine, 8 times.

Crude death rates per 1,000 were high in some years even in the nineteenth century, for example, 54.6 in 1843, 55.8 in 1846, and 48.4 in 1860.

39.4 Faeroe Islands

This small group of islands, between the Shetland Islands and Iceland at 61°N and 62°N, has a rainfall of about 150 cm per annum distributed over 280 rainy days. Seventeen islands were inhabited in 1880. Communications with the mainland are difficult, so that isolation has been a marked feature of their demographic history. Westergaard (1880) gives a table of mortality rates by 5-year age groups and by sex for the years 1855–1874. These rates were lower than comparable rates for the whole kingdom and for the rural districts of Denmark, and were also lower than those for England, except at ages 15–50 years when deaths from injury and accident caused the Faeroe rates to be higher. The rates were particularly favorable to the Faeroes in infancy and early childhood. As Utterström (1954) comments, the Faeroes suffer from an extreme degree of isolation, but the model of a large reservoir of susceptibles because of isolation is also relevant for the study of mortality in Sweden, in which large epidemics of measles and smallpox have occurred.

Panum (1847) established, from an investigation of the epidemic of 1846, that measles was infective from person to person and that an incubation period of about 14 days elapsed between infection and the appearance of an exanthem (i.e. rash) when the patient was infective. He believed that the immunity provoked by the disease was of long standing and that elderly persons, who had had the disease at the time of an epidemic in 1781, were immune. It is now known that a second attack of measles is comparatively rare.

Panum (1847) noted that in the Faeroes, there

TABLE 39.4.1. Drowning in Norden.

	Iceland	Faeroe Islands	Denmark
Total number drowned from 1835–1844	530	41	2,503
Average yearly number drowned	53	4	250
Number of inhabitants on an average of the censuses 1835, 1840, and 1841	57,229	7,314	1,284,817
Drowned out of 100,000 living individuals	92.6	56.1	19.5
Drowned out of 100,000 males living, between 15 and 60 years	351.6	196.9	67.3

From Schleisner (1851).

was an almost complete absence of some infective diseases that had been responsible for the loss of much life in the continental areas and that this was reflected in the mortality rates, so that the expectation of life at birth was 44 years in the Faeroes against 36 years in Denmark. He considered that other aspects of hygiene were not more favorable in the Faeroes than in Denmark.

Some figures on drowning are given in Table 39.4.1.

For more comprehensive studies, see Nordal and Kristinsson (1975) and Tomasson (1977, 1980).

39.5 Norway

Historical notes are available in *Historisk Statistikk* 1978 (Oslo). Organized official statistics date back to the dual monarchy of Denmark and Norway, when a Tables Office was first set up under the auspices of the Exchequer in Copenhagen in 1797. Until 1846 the clergy was responsible for the collection of vital statistics (Backer, 1947/1948, 1961). See also the following section on Sweden and H. Gille (1949) and Ofstad (1949–1950). Official statistical returns of the deaths have been available since 1801.

Life tables have been computed for the years 1846–1855 and for the intercensal periods after 1871. Interesting tables and graphs are available in 40 pages of the *Historisk Statistikk*, including extensive tables for total mortality by 5-year age and calendar groupings since 1866 and special tables of the death rates for such particular causes as tuberculosis, total cancer, cardiovascular disease, and injury and accident. Many tables are available in Backer (1961).

Mortality (all causes). Backer (1961) discusses the Norwegian mortality since 1871. For example, her Table 154 gives the Norwegian rates in the three 10-year age groups from 45 to 74 years as being below the rates of European countries for either sex in almost every case in four representative epochs in 1871–1955. In her Table 151, the rates for other Scandinavian countries and the Netherlands tend to be lower than those of Norway for the three 10-year age groups, 15 to 44 years. Her Table 160 gives the age-specific mortality rates for some dozen cohorts and illustrates how the influenza epidemic of 1918 and the war of 1941–1945 distorted the shape of the curve for the mortality rates of the cohorts.

Tuberculosis. In Backer (1961) mortality rates from tuberculosis are studied by calendar and cohort methods, for which see also §7.9 and Springett (1950). In her Table 53, Backer gives tuberculosis death rates at ages 1–4 years, from 1871 to 1955, from which it seems that 1886 should be chosen as the year of the commencement of the decline in mortality at these ages and, by the cohort theory, as the real date of commencement of the decline in tuberculosis. This is confirmed, to some extent, by the rates for males (females) at ages 15–19, 20–29, and 30–39 years commencing their declines in 1906 (1906), 1916 (1926), and 1921 (1911), respectively, although the choice of the commencement of the decline is rather arbitrary; the same Table also shows that tuberculosis often caused more than half the deaths in the three age groups before 1916.

Backer (1961) states that tuberculosis had been the dominating cause of mortality of young adults until recently (i.e., about 1955)

and that before 1940, variations of the general mortality rates among young adults in different parts of the country were determined largely by tuberculosis and violence death rates.

Leprosy. Vogelsang (1965) gives a historical account of the incidence and therapy of leprosy in Norway. He believes that the first cases appeared ca AD 1100 and that leprosy was associated with poverty. Censuses of the lepers are available: 2,858 in 1856, 1,752 in 1875, 688 in 1896, 577 in 1900, 326 in 1910, 160 in 1920, and 69 in 1930: the disease was practically extinct by 1965. See also Skinsnes (1973), Leprosy Congress (1973), and Irgens (1981).

Smallpox. Inoculations had been successfully carried out in some parishes in the diocese of Bergen before 1800, for which see §11.2. Drake (1969, p.53) quotes some severe epidemics in some Norwegian towns, but there are more data available from Sweden, which we consider in §39.7.

Measles. See §39.7.

Famine. The climate is, after Denmark, milder than in the other nordic countries. According to Drake (1969), there are difficulties in assessing the diet of eighteenth century Norway. Three leading types of diet were fish, grain (mainly barley and oats), and animal products (mainly milk and cheese). The potato had been introduced into Norway before 1735 and by the 1750s enough was produced to feed more than one-fifth of the population; some of it was used to produce alcohol. In western Norway, where the chief item of food was fish, there was failure of the herring and cod in the last few years of the eighteenth century and much disturbance through a blockade by the English fleet in 1807–1814. These events encouraged greater use of the potato in western Norway, although it had been introduced there about 1760.

After 1749 crude death rates increased to more than 29 per 1,000 per annum on few occasions: 38.8, 29.1, 30.2, and 30.4 in 1763–1766, 48.1 in 1773, 33.3 in 1785, 30.6 in 1789, 35.3 in 1809, and after 1815 there were no years of more than 23.0. The grain harvest failed in 1741–1744, 1748, and 1773, and during 1797–

1806, especially 1801, 1803, and 1804. The famine position was complicated by epidemics of typhus and dysentery on the return of the soldiers in 1808, and high mortality was experienced in 1809.

For the historical demography of Norway, see Dyrvik (1972); for the official statistics, see Norway Central Bureau (1974).

39.6 Denmark

References have come to hand more rarely for Denmark than for the other Scandinavian countries. The experience of Denmark is more that of part of a continent, whereas the other Scandinavian countries can be considered rather as a collection of isolated areas. There is a splendid cover of the neoplasms in Clemmesen (1965), and for infant mortality the reader is referred to US National Center for Health Statistics (1967b). The dependencies of Denmark have been treated in other sections.

39.7 Sweden

The Central Bureau publishes the *Statistisk Årsbok för Sverige* (yearbook), *Statistisk Tidskrift* (review), *Statistiska Meddelanden* (reports), and *Historisk Statistik för Sverige* (historical statistics). The last volume summarizes the vital statistics from 1720 to the present time. The National Board of Health publishes an annual report.

According to the official publication *Historisk Statistik för Sverige* (1955), the organization of the official statistics was presribed in the Royal Decree of November 10, 1748. The collection and preparation of the tables were not centralized. Parish data were combined for the rural deaneries, then for the dioceses and counties, and finally for the whole country. This decree had been foreshadowed in a church law of 1686, and the first compilations based on parish registers were made in 1721, although the data remained meager until 1750. Some further impetus to the development of statistics was provided by the misery and distress of the Great Northern War of 1700–1721. The first census for Sweden and Finland was taken in 1749. Causes of death are available

from 1749. See Grönlund (1949) and Hofsten and Lundström (1976). Wargentin (1766) calculated the first national set of age-specific fertility rates; see Dupâquier (1977). Much later work has been expended in extending or creating new tables from the original data. Thus, the Tabellkommission extracted the number of deaths by cause since 1749 (*Bidrag till Sveriges officiella statistik*, 1857); Sundbärg (1907/1970) summarized his studies on the vital statistics of past years, which he had published in the *Statistisk Tidskrift* over a number of years, and Heckscher (1936) made compilations for the years 1720–1750.

The Central Bureau of Statistics, Statistiska Centralbyrån, publishes data on the censuses held in Sweden in years ending in a zero or five (i.e., 1980, 1975, 1970, . . .). See Kock (1959).

TABLE 39.7.1. Crude death rates in Sweden (deaths per 10,000 per annum).

	0	1	2	3	4	5	6	7	8	9
174–										281
175–	269	262	273	240	263	274	277	299	324	263
176–	248	258	312	329	272	277	251	256	272	272
177–	261	278	374	525	224	248	225	249	267	285
178–	217	256	273	281	298	283	259	240	267	331
179–	305	255	239	243	236	279	247	238	231	252
180–	314	261	237	238	249	235	275	262	349	400
181–	316	288	303	274	251	236	227	243	244	274
182–	245	256	226	210	208	205	226	231	267	290
183–	241	260	234	217	257	186	200	247	241	236
184–	204	194	211	215	203	188	218	237	197	198
185–	198	207	227	237	198	215	218	276	217	201
186–	177	185	214	193	203	194	200	196	210	223
187–	198	172	163	172	203	203	196	187	181	169
188–	181	177	174	173	175	178	166	161	160	160
189–	171	168	179	168	164	152	156	154	151	177
190–	168	161	154	151	153	156	144	146	149	137
191–	140	138	142	137	138	147	136	134	180	145
192–	133	124	128	114	120	117	118	127	120	122
193–	117	125	116	112	112	117	120	120	115	115
194–	114	113	99	102	110	108	105	108	98	100
195–	100	99	96	97	96	95	96	99	96	95
196–	100	98	102	101	100	101	101	101	104	104
197–	99	102	104	105	106	108	110	107	108	110
198–	110									

Data from B.R. Mitchell, *European Historical Statistics, 1750–1970*, pp. 104–124. Copyright 1975, The Macmillan Press Ltd., reprinted with permission.

TABLE 39.7.2. Age-specific death rates for Sweden, 1751–1980 (per 100,000 mean population).

Year	1–2 (yr)	3–4	0–4	5–9	10–14	15–19	20–24	25–29	30–34	35–39	40–44	45–49	50–54	55–59	60–64	65–69	70–74	75–79	80–
								Males											
1751–1760	5,159	2,735	8,842	1,306	651	672	924	1,021	1,157	1,237	1,725	1,984	2,538	3,145	4,177	5,275	8,425	12,283	21,413
1761–1770	5,263	2,831	9,228	1,343	697	694	926	1,065	1,202	1,264	1,707	2,028	2,656	3,046	4,347	6,067	8,903	12,263	23,209
1771–1780	6,259	3,274	9,245	1,648	941	830	1,058	1,196	1,333	1,366	1,786	2,089	2,688	3,152	4,549	7,053	10,028	13,114	22,258
1781–1790	5,711	3,016	8,840	1,450	812	814	1,054	1,278	1,382	1,450	1,805	2,095	2,574	3,143	4,573	7,072	9,777	13,923	22,585
1791–1800	4,832	2,339	8,329	1,075	520	564	776	858	986	1,100	1,482	1,863	2,350	2,982	4,512	6,232	10,119	15,450	26,311
1801–1810	5,247	2,381	8,426	1,262	756	768	1,089	1,131	1,228	1,414	1,724	2,168	2,961	3,792	5,277	7,047	10,912	16,012	27,028
1811–1820	5,154	2,021	8,147	1,000	577	620	906	987	1,150	1,386	1,745	2,125	2,786	3,527	5,015	6,972	10,394	15,047	25,699
1821–1830	3,927	1,575	6,766	783	459	502	805	965	1,172	1,396	1,778	2,182	2,756	3,441	4,804	6,574	9,794	14,751	25,506
1831–1840	3,691	1,470	6,469	777	484	510	808	996	1,235	1,491	1,818	2,173	2,814	3,519	4,740	6,651	10,080	14,905	25,767
1841–1850	3,410	1,562	6,129	824	451	480	706	815	988	1,264	1,566	1,918	2,506	3,187	4,228	6,649	9,405	14,214	24,829
1851–1860	4,042	2,142	6,489	1,143	574	568	779	850	1,000	1,179	1,483	1,857	2,389	3,079	4,220	5,996	9,209	13,867	22,209
1861–1870	4,118	2,108	6,098	938	448	487	696	741	818	982	1,216	1,542	2,034	2,744	3,921	5,638	8,610	13,345	23,035
1871–1880	3,406	1,760	5,569	859	410	453	711	755	819	925	1,087	1,335	1,696	2,258	3,164	4,782	7,461	11,798	21,088
1881–1890	2,955	1,538	4,649	782	391	450	657	675	683	769	950	1,160	1,468	1,983	2,791	4,129	6,509	10,587	20,426
1891–1900	2,343	1,130	3,959	591	345	464	674	661	672	759	881	1,073	1,373	1,861	2,613	3,954	6,204	10,127	19,781
1901–1910	1,707	702	3,067	405	292	455	651	622	603	666	806	992	1,285	1,707	2,433	3,631	5,708	9,365	18,313
1911–1920	1,286	568	2,390	355	276	513	809	761	724	712	759	925	1,215	1,659	2,363	3,594	5,722	9,283	18,790
1921–1930	817	309	1,784	204	175	333	471	451	448	483	579	753	1,010	1,459	2,199	3,361	5,350	8,801	18,127
1931–1940	504	219	1,393	151	133	244	347	327	334	391	503	683	982	1,417	2,166	3,406	5,508	9,134	18,606
1941–1950	248	145	836	102	81	159	257	224	231	273	351	528	812	1,248	1,943	3,097	5,004	8,489	17,579
1951–1960	138	90	494	63	46	98	124	125	149	186	264	418	671	1,129	1,839	2,977	4,891	8,100	16,966
1961–1970	84	62	373	47	36	92	111	114	137	183	251	404	653	1,071	1,818	2,986	4,912	8,046	16,259
1971–1980	74	39	228	34	28	79	112	113	133	182	278	428	671	1,068	1,725	2,860	4,729	7,820	16,372
								Females											
1751–1760	4,975	2,559	7,931	1,211	627	612	687	879	1,157	1,068	1,514	1,458	1,861	2,431	3,595	4,818	8,148	11,791	20,476
1761–1770	5,057	2,757	8,331	1,296	615	614	704	882	1,181	1,095	1,541	1,521	1,969	2,325	3,708	5,093	8,600	11,981	22,533
1771–1780	5,979	3,156	8,394	1,489	802	780	863	1,054	1,278	1,316	1,691	1,739	2,231	2,676	4,194	6,238	9,593	12,718	22,802
1781–1790	5,485	2,880	7,978	1,343	731	705	779	946	1,131	1,186	1,492	1,565	1,947	2,446	3,918	6,350	9,206	13,022	21,217
1791–1800	4,579	2,212	7,343	1,005	497	536	631	802	989	1,046	1,387	1,458	1,830	2,408	3,864	5,684	9,377	13,970	24,073
1801–1810	4,869	2,263	7,364	1,164	680	730	823	954	1,112	1,301	1,550	1,702	2,370	3,098	4,631	6,246	9,777	15,282	25,936
1811–1820	4,735	1,938	7,055	934	544	617	756	832	1,014	1,243	1,403	1,553	2,093	2,770	4,156	6,122	9,413	13,498	24,561
1821–1830	3,595	1,520	5,856	732	441	494	639	753	899	1,084	1,277	1,429	1,889	2,490	3,846	5,502	8,408	13,045	22,846
1831–1840	3,413	1,378	5,590	724	447	496	644	776	951	1,119	1,347	1,536	2,023	2,680	3,774	5,684	8,958	13,136	23,273
1841–1850	3,117	1,434	5,222	738	429	477	569	642	795	966	1,143	1,269	1,723	2,335	3,354	5,427	8,279	12,726	22,570
1851–1860	3,707	1,978	5,596	1,045	528	521	586	688	844	1,010	1,162	1,327	1,726	2,382	3,523	5,275	8,224	12,414	20,530
1861–1870	3,854	2,023	5,358	883	424	446	538	617	714	850	1,003	1,141	1,480	2,082	3,107	4,709	7,240	11,480	21,492
1871–1880	3,221	1,706	4,876	839	426	447	549	668	724	822	905	989	1,280	1,732	2,597	4,003	6,356	10,082	18,636
1881–1890	2,800	1,505	4,053	767	415	455	529	607	664	749	819	907	1,124	1,540	2,296	3,570	5,695	9,177	18,247
1891–1900	2,227	1,105	3,416	598	379	475	572	613	651	724	789	859	1,093	1,429	2,129	3,376	5,477	9,009	17,962
1901–1910	1,597	689	2,605	407	340	474	556	601	616	672	726	826	1,012	1,358	1,957	3,050	5,003	8,435	16,978
1911–1920	1,213	552	2,008	347	308	506	614	670	664	670	729	792	1,002	1,325	1,939	3,058	5,065	8,335	17,387
1921–1930	711	282	1,424	192	188	326	414	422	438	471	551	686	920	1,244	1,858	2,976	4,843	8,273	17,297
1931–1940	427	175	1,068	123	121	225	299	305	319	362	446	605	835	1,195	1,826	3,003	5,052	8,541	17,857
1941–1950	202	114	643	66	62	118	166	174	195	232	307	444	658	983	1,570	2,617	4,561	7,826	16,717
1951–1960	113	60	375	37	30	45	55	70	94	133	203	317	498	779	1,291	2,248	4,056	7,120	15,849
1961–1970	61	43	280	33	25	40	46	56	75	110	171	271	412	632	1,040	1,811	3,346	6,159	14,066
1971–1980	67	28	175	23	21	38	42	48	66	97	158	239	367	552	860	1,450	2,596	4,844	12,413

From Historisk Statistik för Sverige, I. Befolkning 1720–1950, Statistiska Centralbyrån, Stockholm (1955).
Tabulation of the last three decades by courtesy of Statistics Sweden.

Crude Death Rate. Table 39.7.1 gives the crude death rate for each year, 1749–1980. The crude deaths rates are also given for epochs in Table 3.11.1. The rate fluctuates widely in the earlier years, but after 1885, in only 1918, the year of the influenza epidemic, did the rate differ considerably from the rates in the neighboring years. Commentators have noted that the crude death rate was far more variable in the years before 1900 than the crude birth rate, which they believe is only seriously disturbed by the effects of war and famines. Some, but not all, of the sharp peaks before 1885 can be identified as due to famines; others are due to or are aggravated by epidemics.

Age-specific Death Rates. We give as Table 39.7.2 the age-specific death rates of Sweden from 1751 to modern times. Striking declines are to be noted at all ages younger than 65 years, and even at ages older than 75 there have been considerable gains.

Infant Mortality. Infant mortality rates are given in Table 32.9.2 and in Mitchell (1975). See also Nybølle (1931).

Famine. Some of the peak years of mortality can be identified as due to famine. Thus, there were crop failures in 1756–1757, 1761–1762, 1771–1772, 1780–1783, 1798–1800, and in 1867–1868, leading to especially high crude death rates per 10,000 per annum of 299 and 324 in 1757 and 1758, 312 and 329 in 1762 and 1763, 374 and 525 in 1772 and 1773, 273, 281, and 298 in 1782, 1783, and 1784, 314 in 1800, and 223 in 1869. This last rate would not be considered high in the earlier years, but, as the Table shows, the general level of the death rate had decreased considerably by that time. In 1773 there were said to be 23,406 deaths from dysentery, but at least some of these deaths may have been due to the noninfective diarrhea often associated with starvation. There were also more than 20,000 deaths from typhus in 1773.

Bowel Diseases and Typhus. Cholera appeared first in 1834 and then again in 1853. Its high case fatality caused especial fear, although dysentery had caused more deaths in some other years. Typhus was not distinguished from the enteric fevers (typhoid) in the early

records. Hendriks (1862) gives a table of the number of deaths from typhus and of the percentage of deaths from typhus and "typhoid" fevers for the quinquennia beginning with 1751–1755 and ending with 1826–1830 in Sweden: these percentages are 6.87, 9.89, 11.59, 8.98, 14.68 (in 1771–1775); 8.36, 9.39, 15.07, 9.46, 7.88 (in 1796–1800); 10.47, 15.32, 9.97, 9.57, 7.82 (in 1821–1825); 11.14. Clearly these two fevers were a great source of mortality.

The graph of Åkesson (1931) and Table 8 of Utterström (1954) indicate that there were many deaths from typhus and enteric fever, 12,850 in 1772, 20,140 in 1773 (1772 and 1773 being famine years), 14,230 in 1789, 11,410 in 1790, 12,530 in 1808, 21,170 in 1809, 9,850 in 1828, and 9,260 in 1829, as against 5,000 in a "normal" year. Next to 1773, the highest crude death rate occurred in 1809, of which Meurk (1932) remarked that in that year there was a fearful neglect of hygiene and sanitation, especially in respect to the mobilized reserves; on demobilization, the reservists carried home with them typhus and dysentery, infecting persons of all ages and both sexes to which is due the small difference, $414 - 367 = 47$ per 10,000 per annum in the crude death rate of the two sexes.

Bubonic Plague. Bubonic plague appeared widely in Scandinavia in 1349–1350, even in the Faeroes in 1349, and then intermittently and principally in Sweden until 1712.

Tuberculosis. See §7.9, Springett (1950), Larsson and Linell (1960), and the following discussion for the general declines in mortality. The Swedish rates were high, for example, Sundbärg (1907/1970) notes that 11.7%, 13.5%, 15.2%, and 15.6% of all deaths in the decades 1861–1870, 1871–1880, 1881–1890, and 1891–1900 were due to tuberculosis.

Generalities on the Infectious Diseases. The great annual variation of total deaths and deaths due to infective diseases caused great interest in England, where the annual variations were much smaller. In particular, Ransome (1880, 1881–1882) gave graphs and a discussion of the Swedish experience; according to him, whooping cough caused about 0.7 deaths per 1,000 per annum over the years

1775–1830, in which year the entries became unavailable. Scarlatina caused somewhat lower rates, 0.6 per 1,000 per annum, and measles about 0.5. It should be noted that, as these infectious diseases affected chiefly the infants and children, the death rates of childhood and infancy from such diseases were great compared with those of recent times. From Ransome's graphs, it appears that the average lengths of the epidemic waves between peaks were 15 years for scarlatina, 8 for measles, and 5 years for smallpox. Whooping cough seemed always to be present.

Utterström (1954) gives a table of the deaths from smallpox, measles, whooping cough, dysentery, and a fifth group (typhus, typhoid fever, and some other infectious diseases, with definitions varying between years, according to Utterström), without giving a commentary on it. Deaths considered are for Sweden (with Finnish figures excluded) for persons *over the age of 1 year precisely*. Let us examine the percentage contributions to the crude death rates so defined, written as 24.6 (185) for 1766, an abbreviated form for 24.6% of deaths in a crude death rate of 185 deaths per 10,000 per annum: 24.6 (185), 20.9 (191), 29.6 (203), 33.0 (205), and 28.7 (197) in 1770; 27.8 (215), 37.4 (312), 54.6 (460), 23.0 (171), and 25.5 (188) in 1775; 20.7 (172), 21.9 (190), 31.5 (198), 41.0 (212), and 19.8 (164) in 1780; . . . 27.0 (204), 21.7 (184), 20.9 (185), 19.7 (195), and 17.8 (184) in 1805; 25.1 (209), 23.6 (209), 34.5 (289), 38,6 (346), and 26.8 (259) in 1810; . . . Large contributions to the 1772 and 1773 rates came from dysentery and the fifth group of diseases, including typhus and enteric fevers; these were 2 years of crop failures. We conclude from these and other data that the famine conditions could contribute largely to mortality, even though the effects might appear indirectly through typhus or, indeed, concealed as due to dysentery or as a high infantile death rate. Troops returning from the 1741–1743 war with Russia brought diseases, mainly typhus and, perhaps, also relapsing fever and typhoid fever. In Värmland in 1742 the crude death rate was 112 per 1,000 per annum, partly due to no crops being sown and the people migrating, then having to return to their homes where they could at least obtain firewood; typhus, dysentery, and typhoid fever all took their toll.

Utterström (1954) believes that

lack of food was seldom the sole cause of increased mortality and far from always the principal cause. Epidemics, whether connected or not with wars and famine, also played a large part; climate, weather, the standard of housing and hygiene were all of importance."

From a population point of view, crop failures were particularly important becase they influenced mortality, marriage, and birth rates in an unfavorable manner; they helped also to spread the epidemics far and wide. Taking a longer view over a thousand years, Utterström (1955, p.47) points out that in the warm intervals between the great glaciations "both economic life and size of the populations have made the greatest advances"; he is now more confident in his hypothesis than in his earlier article.

Smallpox. Although deaths from smallpox are known to have occurred in Sweden earlier, the first severe epidemic of smallpox is reported in Malmö in 1736, from where it spread to other parts of Sweden; it was again very severe in Malmö in 1740–1741. See Utterström (1954, Table 4) for deaths by age from smallpox in the diocese of Linköping during 1776–1790; smallpox and measles are not separated before 1774 in Table 8 of Utterström (1954), but smallpox caused more than 1,000 deaths in each year from 1774 to 1810 and in some years many more; 15,100 in 1779, 12,450 in 1784, and 12,030 in 1800. Vaccination was introduced in 1801 and became compulsory in 1815, after which smallpox caused relatively few deaths. Nevertheless, in 1874 the number of deaths was again high, and commentators such as Prinzing (1916) believe that this increase was due to the unsettled conditions in Europe after the Franco-German War of 1870. See also the tables of Hendriks (1862).

Typhus. See above.

Maternal Mortality. According to Hendriks (1862), the maternal deaths per 10,000 confinements were for the 16 quinquennia 1776–1780 to 1851–1855: 89, 83, 93, 101, and 85 in 1796–1800; 78, 89, 79, 73, and 67 in 1821–1825; 66,

TABLE 39.7.3. Urban-rural differences in mortality in Sweden (death rates by age per 1,000 per annum).

Period	Infancy*			Ages 15–19			Ages 55–59		
	Country	Other towns	Stockholm	Country	Other towns	Stockholm	Country	Other towns	Stockholm
1856–1860	138	181	318	5.27	6.94	7.42	25.4	38.5	48.5
1871–1880	119	166	274	4.30	5.74	6.39	18.5	26.1	33.8
1891–1900	94	116	169	4.57	5.51	4.52	15.3	19.8	23.1

*The rates are the infant mortalities as usually computed, (deaths of infants)/(live births).
Data from A.G. Sundbärg, *Bevölkerungsstatistik Schwedens 1750–1900*. Statistiska Centralbyrån, Stockholm (1970).

57, 51, 44, and 44 in 1846–1850; and 44 in 1851–1855. The rates are not greatly different from modern European rates in the early part of this century. Högberg and Broström (1985) give a rate of 59.5 in seven country parishes for the entire century.

Injury and Accident. Hendriks (1862, Table X) gives suicides by sex and three age groups and deaths by some other causes (Hendriks, 1862, Table Y). In the years 1811–1855, drowning caused more than 2.5% and 1.5% of deaths of males and females, respectively; suffocation from the fumes of charcoal caused far fewer deaths, and destruction by lightning still fewer, the three causes being in the ratios 100:2:0.4, approximately. Suicide, before 1820, caused about 0.1% of all deaths but, by 1850, it was causing up to 0.3% of deaths. For suicide, see Dahlgren (1945).

Alcoholism. Swedish commentators, such as Meurk (1932), Sundbärg (1907/1970), and Sjöstrand and Sahlin (1924), discussing the paper of Greenwood (1924), stress the importance of alcoholism on the mortality rates. In 1775 the Swedish Government set up its own distilleries to produce spirits for revenue. A temperance movement began in the 1830s under the leadership of P. Wieselgren, and alcoholism is believed to have declined in the later years of the century.

Urbanization. There were considerable urban-rural differences in mortality in the nineteenth century in the European states. We give, as an example, extracts from a table of Sund-

bärg (1907/1970) for Sweden as Table 39.7.3. Infant mortality was almost twice as high in Stockholm as in the country districts; at ages 15–19 years, the mortality was again notably higher in the earliest of the 3 decades but in the latest there had been some equalization between the areas. At ages 55–59 years there is a great difference, almost a ratio of 2:1, between the Stockholm rates and the country rates. Again, there is a tendency toward equalization in the latest decade.

It is clear that the long experience of Sweden has to be considered in two parts, and perhaps the year 1850 can be chosen as the division between them, for which see Table 39.7.2. At that time there had been no improvement in the death rates above the age of 35 years. The rates at ages under 10 years were to deteriorate in the next 2 decades. Before 1850 it is illusory to detect trends, for the mortality in 1791–1800 is more favorable than that in either of the neighboring decades. We can state that in the years before 1850 nutrition (or famine conditions) had been the great determinant of mortality levels, either directly or indirectly, as has been argued above. It cannot be argued against this hypothesis that the presence of the epidemics by themselves would be sufficient to explain the changes. The case fatalities of the common infections were obviously higher than have been experienced in more modern times, and this would have been due to diet, care of patients, and other social causes. We note that a crude death rate of 1 per 1,000 per annum for the whole country from any particular disease lasting for, for instance, 40 years, implies that about 4% of the population dies of the disease, if we assume that the expectation of life is 40 years. This sets the minimum estimate for the case fatality rate at 4%, if it is assumed that everyone has an attack of the disease; but of course everyone did not have an attack of each disease, so that a realistic estimate of case fatality would be higher.

Commentaries on the Mortality of Modern Times, after 1850. Meurk (1932) and Dr Folke Lindstedt, medical adviser to the committee of Åkesson (1931), would have agreed on the general reasons for the declines in mortality as set out by Meurk (1932). They are as follows: (*i*) improved food and living, (*ii*) better protection against injurious temperature conditions, (*iii*) reduced physical exertion at work, (*iv*) reduced consumption of alcoholic beverages, (*v*) increased protection against infections, mainly by hygienic improvements, (*vi*) advances in medical science acting through preventive measures, and (*vii*) declines in occupational mortality, for example, mechanization leading to a decline in deaths from drowning and shipwrecks. Meurk's explanations (*v*), (*vi*), and (*vii*) might well be active in reducing the urban mortality.

There have been attempts to estimate the growth rate for years before the initiation of the official series. Heckscher (1954) estimates the annual rate of growth in the century before 1720 as 0.22%. This is lower than for any decade since. There were absolute decreases in 1806–1810, largely due to epidemics of dysentery caused by the Finnish War, and in 1771–1775 because of crop failures and epidemics. At other times there were absolute decreases in population for single years. From Utterström (1954, Table 2) the population increase annually was 1.1% in the years 1735–1750, about 0.5% during the years 1750–1815, and then about 1% from 1815–1860. See also Thomas (1941).

Because Heckscher's work is so often cited, some comments are necessary on his views on mortality. He believes that after 1735 the Swedish population was close to the limits of their food supplies and that the mortality follows harvest conditions and the wars. He is unwilling to admit the importance of epidemics of the common infective diseases, which he regards as endemic, in the sense of perpetuation within the country. However, his hypotheses lead him to regard increased mortality before bad harvests and wars as in some way due to them. He believes also that passing through an epidemic of, for instance, smallpox, hardens the survivors in some way so that they can better resist not only smallpox but other diseases in the future. Utterström (1954), with whom we can agree, gives reasons for not accepting some of Heckscher's interpretations.

For further references on Swedish mortality, see: deaths by cause: Bolander (1981), Boström and Ljungstedt (1981), Henschen (1947), and Prawitz (1960); eighteenth century: Boethius (1953); 1967: Jung (1970); 1951–1968, with special reference to cardiovascular disease: Vedin, Wilhelmson, et al. (1970); Malthusian interpretations: Loschky (1976); risk factors in cardiovascular disease: Böttiger and Carlson (1981) and Wilhelmsen (1981); causes of death 1951–1960: Widén (1962).

Pyörälä and Valkonen (1981) state that the high ischemic heart disease mortality reached peak levels in the 1960s and started to decline in the 1970s; they conclude that decreasing trends in dairy fat consumption and in cigarette smoking and the increase in hypertension control may possibly be the explanation.

See also Utterström (1965).

39.8 Finland

Finland formed part of the kindom of Sweden from 1154 to 1809, when it was united to Russia as an autonomous Grand Duchy. In 1917 it declared its independence. In 1970 6.6% of the population spoke Swedish. Other language speaking minority groups totalled 0.2%. A mention is made of the publications of the Central Statistical Office in the Statistical Yearbook of Finland for 1980 (pp. 489–491), the 76th of the series. There is also a demographic journal.

In earlier times Finland was largely agrarian; the principal cereals grown are barley and oats, as Finland lies at the northern limit of

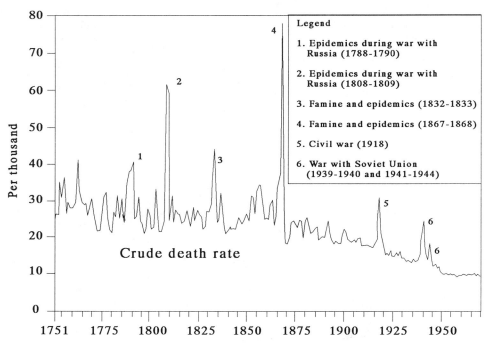

FIGURE 39.8.1. Crude death rates in Finland. (After Turpeinen (1979*a*), p. 102.)

cultivation. Arable land was always in good supply in the seventeenth and eighteenth centuries.

Many numerical data are available for Finland after 1821, but even before that year, there are good statistics of the famine of 1696–1697, in which about one-third of the population of some provinces died, as has already been mentioned in §22.5. Jutikkala (1945) mentions that at ages 60 to 65 years in the census of 1749 (and so among the survivors of the births of 1685–1689), there were 43% more women than men; this is explainable by the mortality of the Great Northern War, 1700–1721. Jutikkala (1945) gives estimates that 60,000 men were levied from Finland for that war and that total losses were 50,000; in spite of these "negative" factors, the population increased by a third betwen 1698 and 1721, "excluding war casualties." In 1710 there had also been bubonic plague. Influenza epidemics were deduced for 1729, partly from the symptoms recorded and partly because influenza had occurred in both Russia and Sweden. A severe epidemic, which began in Åland and the

Turku province in the southwest of the country, spread throughout Finland in 1736 and 1737; it is thought that this was influenza rather than relapsing fever. After 1739 typhus, dysentery, smallpox, measles, and diphtheria were all common causes of death. In 1740 the crude death rate for Finland was 52 per 1,000 and Jutikkala (1945) believes that the main causes of death were dysentery and spotted fever (typhus). According to Jutikkala and Kauppinen (1971), 1867 and 1868 were famine years, but they conclude that many of the large swings, excepting 1696–1697 and 1867–1868, were associated with diagnosable epidemics rather than famine. In "catastrophic" years, defined as having a crude death rate above 30 per 1,000 per annum, 40% of the deaths could be due to the epidemic causes against 25% in a normal year, that is, 2 to 3 against 1 to 3 for the ratio, epidemic to nonepidemic causes. The effects of typhoid, typhus, and dysentery were active in the summer, whereas smallpox and measles appeared to be more active in the winter. Turpeinen (1978) finds that the death rates at ages under 10 years reached maxima usually

TABLE 39.8.1. Number of deaths per 100,000 inhabitants per annum, 1749–1773.

	Smallpox	Burning fever, typhus	Pulmonary tuberculosis	Whooping cough	Dysentery
All Finland (1751–1773)	369	318	232	194	64
Rural parishes with high crude death rate	499	244	241	288	59
Rural parishes with low crude death rate	257	185	115	114	26
Urban parishes	456	555	416	165	25

Data from Turpeinen (1978).

in July or even September. He observes that snow melting gives rise to diarrhea in the spring; it seems from this distance that such epidemics would be indistinguishable from the diarrhea of malnutrition. Turpeinen (1979b) estimates the contribution of measles to the infant mortality rate in 1751–1775 and 1776–1800 as 19.5 and 20.7 deaths per 1,000; smallpox contributed 17.1, 9.4 and 5.4 deaths per 1,000 in 1776–1800, 1801–1825 and 1826–1865, respectively. In general he concludes that the critical factor in infantile mortality is breast feeding.

Turpeinen (1978, 1979a,b, 1980) has given many interesting tables, especially the age-specific mortality rates from 1751 to 1925, enlarging on the discussions of Jutikkala (1945). He is concerned with the high degree of variation in the death rates. Turpeinen (1979a) gives a striking diagram (our Figure 39.8.1) with four peaks in the crude death rates "dwarfing" that of the year of civil war and influenza in 1918; in 1788–1790 and again in 1808–1809 there were epidemics during the wars with Russia. In 1832–1833 and again in 1867–1868 there were famine and epidemics. The crude death rates per 1,000 per annum were 38.2, 38.4, and 40.6 in 1789, 1790, 1791; 61.5 and 59.1 in 1808, 1809; 46.1 in 1833; 38.1 and 77.5 in 1867, 1868; and 30.4 in 1918. The harvest failed in 1807 and this was followed by 2 years of high mortality in 1808 and 1809. In 1832 the harvest was generally poor and almost a total failure in north Finland; early in 1833 there were outbreaks of

dysentery and enteric fever, and later in 1833 cholera was widespread in south Finland, especially in the towns. See also Turpeinen (1980) for explanations of the annual rates. In more recent times the effect of poor harvests as a cause of high mortality has been less clear, according to Turpeinen (1979a).

Turpeinen (1979b) gives a table of infant mortality rates, for which see also Mitchell (1975). The rate per 1,000 was 360 in 1808, 300 was approached in 1756, 1763, and 1833, and 250 was frequently exceeded. He believes that there was little correlation between infant mortality rates and harvest yields. Moreover. "the highest rates of infant mortality figures did not appear in the poorest but in relatively wealthy districts. Infant mortality was higher in towns than in rural areas."

Turpeinen (1973, 1978) gives evidence that mortality in Finland, Russia, and Sweden, in at least the latter decades of the preindustrial era, was highest in and around the large towns and generally wherever there were densely populated districts having active contacts with other countries. His maps show that crude death rates were greatest in those Finnish counties, contiguous in the east to St. Petersburg or in the west to Turku, that were open to sea traffic; further, there was a distinct gradient of mortality downward from the large towns, to the surrounding countryside, and then to the rural areas. Important factors in this gradient were tuberculosis, smallpox, typhus, and whooping cough, for which see Table 39.8.1.

Chapter 40
Asia

40.1 Introduction

There are great difficulties, due to past civil disorganizations and the lack of central statistical bureaus, in obtaining long time series of mortality from many of the Asian countries. This is especially so for China, the world's most populous country. We refer the reader to Banister (1979) for some relevant details and a bibliography on population changes and to Hinton (1979) for more general information. For recent experience, the reader is referred to Ling Riu-Zhu (1981), who reports great declines in infant and child mortality after 1949.

Other more general references for Asia include: disaster in Bangladesh: Chen (1973); recent trends in Asian mortality: Ueda (1983); comparative mortalities in Asia: ECAFE (1973); outlook of Southeast Asia in AD 2000: Hansluwka, Lopez, and Ruzicka (1981); pediatrics in Asia: Bose and Dey (1964); gastrointestinal infections in S.E. Asia: Hiraishi, Kohari, et al. (1977), Kitamoto (1975); viral diseases in S.E. Asia: MacKenzie (1983); infant mortality in Asia and Oceania: Symposium (1961); epidemiology of the Far East: Simmons, Whayne, et al. (1944, 1951, 1954); urbanization: Cassen (1978). For the ten leading causes of death and a decade of health development in Asia, see WHO-underdeveloped (1974, 1978). For the ecology of malnutrition in Asia, see May and Jarcho (1961).

40.2 Japan

For a brief summary of the mortality in Japan, we follow Ohno (1985). Great changes have occurred in the past half century. The crude death rate in 1980 was 6.2 per 1,000; standardized on to a population with the same age-sex distribution as Japan, 1936, the rate was 3.6 per 1,000, lower than those prevailing in Canada, 4.5, and the United States, 4.6, with the same standard population. It was strikingly lower than the crude death rate in Japan for 1936, 17.5. Using the same standard population, the rate for Japan was 25.2 in 1920, 16.8 in 1935, 10.8 in 1950, 6.9 in 1960, 5.1 in 1970, and 3.6 in 1980; the decline was quite regular from 1916 to 1981, if the effects of the wars in 1918–1921 and 1944–1946 are neglected. The decrease in the infant mortality rate was equally striking, the rates per 1,000 for 1921, 1931, . . . , 1981 being 168, 132, 84, 58, 29, 12, and 7.

In Ohno (1985, Figure 3) it is evident that obvious declines in the age-specific mortality rates did not occur in the period 1935–1947. After 1947 the rates at ages 0–4, 5–9, 20–24, and 30–34 decreased at approximately the same rate proportionally (i.e., the slopes of the curves on the semilogarithmic grid are parallel) over the period 1947–1980; at the older age groups the slopes are successively less steep, although even at ages 70–74 years the slope is obviously downward corresponding, indeed, to almost a halving of the death rate in a stretch of 40 years. The behavior of the rates by cause can be considered, noting that some of the rates are of deaths, others of incidence, but that all are per 1,000 per annum.

Enteric Fever. Between 1950 and 1970 the incidence rate for the enteric fevers fell from about 1 per 1,000 per annum to an almost negligible 0.002.

Dysentery. The incidence rate for dysentery fell from about 1 per 1,000 in 1962 to 0.01 in 1980.

Tuberculosis. Tuberculosis death rates fell from about 2 per 1,000 in 1935 to 0.003 in 1980. Causes for the decline are as follows. Control began in 1936; there was BCG inoculation of all primary school pupils after 1942, registration of patients since 1947, compulsory BCG inoculation of those under 30 years since 1948, widespread use of antituberculosis drugs, such as streptomycin, since 1952, free treatment and care since 1951, mass screening since 1955, and free screening after 1957.

Leprosy. Incidence rates fell from 0.02 per 1,000 in 1950 to negligible proportions in 1965.

Diphtheria. Incidence rates fell rapidly from 1 per 1,000 in 1946 to negligible rates in 1980.

Pertussis. Incidence rates for whooping cough had been about 0.8 per 1,000 in 1946; they fell to about 0.002 in 1972, rose to 0.1 in 1979 because of a temporary cessation of the vaccination campaign, and have since declined.

Tetanus. Incidence rates fell from about 0.03 per 1,000 in 1950 to negligible proportions in 1975.

Poliomyelitis. The incidence fluctuated about 0.04 per 1,000 in the years around 1950 but fell to negligible proportions in 1963.

Measles. Incidence rates fluctuated around 1.5 per 1,000 in the early 1950s, falling to about 0.1 in 1980. Remarkably, the graph of incidence has a saw-toothed appearance with a 2-year cycle, as in London (see §11.7). Perhaps the influence of Tokyo, a very large city in a relatively small geographical area, was dominant throughout the years of observation.

Japanese Encephalitis. Incidence rates fluctuated around 0.03 per 1,000 until 1965. By 1970 the rates were negligible. See §12.4.

Neoplasms. The death rates from neoplasms show some tendency to increase, from a level of about 0.8 per 1,000 in 1950 to about 1 per 1,000 in 1980.

Pneumonia and Bronchitis. The death rates decreased from almost 2 per 1,000 in 1950 to about 0.2 in 1980.

Accidents. There was a decline in deaths from 0.4 in 1950 to 0.2 per 1,000 in 1980. There have been special risks from earthquakes, with 77,000 deaths in 1908 and 30,500 in 1915, for example.

Infant Mortality. Measles and pertussis had been important factors in infant mortality. Expectations of life at birth for males (females) were, in years, 50.1 (54.0) in 1947 and 74.2 (79.8) in 1983.

Ohno (1985) explains the great falls in mortality as due to: (*i*) immunization campaigns against the acute infectious diseases of childhood; (*ii*) new drugs including, especially, penicillin, other antibiotics, and other synthetic drugs; (*iii*) general availability of piped water and efficient sewage disposal after World War II; piped water was available to 97% of the great city areas and to 87% of the remainder in 1980, with the coverage of efficient sewage disposal still only 30% but increasing (these two factors were especially important for the control of the gastrointestinal group of infections); (*iv*) almost 100% now have primary school education and 94% have high school education; latest university rates are 41% for males and 33% for females; school lunches have been available since 1954; (*v*) there have been improvements in diet with more fats and proteins appearing, but also too much salt, leading to hypertension and gastric ulcer; and (*vi*) medical, hospital, and allied services have greatly increased.

There is an account of the development of official statistics in the *Review of the International Statistical Institute*, 36 (1968, pp. 332, 333) and an English language *Statistical Yearbook of Japan* is published annually. Taeuber (1958) believes that it is difficult to demonstrate that the mortality was declining before 1920, but the collection and presentation of mortality statistics were improving.

See, for declines in mortality: US National Center for Health Statistics (1968a); cause-specific mortality: Yamaguchi (1982); enteric eradication: Ohashi (1975); smallpox: Suda and Soekawa (1983); western diseases: Hishinuma (1981) and Yamamoto (1981); early Meiji period: Morita (1963); changing patterns of parasitic infections: Kobayashi (1983); parasite control: Kunii (1983); coronary heart disease: Robertson, Kato, Gordon, et al. (1977), Robertson, Kato, Rhoads, et al. (1977).

40.3 India

Climate

The economy of India is dominated by the seasonal rainfall, the monsoon which brings in the rain from the southwest from June to October and from the northeast in January and February, although the rainfall in these winter months is comparatively light. The monsoon rains are variable, but monsoon failure is never universal; a failure can mean that the total rainfall over a large area may be only 20% of the normal expectation (Passmore, 1951).

Considering the Indian subcontinent as a whole, the crops grown and the seasons in which normal rainfall is essential for a good harvest vary greatly. According to Srivastava (1968), the two main harvests in India are the *kharif* and the *rabi*. Rice, millet, and maize, the principal *kharif* crops, are sown in June and July and reaped in September to December, although in some areas with the aid of irrigation it is possible to reap two and even three crops per year. Rice is indeed the predominant staple food of the Indian population. The *rabi* crops, wheat, barley, and oats, are sown in October and November and harvested in March and April; they require less rain than the *kharif* crops and are dependent on the northeast monsoon. It is the summer rain or southwest monsoon that provides the harvests in the rice-producing areas, such as Bengal, Burma, Assam, and the land lying between the Western Ghats and the Persian Gulf.

We can choose only one topic here, but see also cholera in §6.3 and bubonic plague in §8.3.

Famine

In the past, the only areas free of the risk of famine due to drought were those, such as the Punjab and Sind, that were supplied with water by canal systems. There is no case of a drought extending over the whole of India; thus, an improvement in communications lessens the risk of disastrous famines. Subsidiary causes of famine are floods, violent hail storms, diseases of the cereals, and locust swarms.

Floods, cyclones, and violent storms can cause widespread destruction of crops, but often around the affected area there will be bumper crops. Floods caused or augmented by hurricanes in the northern littoral of the Bay of Bengal are to be feared because there may be inroads of the salt water as well. Tsunamis can also have this effect. Locust plagues may follow famines, as in the Rajputana famine of 1868–1869, where they followed the breaking of the rains; the second brood attacked the ripening crop, so that the crop harvested was only one-eighth of the normal yield.

Some specific instances of drought may be mentioned. Thus, according to governmental reports cited by Loveday (1914), about one quarter of the population in Orissa died in 1866. The export of grain in 1864 and 1865 had been excessive. When signs of famine first appeared, approval for the import of grain was delayed. According to Campbell (1893), the magistrate of Cuttack reported in April 1866 that there was no need for the most serious apprehension; a few days later, in May, he and his followers almost starved. There was terrible suffering through the months from May to October. In October the government was pouring in large quantities of grain, but by that time the new crop was coming in. The district officers did their duty as well as could be expected. No serious famine had occurred since 1769–1770. The landlords, often absentee, not the government, were responsible for relief. There was a curious incident in which a vessel beached by an accident could not be unloaded

TABLE 40.3.1. Deaths in the famine year 1900 in the provinces of Gujarat (amended from Cotton, 1976 p. 66).

Province	Fever		Dysentery and diarrhea		Cholera		All causes	
	1900*	DA*	1900	DA	1900	DA	1900	DA
Ahmedabad	111[†]	30	15	1	14	1	173	36
Broach	89	33	16	0[§]	16	2	162	40
Kaira	48	28	24	1	14	1	148	34
Panch Mahála[‡]	168	22	64	0	18	1	281	23
Surat	40	25	4	1	10	2	79	33

* The 1900 rates are compared with a decennial average (DA) in each case.

[†] The deaths are given rounded off per 1,000 per annum.

[‡] Smallpox was 0.5 per 1,000 in Panch Mahála in 1900 but was otherwise a low contributor to the death rate; all other smallpox entries were below 0.2 per 1,000.

[§] 0 means less than 0.5 per 1,000 per annum.

because of doubts about the ownership of the grain carried, causing bureaucratic delays. In the autumn of 1866 the government brought in grain, which was subsequently almost entirely wasted because of rotting. Moreover, with the coming of the new harvest a drop in prices caused a great economic loss to the government. Cotton (1976) reports that in the famine of 1900 Gujarat had the highest mortality figures, and these are given by district in Table 40.3.1.

A modern famine in Bihar in 1966 has already been mentioned in §22.7.

See also:
vital rates in India: Bhat, Preston, and Dyson (1984); historical demography of India: Das Gupta (1972); mortality rates: Hardy (1885, 1905); infant mortality: Chandrasekhar (1959) and Symposium (1961); mortality by age: Das (1974); diseases of India: Annesley (1828); urbanization, population, economy, and science: Cassen (1978); dysenteries: Rogers (1913); population problems in rural Punjab: Wyon and Gordon (1971); maternal mortality in Mysore: Poornapregna, Krishna Sastry, and Madhava (1933).

Chapter 41
Oceania

41.1 Introduction

Oceania is a convenient grouping of Australia, New Zealand and their dependent territories, and Polynesia. The climate varies from tropical in northern Australia and the Polynesian islands through temperate to the southern-most points of Tasmania and New Zealand at 42°S and 43°S, respectively. The region has possessed no large city until the rise of Sydney and Melbourne in Australia to the million mark around 1930. There are many observations on the effects of the small scattered populations on the incidence of infective diseases, for example, Rolleston (1937); poverty and urban overcrowding have not occurred anywhere on the scale of the European states. Although part of Oceania lies in the tropics, "tropical diseases," with the exception of filariasis, have played a small part in the health of the community. In particular, malaria has only been endemic in the far north of Australia, that is, in northern Queensland and the Northern Territory. The influenza pandemic affected most of Oceania. Malaria has not been endemic in Polynesia, neither have the other great pestilences, although plague has occurred in Australia. There has been no parallel in Australia and New Zealand to the frequent importation of epidemics from the West Indies into the eastern seaboard of the United States.

For an epidemiologic survey, see Simmons, Whayne, et al. (1944).

41.2 Aboriginal Australia

Before European settlement in 1788, Australia had been occupied by aboriginal peoples for some 40,000 years. The possible classification of these peoples is still unsettled. There were no important anthropozoonoses if we except the scrub typhus of the present Queensland coastal area. Yaws, gangosa, and filariasis were present in the wet tropical north; malaria if present was sporadic; leprosy was possibly absent; smallpox was normally absent. Of these, malaria, leprosy, and smallpox might have been quite recent arrivals, as there is some slight evidence that the Indonesians and Malays had only begun to visit northern Australia about 1770. An epidemic of smallpox was observed in the Sydney area in 1788–1789 but this probably came down by infections of the aborigines from Indonesians in the north. See Cleland (1928), and 14 other articles in the same volume, and Basedow (1932).

After European settlement there were further epidemics of smallpox, with important mortality. Measles was later introduced at intervals and was responsible for the loss of perhaps up to one half of some tribes. Whooping cough sometimes caused great mortality. Leprosy became established in the northern areas after 1873. Tuberculosis caused many infections, often of the acute glandular and gastrointestinal forms; social customs, such as crowding around the sick, aggravated the havoc caused by the disease. Syphilis was introduced by whalers and sealers into the present South Australia before formal occupation by settlers.

Alcoholism and in some places opium have caused great problems and added to the forces destroying the social structure. Many deaths, of course, were caused by the petty wars, police actions, retribution raids, and so on. Some present views of the problem and a bibliography have been given by Moodie (1973, 1981) and Moodie and Pederson (1971). The first full census of the aboriginal population was taken in 1971. See also for aboriginal man and his environment, Kirk (1981) and Mulvaney and Golson (1971). See also for some favorable modern death rates, Hicks (1985). For a general review of aboriginal mortality, see Lancaster and Gordon (1988).

41.3 Australia, Non-Aboriginal

Before Federation in 1901, each Australian colony published its own statistics, but the colonies were careful to hold their censuses at an agreed common time. After Federation, the separate states (formerly colonies) continued to collect and report on the vital statistics, but since 1907 the statistics of the six states have been aggregated to give Australia-wide totals. These Australian statistics have been analyzed in a series of articles largely in the *Medical Journal of Australia*, and a bibliography and two supplements of the Australian vital statistics have been published (Lancaster, 1964*b*, 1973*b*, 1982*b*).

Table 41.3.1 gives the mortality rates by decades over the stretch of years 1881–1980 and by age and sex. There have been great declines in early childhood, 0–4 years, and in childhood, 5–14 years, and indeed notable declines in both sexes up to the age of 55 years. With increasing age above 55 years the mortality rates of males have declined at an increasingly modest rate, that is, from 32 to 19 at ages 55–64, from 63 to 45 at ages 65–74, and

TABLE 41.3.1. Age-specific death rates in Australia (all causes*) (deaths per 1,000,000 per annum).

	0–4	5–14	15–24	25–34	35–44	45–54	55–64	65–74	75+	All ages
					Males					
1881–1890	45,494	3,221	6,637	8,788	11,287	18,223	32,176	63,169	144,724	16,602
1891–1900	37,775	2,666	4,540	6,910	9,587	15,045	29,916	59,764	146,646	14,259
1901–1910	28,007	2,073	3,539	5,109	8,097	13,547	25,319	58,805	149,640	12,411
1911–1920	23,662	1,971	3,128	5,050	7,450	13,346	25,465	53,796	153,519	12,117
1921–1930	17,691	1,562	2,468	3,509	5,632	11,009	22,443	49,042	134,684	10,417
1931–1940	12,435	1,368	2,099	2,657	4,569	9,624	21,861	50,004	132,434	10,315
1941–1950	9,703	1,021	1,489	1,778	3,421	8,954	22,063	51,638	137,491	10,837
1951–1960	6,445	606	1,642	1,729	2,993	7,972	21,754	51,167	136,199	9,980
1961–1970	5,164	481	1,490	1,546	3,051	8,127	21,544	52,946	133,536	9,787
1971–1980	3,795	380	1,588	1,346	2,552	7,284	18,874	45,345	122,617	8,763
					Females					
1881–1890	40,349	2,979	4,990	7,952	10,281	13,997	23,291	51,501	131,609	13,696
1891–1900	32,759	2,450	3,802	6,382	8,421	11,244	21,893	45,192	128,813	11,521
1901–1910	23,648	1,866	3,201	5,010	7,072	9,581	18,528	45,936	124,417	9,908
1911–1920	19,104	1,711	2,761	4,574	5,843	8,983	16,866	40,964	129,588	9,337
1921–1930	14,161	1,241	2,176	3,505	4,821	7,861	15,379	37,110	117,348	8,312
1931–1940	10,002	993	1,642	2,657	3,875	6,946	14,435	36,451	112,655	8,309
1941–1950	7,686	705	1,036	1,762	2,951	6,248	13,533	35,221	114,146	8,855
1951–1960	5,147	413	605	980	2,089	4,983	11,711	30,483	107,827	7,989
1961–1970	4,040	316	562	814	1,903	4,655	10,802	28,880	99,858	7,836
1971–1980	2,931	251	528	630	1,523	4,000	9,283	23,362	89,531	7,045

*Statistics on the aboriginal population were not available until the epoch 1971–1980, for which they have been included.
From Lancaster (1987).

TABLE 41.3.2. Sex differentials of the total death rates in Australia.*

	0–4	5–14	15–24	25–34	35–44	45–54	55–64	65–74	75+	All ages
				(Age in years)						
1881–1890	113	108	133	111	110	130	138	123	110	121
1891–1900	115	109	119	108	114	134	137	132	114	124
1901–1910	118	111	111	102	114	141	137	128	120	125
1911–1920	124	115	113	110	128	149	151	131	118	130
1921–1930	125	126	113	100	117	140	146	132	115	125
1931–1940	124	138	128	100	118	139	151	137	118	124
1941–1950	126	145	144	101	116	143	163	147	120	122
1951–1960	125	147	271	176	143	160	186	168	126	125
1961–1970	128	152	265	190	160	175	199	183	134	125
1971–1980	129	151	301	214	168	182	203	195	137	124

* 100 × (male death rates)/(female death rates).
From Lancaster (1987).

from 145 to 123 per 1,000 per annum at ages 75 years and older. The female rates have declined more sharply at all these older ages, that is, 23 to 9, 52 to 23, and 132 to 90. These differences can be brought out by Table 41.3.2 showing sex differentials; in 1881–1890 the sex differentials were all in the range of 108–138, but by 1971–1980 they had increased to be in the range of 129–301. In the latter period, the male rates were 3.01 times the female at ages 15–24 and were 2.03 and 1.95 times the female at ages 55–64 and 65–74 years. At ages 15–24 years the explanation is simple; almost all causes of death, particularly the infections generally, and tuberculosis, have been overcome, so the male rate is dominated by deaths from accidents. At ages 55–74 years in the latest period, the male rates are higher because of the diseases caused by smoking, by alcohol, and by occupational hazards.

For comparisons of diseases or classes of diseases over time, it is, of course, necessary to use the age- and sex-specific rates, which would give very bulky tables, or to standardize them. We choose this latter method and use three standard populations; for comparison we include a table of crude death rates by cause, see Tables 41.3.3 to 41.3.6. We can only hope to use groups of diseases and modify the classes of the ICD, because the class definitions have altered with time. In these tables, abbreviated names have been assigned to the classes of the ICD, and some minor changes have been

made; class I of the sixth revision of the ICD has been subdivided into tuberculosis, venereal diseases, and "infections"; influenza has been retained in respiratory diseases; diabetes has been given a separate entry, and the remainder of class III and class IV are combined into "other general" diseases.

In Table 41.3.3, declines in the crude death rates by cause are evident in the groups comprising "infections," tuberculosis, and venereal diseases, and in other classes, such as respiratory, nervous, and skin and cellular diseases in which infections were the important cause of many of the deaths, for example, pneumonia in the class of respiratory diseases. There have been great declines in the class of ill-defined diseases; possibly deaths assigned to this class in the earlier epochs were assigned to the class of cardiovascular diseases in the later epochs. Cancer crude death rates increased over the epochs largely because of the aging of the population. The same increases are not apparent in Tables 41.3.4 and 41.3.5, in which the rates are standardized on to 1,000,000, based on the population of England and Wales as enumerated in 1901 and on the Australian life tables of 1933, respectively.

The England and Wales populations of 1901 were relatively young, for there had been a rapid growth of population in the late nineteenth century, and so standardization of the rates on to them gives emphasis to the mortality at younger ages. The Australian life table

TABLE 41.3.3. Crude death rates in Australia (deaths per 1,000,000 per annum).

Cause of death	1908–1910	1911–1920	1921–1930	1931–1940	1941–1950	1951–1960	1961–1970	1971–1980
				Males				
Infections	1,773	1,796	902	460	280	145	41	44
Tuberculosis	939	837	670	497	404	131	45	10
Venereal	121	117	88	74	37	26	8	1
Cancer	724	808	950	1,123	1,219	1,245	1,495	1,534
Other tumours	31	29	41	94	106	139	14	151
Other general	49	77	60	39	33	24	109	30
Blood-forming	59	60	59	45	36	33	27	19
Rheumatism	55	61	59	50	33	51	62	76
Diabetes	84	93	93	117	127	85	112	112
Respiratory	1,229	1,338	1,187	1,007	826	746	804	739
Nervous	851	830	711	585	982	1,178	769	166
Cardiovascular	1,368	1,477	1,681	2,850	3,762	3,909	4,419	4,412
Alimentary	506	495	470	477	427	333	273	256
Genitourinary	693	732	746	828	741	343	213	117
Skin and cellular	68	61	55	28	13	14	7	4
Bones	22	17	27	30	13	18	25	24
Congenital malformations	89	119	119	106	116	131	110	87
Early infancy	758	860	662	436	440	337	258	143
Ill-defined	1,131	1,150	786	464	363	133	52	61
Violence, accidents, and poisonings	1,211	1,157	1,047	1,002	879	958	933	855
All causes	11,759	12,117	10,417	10,315	10,837	9,980	9,787	8,763
				Females				
Infections	1,524	1,491	775	400	236	123	37	39
Tuberculosis	817	639	494	340	219	46	13	4
Venereal	46	39	26	19	10	8	3	1
Cancer	715	771	907	1,074	1,226	1,149	1,223	1,183
Other tumours	60	52	63	99	105	118	18	125
Other general	59	82	87	79	62	34	89	34
Blood-forming	66	65	69	54	49	50	34	23
Rheumatism	61	73	70	67	48	64	80	59
Diabetes	100	119	146	211	249	157	160	137
Respiratory	899	939	862	733	635	465	401	366
Nervous	761	746	728	664	1,239	1,490	984	137
Cardiovascular	1,092	1,135	1,333	2,237	2,758	2,888	3,449	4,028
Alimentary	442	430	377	345	295	236	204	178
Genitourinary	420	421	508	600	498	195	179	121
Child-bearing	287	265	242	176	97	30	12	4
Skin and cellular	59	49	44	25	14	17	10	6
Bones	13	9	16	15	10	23	37	44
Congenital malformations	74	95	95	84	99	110	94	76
Early infancy	612	670	508	331	324	254	182	101
Ill-defined	878	923	670	439	352	153	66	54
Violence, accidents, and poisonings	378	321	283	318	332	379	432	387
All causes	9,366	9,337	8,312	8,309	8,855	7,989	7,836	7,045

From Lancaster (1978).

417

TABLE 41.3.4. Standardized death rates in Australia, E. & W., 1901* (deaths per 1,000,000 per annum).

Cause of death	1908–1910	1911–1920	1921–1930	1931–1940	1941–1950	1951–1960	1961–1970
				Males			
Infections	1,775	1,810	949	503	287	135	37
Tuberculosis	913	795	616	423	305	92	29
Venereal	118	109	76	59	26	17	3
Cancer	714	742	775	785	765	808	993
Other tumours	31	28	38	83	89	109	8
Other general	47	74	50	37	30	17	81
Blood-forming	58	56	50	38	26	22	17
Rheumatism	54	58	57	46	29	39	42
Diabetes	84	87	79	84	81	54	71
Respiratory	1,197	1,280	1,090	843	592	508	526
Nervous	831	782	613	433	629	753	486
Cardiovascular	1,330	1,371	1,396	1,965	2,293	2,442	2,761
Alimentary	495	473	425	392	309	232	195
Genitourinary	670	679	629	591	471	225	137
Skin and cellular	65	56	61	25	9	9	3
Bones	21	17	28	31	10	14	16
Congenital malformations	90	125	135	144	140	141	122
Early infancy	768	897	756	618	531	367	300
Ill-defined	1,035	1,061	669	302	201	79	35
Violence, accidents, and poisonings	1,178	1,106	983	914	769	888	870
All causes	11,474	11,617	9,475	8,332	7,598	6,959	6,753
				Females			
Infections	1,461	1,481	798	432	232	111	33
Tuberculosis	822	638	492	328	202	37	8
Venereal	45	39	26	16	7	5	1
Cancer	833	828	849	830	818	739	789
Other tumours	65	54	60	86	86	93	14
Other general	61	81	84	69	51	24	62
Blood-forming	72	67	64	45	34	32	20
Rheumatism	65	78	68	57	38	47	53
Diabetes	119	130	139	162	162	91	85
Respiratory	971	992	860	651	467	309	246
Nervous	854	807	702	521	801	878	534
Cardiovascular	1,267	1,242	1,284	1,702	1,704	1,626	1,796
Alimentary	482	446	364	295	222	160	133
Genitourinary	466	445	485	485	346	136	116
Child-bearing	285	261	242	179	101	32	14
Skin and cellular	65	53	45	23	11	11	5
Bones	13	7	16	15	6	12	23
Congenital malformations	67	91	101	110	116	112	103
Early infancy	553	643	542	447	381	266	208
Ill-defined	1,029	1,063	680	326	203	83	30
Violence, accidents, and poisonings	386	326	289	297	269	296	353
All causes	9,994	9,775	8,190	7,076	6,257	5,105	4,626

*E. & W. Standardized on to the male and female populations of England and Wales, 1901.
From Lancaster (1978).

418

TABLE 41.3.5. Standardized death rates in Australia, LTA, 1933* (deaths per 1,000,000 per annum).

Cause of death	1908–1910	1911–1920	1921–1930	1931–1940	1941–1950	1951–1960	1961–1970
				Males			
Infections	1,725	1,724	910	516	285	151	44
Tuberculosis	1,125	969	778	577	475	179	65
Venereal	153	146	110	93	45	38	12
Cancer	1,537	1,624	1,754	1,826	1,789	1,873	2,229
Other tumours	43	38	52	111	124	169	20
Other general	52	181	118	64	61	29	144
Blood-forming	91	95	91	64	50	49	41
Rheumatism	94	100	79	62	42	67	86
Diabetes	152	161	155	188	186	130	175
Respiratory	2,082	2,201	1,884	1,500	1,152	1,119	1,241
Nervous	1,568	1,521	1,265	931	1,447	1,838	1,213
Cardiovascular	2,928	3,028	3,281	4,885	5,730	6,160	6,922
Alimentary	807	728	662	634	555	468	388
Genitourinary	1,453	1,461	1,400	1,371	1,115	535	336
Skin and cellular	130	120	92	37	17	19	11
Bones	24	18	28	34	16	27	38
Congenital malformations	60	80	86	94	89	99	88
Early infancy	488	569	480	393	337	233	191
Ill-defined	2,958	3,210	2,042	951	634	239	82
Violence, accidents, and poisonings	1,511	1,322	1,184	1,117	959	1,092	1,057
All causes	18,984	19,300	16,440	15,457	15,111	14,514	14,383
				Females			
Infections	1,562	1,541	843	476	255	131	40
Tuberculosis	858	657	507	349	227	53	16
Venereal	52	38	29	23	11	10	4
Cancer	1,711	1,733	1,812	1,812	1,795	1,627	1,680
Other tumours	111	84	90	120	122	143	23
Other general	79	95	115	102	80	44	113
Blood-forming	100	108	119	82	73	74	49
Rheumatism	127	139	115	102	69	86	108
Diabetes	240	260	290	376	389	236	234
Respiratory	1,885	1,914	1,666	1,262	965	678	556
Nervous	1,762	1,726	1,601	1,229	1,974	2,310	1,446
Cardiovascular	2,843	2,821	3,182	4,539	4,714	4,657	5,154
Alimentary	821	750	613	514	401	329	278
Genitourinary	818	796	923	992	734	264	244
Child-bearing	251	228	210	153	86	29	12
Skin and cellular	143	120	88	36	19	23	14
Bones	17	10	19	19	15	33	53
Congenital malformations	43	58	64	72	75	81	74
Early infancy	353	411	347	286	243	170	133
Ill-defined	3,164	3,488	2,273	1,135	696	274	99
Violence, accidents, and poisonings	525	452	398	448	443	495	526
All causes	17,466	17,451	15,304	14,127	13,390	11,745	10,859

*LTA, standardized on to the male and female life tables of Australia, 1933. These populations are detailed in Lancaster (1950e).
From Lancaster (1978).

populations of 1933 give more emphasis to the older age groups, and comparisons made with their help are more "biological" in the sense that these populations are roughly the stationary population implied by the total age-specific death rates, see chapter 4. With their use, it is evident that, with the England and Wales 1901 population as base in Table 41.3.4, the standardized rates of males have declined from 11,474 per 1,000,000 per annum to 6,753. A large proportion of this decline is accounted for by the declines in "infections," 1,775 to 37; tuberculosis, 913 to 29; venereal, 118 to 3; and respiratory, 1,197 to 526; with a total for these classes of 4,003 to 595. In other words, out of a total decline of 4,721, the decline in these classes has been 3,408, or about three quarters of the total. For the females, a similar finding is evident; these classes have contributed 3,011 to a total decline of 5,368, or more than one half of the total decline. The largest decline for the deaths from all causes was between the second and third decades, that is, around 1920. The rates from cancers and other tumors showed some tendency to rise. Some of this increase is probably due to more careful certification of the elderly, an observation which is confirmed by referring to Table 41.3.5, which gives different weights to the rates at older ages, but there have been increases in the age-specific death rates from lung cancer and also melanoma. The increase is greater in the "oldest" of these three standard populations and less in the "younger," for the equivalent average death rates of Table 41.3.6 give no weight to the rates at ages over 65 years. The rates in the group of "other general" diseases, which includes allergic diseases, diabetes, diseases of the blood-forming organs, and chronic rheumatic diseases other than cardiac, have declined to about two thirds of their original size, but the diseases included have never been a large cause of mortality. The rates from diseases of the nervous system had already declined by the fourth decade to about half the value in the first. Here again, these declines are largely explained by the improvement in the control of infectious diseases, because "convulsions" deaths were almost always secondary to some infection. These deaths, occurring mainly in children, were classified in the earlier epochs as "diseases of the ear" or "other diseases of the nervous system". There had been some changes in assignment of deaths due to cerebral vascular causes between the fourth and fifth decades, or, in other words, between the fourth and fifth revisions of the ICD and it is probably not really appropriate to discuss "nervous" diseases, cardiovascular diseases, renal diseases, and senility and ill-defined diseases separately in making secular comparisons. The residuum of "alimentary diseases," after the deaths due to gastroenteritis have been reassigned to the class of other infectious diseases, is relatively unimportant. There have been worthwhile declines in the death rates from the genitourinary diseases only since 1940, and these appear to be almost entirely due to the changes in assignment of chronic nephritis, which has tended to become classified with nervous and cardiovascular diseases.

Diseases of the skin, cellular tissues, and organs of locomotion have declined in importance. This is readily explained by the principal diseases in this class being boils, carbuncles, osteomyelitis, and similar diseases.

The death rates from malformations have remained practically stationary since the second decade. The death rates from diseases peculiar to the first year of life have declined, but not as rapidly as the rates from "other causes of infancy"; a longer discussion of this point is given in chapter 32.

Senility and ill-defined causes have declined as an assigned cause of death largely because of the policy of the Bureau of Statistics of not accepting such certificates. Because formerly these vague diagnoses were usually in the elderly, there has been an increase in the deaths apparently due to cardiovascular disease, cerebral accidents, and chronic nephritis.

The death rates from violence, accidental causes, and poisonings had declined steadily from the first to the fifth decade, but there has been a slight increase in the most recent decade.

The general conclusions to be drawn from Tables 41.3.4 to 41.3.6 are that almost all the improvements in mortality in Australia since

TABLE 41.3.6. Equivalent average death rates in Australia* (deaths per 1,000,000 per annum).

Cause of death	1908–1910	1911–1920	1921–1930	1931–1940	1941–1950	1951–1960	1961–1970
				Males			
Infections	1,350	1,472	731	404	226	111	32
Tuberculosis	1,140	1,000	790	566	415	121	31
Venereal	149	145	107	86	39	23	5
Cancer	826	873	838	775	739	802	1,005
Other tumours	34	30	42	98	102	126	13
Other general	51	77	56	39	30	19	96
Blood-forming	76	80	65	34	20	16	14
Rheumatism	46	52	49	40	24	44	57
Diabetes	101	95	86	80	72	45	57
Respiratory	1,004	1,123	960	739	468	381	357
Nervous	744	741	555	389	560	611	341
Cardiovascular	1,271	1,336	1,251	1,643	1,960	2,104	2,412
Alimentary	525	509	480	447	355	254	199
Genitourinary	654	661	574	502	377	173	103
Skin and cellular	49	41	39	23	8	7	4
Bones	18	17	24	27	10	11	16
Congenital malformations	59	82	89	98	93	101	89
Early infancy	501	585	493	403	347	239	195
Ill-defined	323	296	194	70	45	23	21
Violence, accidents, and poisonings	1,368	1,279	1,103	987	811	925	926
All causes	10,290	10,498	8,533	7,444	6,704	6,141	5,972
				Females			
Infections	1,083	1,162	608	336	179	90	27
Tuberculosis	893	688	524	349	215	42	10
Venereal	45	41	28	21	11	5	2
Cancer	962	939	926	870	836	751	823
Other tumours	75	61	68	105	100	99	16
Other general	67	90	93	83	66	24	67
Blood-forming	91	87	77	39	25	22	13
Rheumatism	59	63	57	48	28	49	62
Diabetes	128	134	133	140	124	61	54
Respiratory	651	665	574	444	292	185	145
Nervous	686	651	549	397	608	570	301
Cardiovascular	1,028	994	908	1,033	933	827	891
Alimentary	485	431	363	293	217	148	109
Genitourinary	510	462	470	436	308	138	119
Child-bearing	288	260	241	176	98	33	14
Skin and cellular	43	32	30	20	8	9	4
Bones	11	8	13	12	6	10	15
Congenital malformations	47	63	70	78	82	85	79
Early infancy	384	446	376	310	264	184	145
Ill-defined	224	160	100	28	19	11	12
Violence, accidents, and poisonings	341	293	260	247	207	251	334
All causes	8,103	7,736	6,471	5,469	4,627	3,593	3,243

*Standardized on to a population of equal numbers in each of the 13 5-year age groups, 0 to 65 years. See §3.9.
From Lancaster (1978).

the beginning of the twentieth century have been in diseases due to infective causes; a small fraction of the improvement over these decades has been due to decreased rates from violent and accidental causes. There have been no declines in the total death rates from the cancers.

We now give a summary of the mortality experience in Australia. After 1788 the European and other migrants settled on a continent that was almost entirely free of anthropozoonoses, that is, zoonoses communicable to man. The aboriginal population was free of serious infective disease. There was isolation from the rest of the world; cases of acute infective diseases on ships coming out from Europe would have caused a shipboard epidemic that had run its course long before reaching Australia. In contrast to the experience of the United States, there was little trade with highly populated tropical regions and, so, no importation of diseases from mainland Asia into Australia; in particular, malaria has never been an important problem in the larger centers of Australian population. Of the other classical pestilences, cholera has only entered Australia in recent years by air travel; epidemics of bubonic plague occurred in the years 1900 to 1909, 1921 to 1922, and 1923 to 1925, and its mode of transmission was studied by J. Ashburton Thompson in 1901 and 1906. Cases of murine typhus were studied by F.S. Hone in 1922–1923; smallpox has occurred but with only 18 deaths since 1908; yellow fever has never occurred. Influenza was prevented from reaching Australia until 1919; rabies has never occurred. Tuberculosis was brought in with the Europeans and has been a leading cause of death, although the age-specific rates have been declining since the 1880s and from the earliest cohort, born in 1866, which it is practicable to study. The enteric fevers have been important for mortality, being typical diseases of pioneering and mining communities. Measles has occurred in intense epidemics at irregular intervals but has caused less mortality in Australia than in Europe, where it has tended, as in London, to attack at ages 0 and 1. Accident and injury played a large part under pioneering conditions. There have been no large concen-

trations of poor persons in great cities and no starvation and there have been high standards of literacy. In the early years of this century, mortality rates tended to be lower in Australia and New Zealand than in, for instance, England and Wales, but in recent years there have been only minor differences in the rates. See Cumpston and McCallum (1927), Gandevia (1971b), and Gordon (1976a, b).

For the mortality of individual diseases in Australia, see Lancaster (passim), but note also the references to and tables for Australia in §7.3 for tuberculosis; §10.9 influenza; §11.6 measles; §11.8 rubella; §25.1 circulatory; §26.1 respiratory; §27.1 digestive; §28.1 genitourinary; §29.2 maternal mortality; §32.9 infant mortality; §34.15 convict mortality; and chapters 35 and 36 for mortality by age.

41.4 Maori New Zealand

The Maori population before the visit of James Cook in 1769 was free of the common infective diseases and anthropozoonoses; in particular, it was free of malaria and the other great pestilences; Pool (1977) suggests that there may have been some famine incidents. Possibly all else is speculation; the population size was 125,000 to 175,000. Warfare may have been endemic; Pool (1977, Table 5.4) gives some estimates of deaths from warfare in 1820–1840 of which the lowest is 30,000, about one-fifth of the estimated total population of New Zealand; specifically, 1,572 persons are reported to have been killed in the Atiawa conquest of the Chatham Islands in 1838. Visitors became more frequent after the settlement of the British in Sydney, New South Wales. Whalers had established permanent shore settlements by 1821, and they were joined by escaped convicts from New South Wales. British sovereignty was not established until 1840. Gold was discovered at Otago in 1861 and Westland in 1865, both in the South Island. As a result, the European population rose from 100,000 in 1861 to 250,000 in 1870 and the Maoris became the minority.

With the increasing European population and increased contact from overseas, the possibility of epidemics increased. Pool (1977) lists

12 epidemics of measles in the period 1835 to 1916, 8 epidemics of whooping cough, 16 epidemics of typhoid, 10 epidemics of influenza, and a total of 6 other epidemics, 1 of erysipelas, 2 of scarlet fever, 1 of typhus, 1 of smallpox, and 1 of mumps in the same period. The great influenza pandemic came to the Maoris in 1918. Tuberculosis has been a leading cause of Maori death since 1921. Infant mortality rates have been high but are declining; the related measure, q_0, the probability of dying in the first year of life, is deducible from Pool (1977, Table 6.6); the probabilities are for males (females): 1926, 119 (112); 1936, 119 (86); 1945, 94 (80); 1951, 80 (70); 1956, 67 (51), per 1,000. These rates have evidently improved further, for in 1973 the age-specific mortality rates for males (females) at ages younger than 5 years were 6 (4) per 1,000 per annum, with the rates about 30% (16%) more than the rates for the non-Maoris. At older ages the rates of the non-Maoris are more favorable than those of the Maoris, but the differences between the two groups can be expected to decrease. Pool (1977) provides an extensive bibliography and Pool (1973) gives estimates of vital rates from 1850 to 1914, approximately. Schwimmer (1968) gives an account of the Maoris in the mid-1960s. See Prior and Tasman-Jones (1981) for the influence of western diseases on the Maoris.

41.5 New Zealand: The Non-Maori Population

There are many resemblances in the mortality experiences of the largely European populations of Australia and New Zealand. New Zealand with its more southerly position has been free of tropical diseases; the population has been literate; there have been no great cities and no extremes of poverty. Like Australia, its experience of infective diseases has been greatly influenced by its isolation and small population size. The mortality experience has been reviewed by Lancaster and Donovan (1966, 1967a, 1968) and Donovan (1969a, b; 1970a, b, c), of these 1969a is an extensive bibliography.

Here, we can only pick out a few highlights.

Death rates are available for the usual age groups from 1876–1880 onward. There have been great declines in mortality, especially at the younger ages. Masculinity rates have been high and have been increasing steadily over the period studied; thus, in 1876–1880 (1961–1965) the masculinities were 117(134), 106(160), 101(267), 121(150), and 128(191) at ages, in years, 0–4, 10–14, 20–24, 40–44, and 60–64, respectively. The sex differences are reflected in the cohort life tables, for example, in the expectations of life at birth of males (females) for births by midyear as follows: 52.6(56.3), 1866; 54.7(57.9), 1871; 55.1(58.5), 1876; 56.5(60.4), 1881; 58.1(62.3), 1886; 58.5(63.2), 1891; 60.0(64.8), 1896; 60.7(65.3), 1901. Further, the female cohorts of 1901 and 1906 had net reproduction rates of 0.984 and 0.998, and thus failed to reproduce themselves. Tuberculosis has yielded low masculinity rates below 100, from age 5 up to age 35 years. The peak in young adult life has not been as marked as in Australia or, indeed, as in many other countries (Springett, 1950), when examined by either calendar or cohort methods; there has been a large contribution to the decline in mortality from tuberculosis.

In 1872–1880 the deaths per 1,000,000 per annum were for males (females) as follows: enteric fevers, 442(457); diphtheria, 365(507); whooping cough, 256(401); scarlet fever, 120 (157); measles, 95(134); and influenza, 30(31). Already, by 1891–1900, the mortality rates from enteric fever and whooping cough had declined to less than one-third of these figures and diphtheria to one-half. There were large epidemics of measles in 1893 and 1899, 511 and 137 deaths, respectively; no deaths occurred in 1895. This is behavior typical of measles in small communities. It has been paralleled by that of rubella, of which there were epidemics in 1898 and the years 1938 to 1943, causing high incidences of births of the deaf (Lancaster and Pickering, 1952e). Infant mortality rates have been low; birth weights were early available; for example, the official *Report on the Medical Statistics of New Zealand for the Year 1952* gives a table of perinatal and infant deaths by weight and cause; there have been special campaigns on infant health, notably by F. Truby King. For an early account, see Bannister (1838).

41.6 Other Pacific Islands

In this section, we add a few notes and references for some of the islands of the south Pacific Ocean.

In §5.4, the epidemic of measles in Fiji in 1875 has already been discussed; we add Gordon (1875) and the general demographic text of McArthur (1967). Adels and Gajdusek (1963) have given a general survey of measles patterns in the region.

Symposium (1961) surveys infant mortality rates in Asia and Oceania.

The Polynesians and Maoris in isolated communities and in New Zealand are reviewed by Prior and Tasman-Jones (1981) and Prior, Salmond, et al. (1981), with special note of mortality and the introduction of western diseases.

For Nauru, Tuvalu, and Western Samoa, see Zimmet and Whitehouse (1981); for Papua-New Guinea (Niugini), see Sinnett (1975).

Chapter 42
America: Beginnings and Development

42.1 The Peopling of America

The peopling of America is a recent event. The Aleuts, Eskimos, and the American Indians all arrived via Alaska. The details are available in the monograph by Hopkins (1967a). Müller-Beck (1967) believes that there is only firm evidence of migrations since 30,000 BP in the Bering Sea region and about 13,000 BP in the southwest United States. During the Ice Ages, there was dry land in much of the region occupied by the present Bering Sea, with its coastline corresponding roughly with the present 100 meter depth line, so that the coastline was south of the present Pribilof Islands, then ran in a southeasterly direction toward the tip of the Alaska Peninsula, and turned southwest past the tip of Umnak, for which see Laughlin (1972) and Laughlin, Jørgensen, and Frøhlich (1979, Figure 4.1). Indeed, there was a land bridge more than 1,500 km wide over the period 35,000 to 11,000 BP. The Aleuts are believed to have traveled from an Asian homeland round this large arc of coast not later than 8,000 BP. The more direct sea route via the Commander Islands seems not to have been used before 1741, the date of arrival of the Russian explorers. The artifacts found at Anangula, now an island a few kilometers north of Umnak, are said to resemble preceramic Japanese and other Asian findings of roughly the same date.

The Indians seem to have migrated from Asia through the interior of the temporary land of Beringia, not by coast, as early as 25,000

BP. Some remained in Alaska and others migrated down through an ice-free zone east of the Rocky Mountains. When this ice-free zone was closed off by ice sheets, there were two groups of "Indians." From the southern group developed all the various tribes and nations of Amerindians. See Müller-Beck (1967, pp. 400, 401). A synthesis of the known findings is given in Hopkins (1967b). It is believed that no further migrations into America occurred until after Columbus, if we except the transient settlements of the Norsemen. See Denevan (1976) and Stewart (1973) for the indigenous population of the Americas in 1492 and Crosby (1972) for the exchanges of flora, fauna, and human populations after that date.

42.2 Pre-Columbian America

The route of migration, described in the previous section, was not compatible with the transport of many of the great pestilences to America from the Old World, that is, Africa and Eurasia. We list the diseases in the following.

Cholera. This disease was unknown in America before 1830.

Enteric Fever. From modern experience with enteric fever and its disappearance as soon as high-density living is compensated for by the construction of drains and, above all, the delivery of a pure water supply, it is unlikely that the enteric fevers would have been perpetuated in the great migrations. Salmonellas seem to be ubiquitous among animals and would have been a cause of death in man in pre-Columbian America.

Bubonic Plague. On general principles, we can see that bubonic plague could not have arrived and survived in America before the modern European invasions because the domestic rats were not yet available for its passage. Furthermore, it is known that bubonic plague has only become established in its many present day niduses since the beginning of the 1894 pandemic.

Bartonellosis. This disease must have been endemic in western South America before 1492.

Tularemia and Other Minor Pestilences. Tularemia, as we have seen in §8.4, is now widespread in North America, Japan, Soviet Asia and Europe, and southern Europe and would have had ample opportunity to pass either way across Beringia when that broad bridge was available. The same argument applies to other zoonoses.

Leprosy. According to Skinsnes (1973, p. 223), leprosy spread from Portugal to Brazil in the sixteenth century; other sources were the negro slaves and the indentured Chinese and Indians.

Smallpox, Measles, and Rubella. After these viruses had taken their human-parasitic form, they could not have crossed into America from the Old World because conditions of population size were not suitable for their perpetuation.

Yellow Fever. Because of a historical accident, yellow fever was first recognized as a clinical entity in America in 1648 and not observed in Africa until 1778; doubts arose, therefore, as to whether it existed in pre-Columbian America. The arguments given in §12.1 are conclusive that it arose in Africa and only reached America after transport by ship.

Malaria. The case of pre-Columbian malaria in America is less certain. *Falciparum* malaria certainly has properties not permitting a passage through Beringia. See §15.8 and §42.5.

Leishmaniasis and Trypanosomiasis. Mucocutaneous (American) leishmaniasis (espundia) and Chagas' disease due to *Trypanosoma cruzi* were already endemic in 1492; the former is illustrated in pre-Columbian pottery.

Endemic and Venereal Syphilis. The origins of these diseases are still controversial.

Helminthic Diseases. Schistosomiases caused by the *haematobium* and *mansoni* species were both imported with the slave trade from Africa (Scott, 1943). Among the hookworms, *Necator americanus* was indigenous and the ancylostomes were imported. Among helminths, *Wuchereria bancrofti*, a cause of filariasis, was probably imported from Africa; more certainly so were *Acanthocheilonema perstans*, the cause of loa loa, and *Dracunculus medinensis*, the cause of the guinea worm infection.

For disease in prehistoric America, see Jarcho (1964).

42.3 Aleutians

There are two accessible accounts of the mortality of the Aleutians, Harper (1979), who accepts rather uncritically much of the methodology of Acsádi and Nemeskéri (1970) and of Karl Pearson, and Laughlin (1980), who is more critical of the treatment of the data. Harper (1979) contains many additional observations, particularly those of the Russian priest I.E. Veniaminov (1797–1879), who was stationed in Unalaska for over a decade.

There seems to be agreement on an estimate of 16,000 persons on almost 13,000 km^2 of land in 1741, the year of the Russian discovery of the islands. An epidemic of smallpox occurred in 1838; no man older than 80 survived it, and the children were severely affected. Measles was epidemic in 1848 and 1849 and caused many deaths among the young. Harper (1979) comments that "the Aleut adaptive level had dropped nearly 10 years of life" in the hundred years since first Russian contact. Little information is available before the year 1948, although "intervening bouts of influenza and almost constant tuberculosis ravaged the Aleuts."

But there had been worse shocks than disease to the Aleutians. First, there was the massacre, probably in 1764; according to the account of Laughlin (1980), a party of Cossacks were oppressing villages to the south of Umnak; assassins murdered the Cossack leader as he examined a pelt, then slew his followers in the house on shore and the next day, the cook on the boat. Retaliatory strikes from September 1764 on by the Cossacks resulted in the deaths of the able-bodied hunters and starvation for the other members of the community, for they had no refuge. Laughlin (1980) believes that the population, originally 16,000, was reduced in these early campaigns to two-thirds or even half of its original size. There was also forced labor on the ships, leading to further peril for the men and starvation for their families. Some Aleuts were relocated on the Pribilof Islands with unfavorable results. By 1799 the population probably had been reduced to about 2,000. Beginning in that year, 1799, protective rules were introduced in favor of the Aleuts, but the schools and hospitals came only after the great reduction of population size.

The Aleuts have been mentioned by authors as attaining a very old age, especially in comparison with the Eskimos. Laughlin (1980, Table 2.4) is rather against this reputation. Sixty-eight men took part in the seal catch of 1870, and it is recorded that of these men, 46 were dead, 15 were able men, 6 were healthy old men, and 1 was a confirmed invalid in July 1887; this is an enormous mortality for the experience of young men, presuming the initial mean age was not more than 30 years, no less than 67% dying in those 17 years.

42.4 Amerindians of the United States

Amerindian mortality is treated more conveniently in the following chapter. Some special problems may be mentioned.

Smallpox. Some epidemics are mentioned in §42.8. An extended discussion is available in Hopkins (1983a). Smallpox was the leading cause of the decline in population of the Amerindians within the borders of the present United States. Some estimates of the deaths go as high as 6,000,000 in a population of 12,000,000, see Wishnow and Steinfeld (1976). See also Duffy (1951).

See Williams (1909) for epidemics, Merbs and Miller (1985) for health and disease in the prehistoric southwest, West (1981) for diseases of the western world among the natives, Cook (1976) for the population of California 1769–1970, and Goodchild (1985) for Indian survival skills.

42.5 Epidemiologic Problems Solved

There are now close parallels between the mortality in the United States and the states of Europe and, more generally, the developed world; but this was not always so, as we will see later, especially in this section and in §42.6, which follows. The differences came about partly because of poverty leading to unhygienic conditions that were dangerous in a subtropical region, and so especially in the south, and partly because of the proximity to the West Indies and to Latin America, from which fevers, especially malaria and yellow fever, were frequently reintroduced into cities along the eastern seaboard. It is of interest to compare the American success in combating the resulting epidemics in a generally prosperous country with the experience in Africa, where little progress had been made.

Cholera. Cholera first reached America in 1832 (Rosenberg, 1962, 1972). As elsewhere, the epidemics of 1832, 1849, and 1866 caused an enhanced interest in public health. In 1832 cholera entered the continent by ship through the ports of Quebec and New York. An emigrant ship brought the disease to New Orleans, from whence it was spread widely in the Mississippi Valley. Wain (1970) quotes an estimate that 2.5% of the world's population was attacked, with a case fatality rate approaching 50%. In 1848 cholera was again introduced and spread with the gold seekers to California, killing thousands of them. When the cholera reappeared in 1866, the country was more prepared and boards of health had been set up; Bordley and Harvey (1976) believe that the epidemics were shorter in those cities with improved hygienic conditions. In 1873 cholera again reached the United States, but the epidemic was limited.

Enteric Fevers. Gay (1918) believed that the United States was particularly backward in applying methods of hygienic protection that had long prevailed in other lands; in 1914 typhoid fever remained the ninth among the contributing causes of death and the fifth among the infectious diseases, being exceeded only by tuberculosis, pneumonia, infantile diarrhea, and diphtheria in the United States, although there had been a decline from 359 deaths per 1,000,000 in 1900 to 179 in 1913. In 1910–1919, the death rate from typhoid in the 57 largest cities of the United States was 196 per 1,000,000 per annum, compared with a rate of 65 in the 33 largest European cities in 1901–1910. In other words, the American rates in 1910–1919 were three times those of the European cities 10 years earlier. In the period 1900–1914, an interesting reversal of the urban-rural comparison occurred; during this time, for example, urban New York rates decreased from 206 per 1,000,000 in 1900 to 140 in 1914, whereas the rural New York rates began at 155 but were still at the same level in 1913 and 1914. Gay (1918) gives a table of the enteric fever mortality rates per 1,000,000 per annum in cities, chiefly of the United States, according to type of water supply. These rates range from 40 in Munich and Vienna with pure mountain springs, 96 in European cities with filtered water supplies, 162 with filtered water supplies in the United States, through six more classes, ending with 457 for cities with mixed surface and underground waters, including St. Paul, the Brooklynborough, Columbus, and McKeesport, and finally an average of 616 for river water subject to pollution, with two entries over 1,100 per 1,000,000 per annum, namely, Allegheny and Pittsburg. Gay (1918, Figure 2) shows quite dramatic falls in the mortality rates of such cities as Lawrence, MA, Paterson, NJ, Albany, NY, Binghampton, NY, Lowell, MA, Newark, NJ, and Jersey City, NJ, where a change was made to a purer water supply in 1893, 1902, 1899, 1902, 1894–1895, 1892, and 1896, respectively. See also Wain (1970, pp. 287–289) for the story of "typhoid Mary" and §§6.5 and 6.6 for water supplies.

Yellow Fever. See §§12.1 and 12.2.

Typhus. Recrudescent typhus was first noted among immigrants from Europe to the United States, for which see §14.2.

Malaria. See §15.8. The most deleterious effects of malaria were felt in the south during the Reconstruction era. With a shortage of white overseers and with free but inefficient negro laborers, the land was fallow with great increases in the mosquito population. Malaria continued to increase for 35 years and, with hookworm, was an important cause of the slow economic recovery. Faust (1945) believed that malaria increased with man-made breeding grounds near human habitations, for example, artificial ponds for stock and borrow pits near the railways. There were also natural breeding grounds in the residual ponds after floods. The control of mosquito breeding grounds and quinine therapy ($4.50 per ounce in the 1880s and 25 cents in 1913) were the principal factors in the declines in malaria mortality before World War I. Nevertheless, in 1933 the rates of malaria mortality were 0.5 in Arkansas, 0.35 in Florida, and 0.3 in Mississippi per 1,000 per annum. With the introduction of the new antimalarials and with renewed public health measures, the rates have remained low since World War II.

Hookworm Disease. As a result of a private conversation of C.W. Stiles, who was reporting on the high incidence of hookworm disease in the south of the United States with members of the (Rockefeller) General Education Board, a hookworm campaign was initiated by the Rockefeller Sanitary Commission in 1909. It began with a survey of incidence. In some schools 90% of the pupils were infected, and in a survey covering 11 states, the average prevalence rate was 40% in the schools, 42% in college students, and 32% in the state militia. An educational drive was begun to alert both the laity and the medical practitioners who had not recognized the disease. The principal means of prevention were (*i*) the construction of efficient privies and (*ii*) the wearing of shoes to prevent the larvae reaching the skin. See §19.7.

Pellagra. Pellagra had been observed in areas where maize was a large constituent of the diet, except among the Amerinds, who first steeped it in an alkaline solution before cooking. Pellagra in the United States was first clearly described during the Civil War, probably being one of the causes of the high death rates among prisoners of war in the southern prisoner-of-war camps. It also occurred in the civilian population of the south. In particular, J. Goldberger noticed that it occurred in orphanages, affecting children older than 3 years of age but not those younger and not the attendants, because of differences in their diets. He obtained funds to supplement the diet, and in a few months the pellagra cases disappeared. Goldberger carried out controlled trials and proved that it was not an infectious disease. An addition of casein to the diet did not prevent it, but an addition of dried yeast did; later, it was determined that the important factor was nicotinamide, belonging to the vitamin B complex, for which see §22.13 and Goldberger, Wheeler, and Sydenstricker (1920).

42.6 New York as Entrepôt

Fort (New) Amsterdam (later New York) was founded in 1624 as a trading post of the Dutch West India Company and was taken over by the British in 1664. It was retaken by the Dutch in 1673 but was formally ceded to the British in 1674. In the early years the pioneers existed largely on dried and salted food brought from Europe, according to Duffy (1968). Their first tasks were to build shelters, to construct fortifications against both Indians and possibly European rivals, and to begin agriculture to become self-sufficient in food. They fought a major war in 1641–1645 against the Indians. By 1650 the population was approximately 1,000. At this time there was no serious sanitary problem as the soil was sandy and porous and sewage could be dumped into the nearby rivers.

The absence of acute infective disease was noted by contemporaries, and for some years the mortality rate was minimal, 2 to 3 per 1,000 per annum, such a low rate being possible only because of the youth of the population. Early public health measures regulated the manufacture of bread, the construction of privies, and the throwing of refuse into the canals. Mortality in the earlier years was due largely to Indian depredations; malaria was not epidemic.

In 1664 the city became British and was renamed New York; the population had reached 4,000 by the 1690s. Public health ordinances at this time referred principally to bakers and butchers, to public nuisances, including hogs feeding on the streets, and to the water supply. Private wells were dug, but the chief supply of good water was from outside the city bounds. See also §6.12. With the larger population, epidemics became a possibility. In September 1668 there was a severe epidemic, possibly malaria or typhoid. In 1679–1680 there was an intense epidemic of smallpox with many deaths. In late summer 1702 a yellow fever epidemic appeared and spread widely with "dyeing near 20 persons dayly for some months" and with 570 persons dying in the space of about 3 months in a population of 4,500, and so about 12% (Duffy, 1968).

The city continued to grow—8,600 in 1731 and more than 20,000 by 1776—but yellow fever remained a great problem and reappeared in the early 1740s.

Immigrants. Duffy (1968) mentions that there were regulations requiring that shipowners who were landing immigrants guarantee that they would not become a charge on the city. When the rate of entry became too large, it was impossible to police the regulations, with the result that the immigrants often arrived half-starved and half-sick after a grueling voyage. There was then no one to welcome them, no proper transit camps, and they were robbed, defrauded by rogues, and abused on landing. They were admitted into the overcrowded almshouses or entered the institutions set up by the brokers who had accepted the responsibility of the shipowners; the state of these institutions was notorious. The result was that many migrants lived in abject poverty. Migration was greatest in the 1840s because of political troubles in Germany and the famine in Ireland.

The conditions on the voyages were terrible; one ship lost 1,100 out of 1,916 passengers on a voyage from Liverpool, and a further 100 died after landing, making a mortality rate for the voyage of 63%. During $2\frac{1}{2}$ months in late 1853, 1,118 out of 16,272 passengers to America died at sea. The solution to the problem was to land all immigrants on a small island off Manhattan, in 1855 Castle Garden, and, later on, in 1892 Ellis Island. European nations and the US Federal Government forced shipowners and captains to provide appropriate conditions of water, food, and accommodation on board the ships. Conditions were somewhat alleviated, but the migrants helped to form a large poverty mass. Moreover, they found difficulty in leaving New York to obtain work elsewhere; the formation of slums followed inevitably, with cellar dwellings, poor ventilation, general filth, crowding of many persons into single rooms, low ratio of privies to persons, inadequate drainage, and narrow halls, staircases, and lanes making for fire traps.

Duffy (1968) remarks that the intense Irish immigration caused 15,919 deaths in 1848, there being a great number of deaths due to dysentery 739, typhus 720, and typhoid fever 223, but also consumption 1,869, convulsions 1,193, and marasmus 680. In 1857 the leading causes of death were: consumption 2,814, convulsions 1,589, cholera infantum (i.e., gastrointestinal infections) 1,308, and dropsy in the head 935, the deaths totaling 23,333; deaths of children under 21 years were 15,775, of which almost two thirds occurred in children under 5. The infant mortality reached a record high of 165.8 per 1,000 in 1850–1854, dropping to 102.9 in 1860–1865, "an alarmingly high rate." The rates in the "foreign-born," living mostly in the slums, were much higher than in the native-born, generally living in better circumstances and in the suburbs.

Cholera. Great epidemics occurred in 1832, 1849, and 1866, the last great cholera epidemic in the United States. In 1871 there was a ship-board epidemic of 52 cases with 12 deaths but no spread to the city.

Smallpox. Neglect of vaccination had led to the possibility of epidemics. There were 805 deaths in 1871, 929 in 1872, no mention in 1873, 484 in 1874, and 1,280 in 1875, 451 in 1881, 259 in 1882, 81 in 1892, 102 in 1893, and 154 in 1894.

Diphtheria. After 1866 diphtheria increased in importance with great epidemics in 1873 and 1874 causing 1,151 and 500 deaths, respectively. Duffy (1968) says that the annual number of deaths from diphtheria never fell below 1,000 in the years 1880–1896 and on three occasions was above 2,000.

The experiences of the other eastern seaports were similar; see for New York, Duffy (1974), for Baltimore, Howard (1924), and for Boston, Blake (1959).

42.7 United States of America, Generalities

There are great difficulties in obtaining a historical account of mortality in the United States from its first settlement. During much of the time, even into this century, new states and settlements were being opened, under conditions that were not conducive to the regular collection of statistics of vital events or to the holding of censuses.

According to Meindl and Swedlund (1977), the history of the trends of mortality in the New World is very incomplete prior to 1850. These authors cite other authors, listed below, who attempt to estimate levels of mortality in the years before 1860. All were troubled by the problems of incomplete registration. A tentative hypothesis was that there had been a negative association between population density and life expectancy in colonial times, that is, urban mortality tended to be higher than rural. In the above authors' article, there were only two commonly listed causes of death, "consumption," possibly almost always tuberculosis, and "dysentery," the latter affecting children only and which, the authors suspect, may have been enteric fever, whereas in contemporary Boston there were epidemics of smallpox, measles, and diphtheria; later, urban Massachusetts suffered severely from typhoid and related diseases and the Asiatic cholera. Tuberculosis rates were high in young adult life. Possibly this was typical of rural United States before this century. Among the authors are: Lockridge (1966), writing on Dedham, MA; Jacobson (1957), on expectation of life in the United States in 1850; Jacobson (1964), on survival for generations since 1840; Blake (1959), on public health in Boston, 1630–1822; Shattuck (1841), on Boston; Jaffe and Lourie (1942), on life tables for whites in 1830.

The unsatisfactory state of the statistics for the whole of the United States could only be solved after creation of the United States Bureau of the Census in 1902. Official accounts of the vital statistics rates are available in Linder and Grove (1943) and Grove and Hetzel (1968). A special feature of the mortality statistics is that they cannot conveniently be computed for the country as a whole before 1933. In 1915 pooling of data from the constituent states of the death registration area began and was complete in 1933. The death registration area for 1900 consisted of 10 states, the District of Columbia, and a number of cities located in the nonregistration states. It included 40.5% of the population of continental United States, predominantly urban and white; beginning in 1940, all published statistical series included only data from the registration states up to 1933, when Texas joined the registration states, completing the continental United States. In 1959 Alaska and in 1960 Hawaii were added to the other states. Although estimates of births are available for the entire country from 1909, there are no such mortality tables, but the rates for the death registration states are believed to give good estimates for the whole country. More extended series can be developed by considering only the original death registration states, or those included by 1920 or other time, or some specified state such as Massachusetts.

The Bureau of the Census publishes the *Statistical Abstract of the United States*, *Histor-* *ical Statistics of the United States*, and various *Reports on the Census*. Other official publications include those of the US National Center for Health Statistics, the US Public Health Service, and the US Surgeon-General. See also Anderson (1988). The *Journal of the American Statistical Association* has made available much information of medical or vital statistical interest. The Population Association of America publishes *Demography*. Other journals published in the United States include the *American Journal of Hygiene*, *American Journal of the Diseases of Children*, *American Journal of Epidemiology*, *American Journal of the Medical Sciences*, *Journal of Infective Diseases*, *Biometrics*, *Human Biology*, *American Journal of Public Health*, *Milbank Memorial Fund Quarterly*, and *Population Index*.

Much has been written on mortality in the United States. The small bibliography below may help to direct attention to points not covered in the text or by references cited there.

For a summary, see Erhardt and Berlin (1974) who give many references, including the series of which their book is the conclusion.

Atlantic migration: Crosby (1972); Hansen (1940).

Bibliographies: mortality trends, US National Center (1964a); 1954–1963, US National Center (1966b, c); vital and health statistics, US National Center (1970).

General medical reviews: Ashburn (1947); Dublin and Lotka (1934); Simpson (1954); Winslow (1943, 1952).

Life tables: Dublin and Lotka (1937); Dublin, Lotka, and Spiegelman (1949); Greville (1946).

County health levels: Anderson and Lerner (1960).

Infant mortality: Chase (1967, 1969, 1972, 1977); Preston and Haines (1984).

Childhood: Preston and Haines (1984); WHO-America (1974); history of American pediatrics, Cone (1979).

Chronic diseases: Lilienfeld, Gifford, et al. (1966), including chapters on diabetes (Marks), chronic respiratory disease (Moriyama), cardiovascular disease (Borhani), and general mortality (Dorn).

Health reform: Wharton (1982); Kramer (1948).

Socioeconomic: Stockwell (1961); Wu and Winslow (1933).

Therapy, 1820–1885: Warner (1986).

Urbanization: Clegg and Garlick (1980); Duffy and Carroll (1967); Miles (1970); Puffer and Griffith (1967).

Wars: Ayres (1919); Civil War, Steiner (1968).

42.8 United States Mortality from Infection

We run through the causes of death roughly in the order of the ICD.

Cholera and Enteric Fever. See §§42.5 and 42.6.

Tuberculosis. Doege (1965) analyzed the death rates from tuberculosis in the US Death Registration states to obtain series over the greatest possible stretch of time. Standardized death rates show a marked decline, usually, to a rate in 1960 of less than one-tenth of the rate in 1900. The rates at any epoch are, in order of decreasing magnitude, nonwhite males, nonwhite females, white males, and white females. The mean age at death has increased by about 20 years in each of the four classes mentioned above; for all races and sexes, the mean has gone from 35 years to 55 years. Doege (1965, Figure 3) shows that on a calendar basis, the rates have decreased at all ages, but the shape of the curves has changed, so in 1960 the death rates no longer have maxima at young adult life but increase throughout life after age 10 years to the oldest ages. For a discussion of such changes see chapter 7, in which a similar pattern has been noted in many countries. Sydenstricker (1927, 1974) rejects the theories of the tubercularization of the population and the decline of virulence in the bacillus, neither of which could be tested scientifically; he favors the argument of the survival of the fittest but admits that there may be racial differences. There are, however, trades associated with tuberculosis, namely, those with dust hazards and silicosis; sometimes the effects of occupation are concealed by self-selection for trades,

by which the weaker (perhaps already tuberculous) persons avoid the heavy, dust–affected trades. Sydenstricker (1927) points to the deleterious effects of low diet in the German population after 1919. His general thesis is that the declines have been due largely to factors included in the phrase "amelioration of life." For further views on the causes of the declines in mortality, which were a substantial fraction of the declines from all causes, see Doege (1965) and chapter 7. See also Shryock (1966) for an interesting account of public and medical attitudes to tuberculosis and the formation of the National Tuberculosis Association in 1904. A good popular account is given by Wain (1970). He points out that the crude death rate from tuberculosis in the United States was more than 4 per 1,000 per annum around 1850, about 2 per 1,000 in 1900, and 0.46 in 1940. By 1945 para-aminosalicylic acid (PAS) came into general use, to be followed by isoniazid in 1952. Although these drugs were successful, tuberculosis was already in a decline by this time. The younger cohorts were showing greatly diminished death rates from tuberculosis. E.L. Trudeau (1848–1915) introduced his regimen of rest in the open air in the quiet countryside in 1884 and made the method available for persons of moderate means. See §7.8 for a general discussion.

Bubonic Plague. According to Anderson (1978), the first endemic case of plague in the Americas was noted in Brazil in October 1899 and shortly after in San Francisco, CA, in March 1900. A public investigation reported that plague "did not nor ever did exist in California." By 1904, 118 out of 121 reported cases had died. From May 30, 1907, to June 30, 1908, 159 cases of plague with 77 deaths were reported in California. Some time before 1908 the ground squirrels had become infected. Plague is now enzootic in a number of localities in the United States. Eighty human cases of sylvatic plague were reported from 1903 to 1966. See also Link (1955).

Tularemia. Since 1935 the cases and case fatality rates have declined. See Dauer, Korns, and Schuman (1968).

Other Zoonoses. Anthrax has been reduced to minimal numbers, according to the same authors. Brucellosis, principally due to *Br. abortus*, has been unimportant. Cases of ratbite fever have been few and case fatalities low.

Leprosy. Leprosy was brought into Florida by slaves, and other early cases occurred in the southernmost States. Scandinavian immigrants, mostly Norwegians, introduced leprosy into the upper Mississippi Valley about 1850; 160 cases were discovered in Iowa, Minnesota, and Wisconsin, in first generation migrants. G.H.A. Hansen (1841–1912) personally investigated this focus. Seven and two cases were found in the second and third generation migrants. Leprosy was brought to the Hawaiian Islands early in the nineteenth century; incidence rose until 1890 after which it declined. The leper colony on Molokai, established in 1866, was the only one that continued to be operated; here, Father Damien (1840–1889) worked and died. For leprosy acquired by veterans of wars abroad, see Aycock and Gordon (1947).

Diphtheria. Between 1935 and 1961 there were great declines in the incidence rates but the case fatality rates were rather stable, according to Dauer, Korns, and Schuman (1968, Table 1.20).

Whooping Cough. According to these same authors, the death rates per annum from whooping cough dropped from 313 in 1935–1939 to 9 per 1,000,000 per annum in 1959–1961. About 97% of the deaths were in children younger than 5 years in 1959–1961 and 67% under 1 year of age. Vaccines are widely used for prophylaxis.

Streptococcal Sore Throat and Scarlatina. Death rates were 41 per 1,000,000 per annum in 1935–1939, 118 in 1940–1944, 47 in 1945–1949, and 7 in 1959–1961. The case fatality decreased from 8 per 1,000 in 1935–1939 to 0.3 in 1950–1954 and has been negligible since.

Erysipelas. Death rates have dropped from 172 per 1,000,000 per annum in 1935–1939 to 2 per 1,000,000 per annum in 1959–1961. The introduction of penicillin for treatment in 1945 caused a very rapid decline in the rates.

Meningococcal Infections. Death rates have decreased from 152 per 1,000,000 per annum in 1935–1939 to 36 in 1959–1961. Case fatality rates varied from 42% in 1935–1939, 19% in 1940–1944, to 29% in 1959–1961; this persistence of a high case fatality rate seems to be due to cases being presented for treatment too late.

Tetanus. There have been declines in the death rates from tetanus from 72 per 1,000,000 per annum in 1935–1939 to 14 in 1959–1961. Case fatality rates have been more than 60% in the years 1955–1961, according to Dauer, Korns, and Schuman (1968). Prophylactic toxoid has been given increasingly widely in the United States, and tetanus is decreasing in incidence. As in other countries, once the disease is recognized, it is often too late for serological therapy to be effective.

We could expect that after 1961 the mortality from this subclass of diseases, "other bacterial diseases," has become negligible in the manner of the Australian data, as given in chapter 35, especially because vigorous campaigns have been waged in the United States for the use of toxoid prophylaxis against diphtheria, tetanus, and whooping cough.

Smallpox. The first outbreak of smallpox in the New World occurred on the island of Hispaniola in 1507, according to Hopkins (1983a). After that time smallpox was almost always endemic somewhere in the Americas, although some epidemics were due to fresh importations with the slaves from Africa. The result was that the seaports were especially prone to severe epidemics of smallpox and these epidemics were spread to the countryside. In 1721 there was a serious outbreak in Boston and variolation was used in some instances. By 1750 variolation was practised in varying degrees in all the colonies (Duffy, 1953). New England had epidemics in 1633, 1648, and 1666; New York in 1663, and Virginia in 1667. Ten percent of all deaths in infancy are said to have been from smallpox (Wishnow and Steinfeld, 1976). Smallpox continued to be one of the greatest health problems, even up to the time of the Civil War; Hopkins (1983a, p. 275) mentions that of 61,132 black troops in the United States Union Army, there were 6,716 cases with 2,341 deaths, whereas the 431,237 white troops experienced 12,236 cases and 4,717 deaths from smallpox. Abraham Lincoln delivered the Gettysburg Address at 2 P.M. on November 19, 1863, suffering from the prodromal symptoms of smallpox. It seems that the United States white population, after 1800 at any rate, may have suffered more from smallpox than that of, for instance, England, Sweden, or France, because in America there was an uncontrolled population of Amerindians, much commercial traffic with endemic areas, little control over vaccination levels, much movement of the colonizers, and a civil war. As a comparison, there were few deaths from smallpox in Australia during the nineteenth century, since many of the unfavorable factors mentioned above for the United States were not operative.

Measles. Dauer, Korns, and Schuman (1968) show that the death rate from measles in the United States in 1935–1939 was 173 per 1,000,000 per annum and that in 1959–1961 the rate was 22. Since that time measles is said not to be endemic in the United States, the result of vaccination campaigns.

Influenza. Influenza has visited the United States on many occasions in pandemic form. See §10.10 and Crosby (1976).

Malaria. See §42.5, earlier.

Toxoplasma is a common infection in the United States; it causes some congenital malformations but little mortality.

Hookworm disease has been considered above in §42.5; it has sometimes been reported as a cause of death in the southern states.

Hydatid Disease (echinococcosis). It is now a rare cause of mortality with most of the deaths occurring after 45 years of age.

Yellow Fever. There were devastating epidemics in the seventeenth to nineteenth centuries in America. *Aedes aegypti* was responsible for the great South American epidemics. On occasion, these epidemics were transferred to centers stretching from England to Italy.

For a review of the major infections, see Wishnow and Steinfeld (1976); for colonial epidemics, see Duffy (1953) and Webster (1799); for disease and American history, see Simpson (1954); for public health, see Sartwell (1973) and Last (1980); for parasitic zoonoses, see Schantz (1983); for obstetrics, gynecology, and infant mortality, see W. Smith (1987); for hospital care, see Rosenberg (1987).

42.9 United States Mortality from Cancer

The epidemiology of cancer has been much studied in the United States, where there are ethnic and racial minorities sufficiently large for valid comparisons to be made with the rest of the community. Many such studies are included or quoted in Schottenfeld and Fraumeni (1982). Young and Pollack (1982, Table 1) give the standardized death rates for cancer (sexes combined, all races) as 3,315 per 1,000,000 per annum for the years 1973–1977; but this rate can be broken down for the ethnic groups: whites 3,257, blacks 3,594, Chinese in San Francisco/Oakland 3,060, Chinese in Hawaii 2,593, . . . Hispanics in New Mexico 2,332, Hispanics in Puerto Rico 2,004. By race and sex, the rates are highest for black males, white males, black females, and white females. Cancers of the stomach occurred twice as frequently in males as in females in both whites and blacks. Again the incidence rates of cancers of the respiratory system were much higher in the males. Melanoma accounts for 2% of all cancers among whites and for only 0.2% in the blacks. The authors' Figure 4 shows the high rates for melanoma in the southern states. Breast is the second most commonly diagnosed cancer in females and the rates are higher, especially in the older ages, for the whites. Myers and Hankey (1982) give the cancer survival rates in the United States and conclude that with the most modern treatment there was little improvement in the survival rates of white males with cancers of the lung, stomach, pancreas, or brain, although there were marked improvements with cancers of the bladder, rectum and colon, Hodgkin's disease, and other lymphomata. Similar results were obtained for white females in the cancers listed above; some improvements were noted also with cancer of the uterine cervix and of the ovary. In white males cancers of the prostate also showed improvements. The changes in survival tended to be similar in the blacks.

Geographical differences in cancer incidence (Blot and Fraumeni, 1982) and studies of migrant populations (Haenszel, 1982) have given useful leads as to cancer etiology. For example, skin cancers, melanoma, and dosage of solar ultraviolet radiation all vary in the same direction, according to Lee (1982), Scotto and Fraumeni (1982), and Scotto, Fears, and Fraumeni (1982, 1983); in particular, there are well-marked gradations for melanoma mortality by latitude in the United States, as in Australia, with rates for the entire country increasing over the past 3 decades from 14 to 24 per 1,000,000 per annum for males and 11 to 16 for females. There was an increase in the incidence of nonmelanoma skin cancers during the 1970s.

For cancer in the United States, see also Burbank (1971), Cutler, Ederer, Gordon, et al. (1961), Lilienfeld, Levin, and Kessler (1972), and McKay, Hanson, and Miller (1982).

42.10 Canada

For the evolution of mortality 1851–1931 in Canada, see Bourbeau and Legaré (1982). For the health of the Canadian people, see Kohn (1967). For demographic transition in Quebec, see Henripin and Peron (1972).

Chapter 43
Latin America

43.1 Amerindians

The great pre-Columbian civilizations existed in what is now Latin America, whereas north of the present Mexican border, the Amerindians formed few great concentrations of population. Numerical data on pre-Columbian America have been difficult or impossible to obtain; and even in the most favorable case, central Mexico, there has been much dispute about the size of the population before the Spanish conquest.

There is great difficulty in estimating mortality in aboriginal populations. It is usually impossible to obtain even a distribution by age groups in the precontact peoples; this distribution, if accompanied by an appropriate estimate (one could say impossible to obtain) of population growth, would give some rough idea of population conditions. Cook (1947) believes that the data show that among two aboriginal American tribes, the Paiute and the Washo in 1902, approximately 40% of the population was surviving to age 50 years. He believes that

prior to the advent of disturbing foreign human invaders, most primitive races maintain themselves without serious losses from war or disease. . . . If the food supply is adequate and living conditions reasonably moderate the individual has a fair chance for survival.

He believes that those Amerindians organized as a pueblo or town, supported by a fairly effective agriculture, did better than the hunter-gatherers; the pueblo people had

perhaps 20 more years of life expectation at birth. In an addendum, he finds that the probability of death before 9 years was 27.6%; he believes that the infant mortality might have been no more than 10%, and this is consistent with certain osteologic researches. He further believes that child and infant mortality were higher after contact than before.

A description of mortality in the tribal state has already been given in §1.1. Even when the classical great pestilences, smallpox and malaria, had been controlled, contact with the caucasoids was dangerous, for which see §47.2.

See for diseases among the Aztecs, Cook (1946); for population history, Cook and Borah (1974); for central Mexico and the Spanish conquest, Borah and Cook (1960, 1963).

43.2 Conquest

The population of Latin America was gravely affected by the conquest, partly by the war and disorganization caused, but principally by the introduction of the great pestilences, to be detailed in §§43.3 and 43.4, which follow.

It is now known that the Spaniards at first continued the native system of tribute in central Mexico and that in the 1560s they instituted a reformed, uniform classification that lasted to the end of the colonial period. Borah and Cook (1969) give estimates of the population at years in millions as follows: 1518, 25.2; 1532, 16.8; 1548, 6.3; 1568, 2.65; 1585, 1.9; 1595, 1.375; and 1605, 1.075. The non-Indian population moved from zero in 1518 to 0.2

million in 1605. Estimates are available for the central Mexican population in 1518 stated as multiples of the population in 1568 taken as unity: 48 for the coastal areas up to 3,000 feet, 10 for an intermediate zone from 3,000 to 4,500 feet, and 7 for the plateau above 4,500 feet, where the figures of Borah and Cook (1969) have been rounded. In Peru the corresponding losses at heights of 10,000 to 15,000 feet were smaller still. In Mexico the estimates of Borah and Cook (1969) agreed with those of the Spaniards, made in the years 1577–1585. It is concluded that the 200,000 square miles of central Mexico had an average population density of 125 per square mile. The vast population depended on an efficient production of maize, beans, and squash in an area free of the epidemic diseases of the Old World, but the limits had probably been passed where agriculture could be continued without undue damage to the soil, erosion, and so on. Of course, the conquest came as a catastrophe; the destruction of war and the dislocation of the productive and distributive systems, together with the unwitting introduction of diseases from the Old World, all contributed to the decline. Within a century, the population of central Mexico has shrunk from 25,000,000 to less than 2,000,000 and the tropical coasts were converted to disease-ridden wastes.

For the Amerindians of Brazil, see Baruzzi and Franco (1981). For Mexico City in the eighteenth century, see Cooper (1965).

43.3 Smallpox, Malaria, and Yellow Fever

Smallpox. Smallpox first appeared in the New World on Hispaniola in 1507. In 1518 there was another outbreak on Hispaniola, apparently brought by slaves from West Africa, and it spread to Cuba. Smallpox appeared in Mexico in 1520 and in Peru between 1524 and 1527. Later epidemics reported include Brazil, 1555 and 1562, Mexico, 1576, South America generally, 1588, and Ecuador, 1680, according to Hopkins (1983a). Smallpox appeared in an epidemic on Hispaniola in December 1518 and by May 1519 up to a third of the Amerindians

on the island had died of it; in 1519 smallpox spread to Puerto Rico, where over half the Amerindians died of it within a few months. Hernando Cortés sailed from Cuba and arrived at the Aztec capital in November 1519. A second expedition under Panfilo de Narvaez followed him in April 1520; in this expedition there was an African slave who first introduced smallpox to the American mainland. In Hopkins (1983a, p. 206), a remarkable description is given by a Spanish friar, which would serve as an excellent account of smallpox and explanation of the high case fatality of such a disease in a new environment, making such points as are given for measles in §11.7. By the summer of 1520 smallpox had spread to the edge of Mexico's inland plateau, particularly the towns around the lakes of the Valley of Mexico. Meanwhile, Moctezuma (Montezuma) had been slain by his countrymen, and his successor forced the Spaniards to leave Tenochtitlan; but the successor died of the smallpox when it first reached the city. Worse still, many of the provincial governors also died. The Spaniards were in general immune. Cortés was able to regroup his forces and gather more allies. He returned to besiege Tenochtitlan in May 1521 and retake it 3 months later. Thus, smallpox played a dominant role in the downfall of the Aztecs. It was equally important in the downfall of the Incas. Smallpox remained a great pestilence in America until this century, for which see Hopkins (1983a).

Malaria. Whether malaria was endemic in pre-Columbian America cannot be determined with certainty, although it is generally believed that it was introduced after the conquest, either by the conquerors from Spain and Portugal or by their slaves from Africa. Much of Latin America lies within the tropics, Capricorn passing just south of Rio de Janeiro and Cancer about 4° north of Mexico City. Malaria in the West Indies is a coastal disease, whereas in South America the highest prevalence is inland. The malaria intensity has not been as great as in wet equatorial Africa or the Asian and East Indian tropics. In the southern equatorial zone the disease incidence has a wave of small amplitude. In some areas, such as Garaboso in Venezuela, the death rates from malaria had peaks occurring after intervals of 5 to 10 years. Gabaldon (1949) deplores the lack of information on the incidence of the disease. The worst epidemic of the hemisphere occurred in northeastern Brazil in 1930–1940 following the importation of the vector *Anopheles gambiae* from Africa; this mosquito was eradicated. In many areas malaria is important only in the valleys, although in some areas transmission occurs up to more than 2,700 meters.

Yellow Fever. In §12.1, the African origin of yellow fever has already been mentioned; the first dependable description of the disease was in 1648 in Yucatan. Great epidemics of yellow fever occurred throughout Latin America in the seventeenth to nineteenth centuries, carried by *Aedes aegypti.* Taylor (1951) points out that yellow fever was confined chiefly to urban communities along the coasts or on navigable rivers. He believes that it was endemic in such cities as Guayaquil, Veracruz, and São Salvador do Bahia and the inhabitants of such places had attacks early in life, either dying from the disease or becoming immune to it. A test of its presence was often the occurrence of disastrous epidemics when European troops arrived or when a ship carried the infection to the United States or Europe (Theiler, 1952).

43.4 Other Great Pestilences

Cholera. Cholera epidemics have occurred as part of the pandemic of 1886–1888.

Enteric Fever. See §6.5.

Gastrointestinal Disease. For views on the importance of the gastrointestinal infections, we may quote from authors in the symposia, Elliott and Knight (1976) and Ouchterloney and Holmgren (1980). Rohde and Northrop (1976) believe that, with more than an average of two attacks of intestinal infection per annum in childhood at ages less than 5 years, diarrhea with its attendant dehydration is the greatest single killer in the developing world. Mata, Kronmal, and Villegas (1980) state that intestinal infection is the cause of much mal-

nutrition and premature death. They cite the estimate of 5 to 18 million deaths per annum in the world due to these diseases.

Tuberculosis. McDougall (1949) gives figures suggesting crude mortality rates of the order of 2 to 4 per 1,000 per annum—high rates indeed—in the early 1940s. In the life tables for Chile constructed by Preston, Keyfitz, and Schoen (1972), tuberculosis accounted for about 9% of all deaths in 1909, rather more for females, and it was not until after 1950 that any notable reduction occurred.

Influenza. In the pandemic of 1918–1919, almost half a million died in Mexico. Epidemics occurred in other states, but sound numerical estimates are not available.

Measles. See §11.7 and Borgoño (1983), who reports that 6% of infant mortality and 20% of mortality at ages 1–4 years are due to measles. Measles would have been introduced early and been associated with high case fatality rates. Possibly measles faded out in many regions and was reintroduced from other regions or from Europe from time to time. For measles in Chile, see Ristori, Boccardo, et al. (1962).

Other Vector-borne Virus Infections. These are enzootic and cause some epidemics in man, mostly the encephalitides, for which see §12.4.

American Trypanosomiasis. See §16.3.

Bartonellosis. See §16.7.

43.5 Infancy

In the developed world, infant mortality rates have declined from over 200 per 1,000 in previous centuries to around 10 per 1,000 at the present time for reasons given in chapter 32. Many causes, formerly important, are now well controlled or even abolished, whereas in the developing world, particularly in Latin America, there remain high rates of mortality, documented by Puffer and Serrano (1973, 1976). After an agreement on health signed by the governments of the American states in 1961, it was hoped to halve the death rates under 5 years of age within a decade. This goal was not reached, and it is now agreed that the factors contributing to mortality in infants and children are many and complex and, further, difficult to ameliorate. Often they are due to poverty, both individual and governmental. Under the agreement, surveys of mortality were undertaken in 15 different areas in 10 participating countries. Projects in California and in Sherbrooke, Canada, served as controls to the other projects in Mexico, Jamaica, el Salvador, and 5 of the South American republics. Comparisons were made with the official statistics of the United States and data from World Health Organization publications. Observations were made from local sources by field workers, who were able to show that their figures were some 13% more than the official registrations.

Infant mortality rates were high, 124 per 1,000 at Viacha in Bolivia and 120 in the rural areas of el Salvador; in Jamaica the rate was 39 and in all other areas, higher. The rates appeared to be higher in the country than the city. Even more surprising are the high rates in the second year of life, about 50 per 1,000 per annum in Viacha and el Salvador. Nutritional deficiency was an important factor and was present as the underlying, or a contributory, cause in 57% of all deaths under 5 years of age; it was associated with low birthweight and deficient development. Deaths from this cause reached a peak at the age of 3 months.

Almost half the deaths were assigned to infections, of which some 70% were due to diarrheal conditions and 15% to measles. Measles appears to be more lethal among infants who are not well fed or are previously weakened by other infections or unfavorable conditions.

Excessive numbers of deaths from congenital anomalies were found in el Salvador and in Monterrey, Mexico. No explanation could be determined.

Infant deaths were higher among those who were not breast-fed. The investigators were surprised to find the high proportion (over 50%) of those who were not breast-fed beyond the first month.

The recommended actions were to provide mothers with adequate medical care and good food, to space the births, to breast-feed the infants, and to increase the availability of health care. Various recommendations concerning medical education, the collection of adequate data classified by acceptable WHO definitions, and follow-up research were also outlined.

Puffer and Serrano (1976) surveyed selected areas in Latin America, having a control series in California that we can neglect. Of deaths in the first year of life, 7.6% had not been registered, including 21.5% of deaths in the first month. The authors found that multiple causes of death were frequent. About one quarter of the deaths were associated with immaturity. Proportions of deaths due to nutritional deficiencies ranged from 6% to 38%. If deaths from immaturity and nutritional deficiency are combined, their contribution was over 40 deaths per 1,000 live births; the effects of these causes also were apparent in the age group 1–4 years. Birth order was important; thus, for the maternal age group 20–24 years, the infant mortality rate increased from 44 per 1,000 live births for the first child to over 300 per 1,000 for the fifth. Birthweight was an important determinant of the infant mortality. Extension of the birth interval is important for the next child.

For a bibliography of infant mortality in Latin America, see Farren (1984). For mortality trends in Chile, see US National Center (1964b). See also Baum and Arriaga (1981) and Arriaga and Davis (1969).

43.6 Childhood

To given an idea of principal causes and the magnitude of the mortality rates, some tables are abbreviated from WHO-underdeveloped (1974). Selected countries were asked to give their mortality rates at ages 1–4 and 5–14 years by the 10 principal causes. Since the 10 principal causes did not coincide, there are blanks in the table where the particular country has put the particular cause into "all other causes."

It is clear from Table 43.6.1 that the rates (for all causes combined) are very high at ages 1–4 years in 1970 and, indeed, per 1,000,000 per annum are 3,928 for Chile, 10,858 for Mexico, 7,572 for Panama, and 5,422 for Venezuela. Deaths from the pneumonias and bron-

TABLE 43.6.1. Death rates by cause at ages 1–4 years in selected countries in Latin America, 1970 (sexes combined, deaths per 1,000,000 per annum).

	Chile	Mexico	Panama	Venezuela
Respiratory	1,349	2,576	1,693	783
Bowel diseases	444	2,898	1,120	933
All other external causes	343	122	—	—
Accidents	307	278	281	290
Measles	271	1,144	871	395
Avitaminosis, etc.	128	349	292	178
Meningitis	97	—	97	71
Malignancy	85	—	—	67
Congenital anomalies	67	—	—	75
Heart diseases	61	82	—	—
Whooping cough	—	273	233	—
Anemia	—	123	70	58
Tuberculosis	—	—	173	—
All other	776	3,013	2,742	2,572
Total	3,928	10,858	7,572	5,422

Data from WHO-underdeveloped (1974).

TABLE 43.6.2. Death rates by cause at ages 5–14 years in selected countries in Latin America, 1970 (sexes combined, deaths per 1,000,000 per annum).

	Chile	Mexico	Panama	Venezuela
Accidents	130	128	242	250
All other external causes	128	129	—	—
Respiratory	126	218	139	55
Malignancy	53	35	33	48
Measles	32	131	167	26
Tuberculosis	28	35	—	—
Heart diseases	25	43	—	—
Congenital anomalies	21	—	—	21
Bowel diseases	16	262	157	42
Renal	16	—	31	13
Anemia	—	38	41	18
Whooping cough	—	17	31	—
Avitaminosis, etc.	—	—	31	16
Meningitis	—	—	—	11
All other	206	613	526	478
Total	781	1,649	1,398	978

Data from WHO-underdeveloped (1974).

chitis are included under "respiratory"; the most important group is always either "respiratory" or "alimentary." "Accidents" are usually fifth among the causes. Measles mortality rates are greatly in excess of those in the developed world, as are the avitaminoses (and other malnutritional states). The same applies to whooping cough (pertussis).

Table 43.6.2 shows that in the 5–14 age group the important causes are accidents, respiratory diseases, bowel diseases, and measles. No other cause has an important position.

Baum and Arriaga (1981) conclude that, although improvements in mortality have occurred, the deaths from respiratory, infectious, and communicable diseases are still at a level that, if registered in any developed country, would be considered to be "epidemic." These authors give a table showing that the probability of a child aged 1 year, precisely, dying before his fifth birthday, at rates holding in 1970, is 3, 7, 40, 42, and 81 per 1,000 for Puerto Rico, Trinidad, Mexico, Colombia, and Bolivia, respectively, among many others. Even the second of these would be high by the standards of the developed world. For health and growth, see Mata (1978).

43.7 General Remarks

It is clear that the main problems of Latin America are political instability, unequal distribution of wealth, individual poverty, poorly developed public services of all kinds, and superabundant fertility.

See Arriaga and Davis (1969) for mortality changes; US National Center (1964b) for mortality trends in Chile; Sanchez-Albornoz (1967) and Lodolini (1958) for parish records in Latin America.

Chapter 44
Africa

44.1 Infectious Diseases

Discussions of mortality have usually centered on the experience of the European states and their extensions abroad and overseas, for which much information is available. Europe has been fortunate during the few recent centuries of state-wide statistics in suffering little mortality from the zoonoses and little from parasitic diseases, peculiar to given regions or niduses. The contrast with African experience is marked.

Detailed information on deaths by age, sex, and cause in the African states is not generally available, so we have made use of some authors to convey an idea of the types of disease in Africa. Much information on the great epidemics is available in H.H. Scott (1939); Sabben-Clare, Bradley, and Kirkwood (1980) consider some problems of disease in colonial days; Ransford (1983) uses his experience as an African medical practitioner to give a popularizing account of African diseases. Vogel, Muller, et al. (1974) give a survey of medical problems in Kenya, and D. Scott (1965) gives a survey of epidemic disease in Ghana, 1901–1960; the convention will be adopted that *if Kenya or Ghana is mentioned, there is an implicit reference to one of these authors*. The description below applies principally to the states south of the Sahara. We can do no more than suggest the importance of some individual infective diseases.

Cholera. In the 1816 pandemic cholera was limited to the coastal areas of Tanzania, in 1826,

to Somalia and Kenya, and these areas were again affected in 1865, when the infection came down from Morocco. The latest pandemic, commencing in 1961, for which see §6.2, reached Africa in 1970, and cholera became endemic in many areas. In 1974 cholera appeared to have faded out in most areas, except for coastal Ghana, the Douala-Victoria area of the Cameroons, Montserrado County in Monrovia, Liberia, and the Lagos-Ibadan region in Nigeria. These locations all include areas of lagoon coast (Stock, 1976).

Enteric Fever and Other Salmonelloses. Enteric fevers are common although they may present as gastroenteritis.

Dysentery. At the Kenya National Hospital, Nairobi, 1966–1972, there were 3,060 shigella and 769 salmonella isolations. Some of the diarrheas of infancy were due to enterotoxic *Escherichia coli*. Gastroenteritis and bacillary dysentery are usually leading causes of mortality, although the literature on gastroenteritis in Africa does not seem as large as that produced in Latin America.

Tuberculosis. It seems likely that there was little tuberculosis in tribal Africa before 1880; indeed, it was rare in David Livingstone's experience. At that time, with the opening up of communications, there was more contact with Europeans, for example, in the recruitment of soldiers and policemen, and the use of native carriers and servants. Since 1880 it has become a disease of great importance in Africa, according to Koch (1971) and Kent (1971). Thus, Koch reports that more than half the children at ages 5 to 14 years could be tuberculin positive reactors, and the morbidity rate could be about 0.5% at the same ages, in the territory covered by the Lake Victoria Tuberculosis Scheme. Case fatality rates were high; for example, in Nairobi, Kenya, of 739 patients entering the investigation with positive-sputum cultures for tuberculosis, 13% were known to be dead and 8% were lost to sight after 1 year. As in §7.5, there would be many clinical forms of the disease, gastrointestinal, glandular, meningeal, and miliary, as well as the pulmonary forms commonly seen in the western countries. BCG campaigns are now common.

Bubonic Plague. There are three enzootic areas of plague in Africa, for which see Manson-Bahr and Apted (1982, Figure 20.1) namely, along the northwest coast, in the easterly half of equatorial Africa and, in a wide area in southwest Africa to just south of Basutoland. In §8.2, it is remarked that plague may have been enzootic in Africa in classical times; indeed, the first mention of the plague of Justinian's time was from the Red Sea area. In the latest pandemic, cases first appeared in east Africa, the infection coming from the Orient; extensive outbreaks of plague were common throughout 1900–1914, particularly near townships, for example, Nairobi in 1902, Nakuru and Kisumu in 1904, and Mombasa in 1912. Between 1921 and 1930 annual totals of 2,000 deaths were recorded. Localized outbreaks have occurred in Tanzania as late as 1972. In Ghana over 300 deaths were recorded during 1908 and 1924.

Leprosy. Africa is the probable first home of leprosy and the country with the highest prevalence rates in modern times. It is believed that the disease was prevalent in Egypt in 2400 BC. Toward the end of the nineteenth century, the incidence per 1,000 is given as 61 in the French Ivory Coast, 20 in the Cameroons, 13 in French Equatorial Africa, with 130 in the Ebolawa district, 5 in French Guinea, and 5 in Northern Nigeria. Leprosy was already present among the Hottentots and Bantus in the early eighteenth century.

By 1950 an estimated 1.5 million lepers were living in tropical Africa, especially in the Congo (50% in some villages!). Many cases of leprosy were treated by chaulmoogra oil until the 1940s when the sulfones were introduced. Manson-Bahr and Apted (1982) cite incidence rates of 1 to 43 per 1,000 in parts of Uganda and even higher in west Africa, 12 to 33 per 1,000 in east Africa, about 20% of which were lepromatous. A map of prevalence for Kenya is available in Vogel, Muller, et al. (1974, p. 207). There is a high rate in the areas around Lake Victoria. See also Browne (1980).

Diphtheria. Diphtheria is said to occur in Kenya and may well be a cause of tropical ulcers. There are relatively few deaths.

Whooping Cough. This disease is endemic in Kenya and is the ninth most common cause of hospital admission; the case fatality rate of such patients is 12%. See also §9.4.

Meningitis. Vogel, Muller, et al. (1974) give a table of percentage isolations of bacteria from 381 cases of meningitis as 48.4 *Str. pneumoniae*, 12.6 *H. influenzae*, 3.9 *N. meningitidis*, 7.8 *E. coli*, 9.5 *Klebsiella*, *Proteus*, and *Pseudomonas*, 5.0 *Salmonella* species, 4.4 *Staphylococcus*, 3.7 *Str. faecalis*, and 4.7 *Cryptococcus neoformans*. Kenya is said to be below an "epidemic meningococcal belt" in the hot dry areas. Various reasons, including nutrition, have been proposed for these meningitis frequencies. There have been large epidemics of cerebrospinal meningitis in Ghana over the epoch 1901–1960, with more than 10,000 notifications in 1945, 1948, and 1949 and an estimated 20,000 deaths in 1906 (Scott, 1965).

Tetanus. In 1972 tetanus ranked fourth as a reported cause of death, following lobar pneumonia and cholera; it contributed 10% of all reported deaths from infectious and parasitic diseases. Infections are believed often to follow chigger bites (Vogel, Muller, et al., 1974).

Streptococcal Disease. Although primary infections are not commonly diagnosed, the sequelae such as acute rheumatic fever, chorea, chronic valvular disease, and acute glomerulonephritis are not rare in Kenya.

Tropical Ulcer. An indolent and chronic ulcer, usually called tropical ulcer, occurs in Africa as in many other tropical parts of the developing world. A predisposing cause is chronic malnutrition, especially protein deficiency. Many organisms, including the diphtheria bacillus, have been incriminated. Possibly few deaths occur, but these ulcers can cause great damage and disfigurations and add to the burden of disease.

Poliomyelitis. In Kenya during the years before 1972 over 90% of children in whom the virus was isolated were under three years of age.

Smallpox. There have been great smallpox epidemics in Africa over the centuries, and it was the last continent to be freed of smallpox. See §11.2. In Luanda in 1864 there was a great epidemic with a case fatality rate of 60% and 40,000 dead. In Kenya the disease was endemic from 1911 to 1921, with more than 6,000 deaths in 1916–1918; there were about 1,800 deaths in 1934 and over 8,000 deaths in 1943–1947. From 1955 to 1970 and in 1972 there were a few deaths; the disease was finally eradicated following a vaccination campaign beginning in 1969; see the figure in Vogel, Muller, et al. (1974, p. 262). Scott (1965) states that smallpox was endemic in west Africa over the period 1901–1960; in Ghana notifications could rise to more than a thousand in a year.

Common Childhood Infections. These diseases probably became greater causes of morbidity and mortality after the opening up of the continent with its greater possibilities of travel and spread of these cosmopolitan diseases. Under unfavorable conditions, the case fatality rates can be very high as noted for measles in §11.7 and for chickenpox (varicella) in §11.4.

Measles. Possibly almost all Kenyan children have an attack of measles. The median age at onset is 19 months in the densely populated areas but is higher elsewhere. In an epidemic observed in 1961 by McGregor, Williams, et al. (1966) in West Kiang, Gambia, out of 207 chil-

dren younger than the age of 10 years, 29 (14%) died from measles in one village, Jali, and out of 230 such children, 35 (15%) died at Keneba from measles; case fatalities were particularly high at ages 6 months to 3 years, 30% in Jali and 24% in Keneba. The average of deaths during the entire dry season at Keneba was only about 3 per annum over the years 1949–1960, so that measles killed as many in the 3 months, February to April 1961, as died in 12 consecutive, dry-season half-year intervals. The authors cite other authors who believe that measles is the greatest killing disease of the preschool child, citing case fatalities of from 3% to 22%. See also Aaby, Bukh, et al. (1983).

Rubella. Rubella is a mild and widespread disease in Africa. See André (1979).

Yellow Fever. Almost certainly, yellow fever evolved in Africa; it still exists there in its sylvatic form. Epidemics have occured in recent times, for which see §12.2. It is a rather rare disease in Kenya but seems to be of more importance in Ghana; in Ghana it is of much greater importance south of a line drawn from the southwest corner in a northeasterly direction.

Hepatitis B. Hepatitis B seems also to have evolved in Africa; it can be spread by blood transfusions, injections, inoculations, and presumably also by tribal scarification and ritual circumcision, and perhaps also by an insect vector. Among Kenyan hospital admissions, it is the stated cause of about one quarter of cases of cirrhosis and perhaps more than half the cases of acute hepatitis (Isaacson, 1982) and is also the leading cause of hepatocellular carcinoma; see §13.1 and §20.6.

Malaria. Malaria has been endemic, indeed usually holoendemic, in all of wet tropical Africa since prehistoric times, and, as we have explained in §15.5, its presence has favored the genes responsible for the sickle cell (hemoglobin S) trait and other related traits. D.B. Wilson (1949) and Hackett (1949b) can be consulted for conditions before World War II. Livingstone (1971) believes that the crude death rates from malaria in holoendemic areas have been probably more than 10 per 1,000 per annum. In particular, there is a great burden on the infants, especialy when there may also be endemic yellow fever, as in the past. As an example of modern conditions in an area, West Kiang of the Gambia, McGregor, Williams, et al. (1966) note that the rains begin in late May or early June and end in October or November. The other months are dry throughout. Agricultural work is limited to the wet months; men tend the upland and women the swampland crops—rice, millet, sorghum, maize, and findo (Digitaria sp.) as cereals, and groundnuts as cash crops. In 1962 and 1963 the cash crops had a value of £25–£35 sterling per adult male per annum. Diet is almost entirely vegetarian. Arthropod vectors flourish in the wet months and are quiescent in the dry months. Parasitemia rates rose in the wet season from a low of 59% in July to 85% in November and 81% in January/February. The diet is not deficient by European standards, but the average blood hemoglobin falls below 9 g/100 ml at 18 months. The average hemoglobin value is highest in July but falls in the wet season, which the authors believe is due to malaria.

Leishmaniasis. *Leishmania donovani* is endemic in the Sudan, Ethiopia, and Kenya, and also in parts of western Africa between the equator and 15°N, with *Leishmania tropica* widely spread in this latter region. See Figure 16.1.1.

Trypanosomiasis. See §16.4 and Duggan (1980) and Forsyth and Bradley (1966).

Relapsing Fever. See §16.6 for tick-borne relapsing fever with a note on a widespread epidemic in the Sahel area. See also Scott (1965).

Syphilis. The classical western form of syphilis may not have been common in Africa before this century.

Yaws. Yaws is a disease of great antiquity in Africa and there is a related disease of baboons. Until the 1940s the incidence of yaws was very high with serological positivity over 80% in some populations, according to Hack-

ett (1980), who states that yaws had been a disabling disease with ulcers, contractures, facial destruction, and palm and plantar lesions, although not a killing disease. By the 1950s it was declining in importance as economic conditions improved. Campaigns using bismuth and arsenical preparations and, later, long-acting penicillin brought about a substantial decline in a few years. Hackett (1980) must be read also for his paragraph on the relation of yaws to syphilis and treponarid (endemic syphilis).

Schistosomiasis. See §§19.1 and 19.2.

Filariasis and Dracontiasis. See §19.6

Hookworm Disease and Intestinal Helminthiases. See §19.7.

Helminthiases. In tropical Africa there is a great burden of the helminthiases; some cause death, but deaths are not often assigned to helminthiasis as a cause. The schistosomiases obviously give rise to lesions dangerous to life, but the other helminths are important as causing morbidity and, directly or indirectly, leading to high death rates.

Chigger Flea or Tunga Penetrans. See Beaver, Jung, and Cupp (1984, p. 699) for a description of this flea. Its origin is probably Brazil and it occurs throughout tropical America; in 1872 it reached the east coast of Africa, and by 1900 had reached Bombay and Karachi. The eggs develop in dry, sandy soil, and the adult female burrows into the skin between man's toes and under the toe nails; it reaches the size of a small pea and passes eggs into the environment. In Angola "sepsis following jigger [chigger] infection became only second to smallpox as a cause of death during the decades which followed the fleas' introduction to Africa," wrote Ransford (1983).

For disease in African history, see Patterson (1974) and Hartwig and Patterson (1978); for a recent review of mortality, see Akinkugbe (1981); for salt trade and disease in the northern Great Lakes region, see Good (1972); for infancy and early childhood in Sierra Leone, see WHO-infant (1981); for diseases of children in the tropics, see Jelliffe (1970); for health in Tanzania and transfer of power to local authorities, see Clyde (1980); for maternal and child health in rural Kenya, see Ginneken and Muller (1984). For human environment and helminth infections, see Nwosu (1983). See also WHO-apartheid (1983).

44.2 Malnutrition

Let us begin with Eddy (1980) who recalls that protein-energy malnutrition is the most serious and widespread disorder known to medical and nutritional science. In the Gambia he had seen an "enormous" rejection rate of recruits for service in World War II. Later, he had seen such men return from military service well fed and fit. Soon after, he sat as assessor on pension boards at which time the same men were seen to be unfit because they had resumed their former inadequate diet. A poor diet accounted for the stunting of growth, a principal cause of rejection of recruits.

As an example of the limits imposed by the availability of food on energy expenditure in work, Eddy cites an incident when under his personal supervision some native laborers became exhausted after 2 or 3 hours of light work, because their diet was deficient.

In Gambia there are clearly defined wet and dry seasons; at the onset of the wet season food supplies run low, but the crops have to be planted; this was the "hungry season," because large expenditures of energy were necessary, so much so that the energy value of the food eaten was only 60% of the estimated requirement during the planting operations. As much of the work was done by the women, they were worse affected than the men and there were problems for the infants and small children; less milk was available from the mother, and they were left at home to be looked after by children, often no older than 10 years of age.

Special forms of malnutrition can be described as due to shortages in the diet of protein and total energy. In mild or moderate cases there is leanness with a reduction in subcutaneous tissues; this is associated with reduced physical activity and stamina, frequent episodes of diarrhea, and also mental dullness and short attention spans. A more serious condition is described as marasmus, in which there is also severe muscle wasting and where the body weight may be only 60% of the body weight expected for height; the patient is weak; heart rate, blood pressure, and body temperature may be low; the child's face may be wasted, giving the appearance of an old man. Complicating features are often acute gastroenteritis and respiratory infections, to which there may be no febrile response, and the subject may die as a result. A third condition is named kwashiorkor and has been described by many, for example, Trowell, Davies, and Dean (1954, reprinted 1982). A predominant feature is soft, painless, pitting edema, usually in the feet and legs but extending to the perineum, upper extremities, and face in severe cases. The hair is dry and brittle, sometimes there are skin lesions resembling pellagra and the skin may be peeled off. Sometimes, these signs of marasmus and kwashiorkor are combined.

Of course, it is possible for the child to recover from these diseases if the standards of nutrition improve; but usually there is stunting of growth, because the food available will not allow recovery to proper standards; there may be intercurrent infections leading to death. As Greenwood and Whittle (1981) point out, there have been extensive studies on children with marasmus, kwashiorkor, and the syndrome containing features of each, to test the view held by physicians working in the tropics that infections are more frequent and more severe among children with these conditions than among well-nourished children. In the severely affected, there is good evidence that poor nutrition affects both specific immune mechanisms and more general mechanisms, such as the development of a febrile reaction. Greenwood and Whittle (1981) conclude that, because of a lack of comparable studies on milder degrees of malnutrition, there can still be doubt that the findings on the severely malnourished have relevance to the moderately or minimally malnourished. It seems, however, that it is only common sense to act as though minor differences in malnutrition have at least minor effects and to remember that in one disease, namely, tuberculosis, malnutrition certainly plays an important role.

We may use this discussion to point to the narrow food reserves that exist even in areas not subject to drought.

See §44.3 for remarks on the unsatisfactory nature of the statistics on malnutrition and famine.

44.3 Famine

There has been a great famine in the Sahel, that is, Chad, Mali, Mauritania, Niger, Senegal, and Upper Volta. According to Lamb (1977), this has been due to a narrowing and movement southward of the tropical rain belt; the drought of 1970–1972 followed climatic movements over a period of 20 years. Schove (1977) gives years of reported famine going back to about 1750 BC, with six periods having as little rain as the most recent one in 1965–1973; he concludes that this latter epoch was the worst since the 1830s. See §22.4 for long-term climatic changes. It is convenient to add Sudan and Ethiopia to the Sahel states listed above, so that the famines of recent years have affected a wide strip of Africa between the Tropic of Cancer and the equator. In these eight countries and some others, famine is not sporadic as in India but is an exaggeration of "normal" conditions, for these countries are in low-rainfall areas. Some of the social and political problems, which we have considered above in our §§22.5 to 22.7, appear here again. Perhaps the best treatment of the subject is given by Garcia, et al. (1981–1982).

Of the eight countries mentioned, only Sudan has ever had a population census, and deaths have not been regularly registered. A cursory inspection of the publications of the World Health Organization will often show that the statistics cited from these countries can have little value. There has been no R.R. Kuczynski to submit the statistics of the modern developing world to such an analysis as he applied to the old imperial protectorates. Garcia, et al. (1981–1982) cite Pierre Cantrelle as stating that vital statistics are so inaccurate in the Sahel countries, for example, as to be virtually useless.

Not only are the total deaths difficult to determine but there are difficulties in making comparisons between the modes of death in famines and in normal times. According to the rules of the *International Classification of Diseases*, designed with the needs of the developed countries during peace time in mind, the diagnosis *malnutrition* has a low priority; the rules require the deaths registered to be assigned to one of the infections mentioned on the death certificates. Thus, where records are kept in countries under conditions of low nutrition, there will be high rates of mortality reported for gastroenteritis, measles, bronchopneumonia, and so on. If any natural disaster, including famine, is acting on the population, deaths tend to be referred to the natural disaster. So we cannot tell how many people died as a result of the drought in the Sahel, first, because we cannot obtain the total number of deaths and, second, when the disaster strikes, it is all too obvious that persons are dying from malnutrition and comparisons of deaths with "normal times" will be quite illusory. In line with what is written above, the vital statistics of the Sahel region show no increase in mortality in Table 44.3.1 constructed from WHO statistics.

TABLE 44.3.1 Recent demographic estimates in the Sahel (rates per 10,000 per annum).

Year	State	Live births	Deaths	Increase of population
1978	Chad	442	214	228
1983	Mali	432	181	251
1976	Mauritania	501	209	292
1981	Niger	510	229	281
1980	Senegal	477	212	265
—	Upper Volta	—	—	—

Data from World Health Statistics Annual (1984).

As an example of conflicting views, Caldwell (1977) found that in one area where acceptable statistics were available, there had been no year in the 1970–1974 drought and famine in which the rate of increase (i.e., births less deaths) of the population was below 2.3% per annum. On the other hand, Sterling (1974) reports that rains failed in the Sahel in 1968 and that, by 1974, several hundred thousands had died of famine plus 20 million head of stock. Many boreholes were dug but there were hundreds of cattle dying of starvation. In the present famine in the Sahel the extent of the mortality is still in doubt, and there is much discussion of additional social and economic factors, to which we now turn.

General factors favoring famine are given by various authors as being the burning of vegetation in agricultural control, woodcutting for corrals, cultivation causing desiccation, overstocking, that is, increase of stock for economic and prestige reasons, and deforestation for tsetse fly control. The introduction of wells and the control of trypanosomiasis have allowed greater numbers of cattle to survive, although there may be insufficient crops to feed them. The bad economic conditions of the country may be aggravated by a dependence on one crop, (Ball, 1978). It is evident that there are many economic and social factors leading to disasters when the drought comes. Garcia, et al. (1981–1982) discuss the structure of the population, especially in chapter 5 of their vol. 2. It is pointed out that countries subject to drought may have quite different social structures, so that their abilities to survive a drought will also be quite different. As a generalization, the changes brought about by passing from an agricultural system self-sufficient in food to a system of cash crops grown on large farms, with many rural workers without social security schemes, are unfavorable for large classes of the community.

See for severe droughts in Ethiopia and Somaliland, Hussein (1976) and Pankhurst (1966), for famine in northern Nigeria, Watts (1983). For the economic history of central Niger, see Baier (1980). See also Ormerod (1976), Roch, Hubert, and Ngyrie (1975), Bryson (1973), authors in Dalby, Church, and Bezzaz (1977), Franke and Chasin (1980), Lofchie (1975), and Lofchie and Commins (1982).

44.4 Other Diseases

This section deals with diseases other than the infections and malnutrition and infant mortality.

Cancer

Cancers of the skin, except in albinoes, are rare in Africans, although melanoma of the nonpigmented sole of the foot is well known. In general, there is less cancer in the black African than in the caucasoid, with only a few exceptions, although there is more cancer of the esophagus and liver in the black Africans. Cancers of the liver are often due to an infection by hepatitis B virus with aflatoxins playing some role; the etiology of cancer of the esophagus is still not determined. The incidence of cancers of the large intestine is notably low in black Africans, and this is to be related to their high fiber diet. Isaacson (1982) concludes from autopsy data at Baragwanath Hospital, Soweto, that cancer incidence in black South Africans differs considerably from that in European communities.

Nutritional Diseases

Trowell (1960) cites a general opinion that most infants and children younger than 3 years of age have some degree of malnutrition, and it is probably still true; protein intake is low by European standards at all ages and if too low, kwashiorkor occurs in infancy. Pellagra has been common in both Rhodesia (Zimbabwe) and Nyasaland (Malawi) but seems to be rare in other areas, except in special circumstances, for example, prisons and hospitals, or where the diet contains a very high proportion of maize (over 60% of calories). Scurvy is a problem in the more arid regions but not as a rule in the wet areas. Beriberi appears only in special cases. Rickets probably is rare in Africa because of the high ultraviolet light dosages received throughout the continent.

Anemia. Iron deficiency anemias are common and associated with malnutrition and helminth infections. Megaloblastic anemias also occur, including classical pernicious (Addisonian) anemia; a severe anemia resembling the pernicious type occurs, and can be fatal, in the Bantu and Indians whose food intake contains a large proportion of maize or rice.

Diabetes. Diabetes was rare on the African scene before 1930 but has increased with westernization. See Jackson (1971, 1978) for a worldwide review and an examination of the prevalence in South African blacks.

Neurological Diseases. Trauma is the most common neurological cause of admission to hospital for the black Africans. There is much meningitis, tubercular, pyogenic, and meningococcal. There are many neurological lesions secondary to endemic diseases, for example, malaria, encephalitis, trypanosomiasis, and tetanus. Cerebrovascular lesions are less common than in Europeans, although Trowell (1960) believes that it is difficult to make any useful observations on them. Epilepsy seems to be widespread.

Cardiovascular Diseases. Studies, such as those of Shaper (1972) and Shaper, Hutt, and Coles (1968) in Uganda, and authors, cited by Trowell (1960, Tables 2.2 and 2.3), in South Africa, Southern Rhodesia, and northern Nigeria, agree that rheumatic heart disease has been the most common form of heart disease in children and young adults, and even in older adults. It is less common at low altitudes and latitudes, for example, 1.5% in Ghana compared with 14.7% in Uganda and 23% in northern Nigeria, percentages based on all heart diseases in each case. The disease takes a severe form similar to that seen in European populations 50 years ago. They would also agree with Isaacson (1982), who states that the pattern of heart disease in South African blacks is changing. Some of the special local disease syndromes and syphilitic cardiovascular disease are decreasing in importance, and there has been an increase in the incidence of cardiac infarction. Tubercular and pyogenic, especially pneumococcal, pericarditis is not rare. Acute bacterial endocarditis formed 2%–5% of cardiac cases in some experiences, for which see Trowell (1960, p. 93). Endomyocardial fibrosis is also a common heart disease. Fatal cases of wet beriberi occur, especially among the rice eaters and alcoholics.

Between 1967 and 1978 descriptions became available of small tribal societies, in the members of which blood pressure did not rise with age; now, altogether, 30 such ethnic groups are known (Trowell, 1981); Trowell had worked in Kenya during 1929–1936 and in Uganda during 1935–1958 and revisited both those countries in 1963 and 1970. In the earlier observations there was lifelong low blood pressure; from 1930–1935, physicians in Kenya were unanimous that they had never seen a case of hypertension in an African, although many observations of blood pressure had been made. Further, Vint (1936–1937), very experienced in autopsies of African blacks, had seen no manifestations of essential hypertension or ischemic heart disease. Moreover, he had seen no case of appendicitis and only a single gallstone in one child. By 1941 conditions in Africa had begun to change, and special blood pressure examinations of hospital patients were made that showed blood pressures at the young ages higher than those of 12 years earlier and, further, blood pressures increasing with age. Malignant hypertension had been reported in 1953. Cerebrovascular disease began to be reported in the 1940s. The most important cause of hypertension, then, was renal disease, particularly glomerulonephritis. See also Akinkugbe (1972). Salt consumption may have been important in bringing about the changes. Trowell (1981) points out that Kenya and Uganda have no surface deposits of salt and most black people lived far from the saline lake deposits, and so in the early decades of this century salt intakes were very low; but a change came about and the diet in institutions, influenced by Europeans, came to contain more salt. It is believed that up to 3–4 g of salt can be consumed daily without inducing hypertension, but above this limit an increasing proportion develops high blood pressure, increasing with age. Conversely, transition to a low-salt diet results in a fall in blood pressure. Hypertension is a leading cause of death in the urbanized blacks of South Africa (Isaacson, 1982). It is believed to be now almost always "essential" and not a complication of renal disease. This author states that among urbanized blacks in Zimbabwe over the age of 39 years, hypertension (including cerebrovascular disease) accounts for 15% of total deaths. Ischemic heart disease had been infrequent in black Africa before 1960 but, since then, it has increased with urbanization and the adoption of western-style diet. Anemia is a cause of some heart disease. See also Walker (1981), who compares the diet, health, morbidity, and mortality of black, Indian, and colored populations in South Africa.

Respiratory System. With the wealth of infectious and parasitic diseases in Africa, the common respiratory diseases have tended to be neglected by authors. However, Buck, Anderson, et al. (1970) give tables on 188,416 cases of disease admitted into hospitals in certain areas of Chad; the leading causes of the 890 deaths registered were: leprosy, 155; malaria, 149; measles, 141; amebiasis, 109; infective hepatitis, 100; pneumococcal pneumonia, 73; pulmonary tuberculosis, 55; meningococcal meningitis, 43; and schistosomiasis, 24. In Kenya, Bonte (1974) finds that 20% of all deaths (21,590) from reporting goverment hospitals in 1968 were due to pneumonia and that the case fatality rate from pneumonia in hospital patients was 15%. It is clear from Greenwood and Whittle (1981), Greenwood, Hassan-King, et al. (1980), and Baird, Whittle, and Greenwood (1976) that mortality from *Str. pneumoniae*, whether in the form of pneumonia or of meningitis, constitutes an important proportion of the mortality in the African. Many of the pneumococcal types encountered in Africa are well known in the developed world, but epidemics may also occur from less well known types; this variation causes difficult problems in choice of type for vaccination campaigns. Vaccination was used among African mine workers in South Africa as early as 1911; it is belived that the mere aggregation of such workers is as important a factor as working in the mines. Incidentally, it appears appropriate that infections with *Str. pneumoniae* should be considered as an infectious disease, thus linking infections of the lung with meningitis; it may even be appropriate to consider them so in revising the rules of the ICD.

Liver Diseases. Enlarged liver is not uncommon in endemic malarial regions, and various other infections are followed by liver changes. Some special syndromes occur in Africa. Thus, according to Isaacson (1982), the blacks of South Africa suffer from siderosis (iron deposi-

tion), especially in the liver; this excess of iron intake occurs from the brewing of beers in iron containers. The disease is tending to fall, due perhaps to a decrease in the consumption of traditionally brewed beer. Iron overload may go on to a micronodular form of cirrhosis. The other more common form of cirrhosis is called macronodular; its etiology is probably multifactorial, with hepatitis B and aflatoxin being of special importance; this type is complicated by hepatocellular carcinoma in about half the cases seen at autopsy, according to Isaacson (1982). Peptic ulcer, cholecystitis, and appendicitis appear to have a low prevalence among the rural black Africans. Diverticulosis is beginning to appear with changes of diet.

Genitourinary Diseases. Glomerulonephritis and chronic pyelonephritis are common forms of disease. Stricture of the male urethra due to gonorrhea is not uncommon and gives rise to cystitis and pyelonephritis.

See, for mortality in francophone Africa, Cantrelle (1968), for mortality in selected countries, WHO-underdeveloped (1974), for Zimbabwe, Gelfand (1981). For an epidemiologic survey, see Simmons, Whayne, et al. (1951).

44.5 Emergence of Western Diseases

The patterns of disease in Africa have been extensively used as a foil for studies on the effects of nutrition on disease in the western world. The first revolution in diet occurred in Africa when men started to grow and store cereals. The diet changed toward more carbohydrate and less fat. Possibly, standards of nutrition (particularly energy or calorie requirements) were set too high by nutritionists formerly. Miller (1979) estimated the proportions of various clinical states in 1,750 (1,110) million people in the developing (developed) countries throughout the world (listed here as percentages); he found obesity 3(25), heart disease 2(30), dental caries 10(99), undernutrition 25(3), anemia 30(5), and xerophthalmia 1(0). On the African scene obesity occurs almost exclusively in the wealthy living on a western diet. As against this, in the tribal Africans some malnutrition occurs at almost all ages, especially in the poorer groups and in times of crop failure or famine; there may be avitaminoses, iodine deficiencies causing goiter and anemia, but still there is neither obesity nor hypertension, and body weight remains low throughout life.

Population pressures have forced many peasants into the cities and towns of Africa to live a precarious life in the shanty towns. Here, violence and alcoholism become important problems. Overcrowding in insanitary conditions leads to higher rates of mortality from the cosmopolitan diseases, measles, gastroenteritis, and childhood diseases, generally, but they may be more readily protected against the geographical diseases such as malaria, schistosomiasis, and some of the worm diseases, so that generalizations about the effect of urbanization on mortality can be made only after examination of the special circumstances in the particular type of city. The diet of the migrant to the city deteriorates because his accustomed foods are partly replaced by cheap western foods, especially the cheaper refined flour breads. Protein deficiencies become more important.

44.6 Demography

It is difficult to relate deaths by cause to the population at risk in Africa, even though many studies have been carried out on the epidemiology of the infective diseases. The various colonial powers were responsible for the collection of data up to the times of the declarations of independence and formations of the states. For the colonial era, the difficulties of obtaining statistics in the tropics were well displayed in the works of Kuczynski (1937, 1939, 1947–1948, 1948–1953); he gave many examples of how many of the figures given in reports do not depend on observations but on "judicious" additions to the statistics of the preceding year or epoch. There was, indeed, little incentive to do better, as Lorimer (1968) points out. This author goes on to show that even the total numbers of inhabitants in the colonies (later states) could not be well estimated before the sampling surveys, mostly beginning in the

1950s. There has been little detailed knowledge of population numbers and structures, and so age-specific death rates can hardly be considered. There are encouraging signs, as in the discussions on mortality given by authors mentioned in §44.1 earlier, that such rates may be available in the near future in some states. A few possibilities may be mentioned.

The mortality can be studied in a limited area or group of villages with a recording of the vital events, for example, McGregor, Billewicz, and Thomson (1961) gave an account of village life in Keneba, Gambia; they found that 57% of live births survived to age 7 years, that is, $l_7 = 0.57$; they also found that inadequate maternal care was a leading problem, gastroenteritis was always present, and there were epidemics of measles with high case fatalities and many deaths.

The demographers have used several methods; Clairin (1968) considers the results of questioning women on the birth and survival of children in the previous 12 months. He obtains an infant mortality of 182 per 1,000 in Upper Volta and 160 per 1,000 in Chad but believes the figures for Upper Volta are not consistent; he finds it necessary to use various formulas to "correct" the observations. Clairin (1968) gives estimated infant mortality rates of Upper Volta, Chad, northern Cameroon, western Cameroon, and Dahomey as 182, 160, 197, 139, and 111 per 1,000. These are denoted $_1q_0$ multiplied by 1,000; there are corresponding probabilities of persons, having reached 1 year precisely, dying before age 5 years. These are 0.218, 0.127, 0.173, 0.147, and 0.194 for the same five regions and are denoted by $_4q_1$. The author recalls that in the United States life table series $_4q_1$ is usually small in relation to $_1q_0$. He therefore explores certain "regional life tables" with such pairs to find a life table with similar parameters and to deduce adjusted figures from such a life table. He gives no statement on cause of death, except that difficulties of weaning may be the cause of the high child mortality. The reader is referred to Brass, Coale, et al. (1968) for the results of a special demographic enquiry into Africa, especially Brass (1968) and Romaniuk (1968). These authors make extensive use of mathematical devices to "correct" the data. It is of interest that no estimate of infant mortality is above 250 per 1,000 and no l_5 is as low as the value implied by the l_7 of McGregor, Billewicz, and Thomson (1961). One can only hope that larger and lengthier surveys in the style of these latter authors, taking note of causes of death, will be carried out in the future.

For projections of population by age and sex in francophone Africa, see Gendreau and Nadot (1967), for population, Barbour and Prothero (1961) and Sai (1984), for community approach to disease, Gould (1971).

44.7 Mortality of European Expatriates

We use the account of Bruce-Chwatt and Bruce-Chwatt (1980) on the experience of British expatriates. Many such were military, especially naval, personnel, for whose experience see also Cantlie (1974a, b).

An early incident was an indicator of disasters to come for the Europeans not immune to African diseases. Thomas Wyndham with two ships, visiting Benin on a trading expedition in 1553, stayed too long into "the late time of the yeare"; his men fell ill in large numbers and Wyndham himself died; "of seven score men" setting out, scarcely 40 returned to Plymouth and of them "many died." British naval ships patrolling the Guinea coast to keep watch on possible slave traders in the era 1807–1857 became known as the "coffin squadron," for the mortality of the personnel was 55 per 1,000 per annum. Enormous mortality was sustained during some explorations, as in Mungo Park's second expedition in 1805; he reported that of 45 Europeans leaving the Gambia in health, only 5 were alive at the time of his last letter; but all 5 were drowned soon after in the Niger. Missionaries also had high risk; of 89 missionaries arriving in Sierra Leone in 1804–1825, 54 died and 14 returned to England in ill health. Kuczynski (1948) states that in 1810–1825, out of 541 officers of garrisons in West Africa, 16% died, and among 5,823 other ranks, the death rates were twice as high. Even in 1903–1907, the mean annual case incidence was 721 per 1,000 with a malaria mortality rate of 5.2 per 1,000 per annum. Bruce-Chwatt and Bruce-Chwatt (1980) believe that these high death rates in West Africa were largely due to malaria and yellow fever, not always well distinguished in the earlier days; especially important was blackwater fever, a complication of malaria improperly treated with quinine. Many of the special problems have now been solved; chemotherapy is available for malaria and vaccination for yellow fever. The hazards of bowel infections and the parasitic diseases are now better understood. Possibly, too, the expatriate is less isolated than formerly and there is less alcoholism. See also Carlson (1984).

Chapter 45

The Role of Therapy in the Decline of Mortality

45.1 Surgery

In this chapter, an attempt is made to assess the importance of various groups of therapy, including vaccination, in the declines in the age-specific mortality rates over the past few centuries, especially since 1800. We shall see in §45.11 that there has been a great tendency among authors to antedate the effectiveness of some modern forms of therapy. See also Table 3.6.1.

Let us begin the discussion with a centenary address of a famous British surgeon in the early modern era. Treves (1900) writes:

greater deeds of surgery were limited to cities and the larger towns. The general practitioner seldom took up the scalpel except in minor necessities. Even in London the list of consulting surgeons was meagre. In the hospitals of the metropolis the number of operations performed in the year would be less than is now the quotum for a month.

It is indeed difficult for anyone to believe that the surgeons of 1800 could have made any favorable change in the general mortality. They had great difficulty in checking hemorrhages. Treves (1900) mentions four advances in surgery between 1800 and 1900, which we use as headings, and to which we add a little on modern advances.

(i) An Improved Knowledge of Anatomy. In §2.2, some advances in microscopic anatomy have already been detailed, especially the establishment of the cell as the fundamental anatomical unit and the development of

microscopic methods to study healthy and diseased tissues. On the diagnostic, side, J. Cohnheim introduced quick-frozen sections in 1870 and W.K. Roentgen in 1895 discovered the Roentgen or X rays, invaluable in the treatment of fractures. In many instances observations can be made with the Roentgen rays without modification, for advantage can be taken of the differential absorption of the rays by the tissues; in other instances help is required to visualize the structure of interest if it is composed of soft tissue, for example, peptic ulcer; from 1910 the gastrointestinal tract could be examined after the administration of barium sulfate. Special contrast media were introduced in 1929 for the visualization of the urinary tract by the intravenous injection of a drug, uroselectan (or iodomethamate), that was excreted through the kidneys. Other chemicals have been used for special purposes, such as the iodopaques or organic iodine compounds; sometimes radioactive material selective for a tissue is injected intravenously and it gives an autoradiograph because the rays are emitted by the radioactive material. Direct inspection of organs has become possible, at first with the use of rigid tubes such as the gastroscope and lately with the use of small flexible tubes carrying glass microfibers. Ultrasonic examinations have become common in the 1980s.

(ii) Arrest of Hemorrhage. At the beginning of Treves's hundred years, styptics, local pressure, including the tourniquet, until clotting had occurred, and the use of the cautery were the

principal methods for arresting hemorrhage; but during that hundred years, ligature became increasingly common and special "artery forceps" were introduced to crush the end of the exposed arteries and aid the process of clotting. Great changes had come in that time in both operative techniques and the whole attitude of surgeon to patient; further, trained or practised assistants became available, and the techniques were modified to avoid hemorrhage. In the latter part of the hundred years, the consequences of hemorrhage could be partially overcome by general nursing and measures against shock. Transfusion of blood in a correct manner was only possible in this century after the fundamental work of K. Landsteiner (1868–1943), beginning in 1901. By that time it was realized that blood from other species could not be used in human transfusion; Landsteiner showed that care had to be taken even with human blood, for there were four blood groups, now symbolized by O, A, B, and AB. If the donor possessed any of the latter three of these types, it could not be injected into a recipient who did not possess the donor's symbol, that is, none of the latter three blood types could be transfused into an O-type recipient; A-type blood could not be transfused into a B-type recipient; nor B-type into an A-type, nor AB-type into any other group at all. Such forbidden transfusions would lead to severe symptoms and sometimes death, caused by the agglutination of the donor's red calls. See Diamond (1980a, b) or Race and Sanger (1975). There was also the problem of clotting; this was first counteracted by transfusion from artery of the donor to vein of the recipient, but clotting often occurred and the amount transfused was difficult to assess. Finally, the blood from the vein of a donor was run into a flask containing sodium citrate as an anticoagulant, and this reduced the mechanics of a transfusion to the status of two venesectomies. This new method had not altogether ousted all other methods by the end of World War I. In the late 1930s blood transfusion units had been established in a number of cities throughout the world. By this time it was known that blood could be safely stored at temperatures just above zero centigrade, and with the coming of World War II, blood transfusions could be performed often close to the front. Plasma was a by-product of the blood transfusion units and could be used against surgical shock or after trauma in war or peace. Saline and other similar infusions have also been used.

(iii) Use of Anesthetics. Treves (1900) mentions also the favorable effects of anesthesia on the work of the specialist surgeon. Before the introduction of anesthesia, in the horrible, nightmarish atmosphere of the operating theater, well attested in the literature, the surgeon had to be ruthless toward his patient; he tended to be rough in his speech and manners, he was not well read, and his association with the barbers pointed to his low prestige. The range of his operations was limited to the treatment of wounds and fractures, especially those sustained in wars, amputations, lithotomy (or cutting for the stone), and the treatment of hemorrhages and fistulae.

Under the difficult conditions, some surgeons had attained respectability and even high academic posts, before the middle of the nineteenth century. With the introduction of anesthesia, a more humane relationship of the surgeons with their patients developed; there was no question of strapping down the patient and ignoring his cries; in the operation itself, speed and ruthlessness could be replaced by carefulness and neatness.

The anesthetic properties of nitrous oxide were known in 1800 but no use of it was made until the 1840s. Ether was introduced by W.T.G. Morton (1819–1868) in 1846, and chloroform by J.Y. Simpson in 1847. Chloroform was favored, particularly for childbirth, and remained so until recent times. The use of nitrous oxide was confined to minor operations. The poorly purified ether was irritant, and so induction was far more difficult with ether than with chloroform; ether was seen to be safer for major operations and became the standard anesthetic over the years, 1890 to 1940. In recent times nitrous oxide, used in conjunction with a fluorinated hydrocarbon, has been the standard form of general anesthesia. Local anesthesia became available as follows: regional or strictly local by cocaine in

1884; spinal (subrachnoid) in 1898; epidural in 1899; acupuncture in 1826 (in America). Cocaine was replaced by synthetic drugs, without its undesirable side effects, such as procaine (Novocain) in 1905.

The ease of operating is said to have led to many operations, not justified by the results, in the years before rigid antiseptic or aseptic methods, for "successful" operations might well be followed by death from infection in the wards.

(iv) The Introduction of Antiseptic Methods. See §9.11 for a discussion of sepsis in hospitals and the introduction of antiseptic and aseptic methods, and §33.7 for war wounds. J. Lister introduced antiseptic dressings in 1865 and developed antiseptic surgery in 1867. More refined bacteriologic analysis suggested that bacteria could be excluded from wounds by appropriate methods. A variation on this theme was given by Trueta during the Spanish civil war, who after debridement of the wound would enclose the limb in a plaster cast thus excluding hospital germs, such as the streptococci. It should be pointed out that such surgeons as Lawson Tait (1890) were able to point to good surgical results with scrupulous cleanliness but without Listerian methods, and, indeed, some of the opposition to Listerism came from this school of surgeons.

Hospital Care and Surgical Regimes. We defer a general account of hospitals to §45.8. Besides improvements in the purely surgical techniques, careful preparation of the patient by appropriate rest, sedation, and diet, treatment of concurrent diseases, and induction of anesthesia all have had the effect of reducing the operative case fatality rates. Such support methods as saline intravenous injections, blood transfusions, and postoperative exercises have also helped to reduce the rates and made feasible operations that would have been impossible without them.

Surgery of Neoplasms. The skin cancers, excepting melanoma but including cancer of the lip, have yielded to treatment by radiation in the past, and recently by liquid nitrogen or simple excision, painting with chemicals, electron

desiccation, or other means; in particular, they have been treated at an early stage in more recent years. The huge block dissections of glands of the neck, common in the early years of this century, are now rarely performed. The results of cancers of the alimentary tract are disappointing. Treatment of cancers of the lung is also disappointing. Cancer of the cervix has declined in importance but age-specific mortality rates from cancer of the breast have remained at an almost constant level for over 100 years, for example, McKinnon (1950), so surgery has not solved the problem. In all, the treatment of the *major* cancers has been palliative rather than curative, although hormone therapy and chemotherapy have improved the prognosis in recent years.

Circulatory System. Surgery of chronic rheumatic heart disease has been successful, but now the chronic valve disease no longer develops under treatment with antibiotics and chemotherapy. By-pass surgery of the heart is an important advance, although it is believed now that many such operations are unnecessary. Replacement of the heart is a virtuoso performance having little real value in reducing mortality or even helping the patient. See §25.6.

Digestive System. Hernia and appendicectomy operations now have an operative mortality little above that implied by the taking of an anesthetic. Cholecystectomy is now undertaken with a low case fatality. The long-term view is that the diseases cholecystitis and appendicitis can only be abolished by reform of the diet. See chapter 27 for further details.

Obstetrics and Gynecology. We can agree with the opinion of Peller (1943), already cited in §29.5, that the value of the male (academically trained) obstetrician was not immediately apparent; only in this century have there been clear gains if we consider the maternal death rate. In gynecology, surgical advances have been of importance, for example, the treatment of simple ovarian cysts, of late effects of childbirth such as prolapse, and of uterine cancer.

Traumatic and Orthopedic Surgery. Orthopedic surgery developed late as a specialty, perhaps we should say after 1920. As to direct effects on mortality, deaths due to compound fractures, osteomyelitis, and other pyogenic infections have almost disappeared in recent years because of improved initial surgery, following from war experience in 1914–1918, and the later introductions of antibiotics and chemotherapy. Besides this, we should consider the change of emphasis brought about by the specialization, whereby the conservation of tissue and the restoration of function are considered to be of greatest importance, so that the surgeon must plan to these ends from the earliest moment, and his responsibilities cannot end with the conclusion of a neat operation. Considering the additional hazards brought about by modern automobile traffic, we could conclude that improvements in the treatment of trauma have been numerically more important in reducing death rates than those in any other surgical field.

Organ Transplantation. van Rood (1982) draws the conclusion

up until now only few patients have benefited from organ transplantation. It is unlikely that this number will increase dramatically in the near future, partially through a lack of organs (heart transplantation), diffculties with the surgical procedure (liver, lung, pancreas transplantation) or the severity of complications induced when unrelated donors are used (bone marrow transplantation).

See, for the history of surgery: general, Cartwright (1967), Graham (1939), Meade (1968), Wangensteen and Wangensteen (1978); from 1900 to 1950, Jefferson (1950); America, S. Smith (1906), Moore (1976); Vienna, Lesky (1976), Pitha and Billroth (1865–1882). See for anesthesia, Sykes (1982), Pernick (1985), Rupreht et al. (1985); antisepsis and asepsis, Poynter (1967), Wangensteen, Wangensteen, and Klinger (1973); blood transfusion, Diamond (1980*a*); heat sterilization, Henry (1832); surgical dressings, Elliott and Elliott (1964); costs, risks, and benefits, Bunker, Barnes, and Mosteller (1977), Aitkin, Laird, and Francis (1983); obstetrics and gynecology, Graham

(1950); wound management in the nineteenth century, Cope (1958), Wangensteen (1970).

45.2 Pharmacodynamics

In these two sections the effects of pharmacology on mortality are discussed. Pharmacology is the study of the action of drugs on living cells and has two branches (*i*) chemotherapy, in which the drug is to act on an invading organism, and (*ii*) pharmacodynamics, in which the drug is to act an aberrant cell or tissue in the host (patient). Of course, any drug introduced into a patient can be expected to have side effects, that is, effects other than those desired. It has been the task of modern pharmacology to choose drugs that will have maximum effect against the "uneconomic" cell, that is, the one to be affected, without harm to the "economic" cells of the host. This is the leading motive of a modern text, *Selective Toxicity*, by Albert (1985).

The word "medicinal" covers the traditional drugs of the pharmacopeia and synthetic drugs introduced in modern times. The early medicinals were, almost without exception, of plant or animal origin and rarely in a pure or concentrated form. Under the influence of Paracelsus (ca. 1493–1541), chemicals such as mercury, lead, sulfur, arsenic, and copper sulfate were introduced into the materia medica. Hubbard (1976) points out that although solutions of crude drugs were available from prehistoric times, distillates and so concentrations of the drugs appeared only in the early eighteenth century with the development of camphor gums and the isolation of thymol in 1719.

The first effective remedy against an infectious disease was cinchona bark, introduced into Europe in the first half of the seventeenth century; its effective use countered the old doctrine that acute sicknesses must be treated with remedies against dyscrasia, an abnormal mixture of fluids, and so with blood letting, vomiting, and purging. Even so, there were difficulties in the introduction of cinchona bark because it was not in the galenical tradition; further, fevers were not yet differentiated, so cinchona bark was applied without benefit to fevers other than malaria. Although cinchona bark had been recognized as a specific cure for remittent fever, and in 1765 James Lind had laid down a correct treatment for malaria, namely, full doses of the drug as soon as the disease had been diagnosed, in 1804 James Johnson, after a very limited experience with the disease, recommended that the drug not be given until the fever had subsided, a treatment that became standard in India until 1847 with disastrous results. We may conclude that the reliance on tradition and authority in the pre-scientific age could lead to unfortunate results in medicinal therapy.

Even worse was the formation of schools of opinion not based on observation. Thus, the system of heroic symptomatic treatment, *allopathy*, spread widely under the influence of James Gregory (1753–1821) with blood letting, emetics, purges, leeching, and so on. A reaction against such monstrosities, summed up in the statement that the patient had died cured, was the rise of *homeopathy*, the exhibition of drugs in small doses. The three principles of this system, enunciated by C.F.S. Hahnemann (1755–1843) were (*i*) like is cured by like (*similia similibus curantur*), as the disease depends on a perversion of the purely spiritual powers and is entirely immaterial, it cannot be combated by physical agencies; (*ii*) its symptoms can be treated by substances whose potency is released by dilution and whose action, originally similar to the disease, is reversed by dilution; (*iii*) the medicinal treatment must be supported by dietetic and hygienic measures. Homeopathy probably did much less harm than allopathy but degenerated into absurdities when in 1829 drugs could be exhibited in dosages of one in 10^{60}, with an almost complete certainty that no molecule of the drug administered would reach the patient. The principal lessons of these aberrations were that some drugs had an effect and that the body was often able to cure its own ills.

Critics of the use of medicinals were not lacking. Voltaire claimed that the doctors poured drugs of which they knew little into patients of whom they knew less. Even later, R. Virchow is reported to have said "therapy is in an empirical stage cared for by practical doctors and clinicians, and it is by means of a combination with physiology that it must rise to be a science, which today it is not," see Clark (1940/1975, p. 1). He clearly realized that it was necessary to know the working of the body, the way the body functions are altered in disease, and the mode of action of drugs.

By the time that Virchow made the remark above, an experimental school in pharmacology had arisen, which we now consider. According to Professor Adrien Albert, before 1804 few authorities could contend that crude drugs owed their medicinal effects to a single purifiable chemical, the "active principle," for none had been produced. F.W.A. Sertürner (1783–1841) revolutionized the study of such drugs by obtaining in 1804 a crystalline substance from opium, which possessed the properties of a weak base, being soluble in acid water from which it could be precipitated by ammonia. Sertürner called this substance morphine, after the Greek god of sleep Morpheus. Moreover, he showed by experiment that the crystals produced the well-known physiological effects of opium. Morphine was the first of the alkaloids, a name adopted after 1818, to be obtained in pure form. Sertürner's work, neglected at first in Germany, secured for him the Monthyon Prize of the Institut de France in 1831; but more to the point, other alkaloids such as emetine, strychnine, brucine, piperine, colchicine, quinine, nicotine, and atropine were obtained in pure form by his methods. The production of the active principles of the drugs was a first step toward reform; for thereby, accurate doses could be administered and toxic effects due to impurities avoided. Later, research into the chemical structure became possible, leading, in some cases, to synthesis of the compound itself or related compounds.

Rudolf Buchheim (1820–1879), assistant in the department of anatomy and physiology in Leipzing under E.H. Weber, began his work in pharmacology with a translation into German of *The Elements of Materia Medica and Therapeutics* by J. Pereira. In so doing he eliminated many of the old remedies and introduced discussions on the effects of drugs. As a result, he was called to a chair at the University of Dorpat (Tallinn), Esthonia, in 1846, from whence he went to Giessen, Germany, in 1866. At Dorpat he and his students published many papers on experimental pharmacology, describing the mode of action of drugs, their excretion, the action of heavy metals, etc., and a text on pharmacology incorporating many of the results obtained from his researches. Experimental research was thus introduced to an important branch of medicine and gradually became a part of it, according to his most notable student, J.E.O. Schmiedeberg (1838–1921). Buchheim, in English translation in Holmstedt and Liljestrand (1963, p. 79), states that the investigation of the biology of drugs is a task for a pharmacologist, and not for a chemist or pharmacist. Schmiedeberg succeeded Buchheim at Dorpat and later, in 1872, became professor at Strassburg. He is said to have had more students than any medical professor, excepting only Carl Ludwig and Robert Koch. Pharmacology was thus established as a proper university discipline, and tradition and authority were being replaced by experiment and observation.

Other drugs were added to the pharmacopeia: cocaine and physostigmine in the 1860s, chloral hydrate, a soporific, in 1869, salts of salicylic acid in 1875, acetanilide in 1886, later to be supplemented by the less toxic phenacetin in 1887 and aspirin in 1899, and the barbiturates, beginning with barbitone in 1903.

Besides the experimental pharmacologists, many physicians were attempting to introduce a proper study of drugs, for example, J. Škoda. Often they were regarded by their colleagues as therapeutic nihilists, although Škoda did introduce effective medicines such as chloral hydrate and salicylic acid. But despite such opposition, critical observations of drugs continued, as we shall see in §45.3. We conclude that by the end of the nineteenth century, a number of drugs were known to be effective against symptoms, but very few against the disease itself. Among the former were the salicylates, digitalis, and morphine, and among the latter were quinine (cinchona), the iodides, and mercury.

In §45.12 some further examples of aberrations are noted. See, for general history of therapeutics, Holmstedt and Liljestrand (1963), Ackerknecht (1973), and Leake (1975); pharmacy, Dowling (1970), Doyle (1962), Lasagna (1972), and Poynter (1965); pharmacological basis of therapeutics, Clark (1940/1975), Gilman, Goodman, et al. (1985), and Albert (1985); rational technology, Banta, Behney, and Willems (1981); scientific medicine, Wightman (1971); drugs, medicines, and man, Burn (1963); drug discovery, Sneader (1985). For therapy in America, 1820–1885, see Warner (1986).

45.3 Chemotherapy

Not only the traditional medicinals, whether natural or synthetic, but also the antibiotics are included in chemotherapeutics; for the antibiotics can sometimes be synthesized and in other cases they are submitted to chemical changes to increase their usefulness.

The effectiveness of cinchona bark against malaria has already been noticed in the previous section. In 1891 D.L. Romanovskiĭ was able to observe damage done to the asexual forms of the malaria parasite in the blood of a patient treated by cinchona bark (quinine) for malaria; indeed, their nuclei were seen to disintegrate. He predicted that other therapeutics would be found that would cause maximal damage to the parasite and minimal damage to the host (patient). Paul Ehrlich (1854–1915) turned his attention to problems of chemotherapy in 1899. He had observed that many simple natural and synthetic substances, administered to man, were taken up differentially by the tissues; it might therefore be possible to find substances that were taken up by parasites in concentrations greater than by the host. Therapeutic agents must be sought with a high affinity for the parasites; of course, this is a property of antibodies, but he hoped to find other substances of low molecular weight reaching or tending to this ideal. He was led by his work on dyes to state the principle that drugs do not act unless they are fixed either on the cells of the body or, in the therapy of infectious disease, on the infecting agent.

Ehrlich gave the dictum that the minimal

curative dose must not be too close to the maximal tolerated dose. A simple example can be given where this dictum was not followed; thallium acetate was formerly used for depilation, as in tinea infections, yet the dosage required was possibly over one half of the lethal (or maximal tolerated) dose; it is now no longer used in medicine.

In 1906, according to Parascandola (1981), Ehrlich classified therapy into organotherapy (e.g., hormones), bacteriotherapy (immunology), and experimental chemotherapy. A translation of Ehrlich (1909) is given in Holmstedt and Liljestrand (1963, pp. 283–292), in which he believes that the treatment of myxoedema and cretinism by thyroid preparations has opened the wide field of organotherapy. He says that the protecting agents (antibodies) are products of an animal body that act selectively against the parasite but do not affect the organs of the patient; they are "magic bullets" in fact. Serum therapy, however, is not effective against many diseases, for example, malaria, trypanosomiasis, and infections by "spirilla" (he is thinking here of the trepanoma of syphilis); for these *chemotherapy must replace serum therapy*. He cites an example where R. Koch had failed to cure infected animals with mercuric chloride, and the highest doses killed the animal host, not the parasite; remedies must be sought that have great effect on the parasite and little on the host.

Ehrlich cured trypanosomiasis in mice with trypan red in 1904, but the drug was ineffective in man. The success of English workers against human trypanosomiasis with an arsenical drug, Atoxyl, in 1905 led Ehrlich to experiment with arsenical drugs and to the production of arsphenamine (Salvarsan) and a derivative (Neo-Salvarsan), effective against syphilis. These successes led many workers in other laboratories to search for other effective chemotherapeutics.

Acriflavine and proflavine were introduced as antiseptics in 1913 and together with acridine and a modification, aminacrine (Monacrin), found much use in wound infections during World War I. Tryparsamides and suramin (Bayer 205), effective against sleeping sickness, were introduced in 1920. For a time it

appeared that the synthetic drugs developed were useful only against syphilis and some tropical diseases. Many compounds were tested in the research laboratory of the Bayer company at Elberfeld. Pamaquine (Plasmoquine) in 1926, mepacrine (Atebrin) in 1932, and chloroquine in 1937–1939 were all developed in the Bayer laboratories and were all very successful antimalarials; indeed, they can be said to have been revolutionary in their effects. Further references are given by Bruce-Chwatt and Zulueta (1980), Coatney (1963), Duenschede (1971), Findlay (1950), Grayson (1982), Harrison (1978), and Thompson and Werbel (1972).

In 1935 Gerhard Domagk (1895–1964) reported therapeutic success for prontosil rubrum, the first of the antibacterial sulfonamides and the first of the chemical agents successful against the common bacteria of temperate climates; for example, it was effective against the hemolytic streptococci of puerperal fever and the streptococci (formerly pneumococci) of lobar pneumonia. A sulfone was found to be effective against leprosy in 1941 and isoniazid against tuberculosis in 1952. The search for further chemotherapeutic agents continues to this day.

The first example of an antibiotic, that is, a substance produced by microorganisms in high dilution, was penicillin, discovered in 1929 by Alexander Fleming (1881–1955), who in 1921 had found the antibacterial substance, lysozyme. Howard Florey (1898–1968), together with colleagues including E.B. Chain (1906–1979), began a systematic study of the antibacterial substances produced by living organisms and studied lysozyme in detail. By 1939 René Dubos (1901–1982) and his colleagues had isolated, from a soil organism, tyrothricin, which was effective against the pneumococcus, but it could not be used therapeutically since it caused blindness in a proportion of subjects. Florey and Chain then turned their attention to penicillin, which showed true systematic antibacterial potency combined with very low toxicity. The whole laboratory was then set to the task of producing enough penicillin to enable clinical trials to begin. In 1941 penicillin yielded dramatic cures in 9 human cases. At Florey's insistence, mass production of penicillin was undertaken in the United States, not then at war, and sufficient quantities became available in 1944 for the treatment of war casualties. These statements can be amplified with the aid of authors in Parascandola (1980). Crellin (1980) points out that the general idea of antibiosis was already well known in the nineteenth century and cites many authors, including Pasteur and von Pettenkofer; he gives reasons for failure to follow up the lead of some case reports. Chain (1980) believes that Fleming failed to follow up his two finds—that penicillin is not toxic to animals and that it is an effective antibacterial agent in vitro—by not combining the two ideas into an experiment in which mice would be infected with pneumococci and treated with penicillin, because he was not interested in such a form of therapy. Indeed, active and passive immunization were leading motives of his former Head of Department, A.E. Wright (1861–1947), and Wright's prejudices against chemotherapy were shared by many bacteriologists. As Chain points out, penicillin appeared to be a relatively simple molecule containing 14 to 16 carbon atoms and the leading organic chemists in Britain and the United States strongly believed that penicillin would be synthesized within a few months; this belief was the "most important factor inhibiting any attempt . . . to produce penicillin by fermentation," for such effort would be a complete waste of money, both in manpower and capital cost. Chain goes on to describe the chemical obstacles to the synthesis of penicillin that, indeed, were not overcome before 1953. These difficulties of synthesis are also stressed by Helfand, Woodruff, et al. (1980). Fortunately, American firms were finally persuaded to produce penicillin by fermentation processes; a new, more productive strain of *Penicillium mycelium* was used in a new culture medium, corn steep liquor, a commercial residue left over from the extraction of starch from corn; various other technical improvements were made. Spectacular increases in output are reported; by March 1943 Squibb reported production at a rate of 25 million units a week; Merck produced 24 million units in January 1943 and 2,131 million units in December 1943. By D-day 100 billion units were being produced per month, and there was sufficient penicillin to take care of all American and British casualties. After the war production reached new heights, 25 or 30 trillion (10^{12}) units per month and in April 1978, 384.5 trillion units; 1,000 units is equivalent to 1 mg penicillin G procaine. See also Hobby (1985).

Many new powerful and useful antibiotics have been found, for example, streptomycin in 1944 by S.A. Waksman (1888–1973) and others by his school, through the examination of soil bacteria. New antibiotics have also been obtained by the modification of the molecules of familiar antibiotics; these may have useful properties that render them more widely applicable, easier to administer, longer acting, and so on. For drugs against organismal agents of disease other than bacteria and viruses, see Schönfeld (1981).

Beale (1984) notes that there has been a lack of success in antiviral drugs and supposes that it is due to the close association of host and virus; further, many virus diseases have completed their multiplication phase by the time of diagnosis. Interferon is a natural antibiotic, preventing bacterial multiplication; use of interferon in therapy has usually been disappointing. There have been some recent successes. Topical remedies were available for herpes in the eye from 1971. In 1981 the Wellcome Research Laboratories (North Carolina) produced acyclovir, a systemic remedy for herpes. A possible remedy for AIDS awaits clinical trials. See also Dolin (1985).

Modern texts dealing with chemotherapy are Albert (1985) and Garrod, Lambert, et al. (1981). Finland (1983) is an opening paper on the empiric therapy for bacterial infections. See also Greenwood and O'Grady (1985) and Campbell and Rew (1986) for antimicrobial and antiparasitic therapy, respectively. See Datta (1984) for antibiotic resistance of bacteria.

45.4 Immunologic Methods

The therapeutic and prophylactic methods of immunology can be divided into four groups, (*i*) inoculation, (*ii*) vaccination with living organisms, (*iii*) vaccination with killed organisms, and (*iv*) other, of which the first three are used prophylactically.

Inoculation. This term has come to mean the infection of the healthy subject by organisms causing the disease, usually by the application of infective material from a patient with the disease to a scarified area of skin. The value of this procedure is still under dispute; it became obsolescent with the use of vaccination.

Vaccination (living organisms). In 1796 E. Jenner introduced the procedure of applying material from the lesions of cowpox to the scarified skin of healthy subjects, thus producing an attack of cowpox, which is a localized disease in humans. In §11.2 it has been shown that this procedure was the principal tool of the eradication of smallpox, the greatest triumph of immunology in the therapeutic and prophylactic fields. L. Pasteur generalized Jenner's work by deliberately attenuating the virus of some strains of rabies and other animal diseases in the laboratory. After 1921 BCG (Bacille Calmette-Guérin), an attenuated strain of the tubercle bacillus, was used as a living vaccine successfully against tuberculosis and against the related disease leprosy under appropriate given conditions. In 1961 A.B. Sabin (b. 1906) developed attenuated strains of poliomyelitis that also have been successfully used as vaccines. These are the principal successes of the use of live vaccines. In recent times other attenuated strains of organisms (notably the cholera bacillus) have been developed.

Vaccination (killed organisms). Vaccination with living organisms has not been available for many organisms other than those used above, so injections of killed organisms or their products have been used. Such prophylactic vaccines have been used against the enteric fevers, diphtheria, poliomyelitis, and other diseases, as we show later in this section.

Other Immunological Procedures. Included in this group is serotherapy or therapy directed against the toxin of some organisms, notably, diphtheria and tetanus. Here the antitoxins (called immunoglobins) are produced in animals injected with killed vaccines of the infection, and the titer (concentration) of antitoxin

in the blood is increased as far as possible; the serum of such animals is then injected into the human patient. There are also methods of stimulating the immune system of the subject, perhaps by the use of ultraviolet light, according to Parrish (1983), perhaps by the use of appropriate diet; there seems to be general agreement that diet, rest, and other nonspecific measures, such as good nursing, favor the patient by assisting the immune system.

We now run through the various diseases or disease groups.

Cholera. There is little evidence for the value of killed vaccines provoking a general immune response. Greenwood and Whittle (1981) mention that live vaccines of avirulent strains show promise of producing effective local antibacterial immunity, a more logical aim than immune responses effective through the blood stream. Vaccination is far inferior to other means of prophylaxis (Wilson, 1984*d*).

Enteric Fevers. Vaccines (TAB) were prepared and used in the two World Wars; Topley and Wilson (1975) and many other authorities have doubted their value. Since that time great refinements in theory and technique have occurred, according to Levine, Kaper, et al. (1983). We can expect greater effectiveness. Indeed, modern, killed vaccines are more effective than those formerly prepared. A live oral vaccine has been produced that shows great promise (Greenwood and Whittle, 1981, and Parker, 1984*f*).

Tuberculosis. Treatment with tuberculin had only a small effect on the disease. BCG (Bacille Calmette-Guérin) vaccination has been useful in immunizing special risk groups, especially native races newly exposed to civilization, the tribal peoples of §1.1. Mande (1968, chapter 6) gives some striking examples of the protection against tuberculosis by BCG in a variety of classes of subjects in Denmark, England, Ruanda-Urundi, and south India, among others. Eickhoff (1977) believes that in the United States and other developed countries, BCG vaccination is only justified in persons or groups specially at risk. Fox (1984) is a symposium on the serology of tuberculosis and

BCG vaccination. See also Grange (1984) and Daniel and Janicki (1978).

Leprosy. BCG vaccines have been given with some success, although G.S. Wilson and G. Smith (1984*a*) have reservations.

Diphtheria. In §9.3 it has been concluded that the evidence for the effectiveness of serotherapy is not as strong as has been maintained by some publicists; probably serotherapy has reduced case fatality rates. The argument that the declines in diphtheria population mortality in the early years of this century were due in any large degree to serotherapy can be countered by citing the changes in bacterial types, the existence of which is made all the more plausible by secular variations in the case fatalities in many European hospitals. Active immunization, on the other hand, introduced and becoming general in the years around 1940, has been effective and has reduced diphtheria to a minor role by direct protective effect and by reducing the probabilities of perpetuation. See §9.3 for the recent practical freedom from diphtheria mortality in Europe and North America. See also G.S. Wilson and G. Smith (1984*b*).

Whooping Cough. There have been few claims on the importance of serotherapy. Some reduction due to active immunization is possible, but Topley and Wilson (1975) suggest that it has been of little importance. After apparently successful results in the trials of 1959, it has now been found that vaccines used in the mid-1960s in the United Kingdom gave poor protection, occasionally associated with serious side effects, about 1 in 3,000. See also J.W.G. Smith (1984*b*).

Meningococcal Infections. Early vaccines were ineffective, but Greenwood and Whittle (1981) cite successful controlled trials with serum prepared against the polysaccharide of the meningococcus.

It may be remarked that the virulence of organisms is often associated with the presence of a polysaccharide capsule. This is especially true of the meningococcus, pneumococcus, and *Haemophilus influenzae.* Modern techniques permit the separation of the polysaccharide from other unimportant constituents of the bacterial cell and the use of such purified material for the production of serum in animals. Wilson (1984*c*) states that prophylactic vaccination is still in the experimental stage, although sera that are efficient against *Haemophilus influenzae*, the cause of dangerous infections in children, can now be prepared.

Tetanus. Serotherapy reduced the case fatality rates, but the disease can be eliminated by active immunization. Puerperal and neonatal tetanus can be prevented by better hygiene and by active immunization during pregnancy. J.W.G. Smith (1984*a*) gives good evidence for the success of active immunization campaigns and also for the value of the serotherapy used as a prophylactic.

Poliomyelitis. Inactivated vaccine of the Salk type after 1955 and then attenuated live vaccine of the Sabin type after 1960 have been successful in reducing paralysis and death rates. See Greenwood and Whittle (1981) for the preferred method of vaccination and the difficulties in the tropics.

Smallpox. Immunologic methods have had their greatest triumph in the control and finally the eradication of smallpox from the whole world. Inoculation before 1800 had little impact on the disease. Jennerian vaccination was increasingly applied, after the demonstrations of Jenner in 1796, in the advanced countries of the world. Vaccination was important in protecting individuals and in raising the proportion of immunes in the population, thus making more difficult the passage of the organism through the community. The disease was thus eradicated in the developed countries. It was then seen that eradication from the world was possible and, after a campaign planned by WHO in 1966, the disease was eradicated in 1976.

Measles. Vaccination with an attenuated strain has been used in the United States but has been used little elsewhere. According to Morley (1980), live measles vaccines, first available in 1961, have been successful in reducing invalidity and mortality in the United States but not in west Africa.

Rubella. Effective attenuated live vaccines are available.

Yellow Fever. Yellow fever live vaccines have been highly successful in controlling epidemics; in some west African states, such vaccinations are included in routine immunization schedules. Vaccines now used are safe and effective and do not give rise to encephalitis.

Hepatitis B. Vaccines against this virus are now available and in populations at high risk, as in the tropics, campaigns are justifiable.

Rabies. Some doubts still exist on the efficacy of Pasteurian inoculation with an attenuated strain. We have argued in §13.2 that the low case fatality rate, 0.19%, in treated patients and the high rates for untreated cases suggest very strongly that therapy is effective.

Malaria. See Mitchison (1980) for a review of some modern work on immunology, in particular in malaria and some other diseases not yet subject to effective immunologic therapy. Greenwood and Whittle (1981) also point to some difficulties in the preparation of antimalarial vaccines.

Trypanosomiasis. Difficulties in the preparation of vaccines have not yet been overcome.

Helminthiases. Here again, neither vaccines nor serotherapy are available; but see Butterworth (1984).

Pneumonia. Vaccines have been produced against many of the different types of pneumococci (not less than 83), which are effective. Vaccines against prevalent or local types can be prepared for special groups, such as South African miners.

In conclusion, (passive) immunization, that is, serotherapy, has been of value in tetanus and possibly in diphtheria; active immunization with killed vaccines has been effective in diphtheria, tetanus, pertussis, and poliomyelitis; active immunization with live vaccines has been effective in poliomyelitis, smallpox, measles (in the United States), and rabies.

See Anderson and May (1982b) for a general theory of control of directly transmitted infectious diseases by vaccination. See also Nahmias

and O'Reilly (1982) and Bell and Torrigiani (1984). For vaccines and the law, see Sun (1985b); for a history of vaccination, see Chase (1982).

45.5 Endocrine Therapy

Insulin is of critical importance in the insulin-dependent form of diabetes. It is of less importance in the form appearing late in life, which can be controlled by diet.

Hyperthyroidism has been successfully treated by iodine and thyroxin. Drugs are now available that reduce hyperthyroidism and are successful in either controlling it or making it amenable to surgery.

Endocrine therapy is available for control of Addison's disease, a disease of the suprarenal glands.

See also chapter 21.

45.6 Radiation Therapy

Radiation therapy has not been successful against the major internal cancers. With appropriate indications, that is, choice of case, it has given results equally as good as those due to surgery in cancer of the breast; but in other cancers it is not regularly used and, in general, its use can be said to be merely palliative. Radiation, either by superficial X rays or radium applications, has been used as effective therapy in skin cancers, other than melanoma. See Scotto and Fraumeni (1982) and §20.13. See also §45.12.

45.7 Vitamins and Nutrition

We mention only the most important vitamin deficiency diseases and refer the reader to §22.12.

Beriberi and pellagra are successfully treated by thiamine and niacin, respectively.

Replacement therapy is available for vitamin B12 deficiency, resulting in Addisonian (or pernicious) anemia or subacute combined degeneration of the spinal cord.

Scurvy can be treated with vitamin C (ascorbic acid) or with vegetable products containing a high concentration of it.

The effects of rickets and osteomalacia can be mitigated by vitamin D.

Vitamin deficiencies are usually associated with general food deficiencies.

45.8 Hospitals

It is necessary for us to consider conditions in hospitals, because of unhistorical assertions made by popularizers of history, some of whom are cited in §45.11. We begin with some highlights from the history of the Hôtel-Dieu, Paris, with the aid of Wangensteen and Wangensteen (1978); its history typifies the progress from hospice to modern hospital.

A hospital in Europe was originally an alms-house, providing refuge for the sick and the poor, under the direction of a religious order. A modern definition of a hospital, requiring the provision of bed care with physicians in regular attendance, would imply that the Hôtel-Dieu became a hospital in the early thirteenth century. It was followed by La Charité in 1519 and the Hôpital St. Louis in 1607. It can be seen that the Hôtel-Dieu served largely as a home for the aged and chronically ill in the years 1366–1368, for 7,500 patients died per annum, or about 20 per day, out of a mean hospital population of about 900. D'Alembert wrote in the *Encyclopédie* in 1765, "it is the largest, has the greatest number of patients, and is the richest and most frightful of French hospitals." The labor ward was cellarlike and some 20 steps down from the street and, so, subject to flooding by the Seine; in 1649 it was relocated in a segment of the hospital constructed over the bridge; overcrowding occurred with 4 to 5 women to a bed.

The Hôtel-Dieu was called on in emergencies; in 1592 it is reported that 63,000 died of bubonic plague there. During such emergencies as the Fronde insurrection, overcrowding would be extreme, indeed nearly 4,000 wounded and sick patients. Similar records could be found for great hospitals in other cities, but Paris was early a great city and its experience is possibly best recorded. In common with other such hospitals, charity and a desire to help the poor were important impulses leading to its foundation, but the prob-

lems it faced were too great for the amount of resources allotted to it.

The Hôtel-Dieu rose to eminence in the late eighteenth century as a surgical center. In 1828 overcrowding was still a problem, but by 1843 the double beds had been replaced by single iron bedsteads and the sexes were accommodated in separate wards, with patients assigned to them according to their disease. In the 1860s the French Imperial Academy of Medicine and the Academy of Surgery turned their attention to the hygiene in hospitals; but now the Hôtel-Dieu was passing into the modern period, and we can leave it to consider general themes.

Crowding led inevitably to the spread of ectoparasites, especially important in the spread of typhus. The hospitals were notorious also for the spread of other infectious diseases. The reader is referred to §45.1 and §9.11 for hospital gangrene and to §29.5 for puerperal sepsis. Comments given earlier in this section show that contemporaries were aware of the importance of size as a factor in mortality. Simpson (1868–1869, 1869–1870) believed that hospitals should be limited in size and made of some material that enabled them to be readily dismantled and rebuilt. Furthermore, both he and F. Nightingale favored the pavilion type design of hospital to avoid crowding.

Notwithstanding the known bad effects of size that were largely due to cross infections, some historians have believed that the hospitals had a positive effect on health, helping to reduce mortality; some received opinions are quoted in §45.11. McKeown (1971) believes that, far from having any positive role in reducing mortality, hospitals were responsible for spreading infections. Cherry (1972, 1980) leans toward the received views as a result of his studies on the Norfolk and Norwich Hospital, 1771–1880. There is great difficulty in assessing the efficacy of hospital treatment. We can proceed in another way and ask in what particular diseases were the hospitals able to give help beyond shelter, food, and ordinary nursing or supportive techniques. In some small hospitals we might find exceptionally good surgery for compound fractures, and in other hospitals some other excellence, but a general movement toward lowered case fatality rates would be difficult to demonstrate; indeed, Simpson (1868–1869) remarked that the case fatality rates for amputation of a limb were 8% in Edinburgh and 3% in Glasgow in 1740, but in the "now greatly enlarged and palatial hospitals, . . . the mortality from the same operation has become greater than 1 in 3." See Table 9.11.1. Moreover, the total number of beds, in England, for instance, was small as Tait (1890, p. 270) remarks. We conclude that hospitals played no part in the declines in mortality before the late nineteenth century. Burdett (1893) would possibly agree.

Burdett (1882) had noted that Simpson's survey of operative mortality of amputations had led to much controversy, especially about the selection of cases; he therefore collected all the data from the cottage hospital case books from the time of foundation of each hospital (ca. 1859) up to 1878, a period of approximately 20 years. He obtained results of the same kind as those of Simpson (1868–1869). Robert Lawson (Tait), taking part in the discussion of an article by Burdett (1893), showed that a fairer comparison could be made by standardizing the results of operations classified by limb site of amputation on to the same population, but that the new comparison still favored the cottage hospitals. Tait also noted the disasters of the Peninsular War, in which hospital gangrene caused huge fatality rates because of the hospital system; the same disasters occurred in the Crimean War, although the general conditions of food, stimulants, and housing were good and chloroform was available. Tait cited a 50.2% case fatality rate for amputations of the thigh and leg in 235 operations, almost twice as high as the rate in 1813–1815, which he ascribed to the massing together of patients. Tait cites Dr. Schede writing in Pitha and Billroth's *Handbook of Surgery* (1865–1882), who showed that with the advent of the Lister system, case fatality rates could be reduced to strikingly low levels, 2.9% in "antiseptic" hospitals against the 15.3% of the cottage hospitals.

Let us conclude that there was much nosocomial (i.e., hospital) infection in the hospitals before 1860 and that the larger the hospital the larger the rate of such cross infections. It is difficult to believe that the hospitals, except in rare instances, would tend to reduce the general death rate. Among such rare instances were the hospitals inspired by Charles White in Manchester and, incidentally, in early Vienna under J.L. Boër, for which see §29.4, and cottage hospitals under such direction as that of Edward Bennion in Shropshire in the early 1800s, for which see §9.11.

For accounts of hospitals, see: 1200–1900, Keevil (1957/1958); 1800–1948, Abel-Smith (1964); eighteenth century, Sigsworth (1966); nineteenth and twentieth centuries, Spink (1979); English hospitals, Guy (1856, 1867), Nightingale (1894a,b), Steele (1861, 1877), and Sweeting (1884); Paris, Ackerknecht (1967); United States, Billings and Hurd (1894); Germany, Welch (1877); problems of modern hospitals, Williams and Shooter (1963), Spink (1979), Parker (1984a, b, c, d), and Vogel (1980); hospital architecture of all ages, Thompson and Goldin (1975); France in the eighteenth century, Greenbaum (1975).

45.9 Nursing

Nursing reform began with the work of the Roman Catholic orders, especially the Third Order of St. Francis, in the thirteenth century; other orders were created, among which the Augustinian Sisters served at the Hôtel-Dieu of Paris. The Sisters of Charity founded by St. Vincent de Paul (1576–1660) has been concerned entirely with nursing and is now the largest Roman Catholic nursing order.

The protestant areas of Europe were not as well served; after the dissolution of the monasteries in England in 1535, there was a serious lack of accommodation and attention for the sick who could not be nursed at home. Singer and Underwood (1962, pp. 702, 703) give an account of the lack of staff, low social status, lack of education and expertise of the nurses in a "well-managed English provincial hospital," the Radcliffe Infirmary at Oxford, until after 1850. This particular problem was well understood by John Howard and other reformers. Elizabeth Fry (1780–1845), striving for the improvement of the lot of female prisoners or dependents of prisoners in Newgate and seeing the necessity for training, instituted an order of nursing sisters. Theodor Fliedner (1800–1864) visited England in 1822 and was much impressed by Elizabeth Fry's example. He and his wife later opened a refuge for discharged female convicts and in 1836 they opened a small hospital. Here, at Kaiserswerth in Germany, young women of the "most spotless character" were invited to serve as "deaconesses" and were instructed by visiting physicians. In 1840 Elizabeth Fry visited Kaiserswerth and on her return to London founded the Institute of Nursing Sisters. Later, Florence Nightingale visited Kaiserswerth in 1851 and returned to become superintendent of the Establishment for Gentlewomen during Illness, but further plans had to be deferred until after the Crimean War.

The examples of these hospitals were influential in raising the standards of recruitment in the nursing profession. Some form of state registration became desirable and the first enforcement of registration of nurses came in New Zealand in 1901; later, a nurses registration act became law in Great Britain in 1919. It is quite unhistorical to equate the nurses and hospitals of this century with those before, for instance, 1880.

For hospitals in the United States, see Rosenberg (1987).

45.10 Role of the Medical Practitioner

We now mention the various causes of death, especially those in which we know that substantial declines have occurred, and attempt to assess the roles of the medical practitioners and medical theorists in academic and medical institutions.

Intestinal Infectious Diseases (ICD 001–009). Factors other than therapy have been dominant in these declines, particularly improved hygiene of the supplies of water, milk, and food.

Tuberculosis (ICD 010–018). Effective therapy came quite late when the disease had declined greatly in importance in the developed world, that is, after 1945. Apart from ordering rest and proper nutrition, the medical practitioner could do little. Surgery and immunologic methods have played little part. In the late 1940s, Domagk's thiacetazone (Tibione), Waksman's streptomycin, and *p*-aminosalicylic acid the latter two often used in conjunction, were successful. They were replaced in the 1950s by isoniazid and *p*-aminosalicylic acid used in conjunction, but now all others are discarded and rifamycin and isoniazid together are used.

Zoonotic Bacterial Diseases (ICD 020–027). Plague, the only disease in this subclass causing large numbers of deaths, has been controlled by hygienic measures, principally directed against the rat. The remaining diseases are effectively treated by antibiotics and chemotherapy.

Other Bacterial Diseases (ICD 030–041). Among these, diphtheria and tetanus could be treated by serotherapy. Chemotherapy and antibiotics were available after 1935 and 1945, respectively, for all the diseases of this subclass. General hygienic changes were responsible for declines before 1935; see §9.3 for the variation in frequency of the diphtheria bacterial types.

Poliomyelitis and Related Virus Diseases (ICD 045–049). These diseases have been a minor cause of mortality.

Virus Diseases with Exanthem (ICD 050–057). Smallpox has been eradicated now; defense against it was vaccination after 1800. No special therapy was ever available against it, neither was such available against measles. Rest in bed provided by the home was the only therapy for measles. Indeed, the physicians of the past would have had little interest in such a "trivial" disease.

Arthropod-borne Viral Diseases (ICD 060–066). Of these, yellow fever remained a "plague" until hygienic measures were applied against the carrier mosquito.

Other Diseases due to Viruses and Chlamydias (ICD 070–079). These are rather exotic diseases and not responsible for any large amount of mortality at any time.

Rickettsioses and Other Arthropod-borne Diseases (ICD 080–088). No specific therapy had been available against typhus, which has been overcome by hygienic action against lice. Quinine was introduced into the therapy of malaria in the seventeenth century but, as we have seen in §45.2, a modification of the drug regime in 1804 led to disaster; from 1926 on, increasingly effective chemotherapy has been available in treatment and prophylaxis. Effective chemotherapy became available against leishmaniasis and trypanosomiasis early this century, and, later, antibiotics against relapsing fever.

Syphilis and Other Venereal Diseases (ICD 090–099). Mercury compounds were used against syphilis before 1500 but were too toxic to be continued; after 1850 a more carefully planned regimen of mercury therapy was used with success. Guaiacum and other vegetable compounds were also used. In 1837 potassium iodide was introduced. After 1910 the arsphenamines and mapharside were available until they were superseded by penicillin.

Other Spirochetal Diseases (ICD 100–104). Penicillin and some other antibiotics are effective against leptospirosis.

Mycoses (ICD 110–118), Helminthiases (ICD 120–129), Other Infectious and Parasitic Diseases (ICD 130–136). These have not been important causes of mortality of European-type communities, so that, here too, therapy played little part in reducing mortality. For these diseases, see §46.2.

Neoplasia (ICD 140–239). See §§45.1 and 45.6.

Endocrine, Nutritional, and Metabolic Diseases (ICD 240–279). See §45.5

Diseases of the Blood and Blood-forming Organs (ICD 280–289). See §45.7.

Mental Disorders (ICD 290–294). Little change was effected in mortality of those affected by psychosis. Their condition in hospital or asylum could be improved by good medical supervision and hygiene. Their lot and probably their mortality would have been improved by new drugs, for example, lithium in 1949, which allowed them to spend more time out of institutions.

Diseases of the Nervous System and Sense Organs (ICD 320–389). The infections could be treated, especially after 1935, and surgery was available for the mastoid infections; epilepsy could be controlled with sedative drugs, but in general the hereditary and degenerative diseases have not yielded to treatment; many rubrics do not represent lethal diseases.

Diseases of the Circulatory System (ICD 390–459). The treatment of rheumatic fever and its complications had been largely supportive. After 1935 chemotherapy and antibiotics were effective in the acute and subacute stages and, so, in aborting the disease. The treatment of hypertensive, ischemic heart, and cerebrovascular diseases has been largely supportive but there have been some improvements reported recently, usually thought to be due to changes in diet and life style.

Diseases of the Respiratory System (ICD 460–519). Deaths occurred in this group from influenza, the pneumonias, and bronchiectasis. No effective treatment against influenza is yet available. Chemotherapy was available against the pneumonias after 1935, and surgery was of some value for bronchiectasis and lung abscess; as the diseases antecedent to bronchiectasis and lung abscess are now well recognized, prophylactic treatment has been effective.

Diseases of the Digestive System (ICD 520–579). The treatment of peptic ulcer was improved in the 1920s. The operative results of appendicectomy, cholecystectomy, and herniotomy have been increasingly favorable.

Diseases of the Genitourinary System (ICD 580–630). Although the death rates from chronic nephritis have declined, it is difficult to ascribe these declines to therapy; but improved surgery has led to declines in the mortality from diseases of the prostate.

Complications of Pregnancy, Childbirth, and the Puerperium (ICD 630–676). Following on rather small declines, if any, until 1910, there were improvements up to 1935, when sulfonamides became available; after 1935 there were great declines in the mortality from abortion (often included in the class of Accidental and Violent Causes) and from sepsis in childbirth, generally. In the 1930s effective prophylaxis and therapy were devised against the toxemias of pregnancy and also against hemorrhages.

Diseases of the Skin, Subcutaneous Tissues, Musculoskeletal System, and Connective Tissue (ICD 680–709 and 710–739). In so far as they occur in these classes, deaths are due to infective (that is, septic) diseases. Great improvements have been made by advances in the surgery of trauma and by chemotherapy after 1935.

Congenital Anomalies (ICD 740–759). The mortality from these diseases has remained remarkably steady.

Certain Conditions Originating in the Perinatal Period (ICD 760–779). There have been great improvements in the mortality of the perinatal period, following the general adoption of proper routines of prenatal care, the avoidance of infections, supportive care, and the use of antibiotics, and, we add, a general amelioration of the conditions of life. Prenatal diagnosis and therapeutic abortion could change the rates in some countries.

Symptoms, Signs, and Ill-defined Conditions (ICD 780–796). Few deaths are now assigned to this class; it is often forgotten when authors are assessing the increased death rates from cardiovascular causes.

Injury and Poisoning (ICD 800–999). There have been great improvements in the management and surgery of trauma. Some of these improvements have been brought about by specialization made necessary by the development of large scale industry. Public health measures have increased the safety in some occupations.

Many authors have written on the role of the medical profession in the declines of mortality; for example, it has been noted that death rates from diphtheria have declined as a result, before 1940, of serotherapy, yet the mortality

from measles has decreased, although there have been no specific remedies against it.

For the role of the profession, see Conybeare (1948), Lancaster (1952a, c, 1963, 1967c), McKeown, Brown, and Record (1972), McKeown and Record (1962), McKeown, Record, and Turner (1975), Burnet (1952), and Forbes (1967). For "doctors" in the sixteenth century, see Pelling and Webster (1979); for physicians of the eighteenth century, see MacMichael (1827); for the rise of the standing of the medical profession in the last 100 years, see Brown (1979) and Parry and Parry (1976); for various criticisms, see Barzun (1974) and Bradshaw (1978); for therapeutic nihilism, see Lesky (1960).

45.11 Received Doctrines on the Declines in Mortality

H.J. Habakkuk (1953) complains that

Few generalizations are so well established in the books as that which ascribes the increase in the population of England and Wales in the second half of the eighteenth century to a fall in the death-rate caused primarily by improvements in medicine, medical skill, and public health.

Among those propagating this view was Griffith (1926) who concluded on p. 260 of the reprint in 1967 of his book that the birth rate increased during the eighteenth century, from 1710 to 1790, but the death rate decreased; the more important contribution to growth was from the improvements in the death rates. Marshall (1935) expressed similar views on a supposed decline in mortality during the Industrial Revolution. Krause (1958) believed that variations in the proportion of births and deaths notified rendered illusory any deductions from the data available. We quote the opinions of well-known economic and social historians.

J.R. Hicks (1942, p.43) says:

It seems probable . . . that the more or less stable-sized populations which seem to have been the rule before 1750 were due to a combination of high birth rate with high death rate . . . The principal development which upset this primitive equilibrium was a marked fall in the death rate, due (beyond all doubt) to the improvements in sanitation and medical skill which were beginning to be effective in the north of Europe by the middle of the eighteenth century . . .

G.M. Trevelyan (1944) includes the three following passages. On his p. 341:

In the course of the Eighteenth Century the population of England and Wales rose from about five and a half millions when Queen Anne came to the throne, to nine millions in 1801. . . . The advance in population represented a rather larger birth-rate and a very much reduced death-rate. The survival of many more infants and the prolongation of the average life of adults mark off modern times from the past, and this great change began in the Eighteenth Century. It was due mainly to improved medical service.

On his p. 470:

the good doctors of Great Britain were responsible for the fact that between 1801–1831, the inhabitants of England, Wales and Scotland rose from eleven to sixteen and a half millions.

On his p. 562:

In the 'seventies and 'eighties [1870s and 1800s] . . . The death-rate dropped with the improvement of town sanitation and the constant progress of medical knowledge and practice.

[G.M. Trevelyan, *English Social History: A Survey of Six Centuries, Chaucer to Queen Victoria*. Longmans, Green & Co., London, 1944. Reprinted with permission.] These conclusions should be compared with the discussion of mortality in England and Wales and in Scotland in §§37.2 and 37.3.

J.H. Plumb (1950) could write on his p. 78: "After 1740, however, there was a steady growth of the population due to a marked, if small, decline in the death rate. Almost certainly this was due to improved midwifery . . . and to the foundation of lying-in hospitals and orphanages; the first kept the children alive, the second prevented them being exposed."

Commenting on such opinions, Hall (1967, p. 141) writes that the demographers assumed a constant live birth rate over the eighteenth century, so they had to explain the increase in population by declines in the death rates, especially among infants, which they asserted were due to improvements in medical practice.

45.12 Therapeutic Aberrations

Many therapeutic and some diagnostic measures carry a risk. Some of these risks must be accepted as part of a balancing between the beneficial and harmful results of the particular therapy; for example, all drugs alter the normal physiology in some way, either in the directions sought or in directions not wished for. Here we give examples of disease or accidents caused by therapeutic measures, discussed in the same order as in the earlier sections of this chapter.

Surgery

(a) *Phlebotomy or Venesection.* This simple operation, initially consisting of a cutting down on a vein, but later supplemented or replaced by cupping or the application of leeches, has a long history from Hippocrates to Osler and beyond. The practice was sufficiently common for the medical practitioners to be referred to collectively as "leeches." Excesses were common; according to Wangensteen and Wangensteen (1978), the Italian Botallo, practising in Paris in 1577, recommended bleeding to faintness for almost every disease. In the early days of the Bristol Royal Infirmary, which opened in 1737, 73% of patients underwent phlebotomy; 41.5 million leeches were imported into France in 1833. St. Bartholomew's hospital bought 97,000 leeches in 1832. F.J. Broussais (1772–1838) and his pupil J.B. Bouillaud (1796–1881) were leading exponents of phlebotomy in Paris early in the nineteenth century. Broussais applied his methods to the victims of the cholera epidemic of 1832 with disastrous results that shocked his students (see his notice in the *Dictionary of Scientific Biography*). W. Osler thought that phlebotomy was used too much in the early and too little in the late nineteenth century. These practices persisted into this century despite criticism by Johann G. Wolstein in 1791 (for which see Rosenthal, 1922), by Louis (1835), and by J. Škoda perhaps later (see his notice in the *Dictionary of Scientific Biography*). The obvious dangers were fatal syncope and sepsis, reported in the literature between 1819 and 1828 (for which see the references of note 17, p. 649 of Wangensteen and Wangensteen, 1978). A modern aberration is reported by Eyster and Bernene (1973), who note that patients hospitalized for 3 to 4 weeks at Cornell Medical Center lose an average of half to one liter of blood for diagnostic purposes.

(*b*) *Focal Sepsis.* A distinguished American surgeon F. Billings (1912 and in later papers) believed that many diseases such as arthritis and nephritis were manifestations of a focal infection in some other organ. W. Arbuthnot Lane (1856–1943), a distinguished London surgeon, held the same hypothesis. Billings was regrettably supported by some extraordinary bacteriology carried out by E.C. Rosenow at the Mayo Clinic. Vast numbers of teeth extractions, tonsillectomies, appendicectomies, partial colectomies, and so on, were carried out in the name of this hypothesis, which was finally discredited by the review of Reimann and Havens (1940).

(*c*) *Sepsis in Surgery and Obstetrics.* Surgeons were often reluctant to make changes in routines to avoid sepsis, even in the face of convincing empirical evidence, for example, in obstetrical practice and in surgical amputations. See §§29.4 and 9.11.

Medicinals and Chemotherapeutics

We give now some illustrative examples of adverse drug reactions, as they are now called.

Antimony. According to Davies (1981), antimony was proscribed by the Paris Faculty of Physicians in the seventeenth century but the ban was lifted after it had been credited with the cure of an attack of enteric fever suffered by Louis XIV in 1657.

Mercury. Benjamin Rush (1746–1813) experienced the yellow fever epidemic of 1793 in Philadelphia, during which, it is said, 4,000 of the 27,000 inhabitants died; during this epidemic he prescribed a purgative consisting of ten grains of calomel (mercurous chloride) and

ten grains of jalap, with what appeared to him to be great success. Rush therefore was led to believe that calomel might be a panacea and it passed into general use, against much criticism. Davies (1981, p. 2) suggests that such violent remedies opened the way for gentler systems of healing. This calomel incident is discussed in detail by Jarcho (1957) and Risse (1973). In §17.1, the use of mercury in the treatment of syphilis has already been discussed; it was reintroduced in the middle nineteenth century and a proper scheme of dosage devised.

With the development of powerful and effective medicines, new problems arose; sudden deaths under chloroform anesthesia were investigated in England in 1880; the jaundice following arsphenamine injection was the subject of an enquiry by the Medical Research Council in England in 1922. The American Medical Association established the Council on Pharmacy and Chemistry in the late 1920s and its publication of *New and non-official Remedies* set up criteria for the use of new remedies. A body later to be called the Food and Drug Administration was established in the United States. We give some examples of the toxicity of drugs or their solvents.

Thallium. Poisoning from thallium has already been briefly mentioned in §45.3.

Tin. In France in 1954, 100 persons died from poisoning with Stalinon, an organic compound of tin, administered in the treatment of boils.

Diethylene Glycol. In 1937 107 persons died by poisoning by diethylene glycol used as a solvent for sulfanilamide; this was a needless disaster, for reports of such toxicity were already available in the literature; as a result, it was enacted in the United States that no drug could be marketed there without the approval of the Food and Drug Administration.

The toxicity of simple inorganic compounds and of the breakdown products of metallo-organic substances is now well known, but in recent decades many synthetic organic medicinals have been produced, the toxicity of which can only be tested by animal experimentation or human experience. The following is an outstanding example of unexpected toxicity.

Thalidomide. This is a complex organic synthetic sedative, with no atomic constituent other than hydrogen, carbon, nitrogen, and oxygen, sold under a variety of trade names. In phocomelia (literally seallike limbs) there may be gross deformities of the limbs. Before 1960 phocomelia was an exceedingly rare congenital abnormality, but in 1961 cases of it were displayed in clinical meetings, and W. Lenz noted that 20% of the mothers of such deformed infants had reported taking the sedative contergan (i.e., thalidomide); on requestioning the mothers he found that at least 50% had taken such a sedative. He warned the pharmaceutical firm of the dangers and they withdrew the product from sale within a fortnight. Lenz then attempted a thorough questioning of the mothers of such damaged children and found definite evidence of intake of the drug among them. It is now known that the fetus is susceptible to the action of the drug over a limited period. Taussig (1962) believes that the number of cases of phocomelia throughout the world can be reckoned in hundreds rather than thousands. For the legal aftermath, see Teff and Munro (1976).

Although it was known that "adverse drug reactions" did occur, the first book devoted entirely to this theme was published by Leopold Meyler in 1952, and since that time there has existed an irregular serial of the same purpose and title, see Meyler and Herxheimer (1972). Jick (1980) points to difficulties in the identification of a drug-induced disease, unless it has some effect in a high proportion of cases or a dramatic effect in a few cases, plus the fact that the time to induction of the disease must not be too long. He quotes an estimate of drug-induced deaths in hospitalized medical patients as about 0.9 per 1,000 admissions. This rate is sufficiently low to cause a great problem in estimating the risks, unless there is access to many patients, directly or through information banks. For the pathology of such diseases, see Grundmann (1980).

Antibiotics

Although there are some dangers of disease syndromes, especially anemia and leukopenia, from the use of antibiotics, a greater danger is the development of new resistant strains of virulent bacteria; see Lappé (1982), Whorton (1980), and Reimann (1961).

Immunologic Methods

The dangers of immunologic therapy have been outlined by Wilson (1967); he states that no vaccine or antiserum can be regarded as completely safe. We cite a few examples. Before bacteriologic studies gave a warning, techniques often could be defective so that instruments and vaccines could become infected with dangerous organisms, for example, syphilis and septic organisms. Even as late as 1928, severe incidents could occur in which live staphylococcal colonies could be injected into children in an immunization campaign, leading to many deaths. In 1885, 190 cases of what is now known as hepatitis B were caused by an infected vaccine used in a prophylactic campaign among workers in a factory in Germany. In the early years of antidiphtheria immunization, the diphtheria toxin itself was toxic and could therefore only be used in association with antiserum; but the mixture was often unstable, and a variable quantity of unbound toxin was sometimes injected. Fatal accidents were reported. To avoid them, the mixture was replaced by toxoid, toxin from which the toxicity had been removed by chemical means, and toxoid became the standard form of injection in the final control of diphtheria. It may be noted that some killed vaccines of viruses are also dangerous but killed vaccines, bacterial or viral, are not as effective in provoking immunity as are live vaccines. The first effective vaccines, the vaccinia of E. Jenner and the rabies vaccine of L. Pasteur, were living vaccines related to the viruses of smallpox and rabies, respectively. Both smallpox virus, used before 1800, and vaccinia viruses are capable of causing encephalitis. Similarly, there may be neuroparalyses or other symptoms after rabies vaccination. There are points in the administration of vaccines at which safety may break down; at Lübeck in 1930, virulent tubercle bacilli were grown alongside the live modified strain of tubercle bacilli (BCG) and were injected, causing many deaths from fulminating generalized tuberculosis. Live vaccines also have the disadvantage that they must be kept uncontaminated without the aid of disinfectants; bacterial contamination may occur during storage or during repeated use of the glass bottle containing the vaccine.

Endocrine Therapy

The principal hazard from hormone therapy arises from the use of diethylstilbestrol in contraceptive pills; Stolley and Hibberd (1982) cite figures of 34 per 1,000,000 for hepatocellular adenoma among those using this hormone for contraceptive purposes. Endometrial cancers and cancer of the breast are also unduly common. See also Apfel and Fisher (1984).

Radiation Therapy

Ionizing radiation used diagnostically or therapeutically formerly gave rise to some neoplasms, especially leukemia, for which see §20.3. Following the work of Court Brown and Doll (1965) and others, such radiation is no longer used for therapy except in the treatment of malignancy. With modern equipment, the dosage received for diagnostic purposes is usually minimal.

Vitamins

Little toxicity results from overdosages of the vitamins. It is said that large doses of vitamin C can lead to urinary calculus; vitamin A intoxication can result from rather specialized diets, but rarely from medication; a greater risk is from an excessive intake of D-enriched products (Hambraeus, 1982).

Blood Transfusions

The first difficulties, due to incompatibility between the bloods of donor and recipient, were overcome by the scientific analysis of blood groups by K. Landsteiner and others. The risk of latent syphilis in donors was eliminated by screening. Hepatitis was the next great problem; screening tests eliminated hepatitis B, for which see Gerety (1981, p. 275). Since 1970, 90% of all cases of posttransfusion hepatitis in

the United States have been due to non-A, non-B hepatitis. The spread of AIDS has been enhanced by high transfusion rates. In South America infection with Chagas' disease is said to be common after transfusion.

Conclusions

The aberrations or errors and accidents of therapy can be rearranged in another way, namely:

(*a*) *Iatrogenic Illnesses.* These are due to excesses, deficiencies, or errors in therapy as undertaken by medical attendants.

(*b*) *Nosocomial Illnesses.* These are usually infections acquired from the hospital surroundings, formerly a grave problem and still not completely preventable, for example, hospital strains of resistant bacteria.

(*c*) *Self-medication by the General Public.* It is believed that the volume of potent drugs ordered by physician's prescription or supplied in hospital is approximately equal to that obtained "over the counter."

(*d*) *Patient Noncompliance.* Of this, the medical profession is constantly complaining; it takes two forms (a) not taking a prescribed medicine essential for health, and (b) taking larger doses of a medicine than have been recommended by the physician.

(*e*) *Alternative Forms of Medicine.* Some of these forms are harmless and sometimes even more effective than traditional medicine; however, effective methods of treatment may be passed over in favor of ineffective nonstandard therapy.

See also, for costs, risks, and benefits, Bunker, Barnes, and Mosteller (1977); benefits, risks, vaccines, and the courts, Koshland (1985); technology in medicine, Towers (1971); for a criticism of modern medicine with many references, see Illich (1975). For diseases' of medical progress, see Moser (1959).

45.13 Education in Medicine

In chapter 2, advances in pathology, bacteriology, and diagnosis have been briefly described, so that an idea can be formed as to the possibilities of giving precise modern names to the diseases described by past writers. Until the development of bacteriology and effective medicinals and therapies, the science and the practice of medicine were not closely related. The acceptance of scientific ways of thinking as the basis of medical practice is now traced for the special case of the United States, which is well documented, as in Bowers and Purcell (1976).

Clinical teaching originated in Leyden with H. Boerhaave (1668–1738), whose influence on many other medical centers was profound. Thus, the first four appointees to chairs in 1726 at the Royal Infirmary of the University of Edinburgh had studied at Leyden. Early Edinburgh had the reputation for the teaching of theory, but many Americans rounded their education by walking the wards in the London hospitals where the influence of John Hunter and his brother William Hunter (1718–1783) was dominant. Later, many Americans studied in Paris, especially under P.C.A. Louis. Of course, these graduates of the European hospitals were only a small minority of the physicians (i.e., general practitioners) of America and tended to be concentrated in the cities.

As Starr (1982, p. 82) points out, a medical career in the nineteenth century did not carry the prestige and security of the present time. There were no educational barriers to entry into the profession, and for much of the nineteenth century the chief form of education was the apprenticeship system, sometimes formalized in the cities by the establishment of schools with the local practitioners as instructors; between such schools there could be bitter rivalry; the "medical course" could be of 2 years or even of 1. These unsatisfactory conditions were beginning to improve by 1870, when there was a general move toward an improvement of higher education, especially in the universities, and more attention was being paid to scientific and technical training. See Cooper (1976) and Holden (1976) for further details of medical education and Rothstein (1972) for the status of American medical practitioners.

According to Bowers (1976), there had been early attempts to control the practice of medicine and to foster professional intercourse in science and medicine. Of the colleges formed with such aims, few survived, among which after a change of name we mention the American Philosophical Society and the Massachusetts Medical Society. Although there were sound colleges of medical education at Philadelphia, New York, New Haven, and Baltimore in the early nineteenth century, there was neither the possibility nor the will to control medical practice during the westward expansion at that time.

Further advances in general and, especially, scientific education were required. In 1801 B. Silliman (1779–1864) became Professor of Chemistry and Natural Philosophy at Yale at a time when only Harvard, Pennsylvania, and the College of New Jersey (Yale) had such chairs. In 1846 a research laboratory was established at Yale in which graduate students could carry out research. In 1847 Harvard invited J.L.R. Agassiz (1807–1873) to a chair of zoology and geology. Also in 1847 the Lawrence Scientific School in applied science was initiated at Harvard, the only department there to give advanced instruction in science. From 1846 the Smithsonian Institution was a leading supporter of science.

The American universities had been dominated by the ideal of the classical education but this was to change. First, there was reform in the older universities; C.W. Eliot (1834–1926), President of Harvard 1869–1901, gave the Harvard medical faculty its modern form in 1877. Second, the Morrill Land Grant Act of 1857 decreed that for each representative and senator, the individual state was to set aside 30,000 acres of land to found an agricultural college; a second act of 1890 awarded $25,000 to each land-grant college to teach military subjects; 28 states established separate colleges as a result, and in 15 other states the funds were turned over to the already established state universities. These benefactions strengthened the teaching of general science at the higher levels.

In the basic medical sciences, H.P. Bowditch (1840–1911) founded the first American laboratory at Harvard in 1871. The Johns Hopkins University was founded in 1876 in the German tradition, whereby the emphasis was on creative scholarship with no undergraduate teaching responsibilities. J.S. Billings (1838–1913) became director of the Henry C. Lea Laboratory and Department of Hygiene at the University of Pennsylvania in 1889. In 1882 a school of physiological chemistry was founded at Yale. Thus, by 1900 a number of research institutes had been formed, usually within the universities, by philanthropy and so by influences from outside the universities. But more was to come from the great fortunes made from commerce. As Bowers (1976) has it:

During the last quarter of the nineteenth century the new tycoons were beginning to turn a part of their vast fortunes to social benefit. They established universities such as Vanderbilt (1872) and Stanford (1885); created philanthropic foundations dedicated to the welfare of all Americans such as the Carnegie Foundation for the Advancement of Teaching (1905), the Rockefeller Foundation (1913), and the Julius Rosenwald Fund (1917); and endowed research institutions such as the Rockefeller Institute for Medical Research (1902) and the Carnegie Institution of Washington (1904).

Happily these businessmen chose outstanding men to assist in managing the finances. A critical change was to follow the appointment by the Carnegie Foundation of Abraham Flexner (1866–1959), a nonmedical graduate of Johns Hopkins University. In 1906 A. Flexner consulted his brother Simon Flexner (1863–1946), a pathologist and then Director of the Rockefeller Institute for Medical Research, on what should be done; Abraham Flexner proceeded abroad to study the medical schools of Europe; Heidelberg and Berlin were his preferred models. On his return in 1908, he carefully reviewed and accepted as his model Johns Hopkins School of Medicine; he then visited 148 medical schools in the United States and 7 in Canada. His chief findings, according to Bowers (1976), were

1) at 137 of the schools specified entrance requirements were nonexistent, or if specified were not enforced; 2) at 138 schools teaching staff was composed entirely of practicing physicians; 3) laboratory courses in the first and second years were poorly taught with totally inadequate equipment; and 4) at 140 schools the libraries were either inadequate or nonexistent.

His report classed the schools as A, B, or C, but as A included the well-known schools such as Harvard, Yale, . . . , it was evident that C would be deficient. The classification and report were taken up by the press. As a result, from 160 medical schools, with 32 rated C, in 1905, there remained in 1920 only 85, of which 8 were rated as C. It must be added that the American Medical Association had made attempts over the years to remedy the defects in the schools and Flexner was accompanied by their representative, sympathetic with Flexner, to many of the schools. See Ludmerer (1985).

There were other philanthropies, for example, the Milbank Memorial Fund in 1905, the Commonwealth Fund in 1918, the John and Mary Markle Foundation in 1927, the W.K. Kellogg Foundation in 1930, the Josiah Macy Jr. Foundation in 1930, and the Robert Wood Johnson Foundation and the Ford Foundation in 1950; and to these we can now add a Hughes Foundation. There were also voluntary health agencies for special projects, for example, tuberculosis: the Pennsylvania Society for the Prevention of Tuberculosis in 1892 and, under another name, the National Tuberculosis Association in 1904; the March of Dimes in 1938, leading to the Salk vaccine for poliomyelitis, having collected $4 billion; the American Cancer Society in 1943; the National Heart Association in 1974, with a current income of almost $60 million.

The development of American medical education can be studied in Bordley and Harvey (1976), Cooper (1976), Duffy (1976), Shryock (1966), and Starr (1982). Similar events in the rise of a despised and badly paid profession to a position of respect and affluence can be found in the medical histories of many other developed countries.

The role of the great foundations has been stressed in the discussion of the American scene but some mention should be made of other influences. In §45.8 we have drawn attention to the role of the religious orders in the foundation of the hospitals and the increasing difficulties as cities grew larger. In the Protestant countries some support for the indigent and sick was lost on the dissolution of the monasteries, as in England, but the religious and humanitarian impulse remained. When education became more general and the conditions of life became easier for a wider range of the population, individuals such as John Howard, Elizabeth Fry, Theodor Fliedner, Florence Nightingale, and Jean Henri Dunant began to enquire into the welfare of civil prisoners, prisoners of war, hospital patients, infants, and underprivileged persons. Some of these, such as John Howard and Florence Nightingale, were influential with governing and administrative bodies; others perhaps were influential within the religious communities, giving direction to the religious motivation of J.D. Rockefeller and Andrew Carnegie; others may have influenced governments, who began to accept the responsibility of public health or, more generally, social medicine.

45.14 Medical Theory

Any rational medical theory must depend on the scientific method, including the abandonment of the notion of authority, for example, Aristotle, and use its techniques, such as the provisional acceptance of hypotheses and the submitting of all hypotheses to empirical tests; it must draw on such special relevant fundamental sciences as anatomy, physiology, biochemistry, pathology, including the study of pathogenesis, and bacteriology. It is often forgotten that these fundamental sciences reached a modern form quite recently; indeed, Poynter (1968) finds 1860–1870 as an appropriate decade for the change from the old medicine to the new.

It would be a difficult task to show in detail how the academic doctors failed, but we can recall a few topics.

(a) *Puerperal Sepsis.* This topic has been discussed in §29.4. Thus, it would seem that many workers had given support to the hypothesis that puerperal fever was indeed contagious; yet in America the Professors of Obstetrics C.D. Meigs and H.L. Hodge refused to accept the evidence that the hand of the obstetrician could carry the infection, and the members of the medical faculty in Vienna would not accept the evidence of I.P. Semmelweis that infection

was carried in from the autopsy room; yet they had the evidence that under the first Professor of Obstetrics, J.L. Boër, the maternal mortality rate was 13 per 1,000 confinements as against the rate of 53 per 1,000 confinements under the new Professor, J. Klein, but they would not allow a commission to be set up to examine why such a difference existed. Common sense would dictate that obstetric wards, that could not do better than unattended confinements on the street (Gassengeburten) and certainly not as well as midwives in the homes, should be closed down; even Semmelweis would not consider this solution. Yet J.W.R. Tilanus and K.E.M. Levy, writing in Semmelweis (1861), could see the correct solution, and so could W. Farr.

(b) *Wound Sepsis.* J.Y. Simpson showed how fatality rates from amputation in the great hospitals were higher than in the small country hospitals. Similar observations were made in military practice, and indeed attempts were made to act on such observations, but the academic doctors often would have nothing to do with such ideas.

(c) *Efficacy of Therapy or Drugs.* In general, there was academic resistance to the innovators, such as P.C.A. Louis and later J. Škoda, who cast doubts on the efficacy of venesection or drugs. Yet the therapeutic nihilists were correct; the procedures were not efficacious.

(d) *Comparative Studies.* A.M. Bassi worked out the pathogenesis of "mal del segno" or muscardine in 1835–1836. J.L. Schoenlein repeated Bassi's work and found another fungus that caused the human disease, favus. Yet such observations did not suggest to the academics that other microscopic life might be the cause of human disease.

For sidelights on the reforms in (b) and (c) above, see Youngson (1979).

45.15 Public Health

Authors point to many acts in classical times that can now be interpreted as public health, for example, water toilets in the Minoan civilization and clean water supplies and baths in ancient Rome; but it was not until there was a growth of a sense of social responsibility that public health could develop as a state enterprise. Johann Peter Frank (1745–1821) wrote about public health as social medicine and suggested a special class of health inspectors (or "police") to rid the community of disease. His emphasis was on hospitals and medical care, but he also saw illness as a result of poverty. Edwin Chadwick noted that the Industrial Revolution had remarkably changed the environment and the population in a small island; he, as J.P. Frank and Jeremy Bentham (1748–1832), saw poverty as the main cause of ill health; moreover, it was evident to all these writers that the traditional sources of charity were insufficient when the population of a city grew too large. *The Sanitary Condition of the Labouring Population* of Chadwick (1842) was an indictment of the insanitary living conditions of the poor in a country in which living standards for the other classes had risen so remarkably. An additional stimulus to action was the cholera epidemic of 1832; people were accustomed to thinking that deaths from measles and other common infections belonged to the natural order, but cholera did not seem to them to do so. They were willing to consider that it might be controllable. The Public Health Act of 1848 was the result of such considerations; Chadwick came to consider the environmental more important than the personal (or therapeutic) procedures. Lemuel Shattuck (1793–1859) reported in 1850 on the health conditions of Massachusetts and believed that England and Wales were more advanced in the provision of state medicine. He also showed that there was justification for state action. By 1850 there was sufficiently

wide interest to have an International Health Congress in Paris in 1851. Until the discoveries of Pasteur and Koch there was no theoretical basis for public health, but demonstrations of the bacteriological or organismal causes of disease gave justification for the purification of the water supply, quarantine, and many other public health activities. But there were other problems.

John Simon (1816–1904) began his enquiries in 1858 to determine the causes of the differences in mortality between localities, classes, occupations, and so on; according to Brockington (1979), the enquiries of Simon and other distinguished doctors in the years 1858–1871 have been probably more important than any other episode in the world history of public health, for great advances were made in the knowledge of the distribution of diet, infantile mortality, occupational dust diseases, worm infestations, industrial inorganic poisons, housing, and so on.

The extension of the concept of public health to the entire world is natural, because the infectious diseases know no boundaries, and now the wealthier nations assist the poorer nations either directly or through the international bodies, particularly WHO and FAO. Such cooperation led to the eradication of smallpox from the world.

For the theory and practice of public health, see Hobson (1979), Brockington (1975), and Sartwell (1973); history of public health, Brockington (1956), Corfield (1870), Hobson (1963), Howard-Jones (1975, 1980), Hudson (1983), Katz and Felton (1965), and Wain (1970); in America, Snyder (1976); history of quarantine, Ford (1914).

Chapter 46
Hygiene and Ecology

46.1 Geographical Pathology

In this chapter some factors, less closely related to medical practice than those of the previous chapter, are reviewed with respect to their effects on mortality. Geographical pathology may be defined as the study of the geographical incidence of disease. It is a commonplace observation that diseases often have marked geographical distributions, for example, malaria in tropical Africa. The study seeks to explain why such differences exist. Sometimes the existence of the differences has pointed to possible etiology.

Cosmopolitan and Peculiarly Human Infections. With the opening up of communications, many infections, formerly with a quite regional distribution, have spread worldwide and now may be termed, with propriety, cosmopolitan, as opposed to regional. We may list the cosmopolitan diseases roughly following the order of the ICD as: salmonellosis, other infections of the intestine (excluding cholera), human tuberculosis, leprosy, pertussis, diphtheria, infections with the staphylococci, streptococci (including pneumococci), and meningococci among the principal bacterial diseases; influenza, poliomyelitis, smallpox, chickenpox, herpes simplex and zoster, hepatitis A, measles, rubella, and mumps among the viruses; classical typhus, a borderline case among the rickettsioses; syphilis and gonorrhea among the venereal diseases; and a few relatively unimportant infections among the mycoses, helminthiases, and other parasitic diseases. The regional infectious diseases include: cholera, brucellosis, zoonotic bacterial diseases (including bubonic plague), rabies, typhus other than classical louse-borne, malaria, leishmaniasis and trypanosomiasis, the nonvenereal trepanomiases, and most of the mycoses and helminthiases. Many of these regional diseases are zoonoses. In general, only malaria among these regional diseases would be difficult to control in a developed society, because most of the others are zoonoses, often spread by an arthropod vector. The AIDS and hepatitis B viruses have gone from regional to cosmopolitan status within recent times.

Latitude. The high solar ultraviolet light dosage in the low latitudes (near the equator) lead to melanoma and other cancers of the skin; a deficiency in the high latitudes leads to rickets, bone dystrophies, and bone tuberculosis.

Race. Many comparisons of diseases and mortality between races are invalidated by concomitant differences in social status and customs. On the other hand, melanoma and other skin cancers appear more commonly on white skins than on black, and similarly the white skinned appear to be adapted better to the northern European conditions.

Longitude and Social Custom. Japanese in Hawaii and in Japan suffer from more cancer of the stomach than do Japanese living in the United States and cooking in the American style (Steiner, 1954).

Affluence. Burkitt (1973*a*) points out that there are groups of diseases, formerly rarities in any communities, that are common in the western world; these diseases are now appearing in the affluent classes of the developing world. Cleave (1973) notes that many of these diseases are due, directly or indirectly, to deficiency of fiber in the diet. Burkitt (1973*a*) lists them as: 1. Noninfective diseases of the large bowel (*a*) appendicitis, (*b*) diverticulitis, (*c*) benign tumors, (*d*) cancer of the large bowel, and (*e*) ulcerative colitis. 2. Diseases associated with cholesterol metabolism (*a*) cholelithiasis and cholecystitis and (*b*) coronary heart disease (in part). 3. Obesity and diabetes. 4. Hiatus hernia. 5. Other diseases for which no explanation can be given for the geographical variation, for example, thyrotoxicosis, pernicious anemia, rheumatoid arthritis, multiple sclerosis, and celiac disease.

Racial factors can be put aside as the cause of these diseases, as they occur in the negro population in the United States at rates much higher than the rates of native populations in Africa and sometimes higher than in white Americans. Moreover, there were great differences in the death rates from these causes among American negroes and whites even 30 years ago but the rates are tending to be approximately equal now.

Trowell (1977*c*, p. 53) notes that duodenal ulcer and carcinoma of the lung are the only diseases, common in the western world but rare in African blacks in 1930–1960, that have become common in the blacks during the period 1960–1976.

Trowell and Burkitt (1981*b*) give a summary and discussion of 25 papers in a symposium on the incidence of diseases in a variety of countries and cultures. We mention many of these in other relevant sections.

Geographical Isolation. Isolation may be defined as any condition that leads to a diminished contact between persons. It may result from distance; in this sense, Iceland, New Zealand, Australia, and the many island groups throughout the world are isolated. Small groups of persons may be isolated because of the aridity or difficulties of the terrain. For ex-

amples, see the Scottish Isles in §37.3, Sweden in §39.7, Finland in §39.8, and Australia in §41.3. For isolation as a general theme, see §5.2.

Symposia devoted to population and geographical aspects of disease are: Harrison and Boyce (1972) and Warren and Mahmoud (1984); see also Gordon (1966) and Doll (1984).

46.2 Tropical Medicine

In an article commemorating the progress of medicine since 1900, Boyd (1950) wrote that

the dweller in the Tropics in 1950 faces a very different prospect from his predecessor in 1900. The temporary resident who takes strict precautions can hope to escape infection, or, if he should contract a tropical disease, may expect to be cured without suffering from any grave or permanent ill-effects. Unfortunately, the same cannot always be said of the native population, mainly because of their poverty and 'backwardness'. An improvement in the general standard of health can be expected only if there is a parallel improvement in economic conditions and in education—better agriculture, better food, better housing, intelligent hygiene, and the many other things which form part of evolving civilization. It is perhaps fair to say that, in tropical medicine, knowledge of the methods of prevention and cure of disease has outstripped its practical application.

These sentiments remain true when expressed in later reviews, for example, Bryant (1969) and Smith (1982).

The special diseases of the tropics are often vector-borne and sometimes zoonoses. Malaria is the most important of these diseases and in some regions its influence has been dominant; but the problems of disease do not depend merely on the geographic features, such as the abundance of parasites and their vectors, for there are usually unfavorable social, nutritional, educational, and other environmental factors, following from individual, family, communal, and state poverty. Even the distribution of the parasitic and vector-borne diseases is affected by these factors, among which may be cited: (*i*) population densities of vertebrate and invertebrate hosts and their closeness of contact with the human population, (*ii*) growth of the cities and the urbanization of the population under unfavorable conditions, (*iii*) manmade lakes or smaller dams and irrigation ditches, and (*iv*) deforestation.

In many of the cities of the developing world, more than half the population lives in slums or squatter settlements and only somewhat more than a quarter has access to a safe water supply or to facilities for the safe disposal of human excreta, according to Smith (1982). The result is that the well-known diseases of slums, such as tuberculosis, diarrheal diseases, respiratory diseases, and malnutrition, are leading causes of death and disability; and, especially, there is a high infant mortality rate. In the disorderly array of the shanty towns, dangerous mosquitoes thrive: *Aedes aegypti*, the transmitter of yellow fever, dengue, and hemorrhagic dengue, and *Culex pipiens fatigans*, transmitting filariasis.

As an effect of the poverty, famine occurs in sub-Saharan Africa and in India, but elsewhere malnutrition, especially undernutrition, is common. United Nations publications have estimated that perhaps 10% of the world's population have calorie intakes at or less than their minimum needs for existence; they can be identified as poor farmers, landless and casual laborers, and the urban poor. Within the families of these classes, those worst affected are the pregnant and lactating women, infants, and young children. See also Johnston (1982) for an analysis of the grand strategy of hunger prevention.

The poverty of the typical tropical country leads to a deficiency of the medical services and, even more, to a deficiency in the collection, publication, and use of mortality statistics. As a rule, the most that can be hoped for is a sampling of a village or district within the state.

Cholera. Cholera is endemic principally in India although it is now also endemic in Africa. For this entry and the next, see chapter 6.

Dysentery, Enteric Fever, Other Salmonelloses, and Gastroenteritis. These diseases are widely spread in the tropics and may show special features. The enteric fevers may be overlooked for they are often diseases of childhood.

According to Keusch (1982), the shigellas cause not only frank dysentery symptoms but also diarrhea, and indeed diarrheal symptoms may be more common than the passage of blood and mucus in a shigellosis. The disease itself is common because of the lack of satisfactory sanitation, and symptoms are more severe because of the malnutrition. Various field workers have estimated by longitudinal studies in Guatemala, Egypt, and India that each child at ages 1 to 4 years may experience an average of two attacks of dysentery per year.

Tuberculosis. In the developing world tuberculosis appears in acute forms affecting not only the lungs but the meninges, intestine, and glandular systems. See §§7.7 and 47.2 and Scott (1935). WHO-respiratory (1980) estimates that tuberculosis accounted for 66% of the deaths from respiratory diseases in Asia, 54% in Oceania, and 11% in Africa. Drug resistance is now a special problem.

Bubonic Plague. Plague is often thought of as a tropical disease, but see §8.2.

Brucellosis. *Br. abortus* infects cattle and so is much less important than *Br. melitensis*, which infects goats in the drier tropics. See §8.6.

Leprosy. Leprosy is said to affect 12–15 million persons throughout the world, most commonly in the tropics and subtropics. See also §9.1 for some estimates of incidence.

Diphtheria. This infection occurs in the tropics as faucial diphtheria and as a cutaneous infection with the *mitis* type, sometimes known as "desert sore."

Poliomyelitis. Infection occurs in early childhood and paralyses are rarely seen. See §10.1.

Smallpox. Once a great pestilence and cause of depopulation in the tropics, smallpox is now eradicated.

Measles. Conditions of travel and intertribal war were formerly unfavorable to the perpetuation of measles in many regions. Measles is now often reported with very high case fatality rates. See §§11.6 and 11.7.

Yellow Fever. The origin of yellow fever and of the *Aedes* mosquitoes was Africa; but the sylvatic form is now widely distributed in tropical America. Control has been successful in almost completely abolishing urban yellow fever. See §§12.1 and 12.2.

Hepatitis B. See §§13.1 and 20.6.

Rickettsioses. Classical typhus is endemic in tropical Africa and America. See Figure 14.1.1. Mite typhus occurs in a roughly triangular region with the apexes of the triangle in Japan, Pakistan, and north Queensland. Tick typus is widely distributed in the tropical regions of all the continents except Australia.

Malaria. Malaria, especially that due to *P. falciparum*, is widely distributed in the tropical areas of the world, excluding Australia. Of all the pestilences, malaria remains still the greatest challenge. It is impossible to give an accurate account of its effects on health and well being, because it occurs in the poor countries where there are no fully developed medical and supporting services, such as satisfactory vital statistics.

Leishmaniasis. Kala-azar or visceral leishmaniasis is spread through many parts of tropical America, Africa, and India-Bangladesh. Cutaneous leishmaniasis of the Old World is endemic on both shores of the Red Sea and in a strip across Africa. Cutaneous leishmaniasis of the New World is widely spread in Latin America.

Trypanosomiasis. African trypanosomiasis (sleeping sickness) is widely spread in wet tropical Africa and American trypanosomiasis (Chagas' disease) in South and Central America.

Cancer. Melanoma and cancers of the skin are special hazards for the fair skinned living in the tropics.

Tropical Splenomegaly. It is believed that besides the enlargement of the spleen in malaria, schistosomiasis, and some other diseases, there is a syndrome or disease, tropical splenomegaly, for a discussion of which, see Nayak (1982).

Sprue. See §27.7.

Immune Complex Nephropathy in the Tropics. The rate of this syndrome is said to be 100 times higher in some parts of Africa than in the United States (Ngu and Soothill, 1982). Its etiology is believed to be the high rate of "common parasite-induced immune complex diseases."

The reader is referred to Stürchler (1981), Manson-Bahr and Apted (1982), Beaver, Jung, and Cupp (1984), and to the references in the sections on the special diseases for maps of the distributions of diseases in the tropics; to Kean, Mott, and Russell (1978) for reprints of or abstracts from investigations on tropical diseases; and to Scott (1939) for historical accounts especially informative on the great pestilences. Recent general reviews of diseases in the tropics are C.E.G. Smith (1982), Bruce-Chwatt (1982), Chandra (1982), Gilles (1984), Gilles, Harinasuta, and Bunnag (1984), Woodruff (1974), and Warren and Mahmoud (1984). Warren and Bowers (1983) review parasitology, largely a tropical problem. Greenwood and Whittle (1981) deal with the special problems of immunization in the tropics. For the ecology of tropical diseases, see Gordon (1966), and for pediatrics in the developing world, Morley (1978).

46.3 Climate

Climatic differences are possibly responsible for the diversification of man into races; the cool, cloudy climate of northern Europe seems to have favored the European type, whereas the hot, humid tropics favored the darker skin colorings. The darker skinned are more vulnerable to frost bite, whereas the Europeans suffer from melanoma and skin cancers when they live in the tropics or subtropical regions with their high ultraviolet light dosage. Adaptations in clothes and housing and development of suitable cereals have enabled man to live in any climate, even before the development of the modern technologies. Many diseases are now endemic throughout the world, and infectious disease incidence varies principally in the tropical diseases mentioned in §46.2; the famines of the two types described in §§22.5 and 22.6, affecting especially the marginal lands, are the other great causes of death due to climate, or rather to changes in climate. For general reviews of climate, see Lamb (1972/1977), H.H. L(amb) and K.W. B(utzger) in the sixteenth edition of the *Encyclopaedia britannica*, Budyko (1974, 1982), and some references in §22.3.

For man's impact on climate and environment, see Bach, Pancrath, and Kellogg (1979) and Stanley and Joske (1980).

46.4 Air

Chemical Pollution. Views on the role of air in the production of disease have varied over the centuries. Strange views were held in nineteenth century Britain, for example, where confinements at home took place in darkened rooms. Later, attention was directed toward odors, which led to legislative and administrative action against drains and other nuisances, even in the absence of bacteriologic theory. The smokey atmosphere of the great industrial cities has been blamed for illness, particularly in childhood, and this perhaps may be justified on the grounds of lower ultraviolet light dosage. Warner (1979) mentions that the air over Britain is now sufficiently pure to enable ozone to form in the atmosphere. Smoke and sulfur dioxide have been used as indicators of air pollution, especially when the source has been fossil fuels. In London both indicators have shown a decline, the sulfur dioxide from 220 to 100 and smoke from 105 to 35 micrograms per cubic meter in the period 1962–1974, according to Warner (1979, Figure 4). These indexes were as high as 3,500 and 6,000, respectively, in an incident in December 1952 that led to an estimated 4,000 extra deaths in Greater London, due to respiratory diseases (Logan, 1953).

In recent times, large-scale chemical manufacturing processes have introduced new substances as pollutants. Warner (1979) remarks that industries produce an excess of chlorine in their manufacture of caustic soda and have combined chlorine with various chemicals to make solvents, pesticides, herbicides, and plastics. Many of these compounds, particularly those containing benzene rings, have caused occupational diseases because of high concentrations during manufacture; but some such compounds have passed directly into the air,

and others have done so after, for instance, agricultural use as fertilizers or pesticides. There are now restrictions on the manufacture of these compounds. An example of an industrial accident at Seveso was cited by Warner (1979), for which see §34.7.

Bacteriologic Pollution. See especially the introductory section in Topley and Wilson (1975, p. 2626). These authors believe that little disease is carried over a distance of miles in the outside air. Air-borne bacilli are spread in three ways: attached to dust particles, contained in gross droplets expelled from the nose and mouth, and in droplet nuclei resulting from the evaporation of the smaller droplets expelled from the nose and mouth. Staphylococci, streptococci, the agents of intestinal diseases, of tuberculosis, and of diphtheria are all spread by indoor dust. Respiratory infections are spread by droplets but these tend to fall out of the air rather rapidly. More dangerous as carriers are the droplet nuclei, which may remain air-borne for hours. A proper understanding of the physical properties of dust, droplets, and droplet nuclei has led to satisfactory conditions of ward management in hospitals and ventilation, filtration of air, ultraviolet light sterilization, and cleaning in public buildings, transport, and so on. Besides these formal measures, there has been an improvement in behavior, especially spitting, commented on by Yule (1934) in his remarks in his later years on the amelioration of life.

Quarantine and Deliberate Isolation. Isolation may also be imposed in the form of deliberate isolation in hospitals of certain infections or of quarantine. Indeed, smallpox was eradicated by the joint application of isolation of cases and vaccination of contacts. The effect of the formal isolation of affected persons within a country is not always clear. Isolation from other members of the family would be valuable in leprosy and in tuberculosis, to which children are particularly susceptible, so they must not be submitted to the risk of a massive dose of bacilli. In other diseases, the effect of isolation on epidemic spread may be less than popularly supposed, especially in those epidemic diseases in which the ratio of cases to carriers is low. Thus, although the isolation of poliomyelitis patients possibly does not greatly influence the course of the epidemic, prophylactic isolation can be defended on the grounds that it reduces the possibility of large infective doses being given to other members of the family. The isolation of pneumonia patients can be justified, particularly if there are other members of the same family or group at school who might be expected to be exposed to a high risk of infection and a high initial dose. In such epidemic diseases as meningitis and scarlet fever, the carrier rate is possibly so high that it would be impracticable to isolate all patients and carriers. Although isolation had been beneficial in its applications to most infections, that is not so for poliomyelitis, mumps, and rubella, for which see §10.1, §13.3, and §11.8, respectively. The delay of infection with rubella until adult life has led to the well-known epidemics of congenital defects.

For pollution, see WHO-pollution (1961); microbial pollution, Sykes and Skinner (1971); normal microbial flora of man, Skinner and Carr (1974).

46.5 Water

In §6.12, we have discussed the improvement of water supplies, which has been of critical importance for the control of cholera and enteric fevers but of less importance for the control of the dysenteries, see §6.5. In England and Wales, and possibly in other European countries, a pure supply of water became available earlier in the cities than in the country, and this was reflected in the incidence and mortality rates during the declines in the enteric fever mortality. After the bacteriologic revolution, unpolluted water supplies have been the aim of those planning the construction of railways and great canals, mining, or the maintenance of armies in the field or in barracks.

Personal and household cleanliness are usually attained only when there is an ample supply of water, although there has been some success in desert environments by strict adherence to a code of cleanliness, often supported by religious taboos. Adequate supplies of un-

polluted water are important in fields other than the intestinal infectious diseases.

46.6 Milk

Bovine tuberculosis and brucellosis are the most important zoonoses spread by milk.

Other disease organisms spread by milk are usually of human origin—streptococci (§9.5), staphylococci (§6.8), diphtheria bacilli (§9.3), salmonellae (§§6.4–6.6), and miscellaneous bacilli causing gastroenteritis (§6.11). Pasteurization of milk has become almost universal in the developed countries, successfully preventing the spread of infections by milk and improving its keeping quality. See Topley and Wilson (1975, Table 93.2) for a remarkable change in the incidence of infectious diseases spread by milk during the three epochs between 1912 and 1937; in the most recent epoch only gastroenteritis has been traced to milk and milk products.

46.7 Protection of Food

Laws for the protection of food have been necessary whenever food has not been consumed at its point of preparation. At first, laws were economic in origin, aiming to forbid adulteration; but after 1860 their broader aims were economic, esthetic, and public health, the latter of which is the most important for mortality. In §§46.5, 46.6, and 46.8–46.10, we have pointed to the problems of protecting water and milk and of keeping infectious organisms away from food, but it is clear that there are many problems. Nevertheless, in the large modern cities of the developed world few deaths occur from the infections and intoxications treated in chapter 6. We refer the reader to Krusé (1973) for a detailed discussion.

46.8 Garbage

The cities of the developed world are now freer of nuisances than ever before. Proper garbage disposal has resulted in fewer flies breeding, important for the control of intestinal infections, and fewer rats in the cities. The decline of the fly population has been especially important in the control of gastroenteritis. As an example of the interaction of different factors not usually associated, we mention that the carting away of garbage is greatly assisted by the abundant supply of newsprint, a by-product of heavy advertising campaigns.

For garbage in the cities, see Melosi (1982).

46.9 Sewage

In many city areas, the water closet and the sewer have replaced all other methods of disposal of the excreta. This is not a critical improvement from the point of view of mortality, as the pan system is compatible with a high standard of hygiene, especially if fly control is adequate. The diseases affected by the mode of disposal are the gastrointestinal. Formerly in the great cities of the world, emptying of sewage into rivers polluted the drinking water; in other cases sewage has filtered down through the soil to wells giving rise to enteric fever epidemics. Of course, now in the developing world there are many such examples. See §6.15.

For sewage in hot climates, see Mara (1976).

46.10 Insects

Insects have been of critical importance for the eradication or control of some diseases, especially several of the great pestilences and many of the "tropical" diseases. See §5.5 for the general theory of transmissibility. The role of insect control in the declines of mortality is now mentioned by cause of death in the order of the ICD listing. We use "insect" below in the sense of "arthropod."

Intestinal infectious diseases are sometimes spread by domestic flies and cockroaches. Public health measures have been directed against them.

The transmission of plague is by rat fleas from rat to man and by human ectoparasites from man to man. Insecticides can reduce risks in either case. Similarly, repellents can be used against the tick vector of tularemia.

Possibly the greatest triumph of the control of insects occurred in the eradication of urban yellow fever by the destruction of the *Aedes* mosquitoes and their breeding places.

The residual subclass, ICD 062–066, of the arthropod-borne viral diseases contains zoonoses spread to man by a variety of arthropods. Here also control of the transmitting arthropod is critical.

The rickettsioses, including classical and other forms of typhus and several other diseases less important to man, are all transmitted by insects, and hence transmission can be broken by insecticides or action against the vectors.

The anopheline mosquitoes transmitting malaria have many diverse properties, and many diverse lines of attack have to be used against them. The control of the mosquitoes concerned and the use of antimalarial drugs have eradicated malaria from the United States, Canada, Europe, and Australia. It has been claimed that malaria was eradicated from Spain by drug therapy alone.

Leishmaniasis is transmitted by sandflies of the genus *Phlebotomus* in the Old World and of the genus *Lutzomyia* in the New World. Control is by elimination of nearby breeding grounds by drainage and filling. Stone walls may be faced with mortar. Persons may be protected by insect repellents.

The African forms of human trypanosomiasis have been controlled by campaigns against the vectors, tse-tse flies *Glossina palpalis* and other *Glossina* species, and by breaking down the relationship of man and the tse-tse fly by moving the residences of the people, by clearing land, by the use of insecticides and repellents. Direct therapy has had little effect in reducing the hazards. American trypanosomiasis is transmitted by some dozen species of the subfamily, *Triatomidae*, of reduviid bugs. The chief methods of control are against the bugs and their shelter.

Louse-borne relapsing fever is transmitted by the common body louse, *Pediculus humanus*, and measures have been directed against it, as in typhus, successfully.

Oroya fever and verruga peruana are two stages of a disease caused by *Bartonella bacilli-*

formis. Prophylaxis is directed against the vector *Phlebotomus*.

Filariasis is transmitted by mosquitoes, usually by *Culex pipiens quinquefasciatus*. Control is by antimosquito measures, such as destruction of breeding places and the use of insecticides and larvicides.

For texts on the medical importance of insects, see Busvine (1976, 1980*a,b*), Cloudsley-Thompson (1976), Harwood and James (1979), and Wigglesworth (1976). See also Beaver, Jung, and Cupp (1984), Garnham (1971), Greenberg (1971), Hammon (1965), Manson-Bahr and Apted (1982), and Stanley (1980).

46.11 Animals

In this section we are considering animals either as killing man directly or as being an alternative host to disease and so exclude the protozoa and the helminths.

Direct Attack. Animals making direct attack on man can range from arthropods and fish that sting up to sharks, reptiles, and the great carnivores. These latter were of great importance to primitive man but are now of little numerical importance.

Reservoirs of the Anthropozoonoses. Animals are of importance in bubonic plague, yellow fever, trypanosomiases, leishmaniases, hydatid disease, and other anthropozoonoses. In many of these cases the disease is transmitted to man by a vector, and often attack on the vector has been sufficient to control the disease in man. Sometimes local eradication of the animal disease has been possible by control or slaughter of the animal hosts.

Directly Transmissible Infectious Disease. Glanders, psittacosis, and anthrax are well known examples of infections spread by contact without a vector. Rabies and rat-bite fever are spread by bites.

Diseases of Animals. Epizootics can be harmful to man by removing a source of food or traction energy, for example, trypanosomiasis killing cattle in Africa.

For rats and mice as enemies of mankind, see Hinton (1918).

46.12 Eradication of Infective Diseases

The assertion of the possibility of eradicating diseases could only exist in one who was convinced of the uniqueness of the disease eradicated and who believed that the disease was spread by contagion. J.Y. Simpson (1871–1872) appears to have been the first to consider the possibility seriously, with smallpox as his model. As smallpox became eradicated in some countries, the question began to be asked why not in the entire world. As explained in §11.2, the project was undertaken by WHO and has been successful. The question was then raised, notably by Hinman (1966), Cockburn (1961*b*, 1963), and Dubos (1965), that eradication was possible in other diseases and would be preferable to control. Yekutiel (1980) gives a view of actions taken and the results. He says that the word "eradication" was first introduced in connection with the local elimination of animal and plant diseases in the United States, notably cattle fever (piroplasmosis) and pleuropneumonia in cattle. By 1950 there were effective drugs and vaccines against several diseases and also synthetic insecticides. It was hoped that with planned application of drugs, vaccines, and insecticides, it would now be possible to eradicate some diseases. There is a scale of possibilities from eradication to practical control: (*i*) complete worldwide eradication, for example, smallpox; (*ii*) complete regional eradication, such as bubonic plague in Australia, yellow fever in Gibraltar, endemic malaria in Europe; (*iii*) transmission control in the sense of continued absence of transmission within a specified area, for example, tularemia and bubonic plague in the United States; and (*iv*) practical control in the sense that the disease ceases to be an important public health problem, such as yellow fever in South America.

Eradication is final and complete and no further action is required. Where merely practical control has been attained, continued control measures may be required indefinitely. In the animal world, regional eradication has been brought about in various ways: quarantine and slaughter of animals in rabies and glanders, destruction of an arthropod vector by arsenic cattle-dip in Texas tick fever, and immunization in brucellosis.

The ease of eradication of smallpox can be contrasted with the perpetuation of measles in almost all the countries of the world. Smallpox is less contagious than measles, and there has long been an efficient vaccine against smallpox. Smallpox had a greater case fatality rate and was readily accepted as an important and ever-present problem. The case fatality rates from measles were lower, and the risk of death was less apparent and had long been accepted as a natural hazard of life. It was therefore easy to obtain worldwide support for an eradication program for smallpox.

For measles the case for eradication was not as clear. Under favorable conditions of infection in the developed world, case fatality rates were not high. Moreover, because of its high infectivity, it is seen in the developed world as a disease of childhood and one of the lesser causes of death in recent times, although it is responsible for encephalitis and other acute complications; but opinions have changed and there are comparatively few other infective causes of death at ages 1 to 14. In addition, it is now known that a late complication is subacute sclerosing panencephalitis associated with progressive dementia, and it is possible that some forms of multiple sclerosis are also late complications of measles. There are now campaigns to reduce all these complications by vaccination with attenuated virus, and it can be expected that measles as a cause of mortality can be controlled and in some regions even eradicated, although this will not be possible worldwide for some time.

The infection of yellow fever is spread by *Aedes aegypti* mosquitoes, which cannot survive over winter; in Gibraltar it was found that the epidemic died out in the winter. The habits of *A. aegypti* are well known, for it breeds in water in domestic containers, roof drains, among others, and can readily be destroyed.

The urban variety of the disease has therefore been eradicated from many areas that are not in close contact with jungle; but the jungle or sylvatic forms of yellow fever are, in practice, difficult to eradicate because of the areas involved, especially in Africa.

Yekutiel (1980, Table 1, p. 36) mentions that a global campaign against malaria was in action in 1955–1973 but was later found to be unsuccessful globally although malaria was eradicated from Europe, Australia, and the United States. He gives reasons for its failure.

Of the other great pestilences, it would appear impossible to eradicate bubonic plague because it is a well-established zoonosis in many niduses, but control is possible by measures against the rats and the fleas. Human typhus can be controlled, but there are doubts as to whether the alternative animal hosts are important, and there is the possibility of recrudescences of human cases (Brill's disease) after many years.

It would appear impossible to eradicate influenza from the world, because it is a cosmopolitan disease, does not have a constant antigenic composition, and can appear in virulent forms after long latent periods.

Ohashi (1975) writes of the eradication of enteric fever in Japan. See also Benenson (1985), Evans (1982*a*), Gordon (1965), Spink (1979), and Stuart-Harris (1984*b*) for the control of communicable disease.

46.13 Nutrition

In §46.7, the protection of food principally from bacteriologic agents has been considered. There are many other relationships between the components of food and health. In particular, see: for total amount, chapter 22; general deficiency, §11.7; carbohydrates, §§22.2 and 22.13; fatty acids, §25.3; proteins and amino acids, §§11.7, 32.7; vitamins, §22.12; bran and fiber, §22.13; bacterial toxins, §6.8; and miscellaneous toxins, §22.14.

Chapter 47
Subpopulations and Classes

47.1 Subpopulations

The subpopulations of a national state may not be uniform; sometimes there may be differences between them that are important for the rates of mortality. Perhaps, we could take Sweden and China as examples of populations homogeneous by race; toward the other end of the scale, in the United States there is a large negro minority. In India there are divisions by race and religion, in Ireland there are divisions by religion, in Canada by language and religion, and so on. There are also differences by social class in many countries and by occupation in all countries. In this chapter, we hope to show that important differences within a state may exist between the mortality rates in the subpopulations defined by stated criteria.

Mortality rates are usually given for the entire national population; here, the national rates are averages of the rates in the subpopulations, weighted by the numbers in the subpopulations. It is clear from this that the national rates cannot usually be favorable if there is a sizeable minority subpopulation with unfavorable rates, for example, infant mortality rates for the entire country cannot be favorable if an important proportion of children are born in slums or are neglected. Some technical points arise in theoretical work, for which we refer the reader to §4.2.

There may be interest in comparing the mortality of subpopulations; Farr (1866, 1885) was fond of comparing the healthy districts with the industrial, for example. See also Neison

(1844). In Farr (1885, p. 200) we find that 89.7%, 85.1%, and 76.6% of infants born in healthy districts of England and Wales, England and Wales generally, and Liverpool, respectively, were alive at the end of their first year of life; he deduces, making the hypothesis that the viability of infants under equal conditions would not vary between districts, that social conditions in Liverpool are responsible for a high proportion of infant deaths. He goes on to show that out of every 100 children born, the number dying before the fifth birthday are in Norway 17, Denmark 20, Sweden 20, England 26, Belgium 27, France 29, Prussia 32, Holland 33, Austria 36, Spain 36, Russia 38 and Italy 39; but there is an equal variability within England in which only 18 die in the healthy districts, yet in the 30 large towns, 36 die. Further, according to peerage records, 10 die before their fifth birthday, and among the children of the clergy, nearly the same proportion. Similarly, Farr (1885, p. 404) compares the death rates of metal miners in Cornwall with those of other males, exclusive of miners, for the years 1849–1853; the death rates per 1,000 per annum for the miners (other males) were at ages 15 to 24, 8.90 (7.12); 25 to 34, 8.96 (8.84); 35 to 44, 14.30 (9.99); 45 to 54, 33.51 (14.76); 55 to 64, 63.17 (24.12); and 65 to 74, 111.23 (58.61). He comments that the miners have rates of mortality not materially different from the other males up to the age of 35 years, but after that age there is a large and progressive excess among the miners. He then compares the Cornish metal miners with northern coal miners, whose rates are of the same order as the other Cornish males and thus much lower than the Cornish miners; in a later paragraph, he finds the differences in mortality almost completely due to excesses in the mortality from respiratory diseases. Thus, Farr has been able to demonstrate the great importance of the excess of diseases, including what is now termed pneumoconiosis, to the Royal Commission on the Condition of Mines in 1864.

47.2 Extension of Civilization

The opening up of communications throughout the world has led to many new problems, particularly the incidence of infectious diseases. Some infectious diseases, especially the zoonoses, require some special local conditions to be perpetuated in the wild, sylvatic, or forest form and to be spread to human populations in new areas. But there are cosmopolitan diseases, especially those that are passed directly between persons, without the mediation of an insect vector. Important examples are the bacterial diseases: tuberculosis, leprosy, the bowel infections, diphtheria, whooping cough, and the streptococcal diseases; the spirochetal diseases: syphilis and yaws; and the viral diseases: measles and smallpox. Of these diseases only smallpox has been eradicated. It is usually considered that civilization has brought these diseases to new peoples; but it could equally well be asserted that the civilized world has been afflicted by all the cosmopolitan-type diseases of those countries that it has embraced.

Easier communications have enabled cholera to spread from its natural habitat in the hot, moist, riverine areas of India to the neighboring countries and hence to many parts of the world. Similarly, new strains of the influenza virus appear to develop after certain genetic recombinations in the viruses of southeastern Asia, and now pass almost inevitably to the entire world; such a pandemic spread may well not have occurred before large populations in contact with one another had developed.

Among other viral infections, smallpox required a large population to perpetuate it. It had already been described in Asia and Europe in pre-Christian times; after the great explorations of the sixteenth century it was spread to the Americas, and in the late eighteenth century to Australia. It has been a great cause of depopulation in native tribes. Measles too has been introduced into territories, either bordering on the great population masses or on "virgin soil," such as Iceland, Greenland, northern Sweden, the Americas, Australia, and the islands of the Pacific Ocean, for example, a severe epidemic occurred in Fiji in 1875, for which see §5.4. Malaria had long been endemic in a zone reaching from west Africa to southeast Asia, but there is good reason to believe that the Americas were free of malaria when the first explorers from Europe reached the West Indies and South America. Whether malaria was carried to America by the Europeans or by the transported slaves, or more probably both, is not known; but appropriate anopheline mosquitoes were available for its spread there. In the 1930s air travel enabled *Anopheles gambiae*, a dangerous vector of malaria, to reach Brazil, so that not only disease but its vectors can be transferred to new countries; fortunately, in this case, the subsequent campaign of eradication by international health bodies was completely successful. A more unfortunate invasion by a vector was the introduction of the mosquito *Aedes aegypti* from Africa together with yellow fever, which it transmits. Indeed, because Asia, Europe, and Africa have been joined geographically since prehistoric times, the greatest problems of the mixing of the caucasoids and the tribal people (see §1.1) occurred as a result of the exploration, colonization, and subsequent domination of the Amerindians by the Europeans, beginning in 1492; Crosby (1972) has detailed the resulting Columbian exchange, see also Cook (1947).

Plague may be cited as an example of a vector-borne infection once localized in either an Asian or African region but with the opening up of communications spreading to other regions. The black and brown rats seem to have evolved from a habitat in Java or elsewhere in the East Indies, from whence they spread through Asia, reaching western Europe perhaps in the seventh or eight century AD, most probably transported along the trade routes; this migration of the rats and their fleas made pandemic plague a possibility, with the plague bacilli subsequently established in new niduses in the Americas and the East Indies. See §§8.2 and 8.3.

Since the bacteriologic revolution, beginning in the 1870s, the populations of the civilized world have been able to prevent damage from newly discovered regional diseases with a few exceptions. Dengue fever (ICD 061) has become potentially worldwide in its distribution, whereas the hemorrhagic mosquito-borne dengue (ICD 065.4) could cause problems outside its present range. See §12.3. Marburg, Ebola, and Lassa fevers appear sporadically in the developed world but do not present a great problem. See §12.4. Hepatitis B is potentially a great problem because of its carcinogenic action. See §§13.1 and 20.6. AIDS, introduced into the developed world from an African tribe, may be the greatest challenge of all.

Now we turn to a related problem, the assimilation of the tribal persons or groups into the wider world community. They may be entering the world community, with its variety of diseases, either by their own desires or, more likely, because of pressure from members of the world community, referred to below as the caucasoids.

For the times after the coming of the caucasoids, we may detail the relative importance of some of the factors *numbered as in the list of §1.1*, essentially in the order of the ICD.

(*i*) Intestinal infectious agents, such as typhoid, may be introduced and, at the same time, the hygienic conditions of the tribal people may deteriorate, and thus epidemics of bowel infections may follow.

(*ii*) Epidemics of acute and subacute glandular and gastrointestinal tuberculosis may appear.

(*vi*) Virgin soil epidemics. For reasons given in §5.4, it may happen that a large proportion of the population is susceptible to such diseases as measles and smallpox. After the introduction of a case of measles, for instance, almost every member of the community becomes infected within a few infection cycles. Case fatality rates may be high; this has formerly been almost universally attributed to a lack of genetic immun-

ity. Recently, a contrary view has been expressed more frequently, as by Neel (1977), who believes that the necessary genetic equipment varies little between tribal and caucasoid peoples. In these epidemics, many tribesmen are ill at the same time, with a consequent breakdown of essential family and community services, such as the provision of food and water; in particular, the infant will lack the mother's care and milk at the time of emergency; the passage of secondary invaders is facilitated in such an epidemic. Thus, 10% to 20% of the population was lost in the measles epidemic in Fiji, mentioned in §5.4. Note also the high case fatalities of the caucasoids in similar conditions, namely, in the United States Civil War, mentioned in §33.9. Of course, even graver damage followed the introduction of smallpox into the West Indies in 1507, see Dixon (1962, p.192), and Hopkins (1983a), the Americas, generally, and into Australia.

(*vii*) Arthropod-borne viral diseases may be introduced or ecological changes may occur that increase the danger from them, for example, yellow fever (ICD 060).

(*ix*) Malaria incidence may be affected, as in (*vii*).

(*x*) Influenza (ICD 487) may occur.

(*xi*) Syphilis and gonorrhea may be introduced.

(*xiv*) Respiratory diseases. The caucasoids may introduce respiratory diseases; thus, these seem to have been a leading cause of the halving of the population of the Kren-Akorore, an indigenous tribe in Brazil, moved from their homeland to make way for the construction of a modern highway (Baruzzi, Marcopito, et al., 1977), even though much care was delivered to their needs. Here again the genetic factors are usually overestimated. Neel (1977), on the other hand, points out that it is rare for a caucasoid to come in contact with several new, possibly dangerous, viruses at one time, whereas a number of such viruses may be introduced and circulate in the tribal people simultaneously.

The events detailed above have often been discussed by anthropologists under the heading "clash of culture," in which the social effects of the coming of the caucasoids have been stressed. It is now widely recognized that physical or epidemiologic happenings must be given a role much more important than was formerly assigned by the anthropologists.

47.3 Island and Rural Communities

In §5.4 we have given examples of island experience with the disastrous measles epidemics. Early man and tribal or isolated societies have had similar experiences, as pointed out in §§1.1 and 1.2. In §§11.6 and 11.7, the behavior of measles in the isolated areas is noted. In §11.4 it is shown that varicella can persist in small island communities, in contrast with the other viral exanthemata. Isolated and rural communities occur in Scotland (§37.3) and in the nordic countries of chapter 39, perhaps less so in Denmark than in the other six regions or countries because of its denser population; the epidemics of Sweden, which caught the attention of English epidemiologists in the nineteenth century, occurred because of the isolated nature of many of the Swedish communities. Australia and New Zealand had many experiences resembling those of the smaller islands. See chapter 41. The effect of isolation is apparent, especially in the low mortality rates of infancy and childhood. Similar experiences no doubt could be discovered for the northern communities of the Soviet in Europe and Asia, in mountainous areas of Asia, in the deserts of Africa, among others.

In the nineteenth century, the rural mortality rates were almost uniformly lower than the urban, but when adequate water supplies became available, the hygiene in some cities became superior to that in the country. For the American cities, see §6.5. Possibly no general statement can be made on the urban-rural comparisons of mortality, because the cities now often have advantages that may counterbalance any tendency toward greater mortality from the cosmopolitan diseases, for example, in a highly malarious country it may be possible to control malaria transmissions in the cities and not in the countryside.

47.4 Urbanization

Some special problems of mortality in the cities are now discussed. Food delivery has already been mentioned in §22.1. London or European cities are regarded here as typical examples; New York and Boston are given in §42.6 as examples of the infectious diseases affecting an entrepôt. Latin American cities can be considered as examples of cities attracting excessive immigration from the countryside of the developing nations.

Intestinal Infectious Diseases. Here, the two principal problems are the provision of an adequate water supply and a hygienic disposal of sewage; they cannot be solved without a sophisticated technology as the population increases. For a new city founded in modern times, for example, in the nineteenth century, we can imagine a picture of an isolated block of cottages, each with its own privy, arranged along the two sides of an open drain in an open field with a gentle slope, within convenient distances from a small stream and from the factory, for example, at Preston in Lancashire. This reasonable state would soon be upset when the blocks of houses were replicated, the stream polluted, and, alas, the proportion of privies per person reduced. Cities, such as London, were often built on the bank of a river for commercial, trading, military, or other reasons; with a later increase and density of population, it appeared natural and even necessary to dump the sewage into the river, but then the water supplies became polluted. The water in shallow wells also became polluted. Before 1800 no European city had solved these two principal problems. See §§6.12 and 6.15. It is worthy of note that, as late as the middle of the nineteenth century, the qualities of the water supplies in London were so variable that comparisons between them showed that cholera and the enteric fevers were water-borne; and yet London was rather advanced in its water supply. In the great European cities, crowding and pollution ensured that there would be a high rate of the water- and food-borne diseases, such as the enteric fevers, dysenteries, other salmonelloses, and other bowel infections, these latter being especially dangerous to the aged and to infants.

Tuberculosis. In §§7.6 and 7.7 we discuss personal and hygienic factors important for the spread of tuberculosis; of these, age at infection, size of dose, population density, and housing will all be unfavorably affected in the city.

Bubonic Plague. Although the villages in England appear to have suffered more depopulation than the towns during the Black Death of 1348–1349, after the first great mortalities, independent village pestilences became rare whereas the towns were intermittently or regularly attacked, presumably because the plague was more readily perpetuated by the large rat populations in the towns, because the greater commercial traffic through the towns favored reintroduction of the infection, and perhaps because the bacillus was more readily transmitted by the human fleas in the denser populations of the towns and cities, see §8.2. According to Collis and Greenwood (1921), outbreaks of plague in the villages were rare in the second half of the fourteenth century, and after the beginning of the sixteenth century plague was essentially a town disease, villages only being affected by direct extension. In the towns, or rather cities, plague maintained itself for another 150 years, the last great outbreak in London occurring in 1665–1666.

Other Bacterial Diseases. Diphtheria, pertussis, scarlatina, and streptococcal sore throat, and meningococcal meningitis all spread more readily in the cities; see. for example, Tables 37.3.3 and 37.3.4 for the extraordinary proportion of deaths due to pertussis and scarlatina in Glasgow.

Measles and Smallpox. See the tables just cited also for deaths from measles and smallpox. In Glasgow there were deaths each year with these diseases as cause, and the continuous endemicity ensured that they would be acquired in early childhood as a rule, a factor in producing high mortality rates because of the high case fatality rate at the young ages.

Typhus. Typhus was associated with the great towns and cities in the late eighteenth and early nineteenth centuries. It is a disease of want and overcrowding. Collis and Greenwood (1921)

ascribed a higher fatality of typhus, in the time of the epidemic at Tiverton in 1741, to the many country girls, unexposed previously to such diseases, who flocked into the towns. See §14.2 and the tables in §37.3.

Infant Mortality. Infant mortality was high during the rapid growth of new and old cities alike. There would be feeding difficulties with the mother going out to work and high infection rates with the diseases mentioned above, especially gastroenteritis, measles, pertussis, scarlatina, and, before the coming of vaccination, smallpox.

Authors sometimes suggest that the mortality rates of the old European cities have been exaggerated; however, in Forbes (1971, pp. 60–62), there is clear evidence that deaths greatly outnumbered births in Aldgate, London, during the years 1560 to 1630, even if the deaths in the epidemics of bubonic plague were excluded; similar findings are available for Colchester, in Dyer (1978) and in Doolittle (1975). Graunt (1662) believed that mortality was such in London that its size was only maintained by migration from the country. This fact has a curious consequence, noticed by Russell (1948b), in that London acted as a kind of sink for the surplus population of the English countryside. Many of the misfits or exceptional persons migrated to London from the counties in the sixteenth and seventeenth centuries, and, as a result, the counties were able to maintain their own peculiarities. We can see also that Malthusian notions are satisfied not only by dramatic epidemics, such as bubonic plague, but also by the high death rates from the acute infective diseases, especially measles, smallpox, typhus, infectious respiratory diseases, and pertussis, in the cities, because the epidemics in the cities can be maintained by the constant flow of susceptibles from the countryside. See also Galton (1873).

Many other authors since Graunt have pointed out the importance of the urban-rural gradients in mortality. Of the earlier authors, Suessmilch (1761–1762) comments that "the secret damage done to the state through towns must almost be considered equivalent to a pestilence." Heckscher (1950) cites Sundbärg's paper on tuberculosis that shows that the crude death rates from it were 2 or 2.5 per 1,000 per annum before 1810, at which time the rates began to rise and did not fall again until the twentieth century. Stockholm had rates of 7 to 8.75 per 1,000 per annum before 1810 but in 1941–1945 they were only 0.75 per 1,000. Heckscher (1950) believes that comparisons between countries in the eighteenth or nineteenth centuries were really only between their degrees of urbanization.

William Farr said that the evils of density were domestic overcrowding and atmospheric pollution—infants and middle life being especially gravely affected. Within the city there may be great variation in the population density per unit of ground area, and thus urbanization of itself may introduce social gradients in the mortality rates. Farr (1885, p. 160) compared the mortality in 30 large towns (1851–1860) with that in 63 healthy districts (1849–1853) and found that at ages 0–4, the death rates were in the ratio of 339/135 or 2.5; at ages 5–9, the ratio was 1.6; and at older ages, the mortality was still unfavorable to the towns.

Cassen (1978) writing of India mentions that the biggest city reaches its mortality peak before the rest of the country and cites London in the mid-eighteenth century and Stockholm at the turn of this century. Most western European cities went through a peak in the middle of the nineteenth century. A similar remark applies to Finland, for which see §39.8. The older cities have almost always been situated at or near a center of commerce, with exotic diseases or new pandemics reaching them before the rest of the country. The experience of this feature is most marked in the discussion of Boston and New York in §42.6.

In this century, with the minimization of deaths from most of the infectious diseases, the urban-rural gradient has tended to disappear; in particular, mortality from the enteric fevers lingered in country areas where water was often taken from shallow wells, whereas unpolluted water was available in the cities. Turpeinen (1973) remarks that

mortality in Finland, Russia and Sweden in at least the last decades of the preindustrial era was highest in and around large towns, and generally wherever

there were densely populated districts with active outside contacts and vigorous social intercourse.

Beaujeu-Garnier (1956) and Beaujeu-Garnier and Chabot (1969) believe that the first phase of industrial and urban development is nearly always marked by a temporary increase in the death rate, which is not linked with exceptional occurrences but is a fairly constant increase reflected in the profound misery of the proletariat with the appearance of occupational diseases, child labor, and unsatisfactory housing. Beaujeu-Garnier cites the United Kingdom as passing through such a phase in 1810–1830 and Germany in 1840–1870. In modern times these unsatisfactory conditions can be overcome more readily; thus, he cites the halving of the crude death rate in 110 years in the United Kingdom, whereas the same decrease, 23 to 11.5 per 1,000, only took 29 years in Japan, 1920–1949. It seems that these authors have overlooked the experience of Edinburgh and Glasgow, in which the classic infections of smallpox, measles, typhus, scarlatina, and pertussis were all unduly active because of the expansion of the population.

See also §37.2, where there are references to the experience of cities in England and Wales, other than London. See Miles (1970) for international perspectives of metropolitan problems; Hammond (1928) and Woods and Woodward (1984a) for urban disease and mortality in nineteenth century England and Wales; Federici, Prignano, et al. (1976) for urban-rural differences; Boyden (1970, 1972) and Clegg and Garlick (1980) for ecology; Hennock (1957) for urban sanitary reform.

47.5 Elite Professions

It is inevitable that historical studies on mortality for periods of time, before which the data given by the parish records are available, should be centered on royalty, the peerage, and the propertied classes. There are some defects in the data; first, the number of sovereigns is not large; second, some authors have excluded certain deaths by murder, warfare, or accident because there are special hazards for the elite, especially assassination, war, and sports, particularly military, for example, jousting, hunting, swordplay; and third, the experience is unrepresentative of the whole population. But there are extensive genealogies of the nobility, and so we must use what is available. The records for the Middle Ages have been discussed in §1.6. We add some bibliographies and notes.

Sovereigns and Nobility. British: Guy (1845, 1847), Bailey and Day (1861), Hollingsworth (1965*a*, *b*), and Young and Russell (1927); French: Lévy and Henry (1960); German: Peller (1943, 1944, 1947, 1965), Prinzing (1930–1931), and Diepgen (1938); Swedish and Finnish: Fahlbeck (1903).

Gentry or Bourgeoisie. British: Bailey and Day (1861), Guy (1846, 1859), and Russell (1948*a*); French: Dupâquier (1978); Genevese: Henry (1956); Venetian: Rodenwaldt (1957).

Medicine. In §5.10 we have mentioned some of the occupational hazards of morbid anatomists and epidemiologists; but general medical practitioners naturally come into contact with infectious disease, especially during epidemics. See §16.6 for an example from the Irish famine of 1846. There have been more general studies of the mortality of medical practitioners: American: Dickinson and Martin (1956), Dublin and Spiegelman (1947), Goodman (1975), Williams, Munford, et al. (1971) (physicians), Miller (1975), and Boice and Land (1982) (radiologists); British: Guy (1854, 1857), Ogle (1886*b*), Neison (1852), and Reid (1957*a*,*b*). Doll and Hill (1954, 1964) used the medical practitioners of England and Wales to test the hypothesis that tobacco was an important cause of lung cancer. Here, medical registration was a useful aid to characterizing the population at risk. For British medical students, see Simon (1968); medical laboratories, Reid (1957*b*); see also §5.10. Hunter (1975) points to enteric fever, diphtheria, and bacterial infections from puncture wounds as hazards for medical practitioners.

Veterinary Medicine. Veterinarians suffer especially from zoonoses such as glanders, psittacosis, swine erysipelas, tularemia, and undulant fever. See §7.1 for tuberculosis of veterinarians.

Miscellaneous. English lawyers: Guy (1857); literary figures, scientists: Guy (1859); Danish clergy: Westergaard (1881, 1887); English clergy: Guy (1851, 1857); English dentists: Hill and Harvey (1972); athletes: Schnohr (1971) and Rook (1954).

47.6 Friendly Societies, Insurance Companies, and Religious Groupings

We now give some examples of mortality studies on subgroups not based completely on social standing or profession or trade.

Friendly Societies. Records from friendly societies are often extensive enough to provide useful mortality data (Neison, 1845–1846, 1877; Ratcliffe, 1850).

Insurance Companies. Although the records kept by insurance companies are on selected members of the community, they can yield information of value on occasion, as in Dublin and Lotka (1937) and Dublin (1948) and the *Bulletin* published by the Metropolitan Life Insurance Company.

Religious Groups. The study of the mortality of religious groups is of interest, as in a given population there may be little racial difference from the complementary group, yet they may differ importantly in diet, smoking, or in other social habits. Phillips, Kuzma, and Lotz (1980) found that the death rates from "cigarette-related" cancers and from colon-rectal cancers were lower in the Seventh Day Adventist population than in the non-SDA population in California, both groups being chosen by virtue of them enrolling in the same concurrent, prospective study. Wynder, Lemon, and Bross (1959) found less cancer of the lung and less coronary heart disease among Seventh Day Adventists than among a control group of American whites. Lyon, Gardner, and West (1980) found that the Mormons in Utah, comprising some 70% of the population, had death rates from cancer of the lung and pleura greatly below the national average, whereas the non-Mormons in Utah had rates comparable with it. For the Mormons, see also Skolnick, Bean, et al. (1978). For the Society of Friends, see Fox (1859), Eversley (1981) (Irish), Beeton and Pearson (1901–1902), and Beeton, Yule, and Pearson (1900). Observations on the incumbency of church officers have been used to estimate the mortality from the Black Death, for which see §8.3 and Campbell (1931).

47.7 Occupation

The causes of many deaths can be traced to occupation. It is a large subject; here, it is possible only to suggest which causes of death may have some relation to occupational disease; the causes are, therefore, considered now in the order of the ICD.

ICD 001–009. Intestinal Infectious Diseases. These have been important for pioneers, soldiers, and miners.

ICD 010–018. Silicosis. This is an underlying cause in deaths from tuberculosis in miners. Much tuberculosis occurs in occupations involving brewing, delivering, or selling alcoholic drinks, for example, publicans, barmen, cellarmen, wine waiters, and truck drivers. Local epidemics of tuberculosis occur in those working under unsatisfactory conditions. There are many trades associated with high tuberculosis rates, for example, knife grinding.

ICD 020–027. Zoonotic Bacterial Diseases. There are special risks for veterinarians and farm workers. Anthrax is often known as woolsorters' disease.

ICD 030–041, Other Bacterial Diseases, and ICD 045–049, Poliomyelitis and some Other Virus Diseases. These include the common infectious diseases but are not especially associated with specific occupations.

ICD 060–066, Arthropod-borne Viral Diseases, ICD 070–079, Other Diseases due to Viruses and Chlamydias, and ICD 080–088, Rickettsioses and Other Arthropod-borne Diseases. These are diseases of occupations requiring travel to the tropics and to forest or uncivilized regions. Those affected are explorers, missionaries, medical workers, soldiers, and construction workers; especially important diseases are yellow fever, malaria, trypanosomiasis, typhus, and other rickettsioses.

ICD 090–099. Syphilis and Other Venereal Diseases. The incidence of these diseases depends as a rule more on style of life than occupation.

ICD 120–129. Helminthiases. Schistosomiasis is a very important occupational infection, occurring usually in rice farmers and in the endemic areas. Hookworm disease has caused much invalidity in miners.

The omitted groups of infectious diseases are not important causes of occupational mortality.

ICD 140–239. Neoplasms. There is now a large literature on occupationally caused neoplasms, for example, general: Hueper (1962, 1966), Lassiter (1977), and Peto and Schneiderman (1981); asbestos: Enterline (1978), Selikoff and Lee (1978), and Doll (1966). We have already noted chimney sweepers' cancer in §20.2, the uranium miners' cancers of the Erzgebirge to the northwest of Bohemia, and watchmakers' sarcoma in §20.3; but purely chemical substances such as nickel, chromates and arsenic (in sheep dips), tar substances, the oils used by cotton-mule spinners, and aniline dyes are capable of provoking cancers. Radioactive materials and Roentgen rays can also cause occupational cancers. In some cases the rates are much higher in the heavy smoking classes.

ICD 460–519. Respiratory System. Workers exposed to great heat or to dusts are susceptible to pneumonia; silicosis is very important and is a predisposing cause of tuberculosis. See Parkes (1982).

ICD E800–999. Injury and Poisonings. An inspection of the rubrics E800–999 shows that there must be a large occupational factor in the deaths. For general references on accidents, see Hale and Hale (1972). Various poisonings have been considered in §34.7. Although it is not mentioned in the text of Hunter (1975), drowning has ranked high among the causes of industrial or occupational deaths. About 2% of all deaths in Scotland and in some of the nordic countries during the first half of the nineteenth century were due to drowning, occurring in watermen, fishermen, and sailors. Many serious accidents have occurred in industrial processes, for example, the bursting of a rapidly rotating wheel or grindstone, collapse of cranes, explosions, fires, electrical accidents, falls into boiling fluids or vats, spills of boiling or hot fluids, and so on. It is one of the triumphs of preventive and legislative medical work that many of these hazards have been controlled in modern industry.

For general references, see Registrar-General of England and Wales (1958, 1978) and predecessors; also Collis and Greenwood (1921), Daric (1949), Farr (1885), Gandevia (1971a), Greenwood (1922b, 1939), and Guy (1844).

See, for occupational, economic, and environmental factors: Bertillon (1892), Hill (1929), Huber (1912), Moriyama and Guralnick (1956), Rom (1983), Stocks (1938), and WHO-death (1980); occupational lung diseases: Gee, Morgan, and Brooks (1984); special occupational classes: Actuarial Society of America (1903); gas workers: Doll (1952); nickel workers: Doll (1958); history of factory and mine legislation: Teleky (1948).

47.8 Mining

In the classical world of Greece and Rome, miners were usually slaves and often of the families of slaves. The miners lived miserable and terrible lives. Xenophon in his treatise *Oeconomicus* quotes Socrates as saying that the mechanical arts must carry a social stigma because these arts disfigure a man by compelling him to sit before fires and by denying him proper exercise. This stigma divided society, for a man could not be a citizen if he were a miner or an artisan. Ancient medicine ignored the worker and the study of occupational medicine was neglected.

After the Renaissance a greater interest was shown. Thus, Georg Bauer (Georgius Agricola, 1494–1555) in his *De Re Metallica*, published in 1556, gives a final chapter on accidents and diseases prevalent among miners and the means to guard against them. Paracelsus (1493–1541) wrote on the diseases of miners, smelter workers, and metallurgists in the book, *Von der Bergsucht und anderen Bergkrankheiten*. Bernardino Ramazzini (1633–1714)

studied diseases in a great number of trades and summarized his knowledge in *De Morbis Artificum Diatriba*. See Rosen (1943).

In modern times this interest has led to the discovery of the role of ionizing radiation in causing cancer, for which see §20.3; further, it has led to the importance of the pneumoconioses, for which see §26.4.

William Farr's report before the Royal Commission on the condition of Mines (Lord Kinnaird, Chairman) showed a huge increase in the mortality of miners of Cornwall over the rest of the population and also miners from Durham (see Farr, 1885, pp. 404–411). Farr showed that the difference was due to an excess of pulmonary diseases, especially tuberculosis. He also noted that the differential rates took time to develop. See also his comparisons between occupations in his table (Farr, 1885, p. 397).

The causes of death in coal miners may be classified into accidents, such as explosions of gases, especially methane, rock falls, falls in transit, asphyxiation, and into diseases, such as pulmonary tuberculosis, miners' pulmonary diseases (including ankylostomiasis), miners' asthma, and bronchitis; however, silicosis is not a problem.

In other mines there will be accidents, as in coal mining, but also poisonings by lead, mercury, and arsenical compounds, and radiations from radium and uranium. See Austrian (1985) for deaths from pneumonia among South African black miners.

47.9 Great Constructional Works and Goldmining

There are events which bring about suddenly the conditions of a large city, (*i*) military campaigns, treated in §33.8, and especially in §33.13, (*ii*) large constructional works, such as for the Suez, Panama, and Forth-Clyde Junction canals, and (*iii*) gold rushes, typified by the Klondike; gold is the important word because a gold miner can obtain and carry away much wealth, whereas mining for other minerals does not involve the same mobility or urgency. Food supply is usually adequate for (*i*) and (*ii*), but there are hazards of travel including vitamin deficiencies and starvation in (*iii*).

Increased mortality occurs principally due to infectious diseases. The crowd may bring diseases with them, for example, typhus or enteric fevers in the goldfields, or find them already endemic, such as cholera and malaria in the Suez area or yellow fever and malaria in Panama. The results of the construction work may alter the ecology of the area, for example, a change from salt water to fresh water in Suez, or the provision of ample breeding places for the *Aedes* and anopheline mosquitoes in Panama. Water may be in very short supply and be contaminated because of bad hygiene conditions, as in the Australian goldmines at Bendigo, Ballarat, Kalgoorlie, and Coolgardie.

The Suez Canal was constructed in 1859–1869. The area was arid and free of malaria and typhus, but the indigenes suffered from hepatitis and dysentery. In 1859 the population consisted of 25 Europeans and 125 indigenes; in 1869 there were approximately 23,000 and 20,000, respectively. The crude death rates for the European and indigenous populations remained at satisfactorily low levels until the introduction of cholera in 1865 (Scott, 1939).

The success of de Lesseps in Suez led him to attempt to build a canal through Panama. After 2 years of preliminary work, the main construction was begun in 1880; but Panama is in the wet tropics, and malaria and yellow fever had been endemic. Mortality among the Europeans was high with the crude death rate at 176 per 1,000 per annum in one period; in 9 years there was a loss of 50,000 lives, the chief causes of death being malaria and yellow fever. The company responsible for the project went bankrupt, and de Lesseps fell into disgrace. After several more false starts, the United States occupied the isthmus of Panama in 1904, with Colonel W.C. Gorgas in charge of the Medical Department. In the 8 years, 1904–1912, there were altogether 5,141 deaths of which 1,022 were from accident or injury and 4,119 from disease. For malaria in Panama, see Simmons, Callender, et al. (1939).

The construction of dams may aggravate risks of disease, for example, the construction of the Madden Dam on the Chagres River in Panama intensified mosquito breeding and hence malaria risk. Similarly, irrigation schemes in the Nile valley caused a greater risk of schistosomiasis, for which see §19.2.

47.10 Social Classes, Prosperity and Poverty

Formerly there was usually a great variation in death rates between the classes; this variation was the subject of many remarks by William Farr (1885) and of many articles in, for example, the *Journal of the Royal Statistical Society* (Greenwood, 1936). With less of the population experiencing actual poverty, with the diminution of occupational hazards following legislative action, and with improved socioeconomic conditions generally, there has been a weakening of the nexus between social class and mortality. Indeed, modern writers often suggest that the working class probably has the best mortality rates in contemporary society.

See, for poverty and disease: Frank (1790/1941), Engels (1892/1971), and Chadwick (1842/1965); mortality and social position: Daric (1949/51) and Humphreys (1887); housing, etc.: Bowley (1923); prosperity: de Laveleye (1891); health and economic development: Taylor and Hall (1967).

47.11 Enclaves and Subject Populations

National statistics sometimes combine together all inhabitants within the national boundaries, and this may conceal interesting differences between communities within the particular state. Often enclaves may arise as a result of conquest or migration and persist for centuries, for example, the Croats in Austria. This persistence may be strengthened by religion and caste systems, as in India. A few examples are cited: Hawaiian ethnic groups: Glober and Stemmermann (1981); Finnish Swedes: Jalavisto (1951); Swedish peasants: Lundborg (1913). See also for aboriginal populations becoming enclaves in the countries invaded by the caucasoids, §§41.2, 41.4, 42.3, 42.4, 43.1–43.3.

47.12 Slavery

We can only touch briefly on the history of slavery; slavery in ancient Rome has already been mentioned in §1.5. In the later Roman Empire there were few conquests of new territory, so that few slaves were imported; there was some loss by manumission, and probably the slave population failed to maintain itself. As Bloch (1966) points out, the slave was regarded as a form of capital with a modest return for there were the expense of food, the tendency to ill health, and the danger of escape. It is believed that the Church had little part in the decline of slavery for its attitude was ambivalent, although the maxim was expressed that one Christian could not enslave another Christian.

The general picture of modern slavery, principally of Africans, is now given, with the aid of Scott (1939).

In Africa there were two classes of slaves, domestic and purchased; slaves were often born such but sometimes submitted themselves to slavery in hard times to avoid famine, to work off a debt, or as punishment for a crime. Similarly, a parent might sell a child for gain. A purchased slave had few rights; the lot of the domestic slaves was not notably worse than that of a freeman. The great increase in the slave trade and its abuses occurred after the first European settlement in America; in 1503 Africans were brought over by the Spaniards to work in Hispaniola. In 1517 Charles V of Spain gave a Flemish merchant the exclusive privilege of importing 4,000 slaves a year into America. Sir Richard Hawkins took his first cargo of slaves to the West Indies in 1562. Between 1680 and 1786 more than 2,000,000 slaves were imported into the British-American colonies and, of these, more than 600,000 into Jamaica within 80 years.

There were considerable losses of life in the slave trade. To obtain 5,000 slaves for shipment may have cost as many as 30,000 lives, when allowance is made for deaths at the roadside from disease, deaths while trying to escape and in the jungle, and deaths in the raids on the villages when the slaves were being taken, young persons aged about 9 to 12 being usually preferred. It has been estimated that the slave trade caused a loss of more than half a million annually in Africa. Depopulation occurred as in the Belgian Congo, in which the population was reduced from 20 to 8 million in 15 years.

The "middle passage" might take as long as 6 months, and there was a premium of 3% against loss, not effective if less than 15 died on the voyage. The extreme degree of crowding, the confinement below deck without facilities or, indeed, sufficient air and water, and other horrors, naturally led to a high incidence of dysentery, diarrheas, ulcers, fevers, and suicides. The mortality rate for the voyage was high, perhaps 12% on an average. The sick were often thrown overboard; after the formal abolition of slavery, the slaves were also often thrown overboard when the ship was being pursued. Once they had reached America, the slaves were given some restorative treatment and were then sold. For much on slavery and, in particular, the spread of infections by the slave trade, see Scott (1934, 1943). For Roman slavery, see Finley (1968); for British West Indies, Sheridan (1985).

47.13 Institutions

John Howard (1726–1790) seems to have been the first to give firm evidence of the high mortality in institutions. With hindsight, it can be seen that there are a number of problems for the inmate: (*i*) disciplinary and wanton violence, (*ii*) often, heavy work, (*iii*) insufficient or poor food, (*iv*) overcrowding, (*v*) lack of hygiene, (*vi*) lack of medical supervision, (*vii*) a heavy burden of infection, and (*viii*) depressed states of mind.

Institutional topics already treated include: civil prisoners, §34.15; soldiers in barracks, §33.5; prisoners of war, §33.9; mental asylums, §24.5; foundlings and illegitimacy, §32.1. Classic studies on vitamin deficiencies have been carried out in orphanages, for example, pellagra in Mississippi (Bordley and Harvey, 1976, p. 249).

Chapter 48
Changes in Mortality by Disease

48.1 Great Pestilences

In this chapter we give an overview of mortality by disease, with the intention of marking out those groups of diseases that have diminished or increased in importance as a cause of mortality. It is customary to think of the declines of mortality rates as a national, continental, or even worldwide phenomenon, the result of medical, social, and economic forces. For some eras, it is easy to look back and pick out the salient features as the supposed reasons for the declines; for example, the declines of the last 80 years may be thought of as being part of some general long-term demographic process, temporarily disturbed by the influenza epidemic of 1918–1919; but, over a longer period, there have been many greater pestilences, perhaps only in a region, for example, plague, typhus, smallpox, or even measles, and these ideas of a continuing process may be quite irrelevant. Some of these pestilences have been so intense that it is illusory to speak of a decline or improvement in mortality in any era and region in which they have been fully active; they act as "shocks" to the system. Nevertheless, the mortality rates in the developed world have declined rather consistently, and in many instances generalizations can be made that are relevant to all or to most of the developed countries.

For easy reference we give the name of the pestilence together with the section in which its effects have been analyzed.

(a) *Cholera, §6.3*. Cholera has been responsible for many deaths in India and several times it has caused sharp pandemics in Europe, America, and Africa; its perpetuation seems to depend on the presence of a large human population living in a hot humid climate on a river plain under unhygienic conditions. With this knowledge, it can be readily controlled with the cooperation of the population, by the provision of pure water supplies, and by proper disposal of human feces; clinically, the case fatality rates can be reduced by restorative measures and chemotherapy.

(b) *Enteric Fevers, §6.5*. These fevers have usually been less dramatic in their effects but more widely distributed than cholera. The mortality from enteric fevers has been almost completely abolished in the developed world, principally as a result of the provision of pure water supplies and the protection of water, milk, and other foods from infection. Case fatality rates have been reduced by chemotherapy.

(c) *Gastroenteritis and Related Diseases, §6.11*. This group of diseases has been responsible for many deaths in the now "developed" world up to the beginning of this century; they are still responsible for many deaths, especially of infants and small children, in the developing world, where the infections are usually complicated by malnutrition. These diseases can be overcome by education of the mothers, protection of the foods against infection, and other hygienic measures, some of which are only possible in a relatively prosperous and settled community. Clinically, case fatality rates are still high, especially in the developing countries, and infants and children are exposed to recurrent infections.

It has been in the diseases (a), (b), and (c) that the hygienic aims of municipal services to hinder the passage of organisms from person to person or, more generally, to combat the defects of urbanization, have been successful. In particular, these measures have acted through control of water (see §6.12 and §46.5), milk (see §6.13 and §46.6), food (see §6.14 and §46.7), and filth arthropods (e.g., flies, cockroaches), and proper disposal of garbage (see §46.8) and sewage (see §6.15 and §46.9). These measures have also been useful in protection against infections by tuberculosis, spread sometimes by food, milk, or water.

(d) *Tuberculosis, §7.9.* For many years tuberculosis was the leading cause of mortality in the countries of western Europe and their extensions overseas. Some authors have written about its behavior as an epidemic or pandemic. If "epidemic" were used in the sense of increasing incidence followed by a decline, no harm would ensue, but implications have often followed that it is disappearing under some biological law that was operative from the beginning of the supposed epidemic. It seems that tuberculosis became more common under the conditions of the formation of the great towns and cities, with crowding and poor hygienic conditions permitting a wide spread of the disease, and low standards of food and living conditions permitting its persistence in the individual patient. Mortality in the developed world had already declined by 1945 and thus before the introduction of chemotherapy. In special classes of the population at risk, BCG vaccination was of value. Surgical procedures played little part in the overall declines. War and famine conditions reminded observers of the importance of rest and nutrition. It may be said that the incidence of the disease declined because of an amelioration of life, which reduced the infection rates and favored the individual cases.

(e) *Bubonic Plague, §8.3.* Bubonic plague has caused the deaths of perhaps half the populations of many European states in several vast pandemics. The causal organism can still be found in wild rodent foci in at least four continents. Because the transfer of plague from such foci to man directly is rare and infection usually spreads to man through the two common rats, measures for the control of plague are evident; moreover, no modern technology is needed for such control. It is hard to imagine how another pandemic could occur, unless civil organization had completely broken down. We must reject the notion that there has been any selection of human lines more resistant to plague. The case fatality can be greatly reduced by chemotherapy but this has been unimportant numerically.

(f) *Leprosy, §9.1.* No generally agreed causes for the disappearance of leprosy from the developed world are available. Therapy by sulfones and BCG vaccination as prophylaxis have been effective in many countries.

(g) *Smallpox, §11.2.* Smallpox has not caused such acute, widespread, and disastrous loss of life as has bubonic plague. Yet smallpox was responsible in the seventeenth century for about 3% of all deaths in Sweden and, perhaps, this might be an estimate for Europe as well. Inoculation, never widely practised, probably had little effect on the general mortality from smallpox, for indeed it was soon superseded by vaccination. The spread of infection would have been controlled to some extent by quarantine measures. After vaccination had been introduced, isolation, or quarantine, and vaccination were shown to be effective in control of the infection in Europe, although breakdowns occurred during wars and their aftermaths in Europe in the nineteenth century. An extension of these methods has resulted finally in the global eradication of smallpox in 1976. Related organisms still exist among animals but it is unlikely that they will ever cause such pandemics as did smallpox.

(h) *Measles, §11.7.* This disease, often considered in modern times as one of the diseases of childhood and so unimportant, is worthy to be ranked with the other great pestilences. Infection in the great cities of the developed world has been, until recently, almost universal. Case fatalities have varied with the hygienic and socioeconomic conditions. For some centuries in western Europe, it may have been responsible for some 2% of all deaths. Nursing and other support has reduced the case fatality under settled social conditions. Prophylactic vaccination is now used, and measles causes a minimum of mortality in the developed world. It still presents great problems in the developing world.

(*i*) *Yellow Fever, §12.2.* This is an anthropozoonosis originating in Africa that now must be considered simply as a zoonosis of Africa and South America. Its conquest followed the discovery that it was conveyed by the *Aedes* mosquitoes and by the destruction of the adult mosquitoes and their breeding grounds. Improvements in therapy have been unimportant in overcoming the mortality.

(*j*) *Typhus, §14.2.* Typhus can persist through interepidemic times by lying in a dormant state in human or animal tissues. It possibly has been the most common cause of the "plagues" or pestilences occurring in association with wars or famine, but it has never been responsible for such widespread pandemics as has bubonic plague. Its control requires no modern technology, and it cannot be thought of as a major risk in the future. The other rickettsiae appear as much smaller risks in restricted geographical areas.

(*k*) *Malaria, §§15.5–15.9.* Malaria has been the leading cause of death in the wet tropics generally and in Africa especially. So much so that genes, which protect against malaria in the heterozygous state, have become frequent in some African populations that exist in a state of balanced polymorphism; see §15.5. Some progress has been made in clearing malaria from previously endemic areas, for example, Europe, Australia, and North America as far south as the Mexican border, but in many other regions the results have been disappointing.

(*l*) *American Trypanosomiasis, §16.3.* Chagas' disease occurs principally in rural areas and endemicity is determined largely by low socioeconomic conditions, especially housing; houses of adobe, mud, or cane furnish numerous hiding places for the vector bugs. The disease is also transmitted by blood transfusions and through the placenta. The disease is regional but could be partly controlled by housing reconstruction. The efficiency of therapy is doubtful.

(*m*) *African Trypanosomiasis, §16.4.* There is no effective therapy against this disease caused by *T. gambiense* and transmitted by *Glossina* flies; but the link can be broken by appropriate clearing of vegetation, appropriate siting of dwellings, and the use of insecticides.

(*n*) *Relapsing Fever, §16.5.* As does typhus, relapsing fever has often appeared in time of famine. The louse-borne form has no other host but man. The tick-borne form is a zoonosis. Prevention consists of hygienic measures against human ectoparasites in either form of the infection.

(*o*) *Syphilis, §17.2.* This cosmopolitan disease has been controlled by chemotherapy and antibiotics.

(*p*) *Influenza, §§10.5–10.11.* Much doubt remains as to the causes of many undiagnosable epidemics or pandemics in the past, but it appears plausible to suggest that some of them were due to some strain of the influenza virus. Although the 1918–1919 pandemic came as a surprise to the world, influenza caused less disturbance of the death rates in Europe at that time than did some other causes of death in Sweden and Finland in the nineteenth century. No effective therapy is available against the virus, and control of an epidemic or pandemic is difficult. The possibility always exists that a recombination of genes in some animal virus will lead to the development of an influenzal virus of a type more lethal to the human population.

48.2 Other Infections in ICD Class 1

We now mention the rubrics of the infectious and parasitic diseases of class 1 not already treated. We are reviewing from the point of view of a developed country, so that the diseases are usually cosmopolitan, although it is evident that regional diseases are of great importance in some geographical greas.

§6.6. Other salmonelloses are controlled by appropriate hygiene as are the bacterial dysenteries of §6.7 and other bacterial food poisonings of §6.8, amebiasis of §6.9, and other protozoal infectious diseases of §6.10. Amebiasis has rarely been epidemic in an area with unpolluted water supply.

§8.4. Tularemia, a regional disease, causes few deaths now, as the special areas of risk are well known. Chemotherapy greatly decreases the case fatality.

§8.5. The special risk comes from the improper disposal of carcasses of animals dying of anthrax. Chemotherapy reduces the case fatality.

§8.6. Brucellosis has been controlled by a prohibition of raw milk from infected goats or ungulata. Therapy is unsatisfactory.

The remaining members, ICD 24–27, of the zoonotic bacterial diseases are not numerically important.

§9.2. Other mycobacteria have caused few deaths.

§9.3. Diphtheria causes dramatic complications that have led to some misconceptions and exaggerations of its importance. It has been controlled by active immunization with toxoid. Possibly serotherapy was far less effective than has been believed.

§9.4. Whooping cough was a far more important cause of death in the early nineteenth century than has usually been supposed. The incidence rate has decreased during infancy, and infants in recent times have been better cared for and have enjoyed lower case fatality rates. Vaccines have been an only partly effective prophylaxis, and chemotherapy is of doubtful value.

§9.5. Streptococcal sore throat and scarlatina, erysipelas, septicemia, wound infections. The causes of the decline in the lethality of scarlatina during the nintheenth century are not definitely known, but probably there was a change of type in the streptococci. The septic complications of wound infections have become less important, probably because of improved surgical and hygienic techniques that exclude the streptococci.

§9.7. Meningococcal meningitis rates have decreased because the special conditions of crowding have been avoided. Chemotherapy has been effective.

§9.8. Tetanus has become less important because of changes in hygiene (neonatal and obstetrical) and in surgical techniques. Vaccines have been used against tetanus as a routine in the armies; tetanus toxoid is now part of the triple vaccine administered in infancy. Serotherapy is possibly ineffective because of its application occurring after the appearance of symptoms.

Chapter 10. Poliomyelitis has never been a large cause of mortality. Inactivated vaccine and, later, live attenuated virus have been effective.

Chapters 11–13. The viruses in these groups, other than smallpox and measles, have been the cause of little mortality in the developed world, although some of them have been important as anthropozoonoses in limited areas.

Chapters 14–17. Typhus and related diseases, malaria, leishmaniasis, trypanosomiasis, relapsing fever, and syphilis have all been mentioned in §48.1.

Chapters 18 and 19. Other spirochetal diseases, mycoses, helminthiasis, and other infections and parasitic diseases. Schistosomiasis as a cause of mortality is of importance and perhaps could even rank as a great pestilence. It is only partly controlled by measures against the parasite at susceptible states of the life cycle. Echinococciasis and filariasis also are of some importance over wide geographic areas, and dracontiasis dominates the health of the population over a restricted region in Africa; but few of these diseases are important in the developed world, even if their control in the undeveloped world should be a high priority.

48.3 Infections Not Assigned to Class 1

Although there has been a general tendency after the revisions to take infections into class 1 of the ICD, there are some infections that have remained in other classes. We mention the classes now and use conventions as to subheadings as in §48.2. It will be recalled that although chemotherapeutics and antibiotics have been successful against the bacteria, they have not been so against the viruses.

Chapter 24. Among disorders and diseases of the nervous system and of the sense organs, infections of the mastoid and other sinuses were formerly of some importance.

§25.2. Rheumatic fever, acute and chronic, and subacute bacterial endocarditis, were formerly the principal infective diseases of the cardiovascular system. These diseases had been declining in importance before the introduction of chemotherapy, but since that time they have become a minor problem, because chemotherapy, applied at an early stage, namely of acute rheumatic fever, may abort the disease.

§26.3. Classical lobar pneumonia due to *Str. pneumoniae* is readily treated by chemotherapy.

§§27.4 and 27.7. Although the bacteria in appendicitis, gallbladder, and related diseases can be thought of as secondary invaders, chemotherapy has aided treatment of the fundamental disease.

§28.1. Acute nephritis no longer goes on to chronic nephritis because chemotherapy is effective against the primary infection.

§29.5. The maternal mortality rates have fallen from around 7 per 1,000 confinements in the earlier years of this century to very low figures in recent years. Briefly, after some years of delay, obstetricians accepted the clinical implications of the bacteriologic findings for puerperal fever and septic abortion and attained a degree of asepsis; chemotherapy was introduced in the late 1930s.

§§30.1 and 30.2. Improved surgery followed by chemotherapy have reduced the mortality rates from diseases of the skin and supporting tissues to negligible proportions.

Chapter 34. The mortality from injury and poisoning formerly was often due to septic complications of compound fractures. Without modern surgery, including chemotherapy, mortality would have increased greatly from the extensive injuries caused by the automobile.

We conclude by saying that important contributions to the declines of mortality from the infections have been made in diseases not in class 1 of the ICD.

48.4 Neoplastic Diseases

The importance of various causes of neoplasms must be discussed if conclusions are to be drawn as to the reasons for declines or absence of declines in the mortality rates. See chapter 20.

Factors favoring increase in the rates include: (*i*) increased use of tobacco, indeed, this is a dominant factor in the rates in the developed world; (*ii*) solar ultraviolet light, this is of great importance for the fair skinned, exposing themselves to the sun in the lower latitudes; (*iii*) X radiation, either received as an occupational risk or in therapy; (*iv*) cosmic rays, gamma rays, nuclear or atomic bomb residues; (*v*) inorganic substances, usually received as an occupational hazard, for example, nickel compounds; (*vi*) carcinogenic substances produced in food by fungi, the aflatoxins; (*vii*) substances produced in the bowel during slow passage of food, especially when nitrites are present in the food; (*viii*) substances produced during the preparation of food; (*ix*) infections by *Schistosoma haematobium*; (*x*) hormones; (*xi*) genetic defects.

Of these hazards, (*iii*), (*v*), and (*vii*) can be reduced by legislative action; educational programs have reduced the hazards of (*i*) slightly in the males, but this is possibly more than balanced by the increased use of tobacco in females; there has been no real reduction of the hazard (*ii*); (*iv*) although there were large local casualties after the explosions of the two atom bombs in 1945, the total mean dosage received from all sources since the beginning of the atomic age has not been large; the dosage of aflatoxins in (*vi*) has been reduced by education; similarly changes in cooking styles have reduced the hazard in (*viii*); little progress has been made in (*vii*); (*ix*) requires control of the schistosomes; a minor problem has been posed by the use of hormones to inhibit ovulation in (*x*).

Factors favoring a decrease in the rates include: (*i*) surgery; (*ii*) radiotherapy, all forms; (*iii*) chemotherapy; (*iv*) hormonal therapy;

(*v*) educational programs; (*vi*) public health measures.

It must be conceded that the results of therapy of the major internal cancers have been disappointing from the point of view of either complete cure or of the number of patients alive after 5 years. As examples, we may cite cancers of the stomach §20.10, of the colon §20.10, of the lung §20.11, and of the breast §20.12. Cancers of the uterus have fared rather better §20.13. Nevertheless, much good palliative therapy has been carried out.

With the superficial cancers, more progress has been made. Insolation has led to a great increase in melanoma and other skin cancers since the migration of the fair-skinned to tropical areas. Early surgery has been responsible for cures of many cases of melanoma but the population mortality rates are still increasing in Australia. Other cancers of the skin have been treated with radium plaques with great success and as a rule without severe scarring; indeed, it can be claimed that, if the therapeutic results had not improved, there would be a great proportion of elderly white-skinned residents in the tropical and subtropical regions suffering chronic and incurable ulcers of lips and skin.

48.5 Endocrine Diseases

The mortality from thyrotoxicosis has been greatly reduced by chemical blockade of thyroid hormone synthesis or by surgical ablation, possibly to less than a third of its former levels. There has always been great difficulty in determining the extent of diabetes mortality, but much progress has been made in reducing it, whether insulin dependent or not.

48.6 Food, Malnutrition, Avitaminoses, and Famine

Freedom from famine was necessary if there were to be consistently declining death rates. It can be claimed that there has been no famine and little avitaminosis in the developed world

over the past hundred years, except perhaps under war conditions. On the other hand, there are now diseases increasing in frequency that are due to imbalances in quantity and quality, for example, diabetes, colonic cancer, and heart disease. In the developing world now, there is much shortage of food and, with the surge of population continuing, there are great risks for the future from both famine and malnutrition. With the adoption of western-style diets, the western-style diseases are increasing in the developing world.

There is much clinical lore and a good deal of experimental data to show that states of nutrition and other factors can alter the level of resistance; the relationship between tuberculosis resistance and nutrition is a good example.

48.7 Diseases in the Organ Systems

It is possibly true that there have been few declines of numerical importance in the diseases of the blood forming, mental, nervous, circulatory, respiratory, digestive, genitourinary, skin, bone, connective tissue systems, namely, in the diseases of systems of chapters 23–28 and 30, that are not due to the control and/or therapy of the infective diseases.

48.8 Injury and Poisoning

As remarked in §34.2, age-specific death rates from injury and poisoning decreased, especially in childhood, as pioneering or industrial and urban conditions improved; but, with increasing use of the automobile, the rates have increased since 1951, especially among males at ages 15 to 34 years. More efficient surgery has prevented these increases from being even more marked. Over the past 150 years, death rates from drownings have decreased considerably in many European countries, and, here, changes of power from sail to coal and oil have been chiefly responsible. Many occupational hazards, for example, in mining and industry, have been reduced.

Epilogue

Our studies have led us from early or primitive man, a hunter-gatherer, to modern civilized man. By inference, from studies on modern tribal man, some guesses can be made on the health of early man. He had few organismal agents to contend with; in many parts of the world his only infections would have been anthropozoonoses; for example, in tropical Africa yellow fever would have been an important cause of mortality. Malaria seems to have played an exceptional role in either Africa or Asia, where in the hot tropics man had inherited the disease from his hominid ancestors. The *Salmonella* group of infections, often zoonoses, may have been common; there may have been gastroenteritis and dysentery arising from changes in the normal bowel commensals. Important proportions of mortality were possibly due to injury by large carnivores, hunting accidents, and drownings, as well as infanticide, especially in hard times. Famine may have been important on special occasions. Where man was able to cope with his surroundings, the population would increase. In the Ice Ages, there would have been large displacements of populations with resulting social disorganization.

With the development of agriculture, larger or more dense populations became possible; some of the zoonoses could now develop into epidemic human diseases, for example, smallpox, measles, typhoid fever, and tuberculosis, for the large human populations would permit their perpetuation. Typhus may only have become a human disease after the domestication of animals. Possibly too, tuberculosis must be considered to have been a zoonosis until the development of the great cities. Contact between tribes at the hunter-gatherer stage of man's development would probably not have been effective in spreading the diseases of the measles type of epidemiology. With the larger populations, contact between members of different areas may have been more effective in perpetuation of those diseases. Finally, as the great centers of population became connected by trade, war, or other causes, any such disease would have the chance of becoming pandemic, for example, smallpox, measles, and this process has continued to the present day with the recent spread of hepatitis B and the AIDS viruses. Man's wanderings possibly were the cause of plague spreading from its original focus in either Asia or Africa to a site in the other continent and enabled it to become, after malaria perhaps, the greatest pestilence.

Larger populations in the valleys of the great rivers gave rise to stratified social classes and bureaucracies, leading to wars and to the appearance in the favored classes of those special diseases that we now associate with the western world.

The story must now be considered in two parts, roughly in the developed world, typified by Europe, and in the developing world, typified by Africa or South America. In Europe, with the rise of the great cities, the *Mycobacterium bovis* became adapted to the human species and a leading cause of death; in the cities man was attacked by a greater variety and intensity of organisms than ever before. Often the population of the cities was maintained only by internal migration from the country. Further, there were several great pandemics of bubonic plague. By the end of the seventeenth century there was a more scientific attitude toward disease. Jennerian vaccination was introduced in 1796 but was not widely used until after 1800. We may call on the experience of England and Wales as an example of the reduction in mortality. Legislation was directed toward the mitigation of the worst effects of the industrial revolution, especially as affecting children and women. In England and Wales, mortality at ages 5–20 years was already declining before 1870, at ages 20–35 years about 1877, and at ages 45–55 years about 1900. Infant mortality began to decline around 1900. At ages older than 65 years, the changes were still very small in 1936. Reforms in the water supply began to be important in the middle of the nineteenth century. The effects of industrial legislation came rather later. The amelioration of the conditions of life was possibly the principal cause of the declines of mortality before 1940. Effective remedies against the infectious diseases had been few before 1936, quinine against malaria, mercury and then the sulfarsenides against syphilis. Chemotherapy after 1935 and the antibiotics after 1944 were effective against the bacterial diseases, but no effective therapy of these kinds has been available against the virus diseases. The experience of the developed countries thus has been that mortality from the infectious diseases has been almost entirely eliminated and most of the other declines of mortality have been due to changes in the deaths from injury and poisoning.

Around 1900 an increasing consumption of refined foodstuffs began, especially flour and bread, with low fiber content in the diet, causing many diseases hitherto rare—appendicitis, cholecystitis, diabetes, colonic cancer. These changes in the causes of death were not fully appreciated until comparative international studies, including African native peoples, were made in the interwar years. There were other excesses in diet. Cigarette smoking and tobacco were incriminated as causes of lung cancer, emphysema, and other diseases, and as potentiating factors in the development of other cancers. The products of modern technology were also incriminated as causes of disease but there is still much doubt as to their importance as causes of death.

It is more difficult to give an account of the mortality in the developing world. Possibly no great changes have come about in many of the countries of Africa, for example. They may have gained something from the introduction of modern technology and medicine, but have lost by entering the world of the cosmopolitan diseases. In general, these countries are dominated by increasing urbanization, sometimes favorably but at other times most unfavorably, with the development of the shanty towns and "septic fringes" of the cities. There is increasing pressure on resources, and it is not evident that the cities can ever develop into prosperous and healthy areas. Near famine conditions will hold an increasing area and the diseases of poverty will persist.

In developed and developing areas alike, there will be shortages of land and material. The chief dangers to health beyond poverty and war will remain the virus diseases, against which there is no special therapy.

Bibliography

For ease of reference we have followed UN and WHO by some modifying word, e.g., UN-historical (1979), WHO-epilepsy (1955).

Aaby, P., Bukh, J., Lisse, I.M. and Smits, A.J. 1983. Measles mortality, state of nutrition and family structure: A community study from Guinea-Bissau. *J. Infect. Dis. 147*, 693–701.

Abbey, H. 1952. An examination of the Reed-Frost theory of epidemics. *Hum. Biol. 3*, 201–33.

Abdel-Wahab, M.F. 1982. *Schistosomiasis in Egypt.* CRC Press, Boca Raton, FL. xii + 237.

Abel-Smith, B. 1964. *The hospitals 1800–1948. A study in social administration in England and Wales.* Heinemann, London. xiii + 514.

Abraham, J.J. 1944. The early history of syphilis. *Br. J. Surg. 32*, 226–37.

Acha, P.N. and Szyfres, B. 1980. *Zoonoses and communicable diseases common to man and animals.* Transl. from Spanish edition, 1977. Sci. Publ. No. 354. Pan American Health Org., Washington, DC. xvi + 702.

Ackerknecht, E.H. 1945. Malaria: history of our knowledge. *Ciba Clin. Symp. 7*, 38–68. Ciba Pharmaceutical Co., Summit, NJ.

Ackerknect, E.H. 1948a. Anticontagionism between 1821 and 1867. *Bull. Hist. Med. 22*, 562–93.

Ackerknect, E.H. 1948b. Hygiene in France, 1815–1848. *Bull. Hist. Med. 22*, 117–55.

Ackerknecht, E.H. 1953. *Rudolf Virchow, doctor, statesman, anthropologist.* University of Wisconsin Press, Madison. xv + 304.

Ackerknecht, E.H. 1967. *Medicine at the Paris Hospital, 1794–1848.* Johns Hopkins, Baltimore, MD. xiv + 242.

Ackerknecht, E.H. 1973. *Therapeutics from the primitives to the twentieth century.* With an appendix: History of dietetics. Hafner, New York. 194 pp.

Acsádi, Gy. and Nemeskéri, J. 1970. *History of human life span and mortality.* Akadémiai Kiadó, Budapest. 346 pp.

Actuarial Society of America 1903. *Experience of thirty-four life companies upon ninety-eight special classes of risks.* Actuarial Soc. of America, New York. xiv + 479.

Adams, E.B., Laurence, D.R. and Smith, J.W.G. 1969. *Tetanus.* Blackwell, Oxford. vii + 165.

Adams, M.W., Ellingboe, A.H., and Rossman, E.C. 1971. Biological uniformity and disease epidemics. *Bio-Science 21*, 1067–70.

Adels, B.R. and Gajdusek, D.C. 1963. Survey of measles patterns in New Guinea, Micronesia and Australia. *Am. J. Hyg. 77*, 317–43.

Adler, S. 1964. Leishmania. *Adv. Parasitol. 2*, 35–96.

Agarwal, K.A. 1984. The effects of maternal iron deficiency on the placenta and foetus. *Adv. Internat. Matern. Child Health 4*, 26–35.

Aikawa, J.K. 1966. *Rocky Mountain spotted fever.* C.C. Thomas, Springfield, IL. xvi + 140.

Ainsworth, G.C. 1976. *Introduction to the history of mycology.* Cambridge University Press, London. xi + 359.

Aird, R.B., Masland, R.L. and Woodbury, D.M. 1984. *The epilepsies. A critical review.* Raven, New York. xii + 308.

Aitkin, M., Laird, N., and Francis, B. 1983. A reanalysis of the Stanford heart transplant data. *J. Am. Stat. Assoc. 78*, 264–74.

Åkesson, O.A. 1931. A research concerning mortality assumptions for life annuity and insurance. *Nord. stat. J. 3*, 281–310.

Akinkugbe, O.O. 1972. *High blood pressure in*

the African. Churchill Livingstone, Edinburgh-London. x + 133.

Akinkugbe, O.O. 1981. Mortality studies in the African context. With discussion. pp. 62–72 in Boström and Ljungstedt.

Albach, R.A. and Booden, T. 1978. Amoebae. pp. 455–506 in Kreier, vol. 2.

Alberman, E. 1974. Stillbirths and neonatal mortality in England and Wales by birthweight, 1953–1971. *Health Trends 6*, 14–17.

Albert, A. 1985. *Selective toxicity: The physico-chemical basis of therapy.* 7th edition. Chapman and Hall, London. xiv + 750.

Alderson, M. 1980. The epidemiology of leukemia. *Adv. Cancer Res. 31*, 1–76.

Alderson, M. 1981. *International mortality statistics.* Macmillan, London. ix + 524.

Alderson, M. 1986. *Occupational cancer.* Butterworth, London. 256 pp.

Allison, A.C. 1954. Protection afforded by sickle-cell trait against subtertian malarial infection. *Br. Med. J. 1*, 290–94.

Allison, R.S. 1943. *Sea diseases: The story of a great natural experiment in preventive medicine in the Royal Navy etc.* J. Bale, London. xxiii + 218.

Almeida, J.D. 1984. Morphology: Virus structure. pp. 14–48 in Topley and Wilson, 1984, vol. 4.

Alström, C.H. 1942. Mortality in mental hospitals with especial regard to tuberculosis. *Acta Psychiatr. et Neurol. Scand.*, Suppl. *24*. Copenhagen.

Alvarado, C.A. and Bruce-Chwatt, L.J. 1962. Malaria. *Sci. Am. 206* (May 1962), 86–98.

Ambraseys, N.N. 1969. Earthquake hazards and emergency planning. pp. 187–99 in *Proc. CENTO Conference on Earthquake Hazard Minimization*, Ankara, 1968. L.L. Shields, Ed. Office of US Economic Coordinator for CENTO Affairs, Ankara, Turkey. 204 pp.

Anderson, D.E. 1982. Familial predisposition. pp. 483–93 in Schottenfeld and Fraumeni.

Anderson, E.T. 1978. Plague in the continental United States, 1900–76. *Public Health Rep. 93*, 297–301.

Anderson, J.S., Cooper, K.E., McLeod, J.W., and Thomson, J.G. 1931. On the existence of two forms of diphtheria bacillus—*B. diphtheriae gravis* and *B. diphtheriae mitis*—and a new medium for their differentiation and for the bacteriological diagnosis of diphtheria. *J. Pathol. Bacteriol. 34*, 667–81.

Anderson, M.J. 1988. *The American census. A social history.* Yale University Press, New Haven, CT. xiv + 257.

Anderson, O.W. and Lerner, M. 1960. *Measuring health levels in the United States, 1900–1958.* Health Inform. Found. Res. Ser. No. 11, New York. 38 pp.

Anderson, R.M. (Ed.) 1982. *Population dynamics of infectious diseases. Theory and applications.* Chapman and Hall, London. xii + 376.

Anderson, R.M. and May, R.M. 1979. Population biology of infectious diseases. Parts I and II. *Nature 280*, 361–67 and 455–61.

Anderson, R.M. and May, R.M. 1982a. Coevolution of hosts and parasites. *Parasitology 85*, 411–26.

Anderson, R.M. and May, R.M. 1982b. Directly transmitted infectious diseases: Control by vaccination. *Science 215*, 1053–60.

Anderson, R.M. and May, R.M. (Eds.) 1982c. *Population biology of infectious diseases.* Life Sciences Research Report 25. Springer, New York. vii + 316.

André, F.E. 1979. Epidemiology of rubella in Africa and the Middle East. pp. 171–85 in *New developments in vaccines*, F.E. André, Ed. Smith, Kline, Rixensart, Belgium.

André, R. and Gyselings, R. 1971. *La mortalité infantile en Belgique.* Etudes démographiques. Institut de Sociologie, Université Libre de Bruxelles, Brussels. 169 pp.

André, R. and Pereira-Roque, J. 1974. *La démographie de la Belgique au XIXe siècle.* Etudes démographiques. Institut de Sociologie, Université Libre de Bruxelles, Brussels. 299 pp.

Andrewes, F.W.E. 1920. The bacteriology of influenza. pp. 110–30 in Newman, Greenwood, et al.

Andrewes, F.W., Bulloch, W., Douglas, S.R., Dreyer, G., Fildes, P., Ledingham, J.C.G. and Wolf, C.G.L. 1923. *Diphtheria: Its bacteriology, pathology and immunology.* Med. Res. Council, HMSO, London. 544 pp.

Andrus, E.C., Bronk, D.W., Carden, G.A. Jr, Keefer, C.S., Lockwood, J.S., Wearn, J.T., and Winternitz, M.C. (Eds.) 1948. *Advances in military medicine—made by American investigators working under the sponsorship of the Committee on Medical Research.* Science in World War II Ser. Little, Brown & Co., Boston. 2 vols. liv + 472; xvii + 473–900.

Andvord, K.F. 1921. Is tuberculosis to be regarded from the etiological standpoint as an acute disease of childhood? *Tubercle 3*, 97–116.

Andvord, K.F. 1930. What can we learn by studying tuberculosis by generations? *Norsk. Mag. Laegevid. 91*, 642–60.

Annales de Démographie historique 1969. *Villes et*

villages de l'ancienne France. Société de Démographie historique, Paris. 520 pp.

Annesley, J. 1828. *Researches into the causes, nature, and treatment of the more prevalent diseases of India and of warm climates generally.* Longmans, London. 2 vols.

Annesley, J., Tulloch, A.M., et al. 1840. Report of a Committee of the Statistical Society of London, appointed to collect and enquire into vital statistics, upon the sickness and mortality among the European and native troops serving in the Madras Presidency, from the year 1793 to 1838. *J. Stat. Soc. (London) 3,* 113–43.

Ansari, N. (Ed.) 1973. *Epidemiology and control of schistosomiasis (Bilharziasis).* Karger, Basel. 752 pp.

Anthony, P.P. 1984. Hepatocellular carcinoma: An overview. pp. 3–29 in Williams, O'Conor, et al.

Antonov, A.N. 1947. Children born during the siege of Leningrad in 1942. *J. Pediatr. 30,* 250–59.

Aoki, K. 1978. Cancer of the liver: International mortality trends. *World Health Stat. Q. 31,* 28–50.

Aoki, K. and Ogawa, H. 1978. Cancer of the pancreas: International mortality trends. *World Health Stat. Q. 31,* 2–27.

Apfel, R.J. and Fisher, S.M. 1984. *To do no harm. DES and the dilemmas of modern medicine.* Yale University Press, New Haven, CT. xii + 199.

Arley, N. 1961. Theoretical analysis of carcinogenesis. *Proc. 4th Berkeley Symp. on Math. Stat. and Probab. 4,* 1–18.

Armenian, H.K. and Lilienfeld, A.M. 1983. Incubation period of diseases. *Epidemiol. Rev. 5,* 1–15.

Armitage, P. 1983. Trials and errors: The emergence of clinical statistics. *J. Roy. Stat. Soc. A146,* 321–34.

Armitage, P. and Doll, R. 1961. Stochastic models for carcinogenesis. *Proc. 4th Berkeley Symp. on Math. Stat. and Probab. 4,* 19–38.

Armstrong, B.K., McMichael, A.J., and MacLennan, R. 1982. Diet. pp. 419–44 in Schottenfeld and Fraumeni.

Armstrong, D. 1984. The acquired immune deficiency disease. *Prog. Med. Virol. 30,* 1–13.

Arnon, S.S. 1980. Infant botulism. *Annu. Rev. Med. 31,* 541–60.

Arnon, S.S., Downs, K., and Chin, J. 1981. Infant botulism: Epidemiology and relation to sudden death syndrome. *Epidemiol. Rev. 3,* 45–66.

Arriaga, E.E. and Davis, K. 1969. The pattern of mortality change in Latin America. *Demography 6,* 223–42.

Aschner, B.M. and Post, R.H. 1956–1957. Modern therapy and hereditary diseases. *Acta Genet.*

Stat. Med. 6, 362–69.

Ashburn, P.M. (Ed.) 1947. *The ranks of death: A medical history of the conquest of America.* Coward, McCann, New York. xix + 208.

Ashcroft, M.T. 1964. Typhoid and paratyphoid fevers in the tropics. *J. Trop. Med. Hyg. 67,* 185–89.

Assaad, F. and Ljungars-Esteves, K. 1984. World overview of poliomyelitis: Regional patterns and trends. *Rev. Infect. Dis. 6,* 302–07.

Auguet, R. 1972. *Cruelty and civilization: The Roman games.* Allen & Unwin, London. 222 pp.

Aurelian, L., Manak, M.M., McKinlay, M., Smith, C.C., Klacsmann, K.T., and Gupta, P.K. 1981. "The Herpesvirus hypothesis"—are Koch's postulates satisfield? *Gynecol. Oncol. 12,* S56–87.

Austin, D.F. 1982. Larynx. pp. 554–63 in Schottenfeld and Fraumeni.

Austrian, R. 1968. Current status of bacterial pneumonia with especial reference to pneumococcal infection. *J. Clin. Pathol. 21* (Suppl.), 93–97.

Austrian, R. 1975. Random gleanings from a life with the pneumococcus. *J. Infect. Dis. 131,* 474–84.

Austrian, R. 1977. Prevention of pneumococcal infection by immunization with capsular polysaccharides of *Streptococcus pneumoniae:* Current status of polyvalent vaccines. *J. Infect. Dis. 136* (Suppl.), S38–42.

Austrian, R. 1985. *Life with the pneumococcus. Notes from the bedside, laboratory, and library.* University of Pennsylvania Press, Philadelphia. xii + 168.

Austrian, R. and Gold, J. 1964. Pneumococcal bacteremia with especial reference to bacteremic pneumococcal pneumonia. *Ann. Intern. Med. 60,* 759–76.

Avogari, P., Sitori, C.R., and Tremoli, E. (Eds.) 1979. *Metabolic effects of alcohol. Proc. of the Internatl. Symp. on metabolic effects of alcohol held in Milan (Italy) on June 18–21, 1979.* Elsevier/ North-Holland, Amsterdam. ix + 430.

Awadzi, K. and Duke, B. 1984. Onchocerciasis (a) Clinical aspects (by K. Awadzi); (b) Epidemiological and experimental aspects (by B. Duke). *Rec. Adv. Trop. Med. 1,* 153–70. See Gilles, 1984.

Aycock, W.L. and Gordon, J.E. 1947. Leprosy in veterans of American wars. *Am. J. Med. Sci. 214,* 329–39.

Ayers, K.N. 1969. Maritime disasters. *Adv. of Sci. 25,* 353–56.

Aykroyd, W.R. 1971. Definition of different degrees of starvation. pp. 17–24 in Blix, Hofvander, and Vahlquist.

Aykroyd, W.R. 1974. *The conquest of famine*. Chatto and Windus, London. v + 216.

Ayoola, E.A. 1984. Synergism between Hepatitis B virus and aflatoxin in hepatocellular carcinoma. pp. 167–79 in Williams, O'Conor, et al.

Ayres, L.P. 1919. *The war with Germany: A statistical summary*. US Govt Printing Office, Washington, DC. 154 pp.

Babbott, F.L. and Gordon, J.E. 1954. Modern measles. *Am. J. Med. Sci. 228*, 334–61.

Baca, O.G. and Paretsky, D. 1983. Q fever and *Coxiella burnetii*: A model for host-parasite interactions. *Microbiol. Rev. 47*, 127–49.

Bach, W., Pancrath, J., and Kellogg, W. (Eds.) 1979. *Man's impact on climate: Proceedings of a conference, Berlin, June 1978*. Developments in Atmospheric Science No. 10. Elsevier, New York. xxvi + 328.

Bachman, W. and Savonen, S. 1934. *Keuhkotaudin kulku Suomessa vuosina 1771–1929*. [Cited by Turpeinen, 1973.]

Backer, J.E. 1947/1948. Population statistics and population registration in Norway. The vital statistics of Norway: An historical view. Parts I & II. *Popul. Studies 1*, 212–26 and 2,318–38.

Backer, J.E. 1961. *Dødeligheten og dens årsaker i Norge, 1856–1955*. (Trend of mortality and causes of death in Norway, 1856–1955.) Samfunnsøkonomisk Studier, No. 10. Statistisk Sentralbyrå, Oslo. 246 pp.

Backett, E.M. 1965. *Domestic accidents*. Public Health Papers, 26. WHO, Geneva. 137 pp.

Baer, G.M. (Ed.) 1975. *The natural history of rabies*. Academic Press, New York. 2 vols. xvi + 454 and xvi + 387.

Bagshawe, K.D. and Lawler, S.D. 1982. Chorioncarcinoma. pp. 909–24 in Schottenfeld and Fraumeni.

Baier, S. 1980. *An economic history of central Niger*. Clarendon, Oxford. xiii + 325.

Bailey, A. and Day, A. 1861. On the rate of mortality prevailing amongst the families of the peerage during the 19th century. *J. Instit. Actuar. 9*, 305–26.

Bailey, A.H. 1868. On the rate of mortality at the period of early manhood. *J. Instit. Actuar. 14*, 247.

Bailey, N.T.J. 1975. *The mathematical theory of infectious diseases and its applications*. 2nd edition. Griffin, London. vi + 413.

Baird, D. 1977. Epidemiologic patterns over time. pp. 5–15 in Reed and Stanley.

Baird, D. and Thomson, A.M. 1969a. General factors underlying perinatal mortality rates. pp. 16–35 in Butler and Alberman.

Baird, D. and Thomson, A.M. 1969b. The effects of obstetric and environmental factors on perinatal mortality by clinico-pathological causes. pp. 211–26 in Butler and Alberman.

Baird, D.R., Whittle, H.C., and Greenwood, B.M. 1976. Mortality from pneumococcal meningitis. *Lancet 2*, 1344–46.

Baker, J.R. 1974. Epidemiology of African sleeping sickness, with discussion. pp. 29–50 in Horsfall and Tamm.

Baker, S.J. 1982. Idiopathic small intestinal disease in the tropics. *Crit. Rev. Trop Med. 1*, 197–245. See Chandra, 1982.

Baker, S.P., O'Neill, B., and Karpf, R.S. 1984. *The injury fact book*. Heath, Lexington, MA. xxix + 313.

Balfour, T.G. 1872. Comparative health of seamen and soldiers as shown by the Naval and Military Statistical Reports. *J. Stat. Soc. (London) 35*, 1–24.

Ball, N. 1978. Drought and dependence in the Sahel. *Int. J. Health Serv. 8*, 271–98.

Baltazard, M., Bahmanyar, M., Mostachfi, P., Eftekhari, M., and Mofidi, Ch. 1960. Recherches sur la peste en Iran. *WHO Bull. 23*, 141–55.

Baltazard, M. 1960. Déclin et destin d'une maladie infectieuse: La peste. *WHO Bull. 23*, 247–62.

Banatvala, J.E. 1977. Rubella vaccines. pp. 172–90 in *Recent advances in clinical virology*, Vol. 1, A.P. Waterson, Ed. Churchill Livingstone, Edinburgh-London-New York. ix + 200.

Banatvala, J.E. and Best, J.M. 1984. Rubella. pp. 271–302 in Topley and Wilson, 1984, vol. 4.

Bang, F.B. 1974. Evolutionary aspects of interactions between human host and virus populations. *Am. J. Epidemiol. 99*, 182–89.

Bang, F.B. 1981. The role of disease in the ecology of famine. pp. 61–75 in Robson.

Banister, J. 1979. Recent population changes in China. pp. 33–61 in Hinton.

Banks, A. (Cartographer) and Martin, G. (Ed.) 1970. *First World War atlas. Introduced by Viscount Montgomery of Alamein*. Weidenfeld & Nicolson, London. xxxviii + 159.

Bannister, S. 1838. Account of the changes and present condition of the population of New Zealand. *J. Stat. Soc. (London) 1*, 362–76.

Banta, H.D., Behney, C.J., and Willems, J.S. 1981 *Toward rational technology in medicine. Considerations for health policy*. Ser, on Health Care and Society, vol. 5. Springer, New York. xiv + 242.

Baratier, E. 1961. *La démographie provençale du XIIIe au XVIe siècle avec chiffres de comparaison pour le XVIIIe siècle*. Ecole pratique des Hautes Etudes, Coll. Démographie et Sociétés, No. V. SEVPEN, Paris. 257 pp.

Barbour, K.M. and Prothero, R.M. (Eds.) 1961. *Essays on African population*. Routledge and Kegan Paul, London. x + 336.

Barger, G. 1931. *Ergot and ergotism: a monograph based on the Dohme lectures delivered in Johns Hopkins University, Baltimore*. Gurney and Jackson, London. xvi + 279.

Barham, C. 1841. Remarks on the abstract of the parish register of Tavistock. *J. Stat. Soc. (London) 4*, 34–49.

Barker, B. 1982. Vitamin A. pp. 221–90 in Barker and Bender, vol. 2.

Barker, B.M. and Bender, D.A. 1980–1982. *Vitamins in medicine*. 4th edition. Heinemann, London. 2 vols. vi + 459 and x + 350.

Barker, F. and Cheyne, J. 1821. *An account of the rise, progress and decline of the fever lately epidemical in Ireland, together with communications from physicians in the provinces, and various official documents*. Baldwin, Cradock & Joy, London; Hodges & M'Arthur, Dublin. 2 vols. (Vol. 1, pp. 139–42 especially.)

Barksdale, L. 1970. *Corynebacterium diphtheriae* and its relatives. *Bacteriol. Rev. 34*, 378–422.

Barksdale, L. and Kim, Kwang-Shin 1977. *Mycobacterium. Bacteriol. Rev. 41*, 217–372.

Barnes, J.K. 1870–1888. *The medical and surgical history of the war of the rebellion (1861–5) prepared in accordance with acts of Congress under the direction of Surgeon-General Joseph K. Barnes, United States Army. Part I—medical history. Part II—surgical history*. US Govt. Printing Office, Washington, DC. 6 vols.

Barnes, R.C. and Holmes, K.K. 1984. Epidemiology of gonorrhea: Current perspectives. *Epidemiol. Rev. 6*, 1–30.

Barrett, J.C. 1985. The mortality of centenarians in England and Wales. *Arch. Gerontol. Geriatr. 4*, 211–18.

Bartlett, M.S. 1960. The critical community size for measles in the United States. *J. Roy. Stat. Soc. A123*, 37–44.

Barua, D. and Burrows, W. (Eds.) 1974. *Cholera*. W.B. Saunders Co., Philadelphia, xvii + 458.

Baruzzi, R. and Franco, L. 1981. Amerindians of Brazil. pp. 138–53 in Trowell and Burkitt.

Baruzzi, R.G., Marcopito, L.F., Serra, M.L.C., Souza, F.A.A., and Stabile, C. 1977. The Kren-Akorore: A recently contacted indigenous tribe.

With discussion. pp. 179–211 in Elliott and Whelan.

Barzun, J. 1974. *Clio and the doctors: Psycho-history, quanto-history and history*. University of Chicago Press, Chicago. xi + 173.

Basedow, H. 1932. Diseases of Australian aborigines. *J. Trop. Med. Hyg. 35*, 177–85, 193–98, 209–13, 247–50, 273–78.

Basu, R.N., Jezek, Z., and Ward, N.A. 1979. *The eradication of smallpox from India*. WHO Regional Office for Southeast Asia, New Delhi. xvi + 350.

Bateson, C. 1969. *The convict ships 1787–1868*. 2nd edition. Brown, Son & Ferguson, Glasgow. xi + 421.

Bath, M. 1967. Earthquakes, large, destructive. pp. 417–24 in *Dictionary of Geophysics*, vol. 1, (S.K. Runcorn, ed.), Pergamon Press, Oxford.

Baum, S. and Arriaga, E.E. 1981. Levels, trends, differentials, and causes of infant and early childhood mortality in Latin America. *World Health Stat. Q. 34*, 147–67.

Baxby, D. 1979. Edward Jenner, William Woodville, and the origins of vaccinia virus. *J. Hist. Med. 34*, 134–62.

Baxby, D. 1981. *Jenner's smallpox vaccine: The riddle of vaccinia virus and its origin*. Heinemann, London. xiv + 214.

Baxby, D. 1984. Poxviruses. pp. 163–82 in Topley and Wilson, 1984, vol. 4.

Beale, A.J. 1977. Measles vaccine. pp. 191–97 in *Recent advances in clinical virology*, vol. 1, A.P. Waterson, Ed. Churchill Livingstone, Edinburgh-London-New York. ix + 200.

Beale, A.J. 1984. Vaccines and antiviral drugs. pp. 147–62 in Topley and Wilson, 1984, vol. 4.

Beard, T.C. 1973. The elimination of echinococcosis from Iceland. *WHO Bull. 48*, 653–60.

Beaujeu-Garnier, J. 1956. *Géographie de la population*. vol. 1. Librairie de Médicis, Paris. 435 pp.

Beaujeu-Garnier, J. and Chabot, G. 1969. *Urban geography*. Transl, by G.M. Yglesias and S.H. Beaver. Longmans Green, London. xvi + 470.

Beaver, P.C., Jung, R.C., and Cupp. E.W. 1984. *Clinical parasitology*. Lea & Febiger, Philadelphia. viii + 825.

Bech, V. 1962. Measles epidemics in Greenland 1951–59. *Am. J. Dis. Child. 103*, 252.

Bechelli, L.M. and Domínguez, V.M. 1966. The leprosy problem in the world. *WHO Bull. 34*, 811–26.

Bechelli, L.M., Gallego Garbajosa, P., et al. 1973. B.C.G. vaccinations against leprosy: Seven-year findings of the controlled WHO trial in Burma.

WHO Bull. 48, 232–34.

Beck, M., Greenfield, W.S., McCarthy, J., and Ralfe, C.H. 1879. Report of the committee appointed by the Pathological Society of London to investigate the nature and causes of those infective diseases known as pyaemia, septicaemia and purulent infection. *Trans. Pathol. Soc. London 30*, 1–188.

Becker, T.M. and Nahmias, A.J. 1985. Genital herpes—Yesterday, today, tomorrow. *Annu. Rev. Med. 36*, 185–93.

Beebe, G.W. 1979. Reflections of the work of the Atomic Bomb Casualty Commission in Japan. *Epidemiol. Rev. 1*, 184–210.

Beebe, G.W. and de Bakey, M.E. 1952. *Battle casualties, incidence, mortality and logistic considerations.* C.C. Thomas, Springfield, IL. xxiii + 277.

Beebe, G.W., Kato, H. and Land, C.E. 1978. Studies of the mortality of A-bomb survivors. 6. Mortality and radiation dose, 1950–1974. *Radiat. Res. 75*, 138–201.

Beeton, M. and Pearson, K. 1901–1902. On the inheritance of the duration of life and on the intensity of natural selection in man. *Biometrika 1*, 50–89.

Beeton, M., Yule, G.U., and Pearson, K. 1900. On the correlation between duration of life and number of offspring. *Proc. Roy. Soc. London 67*, 159–79.

Bégin, E. 1879. Bibliographie analytique des écrits sur l'hygiène depuis 1792 jusqu'à nos jours. *J. d'Hyg. (Paris) 4*, 157.

Béhar, L. 1976. Des tables de mortalité aux XVIIe et XVIIIe siècles. Histoire—signification. *Ann. Démog. Hist.* (1976) 173–200.

Béhar, M. 1964. Death and disease in infants and toddlers of preindustrial countries. *Am. J. Public Health 54*, 1100–05.

Behbehani, A.M. 1983. The smallpox story: Life and death of an old disease. *Microbiol. Rev. 47*, 455–509.

Behlmer, G.K. 1979. Deadly motherhood: Infanticide and medical opinion in mid-Victorian England. *J. Hist. Med. 34*, 403–27.

Behr, J.B. (Ed.) 1963. *Research on road safety.* DSIR Road Research Laboratory, HMSO, London. xii + 602.

Bell, A.C. 1937. *A history of the blockade of Germany and of the countries associated with her in the Great War, Austria-Hungary, Bulgaria, and Turkey.* HMSO, London. xvi + 848.

Bell, R. and Torrigiani, G. (Eds.) 1984. *New approaches to vaccine development.* Schwabe, Basel

(WHO, Geneva). viii + 519.

Bell, W.G. 1951. *The great plague in London in 1665.* Bodley Head, London. xii + 361.

Bellanti, J.A. (Ed.) 1983. *Acute diarrhea. Its nutritional consequences in children.* Nestlé Nutrition Workshop Series, vol. 2. Raven, New York. xvi + 224.

Beller, E.A. 1970. The Thirty Years' War. pp. 306–58 in *The New Cambridge Modern History*, vol. IV. Cambridge University Press.

Belletini, A. 1980. La démographie italienne au XVIe siècle: Sources et possibilités de recherche. *Ann. Démog. Hist.*, Pt. 1, 19–38.

Beloch, K.J. 1886. *Die Bevölkerung der griechischrömischen Welt.* Duncker and Humblot, Leipzig. xvi + 520.

Beloch, K.J. 1897. Zur Bevölkerungsgeschichte des Altertums. *Jahrb. f. Nationalökon. u. Statist.* (3) *13*, 321–43.

Beloch, K.J. 1900. Die Bevölkerung Europas in Mittelalter. *Zeitschr. f. Sozialwiss. 3*, 405–23.

Beloch, K.J. 1937–1961. *Bevölkerungsgeschichte Italiens.* De Gruyter, Berlin. 3 vols.

Bemmelen, R.W. van 1956. The influence of geological events upon human history. *Verh. K. ned. geol.-mijnb. Genoot. 16*, 1.

Bender, D.A. 1980. Niacin. pp. 315–47 in Barker and Bender, vol. 1.

Bender, D.A. 1982. Vitamin C. pp. 1–68 in Barker and Bender, vol. 2.

Benenson, A.S. (Ed.) 1985. *Control of communicable diseases in man.* Interdisciplinary Books, Amer. Public Health Assoc., Washington, DC. xxvi + 485.

Bengtsson, T., Fridlizius, G. and Ohlsson, R. (Eds.) 1984. *Pre-industrial population change: The mortality decline and short-term population movements.* Almqvist & Wiksell, Stockholm.

Benjamin, B. 1966. Mortality trends in the world. *J. Roy. Stat. Soc. A129*, 216–21.

Benjamin, B. 1968. *Health and vital statistics.* Allen & Unwin, London. 307 pp.

Benjamin, B. 1973a. *Rates of mortality.* Gregg International, London. 256 pp.

Benjamin, B. 1973b. *Population and disease in early industrial England.* Gregg International, London. 192 pp.

Benjamin, B. 1974, Mortality trends in Europe. *World Health Stat. Rep. 27*, 24–39.

Benjamin, B. 1977. Trends and differentials in lung cancer mortality. *World Health Stat. Rep. 30*, 118–46.

Bennassar, B. 1969. *Recherches sur les grandes épidémies dans le nord de l'Espagne à la fin du XVIe siècle*. SEVPEN, Paris. 192 pp.

Bennett, P.H. 1983. The diagnosis of diabetes: New international classification and diagnostic criteria. *Annu. Rev. Med. 34*, 295–309.

Ben-Porath, Y. 1980. Child mortality and fertility: Issues in the demographic transition of a migrant population. pp. 151–207 in Easterlin.

Berg, A. 1971. Famine contained: Notes and lessons from the Bihar experience. pp. 113–29 in Blix, Hofvander, and Vahlquist.

Berg, A. 1973. *The nutrition factor—its role in national development*. Brookings Institution, Washington, DC. xii + 290.

Berg, B.J. van den 1979. The California Child Health and Development Studies: Twenty years of research. *World Health Stat. Q. 32*, 269–86.

Bergsma, D. (Ed.) 1976. *Cancer and genetics*. The National Foundation—March of Dimes. Birth Defects: Original Article Series, vol. 12, no. 1. Alan R. Liss, New York. x + 202.

Bergues, H. 1948. Répercussions des calamités de guerre sur la première enfance. *Population 3*, 501–18.

Bergues, H., Aries, P., Helin, E., Henry, L., Riquet, R.P., Sauvy, A., and Sutter, J. 1959. *La prévention des naissances dans la famille. Ses origines dans les temps modernes*. Institut National d'Etudes Démographiques, Paris. 400 pp.

Berkson, D.M. and Stamler, J. 1981. Epidemiology of the killer chronic diseases. pp. 17–55 in Winick.

Berkson, J., Harrington, S.W., Clagett, O.T., Kirklin, J.W., Dockerty, M.B., and McDonald, J.R. 1957. Mortality and survival in surgically treated cancer of the breast: A statistical summary of some experience of the Mayo Clinic. *Proc. Staff Meet. Mayo Clinic 32*, 645–70.

Berkson, J., Walters, W., Gray, H.K., and Priestley, J.T. 1952. Mortality and survival in cancer of the stomach: A statistical summary of the experience of the Mayo Clinic. *Proc. Staff Meet. Mayo Clinic 27*, 137–51.

Bernoulli, C. 1841. *Handbuch der Populationistik oder der Völker- und Menschenkunde*. xv + 612. *Nachtrag: Neuere Ergebnisse der Bevölkerungsstatistik*. (1843) 80 pp. Verlag der Stettin'schen Buchhandlung, Ulm.

Bernstein, I.L. 1981. Occupational asthma. pp. 225–72 in Brooks, Lockey, and Harber.

Berry, M.S. and Pentreath, V.W. 1980. The neurophysiology of alcohol. pp. 43–72 in Sandler.

Bertelsen, A. 1920–1921. Some statistics on the native population of Greenland. *Metron 1* (4), 132–36.

Bertillon, J. 1892. Morbidity and mortality according to occupation. (Trans. from *J. Soc. Stat. Paris*, Oct., 1892.) *J. Roy. Stat. Soc. 55*, 559–600.

Beutler, E. 1980. The red cell: A tiny dynamo. pp. 141–68 in Wintrobe.

Beveridge, W.I.B. 1977. *Influenza: The last great plague, an unfinished story of discovery*. Heinemann, London. xii + 124.

Bhat, P.N.M., Preston, S., and Dyson, T. 1984. *Vital rates in India, 1961–1981*. Committee on Population and Demography Report No. 24. National Academy Press, Washington, DC. xvi + 173.

Bhatia, B.M. 1967. *Famines in India: A study in some aspects of the economic history of India, 1860–1955*. 2nd edition. Asia Publ. House, London. ix + 389.

Bickel, W. 1947. *Bevölkerungsgeschichte und Bevölkerungspolitik der Schweiz seit dem Ausgang des Mittelalters*. Gutenberg, Zürich. 333 pp.

Bideau, A., Brunet, G., and Desbos, R. 1978. Variations locales de la mortalité des enfants: L'exemple de la châtellenie de Saint-Trivier-en-Dombes (1730–1869). *Ann. Démog. Hist.*, Pt. 1, 7–29.

Bignall, J.R. 1971. Tuberculosis in England and Wales in the next 20 years. *Postgrad. Med. J. 47*, 759–62.

Bignell, V., Peters, G., and Pym, C. (Eds.) 1977. *Catastrophic failures*. Open University Press. Milton Keynes. 274 pp.

Billings, F. 1912. Chronic focal infections and their etiologic relations to arthritis and nephritis. *Arch. intern. Med. 9*, 484–98.

Billings, J.S. and Hurd, H.M. (Eds.) 1894. Hospitals, dispensaries and nursing. Papers and discussions. In *International Congress of Charities, Correction and Philanthropy, Chicago, 1893. Report of the Proceedings*. Section III (vol. 3). Johns Hopkins, Baltimore. xiv + 719.

Billroth, T. and Winiwarter, A. von 1883. *General surgical pathology and therapeutics in fifty one lectures: A textbook for students and physicians*. (Transl. by C.E. Hackley from the 10th edition.) H.K. Lewis, London. xvi + 835.

Binford, L.R. 1981. *Bones. Ancient men and modern myths*. Studies in Archaeology. Academic Press, New York. xxviii + 322.

Bingel, A. 1918. Über Behandlung der Diphtherie mit gewöhnlichem Pferdeserum. *Deut. Arch. Klin. Med. 125*, 284–332.

Biraben, J.N. 1972. Certain demographic characteristics of the plague epidemic in France, 1720–1722. pp. 233–41 in Glass and Revelle.

Biraben, J.N. 1975–1976. *Les hommes et la peste en France et dans les pays européens et méditerranéens. Vol. I—La peste dans l'histoire. Vol. II—Les hommes face à la peste.* Mouton, Paris. 455 and 416 pp.

Biraben, J.N. and Henry, L. 1957. La mortalité des jeunes enfants dans les pays méditerranéens. *Population 12*, 615–44.

Biraud, Y. and Kaul, P.M. 1947–1948. World distribution and prevalence of cholera in recent years. *WHO Epidemiol. Vital Stat. Rep. 1*, 140–52.

Birch, G.G. and Parker, K.J. (Eds.) 1980. *Food and health: Science and technology.* Applied Science Publ., London. xii + 532.

Bisseru, B. 1967. *Diseases of man acquired from his pets.* Heinemann, London. xiv + 482.

Biswas, M.R. and Biswas, A.K. 1979. *Food, climate and man.* Wiley, New York. xxiii + 285.

Bizzini, B. 1979. Tetanus toxin. *Microbiol. Rev. 43*, 224–40.

Bjarnar, V. 1965. The Laki eruption and the famine of the mist. pp. 410–21 in Bayerschmidt, C.F. and Friis, E.J. (Eds), *Scandinavian studies: Essays presented to Dr. Henry Goddard Leach.* University of Washington Press, Seattle. xi + 458.

Black, F.L. 1966. Measles endemicity in insular populations: Critical community size and its evolutionary implication. *J. Theor. Biol. 11*, 207–11.

Black, F.L. 1975. Infectious diseases in primitive societies. *Science 187*, 515–18.

Black, F.L. 1980. Modern isolated pre-agricultural populations as a source of information on prehistoric epidemic patterns. pp. 37–54 in Stanley and Joske.

Black, F.L. 1982. Measles. pp. 397–418 in Evans.

Black, F.L., Hierholzer, W.J., Pinheiro, F. de P., Evans, A.S., Woodall, J.P., Opton, E.M., Emmons, J.E., West, B.S., Edsall, G., Downs, W.G., and Wallace, G.D. 1974. Evidence for persistence of infectious agents in isolated human populations. *Am. J. Epidemiol. 100*, 230–50.

Black, F.L., Pinheiro, F. de P., Hierholzer, W.J., and Lee, R.V. 1977. Epidemiology of infectious disease: The example of measles. With discussion. pp. 115–35 in Elliott and Whelan.

Black, R.H. 1972. *Malaria in Australia.* Commonwealth Dept. of Health, SPHTM Service Publn. No. 9. Austral. Govt. Publ. Service, Canberra. 222 pp.

Black, W. 1789. *An arithmetical and medical analysis of the diseases and mortality of the human species.* 2nd edition. Reprinted by Gregg International, London, 1973. 304 pp.

Blacklock, N. 1981. Renal stone. pp. 60–70 in Trowell and Burkitt.

Blake, J.B. 1953. Smallpox inoculation in colonial Boston. *J. Hist. Med. 8*, 284–300.

Blake, J.B. 1959. *Public health in the town of Boston 1630–1822.* Harvard University Press, Cambridge, MA. xiv + 278.

Blake, N.M. 1956. *Water for the cities: A history of the urban water supply problem in the United States.* Maxwell School Series—III. Syracuse University Press, Syracuse, NY. x + 341.

Blaser, M.J., Taylor, D.N., and Feldman, R.A. 1983. Epidemiology of *Campylobacter jejuni* infections. *Epidemiol. Rev. 5*, 157–76.

Blaxter, K. and Fowden, L. (Eds.) 1982. *Food, nutrition and climate.* American Scientific Publ., London. ix + 422.

Blix, G. 1964. *Occurrence, causes and prevention of overnutrition.* Swedish Nutrition Foundation, Uppsala. 152 pp.

Blix, G., Hofvander, Y., and Vahlquist, B. (Eds.) 1971. *Famine: A symposium dealing with nutrition and relief operations in times of disaster.* Swedish Nutrition Foundation, Uppsala. 200 pp.

Bloch, M. 1966. The rise of dependent cultivation and seignorial institutions. pp. 235–90 in *Cambridge Economic History of Europe*, Vol. 6. Cambridge University Press. (Especially pp. 246–55, the decline of slavery.)

Blom-Cooper, L.J. (Ed.) 1975. *Progress in penal reform.* Clarendon, Oxford. xii + 288.

Blong, R.J. 1984. *Volcanic hazards. A sourcebook on the effects of eruptions.* Academic Press, Orlando, FL. xvi + 424.

Blot, W.J. and Fraumeni, J.F. Jr 1982. Geographic epidemiology of cancer in the United States. pp. 179–93 in Schottenfeld and Fraumeni.

Blum, H.F. 1959a. *Carcinogenesis by ultraviolet light.* Princeton University Press, Princeton, NJ. xv + 340.

Blum, H.F. 1959b. Environmental radiation and cancer. *Science 130*, 1545–47.

Boak, A.E.R. 1955. *Manpower shortage and the fall of the Roman Empire in the West.* University of Michigan Press, Ann Arbor. vii + 169.

Bodart, G. 1916. Losses of life in modern wars. Austria-Hungary, 1618–1913; France, 1614–1913. pp. 1–156 in Westergaard, 1916.

Bodey, G.P. and Fainstein, V. 1985. *Candidiasis.* Raven, New York. 281 pp.

Boethius, B. 1953. New light on eighteenth century Sweden. *Scand. Econ. Hist. Rev. 1*, 143–77.

Böttiger, L.E. and Carlson, L.A. 1981. Mortality and entry characteristics ("risk factors") in the

Stockholm Prospective Study. With discussion. pp. 89–120 in Boström and Ljungstedt.

Boice, J.D. Jr and Land, C.E. 1982. Ionizing radiation. pp. 231–53 in Schottenfeld and Fraumeni.

Boissier de Sauvages de la Croix, F. 1768/1772. *Nosologia methodica, sistens morborum classes, juxta Sydenhami mentem et botanicorum ordinem . . . 2* vols. 1768. Amsterdam. (French trans. by Gouvion, 1772, Lyon.)

Bolander, A.M. 1981. Mortality statistics in Sweden and its neighbouring countries. pp. 236–58 in Boström and Ljungstedt.

Bolt, B.A., Horn, W.L., Macdonald, G.A., and Scott, R.F. 1975. *Geological hazards: earthquakes, tsunamis, volcanoes, avalanches, landslides and floods.* Springer, New York. viii + 328.

Bonita, R. and Beaglehole, R. 1982. Trends in cerebrovascular disease mortality in New Zealand. *N.Z. Med. J. 95*, 411–14.

Bonney, V. 1918–1919. The continued high maternal mortality of child-bearing: The reason and the remedy. *Proc. Roy. Soc. Med. 12* (3), 75–107.

Bonser, W. 1944. Epidemics during the Anglo-Saxon period. *J. Br. Archaeol. Assoc.*, Ser. 3, 9, 48–71.

Bonser, W. 1963. *The medical background of Anglo-Saxon England: A study in history, psychology and folklore.* Wellcome Historical Medical Library, London. xxxvi + 448.

Bonte, J. 1974. Patterns of mortality and morbidity. pp. 75–90 in Vogel, Muller, et al.

Booth, C. 1902/1903 *Life and labour of the people in London.* Macmillan, London. 17 vols.

Bora, K.C., Douglas, G.R. and Nestleman, E.R. (Eds) 1982. *Chemical mutagenesis, human population monitoring and genetic risk assessment.* Prog. Med. Res., vol. 3. Elsevier, Amsterdam. xxiv + 364.

Borah, W. and Cook, S.F. 1960. *The population of Central Mexico in 1548; an analysis of the Suma de visitas de pueblos.* Ibero-Americana No. 43. University of California Press, Berkeley-Los Angeles. 215 pp.

Borah, W. and Cook, S.F. 1963. *The Aboriginal population of Central Mexico on the eve of the Spanish conquest.* Ibero-Americana No. 45. University of California Press, Berkeley-Los Angeles. 157 pp.

Borah, W. and Cook. SF. 1969. Conquest and population: A demographic approach to Mexican history. *Proc. Am. Philos. Soc. 113*, 177–83.

Bordley, J. III and Harvey, A.McG. 1976. *Two centuries of American medicine, 1776–1976.* W.B. Saunders, Philadelphia. xv + 844.

Borgoño, J.M. 1983. Current impact of measles in Latin America. *Rev. Infect. Dis. 5*, 417–21.

Borhani, N.O. 1966. Magnitude of the problem of cardiovascular-renal diseases. pp. 492–526 in Lilienfeld and Gifford.

Bose, S.K. and Dey, A.K. (Eds.) 1964. *Asian pediatrics.* Proc. 1st All Asian Congress of Pediatrics, New Delhi, 1961. Asia Publ. House, New York. xx + 476.

Boström, H. and Ljungstedt, N. (Eds.) 1981. *Medical aspects of mortality statistics.* Almqvist & Wiksell, Stockholm. 387 pp.

Boué, A., Boué, J. and Gropp, A. 1985. Cytogenetics of pregnancy wastage. *Adv. Hum. Genet. 14*, 1–57.

Boulanger, P.M. and Tabutin, D. 1980. *La mortalité des enfants dans le monde et dans l'histoire.* Département de Démographie, Université Catholique de Louvain. Ordina, Liège. 413 pp.

Bourbeau, R. and Legaré, J. 1982. *Evolution de la mortalité au Canada et au Québec 1851–1931: Essai de mesure par génération.* Presses Universitaires Montréal, Montreal. 140 pp.

Bourdelais, P. and Raulot, J.-Y. 1976. Des risques de la petite enfance à la fin du XVIIe siècle. *Ann. Démog. Hist.*, Pt. E, 305–18.

Bourgeois, J. 1946. De la mesure de la mortalité infantile. *Population 1*, 53–68.

Bourgeois-Pichat, J. 1951. La mesure de la mortalité infantile. I. Principes et méthodes. II. Les causes de décès. *Population 6*, 233–48 and 459–80.

Bourgeois-Pichat, J. 1964. Evolution récente de la mortalité infantile. *Population 19*, 417–38.

Bourgeois-Pichat, J. 1965. The general development of the population of France since the eighteenth century. pp. 474–506 in Glass and Eversley. (Reprinted from *Population 6* (1951) 635–62 and 7 (1952) 319–29.)

Bourne, G.H. (Ed.) 1985. *World nutritional determinants.* World Review of Nutrition and Dietetics, vol. 45. Karger, Basel. x + 225.

Bouvier, M.H. and Guidevaux, M. 1979. Mortality from disorders of the respiratory system throughout the world between 1950 and 1972. *World Health Stat. Q. 32*, 174–97.

Bowerman, W.G. 1939. Centenarians. *Trans. Am. Actuar. Soc. 40*, 22–49.

Bowers, J.Z. 1976. Influences on the development of American medicine. pp. 1–38 in Bowers and Purcell.

Bowers, J.Z. and Purcell, E.F. (Eds.) 1976. *Advances in American medicine: Essays at the bicentennial.* Josiah Macy, Jr Found., New York. 2 vols. viii + 457; v + 459–918.

Bowley, A.L. 1923. Death-rates, density, population and housing. *J. Roy. Stat. Soc. 86*, 516–46.

Boxall, R. 1893. The mortality of childbirth. *Lancet 2*, 9–15.

Boyce, R.W. 1951. *Yellow fever and its prevention.* John Murray, London. xix + 380.

Boyd, J.S.K. 1950. Fifty years of tropical medicine. *Br. Med. J. 1*, 37–43.

Boyd, M.F. (Ed.) 1949. *Malariology: a comprehensive survey of all aspects of this group of diseases from a global standpoint.* W.B. Saunders, Philadelphia-London. 2 vols. xxi + 787 and v + 788–1643.

Boyden, S.V. 1972. Ecology in relation to urban population structure. pp. 411–41 in Harrison and Boyce.

Boyden, S.V. (Ed.) 1970. *The impact of civilisation on the biology of man.* Austral. Natl. University Press, Canberra. xx + 233.

Bracegirdle, B. 1978. *A history of microtechnique: the evolution of the microtome and the development of tissue preparation.* Heinemann, London. xv + 359.

Bracken, M.B. (Ed.) 1984. *Perinatal epidemiology.* Oxford University Press, Oxford-New York. xx + 550.

Bracken, M.B., Brinton, L.A., and Hayashi, K. 1984. Epidemiology of hydatidiform mole and choriocarcinoma. *Epidemiol. Rev. 6*, 52–75.

Brackenridge, R.D.C. 1977. *Medical selection of life risks.* Undershaft Press, London. xii + 765.

Bradley, P.B. 1980. Introduction. pp. xiii–xiv in Sandler.

Bradley, W.H., Massey, A., Logan, W.P.D., Semple, A.B., Benjamin, B., Grist, M.R., Hope-Simpson, R.E., Isaacs, A., Andrewes, C.H., et al. 1951. Discussion: influenza 1951. *Proc. Roy. Soc. Med. 44*, 789–804.

Bradshaw, J.S. 1978. *Doctors on trial.* Paddington Press, New York-London. 320 pp.

Brandt, A.M. 1985. *No magic bullet. A social history of venereal disease in the United States since 1880.* Oxford University Press, New York. x + 245.

Brass, W. 1968. The demography of French-speaking territories covered by special sample inquiries: Upper Volta, Dahomey, Guinea, North Cameroon, and other areas. pp. 342–439 in Brass, Coale, et al.

Brass, W., Coale, A.J., Demeny, P., Heisel, D.F., Lorimer, F., Romaniuk, F., and van de Walle, E. 1968. *The demography of tropical Africa.* Princeton University Press, Princeton, NJ. xxx + 539.

Braude, A.I., Davis, C.E. and Fierer, J. (Eds.) 1986.

Infectious diseases and medical microbiology. 2nd edition. W.B. Saunders, Philadelphia. xvi + 1620.

Brent, R.L. 1980. Radiation-induced embryonic and fetal loss from conception to birth. pp. 177–81 in Porter and Hook.

Brès, P. 1970. Données récentes apportées par les enquêtes sérologiques sur la prévalence des arbovirus en Afrique, avec référence spéciale à la fièvre jaune. *WHO Bull. 43*, 223–67.

Brill, A.B., Tomonaga, M., and Heyssel, R.M. 1962. Leukemia in man following exposure to ionizing radiation: Summary of findings in Hiroshima and Nagasaki, and comparison with other human experience. *Ann. Intern. Med. 56*, 590–609.

Brincker, J.A.H. 1938. A historical, epidemiological and aetiological study of measles (morbilli; rubeola). *Proc. Roy. Soc. Med. 31*, 807–28.

Brockington, C.F. 1956. *A short history of public health.* J. and A. Churchill, London. vii + 235.

Brockington, (C.) F. 1975. *World health.* 3rd edition. Churchill-Livingstone, Edinburgh-London-New York. 345 pp.

Brockington, C.F. 1979. The history of public health. pp. 1–8 in Hobson.

Broders, A.C. 1920. Squamous cell epithelioma of the lip: A study of five hundred and thirty-seven cases. *J. Am. Med. Assoc. 74*, 656–64.

Brodribb, A.J.M. 1980. Dietary fiber in diverticular disease of the colon. pp. 43–66 in Spiller and Kay.

Bronner, M. and Bronner, M. 1971. *Actinomycosis.* 2nd edition. John Wright, Bristol. xix + 355.

Brooke, E.M. 1974. *Suicide and attempted suicide.* Public Health Papers, 58. WHO, Geneva. 127 pp.

Brooks, S.M., Lockey, J.E., and Harber, P. 1981. *Occupational lung diseases, I.* Clinics in Chest Medicine, vol. 2, No. 2. W.B. Saunders, Philadelphia. vii + 169–302. (Separately reprinted.)

Brooks, W.D.W. 1952. Tuberculosis in the Royal Navy. pp. 319–32 in Cope, 1952.

Broome, C.V. and Fraser, D.W. 1979. Epidemiologic aspects of legionellosis. *Epidemiol. Rev. 1*, 1–16.

Brotherston, J.H.F. 1952. *Observations on the early public health movement in Scotland.* Mem. Ser. London School of Hygiene, No. 8. London. xi + 119.

Brothwell, D. 1967. The bio-cultural background to disease. pp. 56–68 in Brothwell and Sandison.

Brothwell, D. and Sandison, A.T. 1967. *Diseases in antiquity: A survey of the diseases, injuries and surgery of early populations.* C.C. Thomas, Springfield, IL. xix + 766.

Brown, A.W.A., Haworth, J., and Zahar, A.R.

1976. Malaria eradication and control from a global standpoint. *J. Med. Entomol. 13*, 1–25.

Brown, E.R. (Ed.) 1979. *Rockefeller medicine men: Medicine and capitalism in America*. University. of California Press, Berkeley. xii + 283.

Brown, F. 1984*a*. The nature of viruses. pp. 1–4 in Topley and Wilson, 1984, vol. 4.

Brown, F. 1984*b*. Classification of viruses. pp. 5–13 in Topley and Wilson, 1984, vol. 4.

Brown, L.R. 1981. World population growth, soil erosion, and food security. *Science 214*, 995–1002.

Brown, P. 1980. An epidemiologic critique of Creutzfeldt-Jakob disease. *Epidemiol. Rev. 2*, 113–35.

Brown, W.J., Donohue, J.F., Axnick, N.W., Blount, J.H., Ewen, N.H., and Jones, O.G. 1970. *Syphilis and other venereal diseases*. Harvard University Press, Cambridge, MA. xx + 241.

Browne, O'D.T.D. 1947. *The Rotunda Hospital 1745–1945*. E. & S. Livingstone, Edinburgh. xx + 286.

Browne, S.G. 1980. Leprosy. pp. 69–79 in Sabben-Clare, Bradley, and Kirkwood.

Brownlee, J. 1915. Investigation into the periodicity of infectious diseases by the application of a method used only in physics. *Public Health 28*, 125-34.

Brownlee, J. 1916*a*. Certain considerations regarding the epidemiology of phthisis pulmonalis. *Public Health 29*, 130–45.

Brownlee, J. 1916*b*. The history of the birth- and death-rates in England and Wales taken as a whole, from 1570 to the present time. *Public Health 29*, 211–22 and 228–38.

Brownlee, J. 1918. *An investigation into the epidemiology of phthisis in Great Britain and Ireland. Part II*. Med. Res. Council Spec. Rep. Series No. 18. HMSO. London. 71 pp.

Brownlee, J. 1919. Notes on the biology of a life table. *J. Roy. Stat. Soc. 82*, 34–77.

Brownlee, J. 1920. *An investigation into the epidemiology of phthisis in Great Britain and Ireland. Part III*. Med. Res. Council Spec. Rep. Series No. 46. HMSO, London. 96 pp.

Brownlee, J. 1925. The health of London in the eighteenth century. *Proc. Roy. Soc. Med. (Epidemiol. Sect.) 18*, 73–85.

Brožek, J., Wells, S., and Keys, A. 1946. Medical aspects of semi-starvation in Leningrad (siege 1941–1942). *Am. Rev. Soviet Med. 4*, 70–86.

Bruce-Chwatt, L.J. 1965. Paleogenesis and paleoepidemiology of primate malaria. *WHO Bull. 32*, 363–87.

Bruce-Chwatt, L.J. 1971. Malaria and its prevention in military campaigns. *Z. Tropenmed. Parasitol. 22*, 370–90.

Bruce-Chwatt, L.J. 1979. Man against malaria: Conquest or defeat. (Manson Oration) *Trans. Roy. Soc. Trop. Med. Hyg. 73*, 605–17. .

Bruce-Chwatt, L.J. 1980. *Essential malariology*. Heinemann, London. xiv + 354.

Bruce-Chwatt, L.J. 1982. The rise of tropical medicine: Milestones of discovery and application. pp. 167–85 in *Science, technology and society in the time of Alfred Nobel*, Nobel Symposium No.52, C.G. Bernhard, E. Crawford, and P. Sörbom (Eds), Pergamon Press, Oxford. xv + 426.

Bruce-Chwatt, L.J. 1987. Malaria and its control: Present situation and future prospects. *Annu. Rev. Public Health 8*, 75–110.

Bruce-Chwatt, L.J. (Ed.) with Black, R.H., Canfield, C.J., Clyde, D.F., Peters, W. and Wernsdorfer, W.H. 1981. *Chemotherapy of malaria*. 2nd edition. WHO, Geneva. 261 pp.

Bruce-Chwatt, L.J. and Bruce-Chwatt, J.M. 1980. Malaria and yellow fever: The mortality of British expatriates in colonial West Africa. pp. 43–66 in Sabben-Clare, Bradley, and Kirkwood.

Bruce-Chwatt, L.J. and Zulueta, J. de 1980. *The rise and fall of malaria in Europe: A historico-epidemiological study*. Oxford University Press, New York. xvi + 240.

Brunt, P.A. 1971. *Italian manpower*, 225 BC–AD 14. Clarendon, Oxford xxi + 750.

Bryan, W.R. 1961. Virus carcinogenesis. *Proc. 4th Berkeley Symp. on Math. Stat. and Probab. 4*, 123–52.

Bryant, J. 1969. *Health and the developing world*. Cornell University Press, Ithaca-London. xxvii + 345.

Bryceson, A.D.M., Parry, E.H.O., Perine, P.L., Warrell, D.A., Vukotich, D., and Leithead, C.S. 1970. Louse-borne relapsing fever. A clinical and laboratory study of 62 cases in Ethiopia and a reconsideration of the literature. *Q. J. Med. (N.S.) 39*, 129–70.

Bryson, R.A. 1973. Drought in Sahelia: Who or what is to blame? *Ecologist 3*, 366–71.

Bryson, R.A. 1974. A perspective on climatic change. *Science 184*, 753–60.

Buck, A.A., Anderson, R.I., Sasaki, T.T. and Kawata, K. 1970. *Health and disease in Chad. Epidemiology, culture and environment in five villages*. Johns Hopkins, Baltimore. xvi + 284.

Budd, W. 1849. *Malignant cholera: Its mode of propagation and its prevention*. John Churchill, London. 30 pp.

Budyko, M.I. 1974. *Climate and life*. English edition, D.H. Miller (Ed.) Internatl. Geophysics Series, Vol. 8. Academic Press, New York-London. xvii + 507.

Budyko, M.I. 1982. *The earth's climate: Past and future*. Internatl. Geophysics Series, Vol. 29. Academic Press, New York. 307 pp.

Buerger, L. 1908. Thromboangiitis obliterans: A study of the vascular lesions leading to presenile spontaneous gangrene. *Am. J. Med. Sci. 136*, 567–80. (See also *Trans. Assoc. Am. Physicians 18* (1908), 200–21.)

Bulla, A. 1977*a*. Global review of tuberculosis morbidity and mortality in the world (1961–1971). *World Health Stat. Rep. 30*, 2–38.

Bulla, A. 1977*b*. Trends in tuberculosis hospital and sanitorium beds throughout the world. *World Health Stat. Rep.* 30, 39–56.

Bullen, J.J. 1976. Iron-binding proteins and other factors in milk responsible for resistance to *Escherichia coli*. pp. 149–62 in Elliott and Knight.

Bulloch, W. 1938. *The history of bacteriology. University of London, Heath Clark Lectures, 1936*. Reprinted 1960. Oxford University Press, London. xii + 422.

Bullough, V.L. 1973. James Lind. In *Dict. Sci. Biog. VIII*, 361–3.

Bundesen, H.N., Connolly, J.I., Gorman, A.E., Hardy, A.V., McCoy, G.W., and Rawlings, I.D. 1936. *Epidemic amebic dysentery. The Chicago outbreak of 1933*. Natl. Instit. Health Bull. No. 166. Govt Printing Office, Washington, DC. xi + 187.

Bunker, J.P., Barnes, B.A., and Mosteller, F. (Eds.) 1977. *Costs, risks and benefits of surgery*. Oxford University Press, New York. xxv + 401.

Burbank, F. 1971. *Patterns in cancer mortality in the United States: 1950–1967*. National Cancer Instit., Bethesda, MD. US Dept. Health, Educ., and Welfare, Washington, DC. xvi + 594.

Burdett, H.C. 1882. On the relative mortality after amputations of large and small hospitals and the influence of the antiseptic (Listerian) system upon such mortality. *J. Stat. Soc. (London) 45*, 444–83.

Burdett, H.C. 1893. *Hospitals and asylums of the world*. 3 vols. J. and A. Churchill, London.

Burgdorfer, W. 1976. The epidemiology of the relapsing fevers. pp. 191–200 in Johnson.

Burgdorfer, W. and Anacker, R.L. (Eds.) 1981. *Rickettsiae and rickettsial diseases*. Academic Press, New York. xxii + 650.

Burkitt, D.P. 1973*a*. Some diseases characteristic of modern western civilization. *Br. Med. J. 1*, 274–78.

Burkitt, D.P. 1973*b*. Epidemiology of large bowel

disease: The role of fibre. *Proc. Nutr. Soc. 32*, 145–49.

Burkitt, D. (P.) 1975*a*. Benign and malignant tumours of the large bowel. pp. 117–33 in Burkitt and Trowell.

Burkitt, D. (P.) 1975*b*. Appendicitis. pp. 87–97 in Burkitt and Trowell.

Burkitt, D.P. 1980. Colon cancer: The emergence of a concept. pp. 75–81 in Spiller and Kay.

Burkitt, D. (P.) 1981. Surgical diseases of the large bowel and other related diseases. pp. 33–43 in Trowell and Burkitt, 1981*a*.

Burkitt, D.P. and Trowell, H.C. (Eds.) 1975. *Refined carbohydrate foods and disease: Some implications of dietary fibre*. Academic Press, London-New York. xv + 356.

Burn, A.R. 1953. Hic Breve Vivitur: A study of the expectation of life in the Roman Empire. *Past and Present 4*, 2–31.

Burn, J.H. 1963. *Drugs, medicines and man*. Allen & Unwin, London. 232 pp.

Burnet, F.M. 1952. The pattern of disease in childhood. *Australas. Ann. Med. 1*, 93–108.

Burnet, F.M. and Clark, E. 1942. *Influenza*. Monograph No. 4, Walter & Eliza Hall Institute, Melbourne. vi + 118.

Burnet, (F.) M. and White, D.O. 1972. *Natural history of infectious disease*. 4th edition. Cambridge University Press. x + 278.

Burnett, J. 1966. *Plenty and want: A social history of diet in England from 1815 to the present day*. Thomas Nelson, London. x + 296.

Burton, G.J. 1982. Parasites. pp. 408–18 in Schottenfeld and Fraumeni.

Burton, I., Kates, R.W., and White, G.F. (Eds.) 1978. *The environment as hazard*. Oxford University Press, London. xvi + 240.

Bushnell, O.A. and Brookhyser, C.S. (Eds.) 1965. *Proceedings of the Cholera Research Symposium*. US Dept. Health, Educ., and Welfare, Public Health Service, Washington, DC. xiv + 397.

Busvine, J.R. 1976. *Insects, hygiene and history*. Athlone Press, London. v + 262.

Busvine, J.R. 1980*a*. *Insects and hygiene: The biology and control of insect pests of medical and domestic importance*. 3rd edition. Chapman and Hall, London, viii + 568.

Busvine, J.R. 1980*b*. The evolution and mutual adaptation of insects, micro-organisms and man. pp. 55–68 in Stanley and Joske.

Butler, N.R. and Alberman, E.D. (Eds.) 1969. *Perinatal problems. The second report of the 1958 British Perinatal Mortality Survey*. E. & S. Livingstone, Edinburgh-London. xx + 395.

Butler, N.R., Alberman, E.D. et al. 1969a. The multiple births, pp. 122–40 in Butler and Alberman.

Butler, N.R., Alberman, E.D., et al. 1969b. Clinico-pathological associations of hyaline membranes, intraventricular haemorrhage, massive pulmonary haemorrhage and pulmonary infection. pp. 184–99 in Butler and Alberman.

Butler, N.R., Alberman, E.D., Schutt, W.H., et al. 1969. The congenital malformations. pp. 283–320 in Butler and Alberman.

Butler, T. 1983. *Plague and other Yersinia infections*. Plenum, New York. xii + 220.

Butterworth, A.E. 1984. Cell-mediated damage to helminths. *Adv. Parasitol. 23*, 143–235.

Bytchenko, B. 1966. Geographical distribution of tetanus in the world, 1951–1960. A review of the problem. *WHO Bull. 34*, 71–104.

Cairns, J., Lyon, J.L. and Skolnick, M. (Eds.) 1980. *Cancer incidence in defined populations*. Banbury Rep. No. 4, Cold Spring Harbor Laboratory. Cold Spring Harbor, NY. xi + 458.

Caldwell, J.C. 1977. Demographic aspects of drought: An examination of the African drought of 1970–74. pp. 93–100 in Dalby, Church, and Bezzaz.

Caldwell, J.C. and Okonjo, C. (Eds.) 1968. *The population of tropical Africa*. Longmans, London. xiii + 457.

Campbell, A.M. 1931. *The Black Death and men of learning*. Columbia University Press, New York. xii + 210.

Campbell, G. 1893. *Memoirs of my Indian career*. Macmillan, London. 2 vols. v + 305, vi + 428.

Campbell, H. 1980. Cancer mortality in Europe: Site-specific patterns and trends 1955 to 1974. *World Health Stat. Q. 33*, 241–80.

Campbell, H., Chiang, R., and Hansluwka, H. 1980. Cancer mortality in Europe: Patterns and trends 1955–1974. *World Health Stat. Q. 33*, 152–84.

Campbell, J.M. 1924. *Maternal mortality*. U.K. Ministry of Health, Reports on Public Health and Medical Subjects No. 25, HMSO, London. vi + 116.

Campbell, J.M. 1927. *The protection of motherhood*. U.K. Ministry of Health, Reports on Public Health and Medical Subjects No. 48, HMSO, London. vii + 87.

Campbell, W.C. and Rew, R.S. (Eds.) 1986. *Chemotherapy of parasitic diseases*. Plenum, New York. xxviii + 655.

Canning, J. (Ed.) 1976. *Great disasters—Catastrophes of the twentieth century*. Octopus Books, London. 124 pp.

Cantaloube, P. 1911. *La fièvre de Malte en France*. A. Maloine, Paris. 223 pp.

Cantlie, N. 1974a. *A history of the Army Medical Department*. Vol. I. Churchill-Livingstone, Edinburgh-London. vi + 519.

Cantlie, N. 1974b. *A history of the Army Medical Department*. Vol. II. Churchill-Livingstone, Edinburgh-London. x + 448.

Cantrelle, P. 1968. Mortalité: Facteurs. Pt. 6, pp. 1–65 in *Afrique Noire, Madagascar, Comores: Démographie comparée*. Vol. 2. Institut National de la Statistique et des Etudes Economiques. Service de Coopération. Institut National d'Etudes Démographiques, Paris.

Carefoot, G.L. and Sprott, E.R. 1969. *Famine on the wind: Plant diseases and human history*. Angus and Robertson, London. 222 pp.

Carlson, D.G. 1984. *African fever: A study of British science, technology and politics in West Africa*. Science History Publ., Watson International, Canton, MA. xix + 108.

Carp, R.I., Warner, H.B., and Merz, G.S. 1978. Viral etiology of multiple sclerosis. *Prog. Med. Virol. 24*, 158–77.

Carpenter, K.J. (Ed.) 1981. *Pellagra*. Benchmark Papers in Biochemistry, Vol. 2. Hutchinson Ross, Stroudsburg, PA. xvi + 394.

Carpenter, K.J. 1986. *The history of scurvy and vitamin C*. Cambridge University Press, New York. viii + 288.

Carroll, V. 1975. *Pacific atoll populations*. Assoc. for Social Anthropology in Oceania Monograph No. 3. University Press of Hawaii, Honolulu. xxii + 528.

Carter, C. and MacCarthy, D. 1951. Incidence of mongolism and its diagnosis in newborn. *Br. J. Soc. Med. 5*, 83–90.

Carter, C.O. 1950. Maternal states in relation to congenital malformations. *J. Obstet. Gynaec. Br. Emp. 57*, 897–911.

Carter, C.O. 1976a. Genetics of common congenital malformations in man. *Proc. Roy. Soc. Med. 69* (1), 38–40.

Carter, C.O. 1976b. Genetics of common single malformations. *Br. Med. Bull. 32*, 21–6.

Carter, C.O. 1981. Genetics. pp. 1–22 in Davis and Dobbing.

Carter, H.R. 1931. *Yellow fever: An epidemiological and historical study of its place of origin*. Williams and Wilkins, Baltimore. 308 pp.

Cartwright, F.F. 1967. *The development of modern surgery*. Arthur Barker, London. x + 323.

Cartwright, F.F. (in collab. with M.D. Biddiss)

1972. *Disease and history*. Crowell, New York. viii + 248.

Case, R.A.M. 1956. Cohort analysis of mortality rates as an historical or narrative technique. *Br. J. Prev. Soc. Med. 10*, 159–71.

Casey, K.R., Rom, W.M., and Moatamed, F. 1981. Asbestos-related diseases. pp. 179–202 in Brooks, Lockey, and Harber.

Cassedy, J. 1973. *Mortality in pre-industrial times: The contemporary verdict*. Gregg International, London. 184 pp.

Cassen, R.H. 1978. *India: Population, economy, society*. Macmillan, London. xiii + 419.

Castellani, A. (Ed.) 1985. *Epidemiology and quantitation of environmental risk in humans from radiation and other agents*. NATO Advanced Science Institutes, Series A, Vol. 96. Plenum, New York. x + 584.

Castle, W.B. 1980. The conquest of pernicious anemia. pp. 283–317 in Wintrobe.

Celli, A. 1933. *The history of malaria in the Roman Campagna from ancient times*. Edited and enlarged by A. Celli-Fraentzel and a preface by A. Castellani. John Bale, Sons and Danielsson, London. viii + 226.

Chadwick, E. 1842/1965. *Report on the sanitary condition of the labouring population of Great Britain*. Reprinted 1965, M.W. Flinn (Ed.) Edinburgh University Press, x + 443.

Chain, E. 1980. A short history of the penicillin discovery from Fleming's early observations in 1929 to the present time. pp. 15–29 in Parascandola.

Chalian, W. 1940. An essay on the history of lockjaw. *Bull. Hist. Med. 8*, 171–201.

Chalmers, A.K. 1930. *The health of Glasgow, 1818–1925: An outline*. The Corporation, Glasgow. xviii + 462.

Chalmers, A.K. Brend, W.A., Findlay, L., and Brownlee, J. 1918. *The mortalities of birth, infancy and childhood*. Med. Res. Council, Spec. Rep. Ser. No. 10, HMSO, London. xvi + 84.

Chambers, J.S. 1938. *The conquest of cholera—America's greatest scourge*. Macmillan, New York. xiv + 366.

Chanarin, I. 1969. *The megaloblastic anaemias*. Blackwell, Oxford-Edinburgh. vii + 1000.

Chanarin, I. 1980. The cobalamins (Vitamin B_{12}). pp. 172–246 in Barker and Bender, vol. 1.

Chandler, F.W., Kaplan, W., and Ajello, L. 1980. *A colour atlas and textbook of the histopathology of mycotic diseases*. Wolfe Medical Publ., London. 333 pp.

Chandra, R.K. (Ed.) 1982. *Critical reviews in tropical medicine*. Vol. 1. Plenum, New York. xv + 396.

Chandrasekhar, S. 1959. *Infant mortality in India. 1901–1955*. Allen & Unwin, London. 175 pp.

Chang, A. 1984. Road transportation hazards to children: A world-wide paediatric problem. *Adv. Int. Matern. Child Health 4*, 1–10.

Chase, A. 1982. *Magic shots. A human and scientific account of the long and continuing struggle to eradicate infectious diseases by vaccination*. Morrow, New York. 576 pp.

Chase, H.C. 1967. *International comparison of perinatal and infant mortality: The United States and six west European countries*. National Center for Health Statistics, Ser. 3, No. 6. US Govt Printing Office, Washington, DC. 97 pp.

Chase, H.C. 1969. Registration completeness and international comparisons of health status. *Demography 6*, 425–33.

Chase, H.C. 1972. The position of the United States in international comparisons of health status. *Am. J. Public Health 62*, 581–89.

Chase, H.C. 1977. Time trends in low birth weight in the United States, 1950–1974. pp. 17–37 in Reed and Stanley.

Chaussinand, R. 1959. Le problème de la nature et de la signification de la réaction à la lépromine de Mitsuda. *Ann. Inst. Pasteur 97*, 125–34.

Cheeseman, E.A. 1950. *Epidemics in schools: An analysis of the data collected during the years 1935 to 1939*. Med. Res. Council Spec. Rep. Series, No. 271, HMSO, London. vii + 96.

Chen, L.C. 1973. *Disaster in Bangladesh*. Oxford University Press, London. xxviii + 290.

Chen, L.C. and Scrimshaw, N.S. (Eds.) 1983. *Diarrhea and malnutrition. Interactions, mechanisms and interventions*. Papers from a conference, Bellagio, Italy, 1981. Plenum, New York. xvi + 318.

Chen, Y., Kam-ling, T., et al. 1988. *The great Tangshan earthquake of 1976. An anatomy of disaster*. Pergamon Press, Oxford. 161 pp.

Cheng, T.C. 1973. *General parasitology*. Academic Press, New York. xxv + 965.

Chernin, E. (Ed.) 1977. Milestones in the history of tropical medicine and hygiene. *Am. J. Trop. Med. Hyg. 26*, 1053–1104.

Cherry, S. 1972. The role of a provincial hospital: The Norfolk and Norwich Hospital, 1771–1880. *Popul. Studies 26*, 291–306.

Cherry, S. 1980. The hospitals and population growth: The voluntary general hospitals, mortality and local populations in the English provinces in the eighteenth and nineteenth centuries. Parts I & II. *Popul. Studies 34*, 59–75 and 251–65.

Chesnais, J.-C. 1976a. *Les morts violentes en France depuis 1826: Comparaisons internationales*. Travaux et Documents No. 75, Institut National d'Etudes Démographiques, Paris. Vol. 1, 346 pp.

Chesnais, J.-C. 1976*b*. Le suicide dans les prisons. *Population 31*, 73–85.

Chesnais, J.-C. and Vallin, J. 1977. Evolution récente de la mortalité et de la morbidité dues aux accidents de la route (1968–1977). *Population 32*, 1239–65.

Christensen, P.E., Schmidt, H., Jenson, O., Bang, H.O., Anderson, V., and Jordal, B. 1953. An epidemic of measles in Southern Greenland, 1951. Measles in virgin soil. I, II, III, and IV. *Acta Med. Scand. 144*, 126–42, 313–22, 430–49, 450–54.

Christie, A.B. 1980. *Infectious diseases: Epidemiology and clinical practice*. 3rd edition. Churchill-Livingstone, Edinburgh. xv + 1033.

Christophers, S.R. 1939. Malaria in war. *Trans. Roy. Soc. Trop. Med. Hyg. 33*, 277–92.

Churchill, F. 1850. *Essays on the puerperal fever and other diseases peculiar to women: Selected from the writings of British authors previous to the close of the eighteenth century*. By request of the Sydenham Society. Lea and Blanchard, Philadelphia. viii + 532.

Ciba Foundation. 1980. *Perinatal infections*. Symposium No. 77 (N.S.). Excerpta Medica, Amsterdam. xi + 292.

Clairin, R. 1968. The assessment of infant and child mortality from the data available in Africa. pp. 199–213 in Caldwell and Okonjo.

Clark, A.J. 1940/1975. *Applied pharmacology*. J. and A. Churchill, London. x + 672. 11th edition, A. Wilson, H.O. Schild, and W. Modell (Eds.). Churchill-Livingstone, 1975.

Clark, P.F. 1961. *Pioneer microbiologists of America*. University of Wisconsin Press, Madison. 369 pp.

Clarke, E. (Ed.) 1971. *Modern Methods in the history of medicine*. Athlone Press, University of London. xiv + 389.

Clarkson, L. 1975. *Death, disease and famine in pre-industrial England*. Gill and Macmillan, Dublin. vii + 188.

Clarkson, L.A. 1981. Irish population revisited, 1687–1821. pp. 13–35 in Goldstrom and Clarkson.

Cleave, T.L. 1973. Diseases of western civilization. *Br. Med. J. 1*, 678–79.

Cleave, T.L. 1974. *The saccharine disease: Conditions caused by the taking of refined carbohydrates such as sugar and white flour*. John Wright, Bristol. xii + 200.

Cleave, T.L. and Campbell, G.D. 1966. *Diabetes, coronary thrombosis and saccharine diseases*. John Wright, Bristol. xi + 146.

Clegg, A.G. and Clegg, P.C. 1973. *Man against disease*. Heinemann, London. vii + 381.

Clegg, E.J. and Garlick, J.P. (Eds.) 1980. *Disease and urbanization*. Symp. Soc. Studies Hum. Biol., No. 20. Taylor and Francis, London. ix + 171.

Cleland, J. 1823. *Statistical tables relating to the City of Glasgow with other matters therewith connected*. J. Lumsden, Glasgow. v + 208.

Cleland, J.B. 1928. Disease among the Australian aborigines. Part IV. Protozoal and helminthic diseases. *J. Trop. Med. Hyg. 31*, 157–60.

Clements, F.W. 1955. Accidental injuries in pre-school children. Part 1: A general survey; Part 2: Traffic accidents; Part 3: Burns and scalds. *Med. J. Austral. 1*, 348–52, 388–91, 421–24.

Clemmesen, J. 1965. *Statistical studies in malignant neoplasms*. Munksgaard, Copenhagen. 3 vols.

Clendinning, J. 1844. Report on the experience of the St. Marylebone Infirmary. . . .*J. Stat. Soc. (London) 7*, 292–310.

Cliff, A.D.,Haggett, P., Ord, J.K., and Versey, G.R. 1981. *Spatial diffusion: An historical geography of epidemic disease in an island community*. Cambridge University Press. xi + 238.

Cloudsley-Thompson, J.L. 1976. *Insects and history*. Weidenfeld & Nicolson, London. ix + 242.

Clyde, D.F. 1980. Tanzania. pp. 98–177 in Sabben-Clare, Bradley, and Kirkwood.

Coale, A.J. 1956. The effect of declines in mortality on age distribution. pp. 125–32 in *Trends and Differentials in Mortality: Papers presented at the 1955 Annual Conf. of the Milbank Memorial Fund*. Milbank Memorial Fund, New York. 165 pp.

Coale, A.J. 1963. Estimates of various demographic measures through the quasi-stable age distribution. pp. 175–93 in *Emerging Techniques in Population Research: Proceedings of a round table at the 1962 Annual Conf. of the Milbank Memorial Fund*. Milbank Memorial Fund, New York. 307 pp.

Coale, A.J. 1972. *The growth and structure of human populations: A mathematical investigation*. Princeton University Press, Princeton, NJ. xvii + 227.

Coale, A.J. and Demeny, P. 1983. *Regional model life tables and stable populations*. 2nd edition. Academic Press, New York. 504 pp.

Coatney, G.R. 1963. The story of chloroquine. *Am. J. Trop. Med. Hyg. 12*, 121–28.

Coatney, G.R., Collins, W.E., Warren, McW., and Contacos, P.G. 1971. *The primate malarias*. US Govt Printing Office, Washington, DC. xi + 366.

Cockburn, T.A. 1961*a*. The origin of the treponematoses. *WHO Bull. 24*, 221–28.

Cockburn. T.A. 1961*b*. Eradication of infectious diseases. *Science* 133, 1050–58.

Cockburn, (T.) A. 1963. *The evolution and eradication of infectious diseases*. Johns Hopkins, Baltimore. xiii + 255.

Cockburn, (T.) A. 1977. Where did our infectious diseases come from? The evolution of infectious disease. (With discussion.) pp. 103–13 in Elliott and Whelan.

Cockburn, (T.) A. and Cockburn, E. (Eds.) 1980. *Mummies, disease and ancient cultures*. Cambridge University Press, London-New York-Sydney. x + 340.

Coghlan, T.A. 1898. Deaths in childbirth in New South Wales. (With discussion.) *J. Roy. Stat. Soc. 61*, 518–33.

Coghlan, T.A. 1899. Reply to criticism on paper "Deaths in childbirth in New South Wales." *J. Roy. Stat. Soc. 62*, 157–59.

Coghlan, T.A. 1900 *Childbirth in New South Wales, a study in statistics*. Govt Printer, N.S.W. 67 pp.

Cohen, M.L. and Tauxe, R.V. 1986. Drug-resistant *Salmonella* in the United States: An epidemiologic perspective. *Science 234*, 964–69.

Cohen, M.N. 1977. *The food crisis in prehistory*. Yale University Press, New Haven, CT. x + 342.

Collier, L.H. and Ridgway, G.L. 1984. Chlamydial diseases. pp. 558–73 in Topley and Wilson, 1984, vol. 3.

Collier, R.J. 1975. Diphtheria toxin: Mode of action and structure. *Bacteriol. Rev. 39*, 54–85.

Collins, C.H. 1983. *Laboratory acquired infections: History, incidence, causes and prevention*. Butterworth, London. ix + 277.

Collins, C.H., Grange, J.M., Noble, W.C., and Yates, M.D. 1984 *Mycobacterium marinum* infections in man. *J. Hyg. Camb. 94*, 135–49.

Collis, E.L. and Greenwood, M. 1921. *The health of the industrial worker, with a chapter by A.J. Collis on "reclamation of the disabled."* J. and A. Churchill, London. xix + 450.

Comfort, A. 1956. *The biology of senescence*. Routledge and Kegan Paul, London. xvi + 365.

Committee Abstract. 1933. Maternal mortality. Abstract of the Report on Maternal Mortality in New York City 1930, 1931, 1932, 1933, *J. Am. Stat. Assoc. 101*, 1826–28.

Committee to Study the Prevention of Low Birthweight, Institute of Medicine. 1985. *Preventing low birthweight*. National Academy Press, Washington, DC. xii + 284.

Committee upon Anaerobic Bacteria and Infections. 1919. *Report on the anaerobic infections of wounds and the bacteriological and serological problems arising therefrom*. Med. Res. Council Spec. Rep. Series, No. 39, HMSO, London. 182 pp.

Compton, P.A. 1985. Rising mortality in Hungary. *Popul. Studies 39*, 71–86.

Comstock, G.W. 1975. Frost revisited: The modern epidemiology of tuberculosis. Third Wade Hampton Frost Lecture. *Am. J. Epidemiol. 101*, 363–82.

Cone, T.E. 1979. *History of American pediatrics*. Little, Brown & Co., Boston. xiv + 278.

Conley, C.L. 1980. Sickle-cell anemia—The first molecular disease. pp. 319–71 in Wintrobe.

Conn, S. (Gen. Ed.) 1965 onward. *United States Army in World War II*. Multivolume series. Office of the Chief of Military History, Dept of the Army, Washington, DC.

Connell, K.H. 1950. *The population of Ireland, 1750–1845*. Oxford University Press, London. xi + 293.

Convit, J.E. and Pinardi, M.E. 1974. Cutaneous leishmaniasis: The clinical and immunopathological spectrum in South America. With discussion. pp. 159–69 in Elliott, O'Connor, and Wolstenholme.

Conybeare, J. 1948. The effects on mortality of recent advances in treatment. With discussion. *J. Inst. Actuar. 74*, 57–81.

Cook, E. 1913. *Life of Florence Nightingale*. Macmillan, London. 2 vols.

Cook, S.F. 1946. The incidence and significance of disease among the Aztecs and related tribes. *Hispanic Am. Hist. Rev. 36*, 320–35.

Cook, S.F. 1947. Survivorship in aboriginal population. *Hum. Biol. 19*, 83–89.

Cook, S.F. 1976. *The population of the Californian Indians: 1769–1970*. University of California Press, Berkeley. xvii + 222.

Cook, S.F. and Borah, W. 1974. *Essays in population history: Mexico and the Caribbean*. Vol. 2. University of California Press, Berkeley-Los Angeles. xv + 472.

Cooper, D.B. 1965. *Epidemic disease in Mexico City, 1761–1813. An administrative, social and medical study*. Latin American Monographs, University of Texas Press, Austin, TX. xi + 236.

Cooper, J.A.D. 1976. Undergraduate medical education. pp. 251–312 in Bowers and Purcell.

Cooper, R., Stamler, J., Dyer, A., and Garside, D. 1978. The decline in mortality from coronary heart disease, USA 1968–1975. *J. Chron. Dis. 31*, 709–20.

Cope, V.Z. (Ed.) 1952. *Medicine and pathology*.

History of the Second World War: United Kingdom Medical Series. A.S. MacNalty (Ed.-in-Chief). HMSO, London. xxix + 565.

Cope, (V.) Z. (Ed.) 1953. *Surgery. History of the Second World War: United Kingdom Medical Series.* A.S. MacNalty (Ed. in Chief). HMSO, London. xix + 772.

Cope, (V.) Z. 1958. The treatment of wounds through the ages. *Med. Hist. 2*, 163–74.

Copeman, W.S.C. 1960. *Doctors and disease in Tudor times.* Dawson, London. xiv + 186.

Corfield, W.H. 1870. Introductory lecture to a course of lectures on hygiene and public health. (Delivered at University College, London, May 10, 1870.) *Br. Med. J. 1*, 617–19, 645–46.

Corfield, W.H. 1871. *The treatment and utilisation of sewage.* 2nd edition. Macmillan, London-New York. xxvi + 343.

Corney, B.G. 1883–1884. The behaviour of certain epidemic diseases in natives of Polynesia, with especial reference to the Fiji Islands. *Trans. Epidemiol. Soc. London 3*, 76–95.

Correa, P. 1977. Hodgkin's disease: International mortality patterns and time trends. *World Health Stat. Rep. 30*, 146–54.

Correa, P. 1982. Morphology and natural history of precursor lesions. pp. 90–115 in Schottenfeld and Fraumeni.

Correa, P. and Haenszel, W. 1975. Colon and rectum. Comparative international incidence and mortality. pp. 386–403 in Schottenfeld.

Corsini, C.A. 1984. L'enfant trouvé: Note de démographie différentielle. *Ann. Démog. Hist.* 1983, 95–102.

Cotton, A.T. 1976. *The Madras famine: With appendix containing a letter from Miss Florence Nightingale, and other papers.* First printed 1877, Simpkin, Marshall & Co., London. 35 pp. Reprinted 1976 as *Famine in India*, together with *Report of the Indian Famine Commission*, 1901, Govt Printer, Calcutta. 133 pp. World Food Supply Series, Arno Press, New York.

Coulter, J.L.S. (Ed.) 1954/1956. *The Royal Navy Medical Service. History of the Second World War, UK Medical Series.* A.S. MacNalty (Ed.-in-Chief). HMSO, London. 2 vols. xvi + 512; xvii + 543.

Counsell, J.N. and Hornig, D.H. (Eds.) 1981. *Vitamin C: Ascorbic acid.* Applied Science Publ., London. xiii + 383.

Court Brown, W.M. and Doll, R. 1965. Mortality from cancer and other causes after radiotherapy for ankylosing spondylitis. *Br. Med. J. 2*, 1327–32.

Cousens, S.H. 1960. Regional death rates in Ireland during the Great Famine. *Popul. Studies 14*, 55–74.

Cousens, S.H. 1963. The regional variation in mortality during the Great Irish Famine. *Proc. Roy. Irish Acad. 63*, C (3), 127–49.

Cousens, S.H. 1964–1965. The regional variations in population changes in Ireland, 1861–1881. *Econ. Hist. Rev. 17*, 301–21.

Covell, G. 1949. Malaria incidence in the Far East. pp. 810–19 in Boyd.

Cowan, R. 1838. *Vital statistics of Glasgow. 1. Statistics of fever and smallpox prior to 1837. 2. Statistics of fever for 1837. 3. Remarks suggested by the mortality bills, etc.* David Robertson, Glasgow. (A. & C. Black, Edinburgh.) 54 pp.

Cowan, R. 1840. Vital statistics of Glasgow, illustrating the sanatory condition of the population. *J. Stat. Soc. (London) 3*, 257–92.

Craddock, C.G. 1980. Defenses of the body: The initiators of defense, the ready reserves, and the scavengers. pp. 417–54 in Wintrobe.

Craig, J.P. 1980. A survey of the enterotoxic enteropathies. pp. 15–25 in Ouchterloney and Holmgren.

Cramer, D.W. 1982. Uterine cervix. pp. 881–900 in Schottenfeld and Fraumeni.

Cramér, H. and Wold, H. 1935. Mortality variations in Sweden: A study in graduation and forecasting. *Skand. Aktuarietidskr. 18*, 161–241. See also *Nord. Stat. J.* (1934), 64–83.

Crawford, E.M. 1981. Indian meal and pellagra in nineteenth-century Ireland. pp. 113–33 in Goldstrom and Clarkson.

Creighton, C. 1965. *A history of epidemics in Britain; with additional material by D.E.C. Eversley (and others).* 2nd edition. Cass. London. Barnes & Noble, New York. 2 vols. xii + 706, xii + 883. (First published 1891/1894 as "A history of epidemics in Britain from A.D. 664 to the extinction of plague," Cambridge University Press.)

Crellin, J. 1980. Antibiosis in the nineteenth century. pp. 5–13 in Parascandola.

Croll, N.A. and Cross, J.H. (Eds.) 1983. *Human ecology and infectious diseases.* Academic Press, New York. xvi + 364.

Cronjé, G. 1984. Tuberculosis and mortality decline in England and Wales, 1851–1910. pp. 79–101 in Woods and Woodward.

Crosby, A.W. Jr 1969. The early history of syphilis: A reappraisal. *Am. Anthropologist 71*, 218–27.

Crosby, A.W. Jr 1972. *The Columbian exchange. Biological and cultural consequences of 1492.* Greenwood Press, Westport, CT. xv + 268.

Crosby, A.W. Jr 1976. *Epidemic and peace, 1918.* Greenwood Press, Westport, CT -London. vi + 337.

Crosby, W.H. 1980. The spleen. pp. 97–138 in Wintrobe.

Crow, J.F. and Denniston, C. 1985. Mutation in human populations. *Adv. Hum. Genet. 14*, 59–123.

Cukor, G. and Blacklow, N.R. 1984. Human viral gastroenteritis. *Microbiol. Rev. 48*, 157–79.

Cullen, L.M. 1981. Population growth and diet, 1600–1850. pp. 89–112 in Goldstrom and Clarkson.

Cullen, W. 1769, *Synopsis nosologiae methodicae, etc.* Edinburgh. iv + 303 + xii.

Cummins, S.L. 1922–1924a. Tetanus in its statistical aspects. pp. 164–87 in *Official History, Medical Services: Pathology* volume.

Cummins, S.L. 1922–1924b. Tuberculosis. pp. 467–84 in *Official History, Medical Services: Pathology* volume.

Cummins, S.L. 1950. *Tuberculosis in history: From the 17th century to our own times.* Baillière, Tindall & Cox, London. xiv + 205.

Cumpston, J.H.L. 1919. *Influenza and maritime quarantine in Australia.* Serv. Publ. No. 18, Quarantine Service, Commonwealth of Australia, Melbourne. v + 176.

Cumpston, J.H.L. 1927. *The history of diphtheria, scarlet fever, measles and whooping cough in Australia.* Serv. Publ. No. 37, Dept Health, Commonwealth of Australia. Govt Printer, Canberra. x + 617.

Cumpston, J.H.L. and McCallum, F. 1927. *The history of the intestinal infections (and typhus fever) in Australia, 1788–1923.* Serv. Publ. No. 36, Dept Health, Commonwealth of Australia. Govt Printer, Melbourne. 738 pp.

Cuny, F.C. 1981. Issues in the provision of food aid following disasters. pp. 89–94 in Robson.

Curran, J.W., Morgan, W.M., Hardy, A.M., Jaffe, H.W., Darrow, W.W., and Dowdle, W.R. 1985. The epidemiology of AIDS: Current status and future prospects. *Science 229*, 1352–57.

Curschmann, F. 1900. *Hungersnöte im Mittelalter. Ein Beitrag zur deutschen Wirtschaftsgeschichte des 8. bis 13. Jahrhunderts.* B.G. Teubner, Leipzig. Reprinted 1970, Scientia Verlag, Aalen.

Cushing, H. 1940. *The life of Sir William Osler.* Oxford University Press, London. xviii + 1417.

Cutler, S.J., Ederer, F., Gordon, T., Crittenden, M., and Haenszel, W. 1961. *End results and mortality trends in cancer.* Natl. Cancer Instit. Mon. No. 6, US Dept Health, Educ., & Welfare. US Govt Printing Office, Washington, DC. 350 pp.

Dacie, J.V. 1980. The life span of the red blood cell and circumstances of its premature death. pp. 211–55 in Wintrobe.

Dahlgren, K.G. 1945. *On suicide and attempted suicide. A psychiatrical and statistical investigation.* P. Lindstedt, Lund. viii + 360.

Dalby, D., Church, R.J.H. and Bezzaz, F. (Eds.) 1977. *Drought in Africa.* Internatl. African Inst., London. viii + 200.

Dalrymple, D. 1964. The Soviet famine of 1932–34. *Soviet Studies XV*, 250–84.

Dalrymple-Champeneys, W. 1960. *Brucella infection and undulant fever in man.* Oxford University Press, London. xii + 196.

d'Alton, E.A. 1910. *History of Ireland from the earliest times to the present day.* Gresham, London. 6 vols.

Dando, W.A. 1980. *The geography of famine.* Scripta Series in Geography. Edward Arnold, London. xii + 209.

Dando, W.A. 1981. Man-made famines: Some geographical insights from an exploratory study of a millenium of Russian famines. pp. 139–54 in Robson.

Daniel, T.M. and Janicki, B.W. 1978. Mycobacterial antigens: A review of their isolation, chemistry and immunological properties. *Microbiol. Rev. 42*, 84–113.

Daniels, M., Ridehalgh, F., Springett, V.H., and Hall, I.M. 1948. *Tuberculosis in young adults.* Report of the Prophit Tuberculosis Survey, 1935–1944, Royal College of Physicians. H.K. Lewis, London. xvi + 227.

Daniels, R. 1981. *Concentration camps in North America: Japanese in the United States and Canada during World War II.* Holt, Rinehard & Winston, New York. 200 pp.

Darby, W.J., Ghalioungui, P., and Grivetti, L. 1977. *Food: the gift of Osiris.* Academic Press, London. 2 vols. xxxiii + 452 + 52; xxxiii 453–877 + 42.

Daric, J. 1949. Mortalité, profession et situation sociale. *Population 4*, 671–94. See also J. Daric, *Mortality, occupation and socio-economic status.* Spec. Rep. *33*, No. 10 (1951). US National Office of Vital Statistics. US Govt Printing Office, Washington, DC.

Daric, J. 1956. L'évolution de la mortalité par suicide en France et à l'étranger. *Population 11*, 673–700.

Das, N.C. 1974. Age pattern of mortality in India. *Sankhyā 36B*, 427–56.

Das Gupta, A. 1972. Study of the historical demography of India. pp. 419–35 in Glass and Revelle.

Datta, N. (Ed.) 1984. Antibiotic resistance in bacteria. *Br. Med. Bull. 40*, 1–111.

Dauer, C.C., Korns, R.F., and Schuman, L.M. 1968. *Infectious diseases*. Harvard University Press, Cambridge, MA. xviii + 262.

Dauer, C.C. and Serfling, R.E. 1961. Mortality from influenza. *Am. Rev. Respir. Dis. 83* (2), 15–28.

Daumas, M. (Ed.) 1962. *A history of technology and invention. Vol. I. The origins of technological civilization*. Presses Universitaires de France. (English transl. by E.B. Hennessy, 1969. Crown, New York. viii + 596.)

Davenport, F.M. 1982. Influenza viruses. pp. 373–96 in Evans.

Davidson, S., Passmore, R., Brock, J.F., and Truswell, A.S. (Eds.) 1979. *Human nutrition and dietetics*. 7th edition. Churchill-Livingstone, Edinburgh. xi + 641.

Davies, D.M. (Ed.) 1981. *Textbook of adverse drug reactions*. Oxford University Press, Oxford-New York-Toronto. xvi + 693.

Davis, A. 1983. The importance of parasitic diseases. pp. 62–74 in Warren and Bowers.

Davis, D.H.S. 1953. Plague in Africa from 1935 to 1949. *WHO Bull. 9*, 665–700.

Davis, J.A. and Dobbing, J. (Eds.) 1981. *Scientific foundations of paediatrics*. 2nd edition. Heinemann, London. xvi + 1095.

Dawber, T.R. 1980. *The Framingham Study. The epidemiology of atherosclerotic disease*. Harvard University Press, Cambridge, MA. xii + 258.

Day, N.E. and Muñoz, N. 1982. Esophagus, pp. 596–623 in Schottenfeld and Fraumeni.

De, S.N. 1961. *Cholera: Its pathology and pathogenesis*. Oliver and Boyd, Edinburgh-London. xi + 141.

Dean, G. 1961. The Turkish epidemic of prophyria. *S. Afr. Med. J. 35*, 509–11.

Deaux, G. 1969. *The Black Death 1347*. Hamish Hamilton, London. ix + 229.

Debus, A.G. (Ed.) 1974. *Medicine in seventeenth century England*. University of California Press, Berkeley. xiii + 485.

Decouflé, P. 1982. Occupation. pp. 318–35 in Schottenfeld and Fraumeni.

Deegan, J.K., Culp, J.E., and Beck, F. 1942. Epidemiology of tuberculosis in a mental hospital. *Am. J. Public Health 32*, 345–51.

Deevey, E.J. 1971. The human population. pp. 49–55 in Ehrlich, Holdren, and Holm.

Delaunay, A. 1971. Charles Edouard Chamberland. In *Dict. Sci. Biog. III*, 188–89.

Delbrueck, H. 1975. *History of the art of war within the framework of political history. I. Antiquity. II. The Germans. III. The Middle Ages*. Transl. from the German by W.J. Renfroe, Jr. Contributions in Military History, Nos. 9, 20, 26. Greenwood Press, Westport, CT. 3 vols.

Demography (Australia) 1907–1971. Nos. 1–87. Commonwealth Bureau of Census and Statistics (later Australian Bureau of Statistics), Canberra.

Denevan, W.M. (Ed.) 1976. *The native population of the Americas in 1492*. University of Wisconsin Press, Madison. xxii + 354.

Deniel, R. and Henry, L. 1965. La population d'un village du Nord de la France, Sainghin-en-Mélantois, de 1665 à 1851. *Population 20*, 563–602.

Dennie, C.C. 1962. *A history of syphilis*. American Lecture Ser. 491. C.C. Thomas, Springfield, IL. x + 137.

Denniston, C. 1982. Low level radiation and genetic risk estimation in man. *Annu. Rev. Genet. 16*, 329–55.

Département de Démographie, Université Catholique de Louvain. 1979. *La mortalité des enfants dans le tiers-monde, orientations et méthodes de recherches*. Ordina, Liège. 226 pp.

Deprez, P. 1969. The demographic development of Flanders in the eighteenth century. pp. 608–30 in Glass and Eversley.

Derrick, V.P.A. 1927. Observations on (1) errors in age in the population statistics of England and Wales, and (2) the changes in mortality indicated by the national records. (With discussion.) *J. Inst. Actuar. 58*, 117–59.

Desai, H.I. and Chandra, R.K. 1982. Giardiasis. *Crit. Rev. Trop. Med. 1*, 109–41. See Chandra, 1982.

Desaive, J.-P., Goubert, J.-P., Le Roy Ladurie, E., Meyer, J., Muller, O., and Peter, J.-P. 1972. *Médecins, climat et épidémies à la fin du XVIIIe siècle*. Mouton, Paris. 254 pp.

Detels, R., Visscher, B.R., Haile, R.W., Malmgren, R.M., Dudley, J.P., and Coulson, A.H. 1978. Multiple sclerosis and age at migration. *Am. J. Epidemiol. 108*, 386–93.

Dharmendra (Ed.) 1985. *Leprosy*. Vol. 2. Samant and Co., Bombay, xvi + 735–1565.

Diamond, E.L., Schmerler, H., and Lilienfeld, A.M. 1973. Relationship of intrauterine radiation to subsequent mortality and the development of leukemia in children. *Am. J. Epidemiol. 97*, 283–313.

Diamond, L.K. 1980a. A history of blood transfusion. pp. 659–88 in Wintrobe.

Diamond, L.K. 1980b. The story of our blood

groups. pp. 691–717 in Wintrobe.

Dickinson, F.G. and Martin, L.W. 1956. Physician mortality, 1949–1951. (Reprinted with additions.) *J. Am. Med. Assoc. 162*, 1462–68.

Dickinson, H.W. 1954. *Water supply of Greater London*. (Memorial volume.) Newcomen Society, London. xvi + 151.

Diehl, H. and Mannerberg, D. 1981. Hypertension, hyperlipidaemia, angina and coronary heart disease. pp. 392–410 in Trowell and Burkitt, 1981*a*.

Diepgen, L. 1938. Statistisches über Fürstenehen, 1500–1900. *Arch. Hyg. Bakteriol. 120*, 192–94.

Dinkel, R.H. 1985. The seeming paradox of increasing mortality in a highly industrialized nation: The example of the Soviet Union. *Popul. Studies 39*, 87–97.

Dissanaike, S. 1984. Filarial infections. *Rec. Adv. in Trop. Med. 1*, 115–52. See Gilles, 1984.

Dixon, C.W. 1962. *Smallpox*. J. and A. Churchill, London. viii + 512.

Dixon, J.M.S. 1984. Diphtheria in North America. *J. Hyg. Camb. 93*, 419–32.

Dobbing, J. (Ed.) 1985. *Maternal nutrition and lactational infertility*. Nestlé Nutrition Workshop Series, vol. 9. Raven, New York. xx + 149.

Dodd, R.Y. and Barker, L.F. (Eds.) 1985. *Infection, immunity and blood transfusion*. Prog. in clin. and biol. Res., vol. 182. Alan R. Liss, New York. xxvi + 464.

Dodson, P. and Humphreys, D. 1981. Hypertension and angina. pp. 411–20 in Trowell and Burkitt, 1981*a*.

Doege, T.C. 1965. Tuberculosis mortality in the United States, 1900 to 1960. *J. Am. Med. Assoc. 192*, 1045–48.

Dolin, R. 1985. Antiviral chemotherapy and chemoprophylaxis. *Science 227*, 1296–1303.

Doll, R. 1952. The causes of death among gas-workers with special reference to cancer of the lung. *Br. J. Indust. Med. 9*, 180–85.

Doll, R. 1958. Cancer of the lung and nose in nickel workers. *Br. J. Indust. Med. 15*, 217–23.

Doll, R. 1966. Occupational lung cancer: A review. pp. 439–52 in Lilienfeld and Gifford.

Doll, R. 1971. Unwanted effects of drugs. *Br. Med. Bull. 27*, 25–31.

Doll, R. 1979. The pattern of disease in the post-infection era: National trends. *Proc. Roy. Soc. London B205*, 47–61. (Reprinted in Doll and McLean.)

Doll, R. (Ed.) 1984. The geography of disease. *Br. Med. Bull. 40*, 309–408.

Doll, R. and Armstrong, B. 1981. Cancer. pp. 93–110 in Trowell and Burkitt, 1981*a*.

Doll, R. and Hill, A.B. 1950. Smoking and carcinoma of the lung. *Br. Med. J. 2*, 739–48.

Doll, R. and Hill, A.B. 1952. Study of the aetiology of cancer of the lung. *Br. Med. J. 2*, 1271–86.

Doll, R. and Hill, A.B. 1954. The mortality of doctors in relation to their smoking habits. *Br. Med. J. 1*, 1451–55.

Doll, R. and Hill, A.B. 1956. Lung cancer and other causes of death in relation to smoking. *Br. Med. J. 2*, 1071–81.

Doll, R. and Hill, A.B. 1964. Mortality in relation to smoking: Ten years' observations of British doctors. *Br. Med. J. 1*, 1399–1410, 1460–67.

Doll, (W.)R. (D.) and McLean, A.E.M. (Eds.) 1979. *Longterm hazards from environmental chemicals*. Royal Society. London. vi + 197.

Doll, R., Muir, C., Waterhouse, J., Correa, P., and Powell, J. (Eds.) 1970. *Cancer incidence in five continents*. IARC Scientific Publ., Geneva. 3 vols.

Doll, R. and Peto, R. 1981. Quantitative estimates of avoidable risks of cancer in America to-day. *J. Natl. Cancer Inst. 66*, 1191–308.

Dolman, C.E. 1970. William Budd. In *Dict. Sci. Biog. II*, 574–76.

Donald, K.W. 1955. Drowning. *Br. Med. J. 2*, 155–60.

Donovan, J.W. 1969*a*. *Bibliography of the epidemiology of New Zealand and its island dependencies*. National Health Statistics Centre, Dept Health, Wellington, N.Z. 94 pp.

Donovan, J.W. 1969*b*. A study in New Zealand mortality: 6. Epidemic diseases. *N.Z. Med. J. 70*, 406–13.

Donovan, J.W. 1970*a*. Measles in Australia and New Zealand, 1834–1835. *Med. J. Austral. 1*, 5–10.

Donovan, J.W. 1970*b*. Cancer mortality in New Zealand: 3. Breast and genital organs. *N.Z. Med. J. 72*, 318–22.

Donovan, J.W. 1970*c*. A study in New Zealand mortality: 7. Infectious diseases (concluded). *N.Z. Med. J. 71*, 143–47.

Doolittle, I.G. 1975. The effects of plague on a provincial town in the sixteenth and seventeenth centuries. *Med. Hist. 19*, 333–41.

Dorn, H.F. 1959. Mortality. pp. 437–71 in Hauser and Duncan.

Dorn, H.F. 1966. Mortality. pp. 23–54 in Lilienfeld and Gifford.

Douglas, C.A. 1966. *Infant and perinatal mortality in Scotland*. US Public Health Serv. Publ. No. 1000, Ser. 3, No. 5. US Govt Printing Office, Washington, DC. 44 pp.

Douglas, R.G. Jr 1975. Influenza in man. pp. 395–

447 in Kilbourne.

Doumenge, J.P. and Mott, K.E. 1984. The global distribution of schistosomiasis: CEGET/WHO atlas. *World Health Stat. Q. 37*, 186–99.

Dowdle, W. and LaPatra, J. 1983. *Informed consent. Influenza facts and myths*. Nelson-Hall, Chicago. x + 136.

Dowling, H.F. 1970. *Medicines for man: The development, regulation, and use of prescription drugs*. Alfred A. Knopf, New York. xiv + 347 + xii.

Downie, A.W. 1965, Poxvirus group. pp. 932–67 in Horsfall and Tamm.

Doyle, P.A. (Ed.) 1962. *Readings in pharmacy*. Interscience Publ., New York. xiv + 429.

Drackett, P. (Compiler) 1977. *The book of great disasters*. Purnell & Sons, Bristol-London. 124 pp.

Drake, M. 1965. The growth of population in Norway, 1735–1855. *Scand. Econ. Hist. Rev. 13*, 97–142.

Drake, M. 1969. *Population and society in Norway, 1735–1865*. Cambridge University Press. xx + 256.

Drew, W.R.M. 1965. The challenge of the rickettsial diseases. *J. Roy. Army Med. Corps 111*, 95–105.

Drummond, J.C. and Wilbraham, A. 1957. *The Englishman's food: A history of five centuries of English diet*. (New edition revised by D. Hollingsworth.) Jonathan Cape, London. 482 pp.

Dublin, L.I. 1948. *Health progress, 1936 to 1945*. (Supplement to Dublin and Lotka, 1937.) Metropolitan Life Insurance Co., New York. vii + 147.

Dublin, L.I. 1963. *Suicide: A sociological and statistical study*. Ronald Press, New York. viii + 240.

Dublin, L.I. and Lotka, A.J. 1934. The history of longevity in the United States. *Hum. Biol. 6*, 43–86.

Dublin, L.I. and Lotka, A.J. 1937. *Twenty-five years of health progress: A study of the mortality experience amongst the industrial policy holders of the Metropolitan Life Insurance Company, 1911–1935*. Metropolitan Life Ins. Co., New York. xi + 611.

Dublin, L.I., Lotka, A.J., and Spiegelman, M. 1949. *Length of life*. 2nd edition. Ronald Press, New York. xxv + 379.

Dublin, L.I. and Spiegelman, M. 1947. The longevity and mortality of American physicians. *J. Am. Med. Assoc. 134*, 1211–15.

Dublin, M. 1936. Maternal mortality and the decline of the birth rate. *Ann Am. Acad. Polit. Soc. Sci. 188*, 107–16.

Dubos, R.J. 1949. Tuberculosis. *Sci. Am. 181*, 30–

41.

Dubos, R.J. 1954. The gold-headed cane in the laboratory. *Public Health Rep. (Wash.) 69*, 365–71.

Dubos, R.J. (Ed.) 1958. *Bacterial and mycotic infections of man*. (Including: The evolution and the ecology of microbial diseases, pp. 14–27, by Dubos.) 3rd edition. Pitman, London. xii + 820.

Dubos, R.(J.) 1960. *Mirage of health: Utopias, progress and biological change*. Allen & Unwin, London. 221 pp.

Dubos, R.(J.) 1961. *The dreams of reason: Science and Utopias*. Columbia University Press, New York-London. xiii + 167.

Dubos, R.J. 1963. *The cultural roots and the social fruits of science*. University of Oregon Press, Eugene, OR. 38 pp.

Dubos, R.J. 1965. *Man adapting*. Yale University Press, New Haven, CT. xxii + 527.

Dubos, R.(J.) 1966. *Man and his environment. Biomedical knowledge and social action*. Scientific Publ. No. 131, Pan-American Health Org., New York. 18 pp.

Dubos, R.J. 1968. *Man, medicine and environment*. Praeger, New York. v + 125.

Dubos, R.(J.) 1970*a*. The biology of civilisation with emphasis on perinatal influences. pp. 219–29 in Boyden.

Dubos, R.(J.) 1970*b*. *Reason awake: Science for man*. Columbia University Press, New York. xix + 280.

Dubos, R.(J.) 1972. *A god within*. Scribner, New York. x + 326.

Dubos, R.J. 1973. Humanizing the earth. *Science 179*, 769–72.

Dubos, R.(J.) 1981. *The wooing of earth*. Scribner, New York. xviii + 184.

Dubos, R.(J.) and Dubos, J. 1952. *The white plague: Tuberculosis, man and society*. Little, Brown & Co., Boston. viii + 277.

Dubreuilh, W. 1907. Epithéliomatose d'origine solaire. *Ann. Dermatol. Syphiligr. (Paris) 8*, 387–416.

Dudgeon, J.A. 1976. Infective causes of human malformations. *Br. Med. Bull. 32*, 77–83.

Dudley, S.F. 1931. Lessons on the infectious diseases in the Royal Navy (The Milroy Lecture). *Lancet 1*, 509–17, 570–78.

Duenschede, H.B. 1971. *Tropenmedizinische Forschung bei Bayer*. Arbeiten für die Geschichte der Medizin, Beihefte No. 2. Michael Triltsch, Dusseldorf. 193 pp.

Duerden, B.I. 1984. Infections due to gram-negative nonsporing anaerobic bacilli. pp. 311–26 in Topley and Wilson, 1984, vol. 3.

Duffy, E.A. and Carroll, R.E. 1967. *United States metropolitan mortality, 1959–1961*. US Public Health Serv. Publ. No. 999-AP-39, National Center for Pollution Control. US Govt Printing Office, Washington, DC. xvii + various pag.

Duffy, J. 1951. Smallpox and the Indians in the American colonies. *Bull. Hist. Med. 25*, 324–41.

Duffy, J. 1953. *Epidemics in colonial America*. (Louisiana) State University Press, Baton Rouge, LA. xi + 274.

Duffy, J. 1968. *A history of public health in New York City, 1625–1866*. Russell Sage Foundation, New York. xix + 619.

Duffy, J. 1974. *A history of public health in New York City, 1866–1966*. Russell Sage Foundation, New York. xxi + 690.

Duffy, J. 1976. *The healers. The rise of the medical establishment*. McGraw-Hill, New York. x + 386.

Duggan, A.J. 1970. An historical perspective. pp. xli–lxxxviii in Mulligan.

Duggan, A.J. 1980. Sleeping sickness epidemics. pp. 19–36 in Sabben-Clare, Bradley, and Kirkwood.

Dumas, S. 1923. Losses of life caused by war. Part I—Up to 1913. pp. 1–127 in Westergaard.

Dunant, J.H. 1862/1959. *Un souvenir de Solferino*. 1st edition. 1862, J.-G. Fick, Geneva, 115 pp. Reprinted 1959, Abbaye du Livre, Lausanne, 134 pp.

Duncan, J.M. 1869–1870. The mortality of childbed. *Edinburgh Med. J. 15*, 399–409.

Duncan, J.M. 1871. *Fecundity, fertility, sterility, and allied topics*. 2nd edition. Black, Edinburgh. 498 pp.

Dunn, F.L. 1965. On the antiquity of malaria in the Western Hemisphere. *Hum. Biol. 37*, 385–93.

Dunn, F.L. 1968. Epidemiological factors: Health and disease in hunter-gatherers. pp. 226–28 in Lee and DeVore.

Dupâquier, J. 1977. Les tables de mortalité de Wargentin. *Ann. Démog. Hist.*, Pt. 7, 385–420.

Dupâquier, J. 1978. Réflexion sur la mortalité du passé: Mesure de la mortalité des adultes d'après les fiches de famille. *Ann. Démog. Hist.*, Pt. 1, 31–48.

Dwyer, T. and Hetzel, B.S. 1980. A comparison of trends of coronary heart disease mortality in Australia, USA and England and Wales with reference to three major risk factors—hypertension, cigarette smoking and diet. *Int. J. Epidemiol. 9*, 65–71.

Dyer, A.D. 1978. The influence of bubonic plague in England, 1500–1667. *Med. Hist. 22*, 308–26.

Dyrvik, S. 1972. Historical demography in Norway 1660–1801: a short survey. *Scand. Econ. Hist. Rev. 20*, 27–44.

Dyson, T. 1977. Levels, trends, differentials and causes of child mortality—a survey. *World Health Stat. Rep. 30*, 282–311.

Easmon, C.S.F. and Adlam, C. (Eds) 1983. *Staphylococci and staphylococcal infections. Vol. 2. The organism in vivo and in vitro*. Academic Press, Orlando, FL. xvi + 385–827.

Easterlin, R.A. 1980. *Population and economic change in developing countries*. University of Chicago Press, Chicago. ix + 581.

Eastwood, M.A., Brydon, W.G., and Tadesse, K. 1980. Effect of fiber on colon function. pp. 1–26 in Spiller and Kay.

Economic Commission for Asia and the Far East (ECAFE) 1973. *Comparative study of mortality trends in ECAFE countries*. Asian Population Studies Ser., No. 14. Economic Commission for Asia and the Far East, Bangkok. vi + 90.

Eddy, P., Potter, E., and Page, B. 1976. *Destination disaster*. Hart-Davis, McGibbon, London. x + 435.

Eddy, T.P. 1980. Food shortage as a health catastrophe. pp. 37–42 in Sabben-Clare, Bradley, and Kirkwood.

Edelstein, S.J. 1986. *The sickled cell. From myths to molecules*. Harvard University Press, Cambridge, MA. xiv + 197.

Ederer, F., Cutler, S.J., Eisenberg, H., and Keogh, J.R. 1960. Survival of patients with cancer of the stomach, Connecticut, 1935–54. *J. Natl. Cancer Inst. 25*, 1005–21.

Edge, P.G. 1926. The growth of mortality due to motor vehicles in England and Wales, 1904–23. (With discussion.) *J. Roy. Stat. Soc. 89*, 405–51.

Edmonds, T.R. 1835–1836. On the mortality of infants in England. *Lancet 1*, 690–94.

Edwards, G. and Grant, M. (Eds.) 1977. *Alcoholism: New knowledge and new responses*. Croom Helm, London. 359 pp.

Edwards, R.D. and Williams, T.D. 1956. *The great famine: Studies in Irish history 1845–1852*. Browne and Nolan, Dublin. xx + 517.

Ehrlich, P. 1909. Ueber den jetzigen Stand der Chemotherapie. *Ber. Deutsch. Chem. Gesellschaft 42*, 17–47. Quoted in translation in Holmstedt and Liljestrand, 1963.

Ehrlich, P.R., Holdren, J.P., and Holm., R.W. (Eds.) 1971. *Man and the ecosphere: Readings from the Scientific American*. Freeman and Co., San Francisco. viii + 307.

Eickhoff, T.C. 1977. The current status of BCG immunization against tuberculosis. *Annu. Rev. Med.* *28*, 411–23.

Eijkman, C. 1921. Pulmonary tuberculosis and the 'curvature of Van Pesch'. *J. Hyg. Camb. 20*, 363–65.

Elliott, I.M.Z. and Elliott, J.R. 1964. *A short history of surgical dressings . . . based on material collected by the late James Rawling Elliott*. Pharmaceutical Press, London. 118 pp.

Elliott, K. and Knight, J. (Eds.) 1976. *Acute diarrhoea in childhood*. Ciba Foundation Symposium 42 (N.S.). Elsevier/Excerpta Medica/North-Holland, Amsterdam. ix + 375.

Elliott, K., O'Connor, M., and Wolstoneholme, G.E.W. (Eds.) 1974. *Trypanosomiasis and leishmaniasis with special reference to Chagas' disease*. Ciba Foundation Symposium 20. Elsevier/ Excerpta Medica/ North-Holland, Amsterdam. xii + 353.

Elliott, K. and Whelan, J. (Eds.) 1977. *Health and disease in tribal societies*. Ciba Foundation Symposium 49. Elsevier/Excerpta Medica/North-Holland, Amsterdam. viii + 344.

Elsdon-Dew, R. 1968. The epidemiology of amoebiasis. *Adv. Parasitol. 6*, 1–62.

Elsdon-Dew, R. 1971. Amebiasis as a world problem. *Bull. N.Y. Acad. Med.* (2) *47*, 438–47.

Engels, F. 1892/1971. *The condition of the working class in England*. (Transl. and edit. by W.O. Henderson and W.H. Chaloner.) Oxford University Press, Oxford. xxxv + 386.

English Plague Commission 1906. XVI. Experimental production of plague epidemics among animals. *J. Hyg. Camb. 6*, 421–35.

Enterline, P.E. (with assistance of N. Sussman and G.M. Marsh) 1978. *Asbestos and cancer: The first thirty years*. Privately published, Pittsburgh, PA. iii + 75.

Epstein, F.H. and Piša, Z. 1979. International comparisons in ischaemic heart disease mortality. pp. 58–90 in Havlik and Feinleib.

Erhardt, C.L. and Berlin, J.E. (Eds.) 1974. *Morbidity and mortality in the United States*. Harvard University Press, Cambridge, MA. xiii + 289.

Erichsen, J. 1859. On the nature and causes of the mortality after surgical operations. *Med. Circ. 14*, 241.

Erichsen, J. 1874. Hospitalism and the causes of death after operations. *Br. Med. J. 1*, 65–67, 97–100, 131–34, 193–96.

Erlandsen, S.L. and Meyer, E.A. (Eds.) 1984. *Giardia and giardiasis. Biology, pathogenesis and epidemiology*. Plenum, New York. xxiv + 407.

Erslev, A.J. 1980. Blood and mountains. pp. 257–80 in Wintrobe.

Estes, M.K., Graham, D.Y., and Dimitrov, D.H. 1983. The molecular epidemiology of *Rotavirus* gastroenteritis. *Prog. Med. Virol. 29*, 1–22.

Euler, L. 1767/1977. A general investigation into the mortality and multiplication of the human species. (Transl. by N. and B. Keyfitz.) pp. 83–91 in Smith and Keyfitz, 1977.

Evans, A.S. 1976. Causation and disease: The Henle-Koch postulates revisited. *Yale J. Biol. Med. 49*, 175–95.

Evans, A.S. (Ed.) 1982a. *Viral infections of humans: Epidemiology and control*. 2nd edition. Plenum, New York-London. xxxvii + 720.

Evans, A.S. 1982b. Viruses. pp. 364–90 in Schottenfeld and Fraumeni.

Evered, D. and Whelan, J. (Eds.) 1983. *Malaria and the red cell*. Ciba Foundation Symposium 94. Pitman Books, London. ix + 257.

Eversley, D.E.C. 1981. The demography of the Irish Quakers, 1650–1850. pp. 57–88 in Goldstrom and Clarkson.

Eyster, E. and Bernene, J. 1973. Nosocomial anemia. *J. Am. Med. Assoc. 223*, 73–74.

Faber, K. 1923. *Nosography in modern internal medicine*. Humphrey Milford, London. xiii + 222.

Fabre, J. 1947–1948. Smallpox prevalence throughout the world during and after the Second World War. *WHO Epidemiol. Vital Stat. Rep. 1*, 262–89.

Fahlbeck, P.E. 1903. *Der Adel Schwedens (und Finnlands). Eine demographische Studie*. G. Fischer, Jena. viii + 361.

Falk, H. 1982. Liver. pp. 668–82 in Schottenfeld and Fraumeni.

Fannin, S.L. 1982. Food infections. pp. 261–80 in Jelliffe and Jelliffe.

Farr, W. 1837. Vital statistics or the statistics of health, sickness, diseases and death. pp. 567–601 in McCulloch. Reprinted in Wall, 1973c.

Farr, W. 1839. p.99 of First Annual Report of the Registrar-General of England and Wales. Cited in Introduction to *International Classification of Diseases*, 1955 revision, WHO, Geneva (1957).

Farr, W. 1866. Mortality of children in the principal states of Europe. *J. Stat. Soc. (London) 29*, 1–35.

Farr, W. 1885/1975. *Vital statistics: A memorial volume of selections from the reports and writings of William Farr*. N.A. Humphreys (Ed.). Offices of the Sanitary Institute, London. Reprinted 1975 under the auspices of the Library of the N.Y. Academy of Medicine, with introd. by M. Susser and A. Adelstein. History of Medicine Ser. No.

46, Scarecrow Press, Metuchen, NJ. xxiv + 563.

Farren, M. (Ed.) 1984. *Infant mortality and health in Latin America. An annotated bibliography from the 1979–82 literature.* Internatl. Development Research Centre, Ottawa. 172 pp.

Faust, E.C. 1945. Clinical and public health aspects of malaria in the United States from an historical point of view. *Am. J. Trop. Med.* 25, 185–201.

Faust, E.C. 1949. Malaria incidence in North America. pp. 748–63 in Boyd.

Faust, E.C. 1954. *Amebiasis.* C.C. Thomas, Springfield, IL. xi + 154.

Faust, E.C. 1955. History of human parasitic infections. *Public Health Rep.* 70, 958–65.

Faust, E.C. and Russell, P.F. 1964. *Craig and Faust's clinical parasitology.* 7th edition. Lea & Febiger, Philadelphia. 1099 pp. For latest edition see Beaver, P.C., Jung, R.C., and Cupp, E.W. (1984).

Feacham, R.G., Bradley, D.J., Garelick, H., Mara, D.D., et al. 1983. *Sanitation and disease: Health aspects of excreta and wastewater management.* Wiley, New York. xxvii + 501.

Federici, N., Prignano, A.S., Pasquali, P., Cariani, G., and Natale, M. 1976. Urban/rural differences in mortality 1950–1970. *World Health Stat. Rep.* 29, 249–378.

Feinstein, A.R. 1967. *Clinical judgment.* Williams and Wilkins, Baltimore. vi + 414.

Feldman, H.A. 1982. Epidemiology of *Toxoplasma* infections. *Epidemiol. Rev. 4*, 204–14.

Felsenfeld, O. 1965. *Borreliae,* human relapsing fever, and parasite-vector-host relationships. *Bacteriol. Rev. 29*, 46–74.

Felsenfeld, O. 1967. *The cholera problem.* Warren H. Green, St. Louis, MO. xiii + 165.

Felsenfeld, O. 1971. *Borrelia. Strains, vectors, human and animal Borreliosis.* Warren H. Green, St. Louis, MO. xii + 180.

Fenjuk, B.K. 1960. Experience in the eradication of enzootic plague in the north-west part of the Caspian Region of the USSR. *WHO Bull. 23*, 263–73.

Fenner, F. 1971. Infectious disease and social change. *Med. J. Austral. 1*, 1043–47 and 1099–1102.

Fenner, F. 1980. Smallpox and its eradication. pp. 215–29 in Stanley and Joske.

Fenner, F. (J.) 1984. Smallpox, "the most dreadful scourge of the human species": its global spread and recent eradication. *Med. J. Austral. 2*, 728–35, 841–46.

Fenner, F., Henderson, D.A., Arita, I., Jezek, Z., and Ladnyi, I.D. 1988. *Smallpox and its eradica-tion.* WHO, Geneva. xvi + 1460.

Fenner, F. and Ratcliffe, F.N. 1965. *Myxomatosis.* Cambridge University Press, New York. xiv + 379.

Fenner, F. and White, D.O. 1976. *Medical virology.* 2nd edition. Academic Press, New York. xviii + 487.

Fibiger, J. 1898. Om Serumbehandlung af Difteri. *Hospitalstidende 4*, Series 6, 309–25, 337–50.

Fiennes, R. 1967. *Zoonoses of primates: The epidemiology and ecology of simian diseases in relation to man.* Weidenfeld & Nicolson, London. ix + 190.

Fiennes, R.N.T.-W. 1978. *Zoonoses and the origins and ecology of human diseases.* Academic Press, London. xv + 196.

Fife, E.H. Jr 1977. *Trypanosoma (Schizotrypanum) cruzi.* pp. 135–73 in Kreier, vol. 1.

Figueroa, M. and Rapp, F. 1980. Herpesviruses and human cancer. *Bull. Pan Am. Health Org. 14*, 269–79.

Figueroa, W.G., Sargent, F., Imperiale, L., Morey, G.R., Paynter, C.R., Vorhaus, L.J., and Kark, R.M. 1952–1953. Lack of avitaminosis among alcoholics: Its relation to fortification of cereal products and the general nutritional status of the population. *J. Clin. Nutr. 1*, 179–99.

Finberg, H.P.R. (Ed.) 1972. *The agrarian history of England and Wales.* Cambridge University Press, New York. xviii + 566.

Findlay, G.M. 1928. Ultraviolet light and skin cancer. *Lancet 2*, 1070–73.

Findlay, G.M. 1950. *Recent advances in chemotherapy.* J. and A. Churchill, London. 2 vols.

Fine, P.E.M. 1982. Leprosy: The epidemiology of a slow bacterium. *Epidemiol. Rev. 4*, 161–88.

Finland, M. 1983. Empiric therapy for bacterial infections: The historical perspective. *Rev. Infect. Dis. 5*, S2–S8.

Finlay, R.A.P. 1978. Gateways to death? London child mortality experience, 1570–1653. *Ann. Démog. Hist.*, Pt. 1, 105–34.

Finley, M.I. 1968. Slavery. In *Int. Encyclop. Soc. Sci. 14*, 307–13. Macmillan, London.

Fisher, H.H. 1927. *The famine in Soviet Russia 1919–1923.* Macmillan, New York. x + 609.

Fitzgerald, T.J. 1981. Pathogenesis and immunology of *Treponema pallidum. Annu. Rev. Microbiol. 35*, 29–54.

Flinn, M. (Ed.) 1977. *Scottish population history from the 17th century to the 1930s.* Cambridge University Press, New York. xxv + 547.

Florey, C. du V., Melia, R.J.W., and Darby, S.C. 1978. Changing mortality from ischaemic heart disease in Great Britain 1968–76 *Br. Med. J. 1*, 635–37.

Foege, W.H. 1971. Famine, infections and epidemics. pp. 64–73 in Blix, Hofvander, and Vahlquist.

Fog-Poulsen, M. 1957. Maeslingeepidemier i Grønland. *Ugeskr. Laeg. 119*, 509–20.

Forbes, T.R. 1971. *Chronicle from Aldgate. Life and death in Shakespeare's London.* Yale University Press, New Haven, CT. London. xx + 251.

Forbes, T.R. 1979. By what disease or casualty: The changing face of death in London. pp. 117–39 in Webster. (See also *J. Hist. Med. 31* (1976), 395–420.)

Forbes, W.H. 1967. Longevity and medical costs. *N. Engl. J. Med. 277*, 71–78.

Ford, J. 1971. *The role of the trypanosomiases in African ecology: A study of the tsetse fly problem.* Clarendon, Oxford. xiv + 568.

Ford, W.L. 1980. The lymphocyte—Its transformation from a frustrating enigma to a model of cellular function. pp. 457–508 in Wintrobe.

Ford. W.W. 1914. Brief history of quarantine. *Bull. Johns Hopkins Hosp. 25*, 80–86.

Ford, W.W. 1939. *Bacteriology.* Hoeber, New York-London. xv + 207. (Reprinted 1964 as Clio Medica Series, Vol. 22. Hafner, New York.)

Forsyth, D.M. and Bradley, D.J. 1966. The consequences of bilharziasis: Medical and public health importance in north-west Tanzania. *WHO Bull. 34*, 715–35.

Fortuine, R. 1971. The health of the Eskimos as portrayed in the earliest written accounts. *Bull. Hist. Med. 45*, 97–114.

Foster, F.H. 1981. Trends in perinatal mortality. *World Health Stat. Q. 34*, 138–46.

Foster, G.M. 1983. *The demands of humanity: Army medical disaster relief.* Spec. stud. series. Center of Med. Hist., US Army. US Govt Printing Office, Washington, DC. x + 188.

Foster, W.D. 1961. *A short history of clinical pathology.* E. & S. Livingstone, Edinburgh-London. ix + 154.

Foster, W.D. 1965. *A history of parasitology.* E. & S. Livingstone, Edinburgh-London. vii + 202.

Foster, W.D. 1970. *A history of medical bacteriology and immunology.* Heinemann, London. xi + 232.

Fowler, R. and McCall, C. 1949. The results of surgical and radiological treatment in primary carcinoma of the breast. *Austral. N.Z. J. Surg. 19*, 142–49.

Fox, A.J. and Goldblatt, P.O. 1982. *Longitudinal study: Socio-demographic mortality differentials.*

HMSO, London. xxii + 227.

Fox, J.J. 1859. On the vital statistics of the Society of Friends. *J. Stat. Soc. (London) 22*, 208–31. Supplementary table. Ibid. 22, 481–83.

Fox, W. (Ed.) 1984. *Serology of tuberculosis and BCG vaccination.* Advances in Tuberculosis Research, vol. 21. Karger, Basel. viii + 251.

Francis, D.P. and Maynard, J.E. 1979. The transmission and outcome of hepatitis A, B, and non-A, non-B. A review. *Epidemiol. Rev. 1*, 17–31.

Francis, T. and Maassab, H.F. 1965. Influenza viruses. pp. 689–740 in Horsfall and Tamm.

Frank, J.P. 1790/1941. The people's misery: Mother of diseases. (Transl. from the Latin and with introd. by H.E. Sigerist.) *Bull. Hist. Med, 9*, 81–100.

Franke, R.W. and Chasin, B.H. 1980. *Seeds of famine. Ecological destruction and the development dilemma in the West African Sahel.* Allanheld, Osmun, Montclair, NJ; Universe, New York. xvi + 268.

Franz, G. 1940/1961. *Der Dreissigjährige Krieg und das deutsche Volk. Untersuchungen zur Bevölkerungs- und Agrargeschichte.* G. Fischer, Stuttgart-Jena. 128 pp. (Reprinted 1961, 114 pp.)

Fraser, K.B. and Martin, S.J. 1978. *Measles virus and its biology.* Academic Press, London-New York-San Francisco. vii + 249.

Fraumeni, J.F. Jr (Ed.) 1975. *Persons at high risk of cancer: An approach to cancer etiology and control.* Academic Press, New York. xvii + 544.

Fraumeni, J.F. Jr and Blot, W.J. 1982. Lung and pleura. pp. 564–82 in Schottenfeld and Fraumeni.

Fraumeni, J.F. Jr, Lloyd, J.W., Smith, E.M., et al. 1969. Cancer mortality among nuns: Role of marital status in etiology of neoplastic disease in women. *J. Natl. Cancer Instit. 42*, 455–68.

Fraumeni, J.F. Jr and Mulvihill, J.J. 1975. Colon and rectum. Who is at risk of colorectal cancer? pp. 404–15 in Schottenfeld.

Freyche, M.J. 1952. World incidence of poliomyelitis in 1951. *WHO Epidemiol. Vital Stat. Rep. 5*, 145–63.

Freyche, M.J. and Deutschman, Z. 1950. Human rickettsioses in Africa. *WHO Epidemiol. Vital Stat. Rep. 3*, 160–95.

Friedberger, E. 1928. Zur Frage der Heilwirkung des antitoxischen Diphtherieserums. *Med. Klin. 24*, 767–71.

Friedlander, J. 1977. Malaria and demography in the lowlands of Mexico: An ethnohistorical approach. pp. 113–19 in Landy.

Friedman, J.M. and Fialkow, P.J. 1980. The genetics of diabetes mellitus. *Prog. Med. Genet.* (N.S.)

4, 199–232.

Frost, W.H. 1920. Statistics of influenza morbidity: With special reference to certain factors in case incidence and case fatality. *Public Health Rep. 35*, 584–97.

Frost, W.H. 1939. The age selection of the mortality from tuberculosis in successive decades. *Am. J. Hyg. 30*, (Nov. Issue), 91–96. (Reprinted in Papers of Wade Hampton Frost, M.D., 1941.)

Fuscaldo, A.A., Erlick, B.J., and Hindman, B. (Eds.) 1980. *Laboratory safety: Theory and practice.* Academic Press, New York. xiv + 357.

Gabaldon, A. 1949. Malaria incidence in the West Indies and South America. pp. 764–87 in Boyd.

Gabaldon, A. and Berti, A.L. 1954. The first large area in the tropical zone to report malaria eradication: North-central Venezuela. *Am. J. Trop. Med. Hyg. 3*, 793–807.

Gabriel, J. 1955. Evolution et tendances actuelles de la mortalité en Belgique. *Proc. World Popul. Conf.* 1954, vol. 1, 89–106.

Gagnon, F. 1950. Contribution to the study of etiology and prevention of cancer of the cervix of the uterus. *Am. J. Obstet. Gynecol. 60*, 516–22.

Gajdusek, D.C. 1977*a*. Urgent opportunistic observations: The study of changing, transient and disappearing phenomena of medical interest in disrupted primitive communities. With discussion. pp. 69–102 in Elliott and Whelan.

Gajdusek, D.C. 1977*b*. Unconventional viruses and the origin and disappearance of Kuru. *Science 197*, 943–60.

Gajdusek, D.C. and Alpers, M. 1965. Definitive bibliography on kuru in New Guinea. pp. 403–09 in Gajdusek, Gibbs, and Alpers.

Gajdusek, D.C., Gibbs, C.J. Jr, and Alpers. M. 1965. *Slow, latent and temperate virus infections.* Public Health Service, U.S. Dept Health, Education, and Welfare, Washington, DC. xx + 489.

Galbraith, N.S., Forbes, P., and Mayon-White, R.T. 1980. Changing patterns of communicable disease in England and Wales. I. Newly recognized diseases; II. Disappearing and declining diseases; III. Increasing infective diseases. *Br. Med. J. 2* (281), 427–30; 489–92; 546–49.

Gale, A.H. 1945. A century of changes in the mortality and incidence of the principal infections of childhood. *Arch. Dis. Child. 20*, 2–21.

Gale, A.H. 1959. *Epidemic diseases.* Pelican Books. London. 159 pp.

Galliano, P. 1966. La mortalité infantile (indigènes et nourissons) dans la banlieue sud de Paris à la fin du XVIIIe siècle (1774–1794). *Ann. Démog. Hist.*

(1966), 139–77.

Galton, F. 1873. The relative supplies from town and country families to the population of future generations. *J. Stat. Soc. (London) 36*, 19–26.

Gamble, D.R. 1984. Enteroviruses: Polio-, ECHO-, and Coxsackie viruses. pp. 394–419 in Topley and Wilson, 1984, vol. 4.

Gandevia, B. 1968. The changing pattern of mortality from asthma in Australia: 2. Mortality and modern therapy. *Med. J. Austral. 1*, 884–91.

Gandevia, B. 1971*a*. Occupation and disease in Australia since 1788. *Bull. Postgrad. Comm. Med. (Sydney) 27*, 157–228.

Gandevia, B. 1971*b*. The medico-historical significance of young and developing countries illustrated by Australian experience. pp. 75–98 in Clarke.

Gangarosa, E.J. 1969. Botulism in the United States, 1899–1967. *J. Infect. Dis. 119*, 308–11.

Gantt, W.H. 1928. *A medical review of Soviet Russia.* British Medical Assoc., London. 112 pp.

Gapp, K.S. 1933. The universal famine under Claudius. *Harvard Theol. Rev. 28*, 258–65.

Garcia, R.V, et al. 1981–1982. *Drought and man: The 1972 case history.* Vol. 1: *Nature pleads not guilty* (R.V. Garcia); Vol. 2: *The constant catastrophe: Malnutrition, famines and drought* (R.V. Garcia and J.C. Escudero); Vol. 3: *The roots of catastrophe* (R.V. Garcia and P. Spitz). Pergamon Press, Oxford-New York. 3 vols.

Garcia-Martin, G. 1972. Status of malaria eradication in the Americas. *Am. J. Trop. Med. Hyg. 21*, 616–34.

Gardner, M.J., Winter, P.D, and Barker, D.J.P. 1984. *Atlas of mortality from selected diseases in England and Wales, 1968–1978.* Wiley, New York. xi + 96.

Garland, J. 1943. Varicella following exposure to herpes zoster. *N. Engl. J. Med. 228*, 336–37.

Garnham, P.C.C. 1963. Distribution of simian malaria parasites in various hosts. *J. Parasitol. 49*, 905–11.

Garnham, P.C.C. 1966. *Malaria parasites and other sporidia.* Blackwell, Oxford. xviii + 1114.

Garnham, P.C.C. 1971. *Progress in parasitology.* University of London Heath Clark Lectures 1968. Athlone Press, University of London. xi + 224.

Garrigues, H.J. 1889. Puerperal infection. pp. 296–313 in *A System of Obstetrics*, by American Authors, Vol. 2. Lea Brothers & Co., Philadelphia. xi + 854.

Garrison, F.H. 1929. *An introduction to the history of military medicine, with medical chronology, suggestions for study and bibliographic data.*

Saunders, London. 996 pp.

Garrison, F.H. 1933. Revised student's check-lists of texts illustrating the history of medicine, with references for collateral reading. *Bull. Hist. Med. 1*, 333–434.

Garrison, F.H. 1966*a. Contributions to the history of medicine.* Hafner, New York. 989 pp.

Garrison, F.H. 1966*b.* The history of drainage, irrigation, sewage-disposal and water supply. pp. 391–442 in Garrison, 1966*a* Reprinted from *Bull. N.Y. Acad. Med. 5* (1929) 887–938.

Garrod, L.P., Lambert, H.P., O'Grady, F, and Waterworth, P.M. 1981. *Antibiotic and chemotherapy.* Churchill-Livingstone, Edinburgh-London. ix + 514.

Garros, B. and Bouvier, M.H. 1978. Excès de la surmortalité masculine en France et causes médicales de décès. *Population 33*, 1077–114.

Garwood, F. and Jeffcoate, G.O. 1960. Comparative death-rates per person-mile associated with various forms of transport. *J. Roy. Stat. Soc. A123*, 59–61.

Gasquet, F.A. 1908. *The Black Death of 1348 and 1349.* 2nd edition. George Bell & Sons, London. xxv + 272.

Gastel, B. 1973. Measles: A potentially finite history. *J. Hist. Med. 28*, 34–44.

Gaud, M., Khalil, M, and Vaucel, M. 1947–1948. The evolution of the epidemic of relapsing fever, 1942–1946. *WHO Bull. 1*, 93–101.

Gaud, M. and Morgan, M.T. 1947–1948. Study of relapsing fever in north Africa. *WHO Bull. 1*, 69–92.

Gautier, E. and Henry, L. 1958. *La population de Crulai, paroisse normande: Étude historique.* Institut National d'Etudes Démographiques, Paris. 272 pp.

Gay, F.P. 1918. *Typhoid fever.* Macmillan, New York. xiii + 286.

Geary, R.C. 1952. Statistical aspects of mortality in early adult life. *Br. Med. J. 2*, 625–31.

Gee, J.B.L., Morgan, W.K.C, and Brooks, S.M. (Eds.) 1984. *Occupational lung disease. From a conference, Chicago, 1982.* Raven, New York. xxxii + 264.

Geigy, R. 1968. Relapsing fevers. pp. 175–216 in Weinman and Ristic.

Geison, G.L. 1974. Louis Pasteur. In *Dict. Sci. Biog. X*, 350–416.

Gelderen, H.H. van 1955. *Pre-school child mortality in the Netherlands.* Publ. No. 28. Netherlands Inst. Prev. Med. H.E. Stenfert Kroese N.V., Leiden. viii + 138.

Gelfand, M. 1981. Zimbabwe. pp. 194–203 in

Trowell and Burkitt, 1981*a.*

Gemmell, A.A., Logan, W.P.D, and Benjamin, B. 1954. Incidence of toxaemia. *J. Obstet. Gynaecol. Br. Emp. 61*, 458–62.

Gendreau, F. and Nadot, R. 1967. Structures par âge, actuelle et future. Nos. 9,10, pp. 1–96 in *Afrique Noire, Madagascar, Comores: Démographie comparée.* vol. 2. Institut National de la Statistique et des Etudes Economiques. Service de Coopération. Institut National d'Etudes Démographiques, Paris.

Génicot, L. 1966. Crisis: From the middle ages to modern times. pp. 660–741 in *Cambridge Economic History of Europe*, vol. 1. Cambridge University Press, New York.

Gerety, R.J. (Ed.) 1981. *Non-A, non-B hepatitis.* Academic Press, New York. xv + 301.

Gerety, R.J. (Ed.) 1984. *Hepatitis A.* Academic Press, Orlando, FL. xiv + 282.

Gerety, R.J. (Ed.) 1985. *Hepatitis B.* Academic Press, New York. xiv + 469.

Gerhard, W.W. 1837. On the typhus fever which occurred at Philadelphia in the spring and summer of 1836. *Am. J. Med. Sci. 20*, 289–322.

Gibbs, J.P. (Ed.) 1968. *Suicide.* Harper & Row, New York-Evanston-London. x + 338.

Gibson, E. and Klein, S. 1961. *Murder: A Home Office research unit report.* HMSO, London. iv + 43.

Gibson, J.R. and McKeown, T. 1950–1952. Observations on all births (23,970) in Birmingham, 1947. Part I. *Br. J. Soc. Med. 4* (1950) 221–33. Part II: Birth weight. Ibid. 5 (1951) 98–112. Part III: Survival. Ibid. 5 (1951) 177–83. Part IV: Sex ratio of stillbirths related to birth rate. Ibid. 5 (1951) 229–35. Part V: Birth weight and economic circumstances of parents. Ibid. 5 (1951) 259–64. Part VI: Birth weight, duration of gestation and survival related to sex. Ibid. 6 (1952) 152–58. Part VII. Effect of changing family size on infant mortality. Ibid. 6 (1952) 183–87.

Gilbert, R.I. Jr and Mielke, J.H. (Eds.) 1985. *The analysis of prehistoric diets.* Academic Press, Orlando, FL. xiv + 440.

Gilbert, R.J., Roberts, D, and Smith, G. 1984. Food-borne diseases and botulism. pp. 477–514 in Topley and Wilson, 1984, vol. 3.

Gille, H. 1949. The demographic history of the northern European countries in the eighteenth century. *Popul. Studies 3*, 3–65.

Gilles, H.M. (Ed.) 1984. *Recent advances in tropical medicine*, vol. 1. Churchill-Livingstone, Edinburgh-London. xiii + 353.

Gilles, H.M., Harinasuta, T, and Bunnag, D. 1984.

Malaria: Clinical aspects. *Rec. Adv. in Trop. Med. 1*, 1–22. See Gilles, 1984.

Gilliam, J.F. 1961. The plague under Marcus Aurelius. *Am. J. Philol. 82*, 225–51.

Gillispie, C.C. (Ed.-in-Chief) 1970–1980. *Dictionary of Scientific Biography*, vols. I–XVI. Scribner, New York.

Gilman, A.G. Goodman, L.S., Rall, T.W, and Murad, F. (Eds.) 1985. *Goodman and Gilman's 'The pharmacological basis of therapeutics'*. 7th edition. Macmillan, New York; Collier Macmillan, London. xvi + 1839.

Ginneken, J.K. van and Muller, A.S. (Eds.) 1984. *Maternal and child health in rural Kenya*. Croom Helm, London-Sydney. vii + 373.

Giraldo, G. and Beth, E. (Eds.) 1980/1984. *The role of viruses in human cancer*. Elsevier, New York. 2 vols. 292 pp.; xvi + 416.

Girard, A., Henry, L, and Nistri, R. 1959. La surmortalité infantile dans le Nord et le Pas-de-Calais. *Population 14*, 221–32.

Gitnick, G. 1984. Non-A, non-B hepatitis: Etiology and clinical course. *Annu. Rev. Med. 35*, 265–78.

Glamann, K. 1977. The changing patterns of trade. pp. 185–289 in *Cambridge Economic History of Europe*, vol. V. Cambridge University Press, New York.

Glass, D.V. 1950. Graunt's life table. *J. Inst. Actuar. 76*, 60–64.

Glass, D.V. 1951. A note on the under-registration in Britain in the nineteenth century. *Popul. Studies 5*, 70–88.

Glass, D.V. 1963. John Graunt and his natural and political observations. (With discussion.) *Proc. Roy. Soc. London B159*, 1–37. See also *Notes Roy. Soc. London 19* (1964), 63–100.

Glass, D.V. 1965a. Gregory King and the population of England and Wales at the end of the seventeenth century. pp. 167–83 in Glass and Eversley. Originally published in *Eugenics Rev.* Jan. 1946. 170–83.

Glass, D.V. 1965b. Population and population movements in England and Wales, 1700 to 1850. pp. 221–46 in Glass and Eversley.

Glass, D.V. 1973a. *Numbering the people: The eighteenth-century population controversy and the development of census and vital statistics in Britain*. Saxon House, Farnborough, Hants. 205 pp.

Glass, D.V. (Ed.) 1973b. *The development of population statistics*. Gregg International, London. 554 pp.

Glass, D.V. and Eversley, D.E.C. (Eds.) 1965. *Population in history: Essays in historical demography*. Edward Arnold, London. ix + 692.

Reprinted 1969.

Glass, D.V. and Grebenik, E. 1965. World population 1800–1950. pp. 56–138 in *Cambridge Economic History of Europe*, vol. VI. Cambridge University Press, New York.

Glass, D.V. and Revelle, R. (Eds.) 1972. *Population and social change*. Edward Arnold, London. viii + 520.

Glatt, M.M. 1958. The English drink problem. Its rise and decline through the ages. *Br. J. Addict. 55*, 51–65.

Glezen, W.P. 1982. Serious morbidity and mortality associated with influenza epidemics. *Epidemiol. Rev. 4*, 25–44.

Glezen, W.P., Payne, A.A., Snyder, D.N, and Downs, T.D. 1982. Mortality and influenza. *J. Infect. Dis. 146*, 313–21.

Glober, G. and Stemmermann, G. 1981. Hawaii ethnic groups. pp. 319–33 in Trowell and Burkitt (1981a).

Glueck, C.J., Larsen, R, et al. 1981. Early feeding patterns and atherosclerosis. pp. 89–97 in Winick.

Glueck, C.J. and Tsang, R.C. 1979. Pediatric nutrition: Potential relationship to the development of atherosclerosis. pp. 363–81 in Winick.

Godfrey, E.S. 1928. The age distribution of communicable disease according to size of community. *Am. J. Public Health 18*, 616–31.

Godkin, J. 1870. *Land war in Ireland; A history for the times*. Macmillan, London. xiv + 436.

Gold, E. and Nankervis, G.A. 1973. Varicella—Zoster viruses. pp. 327–51 in Kaplan.

Goldberg, I.D. and Kurland, L.T. 1962. Mortality in 33 countries from diseases of the nervous system. *World Neurol. 3*, 444–65.

Goldberger, J., Wheeler, G.A, and Sydenstricker, E. 1920. A study of the relation of diet to pellagra incidence in seven textile-mill communities of South Carolina in 1916. *Public Health Rep. 35*, 648–713. Reprinted in Sydenstricker, 1974, pp. 345–69.

Goldstein, S. 1971. The biology of aging. *N. Engl. J. Med. 285*, 1120–29.

Goldstrom, J.M. and Clarkson, L.A. (Eds.) 1981. *Irish population, economy, and society. Essays in honour of the late K.H. Connell*. Clarendon, Oxford. x + 322.

Gomme, A.W. 1933. *The populations of Athens in the fifth and fourth centuries B.C.* Blackwell, Oxford. vii + 87. (Reprinted 1967, Argonaut, Chicago.)

Gompertz, B. 1820. A sketch of an analysis and notation applicable to the study of life contingencies. *Philos. Trans. Roy. Soc. London 110*, 214–

94. Corrig. *115*, 584–85.

Gompertz, B. 1825. On the nature of the function expressive of the law of human mortality; and on a new mode of determining the value of life contingencies. In a letter to Francis Baily. *Philos. Trans. Roy. Soc. London 115*, 513–83.

Gompertz, B. 1860–1861. On one uniform law of mortality from birth to extreme old age, and on the law of sickness. 454–62 + 11 in *Report on Proc. 4th Session Internat. Stat. Congr. (London)*. W. Farr, R. Valpy and J.T. Hammack, Eds. HMSO, London. xix + 548.

Gompertz, B. 1862. A supplement to two papers published in the Transactions of the Royal Society "On the science connected with human mortality," the one published in 1820, the other in 1825. *Philos. Trans. Roy. Soc. London 152*, 511–60.

Gontzea, I. 1974. *Nutrition and anti-infectious defence*. 2nd edition. (Completed with the aid of F.B. Gontzea.) Karger, Basel. vii + 287.

Good, C.N. 1972. Salt, trade and disease: Aspects of development in Africa's northern Great Lakes region. *Int. J. Afr. Hist. Studies 5*, 43–86.

Goodall, E.W., Greenwood, M, and Russell, W.T. 1929. *Scarlet fever, diphtheria and enteric fever 1895–1914: A clinical-statistical study*. Med. Res. Council Spec. Rep. Series No. 137, HMSO, London. 58 pp.

Goodchild, P. 1985. *Survival skills of the North American Indians*. Chicago Review Press, Chicago. vi + 234.

Goodman, H. 1943. *Notable contributions to the knowledge of syphilis*. Froben Press, New York. xii + 144.

Goodman, L.J. 1975. The longevity and mortality of American physicians, 1969–1973. *Milbank Q. 53*, 353–75.

Gordis, L. 1973. *Epidemiology of chronic lung diseases in children*. Johns Hopkins, Baltimore. xi + 137.

Gordon, A. 1795. *A treatise on the epidemic puerperal fever of Aberdeen*. London. (Reprinted by the Sydenham Society in Churchill, 1850, pp. 377–422.)

Gordon, A. 1875. *Official dispatch to the Secretary of State*, C.1624, No. 23. Parliamentary Papers, London.

Gordon, D. 1976a. *Health, sickness and society*. University of Queensland Press, St Lucia, Qld. xvi + 954.

Gordon, D. 1976b. Improvement in health in Australia—1871 to 1971. pp. 1–28 in *The Gordon Symposium*, B.A. Smithurst (Ed.), University of Queensland Press, St Lucia, Qld. ix + 95.

Gordon, J.E. 1962. Chickenpox: An epidemiological review. *Am. J. Med. Sci. 244*, 362–89.

Gordon, J.E. 1965. Communicable disease control: Old principles in a new setting. *Am. J. Med. Sci. 250*, 346–64.

Gordon, J.E. 1966. Ecologic interplay of man, environment and health. *Am. J. Med. Sci. 252*, 341–56.

Gordon, J.E., Wyon, J.B, and Ascoli, W. 1967. The second year death rate in less developed countries. *Am. J. Med. Sci. 254*, 357–80.

Gordon, T., Crittenden, M, and Haenszel, W. 1961. *Cancer mortality trends in the United States, 1930–1955. Part 2*. Natl. Cancer Instit. Mon. No. 6, US Dept Health, Education, and Welfare, Washington, DC. pp. 131–350.

Gorgas, W.C. 1915. *Sanitation in Panama*. D. Appleton & Co., New York-London. iv + 297.

Gottesman, I.I., Shields, J, and Hanson, D.R. 1982. *Schizophrenia: The epigenetic puzzle*. Cambridge University Press. xiii + 258.

Gottfried, R.S. 1978. *Epidemic diseases in fifteenth century England: The medical response and the demographic consequences*. Leicester University Press. xiii + 262.

Gottschalk, L.A. McGuire, F.L., Heiser, J.F., Dinovo, E.C, and Birch, H. 1980. *Drug abuse deaths in nine cities. A survey report*. Research Mon. No. 29, National Institute on Drug Abuse, Rockville, MD. xii + 176.

Goubert, P. 1954. Une richesse historique: les régistres paroissiaux. *Ann. Démog. Hist.* (1954), 92.

Goubert, P. 1960. *Beauvais et le Beauvaisis de 1600 à 1730. Contribution à l'histoire sociale de la France du XVIIe siècle*. SEVPEN, Paris. lxxii + 653. Supplément: Cartes et graphiques, 119 pp.

Goubert, P. 1965a. Recent theories and research in French population between 1500–1700. Transl. by M. Hilton. pp. 457–73 in Glass and Eversley.

Goubert, P. 1965b. Régistres paroissiaux et démographie dans la France du XVIe siècle. *Ann. Démog. Hist.* (1965), 43–48.

Goubert, P. 1968. Legitimate fecundity and infant mortality in France during the eighteenth century: A comparison. *Daedalus 97*, 593–603. Reprinted in Glass and Revelle, 1972, pp. 321–30.

Goubert, (J.) P. 1972. Le phénomène épidémique en Bretagne à la fin du XVIIIe siècle (1770–1787). pp. 225–52 in Desaive, Goubert, et al.

Goubert, (J.) P. 1974. *Malades et médecins en Bretagne, 1770–1790*. Institut Armoricain de Recherches Historiques, Rennes. Klinsieck, Paris. 508 pp.

Goubert, P. 1976. *Clio parmi les hommes*. La Haye-

Mouton, Paris. 310 pp.

Gould, G.C. (Ed.) 1971. *Health and disease in Africa—The community approach. Proc. East African Medical Research Council Scientific Conf., 1970*. East African Literature Bureau, Kampala-Nairobi-Dar es Salaam. xii + 372.

Goure, L. 1962. *The siege of Leningrad*. Stanford University Press, Stanford, CA. xiv + 363.

Government of Bihar 1973. *Bihar Famine Report, 1966–1967*. Superintendent Secretarial Press, Patnar, India. 473 pp.

Goyer, R.A. and Mehlman, M.A. (Eds.) 1977. *Toxicology of trace elements*. Halsted Press (John Wiley), New York. xiv + 303.

Graetzer, J. 1883. *Edmund Halley und Caspar Neumann. Ein Beitrag zur Geschichte der Bevölkerungs-Statistik*. S. Schottlaender, Breslau. 8 + 93 + chart.

Graham, H. 1939. *Surgeons all*. Rich & Cowan, London. xv + 426.

Graham, H. 1950. *Eternal Eve*. Heinemann, Altrincham. xx + 699. (Rev. 2nd edition, 1960.)

Gramiccia, G. and Hempel, J. 1972. Mortality and morbidity from malaria in countries where malaria eradication is not making satisfactory progress. *J. Trop. Med. Hyg.* 75, 187–92.

Grange, J.M. 1984. Tuberculosis. pp. 32–61 in Topley and Wilson, 1984, vol. 3.

Graunt, J. 1662. *Natural and political observations mentioned in a following index, and made upon the Bills of Mortality . . . by John Graunt, fellow of the Royal Society. With reference to the government, religion, trade, growth, ayre, diseases, and the several changes of the said city . . .* J. Martin, J. Allestry and T. Dicas, London. 85 pp. Reprinted in Hull (1899) and in *J. Inst. Actuar.* 90 (384), 4–61 (1964).

Grayson, M. (Ed.) 1982. *Antibiotics, chemotherapeutics, and antibacterial agents for disease control*. Encyclopedia Reprint Series. (From the Kirk-Othmer Encycl. of Chemical Technology.) Wiley-Interscience, New York. xxvi + 514.

Green, F.H.K. and Covell, G. (Eds.) 1953. *Medical research. History of the Second World War: United Kingdom Medical Series*. A.S. MacNalty, Ed.-in-Chief. HMSO, London. xvi + 387.

Greenbaum, C.H. and Beerman, H. 1965. Epidemiology of diseases of the skin. *Am. J. Med. Sci.* 250, 458–71.

Greenbaum, L.S. 1975. 'Measure of civilization,' the hospital thought of Jacques Tenon on the eve of the French Revolution. *Bull. Hist. Med. 49*, 43–56.

Greenberg, B. 1971. *Flies and disease*. Vol. I. *Ecol-*

ogy, classification and biotic associations. Vol. II. *Biology and disease transmission*. Princeton University Press. xi + 856, xi + 447.

Greenberg, M.R. 1983. *Urbanization and cancer mortality. The United States experience, 1950–1975*. Monographs in Epidemiol. and Biostatist., vol. 4. Oxford University Press, New York. xii + 276.

Greenhow, E.H. 1858/1973. *Papers relating to the sanitary state of the people of England*. General Board of Health Papers, 1858. (Reprinted 1973, Gregg International, London, 176 pp.)

Greenhow, E.H. 1859. On the standard of public health for England. *J. Stat. Soc. (London) 22*, 253–70.

Greenwald, P. 1982. Prostate. pp. 938–46 in Schottenfeld and Fraumeni.

Greenwood, B.M., Hassan-King, M., et al. 1980. Pneumococcal serotypes in West Africa. *Lancet 1*, 360.

Greeenwood, B.M. and Whittle, H.C. 1981. *Immunology of medicine in the tropics*. Edward Arnold, London. xiv + 306.

Greenwood, D. and O'Grady, F. (Eds.) 1985. *The scientific basis of antimicrobial chemotherapy*. Symposia of the Soc. for General Microbiology, 38. Cambridge University Press, New York. x + 404.

Greenwood, M. 1920. The history of influenza, 1658–1911. pp. 3–30 in Newman, Greenwood, et al. A general account of influenza in the united Kingdom during 1918–19. Ibid. pp. 35–65.

Greenwood, M. 1922a. Discussion on the value of life-tables in statistical research. *J. Roy. Stat. Soc. 85*, 537–60.

Greenwood, M. 1922b. The Milroy Lecture on the influence of industrial employment upon general health. *Br. Med. J. 1*, 667–72, 708–13, 752–58.

Greenwood, M. 1924. The vital statistics of Sweden and England and Wales: An essay in international comparison. *J. Roy. Stat. Soc. 87*, 493–543.

Greenwood, M. 1926. Communication to the Health Committee of the League of Nations. Quoted at pp. 355–57 of McDougall (1949).

Greenwood, M. 1927. In discussion of Derrick.

Greenwood, M. 1928. 'Laws' of mortality from the biological point of view. *J. Hyg. Camb. 28*, 267–94.

Greenwood, M. 1931. On the statistical measure of infectiousness. *J. Hyg. Camb. 31*, 336–51.

Greenwood, M. 1932. *Epidemiology, historical and experimental. The Herter Lectures for 1931*. Johns Hopkins, Baltimore. x + 80.

Greenwood, M. 1935. *Epidemics and crowd-*

diseases. An introduction to the study of epidemiology. Macmillan, New York. 409 pp.

Greenwood, M. 1936. English death rates, past, present and future. A valedictory address. (With discussion.) *J. Roy. Stat. Soc.* 99, 674–715.

Greenwood, M. 1939. Occupational and economic factors of mortality. *Br. Med. J.* 1, 862–66.

Greenwood, M. 1942. British loss of life in the wars of 1794–1815 and in 1914–1918. *J. Roy. Stat. Soc.* 105, 1–16.

Greenwood, M. 1946. The statistical study of infectious diseases. *J. Roy. Stat. Soc.* 109, 85–110.

Greenwood, M. 1948a. William Farr. pp. 61–68 in M. Greenwood, *Some British Pioneers of Social Medicine,* Oxford University Press, London. ii + 118.

Greenwood, M. 1948b. *Medical statistics from Graunt to Farr. The Fitzpatrick Lectures for the years, 1941 and 1943.* (Reprinted from Biometrika.) Cambridge University Press. v + 73.

Greenwood, M. and Brown, J.W. 1912. An examination of some factors influencing the rate of infant mortality. *J. Hyg. Camb.* 12, 5–45.

Greenwood, M. and Candy, R.H. 1911. The fatality of fractures of the lower extremity and of lobar pneumonia. A study of hospital mortality rates 1751–1901. *J. Roy. Stat. Soc.* 74, 365–97.

Greenwood, M., Hill, A.B., Topley, W.W.C, and Wilson, G.S. 1936. *Experimental epidemiology.* Med. Res. Council Spec. Rep. Series No. 209, HMSO, London. 204 pp.

Greenwood, M. and Irwin, J.O. 1939. The biostatistics of senility. *Hum. Biol.* 11, 1–23.

Greenwood, M. and Newbold, E.M. 1925. On the excess mortality of males in the first years of life. *Biometrika* 17, 327–42.

Greenwood, M. and Russell, W.T. 1937. Bright's disease, nephritis and arteriosclerosis: A contribution to the history of medical statistics. *Biometrika* 29, 249–76.

Greenwood, M. and Topley, W.W.C. 1925. A further contribution to the experimental study of epidemiology. *J. Hyg. Camb.* 24, 45–110.

Gregg, C.T. 1985. *Plague. An ancient disease in the twentieth century.* University of New Mexico Press, Albuquerque, NM. xv + 373.

Gregg, N.M. 1941. Congenital cataract following German measles in the mother. *Trans. Ophthalmol. Soc. Aust.* 3, 35–46.

Greville, T.N.E. 1946. *United States life tables and actuarial tables, 1939–1941. Sixteenth Census of the United States: 1940.* US Govt Printing Office, Washington, DC. iv + 153.

Griffin, D. 1841. An enquiry into the mortality occurring among the poor of the city of Limerick. *J. Stat. Soc. (London)* 3, 305–30.

Griffith, G.T. 1926. *Population problems in the age of Malthus.* Cambridge University Press. 276 pp. Reprinted 1967.

Griffiths, A.G.F. 1884. *The chronicles of Newgate.* Chapman and Hall, London, xii + 596.

Grigg, E.R.N. 1958. The arcana of tuberculosis. With a brief epidemiologic history of the disease in the USA. *Am. Rev. Tuberc. Pulmon. Dis.* 78, 151–72.

Grinblat, J. 1982. Aging in the world: Demographic determinants, past trends and long-term perspectives to 2075. *World Health Stat. Q.* 35, 124–32.

Griswold, M.H., Wilder, C.S., Cutler, S.J, and Pollack, E. 1955. *Cancer in Connecticut, 1935–1951.* Connecticut State Dept. Health, Hartford, CT. 141 pp.

Grmek, M.D. 1969. Maladies et morts: Préliminaires d'une étude historique des maladies. *Ann.: Economies, Sociétés, Civilisations* 24, 1473–83.

Grmek, M.D. 1983. Les maladies à l'aube de la civilisation occidentale. Payot, Paris. 527 pp. English transl. by M. Muellner and L. Muellner, *Diseases in the ancient Greek world.* Johns Hopkins, Baltimore, 1988. xiv + 458.

Grönlund, O. 1949. *Oversikt av befolkningsrörelsen i Sverige under 200 år.* (Survey of vital statistics of Sweden during 200 years.) Norstedt, Stockholm. 50 pp.

Groman, N.B. 1984. Conversion by corynephages and its role in the natural history of diphtheria. *J. Hyg. Camb.* 93, 405–17.

Gross, A.J. and Clark, V.A. 1975. *Survival distributions: Reliability applications in the biomedical sciences.* Wiley-Interscience, New York. xv + 331.

Gross, R.J. 1984. Acute enteritis. pp. 458–76 in Topley and Wilson, 1984, vol. 3.

Grove, R.D. and Hetzel, A.M. 1968. *Vital statistics rates in the United States 1940–1960.* US Dept Health, Education, and Welfare, Washington, DC. ix + 881.

Gruenwald, P. 1969. Stillbirth and early neonatal death. pp. 163–83 in Butler and Alberman.

Grufferman, S. 1982. Hodgkin's disease. pp. 739–53 in Schottenfeld and Fraumeni.

Grufferman, S. and Delzell, E. 1984. Epidemiology of Hodgkin's disease. *Epidemiol. Rev.* 6, 76–106.

Grundmann, E. (Ed.) 1976. *Glomerulonephritis.* Current Topics in Pathology, vol. 61. Springer, Berlin-Heidelberg-New York. iv + 286.

Grundmann, E. (Ed.) 1980. *Drug-induced pathology.* Current Topics in Pathology, vol. 69.

Springer, Berlin-New York. vii + 384.

Grundy, F. and Lewis-Faning, E. (Eds.) 1957. *Morbidity and mortality in the first year of life: A field enquiry in fifteen areas of England and Wales*. The Eugenics Soc., London. 145 pp.

Gruner, E. 1963. Dam disasters. *Proc. Inst. Civ. Engin.* 24, 47–60.

Guillaume, P. 1978. La grippe à Bordeaux en 1918. *Ann. Démog. Hist.*, Pt. 1, 167–73.

Gundersen, P.R. 1967. *Coronary heart disease in Kristiansund, 1959–61: Incidence, prevalence and mortality*. Norwegian monographs on Medical Science. Universitetsforlaget, Oslo. 178 pp.

Guntheroth, W.G. 1982. *Crib death. The sudden infant death syndrome*. Futura, Mount Kisco, NY. xvi + 224.

Gunz, F.W. 1980. The dread leukemias and the lymphomas: Their nature and their prospects. pp. 511–46 in Wintrobe.

Gutmann, M.P. 1977. Putting crises in perspective: The impact of war on civilian populations in the seventeenth century. *Ann. Démog. Hist.*, Pt. 1, 101–28.

Guy, W.A. 1844. A third contribution to a knowledge of the influence of employments upon health. *J. Stat. Soc. (London)* 7, 232–43.

Guy, W.A. 1845. On the duration of life among the families of the peerage and baronetage of the United Kingdom. *J. Stat. Soc. (London)* 8, 69–77.

Guy, W.A. 1846. On the duration of life among the English gentry, with additional observations on the duration of life among the aristocracy. *J. Stat. Soc. (London)* 9, 37–49.

Guy, W.A. 1847. On the duration of life of sovereigns. *J. Stat. Soc. (London)* 11, 62–69.

Guy, W.A. 1851. On the duration of life among the clergy. *J. Stat. Soc. (London)* 14, 289–97.

Guy, W.A. 1854. On the duration of life among medical men. *J. Stat. Soc. (London)* 17, 15–23.

Guy, W.A. 1856. On the nature and extent of the benefits conferred by hospitals on the working classes and the poor. *J. Stat. Soc. (London)* 19, 12–27.

Guy, W.A. 1857. On the duration of life among lawyers; with additional observations on the relative longevity of the members of the three learned professions. *J. Stat. Soc. (London)* 20, 65–71.

Guy, W.A. 1859. On the duration of life as affected by the pursuits of literature, science and arts; with a summary view of the duration of life among the upper and middle classes of society. *J. Stat. Soc. (London)* 22, 337–61.

Guy, W.A. 1867. On the mortality of London hospitals: And incidentally on the deaths in the prison and public institutions of the metropolis. *J. Stat. Soc. (London)* 30, 293–322.

Guy, W.A. 1875. On the executions for murder that have taken place in England and Wales during the last seventy years. *J. Stat. Soc. (London)* 38, 463–86.

Guy, W.A. 1882a. Two hundred and fifty years of smallpox in London. *J. Stat. Soc. (London)* 45, 399–437.

Guy, W.A. 1882b. The smallpox epidemic as affected by the states of war and peace. *J. Stat. Soc. (London)* 45, 577–87.

Gwei-Djen, L. and Needham, J. 1967. Records of diseases in ancient China. pp. 222–37 in Brothwell and Sandison.

Habakkuk, H.J. 1953. English population in the eighteenth century. *Econ. Hist. Rev.* (2) 6, 117–33.

Haber, L.F. 1986. *The poisonous cloud. Chemical warfare in the First World War*. Oxford University Press, London. Clarendon, New York. xiv + 415.

Hackett, C.J. 1963. On the origin of the human trepanomatoses (pinta, yaws, endemic syphilis and venereal syphilis). *WHO Bull.* 29, 7–41.

Hackett, C.J. 1967. The human trepanomatoses. pp. 152–69 in Brothwell and Sandison.

Hackett, C.J. 1980. Yaws. pp. 82–95 in Sabben-Clare, Bradley, and Kirkwood.

Hackett, J. 1983. *The profession of arms*. Sidgwick and Jackson, London. 256 pp.

Hackett, L.W. 1937. *Malaria in Europe*. Oxford University Press, London. xvi + 336.

Hackett, L.W. 1949a. The distribution of malaria. pp. 722–35 in Boyd.

Hackett, L.W. 1949b. Conspectus of malaria incidence in Northern Europe, the Mediterranean region and the Near East. pp. 788–99 in Boyd.

Haenszel, W. 1966. Quantitative evaluation of the etiologic factors in lung cancer. pp. 425–38 in Lilienfeld and Gifford.

Haenszel, W. 1982. Migrant studies. pp. 194–207 in Schottenfeld and Fraumeni.

Härting, F.H. and Hesse, W. 1879. Der Lungenkrebs, die Bergkrankheit in den Schneeberger Gruben. *Vierteljahrsschr. f. gerichtl. Med. u. öffentl. Gesundheitswesen* (N.F.) 30, 296–309; 31, 102–29 and 313–37.

Haeser, H. 1862. *Bibliotheca epidemiographica, sive, Catalogus librorum de historia morborum epidemicorum cum generali tum speciali conscriptorum*. Editio altera aucta et prorsus recognita. Greifswald, Jena. 245 pp.

Haeser, H. 1882. *Lehrbuch der Geschichte der Medizin und der epidemischen Krankheiten*. H.

Dufft, G. Fischer, Jena. 3 vols. First published 1845, under title *Lehrbuch der Geschichte der Medizin und der Volkskrankheiten.*

Hair, P.E.H. 1971. Deaths from violence in Britain: a tentative secular study. *Popul. Studies 25*, 5–24.

Hakulinen, T., Teppo, L, and Saxén, E. 1978. Cancer of the eye: A review of trends and differentials. *World Health Stat. Q. 31*, 143–58.

Hale, A.R. and Hale, M. 1972. *A review of the industrial accidents research literature.* HMSO, London. 95 pp.

Hall, A.R. 1967. Scientific progress and the progress of techniques. pp. 96–154 in *Cambridge Economic History of Europe*, vol. 4. Cambridge University Press.

Hall, C.B. 1983. The nosocomial spread of respiratory syncytial virus infections. *Annu. Rev. Med.* 34, 311–19.

Hall, N.E.L. and Schottenfeld, D. 1982. Penis. pp. 958–67 in Schottenfeld and Fraumeni.

Halley, E. 1693. An estimate of the degrees of the mortality of mankind, drawn from curious tables of the births and funerals at the city of Breslau; with an attempt to ascertain the price of annuities upon lives. *Philos. Trans. Roy. Soc. London 17*, 596–610, 654–56. Reprinted 1942, L.J. Reed (Ed.), Johns Hopkins, Baltimore.

Halley, E., Haygarth, J., Wigglesworth, E., Barton, W, and Milne, J. 1973. *Mortality in pre-industrial times: The contemporary verdict.* [Containing reprints of the above authors, 1694–1837.] Gregg International, London. Various pag.

Halliday, J.L. 1928. *An inquiry into the relationship between housing conditions and the incidence and fatality of measles.* Med. Res. Council Spec. Rep. Series No. 120, HMSO, London. 34 pp.

Hambraeus, L. 1982. Naturally occurring toxicants in food. pp. 13–36 in Jelliffe and Jelliffe.

Hamer, W.H. 1906. The Milroy Lectures on epidemic disease in England—The evidence of variability and persistency of type. *Lancet 1*, 569–74, 655–62, 733–39.

Hamilton, J.A.B. 1967. *British railway accidents of the twentieth century.* Allen & Unwin, London. 180 pp.

Hammon, W. McD. 1965. Diseases transmitted by an arthropod vector. pp. 290–357 in Sartwell.

Hammond, B. 1928. Urban death rates in the early nineteenth century. *Econ. Hist. 1*, 419–28.

Hammond, E.C., Selikoff, I.J, and Seidman, H. 1979. Asbestos exposure, cigarette smoking and death rates. *Ann. N. Y. Acad. Sci. 330*, 473–90.

Hammoud, E.I. 1977. Sex differentials in mortality. An enquiry with reference to the Arab countries and others. *World Health Stat. Rep. 30*, 174–206.

Hansen, M.L. 1940. *The Atlantic migration, 1607–1860.* Harvard University Press, Cambridge, MA. xxii + 386. Reprinted 1961, Harper & Row, New York.

Hansluwka, H. 1978. Cancer mortality in Europe, 1970–1974. *World Health Stat. Q. 31*, 159–94.

Hansluwka, H., Lopez, A.D, and Ruzicka, L.T. 1981. Health outlook for south and east Asia for the year 2000. *World Health Stat. Q. 34*, 168–95.

Harada, M. 1982. Minamata disease: Organic mercury poisoning caused by ingestion of contaminated fish. pp. 135–48 in Jelliffe and Jelliffe.

Hardy, G.F. 1885. The rates of mortality among the natives of India, as deducted from the recent census returns. *J. Inst. Actuar. 25*, 217–45.

Hardy, G.F. 1905. *Memorandum on the age tables and rates of mortality of the Indian census of 1901.* Supt. Govt. Printing, Calcutta. 66 pp.

Harinasuta, C. 1983. Parasitic diseases in the south (developing world). pp. 19–44 in Warren and Bowers.

Harlan, J.R. 1975. *Crops and man.* Foundations for Modern Crop Science Series. Am. Soc. Agronomy, Madison, WI. xi + 295.

Harnett, W.L. 1952. *A survey of cancer in London.* Report of the Clinical Cancer Research Committee, British Empire Cancer Campaign, London. vi + 834.

Harper, A.B. 1979. Life expectancy and population adaptation: The Aleut centenarian approach. pp. 309–27 in Laughlin and Harper.

Harries, J.T. 1976. The problem of bacterial diarrhoea. pp. 3–25 in Elliott and Knight.

Harris, C.C. and Autrup, H.N. (Eds.) 1983. *Human carcinogenesis.* Academic Press, New York. xxiv + 986.

Harrison, G. 1978. *Mosquitoes, malaria and man: A history of the hostilities.* E.P. Dutton, New York. viii + 314.

Harrison, G.A. and Boyce, A.J. (Eds.) 1972. *The structure of human populations.* Oxford University Press, New York. xvi + 448.

Hart, G.D. 1980. Ancient diseases of the blood. pp. 33–55 in Wintrobe.

Hart, G.D. 1984. *Disease in ancient man.* Clarke Irwin, Toronto. xvii + 297.

Hart, P.M.D'A. and Wright, G.P. 1939. *Tuberculosis and social conditions in England, with special reference to young adults.* National Assoc. for the Prevention of Tuberculosis, London. vii + 165.

Hartwig, G.W. and Patterson, K.D. (Eds.) 1978. *Disease in African history: An introductory survey and case studies.* No. 24, Duke University Center for Commonwealth and Comparative Studies. Duke University Press, Durham, NC. xiv + 258.

Harwood, R.F. and James, M.T. 1979. *Entomology in human and animal health*. 7th edition. (Formerly Herm's Medical Entomology.) Macmillan, New York. ix + 548.

Hassall, W.O. (Compiler) 1962. *How they lived. Vol. 1: An anthology of original accounts written before 1485*. Blackwell, Oxford. xvi + 356.

Hathcock, J.N. (Ed.) 1982. *Nutritional toxicology*. Vol. 1. Academic Press, New York. xiii + 515.

Hauser, P.M. 1942. The impact of war on population and vital phenomena. *Am. J. Sociol. 48*, 309–22.

Hauser, P.M. and Duncan, O.D. 1959. *The study of population*. University of Chicago Press, Chicago. IL. xvi + 864.

Hausfater, G. and Hrdy, S.B. (Eds.) 1984. *Infanticide. Comparative and evolutionary perspectives. From a conference, Ithaca, NY, 1982*. Biological Found. of Human Behavior Ser. Aldine, New York. xl + 598.

Havard, J.D.J. 1979. Mortality from motor vehicle accidents in the 15–24 year age group. *World Health Stat. Q. 32*, 225–41.

Havlik, R.J. and Feinleib, M. (Eds.) 1979. *Proceedings of the conference on the decline in coronary heart disease mortality. National Heart, Lung and Blood Institute, Bethesda, 1978*. NIH Publ. No. 79–1610, US Dept Health, Education, and Welfare, Washington, DC. xxvii + 399 + 42.

Hayflick, L. 1973. The biology of aging. *Am. J. Med Sci. 265*, 432–45.

Hayward, T.E. 1901. A series of life-tables for England and Wales for each successive decennium from 1841–50 to 1881–90, calculated by an abbreviated method. *J. Roy. Stat. Soc. 64*, 636–41.

Heaf, F. and Rusby, N.L. 1968. *Recent advances in respiratory tuberculosis*. 6th edition. J. and A. Churchill, London. viii + 234.

Heath, C.W. Jr 1982. The leukemias. pp. 728–38 in Schottenfeld and Fraumeni.

Heaton, K. 1975. The effects of carbohydrate refining on food ingestion, digestion and absorption. pp. 59–67 in Burkitt and Trowell.

Heaton, K. 1981. Gallstones, pp. 47–59 in Trowell and Burkitt, 1981*a*.

Hecker, J.F.K. 1832/1844. *Epidemics of the Middle Ages. Part 1. The Black Death in the fourteenth century. Part 2. The Dancing Mania. Part 3. The English Sweat*. Transl. from the German by B.G. Babington, 1844. Sydenham Society, London. xxiv + 344.

Heckscher, E.F. 1936. Sveriges befolkning från det stora nordiska krigets slut till Tabellverkets början, 1720–1750. pp. 255–85 in E.F. Heckscher, *Ekonomisk-historiska Studier*, Stockholm, 1936. 320 pp.

Heckscher, E.F. 1950. Swedish population trends before the Industrial Revolution. *Econ. Hist. Rev. 2* (2), 266–77.

Heckscher, E.F. 1954. *An economic history of Sweden*. Transl. by G. Ohlin with supplement by G. Heckscher and preface by A. Gerschenkron. Harvard Econ. Stud. Vol. 95. Cambridge, MA. xlii + 308.

Hegyeli, R.J. (Ed.) 1983. *Nutrition and cardiovascular disease, Papers from a symposium, Rome, 1980*. Progress in Biochemical Pharmacology, vol. 19. Karger, Basel. xii + 314.

Heiser, C.B. Jr 1981. *Seed to civilization. The story of food*. 2nd edition. Freeman and Co., San Francisco. xiv + 254.

Heite, H.J. (Ed.) 1967. *Krankheiten durch Aktinomyzeten und verwandte Erreger. Wechselwirkung zwischen pathogenen Pilzen und Wirtsorganismus*. Springer, Berlin. vi + 154.

Helfand, W.H., Woodruff, H.B., Coleman, K.M.H, and Cowen, D.L. 1980. Wartime industrial development of penicillin in the United States. pp. 31–56 in Parascandola.

Helleiner, K.F. 1967. The population of Europe from the Black Death to the eve of the vital revolution. pp. 1–95 in *Cambridge Economic History of Europe*, vol. IV. Cambridge University Press.

Helweg-Larsen, P., Hoffmeyer, H., Kieler, J., Thaysen, E.H., Thaysen, J.H., Thygesen, P, and Wulff, M.H. 1952*a*. Famine disease in German concentration camps: Complications and sequels. With special reference to tuberculosis, mental disorders and social consequences. *Acta Med. Scand. Suppl. 274*, 460 pp.

Helweg-Larsen, P., Hoffmeyer, H., Kieler, J., Thaysen, E.H., Thaysen, J.H., Thygesen, P, and Wulff, M.H. 1952*b*. Tuberculosis. pp. 330–61 in Helweg-Larsen, Hoffmeyer, et al. 1952*a*.

Hendriks, F. 1862. On the vital statistics of Sweden, 1749–1855. *J. Stat. Soc. (London) 25*, 111–74.

Henle, F.G.J. 1840. *Pathologische Untersuchungen, Pt. 1*. Berlin. Reprinted as *Von den Miasmen und Kontagien*, in Sudhoffs Klassiker der Medizin, No. 3, F. Marchand, Leipzing, 1910; and as *On miasma and contagia*, transl. by G. Rosen, *Bull. Hist. Med. 6* (1938), 907–83.

Henle, W., Henle, G, and Lennette, T. 1979. The Epstein-Barr virus. *Sci. Am. 241*, 40–51.

Hennen, J. 1820. *Principles of military surgery:*

Comprising observations on the arrangement, policy, and practice of hospitals, and on the history, treatment and anomalies of variola and syphilis. 2nd edition. Longman, Hurst, Rees, Orme and Brown, Edinburgh. xiii + 580.

Hennock, E.P. 1957. Urban sanitary reform a generation before Chadwick. *Econ. Hist. Rev.* (2) *10*, 113–20.

Henripin, J. and Peron, Y. 1972. The demographic transition of the province of Quebec. pp. 213–31 in Glass and Revelle.

Henry, L. 1956. *Anciennes familles génévoises. Etude démographique, 16ème-20ème siècle.* Institut National d'Etudes Démographiques, Paris. 234 pp.

Henry, L. 1965a. Démographie de la noblesse britannique. *Population 20*, 692–704.

Henry, L. 1965b. The population of France in the eighteenth century. Transl. P. Jimack. pp. 434–56 in Glass and Eversley.

Henry, L. 1976. *Population: Analysis and models.* Transl. E. van der Walle and E.F. Jones. Edward Arnold, London. xiii + 301.

Henry, W. 1832. Further experiments on the disinfecting powers of increased temperatures. *Philos. Mag. 11*, 25–26.

Henschen, F. 1947. *On Förändringar i det sverska sjukdomspanoramat under de sista 50 åren (Changes in causes of mortality in Sweden in the last fifty years).* Bonnier, Stockholm. 80 pp.

Henshaw, P.S. and Hawkins, J.W. 1944. Incidence of leukemia in physicians. *J. Natl. Cancer Instit. 4*, 339–46.

Hercules, J.I., Schechter, A.N., Eaton, W, and Jackson, R.E. (Eds.) 1974. *Proceedings of the first national symposium on sickle cell disease.* DHEW Publn No. (NIH) 75–723, US Nat. Instit. Health, Bethesda, MD. vi + 414.

Herford, G.V.B. 1961. Losses resulting from the infestation of stored products by insects. *Proc. Nutr. Soc. 20*, 11–14.

Hersch, L. 1925–1927. La mortalité causée par la guerre mondiale. *Metron 5* (1), 89–133 and 7 (1), 3–82.

Hershey, D. 1974. *Lifespan and factors affecting it.* C.C. Thomas, Springfield, IL. xiv + 158.

Hess, A.F. 1982. *Scurvy. Past and present.* Reprint 1920 edition with new material. Nutrition Foundation Reprints. Academic Press, New York. xxxiv + 280.

Heyningen, W.E. van and Seal, J.R. 1983. *Cholera. The American scientific experience, 1947–1980.* Westview, Boulder, CO. xviii + 344.

Hicks, D.G. 1985. *Aboriginal mortality rates in Western Australia.* Health Dept of Western Australia, Perth. 160 pp.

Hicks, J.R. 1942. *The social framework.* Clarendon, Oxford. xii + 212.

Higginson, J., Terracini, B., and Agthe, C. 1975. Nutrition and cancer: Ingestion of foodborne carcinogens. pp. 177–206 in Schottenfeld.

Higounet-Naval, A. 1980. La démographie des villes françaises au Moyen-Age. *Ann. Démog. Hist.*, Pt. 2, 187–211.

Hill, A.B. 1929. An investigation of sickness in various industrial occupations. *J. Roy. Stat. Soc. 92*, 183–238.

Hill, A.B. 1933. Some aspects of the mortality from whooping cough. *J. Roy. Stat. Soc. 96*, 240–85.

Hill, A.B. 1936. The recent trend in England and Wales of mortality from phthisis at young adult ages. *J. Roy. Stat. Soc. 99*, 247–96.

Hill, G.B. and Harvey, W. 1972. The mortality of dentists. *Br. Dental J. 132*, 179–82.

Hinde, R.S.E. 1951. *The British penal system 1773–1950.* Duckworth, London. 255 pp.

Hinman, A.R., Brandling-Bennett, A.D., Bernier, R.H., Kirby, C.D., and Eddins, D.L. 1980. Current features of measles in the United States: Feasibility of measles elimination. *Epidemiol. Rev. 2*, 153–70.

Hinman, E.H. 1966. *World eradication of infectious diseases.* C.C. Thomas, Springfield, IL. xvii + 223.

Hinton, H.C. (Ed.) 1979. *The People's Republic of China: A handbook.* Westview, Boulder, CO. xvii + 443.

Hinton, M.A.C. 1918. *Rats and mice as enemies of mankind.* British Museum, London. x + 63.

Hiraishi, K., Kohari, K., Miyairi, M., and Yamamoto, S. (Eds.) 1977. *Gastrointestinal infections in Southeast Asia: Laboratory works and preventive measures.* Southeast Asian Medical Information Center (SEAMIC), Tokyo. xiv + 130.

Hirsch, A. 1883–1886. *Handbook of geographical and historical pathology.* Transl. by C. Creighton. New Sydenham Society, London. 3 vols.

Hirst, B.C. (Ed.) 1889. *A system of obstetrics by American authors.* Lea Brothers, Philadelphia. xi + 854.

Hirst, L.F. 1953. *The conquest of plague: A study of the evolution of epidemiology.* Clarendon, Oxford. xvi + 478.

Hishinuma, S. 1981. Mortality trends in Japan and their possible causes. With discussion. pp. 121–42 in Boström and Ljungstedt.

Historisk Statistik för Sverige. 1955. I. Befolkning, 1720–1950. (Historical statistics of Sweden. I.

Population, 1720–1950.) Statistiska Centralbyrån, Stockholm. 78 + tables.

Historisk Statistikk. 1978. Norges offisielle statistikk. Statistisk Sentralbyrå, Oslo. 650 pp. (Irregular series.)

Hjerman, I., Velve Byre, K., Holme, I., and Leren, P. 1981. Effect of diet and smoking intervention on the incidence of coronary heart disease. Report from the Oslo Study Group of a randomized trial in healthy men. *Lancet 2*, 1303–10.

Hoare, C.A. 1972. *The trypanosomes of mammals: A zoological monography.* Blackwell, Oxford-Edinburgh. xvii + 749.

Hobbs, B.C. 1974. *Food poisoning and food hygiene.* Edward Arnold, London. ix + 308.

Hobby, G.L. 1985. *Penicillin. Meeting the challenge.* Yale University Press, New Haven, CT. xxii + 319.

Hobson, W. 1963. *World health and history.* John Wright, Bristol. xii + 252.

Hobson, W. (Ed.) 1979. *The theory and practice of public health.* 5th edition. Oxford University Press, New York-Toronto. xv + 785.

Hoeden, J. van der (Ed.) 1964. *Zoonoses.* Elsevier, Amsterdam. xi + 774.

Högberg, U. and Broström, G. 1985. The demography of maternal mortality—Seven Swedish parishes in the 19th century. *Int. J. Gynaecol. Obstet. 23*, 489–97.

Hoeppli, R. 1959. *Parasites and parasitic infections in early medicine and science.* University of Malaya Press, Singapore. xiv + 526.

Hoffman, F.L. 1932. Causes of death in primitive races. *Metron 10* (1–2), 153–200.

Hoffman, H.J., Lundin, F.E. Jr. Bakketeig, L.S., and Harley, E.E. 1977. Classification of births by weight and gestational age for future studies of prematurity. pp. 297–333 in Reed and Stanley.

Hofsten, E. and Lundström, H. 1976. *Swedish population history: Main trends from 1750 to 1970.* Statistiska Centralbyrån, Stockholm. 186 pp.

Holden, W.D. 1976. Graduate medical education. pp. 313–44 in Bowers and Purcell.

Holland, C. and Heaton, K.W. 1972. Increasing frequency of gall bladder operations in the Bristol clinical area. *Br. Med. J. 3*, 672–75.

Holland, E. 1922. *The causation of foetal death. Report of an investigation into the factors which determined death in a sample of three hundred foetuses of viable age.* U.K. Ministry of Health, Reports on Public Health and Medical Subjects No. 7, HMSO, London. viii + 159.

Hollingsworth, M. and Hollingsworth, T.H. 1971. Plague mortality rates by age and sex in the Parish of St. Botolph's without Bishopsgate, London, 1603. *Popul. Studies 25*, 131–46.

Hollingsworth, T.H. 1957. A demographic study of the British ducal families. *Popul. Studies 11*, 4–26. Reprinted in Glass and Eversley, 1965, pp. 354–78.

Hollingsworth, T.H. 1965a. The demographic background of the peerage, 1603–1938. *Eugenics Rev. 57*, 56–66.

Hollingsworth, T.H. 1965b. *The demography of the British peerage.* Suppl. to *Popul. Studies*, vol. 18. Population Investigation Council, London. 108 pp.

Hollingsworth, T.H. 1969. *Historical demography.* Hodder & Stoughton, London. 448 pp.

Holm, S.E. and Christensen, P. (Eds.) 1982. *Basic concepts of streptococci and streptococcal diseases.* Internatl. Symp. on Streptococci and Streptococcal Diseases No. 8. Reedbooks, Chertsey, Surrey. 335 pp.

Holman, C.D.J., Mulroney, C.D., and Armstrong, B.K. 1980. Epidemiology of pre-invasive and invasive malignant melanoma in Western Australia. *Int. J. Cancer 25*, 317–23.

Holme, T., Holmgren, J., Merson, M.H., and Möllby, R. (Eds.) 1981. *Acute enteric infections in children. New prospects for treatment and prevention.* Elsevier/North Holland, Amsterdam. xxi + 549.

Holmes, I.H. 1979. Viral gastroenteritis. *Prog. Med. Virol. 25*, 1–36.

Holmes, O.W. 1843. The contagiousness of puerperal fever. *N. Engl. Q. J. Med. Surg.*, 28 pp.

Holmes, O.W. 1855. *Puerperal fever, as a private pestilence.* (Holmes, 1843, reprinted with additions.) Ticknor and Fields, Boston. 60 pp.

Holmstedt, B. and Liljestrand, G. (Eds.) 1963. *Readings in pharmacology.* Pergamon Press. Oxford-London-New York. x + 395.

Holt, S.C. 1978. Anatomy and chemistry of spirochetes. *Microbiol. Rev. 42*, 114–60.

Hoogstraal, H. (with edit. assist. of A.L. Gahin and A. Djigounian) 1970. *Bibliography of ticks and tickborne diseases. From Homer (about 800 BC) to 31 December 1969.* US Naval Medical Res. Unit No. 3, Cairo. vi + 496.

Hoover, H. 1960/1961. *An American epic.* Vol. 2, *Famine in forty-five nations. Organization behind the front 1914–1923.* xii + 489. Vol. 3, *Famine in forty-five nations. The battle on the front line 1914–1923.* xxv + 592. Hoover Institution on War, Revolution and Peace. Henry Regnery, Chicago.

Hope-Simpson, R.E. 1954. Studies on shingles. Is the virus ordinary chickenpox virus? *Lancet 2*,

1299–1302.

Hopkins, D.M. (Ed.) 1967a. *The Bering land bridge*. Stanford University Press, Stanford, CA. xiii + 495.

Hopkins, D.M. 1967b. The cenozoic history of Beringia. pp. 451–84 in Hopkins, 1967a.

Hopkins, D.R. 1983a. *Princes and peasants: Smallpox in history*. University of Chicago Press, Chicago-London. xx + 380.

Hopkins, D.R. 1983b. Dracunculiasis: an eradicable scourge. *Epidemiol. Rev. 5*, 208–19.

Hopkins, M.K. 1966. On the probable age structure of the Roman population. *Popul. Studies 20*, 245–64.

Hornabrook, R.W. 1982. Adverse effects of diet in New Guinea: Kuru and enteritis necroticans. pp. 289–96 in Jelliffe and Jelliffe.

Hornick, R.B., Greisman, S.E., Woodward, T.E., Dupont, H.L., Dawkins, A.T., and Snyder, M.J. 1970. Typhoid fever: Pathogenesis and immunological control. *N. Engl. J. Med. 283*, 686–91; 739–46.

Horsfall, F.L. and Tamm, I. (Eds.) 1965. *Viral and rickettsial infections of man*. J.B. Lippincott, Philadelphia. xvi + 1282.

Horstmann, D.M. 1982. Rubella. pp. 519–39 in Evans, 1982a.

Houdaille, J. 1972. Pertes de l'armée de terre sous le premier Empire, d'après les registres matricules. *Population 27*, 27–50.

Housworth, J. and Langmuir, A.D. 1974. Excess mortality from epidemic influenza. *Am. J. Epidemiol. 100*, 40–48.

Howard, C.R. 1984. Viral hepatitis. pp. 451–71 in Topley and Wilson, 1984, vol. 4.

Howard, J. 1777/1977. *The state of the prisons*. Bicentennial edition, comprising a facsimile reprint of the first edition published in 1777 with a preface by Martin Wright. Professional Books, Abingdon, Oxon. xv + 512.

Howard, M. 1976. *War in European history*. Oxford University Press, Oxford. x + 165.

Howard, W.T. 1924. *Public health administration and the natural history of disease in Baltimore, Maryland, 1797–1920*. Carnegie Instit., Washington, DC. vi + 565.

Howard-Jones, N. 1975. *The scientific background of the International Sanitary Conferences 1851–1938*. Reprinted from *WHO Chron. 28*, 159–71, 229–47, 369–84, 414–26, 455–70, 495–508. WHO, Geneva. 110 pp.

Howard-Jones, N. 1980. Prelude to modern preventive medicine. pp. 69–80 in Stanley and Joske.

Howe, G.M. 1963. *National atlas of disease mortality in the U.K.* Thomas Nelson, London. viii + 111.

Howe, G.M. 1971. The mapping of disease in history. pp. 335–57 in Clarke.

Howe, G.M. 1972. *Man, environment and disease in Britain: A Medical geography of Britain through the ages*. Barnes and Noble, New York; David & Charles, Newton Abbot. xviii + 285.

Hubbard, W.N. Jr 1976. The origins of medicinals. pp. 685–721 in Bowers and Purcell.

Huber, M. 1912. Mortalité suivant la profession, d'après les décès en France en 1907 et 1908. *Bull. Stat. Générale de la France 1* (4), 402–39.

Huckstep, R.L. 1962. *Typhoid fever and other salmonella infections*. E. & S. Livingstone, Edinburgh-London. xvi + 334.

Hudson, R.P. 1983. *Disease and its control. The shaping of modern thought*. Contributions in Medical Hist. No. 12. Greenwood Press, Westport, CT. xviii + 259.

Hueper, W.C. 1962. Symposium on chemical carcinogenesis. Part 1. Environmental and occupational cancer hazards. *Clin. Pharmacol. Ther. 3*, 776–813.

Hueper, W.C. 1966. *Occupational and environmental cancers of the respiratory system*. Springer, Berlin. xi + 214.

Hughes, J.D. and Thirgood, J.V. 1982. Deforestation in ancient Greece and Rome: A cause of collapse. *Ecologist 12*, 196–208.

Hughes, P.H., Canavan, K.P., Jarvis, G., and Arif, A. 1983. Extent of drug abuse: An international review with implications for health planners. *World Health Stat. Q. 36*, 394–497.

Hughes, R. 1987. *The fatal shore: A history of the transportation of convicts to Australia, 1787–1868*. Collins Harvill, London. xvi + 688.

Hull, C.H. (Ed.) 1899. *The economic writings of Sir William Petty. Together with the Observations upon the Bills of Mortality more probably by Captain John Graunt*. Cambridge University Press. 2 vols.

Humphrey, G.T. 1970. Mortality at the oldest ages. *J. Inst. Actuar. 96*, 105–19.

Humphreys, N.A. 1883. The recent decline in the English death-rate and its effect upon the duration of life. With discussion. *J. Stat. Soc. (London) 46*, 189–224.

Humphreys, N.A. 1887. Class mortality statistics. *J. Roy. Stat. Soc. 50*, 255–85.

Hunt, S.A. and Stinson, E.B. 1981. Cardiac transplantation. *Annu. Rev. Med. 32*, 213–20.

Hunter, D. 1975. *The diseases of occupations*. 5th edition. English Universities Press, London. xix

+ 1225.

Hunter, D., Bomford, R.R., and Russel, D.S. 1940. Poisoning by methyl mercury compounds. *Q. J. Med. 9*, 193–213.

Hurley, R. 1983. Virus infections in pregnancy and the puerperium. pp. 19–55 in *Recent advances in clinical virology*, vol. 3. A.P. Waterson, Ed. Churchill-Livingstone, Edinburgh. viii + 278.

Hussein, A.M. (Ed.) 1976. *Rehab: Drought and famine in Ethiopia*. Internatl. African Inst., London. iv + 122.

Hutchinson, J., Clark, J.G.G., Jope, E.M., and Riley, R. (Eds.) 1977. *The early history of agriculture: A joint symposium of the Royal Society and the British Academy*. Oxford University Press, New York. iv + 214. (Reprinted from *Philos. Trans. Roy. Soc. B275*, 1976.)

Iida, K. and Iwasaki, T. (Eds.) 1983. *Tsunamis. Their science and engineering*. From a symposium, Advances in Earth and Planetary Sciences, Japan, 1981. Terra, Tokyo; Reidel, Boston. xiv + 563.

Illich, I. 1975. *Medical nemesis: The expropriation of health*. Ideas in Progress Series. Marion Boyars, London. 184 pp.

Imhof, A.E. 1981. *Die gewonnenen Jahre. Von der Zunahme unserer Lebensspanne seit dreihundert Jahren oder von der Notwendigkeit einer neuen Einstellung zu Leben und Sterben*. C.H. Beck, Munich. 279 pp.

Imhof, A.E. 1983. Man and body in the history of the modern age. Reflections on an international symposium in Berlin 1–3 December 1981. *Med. Hist. 27*, 394–406.

Imhof, A.E. 1984. The amazing simultaneousness of the big differences and the boom in the 19th century—Some facts and hypotheses about infant and maternal mortality in Germany, 18th to 20th century. pp. 191–222 in Bengtsson, Fridlizius, et al.

Imhof, A.E. 1985*a*. From the old mortality pattern to the new: Implications of a radical change from the sixteenth to the twentieth century. The Fielding H. Garrison Lecture, San Francisco, May 1984. *Bull. Hist. Med. 59*, 1–29.

Imhof, A.E. 1985*b*. Mortality problems in Brazil and in Germany: Past, present, future. Learning from each other? *Rev. Saúde pública (S. Paulo) 19*, 233–50.

INED/PUF 1984. *La lutte contre la mort: l'influence des politiques sociales et des politiques de santé sur l'évolution de la mortalité*. INED/PUF Travaux et Documents, Cahier No. 109. Institut National d'Etudes Démographiques, Paris. 538 pp. (For re-

view, see Vallin and Lopez, 1985.)

Ingalls, T.H., Babbott, F.L., Hampson, K.W., and Gordon, J.E. 1960. Rubella: Its epidemiology and teratology. *Am. J. Med. Sci. 239*, 363–83.

Ingalls, T.H. and Klingberg, M.A. 1965. Congenital malformations: Clinical and community considerations. *Am. J. Med. Sci. 249*, 316–44.

Ingalls, T.H., Plotkin, S.A., Meyer, H.M., and Parkman, P.D. 1967. Rubella: Epidemiology, virology and immunology. *Am. J. Med. Sci. 253*, 349–73.

Institut National d'Etudes Démographiques (INED) 1977. Sixième rapport sur la situation démographique de la France. *Population 32*, 253–338.

Institute of Medicine—Panel on Health Services Research. 1973. *Infant death: An analysis by maternal risk and health care*. Contrasts in Health Status, vol. 1. US National Academy of Sciences, Washington, DC. xvii + 203.

Interdisciplinary Panel on Carcinogenicity 1984. Criteria for evidence of chemical carcinogenicity. *Science 225*, 682–87.

Irgens, L.M. 1981. Epidemiological aspects and implications of the disappearance of leprosy from Norway: Some factors contributing to the decline. *Leprosy Rev. 52* Suppl., 147–65.

Isaacson, C. 1982. *Pathology of a black African population*. Current Topics in Pathology, Vol. 72. Springer, Berlin-Heidelberg-New York. 152 pp.

Iskrant, A.P. and Joliet, P.V. 1968. *Accidents and homicide*. Harvard University Press, Cambridge, MA. xvi + 202.

Istituto Centrale di Statistica del Regno d'Italia 1934. La mortalità per malattie puerperali. *Metron 11* (3), 75–165.

Iversen, E. 1971. Epidemiological basis of tuberculosis eradication. II. Mortality among tuberculosis cases and the general population of Greenland. *WHO Bull. 45*, 677–87.

Jackson, W.P.U. 1971. Diabetes mellitus in different countries and different races. Prevalence and major features. *Acta Diabet. Latina 7*, 361–401.

Jackson, W.P.U. 1978. The genetics of diabetes mellitus. *S. Afr. Med. J. 53*, 481–90.

Jacobson, P.H. 1957. An estimation of the expectation of life in the United States in 1850. *Milbank Q. 35*, 197–201.

Jacobson, P.H. 1964. Cohort survival for generations since 1840. *Milbank Q. 42*, 36–53.

Jaffe, A.J. and Lourie, W.I. 1942. An abridged life table for the white population of the United States in 1830. *Hum. Biol. 14*, 352–71.

Jalavisto, E. 1951. Inheritance of longevity according to Finnish and Swedish genealogies. *Ann. Medicinae Internae Fenniae 40* (4), 263–74.

James, S.P. 1920. The general statistics of influenza in Australasia and parts of Africa and Asia. pp. 349–86 in Newman, Greenwood, et al.

James, S.P. and Christophers, S.R. 1922. Malaria. pp. 1500–07 in *Practice of Medicine in the Tropics*, vol. 2, W. Byam and R.G. Archibald, Eds. Hodder & Stoughton, London. 4 vols.

Janerich, D.T. and Polednak, A.P. 1983. Epidemiology of birth defects. *Epidemiol. Rev. 5*, 16–37.

Janeway, C.A. 1980. Plasma, the transport fluid for blood cells and humors. pp. 573–99 in Wintrobe.

Janssens, P.A. 1970. *Palaeopathology. Diseases and injuries of prehistoric man*. John Baker, London; Humanities Press, New York. xiii + 170.

Jarcho, S. 1957. John Mitchell, Benjamin Rush, and yellow fever. *Bull. Hist. Med. 31*, 132–36.

Jarcho, S. 1964. Some observations on diseases in prehistoric America. *Bull. Hist. Med. 38*, 1–19.

Jarcho, S. (Ed.) 1966. *Symposium on human palaeopathology, Washington, 1965*. Yale University Press, New Haven, CT. xiii + 182.

Jefferson, G. 1950. Surgery 1900–1950. *Br. Med. J. 1*, 8–12.

Jeffrey, M.R. and Ball, J. (Eds.) 1963. *The epidemiology of chronic rheumatism. A symposium organized by the Council for International Organization of Medical Sciences*. Blackwell, Oxford. 2 vols.

Jelliffe, D.B. (Ed.) 1970. *Diseases of children in the subtropics and tropics*. 2nd edition. Edward Arnold, London. xx + 1010.

Jelliffe, D.B. and Jelliffe, E.F.P. 1971. The effects of starvation on the function of the family and of society. pp. 54–63 in Blix, Hofvander, and Vahlquist.

Jelliffe, D.B. and Jelliffe, E.F.P. 1978. *Human milk in the modern world: Psychological, nutritional and economic significance*. Oxford University Press, Oxford. x + 500.

Jelliffe, E.F.P. and Jelliffe, D.B. (Eds.) 1982. *Adverse effects of foods*. Plenum, New York-London. xv + 614.

Jensen, O.M. and Bolander, A.M. 1980. Trends in malignant melanoma of the skin. *World Health Stat. Q. 33*, 2–26.

Jick, H. 1980. Epidemiological observation on drug-induced illness. pp. 1–15 in Grundmann.

Johansson, S., Vedin, A., and Wilhelmsson, C. 1983. Myocardial infarction in women. *Epidemiol. Rev. 5*, 67–95.

Johnson, J.H. 1957–1958. The population of Londonderry during the Great Irish Famine. *Econ. Hist Rev.* (2) *10*, 273–85.

Johnson, R.C. (Ed.) 1976. *The biology of parasitic spirochetes*. Academic Press, New York-London. xiii + 402.

Johnson, R.C. 1977. The spirochetes. *Annu. Rev. Microbiol. 31*, 89–106.

Johnston, B.F. 1982. Multisectorial nutrition interventions: A policy analysis perspective. *Crit. Rev. Trop. Med. 1*, 335–65. See Chandra, 1982.

Johnstone, R.W. 1950. Fifty years of midwifery. *Br. Med. J. 1*, 12–16.

Jokl, E. 1985. *Sudden death of athletes*. C.C. Thomas, Springfield, IL. xviii + 124.

Jones, E.L. and Mingay, G.E. (Eds.) 1967. *Land, labour and population in the Industrial Revolution. Essays presented to J.D. Chambers*. Edward Arnold, London. xvii + 286.

Jones, P.E. and Judges, A.V. 1935. London population in the late seventeenth century. *Econ. Hist. Rev.* (1) *6*, 45–63.

Jones, R.E. 1976. Infant mortality in rural North Shropshire, 1561–1810. *Popul. Studies 30*, 305–17.

Jones, R.E. 1980. Futher evidence on the decline in infant mortality in pre-industrial England: North Shropshire 1561–1810. *Popul. Studies 34*, 239–50.

Jones, R.T. 1983. Cannabis and health. *Annu. Rev. Med. 34*, 247–58.

Jones, W.H.S. 1909. *Malaria and Greek history*. pp. ix–136, 157–75. To which is added *The history of Greek therapeutics and the malaria theory*, by E.T. Withington, pp. 137–56. Historical Ser. No. 8, Manchester University Press, Manchester. ix + 175. Edited and reduced in Brothwell and Sandison, 1967.

Jonsson, S. 1944. *Sóttarfar og sjúkdómar á Íslandi, 1400–1800*. (Epidemics in Iceland, 1400–1800.) Íslenzka Bókmenntafélag, Reykjavik. viii + 263.

Joossens, J.V. 1980. Stroke, stomach cancer and salt: A possible clue to the prevention of hypertension. pp. 489–508 in Kesteloot and Joossens.

Jordan, E.O. 1927. The influenza epidemic of 1918. I. Encephalitis and influenza. II & III. Preventive measures. *J. Am. Med. Assoc. 89*, 1603–06, 1689–93, 1779–83.

Joslin, E.P., Root, H.F., White, P., and Marble, A. 1946/1959. *The treatment of diabetes mellitus*. 10th edition, 1959. Henry Kimpton, London. 798 pp. (8th edition, 1946)

Joslin, E.P. and Wilson, J.L. 1950. Lessons from 472 fatalities in diabetic children. *Br. Med. J. 2*, 1293–96.

Juergens, J.L. 1980. Thromboangiitis obliterans (Buerger's disease, TAO). pp. 469–91 in Juergens, Spittell, and Fairbairn.

Juergens, J.L., Spittell, J.A. Jr, and Fairbairn, J.F.II (Eds.) 1980. *Peripheral vascular diseases.* 5th edition. W.B. Saunders, Philadelphia. xiv + 981.

Jung, J. 1970. Mortality in the general population and among the insured in Sweden in 1967. *Skand. Aktuarietidskr. 53,* 131–45.

Juniper, K. Jr 1971. Amebiasis in the U.S. *Bull. N.Y. Acad. Med.* (2) *47,* 448–61.

Jutikkala, E. 1945. Die Bevölkerung Finnlands in den Jahren 1721–49. *Ann. Acad. Sci. Fenn. 55* (4), Transl. and reprinted in Glass and Eversley, 1965, pp. 549–69.

Jutikkala, E. 1955. The Great Finnish Famine in 1696–97. *Scand. Econ. Hist. Rev. 3* (1), 48–63.

Jutikkala, E. and Kauppinen, M. 1971. The structure of mortality during catastrophic years in a preindustrial society. *Popul. Studies 25,* 283–85.

Kagan, A., Harris, B.R., Winkelstein, W. Jr, Johnson, K.G., Kato, H., Syme, S.L., Rhoads, G.G., Gay, M.L., Nichaman, M.Z., Hamilton, H.B., and Tillotson, J. 1974. Epidemiologic studies of coronary heart disease and stroke in Japanese men living in Japan, Hawaii and California: Demographic, physical, dietary and biochemical characteristics. *J. Chron. Dis. 27,* 345–64.

Kalbfleisch, J.D. and Prentice, R.L. 1980. *The statistical analysis of failure time data.* Wiley, New York. xi + 321.

Kalter, H. and Warkany, J. 1983. Congenital malformations: etiologic factors and their role in prevention. *N. Engl. J. Med. 308,* 424–31, 494–97.

Kamal, A.M. 1974. The seventh pandemic of cholera. pp. 1–14 in Barua and Burrows.

Kapadia, C.R. and Donaldson, R.M. 1985. Disorders of cobalamin (Vitamin B_{12}) absorption and transport. *Annu. Rev. Med. 36,* 93–110.

Kaplan, A.S. (Ed.) 1973. *The herpesviruses.* Academic Press, New York. xiv + 739.

Kaplan, M.M., Abdussalam, M., and Bijlenga, G. 1962. Diseases transmitted through milk. pp. 11–74 in WHO-milk.

Kates, R.W., Haas, J.E., Amaral, D.J., Olson, R.A., Ramos, R., and Olson, R. 1973. Human impact of the Managua earthquake. *Science 182,* 981–90.

Kato, H., Tillotson, J., Nichaman, M.Z., Rhoads, G.G., and Hamilton, H.B. 1973. Epidemiologic studies of coronary heart disease and stroke in Japanese men living in Japan, Hawaii and Califor-

nia—Serum lipids and diet. *Am. J. Epidemiol. 97,* 372–85.

Katz, A.H. and Felton, J.S. (Eds.) 1965. *Health and the community. Readings in the philosophy and sciences of public health.* Free Press, New York; Collier-Macmillan, London. xviii + 877.

Kean, B.H., Mott, K.E., and Russell, A.J. 1978. *Tropical medicine and pathology: Classic investigations.* Cornell University Press. Ithaca. xxiii + 677 (2 vols.)

Keatinge, W.R. 1981. Hypothermia. pp. 123–29 in Watt, Freeman, and Bynum.

Keen, H. 1982. Problems in the definition of diabetes mellitus and its subtypes. pp. 1–11 in Koebberling and Tattersall.

Keers, R.Y. 1978. *Pulmonary tuberculosis: A journey down the centuries.* Baillière Tindall, London; Collier-Macmillan, Sydney. 276 pp.

Keevil, J.J. 1957/1958. *Medicine and the navy, 1200–1900. Vol. I—1200–1649. Vol. II—1649–1714.* E. & S. Livingstone, Edinburgh-London. xii + 255; xii + 332. (For later vols. see Lloyd and Coulter, 1961/1963.)

Kehrer, E. 1952. *Anatomie und Physiologie der Schwangerschaft.* pp. 354–55 in Biologie und Pathologie des Weibes, ein Handbuch der Frauenheilkunde und der Geburtshilfe. 2nd edition. L. Seitz and A.I. Amreich, Eds. Urban and Schwarzenburg, Berlin.

Keller, W. and Fillmore, C.M. 1983. Prevalence of protein-energy malnutrition. *World Health Stat. Q. 36,* 129–40.

Kelsey, J.L. 1979. A review of the epidemiology of human breast cancer. *Epidemiol. Rev. 1,* 74–109.

Kennaway, E.L. and Waller, R.E. 1954. Studies on cancer of the lung. In *Cancer of the Lung (Endemiology): a symposium.* J. Clemmesen, Ed. Council Internat. Org. Med. Sci. (CIOMS), Louvain, Belgium. 210 pp. Reprinted from *Acta Un. Int. c. Cancr. 9* (1953), 485–94.

Kent, P.W. 1971. Treatment of pulmonary tuberculosis: A comparison of the one-year results as obtained under routine service and under EA/UK MRC clinical trial conditions (a preliminary report). pp. 310–13 in Gould.

Kent, W. (Ed.) 1951. *An encyclopaedia of London.* J.M. Dent, London. xii + 674.

Kermack, W.O., McKendrick, A.G., and McKinlay, P.L. 1934a. Death rates in Great Britain and Sweden: some general regularities and their significance. *Lancet 1,* 698–703.

Kermack, W.O., McKendrick, A.G., and McKinlay, P.L. 1934b. Death rates in Great Britain and Sweden: Expression of specific mortality rates as products of two factors and some consequences thereof. *J. Hyg. Camb. 34*, 433–57.

Kerr, D.N.S. 1977. Chronic renal failure. pp. 1093–107 in *Textbook of Medicine*, P.B. Beeson and W. McDermott (Eds.), W.B. Saunders, Philadelphia. lxxviii + 1892.

Kessler, I.I. and Lilienfeld, A.M. 1969. Perspectives in the epidemiology of leukemia. *Adv. Cancer Res. 12*, 225–302.

Kesteloot, H. and Joossens, J.V. 1980. *Epidemiology of arterial blood pressure*. Martinus Nijhoff, The Hague. xvi + 515.

Keusch, G. 1982. Shigellosis. *Crit. Rev. Trop. Med.* 1, 77–107. See Chandra, 1982.

Keyfitz, N. and Flieger, W. 1968. *World population: An analysis of vital data*. University of Chicago Press, Chicago. xii + 672.

Keys, A. (Ed.) 1970. Coronary heart disease in seven countries. *Circulation 41*, Suppl. 1, 211 pp.

Keys, A. 1981. Ten-year mortality in the seven countries study. With discussion. pp. 15–61, in Boström and Ljungstedt.

Keys, A., et al. 1980. *Seven countries. A multivariate analysis of death and coronary heart disease*. Harvard University Press, Cambridge, MA. xvi + 382.

Keys, A., Brožek, J., Henschel, A., Mickelsen, O., and Taylor, H.L. 1950. *The biology of human starvation*. University of Minnesota Press, Minneapolis. 2 vols. xxii + 766; ix + 767–1385.

Keyser, E. 1941. *Bevölkerungsgeschichte Deutschlands*. 2nd edition. S, Hirzel, Leipzig. xv + 459.

Kilbourne, E.D. (Ed.) 1975a. *The influenza viruses and influenza*. Academic Press, New York. xi + 573.

Kilbourne, E.D. 1975b. Epidemiology of influenza. pp. 483–538 in Kilbourne, 1975a.

Kilbourne, E.D. 1987. *Influenza*. Plenum, New York, xxii + 359.

Kim, C.W., Campbell, W.C., et al. (Eds.) 1985. *Trichinellosis. Proc. of the Sixth Internat, Conf., July 1984*. State University of New York Press, Albany. xx + 343.

Kimberlin, R.H. 1984. Slow viruses: Conventional and unconventional. pp. 487–510 in Topley and Wilson, 1984, vol. 4.

King, L.S. 1952. Dr. Koch's postulates. *J. Hist. Med. 7*, 350–61.

King, L.S. 1958. *The medical world of the eighteenth century*. University of Chicago Press, Chicago, xix + 346.

Kirk, R.L. 1981. *Aboriginal man adapting: The human biology of Australian aboriginals*. Oxford University Press, New York. xii + 230.

Kisskalt, K. 1929. Laboratoriumsinfektionen mit Typhusbazillen und anderen Bakterien. *Arch. Hyg. Bakteriol. 101*, 137–60.

Kitamoto, O. (Ed.) 1975. *Gastrointestinal infections in Southeast Asia*. Southeast Asian Medical Information Center (SEAMIC), Tokyo. xvii + 251.

Klainer, A.S. and Beisel, W.R. 1969. Opportunistic infection: A review. *Am. J. Med. Sci. 258*, 431–56.

Klayman, D.L. 1985. Qinghaosu (Artemisinin): An antimalarial drug from China. *Science 228*, 1049–55.

Klein, G. 1973. The Epstein-Barr virus. pp. 521–55 in Kaplan.

Klein, G. and Klein, E. 1984. The changing face of EBV research. *Prog. Med. Virol. 30*, 87–106.

Kliks, M.M. 1983. Paleoparasitology: On the origins and impact of human-helminth relationships. pp. 291–313 in Croll and Cross.

Klingberg, F.L. 1945. *Historical studies of war casualties*. Office of the Secretary of War, Washington, DC.

Knibbs, G.H. 1917. *The mathematical theory of population, of its character and fluctuations and of the factors which influence them*. Appendix A, vol. 1, Census of the Commonwealth of Australia. Govt. Printer, Melbourne. xv + 466.

Kobayashi, A. 1983. Changing patterns of parasitic infections in Japan. pp. 137–68 in Croll and Cross.

Koch, A. 1971. Critical views on B.C.G. mass vaccination campaigns. With discussion. pp. 234–42 in Gould.

Koch, R. 1880. *Investigations into the etiology of traumatic infective diseases*. New Sydenham Society Publ., vol. 88, London. 74 + 5 plates.

Koch, R. 1882. Die Aetiologie der Tuberculose. *Berliner klin. Wochenschr.* 19, 221–30. Reprinted in *Medical Classics* 2 (1938) 821–52, with transl. by W. de Rouville, 853–80.

Koch, R. 1890. An address on bacteriological research. *Br. Med. J. 2*, 380–3.

Kock, K. 1959. The Central Bureau of Statistics, 100 years old. *Stat. Rev. (Stockholm)*, No. 7, 363–72.

Koebberling, J. and Tattersall, R. (Eds.) 1982. *The genetics of diabetes mellitus*. Proc. of the Serono Symposia, vol. 47. Academic Press, London. xiii + 293.

Kohn, R. 1967. *The health of the Canadian people. Royal Commission on Health Services*. Queen's Printer, Ottawa. xi + 412.

Kohn, S. and Meyendorff, A.F. 1932. *The cost of the war to Russia: The vital statistics of European Russia during the world War 1914–1917*. Carnegie

Endowment for International Peace. Yale University Press, New Haven, CT. xviii + 219.

Kolata, G. 1985a. The search for a malaria vaccine. *Science 226*, 679–82.

Kolata, G. 1985b. Is the war on cancer being won? *Science 229*, 543–44.

Kolata, G. 1985c. Breast cancer consensus. *Science 229*, 1378.

Korte, W.E. de 1904. Amaas, or kaffir milk-pox. *Lancet 1*, 1273–76.

Koshland, D.E. Jr 1985. Benefits, risks, vaccines, and the courts. *Science 227*, 1289.

Kozel, N.J. and Adams. E.H. 1986. Epidemiology of drug abuse: An overview. *Science 234*, 970–74.

Kramer, H.D. 1948. The germ theory and the early public health program in the United States. *Bull. Hist. Med. 22*, 233–47.

Kraus, J.F. and Conroy, C. 1984. Mortality and morbidity from injuries in sports and recreation. *Annu. Rev. Public Health 5*, 163–92.

Krause, J.T. 1958. Changes in English fertility and mortality, 1781–1850. *Econ. Hist. Rev.* (2) *11*, 52–70.

Kraybill, H.F. and Mehlman, M.A. (Eds.) 1977. *Environmental cancer*. Advances in Modern Toxicology vol. 3. Wiley, New York. xii + 388.

Kreier, J.P. (Ed.) 1977. *Parasitic protozoa*. Academic Press, New York. 4 vols.

Kreier, J.P. (Ed.) 1980. *Malaria. Vol. 1, Epidemiology, chemotherapy, morphology and metabolism; Vol. 2, Pathology, vector studies and culture; Vol. 3, Immunology and immunization*. Academic Press, New York.

Krick, J.A. and Remington, J.S. 1978. Toxoplasmosis in the adult—An overview. *N. Engl. J. Med. 298*, 550–53.

Krusé, C.W. 1973. Sanitary control of food. pp. 1029–63 in Sartwell, 1973.

Kuczynski, R.R. 1937. *Colonial population*. Oxford University Press, London. xiv + 101.

Kuczynski, R.R. 1939. *The Cameroons and Togoland: A demographic study*. Oxford University Press, London. xviii + 582.

Kuczynski, R.R. 1947–1948. R.R. Kuczynski, 1876-1945. A bibliography of the demographic studies of Dr. R.R. Kuczynski, prepared by B. Long and H. Gille. *Popul. Studies 1*, 471–72 and *2*, 125–26.

Kuczynski, R.R. 1948–1953. *Demographic survey of the British Colonial Empire. Vol. 1, West Africa; Vol. 2, South and East Africa; Vol. 3, West Indian and American territories*. Oxford University Press, London.

Kuller, L. 1966. Sudden and unexpected nontraumatic death in adults: A review of epidemiological and clinical studies. *J. Chronic Dis. 19*, 1165–92.

Kulstad, R. (Ed.) 1989. *AIDS: Papers from Science, 1982–1985*. American Assoc. for the Adv. of Science, Washington, DC. 654 pp.

Kunii, C. 1983. Parasite control activities in Japan: Government-expert-private sector partnership. pp. 169–85 in Croll and Cross.

Kurland, L.T. and Reed, D. 1964. Geographic and climatic aspects of multiple sclerosis. *Am. J. Public Health 54*. 588–97.

Kuwert, E., Merieux, C., Koprowski, H., and Bogel, K. (Eds.) 1985. *Rabies in the tropics*. Springer, New York. xviii + 786.

Kwantes, W. 1984. Diphtheria in Europe. *J. Hyg. Camb. 93*, 433–37.

Kyd, J.G. (Ed.) 1975. *Scottish population statistics including Webster's analysis of population 1755*. Scottish Academic Press, Edinburgh. xxxix + 107.

Lajtha, L.G. 1980. The common ancestral cell. pp. 81–95 in Wintrobe.

Lamb, H.H. 1966. *The changing climate*. Methuen, London. xi + 236.

Lamb, H.H. 1972/1977. *Present, past and future. Vol. 1, Fundamentals and climate now; Vol. 2, Climatic history and the future*. Methuen, London. 613 pp.; xxx + 835.

Lamb, H.H. 1977. Some comments on the drought in recent years in the Sahel-Ethiopian zone of North Africa. pp. 33–37 in Dalby, Church, and Bezzaz.

Lamb, H.H. 1982. *Climate, history and the modern world*. Methuen, New York. xx + 388.

Lambert, P.M. 1975. Hypertensive disease, study on mortality. *World Health Stat. Rep. 28*, 401–17.

Lambert, S.M. 1949. Malaria incidence in Australia and the South Pacific. pp. 820–30 in Boyd.

Lambrecht, F.L. 1967. Trypanosomiasis in prehistoric and later human populations: A tentative reconstruction. pp. 132–51 in Brothwell and Sandison.

Lancaster, H.O. (with Maddox J.K.) 1950a. Diabetic mortality in Australia. *Med. J. Austral. 1*, 317–25.

Lancaster, H.O. (with Willcocks W.J.) 1950b. Mortality in Australia: population and mortality data. *Med. J. Austral. 1*, 613–19.

Lancaster, H.O. 1950c. Tuberculosis mortality in Australia, 1908 to 1945. *Med. J. Austral. 1*, 655–62.

Lancaster, H.O. 1950d. Tuberculosis mortality of childhood in Australia. *Med. J. Austral. 1*, 760–65.

Lancaster, H.O. 1950e. Cancer mortality in Australia. *Med. J. Austral.* 2, 501–07.

Lancaster, H.O. (with Willcocks W.J.*) 1951a. Maternal mortality in New South Wales with special reference to age and parity. *J. Obstet. Gynaecol. Br. Emp.* 58, 945–60. *Senior author.

Lancaster, H.O. 1951b. Diabetic prevalence in New South Wales. *Med. J. Austral.* 1, 117–19.

Lancaster, H.O. 1951c. The measurement of mortality in Australia. *Med. J. Austral.* 1, 389–99.

Lancaster, H.O. 1951d. The mortality in Australia from cancers peculiar to the female. *Med. J. Austral.* 2, 1–6.

Lancaster, H.O. 1951e. Australian life tables from a medical point of view. *Med. J. Austral.* 2, 251–58.

Lancaster, H.O. 1951f. Mortality from congenital malformations in Australia. *Med. J. Austral.* 2, 318–20.

Lancaster, H.O. 1951g. Deafness as an epidemic disease in Australia: A note on census and institutional data. *Br. Med. J.* 2, 1429–32.

Lancaster, H.O. 1952a. The mortality in Australia from acute infective disease. *Med. J. Austral.* 1, 175–80.

Lancaster, H.O. 1952b. The mortality in Australia from cancers peculiar to the male. *Med. J. Austral.* 2, 41–44.

Lancaster, H.O. 1952c. The mortality in Australia from measles, scarlatina and diphtheria. *Med. J. Austral.* 2, 272–76.

Lancaster, H.O. 1952d. The mortality from violence in Australia. *Med. J. Austral.* 2, 649–54.

Lancaster, H.O. (with Pickering, H.) 1952e. The incidence of births of the deaf in New Zealand. *N. Z. Med. J.* 51, 184–89.

Lancaster, H.O. 1953a. The mortality in Australia from typhus, typhoid fever and infections of the bowel. *Med. J. Austral.* 1, 576–79.

Lancaster, H.O. 1953b. The mortality from tetanus in Australia. *Med. J. Austral.* 2, 417–18.

Lancaster, H.O. 1953c. The mortality in Australia from influenza and from diseases of the respiratory system. *Med. J. Austral.* 2, 672–76.

Lancaster, H.O. 1953d. The mortality in Australia from cancer of the respiratory system. *Med. J. Austral.* 2, 855–57.

Lancaster, H.O. 1953e. An amoebic survey of Australian soldiers during the Second World War. *Med. J. Austral.* 1, 552–53.

Lancaster, H.O. 1954a. Epidemics of poliomyelitis in New South Wales. *Med. J. Austral.* 1, 245–46.

Lancaster, H.O. 1954b. The mortality in Australia from infective disease (concluded). *Med. J. Austral.* 1, 506–10.

Lancaster, H.O. 1954c. The mortality in Australia from cancer of the pancreas. *Med. J. Austral.* 1, 596–97.

Lancaster, H.O. 1954d. The mortality in Australia from cancers of the alimentary system. *Med. J. Austral.* 1, 744–49.

Lancaster, H.O. 1954e. The mortality in Australia from cancer (concluded). *Med. J. Austral.* 2, 93–97.

Lancaster, H.O. 1954f. Deafness due to rubella. *Med. J. Austral.* 2, 323–24.

Lancaster, H.O. 1954g. Aging in the Australian population. *Med. J. Austral.* 2, 548–54.

Lancaster, H.O. 1954h. The epidemiology of deafness due to maternal rubella. *Acta Genet.* 5, 12–24.

Lancaster, H.O. 1955a. The mortality in Australia from cancer for the period, 1946 to 1950. *Med. J. Austral.* 2, 235–39.

Lancaster, H.O. 1955b. The mortality in Australia from syphilis. *Med. J. Austral.* 2, 895–97.

Lancaster, H.O. 1955c. The mortality in Australia from leuchaemia. *Med. J. Austral.* 2, 1064–65.

Lancaster, H.O. 1955d. Maternal rubella during pregnancy as a cause of deaf-mutism. Some aspects of its incidence in Australia. *Health* (Canberra) 5, 56–58.

Lancaster, H.O. 1956a. The mortality in Australia from diseases of the alimentary system. *Med. J. Austral.* 1, 787–89.

Lancaster, H.O. 1956b. Some geographical aspects of the mortality from melanoma in Europeans. *Med. J. Austral.* 1, 1082–87.

Lancaster, H.O. 1956c. Infant mortality in Australia. *Med. J. Austral.* 2, 100–08

Lancaster, H.O. 1956d. The mortality of childhood in Australia. Part 1. Early childhood. *Med. J. Austral.* 2, 889–94.

Lancaster, H.O. 1956e. Australia and diphtheria immunization. *Med. J. Austral.* 1, 1060.

Lancasrer, H.O. 1957a. The mortality of childhood in Australia. Part 2. The school ages. *Med. J. Austral.* 1, 415–19.

Lancaster, H.O. (with Nelson, J.) 1957b. Sunlight as a cause of melanoma: A clinical survey. *Med. J. Austral.* 1, 452–56.

Lancaster, H.O. 1957c. The mortality in Australia of young adults. *Med. J. Austral.* 2, 821–26.

Lancaster, H.O. 1957d. Mortality in Australia. *Health* (Canberra) 7, 82–87.

Lancaster, H.O. 1957e. Generation death-rates and tuberculosis. *Lancet* 2, 391–92.

Lancaster, H.O. 1958a. Cancer statistics in Australia, Part 1, *Med. J. Austral.* 2, 350–56.

Lancaster, H.O. (with Maddox, J.K.) 1958*b*. Diabetic mortality in Australia. *Australas. Ann. Med. 7*, 144–50.

Lancaster. H.O. 1958*c*. Sunlight and its effects on the human skin in Australia. *Health* (Canberra) *8*, 107–10.

Lancaster, H.O. 1959*a*. Mortality in Australia, 1951 to 1955. *Med. J. Austral. 1*, 350–55.

Lancaster, H.O. 1959*b*. Generation life tables for Australia. *Austral. J. Stat. 1*, 19–33.

Lancaster, H.O. 1960*a*. Australian mortality in the late nineteenth century. *Med. J. Austral. 2*, 84–87.

Lancaster, H.O. 1960*b*. Mortality at young adult ages—A relative maximum. *Austral. J. Stat. 2*, 93–96.

Lancaster, H.O. 1962*a*. Cancer statistics in Australia: Part II. Respiratory system. *Med. J. Austral. 1*, 1007–11.

Lancaster, H.O. 1962*b*. An early statistician—John Graunt (1620–1674). *Med. J. Austral. 2*, 734–38.

Lancaster, H.O. 1962*c*. The epidemiology of skin cancer in Queensland: A methodological note. *Br. J. Cancer 16*, 811–12.

Lancaster, H.O. 1963. Vital statistics as human ecology. *Austral. J. Sci. 25*, 445–53.

Lancaster, H.O. 1964*a*. The mortality from violence in Australia, 1863 to 1960. *Med. J. Austral. 1*, 388–93.

Lancaster, H.O. 1964*b*. Bibliography of vital statistics in Australia and New Zealand. *Austral. J. Stat. 6*, 33–99.

Lancaster, H.O. 1965. Aging of the population in Australia. *Gerontologist 5*, 252–53.

Lancaster, H.O. (with Donovan, J.W.) 1966. A study in New Zealand mortality. 1. Population data. *N.Z. Med. J. 65*, 946–53.

Lancaster, H.O. (with Donovan, J.W.) 1967*a*. A study in New Zealand mortality. 2. Mortality data. *N.Z. Med. J. 66*, 769–77.

Lancaster, H.O. 1967*b*. The infections and population size in Australia. *Bull. Int. Stat. Inst. 42*, 459–71.

Lancaster, H.O. 1967*c*. The causes of the declines in the death rates in Australia. *Med. J. Austral. 2*, 937–41.

Lancaster, H.O. (with Donovan, J.W.) 1968. A study in New Zealand mortality. 3. Cohort life tables. *N.Z. Med. J. 67*, 623–30.

Lancaster, H.O. 1973*a*. The balance of population during historical time. *J. Sydney Univ. Arts Assoc. 8*, 30–42.

Lancaster, H.O. 1973*b*. Bibliography of vital statistics in Australia: A second list. *Austral. J. Stat. 15*, 1–26.

Lancaster, H.O. 1974. *An introduction to medical statistics*. Wiley, New York. xiv + 305.

Lancaster, H.O. 1978. World mortality survey. Address to the Statistical Society of Australia, July 12th, 1977. *Austral. J. Stat. 20*, 1–42.

Lancaster, H.O. 1979. Ageing and mortality statistics in Australia. pp. 28–30 in *Ageing in Australia*, J.M. Donald, A.V. Everitt, and P.J. Wheeler (Eds.), Austral. Assoc. of Gerontology, Sydney.

Lancaster, H.O. 1982*a*. Cohort or generation methods: A priority for John Brownlee (1868–1927). *Am. J. Epidemiol. 115*, 153–54.

Lancaster, H.O. 1982*b*. Bibliography of vital statistics in Australia: A third list. *Austral. J. Stat. 24*, 361–80.

Lancaster, H.O. 1982*c*. A bibliography of statistical bibliographies: A fourteenth list. *Int. Stat. Rev. 50*, 195–217.

Lancaster, H.O. 1983. Re: Cohort or generation methods: A priority for John Brownlee (1868–1927). Letter to the Editor. *Am. J. Epidemiol. 117*, 517–18.

Lancaster, H.O. (with Gordon, D.) 1987. Health and medicine. pp. 314–27 in W. Vamplew (Ed.), *Australians: Historical statistics*, Fairfax, Syme & Weldon, Sydney. xvii + 470.

Lancaster, H.O. 1987. Tables of mortality rates for Australia, 1881–1980. *Reference Australia* No. 1, 3–26.

Lancaster, H.O. (with Gordon, D.) 1988. Health and medicine in Australia, 1788–1988. *Reference Australia* No. 2, 21–49.

Landy, D. (Ed.) 1977. *Culture, disease and healing: Studies in medical anthropology*, Macmillan, New York. xv + 559.

Langer, H. 1980. *The Thirty Years War*. Transl. by C.S.V. Salt. Blandford Press, Poole, Dorset. 262 + 18 pp.

Langman, M.J.S. 1979. *The epidemiology of chronic digestive disease*. Edward Arnold, London. iv + 139.

Langmuir, A.D. 1962. Medical importance of measles. *Am. J. Dis. Child. 103*, 224–26.

Langmuir, A.D., Worthen, T.D., Solomon, J., Ray, C.G., and Petersen, E. 1985. The Thucydides syndrome: A new hypothesis for the cause of the Plague of Athens. *N. Engl. J. Med. 313*, 1027–30.

Lapp, N.L. 1981. Lung disease secondary to inhalation of nonfibrous minerals. pp. 219–33 in Brooks, Lockey, and Harber.

Lappé, M. 1982. *Germs that won't die. Medical con-*

sequences of the misuse of antibiotics. Anchor/ Doubleday, Garden City, NY. xviii + 246.

Larsson, J. and Linell, F. 1960. Tuberkulos och mortalitet. (Tuberculosis and mortality.) *Sv. Läkartidn. 57*: 22.

Larsson, T. 1965. *Mortality in Sweden.* Suppl. to *Acta Genet. Stat. Med. 15.* Karger, Basel. 143 pp.

Lasagna, L. 1972. Research, regulation and development of new pharmaceuticals: Past, present and future. I. *Am. J. Med. Sci. 263*, 8–18.

Lassiter, D.V. 1977. Occupational carcinogenesis. pp. 63–86 in Kraybill and Mehlman.

Last, J.M. (Ed.) 1980. *Maxcy-Rosenau 'Public health and preventive medicine'.* 11th edition. Appleton-Century-Crofts, New York. xxv + 1926.

Latham, B. 1878. *Sanitary engineering: A guide to the construction of works of sewerage and house drainage.* 2nd edition. E. & F.N. Spon, London-New York. xxxii + 559.

Latter, J.H. 1969. Natural disasters. *Adv. of Sci. 25*, 362–80.

Laughlin, W.S. 1972. Ecology and population structure in the arctic. pp. 379–92 in Harrison and Boyce.

Laughlin, W.S 1980. *Aleuts: Survivors of the Bering land bridge.* Holt, Rinehart & Winston, New York. viii + 151.

Laughlin, W.S. and Harper, A.B. (Eds.) 1979. *The first Americans: Origins, affinities, and adaptations.* Gustav Fischer, New York-Stuttgart. xi + 340.

Laughlin, W.S., Jørgensen, J.B., and Frøhlich, B. 1979. Aleuts and Eskimos: Survivors of the Bering land bridge coast. pp. 91–104 in Laughlin and Harper.

Lauritsen, J.G. 1977. Genetic aspects of spontaneous abortion. *Dan. Med. Bull. 24*, 169–88.

Laveleye, E. de 1891. *Luxury.* 2nd edition. Sonnenschein & Co. London. iv + 179.

Laver, W.G. (Ed.) 1983. *The origin of pandemic influenza viruses.* From a workshop, Peking, 1982. Elsevier, New York. xvi + 309.

Lawrence, R.C. and Shulman, L.E. 1985. *Epidemiology of the rheumatic diseases.* Gower Publ., Brookfield, VT. 381 pp.

Lawther, P.J. 1979. Epidemics of non-infectious disease. With discussion. *Proc. Roy. Soc. London B205*, 63–75. Reprinted in Doll and McLean.

Leaf, A. 1973. Every day is a gift when you are over 100. *Natl. Geogr. 143*, 93–118.

Leake, C.D. 1975. *An historical account of pharmacology to the 20th century.* C.C. Thomas, Springfield, IL. xi + 210.

Learmonth, A. 1978. *Patterns of disease and hunger.* David & Charles, Newton Abbot. 256 pp.

Leavitt, J.W. 1986. *Brought to bed. Childbearing in America 1750 to 1950.* Oxford University Press, New York. xii + 284.

Lebenthal, E. (Ed.). 1984. *Chronic diarrhea in children.* Nestlé Nutrition Workshop Series, vol. 6. Vevey and Raven, New York. xx + 568.

Leboutte, R. 1984. L'infanticide dans l'est de la Bretagne aux XVIIIe–XIXe siècles: Une réalité. *Ann. Démog. Hist.* 1983, 163–92.

Lebrun, F. 1971. *Les hommes et la mort en Anjou aux XVIIe et XVIIIe siècles.* Mouton, Paris-La Haye. 562 pp.

Lebrun, F. 1977. Les épidémies en Haute-Bretagne à la fin de l'ancien régime (1770–1789). *Ann. Démog. Hist.*, Pt. 3, 181–206.

Lechevalier, H.A. and Solotorovsky, M. 1965. *Three centuries of microbiology.* McGraw-Hill, New York. 536 pp. Corrected 1974.

Leck, I. 1981a. Epidemiological aspects of paediatrics: The frequency of disorders of early life. pp. 923–46 in Davis and Dobbing.

Leck, I. 1981b. Epidemiological aspects of paediatrics: Insights into the causation of disorders of early life. pp. 947–79 in Davis and Dobbing.

Ledermann, S. 1946. La mortalité des adultes en France. *Population 1*, 663–80.

Ledermann, S. 1956. *Alcool, alcoolisme, alcoolisation. Données scientifiques de caractère physiologique, économique et social.* Institut National d'Etudes Démographiques, Travaux et documents No. 29, Presses Universitaires, Paris. 314 pp.

Ledermann, S. 1958. Mortalité et alcoolisation excessive. *J. Soc. Stat. Paris 99*, 28–42.

Ledermann, S. 1964. *Alcool, alcoolisme, alcoolisation: mortalité, morbidité, accidents du travail.* Institut National d'Etudes Démographiques, Travaux et documents No. 41. Presses Universitaires, Paris. 613 pp.

Ledermann, S. and Metz, B. 1960. Les accidents du travail et l'alcool. *Population 15*, 301–16.

Ledermann, S. and Tabah, F. 1951. Nouvelles données sur la mortalité d'origine alcoolique. *Population 6*, 41–58.

Lee, J.A. and Kean, B.H. 1978. International conference on the diarrhea of travellers—New directions in research: A summary. *J. Infect. Dis 137*, 355–69.

Lee, J.A.H. 1982. Melanoma and exposure to sunlight. *Epidemiol. Rev. 4*, 110–36.

Lee, M. and Leichter, J. 1982. Alcohol and the fetus. pp. 245–52 in Jelliffe and Jelliffe.

Lee, R.B. and DeVore, I. (Eds.). 1968a. *Man the hunter. Proc. Symp. Univ. of Chicago, 1966.* Aldine, Chicago. ix + 415.

Lee, R.B. and DeVore, I. 1968b. Problems in the study of hunters and gatherers. pp. 3–12 in Lee and DeVore, 1968a.

Lee, R.B. and DeVore, I. (Eds.). 1976. *Kalahari hunter-gatherers.* Harvard University Press, Cambridge, MA. xx + 408.

Lehmann, H. and Raper, A.B. 1956. Maintenance of a high sickling rate in an African community. *Br. Med. J. 2*, 233–36.

Lehners, J.-P. 1973. Die Pfarre Stockerau im 17. und 18. Jahrhundert: Erste Resultate einer demographischen Studie. pp. 373–401 in *Beiträge zur Bevölkerungs-und Sozialgeschichte Österreichs*, H. Helczmanovszki (Ed.). Verlag für Geschichte u. Politik, Wien. 448 pp.

Leibowitz, J.O. 1970. *The history of coronary heart disease.* Wellcome Instit. of Hist. Med., London and University of California Press, Berkeley. xvii + 227.

Leichtenstern, O.M.L. 1912. *Influenza, von weil. Prof. Dr. Otto Leichtenstern.* 2nd edition, Dr. G. Sticker (Ed.). A. Hölder, Vienna, vi + 250.

Lelyfeld, H. van and Zoeteman, B.C.J. (Eds.). 1981. *Water supply and health. Proc. Internatl. Symposium, Noordwijkerhout, Netherlands, 1980.* Elsevier, Amsterdam. xxii + 397. See also *Science of the Total Environment*, vol. 18 (1981).

Lenz, W. and Knapp, K. 1962. Thalidomide embryopathy. *Arch. Environ. Health 5*, 100–05.

Leowski, J. 1986. Mortality from acute respiratory infections in children under 5 years of age: Global estimates. *World Health Stat. Q. 39*, 138–44.

Lepes, T. 1974. Review of research on malaria. *WHO Bull. 50*, 151–57.

Leprosy Congress 1973. Centennial festskrift, 1, 1873–1973: presenting a review of progress in the understanding, treatment and control of leprosy in the century just past. *Int. J. Leprosy 41*, 149–797.

Le Roy Ladurie, E. 1966. *Les paysans de Languedoc.* SEVPEN, Paris. 2 vols. Transl. as *The peasants of Languedoc*, by John Day, Illinois University Press, Urbana, IL, 1974, xii + 370.

Le Roy Ladurie, E. 1969. Amenorrhea in time of famine (seventeenth to twentieth century). In *Ann. Démog. Hist.*, Nov.–Dec. 1969. Reprinted in English, pp. 255–71 in Le Roy Ladurie, 1979.

Le Roy Ladurie, E. 1972. *Chaunu, Lebrun, Vovelle: The new history of death.* Address given at the annual meeting of Catholic intellectuals, Paris, 1972. Reprinted in English, pp. 273–84 in Le Roy

Ladurie, 1979.

Le Roy Ladurie, E. 1973. *Times of feast, times of famine: A history of climate since the year 1000.* Doubleday, Garden City, NY. xxiv + 426.

Le Roy Ladurie, E. 1979. *The territory of the historian.* Transl. from the French by B. & S. Reynolds. Harvester Press, Hassocks, Sussex. viii + 345, Orig. published 1973 by Gallimard as *Le territoire de l'historien.*

Le Roy Ladurie, E. and Goy, J. 1982. *Tithe and agrarian history from the 14th to the 19th century: An essay in comparative history.* Cambridge University Press. ix + 206.

Lesky, E. 1960. Von den Ursprüngen des therapeutischen Nihilismus. *Sudhoffs Arch. 44*, 1–20.

Lesky, E. 1964. Ignaz Philipp Semmelweis und die Wiener medizinische Schule. *Sitz.-Ber. Österreich. Akad. Wiss. philos.-hist. Kl. 245* (3), p. 60. Böhlaus, Vienna.

Lesky, E. 1972. Ignaz Philipp Semmelweis, Legende und Historie. *Deut. medizin. Wochenschr. 97*, 627–32.

Lesky, E. 1976. *The Vienna Medical School of the 19th century.* Transl. from the German by L. Williams and I.S. Levij. Johns Hopkins, Baltimore-London. xv + 604.

Levasseur, E. 1889–1892. *La population française. Histoire de la population avant 1789 et démographie de la France comparée à celle des autres nations au XIXe siècle. Précédée d'une introduction sur la statistique.* Arthur Rousseau, Paris. 3 vols.

Levine, D. 1976. The reliability of parochial registration and the representativeness of family reconstitution. *Popul. Studies 30*, 107–22.

Levine, M.M., Kaper, J.B., Black, R.E., and Clements, M.L. 1983. New knowledge on pathogenesis of bacterial enteric infections as applied to vaccine development. *Microbiol. Rev. 47*, 510–50.

Lévy, C. and Henry, L. 1960. Ducs et pairs sous l'ancien régime: Caractéristiques démographiques d'une caste. *Population 15*, 807–30.

Levy, C.E.M. 1861. A report on the lying-in hospitals in London and Dublin. Originally published in Bibliothek for Laeger, Copenhagen, 1847. pp. 153–69 in Semmelweis.

Levy, J.S. 1983. *War in the modern great power system, 1495–1975.* University of Kentucky Press, Lexington. xix + 215.

Levy, R.I. and Moskowitz, J. 1982. Cardiovascular research: Decades of progress, a decade of promise. *Science 217*, 121–29.

Levy, R.I., Rifkind, B.M., Dennis, B.H., and Ernst, N. (Eds.) 1979. *Nutrition, lipids, and coronary heart disease: a global view.* Nutrition in Health and Disease, vol. 1. Raven, New York. x + 566.

Lewis-Faning, E. 1930. A survey of the mortality in Dr. Farr's 63 healthy districts of England and Wales during the period 1851–1925. *J. Hyg. Camb. 30*, 121–53.

Leymond, D. 1967. La communauté de Duravel au XVIIIe siècle (démographie-économie). *Ann. du Midi 79*, 363–85.

Li, F.P. 1982. Cancers in children. pp. 1012–24 in Schottenfeld and Fraumeni.

Lie, J.T. 1963. Acute appendicitis: A review of mortality and a reappraisal of early diagnosis and appendicectomy. *Med. J. Austral. 2*, 846–53.

Lieberman, A.N. 1974. Parkinson's disease: A clinical review. *Am. J. Med. Sci. 267*, 66–80.

Lightdale, C.J., Koepsell, T.D., and Sherlock, P. 1982. Small intestine. pp. 692–702 in Schottenfeld and Fraumeni.

Lilienfeld, A.M. (Ed.) 1980. *Times, places and persons: Aspects of the history of epidemiology.* Henry F. Sigerist Suppl. to *Bull. Hist. Med.*, N.S. No. 4. Johns Hopkins, Baltimore. 160 pp.

Lilienfeld, A.M., Gifford, A.J. (Eds.) (In collaboration with the conference of Chronic Disease Training Program Directors of Schools of Public Health) 1966. *Chronic diseases and public health.* Johns Hopkins, Baltimore. xvii + 846.

Lilienfeld, A.M., Levin, M.L., and Kessler, I.I. 1972. *Cancer in the United States.* Harvard University Press, Cambridge, MA. xxvi + 546.

Lind, J. 1753. *A treatise of the scurvy.* Sands, Murray and Cochran, Edinburgh. Reprinted 1772.

Linder, F.E. and Grove, R.D. 1943. *Vital statistics rates in the United States 1900–1940.* US Govt Printing Office, Washington, DC. vii + 1051.

Lindsay, D.G. and Sherlock, J.C. 1982. Environmental contaminants. pp. 85–110 in Jelliffe and Jelliffe.

Linet, M.S. 1985. *The leukemias. Epidemiologic aspects.* Monogr. in Epidemiol. and Biostatist., vol. 6. Oxford University Press, New York. xiv + 293.

Ling Riu-Zhu 1981. A brief account of 30 years' mortality of Chinese population. *World Health Stat. Q. 34*, 127–34.

Link, V.B. 1955. *A history of plague in the United States.* Public Health Monograph No. 26. US Public Health Service, Washington, DC. viii + 120.

Linnaeus (von Linné), C. 1763. *Genera morborum, in auditorum usu edita.* Upsaliae.

Linnerooth, J. 1979. The value of human life: A review of the models. *Economic Inquiry 17*, 52–74.

Littman, R.J. and Littman, M.L. 1969. The Athenian plague: Smallpox. *Proc. Am. Philol. Assoc. 100*, 261–73.

Littman, R.J. and Littman, M.L. 1973. Galen and the Antonine plague. *Am. J. Philol. 94*, 243–55.

Livingstone, F.B. 1971. Malaria and human polymorphisms. *Annu. Rev. Genet. 5*, 33–64.

Lloyd, C. (Ed.) 1965. *The health of seamen. Selections from the works of Dr. James Lind, Sir Gilbert Blane, and Dr. Thomas Trotter.* The Navy Records Soc., London, vol. 107. x + 320.

Lloyd, C. and Coulter, J.L.S. 1961/1963. *Medicine and the navy, 1200–1900. Vol. III: 1714–1815. Vol. IV: 1815–1900.* E. & S. Livingstone, Edinburgh-London. xiii + 402; xi + 300 (For earlier vols see Keevil, 1957/1958.)

Lockey, J.E. 1981. Nonasbestos fibrous minerals. pp. 203–18 in Brooks, Lockey, and Harber.

Lockridge, K.A. 1966. The population of Dedham, Massachusetts, 1636–1736. *Econ. Hist. Rev.* (2) *19*, 318–44.

Lodolini, E. 1958. Los libros parroquiales y de estado civil en América Latina. *Archivum 8*, 95–113.

Lofchie, M.F. 1975. Political and economic origins of African hunger. *J. Mod. Afr. Stud. 13*, 551–67.

Lofchie, M.F. and Commins, S.K. 1982. Food deficits and agricultural policies in Tropical Africa. *J. Mod. Afr. Stud. 20*, 1–25.

Logan, W.P.D. 1950a. Mortality from diphtheria: The recent trend compared with scarlet fever, whooping cough and measles. *Med. Officer 84*, 217–19.

Logan, W.P.D. 1950b. Mortality in England and Wales from 1848 to 1947. *Popul. Studies 4*, 132–78.

Logan, W.P.D. 1953. Mortality in the London fog incident, 1952. *Lancet 1*, 336–38.

Logan, W.P.D. 1956. Mortality from fog in London, January, 1956. *Br. Med. J. 1*, 722–25.

Logan, W.P.D. 1975. Cancer of the female breast. International mortality trends. *World Health Stat. Rep. 28*, 232–51.

Logan, W.P.D. and Benjamin, B. 1957. *Tuberculosis statistics for England and Wales, 1938–1955: An analysis of trends and geographical distribution.* Stud. Med. Popul. Subj., No. 10. HMSO. London. 56 pp.

Logue, J.N., Melick, M.E., and Hansen, H. 1981. Research issues and directions in the epidemiology of health effects of disasters. *Epidemiol. Rev. 3*, 140–62.

London, I.M. 1980. Iron and heme: Crucial carriers and catalysts. pp. 171–208 in Wintrobe.

London, W.P. and Yorke, J.A. 1973. Recurrent

outbreaks of measles, chickenpox and mumps. I. Seasonal variation in contact rates. II. Systematic differences in contact rates and stochastic effects. (Authors reversed.) *Am. J. Epidemiol.* 98. 453–68, 469–82.

Longrigg, J. 1980. The great plague of Athens. *Hist. Sci. 18*, 209–25.

Loosli, C.G., Portnoy, B., and Myers, E.C. 1978. *International bibliography of influenza, 1930–1959.* University of Southern California, Los Angeles. 348 pp.

Lopez, A.D. and Hanada, K. 1982. Mortality patterns and trends among the elderly in developed countries. *World Health Stat. Q. 35*, 203–24.

Lorimer, F. 1959. The development of demography. pp. 124–79 in Hauser and Duncan.

Lorimer, F. 1968. The present situation of demography in Africa south of the Sahara. pp. 3–11 in Brass, Coale, et al.

Loschky, D.J. 1967. The usefulness of England's parish registers. *Rev. Econ. Stat. 49* (4), 471–79.

Loschky, D.J. 1976. Economic change, mortality and Malthusian theory. *Popul. Studies 30*, 439–52.

Lotka, A.J. 1931. Orphanhood in relation to demographic factors. A study in population analysis. *Metron 9* (2), 37–110.

Loudon, I. 1986a. Deaths in childbed from the eighteenth century to 1935. *Med. Hist. 30*, 1–41.

Loudon, I. 1986b. Obstetric care, social class, and maternal mortality. *Br. Med. J. 293*, 606–08.

Louis, P.C.A. 1835. *Recherches sur les effets de la saignée dans quelques maladies inflammatoires et sur l'action de l'émétique et les vésicatoires dans la pneumonie.* J.B. Baillière, Paris. 120 pp. Transl. by C.G. Putnam as *Researches on the effects of bloodletting in some inflammatory diseases, and on the influence of tartarised antimony and vesication in pneumonitis.* With preface and appendix by J. Jackson. Hilliard, Gray and Co., Boston, 1836. xxxii + 171.

Louis, P.C.A. 1844. *Researches on phthisis, anatomical, pathological and therapeutical.* Transl. by W.H. Walshe. Sydenham Society, London. xxxvi + 571.

Loveday, A. 1914. *The history and economics of Indian famines.* Bell, London. xi + 163.

Low, R.B. 1920a. The incidence of epidemic influenza during 1918–19 in Europe and in the Western Hemisphere. pp. 202–348 in Newman, Greenwood, et al.

Low, R.B. 1920b. *The progress and diffusion of plague, cholera and yellow fever throughout the world 1914–1917.* UK Ministry of Health, Re-

ports on Public Health and Medical Subjects No. 3, HMSO, London. xv + 276.

Lowenberg, M.E., Todhunter, E.N., Wilson, E.D., Savage, J.R., and Lubawski, J.L. 1974. *Food and man.* 2nd edition. Wiley, New York. xi + 459.

Lozoff, B. and Brittenham, G.M. 1977. Field methods for the assessment of health and diseases in pre-agricultural societies. pp. 49–67 in Elliott and Whelan.

Lucas, H.S. 1930. The great European famine of 1315, 1316 and 1317. *Speculum 5*, 343–77.

Luckin, B. 1984. Evaluating the sanitary revolution: Typhus and typhoid in London, 1851–1900. pp. 102–19 in Woods and Woodward.

Ludmerer, K.M. 1985. *Learning to heal. The development of American medical education.* Basic Books, New York. xvi + 346.

Luerman, A. 1885. Eine Icterusepidemie. *Berlin klin. Wochenschr. 22*, 20–3.

Lundborg, H. 1913. *Medizinisch-biologische Familienforschungen innerhalb eines 2,232 köpfigen Bauerngeschlechtes in Schweden (Provinz Blekinge).* G. Fischer, Jena. 2 vols.

Luzatto, L. and Battistuzzi, G. 1985. Glucose-6-phosphate dehydrogenase. *Adv. Hum. Genet. 14*, 217–329.

Lyon, J.L., Gardner, J.W., and West, D.W. 1980. Cancer risk and life style among Mormons from 1967–1975. pp. 3–30 in Cairns, Lyon, and Skolnick.

Lyons, A.S. and Petrucelli, R.J. 1979. *Medicine: An illustrated history.* Macmillan, Sydney. 616 pp.

McArthur, N. 1967. *Island populations of the Pacific.* Austral. Natl. University Press, Canberra. xiv + 381.

MacArthur, W.P. 1927. Old time typhus in Britain. *Trans. Roy. Soc. Trop. Med. Hyg. 20*, 487–503.

MacArthur, W.P. 1952. The occurrence of the rat in early Europe: The plague of the Philistines (1 Sam., 5,6). *Trans. Roy. Soc. Trop. Med. Hyg. 46*, 209–12.

MacArthur, W.P. 1956. Medical history of the famine. pp. 263–315 in Edwards and Williams.

MacArthur, W.(P.) 1957. Epidemic diseases and jaundice in history: Historical notes on some epidemic diseases associated with jaundice. *Br. Med. Bull. 13*, 146–49.

McBean, L.D. and Speckmann, E.W. 1982. Diet, nutrition and cancer. pp. 511–28 in Jelliffe and Jelliffe.

McCarron, D.A., Morris, C.D., Henry, H.J., and Stanton, J.L. 1984. Blood pressure and nutrient intake in the United States. *Science 224*, 1392–98.

McCay, C.M. 1973. *Notes on the history of nutrition*

research. Williams and Wilkins, Baltimore. 234 pp.

McCloskey, B.P. 1950. The relation of prophylactic inoculation to the onset of poliomyelitis. *Lancet 1*, 659–63.

McCollum, E.V. 1956. *A history of nutrition. The sequence of ideas in nutrition investigations*. Houghton Mifflin, Boston. x + 451.

McCormac, B.M. (Ed.). 1983. *Weather and climate responses to solar variations*. From a symp., Boulder, CO., Aug. 1982. Colorado Assoc. University Press, Boulder. x + 626.

MacCulloch, J. 1819. *A description of the Western Islands of Scotland, including the Isle of Man*. London. 2 vols.

McCulloch, J.R. 1837. *A statistical account of the British Empire, exhibiting its strength, physical capacities, population, industry, and civil and religious institutions*. Soc. for Diffusion of Useful Knowledge, Knight, London. 2 vols.

McCutchan, T.F., Dame, J.B., Miller, L.H., and Barnwell, J. 1984. Evolutionary relatedness of *Plasmodium* species as determined by the structure of DNA. *Science 225*, 808–11.

McDougall, J.B. 1949. *Tuberculosis: A global study in social pathology*. E. & S. Livingstone, Edinburgh. viii + 455.

McDougall, J.B. 1950. Tuberculosis mortality 1937 to 1949. *WHO Epidemiol. Vital Stat. Rep. 3*, 240–50.

McEvedy, C. and Jones, R. 1978. *Atlas of world population history*. Penguin, Harmondsworth, Middlesex. 368 pp.

McFarland, R.A. 1957. The role of human factors in accidental trauma. *Am. J. Med. Sci. 234*, 1–27.

Macfarlane, A. and Mugford, M. 1984*a,b. Birth counts: Statistics of pregnancy and childbirth*. National Perinatal Epidemiology Unit (in collab. with OPCS). HMSO, London. 2 vols. xiv + 345; xi + 310.

McGovern, V.J. 1952. Melanoblastoma. *Med. J. Austral. 1*, 139–42.

McGovern, V.J. 1977. Epidemiological aspects of melanoma: A review. *Pathology 9*, 233–41.

McGregor, I.A. 1964. Measles and child mortality in the Gambia. *West Afr. Med. J. 13*, 251–57.

McGregor, I.A., Billewicz, W.Z., and Thomson, A.M. 1961. Growth and mortality in an African village. *Br. Med. J. 2*, 1661–66.

McGregor, I.A., Williams, K., Billewicz, W.Z., and Thomson, A.M. 1966. Haemoglobin concentration and anaemia in young West African (Gambian) children. *Trans. Roy. Soc. Trop. Med. Hyg. 60*, 650–67.

MacIntyre, D. 1926. The serum treatment of diphtheria. *Lancet 1*, 855–58.

Mack, T.M. 1982. Pancreas. pp. 638–67 in Schottenfeld and Fraumeni.

McKay, F.W., Hanson, M.R., and Miller, R.W. 1982. *Cancer mortality in the United States, 1950–1977*. Natl. Cancer Inst. Mon. No. 59, Natl. Inst. Health, Bethesda, MD. vi + 476.

McKendrick, A.G. 1926. Applications of mathematics to medical problems. *Proc. Edinburgh Math. Soc. 44*, 98–130.

McKenzie, A., Case, R.A.M., and Pearson, J.T. 1957. *Cancer statistics for England and Wales 1901–1955*. Stud. Med. Popul. Subj., No. 13. HMSO, London. 99 pp.

MacKenzie, J.S. 1980. Possible future changes in the epidemiology and pathogenesis of human influenza A virus infections. pp. 129–49 in Stanley and Joske.

MacKenzie, J.S. (Ed.) 1983. *Viral diseases in southeast Asia and the western Pacific*. From a seminar, Canberra, Australia, Feb. 1982. Academic Press, New York. xx + 751.

McKeown, T. 1971. Medical issues in historical demography. pp. 57–74 in Clarke.

McKeown, T. 1976. *The modern rise of population*. Edward Arnold, London. 168 pp.

McKeown, T. 1978. Fertility, mortality and causes of death. *Popul. Studies 32*, 535–42.

McKeown, T. and Brown, R.G. 1965. Medical evidence related to English population changes in the eighteenth century. pp. 285–307 in Glass and Eversley. Reprinted from *Popul. Studies 9* (1955), 119–41.

McKeown, T., Brown, R.G., and Record, R.G. 1972. An interpretation of the modern rise of population in Europe. *Popul. Studies 26*, 345–82.

McKeown, T. and Record, R.G. 1952. Observations on foetal growth in multiple pregnancies in man. *J. Endocrinol. 8*, 386–401.

McKeown, T. and Record, R.G. 1962. Reasons for the decline in mortality in England and Wales during the nineteenth century. *Popul. Studies 16*, 94–122.

McKeown, T., Record, R.G., and Turner, R.D. 1975. An interpretation of the decline of mortality in England and Wales during the twentieth century. *Popul. Studies 29*, 391–422.

MacKie, R.M. (Ed.) 1983. *Malignant melanoma. Advances of a decade*. Pigment Cell, Vol. 6. Karger, Basel. viii + 201.

Mackie, T.J. and McLachlan, D.G.S. (with section by Percival, G.H.) 1929. Role of haemolytic streptococci in human disease. pp. 71–99 in vol. 2

of *A System of Bacteriology in relation to Medicine*, P. Fildes and J.C.G. Ledingham (Gen. Eds.), Med. Res. Council, Great Britain. HMSO, London, 1929–1931.

McKinlay, P.L. 1929. The influence of the age of the mother and associated factors on the mortality rates in childbearing. *J. Hyg. Camb. 29*, 160–90.

McKinlay, P.L. 1947. Maternal mortality in Scotland, 1911–1945. In *91st Annual Rep. of Registrar-General for Scotland*. HMSO, Edinburgh.

McKinnon, N.E. 1949. Breast cancer mortality, Ontario, 1909–1947. *Can. J. Public Health 40*, 257–69.

McKinnon, N.E. 1950. Cancer mortality trends in different countries. *Can. J. Public Health 41*, 230–40.

McKinnon, N.E. 1952. Cancer of the breast: Invalid evidence of increase. *Can. J. Public Health 43*, 10–13.

McLachlan, G. and McKeown, T. (Eds.) 1971. *Medical history and medical care*. Oxford University Press, London. xiii + 244.

McLaren, D.S. 1982. Excessive nutrient intakes. pp. 367–88 in Jelliffe and Jelliffe.

MacLennan, J.D. 1962. The histotoxic clostridial infections of man. *Bacteriol. Rev. 26*, 177–274.

McLeod, J.W. 1943. The types *mitis, intermedius* and *gravis* of *Corynebacterium diphtheriae*: A review of observations during the past ten years. *Bacteriol. Rev. 7*, 1–56.

MacLeod, R.M. 1967. The edge of hope: social policy and chronic alcoholism. *J. Hist. Med. 22*, 215–45.

MacMahon, S.W. and Leeder, S.R. 1984. Blood pressure levels and mortality from cerebrovascular disease in Australia and the United States. *Am. J. Epidemiol. 120*, 865–75.

MacMichael, W. 1827/1968. *The gold-headed cane*. Facsimile copy. Roy. Coll. Physicians, London. iv + 26 + 179.

MacNalty, A.S. (Ed.-in-chief). 1952 onward. *History of the Second World War: United Kingdom Medical Series*. HMSO, London. (Multivolume series.)

MacNalty, A.S. (Ed.). 1953–1955. *The civilian health and medical services. History of the Second World War: United Kingdom, Medical Series*. HMSO, London. 2 vols. x + 441, xi + 406.

MacNalty, A.S. and Mellor, W.F. (Eds.) 1968. *Medical services in war: The principal medical lessons of the Second World War based on the official medical histories of the United Kingdom, Canada, Australia, New Zealand and India. History of the*

Second World War: United Kingdom, Medical Series. HMSO, London. xviii + 781.

McNamara, R. 1982. Mortality trends. pp. 459–61 in *International Encyclopedia of Population*, Free Press, New York.

McNee, J.W. 1952. Medicine in the Royal Navy. pp. 1–8 in Cope.

McNeill, W.H. 1976. *Plagues and peoples*. Anchor Doubleday, Garden City, NY. viii + 369.

Madeley, C.R. 1984. Other enteric viruses. pp. 420–50 in Topley and Wilson. 1984, vol. 4.

Madsen, Th. and Madsen, S. 1956. Diphtheria in Denmark. From 23,695 to 1 case—Post or propter. I. Serum therapy. II. Diphtheria immunization. *Dan. Med. Bull. 3*, 112–21.

Mahboubi, E. and Sayed, G.M. 1982. Oral cavity and pharynx. pp. 583–95 in Schottenfeld and Fraumeni.

Mahmoud, A.A.F. 1984. Schistosomiasis. *Rec. Adv. in Trop. Med. 1*, 179–206. See Gilles, 1984.

Makeham, W.M. 1860. On the law of mortality and construction of annuity tables. *J. Inst. Actuar. 8*, 301–10.

Makeham, W.M. 1867. On the law of mortality. *J. Inst. Actuar. (Assur. Mag.) 13*, 325–58.

Makeham, W.M. 1890. On the further development of Gompertz's law. *J. Inst. Actuar. 28*, 152–59; 185–92; 316–32.

Malaurie, J., Tabah, L., and Sutter, J. 1952. L'isolat esquimau de Thulé (Groenland). *Population 7*, 675–92.

Mande, R. (in collab. with Fillastre, C. and Rouillon, A.) 1968. *B.C.G. vaccination*. Dawsons of Pall Mall, London. 280 pp.

Manning, D.H. 1976. *Disaster technology: An annotated bibliography*. Pergamon Press, Oxford. vi + 282.

Manson, P. 1899. The need for special training in tropical diseases. *J. Trop. Med. 2*, 57–62.

Manson-Bahr, P. 1963. The story of malaria: The drama and the actors. pp. 329–90 in *International Review of Tropical Medicine*, vol. 2, D.R. Lincicome, Ed. Academic Press, New York-London. xiv + 425.

Manson-Bahr, P.E.C. and Apted, F.I.C. 1982. *Manson's tropical diseases*. 18th edition. Baillière Tindall, London. xiv + 843.

Manton, K.G. and Stallard, E. 1984. *Recent trends in mortality analysis*. Studies in Population. Academic Press, Orlando, FL. x + 344.

Mao, S.-P. and Shao, B.-R. 1982. Schistosomiasis control in the People's Republic of China. *Am. J. Trop. Med. Hyg. 31*, 92–99.

Mara, D. 1976. *Sewage treatment in hot climates*.

Wiley, New York. xv + 168.

Marcusson, H. and Oehmisch, W. 1977. Accident mortality in childhood in selected countries of different continents, 1950–1971. *World Health Stat. Rep. 30*, 57–92.

Margulies, E. (Ed.) 1983. *Myocardial infarction and cardiac death*. Academic Press, New York. xiv + 220.

Mari Bhat, P.N., Preston, S., and Dyson, T. 1984. *Vital rates in India, 1961–1981*. US Natl. Res. Council Comm. on Popul. and Demogr., National Academy Press, Washington, DC. 173 pp.

Marks, H.H. 1966. Vital statistics. pp. 622–35 in Lilienfeld, Gifford, et al.

Marmion, B.P. 1984. Rickettsial diseases of man and animals. pp. 574–90 in Topley and Wilson, 1984, vol. 3.

Marsden, J.P. 1948. Variola minor: A personal analysis of 13,686 cases. *Bull. Hyg. 23*, 735–46.

Marsden, P.D. 1983. The transmission of *Trypanosoma cruzi* infection to man and its control. pp. 253–89 in Croll and Cross.

Marsden, P.D. 1984. Chagas' disease: Clinical aspects. *Rec. Adv. Trop. Med. 1*, 63–77. See Gilles, 1984.

Marshall, E. 1984. Juarez: An unprecedented radiation accident. *Science 223*, 1152–54.

Marshall, J.L. 1973. *Lightning protection*. Wiley-Interscience, New York. xvi + 190.

Marshall, T.H. 1935. The population of England and Wales from the industrial revolution to the world war. *Econ. Hist Rev. 5*, 65–78.

Martin, L. 1919. Vingt-cinq années de sérothérapie antidiphthérique. *Bull. Acad. Méd. (Paris) 82*, 173–79.

Martin, W.J. 1935. The decrease in mortality during early adult male life in England and Wales. *J. Hyg. Camb. 35*, 375–87.

Martin, W.J. 1950. Recent changes in the death rates from influenza. *Br. Med. J. 1*, 267–68.

Martland, H.S. 1931. The occurrence of malignancy in radioactive persons: A general review of data gathered in the study of the radium dial painters, with special reference to the occurrence of osteogenic sarcoma and the inter-relationship of certain blood diseases. *Am. J. Cancer 15*, 2435–516.

Martland, H.S. and Humphries, R.E. 1929. Osteogenic sarcoma in dial painters using luminous paint. *Arch. Pathol. 7*, 406–17.

Marx, J.L. 1982. New disease baffles medical community. *Science 217*, 618–21.

Mass, M.J. et al. (Eds.) 1985. *Cancer of the respiratory tract. Predisposing factors*. Carcinogenesis: a comprehensive survey, vol. 8. Raven, New York,

xxviii + 468.

Masse, L., Juillan, J.M., and Chisloup, A. 1976. Trends in mortality from cirrhosis of the liver, 1950–1971. *World Health Stat. Rep. 29*, 40–67.

Mastromatteo, E. 1967. Nickel: A review of its occupational health aspects. *J. Occup. Med. 9*, 127–36.

Masuy-Stroobant, G. 1983. *Les déterminants individuels et régionaux de la mortalité infantile. La Belgique d'hier et d'aujourd'hui*. Dépt. de Démog., Université Catholique, Louvain-la-neuve. 540 pp.

Mata, L.J. 1978. *The children of Santa Maria Cauqué. A prospective field study of health and growth*. International Nutrition Policy Series No. 2. MIT Press, Cambridge, MA. xvii + 395.

Mata, L.J., Kronmal, R.A., Garcia, B., Butler, W., Urrutia, J.J., and Murillo, S. 1976. Breast-feeding, weaning and the diarrhoeal syndrome in a Guatemalan Indian village. pp. 311–38 in Elliott and Knight.

Mata, L.(J.), Kronmal, R.A., and Villegas, H. 1980. Diarrheal diseases: A leading world health problem. pp. 1–14 in Ouchterlony and Holmgren.

Matossian, R.M., Rickard, M.D. and Smyth, J.D. 1977. Hydatidosis: A global problem of increasing importance. *WHO Bull. 55*, 499–507.

Matumoto. M. 1969. Mechanism of perpetuation of animal viruses in nature. *Bacteriol. Rev. 33*, 404–18.

Maxcy, K.F. 1923. The distribution of malaria in the United States as indicated by mortality reports. *Public Health. Rep. (USA)* 38, 1125–38.

Maxted, W.R. 1978. Group A streptococci: Pathogenesis and immunity. pp. 107–25 in Skinner and Quesnel.

May, J.M. (Ed.). 1961. *Studies in disease ecology*. Hafner, New York. xx + 613.

May, J.M. and Jarcho, I.S. 1961. *The ecology of malnutrition in the Far and Near East*. Hafner, New York. xvi + 688.

Mayhew, H. 1851/1861/1968. *London labour and the London poor: A cyclopaedia of the condition and earnings of those that will work, those that cannot work and those that will not work*. 2 vols. 1851; reprinted, 4 vols., 1861. Griffin, London. Reprinted 1968 by Dover, New York. 4 vols.

Mazuzan, G.T. and Walker, J.S. 1985. *Controlling the atom. The beginnings of nuclear regulation, 1946–1962*. University of California Press, Berkeley. x + 530.

Meade, R.H. 1968. *An introduction to the history of general surgery*. W.B. Saunders, Philadelphia-London-Toronto. xi + 403.

Meegama, S.A. 1982. Aging in developing countries. *World Health Stat. Q. 35*, 239–45.

Meehan, R.L. 1984. *The atom and the fault. Experts, earthquakes, and nuclear power*. MIT Press, Cambridge, MA. xvi + 161.

Meerwarth, R. 1932. Die Entwicklung der Bevölkerung in Deutschland während der Kriegs-und Nachkriegszeit. pp. 1–97 in Meerwarth, Günther, and Zimmermann.

Meerwarth, R. Günther, A., and Zimmermann, W. 1932. *Die Einwirkung des Krieges auf Bevölkerungsbewegung, Einkommen und Lebenshaltung in Deutschland. Wirtschafts- und Sozialgeschichte des Weltkrieges*. Deutsche Serie. J.T. Shotwell, Gen. Ed. Veröffentlichungen der Carnegie Stifung für Internationalen Frieden. Deutsche Verlagsanstalt, Stuttgart-Berlin-Leipzig. xv + 474.

Meiklejohn, A. 1960. Industrial pulmonary diseases in Great Britain. pp. 1–22 in *Industrial pulmonary diseases*, E.J. King and C.M. Fletcher, Eds. J. and A. Churchill, London. viii + 273.

Meindl, R.S. and Swedlund, A.C. 1977. Secular trends in mortality in the Connecticut Valley 1700–1850. *Hum. Biol. 49*, 389–414.

Meleney, F.L. 1924. Hemolytic streptococcus gangrene. *Arch. Surg. 9*, 317–64.

Melia, R.J.W. and Swan, A.V. 1986. International trends in mortality rates for bronchitis, emphysema and asthma during the period 1971–1980. *World Health Stat. Q. 39*, 206–17.

Mellor, J.W. and Gavian, S. 1987. Famine: Causes, prevention, and relief. *Science 235*, 539–45.

Mellor, W.F. (Ed.). 1972. *Casualties and medical statistics. History of the Second World War: United Kingdom, Medical Series*. A.S. MacNalty, Ed.-in-Chief. HMSO, London. 908 pp.

Melosi, M.V. 1982. *Garbage in the cities. Refuse, reform and the environment, 1880–1980*. Environmental Hist. Series No. 4. Texas A. & M. University Press, College Station, TX. xvi + 268.

Merbs, C.F. and Miller, R.J. (Eds.). 1985. *Health and disease in the prehistoric south-west*. Anthropology Res. Papers, No. 34. Arizona State University, Tempe, AZ. xxii + 404.

Mettler, C.C. 1947. *History of medicine. A correlative text, arranged according to subjects*. F.A. Mettler, Ed. Blakiston Co., Philadelphia-Toronto. xxix + 1215.

ter Meulen, V. and Carter, M.J. 1984. Measles virus persistency and disease. *Prog. Med Virol. 30*, 44–61.

Meurk, B.E. 1932. New Swedish mortality tables for annuity insurance. *Skand. Aktuarietidskr. 15*, 251–77.

Meuvret, J. 1946. Les crises de subsistances et la démographie de la France d'ancien régime. *Population 1*, 643–50.

Meuvret, J. 1965. Demographic crisis in France from the sixteenth to the eighteenth century. Transl. by M. Hilton. pp. 507–22 in Glass and Eversley.

Meyer, H.M., Brooks, B.E., Douglas, R.D., and Rogers, N.G. 1962. Ecology of measles in monkeys. *Am. J. Dis. Child. 103*, 307–13.

Meyer, K.F. 1956. The status of botulism as a world health problem. *WHO Bull. 15*, 281–98.

Meyer, P. 1980. *Hypertension: Mechanisms and clinical and therapeutic aspects*. Transl. by M.J. Osborne-Pellegrin. Oxford University Press, New York-Toronto. 199 pp.

Meyer, R.D. 1983. Legionella infections: A review of five years of research. *Rev. Infect. Dis. 5*, 258–78.

Meyler, L. 1952. *Side effects of drugs*. Elsevier, Amsterdam. xii + 268.

Meyler, L. and Herxheimer, A. 1972. *Side effects of drugs: Vol. 7. A survey of unwanted effects of drugs reported in 1968–1971*. Excerpta Medica, Amsterdam. x + 758.

Michell, A.R. 1977. The European fisheries in early modern history. pp. 133–84 in *Cambridge Economic History of Europe*, Vol. 5. Cambridge University Press.

Miles, A. 1967. Lister's contribution to microbiology. *Br. J. Surg. 54*, 415–18.

Miles, S.R. (Ed.). 1970. *Metropolitan problems: International perspectives. a search for comprehensive solutions*. Intermet Metropolitan Studies Series. Methuen, London. xv + 534.

Millar, W.H. 1874. Statistics of deaths by suicide among Her Majesty's British troops serving at home and abroad during the ten years 1862–71. *J. Stat. Soc. (London) 37*, 187–90.

Miller, D.L., Alderslade, R., and Ross, E.M. 1982. Whooping cough and whooping cough vaccine: The risks and benefits debate. *Epidemiol. Rev. 4*, 1–24.

Miller, D.S. 1979. Prevalence of nutritional problems in the world. *Proc. Nutr. Soc. 38*, 197–205.

Miller, R.W. 1975. Radiation. pp. 93–101 in Schottenfeld.

Millman, I., Eisenstein, T.K., and Blumberg, B.S. (Eds.) 1984. *Hepatitis B. The virus, the disease, and the vaccine. From a symp., Philadelphia, 1982*. Plenum, New York. xii + 251.

Millous, M. 1936. Une épidémie de varicelle maligne au Caméroun. *Bull. Acad. Méd (Paris) 115*, 840–43.

Milne, J. 1911. *Catalogue of destructive earthquakes AD 7 to AD 1899*. Br. Assoc. Adv. Sci., Seismological Committee, London. 92 pp.

Minor, T.C. 1874. *Erysipelas and childbed fever*. Cincinnati.

Mitchell, B.R. 1975. *European historical statistics, 1750–1970*. Macmillan, London. xx + 827.

Mitchison, N.A. 1980. The impact of immunology. pp. 567–92 in Stanley and Joske.

Modan, B. and Lubin, F. 1980. Epidemiology of colon cancer: Fiber, fats, fallacies and facts. pp. 119–35 in Spiller and Kay.

Moine, M. and Oudet, P. 1947. Etude, selon les générations et le sexe, de la mortalité parisienne par tuberculose toutes formes entre 1888 et 1938. *Rev. Tuberculose 11*, 488–501.

Moivre, A. de 1725. *Annuities upon Lives; or, the valuation of Annuities upon any number of lives; as also, of Reversions. To which is added, an appendix concerning the expectations of life and probabilities of survivorship*. W. Pearson, London. viii + 108. 2nd ed., 1731, S. Fuller, Dublin, viii + 122; 2nd ed., 1743, H. & G. Woodfall, London, xii + 117; 3rd ed., 1750, A. Millar, London, xii + 117; 4th ed., 1752, A. Millar, London, 133 pp.

Molin, G. da 1984. Les enfants abandonnés dans les villes italiennes aux XVIIIe et XIXe siècles. *Ann. Démog, Hist*. 1983, 103–24.

Møller-Christensen, V. 1966. Evidence of tuberculosis, leprosy and syphilis in antiquity and the Middle Ages. pp. 229–37 in *Proc. XIX internat. Congress Hist. Med. (Verh. XIX int. Kongr. Gesch. Med.)*, Basel 1964. Karger, Basel. xxvii + 687.

Møller-Christensen, V. 1967. Evidence of leprosy in earliest peoples. pp. 295–306 in Brothwell and Sandison.

Mollison, P.L. 1946. Observations on starvation in Belsen. *Br. Med. J. 1*, 4–8.

Mols, R. 1954–1956. *Introduction à la démographie historique des villes d'Europe, du XIVe au XVIIIe siècle*. Recueil de travaux d'histoire et de philologie, Ser. 4, fasc. 1–3. Publications Universitaires, Louvain. 3 vols.

Molyneux, D.H., de Raadt, P., and Seed, J. 1984. African human trypanosomiasis. *Rec. Adv. Trop Med. 1*, 39–62. See Gilles, 1984.

Molz, G. 1973. Perinatal and newborn deaths (necropsy findings in 970 term, pre-term and small-for-date births). *Curr. Top. Pathol. 58*, 149–64.

Monnier, A. 1974. La mortalité. pp. 81–114 in *La population de la France. Population* (spec. issue), 29th year. 356 pp.

Montandon, F. 1959. Quelle est la moyenne annuelle des morts causées par les tremblements de terre? *Rev. Etude Calam*. (Geneva) *36*, 61–

Montandon, R. 1924. La géographie des calamités. *Matér. Etude Calam*. (Geneva) *1*, 13–

Montezambert, F. 1901. Notes on a mild type of small-pox (variola ambulans). *Br. Med. J. 1*, 1134.

Moodie, P.M. 1973. *Aboriginal health*. Aborigines in Australian Society, 9. Austral. Natl. Univ. Press, Canberra. xvii + 307.

Moodie, P. (M.) 1981. Australian aborigines. pp. 154–67 in Trowell and Burkitt.

Moodie, P.M. and Pederson, E.B. 1971. *The health of Australian aborigines: An annotated bibliography*. Service Publn. No. 8, Commonwealth Dept of Health, School of Public Health and Tropical Medicine, Univ. of Sydney. Austral. Govt Publ. Service, Canberra. 248 pp.

Moore, D.V., Collins, W.E., and Young, M.D. 1976. Fifty years of American parasitology: Some fulgent personalities in helminthology, arthropodology, protozoology. *J. Parasitol. 62*, 498–514.

Moore, F.D. 1976. Surgery. pp. 614–84 in Bowers and Purcell.

Moraes, N.L.deA. 1962. Medical importance of measles in Brazil. *Am. J. Dis. Child. 103*, 233–36.

Morgan, A.E. 1971. *Dams and other disasters. A century of the Army Corps of Engineers in civil works*. Porter Sargent, Boston xxvi + 422.

Morgan, E.M. and Rapp, F. 1977. Measles virus and its associated diseases. *Bacteriol. Rev. 41*, 636–66.

Moriceau, J.-M. 1980. Les crises démographiques dans le sud de la région parisienne de 1560 à 1670. *Ann. Démog. Hist.*, Pt. 1, 105–23.

Morita, Y. 1963. An estimation on the actual birth and death rates in the early Meiji period of Japan. *Popul. Studies 17*, 33–56.

Moriyama, I.M. 1948. Is diabetes mortality increasing? *Public Health Rep. 63*, 1334–39.

Moriyama, I.M. 1966. Chronic respiratory disease mortality in the United States. pp. 706–11 in Lilienfeld and Gifford.

Moriyama, I.M., Baum, W.S., Haenszel, W.M., and Mattison, B.F. 1966. Inquiry into diagnositic evidence supporting medical certifications of death. pp. 55–65 in Lilienfeld and Gifford.

Moriyama, I.M. and Guralnick, L. 1956. Occupational and social class differences in mortality. pp. 61–73 in *Trends and Differentials in Mortality. Papers presented at the 1955 Annual Conf. of the Milbank Memorial Fund*. Milbank Memorial Fund, New York. 166 pp.

Moriyama, I.M., Krueger, D.E., and Stamler, J.

1971. *Cardiovascular diseases in the United States.* Harvard University Press, Cambridge, MA. xxvi + 496.

Morley, D.C. 1962. Measles in Nigeria. *Am. J. Dis. Child. 103*, 230–33.

Morley D.(C.) 1978. *Paediatric priorities in the developing world.* Butterworth, London. xiii + 470.

Morley, D.(C.) 1980. Severe measles. pp. 115–28 in Stanley and Joske.

Morley, D.(C.), Woodland, M., and Martin, W.J. 1963. Measles in Nigeria: A study of the disease in West Africa, and its manifestations in England and other countries during different epochs. *J. Hyg. Camb. 61*, 115–34.

Morley, D.C., Woodland, M., and Martin, W.J. 1966. Whooping cough in Nigerian children. *Trop. Geogr. Med. 18*, 169–82.

Morris, C. 1751. *Observations on the past growth and present state of the City of London. To which are annexed a complete table of the christnings and burials within this City from 1601 to 1750; . . . together with a table of the numbers which have annually died of each disease from 1675 to the present time.* London.

Morris, C. 1971. The plague in Britain. (A review of Shrewsbury, 1970.) *Hist. J. 14*, 205–15.

Morris, J.M, et al. 1955. Social and biological factors in infant mortality. *Lancet 1*, 343–49, 395–97, 445–48, 499–503, 554–59.

Morris, J.V. 1955. *Fires and fire-fighters.* Little, Brown & Co., Boston. x + 393.

Morrison, A.S. and Cole, P. 1982. Urinary tract. pp. 925–37 in Schottenfeld and Fraumeni.

Morrow, R.H. Jr 1982. Burkitt's lymphoma. pp. 779–94 in Schottenfeld and Fraumeni.

Morse, D. 1967. Tuberculosis. pp. 249–71 in Brothwell and Sandison.

Morse, D., Brothwell, D., and Ucko, P.J. 1964. Tuberculosis in ancient Egypt. *Am. Rev. Respir. Dis. 90*, 524–30.

Morton, L.T. 1983. *A medical bibliography (Garrison and Morton). An annotated check-list of texts illustrating the history of medicine.* 4th edition. Andre Deutsch, London. 950 pp.

Moschella, S.L. and Hurley, H.J. (Eds.) 1985. *Dermatology.* W.B. Saunders, Philadelphia. 2 vols. xxvi + 2216 + lxxviii.

Moser, R. 1959. *Diseases of medical progress: A survey of diseases and syndromes unintentionally induced as a result of properly indicated, widely accepted therapeutic procedures.* C.C. Thomas, Springfield, IL. 131 pp.

Mostofi, F.K. (Ed.) 1967. *Bilharziasis.* Internatl. Acad. Pathology. Springer, New York. viii + 357.

Motulsky, A.G. 1960. Metabolic polymorphisms and the role of infectious diseases in human evolution. *Hum. Biol. 32*, 28–62.

Mould, R.F. 1983. *Cancer statistics.* Adam Hilger, Bristol. xiv + 286.

Mourant, A.E., Kopeć, A.C., and Domaniewska-Sobczak, K. (with an appendix by Ryder, L.P. and Svejgaard, A.) 1978. *Blood groups and disease: a study of associations of diseases with blood group and other polymorphisms.* Oxford University Press, New York. x + 328.

Mudge, G.A. 1970. Starvation as a means of warfare. *Int. Lawyer 4* (2), 228–68.

Mueller, F.H. 1939. Tabakmissbrauch und Lungencarcinom. *Z. Krebsforsch. 49*, 57–85.

Müller-Beck, H. 1967. On migrations of hunters across the Bering land bridge in the Upper Pleistocene. pp. 373–408 in Hopkins.

Muir, C.S. and Nectoux, J. 1978. Ovarian cancer: Some epidemiological features. *World Health Stat. Q. 31*, 51–61.

Muir, C.S. and Nectoux, J. 1982. International patterns of cancer. pp. 119–37 in Schottenfeld and Fraumeni.

Mukerjee, S., Basu, S., and Bhattacharya, P. 1965. A new trend in cholera epidemiology. *Br. Med. J. 2*, 837–39.

Muller, H.J. 1950. Our load of mutation. *Am. J. Hum. Genet. 2*, 111–76.

Mullett, C.F. 1956. *The bubonic plague and England. An Essay in the history of preventive medicine.* University of Kentucky Press, Lexington. ix + 401.

Mulligan, H.W. (Ed.) 1970. *The African trypanosomiases.* Allen & Unwin, London. lxxxviii + 950.

Mulvaney, D.J. and Golson, J. 1971. *Aboriginal man and environment in Australia.* Austral. Natl. University Press, Canberra. xxii + 390.

Munby, L. 1964. *Hertfordshire population statistics, 1563–1801.* Hertfordshire Local History Council, Hitchin, Herts.

Mundkur, M., Yurchyshyn, L.L. and de Luca, L. 1978. *Aging: A guide to reference sources, journals and government publications.* Bibliographic Series No. 11. University of Connecticut Library, Storrs, CT. xii + 162.

Munoz, J.J. and Bergman, R.K. 1977. *Bordetella pertussis. Immunological and other biological activities.* Dekker, New York. xii + 236.

Munro-Kerr, J.M., Johnstone, R.W., and Phillips, M.H. (Eds.) 1954. *Historical review of British obstetrics and gynaecology, 1800–1950.* E. & S. Livingstone, Edinburgh-London. viii + 420.

Murchison, C. 1862. *A treatise on the continued*

fevers of Great Britain. Parker, Son and Bourn, London. xiv + 638.

Murphy, F.A. 1979. Control and eradication of exotic viruses affecting man. *Prog. Med. Virol. 25*, 69–82.

Murray, L.H. 1951. A world review of smallpox incidence. *WHO Epidemiol. Vital Stat. Rep. 4*, 394–420.

Muschel, L.H. 1966. Blood groups, disease and selection. *Bacteriol. Rev. 30*, 427–41.

Mustacchi, P. and Shimkin, M.B. 1958. Cancer of the bladder and infestation with *Schistosoma hematobium*. *J. Natl. Cancer Inst. 20*, 825–42.

Myers, G.C. 1978. Cross-national trends in mortality rates among the elderly. *Gerontologist 18*, 441–48.

Myers, J.A. 1974. Development of knowledge of unity of tuberculosis and of the portals of entry of tubercle bacilli. *J. Hist. Med. 29*, 213–28.

Myers, J.A. and Steele, J.H. 1969. *Bovine tuberculosis. Control in man and animals*. Warren H. Green, St. Louis, MO. xxvii + 403.

Myers, M.H. and Hankey, B.F. 1982. Cancer patient survival in the United States. pp. 166–78 in Schottenfeld and Fraumeni.

Myers, R.J. 1965. Analysis of mortality in the Soviet Union according to 1958–59 life tables. *Trans. Soc. Actuar. 16*, 309–17.

Nabarro, D. 1954. *Congenital syphilis*. Edward Arnold, London. xii + 470.

Nace, E.P. 1984. Epidemiology of alcoholism and prospects for treatment. *Annu. Rev. Med. 35*, 293–309.

Nagano, Y. and Davenport, F.M. (Eds.) 1972. *Rabies. Proc. of a working conference on rabies*. Harvard University Press, Cambridge, MA. viii + 406.

Nahmias, A.J. and O'Reilly, R.J. 1982. *Immunology of human infections. Part 1. Bacteria, Mycoplasmae, Chlamydiae and Fungi. Part 2. Viruses and Parasites, immunodiagnosis and presentation of infectious disease*. Comprehensive Immunology Series, 8 and 9. Plenum, New York. 632 pp.

Namfua, P., Kim, Y.J., and Mosley, W.H. 1978. An estimation of the impact of smallpox eradication on the expectation of life in selected less developed countries. *World Health Stat. Q. 31*, 110–19.

Napalkov, N.P., Tserkovny, G.F. et al. (Eds.) 1983. *Cancer incidence in the USSR*. (Supplement to *Cancer Incidence in Five Continents*, vol. 3.) 2nd rev. edition. Internatl. Agency for Research on Cancer, Lyon. 74 pp.

Naranjo, J.L., Sigurdsson, H., Carey, S.N., and

Fritz, W. 1986. Eruption of the Nevado del Ruiz volcano, Colombia, on 13 November 1985: Tephra falls and lahars. *Science 233*, 961–63.

Nash, T.E. (Moderator) 1982. Schistosome infections in humans: Perspectives and recent findings. *Ann. Intern. Med. 97*, 740–54.

Nathanson, N. 1984. Epidemiologic aspects of poliomyelitis eradication. *Rev. Infect. Dis. 6*, S308–12.

National Academy 1980. *Disasters and the mass media. Proc. of a workshop, Washington, DC., 1979*. National Academy of Sciences, Washington, DC. xiv + 302.

National Academy 1985a. *Safety of dams. Flood and earthquake criteria*. National Academy of Sciences, Washington, DC. xviii + 276.

National Academy 1985b. *Injury in America. A continuing public health problem*. National Academy of Sciences, Washington, DC. xii + 164.

National Diabetes Data Group 1985. *Diabetes in America*. NIH Publ. No. 85–1468, US Dept. Health and Human Services, Nat. Instit. Health, Bethesda, MD. Variously paged.

Nayak, N.C. 1982. Tropical splenomegaly. *Crit. Rev. Trop. Med. 1*, 247–73. See Chandra, 1982.

Neel, J.V. 1977. Health and disease in unacculturated Amerindian populations. With discussion. pp. 155–77 in Elliott and Whelan.

Neel, J.V. (Moderator), Spielman, R.S., Cudworth, A.G., Svejgaard, A., and Rotter, J.I. 1982. A discussion of contrasting viewpoints on the genetics of insulin-dependent diabetes. pp. 137–47 in Koebberling and Tattersall.

Neison, F.G.P. 1844. On a method recently proposed for conducting inquiries into the comparative sanatory conditions of various districts with illustrations derived from numerous places in Great Britain at the period of the last census. *J. Stat. Soc. (London) 7*, 40–68.

Neison, F.G.P. 1845–1846. Contributions to vital statistics, especially designed to elucidate the rate of mortality, the laws of sickness, and the influences of trade and locality on health, derived from an extensive collection of original data supplied by Friendly Societies, and proving their frequent instability. *J. Stat. Soc. (London) 8*, 290–343; *9*, 50–76.

Neison, F.G.P. 1852. On the rate of mortality in the medical profession. *J. Stat. Soc. (London) 15*, 193–222.

Neison, F.G.P. 1877. Some statistics of the affiliated orders of Friendly Societies (Odd Fellows and Foresters). *J. Stat. Soc. (London) 40*, 42–81.

Nelson, W. 1982. *Applied life data analysis*. Wiley

Series in Probability and Math. Statistics. Wiley, New York. xvi + 634.

Ness, G.B. van 1971. Ecology of anthrax. *Science* 172, 1303–07.

Nettleship, M.A., Givens, R.D., and Nettleship, A. 1975. *War, its causes and correlates*. Mouton, The Hague-Paris. xviii + 813.

Neva, F.A., Alford, C.A., and Weller, T.H. 1964. Emerging perspective of rubella. *Bacteriol. Rev.* 28, 444–51.

Newell, G.R. and Ellison, N.M. (Eds.) 1981. *Nutrition and cancer. Etiology and treatment*. Progress in Cancer Research and Therapy, vol. 17. Raven, New York. xiv + 446.

Newman, G., Greenwood, M., Carnwath, T., French, H., Andrewes, F., Low, R.B., and James, S.P. 1920. *Report on the pandemic of influenza 1918–9. I, Influenza in Great Britain and Ireland; II, Influenza in foreign countries 1918–9; III, Appendices*. UK Ministry of Health, Reports on Public Health and Medical Subjects No. 4, HMSO, London. xxiii + 577.

Newsholme, A. 1918. Discussion on influenza. *Br. Med. J. 2*, 574–75.

Newsholme, A. 1918–1919. Discussion on influenza. *Proc. Roy. Soc. Med. 12* (1), 15–102.

Ngu, J.L. and Soothill, J.F. 1982. Immune complex nephropathy in the tropics. *Crit. Rev. Trop Med. 1*, 275–306. See Chandra, 1982.

Nicholas, L. and Beerman, H. 1967. Late syphilis: A review of some of the recent literature. *Am. J. Med. Sci. 255*, 549–69.

Nichols, B.L. and Soriano, H.A. 1977. A critique of oral therapy of dehydration due to diarrheal syndromes. *Am. J. Clin. Nutr. 30*, 1457–72.

Nicolini, C. (Ed.) 1982. *Chemical carcinogenesis. Proc. of an institute, Erice, Italy, 1981*. NATO Advanced Study Institutes Series A, vol. 52. Plenum, New York. xii + 492.

Nielsen, J. and Sillesen, I. 1975. Incidence of chromosome aberrations among 11,148 newborn children. *Hum. Genet. 30*, 1–12.

Nightingale, F. 1894a. Sick nursing and health nursing. p.449 in Billings and Hurd.

Nightingale, F. 1894b. *Health teaching in towns and villages. Rural hygiene*. Spottiswoode, London. 27 pp.

Niswander, K.R. 1977. Obstetric factors related to prematurity. pp. 249–68 in Reed and Stanley.

Nixon, J.W. 1960. *A history of the Internatinal Statistical Institute, 1885–1960*. Internatl. Stat. Inst., The Hague. viii + 188.

Nomura, A. 1982. Stomach. pp. 624–37 in Schottenfeld and Fraumeni.

Noorden, S.K. and Lopez Bravo, L. 1986. The world leprosy situation. *World Health Stat. Q. 39*, 122–37.

Nora, J.J. and Fraser, F.C. 1974. *Medical genetics: Principles and practice*. Lea & Febiger, Philadelphia. xii + 399.

Nordal, J. and Kristinsson, V. 1975. *Iceland, 874–1974: handbook published by the Central Bank of Iceland on the occasion of the eleventh centenary of the settlement of Iceland*. Central Bank of Iceland, Reykjavik. xv + 416.

Nordiska Rådet 1978. *Nordisk statistisk årsbok (Yearbook of Nordic statistics)*. Vol. 17. Norstedts Tryckeri, Stockholm. 352 pp.

Norman, C. 1985. AIDS virology: A battle on many fronts. *Science 230*, 518–21.

Norman, L.G. 1962. *Road traffic accidents: Epidemiology, control and prevention*. Public Health Papers No. 12, WHO, Geneva. 110 pp.

Nørregaard, C. and Schmidt, G. 1975. Mortality and fertility in Arctic communities: Greenland—A case study. *Popul. Studies 29*, 37–51.

Norway Central Bureau 1974. *Dødelighetsutvikling og dødsårsaksmønster 1951–1970*. Central Bureau of Statistics (Statistisk Sentralbyrå), Oslo. 208 pp.

Norwood, W.D. 1975. *Health protection of radiation workers*. C.C. Thomas, Springfield, IL. xi + 442.

Nriagu, J.O. 1983. *Lead and lead poisoning in antiquity*. Wiley, New York. xv + 437.

Nunneley, T. 1841. *A treatise on the nature, causes, and treatment of erysipelas*. John Churchill, London. xii + 307.

Nurse, G.T. and Jenkins, T. 1977. *Health and the hunter-gatherer*. Monographs in Human Genetics, vol. 8. Karger, Basel. x + 126.

Nwosu, A.B.C. 1983. The human environment and helminth infections: A biomedical study of four Nigerian villages. pp. 225–52 in Croll and Cross.

Nybølle, H.C. 1931. Infant mortality in the northern countries. *Nord. Stat. J. 3*, 311–41.

O'Brien, G.A.T. 1918 *Economic history of Ireland in the eighteenth century*. Maunsel, Dublin. viii + 437.

O'Brien, G.A.T. 1919. *Economic history of Ireland in the seventeenth century*. Maunsel, Dublin. 283 pp.

O'Brien, G.A.T. 1921. *Economic history of Ireland, from the union to the famine*. Longmans, London. xii + 589.

Official History of the War 1922–1924. *History of the Great War based on official documents*. Vols. 1 & 2. *Medical services, diseases of the war*. W.G. Macpherson, W.P. Herringham, T.R. Elliott, and A. Balfour (Eds.) 1922; 1923. viii + 550; viii +

621. Vol. (unnumbered) *Medical services, pathology*. W.G. Macpherson, W.B. Leishman., and S.L. Cummins (Eds.). 1923. vii + 600. HMSO, London. 7 vols.

Ofstad, K. 1949–1950. Population statistics and population registration in Norway. Part 3, Population censuses. *Popul. Studies 3*, 66–75.

Ogle, W. 1886*a*. Suicides in England and Wales in relation to age, sex, season and occupation. *J. Stat. Soc. (London) 49*, 101–26.

Ogle, W. 1886*b*. Mortality in the medical profession. *J. Stat. Soc. (London) 49*, 164–70.

Ogra, P.L. (Ed.) 1984. *Neonatal infections. Nutritional and immunologic interactions*. Grune and Stratton, Orlando, FL. xx + 352.

Ogston, A. 1881. Report upon micro-organisms in surgical diseases. *Br. Med. J. 1*, 369–74; corrig. 453.

Ohashi, M. 1975. Enteric fever eradication program in Japan. pp. 26–47 in Kitamoto.

Ohlin, L.E. (Ed.) 1973. *Prisoners in America: Perspectives on our correctional system*. Prentice-Hall, Englewood Cliffs, NJ. iv + 216.

Ohno, Y. 1985. Health development in Japan. *World Health Stat. Q. 38*, 176–92.

Okuno, T. 1978. An epidemiological review of Japanese encephalitis. *World Health Stat. Q. 31*, 120–33.

Olitzki, A. 1972. *Enteric fevers: Causing organisms and hosts reactions*. Karger, Basel. x + 486.

Opitz, J.M., Jürgen, H., Pettersen, J.C., Bersu, E.T., and Colacino, S.C. 1979. Terminological, diagnostic, nosological, and anatomical-developmental aspects of developmental defects in man. *Adv. Hum. Genet. 9*, 71–164.

Ordish, G. 1952. *Untaken harvest: Man's loss of crops from pest, weed and disease*. Constable, London. xii + 171.

Ormerod, W.E. 1976. Ecological effect of control of African trypanosomiasis. *Science 191*, 815–21.

O'Rourke, J. 1875. *History of the great Irish famine*. McGlashan & Gill, Dublin. xxiv + 559.

Osler, W. 1897*a*. On certain features in the prognosis of pneumonia. *Am. J. Med. Sci. 113*, 1–10.

Osler, W. 1897*b*. Pneumonia: A review of cases studied by the third and fourth year classes, Johns Hopkins Hospital, session of 1896–97. *Natl. Med. Rev. 7*, 177–80.

Osler, W. 1899. On the study of pneumonia. *St. Paul Med. J. 1*, 5–9.

Osler, W. 1921. *The evolution of modern medicine*. Yale University Press, New Haven, CT. xiv + 243.

Ostfeld, A.M. 1980. A review of stroke epidemiology. *Epidemiol. Rev. 2*, 136–52.

Osunkoya, B.O. 1982. Burkitt's lymphoma. *Crit. Rev. Trop. Med. 1*, 367–96. See Chandra, 1982.

Ouchterlony, Oe. and Holmgren, J. (Eds.) 1980. *Cholera and related diarrheas: Molecular aspects of a global health problem*. 43rd Nobel Symp. co-sponsored by WHO. Karger, Basel. xi + 251.

Ovčarov, V.K. and Bystrova, V.A. 1978. Present trends in mortality in the age group 35–64 in selected developed countries between 1950–1973. *World Health Stat. Q. 31*, 208–346.

Oxford, J.S. and Öberg, B. 1985. *Conquest of viral diseases. A topical review of drugs and vaccines*. Elsevier, New York. xxx + 708.

Oye, E. van (Ed.). 1964. *The world problem of salmonellosis*. Dr. W. Junk Publ., The Hague. 606 pp.

Paccaud, M.F. 1979. World trends in poliomyelitis morbidity and mortality, 1951–1975. *World Health Stat. Q. 32*, 198–224.

Paffenbarger, R.S. Jr, Hyde, R.T., Wing, A.L., and Hsieh, Chung-Cheng. 1986. Physical activity, all-cause mortality, and longevity of college alumni. *N. Engl. J. Med. 314*, 605–13.

Page, M. 1948. Surgical records. President's Address. *Proc. Roy. Soc. Med. 41*, 113–18.

Pagès, G. 1970. *The Thirty Years War, 1618–1648*. Transl. by D. Maland and J. Hooper from the French, *La Guerre de Trente Ans*, Payot, Paris. R. & R. Clark, Edinburgh. 269 pp.

PAHO/WHO 1973. *The control of lice and louse-borne diseases*. Proc. Internatl. Symp., Washington, DC., 1972. Sci. Publ. No. 263, Pan American Health Org., Washington, DC. ix + 311.

Painter, N. and Burkitt, D. 1975. Diverticular disease of the colon. pp. 99–116 in Burkitt and Trowell.

Pakter, J. and Nelson, F. 1974. Factors in the unprecedented decline in infant mortality in New York City. *Bul. N.Y. Acad. Med. 50*, 839–68.

Palloni, A. 1981. A review of infant mortality trends in selected underdeveloped countries: Some new estimates. *Popul. Studies 35*, 100–19.

Palo, G. de, Rilke, F., and zur Hausen, H. (Eds.) 1986. *Herpes and papilloma virus. Their role in the carcinogenesis of the lower genital tract*. Serono Symp. Publ., vol. 31. Raven, New York. xiv + 368.

Paltridge, G.W. and Barton, I.J. 1978. *Erythemal ultraviolet radiation distribution over Australia— The calculations, detailed results and input data, including frequency analysis of observed Australian cloud cover*. Tech. Paper No. 33, CSIRO

Div. of Atmospheric Physics, Melbourne. 48pp.

Pampana, E.J. and Russell, P.F. 1955. Malaria: A world problem. *WHO Chron. 9* (2–3), 72 pp.

Pamuk, E.R. 1985. Social class inequality in mortality from 1921 to 1972 in England and Wales. *Popul. Studies 39*, 17–31.

Pankhurst, R. 1966. The great Ethiopian famine of 1888–1892: a new assessment. *J. Hist. Med. 21*, 95–124 and 271–94.

Panum, P.L. 1847. *Iagttagelser, anstillende under Maeslinge-Epidemien paa Faerøerne i Aaret 1846.* Transl. by A.S. Hatcher as *Observations made upon the epidemic of measles in the Faroe Islands in the year 1846.* With a biographical memoir by J.J. Petersen, transl. by J. Dimont. Delta Omega Soc. and Am. Public Health Assoc., New York, 1940. xxxvii + 111.

Pappenheimer, A.M. 1984. The diphtheria bacillus and its toxin: A model system. *J. Hyg. Camb. 93*, 397–404.

Parain, C. 1966. The evolution of agricultural technique. pp. 125–204 in *The agrarian life of the Middle Ages*, M.M Postan, Ed. Vol. 1, *Cambridge Economic History of Europe*. Cambridge University Press.

Parascandola, J. (Ed.) 1980. *The history of antibiotics: A symposium.* American Institute of the History of Pharmacy, Madison, WI. vi + 137.

Parascandola, J. 1981. The theoretical basis of Paul Ehrlich's chemotherapy. *J. Hist. Med. 36*, 19–43.

Park, W.H., Krumwiede, C., Anthony, B., et al. 1910–1911. The relative importance of the bovine and human types of tubercle bacilli in the different forms of human tuberculosis. *J. Med. Res. (Boston) 23*, 205–68.

Parker, G. 1979. Warfare. pp. 201–19 in *Companion Volume to Vol. 13* (P. Burke,Ed.) *The New Cambridge Modern History*. Cambridge University Press.

Parker, M. le M. 1964. Christmas Island, Indian Ocean: the pattern of disease in an isolated community. *Med. J. Austral. 2*, 1000–03.

Parker, M.T. 1978. The pattern of streptococcal disease in man. pp. 71–106 in Skinner and Quesnel.

Parker, M.T. 1984a. Pyogenic infections, generalized and local. pp. 170–91 in Topley and Wilson, 1984, vol. 3.

Parker, M.T. 1984b. Hospital-acquired infections. pp. 192–224 in Topley and Wilson, 1984, vol. 3.

Parker, M.T. 1984c. Streptococcal diseases. pp. 225–53 in Topley and Wilson, 1984, vol. 3.

Parker, M.T. 1984d. Staphylococcal diseases. pp. 254–78 in Topley and Wilson, 1984, vol. 3.

Parker, M.T. 1984e. Septic infections due to gram-negative aerobic bacilli. pp. 279–310 in Topley and Wilson, 1984, vol. 3.

Parker, M.T. 1984f. Enteric infections: Typhoid and paratyphoid fever. pp. 407–33 in Topley and Wilson, 1984, vol. 3.

Parker, M.T. 1984g. Bacillary dysentery. pp. 434–45 in Topley and Wilson, 1984, vol. 3.

Parkes, W.R. 1982. *Occupational lung disorders.* 2nd edition. Butterworth, London. xv + 529.

Parkin, D.M. (Ed.) 1986. *Cancer occurrence in developing countries.* Internatl. Agency for Research on Cancer, Lyon. xi + 339.

Parkinson, R. 1977. *Encyclopedia of modern war.* Routledge and Kegan Paul, London. ix + 226.

Parrish, J.A. (Ed.) 1983. *The effect of ultraviolet radiation on the immune system. A scientific round table.* Johnson and Johnson Baby Products Co., Skillman, NJ. viii + 424.

Parry, J.H. 1967. Transport and trade routes. pp. 155–222 in *Cambridge Economic History of Europe*, Vol. 4. Cambridge University Press.

Parry, N. and Parry, J. 1976. *The rise of the medical profession.* Croom Helm, London. v + 282.

Parsons, H.F. 1898–1899. Half a century of sanitary progress, and its results. *Trans. Epidemiol. Soc. London 18*, 1–38.

Parsons, H.F. 1899–1900. On the comparative mortality of English districts. *Trans, Epidemiol. Soc. London 19*, 1–24.

Pascua, M. 1948. Diversity of stillbirth definitions and some statistical repercussions. *WHO Epidemiol. Vital Stat. Rep. 1*, 210–20.

Passmore, R. 1951. Famine in India. An historical survey. *Lancet 2*, 303–07.

Passmore, R. 1962. Food supplies and population growth. Estimation of food requirements. With discussion. *J. Roy. Stat. Soc. A125*, 387–98.

Pasteur, L. (with collab. of J.F. Joubert and C.E. Chamberland) 1878. La théorie des germes et ses applications à la médecine et à la chirurgie. *C.R. Acad. Sci. 86*, 1037–43 (*Oeuvres, 6:* 112–30).

Patterson, K.D. 1974. Disease and medicine in African history. *History in Africa 1*, 142–48.

Patterson, K.D. 1986. *Pandemic influenza 1700–1900. A study in historical epidemiology.* Rowman and Littlefield, Totowa, NJ. xviii + 118.

Paul, J.R. 1971. *A history of poliomyelitis.* Yale University Press, New Haven, CT. xv + 486.

Pavlovsky, E.N. (Ed.) 1963. *Human diseases with natural foci.* Transl. from Russian. Foreign Languages Publ. House, Moscow. 346 pp.

Pavlovsky, E.N. 1966. *Natural nidality of transmissible diseases with special reference to the landscape epidemiology of zooanthroponoses.* Transl. by

F.K. Plous, Jr and edited by N.D. Levine. University of Illinois Press, Urbana-London. xiv + 261.

Paxman, J. and Harris, R. 1982. *A higher form of killing: The secret story of gas and germ warfare.* Farrar, Straus & Giroux, New York. 276 pp. Straus & Giroux, New York. 276 pp.

Payne, D., Grab, B., Fontaine, R.E., and Hempel, J.H.G. 1976. Impact of control measures on malaria transmission and general mortality. *WHO Bull. 54*, 369–77.

Pearl, R. 1919. On the mean age at death of centenarians. *Proc. Natl. Acad. Sci. 5*, 83–86.

Pearl, R. 1922. *The biology of death.* J.B. Lippincott, Philadelphia. 275 pp.

Pearson, D. and Shaw, S. 1982. *Life extension: A practical scientific approach.* Warner, New York. xxxviii + 858.

Peart, A.F.W. and Nagler, F.P. 1954. Measles in the Canadian Arctic. *Can. J. Public Health 45*, 146–56.

Peckham, C.H. 1935. A brief history of puerperal fever. *Bull. Hist. Med. 3*, 187–212.

Pel, J.Z.S. 1962. Common infections during the first five years of life. *J. Hyg. Camb. 60*, 163–74.

Peller, S. 1920. Zur Kenntnis der städtischen Mortalität im 18. Jahrhundert mit besonderer Berücksichtigung der Säuglings- und Tuberkulosesterblichkeit. *Z. Hyg. u. Infektionskrank. 9*, 227–62.

Peller, S. 1939. Lung cancer among mine workers in Joachimsthal. *Hum. Biol. 11*, 130–43.

Peller, S. 1943. Studies on mortality since the Renaissance. A. General mortality of women; B. Maternal mortality; C. Infancy and childhood. *Bull. Hist. Med. 13*, 427–61.

Peller, S. 1944. Studies on mortality since the Renaissance. D. Twins and singletons. *Bull. Hist. Med. 16*, 362–81.

Peller, S. 1947. Studies on mortality since the Renaissance. E. Men's reproductive activity; F. Men's mortality. *Bull. Hist. Med. 21*, 51–101.

Peller, S. 1948. Mortality, past and future. *Popul. Studies 1*, 405–56.

Peller, S. 1965. Births and deaths among Europe's ruling families since 1500. Revised from three papers in *Bull. Hist. Med. 13* (1943), *16* (1944), and *21* (1947). pp. 87–100 in Glass and Eversley.

Peller, S. 1979. *Cancer research since 1900: An evaluation.* Philosophical Library, New York. xv + 394.

Peller, S. and Pick, P. 1952. Leukaemia and other malignancies in physicians. *Am. J. Med. Sci. 224*, 154–59.

Pelling, M. 1978. *Cholera, fever and English medicine: 1825–1865.* Oxford Hist. Monogr. Oxford University Press, Oxford. 342 pp.

Pelling, M. and Webster, C. 1979. Medical practitioners. pp. 165–235 in Webster.

Peltokallio, P. and Tykkä, H. 1981. Evolution of the age distribution and mortality of acute appendicitis. *Arch. Surg. 116*, 153–56.

Peltola, H. 1983. Meningococcal disease: Still with us. *Rev. Infect. Dis. 5*, 71–91.

Pemberton, J.E. 1971. *British official publications.* Pergamon Press, Oxford. xiii + 315.

Penrose, L.S. 1963. Limitations of eugenics. *Proc. Roy. Inst. Gt. Brit. 39*, 506–19.

Percival, T. and Heberden, W. 1973. *Population and disease in early industrial England.* Facsimile reprints of Percival, *Observations on the state of population in Manchester and other adjacent places*, Philos. Trans. Roy. Soc. London 44, 45, 46 (1789) 67 pp. and Heberden, *Observations on the increase and decrease of different diseases and particularly of the plague* (1801), vii + 84. Introd. by B. Benjamin, Pioneers of Demography Series, Gregg International, Westmead, England.

Perine, P.L., Hopkins, D.R., Niemel, P.L.A., St John, R.K., Causse, G., and Antal, G.M. 1984. *Handbook of endemic treponematoses. Yaws, endemic syphilis, and pinta.* WHO, Geneva. vi + 60.

Pernick, M.S. 1985. *A calculus of suffering. Pain, professionalism, and anesthesia in nineteenth-century America.* Columbia University Press, New York. xvi + 421.

Perrenoud, A. 1978. La mortalité à Genève de 1625 à 1825. *Ann. Démog. Hist.*, Pt. 1, 209–33.

Perrenoud, A. 1979. *La population de Genève du seizième au début du dix-neuvième siècle. Etude démographique. Tome 1, Structures et mouvements.* Edit. Société d'Histoire et d'Archéologie de Genève, Geneva. xv + 611.

Perrow, C. 1984. *Normal accidents. Living with high-risk technologies.* Basic Books, New York. x + 386.

Perroy, E. 1951. *The Hundred Years War.* Indiana University Press, Bloomington, IN. 376 pp.

Perry, C.B. 1936. *Bacterial endocarditis.* John Wright, London. viii + 137.

Pesch, A.J. van 1885. Sterftetafels voor Nederland afgeleid uit de waarnemingen over het tijdvak 1870–1880. *Bijdragen van het Statistisch Instituut*, No. 3. Harlem.

Peters, R.S., Gitlin, N., and Libke, R.D. 1981. Amebic liver abscess. *Annu. Rev. Med. 32*, 161–74.

Petersen, W. 1975. *Population.* 3rd edition. Macmillan, New York. xi + 784.

Peterson, D.R. 1980. Evolution of the epidemiology of sudden infant death syndrome. *Epidemiol. Rev. 2*, 97–112.

Peterson, D.R. 1984. Sudden infant death syndrome. pp. 339–54 in Bracken.

Peto, R. and Schneiderman, M. (Eds.) 1981. *Quantification of occupational cancer. Papers from a conf., 1981*. Banbury Rep. No. 9. Cold Spring Harbor Laboratory, NY. xx + 756.

Petrakis, N.L., Ernster, V.L., and King, M.-C. 1982. Breast. pp. 855–70 in Schottenfeld and Fraumeni.

Petty, C.S. 1965. Botulism: The disease and its toxin. *Am. J. Med. Sci. 249*, 345–59.

Pharoah, P.O.D. and Morris, J.N. 1979. Post-neonatal mortality. *Epidemiol. Rev. 1*, 170–83.

Philip, C.B. 1948. Tsutsugamushi disease (scrub typhus) in World War II. *J. Parasitol. 34*, 169–91.

Philip, R., Willoughby, W.M., Collis, E.L., and Greenwood, M. 1928. Causes of the decline in tuberculosis mortality. *Public Health (London) 41*, 336–57.

Phillips, R.A. 1964. Water and electrolyte losses in cholera. *Fed. Proc. Am. Soc. Exp. Biol.* 23, 705–12.

Phillips, R., Lemon, F., and Kuzma, J. 1978. Coronary heart disease mortality among Seventh-Day Adventists with differing dietary habits. *Am. J. Clin. Nutr. 31* Suppl., 191–98.

Phillips, R.L., Kuzma, J.W., and Lotz, T.M. 1980. Cancer mortality among comparable members versus nonmembers of the Seventh-day Adventist Church. pp. 93–108 in Cairns, Lyon, and Skolnick.

Phillips, S. 1908. A review of mortality statistics during the last half century. *Clin. J. 32*, 55–61, 73–80.

Pickles, W.N. 1939. *Epidemiology in country practice*. John Wright, Bristol. viii + 110.

Pièry, M. and Roshem, J. 1931. *Histoire de la tuberculose*. G. Doin, Paris. xv + 479.

Pike, R.M. 1976. Laboratory associated infections: Summary and an analysis of 3921 cases. *Health Lab. Sci. 13*, 105–14.

Pike, R.M. 1979. Laboratory-associated infections: Incidence, fatalities, causes, and prevention. *Annu. Rev. Microbiol. 33*, 41–66.

Pinel, P. 1798. *Nosologie philosophique ou la méthode de l'analyse appliquée à la médecine*. Richard, Caille et Ravier, Paris. 2 vols.

Piot, P., Plummer, F.A., Mhalu, F.S., Lamboray, J.-L., Chin, J., and Mann, J.M. 1988. AIDS: An international perspective. *Science 239*, 573–79. [Articles up to p. 622 give further details on the AIDS virus.]

Pirie, N.W. (Chairman) 1961. Food losses in field and store. A symposium. *Proc. Nutr. Soc. 20*, 1–24.

Pirie, N.W. 1969. *Food resources, conventional and novel*. Penguin, Harmondsworth, Middlesex. 208 pp.

Piša, Z. and Uemura, K. 1982. Trends of mortality from ischaemic heart disease and other cardio-vascular diseases in 27 countries, 1968–1977. *World Health Stat. Q. 35*, 11–47.

Pitha, F. and Billroth, T. (Eds.) 1865–1882. *Handbuch der allgemeinen und speziellen Chirurgie mit Einschluss der topographischen Anatomie, Operations- und Verbandlehre*. F. Enke, Erlangen. 4 vols.

Pizzi, M. 1952. Prevalence of leprosy in the world. *WHO Epidemiol. Vital Stat. Rep. 5*. 263–82.

Playfair, W.S. 1882. Puerperal septicaemia. pp. 328–62 in vol. 2. of Playfair, *A treatise on the science and practice of midwifery*, 4th edition, Smith Elder, London. 2 vols.

Plenčič, M.A. 1762. *Opera medico-physica in quattuor tractatus digesta, quorum primus contagii morborum ideam novam una cum additamento de lue bovine anno 1761. Epidemice grassante, sistit. Secundus de variolis, tertius de scarlatina, quartus de terremotu, sed praecipue illo horribili agit. Qui primo novembris anno 1755 Europam, Africam, et Americam conquassabat*. J.T. Trattner, Vienna.

Plumb, J.H. 1950. *England in the eighteenth century*. Penguin, Harmondsworth, Middlesex. 224 pp.

Poitou, C. 1978. La mortalité en Sologne orléanaise de 1670 à 1870. *Ann. Démog. Hist.*, Pt. 1, 235–64.

Polednak, A.P., Stehney, A.F. and Rowland, R.E. 1978. Mortality among women first employed before 1930 in the U.S. radium dial-painting industry. *Am. J. Epidemiol. 107*, 179–95.

Pollard, A.H. 1949. Methods of forecasting mortality using Australian data. *J. Inst. Actuar. 75*, 151–82.

Pollitzer, R. 1954. *Plague*. World Health Org. Monogr. Series No. 22. WHO, Geneva. 698 pp.

Pollitzer, R. 1959. *Cholera*. World Health Org. Monogr. Series No. 43. WHO, Geneva. 1019 pp.

Pollitzer, R. 1960. A review of recent literature on plague. *WHO Bull. 23*, 313–400.

Polunin, I.V. 1967. Health and disease in contemporary primitive societies. pp. 69–97 in Brothwell and Sandison.

Pongrácz, M. 1972. Some characteristics of infant mortality in Central and Eastern Europe. pp. 225–31 in Törö, Szabady, Nemeskéri, and Eiben.

Pool, D.I. 1973. Estimates of New Zealand Maori vital rates from the mid-nineteenth century to

World War I. *Popul. Studies 27*, 117–25.

Pool, D.I. 1977. *The Maori population of New Zealand 1769–1971*. Auckland University Press, Auckland. 266 pp.

Pooley, M.E. and Pooley, C.G. 1984. Health, society and environment in nineteenth-century Manchester. pp. 148–75 in Woods and Woodward.

Poornapregna, V.N., Krishna Sastry, K.V., and Madhava, K.B. 1933. Maternity statistics from Mysore. *Sankhyā 1*, 63–75.

Porter, A. 1889. *The diseases of the Madras famine of 1877–79*. Government Press, Madras. 243 pp.

Porter, I.H. and Hook, E.B. (Eds.) 1980. *Human embryonic and fetal death. Proc. Tenth Annual New York State Health Dept. Birth Defects Symp., 1979*. Academic, New York-London. xvi + 371.

Porterfield, J.S. 1984. *Bunyaviridae*. pp. 250–54 in Topley and Wilson, 1984, vol. 4.

Pott, P. 1775. *Chirurgical observations relative to the cataract, the polypus of the nose, the cancer of the scrotum, the different kinds of ruptures, and the mortification of the toes and feet*. Hawes, Clarke and Collins, London. xi + 208.

Potter, H.P. 1880. The oriental plague in its social, economical, political and international relations, special reference being made to the labours of John Howard on the subject. *J. Stat. Soc. (London) 43*, 605–42.

Pouthas, Ch.H. 1956. *La population française pendant la première moitié du XIXe siècle*. Institut National d'Etudes Démographiques, Paris. 224 pp.

Poynter, F.N.L. (Ed.) 1965. *The evolution of pharmacy in Britain*. C.C. Thomas, Springfield, IL. 240 pp.

Poynter, F.N.L. 1967. The contemporary scientific background of Lister's achievement. *Br. J. Surg. 54*, 410–15.

Poynter, F.N.L. (Ed.) 1968. *Medicine and science in the 1860s*. Wellcome Inst. of Hist. Med., London. xiii + 324.

Prawitz, H. 1960. Mortality in Sweden from different causes of death. pp. 639–57 in *Comptes rendus du XVIe Congrès international d'Actuaires*, vol. 2. Georges Thone, Liege.

Preblud, S.R., Serdula, M.K., Frank, J.A. Jr, Brandling-Bennett, A.D., and Hinman, A.R. 1980. Rubella vaccination in the United States. *Epidemiol. Rev. 2*, 171–94.

Pressat, R. 1954. Vues générales sur la mortalité française depuis la guerre. *Population 9*, 477–506.

Pressat, R. 1963. Les premières tables de mortalité de l'Union Soviétique (1958–1959). *Population 18*, 65–92.

Pressat, R. 1972. *Demographic analysis: Methods, results, applications*. Transl. from the French. Edward Arnold, London. xx + 498.

Pressat, R. 1974a. *A workbook in demography*. Transl. from the French by E. Grebenik and C.A.M. Sym. Methuen, London. 294 pp.

Pressat, R. 1974b. Mortality projections and actual trends. A comparative study. *World Health Stat. Rep. 27*, 516–39.

Pressat, R. 1978. *Statistical demography*. Transl. from the French and adapted by D.A. Courtney. Methuen, London. vii + 150.

Pressat, R. 1981. L'Analyse par cohorte: Origine et champ d'application. *Population 36*, 634–40.

Preston, S.H. 1974. An evaluation of postwar mortality projections in Australia, Canada, Japan, New Zealand and the United States. *World Health Stat. Rep. 27*, 719–45.

Preston, S.H. 1975. The changing relation between mortality and level of economic development. *Popul. Studies 29*, 231–48.

Preston, S.H. 1976. *Mortality patterns in national populations: With special reference to recorded causes of death*. Academic Press, New York. xii + 202.

Preston, S.H. 1977a. Mortality trends. *Annu. Rev. Sociol. 3*, 163–78.

Preston, S.H. (Ed.) 1977b. *The effects of infant and child mortality on fertility*. Academic Press, New York. x + 262.

Preston, S.H. 1980. Causes and consequences of mortality declines in less developed countries during the twentieth century. pp. 289–360 in Easterlin.

Preston, S.H. and Haines, M.R. 1984. New estimates of child mortality in the United States at the turn of the century. *J. Am. Stat. Assoc. 79*, 272–81.

Preston, S.H., Keyfitz, N., and Schoen, R. with collab. of Nelson, V.E. 1972. *Causes of death: Life tables for national populations*. Studies in Population, Seminar Press, New York. xii + 788.

Preston, S.H. and Nelson, V.E. 1974. Structure and change in causes of death: An international summary. *Popul. Studies 28*, 19–51.

Preston, S.H. and van de Walle, E. 1978. Urban French mortality in the nineteenth century. *Popul. Studies 32*, 275–97.

Preston, S.H. and Weed, J.A. 1976. Causes of death responsible for international and intertemporal variations in sex mortality differentials. *World Health Stat. Rep. 29*, 144–88.

Preto, P. 1978. *Peste e società a Venezia nel 1576*. La Grafica & Stampa, Vicenza. 25 pp.

Price, D.L., Whitehouse, P.J., and Struble, R.G.

1985. Alzheimer's disease. *Annu. Rev. Med. 36*, 349–56.

Price, T.D. and Brown, J.A. (Eds) 1985. *Prehistoric hunter-gatherers. The emergence of cultural complexity*. Studies in Archaeology. Academic Press, Orlando, FL. xviii + 454.

Price, W.H., Emerson, H., Nagel, H., Blumberg, R., and Talmadge, S. 1958. Ecological studies on the interepidemic survival of louse-borne epidemic typhus fever. *Am. J. Hyg. 67*, 154–78.

Pringle, C.R. 1984. The genetics of viruses. pp. 59–93 in Topley and Wilson, 1984, vol. 4.

Pringle, J. 1761. *Observations on the diseases of the army in camp and garrison*. 3rd edition. Millar, Wilson, Durham & Payne, London.

Prinzing, F. 1895. *Trunksucht und Selbstmord und deren gegenseitige Beziehungen*. J.C. Hinrichs, Leipzig. 94 pp.

Prinzing, F. 1916. *Epidemics resulting from wars*. H. Westergaard, Ed. Carnegie Endowment for International Peace. Clarendon, Oxford. xii + 340.

Prinzing, F. 1930–1931. *Handbuch der medizinischen Statistik*. Revised edition. G. Fischer, Jena. 2 vols.

Prior, I. and Tasman-Jones, C. 1981. New Zealand Maori and Pacific Polynesians. pp. 227–67 in Trowell and Burkitt, 1981a.

Prior, I.A.M., Salmond, C.E., Clements, J., Beaglehole, R., Stanhope, J., Rees, R., and Tuia, H. 1981. Mortality in Polynesians in isolated communities and New Zealand. With discussion. pp. 143–64 in Boström and Ljungstedt.

Prusiner, S.B. and Hadlow, W.J. (Eds.) 1979. *Slow transmissible diseases of the nervous system. Clinical, epidemiological, genetic and pathological aspects of the spongiform encephalopathies*. Academic Press, New York. xxiv + 472.

Puffer, R.R. and Griffith, G.W. 1967. *Patterns of urban mortality: Report of the Inter-American Investigation of Mortality*. Scientific Publ. No. 151, Pan-American Health Org., Washington, DC. xiv + 353.

Puffer, R.R. and Serrano, C.V. 1973. *Patterns of mortality in childhood: Report of the Inter-American Investigation of Mortality in Childhood*. Scientific Publ. No. 262, Pan-American Health Org., Washington, DC. xix + 470.

Puffer, R.R. and Serrano, C.V. 1976. The inter-American investigation of mortality in childhood. *World Health Stat. Rep. 29*, 493–520.

Puffer, R.R. and Verhoestraete, M.D. 1958. Mortality from cardiovascular diseases in various countries, with special reference to atherosclerotic heart disease. *WHO Bull. 19*, 315–24.

Pullen, R.L. (Ed.) 1950. *Communicable diseases*. Lea & Febiger, Philadelphia. 1035 pp.

Pyörälä, K. and Valkonen, T. 1981. The high ischaemic heart disease mortality in Finland—International comparisons, regional differences, trends and possible causes. With discussion. pp. 37–61 in Boström and Ljungstedt.

Quetelet, L.A.J. 1827. *Recherches sur la population, les naissances, les décès, les prisons, les dépôts de mendicité, etc. dans le royaume des Pays-Bas*. H. Tarlier, Bruxelles. 90 pp.

Quetelet, (L.) A. (J.) 1849. Nouvelles tables de la mortalité pour la Belgique. *Bull. Comm. Centrale de Stat. 4*. F. Hayez, Bruxelles. 22 pp.

Quetelet, L.A.J. 1870. *Mémoires et communications. Tables de mortalité et leur développement*. F. Hayez, Bruxelles. 39 pp.

Quinn, T.C., Mann, J.M., Curran, J.W., and Piot, P. 1986. AIDS in Africa: An epidemiologic paradigm. *Science 234*, 955–63.

Raab, W. 1932. Alimentäre Faktoren in der Entstehung von Arteriosklerose und Hypertonie. *Med. Klin. 28*, 487 and 521.

Raadt, P. de and Seed, J.R. 1977. Trypanosomes causing disease in man in Africa. pp. 176–237 in Kreier, vol. 1.

Race, R.R. and Sanger, R. 1975. *Blood groups in man*. 6th edition. Blackwell, Oxford-London-Edinburgh. xix + 659.

Rail, C.D. 1985. *Plague ecotoxicology. Including historical aspects of the disease in the Americas and the Eastern Hemisphere*. C.C. Thomas, Springfield, IL. xxii + 210.

Ramalingaswami, V., Deo, M.G., Guleria, J.S., Malhotra, K.K., Sood, S.K., Prakash, O., and Sinha, R.V.N. 1971. Studies of the Bihar famine of 1966–67. pp. 94–112 in Blix, Hofvander, and Vahlquist.

Ramsden, J.M. 1976. *The safe airline*. MacDonald and Jane's Publ., London. vi + 231.

Ransford, O. 1983. *'Bid the sickness cease': Disease in the history of black Africa*. John Murray, London. x + 235.

Ransome, A. 1877. Losses and gains in the death-toll of England and Wales during the last thirty years. *Manchester Lit. Philos. Soc. Proc. 16*, 194–208. Also in the *Memoirs* of the same, vol. 6 (1879), 126–40.

Ransome, A. 1880. On epidemic cycles. *Manchester Lit. Philos. Soc. Proc. 19*, 75–95.

Ransome, A. 1881–1882. On the form of the epidemic wave, and some of its probable causes.

Trans. Epidemiol. Soc. London 1, 96–111.

Rapmund, G. 1984. Rickettsial diseases of the Far East: New perspectives. *J. Infect. Dis. 149*, 330–38.

Rapp, F. and Jerkovsky, M.A. 1973. Persistent and latent infections. pp. 271–89 in Kaplan.

Rashkind, W.J. (Ed.) 1982. *Congenital heart disease*. Hutchinson Ross, Stroudsburg, PA. xviii + 392.

Ratcliffe, H. 1850/1974. *Observations on the rate of mortality and sickness existing amongst friendly societies*. George Falkner, Manchester. Reprinted 1974 in *Mortality in mid 19th century Britain*, R. Wall, Ed. Gregg International, D.C. Heath Limited, London. viii + 168.

Rather, L.J. 1974. Pathology at mid-century: A reassessment of Thomas Willis and Thomas Sydenham. pp. 79–83 in Debus.

Ratnoff, O.D. 1980. Why do people bleed? pp. 601–57 in Wintrobe.

Rawls, W.E. 1973. Herpes simplex virus. pp. 291–325 in Kaplan.

Razzell, P. (E.) 1965. Population change in eighteenth-century England: A reappraisal. *Econ. Hist. Rev.* (2) *18*, 312–32.

Razzell, P.E. 1967. Population growth and economic change in 18th and early 19th century England and Ireland. pp. 260–81 in Jones and Mingay.

Razzell, P.E. 1974. An interpretation of the modern rise of population in Europe—A critique. *Popul. Studies 28*, 5–17.

Razzell, P. (E.) 1977. *The conquest of smallpox*. Firle, Lewes, Sussex. x + 190.

Read, P.P. 1974. *Alive: The story of the Andes survivors*. Martin Secker & Warburg and Pan Books, London. xii + 308.

Reddy, B.S. and Cohen, L.A. (Eds.) 1986. *Diet, nutrition and cancer. A critical evaluation*. Vol. 1: *Macronutrients and cancer*. Vol. 2: *Macronutrients, nonnutritive dietary factors and cancer*. CRC Press, Boca Raton, FL. viii + 175; viii + 181.

Redmond, D.E. 1970. Tobacco and cancer: The first clinical report, 1761. *N. Engl. J. Med. 282*, 18–23.

Reed, D.M. and Stanley, F.J. (Eds.) 1977. *The epidemiology of prematurity*. Urban & Schwarzenberg, Baltimore-Munich. xiv + 370.

Rees, W. 1923. The Black Death in England and Wales, as exhibited in manorial documents. *Proc. Roy. Soc. Med. (Med. Hist.) 16*, 27–45.

Registrar-General of England and Wales

1920. 81st Annual Report for year 1918.

1920. Supplement to the 81st Annual Report. 119 pp.

1920. 82nd Annual Report for year 1919.

1949. Statistical Review of England and Wales for the six years 1940–1945. Vol. 1. xi + 388.

1950. Statistical Review of England and Wales for the two years 1948–1949. vi + 370.

1952. Decennial Supplement, England and Wales, 1931. Part III. Estimates of population, statistics of marriages, births and deaths, 1921–1930. vi + 574.

1958. Decennial Supplement, England and Wales, 1951. Occupational mortality Part II. 2 vols.

1963. Statistical Review of England and Wales for the year 1961. Part 1. Tables, medical. xi + 368; Part 2. Tables, population. xiii + 189; Part 3. Commentary. xvii + 362.

1978. Occupational mortality—Decennial Supplement to the Registrar-General's Statistical Review for England and Wales, 1970–72. Series D5, No. 1. xviii + 224.

1982. Mortality statistics: Childhood. Review of the Registrar-General on deaths in England and Wales, 1980. Series DH3, No. 8. ii + 71. HMSO, London.

Reid, D.D. 1957a. Incidence of tuberculosis among workers in medical laboratories. *Br. Med. J. 2*, 10–14.

Reid, D.D. 1957b. Records and research in occupational medicine. *J. Roy. Soc. Promot. Health 77*, 675–80.

Reilly, C. 1980. *Metal contamination of food*. Applied Science Publ., London. xvi + 235.

Reimann, H. 1961. The misuse of antibiotics. *Med. Clin. North Am. 45*, 849–56.

Reimann, H.A. and Havens, W.P. 1940. Focal infection and systemic disease: A critical appraisal. *J. Am. Med. Assoc. 114*. 1–6.

Reinhard, M., Armengaud, A. and Dupâquier, J. 1961. *Histoire générale de la population mondiale*. Montchrestien, Paris. v + 597. Reprinted 1968.

Reiser, S.J. 1978. *Medicine and the reign of technology*. Cambridge University Press, New York. xi + 378.

Reister, F.A. (Ed.) 1976. *Medical statistics in World War II*. US Army Medical Dept., Office of the Surgeon General, Dept. of the Army, Washington, DC. xvii + 1215.

Remein, Q.R. 1959. A current estimate of the prevalence of diabetes mellitus in the United States. *Ann. N. Y. Acad. Sci. 82*, 229–35.

Remington, J.S. and Klein, J.O. (Eds.) 1983. *Infectious diseases of the fetus and newborn infant*. W.B. Saunders, Philadelphia. xvi + 1147.

Renouard, Y. 1948. Conséquences et intérêt

démographiques de la peste de 1348. *Population* 3, 459–66.

Retherford, R.D. 1975. *The changing sex differential in mortality*. Studies in Population and urban Demography, No. 1. Greenwood Press, Westport, CT. xi + 139.

Rhodes, E.C. 1941. Secular changes in death rate. *J. Roy. Stat. Soc. 104*, 15–33.

Richardson, R.G. 1974. *Larrey: Surgeon to Napoleon's Imperial Guard*. John Murray, London. x + 266.

le Riche, W.H. and Milner, J. 1971. *Epidemiology as medical ecology*. Churchill-Livingstone, Edinburgh-London. xii + 460.

Rieckmann, K.H. 1983. *Falciparum* malaria: The urgent need for safe and effective drugs. *Annu. Rev. Med.* 34, 321–35.

Rieckmann, K.H. and Silverman, P.H. 1977. *Plasmodia* of man. pp. 493–527 in Kreier, vol. 3.

Riemann, H. 1969. *Food-borne infections and intoxications*. Academic Press, New York-London. xxviii + 698.

Risse, G.B. 1973. Calomel and the American medical sects during the nineteenth century. *Mayo Clin. Proc.* 48, 57–64.

Ristic, M. and Lewis, G.E. 1977. Babesia in man and wild and laboratory-adapted mammals. pp. 53–76 in Kreier, vol. 4.

Ristori, C., Boccardo, H., Borgoño, J.M., and Armijo, R. 1962. Medical importance of measles in Chile. *Am. J. Dis. Child. 103*, 236–41.

Ritson, B. 1977. Alcoholism and suicide. pp. 271–8 in Edwards and Grant.

Rivers, T.M. 1937. Viruses and Koch's postulates. *J. Bacteriol. 33*, 1–12.

Roberts, H.R. (Ed.) 1981. *Food safety*. Wiley-Interscience, New York. xiii + 339.

Robertson, T.L., Kato, H., Gordon, T., Kagan, A., Rhoads, G.G., Land, C.E., Worth, R.M., Belsky, J.L., Dock, D.S., Miyanishi, M., and Kawamoto, S. 1977. Epidemiologic studies of coronary heart disease and stroke in Japanese men living in Japan, Hawaii and California. Coronary heart disease risk factors in Japan and Hawaii. *Am. J. Cardiol.* 39, 244–49.

Robertson, T.L., Kato, H., Rhoads, G.G., Kagan, A., Marmot, M., Syme, S.L., Gordon, T., Worth, R.M., Belsky, J.L., Dock, D.S., Miyanishi, M., and Kawamoto, S. 1977. Epidemiologic studies of coronary heart disease and stroke in Japanese men living in Japan, Hawaii and California. Incidence of myocardial infarction and death from coronary heart disease. *Am. J. Cardiol. 39*, 239–43.

Robins, F.W. 1946. *The story of water supply*. Oxford University Press, London. xi + 207.

Robson, J.R.K. (Ed.) 1981. *Famine: Its causes, effects and management*. Food and Nutrition in History and Anthropology, vol. 2. Gordon and Breach, New York. x + 170.

Roch, J., Hubert, B., Ngyrie, E., and Richard, P. 1975. Selective bibliography of the famines and the drought in the Sahel. *Afr. Environ. 1* (2), 94–116.

Rochat, R.W. 1981. Maternal mortality in the United States of America. *World Health Stat. Q. 34*, 2–13.

Rodenwaldt, E. 1953. Pest in Venedig, 1575–77: Ein Beitrag zur Frage der Infektkette bei den Pestepidemien West Europas. *Sitzungsber. Heidelberg. Akad. Wiss. Math.-naturw. Kl.*, Jahrg. 1952, Abh. 2. 263 pp.

Rodenwaldt, E. 1957. Untersuchungen über die Biologie des venezianischen Adels. *Homo 8*, I, 1–26.

Roe, D.A. 1973. *A plague of corn: The social history of pellagra*. Cornell University Press, Ithaca, NY. xiii + 217.

Roe, D.A. (Ed.) 1983. *Diet, nutrition and cancer. From basic research to policy implications*. Current Topics in Nutrition and Disease, vol. 9. Liss, New York. x + 294.

Roe, F.J.C. and Lancaster, M.C. 1964. Natural, metallic and other substances as carcinogens. *Br. Med. Bull. 20*, 127–33.

Roelants, G.E. and Williams, R.O. 1982. Shigellosis. *Crit. Rev. Trop. Med. 1*, 31–75. See Chandra, 1982.

Rogers, L. 1913. *Dysenteries: Their differentiation and treatment*. Oxford University Press, London. xi + 336.

Rohde, J.E. and Northrup, R.S. 1976. Taking science where the diarrhoea is. pp. 339–66 in Elliott and Knight.

Roht, L.H., Sherwin, R., and Henderson, M.M. 1974. The impact of legal abortion: Redefining the maternal mortality rate. *Health Serv. Rep. 89*, 267–73.

Roizman, B. (Ed.) (with Lopez, C.) 1982–1985. *The herpesviruses*. Plenum, New York. 4 vols.

Rolleston, J.D. 1937. *History of the acute exanthemata*. Heinemann, London. x + 114.

Rolt, L.T.C. 1955. *Red for danger: A history of railway accidents and railway safety precautions*. 3rd edition, revised. J. Lane, London. 297 pp.

Rom, W.N. (Ed.) 1983. *Environmental and occupational medicine*. Little, Brown & Co., Boston. xxv + 1015.

Romaniuk, A. 1968. The demography of the Democratic Republic of the Congo. pp. 241–341 in Brass, Coale, et al.

Romeder, J.M. and McWhinney, J.R. 1977. Potential years of life lost between 1 and 70: An indicator of premature mortality for health planning. *Int. J. Epidemiol. 6*, 143–51.

Rood, J.J. van 1982. Organ transplantation. pp. 229–44 in *Proceedings of the Royal College of Physicians of Edinburgh Tercentenary Congress.* Publ. No. 56, Royal College of Physicians of Edinburgh. xvi + 416.

Rook, A. 1954. An investigation into the longevity of Cambridge sportsmen. *Br. Med. J. 1*, 773–77.

Rook, A. 1959. Student suicides. *Br. Med. J. 1*, 599–603.

Ropp, T. 1959. *War in the modern world.* Duke University Press, Durham, NC. xv + 400.

Rosahn, P.D. 1960. *Autopsy studies in syphilis.* US Public Health Serv. Publ. No. 433, US Govt. Printing Office, Washington, DC. vii + 67.

Rose, G., Reid, D.D., Hamilton, P.J.S., McCarthy, P., Keen, H., and Jarrett, R.J. 1977. Myocardial ischaemia, risk factors and death from coronary heart disease. *Lancet 1*, 105–09.

Rosen, G. 1943. *The history of miners' diseases: A medical and social interpretation.* With introd. by H.E. Sigerist. Schumans, New York. xii + 490.

Rosen, G. 1958. *A history of public health.* MD Publications, New York. 551 pp.

Rosenberg, C.E. 1962. *The cholera years: The United States in 1832, 1849 and 1866.* University of Chicago Press, Chicago, IL. x + 257.

Rosenberg, C.E. (Ed.) 1972. *The cholera bulletin: Conducted by an association of physicians. Vol. 1, Numbers 1–24, 1832.* Arno Press and The New York Times, New York. vii + 8 + 192.

Rosenberg, C.E. 1987. *The care of strangers. The rise of America's hospital system.* Basic Books, New York. x + 437.

Rosenberg, H.M. and Klebba, A.J. 1979. Trends in cardiovascular mortality with a focus on ischemic heart disease: United States, 1950–1976. pp. 11–41 in Havlik and Feinleib.

Rosenthal, R. 1922. An early opponent of venesection. [Johann G. Wolstein]. *Med. Life (New York) 29*, 585–90.

Rosenthal, S.R. 1934. Studies in atherosclerosis: Chemical, experimental and morphologic. *Arch. Pathol. 18*, 473–506, 660–98, 827–42.

Ross, R. 1906. Malaria in Greece. *J. Trop. Med. 9*, 341–56.

Rossignol, J.-F. 1984. Soil-transmitted helminths: Treatment. *Rec. Adv. Trop. Med. 1*, 207–22. See Gilles, 1984.

Rothschild, H. and Chapman, C.F. (Eds.) 1981. *Biocultural aspects of disease.* Academic Press, New York, xix + 653.

Rothstein, W.G. 1972. *American physicians in the nineteenth century. From the sects to science.* Johns Hopkins, Baltimore. xvi + 362.

Rouquette, C. and Corone, J. 1965. Evolution récente de la mortalité chez les enfants de 1 à 14 ans. *Bull. Inst. Nat. Santé Rech. Méd. 20*, 183–202.

Routh, C.H.F. 1848. On the causes of the endemic puerperal fever of Vienna. (Read before the Roy. Med. and Chir. Soc. in 1848.) *Med. Chir. Trans.* xxxii, 27–40.

Royal Commission on Population 1949–1950. *Report. Command Paper 7695. Papers: Vol. 1—Family limitation; Vol. 2—Reports and selected papers of the Statistics Committee; Vol. 3—Report of the Economics Committee; Vol. 4—Reports of the Biological and Medical Committees; Vol. 5—Memoranda presented to the Royal Commission.* HMSO, London.

Royston, E. 1982. The prevalence of nutritional anaemia in women in developing countries. *World Health Stat. Q. 35*, 52–91.

Rubin, E. and Damjanov, I. 1984. *Advances in the biology of disease, vol. 1.* Williams and Wilkins, Baltimore. viii + 208.

Rupreht, J., van Lieburg, M.J., Lee, J.A., and Erdmann, W. (Eds.) 1985. *Anaesthesia: Essays on its history.* Springer, Berlin-New York. xxi + 409.

Russell, J.C. 1941. The Ecclesiastical Age. A demographic interpretation of the period A.D. 200–900. *Rev. Religion 5*, 137–47.

Russell, J.C. 1948a. *Medieval British population.* University of New Mexico, Albuquerque, NM. xvi + 389.

Russell, J.C. 1948b. Demographic pattern in history. *Popul. Studies 1*, 388–404.

Russell, J.C. 1958. Late ancient and medieval population. *Trans. Am. Philos. Soc. N.S. 48*, Pt. 3. 152 pp.

Russell, J.C. 1966. Effects of pestilence and plague, 1315–1385. *Comp. Studies Soc. Hist. 8*, 464–73.

Russell, J.C. 1968. That earlier plague. *Demography 5*, 174–84.

Russell, P.F. 1955. *Man's mastery of malaria. University of London Heath Clark Lectures 1953.* Oxford University Press, London. xv + 308.

Russell, W.T. 1933. The statistics of erysipelas in England and Wales. *J. Hyg. Camb. 33*, 421–34.

Russell, W.T. 1943. *The epidemiology of diphtheria during the last forty years.* Med. Res. Council

Spec. Rep. Series No. 247, HMSO, London. 52 pp.

Rutstein, D.D., Nickerson, R.J., and Heald, F.P. 1952. Seasonal incidence of patent ductus arteriosus and maternal rubella. *Am. J. Dis. Child. 84*, 199–213.

Ruttenberg, A.J. and Luke, J.L. 1984. Heroin-related deaths: New epidemiologic insights. *Science 226*, 14–20.

Ruwet, J. 1954. Crises démographiques: Problèmes économiques ou crises morales? *Population 9*, 451–76.

Ruwet, J. 1957. La population de Saint-Trond en 1635. *Bull. Soc. Art Hist. Diocèse de Liège 40*, 151–93.

Ruzicka, L.T. 1976. Suicide, 1950 to 1971. *World Health Stat. Rep. 29*, 396–413.

Ryan, G.A. 1980. The automobile and human health. pp. 467–90 in Stanley and Joske.

Sabben-Clare, E.E., Bradley, D.J., and Kirkwood, K. (Eds.) 1980. *Health in tropical Africa during the colonial period*. Clarendon, Oxford. ix + 276.

Sack, R.B. 1975. Human diarrheal disease caused by enterotoxigenic *Escherichia coli*. *Annu. Rev. Microbiol. 29*, 333–53.

Sai, F.T. 1984. The population factor in Africa's development dilemma. *Science 226*, 801–05.

Sainsbury, P. 1955. *Suicide in London: An ecological study*. Chapman and Hall, London. 116 pp.

Sainsbury, P. 1983. Validity and reliability of trends in suicide statistics. *World Health Stat. Q. 36*, 339–45.

Salaman, R.N. 1949. *The history and social influence of the potato*. Cambridge University Press. xxiv + 685.

Saltmarsh, J. 1941. Plague and economic decline in England in the later Middle Ages. *Cambridge Hist. J. 7* (1), 23–41.

Saltzman, B. (Ed.) 1983. *Theory of climate. From a symposium, Lisbon, 1981*. Advances in Geophysics, vol. 25. Academic Press, New York. xiv + 505.

Sanchez-Albornoz, N. 1967. Les registres paroissiaux en Amérique latine. Quelques considérations sur leur exploitation pour la démographie historique. *Rev. Suisse d'Hist. 17* (1), 60–71.

Sandison, A.T. 1980. Diseases in ancient Egypt. pp. 29–44 in Cockburn and Cockburn.

Sandler, M. (Ed.) 1980. *Psychopharmacology of alcohol*. Raven, New York. xiv + 280.

Sansarricq, H. 1981. Leprosy in the world today. *Leprosy Rev. (Special issue) 52*, Suppl. 15–31.

Sargant, W.L. 1866. On the vital statistics of Bir-

mingham and seven other large towns. *J. Stat. Soc. (London) 29*, 92–111.

Sartwell, P.E. 1950. The distribution of incubation periods of infectious disease. *Am. J. Hyg. 51*, 310–18.

Sartwell, P.E. 1966. The incubation period and the dynamics of infectious disease. *Am. J. Epidemiol. 83*, 204–16.

Sartwell, P.E. (Ed.) 1973. *Maxcy-Rosenau: Preventive medicine and public health*. 10th edition. Appleton-Century-Crofts, New York. xiv + 1189.

Sasa, M. 1976. *Human filariasis. A global survey of epidemiology and control*. University Park Press, Baltimore-London-Tokyo. vii + 819.

Sax, N.I. 1979. *Dangerous properties of industrial materials*. Van Nostrand Reinhold, New York. xi + 1118.

Saylor, L.F. and Gordon, J.E. 1957. The medical component of natural disasters. *Am. J. Med. Sci. 234*. 342–62.

Scarborough, J. 1984. The myth of lead poisoning among the Romans: An essay review. *J. Hist. Med. Allied Subj. 39*, 469–75.

Scardovi, I. 1960. Indagini statistiche sul peso fetale. *Statistica (Bologna) 20*, 49–90.

Schachter, J. 1978. Chlamydial infections. *N. Engl. J. Med. 298*, 429–35, 490–95, 540–49.

Schachter, J. and Grossman, M. 1981. Chlamydial infections. *Annu. Rev. Med. 32*, 45–61.

Schad, G.A., Nawalinski, T.A., and Kochar, V. 1983. Human ecology and the distribution and abundance of hookworm populations. pp. 187–223 in Croll and Cross.

Schaefer, O. 1981. Eskimos (Inuit). pp. 113–28 in Trowell and Burkitt, 1981*a*.

Schantz, P.M. 1983. Human behavior and parasitic zoonoses in North America. pp. 21–48 in Croll and Cross.

Schardein, J.L. 1985. *Chemically induced birth defects*. Drug and Chemical Toxicology, vol. 2. Dekker, New York. xiv + 879.

Scheinberg, L. and Raine, C.S. (Eds.) 1984. *Multiple sclerosis. Experimental and clinical aspects*. Ann. New York Acad. Sci., vol. 436. New York Academy of Sciences, New York. xii + 518.

Schernthaner, G. 1982. The relationship between clinical, immunological and genetic factors in insulin-dependent diabetes. pp. 99–114 in Koeberling and Tattersall.

Schild, G.C. 1984. Influenza. pp. 315–44 in Topley and Wilson, 1984, vol. 4.

Schinz, H.R. and Reich, T. 1959. Changes in the carcinoma hazard in England and Wales in comparison with the Federal Republic of Germany,

France and Switzerland. (German) *Oncologia 12*, 257–67.

Schleisner, P.A. 1851. Vital statistics of Iceland. [A summary of *Island undersögt fra et large-videnskabeligt Synspunkt af*, Medlem, 1849.] *J. Stat. Soc. (London) 14*, 1–10.

Schlink, H. 1960. Cancer of the female pelvis. *J. Obstet. Gynaecol. Br. Emp. 67*, 402–10.

Schmähl, D. and Habs, M. 1980. Drug-induced cancer. *Curr. Top. Pathol. 69*, 333–69.

Schmidt, W. 1977. Cirrhosis and alcohol consumption: An epidemiological perspective. pp. 15–47 in Edwards and Grant.

Schmidt, W. and de Lint, J.E.E. 1972. Causes of death of alcoholics. *Q. J. Studies Alcohol. 33*, 171–85.

Schneider, S.H. and Londer, R. 1984. *The coevolution of climate and life*. Sierra Club Books, San Francisco. xii + 563.

Schneidman, E.S. (Ed.) 1972. *Death and the college student*. Behavioural Publ., New York. xx + 208.

Schnohr, P. 1971. Longevity and cause of death in male athletic champions. *Lancet 2*, 1364–66.

Schönfeld, H. 1981. *Antiparasitic chemotherapy*. Antibiotics and Chemotherapy, vol. 30. Karger, Basel. vii + 287.

Schofield, R. and Wrigley, E.A. 1979. Infant and child mortality in England in the late Tudor and early Stuart period. pp. 61–95 in Webster, 1979.

Schonland, B.F.J. 1950. *Flight of thunderbolts*. Clarendon, Oxford. viii + 152. 2nd edition, 1964.

Schottenfeld, D. (Ed.) 1975. *Cancer epidemiology and prevention*. C.C. Thomas, Springfield, IL. xii + 574.

Schottenfeld, D. and Fraumeni, J.F. Jr (Eds.) 1982. *Cancer epidemiology and prevention*. W.B. Saunders, Philadelphia. xxiv + 1173.

Schottenfeld, D. and Warshauer, M.E. 1982. Testis. pp. 947–57 in Schottenfeld and Fraumeni.

Schottenfeld, D. and Winawer, S.J. 1982. Large intestine. pp. 703–27 in Schottenfeld and Fraumeni.

Schove, D.J. 1977. African droughts and the spectrum of time. pp. 38–53 in Dalby, Church, and Bezzaz.

Schultweiss, E. and Tardy, L. 1966. Short history of epidemics in Hungary until the Great Cholera Epidemic of 1831. *Centaurus 11*, 279–301.

Schultz, A.H. 1939. Notes on diseases and healed fractures of wild apes and their bearing on the antiquity of pathological conditions in man. *Bull. Hist. Med. 7*, 571–82.

Schulze, R. and Grafe, K. 1969. Consideration of sky ultraviolet radiation in the measurement of solar ultraviolet radiation. pp. 359–73 in *The biologic effects of ultra-violet radiation*, F. Urbach (Ed.), Pergamon Press, Oxford. 650 pp.

Schwarz, E. 1960. Classification, origin and distribution of commensal rats. *WHO Bull. 23*, 411–16.

Schwimmer, E.G. (Ed.) 1968. *The Maori people in the nineteen sixties*. Blackwood and Janet Paul, Auckland. 396 pp.

Scott, D. 1965. *Epidemic disease in Ghana, 1901–1960*. Oxford University Press, London. xviii + 208.

Scott, G. 1976. *Building disasters and failures: A practical report*. Construction Press, Lancaster. 169 pp.

Scott, H.H. 1934. *Some notable epidemics*. Edward Arnold, London. xix + 272.

Scott, H.H. 1935. Tuberculosis in man in the tropics. *Proc. Roy. Soc. Med. 28*, 1343–52.

Scott, H.H. 1939. *A history of tropical medicine. Based on the Fitzpatrick Lectures delivered before the Royal College of Physicians of London 1937–38*. Edward Arnold, London. 2 vols. xix + 648, iv + 649–1165.

Scott, H.H. 1943. The influence of the slave trade in the spread of tropical disease. *Trans. Roy. Soc. Trop. Med. Hyg. 37*, 169–88.

Scotto, J., Fears, T.R., and Fraumeni, J.F. Jr 1982. Solar radiation. pp. 254–76 in Schottenfeld and Fraumeni.

Scotto, J., Fears, T.R., and Fraumeni, J.F. Jr 1983. *Incidence of nonmelanoma skin cancer in the United States*. NIH Publ. No. 83-2433, National Cancer Inst., Bethesda, MD. xvi + 113.

Scotto, J. and Fraumeni, J.F. Jr 1982. Skin (other than melanoma). pp. 996–1011 in Schottenfeld and Fraumeni.

Scrimshaw, N.S. 1966. Ecological factors in nutritional disease. pp. 114–24 in Lilienfeld and Gifford.

Scrimshaw, N.S., Taylor, C.E., and Gordon, J.E. 1968. *Interactions of nutrition and infection*. WHO, Geneva. 329 pp.

Seal, H.L. 1978. *Survival probabilities: The goal of risk theory*. Wiley, New York. x + 103.

Seal, S.C. 1960. Epidemiological studies of plague in India. 1. The present position. 2. The changing pattern of rodents and fleas in Calcutta and other cities. *WHO Bull. 23*, 283–92, 293–300.

Seaman, J., Leivesley, S., and Hogg, C. 1984. *Epidemiology of natural disasters*. Contributions to Epidemiology and Biostatistics, vol. 5. Karger, Basel. viii + 177.

Segerberg, O. Jr 1982. *Living to be 100. 1200 who did and how they did it*. Scribner, New York. x + 406.

Segi, M., Fukushima, I, et al. 1955. *Cancer mortality statistics in Japan, 1900–1954*. Dept Publ. Health, Sendai, Japan. 42 pp.

Segi, M., Kurihara, M., and Matsuyama, T. 1969. *Cancer mortality for selected sites in 24 countries. No. 5 (1964–1965)*. [See also No. 4 and No. 6] Dept. Publ. Health, Tohoku University, Japan.

Sekura, R.D., Moss, J., and Vaughan, M. (Eds.) 1985. *Pertussis toxin. From a conference, Bethesda, Md., 1984*. Academic Press, Orlando, FL. xii + 255.

Selby, P. 1974. *Health in 1980–1990*. Perspectives in Medicine. Karger, Basel. x + 88.

Select Committee on Nutrition 1977. *Diet related to killer diseases, IV. Hearings before the Select Committee on Nutrition and Human needs of the US Senate, 95th Congress, 1st Session. Dietary Fiber and Health*. US Govt. Printing Office, Washington, DC. iii + 239.

Seligsohn, U., Rimon, A., and Horoszowski, H. (Eds.) 1981. *Haemophilia. Based on symposia held during XIIIth Congress of World Federation of Haemophilia, Tel-Aviv, 1979*. Castle House Publ., Tunbridge Wells, Kent. x + 245.

Selikoff, I.J., Bader, R., Bader, M, et al. 1967. Asbestos and neoplasia. *Am. J. Med.* 42, 487–96.

Selikoff, I.J., Hammond, E.C., and Churg, J. 1968. Asbestos exposure, smoking and neoplasia. *J. Am. Med. Assoc.* 204, 106–12.

Selikoff, I.J. and Lee, D.H.K. 1978. *Asbestos and disease*. Academic Press, New York. xviii + 552.

Selikoff, I.J., Teirstein, A.S., and Hirschman, S.Z. (Eds.) 1984. *Aquired immune deficiency syndrome*. Ann. New York Acad. Sci., vol. 437. New York Academy of Sciences, New York. xiv + 622.

Sellers, R.F. 1984a. Vesicular viruses. pp. 213–32 in Topley and Wilson, 1984, vol. 4.

Sellers, R.F. 1984b. Orbiviruses. pp. 303–14 in Topley and Wilson, 1984, vol. 4.

Sellers, R.F. 1984c. The *Paramyxoviridae*. pp. 376–93 in Topley and Wilson, 1984, vol. 4.

Semmelweis, I.P. 1861/1941/1966. *Die Aetiologie, der Begriff und die Prophylaxis des Kindbettfiebers*. Reprinted from the 1861 edition. Sources of Science, No. 19. Johnson Reprint Corp., New York-London, 1966. xxxii + 543. Translated by F.P. Murphy as *The etiology, the concept and prophylaxis of childbed fever*. Medical Classics 5 (1941), 350–773.

Semple, D. 1919. On the nature of rabies and antirabic treatment. *Br. Med. J.* 2, 333–36, 371–73.

Sever, J.L. 1980. Infectious causes of human reproductive loss. pp. 169–75 in Porter and Hook.

Shaffer, J.G., Shlaes, W.H., and Radke, R.A. 1965. *Amebiasis: A biomedical problem*. C.C. Thomas, Springfield, IL. xiii + 172.

Shanmugaratnam, K. 1982. Nasopharynx. pp. 536–53 in Schottenfeld and Fraumeni.

Shaper, A.G. 1972. Cardiovascular disease in the tropics. I. Rheumatic heart. II. Endomyocardial fibrosis. III. Blood pressure and hypertension. IV. Coronary heart disease. *Br. Med. J. 3*, 683–86, 743–46, 805–07; 4, 32–6.

Shaper, A.G., Hutt, M.S., and Coles, R.M. 1968. Necropsy study of endomyocardial fibrosis and rheumatic heart disease in Uganda 1950–1965. *Br. Heart J. 30*, 390–401.

Shapiro, S., Schlesinger, E.R., and Nesbitt, R.E.L. 1968. *Infant, perinatal, maternal, and childhood mortality in the United States*. Harvard University Press, Cambridge, MA. xix + 388.

Shattuck, L. 1841. *The vital statistics of Boston; Containing an abstract of the bills of mortality for the last twenty-nine years, and a general view of the population and health of the city at other periods of its history*. Lea and Blanchard, Philadelphia. 35 pp.

Sheldon, J.H. 1948. *The social medicine of old age: Report of an enquiry at Wolverhampton*. Oxford University Press, London. x + 239.

Sheldon, J.H. 1960. On the natural history of falls in old age. *Br. Med. J. 2*, 1685–90.

Sheridan, R.B. 1985. *Doctors and slaves. A medical and demographic history of slavery in the British West Indies, 1680–1834*. Cambridge University Press. xxii + 420.

Shimada, K. 1971. The last rabies outbreak in Japan. With discussion. pp. 11–35 in Nagano and Davenport.

Shine, I. (with R. Gold) 1970. *Serendipity in St. Helena: A genetical and medical study of an isolated community*. Pergamon Press, Oxford. xvi + 187.

Shirley-Smith, H. 1969. Disasters in bridges and dams. *Adv. Sci. 25*, 386–90.

Short, A.R. 1920–1921. The causation of appendicitis. *Br. J. Surg. 8*, 171–88.

Short, R.V. 1983. The biological basis for the contraceptive effects of breast-feeding. *Adv. Int. Matern. Child Health 3*, 27–39.

Short, R.V. 1984. Breast feeding. *Sci. Amer. 250* (4), 35–41.

Short, T. 1750. *New observations on city, town and country bills of mortality*. Reprinted, 1973. Gregg International, London. 532 pp.

Shrewsbury, J.F.D. 1970. *A history of bubonic plague in the British Isles*. Cambridge University Press. xi + 661. (See Morris, 1971.)

Shrivastava, P. 1987. *Bhopal. Anatomy of a crisis*.

Ballinger Ser. In Business in a global Environment. Ballinger, Cambridge, MA. 185 pp.

Shryock, R.H. 1966. *Medicine in America. Historical essays.* Johns Hopkins, Baltimore. xviii + 346.

Shy, C.M. and Struba, R.J. 1982. Air and water pollution. pp. 336–63 in Schottenfeld and Fraumeni.

Siegel, J.S. and Hoover, S.L. 1982. Demographic aspects of the health of the elderly to the year 2000 and beyond. *World Health Stat. Q. 35*, 133–202.

Sievert, R.M., Swedjemark, G.A., and Wilson, J.C. 1966. Exposure of man to ionizing radiation from natural and artificial sources. pp. 334–71 in Zuppinger, vol. 2.

Sigma 1986. International survey of major losses and catastrophes 1970–1985. *Sigma* No. 11 (1986). Swiss Reinsurance Co., Zürich. 17 pp.

Sigsworth, E. 1966. A provincial hospital in the eighteenth and early nineteenth centuries. *Coll. Gen. Practitioners, Yorkshire Faculty J.* (1966) 1–8.

Sigurdsson, S. and Tomasson, B. 1968. Public health in Iceland. *World Med. J. 15*, 97–100.

Sigurjonsson, J. 1961. Rubella and congenital deafness. *Am. J. Med. Sci. 242*, 712–20.

Sigurjonsson, J. 1962. Rubella and congenital cataract blindness. *Med. J. Austral. 1*, 588–90.

Silverstein, A. 1979. *Conquest of death.* Macmillan, New York. xiv + 242.

Simkin, T. and Fiske, R.S. (with S. Melcher and E. Nielsen) 1983. *Krakatau 1883. The volcanic eruption and its effect.* Smithsonian Inst. Press, Washington, DC. 464 pp.

Simmonds, N.W. (Ed.) 1976. *Evolution of crop plants.* Longmans, London. xii + 339.

Simmons, J.S., Callender, G.R., Curry, D.P., Schwartz, S.C., and Randall, R. 1939. *Malaria in Panama.* Johns Hopkins, Baltimore. xv + 326.

Simmons, J.S., Whayne, T.F., Anderson, G.W., and Horack, H.M. 1944/1951/1954. *Global epidemiology. I. Pt. 1, India and the Far East; Pt. 2, The Pacific area. II. Africa and adjacent islands. III. The Near and Middle East.* J.B. Lippincott, Philadelphia. 3 vols.

Simon, H.J. 1968. Mortality among medical students, 1947–1967. *J. Med. Educ. 43*, 1175–82.

Simpson, D.I.H. 1984a. *Togaviridae.* pp. 233–49 in Topley and Wilson, 1984, vol. 4.

Simpson, D.I.H. 1984b. *Arenaviridae.* pp. 255–65 in Topley and Wilson, 1984, vol. 4.

Simpson, D.I.H. 1984c. Marburg and Ebola viruses. pp. 266–70 in Topley and Wilson, 1984, vol. 4.

Simpson, H.N. 1954. The impact of disease on American history. *N. Engl. J. Med. 250*, 679–87.

Simpson, J.Y. 1850. On the analogy between puerperal and surgical fever. *Edinburgh Mon. J. Med. Sci. 11*, Nov. 1850, 414–29. Reprinted in *Obstetric Memoirs II*, 1–19 (1856).

Simpson, J.Y. 1851. On the communicability and propagation of puerperal fever. *Edinburgh Mon. J. Med. Sci. 12*, July 1851, 72 pp. Reprinted in *Obstetric Memoirs II*, 20–33 (1856).

Simpson, J.Y. 1855–1856. *The obstetric memoirs and contributions of James Y. Simpson, M.D. F.R.S.E.* W.O. Priestley and H.R. Storer, Eds. Adam and Charles Black, Edinburgh. xv + 857, xii + 819.

Simpson, J.Y. 1868–1869 and 1869–1870. Our existing system of hospitalism and its effects. *Edinburgh Mon. J. Med. Sci. 14*, 816–30, 1084–115; *15*, 523–32. Reprinted in *Works 2*, 288–405 (1871).

Simpson, J.Y. 1871–1872. *The works of Sir J.Y. Simpson, Bart.* Vol. 1, *Selected obstetrical and gynaecological works* . . . J.W. Black, Ed. Vol. 2, *Anaesthesia, hospitalism, hermaphroditism* . . . W.G. Simpson, Ed. Vol. 3, *Clinical lectures on the disease of women* . . . A.R. Simpson, Ed. Adam and Charles Black, Edinburgh. 3 vols.

Simpson, W.J. 1905. *A treatise on plague; dealing with the historical, epidemiological, clinical, therapeutic and preventive aspects of the disease.* Cambridge University Press. xxiv + 466.

Sinclair, C.G. and Maxcy, K.F. 1925. Mild typhus (Brill's disease) in the lower Rio Grande Valley. *Public Health Rep. 40*, 241–48.

Sinclair, H.M. 1982. Thiamin. pp. 114–67 in Barker and Bender.

Sinclair, J. 1791–1799. *The statistical account of Scotland; drawn up from the communications of the Ministers of the different Parishes.* Edinburgh. 21 vols.

Sinclair, J. 1831. *Analysis of the statistical account of Scotland.* Edinburgh.

Singer, C. and Underwood, E.A. 1962. *A short history of medicine.* Clarendon, Oxford. xvi + 854.

Singer, J.D. and Small, M. 1972. *The wages of war, 1816–1965: A statistical handbook.* Wiley, New York. xii + 419.

Sinnett, P.F. 1975. *The peopling of Murafin.* Monogr. Ser. No. 4, Institute of Medical Research, Papua New Guinea. E.W. Classey, Faringdon, Oxon. xii + 208.

Sisley, R. 1891. *Epidemic influenza: Notes on its origin and method of spread.* Longmans Green, London. xi + 150.

Sjostrand and Sahlin 1924, See Greenwood, 1924 (discussion).

Skehel, J.J. 1984. Virus replication. pp. 49–58 in Topley and Wilson, 1984, vol. 4.

Skinner, F.A. and Carr, J.G. 1974. *The normal microbial flora of man.* Academic Press, London. xv + 264.

Skinner, F.A. and Quesnel, L.B. (Eds.) 1978. *Streptococci.* Academic Press, New York. xiii + 415.

Skinner, F.A., Walker, P.D., and Smith, H. 1977. *Gonorrhea: Epidemiology and pathogenesis.* Federation of European Microbiological Societies. Academic Press, London. xiii + 255.

Skinsnes, O.K. 1973. Notes from the history of leprosy. *Int. J. Leprosy 41*, 220–37.

Skinsnes, O.K. 1982. Infectious granulomas: Exposit from the leprosy model. *Annu. Rev. Med. 33*, 47–67.

Skolnik, M., Bean, L., May, D., Arbon, V., de Nevers, K., and Cartwright, P. 1978. Mormon demographic history, I. *Popul. Studies 32*, 5–19.

Sladen, B.K. and Bang, F.B. (Eds.) 1969. *Biology of populations: The biological basis of public health.* American Elsevier, New York. xxii + 449.

Slicher van Bath, B.H. 1963. *The agrarian history of Western Europe, A.D. 500–1850.* Transl. by O. Ordish. Edward Arnold, London. iv + 364.

Slicher van Bath, B.H. 1977. Agriculture in the vital revolution. pp. 42–132 in *Cambridge Economic History of Europe*, Vol. 5. Cambridge University Press.

Small, M. and Singer, J.D. 1982. *Resort to arms: International and civil wars. 1816–1980.* Sage, Beverly Hills. 288 pp.

Smith, A.D.M. 1983. Epidemiology patterns in directly transmitted human infections. pp. 333–53 in Croll and Cross.

Smith, A.L. 1985. *Principles of microbiology.* 10th edition. Times Mirror/Mosby College, St. Louis-Toronto-Santa Clara. xx + 929 + 16 + 31.

Smith, C.A. 1947a. The effect of wartime starvation in Holland upon pregnancy. *Am. J. Obstet. Gynecol.* (Apr. 1947) 599–608.

Smith, C.A. 1947b. Effects of maternal undernutrition upon the new-born infant in Holland (1944–45). *J. Pediatr 30*, 229–43.

Smith, C.E.G. 1982. Priorities for medicine and health in the tropics. *Crit. Rev. Trop. Med. 1*, 1–29. See Chandra, 1982.

Smith, D.H., Manson-Bahr, P.E.C., and Chance, M.L. 1984. Leishmaniasis. (a) Visceral leishmaniasis—Human aspects (by D.H. Smith); (b) Cutaneous leishmaniasis (by P.E.C. Manson-Bahr); (c) Experimental studies of visceral and cutaneous leishmaniasis (by M.L. Chance). *Rec. Adv. Trop. Med. 1*, 79–113. See Gilles, 1984.

Smith, D.P. and Keyfitz, N. 1977. *Mathematical demography.* Springer, Berlin-Heidelberg-New York. xi + 514.

Smith, G. 1984. *Mycoplasma* diseases of animals and man. pp. 591–601 in Topley and Wilson, 1984, vol. 3.

Smith, G. and Wilson, G.(S.) 1984a. *Erysipelothrix* and *Listeria* infections. pp. 23–31 in Topley and Wilson, 1984, vol. 3.

Smith, G. and Wilson, G.(S.) 1984b. Plague and other yersinial diseases, *Pasteurella* infections, and tularaemia. pp. 114–40 in Topley and Wilson, 1984, vol. 3.

Smith, J.W. and Wolfe, M.S. 1980. Giardiasis. *Annu. Rev. Med. 31*, 373–83.

Smith, J.W.G. 1984a. Tetanus. pp. 345–68 in Topley and Wilson, 1984, vol. 3.

Smith, J.W.G. 1984b. Bacterial infections of the respiratory tract. pp. 391–406 in Topley and Wilson, 1984, vol. 3.

Smith, J.W.G. and Smith, G. 1984. Gas gangrene and other clostridial infections of man and animals. pp. 327–44 in Topley and Wilson, 1984, vol. 3.

Smith, N. 1976. *Man and water: A history of hydrotechnology.* Peter Davies, London. xiv + 239.

Smith, P.D. 1985. Pathophysiology and immunology of giardasis. *Annu. Rev. Med. 36*, 295–307.

Smith, S. 1906. The evolution of American surgery. pp. 3–67 in *American Practice of Surgery, vol. 1.* J.D. Bryant and A.H. Buck, Eds. William Wood, New York, 1906–11. 8 vols.

Smith, S. 1973. *The city that was. (Incorporating the Report of the General Committee of Health, New York City, 1806.)* Scarecrow Reprint Corp., Metuchen, NJ. xii + 211 + 101.

Smith, W(rynn) 1987. *Obstetrics, gynecology, and infant mortality.* A Profile of Health and Disease in America, 3. Facts on File, New York. xiv + 146.

Sneader, W. 1985. *Drug discovery. The evolution of modern medicines.* Wiley, New York. x + 435.

Snow, J. 1936. *Snow on cholera: Being a reprint of two papers by John Snow. Together with a biographical memoir by B.W. Richardson and an introduction by W.H. Frost.* Commonwealth Fund, New York. xlviii + vii + 191.

Snyder, J.C. 1965. Typhus fever rickettsiae. pp. 1095–129 in Horsfall and Tamm.

Snyder, J.C. 1976. Public health and preventive medicine. pp. 384–457 in Bowers and Purcell.

Soest, P.J. van 1977. Statement (on dietary fiber).

pp. 61–72 in Select Committee on Nutrition.

Solomons, B. 1958. The history of infant welfare. *J. Pediatr. (St Louis) 53*, 360–77.

Sømme, A. (Ed.) 1968. *A geography of Norden: Denmark, Finland, Iceland, Norway and Sweden.* Heinemann, London. 343 pp.

Soper, F.L. (Chairman) 1955. Yellow fever conference. *Am. J. Trop. Med. Hyg. 4*, 571–661.

Soper, F.L., Davis, W.A., Markham, F.S., and Riehl, L.A. 1947. Typhus fever in Italy, 1943–1945, and its control with louse powder. *Am. J. Hyg. 45*, 305–34.

Spaet, T.H. 1980. Platelets: The blood dust. pp. 549–71 in Wintrobe.

Sparks, R.S.J. 1979. The Santorini eruption and its consequences. *Endeavour N.S. 3*, 27–31.

Special Committee 1913. Report of the special committee on infantile mortality. *J. Roy. Stat. Soc. 76*, 27–87.

Special Report 1918. *The mortalities of birth, infancy and childhood.* Med. Res. Council Spec. Rep. Series No. 10, HMSO, London. 84 pp.

Speizer, F.E., Doll, R., and Heaf, P. 1968. Observations on the recent increase in mortality from asthma. *Br. Med. J. 1*, 335–39.

Spencer, H.A. 1932. *Lightning, lightning stroke and its treatment.* Baillière, Tindall & Cox, London. ix + 91.

Spencer, H.R. 1927a. History of British midwifery. *Br. Med. J. 2*, 853–56.

Spencer, H.R. 1927b. The history of British midwifery, 1650–*1800. The Fitzpatrick Lectures.* John Bale, Sons and Danielsson, London. xxiv + 185.

Spiegelman, M. 1955. *Introduction to demography.* Society of Actuaries, Chicago, IL. xxi + 309.

Spiller, G.A. and Amen, R.J. (Eds.) 1976. *Fiber in human nutrition.* Plenum, New York. xvii + 278.

Spiller, G.A. and Kay, R.M. (Eds.) 1980. *Medical aspects of dietary fibre.* Plenum, New York. xix + 299.

Spink, W.W. 1956. *The nature of brucellosis.* University of Minnesota Press, Minneapolis. xiv + 464.

Spink, W.W. 1979. *Infectious diseases: Prevention and treatment in the nineteenth and twentieth centuries.* University of Minnesota Press, Minneapolis; Dawson, Folkstone. xx + 577.

Sprengell, C.J. 1723. Bills of mortality of several considerable towns in Europe. Beginning with the year 1717, i.e., from Christmas 1716 to Christmas 1717. Extracted from the Acta Breslaviensia. *Philos. Trans. Roy. Soc. London 32* (380), 454–69.

Sprengell, C.J. 1733. The bills of mortality from the town of Dresden, for a whole century, viz., from the year 1617 to 1717, containing the numbers of marriages, births, burials and communicants. *Philos. Trans. Roy. Soc. London 38* (428), 89–92.

Springett, V.H. 1950. A comparative study of tuberculosis mortality rates. *J. Hyg. Camb. 48*, 361–95.

Springett, V.H. 1952. An interpretation of statistical trends in tuberculosis. *Lancet 1*, 521–25, 575–79.

Squire, W. 1875–1877. On measles in Fiji. *Trans. Epidemiol. Soc. London 4*, 72–74.

Srivastava, H.S. 1968. *The history of Indian famines and development of famine policy (1858–1918).* Sri Ram Mehra & Co., Agra. 9 + x + 417.

Stallones, R.A. 1965. Epidemiology of cerebrovascular disease. A review. *J. Chronic Dis. 18*, 859–72.

Stamler, J. 1973. Epidemiology of coronary heart disease. *Med. Clin. North Am. 57*, 5–46.

Stamler, J. 1979. Population studies. pp. 25–88 in Levy, Rifkind, et al.

Stanbury, J.B., Wyngaarden, J.B., and Fredrickson, D.S. 1976. *The metabolic basis of inherited disease.* 3rd edition. McGraw-Hill, New York. xiv + 1778.

Stanley, F.J. 1977. Medical care of the fetus and the risk of prematurity. pp. 269–79 in Reed and Stanley.

Stanley, N.F. 1980. Man's role in changing patterns of arbovirus infections. pp. 151–73 in Stanley and Joske.

Stanley, N.F. and Alpers, M.P. 1975. *Man-made lakes and human health.* Academic Press, London-New York. xvi + 495.

Stanley, N.F. and Joske, R.A. (Eds.) 1980. *Changing disease patterns and human behaviour.* Academic Press, New York. xiv + 666.

Stark, J. 1851. Contribution to the vital statistics of Scotland. *J. Stat. Soc. (London) 14*, 48–87.

Stark, J. 1857. *Inquiry into some points of the sanitary state of Edinburgh, etc.* Edinburgh. 45 pp.

Stark, J. 1869–1870. Contribution to vital statistics. I. On the general mortality of the town and rural districts of Scotland. II. Are any deaths preventable? If so, are they caused by any particular class of diseases? Is there any probability of the mortality of the towns being reduced to that of the rural districts? *Edinburgh Med. J. 14*, 481–87, 593–605.

Starr, P. 1982. *The social transformation of American medicine.* Basic Books, New York, xiv + 514.

Staszewski, J. 1980a. Cancer of the urinary bladder: International mortality patterns and trends. *World Health Stat. Q. 33*, 27–41.

Staszewski, J. 1980b. Cancer of the kidney: International mortality patterns and trends. *World Health*

Stat. Q. 33, 42–55.

Statistics—alcohol and drug use 1985. *Statistics on alcohol and drug use in Canada and other countries. Data available by September 1984. Vol. 1, Statistics on alcohol use.* xxii + 316. *Vol. 2, Statistics on drug use.* xxiv + 370. Addiction Research Foundation, Toronto.

Steele, J.C. 1861. Numerical analysis of the patients treated in Guy's Hospital for the last seven years, from 1854 to 1861. *J. Stat. Soc. (London) 24*, 374–401.

Steele, J.C. 1877. The mortality of hospitals, general and special, in the United Kingdom, in times past and present. *J. Stat. Soc. (London) 40*, 177–261.

Steele, J.H. 1975. History of rabies. pp. 1–29 in Baer.

Steele, J.H. (Ed.-in-Chief) 1982. *CRC Handbook Series in Zoonoses. Section C: Parasitic zoonoses.* 3 vols. CRC Press, Boca Raton, FL.

Stefansson, V. 1958. Eskimo longevity in northern Alaska. *Science 127*, 16–19.

Stein, Z., Susser, M., Saenger, G., and Marolla, F. 1975. *Famine and human development: The Dutch hunger winter of 1944–1945.* Oxford University Press, New York. xx + 284.

Steinberg, A.G. and Wilder, R.M. 1952. A study of the genetics of diabetes mellitus. *Am. J. Hum. Genet. 3*, 113–35.

Steiner, P.E. 1954. *Cancer: Race and geography.* Williams and Wilkins, Baltimore. xiii + 363.

Steiner, P.E. 1968. *Disease in the Civil War. Natural biological warfare in 1861–1865.* C.C. Thomas, Springfield, IL. xv + 243.

Sterling, C. 1974. The making of the sub-Saharan wasteland. *Atlantic Monthly 233* (May 1974) 98–105.

Stevens, P.J. 1970. *Fatal civil aircraft accidents: Their medical and pathological investigation.* John Wright, Bristol. 218 pp.

Stevenson, T.H.C. 1921. The incidence of mortality upon the rich and poor districts of Paris and London. *J. Roy. Stat. Soc. 84*, 90–99.

Stevenson, T.H.C. 1923. The social distribution of mortality from different causes in England and Wales, 1910–12. *Biometrika 15*, 382–400.

Stevenson, T.H.C. 1928. The vital statistics of wealth and poverty. *J. Roy. Stat. Soc. 91*, 207–30.

Stewart, A., Webb, J., and Hewitt, D. 1958. A survey of childhood malignancies. *Br. Med. J. 1*, 1495–1508.

Stewart, A.P. and Jenkins, E. 1867/1969. *The medical and legal aspects of sanitary reform.* Reprinted 1969 with an introd. by M.W. Flinn.

Leicester University Press, Leicester; Humanities Press, New York, 25 + 100.

Stewart, T.D. 1973. *The people of America.* Scribner, New York. xiv + 261.

Stewart, T.D. and Spoehr, A. 1952. Evidence on the paleopathology of yaws. *Bull. Hist. Med. 26*, 538–53.

Sticker, G. 1908/1912. *Abhandlungen aus der Seuchengeschichte und Seuchenlehre. Vol. I (in 2 parts)—Die Pest.* viii + 478 and 542. *Vol. II—Die Cholera.* iv + 592. A Töpelmann, Giessen.

Stinnett, J.D. 1983. *Nutrition and the immune response.* CRC Press, Boca Raton, FL. viii + 150.

Stock, R.F. 1976. *Cholera in Africa: Diffusion of the disease 1970–1975 with special emphasis on West Africa.* African Environment Spec. Rep. 3, Internatl. African Inst., London. vii + 127.

Stocks, P. 1935. The effect of influenza epidemics on the certified causes of death. *Lancet 2*, 386–95.

Stocks, P. 1938. The effects of occupation and its accompanying environment on mortality. *J. Roy. Stat. Soc. 101*, 668–708.

Stocks, P. 1941. Diphtheria and scarlet fever incidence during the dispersal of 1939–40. *J. Roy. Stat. Soc. 104*, 311–45.

Stocks, P. 1942. Measles and whooping-cough incidence before and during the dispersal of 1939–1941. *J. Roy. Stat. Soc. 105*, 259–91.

Stocks, P. 1944. Diabetes mortality in 1861–1942 and some of the factors affecting it. *J. Hyg. Camb. 43*, 242–47.

Stocks, P. 1949. A study of tuberculosis mortality in England and Wales. *Tubercle 30*, 50–61.

Stocks, P. 1950. Fifty years of progress as shown by vital statistics. *Br. Med. J. 1*, 54–57.

Stockwell, E.G. 1961. Socio-economic status and mortality in the United States. *Public Health Rep. 76*, 1081–86.

Stollerman, G.H. 1975. *Rheumatic fever and streptococcal infection.* Grune and Stratton, New York. xv + 336.

Stolley, P.D. and Hibberd, P.L. 1982. Drugs. pp. 304–17 in Schottenfeld and Fraumeni.

Stolnitz, G.J. 1955. A century of international mortality trends. *Popul. Studies 9*, 24–55.

Stolnitz, G.J. 1956a. Comparison between some recent mortality trends in underdeveloped areas and historical trends in the West. pp. 26–34 in *Trends and Differentials in Mortality. Papers presented at the 1955 Annual Conf. of the Milbank Memorial Fund.* Milbank Memorial Fund, New York. 166 pp.

Stolnitz, G.J. 1956b. *Life tables from limited data: A demographic approach.* Office of Population Research, Princeton University, Princeton, NJ. xii + 164.

Stolnitz, G.J. 1957. A century of international mortality trends, II. *Popul. Studies 10*, 17–42.

Stolnitz, G.J. 1975. International mortality trends: Some main facts and implications. pp. 220–36 in *The population debate: Dimensions and perspectives, vol. 1. Papers of the World Population Conf., Bucharest, 1974*. United Nations, New York. viii + 676.

Stothers, R.B. 1984. The great Tambora eruption in 1815 and its aftermath. *Science 224*, 1191–98.

Stott, E.J. and Garwes, D.J. 1984. Respiratory disease: *Rhinoviruses, Adenoviruses* and *Coronaviruses*. pp. 345–75 in Topley and Wilson, 1984, vol. 4.

Stowman, K. 1947–1948a. Post-war death rates. *WHO Epidemiol. Vital Stat. Rep. 1*, 88–93.

Stowman, K. 1947–1948b. The declining death-rate. *WHO Epidemiol. Vital Stat. Rep. 1*, 412–18.

Stowman, K. 1947–1948c. Recrudescence of typhoid fever in Europe. *WHO Epidemiol. Vital Stat. Rep. 1*, 166–72.

Stowman, K. 1947–1948d. Downward trend of infant mortality persists. *WHO Epidemiol. Vital Stat. Rep. 1*, 188–94.

Strauss, E. 1954. *Sir William Petty, portrait of a genius*. Bodley Head, London. 260 pp.

Strehler, B.L. and Mildwan, A.S. 1960. General theory of mortality and ageing. *Science 132*, 14–21.

Strode, G.K. (Ed.) 1951. *Yellow fever*. McGraw-Hill, New York. xv + 710.

Strong, L.C. 1982. Genetic-environmental interactions. pp. 506–16 in Schottenfeld and Fraumeni.

Strong, R.P., Shattuck, G.C., Sellards, A.W., Zinsser, H., and Hopkins, J.G. 1920. *Typhus fever with particular reference to the Serbian epidemic*. Harvard University Press, Cambridge, MA. viii + 273.

Strong, R.P., Tyzzer, E.E., Brues, C.T., Sellards, A.W., and Gastiaburú, J.C. 1915a. *Report of first expedition to South America, 1913*. Harvard University Press, Cambridge, MA. xiv + 200 + xlvi plates.

Strong, R.P., Tyzzer, E.E., and Sellards, A.W. 1915b. Oroya fever, second report. *J. Am. Med. Assoc. 64*, 806–08.

Stroop, W.G. and Baringer, J.R. 1982. Persistent, slow and latent infections. *Prog. Med. Virol. 28*, 1–43.

Stuart-Harris, C.H. 1953/1965. *Influenza and other viral infections of the respiratory tract*. Edward Arnold, London. v + 235. 2nd edition 1965. Wil-

liams and Wilkins, Baltimore.

Stuart-Harris, C.H. 1970. Pandemic influenza: An unresolved problem in prevention. *J. Infect. Dis. 122*, 108–15.

Stuart-Harris, C. (H.) 1973. Influenza—The problems and the future. Special supplement: Symposium on influenza. *Med. J. Austral. 1*, 42–46.

Stuart-Harris, C. (H.) 1984a. Epidemiology of viral infections. pp. 124–46 in Topley and Wilson, 1984, vol. 4.

Stuart-Harris, C. (H.) 1984b. Prospects for the eradication of infectious diseases. *Rev. Infect. Dis. 6*, 405–11.

Stuart-Harris, C.H. and Oxford, J. (Eds.) 1984. *Problems of antiviral therapy*. Academic Press, Orlando, FL. x + 347.

Stuart-Harris, C.H. and Schild, G.C. 1976. *Influenza. The viruses and the disease*. Edward Arnold, London. x + 242.

Stuckey, W.J. 1966. Hemolytic anaemia and erythrocyte glycose-6-phosphate dehydrogenase deficiency. *Am. J. Med. Sci. 251*, 105–15.

Study Committee of the National Academy of Sciences 1971. *Rapid population growth: consequences and policy implications*. National Academy of Sciences. Johns Hopkins, Baltimore. xii + 696.

Stürchler, D. 1981. *Endemiegebiete tropischer Infektionskrankheiten: Karten und Texte für die Praxis*. Hans Huber, Bern. 246 pp.

Suda, K. and Soekawa, M. 1983. Smallpox mortality in a mountainous district in Japan where neither variolation nor vaccination had been performed. *J. Jap. Soc. Med. Hist.* (Nihon Ishigaku Zasshi) *29*, 83–94.

Suessmilch, J.P. 1761–1762. *Die göttliche Ordnung in den Veränderungen des menschlichen Geschlechts, aus der Geburt, dem Tode und der Fortpflanzung desselben erwiesen*. Verlag des Buchladens der Realschule, Berlin. 2 vols. 2nd edition; original 1741–42.

Sugiyama, H. 1980. *Clostridium botulinum* neurotoxin. *Microbiol. Rev. 44*, 419–48.

Sulkin, S.E. and Pike, R.M. 1951. Survey of laboratory acquired infections. *Am. J. Public Health 41*, 769–81.

Sullivan, F.M. and Barlow, S.M. 1979. Congenital malformations and other reproductive hazards from environmental chemicals. *Proc. Roy. Soc. London B205*, 91–110. Reprinted in Doll and McLean.

Summer, W. and Haponik, E. 1981. Inhalation of irritant gases. pp. 273–87 in Brooks, Lockey, and Harber.

Sun, M. 1985*a*. Illinois traces cause of *Salmonella* outbreak. *Science 228*, 972–73.

Sun, M. 1985*b*. The vexing problems of vaccine compensation: Whooping cough vaccine research revs up. *Science 227*, 1012–14, 1184–86.

Sundbärg, A. G. 1907/1970. *Bevölkerungsstatistik Schwedens, 1750–1900*. [A photographic reproduction of the book of 1907.] Central Bureau of Statistics, Stockholm. x + 170.

Sundby, P. 1967. *Alcoholism and mortality*. Universitets-forlaget, Oslo. 207 pp.

Susser, M. and Stein, Z. 1977. Prenatal nutrition and subsequent development. pp. 177–92. in Reed and Stanley.

Sussman, M. (Ed.) 1985. *The virulence of Escherichia coli. Reviews and methods*. Academic Press, Orlando, FL. 473 pp.

Sutherland, I. 1972. When was the great plague? Mortality in London, 1563–1665. pp. 287–320 in Glass and Revelle.

Sutherland, J.M. 1969. Geography and diseases of the nervous system. *Med. J. Austral. 2*, 885–91.

Sutter, J. and Tabah, L. 1952. La mortalité, phénomène biométrique. *Population 7*, 69–94.

Sutton, W. 1872. Lectures: A course of three lectures for the second year examination of the Institute of Actuaries. *J. Inst. Actuar. 16*, 434–64.

Swaroop, S. (assisted by R. Pollitzer)1952. World distribution of cholera endemicity. *WHO Epidemiol. Vital Stat. Rep. 5*, 569–89.

Sweany, H.C. (Ed.) 1960. *Histoplasmosis*. C.C. Thomas, Springfield, IL. xiv + 538.

Sweet, C. and Smith, H. 1980. Pathogenicity of influenza virus. *Microbiol. Rev. 44*, 303–30.

Sweeting, R.D.R. 1884. The experiences and opinions of John Howard on the preservation and improvement of the health of the inmates of schools, prisons, workhouses, hospitals, and other public institutions as far as health is affected by structural arrangements relating to supplies of air and water, drainage, etc. *J. Stat. Soc. (London) 47*, 125–41.

Sweitzer, S.E. and Ikeda, K. 1927. Variola: A clinical study of the Minneapolis epidemic of 1924–1925. *Arch. Dermatol. Syph. 15*, 19–29.

Swift, M. 1982. Single gene syndromes. pp. 475–82 in Schottenfeld and Fraumeni.

Sydenstricker, E. 1918. Preliminary statistics of the influenza epidemic. *Public Health Rep. 33*, 2305–21.

Sydenstricker, E. 1921. Variations in case fatality during the influenza epidemic of 1918. *Public Health Rep. 36*, 2201–10.

Sydenstricker, E. 1927. The declining death rate from tuberculosis. *Trans. Natl. Tuberc. Assoc. 23*, 102–24. Reprinted in Sydenstricker, 1974.

Sydenstricker, E. 1929. Trends of tuberculosis mortality in rural and urban areas. *Am. Rev. Tuberc. 19*, 461–82.

Sydenstricker, E. 1974. *The challenge of facts: Selected public health papers of Edgar Sydenstricker*. R.V. Kasius, Ed. Prodist (Neale Watson Academic Publ.), New York. xi + 386.

Sydenstricker, V.P. 1958. The history of pellagra, its recognition as a disease of nutrition and its conquest. *Am. J. Clin. Nutr. 24*, 655–851.

Sykes, G. and Skinner, F.A. (Eds.) 1971. *Microbial aspects of pollution*. Society for Applied Bacteriology Symp. Ser. No. 1. Academic Press, London. xiii + 289.

Sykes, G. and Skinner, F.A. (Eds.) 1973. *Actinomycetales: Characteristics and practical importance*. Society for Applied Bacteriology Symp. Ser. No. 2. Academic Press, London. xv + 339.

Sykes, W.S. 1982. *Essays on the first hundred years of anaesthesia*. 3 vol. Vol. 3 edited by R.H. Ellis. Churchill-Livingstone, Edinburgh. 171, 187, and 272 pp.

Symposium 1961. Trends in infant mortality in Asia and Oceania. A symposium. *J. Philippine Med. Assoc. 37*, 581–613.

Tabah, L. 1955. La mortalité sociale: Enquête nouvelle en Angleterre. *Population 10*, 57–78.

Tabutin, D. 1978. La surmortalité féminine en Europe avant 1940. *Population 33*, 121–48.

Taeuber, I.B. 1958. *The population of Japan*. Princeton University Press, Princeton, NJ. xx + 461.

Taffel, S. 1978. *Congenital anomalies and birth injuries among live births: United States, 1973–74*. DHEW Publn. No. (PHS) 79-1909, Ser. 21, No. 31. US Dept. Health, Education and Welfare, Hyattsville, MD. vi + 58.

Tait, L. 1890. Address in surgery: Surgical training, surgical practice, surgical results. *Br. Med. J. 2*, 267–73.

Takahashi, K. and Yoshina, M.M. (Eds.) 1978. *Climatic change and food production. Papers from a symposium, Tsukuba and Tokyo, 1976*. University of Tokyo Press, Tokyo. xii + 434.

Tandy, E.C. 1935. *Comparability of maternal mortality rates in the United States and certain foreign countries; a study of the effects of variations in assignment procedures, definitions of live births, and completeness of birth registration*. Pub. No. 229, Children's Bureau, US Dept. Labor. US Govt. Printing Office, Washington, DC. v + 24.

Taneja, P.N., Ghai, O.P., and Bhakoo, O.N. 1962.

Importance of measles to India. *Am. J. Dis. Child. 103*, 226–29.

Taussig, H.B. 1962/1965. A study of the German outbreak of Phocomelia: The thalidomide syndrome. pp. 812–24 in Katz and Felton. Reprinted from *J. Am. Med. Assoc. 180* (1962), 1106–14.

Tavassoli, M. 1980. Bone marrow: the seed bed of blood. pp. 57–79 in Wintrobe.

Taylor, A.E.R. and Muller, R. (Eds.) 1978. *The relevance of parasitology to human welfare today*. Symposia of the British Soc. for Parasitology, vol. 16. Blackwell, Oxford. viii + 135.

Taylor, C.E. and Hall, M.F. 1967. Health, population and economic development. *Science 157*, 651–57.

Taylor, D.W. and Siddiqui, W.A. 1982. Recent advances in malarial immunity. *Annu. Rev. Med. 33*, 69–96.

Taylor, R.M. 1951. Epidemiology. pp. 427–538 in Strode.

Taylor, W. 1951. Changing mortality from 1841 to 1947 measured by the life table. *Br. J. Prev. Soc. Med. 5*, 162–76.

Taylor, W.F. 1961. On the methodology of studying aging in humans. *Proc. 4th Berkeley Symp. on Math. Stat. and Probab. 4*, 347–68.

Teff, H. and Munro, C.R. 1976. *Thalidomide: The legal aftermath*. Saxon House, Farnborough, Hants. xiii + 154.

Teleky, L. 1948. *History of factory and mine legislation*. Columbia University Press, New York. xvii + 342.

Temkin, O. 1977. *The double face of Janus and other essays in the history of medicine*. Johns Hopkins, Baltimore-London. 592 pp.

de-Thé, G. 1979. The epidemiology of Burkitt's lymphoma: Evidence for a causal association with Epstein-Barr virus. *Epidemiol. Rev. 1*, 32–54.

Theiler, M. 1952. Yellow fever. pp. 343–60 in *Viral and rickettsial diseases of man*, T.M. Rivers and F.L. Horsfall (Eds.). 3rd edition. J.B. Lippincott, Philadelphia. xviii + 967.

Theodor, O. 1964. Pathological conditions caused by arthropod parasites. pp. 720–39 in van der Hoeden.

Thom, J. and Kannel, W.B. 1981. Downward trend in cardiovascular mortality. *Annu. Rev. Med. 32*, 427–34.

Thomas, D.S. 1941. *Social and economic aspects of Swedish population movements, 1750–1933*. Macmillan, New York. xxiii + 487.

Thompson, B. 1984. Infant mortality in nineteenth-century Bradford. pp. 120–47 in Woods and Woodward.

Thompson, E.S. 1890. *Influenza or epidemic catarrhal fever: An historical survey of past epidemics in Great Britain from 1510 to 1890*. Percival & Co., London. xv + 490.

Thompson, J.D. and Goldin, G. 1975. *The hospital: A social and architectural history*. Yale University Press, New Haven, CT. xxvii + 349.

Thompson, J.M.T. 1982. *Instabilities and catastrophes in science and engineering*. Wiley-Interscience, New York. xvi + 226.

Thompson, J.W. 1966. *Economic and social history of the Middle Ages (300–1300)*. Frederick Ungar, New York. ix + 900.

Thompson, P.E. and Werbel, L.M. 1972. *Antimalarial agents*. Academic Press, London. xii + 395.

Thompson, R.C.A. (Ed.) 1986. *The biology of Echinococcus and hydatid disease*. Allen & Unwin, Boston. xiv + 290.

Thornsberry, C., Balows, A., Feeley, J.C., and Jakubowski, W. (Eds.) 1984. *Legionella: Proceedings of the 2nd International Symposium*. American Soc. for Microbiology, Washington, DC. xiii + 371.

Thorsteinsson, T. 1929. The census of Iceland in 1703. *Nord. Stat. J. 1*, 362–70.

Thrupp, S.L. 1965. The problem of replacement-rates in late medieval England. *Econ. Hist. Rev.* (2) *18*, 101–19.

Thrupp, S.(L.) 1966. Plague effects in medieval Europe. *Comp. Studies Soc. Hist. 8*, 474–83.

Tickner, F.J. and Medvei, V.C. 1958. Scurvy and the health of European crews in the Indian Ocean in the seventeenth century. *Hist. Med. 2*, 36–46.

Tierkel, E.S. 1972. Historical review of rabies in Asia. pp. 3–9, with discussion pp. 29–35 in Nagano and Davenport.

Tietze, C. 1977. Maternal mortality(excluding abortion mortality). *World Health Stat. Rep. 30*, 312–39.

Tiselius, H. 1904. Om dödligheten bland svenska arméns officerare och underofficerare. *Aktuaren 1*, 51–56.

Todd, J.K. 1985. Staphylococcal toxin syndromes. *Annu. Rev. Med. 36*, 337–47.

Tomasson, R.F. 1977. A millenium of misery: The demography of the Icelanders. *Popul. Studies 31*, 405–27.

Tomasson, R.F. 1980. *Iceland, the first new society*. University of Minnesota Press, Minneapolis. xix + 247.

Tomatis, L., Breslow, N.E., and Bartsch, H. 1982. Experimental studies in the assessment of human risk. pp. 44–73 in Schottenfeld and Fraumeni.

Tomkins, A. 1984. Diarrhoeal diseases. *Rec. Adv.*

Trop. Med. 1, 253–66. See Gilles, 1984.

Topley, W.W.C. 1919. The Goulstonian Lectures on the spread of bacterial infection. *Lancet 2*, 1–5, 45–49, 91–96.

Topley, W.W.C. and Wilson, G.S. 1975. *Topley and Wilson's 'Principles of bacteriology, virology and immunity'*. G.S. Wilson, A. Miles, et al. (Eds.) 6th edition. Edward Arnold, London. 2 vols. (2nd edition, 1936)

Topley, W.W.C. and Wilson, G.S. 1983–1984. *Topley and Wilson's 'Principles of bacteriology, virology and immunity'*. G.S. Wilson, A. Miles, and M.T. Parker (Gen. Eds.) 7th edition. Edward Arnold, London. Williams and Wilkins, Baltimore. 4 vols.

Torchia, M.M. 1977. Tuberculosis among American negroes: Medical research on a racial disease, 1830–1950. *J. Hist. Med. 32*, 252–79.

Törö, I., Szabady, E., Nemeskéri, J., and Eiben, O.G. 1972. *Advances in the biology of human populations*. Akadémiai Kiadó, Budapest. v + 508.

Towers, B. 1971. The influence of medical technology on medical services. pp. 159–77 in McLachlan and McKeown.

Trevelyan, C.E. 1848. *The Irish crisis*. Longman, Brown, Green & Longmans, London. 201 pp.

Trevelyan, G.M. 1944. *English social history: A survey of six centuries, Chaucer to Queen Victoria*. Longmans, Green & Co., London. xii + 628. Reprinted, 1948.

Treves, F. 1900. Address in surgery: The surgeon in the nineteenth century. *Br. Med. J. 2*, 285–89.

Trewartha, G.T. 1969. *A geography of population: World patterns*. Wiley, New York. iii + 186.

Trowell, H. (C.) 1960. *Non-infective disease in Africa: The peculiarities of medical non-infective diseases in the indigenous inhabitants of Africa south of the Sahara*. Edward Arnold, London. viii + 481.

Trowell, H. (C.) 1975. Diabetes mellitus and obesity. pp. 227–49 in Burkitt and Trowell.

Trowell, H. (C.) 1977a. Diabetes mellitus and the dietary fiber of the starchy foods. pp. 116–21 in Select Committee on Nutrition.

Trowell, H.C. 1977b. Dietary fiber and colonic diseases. pp. 123–48 in Select Committee on Nutrition.

Trowell, H. (C.) 1977c. Statement of Dr. Hugh Trowell. pp. 50–57 in Select Committee on Nutrition.

Trowell, H. (C.) 1981. Hypertension, obesity, diabetes mellitus and coronary heart disease. pp. 3–32 in Trowell and Burkitt, 1981a.

Trowell, H. (C.) and Burkitt, D.P. (Eds.) 1981a. *Western diseases: Their emergence and prevention*. Edward Arnold, London. xix + 456.

Trowell, H. (C.) and Burkitt, D. (P.) 1981b. Contributors' reports. pp. 427–35 in Trowell and Burkitt. 1981a.

Trowell, H. (C.), Burkitt, D. and Heaton, K. (Eds.) 1985. *Dietary fibre, fibre-depleted foods and disease*. Academic Press, Orlando, FL. xvi + 433.

Trowell, H.C., Davies, J.N.P., and Dean, R.F.A. 1982. *Kwashiorkor*. Nutrition Foundation Reprints. Academic Press, New York. xlii + 308. Reprint with new material of 1954 edition.

Truswell, A.S. 1977. Diet and nutrition of hunter-gatherers. With discussion. pp. 213–26 in Elliott and Whelan.

Truswell, A.S. and Apeagyei, F. 1982. Alcohol and cerebral thiamine deficiency. pp. 253–60 in Jelliffe and Jelliffe.

Tsubaki, T. and Irukayama, K. (Eds.) 1977. *Minamata disease: Methyl mercury poisoning in Minamata and Niigata, Japan*. Kodansha Ltd., Tokyo; Elsevier, Amsterdam. ix + 317.

Tucker, H.G. 1961. A stochastic model for a two-stage theory of carcinogenesis. *Proc. 4th Berkeley Symp. on Math. Stat. and Probab. 4*, 387–413.

Tulloch, A.M. 1841. Comparison of sickness, mortality, and prevailing diseases among seamen and soldiers, as shown by the naval and military statistical reports. *J. Stat. Soc. (London) 4*, 1–16.

Turner, G.S. 1984. Rabies. pp. 472–86 in Topley and Wilson, 1984, vol. 4.

Turner, H.H. (Compiler) 1928. *Catalogue of earthquakes, 1918–1924 (being a digest of the International Seismological Survey)*. British Assoc. for the Advancement of Science, London. 64 pp.

Turpeinen, O. 1973. Regional differentials in Finnish mortality rates, 1816–1865. *Scand. Econ. Hist. Rev. 21*, 145–63.

Turpeinen, O. 1978. Infectious diseases and regional differences in Finnish death rates, 1749–1773. *Popul. Studies 32*, 523–33.

Turpeinen, O. 1979a. Fertility and mortality in Finland since 1750. *Popul. Studies 33*, 101–14.

Turpeinen, O. 1979b. Infant mortality in Finland 1749–1865. *Scand. Econ. Hist. Rev. 27*, 1–21.

Turpeinen, O. 1980. Les causes des fluctuations annuelles du taux de mortalité finlandais entre 1750 et 1806. *Ann. Démog. Hist.*, Pt. 2, 287–96.

Tuyns, A.J. 1982. Alcohol. pp. 293–303 in Schottenfeld and Fraumeni.

Tye, W. 1969. Air transport disasters. *Adv. of Sci. 25*, 357–61.

Tyrrell, D.A.J. 1977. Aspects of infection in isolated communities. With discussion. pp. 137–53 in Elliott and Whelan.

Ueda, K. 1983. *Recent trends of mortality in Asian countries*. Publ. No. 34, Southeast Asian Medical Information Center and Internat. Medical Foundation of Japan, Tokyo. ix + 158.

Uemura, K. and Piša, Z. 1985. Recent trends in cardiovascular disease mortality in 27 industrialized countries. *World Health Stat. Q. 38*, 142–62.

UK Ministry of Health 1931. *A memorandum on bovine tuberculosis in man. With special reference to infection by milk*. UK Ministry of Health, Reports on Public Health and Medical Subjects No. 63, HMSO, London. 25 pp.

UK Ministry of Health 1932. *Final report of the Departmental Committee on maternal mortality and morbidity*. HMSO, London. 156 pp.

UN-historical 1979. *Demographic yearbook: Historical supplement*. United Nations, New York. vii + 1169.

UN Population Studies 1954. *Foetal, infant and early childhood mortality. Vol. 1, The statistics; Vol. 2, Biological, social and economic factors*. UN Population Studies No. 13, United Nations, New York.

UN Population Studies 1984. *Data bases for mortality measurement. From a meeting, Bangkok, 1981*. Dept. of International Economic and Social Affairs Population Studies No. 84. United Nations, New York. x + 164.

UN Population Studies 1985. *World population prospects. Estimates and projections as assessed in 1982*. Dept. of International Economic and Social Affairs Population Studies No. 86. United Nations, New York. xii + 521.

UN/WHO-mortality 1970. *Programmes of analysis of mortality trends and levels. Report of a joint UN/WHO meeting, Geneva, 1968*. Tech. Rep. Ser. No. 440. UN/WHO, Geneva. 30 pp.

Underwood, E.A. (Ed.) 1953. *Science, medicine and history*. Oxford University Press, London. 2 vols, xxxii + 563, viii + 646.

Urbistondo, R. (Ed.) 1985. Safe water for all. From a congress, Monastir, Tunisia, 1984. *Water Supply 2*, Nos. 3–4. Pergamon Press, New York. (variously paged)

Urlanis, B.Ts. (or C.) 1960. *Wars and population in Europe. Losses of human lives in the armed forces of European countries during the last three and a half centuries*. (Russian) Izdat. Social Econ. Lit., Moscow. 567 pp.

Urlanis, B.Ts. (or C.) 1971. *Wars and population*. (Russian) Progress Publishers, Moscow. 320 pp.

US National Academy of Sciences 1988. *Confront-ing AIDS. Update 1988*. National Academy Press, Washington, DC. xii + 239.

US National Center for Health Statistics, US Dept. Health, Education and Welfare, Washington, DC. and Rockville, MD.

——1964a. *The change in mortality trend in the United States*. Ser. 3, No. 1. 43 pp.

——1964b. *Recent mortality trends in Chile*. Ser. 3, No. 2. 34 pp.

——1965a. *Changes in mortality trends in England and Wales 1931–1961*. (Hubert Campbell) Ser. 3, No. 3. 49 pp.

——1965b. *Infant and perinatal mortality in the United States*. Ser. 3, No. 4. iv + 87.

——1965c. *Infant mortality trends, United States and each state, 1930–1964*. Ser. 20, No. 1. ii + 70.

——1965d. *Weight at birth and survival of the newborn in the United States, early 1950*. Ser. 21, No. 3. 33 pp.

——1965e. *Weight at birth and survival of the newborn by age of mother and total birth order, United States, early 1950*. Ser. 21, No. 5. pp. 21–73.

——1965f. *Weight at birth and cause of death in the neonatal period, United States, early 1950*. Ser. 21, No. 6. pp. 223–99.

——1966a. *Infant and perinatal mortality in Scotland*. (Charlotte A. Douglas) Ser. 3, No. 5. 44 pp.

——1966b. *Mortality trends in the United States, 1954–1963*. Ser. 20, No. 2. vi + 57.

——1966c. *Infant, fetal, and maternal mortality, United States, 1963*. Ser. 20, No. 3. vi + 64.

——1967a. *Infant mortality problems in Norway*. Ser. 3, No. 8. 40 pp.

——1967b. *Infant and perinatal mortality in Denmark*. Ser. 3, No. 9. 67 pp.

——1967c. *Multiple births, United States, 1964*. Ser. 21, No. 14. ii + 49.

——1968a. *Recent retardation of mortality trends in Japan*. Ser. 3, No. 10. vi + 28.

——1968b. *Infant loss in the Netherlands*. Ser. 3, No. 11. 63 pp.

——1968c. *Infant and perinatal mortality in England and Wales*. Ser. 3, No. 12. 77 pp.

——1969. *Mortality trends in Czechoslovakia*. Ser. 3, No. 13. ii + 26.

——1970. *Annotated bibliography on vital and health statistics*. Public Health Serv. Publ. No. 2094. vii + 143.

——1972. *Cohort mortality and survivorship: United States death-registration States, 1900–1968*. Ser. 3, No. 16. iii + 36.

US Office on Smoking and Health 1983. *Bibliography on smoking and health*. (In collaboration with WHO.) Public Health Serv. Bibliog. Ser. No. 45,

DHHS (PHS) 84-50196. US Govt Printing Office, Rockville, MD. v + 573.

US Public Health Service 1972. *Bibliography on smoking and health.* Natl. Clearinghouse for Smoking and Health, Bethesda, MD. Supt Documents, Washington, DC. iv + 314.

US Public Health Service 1974. *Bibliography on smoking and health 1973.* DHEW No. 74-8719. Supt Documents, Washington, DC. iv + 330.

US Surgeon-General 1964. *Smoking and health. Report of the Advisory Committee to the Surgeon-General of the Public Health Service.* US Dept Health, Education and Welfare, Washington, DC. xvii + 387.

US Surgeon-General 1979. *Smoking and health: A report of the Surgeon-General.* DHEW No. (PHS) 79-50066. Supt Documents, Washington, DC. xxxi + variously paged.

US Surgeon-General 1982. *The health consequences of smoking. Cancer.* US Dept Health and Human Services, Washington, DC. xix + 322.

USA/USSR Joint Symposium 1980. *Sudden cardiac death. Second USA/USSR Joint Symposium, Indianapolis, Ind., 1979.* NIH Publ. No. 81-2101, National Heart, Lung and Blood Institute, Bethesda, MD. xiii + 323.

Utterström, G.O. 1954. Some population problems in preindustrial Sweden. *Scand. Econ. Hist. Rev.* 2, 103–65.

Utterström, G. (O.) 1955. Climatic fluctuations and population problems in early modern history. *Scand. Econ. Hist. Rev.* 3, 1–47.

Utterström, G. (O.) 1961. Population and agriculture in Sweden circa 1700–1830. *Scand. Econ. Hist. Rev. 9*, 176–94.

Utterström, G. (O.) 1965. Two essays on population in eighteenth-century Scandinavia. I. A survey of some recent work and current problems. II. An outline of some population changes in Sweden ca 1660–1750 and a discussion of some current issues. pp. 523–48 in Glass and Eversley.

Uwaifo, A.O. and Bababunmi, E.A. 1984. Liver carcinogenesis in tropical Africa. pp. 59–88 in Williams, O'Conor, et al.

Vaeth, J.M. (Ed.) 1985. *Cancer and AIDS. From a symposium, San Francisco, 1984.* Frontiers of Radiation Therapy and Oncology, vol. 19. Karger, Basel. x + 184.

Vainio, H., Sorsa, M., and Hemminki, K. (Eds.) 1979. *Occupational cancer and carcinogenesis.* Hemisphere, Washington, DC. vi + 422.

Valberg, L.S. and Ghent, C.N. 1985. Diagnosis and management of hereditary hemochromatosis. *Annu. Rev. Med. 36*, 27–37.

Vallaux, C. 1924. Les raz de marée. *Matér. Etude Calam.* (Geneva) *4*, 333–

Vallin, J. 1972. La mortalité par génération en France depuis 1899: Présentation d'un cahier de l'INED. *Population 27*, 979–84.

Vallin, J. 1974. La table de mortalité française 1966–1970. *Population 29*, 553–77.

Vallin, J. 1976a. World trends in infant mortality since 1950. *World Health Stat. Rep. 29*, 646–74.

Vallin, J. 1976b. La mortalité infantile dans le monde. Evolution depuis 1950. *Population 31*, 801–38.

Vallin, J. and Chesnais, J.-C. 1975. Les accidents de la route en France. Mortalité et morbidité depuis 1953. *Population 30*, 433–78.

Vallin, J. and Lopez, A. 1985. La lutte contre la mort: l'Influence des politiques sociales et des politiques de santé sur l'évolution de la mortalité. (A review of INED/PUF, 1984.) *Population 40*, 347–55.

Vallin, J. and Nizard, A. 1978. Les causes de décès en France, I. Pour une typologie simple et homogène; application à la période 1968–1974. *Population 33*, 547–608.

Vallois, H.V. 1937. La durée de la vie chez l'homme fossile. *L'Anthropologie 47*, 499–532.

Valpy, R. 1851. Vital statistics of Geneva: An abridged translation from the French of M. Edouard Mallet. *J. Stat. Soc. (London) 14*, 298–337.

Valverius, M.R. 1981. Alcohol and mortality. With discussion. pp. 314–27 in Boström and Ljungstedt.

Vasiliev, K.G. and Segal, A.E. 1960. *History of epidemics in Russia.* (Russian) State Publ. Med. Lit., Moscow. 396 pp.

Vaughan, W.E. and Fitzpatrick, A.J. 1978. *Irish historical statistics: Population, 1812–1971.* Royal Irish Academy, Dublin. xxiii + 372.

Vaughan, W.T. 1921. *Influenza: An epidemiological study.* Am. J. Hyg. Monograph Ser. No. 1. 260 pp.

Vedel-Petersen, K.O. 1923. Losses of life caused by war. Part II—the World War. pp. 129–91 in Westergaard.

Vedin, J.A., Wilhelmsson, C.E., Bolander, A.M., and Werkö, L. 1970. Mortality trends in Sweden 1951–1968 with special reference to cardiovascular causes of death. *Acta. Med. Scand.* Suppl. 515, 76 pp.

Vedrenne-Villeneuve, E. 1961. L'inégalité sociale devant la mort dans la première moitié du XIXe siècle. *Population 16*, 665–98.

Verkko, V. 1951. *Homicides and suicides in Finland and their dependence on national character.* G.E.C. Gad, Copenhagen. 189 pp.

Villermé, L.R. 1828. Mémoire sur la mortalité en France, dans la classe aisée et dans la classe indigène. *Mém. de l'Acad. Roy. de Méd.* 1, 51 ff.

Vilquin, E. 1978. La mortalité infantile selon le mois de naissance. Le cas de la Belgique au XIXe siècle. *Population 33*, 1137–53.

Vincent, P. 1946. Conséquences de six années de guerre sur la population française. *Population 1*, 429–40.

Vincent, P. 1947. Guerre et population. *Population 2*, 9–30.

Vincent, P. 1951. La mortalité des vieillards. *Population 6*, 181–204.

Vincent, P. 1973. La mortalité des grands vieillards. *Population 28*, 755–92.

Vint, F.W. 1936–1937. Postmortem findings in the natives of Kenya. *East Afr. Med. J. 13*, 332–40.

Vita, V.T. de, Hellman, S. and Rosenburg, S.A. (Eds.) 1985. *AIDS: Etiology, diagnosis, treatment and prevention.* J.B. Lippincott, Philadelphia, xiv + 352.

Vlodaver, Z., Amplatz, K., Burchell, H.B., and Edwards, J.E. 1976. *Coronary heart disease.* Springer, New York. xvi + 584.

Voe, I.W. de 1982. The meningococcus and mechanisms of pathogenicity. *Microbiol. Rev. 46*, 162–90.

Vogel, F. 1979. 'Our load of mutation': Reappraisal of an old problem. *Proc. Roy. Soc. London B205*, 77–90. Reprinted in Doll and McLean.

Vogel, F. and Motulsky, A.G. 1982. *Human genetics. Problems and approaches.* Springer, Berlin-Heidelberg-New York. xxviii + 700.

Vogel, L.C., Muller, A.S., Odingo, R.S., Onyango, Z., and de Geus, A. (Eds.) 1974. *Health and disease in Kenya.* East African Literature Bureau, Nairobi-Dar es Salaam-Kampala. xvi + 529.

Vogel, M.J. 1980. *The invention of the modern hospital.* University of Chicago Press, Chicago. x + 172.

Vogelsang, Th. M. 1965. Leprosy in Norway. *Med. Hist. 9*, 30–35.

Voight, B. (Ed.) 1978. *Rockslides and avalanches. Part 1. Natural phenomena.* Dev. in Geotech. Eng. 14A. Elsevier, New York. xviii + 834.

Volk, B.W. and Arquilla, E.R. (Eds.) 1985. *The diabetic pancreas.* 2nd edition. Plenum, New York. xxiv + 628.

Waard, F. de 1982. Uterine corpus. pp. 901–08 in Schottenfeld and Fraumeni.

Wagoner, J.K., Archer, V., Carol, B.E., Holaday, D.A., and Lawrence, P.A. 1964. Cancer mortality patterns among United States uranium miners and millers, 1950 through 1962. *J. Natl. Cancer Inst. 32*, 787–801.

Wain, H. 1970. *A history of preventive medicine.* C.C. Thomas, Springfield, IL. x + 407.

Waksman, S.A. 1964. *The conquest of tuberculosis.* University of California Press, Berkeley. xiv + 241.

Walcher, D.N. and Kretchmer, N. (Eds.) 1981. *Food, nutrition and evolution: Food as an environmental factor in the genesis of human variability.* Masson, New York. xi + 234.

Walcher, D.N., Kretchmer, N., and Barnett, H.L. (Eds.) 1976. *Food, man, and society.* Plenum, New York. xv + 288.

Wald, N.J. 1976. Mortality from lung cancer and coronary heart disease in relation to changes in smoking habits. *Lancet 1*, 136–38.

Walford, C. 1878–1879/1970. *The famines of the world: Past and present.* [Being two papers read before the Statistical Society of London in 1878 and 1879 respectively and reprinted from its Journal.] Burt Franklin, New York. 303 pp.

Walford, C. 1881. On the number of deaths from accident, negligence, violences, and misadventure in the United Kingdom and some other countries. *J. Stat. Soc. (London) 44*, 444–527.

Walford, R.L. 1983. *Maximum life span.* Avon, New York. xvi + 256.

Walker, A. 1981. South African black, Indian and coloured populations. pp. 285–318 in Trowell and Burkitt, 1981a.

Walker, J.B. 1964. Diabetes in a village community. pp. 5–17 in *Aetiology of diabetes mellitus and its complications.* M.P. Cameron and M. O'Connor, Eds. Ciba Foundation Colloquia on Endocrinology, vol. 15. Churchill, London. xiv + 405.

Walker, W.J. 1977. Changing United States lifestyle and declining vascular mortality: Cause or coincidence? *N. Engl. J. Med. 297*, 163–65.

Wall, R. (Ed.) 1973a. *Comparative statistics in the 19th century.* Gregg International, London. 400 pp.

Wall, R. (Ed.) 1973b. *Slum conditions in London and Dublin.* Gregg International, London. 256 pp.

Wall, R. (Ed.) 1973c. *Mortality in mid 19th century Britain.* Gregg International, London. 212 pp.

Wallace, R. 1753. *A dissertation on the numbers of mankind in ancient and modern times . . . with an appendix . . . containing . . . additional observations, and some remarks on Mr. Hume's political* discourse, Of the Populousness of Ancient Nations. G. Hamilton and J. Balfour, Edinburgh. iv + 331.

Wallace, R. 1761. *Various prospects of mankind, nature and Providence*. A. Millar, London. viii + 406.

Walle, E. van de 1974. Mortalité de l'enfance au XIXe siècle à Paris et dans le Département de la Seine. *Population 29*, 89–107.

Walsh, B. and Grant, M. 1985. International trends in alcohol production and consumption: Implications for public health. *World Health Stat. Q. 38*, 130–41.

Walsh, J. 1983. Human helminthic and protozoan infections in the north. pp. 45–61 in Warren and Bowers.

Walsh, J.A. and Warren, K.S. 1979. Selective primary health care: An interim strategy for disease control in developing countries. *N. Engl. J. Med. 301*, 967–74.

Wangensteen, O.H. 1970. Nineteenth century wound management of the parturient uterus and compound fracture: The Semmelweis-Lister priority controversy. *Bull. N.Y. Acad. Med. 46*, 565–96.

Wangensteen, O.H. and Wangensteen, S.D. 1978. *The rise of surgery. From empiric craft to scientific discipline*. Dawson, Folkstone; University of Minnesota Press, Minneapolis. xviii + 785.

Wangensteen, O.H., Wangensteen, S.D., and Klinger, C.F. 1973. Some pre-Listerian and post-Listerian antiseptic wound practices and the emergence of asepsis. *Surg. Gynecol. Obstet. 137*, 677–702.

War Office 1948. *Statistical report on the health of the Army, 1943–1945*. HMSO, London. 204 pp.

Ward, A.A. Jr, Penry, J.K., and Purpura, D.P. (Eds.) 1983. *Epilepsy*. Research Publns: Assoc. for Research in Nervous and Mental Disease, vol. 61. Raven, New York. xii + 404.

Wargentin, P.W. 1766/1930. Mortaliteten i Sverige, i anledning af Tabell-Verket. *Kongl. Vetenskaps Acad. Handlingar 27*. Reprinted as *Tables of mortality based upon the Swedish population, prepared and presented in 1766 by Per Wilhelm Wargentin*, 1930. Thule Life Insurance Co., I. Haeggström, Stockholm. 68 pp.

Warkany, J. and Kalter, H. 1961. Congenital malformations. *N. Engl. J. Med. 265*. 993–1001, 1046–52.

Warner, F. 1979. Sources and extent of pollution. *Proc. Roy. Soc. London B205*, 5–15. Reprinted in Doll and McLean.

Warner, J.H. 1986. *The therapeutic perspective.*

Medical practice, knowledge and identity in America, 1820–1885*. Harvard University Press, Cambridge, MA. xii + 367.

Warren, K.S. and Bowers, J.Z. (Eds.) 1983. *Parasitology. A global perspective*. Springer, New York-Berlin-Heidelberg-Tokyo. vii + 292.

Warren, K.S. and Mahmoud, A.A.F. (Eds.) 1984. *Tropical and geographical medicine*. McGraw-Hill, New York. xvii + 1175.

Warren, K.S. and Purcell, E.F. (Eds.) 1982. *The current status and future of parasitology*. Josiah Macy Jr Found., New York. 298 pp.

Washington, A.E., Mandell, G.L., and Wiesner, P.J. 1982. Editorial (to a Symposium). Treatment of sexually transmitted diseases: New additions to an old tradition. *Rev. Infect. Dis. 4*, S727–S728.

Water Development 1978. *Water development and management: Proceedings of a conference, Mar del Plata, Argentina, 1977*. Water Development, Supply and Management, vol. 1. Pergamon Press, New York. lxxxviii + 2646.

Waterhouse, J., Shanmugaratnam, K., Muir, C., and Powell, J. (Eds.) 1982. *Cancer incidence in five continents*. Vol. 4. IARC Sci. Publn No. 42. International Agency for Research on Cancer, Lyon. WHO Publns Center USA, Albany NY. 812 pp.

Waterlow, J.C. (Scientific Ed.) 1981. Nutrition of man. *Br. Med. Bull. 37*, 1–103.

Waters, M.F.R. 1984. Leprosy (Hansen's disease). *Rec. Adv. Trop. Med. 1*, 229–51. See Gilles, 1984.

Waterson, A.P. and Wilkinson, L. 1978. *An introduction to the history of virology*. Cambridge University Press, London. xiv + 237.

Watson, D.H. 1984. The herpesviruses. pp. 183–212 in Topley and Wilson, 1984, vol. 4.

Watson Cheyne, W. (Ed.) 1886. *Recent essays by various authors on bacteria in relation to disease*. New Sydenham Society, London. xvi + 650.

Watt, J., Freeman, E.J., and Bynum, W.F. (Eds.) 1981. *Starving sailors: The influence of nutrition upon naval and maritime history*. National Maritime Museum, London. xiv + 212.

Watt, R. 1813. *Treatise on the history, nature and treatment of chincough: Including a variety of cases and dissections. To which is subjoined, an inquiry into the relative mortality of the principal diseases of children, and the numbers who have died under ten years of age, in Glasgow, during the last thirty years*. John Smith & Son, Glasgow. 392 pp.

Watts, M. 1983. *Silent violence: Food, famine and peasantry in Northern Nigeria*. University of California Press, Berkeley. xxxii + 687.

Weatherall, D.J. 1980. Toward an understanding of the molecular biology of some common inherited anemias: The story of thalassemia. pp. 373–414 in Wintrobe.

Weatherall, D.J., Abdalla, S. and Pippard, M.J. 1983. The anaemia of *Plasmodium falciparum* malaria. pp. 74–97 in Evered and Whelan.

Weatherall, D.J. and Clegg, J.B. 1981. *The Thalassaemia syndromes.* 3rd edition. Blackwell, Oxford. xii + 875.

Webb, S. and Webb, B. 1922. *English prisons under local government.* (With preface by Bernard Shaw). Longmans, London. lxxvi + 261.

Webster, C. (Ed.) 1979. *Health, medicine and mortality in the sixteenth century.* Cambridge University Press, New York. xiv + 394.

Webster, L.T. 1946. Experimental epidemiology. *Medicine 25,* 77–109.

Webster, N. 1799. *A brief history of epidemic and pestilential diseases, with the principal phenomena of the physical world which precede and accompany them and observations deduced from the facts stated.* Hudson and Goodwin, Hartford. 2 vols.

Wedeen, R.P. 1984. *Poison in the pot. The legacy of lead.* Southern Illinois University Press, Carbondale, IL. xii + 275.

Weill, H. and Diem, J. 1978. Relationships between cigarette smoking and occupational pulmonary disease. *Bull. Eur. Physiopathol. Respir. 14,* 137–43. Reprinted in Brooks, Lockey, and Harber, 1981.

Weill, H. and Turner-Warwick, M. (Eds.) 1981. *Occupational lung diseases: Research approaches and methods.* Lung Biology in Health and Disease, vol. 18. Dekker, New York. 504 pp.

Weinberg, E.D. 1978. Iron and infection. *Microbiol. Rev. 42,* 45–66.

Weinman, D. 1944. Infectious anemias due to *Bartonella* and related red cell parasites. *Trans. Am. Philos. Soc.* N.S. *33* (3), 242–350.

Weinman, D. 1977. Trypanosomiases of man and macaques in South Asia. pp. 329–55 in Kreier, vol. 1.

Weinman, D. and Kreier, J.P. 1977. *Bartonella and Grahamella.* pp. 197–233 in Kreier, vol. 4.

Weinstein, L. (Ed.) 1976. *Teratology and congenital malformations: A comprehensive guide to the literature.* Plenum, New York. 3 vols. 1598 pp.

Weisman, A.I. 1966. Syphilis: Was it endemic in pre-Columbian America or was it brought here from Europe? *Bull. N.Y. Acad. Med. 42,* 284–300.

Weiss, N.S. 1976. Recent trends in violence deaths among young adults in the United States. *Am. J. Epidemiol. 103,* 416–22.

Weiss, N.S. 1982. Ovary. pp. 871–80 in Schottenfeld and Fraumeni.

W(elch), W.H. 1877. The hospitals of Berlin. *Clinic (Cincinnati). 13,* 130–32.

Weller, T.H. 1982. Varicella-herpes zoster virus. pp. 569–95 in Evans.

Wells, C. 1964. *Bones, bodies and disease.* Ancient Peoples and Places, 37. Thames and Hudson, London. 288 pp.

Welton, T.A. 1875. The effect of migrations upon death-rates. *J. Stat. Soc. (London) 38,* 324–34.

Welton, T.A. 1880. On certain changes in the English rates of mortality. With discussion. *J. Stat. Soc. (London) 43,* 65–94.

Welton, T.A. 1897. Local death-rates in England and Wales in the ten years 1881–90. *J. Roy. Stat. Soc. 60,* 33–75.

Welton, T.A. 1911. *England's recent progress: An investigation of the statistics of migration, mortality, etc. in the twenty years from 1881 to 1901, as indicating tendencies towards the growth or decay of particular communities.* Chapman and Hall, London. lxiv + 742.

Welton, T.A. 1916a. On the birth-rates in various parts of England and Wales in 1911, 1912 and 1913. *J. Roy. Stat. Soc. 79,* 18–36.

Welton, T.A. 1916b. On the death-rates in various parts of England and Wales in 1913. *J. Roy. Stat. Soc. 79,* 37–54.

Welton, T.A. 1917. Note on the birth- and death-rates in various parts of England and Wales in 1915. *J. Roy. Stat. Soc. 80,* 521–28.

Wenger, N.K. 1985. Coronary disease in women. *Annu. Rev. Med. 36,* 285–94.

Wentworth, B.B. 1955. Historical review of the literature on Q fever. *Bacteriol. Rev. 19,* 129–49.

Wernsdorfer, W.H. 1984. Drug resistant malaria. *Endeavour 8,* 166–71.

West, K. 1981. North American Indians. pp. 129–37 in Trowell and Burkitt, 1981a.

West, R. 1984. Childhood cancer mortality: International comparisons 1955–1974. *World Health Stat. Q. 37,* 98–127.

Westergaard, H. 1880. Mortality in remote corners of the world. *J. Stat. Soc. (London) 43,* 509–20.

Westergaard, H. 1881. Notes on the mortality of the Danish clergy, from 1650 to 1878. *J. Inst. Actuar. 23,* 29–40.

Westergaard, H. 1882. *Die Lehre von der Mortalität und Morbilität, anthropologisch-statistische Untersuchungen.* G. Fischer, Jena. vii + 504. 2nd edition, 1901.

Westergaard, H.(L.) 1887. *Kirkelig statistik, med saerligt henblik paa Danmark.* [Ecclesiastical statistics with special reference to Denmark.] Copenhagen. 54 pp.

Westergaard, H.(L.) 1899. Mortality in extreme old age. *Econ. J. 9*, 315–22.

Westergaard, H. (Ed.) 1916. *Losses of life in modern wars. Austria-Hungary, 1618–1913* (G. Bodart); *France, 1614–1913* (G. Bodart); *Military selection and race deterioration* (V.L. Kellogg). Carnegie Endowment for International Peace. Clarendon, Oxford. 207 + 6.

Westergaard. H. (Ed.) 1923. *Losses of life caused by war.* (S. Dumas and K.O. Vedel-Petersen). Carnegie Endowment for International Peace. Clarendon, Oxford. 191 pp.

Westergaard, H. 1932. *Coontributions to the history of statistics.* P.S. King & Son, London. vii + 280. Reprinted 1969, Mouton, Paris, and S.R. Publishers, Wakefield, England.

Westermann, W.L. 1942. Industrial slavery in Roman Italy. *J. Econ. Hist. 2*, 149–63.

Westermanns Atlas 1956. *Westermanns Atlas zur Weltgeschichte.* H.-E. Stier, et al. (Eds.). Georg Westermann Verlag, Braunschweig. viii + 160.

Western, K.A. 1972. *The epidemiology of natural and manmade disasters: The present state of the art.* Dissertation for Academic Diploma in Tropical Public Health, London School of Hygiene and Tropical Medicine. 123 pp. Unpublished. See D.H. Manning (1976), *Disaster technology: An annotated bibliography*, Pergamon Press, Oxford. pp. 5–8.

Wharton, J.C. 1982. *Crusaders for fitness. The history of American health reformers.* Princeton University Press, Princeton, NJ. xii + 360.

Wheatcroft, S.G. 1984. Famine and epidemic crises in Russia, 1918–1922: The case of Saratov. *Ann. Démog. Hist. 1983*, 329–52.

White, C. 1773. *A treatise on the management of pregnant and lying-in women.* Reprinted 1777, 1784, 1791. Also reprinted in J.G. Adami, *Charles White of Manchester (1728–1813) and the arrest of puerperal fever*, Hodder & Stoughton, London, 1922, 142 pp. and in Churchill, 1850.

White, P.J. 1958. Mortality from hydatid disease in Victoria, 1853–1956. *Med. J. Austral. 2*, 378–81.

Whitelegge, B.A. 1892–1983. Measles epidemics, major and minor. *Trans. Epidemiol. Soc. London* N.S. *12*, 37–54.

Whitford, H.W. 1979. Anthrax. pp. 31–66 in *CRC Handbook Series in Zoonoses. Section A. Vol. 1.* J.H. Steele, Ed. CRC Press, Boca Raton, FL.

WHO-accidents 1965. Mortality from accidents, with special details of motor vehicle accidents, 1950–1962. *WHO Epidemiol. Vital Stat. Rep. 18*, 117–24.

WHO-America 1974. Childhood mortality in the Americas. *WHO Chron. 28*, 276–82.

WHO-apartheid 1983. *Apartheid and health. From a conference, Brazzaville, People's Republic of the Congo, 1981.* WHO, Geneva: WHO Publns Center USA, Albany, NY. 258 pp.

WHO-bibliography 1958. *Publications of the World Health Organization, 1947–1957.* WHO, Geneva; Columbia University Press, New York. 128 pp.

WHO-bibliography 1964. *Publications of the World Health Organization, 1958–1962.* WHO, Geneva. 125 pp.

WHO-bibliography 1969. *Publications of the World Health Organization, 1963–1967.* WHO, Geneva. 152 pp.

WHO-bibliography 1974. *Publications of the World Health Organization, 1968–1972: A bibliography.* WHO, Geneva. 158 pp.

WHO-bibliography 1980. *World Health Organization publications: catalogue 1947–1979.* WHO, Geneva. v + 132.

WHO-bibliography 1984. *World Health Organization publications: Catalogue 1947–1979. Supplement 1980–1984*, 2nd edition. WHO, Geneva. 113 pp.

WHO-breast feeding 1982. The prevalence and duration of breast feeding: A critical review of available information (by the Division of Family Health, WHO). *World Health Stat. Q. 35*, 92–116.

WHO-Chagas' disease 1960. *Chagas' disease: Report of a study group.* WHO Tech. Rep. Ser. No. 202. WHO, Geneva. 21 pp.

WHO-death 1980. The inequality of death: Assessing socioeconomic influences on mortality. *WHO Chron. 34*, 9–15.

WHO-developed 1974. The ten leading causes of death for selected countries in North America, Europe and Oceania, 1969, 1970, and 1971. *World Health Stat. Rep. 27*, 563–652.

WHO-diabetes 1955. Diabetes mellitus: A critical note on mortality statistics. Annex II: Comments referring to particular countries. *WHO Epidemiol. Vital Stat. Rep. 8*, 467–512

WHO-diphtheria 1952. World incidence of diphtheria during recent years. *WHO Epidemiol. Vital Stat. Rep. 5*, 223–42.

WHO-Director-General 1970. *The work of WHO, 1970: Annual Report of the Director-General to the World Health Assembly and to the United Nations.* WHO, Geneva. xvii + 306.

WHO-epilepsy 1955. Some numerical data on epilepsy: Critical note on the available statistics. *WHO Epidemiol. Vital Stat. Rep. 8*, 169–93.

WHO-Europe 1952. Deaths by cause, sex and age in Europe and in some non-European countries. *WHO Epidemiol. Vital Stat. Rep. 5*, 371–568.

WHO-family health 1980. The incidence of low birth weight: A critical survey of available information. *World Health Stat. Q. 33*, 197–224.

WHO-forecast 1974. Health trends and prospects, 1950–2000. *World Health Stat. Rep. 27*, 670–706.

WHO-genetics 1964. *Human genetics and public health. Second report of the Expert Committee on Human Genetics*. WHO Tech. Rep. Ser. No. 282. WHO, Geneva. 38 pp.

WHO-goitre 1960. *Endemic goitre*. WHO Monogr. Ser. No. 44. WHO, Geneva. 471 pp.

WHO-health statistics 1969. *Statistics of health services and of their activities: Thirteenth report of WHO Expert Committee on Health Statistics*. WHO Tech. Rep. Ser. No. 429. WHO, Geneva. 36 pp.

WHO-Hodgkin's disease 1955. Mortality from Hodgkin's disease and from leukaemia and aleukaemia. *WHO Epidemiol. Vital Stat. Rep. 8*, 81–114.

WHO-infant 1970. Infant mortality. *World Health Stat. Rep. 23*, 777–835.

WHO-infant 1976. Mortality and the life cycle of the family: Some implications of recent research. *World Health Stat. Rep. 29*, 220–34.

WHO-infant 1981. Summary of the ad hoc survey on infant and early childhood mortality in Sierra Leone. *World Health Stat. Q. 34*, 220–38.

WHO-influenza 1953. 1952–53 influenza epidemic in the Northern Hemisphere. *WHO Epidemiol. Vital Stat. Rep. 6*, 203–19.

WHO-malaria 1969. *Parasitology of malaria*. WHO Tech. Rep. Ser. No. 433. WHO, Geneva. 70 pp.

WHO-malaria 1974. The malaria situation in 1973. *WHO Chron. 28*, 479–87.

WHO-malaria 1975*a*. The malaria situation in 1974. *WHO Chron. 29*, 474–81.

WHO-malaria 1975*b*. Six-monthly information on the world malaria situation, January–December 1973. *WHO Weekly Epidemiol. Rec. 50*, Nos. 6–7, pp. 53–69, 76–86.

WHO-malaria 1978. The malaria situation in 1976. *WHO Chron. 32*, 9–17.

WHO-malaria 1983. World malaria situation 1981. *WHO Weekly Epidemiol. Rec. 58*, Nos. 25–30, pp. 189–92. 198–99, 206–09, 214–16, 222–24, 232–33.

WHO-malaria 1984. The world malaria situation, 1982. *World Health Stat. Q. 37*, 130–61.

WHO-malaria 1985. World malaria situation 1983. Malaria Action Programme, WHO, Geneva. *World Health Stat. Q. 38*, 193–231.

WHO-malaria 1986. World malaria situation 1984. *World Health Stat. Q. 39*, 171–205.

WHO-manual 1948–1949. *Manual of the International Statistical Classification of Diseases, Injuries and Causes of Death: Sixth Revision of the International Lists of Diseases and Causes of Death as Adopted, 1948*. Vol. 1, 1948; vol. 2, *Alphabetical Index*, 1949. WHO, Geneva. xxxix + 376, xxviii + 524.

WHO-manual 1967–1969. *Manual of the International Statistical Classification of Diseases, Injuries and Causes of Death: Eighth Revision, 1965*. Vol. 1, 1967; vol. 2, 1969. WHO, Geneva. xxxiii + 478; xiv + 616.

WHO-manual 1977–1978. *Manual of the International Statistical Classification of Diseases, Injuries and Causes of Death. Based on the recommendations of the Ninth Revision Conference, 1975, and adopted by the twenty-ninth World Health Assembly*. Vol. 1, 1977; vol. 2, *Alphabetical Index*, 1978. WHO, Geneva. xxxiii + 773; xii + 659.

WHO-measles 1952. Measles, its recent trend. *WHO Epidemiol. Vital Stat. Rep. 5*, 332–42.

WHO-meningitis 1952. Cerebro-spinal meningitis, its recent trend. *WHO Epidemiol. Vital Stat. Rep. 5*, 617–23.

WHO-milk 1962. *Milk hygiene: Hygiene in milk production, processing and distribution*. WHO Monogr. Ser. No. 48. WHO, Geneva. 782 pp.

WHO-mortality 1977. *Manual of mortality analysis. WHO, Geneva. 245 pp.*

WHO-mortality 1978. Life table and mortality analysis. WHO, Geneva. xiv + 399.

WHO-neoplasms 1963. *Bibliography on the epidemiology of cancer, 1946–1960*. WHO, Geneva. 168 pp.

WHO-neoplasms 1970. *Mortality from malignant neoplasms, 1955–1965*. WHO, Geneva. 1147 pp.

WHO-neoplasms 1974. Malignant neoplasms according to site, by sex and age—Morbidity statistics. Parts I & II. *World Health Stat. Rep. 27*, 239–361, 393–487.

WHO-paralysis agitans 1955. Mortality from paralysis agitans (Parkinson's disease). *WHO Epidemiol. Vital Stat. Rep. 8*, 320–31.

WHO-parasitic 1986. Major parasitic infections: A global review. *World Health Stat. Q. 39*, 145–60.

WHO-perinatal 1970. *Report of the WHO Expert Committee on the Prevention of Perinatal Mortality and Morbidity*. WHO Tech. Rep. Ser. No.

457. WHO, Geneva. 60 pp.

WHO-perinatal 1972. *The prevention of perinatal morbidity and mortality*. Public Health Paper No. 42. WHO, Geneva. Amer. Publ. Hlth Assoc., Washington, DC. 100 pp.

WHO-perinatal 1976. Comparative study of social and biological effects on perinatal mortality. *World Health Stat. Rep. 29*, 228–34.

WHO-perinatal 1978. Main findings of the comparative study of social and biological effects on perinatal mortality. *World Health Stat. Q. 31*, 74–83.

WHO-perinatal 1980. The incidence of low birth weight: A critical review of available information. *World Health Stat. Q. 33*, 197–224.

WHO-perinatal and child 1976. Commentary on the ad hoc surveys on foetal, infant and early childhood mortality and fertility patterns. *World Health Stat. Rep. 29*, 438–57.

WHO-plague 1979. Human plague in 1958–1978: Incidence down but urgent tasks remain. *WHO Chron. 33*, p. 426.

WHO-plague 1980. Plague surveillance and control. *WHO Chron. 34*, 139–43.

WHO-poliomyelitis 1951. The incidence of poliomyelitis in the world in 1950. *WHO Epidemiol. Vital Stat. Rep. 4*, 2–11.

WHO-poliomyelitis 1953. World incidence of poliomyelitis in 1952. *WHO Epidemiol. Vital Stat. Rep. 6*, 87–99.

WHO-pollution 1961. *Air pollution*. WHO Monogr. Ser. No. 46. WHO, Geneva. 442 pp. (esp. pp. 159–220).

WHO-respiratory 1980. *Viral respiratory diseases*. WHO Tech. Rep. Ser. No. 642. WHO, Geneva. 63 pp.

WHO-rheumatic 1963. Mortality and morbidity from chronic rheumatic diseases in the United Kingdom and Western Europe. pp. 1–11 in Jeffrey and Ball.

WHO-scarlet fever. 1951. The trend of scarlet fever in recent years. *WHO Epidemiol. Vital Stat. Rep. 4*, 354–66.

WHO-scarlet fever 1952. Scarlet fever, its recent trend. *WHO Epidemiol. Vital Stat. Rep. 5*, 624–29.

WHO-schistosomiasis 1959. Nature and extent of the problem of bilharziasis. *WHO Chron. 13*, 2–56.

WHO-schistosomiasis 1980. *Epidemiology and control of schistosomiasis. Report of a WHO Expert Committee*. WHO Tech. Rep. Ser. No. 643. WHO, Geneva. 63 pp.

WHO-schizophrenia 1975. *Schizophrenia: A multinational study*. [A summary of: *Report of the International Pilot Study of Schizophrenia. Vol. 1, Results of the initial evaluation phase*. WHO Offset Publn No. 2. 427 pp. (1973).] Publ. Hlth Paper No. 63. WHO, Geneva. 151 pp.

WHO-smallpox 1953. A study of smallpox endemicity in the world during 1936–1950. *WHO Epidemiol. Vital Stat. Rep. 6*, 227–43.

WHO-smallpox 1955. Deaths from smallpox in certain countries since the beginning of the century. *WHO Epidemiol. Vital Stat. Rep. 8*, 57–72.

WHO-smallpox 1975. Smallpox in 1974. *WHO Chron. 29*, 134–39.

WHO-smallpox 1980. *The global eradication of smallpox. Final report of the Global Commission for the Certification of Smallpox Eradication*. History of International Public Health, No. 4. WHO, Geneva. 121 pp.

WHO-tuberculosis 1980. Recent advances in the chemotherapy of tuberculosis. *WHO Chron. 34*, 101–03.

WHO-typhoid 1950. The incidence of typhoid and paratyphoid fevers in the world since 1947. *WHO Epidemiol. Vital Stat. Rep. 3*, 296–302.

WHO-ultraviolet 1979. *Ultraviolet radiation*. WHO, Geneva. 110 pp.

WHO-underdeveloped 1974. The ten leading causes of death for selected countries in Africa, South and Central America and Asia, 1969–1971. *World Health Stat. Rep. 27*, 150–88.

WHO-underdeveloped 1978. *A decade of health development in South-East Asia*. WHO Regional Office for South-East Asia, New Delhi. xx + 418.

WHO-venereal disease 1954. Some statistical data on venereal diseases: Syphilis, gonorrhoea, lymphogranuloma venereum. *WHO Epidemiol. Vital Stat. Rep. 7*, 373–418.

WHO-vital statistics 1985. Section B: Vital statistics and life tables. pp. 16–38 in *World Health Statistics Annual*. WHO, Geneva.

WHO-water 1976. Community water supply and excreta disposal in developing countries. Review of progress. *World Health Stat. Rep. 29*, 544–603.

WHO-whooping cough 1952. Whooping cough, its recent trend. *WHO Epidemiol. Vital Stat. Rep. 5*, 323–31.

WHO-world 1980. *Sixth Report on World Health Situation, 1973–77*. 1. *Global analysis*. vii + 290. 2. *Review by country and area*. vi + 412. WHO, Geneva.

WHO-yaws 1953. *First international symposium on yaws control, Bangkok, 1952*. WHO Monogr. Ser. No. 15. WHO Geneva. 418 pp.

WHO-yellow fever 1971. *WHO Expert Committee on Yellow Fever: Third report*. WHO Tech. Rep.

Ser. No. 479. WHO, Geneva. 56 pp.

Whorton, J. 1980. "Antibiotic abandon": The resurgence of therapeutic rationalism. pp. 125–36 in Parascandola.

Wicksell, S. 1934. Självmorden i statistisk belysning. [Suicides from the statistical point of view.] In *Om självmord* [On suicide] by S. Wicksell and T. Sondén. Svenska föreningens för psykisk hälsovård småskrifter, 7. Stockholm.

Widén, L. 1962. The development of mortality within different groups of causes of death in Sweden, 1951–1960. *Stat. Tidskrift 11*, 1–14.

Wigglesworth, V.B. 1976. *Insects and the life of man: Collected essays on pure science and applied biology*. Chapman and Hall, London, vi + 217.

Wightman, W.P.D. 1971. *The emergence of scientific medicine*. Oliver and Boyd, Edinburgh. 109 pp.

Wigley, T.M.L., Ingram, M.J., and Farmer, G. (Eds.) 1981. *Climate and history: Studies in past climates and their impact on man*. Cambridge University Press. xii + 530.

Wilbur, C.L. 1913. Correspondence: Still-births in relation to infantile mortality. *J. Roy. Stat. Soc. 76*, 544–46.

Wilcocks, C. 1962. *Aspects of medical investigation in Afrcia*. Oxford University Press, London. xiii + 120.

Wilhelmsen, L. 1981. Risk factors for disease according to population studies in Göteborg, Sweden. With discussion. pp. 73–88 in Boström and Ljungstedt.

Wilhelmsson, C., Vedin, A., Ulvenstam, G., Åberg, A., Johansson, S., and Wilhelmsen, L. 1981. Tobacco smoking and mortality from various causes. With discussion. pp. 328–44 in Boström and Ljungstedt.

Wilkerson, H.L.C. and Krall, L.P. 1947. Diabetes in a New England town: Study of 3, 516 persons in Oxford, Mass. *J. Am. Med. Assoc. 135*, 209–16.

Wilkerson, H.L.C. and Krall, L.P. 1953. Diabetes in a New England town: Report of 4 years progress study of Oxford, Mass. diabetes survey of 1946–1947. *J. Am. Med. Assoc. 152*, 1322–29.

Wilkerson, H.L.C., Krall, L.P. and Butler, F.K. 1959. Diabetes in a New England town. III. A comprehensive baseline study in Oxford, Mass. *J. Am. Med. Assoc. 169*, 910–14.

Wilkinson, A.E. 1984*a*. Gonorrhoea. pp. 382–90 in Topley and Wilson, 1984, vol. 3.

Wilkinson, A.E. 1984*b*. Syphilis, rabbit syphilis, yaws and pinta. pp. 543–57 in Topley and Wilson, 1984, vol. 3.

Wilkinson, L. 1981. Glanders: Medicine and veterinary medicine in common pursuit of a contagious disease. *Med. Hist. 25*, 363–84.

Willcox, W.F. 1918. The development of military sanitary statistics. *Am. Stat. Assoc. Q. Publ. 16*, 907–20.

Willcox, W.F. 1923. Population and the world war: A preliminary survey. *J. Am. Stat. Assoc. 18*, 699–712.

Willcox, W.F. 1928. Military losses in the World War. *J. Am. Stat. Assoc. 23*, 304–05.

Williams, A.O., O'Conor, G.T., de-Thé, G.B., and Johnson, C.A. 1984. *Virus-associated cancers in Africa*. Internatl. Agency for Research on Cancer, Lyon. xxxi + 774.

Williams, C.K.O. 1984. Some biological and epidemiological characteristics of human leukaemia in Africans. pp. 687–712 in Williams, O'Conor, et al.

Williams, C.K.O., Johnson, A.O.K., and Blattner, W.A. 1984. Human T-cell leukaemia virus in Africa: Possible roles in health and disease. pp. 713–44 in Williams, O'Conor, et al.

Williams, H.U. 1909. Epidemic among Indians, 1616–1620. *Johns Hopkins Hosp. Bull. 20* (224), 340–49.

Williams, R. and Davis, M. 1977. Alcoholic liver diseases — Basic pathology and clinical variants. pp. 157–78 in Edwards and Grant.

Williams. R.E.O. and Shooter, R.A. 1963. *Infections in hospitals: Epidemiology and control*. Blackwell, Oxford. xviii + 355.

Williams, S.V., Munford, R.S., Colton, T., Murphy, D.A., and Poskanzer, D.C. 1971. Mortality among physicians: A cohort study. *J. Chron. Dis. 24*, 393–401.

Williamson, J.G. 1984. British mortality and the value of life, 1781–1931. *Popul. Studies 38*, 157–72.

Willis, A.T. 1969. *Clostridia of wound infection*. Butterworth, London. ix + 470.

Wilson, B.J. and Hayes, A.W. 1973. Microbial toxins. pp. 372–423 in *Toxicants occurring naturally in foods*, 2nd edition, US Committee on Food Protection, Food and Nutrition Board, National Research Council. National Academy of Sciences, Washington, DC. vii + 624.

Wilson, C.A. 1974. *Food and drink in Britain: From the Stone Age to recent times*. Harper & Row, New York. 472 pp.

Wilson, D.B. 1949. Malaria incidence in Central and South Africa. pp. 800–09 in Boyd.

Wilson, E.B. 1947. The spread of measles in the family. *Proc. Natl. Acad. Sci. (USA). 33*, 68–72.

Wilson, E.B., Bennett, C., Allen, M., and Worcester, J. 1939. Measles and scarlet fever in Providence, R.I., 1929–1934 with respect to age and size of family. *Proc. Am. Philos. Soc. (Philadelphia) 80*, 357–476.

Wilson, G.N. 1905. Measles: Its prevalence and mortality in Aberdeen . *Public Health 18*, 65–82.

Wilson, G.S. 1962. Measles as a universal disease. *Am. J. Dis. Child. 103*, 219–24.

Wilson, G.S. 1967. *The hazards of immunization.* Athlone Press, University of London. x + 324.

Wilson, G.(S.) 1984a. General epidemiology. pp. 1–9 in Topley and Wilson, 1984, vol. 3.

Wilson, G.(S.) 1984b. Actinomycosis, actinobacillosis, and related diseases. pp. 10–22 in Topley and Wilson, 1984, vol. 3.

Wilson, G.(S.) 1984c. Bacterial meningitis. pp. 369–81 in Topley and Wilson, 1984, vol. 3.

Wilson, G.(S.) 1984d. Cholera. pp. 446–57 in Topley and Wilson, 1984, vol. 3.

Wilson, G.(S.) 1984e. Miscellaneous diseases: Granuloma venereum, soft chancre, cat-scratch fever, Legionnaires' disease, bartonella infections, and Lyme disease. pp. 515–22 in Topley and Wilson, 1984, vol. 3.

Wilson, G.(S.) and Coghlan, J. 1984. Spirochaetal and leptospiral diseases. pp. 523–42 in Topley and Wilson 1984, vol. 3.

Wilson, G.(S.) and Smith, G. 1984a. Leprosy, rat leprosy, sarcoidosis, and Johne's disease. pp. 62–72 in Topley and Wilson, 1984, vol. 3.

Wilson, G.(S.) and Smith, G. 1984b. Diphtheria and other diseases due to *Corynebacteria.* pp. 73–101 in Topley and Wilson, 1984, vol. 3.

Wilson, G.(S.) and Smith, G. 1984c. Anthrax. pp. 102–13 in Topley and Wilson, 1984, vol. 3.

Wilson, G.(S.) and Smith, G. 1984d. *Brucella* infections of man and animals, *Campylobacter* abortion, and contagious equine metritis. pp. 141–69 in Topley and Wilson, 1984, vol. 3.

Wilson, J.G. and Fraser, F.C. (Eds.) 1977–1978. *Handbook of teratology. Vol. 1, General principles and etiology; Vol. 2, Mechanisms and pathogenesis; Vol. 3, Comparative maternal and epidemiologic aspects; Vol. 4, Research procedures and data analysis.* Plenum, New York. 4 vols.

Wilson, L.G. 1978. Fevers and science in early nineteenth century medicine. *J. Hist. Med. 33*, 386–407.

Wilson, L.G. 1984. The internal secretions in disease: The historical relations of clinical medicine and scientific physiology. *J. Hist. Med. Allied Subj. 39*, 263–302.

Wilson, W.R. and Geraci, J.E. 1983. Antibiotic treatment of infective endocarditis. *Annu. Rev. Med. 34*, 413–27.

Wiltse, C.M. 1965. *The Medical Department: Medical service in the Mediterranean and minor theaters.* Part of *United States Army in World War II*, S. Conn, Gen. Ed., Subseries: *The Technical Services.* Office of Chief of Military History, Dept of the Army, Washington, DC. xxvi + 664.

Wing, E.S. and Brown, A.B. 1979. *Paleonutrition: Method and theory in prehistoric foodways.* Academic Press, London. xiv + 202.

Wingard, D.L. 1984. The sex differential in morbidity, mortality and lifestyle. *Annu. Rev. Public Health 5*, 433–58.

Winick, M. (Ed.) 1979. *Nutrition: pre- and postnatal development.* Vol. 1 of *Human nutrition: A comprehensive treatise*, R.B. Alfin-Slater and D. Kritchevsky, Gen. Eds. Plenum, New York. ix + 496.

Winick, M. (Ed.) 1981. *Nutrition and the killer diseases.* Wiley-Interscience, New York. viii + 191.

Winslow, C.E.A. 1943. *The conquest of epidemic diseases.* Princeton University Press, Princeton, NJ. 411 pp.

Winslow, C.E.A. 1952. *Man and epidemics.* Princeton University Press. Princeton, NJ. 246 pp.

Winslow, R.M. 1984. High altitude polycythemia. pp. 163–72 in *High altitude and man*, J.B. West and S. Lahiri, Eds. Am. Physiological Soc., Bethesda, MD. viii + 199.

Winter, J.M. 1977. Britain's 'Lost Generation' of the First World War. *Popul. Studies 31*, 449–66.

Wintrobe, M.M. (Ed.). 1980a. *Blood, pure and eloquent: A story of discovery, of people, and of ideas.* McGraw-Hill, New York, xxiii + 771.

Wintrobe, M.M. 1980b. Milestones on the path of progress. pp. 1–31 in Wintrobe, 1980a.

Wintrobe, M.M. 1980c. The lessons of history. pp. 719–26 in Wintrobe, 1980a.

Wishnow, R.M. and Steinfeld, J.L. 1976. The conquest of the major infectious diseases in the United States: A bicentennial retrospect. *Annu. Rev. Microbiol. 30*, 427–50.

Witenberg, G.G. 1964. Cestodiases. pp. 649–707 in van der Hoeden.

Witting, C. 1976. The terminology of glomerulonephritis. A review. pp. 45–60 in Grundmann (1976).

Wogen, G.N. (Ed.) 1965. *Mycotoxins in foodstuffs. Proceedings of a symposium, Massachusetts Institute of Technology, 1964.* MIT Press, Cambridge, MA. xii + 291.

Wogan, G.N. 1969. Naturally occurring carcinogens in foods. *Prog. Exp. Tumor Res. 11*, 134–62.

Wohl, A.S. 1983. *Endangered lives: Public health in Victorian Britian*. Harvard University Press, Cambridge, MA. viii + 440.

Woodham-Smith, C. 1962. *The Great Hunger*. Hamish Hamilton, London, 510 pp.

Woodruff, A.W. (Ed.) 1974. *Medicine in the tropics*. Churchill-Livingstone, Edinburgh-London. xii + 623.

Woods, H.M. 1933. *Epidemiological study of scarlet fever in England and Wales since 1900*. Med. Res. Council Spec. Rep. Series No. 180. HMSO, London, 61 pp.

Woods, R. 1984*a*. Mortality patterns in the nineteenth-century. pp. 37–64 in Woods and Woodward.

Woods, R. 1984*b*. Mortality and sanitary conditions in late nineteenth-century Birmingham. pp. 176–202 in Woods and Woodward.

Woods, R. and Woodward, J. 1984*a*. *Urban disease and mortality in nineteenth-century England*. Batsford Acad. & Educ., London. 255 pp.

Woods, R. and Woodward, J. 1984*b*. Mortality, poverty and the environment. pp. 19–36 in Woods and Woodward.

Woodward, J. 1984. Medicine and the city: The nineteeth-century experience. pp. 65–78 in Woods and Woodward.

Woodward, T.E. 1973. A historical account of the Rickettsial diseases with a discussion of unsolved problems. *J. Infect. Dis. 127*, 583–94.

Worboys, M. 1983. The emergence and early development of parasitology. pp. 1–18 in Warren and Bowers.

Wright, H.D. 1939. The clinical severity of diphtheria in certain cities in Great Britain. *J. Pathol. Bacteriol. 49*, 135–55.

Wright, H.T. 1973. *Cytomegalovirus*. pp. 353–88 in Kaplan.

Wright, J.W., Fritz, R.F., and Haworth, J. 1972. Changing concepts of vector control in malaria eradication. *Annu. Rev. Entomol. 17*, 75–102.

Wright, Q. 1965. *A study of war*. University of Chicago Press, Chicago, IL. 2 vols. xliii + 1637.

Wrigley, E.A. 1968. Mortality in pre-industrial England: The example of Colyton, Devon, over three centuries. *Daedalus* (Cambridge, MA) 97, 546–80. Reprinted in Glass and Revelle, 1972.

Wrigley, E.A. 1969. *Population and history*. World University Library, Weidenfeld & Nicholson, London. 256 pp.

Wrigley, E.A. (Ed.). 1972. *Nineteenth-century society: Essays in the use of quantitative methods for the study of social data*. Cambridge University Press, New York. vii + 448.

Wrigley, E.A. and Schofield, R. S. (with contributions by R. Lee and J. Oeppen) 1981. *The population history of England, 1541–1871. A reconstruction*. Studies in Social and Demographic History. Harvard University Press, Cambridge, MA.; Edward Arnold, London. xvi + 780.

Wu, C.K. and Winslow, C.E.A. 1933. Mortality, prosperity in United States counties. *Am. J. Hyg. 18*, 491–542.

Wyke, J.A. 1984. Oncogenic viruses. pp. 511–37 in Topley and Wilson, 1984, vol. 4.

Wynder, E.L. 1967. On the epidemiology of gastric cancer. pp. 37–65 in *Racial and geographical factors in tumour incidence*, A.A. Shivas (Ed.), Edinburgh University Press, Edinburgh. viii + 291.

Wynder, E.L. 1972. Etiology of lung cancer. Reflections of two decades of research. *Cancer 30*, 1332–39.

Wynder, E.L. and Bross, I.J. 1961. A study of etiological factors in cancer of the esophagus. *Cancer 14*, 389–413.

Wynder, E.L. Bross, I.J., and Day, E. 1956. A study of environmental factors in cancer of the larynx. *Cancer 9*, 86–110.

Wynder, E.L. and Goodman, M.T. 1983. Smoking and lung cancer: Some unresolved issues. *Epidemiol. Rev. 5*, 177–207.

Wynder, E.L. and Graham, E.A. 1950. Tobacco smoking as a possible etiologic factor in bronchiogenic carcinoma. *J. Am. Med. Assoc. 143*, 329–36.

Wynder, E.L. and Graham, E.A. 1951. Etiologic factors in bronchogenic carcinoma with special references to industrial exposures—Report on 857 proved cases. *AMA Arch. Ind. Hyg. Occup. Med. 4*, 221–35.

Wynder, E.L., Hertzberg, S., and Parker, E. (Eds.) 1981. *The book of health*. American Health Foundation. Franklin Watts, New York. 732 pp.

Wynder, E.L. and Hoffmann, D. 1964. Experimental tobacco carcinogenesis. *Adv. Cancer Res. 8*, 250–453.

Wynder, E.L. and Hoffmann, D. 1982. Tobacco. pp. 277–92 in Schottenfeld and Fraumeni.

Wynder, E.L., Kmet, J., Dungal, N., and Segi, M. 1963. An epidemiological investigation of gastric cancer. *Cancer 16*, 1461–96.

Wynder, E.L., Lemon, F.R., and Bross, I.J. 1959. Cancer and coronary artery disease among Seventh-Day Adventists. *Cancer 12*, 1016–28.

Wyon, J.B. and Gordon, J.E. 1971. *The Khanna Study: Population problems in the rural Punjab*. Harvard University Press, Cambridge, MA, xxiii + 437.

Yamaguchi, K. 1982. *Cause-specific mortality.* (Japanese) IDE Res. Publn Ser. No. 310, Tokyo. Translation pp. 93–119 in Ueda, 1983.

Yamamoto, S. 1981. Japan. pp. 337–51 in Trowell and Burkitt, 1981*a*.

Yekutiel, P. 1980. *Eradication of infectious diseases: A critical study.* Contributions to Epidemiology and Biostatistics, vol. 2. Karger, Basel. x + 164.

Yelton, S.E. 1946. Tuberculosis throughout the world. I. The prewar distribution of tuberculosis throughout the world. *Public Health Rep. (Wash.) 61*, 1144–60.

Yerushalmy. J. 1938. Neonatal mortality by order of birth and age of parents. *Am. J. Hyg. 28*, 244–70.

Yerushalmy, J., van den Berg, B.J., Erhardt, C.L., and Jacobziner, H. 1965. Birth weight and gestation as indices of "immaturity." *Am. J. Dis. Child. 109*, 43–57.

Yerushalmy, J. 1967. The classification of newborn infants by birth weight and gestational age. *J. Pediatr. 71*, (2), 164–72.

Yokogawa, M. 1976*a*. Review of prevalence and distribution of schistosomiasis in Japan. *Southeast Asian J. Trop. Med. Public Health 7*, 137–43.

Yokogawa, M. 1976*b*. Programme of schistosomiasis control in Japan. *Southeast Asian J. Trop. Med. Public Health 7*, 322–29.

Yorke, J.A., Nathanson, N., Pianigiani, G., and Martin, J. 1979. Seasonality and the requirements for perpetuation of viruses in populations. *Am. J. Epidemiol. 109*, 103–23.

Young, E.J. 1983. Human brucellosis. *Rev. Infect. Dis. 5*, 821–42.

Young, J.L. Jr and Pollack, E.S. 1982. The incidence of cancer in the United States. pp. 138–65 in Schottenfeld and Fraumeni.

Young, M. and Russell, W.T. 1927. Historical expectation of life: A study of the longevity of males at different periods in the history of Great Britain and Ireland from the sixteenth to the beginning of the nineteenth century, based on data from the "Dictionary of National Biography" and "Burke's Peerage and Baronetage." *J. Hyg. Camb. 25*, 256–72.

Young, M. and Russell, W.T. 1939. *Appendicitis, a statistical study.* Med. Res. Council Spec. Rep. Series No. 233. HMSO, London, 64 pp.

Youngson, A.J. 1979. *The scientific revolution in Victorian medicine.* Holmes & Meier, New York. 237 pp.

Yule, G.U. 1895–1896. On the correlation of total pauperism with proportion of out-relief. I. All ages. II. Males over sixty-five. *Econ. J. 5*, 603–608 and *6*, 613–23.

Yule, G.U. 1934. On some points relating to vital statistics, more especially statistics of occupational mortality. *J. Roy. Stat. Soc. 97*, 1–84.

Yunes, J. 1981. Evolution of infant mortality and proportional infant mortality in Brazil. *World Health Stat. Q. 34*, 200–20.

Zaman, V. 1978. *Balantidium coli.* pp. 633–53 in Kreier, vol. 2.

Zbořilová, J. 1977. Les tables de mortalité infantile par cause. Application à la Tchécoslovaquie et à la France, 1968–1972. *Population 32*, 555–78.

Zdrodovskiǐ, P.F. and Golinevich, H.M. 1960. *The Rickettsial disease.* Transl. from the Russian by B. Haigh. Pergamon Press, London, xii + 629.

Zentner, H.M. 1942. *Human plague in the United States from 1900 to 1940.* Tulane University Press, New Orleans. 36 pp.

Zeuner, F.E. 1963. *A history of domesticated animals.* Hutchinson, London, 560 pp.

Ziegler, J. 1971. *World War II: Books in English, 1945–65.* Hoover Bibliographical Ser., 45. Hoover Inst. Press, Stanford University, Stanford, CA. xvii + 194.

Ziegler, P. 1969. *The Black Death.* Collins, London. 319 pp.

Zimmerman, M.R. and Kelley, M.A. 1982. *Atlas of human paleopathology.* Praeger, New York. xiv + 220.

Zimmermann, E.L. 1935. The pathology of syphilis as revealed by autopsies performed between 1563 and 1761. *Bull. Hist. Med. 3*, 355–99.

Zimmet, P. and Whitehouse, S. 1981. Pacific islands of Nauru, Tuvalu and Western Samoa. pp. 204–24 in Trowell and Burkitt, 1981*a*.

Zinsser, H. 1934. Varieties of typhus virus and the epidemiology of the American form of European typhus fever (Brill's disease). *Am. J. Hyg. 20*, 513–32.

Zinsser, H. 1935. *Rats, lice and history.* George Routledge & Sons, London. xii + 301.

Zuckerman, A. and Lainson, R. 1977. Leishmania. pp. 58–133 in Kreier, vol. 1.

Zuckerman, A.J. 1979. The chronicle of viral hepatitis. *Abstr. Hyg. 54*, 1113–35.

Zulueta, J. de 1973. Malaria and Mediterranean history. *Parassitologia 15*, 1–15.

Zuppinger, A. (Ed.) 1966. *Encyclopedia of medical radiology.* English edition. Vol. 2. Pt. 1, P. Alexander, et al. (Eds.) xiv + 726. Pt. 2, A. Catsch, et al. (Eds.), xii + 668. Springer, Berlin.

Index of Persons

*Denotes inclusion in *Dictionary of Scientific Biography*, C. C. Gillispie, Ed. in Chief. Charles Scribner's Sons, New York (1970–1980).
† Denotes dates differing from *Dictionary of Scientific Biography*.

General Index